Lecture Notes in Computer S

T0238667

Commenced Publication in 1973
Founding and Former Series Editors:
Gerhard Goos, Juris Hartmanis, and Jan van Leeuwen

Lecture Notes in Computer Science

Commenced Publication in 1973
Founding and Former Series Editors:
Gerhard Goos, Juris Hartmanis, and Jan van Leeuwen

Editorial Board

David Hutchison
Lancaster University, UK
Takeo Kanade
Carnegie Mellon University, Pittsburgh, PA, USA
Josef Kittler
University of Surrey, Guildford, UK
Jon M. Kleinberg
Cornell University, Ithaca, NY, USA
Alfred Kobsa
University of California, Irvine, CA, USA
Friedemann Mattern
ETH Zurich, Switzerland
John C. Mitchell
Stanford University, CA, USA
Moni Naor
Weizmann Institute of Science, Rehovot, Israel
Oscar Nierstrasz
University of Bern, Switzerland
C. Pandu Rangan
Indian Institute of Technology, Madras, India
Bernhard Steffen
TU Dortmund University, Germany
Demetri Terzopoulos
University of California, Los Angeles, CA, USA
Doug Tygar
University of California, Berkeley, CA, USA
Gerhard Weikum
Max Planck Institute for Informatics, Saarbruecken, Germany

Phong Q. Nguyen   Elisabeth Oswald (Eds.)

Advances in Cryptology – EUROCRYPT 2014

33rd Annual International Conference
on the Theory and Applications of Cryptographic Techniques
Copenhagen, Denmark, May 11-15, 2014
Proceedings

 Springer

Volume Editors

Phong Q. Nguyen
Ecole normale supérieure
Départment d'informatique
45, rue d'Ulm, 75230 Paris Cedex 05, France
E-mail: phong.nguyen@inria.fr

Elisabeth Oswald
University of Bristol
Department of Computer Science
Merchant Venturers Building, Woodland Road, Bristol BS8 1UB, UK
E-mail: elisabeth.oswald@bristol.ac.uk

ISSN 0302-9743   e-ISSN 1611-3349
ISBN 978-3-642-55219-9   e-ISBN 978-3-642-55220-5
DOI 10.1007/978-3-642-55220-5
Springer Heidelberg New York Dordrecht London

Library of Congress Control Number: 2014936637

LNCS Sublibrary: SL 4 – Security and Cryptology

Typesetting: Camera-ready by author, data conversion by Scientific Publishing Services, Chennai, India

Printed on acid-free paper

Springer is part of Springer Science+Business Media (www.springer.com)

Preface

These are the proceedings of Eurocrypt 2014, the 33rd annual IACR Eurocrypt conference on the theory and applications of cryptographic techniques. The conference was held May 11–15, 2014, in Copenhagen, Denmark, and sponsored by the International Association for Cryptologic Research (IACR). Responsible for the local organization were Lars Knudsen, from the Technical University of Denmark, and Gregor Leander, from the Ruhr University Bochum. We are indebted to them for their support.

The Eurocrypt 2014 Program Committee (PC) consisted of 32 members. Each paper was reviewed by at least three reviewers. Submissions co-authored by PC members were reviewed by at least five reviewers. All reviews were conducted double-blind and we excluded PC members from discussing submissions for which they had a possible conflict of interest.

We received a total of 197 submissions, many were of high-quality. From these, after in-depth discussions among the PC, we eventually selected 40 papers, four of which the PC recommended merging. Hence, in total 38 papers were presented during the conference and the revised versions of these papers are included in these proceedings. Because revisions were not reviewed again, the authors (and not the committee) bear full responsibility for the contents of their papers.

The review process would have been impossible without the hard work of the PC members and 227 external reviewers, whose effort we would like to commend here. It has been an honor to work with everyone. The process was enabled by the Web Submission and Review Software written by Shai Halevi and the server was hosted by IACR. We would like to thank Shai for setting up the service on the server and helping us whenever needed.

The PC decided to honor two submissions with the Best Paper Award this year. These were "Unifying Leakage Models: From Probing Attacks to Noisy Leakage," authored by Alexandre Duc, Stefan Dziembowski, and Sebastian Faust, and "A Heuristic Quasi-polynomial Algorithm for Discrete Logarithm in Finite Fields of Small Characteristic" authored by Razvan Barbulescu, Pierrick Gaudry, Antoine Joux, and Emmanuel Thomé.

In addition to the contributed talks, there were two invited talks given by Jeff Hoffstein and Adi Shamir. Jeff Hoffstein talked about "A Mathematical History of NTRU and Some Related Cryptosystems." Adi Shamir talked about "The Security and Privacy of Bitcoin Transactions." We would like to thank them both for accepting our invitation and for their contribution to the program of Eurocrypt 2014.

Last, we dedicated the conference to James L. Massey (former president of IACR and IACR Fellow 2009, 1934–2013), who lived near the conference venue at the end of his life, and whose many contributions including cipher design and analysis were inspiring to many of us. We remembered Scott Vanstone (IACR

Fellow 2011, 1947–2014), whose contributions to the deployment of Elliptic Curve Cryptography, as well as sustained educational leadership in applied cryptology, shaped a whole new generation of cryptographers.

May 2014   Phong Q. Nguyen
                                                     Elisabeth Oswald

EUROCRYPT 2014

The 33rd Annual International Conference on the Theory and Applications of Cryptographic Techniques

Copenhagen, Denmark, May 11–15, 2014

Dedicated to the Memory of James L. Massey, 1934–2013.

General Chairs

Lars Knudsen   Technical University of Denmark
Gregor Leander   Ruhr University Bochum, Germany

Program Co-chairs

Phong Q. Nguyen   Inria, France and Tsinghua University, China
Elisabeth Oswald   University of Bristol, UK

Program Committee

Masayuki Abe   NTT, Japan
Joël Alwen   ETH Zurich, Switzerland
Zvika Brakerski   Weizmann Institute of Science, Israel
David Cash   Rutgers University, USA
Dario Catalano   Università di Catania, Spain
Jean-Sébastien Coron   University of Luxembourg, Luxembourg
Serge Fehr   CWI Amsterdam, The Netherlands
Pierre-Alain Fouque   Université de Rennes, France
Marc Joye   Technicolor, USA
Charanjit Jutla   IBM Research, USA
Alexander May   Ruhr University Bochum, Germany
Florian Mendel   TU Graz, Austria
Ilya Mironov   Microsoft Research, USA
Payman Mohassel   University of Calgary, Canada
Shiho Moriai   NICT, Japan
María Naya-Plasencia   INRIA, France
Adam O'Neill   Georgetown University, USA
Rafael Pass   Cornell University, USA
Ludovic Perret   UPMC/Inria/CNRS/LIP6, France

Emmanuel Prouff   ANSSI, France
Thomas Ristenpart   University of Wisconsin, USA
Pankaj Rohatgi   Cryptography Research Inc., USA
Mike Rosulek   Oregon State University, USA
Francois-Xavier Standaert   Université catholique de Louvain, Belgium
Ron Steinfeld   Monash University, Australia
Dominique Unruh   University of Tartu, Estonia
Serge Vaudenay   EPFL, Switzerland
Frederik Vercauteren   KU Leuven, Belgium
Ivan Visconti   Università di Salerno, Italy
Lei Wang   NTU, Singapore
Bogdan Warinschi   University of Bristol, UK
Stefan Wolf   USI Lugano, Switzerland

External Reviewers

Michel Abdalla	Sandro Coretti	Peter Gazi
Arash Afshar	Dana Dachman-Soled	Essam Ghadafi
Martin Albrecht	Gareth Davies	Hannes Gross
Jacob Alperin-Sheriff	Cécile Delerablée	Vincent Grosso
Paulo Barreto	Gregory Demay	Aurore Guillevic
Carsten Baum	Jean-François Dhem	Sylvain Guilley
Aemin Baumeler	Laurent-Stéphane Didier	Jian Guo
Aslı Bay	Itai Dinur	Benoît Gérard
Mihir Bellare	Nico Dottling	Robbert de Haan
Fabrice Benhamouda	Chandan Dubey	Michael Hamburg
Olivier Billet	Alexandre Duc	Helena Handschuh
Olivier Blazy	François Durvaux	Christian Hanser
Johannes Blomer	Helen Ebbe	Kristiyan Haralambiev
Céline Blondeau	Maria Eichlseder	Jens Hermans
Sonia Bogos	Keita Emura	Gottfried Herold
Florian Bohl	Sebastian Faust	Shoichi Hirose
Joppe Bos	Matthieu Finiasz	Dennis Hofheinz
Elette Boyle	Dario Fiore	Jialin Huang
Christina Brzuska	Marc Fischlin	Michael Hutter
Anne Canteaut	Jean-Pierre Flori	Vincenzo Iovino
Angelo De Caro	Georg Fuchsbauer	Yuval Ishai
Xavier Carpent	Benjamin Fuller	Tetsu Iwata
Ignacio Cascudo	Philippe Gaborit	Malika Izabachene
Wouter Castryck	Steven Galbraith	Stanislaw Jarecki
Melissa Chase	David Galindo	Eliane Jaulmes
Kai-min Chung	Nicolas Gama	Mahabir Jhanwar
Christophe Clavier	Sanjam Garg	Pascal Junod
Henry Cohn	Lubos Gaspar	Yael Kalai
Baudoin Collard	Pierrick Gaudry	Pierre Karpman

Sriram Keelveedhi
Marcel Keller
Elena Kirshanova
Susumu Kiyoshima
Ilya Kizhvatov
Thorsten Kleinjung
François Koeune
Vladimir Kolesnikov
Yuichi Komano
Thomas Korak
Ranjit Kumaresan
Eyal Kushilevitz
Adeline Langlois
Gregor Leander
Tancréde Lepoint
Gaëtan Leurent
Allison Lewko
Huijia Lin
Yiyuan Luo
Vadim Lyubashevsky
Stefan Mangard
Antonio Marcedone
Joana Treger Marim
Mark Marson
Takahiro Matsuda
Christian Matt
Marcel Medwed
Alfred Menezes
Bart Mennink
Kazuhiko Minematsu
Rafael Misoczki
Shigeo Mitsunari
Amir Moradi
Kirill Morozov
Nicky Mouha
Elke De Mulder
Yusuke Naito
Khoa Nguyen
Antonio Nicosi
Jesper Buus Nielsen
Valeria Nikolaenko
Ivica Nikolić
Ryo Nishimaki
Ryo Nojima
Miyako Ohkubo

Tatsuaki Okamoto
Thomaz Oliveira
Claudio Orlandi
Ilya Ozerov
Jiaxin Pan
Anat
    Paskin-Cherniavsky
Kenny Paterson
Chris Peikert
Giuseppe Persiano
Edoardo Persichetti
Thomas Peters
Christophe Petit
Thomas Peyrin
Marcel Pfaffhauser
Le Trieu Phong
Krzysztof Pietrzak
Jérôme Plût
Orazio Puglisi
Ananth Raghunathan
Mario Di Raimondo
Vanishree H. Rao
Jibran Rashid
Pavel Raykov
Mariana Raykova
Francesco Regazzoni
Guenael Renault
Reza Reyhanitabar
Ben Riva
Matthieu Rivain
Damien Robert
Thomas Roche
Francisco
    Rodríguez-Henríquez
Guy Rothblum
Yannis Rouselakis
Sujoy Sinha Roy
Saeed Sadeghian
Louis Salvail
Yu Sasaki
Alessandra Scafuro
Christian Schaffner
Martin Schläffer
Berry Schoenmakers
Dominique Schröder

Lior Seeman
Igor Semaev
Nicolas Sendrier
Jae Hong Seo
Karn Seth
Yannick Seurin
Hovav Shacham
Abhi Shelat
Elaine Shi
Igor Shparlinski
Daniel Slamanig
Nigel Smart
Ben Smith
Florian Speelman
Raphael Spreitzer
Martijn Stam
Emil Stefanov
Damien Stehlé
John Steinberger
Koutarou Suzuki
Petr Sušil
Alan Szepieniec
Bjoern Tackmann
Sidharth Telang
Isamu Teranishi
Stefano Tessaro
Susan Thomson
Emmanuel Thomé
Mehdi Tibouchi
Daniel Tschudi
Michael Tunstall
Muthu
    Venkitasubramaniam
Damien Vergnaud
Camille Vuillaume
Huaxiong Wang
Gaven Watson
Hoeteck Wee
Carolyn Whitnall
Keita Xagawa
Kan Yasuda
Arkady Yerukhimovich
Scott Yilek
Kazuki Yoneyama
Xiaoli Yu

Yu Yu
Rina Zeitoun
Mark Zhandry

Liting Zhang
Hong-Sheng Zhou
Vassilis Zikas

Joe Zimmerman

Table of Contents

Obfuscation and Multilinear Maps

Authenticated Encryption

Symmetric Encryption

Multi-party Computation

Side-Channel Attacks

Signatures and Public-Key Encryption

Functional Encryption

Foundations

Multi-party Computation

A Heuristic Quasi-Polynomial Algorithm for Discrete Logarithm in Finite Fields of Small Characteristic

Razvan Barbulescu[1], Pierrick Gaudry[1], and Antoine Joux[2,3], and Emmanuel Thomé[1]

[1] Inria, CNRS, University of Lorraine, France
[2] CryptoExperts, Paris, France
[3] Chaire de Cryptologie de la Fondation UPMC
Sorbonne Universités, UPMC Univ Paris 06, CNRS UMR
7606, LIP 6, France

Abstract. The difficulty of computing discrete logarithms in fields $\mathbb{F}_{q^k}$ depends on the relative sizes of k and q. Until recently all the cases had a sub-exponential complexity of type $L(1/3)$, similar to the factorization problem. In 2013, Joux designed a new algorithm with a complexity of $L(1/4 + \epsilon)$ in small characteristic. In the same spirit, we propose in this article another heuristic algorithm that provides a quasi-polynomial complexity when q is of size at most comparable with k. By quasi-polynomial, we mean a runtime of $n^{O(\log n)}$ where n is the bit-size of the input. For larger values of q that stay below the limit $L_{q^k}(1/3)$, our algorithm loses its quasi-polynomial nature, but still surpasses the Function Field Sieve. Complexity results in this article rely on heuristics which have been checked experimentally.

1 Introduction

The discrete logarithm problem (DLP) was first proposed as a hard problem in cryptography in the seminal article of Diffie and Hellman [7]. Since then, together with factorization, it has become one of the two major pillars of public key cryptography. As a consequence, the problem of computing discrete logarithms has attracted a lot of attention. From an exponential algorithm in 1976, the fastest DLP algorithms have been greatly improved during the past 35 years. A first major progress was the realization that the DLP in finite fields can be solved in subexponential time, i.e. $L(1/2)$ where $L_N(\alpha) = \exp\left(O((\log N)^\alpha (\log \log N)^{1-\alpha})\right)$. The next step further reduced this to a heuristic $L(1/3)$ running time in the full range of finite fields, from fixed characteristic finite fields to prime fields [2,6,11,3,17,18].

Recently, practical and theoretical advances have been made [15,10,16] with an emphasis on small to medium characteristic finite fields and composite degree extensions. The most general and efficient algorithm [16] gives a complexity of $L(1/4 + o(1))$ when the characteristic is smaller than the square root of the extension degree. Among the ingredients of this approach, we find the use of a very

P.Q. Nguyen and E. Oswald (Eds.): EUROCRYPT 2014, LNCS 8441, pp. 1–16, 2014.

particular representation of the finite field; the use of the so-called *systematic equation*[1]; and the use of algebraic resolution of bilinear polynomial systems in the individual logarithm phase.

In this work, we present a new discrete logarithm algorithm, in the same vein as in [16] that uses an asymptotically more efficient descent approach. The main result gives a *quasi-polynomial* heuristic complexity for the DLP in finite fields of small characteristic. By quasi-polynomial, we mean a complexity of type $n^{O(\log n)}$ where n is the bit-size of the cardinality of the finite field. Such a complexity is smaller than any $L(\epsilon)$ for $\epsilon > 0$. It remains super-polynomial in the size of the input, but offers a major asymptotic improvement compared to $L(1/4 + o(1))$.

The key features of our algorithm are the following.

- We keep the field representation and the systematic equations of [16].
- The algorithmic building blocks are elementary. In particular, we avoid the use of Gröbner basis algorithms.
- The complexity result relies on three key heuristics: the existence of a polynomial representation of the appropriate form; the fact that the smoothness probabilities of some non-uniformly distributed polynomials are similar to the probabilities for uniformly random polynomials of the same degree; and the linear independence of some finite field elements related to the action of $\mathrm{PGL}_2(\mathbb{F}_q)$.

The heuristics are very close to the ones used in [16]. In addition to the arguments in favor of these heuristics already given in [16], we performed some experiments to validate them on practical instances.

Although we insist on the case of finite fields of small characteristic, where quasi-polynomial complexity is obtained, our new algorithm improves the complexity of discrete logarithm computations in a much larger range of finite fields.

More precisely, in finite fields of the form $\mathbb{F}_{q^k}$, where q grows as $L_{q^k}(\alpha)$, the complexity becomes $L_{q^k}(\alpha + o(1))$. As a consequence, our algorithm is asymptotically faster than the Function Field Sieve algorithm in almost all the range previously covered by this algorithm. Whenever $\alpha < 1/3$, our new algorithm offers the smallest complexity. For the limiting case $L(1/3, c)$, the Function Field Sieve remains more efficient for small values of c, and the Number Field Sieve is better for large values of c (see [18]).

This article is organized as follows. In Section 2, we state the main result, and discuss how it can be used to design a complete discrete logarithm algorithm. In Section 3, we analyze how this result can be interpreted for various types of finite fields, including the important case of fields of small characteristic. Section 4 is devoted to the description of our new algorithm. It relies on heuristics that are discussed in Section 5, from a theoretical and a practical point of view. Before getting to the conclusion, in Section 6, we propose a few variants of the algorithm.

---

[1] While the terminology is similar, no parallel is to be made with the systematic equations as defined in early works related to the computation discrete logarithms in $\mathbb{F}_{2^n}$, as [4].

2   Main Result

We start by describing the setting in which our algorithm applies. It is basically the same as in [16]: we need a large enough subfield, and we assume that a sparse representation can be found. This is formalized in the following definition.

Definition 1. *A finite field K admits a sparse medium subfield representation if*

- *it has a subfield of q^2 elements for a prime power q, i.e. K is isomorphic to $\mathbb{F}_{q^{2k}}$ with $k \geq 1$;*
- *there exist two polynomials h_0 and h_1 over $\mathbb{F}_{q^2}$ of small degree, such that $h_1 X^q - h_0$ has a degree k irreducible factor.*

In what follows, we will assume that all the fields under consideration admit a sparse medium subfield representation. Furthermore, we assume that the degrees of the polynomials h_0 and h_1 are uniformly bounded by a constant δ. Later, we will provide heuristic arguments for the fact that any finite field of the form $\mathbb{F}_{q^{2k}}$ with $k \leq q+2$ admits a sparse medium subfield representation with polynomials h_0 and h_1 of degree at most 2. But in fact, for our result to hold, allowing the degrees of h_0 and h_1 to be bounded by any constant δ independent of q and k or even allowing δ to grow slower than $O(\log q)$ would be sufficient.

In a field in sparse medium subfield representation, elements will always be represented as polynomials of degree less than k with coefficients in $\mathbb{F}_{q^2}$. When we talk about the discrete logarithm of such an element, we implicitly assume that a basis for this discrete logarithm has been chosen, and that we work in a subgroup whose order has no small irreducible factor (we refer to the Pohlig-Hellman algorithm [20] to limit ourselves to this case).

Proposition 2. *Let $K = \mathbb{F}_{q^{2k}}$ be a finite field that admits a sparse medium subfield representation. Under the heuristics explained below, there exists an algorithm whose complexity is polynomial in q and k and which can be used for the following two tasks.*

1. *Given an element of K represented by a polynomial $P \in \mathbb{F}_{q^2}[X]$ with $2 \leq \deg P \leq k - 1$, the algorithm returns an expression of $\log P(X)$ as a linear combination of at most $O(kq^2)$ logarithms $\log P_i(X)$ with $\deg P_i \leq \lceil \frac{1}{2} \deg P \rceil$ and of $\log h_1(X)$.*
2. *The algorithm returns the logarithm of $h_1(X)$ and the logarithms of all the elements of K of the form $X + a$, for a in $\mathbb{F}_{q^2}$.*

Before the presentation of the algorithm, which is made in Section 4, we explain how to use it as a building block for a complete discrete logarithm algorithm.

Let $P(X)$ be an element of K for which we want to compute the discrete logarithm. Here P is a polynomial of degree at most $k - 1$ and with coefficients in $\mathbb{F}_{q^2}$. We start by applying the algorithm of Proposition 2 to P. We obtain a relation of the form

$$\log P = e_0 \log h_1 + \sum e_i \log P_i,$$

where the sum has at most $\kappa q^2 k$ terms for a constant κ and the P_i's have degree at most $\lceil \frac{1}{2} \deg P \rceil$. Then, we apply recursively the algorithm to the P_i's, thus creating a descent procedure where at each step, a given element P is expressed as a product of elements, whose degree is at most half the degree of P (rounded up) and the arity of the descent tree is in $O(q^2 k)$.

At the end of the process, the logarithm of P is expressed as a linear combination of the logarithms of h_1 and of the linear polynomials, for which the logarithms are computed with the algorithm in Proposition 2 in its second form.

We are left with the complexity analysis of the descent process. Each internal node of the descent tree corresponds to one application of the algorithm of Proposition 2, therefore each internal node has a cost which is bounded by a polynomial in q and k. The total cost of the descent is therefore bounded by the number of nodes in the descent tree times a polynomial in q and k. The depth of the descent tree is in $O(\log k)$. The number of nodes of the tree is then less than or equal to its arity raised to the power of its depth, which is $(q^2 k)^{O(\log k)}$. Since any polynomial in q and k is absorbed in the $O()$ notation in the exponent, we obtain the following result.

Theorem 3. *Let $K = \mathbb{F}_{q^{2k}}$ be a finite field that admits a sparse medium subfield representation. Assuming the same heuristics as in Proposition 2, any discrete logarithm in K can be computed in a time bounded by*

$$\max(q, k)^{O(\log k)}.$$

3   Consequences for Various Ranges of Parameters

We now discuss the implications of Theorem 3 depending on the properties of the finite field $\mathbb{F}_Q$ where we want to compute discrete logarithms in the first place. The complexities will be expressed in terms of $\log Q$, which is the size of the input.

Three cases are considered. In the first one, the finite field admits a sparse medium subfield representation, where q and k are almost equal. This is the optimal case. Then we consider the case where the finite field has small (maybe constant) characteristic. And finally, we consider the case where the characteristic is getting larger so that the only available subfield is a bit too large for the algorithm to have an optimal complexity.

In the following, we always assume that for any field of the form $\mathbb{F}_{q^{2k}}$, we can find a sparse medium subfield representation.

3.1   Case Where the Field is $\mathbb{F}_{q^{2k}}$, with $q \approx k$

The finite fields $\mathbb{F}_Q = \mathbb{F}_{q^{2k}}$ for which q and k are almost equal are tailored for our algorithm. In that case, the complexity of Theorem 3 becomes $q^{O(\log q)}$.

Since $Q \approx q^{2q}$, we have $q = (\log Q)^{O(1)}$. This gives an expression of the form $2^{O((\log \log Q)^2)}$, which is sometimes called quasi-polynomial in complexity theory.

Corollary 4. *For finite fields of cardinality $Q = q^{2k}$ with $q + O(1) \geq k$ and $q = (\log Q)^{O(1)}$, there exists a heuristic algorithm for computing discrete logarithms in quasi-polynomial time*

$$2^{O((\log \log Q)^2)}.$$

We mention a few cases which are almost directly covered by Corollary 4. First, we consider the case where $Q = p^n$ with p a prime bounded by $(\log Q)^{O(1)}$, and yet large enough so that $n \leq (p + \delta)$. In this case $\mathbb{F}_Q$, or possibly $\mathbb{F}_{Q^2}$ if n is odd, can be represented in such a way that Corollary 4 applies.

Much the same can be said in the case where n is composite and factors nicely, so that $\mathbb{F}_Q$ admits a large enough subfield $\mathbb{F}_q$ with $q = p^m$. This can be used to solve certain discrete logarithms in, say, $\mathbb{F}_{2^n}$ for adequately chosen n (much similar to records tackled by [12,8,13,9,14]).

3.2 Case Where the Characteristic is Polynomial in the Input Size

Let now $\mathbb{F}_Q$ be a finite field whose characteristic p is bounded by $(\log Q)^{O(1)}$, and let $n = \log Q / \log p$, so that $Q = p^n$. While we have seen that Corollary 4 can be used to treat some cases, its applicability might be hindered by the absence of an appropriately sized subfield: p might be as small as 2, and n might not factor adequately. In those cases, we use the same strategy as in [16] and embed the discrete logarithm problem in $\mathbb{F}_Q$ into a discrete logarithm problem in a larger field.

Let k be n if n is odd and $n/2$ if n is even. Then, we set $q = p^{\lceil \log_p k \rceil}$, and we work in the field $\mathbb{F}_{q^{2k}}$. By construction this field contains $\mathbb{F}_Q$ (because $p|q$ and $n|2k$) and it is in the range of applicability of Theorem 3. Therefore, one can solve a discrete logarithm problem in $\mathbb{F}_Q$ in time $\max(q, k)^{O(\log k)}$. Rewriting this complexity in terms of Q, we get $\log_p(Q)^{O(\log \log Q)}$. And finally, we get a similar complexity result as in the previous case. Of course, since we had to embed in a larger field, the constant hidden in the $O()$ is larger than for Corollary 4.

Corollary 5. *For finite fields of cardinality Q and characteristic bounded by $\log(Q)^{O(1)}$, there exists a heuristic algorithm for computing discrete logarithms in quasi-polynomial time*

$$2^{O((\log \log Q)^2)}.$$

We emphasize that the case $\mathbb{F}_{2^n}$ for a prime n corresponds to this case. A direct consequence of Corollary 5 is that discrete logarithms in $\mathbb{F}_{2^n}$ can be computed in quasi-polynomial time $2^{O((\log n)^2)}$.

3.3 Case Where $q = L_{q^{2k}}(\alpha)$

If the characteristic of the base field is not so small compared to the extension degree, the complexity of our algorithm does not keep its nice quasi-polynomial form. However, in almost the whole range of applicability of the Function Field Sieve algorithm, our algorithm is asymptotically better than FFS.

We consider here finite fields that can be put into the form $\mathbb{F}_Q = \mathbb{F}_{q^{2k}}$, where q grows not faster than an expression of the form $L_Q(\alpha)$. In the following, we assume that there is equality, which is of course the worst case. The condition can then be rewritten as $\log q = O((\log Q)^{\alpha}(\log\log Q)^{1-\alpha})$ and therefore $k = \log Q/\log q = O((\log Q/\log\log Q)^{1-\alpha})$. In particular we have $k \leq q + \delta$, so that Theorem 3 can be applied and gives a complexity of $q^{O(\log k)}$. This yields the following result.

Corollary 6. *For finite fields of the form $\mathbb{F}_Q = \mathbb{F}_{q^{2k}}$ where q is bounded by $L_Q(\alpha)$, there exists a heuristic algorithm for computing discrete logarithms in subexponential time*
$$L_Q(\alpha)^{O(\log\log Q)}.$$

This complexity is smaller than $L_Q(\alpha')$ for any $\alpha' > \alpha$. Hence, for any $\alpha < 1/3$, our algorithm is faster than the best previously known algorithm, namely FFS and its variants.

4   Main Algorithm: Proof of Proposition 2

The algorithm is essentially the same for proving the two points of Proposition 2. The strategy is to find relations between the given polynomial $P(X)$ and its translates by a constant in $\mathbb{F}_{q^2}$. Let D be the degree of $P(X)$, that we assume to be at least 1 and at most $k - 1$.

The key to find relations is the *systematic equation*, which is valid on any $\mathbb{F}_q$-algebra:
$$X^q - X = \prod_{a\in\mathbb{F}_q}(X - a). \tag{1}$$

We like to view Equation (1) as involving the projective line $\mathbb{P}^1(\mathbb{F}_q)$. Let $S = \{(\alpha, \beta)\}$ be a set of representatives of the $q + 1$ points $(\alpha : \beta) \in \mathbb{P}^1(\mathbb{F}_q)$, chosen adequately so that the following equality holds.

$$X^q Y - XY^q = \prod_{(\alpha,\beta)\in S}(\beta X - \alpha Y). \tag{2}$$

To make translates of $P(X)$ appear, we consider the action of *homographies*. Any matrix $m = \begin{pmatrix} a & b \\ c & d \end{pmatrix}$ acts on $P(X)$ with the following formula:

$$m \cdot P = \frac{aP + b}{cP + d}.$$

In the following, this action will become trivial if the matrix m has entries that are defined over $\mathbb{F}_q$. This is also the case if m is non-invertible. Finally, it is clear that multiplying all the entries of m by a non-zero constant does not change its action on $P(X)$. Therefore the matrices of the homographies that we consider are going to be taken in the following set of cosets:

$$\mathcal{P}_q = \mathrm{PGL}(\mathbb{F}_{q^2})/\mathrm{PGL}(\mathbb{F}_q).$$

(Note that in general $\mathrm{PGL}_2(\mathbb{F}_q)$ is not a normal subgroup of $\mathrm{PGL}_2(\mathbb{F}_{q^2})$, so that $\mathcal{P}_q$ is not a quotient group.)

To each element $m = \begin{pmatrix} a & b \\ c & d \end{pmatrix} \in \mathcal{P}_q$, we associate the equation (E_m) obtained by substituting $aP + b$ and $cP + d$ in place of X and Y in Equation (2).

$$(aP + b)^q(cP + d) - (aP + b)(cP + d)^q = \prod_{(\alpha,\beta)\in\mathcal{S}} \beta(aP + b) - \alpha(cP + d) \quad (E_m)$$

$$= \prod_{(\alpha,\beta)\in\mathcal{S}} (-c\alpha + a\beta)P - (d\alpha - b\beta)$$

$$= \lambda \prod_{(\alpha,\beta)\in\mathcal{S}} P - \mathrm{x}(m^{-1} \cdot (\alpha : \beta)).$$

This sequence of formulae calls for a short comment because of an abuse of notation in the last expression. First, λ is the constant in $\mathbb{F}_{q^2}$ which makes the leading terms of the two sides match. Then, the term $P - \mathrm{x}(m^{-1} \cdot (\alpha : \beta))$ denotes $P - u$ when $m^{-1} \cdot (\alpha : \beta) = (u : 1)$ (whence we have $u = \frac{d\alpha - b\beta}{-c\alpha + a\beta}$), or 1 if $m^{-1} \cdot (\alpha : \beta) = \infty$. The latter may occur since when a/c is in $\mathbb{F}_q$, the expression $-c\alpha + a\beta$ vanishes for a point $(\alpha : \beta) \in \mathbb{P}^1(\mathbb{F}_q)$ so that one of the factors of the product contains no term in $P(X)$.

Hence the right-hand side of Equation (E_m) is, up to a multiplicative constant, a product of $q + 1$ or q translates of the target $P(X)$ by elements of $\mathbb{F}_{q^2}$. The equation obtained is actually related to the set of points $m^{-1} \cdot \mathbb{P}^1(\mathbb{F}_q) \subset \mathbb{P}^1(\mathbb{F}_{q^2})$.

The polynomial on the left-hand side of (E_m) can be rewritten as a smaller degree equivalent. For this, we use the special form of the defining polynomial: in K we have $X^q \equiv \frac{h_0(X)}{h_1(X)}$. Let us denote by $\tilde{a}$ the element a^q when a is any element of $\mathbb{F}_{q^2}$. Furthermore, we write $\tilde{P}(X)$ the polynomial $P(X)$ with all its coefficients raised to the power q. The left-hand side of (E_m) is

$$(\tilde{a}\tilde{P}(X^q) + \tilde{b})(cP(X) + d) - (aP(X) + b)(\tilde{c}\tilde{P}(X^q) + \tilde{d}),$$

and using the defining equation for the field K, it is congruent to

$$\mathcal{L}_m := \left(\tilde{a}\tilde{P}\left(\frac{h_0(X)}{h_1(X)}\right) + \tilde{b}\right)(cP(X) + d) - (aP(X) + b)\left(\tilde{c}\tilde{P}\left(\frac{h_0(X)}{h_1(X)}\right) + \tilde{d}\right).$$

The denominator of $\mathcal{L}_m$ is a power of h_1 and its numerator has degree at most $(1 + \delta)D$ where $\delta = \max(\deg h_0, \deg h_1)$. We say that $m \in \mathcal{P}_q$ yields a relation if this numerator of $\mathcal{L}_m$ is $\lceil D/2 \rceil$-smooth.

To any $m \in \mathcal{P}_q$, we associate a row vector $v(m)$ of dimension $q^2 + 1$ in the following way. Coordinates are indexed by $\mu \in \mathbb{P}^1(\mathbb{F}_{q^2})$, and the value associated to $\mu \in \mathbb{F}_{q^2}$ is 1 or 0 depending on whether $P - \mathrm{x}(\mu)$ appears in the right-hand side of Equation (E_m). Note that exactly $q + 1$ coordinates are 1 for each m. Equivalently, we may write

$$v(m)_{\mu \in \mathbb{P}^1(\mathbb{F}_{q^2})} = \begin{cases} 1 \text{ if } \mu = m^{-1} \cdot (\alpha : \beta) \text{ with } (\alpha : \beta) \in \mathbb{P}^1(\mathbb{F}_q), \\ 0 \text{ otherwise.} \end{cases} \qquad (3)$$

We associate to the polynomial P a matrix $H(P)$ whose rows are the vectors $v(m)$ for which m yields a relation, taking at most one matrix m in each coset of $\mathcal{P}_q$. The validity of Proposition 2 crucially relies on the following heuristic.

Heuristic 7. *For any $P(X)$, the set of rows $v(m)$ for cosets $m \in \mathcal{P}_q$ that yield a relation form a matrix which has full rank $q^2 + 1$.*

As we will note in Section 5, the matrix $H(P)$ is heuristically expected to have $\Theta(q^3)$ rows, where the implicit constant depends on δ. This means that for our decomposition procedure to work, we rely on the fact that q is large enough (otherwise $H(P)$ may have less than $q^2 + 1$ rows, which precludes the possibility that it have rank $q^2 + 1$).

The first point of Proposition 2, where we descend a polynomial $P(X)$ of degree D at least 2, follows by linear algebra on this matrix. Since we assume that the matrix has full rank, then the vector $(\ldots, 0, 1, 0, \ldots)$ with 1 corresponding to $P(X)$ can be written as a linear combination of the rows. When doing this linear combination on the equations (E_m) corresponding to P we write $\log P(X)$ as a linear combination of $\log P_i$ where $P_i(x)$ are the elements occurring in the left-hand sides of the equations. Since there are $O(q^2)$ columns, the elimination process involves at most $O(q^2)$ rows, and since each row corresponds to an equation (E_m), it involves at most $\deg \mathcal{L}_m \leq (1 + \delta)D$ polynomials in the left-hand-side[2]. In total, the polynomial D is expressed by a linear combination of at most $O(q^2 D)$ polynomials of degree less than $\lceil D/2 \rceil$. The logarithm of $h_1(X)$ is also involved, as a denominator of $\mathcal{L}_m$. We have not made precise the constant in $\mathbb{F}_{q^2}^*$ which occurs to take care of the leading coefficients. Since discrete logarithms in $\mathbb{F}_{q^2}^*$ can certainly be computed in polynomial time in q, this is not a problem.

Since the order of $\mathrm{PGL}_2(\mathbb{F}_{q^i})$ is $q^{3i} - q^i$, the set of cosets $\mathcal{P}_q$ has $q^3 + q$ elements. For each $m \in \mathcal{P}_q$, testing whether (E_m) yields a relation amounts to some polynomial manipulations and a smoothness test. All of them can be done in polynomial time in q and the degree of $P(X)$ which is bounded by k. Finally, the linear algebra step can be done in $O(q^{2\omega})$ using asymptotically fast matrix multiplication algorithms, or alternatively $O(q^5)$ operations using sparse matrix techniques. Indeed, we have $q + 1$ non-zero entries per row and a size of $q^2 + 1$. Therefore, the overall cost is polynomial in q and k as claimed.

---

[2] This estimate of the number of irreducible factors is a pessimistic upper bound. In practice, one expects to have only $O(\log D)$ factors on average. Since the crude estimate does not change the overall complexity, we keep it that way to avoid adding another heuristic.

For the second part of Proposition 2 we replace P by X during the construction of the matrix. In that case, both sides of the equations (E_m) involve only linear polynomials. Hence we obtain a linear system whose unknowns are $\log(X + a)$ with $a \in \mathbb{F}_{q^2}$. Since Heuristic 7 would give us only the full rank of the system corresponding to the right-hand sides of the equations (E_m), we have to rely on a specific heuristic for this step:

Heuristic 8. *The linear system constructed from all the equations (E_m) for $P(X) = X$ has full rank.*

Assuming that this heuristic holds, we can solve the linear system and obtain the discrete logarithms of the linear polynomials and of $h_1(X)$.

5 Supporting the Heuristic Argument in the Proof

We propose two approaches to support Heuristic 7. Both allow to gain some confidence in its validity, but of course none affect the heuristic nature of the statement.

For the first line of justification, we denote by $\mathcal{H}$ the matrix of all the $\#\mathcal{P}_q = q^3 + q$ vectors $v(m)$ defined as in Equation (3). Associated to a polynomial P, Section 4 defines the matrix $H(P)$ formed of the rows $v(m)$ such that the numerator of $\mathcal{L}_m$ is smooth. We will give heuristics that $H(P)$ has $\Theta(q^3)$ rows and then prove that $\mathcal{H}$ has rank $q^2 + 1$, which of course does not prove that its submatrix $H(P)$ has full rank.

In order to estimate the number of rows of $H(P)$ we assume that the numerator of $\mathcal{L}_m$ has the same probability to be $\lceil \frac{D}{2} \rceil$-smooth as a random polynomial of same degree. In this paragraph, we assume that the degrees of h_0 and h_1 are bounded by 2, merely to avoid awkward notations; the result holds for any constant bound δ. The degree of the numerator of $\mathcal{L}_m$ is then bounded by $3D$, so we have to estimate the probability that a polynomial in $\mathbb{F}_{q^2}[X]$ of degree $3D$ is $\lceil \frac{D}{2} \rceil$-smooth. For any prime power q and integers $1 \le m \le n$, we denote by $N_q(m, n)$ the number of m-smooth monic polynomials of degree n. Using analytic methods, Panario et al. gave a precise estimate of this quantity (Theorem 1 of [19]):

$$N_q(n, m) = q^n \rho\left(\frac{n}{m}\right)\left(1 + O\left(\frac{\log n}{m}\right)\right),\tag{4}$$

where ρ is Dickman's function defined as the unique continuous function such that $\rho(u) = 1$ on $[0, 1]$ and $u\rho'(u) = \rho(u - 1)$ for $u > 1$. We stress that the constant κ hidden in the $O()$ notation is independent of q. In our case, we are interested in the value of $N_{q^2}(3D, \lceil \frac{D}{2} \rceil)$. Let us call D_0 the least integer such that $1 + \kappa\left(\frac{\log(3D)}{\lceil D/2 \rceil}\right)$ is at least $1/2$. For $D > D_0$, we will use the formula (4); and for $D \le D_0$, we will use the crude estimate $N_q(n, m) \ge N_q(n, 1) = q^n/n!$. Hence the smoothness probability of $\mathcal{L}_m$ is at least $\min\left(\frac{1}{2}\rho(6), 1/(3D_0)!\right)$.

More generally, if $\deg h_0$ and $\deg h_1$ are bounded by a constant δ then we have a smoothness probability of $\rho(2\delta + 2)$ times an absolute constant. Since we have $q^3 + q$ candidates and a constant probability of success, $H(P)$ has $\Theta(q^3)$ rows.

Now, unless some theoretical obstruction occurs, we expect a matrix over $\mathbb{F}_\ell$ to have full rank with probability at least $1 - \frac{1}{\ell}$. The matrix $\mathcal{H}$ is however peculiar, and does enjoy regularity properties which are worth noticing. For instance, we have the following proposition.

Proposition 9. *Let ℓ be a prime not dividing $q^3 - q$. Then the matrix $\mathcal{H}$ over $\mathbb{F}_\ell$ has full rank $q^2 + 1$.*

Proof. We may obtain this result in two ways. First, $\mathcal{H}$ is the incidence matrix of a $3 - (q^2 + 1, q + 1, 1)$ combinatorial design called *inversive plane* (see e.g. [21, Theorem 9.27]). As such we obtain the identity

$$\mathcal{H}^T \mathcal{H} = (q + 1)(J_{q^2+1} - (1 - q)I_{q^2+1})$$

(see [21, Theorem 1.13 and Corollary 9.6]), where J_n is the $n \times n$ matrix with all entries equal to one, and I_n is the $n \times n$ identity matrix. This readily gives the result exactly as announced.

We also provide an elementary proof of the Proposition. We have a bijection between rows of $\mathcal{H}$ and the different possible image sets of the projective line $\mathbb{P}^1(\mathbb{F}_q)$ within $\mathbb{P}^1(\mathbb{F}_{q^2})$, under injections of the form $(\alpha : \beta) \mapsto m^{-1} \cdot (\alpha : \beta)$. All these $q^3 + q$ image sets have size $q + 1$, and by symmetry all points of $\mathbb{P}^1(\mathbb{F}_{q^2})$ are reached equally often. Therefore, the sum of all rows of $\mathcal{H}$ is the vector whose coordinates are all equal to $\frac{1}{1+q^2}(q^3 + q)(q + 1) = q^2 + q$.

Let us now consider the sum of the rows in $\mathcal{H}$ whose first coordinate is 1 (as we have just shown, we have $q^2 + q$ such rows). Those correspond to image sets of $\mathbb{P}^1(\mathbb{F}_q)$ which contain one particular point, say $(0 : 1)$. The value of the sum for any other coordinate indexed by e.g. $Q \in \mathbb{P}^1(\mathbb{F}_{q^2})$ is the number of image sets $m^{-1} \cdot \mathbb{P}^1(\mathbb{F}_q)$ which contain both $(0 : 1)$ and Q, which we prove is equal to $q + 1$ as follows. Without loss of generality, we may assume $Q = \infty = (1 : 0)$. We need to count the relevant homographies $m^{-1} \in \mathrm{PGL}_2(\mathbb{F}_{q^2})$, modulo $\mathrm{PGL}_2(\mathbb{F}_q)$-equivalence $m \equiv hm$. By $\mathrm{PGL}_2(\mathbb{F}_q)$-equivalence, we may without loss of generality assume that m^{-1} fixes $(0 : 1)$ and $(1 : 0)$. Letting $m^{-1} = \begin{pmatrix} a & b \\ c & d \end{pmatrix}$, we obtain $(b : d) = (0 : 1)$ and $(a : c) = (1 : 0)$, whence $b = c = 0$, and both $a, d \neq 0$. We may normalize to $d = 1$, and notice that multiplication of a by a scalar in $\mathbb{F}_q^*$ is absorbed in $\mathrm{PGL}_2(\mathbb{F}_q)$-equivalence. Therefore the number of suitable m is $\#\mathbb{F}_{q^2}^*/\mathbb{F}_q^* = q + 1$.

These two facts show that the row span of $\mathcal{H}$ contains the vectors $(q^2 + q, \ldots, q^2 + q)$ and $(q^2 + q, q + 1, \ldots, q + 1)$. The vector $(q^3 - q, 0, \ldots, 0)$ is obtained as a linear combination of these two vectors, which suffices to prove that $\mathcal{H}$ has full rank, since the same reasoning holds for any coordinate. $\qquad\square$

Proposition 9, while encouraging, is clearly not sufficient. We are, at the moment, unable to provide a proof of a more useful statement. On the experimental side, it is reasonably easy to sample arbitrary subsets of the rows of $\mathcal{H}$ and check for their rank. To this end, we propose the following experiment. We have considered small values of q in the range $[16, \ldots, 64]$, and made 50 random picks of

Table 1. Prime factors appearing in determinant of random square submatrices of $\mathcal{H}$ (for one given set of random trials)

q	#trials	in gcd($\{\delta_i\}$)	in gcd(δ_i, δ_j)	q	#trials	in gcd($\{\delta_i\}$)	in gcd(δ_i, δ_j)
16	50	17	691	37	50	2, 19	2879
17	50	2, 3	431, 691	41	50	2, 3, 7	none above q^2
19	50	2, 5	none above q^2	43	50	2, 11	none above q^2
23	50	2, 3	none above q^2	47	50	2, 3	none above q^2
25	50	2, 13	none above q^2	49	50	2, 5	none above q^2
27	50	2, 7	1327	53	50	2, 3	none above q^2
29	50	2, 3, 5	none above q^2	59	50	2, 3, 5	none above q^2
31	50	2	1303, 3209	61	50	2, 31	none above q^2
32	50	3, 11	none above q^2	64	50	5, 13	none above q^2

subsets $S_i \subset \mathcal{P}_q$, all of size exactly $q^2 + 1$. For each we considered the matrix of the corresponding linear system, which is made of selected rows of the matrix $\mathcal{H}$, and computed its determinant δ_i. For all values of q considered, we have observed the following facts.

– First, all square matrices considered had full rank over $\mathbb{Z}$. Furthermore, their determinants had no common factor apart possibly from those appearing in the factorization of $q^3 - q$ as predicted by Proposition 9. In fact, experimentally it seems that only the factors of $q + 1$ are causing problems.
– We also explored the possibility that modulo some primes, the determinant could vanish with non-negligible probability. We thus computed the pairwise GCD of all 50 determinants computed, for each q. Again, the only prime factors appearing in the GCDs were either originating from the factorization of $q^3 - q$, or sporadically from the birthday paradox.

These results are summarized in table 1, where the last column omits small prime factors below q^2. Of course, we remark that considering square submatrices is a more demanding check than what Heuristic 7 suggests, since our algorithm only needs a slightly larger matrix of size $\Theta(q^3) \times (q^2 + 1)$ to have full rank.

A second line of justification is more direct and natural, as it is possible to implement the algorithm outlined in Section 4, and verify that it does provide the desired result. A MAGMA implementation validates this claim, and has been used to implement descent steps for an example field of degree 53 over $\mathbb{F}_{53^2}$. An example step in this context is given for applying our algorithm to a polynomial of degree 10, attempting to reduce it to polynomials of degree 6 or less. Among the 148,930 elements of $\mathcal{P}_q$, it sufficed to consider only 71,944 matrices m, of which about 3.9% led to relations, for a minimum sufficient number of relations equal to $q^2 + 1 = 2810$ (as more than half of the elements of $\mathcal{P}_q$ had not even been examined at this point, it is clear that getting more relations was easy— we did not have to). As the defining polynomial for the finite field considered was constructed with $\delta = \deg h_{0,1} = 1$, all left-hand sides involved had degree 20. The polynomials appearing in their factorizations had the following degrees (the number in brackets give the number of distinct polynomials found for each degree): 1(2098), 2(2652), 3(2552), 4(2463), 5(2546), 6(2683). Of course this tiny example size uses no optimization, and is only intended to check the validity of Proposition 2.

As for Heuristic 8, it is already present in [16] and [10], so this is not a new heuristic. Just like for Heuristic 7, it is based on the fact that the probability that a left-hand side is 1-smooth and yields a relation is constant. Therefore, we have a system with $\Theta(q^3)$ relations between $O(q^2)$ indeterminates, and it seems reasonable to expect that it has full rank. On the other hand, there is not as much algebraic structure in the linear system as in Heuristic 7, so that we see no way to support this heuristic apart from testing it on several inputs. This was already done (including for record computations) in [16] and [10], so we do not elaborate on our own experiments that confirm again that Heuristic 8 seems to be valid except for tiny values of q.

An obstruction to the heuristics. As noted by Cheng, Wan and Zhuang [5], the irreducible factors of $h_1 X^q - h_0$ other than the degree k factor that is used to define $\mathbb{F}_{q^{2k}}$ are problematic. Let P be such a problematic polynomial. The fact that it divides the defining equation implies that it also divides the $\mathcal{L}_m$ quantity that is involved when trying to build a relation that relates P to other polynomials. Therefore the first part of Proposition 2 can not hold for this P. Similarly, if P is linear, its presence will prevent the second part of Proposition 2 to hold since the logarithm of P can not be found with the strategy of Section 4. We present here a technique to deal with the problematic polynomials. (The authors of [5] proposed another solution to keep the quasi-polynomial nature of algorithm.)

Proposition 10. *For each problematic polynomial P of degree D, we can find a linear relation between $\log P$, $\log h_1$ and $O(D)$ logarithms of polynomials of degree at most $(\delta - 1)D$ which are not problematic.*

Proof. Let P be an irreducible factor of $h_1 X^q - h_0$ of degree D. Let us consider P^q; by reducing modulo $h_1 X^q - h_0$ and clearing denominators, there exists a polynomial $A(X)$ such that

$$h_1^D P^q = h_1^D \tilde{P}\left(\frac{h_0}{h_1}\right) + (h_1 X^q - h_0)A(X). \tag{5}$$

Since P divides two of the terms of this equality, it must also divide the third one, namely the polynomial $\mathcal{R} = h_1^D \tilde{P}(h_0/h_1)$. Let $v_P \geq 1$ be the valuation of P in $\mathcal{R}$. In the finite field $\mathbb{F}_{q^{2k}}$ we obtain the following equalities between logarithms:

$$(q - v_P) \log P = -D \log h_1 + \sum_i e_i \log Q_i,$$

where Q_i are the irreducible factors of $\mathcal{R}$ other than P and e_i their valuation in $\mathcal{R}$. A polynomial Q_i can not be problematic. Otherwise, it would divide the right-hand side of Equation (5), and therefore, also the left-hand side, which is impossible. Since $v_P \leq \frac{\deg \mathcal{R}}{\deg P} \leq \delta < q$, the quantity $q - v_P$ is invertible modulo ℓ (we assume, as usual that ℓ is larger than q) and we obtain a relation between

$\log P$, $\log h_1$ and the logarithms of the non-problematic polynomials Q_i. The degree of $\mathcal{R}/P^{v_P}$ is at most $(\delta - 1)D$, which gives the claimed bound on the degrees of the Q_i.   □

If $\delta \leq 2$, this proposition solves the issues raised by [5] about problematic polynomials. Indeed, for each problematic polynomial of degree $D > 1$, it will be possible to rewrite its logarithm in terms of logarithms of non-problematic polynomials of at most the same degree that can be descended in the usual way. Similarly, each problematic polynomial of degree 1 can have its logarithm rewritten in terms of the logarithms of other non-problematic linear polynomials. Adding these relations to the ones obtained in Section 4, we expect to have a full-rank linear system.

If $\delta > 2$, we need to rely on the additional heuristic. Indeed, when descending the Q_i that have a degree potentially larger than the degree of D, we could hit again the problematic polynomial we started with, and it could be that the coefficients in front of $\log P$ in the system vanishes. More generally, taking into account all the problematic polynomials, if when we apply Proposition 10 to them we get polynomials Q_i of higher degrees, it could be that descending those we creates loops so that the logarithms of some of the problematic polynomials could not be computed. We expect this event to be very unlikely. Since in all our experiments it was always possible to obtain $\delta = 2$, we did not investigate further.

Finding appropriate h_0 and h_1. One key fact about the algorithm is the existence of two polynomials h_0 and h_1 in $\mathbb{F}_{q^2}[X]$ such that $h_1(X)X^q - h_0(X)$ has an irreducible factor of degree k. A partial solution is due to Joux [16] who showed how to construct such polynomials when $k \in \{q - 1, q, q + 1\}$. No such deterministic construction is known in the general case, but experiments show that one can apparently choose h_0 and h_1 of degree at most 2. We performed an experiment for every odd prime power q in $[3, \ldots, 1000]$ and every $k \leq q$ and found that we could select $a \in \mathbb{F}_{q^2}$ such that $X^q + X^2 + a$ has an irreducible factor of degree k. Finally, note that the result is similar to a commonly made heuristic in discrete logarithm algorithms: for fixed $f \in \mathbb{F}_{q^2}[X, Y]$ and random $g \in \mathbb{F}_{q^2}[X, Y]$, the polynomial $\mathrm{Res}_Y(f, g)$ behaves as a random polynomial of same degree with respect to the degrees of its irreducible factors.

6   Some Directions of Improvement

The algorithm can be modified in several ways. On the one hand one can obtain a better complexity if one proves a stronger result on the smoothness probability. On the other hand, without changing the complexity, one can obtain a version which should behave better in practice.

6.1   Complexity Improvement

Heuristic 7 tells that a rectangular matrix with $\Theta(q)$ times more rows than columns has full rank. It seems reasonable to expect that only a constant times more rows than columns would be enough to get the full rank properties (as is suggested by the experiments proposed in Section 5). Then, it means that we expect to have a lot of choices to select the best relations, in the sense that their left-hand sides split into irreducible factors of degrees as small as possible.

On average, we expect to be able to try $\Theta(q)$ relations for each row of the matrix. So, assuming that the numerators of $\mathcal{L}_m$ behave like random polynomials of similar degrees, we have to evaluate the expected smoothness that we can hope for after trying $\Theta(q)$ polynomials of degree $(1 + \delta)D$ over $\mathbb{F}_{q^2}$. Set $u = \log q / \log \log q$, so that $u^u \approx q$. According to [19] it is then possible to replace $\lceil D/2 \rceil$ in Proposition 2 by the value $O(D \log \log q / \log q)$.

Then, the discussion leading to Theorem 3 can be changed to take this faster descent into account. We keep the same estimate for the arity of each node in the tree, but the depth is now only in $\log k / \log \log q$. Since this depth ends up in the exponent, the resulting complexity in Theorem 3 is then

$$\max(q, k)^{O(\log k / \log \log q)}.$$

6.2   Practical Improvements

Because of the arity of the descent tree, the breadth eventually exceeds the number of polynomials below some degree bound. It makes no sense, therefore, to use the descent procedure beyond this point, as the recovery of discrete logarithms of all these polynomials is better achieved as a pre-computation. Note that this corresponds to the computations of the $L(1/4 + \epsilon)$ algorithm which starts by pre-computing the logarithms of polynomials up to degree 2. In our case, we could in principle go up to degree $O(\log q)$ without changing the complexity.

We propose another practical improvement in the case where we would like to spend more time descending a given polynomial P in order to improve the quality of the descent tree rooted at P. The set of polynomials appearing in the right-hand side of Equation (E_m) in Section 4 is $\{P - \lambda\}$, because in the factorization of $X^q - X$, we substitute X with $m \cdot P$ for homographies m. In fact, we may apply m to $(P : P_1)$ for any polynomial P_1 whose degree does not exceed that of P. In the right-hand sides, we will have only factors of form $P - \lambda P_1$ for λ in $\mathbb{F}_{q^2}$. On the left-hand sides, we have polynomials of the same degree as before, so that the smoothness probability is expected to be the same. Nevertheless, it is possible to test several P_1 polynomials, and to select the one that leads to the best tree.

This strategy can also be useful in the following context (which will not occur for large enough q): it can happen that for some triples (q, D, D') one has $N_{q^2}(3D, D')/q^n \approx 1/q$. In this case we have no certainty that we can descend a degree-D polynomial to degree D', but we can hope that at least one of the P_1 allows to descend.

Finally, if one decides to use several auxiliary P_1 polynomials to descend a polynomial P, it might be interesting to take a set of polynomials P_1 with an arithmetic structure, so that the smoothness tests on the left-hand sides can benefit from a sieving technique.

7   Conclusion

The algorithm presented in this article achieves a significant improvement of the asymptotic complexity of discrete logarithm in finite fields, in almost the whole range of parameters where the Function Field Sieve was presently the most competitive algorithm. Compared to existing approaches, and in particular to the line of recent works [15,10], the practical relevance of our algorithm is not clear, and will be explored by further work.

We note that the analysis of the algorithm presented here is heuristic, as discussed in Section 5. Some of the heuristics we stated, related to the properties of matrices $H(P)$ extracted from the matrix $\mathcal{H}$, seem accessible to more solid justification. It seems plausible to have the validity of algorithm rely on the sole heuristic of the validity of the smoothness estimates.

The crossing point between the $L(1/4)$ algorithm and our quasi-polynomial one is not determined yet. One of the key factors which hinders the practical efficiency of this algorithm is the $O(q^2 D)$ arity of the descent tree, compared to the $O(q)$ arity achieved by techniques based on Gröbner bases [15] at the expense of a $L(1/4 + \epsilon)$ complexity. Adj et al. [1] proposed to mix the two algorithms and deduced that the new descent technique must be used for cryptographic sizes. Indeed, by estimating the time required to compute discrete logarithms in $\mathbb{F}_{3^{6\cdot509}}$, they showed the weakness of some pairing-based cryptosystems.

Acknowledgements. The authors would like to thank Daniel J. Bernstein for his comments on an earlier version of this work, and for pointing out to us the possible use of asymptotically fast linear algebra for solving the linear systems encountered.

References

1. Adj, G., Menezes, A., Oliveira, T., Rodríguez-Henríquez, F.: Weakness of $\mathbb{F}_{3^{6\cdot509}}$ for discrete logarithm cryptography. In: Cao, Z., Zhang, F. (eds.) Pairing 2013. LNCS, vol. 8365, pp. 20–44. Springer, Heidelberg (2014)
2. Adleman, L.: A subexponential algorithm for the discrete logarithm problem with applications to cryptography. In: 20th Annual Symposium on Foundations of Computer Science, pp. 55–60. IEEE (1979)
3. Adleman, L.: The function field sieve. In: Huang, M.-D.A., Adleman, L.M. (eds.) ANTS 1994. LNCS, vol. 877, pp. 108–121. Springer, Heidelberg (1994)
4. Blake, I.F., Fuji-Hara, R., Mullin, R.C., Vanstone, S.A.: Computing logarithms in finite fields of characteristic two. SIAM J. Alg. Disc. Meth. 5(2), 276–285 (1984)
5. Cheng, Q., Wan, D., Zhuang, J.: Traps to the BGJT-algorithm for discrete logarithms. Cryptology ePrint Archive, Report 2013/673 (2013),
   http://eprint.iacr.org/2013/673/
6. Coppersmith, D.: Fast evaluation of logarithms in fields of characteristic two. IEEE Transactions on Information Theory 30(4), 587–594 (1984)
7. Diffie, W., Hellman, M.: New directions in cryptography. IEEE Transactions on Information Theory 22(6), 644–654 (1976)

8. Göloglu, F., Granger, R., McGuire, G., Zumbrägel, J.: Discrete logarithm in GF(2^{1971}) (February 2013), Announcement to the NMBRTHRY list
9. Göloglu, F., Granger, R., McGuire, G., Zumbrägel, J.: Discrete logarithm in GF(2^{6120}) (April 2013), Announcement to the NMBRTHRY list
10. Göloğlu, F., Granger, R., McGuire, G., Zumbrägel, J.: On the Function Field Sieve and the Impact of Higher Splitting Probabilities. In: Canetti, R., Garay, J.A. (eds.) CRYPTO 2013, Part II. LNCS, vol. 8043, pp. 109–128. Springer, Heidelberg (2013)
11. Gordon, D.M.: Discrete logarithms in GF(p) using the number field sieve. SIAM Journal on Discrete Mathematics 6(1), 124–138 (1993)
12. Joux, A.: Discrete logarithm in GF(2^{1778}) (February 2013), Announcement to the NMBRTHRY list
13. Joux, A.: Discrete logarithm in GF(2^{4080}) (March 2013), Announcement to the NMBRTHRY list
14. Joux, A.: Discrete logarithm in GF(2^{6168}) (May 2013), Announcement to the NMBRTHRY list
15. Joux, A.: Faster index calculus for the medium prime case application to 1175-bit and 1425-bit finite fields. In: Johansson, T., Nguyen, P.Q. (eds.) EUROCRYPT 2013. LNCS, vol. 7881, pp. 177–193. Springer, Heidelberg (2013)
16. Joux, A.: A new index calculus algorithm with complexity L(1/4 + o(1)) in very small characteristic. Cryptology ePrint Archive, Report 2013/095 (2013)
17. Joux, A., Lercier, R.: The function field sieve in the medium prime case. In: Vaudenay, S. (ed.) EUROCRYPT 2006. LNCS, vol. 4004, pp. 254–270. Springer, Heidelberg (2006)
18. Joux, A., Lercier, R., Smart, N., Vercauteren, F.: The number field sieve in the medium prime case. In: Dwork, C. (ed.) CRYPTO 2006. LNCS, vol. 4117, pp. 326–344. Springer, Heidelberg (2006)
19. Panario, D., Gourdon, X., Flajolet, P.: An analytic approach to smooth polynomials over finite fields. In: Buhler, J.P. (ed.) ANTS 1998. LNCS, vol. 1423, pp. 226–236. Springer, Heidelberg (1998)
20. Pohlig, S., Hellman, M.: An improved algorithm for computing logarithms over GF(p) and its cryptographic signifiance. IEEE Transactions on Information Theory 24(1), 106–110 (1978)
21. Stinson, D.R.: Combinatorial designs: constructions and analysis. Springer (2003)

Polynomial Time Attack on Wild McEliece over Quadratic Extensions

Alain Couvreur[1], Ayoub Otmani[2], and Jean–Pierre Tillich[3]

[1] GRACE Project — INRIA Saclay & LIX, CNRS UMR 7161 — École
Polytechnique, 91120 Palaiseau Cedex, France
alain.couvreur@lix.polytechnique.fr
[2] Normandie Univ, France, UR, LITIS, F-76821 Mont-Saint-Aignan, France
ayoub.otmani@univ-rouen.fr
[3] SECRET Project — INRIA Rocquencourt, 78153 Le Chesnay Cedex, France
jean-pierre.tillich@inria.fr

Abstract. We present a polynomial time structural attack against the
McEliece system based on Wild Goppa codes from a quadratic finite field
extension. This attack uses the fact that such codes can be distinguished
from random codes to compute some filtration, that is to say a family of
nested subcodes which will reveal their secret algebraic description.

Keywords: public-key cryptography, wild McEliece cryptosystem,
filtration, cryptanalysis.

1 Introduction

The McEliece Cryptosystem and its Security. The McEliece encryption
scheme [35] which dates backs to the end of the seventies still belongs to the
very few public-key cryptosystems which remain unbroken. It is based on the
famous Goppa codes family. Several proposals which suggested to replace binary Goppa codes with alternative families did not meet a similar fate. They
all focus on a specific class of codes equipped with a decoding algorithm: generalized Reed–Solomon codes (GRS for short) [38] or subcodes of them [4],
Reed–Muller codes [43], algebraic geometry codes [22], LDPC and MDPC codes
[2,37] or convolutional codes [28]. Most of them were successfully cryptanalyzed
[44,48,36,19,39,13,24,14]. Each time a description of the underlying code suitable for decoding is efficiently obtained. But some of them remain unbroken,
namely those relying on MDPC codes [37] and their cousins [2], the original
binary Goppa codes of [35] and their non-binary variants as proposed in [6,7].

Concerning the security of the McEliece proposal based on Goppa codes,
weak keys were identified in [21,27] but they can be easily avoided. There also
exist generic attacks by exponential decoding algorithms [25,26,45,10,5,34,3].
More recently, it was shown in [18,20] that the secret structure of Goppa codes
can be recovered by an algebraic attack using Gröbner bases. This attack is
of exponential nature and is infeasible for the original McEliece scheme (the
number of unknowns is linear in the length of the code), whereas for variants

P.Q. Nguyen and E. Oswald (Eds.): EUROCRYPT 2014, LNCS 8441, pp. 17–39, 2014.

using Goppa codes with a quasi-dyadic or quasi-cyclic structure it was feasible due to the huge reduction of the number of unknowns.

Distinguisher for Goppa and Reed-Solomon Codes. None of the existing strategies is able to severely dent the security of [35] when appropriate parameters are taken. Consequently, it has even been advocated that the generator matrix of a Goppa code does not disclose any visible structure that an attacker could exploit. This is strengthened by the fact that Goppa codes share many characteristics with random codes. However, in [16,17], an algorithm that manages to distinguish between a random code and a high rate Goppa code has been introduced.

Code Product. [33] showed that the distinguisher given in [16] has an equivalent but simpler description in terms of component-wise product of codes. This product allows in particular to define the square of a code; This can be used to distinguish a high rate Goppa code from a random one because the dimension of the square of the dual is much smaller than the one obtained with a random code. The notion of component-wise product of codes was first put forward to unify many different algebraic decoding algorithms [40,23], then exploited in cryptology in [48] to break a McEliece variant based on random subcodes of GRS codes [4] and in [30,32] to study the security of encryption schemes using algebraic-geometric codes. Component-wise powers of codes are also studied in the context of secret sharing and secure multi-party computation [11,12].

Distinguisher-Based Key-Recovery Attacks. The works [16,17], without undermining the security of [35], prompts to wonder whether it would be possible to devise an attack exploiting the distinguisher. That was indeed the case in [13] for McEliece-like public-key encryption schemes relying on modified GRS codes [8,1,47]. Additionnally, [13] has shown that the unusually low dimension of the square code of a generalized GRS code enables to compute a nested sequence of subcodes – we call this a filtration – allowing the recovery of its algebraic structure. This gives a completely different attack from [44] of breaking GRS-based encryption schemes. In particular, compared to the attack of [44] on GRS codes and to the attack of [36,19] on binary Reed–Muller codes and low-genus algebraic geometry codes, this new way of cryptanalyzing does not require as a first step the computation of minimum weight codewords, which is polynomial in time only for the very specific case of GRS codes.

Our Contribution. The purpose of this article is to show that the filtration attack of [13] which gave a new way of attacking a McEliece scheme based on GRS codes can be generalized to other families of codes. It leads for instance to a successful attack of McEliece based on high genus algebraic geometry codes [14]. A tantalizing project would be to attack Goppa code based McEliece schemes, or more generally alternant code based schemes. The latter family of codes are subfield subcodes defined over some field $\mathbb{F}_q$ of GRS codes defined over a field extension $\mathbb{F}_{q^m}$. Even the smallest field extension, that is $m = 2$, for which these subfield subcodes are not GRS codes is a completely open question. Codes of this kind have indeed been proposed as possible improvements of the original

McEliece scheme, under the form of wild Goppa codes in [6]. Such codes are Goppa codes associated to polynomials of the form γ^{q-1} where γ is irreducible. Notice that all irreducible binary Goppa codes of the original McEliece system are actually wild Goppa codes. Interestingly enough, it turns out that these wild Goppa codes for $m = 2$ can be distinguished from random codes for a very large range of parameters by observing that the square code of some of their shortenings have an abnormally small dimension.

We show here that this distinguishing property can be used to compute a filtration of the public code, that is to say a family of nested subcodes of the public Goppa code. This filtration can in turn be used to recover the algebraic description of the Goppa code as an alternant code, which yields an efficient key recovery attack. This attack has been implemented in Magma [9] and allowed to break completely all the schemes with a claimed 128 bit security in Table 7.1 of [6] corresponding to $m = 2$ when the degree of γ is larger than 3. This corresponds precisely to the case where these codes can be distinguished from random codes by square code considerations. The filtration attack has a polynomial time complexity and basically boils down to linear algebra. This is the first time in the 35 years of existence of the McEliece scheme based on Goppa codes that a polynomial time attack has been found on it. It questions the common belief that GRS codes are weak for a cryptographic use while Goppa codes are secure as soon as $m \geqslant 2$ and that for the latter only generic information-set-decoding attacks apply. It also raises the issue whether this algebraic distinguisher of Goppa and more generally alternant codes (see [17]) based on square code considerations can be turned into an attack in the other cases where it applies (for instance for Goppa codes of rate close enough to 1). Finally, it is worth pointing out that our attack works against codes without external symmetries confirming that the mere appearance of randomness is far from being enough to defend codes against algebraic attacks.

Note that due to space constraints, the results are given here without proofs. For more details we refer to a forthcoming paper.

2   Notation, Definitions and Prerequisites

We introduce in this section notation we will use in the sequel. We assume that the reader is familiar with notions from coding theory. We refer to [29] for the terminology.

Star Product. Vectors and matrices are respectively denoted in bold letters and bold capital letters such as $\boldsymbol{a}$ and $\boldsymbol{A}$. We always denote the entries of a vector $\boldsymbol{u} \in \mathbb{F}_q^n$ by $u_0, \ldots, u_{n-1}$. Given a subset $\mathcal{I} \subset \{0, \ldots, n-1\}$, we denote by $\boldsymbol{u}_{\mathcal{I}}$ the vector $\boldsymbol{u}$ *punctured* at $\mathcal{I}$, that is to say, *indexes that are in $\mathcal{I}$ are removed*. When $\mathcal{I} = \{j\}$ we allow ourselves to write $\boldsymbol{u}_j$ instead of $\boldsymbol{u}_{\{j\}}$. The component-wise product $\boldsymbol{u} \star \boldsymbol{v}$ of two vectors $\boldsymbol{u}, \boldsymbol{v} \in \mathbb{F}_q^n$ is defined as: $\boldsymbol{u} \star \boldsymbol{v} \stackrel{\text{def}}{=} (u_0 v_0, \ldots, u_{n-1} v_{n-1})$. The i–th power $\boldsymbol{u} \star \cdots \star \boldsymbol{u}$ is denoted by $\boldsymbol{u}^i$. When every entry u_i of $\boldsymbol{u}$ is nonzero, we denote by $\boldsymbol{u}^{-1} \stackrel{\text{def}}{=} (u_0^{-1}, \ldots, u_{n-1}^{-1})$, and more generally for all i, we define $\boldsymbol{u}^{-i}$

in the same manner. The operation $\star$ has an identity element, which is nothing but the all-ones vector $(1, \ldots, 1)$ denoted by $\mathbf{1}$. To a vector $\boldsymbol{x} \in \mathbb{F}_q^n$, we associate the set $\mathcal{L}_{\boldsymbol{x}} \overset{\text{def}}{=} \{x_i \mid i \in \{0, \ldots, n-1\}\}$ which is defined as the set of entries of $\boldsymbol{x}$. We always have $|\mathcal{L}_{\boldsymbol{x}}| \leqslant n$ and equality holds when the entries of $\boldsymbol{x}$ are pair-wise distinct.

The ring of polynomials with coefficients in $\mathbb{F}_q$ is denoted by $\mathbb{F}_q[z]$, while the subspace of $\mathbb{F}_q[z]$ of polynomials of degree less than t is denoted by $\mathbb{F}_q[z]_{<t}$. For every polynomial $P \in \mathbb{F}_q[z]$, $P(\boldsymbol{u})$ stands for $(P(u_0), \ldots, P(u_{n-1}))$. In particular for all $a, b \in \mathbb{F}_q$, $a\boldsymbol{u} + b$ is the vector $(au_0 + b, \ldots, au_{n-1} + b)$. To each vector $\boldsymbol{x} = (x_0, \ldots, x_{n-1}) \in \mathbb{F}_q^n$, we associate its *locator polynomial* denoted as $\pi_{\boldsymbol{x}}$ and defined as $\pi_{\boldsymbol{x}}(z) \overset{\text{def}}{=} \prod_{i=0}^{n-1}(z - x_i)$. Its first derivative is denoted as $\pi'_{\boldsymbol{x}}$ and one shows easily that its evaluation at the entries of $\boldsymbol{x}$ yields the vector
$$\pi'_{\boldsymbol{x}}(\boldsymbol{x}) = \left(\prod_{j \neq i}(x_i - x_j) \right)_{0 \leqslant i < n}.$$

The *norm* and *trace* from $\mathbb{F}_{q^2}$ to $\mathbb{F}_q$ when applied to any $\boldsymbol{x} \in \mathbb{F}_{q^2}^n$ are respectively $N(\boldsymbol{x})$ and $\operatorname{Tr}(\boldsymbol{x})$ with by definition $N(\boldsymbol{x}) \overset{\text{def}}{=} \left(x_0^{q+1}, \ldots, x_{n-1}^{q+1} \right)$ and $\operatorname{Tr}(\boldsymbol{x}) \overset{\text{def}}{=} \left(x_0^q + x_0, \ldots, x_{n-1}^q + x_{n-1} \right)$.

Shortening and Puncturing Codes. For a given code $\mathscr{D} \subset \mathbb{F}_q^n$ and a subset $\mathcal{I} \subset \{0, \ldots, n-1\}$ the *punctured* code $\mathscr{D}_{\mathcal{I}}$ and *shortened* code $\mathscr{D}^{\mathcal{I}}$ are defined as:
$$\mathscr{D}_{\mathcal{I}} \overset{\text{def}}{=} \{(c_i)_{i \notin \mathcal{I}} \mid \boldsymbol{c} \in \mathscr{D}\};$$
$$\mathscr{D}^{\mathcal{I}} \overset{\text{def}}{=} \{(c_i)_{i \notin \mathcal{I}} \mid \exists \boldsymbol{c} = (c_i)_i \in \mathscr{D} \text{ such that } \forall i \in \mathcal{I}, \ c_i = 0\}.$$

Instead of writing $\mathscr{D}_{\{j\}}$ and $\mathscr{D}^{\{j\}}$ when $\mathcal{I} = \{j\}$ we rather use the notation $\mathscr{D}_j$ and $\mathscr{D}^j$. The following classical results will be used repeatedly.

Lemma 1. *Let $\mathscr{A} \subset \mathbb{F}_q^n$ be a code and $\mathcal{I} \subset \{0, \ldots, n-1\}$ be a set of positions. Then,*
$$\left(\mathscr{A}^{\mathcal{I}} \right)^{\perp} = \mathscr{A}_{\mathcal{I}}^{\perp} \quad \text{and} \quad \left(\mathscr{A}_{\mathcal{I}} \right)^{\perp} = \left(\mathscr{A}^{\perp} \right)^{\mathcal{I}}.$$

Diagonal Equivalence of Codes. Two q-ary codes $\mathscr{A}, \mathscr{B} \subset \mathbb{F}_q^n$ are said to be $\mathbb{F}_q$-*diagonally equivalent*, and we will write $\mathscr{B} \sim_{\mathbb{F}_q} \mathscr{A}$, if there exists $\boldsymbol{u} \in \left(\mathbb{F}_q^{\times} \right)^n$ such that:
$$\mathscr{B} = \boldsymbol{u} \star \mathscr{A} = \{\boldsymbol{u} \star \boldsymbol{a} \mid \boldsymbol{a} \in \mathscr{A}\}.$$

It is equivalent to say that $\mathscr{A}$ and $\mathscr{B}$ are $\mathbb{F}_q$-equivalent if $\mathscr{B}$ is the image of $\mathscr{A}$ by an invertible diagonal matrix whose diagonal is $\boldsymbol{u}$.

Generalized Reed–Solomon, Alternant and Classical Goppa Codes

Definition 1 (Generalized Reed-Solomon code). *Let q be a prime power and k, n be integers such that $1 \leqslant k < n \leqslant q$. Let $\boldsymbol{x}$ and $\boldsymbol{y}$ be two n-tuples such that the entries of $\boldsymbol{x}$ are pairwise distinct elements of $\mathbb{F}_q$ and those of $\boldsymbol{y}$*

are nonzero elements in $\mathbb{F}_q$. The generalized Reed-Solomon code $\mathbf{GRS}_k(\boldsymbol{x}, \boldsymbol{y})$ of dimension k associated to $(\boldsymbol{x}, \boldsymbol{y})$ is the k-dimensional vector space

$$\mathbf{GRS}_k(\boldsymbol{x}, \boldsymbol{y}) \overset{def}{=} \left\{ \left(y_0 p(x_0), \ldots, y_{n-1} p(x_{n-1}) \right) \ \big| \ p \in \mathbb{F}_q[z]_{<k} \right\}.$$

Reed-Solomon codes correspond to the case where $y_i = 1$ for all $i \in \{0, \ldots, n-1\}$ and are denoted as $\mathbf{RS}_k(\boldsymbol{x})$. The vector $\boldsymbol{x}$ is called the support *of the code.*

Proposition 1. *Let $\boldsymbol{x}, \boldsymbol{y}$ be as in Definition 1. Then,*

$$\mathbf{GRS}_k(\boldsymbol{x}, \boldsymbol{y})^\perp = \mathbf{GRS}_{n-k}(\boldsymbol{x}, \boldsymbol{y}^{-1} \star \pi'_{\boldsymbol{x}}(\boldsymbol{x})^{-1}).$$

This leads to the definition of alternant codes ([29, Chap. 12, §2]).

Definition 2 (Alternant code). *Let $\boldsymbol{x}, \boldsymbol{y} \in \mathbb{F}_{q^m}^n$ be two vectors such that the entries of $\boldsymbol{x}$ are pairwise distinct and those of $\boldsymbol{y}$ are all nonzero. The* alternant code $\mathscr{A}_r(\boldsymbol{x}, \boldsymbol{y})$ *defined over $\mathbb{F}_q$ where $\boldsymbol{x}, \boldsymbol{y} \in \mathbb{F}_{q^m}^n$ is the subfield subcode over $\mathbb{F}_q$ of the code $\mathbf{GRS}_r(\boldsymbol{x}, \boldsymbol{y})^\perp$ defined over $\mathbb{F}_{q^m}$, that is:*

$$\mathscr{A}_r(\boldsymbol{x}, \boldsymbol{y}) \overset{def}{=} \mathbf{GRS}_r(\boldsymbol{x}, \boldsymbol{y})^\perp \cap \mathbb{F}_q^n.$$

The integer r is referred to as the degree *of the alternant code, the integer m as its* extension degree *and the vector $\boldsymbol{x}$ as its* support.

From this definition, it is clear that alternant codes inherit the decoding algorithms of the underlying GRS codes. The key feature of an alternant code is the following fact (see [29, Chap. 12, §9]):

Fact 1. *There exists a polynomial time algorithm decoding all errors of Hamming weight at most $\lfloor \frac{r}{2} \rfloor$ once the vectors $\boldsymbol{x}$ and $\boldsymbol{y}$ are known.*

The following description of alternant codes, will be extremely useful in this article.

Proposition 2

$$\mathscr{A}_r(\boldsymbol{x}, \boldsymbol{y}) = \left\{ \left(\frac{f(x_i)}{y_i \pi'_{\boldsymbol{x}}(x_i)} \right)_{0 \leqslant i < n} \ \Bigg| \ f \in \mathbb{F}_{q^m}[z]_{<n-r} \right\} \cap \mathbb{F}_q^n$$

$$= \left\{ f(\boldsymbol{x}) \star \boldsymbol{y}^{-1} \star \pi'_{\boldsymbol{x}}(\boldsymbol{x})^{-1} \ \big| \ f \in \mathbb{F}_{q^m}[z]_{<n-r} \right\} \cap \mathbb{F}_q^n.$$

Definition 3 (Classical Goppa code). *Let $\boldsymbol{x}$ be an n-tuple of distinct elements of $\mathbb{F}_{q^m}$, let r be a positive integer and $\Gamma \in \mathbb{F}_{q^m}[z]$ be a polynomial of degree r such that $\Gamma(x_i) \neq 0$ for all $i \in \{0, \ldots, n-1\}$. The* classical Goppa code $\mathscr{G}(\boldsymbol{x}, \Gamma)$ *over $\mathbb{F}_q$ associated to Γ and supported by $\boldsymbol{s}$ is defined as*

$$\mathscr{G}(\boldsymbol{x}, \Gamma) \overset{def}{=} \mathscr{A}_r(\boldsymbol{x}, \Gamma(\boldsymbol{x})^{-1}).$$

We call Γ the Goppa polynomial, $\boldsymbol{x}$ *the* support *and m the* extension degree *of the Goppa code.*

As for alternant codes, the following description of Goppa codes, which is due to Proposition 2 will be extremely useful in this article.

Lemma 2

$$\mathscr{G}\left(\boldsymbol{x}, \Gamma\right) = \left\{ \left(\frac{\Gamma(x_i) f(x_i)}{\pi'_{\boldsymbol{x}}(x_i)} \right)_{0 \leqslant i < n} \middle| f \in \mathbb{F}_{q^2}[z]_{<n-\deg(\Gamma)} \right\} \cap \mathbb{F}_q^n$$
$$= \left\{ \Gamma(\boldsymbol{x}) \star f(\boldsymbol{x}) \star (\pi'_{\boldsymbol{x}}(\boldsymbol{x}))^{-1} \middle| f \in \mathbb{F}_{q^2}[z]_{<n-\deg(\Gamma)} \right\} \cap \mathbb{F}_q^n$$

The interesting point about this subfamily of alternant codes is that under some conditions, Goppa codes can correct more errors than a generic alternant code.

Proposition 3 ([46]). *Let γ be a monic and square free polynomial of degree r. Let $\boldsymbol{x}$ be an n-tuple of distinct elements of $\mathbb{F}_{q^m}$ satisfying $\gamma(x_i) \neq 0$ for all i in $\{0, \ldots, n-1\}$, then:*

$$\mathscr{G}\left(\boldsymbol{x}, \gamma^{q-1}\right) = \mathscr{G}\left(\boldsymbol{x}, \gamma^q\right).$$

From Fact 1, these Goppa codes correct up to $\lfloor \frac{qr}{2} \rfloor$ errors in polynomial-time instead of just $\lfloor \frac{(q-1)r}{2} \rfloor$ if seen as $\mathscr{A}_{(q-1)r}(\boldsymbol{x}, \gamma^{-(q-1)}(\boldsymbol{x}))$. Notice that when $q = 2$, this amounts to double the error correction capacity. It is one of the reasons why binary Goppa codes have been chosen in the original McEliece scheme or why Goppa codes with Goppa polynomials of the form γ^{q-1} (called *wild Goppa codes*) are proposed in [6,7].

McEliece Encryption Scheme. We recall here the general principle of McEliece's public-key scheme [35]. The key generation algorithm picks a random $k \times n$ generator matrix $\boldsymbol{G}$ of a code $\mathscr{C}$ over $\mathbb{F}_q$ which is itself randomly picked in a family of codes for which t errors can be corrected efficiently. The *secret* key is the decoding algorithm $\mathcal{D}$ associated to $\mathscr{C}$ and the *public* key is $\boldsymbol{G}$. To encrypt $\boldsymbol{u} \in \mathbb{F}_q^k$, the sender chooses a random vector $\boldsymbol{e}$ in $\mathbb{F}_q^n$ of Hamming weight t and computes the ciphertext $\boldsymbol{c} \overset{\text{def}}{=} \boldsymbol{u}\boldsymbol{G} + \boldsymbol{e}$. The receiver then recovers the plaintext by applying $\mathcal{D}$ on $\boldsymbol{c}$.

This describes the general scheme suggested by McEliece. From now on, we will say that $\boldsymbol{G}$ is the *public generator matrix* and that the vector space $\mathscr{C}$ spanned by its rows is the *public code* i.e. $\mathscr{C} \overset{\text{def}}{=} \{\boldsymbol{u}\boldsymbol{G} \mid \boldsymbol{u} \in \mathbb{F}_q^k\}$. McEliece based his scheme solely on binary Goppa codes. In [6,7], it is advocated to use q-ary Goppa codes with Goppa polynomials of the form γ^{q-1} because of their better error correction capability (see Proposition 3). Such codes are then named wild Goppa codes. In this paper, we precisely focus on these codes but defined over quadratic extensions ($m = 2$). We shall see how it is possible to fully recover their secret structure.

3   A Distinguisher Based on Square Codes

From now on, and until the end of the article, $\mathscr{C}$ denotes the public code of the wild McEliece scheme we want to attack, that is $\mathscr{C} \overset{\text{def}}{=} \mathscr{G}\left(\boldsymbol{x}, \gamma^{q-1}\right)$ and we want to recover the *secret* support vector $x \in \mathbb{F}_{q^2}^n$ and the *secret* irreducible polynomial $\gamma \in \mathbb{F}_{q^2}[z]$ that is assumed to be of degree $r > 1$. Such a Goppa code has extension degree 2 and we will first show in this section that it displays some peculiarities which allows to distinguish such codes from random ones. As in [16,33], the main tool for achieving this purpose is given by square product considerations. It will turn out later on in Section 4 that the very reason which allows to distinguish these wild Goppa codes is also the fundamental reason which enables to compute a nested family of codes and hence used to reveal their algebraic structure.

3.1 Square Code

One of the keys for the distinguisher presented here and the attack oulined in Section 4 is a special property of certain alternant codes with respect to the component-wise product.

Definition 4 (Product of codes, square code). *Let $\mathscr{A}$ and $\mathscr{B}$ be two codes of length n. The star product code denoted by $\mathscr{A} \star \mathscr{B}$ is the vector space spanned by all products $a \star b$ for all $(a, b) \in \mathscr{A} \times \mathscr{B}$. When $\mathscr{B} = \mathscr{A}$ then $\mathscr{A} \star \mathscr{A}$ is called the square code of $\mathscr{A}$ and is denoted by $\mathscr{A}^{\star 2}$.*

The dimension of the star product is easily bounded by:

Proposition 4. *Let $\mathscr{A}$ and $\mathscr{B}$ be two linear codes $\subseteq \mathbb{F}_q^n$, then*

$$\dim (\mathscr{A} \star \mathscr{B}) \leqslant \min \left\{ n, \ \dim \mathscr{A} \dim \mathscr{B} - \binom{\dim(\mathscr{A} \cap \mathscr{B})}{2} \right\} \tag{1}$$

$$\dim (\mathscr{A}^{\star 2}) \leqslant \min \left\{ n, \ \binom{\dim(\mathscr{A}) + 1}{2} \right\}. \tag{2}$$

Proof. Let $(e_1, \ldots, e_s)$ be a basis of $\mathscr{A} \cap \mathscr{B}$. Complete it as two bases $B_{\mathscr{A}} = (e_1, \ldots, e_s, a_{s+1}, \ldots, a_k)$ and $B_{\mathscr{B}} = (e_1, \ldots, e_s, b_{s+1}, \ldots, b_\ell)$ of $\mathscr{A}$ and $\mathscr{B}$ respectively. The star products $u \star v$ where $u \in B_{\mathscr{A}}$ and $v \in B_{\mathscr{B}}$ span $\mathscr{A} \star \mathscr{B}$. The number of such products is $k\ell = \dim \mathscr{A} \dim \mathscr{B}$ minus the number of products which are counted twice, namely the products $e_i \star e_j$ with $i \neq j$. This proves (1). The inequality given in (2) is a consequence of (1). $\qquad\square$

Most codes of a given length and dimension reach these bounds while GRS codes behave completely differently when they have the same support.

Proposition 5. *Let x be an n–tuple of pairwise distinct elements of $\mathbb{F}_q$ and y, y' be two n–tuples of nonzero elements of $\mathbb{F}_q$. Then,*

(i) $\mathbf{GRS}_k(x, y) \star \mathbf{GRS}_{k'}(x, y') = \mathbf{GRS}_{k+k'-1}(x, y \star y')$;
(ii) $\mathbf{GRS}_k(x, y)^{\star 2} = \mathbf{GRS}_{2k-1}(x, y \star y)$.

Remark 1. This proposition shows that the dimension of $\mathbf{GRS}_k(x, y) \star \mathbf{GRS}_{k'}(x, y')$ does not scale multiplicatively as kk' but additively as $k + k' - 1$. It has been used the first time in cryptanalysis in [48] and appears for instance explicitly as Proposition 10 in [31]. We provide the proof here because it is crucial for understanding why the star products of GRS codes and some alternant codes behave in a non generic way.

Proof. Let $c = (y_0 f(x_0), \ldots, y_{n-1} f(x_{n-1})) \in \mathbf{GRS}_k(\boldsymbol{x}, \boldsymbol{y})$ and $c' = (y_0' g(x_0), \ldots, y_{n-1}' g(x_{n-1})) \in \mathbf{GRS}_{k'}(\boldsymbol{x}, \boldsymbol{y}')$ where $\deg(f) \leqslant k - 1$ and $\deg(g) \leqslant k' - 1$. Then, $c \star c'$ is of the form:

$$c \star c' = (y_0 y_0' f(x_0) g(x_0), \ldots, y_{n-1} y_{n-1}' f(x_{n-1}) g(x_{n-1})) = (y_0 y_0' r(x_0), \ldots, y_{n-1} y_{n-1}' r(x_{n-1}))$$

where $\deg(r) \leqslant k + k' - 2$. Conversely, any element $(y_0 y_0' r(x_0), \ldots, y_{n-1} y_{n-1}' r(x_{n-1}))$ where $\deg(r) \leqslant k + k' - 2$, is a linear combination of star products of two elements of $\mathbf{GRS}_k(\boldsymbol{x}, \boldsymbol{y})$. Statement (ii) is a consequence of (i) by putting $\boldsymbol{y}' = \boldsymbol{y}$ and $k' = k$. $\qquad\square$

Since an alternant code is a subfield subcode of a GRS code, we might suspect that products of alternant codes have also an abnormal low dimension. This is is true but in a very attenuated form as shown by:

Theorem 2. *Let $\boldsymbol{x}$ be an n–tuple of distinct elements of $\mathbb{F}_{q^m}$, with $m \geqslant 1$. Let $\boldsymbol{y}, \boldsymbol{y}'$ be two n–tuples of nonzero elements of $\mathbb{F}_{q^m}$. There exists then $\boldsymbol{y}'' \in \mathbb{F}_{q^m}^n$ such that:*

$$\mathscr{A}_s(\boldsymbol{x}, \boldsymbol{y}) \star \mathscr{A}_{s'}(\boldsymbol{x}, \boldsymbol{y}') \subseteq \mathscr{A}_{s+s'-n+1}(\boldsymbol{x}, \boldsymbol{y}''). \tag{3}$$

Proof. Let c, c' be respective elements of $\mathscr{A}_s(\boldsymbol{x}, \boldsymbol{y})$ and $\mathscr{A}_{s'}(\boldsymbol{x}, \boldsymbol{y}')$. From Proposition 2,

$$c = f(\boldsymbol{x}) \star \boldsymbol{y}^{-1} \star \pi_{\boldsymbol{x}}'(\boldsymbol{x})^{-1} \quad \text{and} \quad c' = g(\boldsymbol{x}) \star \boldsymbol{y}'^{-1} \star \pi_{\boldsymbol{x}}'(\boldsymbol{x})^{-1}$$

for some polynomials f, g of respective degrees $< n - s$ and $< n - s'$. This implies that

$$c \star c' = h(\boldsymbol{x}) \star \boldsymbol{y}^{-1} \star \boldsymbol{y}'^{-1} \star \pi_{\boldsymbol{x}}'(\boldsymbol{x})^{-2}$$

where $h \overset{\text{def}}{=} fg$ is a polynomial of degree $< 2n - (s + s') - 1$. Moreover, since c, c' have their entries in $\mathbb{F}_q$, then, so has $c \star c'$. Consequently,

$$c \star c' \in \mathbf{GRS}_{2n-(s+s')-1}(\boldsymbol{x}, \boldsymbol{y}^{-1} \star \boldsymbol{y}'^{-1} \star \pi_{\boldsymbol{x}}'(\boldsymbol{x})^{-2}) \cap \mathbb{F}_q^n$$

and, from Definition 2, the above code equals $\mathscr{A}_{s+s'-n+1}(\boldsymbol{x}, \boldsymbol{y}'')$ for $\boldsymbol{y}'' = \boldsymbol{y} \star \boldsymbol{y}' \star \pi_{\boldsymbol{x}}'(\boldsymbol{x})$. $\qquad\square$

Remark 2. This theorem generalizes Proposition 5: it corresponds to the particular case $m = 1$. However, when $m > 1$, the right hand term of (3) is in general the full space $\mathbb{F}_q^n$. Indeed, assume that $m > 1$ and that the dimension of $\mathscr{A}_s(\boldsymbol{x}, \boldsymbol{y})$ is $n - sm$ whereas the dimension of $\mathscr{A}_{s'}(\boldsymbol{x}, \boldsymbol{y}')$ is equal to $n - s'm$. If we assume that both codes have non trivial dimension then we should have $n - sm > 0$ and $n - s'm > 0$ which implies that $s < \frac{n}{m} \leqslant n/2$. Therefore we have $s \leqslant n/2 - 1$ and $s' \leqslant n/2 - 1$. This implies that $(s + s') - n + 2 \leqslant 0$, which entails that $\mathscr{A}_{s+s'-n+1}(\boldsymbol{x}, \boldsymbol{y}'')$ is the full space $\mathbb{F}_q^n$.

However, in the case $m = 2$ and when either (i) at least one of the codes $\mathscr{A}_s(\boldsymbol{x}, \boldsymbol{y})$ and $\mathscr{A}_{s'}(\boldsymbol{x}, \boldsymbol{y}')$ has dimension greater than the designed dimension, or (ii) when one of these codes is actually an alternant code for a larger degree i.e. $\mathscr{A}_s(\boldsymbol{x}, \boldsymbol{y}) = \mathscr{A}_{s''}(\boldsymbol{x}, \boldsymbol{y})$ for $s'' > s$, then the right-hand term of (3) can be smaller than the full space (at least for small dimensions). This is precisely what happens for our wild Goppa codes of extension degree 2 as shown by:

Proposition 6 ([15]). *Let $\mathscr{G}\left(\boldsymbol{x}, \gamma^{q-1}\right)$ be a wild Goppa code of length n, defined over $\mathbb{F}_q$ with support $\boldsymbol{x} \in \mathbb{F}_{q^2}^n$ where $\gamma \in \mathbb{F}_{q^2}[z]$ is assumed to be irreducible of degree $r > 1$. Then*

(i) $\mathscr{G}\left(\boldsymbol{x}, \gamma^{q-1}\right) = \mathscr{G}\left(\boldsymbol{x}, \gamma^{q+1}\right)$;
(ii) $\dim(\mathscr{G}\left(\boldsymbol{x}, \gamma^{q+1}\right)) \geqslant n - 2r(q-1) + r(r-2)$;
(iii) $\mathscr{G}\left(\boldsymbol{x}, \gamma^{q+1}\right) \sim_{\mathbb{F}_q} \mathscr{A}_{r(q+1)}(\boldsymbol{x}, \boldsymbol{1})$.

The results (i) and (ii) are respective straighforward consequences of Theorems 1 and 24 of [15]. Only (iii) which is used later on, requires further details, see the forthcoming long version of this article.

3.2 A Distinguisher Obtained by Shortening

As explained in Remark 2 the square code of an alternant code of extension degree 2 may have an unusually low dimension when its dimension is larger than its designed rate. This is precisely what happens for wild Goppa codes as explained by Proposition 6.

Taking directly the square of the Goppa code does not work unless the rate of the code is close to 0. However, one can reduce to this case by the shortening operation:

Proposition 7. *Let $\boldsymbol{x}$ be an n–tuple of pairwise distinct elements in $\mathbb{F}_{q^m}$ and let $\boldsymbol{y}$ be an n–tuple of nonzero elements of $\mathbb{F}_{q^m}$ then $\mathscr{A}_r(\boldsymbol{x}, \boldsymbol{y})^{\mathcal{I}} = \mathscr{A}_r(\boldsymbol{x}_{\mathcal{I}}, \boldsymbol{y}_{\mathcal{I}})$.*

Proof. This proposition follows on the spot from the definition of the alternant code $\mathscr{A}_r(\boldsymbol{x}, \boldsymbol{y})$: there is a parity-check $\boldsymbol{H}$ for it with entries over $\mathbb{F}_{q^m}$ which is the generating matrix of $\mathbf{GRS}_r(\boldsymbol{x}, \boldsymbol{y})$. A parity-check matrix of the shortened code $\mathscr{A}_r(\boldsymbol{x}, \boldsymbol{y})^{\mathcal{I}}$ is obtained by throwing away the columns of $\boldsymbol{H}$ that belong to $\mathcal{I}$. That is to say, by puncturing $\mathbf{GRS}_r(\boldsymbol{x}, \boldsymbol{y})$ at $\mathcal{I}$. This parity-check matrix is therefore the generator matrix of $\mathbf{GRS}_r(\boldsymbol{x}_{\mathcal{I}}, \boldsymbol{y}_{\mathcal{I}})$ and the associated code is $\mathscr{A}_r(\boldsymbol{x}_{\mathcal{I}}, \boldsymbol{y}_{\mathcal{I}})$. □

This shortening trick, together with Proposition 6 (ii) explain that the square of a shortened wild Goppa code of extension degree 2 is contained in an alternant code of non trivial dimension.

Proposition 8. *Let $\mathcal{I} \subseteq \{0, \ldots n-1\}$ and $r' \overset{def}{=} 2r(q+1) - (n - |\mathcal{I}|) + 1$. Then there exists some $\boldsymbol{y} \in \left(\mathbb{F}_{q^2}^{\times}\right)^{n - |\mathcal{I}|}$ such that:*

$$\mathscr{C}^{\mathcal{I}} \star \mathscr{C}^{\mathcal{I}} \subseteq \mathscr{A}_{r'}(\boldsymbol{x}_{\mathcal{I}}, \boldsymbol{y}) \tag{4}$$

Proof. By Proposition 6, we know that $\mathscr{C} = \mathscr{G}\left(\boldsymbol{x}, \gamma^{q-1}\right) = \mathscr{G}\left(\boldsymbol{x}, \gamma^{q+1}\right)$ which can therefore be viewed as an alternant code $\mathscr{A}_{r(q+1)}(\boldsymbol{x}, \boldsymbol{y})$ for $\boldsymbol{y} = \gamma(\boldsymbol{x})^{-(q+1)}$. By applying Proposition 7 to it, we know that $\mathscr{C}^{\mathcal{I}}$ is an alternant code of degree $r(q+1)$ and length $n - |\mathcal{I}|$. We then finish the proof by applying Theorem 2 to it.   □

Let us bring in now the quantities:

$$k(a) \stackrel{\text{def}}{=} n - a - 2r(q-1) + r(r-2)$$

$$k_{\text{Alt}}(a) \stackrel{\text{def}}{=} 3(n-a) - 4r(q+1) - 2$$

$$k_{\text{Rand}}(a) \stackrel{\text{def}}{=} \min\left\{n-a, \binom{k(a)+1}{2}\right\}$$

$$a^- \stackrel{\text{def}}{=} n - 2r(q+1) - 1.$$

$$a^+ \stackrel{\text{def}}{=} \sup\left\{a \in \{0, k(0) - 1\} \mid k_{\text{Alt}}(a) \leqslant k_{\text{Rand}}(a)\right\}.$$

Let $\mathscr{R}$ be a random code of the same length and dimension as $\mathscr{C}^{\mathcal{I}}$. Then for $a = |\mathcal{I}|$, $k(a)$ and $k_{\text{Rand}}(a)$ would be the dimensions we expect for $\mathscr{C}^{\mathcal{I}}$ and $\mathscr{R}^{\star 2}$. The quantity $k(0)$ is the dimension we expect for $\mathscr{C}$. In our experiments we never found a case where the dimensions of $\mathscr{C}^{\mathcal{I}}$ and $\mathscr{A}^{\star 2}$ differ from $k(a)$ and $k_{\text{Rand}}(a)$ respectively. On the other hand, notice that from Proposition 8, $k_{\text{Alt}}(a)$ can be viewed as an upper bound on the dimension of $(\mathscr{C}^{\mathcal{I}})^{\star 2}$. In other words, as soon as $k_{\text{Alt}}(a) < k_{\text{Rand}}(a)$, we expect to distinguish $\mathscr{C}^{\mathcal{I}}$ from $\mathscr{R}$. It also turns out in our experiments that the observed dimension of $(\mathscr{C}^{\mathcal{I}})^{\star 2}$ is equal to $k_{\text{Alt}(a)} - 1$ when $k_{\text{Alt}}(a) \leqslant k_{\text{Rand}}(a)$. We can therefore include the a's for which $k_{\text{Alt}}(a) = k_{\text{Rand}}(a)$ in the choices for a for which we distinguish $\mathscr{C}^{\mathcal{I}}$ from $\mathscr{R}$. This motivates to define the *distinguisher interval* as the set of $a \in \{0, \ldots, k(0) - 1\}$ such that $k_{\text{Alt}}(a) \leqslant k_{\text{Rand}}(a)$. Finally a^- corresponds to the critical value of a for which $k_{\text{Alt}}(a) = n - a$. It turns out that there is a simple characterization of the distinguisher interval, namely

Proposition 9. *The distinguisher interval is empty if* $\binom{r(r+2)+2}{2} < 2r(q+1)+1$. *On the other hand if* $\binom{r(r+2)+2}{2} \geqslant 2r(q+1)+1$ *and* $a^- \geqslant 0$, *then it is non empty and is an interval of the form* $[a^-, a^+]$.

We checked that this allows to distinguish all the wild Goppa codes of extension degree 2 suggested in [6] from random codes when $r > 3$. For instance, consider the first entry in Table 7.1 in [6] which is a code of this kind. It has length 794, dimension 529, is defined over $\mathbb{F}_{29}$ and is associated to a Goppa polynomial $\gamma(x)^{29}$ where γ has degree 5. Table 1 shows that for a in the range $\{493, \ldots, 506\}$ the dimensions of $(\mathscr{C}^{\mathcal{I}})^{\star 2}$ differ when $\mathscr{C}$ is the aforementioned wild Goppa code or is a random code with the same parameters. Note that for this example $a^- = 493$. This is a typical behavior and it is only when the degree of γ is very small and the field size is large that we cannot distinguish the Goppa code in this way. More precisely, we have gathered in Table 2 upper bounds on the field size for which we expect to distinguish $\mathscr{G}\left(\boldsymbol{x}, \gamma^{q-1}\right)$ from a random code in terms of r, the degree of γ.

Table 1. Dimension of $(\mathscr{C}^{\mathcal{I}})^{\star 2}$ when $\mathscr{C}$ is either the aforementioned wild Goppa code or a random code of the same length and dimension for various values of the size of $\mathcal{I}$. We can notice that for all $|\mathcal{I}| \in \{493, \ldots, 506\}$ the dimension of the square of the random code and that of the square of the Goppa code differ.

$|\mathcal{I}|$	493	494	495	496	497	498	499	500	501	502	503	504
Goppa	300	297	294	291	288	285	282	279	276	273	270	267
random	301	300	299	298	297	296	295	294	293	292	291	290

$|\mathcal{I}|$	505	506	507	508	509	510	511	512	513	514
Goppa	264	261	253	231	210	190	171	153	136	120
random	289	276	253	231	210	190	171	153	136	120

Table 2. Largest field size q for which we can expect to distinguish $\mathscr{G}\left(\boldsymbol{x}, \gamma^{q-1}\right)$ when γ is an irreducible polynomial in $\mathbb{F}_{q^2}[z]$ of degree r

r	2	3	4	5
q	9	19	37	64

4 The Code Filtration

4.1 Main Tool

We bring in here the crucial ingredient of our attack which is the following family of nested codes defined for any a in $\{0, \ldots, n-1\}$:

$$\mathscr{C}^a(0) \supseteq \mathscr{C}^a(1) \supseteq \cdots \mathscr{C}^a(i) \supseteq \mathscr{C}^a(i+1) \supseteq \cdots \supseteq \mathscr{C}^a(q+1).$$

Roughly speaking, $\mathscr{C}^a(j)$ (see Definition 5 below) consists in the codewords of $\mathscr{C}$ which correspond to polynomials which have a zero of order j at position a. Using a common terminology in algebra, we will call this family of nested codes a *filtration*. It turns out that the first two elements of this filtration are just punctured and shortened versions of $\mathscr{C}$ and the rest of them can be computed from $\mathscr{C}$ only by computing star products and solving linear systems. The key point is that this nested family of codes reveals a lot about the algebraic structure of $\mathscr{C}$. In particular, we will be able to recover the support from it. This is a consequence of the following proposition:

Proposition 10. *For all $a \in \{0, \ldots, n-1\}$, we have*[1]:

$$(\boldsymbol{x}_a - \boldsymbol{x}_a)^{-(q+1)} \star \mathscr{C}^a(q+1) \subseteq \mathscr{C}_a.$$

Without loss of generality, one can assume that the first two entries of $\boldsymbol{x}$ are $x_0 = 0$ and $x_1 = 1$. As explained further, this will in particular make possible

---

[1] Recall that by $(\boldsymbol{x}_a - \boldsymbol{x}_a)^{-(q+1)}$ we mean the vector $\left((x_i - x_a)^{-(q+1)}\right)_{i \in \{0, \ldots, n-1\} \setminus \{a\}}$.

the computation of the vectors $x_0^{-(q+1)}$ and $(x_1 - 1)^{q+1}$ and we prove further that the knowledge of these two vectors provides that of x up to some Galois action. Let us now define precisely these codes $\mathscr{C}^a(j)$. They are defined for any $a \in \{0, \ldots, n-1\}$ and for any integer j as follows:

Definition 5. *For all $a \in \{0, \ldots, n-1\}$ and for all $j \in \mathbb{Z}$, we define the code $\mathscr{C}^a(j)$ as:*

$$\mathscr{C}^a(j) \stackrel{def}{=} \left\{ \left(\frac{\gamma^{q+1}(x_i)}{\pi'_x(x_i)} (x_i - x_a)^j f(x_i) \right)_{i \in \{0,\ldots,n-1\}\setminus\{a\}} \middle| f \in \mathbb{F}_{q^2}[z]_{<n-r(q+1)-j} \right\} \cap \mathbb{F}_q^{n-1}.$$

The link with $\mathscr{C}$ becomes clearer if we use Proposition 6, which gives that $\mathscr{C} = \mathscr{G}(x, \gamma^{q-1}) = \mathscr{G}(x, \gamma^{q+1})$. Viewing now $\mathscr{C}$ as a subfield subcode of a GRS code, and thanks to Lemma 2, we have:

$$\mathscr{C} = \left\{ \left(\frac{\gamma^{q+1}(x_i) f(x_i)}{\pi'_x(x_i)} \right)_{0 \leqslant i < n} \middle| f \in \mathbb{F}_{q^2}[z]_{<n-r(q+1)} \right\} \cap \mathbb{F}_q^n. \tag{5}$$

From this definition, it is clear that $\mathscr{C}^a(1)$ is $\mathscr{C}$ shortened in a.

4.2   The Computation of the Filtration

This filtration is strongly related to $\mathscr{C}$ since, as explained in the following statement, its two first elements are respectively obtained by puncturing and shortening $\mathscr{C}$ at a.

Theorem 3. *For all $a \in \{0, \ldots, n-1\}$, we have:*

(i) $\mathscr{C}^a(0) = \mathscr{C}_a$;
(ii) $\mathscr{C}^a(1) = \mathscr{C}^a$;
(iii) $\mathscr{C}^a(q-r) = \mathscr{C}^a(q+1)$;
(iv) $\mathscr{C}^a(-r) = \mathscr{C}^a(0)$.

After the computation of the two first elements and for the same reason we need to take shortened versions of the public code to distinguish it from a random code, the rest of the filtration relies in a crucial way on taking star products of shortened versions of the codes $\mathscr{C}^0(s)$ that we denote by $\mathscr{C}^{0,\mathcal{I}}(s)$ which stands for the code $\mathscr{C}^0(s)$ shortened in the positions belonging to $\mathcal{I} \subset \{1, \ldots, n-1\}$. It is readily checked that such a code can be written as:

$$\mathscr{C}^{0,\mathcal{I}}(s) = \left\{ \left(\frac{x_i^s \gamma^{q+1}(x_i) f(x_i)}{\pi'_{x_\mathcal{I}}(x_i)} \right)_{i \in \{1,\ldots,n-1\}\setminus\mathcal{I}} \middle| f \in \mathbb{F}_{q^2}[z]_{<n-r(q+1)-s-|\mathcal{I}|} \right\} \cap \mathbb{F}_q^{n-1-|\mathcal{I}|} \tag{6}$$

where we recall that $x_\mathcal{I}$ denotes the vector x punctured at $\mathcal{I}$. From this form, it is clear that by applying the equivalent definition of an alternant code given in Definition 2, that we have:

Lemma 3. *For some* $y \in (\mathbb{F}_{q^2}^{\times})^{n-|\mathcal{I}|-1}$ *we have* $\mathscr{C}^{0,\mathcal{I}}(s) = \mathscr{A}_{r(q+1)+s-1}(x_{\mathcal{I}\cup\{0\}}, y)$.

Since such codes are alternant codes, a simple consequence of Lemma 3 is:

Proposition 11. *Let* $\mathcal{I}$ *be a subset of* $\{1, \ldots, n-1\}$ *and let us define* $r(s,t) \overset{def}{=} 2r(q+1) + s + t - n + |\mathcal{I}|$ *then there exists some* $y \in \mathbb{F}_{q^2}^{n-1-|\mathcal{I}|}$ *such that:*

$$\mathscr{C}^{0,\mathcal{I}}(s) \star \mathscr{C}^{0,\mathcal{I}}(t) \subseteq \mathscr{A}_{r(s,t)}(x_{\mathcal{I}\cup\{0\}}, y) \tag{7}$$

Proof. This follows at once from Lemma 3 which says that $\mathscr{C}^{0,\mathcal{I}}(s)$ and $\mathscr{C}^{0,\mathcal{I}}(t)$ are alternant codes of respective degrees $r(q+1) + s - 1$ and $r(q+1) + t - 1$. From Theorem 2, we know that their star product is included in an alternant code with support $x_{\mathcal{I}\cup\{0\}}$ and of degree r' with:

$$r' = r(q+1) + s - 1 + r(q+1) + t - 1 - (n - |\mathcal{I}| - 1) + 1 = r(s,t)$$

□

This suggests that the product $\mathscr{C}^{0,\mathcal{I}}(s) \star \mathscr{C}^{0,\mathcal{I}}(t)$ might only depend on $s+t$. In order to find $\mathscr{C}^{0,\mathcal{I}}(t)$ once $\mathscr{C}^{0,\mathcal{I}}(0), \mathscr{C}^{0,\mathcal{I}}(1), \ldots, \mathscr{C}^{0,\mathcal{I}}(t-1)$ have been found, we might be tempted to use the "Equation":

$$\mathscr{C}^{0,\mathcal{I}}(0) \star \mathscr{C}^{0,\mathcal{I}}(t) = \mathscr{C}^{0,\mathcal{I}}(\lfloor t/2 \rfloor) \star \mathscr{C}^{0,\mathcal{I}}(\lceil t/2 \rceil).$$

Unfortunately, this equality does not hold in general. However, we have the following related statement.

Lemma 4. *Let* $\mathcal{I}$ *be a subset of* $\{1, \ldots, n-1\}$ *such that* $r' \overset{def}{=} r(\lfloor t/2 \rfloor, \lceil t/2 \rceil) = -n + |\mathcal{I}| + 2r(q+1) + t > 0$. *We have:*

(i) *Any codeword* s *in* $\mathscr{C}^{0,\mathcal{I}}(t-1)$ *such that* $s \star \mathscr{C}^{0,\mathcal{I}}(0) \subseteq \mathscr{C}^{0,\mathcal{I}}(\lfloor t/2 \rfloor) \star \mathscr{C}^{0,\mathcal{I}}(\lceil t/2 \rceil)$, *necessarily belongs to* $\mathscr{C}^{0,\mathcal{I}}(t)$.

(ii) *Conversely,* $\mathscr{C}^{0,\mathcal{I}}(t)$ *is equal to the set of codewords* s *in* $\mathscr{C}^{0,\mathcal{I}}(t-1)$ *such that*

$$s \star \mathscr{C}^{0,\mathcal{I}}(0) \subseteq \mathscr{A}_{r'}(x_{\mathcal{I}\cup\{0\}}, y).$$

for some $y \in \mathbb{F}_q^{n-1-|\mathcal{I}|}$.

Thus, one expects to find $\mathscr{C}^{0,\mathcal{I}}(t)$ by solving the following problem, which has already been considered in [13].

Problem 1. *Given* $\mathscr{A}$, $\mathscr{B}$, *and* $\mathscr{D}$ *be three codes in* $\mathbb{F}_q^n$, *find the subcode* $\mathscr{S}$ *of elements* s *in* $\mathscr{D}$ *satisfying* $s \star \mathscr{A} \subseteq \mathscr{B}$.

Such a space can be computed by linear algebra or equivalently by computing dual codes and code products. More precisely, we have:

Proposition 12. *The solution space* $\mathscr{S}$ *of Problem 1 is* $\mathscr{S} = (\mathscr{A} \star \mathscr{B}^{\perp})^{\perp} \cap \mathscr{D}$.

Proof. Let $s \in \mathscr{S}$, $a \in \mathscr{A}$ and $b^{\perp} \in \mathscr{B}^{\perp}$. Then $s \in \mathscr{D}$ and $\langle s, a \star b^{\perp} \rangle = \sum_{i=0}^{n-1} s_i a_i b_i^{\perp} = \langle s \star a, b^{\perp} \rangle$ This last term is zero by definition of $\mathscr{S}$. This proves $\mathscr{S} \subseteq (\mathscr{A} \star \mathscr{B}^{\perp})^{\perp} \cap \mathscr{D}$. The converse inclusion is proved in the same way. □

This allows to find several of these $\mathscr{C}^{0,\mathcal{I}}(t)$'s associated to different subsets of $\mathcal{I}$. It is straightforward to use such sets in order to recover $\mathscr{C}^0(t)$. Indeed, from the characterization of $\mathscr{C}^{0,\mathcal{I}}(t)$ given in (6) we clearly expect that:

$$\mathscr{C}^{0,\mathcal{I}\cap\mathcal{J}}(t) = \mathscr{C}^{0,\mathcal{J}}(t) + \mathscr{C}^{0,\mathcal{I}}(t) \tag{8}$$

where with an abuse of notation we mean by $\mathscr{C}^{0,\mathcal{J}}(t)$ and $\mathscr{C}^{0,\mathcal{I}}(t)$ the code $\mathscr{C}^{0,\mathcal{J}}(t)$ and $\mathscr{C}^{0,\mathcal{J}}(t)$ whose set of positions has been completed such as to also contain the positions belonging to $\mathcal{I} \setminus \mathcal{J}$ and $\mathcal{J} \setminus \mathcal{I}$ respectively and which are set to 0. Such an equality does not always hold of course, but apart from rather pathological cases it typically holds when $\dim\left(\mathscr{C}^{0,\mathcal{I}}(t)\right)+\dim\left(\mathscr{C}^{0,\mathcal{J}}(t)\right) \geqslant \dim\left(\mathscr{C}^{0,\mathcal{I}\cap\mathcal{J}}(t)\right)$. These considerations suggest the following Algorithm 1 for computing the $\mathscr{C}^0(t)$'s.

Algorithm 1. Algorithm for computing $\mathscr{C}^0(q+1)$

---

  for $t = 2$ to $q+1$ **do**
    $\mathscr{C}^0(t) \leftarrow \{0\}$
    while $\dim \mathscr{C}^0(t) \neq k(t)$ **do**
      $\{k(t)$ is obtained "offline" by computing the true dimension of a $\mathscr{C}^0(t)$ for an
      arbitrary choice of γ and $\boldsymbol{x}.\}$
      $\mathcal{I} \leftarrow$ rand. subset of $\{1, \ldots, n-1\}$ of size $a(t)$ {We explain in (11) how $a(t)$ is
      obtained.}
      $\mathscr{A} \leftarrow \mathscr{C}^{0,\mathcal{I}}(0)$
      $\mathscr{B} \leftarrow \mathscr{C}^{0,\mathcal{I}}(\lfloor \frac{t}{2} \rfloor) \star \mathscr{C}^{0,\mathcal{I}}(\lceil \frac{t}{2} \rceil)$
      $\mathscr{D} \leftarrow \mathscr{C}^{0,\mathcal{I}}(t-1)$
      $\mathscr{C}^{0,\mathcal{I}}(t) \leftarrow \mathscr{D} \cap \left(\mathscr{A} \star \mathscr{B}^{\perp}\right)^{\perp}$ {Problem 1.}
      $\mathscr{C}^0(t) \leftarrow \mathscr{C}^0(t) + \mathscr{C}^{0,\mathcal{I}}(t)$
    end while
  end for
  return $\mathscr{C}^0(q+1)$

In Algorithm 1 it is essential to choose the sizes $a(t)$ of the set of indices $\mathcal{I}$ used to compute $\mathscr{C}^{0,\mathcal{I}}(t)$ appropriately. Let us denote by k the dimension of $\mathscr{C}$ and bring in the quantity:

$$k_{\mathrm{Alt}}(s,t,a) \overset{\text{def}}{=} 3(n-a) - 4r(q+1) - 2(s+t) - 1 \tag{9}$$

$$k_{\mathrm{Rand}}(s,t,a) \overset{\text{def}}{=} \frac{1}{2}(k - 2s - a + 1)(k - 4t + 2s - a + 2) \tag{10}$$

then we choose we choose $a(t)$ such that:

$$a(t) > n - 2r(q+1) - t \tag{11}$$
$$k_{\mathrm{Alt}}(\lceil t/2 \rceil, \lfloor t/2 \rfloor, a(t)) < k_{\mathrm{Rand}}(\lceil t/2 \rceil, \lfloor t/2 \rfloor, a(t)) \tag{12}$$

The reasons for this choice are explained in a forthcoming long version of this paper.

5   An Efficient Attack Using the Distinguisher

The attack consists in 5 steps which are outlined below.

Step 1. Compute $\mathscr{C}^0(q+1)$ and $\mathscr{C}^1(q+1)$ using the distinguisher–based methods developed in Section 4. Thanks to Theorem 3(iii), it is sufficient to compute $\mathscr{C}^0(q-r)$ and $\mathscr{C}^1(q-r)$.

Step 2. From $\mathscr{C}^0(q+1)$ and $\mathscr{C}^1(q+1)$ respectively, we compute two sets of vectors in $\mathbb{F}_q^{n-1}$ which are the respective solution sets of the systems:

$$(S_0): \begin{cases} \boldsymbol{z} \star \mathscr{C}^0(q+1) \subseteq \mathscr{C}_0 \\ \forall i \in \{0 \dots n-2\}, \ z_i \neq 0 \\ z_0 = 1 \end{cases} \quad \text{and} \quad (S_1): \begin{cases} \boldsymbol{z} \star \mathscr{C}^1(q+1) \subseteq \mathscr{C}_1 \\ \forall i \in \{0 \dots n-2\}, \ z_i \neq 0 \\ z_0 = 1 \end{cases}$$

$$(13)$$

From Proposition 10, $\boldsymbol{x}_0^{-(q+1)}$ is a solution of (S_0) and $(\boldsymbol{x}_1-1)^{-(q+1)}$ is a solution of (S_1). In addition, from Proposition 12, the sets of solutions of the above systems are the respective full-weight codewords whose first entry is 1 of the following codes:

$$\mathscr{D} \stackrel{\text{def}}{=} \left(\mathscr{C}^0(q+1) \star (\mathscr{C}_0)^{\perp}\right)^{\perp} \quad \text{and} \quad \mathscr{D}' \stackrel{\text{def}}{=} \left(\mathscr{C}^1(q+1) \star (\mathscr{C}_1)^{\perp}\right)^{\perp}. \quad (14)$$

Experimentally we found out that $\mathscr{D} \ \mathscr{D}'$ have dimension 4. A heuristic explaining this observation is given in the forthcoming full version of this paper. Therefore an exhaustive search can be performed to find the full-weight codewords. In addition, we have a complete description of these sets.

Proposition 13. *There are at least $q^2 - n + 2$ solutions for (S_0) which are 1, $\boldsymbol{x}_0^{-(q+1)}$ and the following vectors $(1-a)^{-(q+1)}\left((\boldsymbol{x}_0 - a)^{q+1} \star \boldsymbol{x}_0^{-(q+1)}\right)$ obtained with $a \in \mathbb{F}_{q^2} \setminus \mathcal{L}_{\boldsymbol{x}}$. Similarly, there at least $q^2 - n + 2$ solutions for (S_1) which are 1, $(\boldsymbol{x}_1 - 1)^{-(q+1)}$ and the vectors $a^{-(q+1)}\left((\boldsymbol{x}_1 - a)^{q+1} \star (\boldsymbol{x}_1 - 1)^{-(q+1)}\right)$ also obtained with $a \in \mathbb{F}_{q^2} \setminus \mathcal{L}_{\boldsymbol{x}}$:*

Remark 3. It is possible to give a lower-bound for the probability P that (S_0) (and (S_1)) has no other solution:

$$P \geqslant 1 - (q^3 + q)\frac{(q^2 - n)!}{(q^2 - n - q)!} \cdot \frac{(q^2 - q)!}{q^2!}.$$

In [6, Table 7.1], the authors propose a code over $\mathbb{F}_{32}$, with $m = 2, t = 4$ of length 841. For such parameters, the above probability is lower than $3.52 \ 10^{-21}$. Table 3 summarizes this probability for other parameters proposed in [6] for $m = 2$ and $t > 3$.

Table 3. Estimates of $1 - P$, where P denotes the probability of Remark 3, for some explicit parameters

$q = 29, n = 791$	$q = 31, n = 892$	$q = 31, n = 851$	$q = 31, n = 813$	$q = 31, n = 795$
$3.6 \ 10^{-36}$	$5.5 \ 10^{-35}$	$3 \ 10^{-27}$	$1.08 \ 10^{-22}$	$5.6 \ 10^{-21}$

Step 3. First, notice that the vectors x_0 and x_1 punctured at the first position are both equal to the vector $x_{01} \stackrel{\text{def}}{=} (x_2, \ldots, x_{n-1}) \in \mathbb{F}_{q^2}^{n-2}$. From the previous step, one can obtain the two following sets of vectors:

$$L_0 \stackrel{\text{def}}{=} \left\{ x_{01}^{q+1} \right\} \cup \left\{ (1 - a)^{q+1} \left(x_{01}^{q+1} \star (x_{01} - a)^{-(q+1)} \right) \ \middle| \ a \in \mathbb{F}_{q^2} \setminus \mathcal{L}_x \right\}$$

$$L_1 \stackrel{\text{def}}{=} \left\{ (x_{01} - 1)^{q+1} \right\} \cup \left\{ a^{q+1} \left((x_{01} - 1)^{q+1} \star (x_{01} - a)^{-(q+1)} \right) \ \middle| \ a \in \mathbb{F}_{q^2} \setminus \mathcal{L}_x \right\}. \tag{15}$$

They are computed by puncturing the first entry of each solution vector and taking the inverse for the star product. Note that the trivial solution $\mathbf{1}$ is always removed. The problem now is to identify x_0^{q+1} and $(x_1 - 1)^{q+1}$ among them.

Proposition 14. *If $n > 2q + 4$, then there exists a one-to-one map $\phi : L_0 \to L_1$ such that $\phi(x_{01}^{q+1}) = (x_{01} - 1)^{q+1}$ and for all $s \in L_0$, the vector $\phi(s)$ is the unique element of L_1 such that every element of $s \star L_1$ is collinear to a unique element of $\phi(s) \star L_0$.*

The end of the attack works as follows: for $s_0 \in L_0$, compute $s_1 = \phi(s_0)$, then apply Steps 4 of the attack. If $s_0 \neq x_0^{q+1}$, then the Final Step will fail to find a nontrivial solution. In such situation, choose another $s_0 \in L_0$. Therefore, in the worst case, Step 4 and Final Step will be iterated $|L_0| = q^2 - n + 1$ times.

Step 4. This step is better explained when we have a valid $(s_0, s_1) = (x_0^{q+1}, (x_1 - 1)^{q+1})$. Recall that $N(t) = t^{q+1}$ is the norm of t over $\mathbb{F}_q$ for all $t \in \mathbb{F}_{q^2}$. The following lemma shows that the minimal polynomial $P_{x_i} \in \mathbb{F}_q[z]$ of x_i can be computed using: if $N(x_i)$ and $N(x_i - 1)$ are known:

Lemma 5. *Let t be an element of $\mathbb{F}_{q^2}$ and $P_t(z) \stackrel{\text{def}}{=} z^2 - (N(t) - N(t - 1) - 1)z + N(t)$. Then, either P_t is irreducible and is the minimal polynomial of t over $\mathbb{F}_q$, or P_t is reducible and in this case $P_t(z) = (z - t)^2$.*

Proof. First, notice that $N(t - 1) = (t - 1)(t^q - 1) = t^{q+1} - t^q - t + 1 = N_{\mathbb{F}_{q^2}/\mathbb{F}_q}(t) - \text{Tr}_{\mathbb{F}_{q^2}/\mathbb{F}_q}(t) + 1$. Therefore, $P_t(z) = z^2 - \text{Tr}(z) + N(z)$, which is known to be the minimal polynomial of t whenever $t \in \mathbb{F}_{q^2} \setminus \mathbb{F}_q$. On the other hand, when $t \in \mathbb{F}_q$, then $P_t(z) = z^2 - 2tz + t^2$ which factorizes as $(z - t)^2$.

Final Step. For the sake of simplicity we will assume in what follows that x is full, that is to say that $n = q^2$. Since the support x is known up to Galois action, after applying some permutation to $\mathscr{C}$, one can assume that

- the q first entries of $\boldsymbol{x}$ are the elements of $\mathbb{F}_q$;
- in the $q^2 - q$ remaining entries, two conjugated elements a, a^q of $\mathbb{F}_{q^2} \setminus \mathbb{F}_q$ are consecutive entries in $\boldsymbol{x}$.

Next, we compute a vector $\boldsymbol{x}' \in \mathbb{F}_{q^2}^{q^2}$ such that for all $0 \leqslant i < q^2$, the minimal polynomial of x_i' equals that of x_i. Thus, $\boldsymbol{x}'$ is the image of $\boldsymbol{x}$ by a product of transpositions with pairwise disjoint supports. Moreover, the possible supports for these transpositions are pairs $(i, i+1)$ such that $x_i^q = x_{i+1}$. We denote by τ this permutation. Its matrix is of the form

$$\mathbf{R}_\tau \overset{\text{def}}{=} \begin{pmatrix} \mathbf{I}_q & (0) \\ (0) & \mathbf{B} \end{pmatrix}, \tag{16}$$

where $\mathbf{B} \in \mathfrak{M}_{q^2-q}(\mathbb{F}_q)$ is 2×2–block diagonal with blocks of the form $\begin{pmatrix} 1 & 0 \\ 0 & 1 \end{pmatrix}$ or $\begin{pmatrix} 0 & 1 \\ 1 & 0 \end{pmatrix}$.

From Proposition 6(iii), $\mathscr{G}\left(\boldsymbol{x}', \gamma^{q+1}\right) = \boldsymbol{u} \star \mathscr{A}_{r(q+1)}(\boldsymbol{x}', 1)$ for some vector $\boldsymbol{u}$ with no zero entry. Therefore, if we denote by $\mathbf{D}_{\boldsymbol{u}}$ the diagonal matrix whose diagonal entries are those of $\boldsymbol{u}$, we see that

$$\mathscr{C} \mathbf{R}_\tau \mathbf{D}_{\boldsymbol{u}} = \mathscr{A}_{r(q+1)}(\boldsymbol{x}', 1). \tag{17}$$

Thus, since $\boldsymbol{x}'$ is known, we can recover τ and $\boldsymbol{u}$ by solving

Problem 2. *Compute the space of matrices $\mathbf{M}$ of the form*

$$\mathbf{M} = \begin{pmatrix} \mathbf{E} & (0) \\ (0) & \mathbf{F} \end{pmatrix}$$

such that $\mathbf{E}$ is diagonal, $\mathbf{F}$ si 2×2 blockdiagonal and which satisfy

$$\mathscr{C}\mathbf{M} \subseteq \mathscr{A}_{r(q+1)}(\boldsymbol{x}', 1). \tag{18}$$

The solution space is computed by solving a linear system whose unknowns are the entries of $\mathbf{M}$. Since $\mathbf{M}$ is block diagonal, the number of unknowns is linear in n while the number of equations is $\dim(\mathscr{C}) \times \dim(\mathscr{A}_{r(q+1)}(\boldsymbol{x}', 1)^\perp) = k(n-k)$ and hence is quadratic in n. Therefore, the solution space will have a very low dimension. Experimentally, this dimension is observed to be 2. Therefore, by exhaustive search in this low-dimensional solution space one finds easily a matrix $\mathbf{M}$ of the form $\mathbf{RD}$, where $\mathbf{R}$ is a permutation matrix and $\mathbf{D}$ is invertible and diagonal. This yields $\boldsymbol{u}$ and τ and hence $\boldsymbol{x}$ and the description of $\mathscr{C}$ as an alternant code.

6   Improvement of the Attack

For some parameters, the computation of the filtration up to $\mathscr{C}^a(q+1)$ or actually up to $\mathscr{C}^a(q - r)$ (thanks to Theorem 3 (iii)) is not possible, while it is still

---

Algorithm 2. Algorithm of the attack

Compute $\mathscr{C}^0(q+1)$, $\mathscr{C}^1(q+1)$ using Algorithm 1.
$L_0 \leftarrow$ List of candidates for $\boldsymbol{x}_0^{q+1}$ (Obtained by solving System (S_0) in (13))
$L_1 \leftarrow$ List of candidates for $(\boldsymbol{x}_1 - 1)^{q+1}$ (Obtained by solving System (S_1) in (13))
$\boldsymbol{M}_0 \leftarrow 0$
while $M_0 = 0$ and $L_0 \neq \emptyset$ **do**
    Pick a random element $\boldsymbol{a}_0$ in L_0.
    $\boldsymbol{a}_1 \leftarrow \phi(\boldsymbol{a}_0)$ {where ϕ is the map obtained thanks to Proposition 14}
    $L_0 \leftarrow L_0 \setminus \{\boldsymbol{a}_0\}$
    $L_1 \leftarrow L_1 \setminus \{\boldsymbol{a}_1\}$
    Compute the minimal polynomials P_{x_i} of the positions using Lemma 5.
    Compute, an arbitrary vector $\boldsymbol{x}'$ as explained in Final Step.
    $V \leftarrow$ Space of solutions of Problem 2.
    if dim $V > 0$ and $\exists M \in V$ of the form **RD** as in Final Step **then**
        $M_0 \leftarrow M$
    end if
end while
if $M_0 = 0$ **then**
    return "error"
else
    Recover $\boldsymbol{x}$ and $\boldsymbol{u}$ from M as described in Final Step.
    return $\boldsymbol{x}, \boldsymbol{u}$
end if

---

possible to compute the filtration up to $\mathscr{C}^a(q+1-s)$ for some s satisfying $r+1 < s \leqslant (q+1)/2$. This for instance what happens for codes over $\mathbb{F}_{32}$, with $t = 4$. In such situation, $\mathscr{C}^a(s)$ is known since by assumption $s \leqslant q+1-s$ and then, we can compute $\mathscr{C}^a(-s)$ from the knowledge of $\mathscr{C}_a$ and $\mathscr{C}^a(s)$. This computation consists in solving a problem very similar to Problem 1. Then, as a generalization of Proposition 10, we have $(\boldsymbol{x}_a - \boldsymbol{x}_a)^{-(q+1)} \star \mathscr{C}^a(q+1-s) \subseteq \mathscr{C}^a(-s)$ and the rest of the attack runs in a very same manner.

7   Complexity and Implementation

In what follows, by "$\mathcal{O}(P(n))$" for some function $P : \mathbb{N} \to \mathbb{R}$, we mean "$\mathcal{O}(P(n))$ operations in $\mathbb{F}_q$". We clearly have $n \leqslant q^2$ and we also assume that $q = \mathcal{O}(\sqrt{n})$.

7.1   Computation of a Code Product

Given two codes $\mathscr{A}, \mathscr{B}$ of length n and respective dimensions a and b, the computation of $\mathscr{A} \star \mathscr{B}$ consists first in the computation of a generator matrix of size $ab \times n$ whose computation costs $\mathcal{O}(nab)$ operations. Then, the Gaussian elimination costs $\mathcal{O}(nab \min(n, ab))$. Thus, the cost of Gaussian elimination dominates that of the construction step. In particular, for a code $\mathscr{A}$ of dimension $k \geqslant \sqrt{n}$, the computation of $\mathscr{A}^{\star 2}$ costs $\mathcal{O}(n^2 k^2)$. Thanks to Proposition 12, one shows that the dominant part of the resolution of Problem 1, consists in computing $\mathscr{A} \star \mathscr{B}^\perp$ and hence costs $\mathcal{O}(na(n-b) \min(n, a(n-b)))$.

7.2 Computation of the Filtration

Let us first evaluate the cost of computing $\mathscr{C}^{a,\mathcal{I}}(s+1)$ from $\mathscr{C}^{a,\mathcal{I}}(s)$. Equations (9) to (12) suggest that the dimension of $\mathscr{C}^{a,\mathcal{I}}(s)$ used to compute the filtration is in $\mathcal{O}(\sqrt{n})$. From §7.1, the computation of the square of $\mathscr{C}^{a,\mathcal{I}}(s)$ costs $\mathcal{O}(n^3)$ operations in $\mathbb{F}_q$. Then, the resolution of Problem 12 in the context of Lemma 4, costs $\mathcal{O}(na(n-b)\min(n, a(n-b)))$, where $a = \dim \mathscr{C}^{a,\mathcal{I}}(s) = \mathcal{O}(\sqrt{n})$ and $b = \dim \mathscr{A}_{r'}(\boldsymbol{x}_{\mathcal{I}\cup\{0\}}, \boldsymbol{y})$. We have $n - b = \mathcal{O}(n)$, hence we get a cost of $\mathcal{O}(n^3\sqrt{n})$.

The heuristic below Proposition 12, suggests that we need to perform this computation for $\mathcal{O}(\sqrt{n})$ choices of $\mathcal{I}$. Since addition of codes is negligible compared to $\mathcal{O}(n^3\sqrt{n})$ this leads to a total cost of $\mathcal{O}(n^4)$ for the computation of $\mathscr{C}^a(s+1)$. This computation should be done $q+1$ times (actually $q-r$ times from Theorem 3 (iii)) and, we assumed that $q = \mathcal{O}(\sqrt{n})$. Thus, the computation of $\mathscr{C}^a(q+1)$ costs $\mathcal{O}(n^4\sqrt{n})$.

7.3 Other Computations

The resolution of Problems (13) in Step 2, costs $\mathcal{O}(n^4)$ (see (14)). Since the solution spaces $\mathscr{D}$ and $\mathscr{D}'$ in (14) have $\mathbb{F}_q$–dimension 4, the exhaustive search in them costs $\mathcal{O}(q^4) = \mathcal{O}(n^2)$ which is negligible. The computation of the map ϕ and that of minimal polynomials is also negligible. Finally, the resolution of Problem 2 costs $\mathcal{O}(n^4)$ since it is very similar to Problem 1. Since Final step should be iterated $q^2 - n + 1$ times in the worst case, we see that the part of the attack after the computation of the filtration costs at worst $\mathcal{O}(n^5)$. Thus, the global complexity of the attack is in $\mathcal{O}(n^5)$ operations in $\mathbb{F}_q$.

7.4 Implementation

This attack has been implemented with MAGMA [9] and run over random examples of codes corresponding to the seven entries [6, Table 1] for which $m = 2$ and $r > 3$. For all these parameters, our attack succeeded. We summarize here the average running times for at least 50 random keys per 4–tuple of parameters, obtained with an Intel® Xeon 2.27GHz.

(q, n, k, r)	(29,781, 516,5)	(29, 791, 575, 4)	(29,794,529,5)	(31, 795, 563, 4)
Average time	16min	19.5min	15.5min	31.5min

(q, n, k, r)	(31,813, 581,4)	(31, 851, 619, 4)	(32,841,601,4)
Average time	31.5min	27.2min	49.5min

Remark 4. In the above table the code dimensions are not the ones mentioned in [6]. What happens here is that the formula for the dimension given [6, p.153,§1] is wrong for such cases: it understimates the true dimension for wild Goppa codes over quadratic extensions when the degree r of the irreducible polynomial γ is larger than 2 as shown by Proposition 6 (ii).

All these parameters are given in [6] with a 128-bit security that is measured against information set decoding attack which is described in [6, p.151, Information set decoding §1] as the *"top threat against the wild McEliece cryptosystem for* $\mathbb{F}_3$, $\mathbb{F}_4$, *etc."*. It should be mentioned that these parameters are marked in [6] by the biohazard symbol ☣ (together with about two dozens other parameters). This corresponds, as explained in [6], to parameters for which the number of possible monic Goppa polynomials of the form γ^{q-1} is smaller than 2^{128}. The authors in [6] choose in this case a support which is significantly smaller than q^m (q^2 here) in order to avoid attacks that fix a support of size q^m and then enumerate all possible polynomials. Such attacks exploit the fact that two Goppa codes of length q^m with the same polynomial are *permutation equivalent*. We recall that the *support-splitting* algorithm [42], when applied to permutation equivalent codes, generally finds in polynomial time a permutation that sends one code onto the other. The authors of [6] call this requirement on the length the *second defense* and write [6, p.152].

"The strength of the second defense is unclear: we might be the first to ask whether the support-splitting idea can be generalized to handle many sets $\{a_1, \ldots, a_n\}$ [2] *simultaneously, and we would not be surprised if the answer turns out to be yes."* The authors also add in [6, p.154,§1] that *"the security of these cases* [3] *depends on the strength of the second defense discussed in Section 6"*. We emphasize that our attack has nothing to do with the strength or a potential weakness of the second defense. Moreover, it does not exploit at all the fact that there are significantly less than 2^{128} Goppa polynomials. This is obvious from the way our attack works and this can also be verified by attacking parameters which were not proposed in [6] but for which there are more than 2^{128} monic wild Goppa polynomials to check. As an illustration, we are also able to recover the secret key in an average time of 24 minutes when the public key is a code over $\mathbb{F}_{31}$, of length 900 and with a Goppa polynomial of degree 14. In such case, the number of possible Goppa polynomials is larger than 2^{134} and according to Proposition 6, the public key has parameters $[n = 900, k \geqslant 228, d \geqslant 449]_{31}$. Note that security of such a key with respect to information set decoding [41] is also high (about 2^{125} for such parameters).

8   Conclusion

The McEliece scheme based on Goppa codes has withstood all cryptanalytic attempts up to now, even if a related system based on GRS codes [38] was successfully attacked in [44]. Goppa codes are subfield subcodes of GRS codes and it was advocated that taking the subfield subcode hides a lot about the structure of the underlying code and also makes these codes more random-like. This is sustained by the fact that the distance distribution becomes indeed random [29] by this operation whereas GRS codes behave differently from random codes with respect to this criterion. We provide the first example of a cryptanalysis which questions this belief by providing an algebraic cryptanalysis which is of polynomial complexity

---

[2] $\{a_1, \ldots, a_n\}$ means here the support of the Goppa code.
[3] Meaning here the cases marked with ☣.

and which applies to many "reasonable parameters" of a McEliece scheme when the Goppa code is the $\mathbb{F}_q$-subfield subcode of a GRS code defined over $\mathbb{F}_{q^2}$.

It could be argued that this attack applies to a rather restricted class of Goppa codes, namely wild Goppa codes of extension degree two. This class of codes also presents certain peculiarities as shown by Proposition 6 which were helpful for mounting an attack. However, it should be pointed out that the crucial ingredient which made this attack possible is the fact that such codes could be distinguished from random codes by square code considerations. A certain nested family of subcodes was indeed exhibited here and it turns out that shortened versions of these codes were related together by the star product. This allowed to reconstruct the nested family and from here the algebraic description of the Goppa code could be recovered. The crucial point here is really the existence of such a nested family whose elements are linked together by the star product. The fact that these codes were linked together by the star product is really related to the fact that the square code of certain shortened codes of the public code were of unusually low dimension which is precisely the fact that yielded the aforementioned distinguisher. This raises the issue whether other families of Goppa codes or alternant codes which can be distinguished from random codes by such square considerations [17] can be attacked by techniques of this kind. This covers high rate Goppa or alternant codes, but also other Goppa or alternant codes when the degree of extension is equal to 2. All of them can be distinguished from random codes by taking square codes of a shortened version of the dual code.

References

1. Baldi, M., Bianchi, M., Chiaraluce, F., Rosenthal, J., Schipani, D.: Enhanced public key security for the McEliece cryptosystem. arxiv:1108.2462v2[cs.IT] (2011) (submitted)
2. Baldi, M., Bodrato, M., Chiaraluce, F.: A new analysis of the McEliece cryptosystem based on QC-LDPC codes. In: Ostrovsky, R., De Prisco, R., Visconti, I. (eds.) SCN 2008. LNCS, vol. 5229, pp. 246–262. Springer, Heidelberg (2008)
3. Becker, A., Joux, A., May, A., Meurer, A.: Decoding random binary linear codes in $2^{n/20}$: How $1 + 1 = 0$ improves information set decoding. In: Pointcheval, D., Johansson, T. (eds.) EUROCRYPT 2012. LNCS, vol. 7237, pp. 520–536. Springer, Heidelberg (2012)
4. Berger, T.P., Loidreau, P.: How to mask the structure of codes for a cryptographic use. Des. Codes Cryptogr. 35(1), 63–79 (2005)
5. Bernstein, D.J., Lange, T., Peters, C.: Attacking and defending the McEliece cryptosystem. In: Buchmann, J., Ding, J. (eds.) PQCrypto 2008. LNCS, vol. 5299, pp. 31–46. Springer, Heidelberg (2008)
6. Bernstein, D.J., Lange, T., Peters, C.: Wild mcEliece. In: Biryukov, A., Gong, G., Stinson, D.R. (eds.) SAC 2010. LNCS, vol. 6544, pp. 143–158. Springer, Heidelberg (2011)
7. Bernstein, D.J., Lange, T., Peters, C.: Wild mcEliece incognito. In: Yang, B.-Y. (ed.) PQCrypto 2011. LNCS, vol. 7071, pp. 244–254. Springer, Heidelberg (2011)
8. Bogdanov, A., Lee, C.H.: Homorphic encryption from codes. In: Proceedings of the 44th ACM Symposium on Theory of Computing (STOC) (2012) (to appear)
9. Bosma, W., Cannon, J.J., Playoust, C.: The Magma algebra system I: The user language. J. Symbolic Comput. 24(3/4), 235–265 (1997)

10. Canteaut, A., Chabaud, F.: A new algorithm for finding minimum-weight words in a linear code: Application to McEliece's cryptosystem and to narrow-sense BCH codes of length 511. IEEE Trans. Inform. Theory 44(1), 367–378 (1998)

11. Cascudo, I., Chen, H., Cramer, R., Xing, C.: Asymptotically Good Ideal Linear Secret Sharing with Strong Multiplication over *Any* Fixed Finite Field. In: Halevi, S. (ed.) CRYPTO 2009. LNCS, vol. 5677, pp. 466–486. Springer, Heidelberg (2009)

12. Cascudo, I., Cramer, R., Xing, C.: The Torsion-Limit for Algebraic Function Fields and Its Application to Arithmetic Secret Sharing. In: Rogaway, P. (ed.) CRYPTO 2011. LNCS, vol. 6841, pp. 685–705. Springer, Heidelberg (2011)

13. Couvreur, A., Gaborit, P., Gauthier-Umaña, V., Otmani, A., Tillich, J.-P.: Distinguisher-based attacks on public-key cryptosystems using Reed-Solomon codes. ArXiv:1307.6458 (2014) To appear in Des. Codes Cryptogr.

14. Couvreur, A., Márquez-Corbella, I., Pellikaan, R.: A polynomial time attack against algebraic geometry code based public key cryptosystems. ArXiv:1401.6025 (January 2014)

15. Couvreur, A., Otmani, A., Tillich, J.-P.: New identities relating Wild Goppa codes. ArXiv:1310.3202v2 (2013)

16. Faugère, J.-C., Gauthier-Umaña, V., Otmani, A., Perret, L., Tillich, J.-P.: A distinguisher for high rate McEliece cryptosystems. In: Proceedings of the Information Theory Workshop 2011, ITW 2011, Paraty, Brasil, pp. 282–286 (2011)

17. Faugère, J.-C., Gauthier-Umaña, V., Otmani, A., Perret, L., Tillich, J.-P.: A distinguisher for high rate McEliece cryptosystems. IEEE Trans. Inform. Theory 59(10), 6830–6844 (2013)

18. Faugère, J.-C., Otmani, A., Perret, L., Tillich, J.-P.: Algebraic cryptanalysis of mcEliece variants with compact keys. In: Gilbert, H. (ed.) EUROCRYPT 2010. LNCS, vol. 6110, pp. 279–298. Springer, Heidelberg (2010)

19. Faure, C., Minder, L.: Cryptanalysis of the McEliece cryptosystem over hyperelliptic curves. In: Proceedings of the Eleventh International Workshop on Algebraic and Combinatorial Coding Theory, Pamporovo, Bulgaria, pp. 99–107 (June 2008)

20. Gauthier-Umaña, V., Leander, G.: Practical key recovery attacks on two McEliece variants. IACR Cryptology ePrint Archive 509 (2009)

21. Gibson, J.K.: Equivalent Goppa codes and trapdoors to McEliece's public key cryptosystem. In: Davies, D.W. (ed.) EUROCRYPT 1991. LNCS, vol. 547, pp. 517–521. Springer, Heidelberg (1991)

22. Janwa, H., Moreno, O.: McEliece public key cryptosystems using algebraic-geometric codes. Des. Codes Cryptogr. 8(3), 293–307 (1996)

23. Kötter, R.: A unified description of an error locating procedure for linear codes. In: Proc. Algebraic and Combinatorial Coding Theory, Voneshta Voda, pp. 113–117 (1992)

24. Landais, G., Tillich, J.-P.: An efficient attack of a mcEliece cryptosystem variant based on convolutional codes. In: Gaborit, P. (ed.) PQCrypto 2013. LNCS, vol. 7932, pp. 102–117. Springer, Heidelberg (2013)

25. Lee, P.J., Brickell, E.F.: An observation on the security of McEliece's public-key cryptosystem. In: Günther, C.G. (ed.) EUROCRYPT 1988. LNCS, vol. 330, pp. 275–280. Springer, Heidelberg (1988)

26. Leon, J.S.: A probabilistic algorithm for computing minimum weights of large error-correcting codes. IEEE Trans. Inform. Theory 34(5), 1354–1359 (1988)

27. Loidreau, P., Sendrier, N.: Weak keys in the McEliece public-key cryptosystem. IEEE Trans. Inform. Theory 47(3), 1207–1211 (2001)

28. Löndahl, C., Johansson, T.: A new version of mcEliece PKC based on convolutional codes. In: Chim, T.W., Yuen, T.H. (eds.) ICICS 2012. LNCS, vol. 7618, pp. 461–470. Springer, Heidelberg (2012)

29. MacWilliams, F.J., Sloane, N.J.A.: The Theory of Error-Correcting Codes, 1st edn. North–Holland, Amsterdam (1986)
30. Márquez-Corbella, I., Martínez-Moro, E., Pellikaan, R.: Evaluation of public-key cryptosystems based on algebraic geometry codes. In: Borges, J., Villanueva, M. (eds.) Proceedings of the Third International Castle Meeting on Coding Theory and Applications, Barcelona, Spain, September 11-15, pp. 199–204 (2011)
31. Márquez-Corbella, I., Martínez-Moro, E., Pellikaan, R.: The non-gap sequence of a subcode of a Generalized Reed–Solomon code. In: Des. Codes Cryptogr, pp. 1–17 (2012)
32. Márquez-Corbella, I., Martínez-Moro, E., Pellikaan, R.: On the unique representation of very strong algebraic geometry codes. Des. Codes Cryptogr., 1–16 (2012) (in press)
33. Márquez-Corbella, I., Pellikaan, R.: Error-correcting pairs for a public-key cryptosystem (2012) (preprint)
34. May, A., Meurer, A., Thomae, E.: Decoding random linear codes in $\tilde{O}(2^{0.054n})$. In: Lee, D.H., Wang, X. (eds.) ASIACRYPT 2011. LNCS, vol. 7073, pp. 107–124. Springer, Heidelberg (2011)
35. McEliece, R.J.: A Public-Key System Based on Algebraic Coding Theory. Jet Propulsion Lab., 114–116 (1978), DSN Progress Report 44
36. Minder, L., Shokrollahi, M.A.: Cryptanalysis of the Sidelnikov Cryptosystem. In: Naor, M. (ed.) EUROCRYPT 2007. LNCS, vol. 4515, pp. 347–360. Springer, Heidelberg (2007)
37. Misoczki, R., Tillich, J.-P., Sendrier, N., Barreto, P.S.L.M.: MDPC-McEliece: New McEliece variants from moderate density parity-check codes. IACR Cryptology ePrint Archive, 2012:409 (2012)
38. Niederreiter, H.: Knapsack-type cryptosystems and algebraic coding theory. Problems of Control and Information Theory 15(2), 159–166 (1986)
39. Otmani, A., Tillich, J.-P., Dallot, L.: Cryptanalysis of two McEliece cryptosystems based on quasi-cyclic codes. Special Issues of Mathematics in Computer Science 3(2), 129–140 (2010)
40. Pellikaan, R.: On decoding by error location and dependent sets of error positions. Discrete Math. 107, 368–381 (1992)
41. Peters, C.: Information-set decoding for linear codes over $\mathbf{f}_q$. In: Sendrier, N. (ed.) PQCrypto 2010. LNCS, vol. 6061, pp. 81–94. Springer, Heidelberg (2010)
42. Sendrier, N.: Finding the permutation between equivalent linear codes: The support splitting algorithm. IEEE Trans. Inform. Theory 46(4), 1193–1203 (2000)
43. Sidelnikov, V.M.: A public-key cryptosytem based on Reed-Muller codes. Discrete Math. Appl. 4(3), 191–207 (1994)
44. Sidelnikov, V.M., Shestakov, S.O.: On the insecurity of cryptosystems based on generalized Reed-Solomon codes. Discrete Math. Appl. 1(4), 439–444 (1992)
45. Stern, J.: A method for finding codewords of small weight. In: Wolfmann, J., Cohen, G. (eds.) Coding Theory 1988. LNCS, vol. 388, pp. 106–113. Springer, Heidelberg (1989)
46. Sugiyama, Y., Kasahara, M., Hirasawa, S., Namekawa, T.: Further results on Goppa codes and their applications to constructing efficient binary codes. IEEE Trans. Inform. Theory 22, 518–526 (1976)
47. Wieschebrink, C.: Two NP-complete problems in coding theory with an application in code based cryptography. In: 2006 IEEE International Symposium on Information Theory, pp. 1733–1737 (2006)
48. Wieschebrink, C.: Cryptanalysis of the Niederreiter public key scheme based on GRS subcodes. In: Sendrier, N. (ed.) PQCrypto 2010. LNCS, vol. 6061, pp. 61–72. Springer, Heidelberg (2010)

Symmetrized Summation Polynomials: Using Small Order Torsion Points to Speed Up Elliptic Curve Index Calculus[*]

Jean-Charles Faugère[1,2,3], Louise Huot[2,1,3], Antoine Joux[4,5,2,3], Guénaël Renault[2,1,3], and Vanessa Vitse[6]

[1] INRIA, POLSYS, Centre Paris-Rocquencourt, F-78153, Le Chesnay, France
[2] Sorbonne Universités, UPMC Univ Paris 06, LIP6 UPMC, F-75005, Paris, France
[3] CNRS, UMR 7606, LIP6 UPMC, F-75005, Paris, France
[4] CryptoExperts, Paris, France
[5] Chaire de Cryptologie de la Fondation UPMC
[6] Institut Fourier, Université Joseph Fourier, Grenoble I, France
jean-charles.faugere@inria.fr, {louise.huot,guenael.renault}@lip6.fr,
antoine.joux@m4x.org, vanessa.vitse@ujf-grenoble.fr

Abstract. Decomposition-based index calculus methods are currently efficient only for elliptic curves E defined over non-prime finite fields of very small extension degree n. This corresponds to the fact that the Semaev summation polynomials, which encode the relation search (or "sieving"), grow over-exponentially with n. Actually, even their computation is a first stumbling block and the largest Semaev polynomial ever computed is the 6-th. Following ideas from Faugère, Gaudry, Huot and Renault, our goal is to use the existence of small order torsion points on E to define new summation polynomials whose symmetrized expressions are much more compact and easier to compute. This setting allows to consider smaller factor bases, and the high sparsity of the new summation polynomials provides a very efficient decomposition step. In this paper the focus is on 2-torsion points, as it is the most important case in practice. We obtain records of two kinds: we successfully compute up to the 8-th symmetrized summation polynomial and give new timings for the computation of relations with degree 5 extension fields.

Keywords: ECDLP, elliptic curves, decomposition method, index calculus, Semaev polynomials, multivariate polynomial systems, invariant theory.

1 Introduction

In the past decade, the resolution of the discrete logarithm problem (DLP) on elliptic curves defined over extension fields has made important theoretical advances. Besides transfer attacks such as GHS [7], a promising approach is the

---

[*] This work has been partially supported by the LabExPERSYVAL-Lab(ANR-11-LABX-0025) and the HPAC grant of the French National Research Agency (HPAC ANR-11-BS02-013).

P.Q. Nguyen and E. Oswald (Eds.): EUROCRYPT 2014, LNCS 8441, pp. 40–57, 2014.

decomposition-based index calculus method pioneered by Gaudry and Diem [6,2], following ideas from Semaev [13]. As in any index calculus, this method is composed of two main steps: the relation search during which relations between elements of a factor base are collected, and the linear algebra stage during which the discrete logarithms are extracted using sparse matrix techniques. Since this second step is not specific to curve-based DLP, this article mainly focuses on the relation search.

In the standard decomposition method, relations are obtained by solving, for given points $R \in E(\mathbb{F}_{q^n})$ related to the challenge, the equation

$$R = P_1 + \cdots + P_n, \quad P_i \in \mathcal{F} \tag{1}$$

where $\mathcal{F} \subset E(\mathbb{F}_{q^n})$ is the factor base (this is the so-called *point decomposition problem*). The resolution of this problem relies critically on the Weil restriction structure of E relative to the extension $\mathbb{F}_{q^n}/\mathbb{F}_q$. In almost all preceding works [6,11,4], the usual factor base is defined as $\mathcal{F} = \{P \in E(\mathbb{F}_{q^n}) : x(P) \in \mathbb{F}_q\}$, where $x(P)$ stands for the abscissa of P, possibly after a change of equation of E. Then (1) translates algebraically using the *Semaev polynomial* $\mathrm{Sem}_{n+1} \in \mathbb{F}_{q^n}[X_1, \ldots, X_{n+1}]$ as

$$\mathrm{Sem}_{n+1}(x_1, \ldots, x_n, x(R)) = 0 \tag{2}$$

where the unknowns are $x_i = x(P_i) \in \mathbb{F}_q$. It is worth noticing that the resolution of this equation is the keystone of the relation search step. Thus, computing Semaev polynomials for larger values of n or finding ways to increase the efficiency of this resolution will undoubtedly enhance the practical impact of decomposition attacks and is the main goal of this paper.

Equation (2) is equivalent through a restriction of scalars to a multivariate polynomial system of n equations and n variables over $\mathbb{F}_q$, see [6]. The resolution of many instances of the multivariate polynomial systems arising from (2) (using for example Gröbner bases) is by far the main bottleneck of this index calculus approach. Recently Faugère *et al.* [4] have proposed to speed up the relation search using a 2-torsion point T naturally present on elliptic curves in the Edwards or Jacobi models. Their approach is based on the observation that in these models, the translation by T corresponds to a simple symmetry of the curve. This implies that the corresponding multivariate polynomial systems also admit an additional symmetry, allowing an easier resolution.

In this work, this approach is taken a step further as we investigate how to take advantage of the existence of some small order torsion points. To achieve this, we generalize ideas from Diem [2] who replaces the map $x : E \to \mathbb{F}_{q^n}$ by morphisms $\varphi : E \to \mathbb{P}^1$ of degree two. More precisely, we highlight new morphisms φ which let us take into account the existence of a torsion point T of small order m. The main idea relies on the construction of morphisms φ of degree divisible by m that satisfy the *equivariance property* $\varphi \circ \tau_T = f_T \circ \varphi$ for some homography (i.e. an automorphism of $\mathbb{P}^1$) $f_T \in \mathrm{PGL}_2(\mathbb{F}_q)$, where τ_T stands for the translation-by-T map $P \mapsto P+T$. A first important practical consequence of this setting is that the corresponding summation polynomials admit an additional invariance property, besides the classical one under any permutation of the variables: this comes from the fact that if $(P_1, \ldots, P_n) \in \mathcal{F}^n$ is a solution to the point decomposition problem (1), then $(P_1 + [k_1]T, \ldots, P_n + [k_n]T)$ is also a solution as soon as $\sum_i k_i = 0 \; [m]$. Using invariant theory, it is possible to express the summation polynomials in term of fundamental invariants. This new representation of the summation polynomials makes them very sparse and much easier to compute, and in particular we succeeded in computing new summation polynomials. This sparsity also leads to a significant simplification of the multivariate systems arising from the analog of (2). A second consequence is that the associated factor base $\mathcal{F} = \{P \in E : \varphi(P) \in \mathbb{P}^1(\mathbb{F}_q)\}$ becomes invariant under translations by multiples of T: this allows a division of the size of the factor base by the order m of T, thus speeding up by a factor m^2 the linear algebra step.

We begin in the next section by defining the summation polynomials associated to arbitrary morphisms $\varphi : E \to \mathbb{P}^1$ and explaining their use for index calculus. In section 3, we investigate the equivariance property satisfied by φ and explain the expected benefit when the small order points are accounted for. Then we focus in Section 4 on the fundamental case of degree 2 morphisms and their equivariance property with respect to translations by order 2 points. We finally give explicit examples of symmetrized summation polynomials and applications to the point decomposition problem on elliptic curves defined over degree 5 extension fields.

2   Summation Polynomials and Index Calculus

Let E be a given elliptic curve defined over an extension $\mathbb{F}_{q^n}$ of degree $n > 2$ of $\mathbb{F}_q$, and let $\varphi : E \to \mathbb{P}^1$ be a morphism defined over $\mathbb{F}_{q^n}$. We recall that in order to perform a decomposition-based index calculus, we consider the factor base $\mathcal{F} = \{P \in E : \varphi(P) \in \mathbb{P}^1(\mathbb{F}_q)\}$ which has approximately q elements, and try to find relations (decompositions) of the form $R = P_1 + \cdots + P_n$, $P_i \in \mathcal{F}$ where R is a given point related to the challenge. Alternatively, it is possible to consider other types of relations, for instance of the form $R = P_1 + \cdots + P_{n-1}$ (see [11]) or of the form $P_1 + \cdots + P_{n+2} = \mathcal{O}$ (see [10]). To do so, we introduce the summation polynomials related to φ (which can be seen as a generalization of those described in [2]):

Definition 1. *Let $E_{|K}$ be an elliptic curve defined over a field K and $\varphi : E \to \mathbb{P}^1$ be a non constant morphism. A polynomial $S \in K[X_1, \ldots, X_n]$ is called an n-th summation polynomial associated to φ if it satisfies*

$$S(a_1, \ldots, a_n) = 0 \Leftrightarrow \exists P_i \in E(\bar{K}), \; \varphi(P_i) = a_i \; and \; \sum_{i=1}^{n} P_i = \mathcal{O}. \quad (3)$$

Note that in the following, we will always explicitly identify $\mathbb{P}^1(K)$ with $K \cup \{\infty\}$, so that it makes sense to consider $\varphi(P)$ as an element of K (unless P is a pole of φ). Also note that this definition, and in fact a large part of what follows, is actually independent of the index calculus context. A first result is that summation polynomials always exist and are uniquely determined by the considered morphism.

Proposition 2. *For a given non-constant morphism* $\varphi : E \to \mathbb{P}^1$ *defined over a field* K, *the set of polynomials satisfying* (3) *is of the form* $\{cP_{\varphi,n}^k : c \in K^*, k \in \mathbb{N}^*\}$ *where* $P_{\varphi,n} \in K[X_1, \ldots, X_n]$. *The polynomial* $P_{\varphi,n}$ *is irreducible, unique up to multiplication by a constant, symmetric when* $n \geq 3$, *and is called the* n-*th summation polynomial associated to* φ.

Proof. Let $\psi : E^{n-1} \to K^n$ be the rational map such that $\psi(P_1, \ldots, P_{n-1}) = (\varphi(P_1), \ldots, \varphi(P_{n-1}), \varphi(-P_1 - \cdots - P_{n-1}))$. Then clearly $\psi(E^{n-1})$ is irreducible since E^{n-1} is irreducible, and has dimension $n - 1$ since φ is surjective. This classically implies the existence of an irreducible polynomial $P_{\varphi,n}$, unique up to a multiplicative constant, such that $\psi(E^{n-1}) = V(P_{\varphi,n})$, and it is easy to check that it satisfies (3).

To prove that $P_{\varphi,n}$ is symmetric, we consider the morphism c from the group of permutations of n elements $\mathfrak{S}_n$ to K^*, such that $c(\sigma)$ is the constant satisfying $P_{\varphi,n}^\sigma(X_1, \ldots, X_n) = c(\sigma)P_{\varphi,n}(X_1, \ldots, X_n)$. This morphism is well-defined since $P_{\varphi,n}^\sigma(X_1, \ldots, X_n) = P_{\varphi,n}(X_{\sigma(1)}, \ldots, X_{\sigma(n)})$ is clearly an irreducible solution of (3). It is well-known that the only morphisms from $\mathfrak{S}_n$ to a commutative group are the identity map or the signature map; this means that $P_{\varphi,n}$ is symmetric or alternating. But this last case is incompatible with (3) as soon as $n \geq 3$: indeed, let $a, a_3 \ldots, a_{n-1} \in K$ and $B = \{P_1 + \cdots + P_{n-1} : \varphi(P_1) = \varphi(P_2) = a, \varphi(P_i) = a_i \text{ for } i \geq 3\}$. This set is obviously finite, of cardinality bounded by $\deg(\varphi)^{n-1}$. However if $P_{\varphi,n}$ is alternating, then $P_{\varphi,n}(a, a, a_3, \ldots, a_{n-1}, a_n)$ is always zero, and (3) implies that for all $a_n \in \bar{K}$, there exist $P \in B$ and $P_n \in E(\bar{K})$ such that $\varphi(P_n) = a_n$ and $P + P_n = \mathcal{O}$; thus B is infinite, which is a contradiction.

It is always possible to compute summation polynomials inductively as it is done for the classical Semaev polynomials by using resultants. For $\varphi(P) = x(P)$ (in a Weierstrass model) we recover of course the polynomials introduced by Semaev [13]. Heuristically, it is possible to estimate the degree of $P_{\varphi,n}$ in each variable (which is clearly the same for all variables by symmetry). Let $(a_1, \ldots, a_{n-1}) \in \bar{K}^{n-1}$. The set of solutions of $P_{\varphi,n}(a_1, \ldots, a_{n-1}, X_n) = 0$ can be obtained as in the following diagram, by considering the preimage A of $\{(a_1, \ldots, a_{n-1})\}$ by φ^{n-1} and taking its image by $\varphi \circ (-\sum)$.

$$\{(P_1, \ldots, P_{n-1}) \in E(\bar{K})^{n-1} : \varphi(P_i) = a_i\} \xrightarrow{\ -\sum\ } \{-(P_1 + \cdots + P_{n-1}) : \varphi(P_i) = a_i\}$$
$$\downarrow{\scriptstyle \varphi \times \cdots \times \varphi} \qquad\qquad\qquad\qquad\qquad \downarrow{\scriptstyle \varphi}$$
$$\{(a_1, \ldots, a_{n-1})\} \qquad\qquad\qquad \{a_n : P_{\varphi,n}(a_1, \ldots, a_{n-1}, a_n) = 0\}$$

If φ is separable, then for most $(n - 1)$-tuples $(a_1, \ldots, a_{n-1})$, the cardinality of $A = \{(P_1, \ldots, P_{n-1}) \in E(\bar{K})^{n-1} : \varphi(P_i) = a_i\}$ is $(\deg \varphi)^{n-1}$. The map $-\sum : E^{n-1} \to E$ is of course not injective, but heuristically, if φ is a morphism with no special property, the restriction of $-\sum$ to A should be injective in general and the same holds for φ restricted to $-\sum(A)$. For a random map φ, the expected degree of $P_{\varphi,n}$ in each variable should be $(\deg\varphi)^{n-1}$. This is in any case an upper bound on the degree of $P_{\varphi,n}$. In the applications we need to be able to solve (4) below easily, and so we want the degree of $P_{\varphi,n}$ to be rather small; therefore most of this article focuses on the case where $\deg\varphi = 2$.

We detail two important cases where the degree is actually smaller than the bound given above.

1. The first case is when $\varphi(P) = \varphi(-P)$ and occurs in particular for Semaev polynomials (i.e. when $\varphi(P) = x(P)$). Then it is clear that $(P_1,\ldots,P_{n-1}) \in A$ if and only if $(-P_1,\ldots,-P_{n-1}) \in A$, thus $-\sum(A)$ is stable under $[-1] \in \mathrm{End}(E)$ and $\varphi_{|-\sum(A)}$ is 2-to-1. An upper bound on the degree $P_{\varphi,n}$ is then $(\deg\varphi^{n-1})/2$.

2. The second case is when φ factors through an isogeny $\psi : E \to E'$, i.e. $\varphi = \varphi' \circ \psi$ where $\varphi' : E' \to \mathbb{P}^1$. Then it is easy to check that $P_{\varphi,n} = P_{\varphi',n}$, and an upper bound on the degree is given by $(\deg\varphi')^{n-1}$.

In this second case, it is actually equivalent to perform the decomposition attack on E using φ or on E' using φ'. For this reason, we will usually only consider morphisms that do not factor through an isogeny.

For index calculus purposes, in order to compute a decomposition $R = P_1 + \cdots + P_n$, $P_i \in \mathcal{F}$, we use the $(n+1)$-th summation polynomial $P_{\varphi,n+1}$ associated to φ and try to find a solution $(a_1,\ldots,a_n) \in (\mathbb{F}_q)^n$ of the equation

$$P_{\varphi,n+1}(a_1,\ldots,a_n,\varphi(-R)) = 0. \tag{4}$$

We then look for points $P_1,\ldots,P_n \in E(\mathbb{F}_{q^n})$ such that $\varphi(P_i) = a_i$ and $P_1 + \cdots + P_n = R$. To solve the equation (4), we take the scalar restriction with respect to a linear basis of the extension $\mathbb{F}_{q^n}/\mathbb{F}_q$, leading to a multivariate polynomial system defined over $\mathbb{F}_q$.

3 Action of Torsion Points

3.1 Equivariant Morphisms

We investigate in this section how the existence of a rational m-torsion point on an elliptic curve E can speed up the decomposition attack. Let $T \in E[m]$; as mentioned in the introduction, our goal is to construct equivariant morphisms $\varphi : E \to \mathbb{P}^1$, i.e. such that there exists $f_T \in \mathrm{Aut}(\mathbb{P}^1)$ satisfying $\varphi(P + T) = f_T(\varphi(P))$ for all $P \in E$: $\varphi \circ \tau_T = f_T \circ \varphi$.

Let d be the order of f_T; clearly d divides m. If d is strictly smaller than m, then $\varphi \circ \tau_{[d]T} = f_T^{\circ d} \circ \varphi = \varphi$. This implies that φ can be factorized through the quotient isogeny $\pi : E \to E/\langle[d]T\rangle$ as $\varphi = \varphi' \circ \pi$. In particular, the relation search on E using φ and T is equivalent to the relation search on $E' = E/\langle[d]T\rangle$ using φ' and $\pi(T) \in E'[d]$, which does not fully exploit the property of T being a m-torsion point. This condition that the homography f_T has order m implies some restriction about the degree of φ.

Proposition 3. *Let* $T \in E[m]$ *be an* m-*torsion point and* $f_T \in \mathrm{Aut}(\mathbb{P}^1)$ *a homography of order* m. *Suppose there exists* $\varphi : E \to \mathbb{P}^1$ *such that* $\varphi \circ \tau_T = f_T \circ \varphi$. *Then* m *divides the degree of* φ.

Proof. Let us denote $e_\psi(P)$ the ramification index of a curve morphism $\psi :$ $\mathcal{C}_1 \to \mathcal{C}_2$ at a point $P \in \mathcal{C}_1$. Then for any point $P \in E$, we have $e_{\varphi \circ \tau_T}(P) =$ $e_{\tau_T}(P) \cdot e_\varphi(\tau_T(P)) = e_\varphi(P+T)$ and $e_{\varphi \circ \tau_T}(P) = e_{f_T \circ \varphi}(P) = e_\varphi(P) \cdot e_{f_T}(\varphi(P)) =$ $e_\varphi(P)$ since f_T and τ_T are isomorphisms. In particular φ has the same ramification index at P and its translates $P+T, \ldots, P+[m-1]T$. We consider now a fixed point $z \in \mathbb{P}^1$ of f_T (which always exists in an extension of K). Then $\varphi^{-1}(\{z\})$ is stable under translation by T, so that for each point P in $\varphi^{-1}(\{z\})$, its m translates $P, P+T, \ldots, P+[m-1]T$ also belong to $\varphi^{-1}(\{z\})$ and have the same ramification index. Since $\deg(\varphi) = \sum_{P \in \varphi^{-1}(z)} e_\varphi(P)$, the degree of φ is necessarily a multiple of m.

More generally, if $E(K)$ has a subgroup G of small order, we would like to find an equivariant morphism $\varphi : E \to \mathbb{P}^1$ such that for any $T \in G$, there exists $f_T \in \mathrm{Aut}(\mathbb{P}^1(K)) \simeq \mathrm{PGL}_2(K)$ such that $\varphi \circ \tau_T = f_T \circ \varphi$. Then the map $\chi : T \mapsto f_T$ is a group morphism from G to $\mathrm{PGL}_2(K)$ that we want to be injective by the above remark (since otherwise φ would factorize through $E/\ker(\chi)$). Unfortunately the set of possible subgroups relevant for our purpose is very restricted.

Proposition 4. *Let* G *be a finite subgroup of* $E(K)$ *and* $\chi : G \to \mathrm{PGL}_2(K)$ *an injective group morphism. Then* G *is of one of the following forms:*
1. $G = E[2]$,
2. $G = \langle T \rangle$ *where* $T \in E[m]$ *with* m *coprime to* $\mathrm{char}(K)$,
3. $G = E[\mathrm{char}(K)]$.

Proof. Since χ is injective, the commutative group G is isomorphic to a subgroup of $\mathrm{PGL}_2(K)$. It follows from the list in [14] that the only finite commutative subgroups of $\mathrm{PGL}_2(K)$ of order prime to the characteristic are either cyclic or isomorphic to $\mathbb{Z}/2\mathbb{Z} \times \mathbb{Z}/2\mathbb{Z}$; furthermore, it is easy to see that $\mathrm{PGL}_2(K)$ has no element whose order is a strict multiple of the characteristic. Thus the only subgroups of $E(K)$ that are of interest for our construction are either $E[2]$ or cyclic, generated by a point of order $\mathrm{char}(K)$ or prime to $\mathrm{char}(K)$.

In what follows, we only deal with the case where the homography f_T has order exactly m. Besides small torsion points, we would also like to take into account the automorphisms of the curve E; for most curves this only means the involution $[-1] : P \mapsto -P$. The group of permutations of E generated by the translation by T and $[-1]$ is isomorphic to the dihedral group $D_m = \mathbb{Z}/m\mathbb{Z} \rtimes \mathbb{Z}/2\mathbb{Z}$, so an equivariant morphism φ (if it exists) would give rise to an action on $\mathbb{P}^1$, i.e. a group morphism from D_m to $\mathrm{PGL}_2(K)$. As noted above, this map should be injective when restricted to the subgroup $\mathbb{Z}/m\mathbb{Z}$ generated by τ_T, since otherwise φ can be factorized through an isogeny. For $m > 2$, it is an easy exercise to show that such a group morphism is necessarily injective; in contrast, for $m = 2$ it is possible to impose the additional property $\varphi(-P) = \varphi(P)$ for all $P \in E$. Note that in the finite field case, $\mathrm{PGL}_2(\mathbb{F}_q)$ has a subgroup isomorphic to D_m if and only if $m|(q-1)$ or $m|(q+1)$ or $m = \mathrm{char}(\mathbb{F}_q)$ when $m > 2$.

3.2   Reducing the Factor Base

We consider an elliptic curve E defined over $\mathbb{F}_{q^n}$ with an m-torsion point T and denote by $\sim$ the equivalence relation given by $P \sim P'$ if and only if $P - P' \in \langle T \rangle$. Assume that there exists an equivariant morphism $\varphi : E \to \mathbb{P}^1(\mathbb{F}_{q^n})$ such that the associated homography f_T is in $\mathrm{PGL}_2(\mathbb{F}_q)$. Then the associated choice of factor base $\mathcal{F} = \{P \in E(\mathbb{F}_{q^n}) : \varphi(P) \in \mathbb{P}^1(\mathbb{F}_q)\}$ is invariant with respect to the translation by T, i.e. if $P \sim P'$ and $P \in \mathcal{F}$ then $P' \in \mathcal{F}$. Therefore, it is possible to divide the size of the factor base by m, by considering a reduced factor base $\mathcal{F}'$ that includes only one element for each equivalence class of elements of $\mathcal{F}$.

This modifies slightly the relation search. Each decomposition $R = P_1 + \cdots + P_n$, $P_i \in \mathcal{F}$ can be rewritten as $R = (Q_1 + [k_1]T) + \cdots + (Q_n + [k_n]T)$ with $0 \le k_i < m$ and where $Q_i \in \mathcal{F}'$ satisfies $Q_i \sim P_i$. We then just store the essentially equivalent relation $[m]R = [m]Q_1 + \cdots + [m]Q_n$. The important fact is that subsequently we only need about $\#\mathcal{F}/m$ relations to compute the discrete logarithms, and that the dimension of the relation matrix used in the resulting linear algebra step is also divided by m providing a speed-up by a factor m^2. On the other hand, this decreases the probability that a random point R decomposes by a factor m^{n-1} (there are more tuples in each preimage of the map $\mathcal{F}^n \to E$, $(P_1, \ldots, P_n) \mapsto \sum_i P_i$, so there are less points in the image), but this is more than compensated by the improved resolution of the associated polynomial systems as explained below.

Of course, if φ is also equivariant with respect to the automorphism $[-1]$ then it is possible to further reduce the factor base by 2. If $m = 2$ and E has full 2-torsion it is often possible to construct a morphism φ equivariant with respect to $[-1]$ and translations by any 2-torsion points, thus allowing a division by 8 of the size of the factor base.

3.3   Symmetries of Summation Polynomials

We have seen in Prop.2 that the summation polynomials are always symmetric for $n \ge 3$. In particular, they can be expressed in terms of the elementary symmetric polynomials $e_1, \ldots, e_n$ in the variables $X_1, \ldots, X_n$. This allows a reduction of the size and the total degree of the summation polynomials, thus simplifying their computation (for instance, it is possible to compute resultants of already partially symmetrized polynomials as was done in [11]). More importantly, this reduction has an impact on the resolution of the multivariate polynomial systems: instead of solving (4), we rather consider the (partially) symmetrized equation $P_{\varphi,n+1}(e_1, \ldots, e_n, \varphi(-R)) = 0, e_1, \ldots, e_n \in \mathbb{F}_q$. Of course, this adds a simple desymmetrization step in order to recover the corresponding solutions of (4) whenever they exist.

This approach can be extended when φ is equivariant with respect to translations by an m-torsion point T. Let $(a_1, \ldots, a_n)$ be a solution of $P_{\varphi,n}(a_1, \ldots, a_n) = 0$, so that there exist points $P_1, \ldots, P_n \in E(\bar{K})$ such that $\varphi(P_i) = a_i$ and $\sum P_i = \mathcal{O}$. Then for any $k_1, \ldots, k_n$ such that $m | \sum k_i$, we have $\sum (P_i + [k_i]T) = \mathcal{O}$. Thus $P_{\varphi,n}(f_T^{k_1}(a_1), \ldots, f_T^{k_n}(a_n)) = 0$. In particular $P_{\varphi,n}(f_T^{k_1}(X_1), \ldots, f_T^{k_n}(X_n))$ is also a solution of (3), except that it is a rational function instead of a polynomial if f_T is not an affine homography. We will see that $P_{\varphi,n}$, or an associated rational fraction $Q_{\varphi,n}$, is actually often invariant under this transformation; more formally, and taking into account Prop.2, it is invariant under an action of the group $G = (\mathbb{Z}/m\mathbb{Z})^{n-1} \rtimes \mathfrak{S}_n$. Then $P_{\varphi,n}$, resp. $Q_{\varphi,n}$, belongs to the invariant ring $K[X_1, \ldots, X_n]^G$ or the invariant field $K(X_1, \ldots, X_n)^G$. In particular, it can be expressed in terms of generators of the invariant ring or field allowing a further reduction of the size and the total degree of the systems; this will be detailed in the next section for $m = 2$. For index calculus purpose when $K = \mathbb{F}_{q^n}$, it is necessary that these invariant generators lie in $\mathbb{F}_q(X_1, \ldots, X_n)$. This means that the action of G restricts to an action on $\mathbb{F}_q(X_1, \ldots, X_n)$.

4   Summation Polynomials Associated to Degree Two Morphisms

We consider the simplest case where φ has degree 2 (note that in this case φ is necessarily separable).

Proposition 5. *Let E be an elliptic curve defined over a field K with Weierstrass coordinate functions x, y such that $[K(E) : K(x)] = 2$, and let $\varphi : E \to \mathbb{P}^1$ be a morphism of degree 2. Then there exist a homography $h \in \mathrm{PGL}_2(\bar{K})$ and a point $Q \in E(\bar{K})$ such that $\varphi = h \circ x \circ \tau_{-Q}$, i.e. $\varphi(P) = h(x(P - Q))$.*

Proof. Let $\mathcal{R}$ be the set of ramification points of φ, that is the set of points $P \in E$ such that the ramification index $e_\varphi(P)$ is strictly greater than 1. We easily deduce from the Hurwitz formula that the set $\mathcal{R}$ is non empty. For a given ramification point $Q \in E$, we consider a homography $\psi \in \mathrm{Aut}(\mathbb{P}^1)$ sending the point $\varphi(Q)$ to the point at infinity $[1 : 0]$ of $\mathbb{P}^1$. Let $\tau_Q : E \to E$ denote the translation by Q, then the morphism $\varphi' = \psi \circ \varphi \circ \tau_Q$ is ramified at $\mathcal{O} = [0 : 1 : 0]$. In particular, since φ has degree 2, φ' has a unique pole at $\mathcal{O}$ of order 2, so that there exist $a, b \in K$ such that $\varphi' = ax + b$. This shows that there exists a homography $h \in \mathrm{Aut}(\mathbb{P}^1)$ such that $\varphi(P) = h(x(P - Q))$.

To compute the associated summation polynomial, it is easy to check that the numerator of the rational fraction $\mathrm{Sem}_{n+1}(h^{-1}(X_1), \ldots, h^{-1}(X_n), x([n]Q))$ where Sem_{n+1} stands for $(n+1)$-th Semaev polynomial, satisfies the property (3). In the case where $Q = \mathcal{O}$ or more generally $Q \in E[n]$, the above expression can be simplified by considering the numerator of $\mathrm{Sem}_n(h^{-1}(X_1), \ldots, h^{-1}(X_n))$. The degree of $P_{\varphi,n}$ in each variable is then equal to 2^{n-1} if $Q \notin E[n]$ and 2^{n-2} otherwise. For index calculus, it is clear that φ should be of the form $h \circ x$: not only is the degree of P_φ smaller, but we also have $\forall P \in E, \varphi(-P) = \varphi(P)$. As mentioned above, this allows to reduce by a further 2 the size of the factor base.

4.1   Speeding Up the Relation Search Using One 2-Torsion Point

It turns out that every degree 2 morphism satisfies an equivariance property with respect to 2-torsion points; this is specific to the degree 2 case.

Lemma 6. *Let E be an elliptic curve defined over K with a 2-torsion point T, and let $\varphi : E \to \mathbb{P}^1$ be a morphism of degree 2. Then there exists $f_T \in \mathrm{PGL}_2(K)$ such that $\varphi(P + T) = f_T(\varphi(P))$ for all $P \in E$.*

Proof. In the special case of $\varphi = x$ where x is a Weierstrass coordinate function such that $[K(E) : K(x)] = 2$, the existence is given directly by the addition formula on E. Let $g_T \in \mathrm{PGL}_2(K)$ be this homography such that $x(P + T) = g_T(x(P))$ for all $P \in E$. For a more general morphism $\varphi = h \circ x \circ \tau_{-Q}$, the homography $f_T = h \circ g_T \circ h^{-1}$ satisfies the property.

In the remainder of this section, we denote by T a rational 2-torsion point, $\varphi : E \to \mathbb{P}^1$ a degree 2 rational map such that $\varphi(P) = \varphi(-P)$, and f_T the involution of $\mathbb{P}^1$ such that $\varphi(P + T) = f_T(\varphi(P))$ for all $P \in E$.

Let $W = \{(P_1, \ldots, P_n) : \sum P_i = \mathcal{O}\} \subset E^n$. This subvariety has many symmetries besides the action of the symmetric group. As mentioned above, we consider the group $G_2 = (\mathbb{Z}/2\mathbb{Z})^{n-1} \rtimes \mathfrak{S}_n$, (called *dihedral Coxeter group* in [4]). It is an abstract reflexion group, corresponding to the Coxeter diagram D_n, and its elements will be denoted by $((\epsilon_1, \ldots, \epsilon_n), \sigma) \in \{0; 1\}^n \times \mathfrak{S}_n$ where $\epsilon_1 + \cdots + \epsilon_n = 0 \mod 2$ (i.e. we explicitly identify G_2 with a subgroup of the group $(\mathbb{Z}/2\mathbb{Z})^n \rtimes \mathfrak{S}_n$ of isometries of the hypercube). The group G_2 acts on E^n by $((\epsilon_1, \ldots, \epsilon_n), \sigma) \cdot (P_1, \ldots, P_n) = ([\epsilon_1]T + P_{\sigma(1)}, \ldots, [\epsilon_n]T + P_{\sigma(n)})$ and leaves W globally invariant.

The image of W by φ^n is $V = V(P_{\varphi,n}) \subset (\mathbb{P}^1)^n$, the set of zeroes of the summation polynomial associated to φ. This set is also left globally invariant by the rational action of G_2 on $(\mathbb{P}^1)^n$ given by $((\epsilon_1, \ldots, \epsilon_n), \sigma) \cdot (a_1, \ldots, a_n) = (f_T^{\epsilon_1}(a_{\sigma(1)}), \ldots, f_T^{\epsilon_n}(a_{\sigma(n)}))$. This means that for any $g \in G_2$, $P_{\varphi,n}^g(X_1, \ldots, X_n) = P_{\varphi,n}(f_T^{\epsilon_1}(X_{\sigma(1)}), \ldots, f_T^{\epsilon_n}(X_{\sigma(n)}))$ is still a solution of (3), except that it is a rational fraction and no longer a polynomial unless f_T is affine. In particular, the summation polynomials associated to φ have additional symmetries, that are simple to handle only when f_T is affine, i.e. when we stay within the framework of polynomials and invariant rings.

Proposition 7. *Assume the involution $f_T \in \mathrm{PGL}_2(K)$ affine. Then for $n \geq 3$ the n-th summation polynomial $P_{\varphi,n}$ is invariant under the action of G_2 i.e. for all $g = (\underline{\epsilon}, \sigma) \in G_2$, $P_{\varphi,n}(X_1, \ldots, X_n) = P_{\varphi,n}(f_T^{\epsilon_1}(X_{\sigma(1)}), \ldots, f_T^{\epsilon_n}(X_{\sigma(n)}))$.*

Proof. A special case of this proposition has already been proved in [4]; for the sake of completeness, we rephrase the demonstration in our more general setting. Since $P_{\varphi,n}^g$ is again an irreducible summation polynomial associated to φ, there exist $c(g) \in K^*$ such that $P_{\varphi,n}^g = c(g)P_{\varphi,n}$. This gives us a morphism $c : G_2 = (\mathbb{Z}/2\mathbb{Z})^{n-1} \rtimes \mathfrak{S}_n \to K^*$ and from Prop.2 $c(\mathfrak{S}_n) = 1$. Let $u = ((1, 1, 0, \ldots, 0), e)$ where $e \in \mathfrak{S}_n$ is the neutral element, and $v = (\underline{0}, (1\ 2\ 3))$. It is clear that G_2 is generated by u together with $\mathfrak{S}_n$, so that the image of c is completely determined by the value of u. Since $u^2 = 1$, we have $c(u) = \pm 1$. Now an easy computation shows that $(uv)^3 = 1$, so $1 = c(uv)^3 = c(u)^3 c(v)^3 = c(u)^3 = c(u)$.

This means that $P_{\varphi,n} \in K[X_1, \ldots, X_n]^{G_2}$, the ring of invariants of G_2. Since the action of G_2 is generated by pseudo-reflections, the Chevalley-Shephard-Todd theorem states that $K[X_1, \ldots, X_n]^{G_2}$ is itself a polynomial ring when the characteristic of K is greater than n; we will show later that it is in fact true in any characteristic. But first, we give a condition on E and T to assure the existence of a degree 2 morphism φ such that the corresponding homography f_T is affine. Moreover when this condition is satisfied, we can take without loss of generality f_T equal to $x \mapsto -x$ in odd characteristic or $x \mapsto x + 1$ in characteristic 2.

Proposition 8. *Let E be an elliptic curve defined over a field K.*
(i) If $char(K) \neq 2$, then there exist $T \in E(K)[2]$ and $\varphi : E \to \mathbb{P}^1$ a degree 2 morphism such that $\varphi(P + T) = -\varphi(P)$ and $\varphi(-P) = \varphi(P)$ if and only if there exist $T' \in E[4]$ such that $x(T') \in K$. In this case $T = [2]T'$ and the curve E has an equation of the form $y^2 = x^3 + ax^2 + bx$ where $T = (0,0)$ and b is a square in K; moreover, φ is of the form

$$\lambda \frac{x(P) + \sqrt{b}}{x(P) - \sqrt{b}},$$

for a choice of the square root of b and $\lambda \in K$.
(ii) If $char(K) = 2$ and $j(E) \neq 0$, then E admits an equation of the form $y^2 + xy = x^3 + ax^2 + b$ with a unique non-trivial 2-torsion point $T = (0, \sqrt{b})$. Then the morphisms φ such that $\varphi(-P) = \varphi(P)$ and $\varphi(P + T) = \varphi(P) + 1$ are of the form

$$\frac{b^{1/4}}{x(P) + b^{1/4}} + \lambda, \text{ where } \lambda \in K.$$

If $char(K) = 2$ and $j(E) = 0$, there is no non-trivial 2-torsion point.

Proof. (i) Suppose there exists a 2-torsion point $T \in E(K)[2]$, then up to a translation we can assume that $T = (0,0)$ and that E has an equation of the form $y^2 = x^3 + ax^2 + bx$. From the addition formula, we get $x(P + T) = g_T(x(P)) = b/x(P)$. Let φ be a degree 2 morphism such that $\varphi(-P) = \varphi(P)$. From Prop.5, there exists $h \in PGL_2(K)$ such that $\varphi = h \circ x$, and $\varphi(P + T) = f_T(\varphi(P))$ where $f_T = h \circ g_T \circ h^{-1}$. Thus we are looking for a homography $h \in PGL_2(K)$ conjugating g_T to $z \mapsto -z$. By considering the associated matrices or the set of fixed points, it is easy to see that there exists such an $h \in PGL_2(K)$ if and only if b is a square, and that all such h are of the form $h(x) = \lambda \left(\frac{x - \sqrt{b}}{x + \sqrt{b}} \right)^{-1}$.

Now, if b is a square in K, then any of the points $T' \in E(\bar{K})$ of abscissa $\pm \sqrt{b}$ satisfies $[2]T' = T$, and are thus in $E[4]$. Reciprocally, if there exists $T' \in E[4]$ such that $x(T') \in K$, then $[2]T'$ is in $E(K)[2]$, and up to a translation E has an equation as above with b square in K.

(ii) It is already well-known that in characteristic 2 an elliptic curve has a non-trivial 2-torsion point if and only if $j(E) \neq 0$. If E has an equation of the form $y^2 + xy = x^3 + ax^2 + b$ and $T = (0, \sqrt{b})$, the addition formula gives $x(P + T) = g_T(x(P)) = \sqrt{b}/x(P)$. Now in characteristic 2, there always exists $h \in \mathrm{PGL}_2(K)$ that conjugates the homography $g_T(x) = \frac{\sqrt{b}}{x}$ to $x \mapsto x + 1$, and it is easy to see that all such h are of the form $x \mapsto \frac{b^{1/4}}{x + b^{1/4}} + \lambda$, $\lambda \in K$.

The first part of Prop.8 generalizes the results given in [4], where the morphism φ is obtained as a projection onto a coordinate for curves in twisted Edwards form. The fact that the morphism φ depends of a parameter $\lambda \in K$ is important for index calculus applications, since it allows to define different factor bases depending on the choice of λ.

Remark 9. *Lemma 6 shows that every degree 2 morphism satisfies an equivariance property $\varphi(P + T) = f_T(\varphi(P))$; the above proposition only describes the cases for which f_T is as simple as possible. In odd characteristic, about half of the curves with a 2-torsion point have a coefficient b that is a square, and thus satisfies directly the hypotheses of the proposition. However if the curve has full 2-torsion (i.e. $a^2 - 4b$ is a square) then it is 2-isogenous to a curve with a rational 4-torsion point, again satisfying the hypotheses. Overall, this proposition applies in odd characteristic to about 3/4 of curves with a 2-torsion point.*

4.2   Action of the Full 2-Torsion

In this subsection, K is a field of characteristic different from 2. Let E be an elliptic curve having a complete rational 2-torsion (in the finite field case, this is equivalent up to a 2-isogeny to the cardinality of E being divisible by 4). Let T_0, T_1 and $T_2 = T_0 + T_1$ be the three non-trivial 2-torsion points of E. According to Lem.6, for any degree 2 morphism φ, there exist homographic involutions f_0, f_1 and $f_2 = f_0 \circ f_1$ such that $\forall P \in E, \forall i \in \{0; 1; 2\}, \varphi(P + T_i) = f_i(\varphi(P))$. In the same way as before, we can consider the action on $(\mathbb{P}^1)^n$ of the reflexion group $G_4 = (\mathbb{Z}/2\mathbb{Z} \times \mathbb{Z}/2\mathbb{Z})^{n-1} \rtimes \mathfrak{S}_n$ seen as a subgroup of $(\mathbb{Z}/2\mathbb{Z} \times \mathbb{Z}/2\mathbb{Z})^n \rtimes \mathfrak{S}_n$ which is given by

$$((\epsilon_1, \ldots, \epsilon_n), (\epsilon'_1, \ldots, \epsilon'_n), \sigma) \cdot (a_1, \ldots, a_n) = (f_0^{\epsilon_1} \circ f_1^{\epsilon'_1}(a_{\sigma(1)}), \ldots, f_0^{\epsilon_n} \circ f_1^{\epsilon'_n}(a_{\sigma(n)})).$$

This means that for any $g \in G_4$, the rational fraction

$$P_{\varphi,n}^g(X_1, \ldots, X_n) = P_{\varphi,n}(f_0^{\epsilon_1} \circ f_1^{\epsilon'_1}(X_{\sigma(1)}), \ldots, f_0^{\epsilon_n} \circ f_1^{\epsilon'_n}(X_{\sigma(n)}))$$

satisfies again (3). But it is no longer possible that $P_{\varphi,n}^g$ is a polynomial for all $g \in G_4$. Indeed, f_0, f_1 and f_2 must commute because of the commutativity of the group law on E, but it is easy to check that two distinct affine involutions cannot commute. Thus the best we can hope is that one of the three involutions is affine, without loss of generality equal to $z \mapsto -z$; then the two remaining involutions are necessarily of the form $z \mapsto c/z$ and $z \mapsto -c/z$ since they all commute. We give below a condition for the best case where $c = 1$.

Proposition 10. *Let E be an elliptic curve in twisted Legendre form $y^2 = cx(x-1)(x-\lambda)$. Let $\Delta_0 = \lambda$, $\Delta_1 = (1-\lambda)$ and $\Delta_2 = -\lambda(1-\lambda)$. Then there exists a degree 2 morphism φ such that $\varphi(-P) = \varphi(P)$ and the associated involutions are $\{f_0; f_1; f_2\} = \{z \mapsto -z; z \mapsto \frac{1}{z}; z \mapsto -\frac{1}{z}\}$ if and only if there are at least two squares among $\{\Delta_0; \Delta_1; \Delta_2\}$.*

Proof. Let $T_0 = (0,0)$, $T_1 = (1,0)$ and $T_2 = (\lambda,0)$ be the non-trivial 2-torsion points of E. Then the abscissa of $P + T_i$ is equal to $g_i(x_P)$, where

$$g_0(x) = \frac{\lambda}{x}, \quad g_1(x) = \frac{x-\lambda}{x-1}, \quad g_2 = g_0 \circ g_1 = g_1 \circ g_0.$$

To determine if these involutions can be conjugated to $z \mapsto -z$, $z \mapsto \frac{1}{z}$ and $z \mapsto -\frac{1}{z}$, we look at their fixed points. Let Fix_i be the set of fixed points of g_i for $i = 0,1,2$; then Fix_i is non empty if and only if Δ_i is a square. As $\{0; \infty\}$ and $\{\pm 1\}$ are the set of fixed points of $z \mapsto -z$ and $z \mapsto \frac{1}{z}$ respectively, we deduce easily that there must be at least two squares among $\{\Delta_0; \Delta_1; \Delta_2\}$. Reciprocally, if there are two squares among $\{\Delta_0; \Delta_1; \Delta_2\}$, then it is possible to find a homography $h \in \mathrm{PGL}_2(K)$ sending the fixed points of the corresponding involutions to $\{0; \infty\}$ and $\{\pm 1\}$, and we can take $\varphi(P) = h(x(P))$.

Remark 11. *The condition that Δ_i is a square in K is equivalent to the existence of a 4-torsion point T_i' with a rational x-coordinate such that $[2]T_i' = T_i$. If $p \equiv 1$ [4] then $\Delta_0\Delta_1\Delta_2$ is a square so there are exactly one or three squares among $\{\Delta_0; \Delta_1; \Delta_2\}$, and heuristically the latter should occur for about one curve out of four. Similarly if $p \equiv 3$ [4] then there are exactly zero or two squares among the Δ_i, the latter occurring heuristically for $3/4$ of the curves. Overall about half of the curves in twisted Legendre form will satisfy the hypotheses of the above proposition. For the remaining curves one has to work with degree 2 morphisms whose equivariance property has a less simple expression.*

Proposition 12. *Suppose that the hypotheses of Prop. 10 are satisfied. Then the rational fraction*

$$Q_{\varphi,n}(X_1, \ldots, X_n) = \frac{P_{\varphi,n}(X_1, \ldots, X_n)}{(X_1 \cdots X_n)^{2^{n-3}}}$$

is invariant under the action of G_4 for $n \geq 3$, i.e. for all $g = ((\underline{\epsilon}, \underline{\epsilon}'), \sigma) \in G_4$,

$$Q_{\varphi,n}(X_1, \ldots, X_n) = Q_{\varphi,n}(f_0^{\epsilon_1} \circ f_1^{\epsilon'_1}(X_{\sigma(1)}), \ldots, f_0^{\epsilon_n} \circ f_1^{\epsilon'_n}(X_{\sigma(n)}))$$

$$= Q_{\varphi,n}((-1)^{\epsilon_1} X_{\sigma(1)}^{(-1)^{\epsilon'_1}}, \ldots, (-1)^{\epsilon_n} X_{\sigma(n)}^{(-1)^{\epsilon'_n}}).$$

Proof. From Prop. 7 the polynomial $P_{\varphi,n}$ is invariant under the action of G_2 (identified with the subgroup of G_4 whose elements are of the form $(\underline{\epsilon}, \underline{0}, \sigma)$), and it is also obviously true for the denominator $(X_1 \cdots X_n)^{2^{n-3}}$. Since G_4 is generated by G_2 and $u' = (\underline{0}, (1,1,0,\ldots,0), e)$ (where $e \in \mathfrak{S}_n$ is the neutral element), it is sufficient to check that $Q_{\varphi,n}^{u'} = Q_{\varphi,n}$. The degree of $P_{\varphi,n}$ is 2^{n-2} in each variable, so $P'(X_1, \ldots, X_n) = (X_1 X_2)^{2^{n-2}} P_{\varphi,n}(1/X_1, 1/X_2, X_3, \ldots, X_n)$ is an irreducible polynomial of $K[X_1, \ldots, X_n]$ satisfying (3); in particular, there exists $c \in K$ such that $P' = c \cdot P_{\varphi,n}$ and consequently

$$Q_{\varphi,n}^{u'}(X_1, \ldots, X_n) = Q_{\varphi,n}(1/X_1, 1/X_2, X_3, \ldots, X_n) = c \cdot Q_{\varphi,n}(X_1, \ldots, X_n).$$

Now the same reasoning as in the proof of Prop.7 shows that $c = 1$.

4.3   Invariant Fields and Invariant Rings

We have seen that when the action of the 2-torsion points is taken into account in the choice of the morphism φ, the associated summation polynomial $P_{\varphi,n}$ and rational fraction $Q_{\varphi,n}$ belong respectively to the invariant ring $K[X_1, \ldots, X_n]^{G_2}$ and the invariant field $K(X_1, \ldots, X_n)^{G_4}$. Hilbert's finiteness theorem implies that the invariant ring $K[X_1, \ldots, X_n]^{G_2}$ is finitely generated, and Galois theory states that $K(X_1, \ldots, X_n)^{G_4}$ is a subfield of $K(X_1, \ldots, X_n)$ with corresponding extension degree $|G_4| = 4^{n-1}n!$. The goal of this section is to determine generators for these two structures.

We recall that the action of G_2 on $K[X_1, \ldots, X_n]$ and $K(X_1, \ldots, X_n)$ is given by permutations of variables and any even change of signs, while the action of G_4 on $K(X_1, \ldots, X_n)$ also includes taking the inverse of an even number of variables. As already mentioned, the group G_2 is a normal subgroup of $G_2' = (\mathbb{Z}/2\mathbb{Z})^n \rtimes \mathfrak{S}_n$, as is $(\mathbb{Z}/2\mathbb{Z})^n$, and the action of G_2 trivially extends to an action on G_2' by allowing any number of sign changes. This means that we have the following diagram of Galois extensions:

$$
\begin{array}{ccccc}
 & & K(X_1, \ldots, X_n) & & \\
 & \overset{2^n}{\diagup} & & \overset{2^{n-1}n!}{\diagdown} & \\
K(X_1, \ldots, X_n)^{(\mathbb{Z}/2\mathbb{Z})^n} & & & & K(X_1, \ldots, X_n)^{G_2} \\
 & \underset{n!}{\diagdown} & & \underset{2}{\diagup} & \\
 & & K(X_1, \ldots, X_n)^{G_2'} & &
\end{array}
$$

It is easy to verify that $K(X_1, \ldots, X_n)^{(\mathbb{Z}/2\mathbb{Z})^n}$ is equal to $K(X_1^2, \ldots, X_n^2)$ in odd or zero characteristic and equal to $K(X_1^2 + X_1, \ldots, X_n^2 + X_n)$ in characteristic 2, since the latter is clearly invariant and has the correct extension degree. Let $Y_i = X_i^2 + X_i$ if $\text{char}(K) = 2$ or $Y_i = X_i^2$ otherwise. Then $K(X_1, \ldots, X_n)^{G_2'} = K(Y_1, \ldots, Y_n)^{\mathfrak{S}_n}$ since $G_2'/(\mathbb{Z}/2\mathbb{Z})^n \simeq \mathfrak{S}_n$, so this invariant field consists of symmetric rational fractions in the Y_i, which are known to be generated by the elementary symmetric polynomials $s_1 = Y_1 + \cdots + Y_n, \ldots, s_n = Y_1 \cdots Y_n$. Now let $e_1 = X_1 + \cdots + X_n$ in characteristic 2 and $e_n = X_1 \cdots X_n$ otherwise; we have $e_1^2 + e_1 = s_1$, resp. $e_n^2 = s_n$. Then $K(e_1, s_2, \ldots, s_n)$, resp. $K(s_1, \ldots, s_{n-1}, e_n)$, is invariant under G_2 and a degree 2 extension of $K(s_1, \ldots, s_n) = K(X_1, \ldots, X_n)^{G_2'}$, hence is equal to the invariant field $K(X_1, \ldots, X_n)^{G_2}$. Finally, since $s_1, \ldots, s_n$ and e_1 (resp. e_n) belong to $K[X_1, \ldots, X_n]$, we have the following proposition.

Proposition 13. $K[X_1, \ldots, X_n]^{G_2} = \begin{cases} K[e_1, s_2, \ldots, s_n] & \text{in characteristic 2,} \\ K[s_1, \ldots, s_{n-1}, e_n] & \text{otherwise.} \end{cases}$

We can use the same argument for the action of G_4 on $K(X_1, \ldots, X_n)$, which extends to an action of $G_4' = (\mathbb{Z}/2\mathbb{Z} \times \mathbb{Z}/2\mathbb{Z})^n \rtimes \mathfrak{S}_n$, by considering the normal subgroups G_4 and $(\mathbb{Z}/2\mathbb{Z} \times \mathbb{Z}/2\mathbb{Z})^n$.

$$K(X_1,\ldots,X_n)^{(\mathbb{Z}/2\mathbb{Z}\times\mathbb{Z}/2\mathbb{Z})^n} \overset{4^n}{\underset{n!}{\rule{0pt}{1em}}} K(X_1,\ldots,X_n) \overset{4^{n-1}n!}{\underset{4}{\rule{0pt}{1em}}} K(X_1,\ldots,X_n)^{G_4}$$

$$K(X_1,\ldots,X_n)^{G_4'}$$

The leftmost field $K(X_1,\ldots,X_n)^{(\mathbb{Z}/2\mathbb{Z}\times\mathbb{Z}/2\mathbb{Z})^n}$ is easily seen to be equal to $K(Z_1,\ldots,Z_n)$ where $Z_i = X_i^2 + X_i^{-2}$, and the bottom field $K(X_1,\ldots,X_n)^{G_4'}$ is then generated by the elementary symmetric polynomials $\sigma_1 = Z_1 + \cdots + Z_n,\ldots,\sigma_n = Z_1\cdots Z_n$. Finding generators for the invariant field of G_4 is less obvious. Let s_i be the i-th elementary symmetric polynomial in $X_1^2,\ldots,X_n^2$ (with the convention that $s_0 = 1$), $w_0 = \sum_{i=0}^{\lfloor n/2\rfloor} s_{2n}/(X_1\cdots X_n)$ and $w_1 = \sum_{i=1}^{\lfloor(n-1)/2\rfloor} s_{2n+1}/(X_1\cdots X_n)$. Then it is only a matter of computation to check that w_0 and w_1 are indeed invariant under the action of G_4; actually, replacing an odd number of variables by their inverse exchanges w_0 and w_1. Moreover, direct computations show that w_0 and w_1 are roots of the polynomial

$$Z^4 - \left(\sum_{i=0}^{\lfloor n/2\rfloor} 2^{2i}\sigma_{n-2i}\right) Z^2 + \left(\sum_{i=0}^{\lfloor(n-1)/2\rfloor} 2^{2i}\sigma_{n-(2i+1)}\right)^2 \in K(X_1,\ldots,X_n)^{G_4'}[Z]$$

so they are algebraic of degree 4 over $K(X_1,\ldots,X_n)^{G_4}$. This shows the following proposition.

Proposition 14. $K(X_1,\ldots,X_n)^{G_4} = K(\sigma_1,\ldots,\sigma_n,w_0) = K(\sigma_1,\ldots,\sigma_n,w_1) = K(\sigma_1,\ldots,\sigma_n,w_0,w_1)$.

These families of generators are of course not algebraically independent. We can in fact choose n generators among them: either removing from the first two families any generator of the form σ_{n-2i}, or removing in the last family any two generators of the σ_i's. From an algorithmic point of view, it is not clear which set of generators is the most efficient for computations of summation polynomials.

5   Examples and Applications

5.1   Computation of Summation Polynomials

Characteristic 2. Let $E : y^2 + xy = x^3 + ax^2 + b$ be an elliptic curve defined over a characteristic 2 field and $\varphi : P \mapsto \frac{\gamma}{x(P)+\gamma} + \lambda$ where $\gamma^4 = b$, as in Prop.8. Then the first summations polynomials associated to φ, expressed in term of the generators $e_1, s_2,\ldots,s_n$ of the invariant ring $K[X_1,\ldots,X_n]^{G_2}$, are equal to

$$P_{\varphi,3} = s_3 + Ls_2 + L^2(e_1^2 + e_1) + L^3 + \gamma(e_1 + \lambda)^2,$$

$$P_{\varphi,4} = e_1^2(s_4 + Ls_3 + L^2 s_2 + L^3(e_1^2 + e_1) + L^4) + (s_3 + (e_1^2 + e_1)L^2 + e_1^2\gamma)^2,$$

where $L = \lambda^2 + \lambda$. The next polynomials become too large to be reproduced with λ and γ as formal parameters, so we give them for $\lambda = 0$. Note that it is possible to recover the general expression for a different value of λ by replacing X_i by $X_i + \lambda$, which corresponds to replacing e_1 by $e_1 + n\lambda$ and s_k by $\sum_{j=0}^{k} \binom{n-j}{k-j} L^{k-j} s_j$. For $n = 5$, we obtain

$$P_{\varphi,5} = e_1^8 \gamma^8 + e_1^6 s_5 \gamma^5 + e_1^4 s_4^2 \gamma^4 + e_1^2 s_3^2 s_5 \gamma^3 + s_3^4 \gamma^4 + e_1^2 s_5^3 \gamma + s_2^2 s_5^2 \gamma^2 + s_5^4 + s_5^3 \gamma.$$

Again, the next polynomials become too large to be reproduced in their entirety; for example, we obtain

$$P_{\varphi,6} = s_5^8 + e_1^2 s_5^6 s_6 + s_5^6 s_6 + \cdots + e_1^{12} s_5^2 \gamma^{10} + e_1^{14} s_6 \gamma^{12} + e_1^{16} \gamma^{16},$$

which has 50 terms in $\mathbb{F}_2(\gamma)[e_1, s_2, \ldots, s_6]$. We observe that when $\lambda = 0$ or 1, the polynomials $P_{\varphi,3}, P_{\varphi,4}$ and $P_{\varphi,5}$ only involve even exponents of the $n - 1$ first variables. This fact is true in general: for $L = 0$, $P_{\varphi,n}(e_1, s_1, \ldots, s_n) = \tilde{P}_{\varphi,n}(e_1^2, s_2^2, \ldots, s_{n-1}^2, s_n)$, which simplifies the inductive computation of these polynomials in characteristic 2.

We sum up in Table 1 the number of monomials of Semaev polynomials and our symmetrized summation polynomials (for $\lambda = 0$), as well as the timings of their computation. For $n \leq 7$, we used resultants of partially symmetrized polynomials followed by a symmetrization at each step. The computation was intractable in this way for $n = 8$. Thus, we implemented a dedicated interpolation algorithm to compute this new record. Here we briefly describe this computation. The 8-th symmetrized polynomial is the result of the symmetrized version of the relation

$$P_{\varphi,8}(X_1, \ldots, X_8) = \mathrm{Res}_X(P_{\varphi,6}(X_1, \ldots, X_5, X), P_{\varphi,4}(X_6, \ldots, X_8, X)),$$

but with $P_{\varphi,4}$ and especially $P_{\varphi,6}$ already in partially symmetrized form. We thus begin by evaluating $P_{\varphi,8}(e_1, s_2, \ldots, s_8)$ on a very large sample of points, which can be done by computing the above resultant with all variables (except X) instantiated. However, in order to apply fast sparse evaluation-interpolation techniques [15], we have to precisely control the instantiations of $e_1, s_2, \ldots, s_8$; thus we cannot simply evaluate the X_i to deduce a sample point, but have to do the converse instead. Moreover, because of the huge size of the sample, each of these evaluations has to be done as efficiently as possible. Actually, since we work with symmetrized polynomials, each instantiation corresponds to the computation of the values of the generators of the invariant ring in $X_1, \ldots, X_5$ and $X_6, \ldots, X_8$ respectively, from an instantiation of $e_1, s_2, \ldots, s_8$. Such a computation is not at all straightforward; it can be done by solving a polynomial system but, even by using the most efficient existing implementations, the timings are too slow to obtain $P_{\varphi,8}$ in a reasonable time. Thus, we investigated new methods to solve this problem and finally reduced it, by using the underlying symmetries, to the almost instantaneous resolution of a univariate polynomial. This efficient resolution is mainly based on a careful study of the factorization of this polynomial and a clever choice of the sample points, which let us avoid half of the most time-consuming steps of the algorithm. The sparse-interpolation step is less tricky but we need also a careful implementation in order to obtain the required efficiency. The complete computation of the 8-th symmetrized summation

Table 1. Comparison of the number of terms of symmetrized Semaev polynomials and summation polynomials using a 2-torsion point in characteristic 2 ($\lambda = 0$). The crosses correspond to computations that stopped unsuccessfully after several weeks.

n		3	4	5	6	7	8
Semaev	nb of monomials	3	6	39	638	–	–
polynomials	timings	0 s	0 s	26 s	725 s	×	×
$P_{\varphi,n}$	nb of monomials	2	3	9	50	2 247	470 369
	timings	0 s	0 s	0 s	1 s	383 s	40.5 h

polynomial was achieved in about 40.5 CPU.hours using MAGMA [1], whereas previous attempts using the direct approach were all stopped after at least one month of computations.

Odd Characteristic. Let $E : y^2 = cx(x-1)(x-\lambda)$ be an elliptic curve in twisted Legendre form over an odd characteristic field K. As in Prop.10, we assume that λ and $1 - \lambda$ are squares, so that there exists $t \in K$ such that $\sqrt{\lambda} = (1-t^2)/(1+t^2)$ and $\sqrt{1-\lambda} = 2t/(1+t^2)$. Let $T_0 = (0,0)$ and $T_1 = (1,0)$; then a map $\varphi : E \to \mathbb{P}^1$ satisfying $\varphi(-P) = \varphi(P)$, $\varphi(P+T_0) = -\varphi(P)$ and $\varphi(P+T_1) = 1/\varphi(P)$ is given by

$$\varphi(P) = \frac{\sqrt{\lambda}+1}{\sqrt{1-\lambda}} \frac{x(P) - \sqrt{\lambda}}{x(P) + \sqrt{\lambda}}.$$

We can compare the summation polynomials $P_{\varphi,n}$ symmetrized with respect to G_2 (corresponding to the action of a single 2-torsion point T_0), the associated rational fractions $Q_{\varphi,n}$ symmetrized with respect to G_4 (corresponding to the action of the complete 2-torsion), and the classical Semaev polynomials, expressed with the elementary symmetric polynomials $e_1, \ldots, e_n$ in the variables $X_1, \ldots, X_n$. For $n = 3$ and 4, we have

$$\text{Sem}_3 = e_2^2 - 4e_1e_3 + 2e_2\lambda - 4e_3(\lambda+1) + \lambda^2,$$
$$P_{\varphi,3} = t^3 e_3^2 + 2(1-t^4)e_3 + t^3 s_1 - ts_2 - t,$$
$$Q_{\varphi,3} = t^3 w_1 - tw_0 - 2t^4 + 2.$$

$$P_{\varphi,4} = t^2(s_1^2 - 2s_1s_3 - 4s_2e_4^2 + 8s_2e_4 - 4s_2 + s_3^2 + 8e_4^3 - 16e_4^2 + 8e_4) + 4(t^4+1)(s_1e_4^2 - s_1e_4 - s_3e_4 + s_3),$$
$$Q_{\varphi,4} = 4(t^4+1)\sigma_1 - 4t^2\sigma_2 + t^2 w_1^2 - 4(t^4+1)w_1 + 8t^2 w_0 - 32t^2.$$

Table 2 sums up the number of terms of the computable polynomials for comparison.

5.2   Index Calculus on $E(\mathbb{F}_{q^5})$

IPSEC Oakley Key Determination 'Well Know Group' 3 Curve An interesting target for the decomposition attack is the IPSEC Oakley key determination 'Well Know Group' 3 curve [9] defined over the binary field $\mathbb{F}_{2^{155}} = \mathbb{F}_{(2^{31})^5}$.

Table 2. Comparison of the number of terms of symmetrized classical Semaev polynomials and summation polynomials in odd characteristic using either a single 2-torsion point or the complete 2-torsion

n	3	4	5	6
Semaev polynomial	5	36	940	–
$P_{\varphi,n}(s_1, \ldots, s_{n-1}, e_n)$	5	13	182	4125
$Q_{\varphi,n}(\sigma_1, \ldots, \sigma_{n-2}, w_0, w_1)$	3	6	32	396

Since this is a degree 5 extension field, the decomposition-based index calculus uses a 6-th summation polynomial. The cardinality of the curve is 12 times a prime number; according to Prop.4, we can only consider the action of the 2-torsion or the 3-torsion points. With the 2-torsion point and the morphism φ of Prop.8 for $\lambda = 0$, the reduced factor base has 536 864 344 elements, which as expected is very close to $2^{31}/4$. Using the corresponding 6-th symmetrized summation polynomial computed above, a decomposition test takes 10.28 sec (3.44 sec for the Gröbner basis computation for a well-chosen order and 6.84 sec for the change of order with FGLM [5]) using FGb [3] on a Intel Core i7-4650U CPU at 1.70 GHz. Alternatively, the same computation with MAGMA V2.18-3 (on an AMD Opteron 6176 SE at 2.3 GHz) takes 995 sec for the Gröbner basis and about 6 hours for the order change[1].

To put this in perspective, we can compare to the only other existing method computing decompositions on this curve, namely the "$n - 1$" approach of [11]: the computation of only one relation was estimated in [8] to take about 37 years on a single core, whereas with our results the expected time to get one relation is $2^4 \times 5! \times 10.28$ sec ≈ 5.5 hr. Even if it is still too slow to seriously threaten the DLP on this IPSEC standard, these experiments show that other non-standard problems like the oracle-assisted static Diffie-Hellman problem [12] are no longer secure on this curve.

Random Curve in Odd Characteristic with Full 2-Torsion To test the speed-up provided by the presence of the full 2-torsion subgroup, we considered a random curve in Legendre form over the optimal extension field $\mathbb{F}_{(2^{31}+413)^5}$, with a near-prime cardinality and satisfying the condition of Prop.10. Using the 6-th symmetrized summation polynomial as computed above, a decomposition test takes only 6.66 sec (2.82 sec for the Gröbner basis and 3.84 sec for FGLM) using FGb on a 3.47 GHz Intel Xeon X5677 CPU, or about 5 hours (55 min for the GB and 4h25 for FGLM) using MAGMA. By comparison, in [4] only one 2-torsion was accounted for (in a twisted Edwards model) and the authors reported a timing of 2 732 sec for one decomposition test. Once again, this shows the total weakness of some non-standard problems on such curves.

---

[1] The performance gap between MAGMA and FGb can be partially explained by the non-optimized arithmetic operations of MAGMA when the field size exceeds 25 bits. Experiments on smaller fields showed a significantly smaller gap.

6   Conclusion

The introduction of summation polynomials associated to any morphism φ from an elliptic curve E to $\mathbb{P}^1$ opens new perspectives for the decomposition-based index calculus. In particular, we have been able to use equivariant morphisms to take advantage of 2-torsion points in any characteristic. As demonstrated by our examples and timings, the speed-up over the classical approach is far from negligible and allows to seriously threaten more curves. The framework we have developed also applies to higher order torsion points, which will be more detailed in an extended version of this article.

References

1. Bosma, W., Cannon, J., Playoust, C.: The Magma algebra system. I. The user language. J. Symbolic Comput. 24(3-4), 235–265 (1997); Computational algebra and number theory, London (1993)
2. Diem, C.: On the discrete logarithm problem in elliptic curves. Compos. Math. 147(1), 75–104 (2011)
3. Faugère, J.-C.: FGb: A Library for Computing Gröbner Bases. In: Fukuda, K., van der Hoeven, J., Joswig, M., Takayama, N. (eds.) ICMS 2010. LNCS, vol. 6327, pp. 84–87. Springer, Heidelberg (2010)
4. Faugère, J.-C., Gaudry, P., Huot, L., Renault, G.: Using symmetries in the index calculus for elliptic curves discrete logarithm. J. Cryptology, 1–41 (2013), doi:10.1007/s00145-013-9158-5.
5. Faugère, J.-C., Gianni, P., Lazard, D., Mora, T.: Efficient computation of zero-dimensional Gröbner bases by change of ordering. J. Symbolic Comput. 16(4), 329–344 (1993)
6. Gaudry, P.: Index calculus for abelian varieties of small dimension and the elliptic curve discrete logarithm problem. J. Symbolic Comput. 44(12), 1690–1702 (2008)
7. Gaudry, P., Hess, F., Smart, N.P.: Constructive and destructive facets of Weil descent on elliptic curves. J. Cryptology 15(1), 19–46 (2002)
8. Granger, R., Joux, A., Vitse, V.: New timings for oracle-assisted SDHP on the IPSEC Oakley 'Well Known Group' 3 curve. Announcement on the NBRTHRY Mailing List (July 2010), http://listserv.nodak.edu/archives/nmbrthry.html
9. IETF. The Oakley key determination protocol. IETF RFC 2412 (1998)
10. Joux, A., Vitse, V.: Cover and Decomposition Index Calculus on Elliptic Curves made practical: Application to a seemingly secure curve over $\mathbb{F}_{p^6}$. In: Pointcheval, D., Johansson, T. (eds.) EUROCRYPT 2012. LNCS, vol. 7237, pp. 9–26. Springer, Heidelberg (2012)
11. Joux, A., Vitse, V.: Elliptic curve discrete logarithm problem over small degree extension fields. J. Cryptology 26(1), 119–143 (2013)
12. Koblitz, N., Menezes, A.: Another look at non-standard discrete log and Diffie-Hellman problems. J. Math. Cryptol. 2(4), 311–326 (2008)
13. Semaev, I.A.: Summation polynomials and the discrete logarithm problem on elliptic curves. Cryptology ePrint Archive, Report 2004/031 (2004)
14. Serre, J.-P.: Propriétés galoisiennes des points d'ordre fini des courbes elliptiques. Invent. Math. 15(4), 259–331 (1972)
15. Zippel, R.: Interpolating polynomials from their values. Journal of Symbolic Computation 9(3), 375–403 (1990)

Why Proving HIBE Systems Secure Is Difficult

Allison Lewko[1,*] and Brent Waters[2,**]

[1] Columbia University
alewko@cs.columbia.edu
[2] University of Texas at Austin
bwaters@cs.utexas.edu

Abstract. Proving security of Hierarchical Identity-Based Encryption (HIBE) and Attribution Based Encryption scheme is a challenging problem. There are multiple well-known schemes in the literature where the best known (adaptive) security proofs degrade exponentially in the maximum hierarchy depth. However, we do not have a rigorous understanding of why better proofs are not known. (For ABE, the analog of hierarchy depth is the maximum number of attributes used in a ciphertext.)

In this work, we define a certain commonly found checkability property on ciphertexts and private keys. Roughly the property states that any two different private keys that are both "supposed to" decrypt a ciphertext will decrypt it to the same message. We show that any simple black box reduction to a non-interactive assumption for a HIBE or ABE system that contains this property will suffer an exponential degradation of security.

1 Introduction

In recent years, there has been emerging interest in increasing the expressiveness of encryption systems in terms of targeting ciphertexts to certain groups of users. First examples included Hierarchical Identity-Based Encryption (HIBE) [HL02] and Attribute-Based Encryption (ABE) [SW05]. The early difficulty in HIBE and ABE research was to obtain systems that were provably secure under robust security definitions. Initial constructions of HIBE [GS02, CHK03, BB04, BBG05] and ABE [SW05, GPSW06] had the drawback that their security reductions degraded *exponentially* in the depth of the hierarchy when encrypting an HIBE ciphertext or number of attributes used when creating an ABE ciphertext. For this reason, the first (standard model) security proofs were done in the selective

---

* Work done while this author was at Microsoft Research.
** Supported by NSF CNS-0915361 and CNS-0952692, CNS-1228599 DARPA through the U.S. Office of Naval Research under Contract N00014-11-1-0382, DARPA N11AP20006, Google Faculty Research award, the Alfred P. Sloan Fellowship, Microsoft Faculty Fellowship, and Packard Foundation Fellowship. Any opinions, findings, and conclusions or recommendations expressed in this material are those of the author(s) and do not necessarily reflect the views of the Department of Defense or the U.S. Government.

P.Q. Nguyen and E. Oswald (Eds.): EUROCRYPT 2014, LNCS 8441, pp. 58–76, 2014.
© International Association for Cryptologic Research 2014

model, a term coined by Canetti, Halevi and Katz [CHK03]. In this weaker model, an attacker (artificially) declared the challenge identity he was attacking *before* seeing the public parameters of the system.

At the time, researchers identified achieving standard (sometimes called adaptive or full) security for these systems as an important open problem. However, it was not well understood whether there existed full security reductions for the already proposed constructions without exponential decay, and if not, why. While there was general intuition about the limitations of what were called *partitioning* proofs (e.g., see discussion in [Wat09]), there was no rigorous explanation of these difficulties.

In 2009, Gentry and Halevi [GH09] gave an HIBE construction and proved it fully secure without an exponential degradation in the depth. Their construction made use of projective hash techniques from [CS02, Gen06]. One tradeoff is that it required the use of non-static or q-type assumptions to prove security where the size of the assumption grew with the number of key queries. Later, Waters [Wat09] described a new and more systematic approach to proving full security called dual system encryption. Using dual system encryption, he proved an HIBE system fully secure under simple assumptions. Dual system encryption was subsequently used to prove full security of ABE and other related systems [LOS+10, OT10, LW12].

While these new proof techniques represent an advance in proving security, they still leave us with an incomplete picture about the security of the initial selectively secure constructions. *Can these systems only be proven selectively secure? If so, why?* Coming to a better understanding is important for multiple reasons. First, the earlier systems are typically more practically efficient than the recent dual system encryption counterparts. If they could be proven fully secure, they might be more desirable to use. Second, it is valuable to have a more rigorous characterization of what properties of a construction make it difficult to prove security, as identifying these properties can potentially inspire new construction and proof methods for encryption systems.

Understanding Partitioning Proofs. We organize our investigation around the goal of understanding partitioning proofs. Intuitively, these are proofs where a reduction algorithm (when creating a set of public parameters) splits ciphertext descriptors or "identities" into two disjoint sets. Those it can leverage for the challenge ciphertext (we call this the "challenge set") and those it cannot. If a certain identity x is in the challenge set, then the reduction cannot issue a private key for y if a private key for y should be allowed to decrypt a ciphertext associated with x.

We begin by asking the following two questions:

1. *Are there functionalities where a partitioning proof cannot work? (I.e. No reduction with a polynomial security loss exists.)*
2. *Under what circumstances are we stuck with a partitioning proof?*

To begin to answer the first question, we try to think of a basic case where partitioning will fail. To this end, we introduce a prefix encryption functionality.

In a prefix encryption system, a private key is associated with a binary string y and a ciphertext with a binary string x. One can decrypt the ciphertext to reveal a hidden message M if and only if y is a prefix of x. The point of introducing this primitive is to describe a simple primitive which distills the core features needed for our impossibility result. HIBE and most expressive ABE systems imply prefix encryption in a straightforward way.

To be successful, any partitioning reduction algorithm must have the set of challenge ciphertext descriptors cover at least a non-negligible fraction of the descriptors, else one would almost never get chosen by an attacker. In addition, there must be some non-negligible chance that the private keys requested by the attacker do not violate this partition. Immediately, we see this cannot work with a prefix encryption system. Consider an attacker $\mathcal{A}$ that chooses a random length n string x (for security parameter n) to be associated with the challenge ciphertext. In addition, it asks for private keys for strings $y_1, \ldots, y_n$, where string y_i is the length i string that matches x in the first $i-1$ bits and is different in the last bit. This small number of private keys can be used to decrypt a ciphertext associated with *any* string *except* x. Thus, any partitioning reduction that has more than one string in its challenge set will not be able to answer all the key queries for this attacker. Consequently, its best strategy is to pick one string for its challenge set, which will match $\mathcal{A}$'s choice with only 2^{-n} probability.

Next, we want to understand what properties of a construction force us to be "stuck with" a partitioning proof, in the sense that there is nothing to be gained from considering different reduction techniques. For prefix encryption, it was problematic for a partitioning proof that a large number of ciphertexts types could be covered by a small number of keys. Intuitively, one might be stuck with a partitioning proof if any authorized key can "equally decrypt" a ciphertext. We consider prefix encryption constructions that implicitly allow a pair of efficient algorithms for respectively checking an acceptability condition of a key and a ciphertext. If a ciphertext associated with a string x is determined to be acceptable by this check, then *all* acceptable keys for any prefix y will decrypt to the *same* message (or all fail decryption). We refer to constructions that allow such decisive checks as "checkable" schemes.

Essentially, this says that all keys that should be able to decrypt an acceptable ciphertext will decrypt it the same way. It is notable that early constructions of HIBE [GS02, CHK03, BB04, BBG05] and ABE [SW05, GPSW06] which were only proved selectively secure all have this property when instantiated under typically used prime order bilinear groups. This matches our intuition that they are in some sense stuck with partitioning proofs. However, constructions using the techniques of Gentry [Gen06] and dual system encryption do not meet this criteria. For example, in dual system encryption proofs, a normal secret key will decrypt a semi-functional ciphertext differently than a semi-functional secret key will.

Our Result. In this work, we formalize this intuition by showing that there are no simple black box reductions from the full security of checkable prefix encryption schemes to non-interactive decisional assumptions [1]. This result extends to HIBE and ABE as we show that these both can embed prefix encryption systems. (For the ABE case, see the full version.)

We capture our result in a somewhat similar manner to Coron [Cor02] and Hofheinz, Jager, and Knapp [HJK12] who showed that no unique [Cor02] or rerandomizable [HJK12] signatures can have black box proofs to non-interactive assumptions. While their focus was on showing the necessity of a polynomial loss (in the number of signature queries) for a class of signatures, we show the necessity of a drastic exponential loss of security for HIBE and ABE schemes.

At a high level, we construct an algorithm $\mathcal{B}$ that runs the reduction algorithm $\mathcal{R}$, where $\mathcal{B}$ acts as an computationally unbounded attacker. Since $\mathcal{B}$ is actually not a "real" attacker it will need to find a way to look like one.

To do this, $\mathcal{B}$ will first wait for the reduction algorithm to commit to a set of public parameters. Next, it will run $\mathcal{R}$ with the same public parameters multiple times (we specify more precisely the number of times in Section 3), each time choosing a random string x and collecting private keys $y_1, \ldots, y_n$ for the n strings that are prefixes of x except in their last bits. After each run, $\mathcal{B}$ rewinds $\mathcal{R}$ to the point where it published the system parameters. The point of these runs is to collect private key information relative to the committed public parameters. If any of these runs for a particular x value does not abort, then $\mathcal{B}$ has the private key information to decrypt a ciphertext for any string but x.

Finally, $\mathcal{B}$ will request a challenge ciphertext for a new random string z. If $x \neq z$ for some x used in a prior run where $\mathcal{B}$ successfully collected keys, then $\mathcal{B}$ has a private key that allows it to decrypt the challenge ciphertext and act as an attacker. If $\mathcal{R}$ is an efficient reduction, it will then break the assumption with non-negligible advantage. We can generalize this to reductions that run the attacker a polynomial number of times in sequence, but like [Cor02, HJK12] we do not cover reductions that concurrently run executions of the attack algorithm.

Future Directions. Multiple interesting questions arise from this work. Perhaps the most exciting direction is to see if limitations of our impossibility result can lead to new proof techniques in the positive direction. For example, in the course of this work we discovered that one can build prefix encryption from any IBE scheme. The proof is an easy hybrid reduction. This construction lies outside of impossibility result since two keys for *different* prefixes y and y' of some string z might decrypt a (malformed) ciphertext to different values. This is different than dual system encryption techniques, which rely on giving a different key structure for the same key value. A parallel goal is of course to strengthen our impossibility results. An natural target is to see if either our impossibility results can be extended to handle reductions that run attack algorithms concurrently or alternatively if building reductions that run attack algorithms concurrently can be leveraged for new positive results. By expanding our knowledge from both

---

[1] The restriction to non-interactive assumptions is natural and arguably necessary. Any scheme can be proven secure under the (possibly interactive) assumption that it is secure. The work of [BSW07] essentially does this, but with the mitigating factor of proving generic group security.

ends of the spectrum, we can hope to get a more complete understanding of the space of possible security proofs for functional encryption systems.

Another direction is to examine how recent selectively secure lattice HIBE [CHKP10, ABB10] constructions fit into this framework. These constructions allow some form of key rerandomization in that an algorithm can sample a new short basis, however, the "quality" of this basis is not as good as the original and in general higher quality private keys are not reachable from lower quality private keys. One possibility is that this quality of key difference can be leveraged to prove full security of these existing schemes.

2   Preliminaries

2.1   Prefix Encryption

We present the functionality of prefix encryption as the simplest functionality that captures the core structure of hierarchical identity-based encryption. Essentially, we strip off the usual trappings of HIBE schemes that are not relevant to our purposes. In particular, we do not require explicit delegation capabilities, and we do not use "identity vectors" with large sets of potential values for each coordinate. Instead, keys and ciphertexts in a prefix encryption scheme will be associated with binary strings, and a key will be able to decrypt a ciphertext if and only if the binary string associated to the key is a prefix of the binary string associated to the ciphertext. We observe that such a functionality can be easily derived from any HIBE scheme by designating fixed identities in each coordinate to play the role of "0" and "1".

We formally define a Prefix Encryption scheme as having the following algorithms:

$Setup(\lambda) \rightarrow$ PP, MSK. The setup algorithm takes in the security parameter λ and outputs the public parameters PP and a master secret key MSK.

$Encrypt(x, M, \text{PP}) \rightarrow$ CT. The encryption algorithm takes in a binary string x, a message M, and the public parameters PP. It outputs a ciphertext CT.

$KeyGen(\text{MSK}, y) \rightarrow$ SK. The key generation algorithm takes in the master secret key MSK and a binary string y. It outputs a secret key SK.

$Decrypt(\text{CT}, \text{SK}) \rightarrow M$. The decryption algorithm takes in a ciphertext CT and a secret key SK. If the binary string y of the secret key is a prefix of the binary string x of the ciphertext, it outputs the message M.

As we will study how security reductions behave as the binary strings involved grow longer, we will allow public parameters to specify a maximum length, q, for the indexing strings of the keys and ciphertexts. Our lower bound on the provable security degradation as an exponential function of the maximum string length will only apply to schemes that are suitably "checkable." In order to define this precisely, we will restrict our consideration to schemes can be augmented with two additional algorithms:

CTCheck(PP, CT, x) → {True, False}. The ciphertext checking algorithm takes in public parameters PP, a ciphertext CT, and a binary string x. It outputs either True or False.

KeyCheck(PP, SK, y) → {True, False}. The key checking algorithm takes in public parameters PP, a secret key SK, and a binary string y. It outputs either True or False.

We note that these additional algorithms are required to be efficient (just like the more standard algorithms above). We also require them to be deterministic.

For correctness, we require that CTCheck(PP, CT, x) outputs True whenever PP is honestly generated and CT is an honestly generated ciphertext for x from PP. Similarly, we require that KeyCheck(PP, SK, y) outputs True whenever PP, MSK are honestly generated and SK is an honestly generated key for y from MSK.

Definition 1. *We say a prefix encryption scheme is* **checkable** *if for any* PP, CT, x, SK_1, y_1, SK_2, y_2 *such that CTCheck(PP, CT, x) = True, KeyCheck(PP, SK_1, y_1) = True, KeyCheck(PP, SK_2, y_2) = True, and y_1, y_2 are both prefixes of x, then Decrypt(CT, SK_1) = Decrypt(CT, SK_2).*

Security Definition. We now define full security for a prefix encryption scheme in terms of the following game between a challenger and an attacker. This is essentially the definition of full IND-CPA security for HIBE schemes, but the case of prefix encryption is a bit simpler as there is no need to track the delegation of keys. The game proceeds in the following phases:

Setup Phase. The challenger runs Setup(λ) to produce MSK and PP. It gives PP to the attacker.

Key Query Phase I. The attacker adaptively chooses binary strings y and queries the challenger for corresponding secret keys. For each queried string y, the challenger runs KeyGen(MSK, y) to produce a secret key SK, which it gives to the attacker.

Challenge Phase. The attacker declares to equal length messages M_0, M_1, and a binary string x. It is required that for all strings y queried in the previous phase, y is **not** a prefix of x. The challenger chooses a uniformly random bit $b \in \{0, 1\}$ and creates a ciphertext CT by running Encrypt(x, M_b, PP). It gives CT to the attacker.

Key Query Phase II. This is the same as the first key query phase, except that any queried y must not be a prefix of the challenge string x.

Guess. The attacker submits a guess b' for the bit b.

Definition 2. *We define the advantage of an attacker in this game to be $|Pr[b = b'] - \frac{1}{2}|$. We say an algorithm $\mathcal{A}$ (t, ϵ, q)-breaks a prefix encryption scheme if it runs in time t, achieves advantage ϵ, and makes at most q total key queries.*

We say a prefix encryption scheme is secure if no algorithm (t, ϵ, q)-breaks for parameters t, q, ϵ where t, q are polynomial in the security parameter and ϵ is non-negligible.

The weaker notion of selective security would be obtained by modifying the security game above by having the attacker declare the binary string x for the challenge at the very beginning of the game, *before* seeing the public parameters.

2.2 Hierarchical Identity-Based Encryption

The relevant definitions for HIBE schemes are standard, and can be found in the full version. As we will study how security reductions behave as the identity vectors involved grow longer, we will allow public parameters to specify a maximum length, q, for the identity vectors associated with the keys and ciphertexts.

Similarly to our definitions for Prefix Encryption schemes, we consider HIBE schemes equipped with two additional algorithms:

CTCheck$(\text{PP}, \text{CT}, \boldsymbol{I}) \to \{\text{True}, \text{False}\}$. The ciphertext checking algorithm takes in public parameters PP, a ciphertext CT, and an identity vector $\boldsymbol{I}$. It outputs either True or False.

KeyCheck$(\text{PP}, \text{SK}, \boldsymbol{I}) \to \{\text{True}, \text{False}\}$. The key checking algorithm takes in public parameters PP, a secret key SK, and an identity vector $\boldsymbol{I}$. It outputs either True or False.

We note that these additional algorithms are required to be efficient (just like the more standard algorithms above). We also require them to be deterministic.

For correctness, we require that $\text{CTCheck}(\text{PP}, \text{CT}, \boldsymbol{I})$ outputs True whenever PP is honestly generated and CT is an honestly generated ciphertext for $\boldsymbol{I}$ from PP. Similarly, we require that $\text{KeyCheck}(\text{PP}, \text{SK}, \boldsymbol{I})$ outputs True whenever PP, MSK are honestly generated and SK is an honestly generated key for $\boldsymbol{I}$ from MSK.

Definition 3. *We say a HIBE scheme is **checkable** if for any* $\text{PP}, \text{CT}, \boldsymbol{I}^*, \text{SK}_1,$ $\boldsymbol{I}^1, \text{SK}_2, \boldsymbol{I}^2$ *such that* $\text{CTCheck}(\text{PP}, \text{CT}, \boldsymbol{I}^*) = \text{True}, \text{KeyCheck}(\text{PP}, \text{SK}_1, \boldsymbol{I}^1) = \text{True}, \text{KeyCheck}(\text{PP}, \text{SK}_2, \boldsymbol{I}^2) = \text{True}, \text{and } \boldsymbol{I}^1, \boldsymbol{I}^2 \text{ are both prefixes of } \boldsymbol{I}^*, \text{ then } \text{Decrypt}(\text{CT}, \text{SK}_1) = \text{Decrypt}(\text{CT}, \text{SK}_2).$

We note the full security definition for a HIBE scheme can be found in [SW08].

2.3 Non-interactive Decisional Problems and Simple Black Box Reductions

We now formally define the kinds of decisional problems and reductions we will consider. We start by describing the non-interactive decisional problems we allow:

Definition 4. *A non-interactive decisional problem $\Pi = (C, \mathcal{D})$ is described by a set C and a distribution $\mathcal{D}$ on C. We refer to C as the set of challenges, and each $c \in C$ is associated with a bit $b(c) \in \{0, 1\}$. We say that an algorithm $\mathcal{A}$ (ϵ, t)-solves Π if $\mathcal{A}$ runs in time t and*

$$Pr[\mathcal{A}(c) = b(c) : c \xleftarrow{\mathcal{D}} C] \geq \frac{1}{2} + \epsilon.$$

Here, $c \xleftarrow{\mathcal{D}} C$ denotes that c is chosen randomly from C according to the distribution $\mathcal{D}$.

Decisional problems used as cryptographic hardness assumptions are actually families of such problems, parameterized by a security parameter λ. Below, we will abuse notation mildly and write only Π while λ is implicit. We will write $poly(\lambda)$ and $neg(\lambda)$ to denote functions that are polynomial functions of λ and negligible functions in λ, respectively.

We next define the type of reductions we will address. We do not consider reductions in full generality - instead we restrict our consideration to black box reductions that satisfy additional requirements. Namely, we require simple reductions that only run the attacker once in a straight line fashion - meaning that the reduction simulates the security game exactly once with the attacker, who it interacts with as a black box. Note that this does not allow the reduction to rewind the attacker or supply its randomness, etc.

Definition 5. *An algorithm $\mathcal{R}$ is a simple $(t, \epsilon, q, \delta, t')$-reduction from a decisional problem Π to breaking the security of a prefix encryption scheme $Prefix$ if, when given black box access to any attacker $\mathcal{A}$ that (t, ϵ, q)-breaks the scheme $Prefix$, the algorithm $\mathcal{R}$ (δ, t')-solves the problem Π after simulating the security game once for $\mathcal{A}$.*

We note that the original selective security reductions given for prior HIBE and ABE schemes are simple reductions in the sense of Definition 5 (e.g. [BB04, GPSW06]).

Remark 1. Many security proofs for cryptographic systems also employ a hybrid technique, where the proof is broken into several smaller steps and the attacker's inability to distinguish in each hybrid step is proven from a computational assumption (typically with a simple reduction). At first glance, hybrid arguments might seem slightly incongruous with our setting where we consider showing that no single reduction can be performed for an attacker. However, we note that any fixed attacker (in particular, the hypothetical attacker we simulate in our proof) will be successful in distinguishing between (at least) one particular hybrid step. Thus, there will be a single (simple) reduction for such an attacker. Or looked at another way, a proof of security using the hybrid method is actually a collection of reductions, where the reduction used will depend on the particular attacker.

2.4   Obtaining Prefix Encryption from HIBE

Given a HIBE scheme with algorithms Setup_{HIBE}, KeyGen_{HIBE}, Encrypt_{HIBE}, Delegate_{HIBE}, and Decrypt_{HIBE}, we will derive a prefix encryption scheme with algorithms Setup_{Pre}, KeyGen_{Pre}, Encrypt_{Pre}, and Decrypt_{Pre}. To accomplish this, we only require that there are at least two possible values for each component of the identity vectors allowed in the HIBE scheme.

We let $\text{Setup}_{Pre} := \text{Setup}_{HIBE}$. We then suppose that $\{I_1^0, I_1^1\}$, $\{I_2^0, I_2^1\}$, ..., $\{I_q^0, I_q^1\}$ are sets of values such that taking any combination $(I_1^{b_1}, I_2^{b_2}, \ldots, I_q^{b_q})$ for bits $b_1, \ldots, b_q \in \{0, 1\}$ forms a valid identity vector (and $I_j^0 \neq I_j^1$ for all j). We define KeyGen_{Pre} to generate a key for a binary string $y = (y_1, y_2, \ldots, y_k)$ for $k \leq q$ by running KeyGen_{HIBE} on the identity $(I_1^{y_1}, I_2^{y_2}, \ldots, I_k^{y_k})$. We similarly define Encrypt_{Pre} to encrypt to a binary vector $x = (x_1, \ldots, x_j)$ by running Encrypt_{HIBE} to encrypt to $(I_1^{x_1}, \ldots, I_j^{x_j})$. We can then set $\text{Decrypt}_{Pre} = \text{Decrypt}_{HIBE}$.

We now observe that if we start with a checkable HIBE, then the derived prefix encryption scheme will also be checkable:

Lemma 1. *If $Setup_{HIBE}$, $KeyGen_{HIBE}$, $Encrypt_{HIBE}$, $Delegate_{HIBE}$, and $Decrypt_{HIBE}$ is a checkable HIBE scheme, than $Setup_{Pre}$, $KeyGen_{Pre}$, $Encrypt_{Pre}$, and $Decrypt_{Pre}$ obtained from it as described above is a checkable prefix encryption scheme.*

Finally, we observe that simple security reductions for the initial HIBE scheme can be translated into simple security reductions for the derived prefix encryption scheme:

Lemma 2. *If $\mathcal{R}_{HIBE}$ is a simple $(t, \epsilon, q, \delta, t')$-reduction from a decisional problem Π to breaking the security of a HIBE encryption scheme, then we can obtain from $\mathcal{R}$ a new reduction $\mathcal{R}_{Pre}$ that is a simple $(t, \epsilon, q, \delta, t')$-reduction from the same decisional problem Π to breaking the security of the derived prefix encryption scheme.*

The proofs of these lemmas are relatively straightforward and can be found in the full version.

3   Main Result

We now prove our main result, establishing that any polynomial time simple black box reduction between the security of a checkable prefix encryption scheme and a hard, non-interactive decisional problem can only achieve an advantage that degrades exponentially in q, where q is the maximum string length of the scheme.

Essentially, we leverage the fact that the reduction can be run to obtain secret keys and then be rewound to "forget" these keys were produced. We can then use the secret keys obtained during the first runs of the reduction to simulate a successful attacker against a different challenge in a final run. The checking algorithms play a pivotal role in ensuring that the unorthodox manner in which these keys are obtained does not compromise their effectiveness. Intuitively, for keys and ciphertexts that pass the (publicly computable) checks, the result of a successful decryption is guaranteed to be independent of the origins of the key.

It is interesting to consider what happens if one tries to apply such techniques to more complicated reductions. A first example would be reductions that sequentially run the attacker a bounded number of times. In such a case, our result should extend easily via an application of the union bound, analogously to the extensions in [Cor02, HJK12]. However, it is not clear how to extend our argument to reductions that may run interleaved instances of the attacker, using concurrency in an arbitrary way. We observe that the arguments in [Cor02, HJK12] also do not address this case.

Theorem 1. *Let* $Prefix = (Setup, Encrypt, KeyGen, Decrypt, CTCheck, Key\text{-}Check)$ *denote a checkable prefix encryption scheme, and let* $\Pi(\lambda)$ *denote a decisional problem such that no algorithm running in time* $t = poly(\lambda)$ *can obtain an advantage that is non-negligible in* λ. *Then any simple* $(t, \epsilon, q, \delta, t')$-*reduction* $\mathcal{R}$ *from* Π *to the security of* $Prefix$ *with* $t = poly(\lambda)$, $t' = poly(\lambda)$ *must have a value of* δ *such that* δ *vanishes exponentially as a function of* q *(up to terms that are negligible in* λ).

Proof. We let $Prefix = (Setup, Encrypt, KeyGen, Decrypt, CTCheck, Key\text{-}Check)$ denote a checkable prefix encryption scheme. We suppose that $\mathcal{R}$ is a simple $(t, \epsilon, q, \delta, t')$-reduction from a decisional problem Π to breaking the security of this prefix encryption scheme. We now design an algorithm $\mathcal{B}$ to solve Π.

A Hypothetical Attacker We first define a hypothetical attacker $\mathcal{A}$ that (t, ϵ, q)-breaks the security of the prefix encryption scheme for some time t. $\mathcal{A}$ proceeds as follows: it first receives PP as input (we assume this also implicitly includes λ). It chooses a random binary string x of length q. In the first key query phase, it requests keys for strings $y_1, \ldots, y_q$ where each y_i is the binary string of length i formed by taking the first $i - 1$ bits of x and then the opposite of the ith bit of x. Note that each y_i is not a prefix of x. It receives the corresponding keys $SK_1, \ldots, SK_q$ from the challenger. For each, it runs KeyCheck(PP, SK_i, y_i). If any of these checks outputs False, it quits.

Next, the attacker $\mathcal{A}$ declares two messages M_0, M_1 (we suppose these are fixed, distinct messages) and x as the challenge string. It receives the ciphertext CT from the challenger. It then runs CTCheck(PP, CT, x). If this outputs False, it quits. Otherwise, it samples SK^* uniformly from the set of all values of SK such that KeyCheck(PP, SK, x_i) = True for any prefix x_i of x. (Of course, this step may not be efficient.) After obtaining SK^*, it decrypts CT with SK^*. If the result is $M_{b'}$ for some $b' \in \{0, 1\}$, it guesses b' with probability $\frac{1}{2} + \epsilon$ and guesses the opposite with probability $\frac{1}{2} - \epsilon$. If the result is not M_0 or M_1, it guesses randomly.

For ease of analysis we will view the hypothetical attacker's set of coins as drawn from a space $Z \times F$. The set Z is the set of possible choices of the challenge string x, and we let F denote the set of all other random coins used.

We now verify that attacker $\mathcal{A}$ has advantage ϵ in the real security game. In this case, since the public parameters and ciphertext are honestly generated, then SK* properly decrypts the challenge ciphertext, and hence the result will always be M_b. $\mathcal{A}$ then guesses b correctly with probability $\frac{1}{2} + \epsilon$.

Using the Reduction. We are assuming that the reduction $\mathcal{R}$ runs the attacker once in a straight-line fashion (e.g. no rewinding). We now create an algorithm $\mathcal{B}$ to solve Π by using $\mathcal{R}$. (Note that $\mathcal{B}$ can rewind $\mathcal{R}$: we just do not allow $\mathcal{R}$ to rewind the attacker.)

$\mathcal{B}$ first receives a problem instance c, which it gives as input to $\mathcal{R}$. $\mathcal{R}$ then outputs public parameters PP. Now $\mathcal{B}$ will simulate the hypothetical attacker described above as follows. First, it will run $\mathcal{R}$ several times in an attempt to collect secret keys. Then it will use the collected keys to simulate the attacker on a new run of $\mathcal{R}$.

More precisely, we let τ be a parameter to be specified later (it will be polynomial in the string length q and the security parameter). $\mathcal{B}$ will choose τ independent random binary strings $x^1, x^2, \ldots, x^\tau$ of length q. It will then query keys for strings $y_1^1, \ldots, y_q^1$ derived from x^1 as described above (note this behavior is identical to the hypothetical attacker $\mathcal{A}$). After receiving each key, it runs the KeyCheck algorithm. If this check ever outputs False, then $\mathcal{B}$ considers this run to be an "aborting run". In addition, $\mathcal{B}$ receives a challenge ciphertext CT. If the CTCheck algorithm run on CT returns false, then it is is also considered to be an "aborting run."[2] If the run was not aborting, then $\mathcal{B}$ successfully received a corresponding key SK_i^1 for each i from 1 to q such that KeyCheck(PP, SK_i^1, y_i^1) = True. It then stores these $SK_1^1, \ldots, SK_q^1$ values.

Next, it rewinds the reduction $\mathcal{R}$ to the point just after it output the public parameters. It will then run $\mathcal{R}$ again (using fresh random coins) and querying keys for strings $y_1^2, \ldots, y_q^2$ derived from x_2. It continues in this way until it has run $\mathcal{R}$ exactly τ times on these same PP. If *all* τ runs were aborting runs, then $\mathcal{B}$ stops and guesses randomly. Otherwise, it continues.

Next, it chooses a new random binary string z of length q. If $z = x^i$ for any i from 1 to τ, then $\mathcal{B}$ stops and guesses randomly. Otherwise, it runs $\mathcal{R}$ one more time on these same PP with fresh random coins, querying keys for strings $w_1, \ldots, w_q$ derived from z. Upon receiving each key for $w_1, \ldots, w_q$, it runs the KeyCheck algorithm as before. If any of these checks fail, it stops and guesses randomly. Otherwise, $\mathcal{B}$ submits the fixed, distinct messages M_0, M_1 and the challenge string z to the reduction. $\mathcal{B}$ receives CT in return. It runs the CTCheck algorithm. If this check fails, $\mathcal{B}$ stops and guesses randomly. If the check passes, it fixes and index j from 1 to τ such that the jth run was not aborting. Then, it considers the unique y_i^j that is a prefix of z (note that the index i is defined as the first bit where z and x^j differ).

---

[2] We observe that for the purposes of collecting private keys, it is not important for the reduction algorithm to return a valid challenge ciphertext. However, we choose to require this to maintain a uniform definition of an "aborting run" in our analysis.

$\mathcal{B}$ now decrypts CT with SK_i^j. If the result is $M_{b'}$ for some $b' \in \{0, 1\}$, it guesses b' with probability $\frac{1}{2} + \epsilon$ and guesses the opposite with probability $\frac{1}{2} - \epsilon$. If the result is not M_0 or M_1, it guesses randomly. It gives b' to $\mathcal{R}$, and finally copies the output of $\mathcal{R}$ as its own output.

It is crucial to observe here that $\mathcal{B}$ is decrypting the challenge ciphertext with a secret key that may not be equivalently distributed to the key that the hypothetical attacker $\mathcal{A}$ would use. Nonetheless, since decryption only occurs when the key SK_i^j and the challenge ciphertext CT have passed their respective checks, it must be the case that the decryption of CT by SK_i^j produces the *same result* as decryption of CT by any other acceptable key, hence $\mathcal{B}$ correctly simulates the decryption output that $\mathcal{A}$ would obtain, despite the fact that it is not simulating the proper key distribution.

Analyzing Algorithm $\mathcal{B}$. We recall that C denotes the set of challenges. We let R denote the set of possible random coins chosen by $\mathcal{R}$ for a single run. We introduce the following notation for the coins used by $\mathcal{B}$ during its final run of the reduction algorithm $\mathcal{R}$. Recall, that in a single run the hypothetical attacker's coins is draw from a space $Z \times F$, Z is the choice of possible challenge strings and F is the set of other coins used. For the final run, we let $z \in Z$ and $f \in F$ denote the simulated choice of these coins.

Fixing $c \in C$, $r \in R$, $z \in Z$, and $f \in F$, we define that the tuple (c, r, z, f) belongs to the event W if running the reduction once with this c and these coins r and an attacker using coins z, f results in all the key and ciphertext checks passing and the reduction correctly solving the challenge. (I.e. W is the set of coins for the final run where the final run does not abort and it gives the correct answer.)

We partition the tuples $(c, r, z, f) \in W$ into two disjoint sets. For notational convenience, we split $r \in R$ into substrings r_1 and r_2 such that r_1 are the coins used to determine PP and r_2 are the remaining coins used by the reduction. We let U denote the set of tuples in W such that, fixing c and r_1, replacing the remaining coins for $\mathcal{R}$ and the attacker with freshly sampled coins results in a non-aborting run with probability $\geq \rho$ (where ρ is a threshold we will specify later). We let V denote the set of tuples in W such that this results in a non-aborting run with probability $< \rho$. Note that by definition, W is a disjoint union of U and V. Hence $\mathbb{P}[W] = \mathbb{P}[U] + \mathbb{P}[V]$.

Note that any two runs that share the same c and r_1 coins also share the same challenge and public parameters generated by the reduction. This is the point to which $\mathcal{B}$ rewinds when conducting multiple runs. We can think of these are being "neighboring" sets of runs. Intuitively, we are partitioning the set W into the set U where a neighbor of $u \in U$ is more likely to be non-aborting and the set V where a neighbor of $v \in V$ is less likely to be non-aborting.

Claim. $\mathbb{P}[V] < \rho$.

The proof of this claim follows in a similar vein to the heavy row lemma [OO98].

Proof. Given c, r_1, we can define $p(c, r_1)$ to be the probability of a non-aborting run when independent random values of r_2, z, f are chosen and $p'(c, r_1)$ to be the probability of a non-aborting and correct run when independent random values of r_2, z, f are chosen. Then we observe:

$$\mathbb{P}[V] = \sum_{c,r_1 \text{ s.t. } p'(c,r_1)<\rho} \mathbb{P}[c,r_1]p'(c,r_1) \leq \sum_{c,r_1 \text{ s.t. } p(c,r_1)<\rho} \mathbb{P}[c,r_1]p(c,r_1)$$

which is $< \rho \sum_{c,r_1} \mathbb{P}[c,r_1] < \rho$.

We define the event A to be the collection of tuples (c, r, z, f) such that an aborting run is produced (here, we consider an aborting run to include any key check or ciphertext check failure). We note that A is disjoint from W. We let S denote the event that the reduction solves the challenge correctly.

Claim. If Π is computationally hard, then $\mathbb{P}[A]\left|\left(\mathbb{P}[S|A] - \frac{1}{2}\right)\right| = negl(\lambda)$.

Proof. Suppose that $\mathbb{P}[A]\left(\mathbb{P}[S|A] - \frac{1}{2}\right) = \epsilon' > 0$. We then define the following algorithm $\mathcal{B}'$ to solve Π. $\mathcal{B}'$ chooses random coins for the attacker and runs $\mathcal{R}$ once until either an abort occurs or it reaches the end where the attacker should provide a response. If an abort occurs, then $\mathcal{B}'$ copies the output of the reduction as its own. Otherwise, it guesses randomly.

The success probability of $\mathcal{B}'$ is $\frac{1}{2}(1 - \mathbb{P}[A]) + \mathbb{P}[A]\mathbb{P}[S|A] = \frac{1}{2} + \mathbb{P}[A]\left(\mathbb{P}[S|A] - \frac{1}{2}\right) = \frac{1}{2} + \epsilon'$. Thus, we must have $\epsilon' = negl(\lambda)$ if Π is computationally hard. The case when $\mathbb{P}[A]\left(\frac{1}{2} - \mathbb{P}[S|A]\right) = \epsilon' > 0$ is analogous, except that $\mathcal{B}'$ should flip the output of the reduction in the case of an abort.

We observe that the success probability of the reduction (with one run of the hypothetical attacker) is $= \mathbb{P}[A]\mathbb{P}[S|A] + \mathbb{P}[W] = \frac{1}{2} + \delta$. Combining this with Claim 3 and Claim 3, we see that

$$\frac{1}{2} \cdot \mathbb{P}[A] + \mathbb{P}[U] \geq \frac{1}{2} + \delta - \rho - negl(\lambda). \tag{1}$$

We let X_i, F_i denote the sets of possible coins for the attacker that $\mathcal{B}$ will use during the ith run of $\mathcal{R}$, and we let R_2^i denote the set of possible coins the reduction will use for the ith run. For each i, we define A_i to be the event that $(c, r_1, r_2^i, x_i, f_i)$ produces an aborting run. We define E_i to be the event that $z = x_i$. We let $\overline{A_i}$ and $\overline{E_i}$ denote their complements.

We now consider the probability that $\mathcal{B}$ solves the decisional problem Π. We observe that this is:

$$\geq \frac{1}{2} \cdot \mathbb{P}[A] + \sum_{(c,r,z,f)\in U} \mathbb{P}[c, r, z, f] \cdot \mathbb{P}\left[\bigcup_{i=1}^{\tau} \overline{A_i} \cap \overline{E_i} \mid c, r, z, f\right]. \tag{2}$$

We consider a tuple $(c, r, z, f) \in U$. We observe

$$\mathbb{P}\left[\bigcup_{i=1}^{\tau} \overline{A_i} \cap \overline{E_i} \mid c, r, z, f\right] \geq 1 - \mathbb{P}\left[\bigcup_{i=1}^{\tau} E_i | c, r, z, f\right] - \mathbb{P}\left[\bigcap_{i=1}^{\tau} A_i | c, r, z, f\right].$$

By the union bound, $\mathbb{P}\left[\bigcup_{i=1}^{\tau} E_i | c, r\right] \leq \tau 2^{-q}$. Since the events A_i are independent once c, r, z, f are fixed, we have $\mathbb{P}\left[\bigcap_{i=1}^{\tau} A_i | c, r, z, f\right] \leq (1-\rho)^\tau$ (here we have also used that $(c, r, z, f) \in U$). Thus, $\mathbb{P}\left[\bigcup_{i=1}^{\tau} \overline{A_i} \cap \overline{E_i} \mid c, r, z, f\right] \geq 1 - \tau 2^{-q} - (1-\rho)^\tau$.

Combining this with (2), we see that $\mathcal{B}$ solves the decisional problem Π with probability $\geq \frac{1}{2} \cdot \mathbb{P}[A] + \mathbb{P}[U](1 - \tau 2^{-q} - (1-\rho)^\tau)$. Considering (1), we see this is $\geq \frac{1}{2} + \delta - \rho - negl(\lambda) - \tau 2^{-q} - (1-\rho)^\tau$. Hence, if we set $\rho = \frac{\delta}{4}$, the advantage of $\mathcal{B}$ is at least

$$\frac{3}{4}\delta - negl(\lambda) - \tau 2^{-q} - \left(1 - \frac{\delta}{4}\right)^\tau. \tag{3}$$

We now set $\tau = \frac{4}{\delta}$. We observe that $\left(1 - \frac{\delta}{4}\right)^{\frac{4}{\delta}}$ is upper bounded by a constant strictly less than 1, since $\lim_{n \to \infty} \left(1 - \frac{1}{n}\right)^n = \frac{1}{e}$. Hence we see that (3) is $= \frac{3}{4}\delta - \frac{4}{\delta}2^{-q} - negl(\lambda)$. This shows that δ must be exponentially small as a function of q when Π is computationally hard.

4 Implications for Existing Constructions

Our result can be applied to explain why the first HIBE schemes that were proven secure in the standard model relied on the weaker notion of selective security. Of course, one can easily translate selective security into full security for the same schemes while incurring a loss that is exponential as a function of the hierarchy depth, as we have shown to be inherent for checkable schemes when using a typical class of reductions.

As an illustrative example, we show that the selectively secure HIBE scheme of Boneh and Boyen [BB04] is checkable. We first review the scheme. Below, λ denotes the security parameter and q denotes the maximum depth. The scheme will be constructed in a bilinear group G of prime order p. We will assume that identities $\boldsymbol{I}$ are vectors of length $\leq q$ whose components are elements of $\mathbb{Z}_p$ and that messages M are elements of G_T. We will also assume that G comes equipped with group membership tests for G and its target group G_T.

4.1   The Boneh-Boyen HIBE Construction

$Setup(\lambda, q) \to \text{MSK}, \text{PP}$ The setup algorithm chooses a bilinear group G of sufficiently large prime order p. We let g denote a generator of G and $e : G \times G \to G_T$ denote the bilinear map. The algorithm chooses a uniformly random exponent $\alpha \in \mathbb{Z}_p$ and sets $g_1 = g^\alpha$. The algorithm also chooses random generators $g_2, h_1, \ldots, h_q \in G$. The MSK is g_2^α, while the public parameters are: $\text{PP} := \{G, p, e, g, g_1, g_2, h_1, \ldots, h_q\}$.

$Encrypt(M, \boldsymbol{I} = (I_1, \ldots, I_k)) \to \text{CT}$. The encryption algorithm chooses a uniformly random exponent $s \in \mathbb{Z}_p$ and forms the ciphertext as:

$\text{CT} := \left\{ Me(g_1, g_2)^s, \ g^s, \ \left(g_1^{I_1} h_1\right)^s, \ \ldots, \ \left(g_1^{I_k} h_k\right)^s \right\}.$

KeyGen(I $= (I_1, \ldots, I_k),$ MSK$) \rightarrow$ SK$_I$. The key generation algorithm chooses uniformly random exponents $r_1, \ldots, r_k$ and produces a secret key for identity I as: SK$_I := \left\{ g_2^\alpha \prod_{i=1}^K \left(g_1^{I_i} h_i \right)^{r_i}, \ g^{r_1}, \ \ldots, \ g^{r_k} \right\}.$

We note that delegation here is rather natural, as one can add on a new coordinate I_{k+1} to the identity vector by sampling a new exponent $r_{k+1} \in \mathbb{Z}_p$, multiplying $\left(g_1^{I_{k+1}} h_{k+1} \right)^{r_{k+1}}$ into the first group element, and appending the extra element $g^{r_{k+1}}$ to the current key. However, we will not need to refer to delegation in order to apply our result.

Decrypt(CT, SK$_I) \rightarrow \{M, \perp\}$. The decryption algorithm takes in a ciphertext encrypted to an identity vector $I^* = (I_1^*, \ldots, I_j^*)$ and a secret key for an identity vector $I = (I_1, \ldots, I_k)$. If I is not a prefix of I^*, it outputs $\perp$. Otherwise, it computes the message as follows. We let $\{C, C_0, C_1, \ldots, C_j\}$ denote the elements of the ciphertext, ordered as in the description above. We let $\{K, K_1, \ldots, K_k\}$ similarly denote the elements of the secret key. Then the decryption algorithm computes: $M = C \cdot \frac{\prod_{i=1}^k e(C_i, K_i)}{e(C_0, K)}.$

To show this HIBE scheme is checkable, we must specify appropriate efficient algorithms for ciphertext checking and key checking. Our checking algorithms will assume that the bilinear group G comes equipped with an efficient membership testThis test is assumed to be perfect (error-free).

CTCheck(PP, CT, I). The ciphertext check algorithm first tests that PP and CT are comprised of the appropriate number and type of group elements (using the group membership tests for G and G_T). If any of these tests fail, it outputs False. Otherwise, we let $C, C_0, C_1, \ldots, C_j$ denote the group elements comprising the ciphertext (where I has length j) and we let $g, g_1, g_2, h_1, \ldots, h_q$ denote the group elements contained in PP. It is checked that none of PP elements are the identity element. It is then checked that $e(C_i, g) = e(C_0, g_1^{I_i} h_i)$ for each i from 1 to j. If any of these checks fail, output False. Otherwise, output True.

KeyCheck(PP, SK$_I$, $I = (I_1, \ldots, I_k))$. The key check algorithm tests that PP and the secret key each contain the correct number of elements, and that all the elements of both are in fact elements of the group G by performing membership tests. If any of these tests fail, the algorithm outputs *False*. Otherwise, we let $K, K_1, \ldots, K_k$ denote the group elements comprising the secret key, and we let $g, g_1, g_2, h_1, \ldots, h_q$ denote the group elements contained in PP. It is checked that none of PP elements are the identity element. Since each of $K_1, \ldots, K_k$ is an element of the cyclic group G and g is a generator, there must exists values $r_1, \ldots, r_k \in \mathbb{Z}_p$ such that $K_1 = g^{r_1}, \ldots, K_k = g^{r_k}$. It remains to check that K is properly formed with respect to these r_i's. To test this, the algorithm computes $A := e(g, K), \ B := e(g_1, g_2) \prod_{i=1}^k e(K_i, g_1^{I_i} h_i)$. If $A = B$, the algorithm outputs True. Otherwise, it outputs *False*.

Proposition 1. *The HIBE scheme in Section 4.1 is checkable.*

Proof. We observe that the checking algorithms always output True when parameters, keys, and ciphertexts are honestly generated. Furthermore, when the public parameters and a secret key pass all of the checks, it must be the case that the secret key is correctly formed for some values of $r_1, \ldots, r_k \in \mathbb{Z}_p$. Thus, the secret key will correctly decrypt any honestly generated ciphertext. To see this, note that $A = B$ in the key check if and only if $K = g_2^\alpha \prod_{i=1}^k (g_1^{I_i} h_i)^{r_i}$ for the r_i values defined from $K_1, \ldots, K_k$. This again relies on the fact that G is a cyclic group generated by g and G_T is also a cyclic group, generated by $e(g, g)$. Hence, $A, B \in G_T$ can only be equal if there discrete logarithms base $e(g, g)$ modulo p are equal. Similarly, a ciphertext can only pass the check if it is properly formed for some value of $s \in \mathbb{Z}_p$.

Hence, for any PP that pass the checks, the set of possible secret keys that pass the key check for a given identity vector is indexed precisely by the p^k possible values of $r_1, \ldots, r_k$, and the possible ciphertexts for a given identity vector are indexed precisely by the p possible vales of s. As a consequence, we see that any two acceptable keys for authorized identity vectors decrypt any acceptable ciphertext to the same message.

Other Schemes. The reasoning employed above to analyze the checking algorithms of the Boneh-Boyen HIBE scheme is also applicable to other schemes with similar structure. More specifically, we can apply the same kind of analysis to any scheme with perfect correctness where the sets of possible keys and ciphertexts output by the key generation and encryption algorithms are parameterized by discrete log relationships that can be tested by pairing with public group elements. Other schemes displaying these properties include the Waters IBE and HIBE schemes in [Wat05], the HIBE construction by Boneh, Boyen, and Goh in [BBG05] that achieves compact ciphertexts, the HIBE scheme of Canetti, Halevi, and Katz [CHK03], the HIBE scheme of Gentry and Silverberg [GS02], and the ABE schemes of Goyal, Pandey, Sahai, and Waters [GPSW06] and Waters [Wat11]. Thus, all of these schemes are checkable. (A checkable ABE scheme can be defined analogously to a checkable HIBE scheme, and we show in the full version that a checkable ABE scheme can be used to build a checkable prefix encryption scheme.)

The HIBE construction of Gentry and Halevi [GH09] does not conform to this structure and is not checkable (under some computational assumption) - this is why it can avoid exponential degradation in security as the hierarchy depth grows. The later HIBE constructions in [Wat09, LW10] and ABE constructions in [LOS+10, OT10, LW12] that are proven fully secure through the dual system encryption methodology also avoid the basic structure that leads to checkability, even though they can be viewed as alternate instantiations of the intuitive mechanisms of the prior Boneh-Boyen, Boneh-Boyen-Goh, and Goyal-Pandey-Sahai-Waters schemes. More concretely, schemes designed for dual system encryption come equipped with additional dimensions that complicate the landscape of possible keys and ciphertexts. As a consequence of this alteration to the scheme structure, they fall outside the rubric of simple discrete log relation-ships between pairs of elements in a prime order cyclic group that can be checked by pairing with public elements. (Some dual system constructions use compos-ite order groups for this purpose, and some replace single group elements with larger tuples of group elements.) The additional dimensions that prevent such checks are designed to enable a simulator to produce "semi-functional" keys that still function like honestly generated keys when decrypting honestly generated ciphertexts, but behave differently when decrypting "semi-functional" cipher-texts that cannot be efficiently distinguished from honestly generated ones. This circumvents our lower bound. The situation for the lattice-based HIBE construc-tions [ABB10, CHKP10] and recent ABE construction [Boy13] is not clear: it would be interesting to determine if they are checkable or not.

In the full version, we additionally show a result in the positive direction; that prefix encryption can actually be built from the simpler primitive of IBE. We prove the reduction secure relative to the IBE scheme with a polynomial loss of security. Since there are known IBE constructions [BF01, Wat05] that are both checkable and have polynomial security reductions to decision assumptions, this might at first seem like a contradiction to our main result. The catch is that our IBE to prefix encryption will not preserve the checkability property (if it existed) of the underlying IBE system.

Acknowledgements. We thank the anonymous reviewers for their important points regarding our analysis.

References

[ABB10]   Agrawal, S., Boneh, D., Boyen, X.: Efficient lattice (H)IBE in the stan-dard model. In: Gilbert, H. (ed.) EUROCRYPT 2010. LNCS, vol. 6110, pp. 553–572. Springer, Heidelberg (2010)

[BB04]   Boneh, D., Boyen, X.: Efficient selective-ID secure identity-based encryp-tion without random oracles. In: Cachin, C., Camenisch, J.L. (eds.) EURO-CRYPT 2004. LNCS, vol. 3027, pp. 223–238. Springer, Heidelberg (2004)

[BBG05]   Boneh, D., Boyen, X., Goh, E.: Hierarchical identity based encryption with constant size ciphertext. In: Cramer, R. (ed.) EUROCRYPT 2005. LNCS, vol. 3494, pp. 440–456. Springer, Heidelberg (2005)

[BF01]   Boneh, D., Franklin, M.: Identity-based encryption from the weil pairing. In: Kilian, J. (ed.) CRYPTO 2001. LNCS, vol. 2139, pp. 213–229. Springer, Heidelberg (2001)

[Boy13]   Boyen, X.: Attribute-based functional encryption on lattices. In: Sahai, A. (ed.) TCC 2013. LNCS, vol. 7785, pp. 122–142. Springer, Heidelberg (2013)

[BSW07]   Bethencourt, J., Sahai, A., Waters, B.: Ciphertext-policy attribute-based encryption. In: Proceedings of the IEEE Symposium on Security and Pri-vacy, pp. 321–334 (2007)

[CHK03]   Canetti, R., Halevi, S., Katz, J.: A forward-secure public-key encryp-tion scheme. In: Biham, E. (ed.) EUROCRYPT 2003. LNCS, vol. 2656, pp. 255–271. Springer, Heidelberg (2003)

[CHKP10] Cash, D., Hofheinz, D., Kiltz, E., Peikert, C.: Bonsai trees, or how to delegate a lattice basis. In: Gilbert, H. (ed.) EUROCRYPT 2010. LNCS, vol. 6110, pp. 523–552. Springer, Heidelberg (2010)

[Cor02] Coron, J.-S.: Optimal security proofs for PSS and other signature schemes. In: Knudsen, L.R. (ed.) EUROCRYPT 2002. LNCS, vol. 2332, pp. 272–287. Springer, Heidelberg (2002)

[CS02] Cramer, R., Shoup, V.: Universal hash proofs and a paradigm for adaptive chosen ciphertext secure public-key encryption. In: Knudsen, L.R. (ed.) EUROCRYPT 2002. LNCS, vol. 2332, pp. 45–64. Springer, Heidelberg (2002)

[Gen06] Gentry, C.: Practical identity-based encryption without random oracles. In: Vaudenay, S. (ed.) EUROCRYPT 2006. LNCS, vol. 4004, pp. 445–464. Springer, Heidelberg (2006)

[GH09] Gentry, C., Halevi, S.: Hierarchical identity based encryption with polynomially many levels. In: Reingold, O. (ed.) TCC 2009. LNCS, vol. 5444, pp. 437–456. Springer, Heidelberg (2009)

[GPSW06] Goyal, V., Pandey, O., Sahai, A., Waters, B.: Attribute based encryption for fine-grained access control of encrypted data. In: ACM Conference on Computer and Communications Security, pp. 89–98 (2006)

[GS02] Gentry, C., Silverberg, A.: Hierarchical ID-based cryptography. In: Zheng, Y. (ed.) ASIACRYPT 2002. LNCS, vol. 2501, pp. 548–566. Springer, Heidelberg (2002)

[HJK12] Hofheinz, D., Jager, T., Knapp, E.: Waters signatures with optimal security reduction. In: Fischlin, M., Buchmann, J., Manulis, M. (eds.) PKC 2012. LNCS, vol. 7293, pp. 66–83. Springer, Heidelberg (2012)

[HL02] Horwitz, J., Lynn, B.: Toward hierarchical identity-based encryption. In: Knudsen, L.R. (ed.) EUROCRYPT 2002. LNCS, vol. 2332, pp. 466–481. Springer, Heidelberg (2002)

[LOS+10] Lewko, A., Okamoto, T., Sahai, A., Takashima, K., Waters, B.: Fully secure functional encryption: Attribute-based encryption and (Hierarchical) inner product encryption. In: Gilbert, H. (ed.) EUROCRYPT 2010. LNCS, vol. 6110, pp. 62–91. Springer, Heidelberg (2010)

[LW10] Lewko, A., Waters, B.: New techniques for dual system encryption and fully secure HIBE with short ciphertexts. In: Micciancio, D. (ed.) TCC 2010. LNCS, vol. 5978, pp. 455–479. Springer, Heidelberg (2010)

[LW12] Lewko, A., Waters, B.: New proof methods for attribute-based encryption: Achieving full security through selective techniques. In: Safavi-Naini, R., Canetti, R. (eds.) CRYPTO 2012. LNCS, vol. 7417, pp. 180–198. Springer, Heidelberg (2012)

[OO98] Ohta, K., Okamoto, T.: On concrete security treatment of signatures derived from identification. In: Krawczyk, H. (ed.) CRYPTO 1998. LNCS, vol. 1462, pp. 354–369. Springer, Heidelberg (1998)

[OT10] Okamoto, T., Takashima, K.: Fully secure functional encryption with general relations from the decisional linear assumption. In: Rabin, T. (ed.) CRYPTO 2010. LNCS, vol. 6223, pp. 191–208. Springer, Heidelberg (2010)

[SW05] Sahai, A., Waters, B.: Fuzzy identity-based encryption. In: Cramer, R. (ed.) EUROCRYPT 2005. LNCS, vol. 3494, pp. 457–473. Springer, Heidelberg (2005)

[SW08]   Shi, E., Waters, B.: Delegating capabilities in predicate encryption systems. In: Aceto, L., Damgård, I., Goldberg, L.A., Halldórsson, M.M., Ingólfsdóttir, A., Walukiewicz, I. (eds.) ICALP 2008, Part II. LNCS, vol. 5126, pp. 560–578. Springer, Heidelberg (2008)

[Wat05]   Waters, B.: Efficient identity-based encryption without random oracles. In: Cramer, R. (ed.) EUROCRYPT 2005. LNCS, vol. 3494, pp. 114–127. Springer, Heidelberg (2005)

[Wat09]   Waters, B.: Dual system encryption: Realizing fully secure IBE and HIBE under simple assumptions. In: Halevi, S. (ed.) CRYPTO 2009. LNCS, vol. 5677, pp. 619–636. Springer, Heidelberg (2009)

[Wat11]   Waters, B.: Ciphertext-policy attribute-based encryption: An expressive, efficient, and provably secure realization. In: Catalano, D., Fazio, N., Gennaro, R., Nicolosi, A. (eds.) PKC 2011. LNCS, vol. 6571, pp. 53–70. Springer, Heidelberg (2011)

Identity-Based Encryption Secure against Selective Opening Chosen-Ciphertext Attack

Junzuo Lai[1], Robert H. Deng[2], Shengli Liu[3,*],
Jian Weng[1], and Yunlei Zhao[4]

[1] Department of Computer Science, Jinan University, China
{laijunzuo,cryptjweng}@gmail.com
[2] School of Information Systems,
Singapore Management University, Singapore
robertdeng@smu.edu.sg
[3] Department of Computer Science and Engineering,
Shanghai Jiao Tong University, China
slliu@sjtu.edu.cn
[4] Software School, Fudan University,
SKLOIS (Beijing) and KLAISTC (Wuhan), China
yunleizhao@gmail.com

Abstract. Security against selective opening attack (SOA) requires that in a multi-user setting, even if an adversary has access to all ciphertexts from users, and adaptively corrupts some fraction of the users by exposing not only their messages but also the random coins, the remaining unopened messages retain their privacy. Recently, Bellare, Waters and Yilek considered SOA-security in the identity-based setting, and presented the first identity-based encryption (IBE) schemes that are proven secure against selective opening chosen plaintext attack (SO-CPA). However, how to achieve SO-CCA security for IBE is still open.

In this paper, we introduce a new primitive called extractable IBE and define its IND-ID-CCA security notion. We present a generic construction of SO-CCA secure IBE from an IND-ID-CCA secure extractable IBE with "One-Sided Public Openability"(1SPO), a collision-resistant hash function and a strengthened cross-authentication code. Finally, we propose two concrete constructions of extractable 1SPO-IBE schemes, resulting in the first simulation-based SO-CCA secure IBE schemes without random oracles.

Keywords: identity-based encryption, chosen ciphertext security, selective opening security.

1   Introduction

Security against chosen-plaintext attack (CPA) and security against chosen-ciphertext attack (CCA) are now well-accepted security notions for encryption.

---

* Corresponding author.

P.Q. Nguyen and E. Oswald (Eds.): EUROCRYPT 2014, LNCS 8441, pp. 77–92, 2014.

However, they may not suffice in some scenarios. For example, in a secure multi-party computation protocol, the communications among parties are encrypted, but an adversary may corrupt some parties to obtain not only their messages, but also the random coins used to encrypt the messages. This is the so-called "selective opening attack" (SOA). The traditional CPA (CCA) security does not imply SOA-security [1].

IND-SOA Security vs. SIM-SOA Security. There are two ways to formalize the SOA-security notion [2,4,18] for encryption, namely IND-SOA and SIM-SOA. IND-SOA security requires that no probabilistic polynomial-time (PPT) adversary can distinguish an unopened ciphertext from an encryption of a fresh message, which is distributed according to the conditional probability distribution (conditioned on the opened ciphertexts). Such a security notion requires that the joint plaintext distribution should be "efficiently conditionally re-samplable", which restricts SOA security to limited settings. To eliminate this restriction, the so-called full-IND-SOA security [5] was suggested. Unfortunately, there have been no known encryption schemes with full-IND-SOA security up to now. On the other hand, SIM-SOA security requires that anything that can be computed by a PPT adversary from all the ciphertexts and the opened messages together with the corresponding randomness can also be computed by a PPT simulator with only the opened messages. SIM-SOA security imposes no limitation on the message distribution, and it implies IND-SOA security.

The SOA-security (IND-SOA vs. SIM-SOA) is further classified into two notions, security against selective opening chosen-plaintext attacks (IND-SO-CPA vs. SIM-SO-CPA) and that against selective opening chosen-ciphertext attacks (IND-SO-CCA vs. SIM-SO-CCA), depending on whether the adversary has access to a decryption oracle or not.

SOA for PKE. The initial work about SOA security for encryption was done in the traditional public-key encryption (PKE) field. In [2], Bellare, Hofheinz and Yilek showed that any lossy encryption is able to achieve IND-SO-CPA security, and SIM-SOA security is achievable as well if the lossy encryption is "efficiently openable". This result suggests the existence of many IND-SO-CPA secure PKEs based on number-theoretic assumptions, such as the Decisional Diffie-Hellman (DDH), Decisional Composite Residuosity (DCR) and Quadratic Residuosity (QR), and lattices-related assumptions [25,14,16,17,6,26,22]. Later, Hemenway et al. [15] showed that both re-randomizable public-key encryption and statistically-hiding $\binom{2}{1}$-oblivious transfer imply lossy encryption.

In [15], Hemenway et al. also proposed a paradigm of constructing IND-SO-CCA secure PKE from selective-tag weakly secure and separable tag-based PKE with the help of chameleon hashing. Hofheinz [19] showed how to get SO-CCA secure PKE with compact ciphertexts. Fehr et al. [13] proved that sender-equivocable (NC-CCA) security implies SIM-SO-CCA security, and showed how to construct PKE schemes with NC-CCA security based on hash proof systems with explainable domains and L-cross-authentication codes (L-XAC, in short).

Recently, Huang et al. [20,21] showed that using the method proposed in [13] to construct SIM-SO-CCA secure PKE, L-XAC needs to be *strong*.

SOA for IBE. Compared with SOA security for PKE, SOA-secure IBE is lagged behind. The subtlety of proving security for IBE comes from the fact that a key generation oracle should be provided to an adversary to answer private key queries with respect to different identities, and the adversary is free to choose the target identity. It was not until 2011 that the question how to build SOA-secure IBE was answered by Bellare et al. in [3]. Bellare et al. [3] proposed a general paradigm to achieve SIM-SO-CPA security from IND-ID-CPA secure and "One-Sided Publicly Openable" (1SPO) IBE schemes. They also presented two 1SPO IND-ID-CPA IBE schemes without random oracles, one based on the Boyen-Waters anonymous IBE [8] and the other based on Water's dual-system approach [27], yielding two SIM-SO-CPA secure IBE schemes. The second SIM-SO-CPA secure IBE scheme proposed in [3] can be extended to construct the first SIM-SO-CPA secure hierarchical identity-based encryption (HIBE) scheme without random oracles. One may hope to obtain SIM-SO-CCA secure IBEs by applying the BCHK transform [7] to SIM-SO-CPA secure HIBEs. Unfortunately, as mentioned in [3], the BCHK transform [7] does not work in the SOA setting. Consequently, how to construct SIM-SO-CCA secure IBEs has been left as an open question.

Our Contribution. We answer the open question of achieving SIM-SO-CCA secure IBE with a new primitive called extractable IBE with One-Sided Public Openability (extractable 1SPO-IBE, in short) and a *strengthened* cross authentication codes (XAC).

- We define a new primitive named extractable 1SPO-IBE and its IND-ID-CCA security notion.
- We define a new property of XAC: *semi-uniqueness*. If an XAC is strong and semi-unique, we say it is a *strengthened* XAC. We also show that the efficient construction of XAC proposed by Fehr et al. [13] is a strengthened XAC actually.
- We propose a paradigm of building SIM-SO-CCA secure IBE from IND-ID-CCA secure extractable 1SPO-IBE, collision-resistant hash function and strengthened XAC. Actually, we can define the notion of extractable 1SPO-PKE similarly, and use the same method to provide a paradigm of building SIM-SO-CCA secure PKE from IND-CCA secure extractable 1SPO-PKE, collision-resistant hash function and strengthened XAC, which is different from the paradigm proposed by Fehr et al. [13].
- We construct extractable 1SPO-IBE schemes without random oracles by adapting anonymous IBEs, including the anonymous extension of Lewko-Waters IBE scheme [23] by De Caro, Iovino and Persiano [11] and the Boyen-Waters anonymous IBE [8].

EXTRACTABLE 1SPO-IBE. Extractable IBE combines one-bit IBE and identity-based key encapsulation mechanism (IB-KEM). The message space of extractable

IBE is $\{0, 1\}$. An encryption of 1 under identity ID also encapsulates a session key K, behaving like IB-KEM. More precisely, $(C, K) \leftarrow \mathsf{Encrypt}_{ex}(\mathsf{PK}_{ex}, \mathsf{ID}, 1; R)$ and $C \leftarrow \mathsf{Encrypt}_{ex}(\mathsf{PK}_{ex}, \mathsf{ID}, 0; R')$, where PK_{ex} is the public parameter and R, R' are the randomness used in encryption. If C is from the encryption of 1 under ID, the decryption algorithm, $(b, K) \leftarrow \mathsf{Decrypt}_{ex}(\mathsf{PK}, \mathsf{SK}_{\mathsf{ID}}, C)$, is able to use the private key $\mathsf{SK}_{\mathsf{ID}}$ to recover message $b = 1$ as well as the encapsulated session key K. As for an encryption of 0, say $C = \mathsf{Encrypt}_{ex}(\mathsf{PK}_{ex}, \mathsf{ID}, 0; R')$, the decryption algorithm can recover message $b = 0$ but generate a *uniformly random* key K as well.

The security of extractable IBE requires that given a challenge ciphertext C^* and a challenge key K^* under some identity ID^*, no PPT adversary can distinguish, except with negligible advantage, whether C^* is an encryption of 1 under identity ID^* and K^* is the encapsulated key of C^*, or C^* is an encryption of 0 under identity ID^* and K^* is a uniformly random key, even if the adversary has access to a key generation oracle for private key $\mathsf{SK}_{\mathsf{ID}}$ with $\mathsf{ID} \neq \mathsf{ID}^*$ and a decryption oracle to decrypt ciphertexts other than C^* under ID^*. Obviously, the security notion of extractable IBE inherits IND-ID-CCA security of one-bit IBE and IND-ID-CCA security of IB-KEM.

An extractable IBE is called *one-sided publicly openable* (1SPO), if there exists a PPT *public* algorithm POpen as follows: given $C = \mathsf{Encrypt}_{ex}(\mathsf{PK}_{ex}, \mathsf{ID}, 0; R)$, it outputs random coins R' which is uniformly distributed subject to $C = \mathsf{Encrypt}_{ex}(\mathsf{PK}_{ex}, \mathsf{ID}, 0; R')$. One-sided public openability [3] is an IBE-analogue of a weak form of deniable PKE [9] (which plays an essential role in the construction of NC-CPA/CCA secure PKE in [13], consequently achieving SIM-SO-CPA/CCA secure PKE). In [3], Bellare et al. used one-bit 1SPO-IBE to construct SIM-SO-CPA secure IBE.

SIM-SO-CCA SECURE IBE FROM EXTRACTABLE 1SPO-IBE. We follow the line of [13], which achieves SIM-SO-CCA secure PKE from sender-equivocable or weak deniable encryption and XAC. We give a high-level description on how to construct a SIM-SO-CCA secure IBE scheme from an extractable 1SPO-IBE scheme characterized by $(\mathsf{Encrypt}_{ex}, \mathsf{Decrypt}_{ex})$, with the help of a collision-resistant hash function H and a strengthened $\ell + 1$-cross-authentication code XAC.

First, we roughly recall the notion of cross-authentication code XAC, which was introduced in [13]. In an $\ell + 1$-cross-authentication code XAC, an authentication tag T can be computed from a *list* of random keys $K_1, \ldots, K_{\ell+1}$ (without a designated message) using algorithm XAuth. The XVer algorithm is used to verify the correctness of the tag T with *any* single key K. If K is from the list, XVer will output 1. If K is uniformly randomly chosen, XVer will output 1 with negligible probability. If an XAC is *strong* and *semi-unique*, we say it is a strengthened XAC. Strongness of XAC means given $(K_i)_{1 \leq i \leq \ell+1, i \neq j}$ and T, a new key $\hat{K}_j$ which is statistically indistinguishable to K_i, can be efficiently sampled. Semi-uniqueness of XAC requires that K can be parsed to (K_a, K_b) and for a fixed T and K_a, there is at most one K_b satisfying $\mathsf{XVer}((K_a, K_b), T) = 1$.

Our cryptosystem has message space $\{0, 1\}^\ell$, and encryption of an ℓ-bit message $M = m_1 \| \cdots \| m_\ell$ for an identity ID is performed bitwise, with one ciphertext element per bit. For each bit m_i, the corresponding ciphertext element C_i is an encryption of m_i under ID, which is generated by the encryption algorithm of the extractable 1SPO-IBE scheme. As shown in [24], a scheme which encrypts long message bit-by-bit is vulnerable to *quoting attacks*. Hence, we use a collision-resistant hash function and a strengthened $\ell+1$-cross-authentication code XAC to bind $C_1, \ldots, C_\ell$ together to resist quoting attacks.

Specifically, let K_a be a public parameter, in our SIM-SO-CCA secure IBE scheme, encryption of an ℓ-bit message $M = m_1 \| \cdots \| m_\ell \in \{0,1\}^\ell$ for an identity ID is given by the ciphertext $CT = (C_1, \ldots, C_\ell, T)$, where

$$\begin{cases} (C_i, K_i) \leftarrow \mathsf{Encrypt}_{ex}(\mathsf{PK}_{ex}, \mathsf{ID}, 1) & \text{if } m_i = 1 \\ C_i \leftarrow \mathsf{Encrypt}_{ex}(\mathsf{PK}_{ex}, \mathsf{ID}, 0), \ K_i \leftarrow \mathcal{K} & \text{if } m_i = 0 \end{cases},$$
$$K_b = \mathsf{H}(\mathsf{ID}, C_1, \ldots, C_\ell), \quad K_{\ell+1} = (K_a, K_b), \quad \dot{T} = \mathsf{XAuth}(K_1, \ldots, K_{\ell+1}).$$

Here C_i is from the extractable 1SPO-IBE encryption of bit m_i, and K_i is the encapsulated key or randomly chosen key depending on $m_i = 1$ or 0. Finally, XAC tag T glues all the C_is together. Given a ciphertext $CT = (C_1, \ldots, C_\ell, T)$ for identity ID, the decryption algorithm first checks whether $\mathsf{XVer}(K'_{\ell+1}, T) = 1$ or not, where $K'_{\ell+1} = (K_a, \mathsf{H}(\mathsf{ID}, C_1, \ldots, C_\ell))$. If not, it outputs message $\overbrace{0 \cdots 0}^{\ell}$. Otherwise, it uses $\mathsf{Decrypt}_{ex}$ of the extractable 1SPO-IBE scheme to recover bit m'_i and a session key K'_i from each C_i. If $m'_i = 0$, set $m''_i = 0$, otherwise set $m''_i = \mathsf{XVer}(K'_i, T)$. Finally, it outputs $M'' = m''_1 \| \cdots \| m''_\ell$. We assume that the key space $\mathcal{XK}$ of the strengthened XAC and the session key space $\mathcal{K}$ of the extractable 1SPO-IBE are identical (i.e., $\mathcal{K} = \mathcal{XK}$), and $\mathcal{K}$ is efficiently samplable and explainable domain.

As for the SIM-SO-CCA security of the IBE scheme, the proving line is to show that encryptions of ℓ ones are "equivocable" ciphertexts, which can be opened to arbitrary messages, and the "equivocable" ciphertexts are computationally indistinguishable from real challenge ciphertexts in an SOA setting, i.e., even if the adversary is given access to a corruption oracle to get the opened messages and randomness, a decryption oracle to decrypt ciphertexts and a key generation oracle to obtain private keys. If so, a PPT SOA-simulator can be constructed to create "equivocable" ciphertexts (i.e., encryptions of ℓ ones) as challenge ciphertexts, then open them accordingly, and SIM-SO-CCA security follows.

To prove a challenge ciphertext $CT = (C_1, \ldots, C_\ell, T)$ under ID, which encrypts $m_1 \| \cdots \| m_\ell$, is indistinguishable from encryption of ℓ ones in the SOA setting, we use hybrid argument. For each $m_i = 0$, we replace (C_i, K_i) (which is used to create CT under ID) with an extractable 1SPO-IBE encryption of 1. If this replacement is distinguishable to an adversary $\mathcal{A}$, then another PPT algorithm $\mathcal{B}$ can simulate SOA-environment for $\mathcal{A}$ by setting (C_i, K_i) to be its own challenge (C^*, K^*) under ID, and use $\mathcal{A}$ to break the IND-ID-CCA security of the extractable 1SPO-IBE. The subtlety lies in how $\mathcal{B}$ deals with $\mathcal{A}$'s decryption query $\widetilde{CT} = (\widetilde{C}_1, \ldots, \widetilde{C}_l, \widetilde{T})$ under ID with $\widetilde{C}_j = C^*$ for some $j \in [\ell]$. Recall that $\mathcal{B}$ is not allowed to issue a private key query $\langle \mathsf{ID} \rangle$ or a decryption query $\langle \mathsf{ID}, C^* \rangle$ to it's own challenger in the extractable 1SPO-IBE security game. In this case, $\mathcal{B}$ will resort to XAC to set $\widetilde{m}_j'' = \mathsf{XVer}(K^*, \widetilde{T})$. Observe that, if $(C^*, K^*) = \mathsf{Encrypt}_{ex}(\mathsf{PK}_{ex}, \mathsf{ID}, 1)$, then $\widetilde{m}_j'' = \mathsf{XVer}(K^*, \widetilde{T}) = 1$, which is exactly the same as the output of Decrypt algorithm. If $C^* = \mathsf{Encrypt}_{ex}(\mathsf{PK}_{ex}, \mathsf{ID}, 0)$ and K^* is random, then $\widetilde{m}_j'' = \mathsf{XVer}(K^*, \widetilde{T}) = 0$ except with negligible probability, due to XAC's security against substitution attacks. This is also consistent with the output of the decryption algorithm, except with negligible probability. Hence, with overwhelming probability, $\mathcal{B}$ simulates SOA-environment for $\mathcal{A}$ properly. Note that to apply XAC's security against substitution attacks, we require:

1. $\widetilde{T} \neq T$, which is guaranteed by XAC's *semi-unique* property and *collision resistance* of hash function.
2. K^* should not be revealed to adversary $\mathcal{A}$. Therefore, in the corruption phase, if $\mathcal{B}$ is asked to open (C^*, K^*), it first resamples a $\hat{K}$, which is statistically indistinguishable from K^*. This is guaranteed by the *strongness* of XAC. Then, C will be opened to 0 with algorithm POpen, and $\hat{K}$ (instead of K^*) is opened with a suitable randomness.

CONSTRUCTION OF EXTRACTABLE 1SPO-IBE. In [3], Bellare et al. proposed two one-bit 1SPO-IBEs, one based on the anonymous extension of Lewko-Waters IBE scheme [23] by De Caro, Iovino and Persiano [11] and the other based on the Boyen-Waters anonymous IBE [8]. Both schemes rely on a pairing $e : \mathbb{G} \times \mathbb{G} \to \mathbb{G}_T$. The 1SPO property of the two one-bit IBE schemes is guaranteed by the fact that $\mathbb{G}$ is an *efficiently samplable and explainable domain*, which is characterized by two PPT algorithms Sample and Sample^{-1} for group $\mathbb{G}$. More precisely, Sample chooses an element g from $\mathbb{G}$ uniformly at random, and Sample$^{-1}(\mathbb{G}, g)$ will output a uniformly distributed R subject to $g = \mathsf{Sample}(\mathbb{G}; R)$. Details of algorithms Sample and Sample^{-1} are given in [3].

Unfortunately, the one-bit 1SPO-IBE schemes in [3] are not extractable IBEs. No session keys can be extracted from encryptions of 1, and the schemes are vulnerable to chosen-ciphertext attacks. Therefore, we have to resort to new techniques for extractable 1SPO-IBE.

We start from anonymous IBE schemes in [11,8]. Recall that an encryption of a message M for an identity ID in anonymous IBEs [11,8] takes the form of $(c_0 = f_0(\mathsf{PK}, s, s_0), c_1 = f_1(\mathsf{PK}, \mathsf{ID}, s, s_1), c_2 = e(g, g)^{\alpha s} \cdot M)$, where PK denotes the system's public parameter, α is the master secret key, s, s_0, s_1 are the randomness used in the encryption algorithm, f_0, f_1 are two efficient functions and each of c_0, c_1 denotes one or several elements in $\mathbb{G}$. The private key $\mathsf{SK}_{\mathsf{ID}}$ is structured such that pairings with group elements of (c_1, c_2) result in $e(g, g)^{\alpha s}$, hence the message M can be recovered from c_2.

The idea of constructing extractable 1SPO-IBE is summerized as follows. Firstly, we generate ciphertexts of the form $(c_0' = f_0'(\mathsf{PK}, s, s_0), c_1' = f_1'(\mathsf{PK}, \mathsf{ID}, \mathsf{ID}', s, s_1))$, where $\mathsf{ID}' = \mathsf{H}(\mathsf{ID}, c_0')$ and H is a collision-resistant hash function. The structure of (c_0', c_1') is characterized by the shared randomness s and this structure can be publicly verified. The master secret key is now (α, β). Correspondingly the private key $\mathsf{SK}_{\mathsf{ID}} = (\mathsf{SK}_{\mathsf{ID},1}, \mathsf{SK}_{\mathsf{ID},2})$, and $\mathsf{SK}_{\mathsf{ID},i}(i = 1, 2)$ are generated by the master secret key α and β respectively, in a similar way as that in the anonymous IBEs [11,8]. Consequently, $\mathsf{SK}_{\mathsf{ID},1}$ and $\mathsf{SK}_{\mathsf{ID},2}$ help generate $e(g,g)^{\alpha s}$ and $e(g,g)^{\beta s}$ from (c_0', c_1').

Next, we use $e(g,g)^{\alpha s}$ to blind (c_0', c_1') and obtain $(c_0'' = f_1''(\mathsf{PK}, s, s_0), c_1'' = f_1''(\mathsf{PK}, \mathsf{ID}, \mathsf{ID}', s, s_1))$, which satisfies the following properties:

1. Without the private key $\mathsf{SK}_{\mathsf{ID}} = (\mathsf{SK}_{\mathsf{ID},1}, \mathsf{SK}_{\mathsf{ID},2})$ for ID, the relationship between c_0'' and c_1'' (that they share the same s) is hidden from any PPT adversary.
2. With $\mathsf{SK}_{\mathsf{ID},1}$ and $\mathsf{SK}_{\mathsf{ID},2}$, it is still possible to generate $e(g,g)^{\alpha s}$ and $e(g,g)^{\beta s}$ from the blinded ciphertext (c_0'', c_1'').
3. Given the blinded factor $e(g,g)^{\alpha s}$, (c_0'', c_1'') can be efficiently changed back to (c_0', c_1').

Finally, we obtain the extractable 1SPO-IBE with the following features:

$\mathsf{Encrypt}_{ex}(\mathsf{PK}_{ex}, \mathsf{ID}, b) =$
$$\begin{cases} ((c_0'', c_1''), K) = ((f_1''(\mathsf{PK}, s, s_0), f_1''(\mathsf{PK}, \mathsf{ID}, \mathsf{ID}', s, s_1)), e(g,g)^{\beta s})) & b = 1 \\ (c_0'', c_1'') \leftarrow \mathsf{Sample}(\mathbb{G}) & b = 0 \end{cases}.$$

- Given a ciphertext $C = (c_0'', c_1'')$ for ID, the decryption algorithm first uses $\mathsf{SK}_{\mathsf{ID},1}$ to compute a blinding factor from (c_0'', c_1''). Then, it uses the blinding factor to retrieve (c_0', c_1') from (c_0'', c_1''). Next, it checks whether (c_0', c_1') have a specific structure. If yes, it outputs message 1 and computes the encapsulated session key from (c_0'', c_1'') using $\mathsf{SK}_{\mathsf{ID},2}$; otherwise, it outputs message 0 and a uniformly random session key.
- Algorithm POpen for 1SPO can be implemented with Sample^{-1}.

We emphasize that the 2-hierarchical IBE structure (when encrypting 1) helps to answer decryption queries in the IND-ID-CCA security proof of the above extractable 1SPO-IBE. In the private key $\mathsf{SK}_{\mathsf{ID}} = (\mathsf{SK}_{\mathsf{ID},1}, \mathsf{SK}_{\mathsf{ID},2})$, $\mathsf{SK}_{\mathsf{ID},2}$ is used to generate the encapsulated key $e(g,g)^{\beta s}$ when encrypting 1, and $\mathsf{SK}_{\mathsf{ID},1}$ is used to generate a blind factor $e(g,g)^{\alpha s}$, which helps to convert the publicly verifiable structure of (c_0', c_1') to a privately verifiable structure, resulting in IND-ID-CCA secure extractable 1SPO-IBE.

Organization. The rest of the paper is organized as follows. Some preliminaries are given in Section 2. We introduce the notion and security model of extractable 1SPO-IBE in Section 3. The notion of strengthened XAC and its efficient construction are given in Section 4. We propose a paradigm of building SIM-SO-CCA secure IBE from IND-ID-CCA secure extractable 1SPO-IBE, collision-resistant hash function and strengthened XAC in Section 5. We present two IND-ID-CCA secure extractable 1SPO-IBE schemes in Section 6.

2 Preliminaries

If S is a set, then $s_1, \ldots, s_t \leftarrow S$ denotes the operation of picking elements $s_1, \ldots, s_t$ uniformly at random from S. If $n \in \mathbb{N}$ then $[n]$ denotes the set

$\{1, \ldots, n\}$. For $i \in \{0, 1\}^*$, $|i|$ denotes the bit-length of i. If $x_1, x_2, \ldots$ are strings, then $x_1 \| x_2 \| \cdots$ denotes their concatenation. For a probabilistic algorithm A, we denote $y \leftarrow A(x; R)$ the process of running A on input x and with randomness R, and assigning y the result. Let $\mathcal{R}_A$ denote the randomness space of A, and we write $y \leftarrow A(x)$ for $y \leftarrow A(x; R)$ with R chosen from $\mathcal{R}_A$ uniformly at random. A function $f(\kappa)$ is *negligible*, if for every $c > 0$ there exists a κ_c such that $f(\kappa) < 1/\kappa^c$ for all $\kappa > \kappa_c$.

2.1 Key Derivation Functions

A family of *key derivation functions* [12] $\mathcal{KDF} = \{\mathsf{KDF}_i : \mathcal{X}_i \to \mathcal{K}_i\}$, indexed by $i \in \{0, 1\}^*$, is *secure* if, for all PPT algorithms $\mathcal{A}$ and for sufficiently large i, the distinguishing advantage $Adv_{\mathcal{KDF}}^{\mathcal{A}}(i)$ is negligible (in $|i|$), where

$$Adv_{\mathcal{KDF}}^{\mathcal{A}}(i) = |\Pr[\mathcal{A}(\mathsf{KDF}_i, \mathsf{KDF}_i(x)) = 1 \,|\, \mathsf{KDF}_i \leftarrow \mathcal{KDF}, x \leftarrow \mathcal{X}_i] -$$
$$\Pr[\mathcal{A}(\mathsf{KDF}_i, K) = 1 \,|\, \mathsf{KDF}_i \leftarrow \mathcal{KDF}, K \leftarrow \mathcal{K}_i]| \,.$$

The above definition is for presentation simplicity. In general, the index i should be generated by a PPT sampler algorithm on the security parameter κ. For notational convenience, we ignore the index i of a key derivation function.

2.2 Efficiently Samplable and Explainable Domain

A domain $\mathcal{D}$ is *efficiently samplable and explainable* [13] iff there exist two PPT algorithms:

- $\mathsf{Sample}(\mathcal{D}; R)$: On input random coins $R \leftarrow \mathcal{R}_{\mathsf{Sample}}$ and a domain $\mathcal{D}$, it outputs an element uniformly distributed over $\mathcal{D}$.
- $\mathsf{Sample}^{-1}(\mathcal{D}, x)$: On input $\mathcal{D}$ and *any* $x \in \mathcal{D}$, this algorithm outputs R that is uniformly distributed over the set $\{R \in \mathcal{R}_{\mathsf{Sample}} \,|\, \mathsf{Sample}(\mathcal{D}; R) = x\}$.

3 Extractable IBE with One-Sided Public Openability (Extractable 1SPO-IBE)

Formally, an extractable identity-based encryption (extractable IBE) scheme consists of the following four algorithms:

$\mathsf{Setup}_{ex}(1^{\kappa})$ takes as input a security parameter κ. It generates a public parameter PK and a master secret key MSK. The public parameter PK defines an identity space $\mathcal{ID}$, a ciphertext space $\mathcal{C}$ and a session key space $\mathcal{K}$.

$\mathsf{KeyGen}_{ex}(\mathsf{PK}, \mathsf{MSK}, \mathsf{ID})$ takes as input the public parameter PK, the master secret key MSK and an identity $\mathsf{ID} \in \mathcal{ID}$. It produces a private key $\mathsf{SK}_{\mathsf{ID}}$ for the identity ID.

$\mathsf{Encrypt}_{ex}(\mathsf{PK}, \mathsf{ID}, m)$ takes as input the public parameter PK, an identity $\mathsf{ID} \in \mathcal{ID}$ and a message $m \in \{0, 1\}$. It outputs a ciphertext C if $m = 0$, and outputs a ciphertext and a session key (C, K) if $m = 1$. Here $K \in \mathcal{K}$.

$\mathsf{Decrypt}_{ex}(\mathsf{PK}, \mathsf{SK}_{\mathsf{ID}}, C)$ takes as input the public parameter PK, a private key $\mathsf{SK}_{\mathsf{ID}}$ and a ciphertext $C \in \mathcal{C}$. It outputs a message $m' \in \{0, 1\}$ and a session key $K' \in \mathcal{K}$.

Correctness. An extractable IBE scheme has completeness error ϵ, if for all κ, ID $\in$ $\mathcal{ID}$, $m \in \{0,1\}$, (PK, MSK) $\leftarrow$ Setup$_{ex}(1^\kappa)$, $C/(C,K) \leftarrow$ Encrypt$_{ex}(\text{PK}, \text{ID}, m)$, SK$_{\text{ID}} \leftarrow$ KeyGen$_{ex}(\text{PK}, \text{MSK}, \text{ID})$ and $(m', K') \leftarrow$ Decrypt$_{ex}(\text{PK}, \text{SK}_{\text{ID}}, C)$:

- The probability that $m' = m$ is at least $1 - \epsilon$, where the probability is taken over the coins used in encryption.
- If $m = 1$ then $m' = m$ and $K' = K$. If $m' = 0$, K' is uniformly distributed in $\mathcal{K}$.

Security. The IND-ID-CCA security of extractable IBE is twisted from IND-ID-CCA security of one-bit IBE and IND-ID-CCA security of identity-based key encapsulation mechanism (IB-KEM). The security notion is defined using the following game between a PPT adversary $\mathcal{A}$ and a challenger.

Setup. The challenger runs Setup$_{ex}(1^\kappa)$ to obtain a public parameter PK and a master secret key MSK. It gives the public parameter PK to the adversary.

Query phase 1. The adversary $\mathcal{A}$ adaptively issues the following queries:
- Key generation query $\langle \text{ID} \rangle$: the challenger runs KeyGen$_{ex}$ on ID to generate the corresponding private key SK$_{\text{ID}}$, which is returned to $\mathcal{A}$.
- Decryption query $\langle \text{ID}, C \rangle$: the challenger runs KeyGen$_{ex}$ on ID to get the private key, then use the key to decrypt C with Decrypt$_{ex}$ algorithm. The result is sent back to $\mathcal{A}$.

Challenge. The adversary $\mathcal{A}$ submits a challenge identity ID*. The only restriction is that, $\mathcal{A}$ did not issue a private key query for ID* in Query phase 1. The challenger first selects a random bit $\delta \in \{0,1\}$. If $\delta = 1$, the challenger computes $(C^*, K^*) \leftarrow$ Encrypt$_{ex}(\text{PK}, \text{ID}^*, 1)$. Otherwise (i.e., $\delta = 0$), the challenger computes $C^* \leftarrow$ Encrypt$_{ex}(\text{PK}, \text{ID}^*, 0)$ and chooses $K^* \leftarrow \mathcal{K}$. Then, the challenge ciphertext and session key (C^*, K^*) are sent to the adversary by the challenger.

Query phase 2. This is identical to Query phase 1, except that the adversary does not request a private key for ID* or the decryption of $\langle \text{ID}^*, C^* \rangle$.

Guess. The adversary $\mathcal{A}$ outputs its guess $\delta' \in \{0,1\}$ for δ and wins the game if $\delta = \delta'$.

The advantage of the adversary in this game is defined as $\text{Adv}^{\text{cca}}_{\text{ex-IBE},\mathcal{A}}(\kappa) = |\Pr[\delta' = 1|\delta = 1] - \Pr[\delta' = 1|\delta = 0]|$, where the probability is taken over the random bits used by the challenger and the adversary.

Definition 1. *An extractable IBE scheme is IND-ID-CCA secure, if the advantage in the above security game is negligible for all PPT adversaries.*

We say that an extractable IBE scheme is IND-sID-CCA secure if we add an **Init** stage before setup in the above security game where the adversary commits to the challenge identity ID*.

Definition 2. (Extractable 1SPO-IBE) *An extractable IBE scheme is One-Sided Publicly Openable if it is associated with a PPT public algorithm POpen such that for all PK generated by $(PK, MSK) \leftarrow Setup_{ex}(1^\kappa)$, for all $ID \in \mathcal{ID}$ and any $C \leftarrow Encrypt_{ex}(PK, ID, 0)$, it holds that: the output of POpen(PK, ID, C) distributes uniformly at random over Coins$(PK, ID, C, 0)$, where Coins$(PK, ID, C, 0)$ denotes the set of random coins $\{\tilde{R} \mid C = Encrypt_{ex}(PK, ID, 0; \tilde{R})\}$.*

4   Strengthened Cross-authentication Codes

In this section, we first review the notion and security requirements of cross-authentication codes introduced in [13]. Then we define a new property of cross-authentication codes: *semi-unique*. If a cross-authentication code is *strong* and *semi-unique*, we say it is a *strengthened* cross-authentication code, which will play an important role in our construction of SIM-SO-CCA secure IBE. Finally, we will show that the efficient construction of cross-authentication code proposed by Fehr et al. [13] is actually a strengthened cross-authentication code.

Definition 3 (*L*-Cross-authentication code.). *For $L \in \mathbb{N}$, an L-cross-authentication code XAC is associated with a key space $\mathcal{XK}$ and a tag space $\mathcal{XT}$, and consists of three PPT algorithms XGen, XAuth and XVer. $XGen(1^\kappa)$ produces a uniformly random key $K \in \mathcal{XK}$, deterministic algorithm $XAuth(K_1, \ldots, K_L)$ outputs a tag $T \in \mathcal{XT}$, and deterministic algorithm $XVer(K,T)$ outputs a decision bit[1]. The following is required:*

Correctness. *For all $i \in [L]$, the probability*

$$fail_{XAC}(\kappa) := \Pr[XVer(K_i, XAuth(K_1, \ldots, K_L)) \neq 1],$$

is negligible, where $K_1, \ldots, K_L \leftarrow XGen(1^\kappa)$ in the probability.

Security against impersonation and substitution attacks. *$Adv_{XAC}^{imp}(\kappa)$ and $Adv_{XAC}^{sub}(\kappa)$ as defined below are both negligible:*

$$Adv_{XAC}^{imp}(\kappa) := \max_{T'} \Pr[XVer(K, T') = 1 | K \leftarrow XGen(1^\kappa)],$$

where the max is over all $T' \in \mathcal{XT}$, and

$$Adv_{XAC}^{sub}(\kappa) := \max_{i, K_{\neq i}, F} \Pr \left[\begin{array}{c} T' \neq T \wedge \\ XVer(K_i, T') = 1 \end{array} \middle| \begin{array}{c} K_i \leftarrow XGen(1^\kappa), \\ T = XAuth(K_1, \ldots, K_L), \\ T' \leftarrow F(T) \end{array} \right]$$

where the max is over all $i \in [L]$, all $K_{\neq i} = (K_j)_{j \neq i} \in \mathcal{XK}^{L-1}$ and all (possibly randomized) functions $F : \mathcal{XT} \to \mathcal{XT}$.

Definition 4 (Strengthened XAC.). *An L-cross-authentication code XAC is a strengthened XAC, if it enjoys the following additional properties.*

Strongness [20]: *There exists another PPT public algorithm ReSamp, which takes as input i, $(K_j)_{j \neq i}$ and T, with $K_1, \ldots, K_L \leftarrow XGen(1^\kappa)$ and $T \leftarrow$*

---

[1] In Fehr et al.'s original definition [13], algorithm XVer includes an additional input parameter: index i. Let $K_1, \ldots, K_L \leftarrow XGen(1^\kappa)$ and $T \leftarrow XAuth(K_1, \ldots, K_L)$. Since $XVer(K_i, i, T) = XVer(K_i, j, T)$ in their efficient construction, we only take a key and a tag as input of algorithm XVer for notational convenience.

XAuth($K_1, \ldots, K_L$), outputs $\hat{K}_i$ (i.e., $\hat{K}_i \leftarrow$ ReSamp($K_{\neq i}, T$)), such that $\hat{K}_i$ is statistically indistinguishable with K_i, i.e., the statistical distance

$$Dist(\kappa) := \frac{1}{2} \cdot \sum_{K \in \mathcal{XK}} \left| \Pr[\hat{K}_i = K \,|(K_{\neq i}, T)] - \Pr[K_i = K \,|(K_{\neq i}, T)] \right|$$

is negligible.

Semi-uniqueness: *The key space* $\mathcal{XK} = \mathcal{K}_a \times \mathcal{K}_b$. *Given an authentication tag* T *and* $K_a \in \mathcal{K}_a$, *there exists at most one* $K_b \in \mathcal{K}_b$ *such that* XVer($(K_a, K_b), T$) = 1.

Next, we review the efficient construction of L-cross-authentication code secure against impersonation and substitution attacks proposed by Fehr et al. [13], and show that it is *strong* and *semi-unique* as well, i.e. it is a *strengthened* XAC.

- $\mathcal{XK} = \mathcal{K}_a \times \mathcal{K}_b = \mathbb{F}_q^2$ and $\mathcal{XT} = \mathbb{F}_q^L \cup \{\bot\}$.
- XGen outputs (a, b), which is chosen from $\mathbb{F}_q^2$ uniformly at random.
- $T \leftarrow$ XAuth($(a_1, b_1), \ldots, (a_L, b_L)$). Let $\mathbf{A} \in \mathbb{F}_q^{L \times L}$ be a matrix with its i-th row $(1, a_i, a_i^2, \ldots, a_i^{L-1})$ for $i \in [L]$. Let $b_1, \ldots, b_L \in \mathbb{F}_q^L$ constitute the column vector $\mathbf{B}$. If $\mathbf{AT} = \mathbf{B}$ has no solution or more than one solution, set $T = \bot$. Otherwise $\mathbf{A}$ is a Vandermonde matrix, and the tag $T = (T_0, \ldots, T_{L-1})$ can be computed efficiently by solving the linear equation system $\mathbf{AT} = \mathbf{B}$.
- Define $poly_T(x) = T_0 + T_1 x + \cdots + T_{L-1} x^{L-1} \in \mathbb{F}_q[x]$ with $T = (T_0, \ldots, T_{L-1})$. XVer($(a, b), T$) outputs 1 if and only if $T \neq \bot$ and $poly_T(a) = b$.
- $(a, b) \leftarrow$ ReSamp($(a_j, b_j)_{j \neq i}, T$). Choose $a \leftarrow \mathbb{F}_q$ such that $a \neq a_j$ ($1 \leq j \leq \ell, j \neq i$) and compute $b = poly_T(a)$. Conditioned on $T =$ XAuth($(a_1, b_1), \ldots, (a_L, b_L)$) ($T \neq \bot$) and $(a_j, b_j)_{j \neq i}$, both of (a, b) and (a_i, b_i) are uniformly distributed over the same support.
- Fixing $a \in \mathbb{F}_q$ results in a unique $b = poly_T(a)$ such that XVer($(a, b), T$) = 1, if $T \neq \bot$.

5   Proposed **SIM-SO-CCA** Secure IBE Scheme

Let (Setup$_{ex}$, KeyGen$_{ex}$, Encrypt$_{ex}$, Decrypt$_{ex}$) be an extractable 1SPO-IBE scheme with identity space $\mathcal{ID}$, ciphertext space $\mathcal{C}$ and session key space $\mathcal{K} = \mathcal{K}_a \times \mathcal{K}_b$, and (XGen, XAuth, XVer) be a strengthened $\ell + 1$-cross-authentication code XAC with key space $\mathcal{XK} = \mathcal{K} = \mathcal{K}_a \times \mathcal{K}_b$ and tag space $\mathcal{XT}$. We require that key space $\mathcal{K}$ is also an *efficiently samplable and explainable domain*[2] associated with algorithms Sample' and Sample'$^{-1}$. Our cryptosystem has message space $\{0, 1\}^\ell$.

---

[2] As mentioned in [13], the *efficiently samplable and explainable* key space $\mathcal{K}$ can be assumed without loss of generality, because $\mathcal{K}$ can always be efficiently mapped into $\mathcal{K}' = \{0, 1\}^l$ by means of a suitable (almost) balanced function, such that uniform distribution in $\mathcal{K}$ induces (almost) uniform distribution in $\mathcal{K}'$, and where l is linear in $\log(|\mathcal{K}|)$.

Our scheme consists of the following algorithms:

Setup(1^κ) : The setup algorithm first chooses $K_a \leftarrow \mathcal{K}_a$ and a collision-resistant hash function $\mathsf{H} : \mathcal{ID} \times \overbrace{\mathcal{C} \times \cdots \times \mathcal{C}}^{\ell} \rightarrow \mathcal{K}_b$, and calls Setup_{ex} to obtain $(\mathsf{PK}_{ex}, \mathsf{MSK}_{ex}) \leftarrow \mathsf{Setup}_{ex}(1^\kappa)$. It sets the public parameter $\mathsf{PK} = (\mathsf{PK}_{ex}, \mathsf{H}, K_a)$ and the master secret key $\mathsf{MSK} = \mathsf{MSK}_{ex}$.

KeyGen($\mathsf{PK}, \mathsf{MSK}, \mathsf{ID} \in \mathcal{ID}$) : The key generation algorithm takes as input the public parameter $\mathsf{PK} = (\mathsf{PK}_{ex}, \mathsf{H}, K_a)$, the master secret key $\mathsf{MSK} = \mathsf{MSK}_{ex}$ and an identity ID. It calls KeyGen_{ex} to get $\mathsf{SK}_{\mathsf{ID}} \leftarrow \mathsf{KeyGen}_{ex}(\mathsf{PK}_{ex}, \mathsf{MSK}_{ex}, \mathsf{ID})$, and outputs the private key $\mathsf{SK}_{\mathsf{ID}}$.

Encrypt($\mathsf{PK}, \mathsf{ID} \in \mathcal{ID}, M$) : The encryption algorithm takes as input the public parameter $\mathsf{PK} = (\mathsf{PK}_{ex}, \mathsf{H}, K_a)$, an identity ID and a message $M = m_1\|\cdots\|m_\ell \in \{0,1\}^\ell$. For $i \in [\ell]$, it computes

$$\begin{cases} (C_i, K_i) \leftarrow \mathsf{Encrypt}_{ex}(\mathsf{PK}_{ex}, \mathsf{ID}, 1) & \text{if } m_i = 1 \\ C_i \leftarrow \mathsf{Encrypt}_{ex}(\mathsf{PK}_{ex}, \mathsf{ID}, 0),\ K_i \leftarrow \mathsf{Sample}'(\mathcal{K}; R_i^K) & \text{if } m_i = 0 \end{cases},$$

where $R_i^K \leftarrow \mathcal{R}_{\mathsf{Sample}'}$. Then, it sets $K_{\ell+1} = (K_a, K_b)$ where $K_b = \mathsf{H}(\mathsf{ID}, C_1, \ldots, C_\ell)$, and computes the tag $T = \mathsf{XAuth}(K_1, \ldots, K_{\ell+1})$. Finally, it outputs the ciphertext $CT = (C_1, \ldots, C_\ell, T)$.

Decrypt($\mathsf{PK}, \mathsf{SK}_{\mathsf{ID}}, CT$) : The decryption algorithm takes as input the public parameter $\mathsf{PK} = (\mathsf{PK}_{ex}, \mathsf{H}, K_a)$, a private key $\mathsf{SK}_{\mathsf{ID}}$ for identity ID and a ciphertext $CT = (C_1, \ldots, C_\ell, T)$. This algorithm first computes $K_b' = \mathsf{H}(\mathsf{ID}, C_1, \ldots, C_\ell)$ and checks whether $\mathsf{XVer}(K_{\ell+1}', T) = 1$ with $K_{\ell+1}' = (K_a, K_b')$. If not, it outputs $M'' = \overbrace{0\cdots0}^{\ell}$. Otherwise, for $i \in [\ell]$, it computes $(m_i', K_i') \leftarrow \mathsf{Decrypt}_{ex}(\mathsf{PK}_{ex}, \mathsf{SK}_{\mathsf{ID}}, C_i)$ and sets

$$m_i'' = \begin{cases} \mathsf{XVer}(K_i', T) & \text{if } m_i' = 1 \\ 0 & \text{if } m_i' = 0 \end{cases}.$$

Then, it outputs the message $M'' = m_1''\|\cdots\|m_\ell''$.

Correctness. If $m_i = 1$, then $(m_i', K_i') = (m_i, K_i)$ by correctness of extractable 1SPO-IBE scheme, so $\mathsf{XVer}(K_i', T) = 1$ (hence $m_i'' = 1$) except with probability $\mathsf{fail}_{\mathsf{XAC}}$ by correctness of XAC. On the other hand, if $m_i = 0$, the ϵ-completeness of the extractable 1SPO-IBE guarantees $m_i' = 0$ (hence $m_i'' = 0$) with probability at least $1 - \epsilon$. Consequently, for any $CT \leftarrow \mathsf{Encrypt}(\mathsf{PK}, \mathsf{ID}, M)$, we have $\mathsf{Decrypt}(\mathsf{PK}, \mathsf{SK}_{\mathsf{ID}}, CT) = M$ except with probability at most $\ell \cdot \max\{\mathsf{fail}_{\mathsf{XAC}}, \epsilon\}$.

Theorem 1. *If the extractable 1SPO-IBE scheme is IND-ID-CCA secure, the hash function H is collision-resistant and the strengthened $\ell + 1$-cross-authentication code XAC is secure against substitution attacks, then our proposed IBE scheme is SIM-SO-CCA secure.*

Proof. See the full version of this paper.

6   Proposed IND-ID-CCA Secure Extractable 1SPO-IBE Scheme

In this section, we propose a concrete construction of extractable 1SPO-IBE from the anonymous IBE [11] in a composite order bilinear group. (In the full version of this paper, we show how to construct an extractable 1SPO-IBE from Boyen-Waters anonymous HIBE [8], which is based on a prime order bilinear group.) The design principle has already been described in the introduction.

The proposed scheme consists of the following algorithms:

$\mathsf{Setup}_{ex}(1^\kappa)$: Run an N-order group generator $\mathcal{G}(\kappa)$ to obtain a group description $(p_1, p_2, p_3, p_4, \mathbb{G}, \mathbb{G}_T, e)$, where $\mathbb{G} = \mathbb{G}_{p_1} \times \mathbb{G}_{p_2} \times \mathbb{G}_{p_3} \times \mathbb{G}_{p_4}$, $e : \mathbb{G} \times \mathbb{G} \to \mathbb{G}_T$ is a non-degenerate bilinear map, $\mathbb{G}$ and $\mathbb{G}_T$ are cyclic groups of order $N = p_1 p_2 p_3 p_4$. Next choose $g, u, v, h \leftarrow \mathbb{G}_{p_1}$, $g_3 \leftarrow \mathbb{G}_{p_3}$, $g_4, W_4 \leftarrow \mathbb{G}_{p_4}$ and $\alpha, \beta \leftarrow \mathbb{Z}_N$. Then choose a collision-resistant hash function $\mathsf{H} : \mathbb{Z}_N \times \mathbb{G} \to \mathbb{Z}_N$, and a key derivation function $\mathsf{KDF} : \mathbb{G}_T \to \mathbb{Z}_N$. The public parameter is $\mathsf{PK} = ((\mathbb{G}, \mathbb{G}_T, e, N), u, v, h, W_{14} = gW_4, g_4, e(g,g)^\alpha, e(g,g)^\beta, \mathsf{H}, \mathsf{KDF})$. The master secret key is $\mathsf{MSK} = (g, g_3, \alpha, \beta)$. We require the group $\mathbb{G}$ be an *efficiently samplable and explainable domain* associated with algorithms Sample and Sample^{-1}. Details on how to instantiate such groups are given in [3].

$\mathsf{KeyGen}_{ex}(\mathsf{PK}, \mathsf{MSK}, \mathsf{ID} \in \mathbb{Z}_N)$: Choose $r, \bar{r} \leftarrow \mathbb{Z}_N$ and $R_3, R_3', R_3'', \bar{R}_3, \bar{R}_3', \bar{R}_3'' \leftarrow \mathbb{G}_{p_3}$ (this is done by raising g_3 to a random power). Output the private key $\mathsf{SK}_{\mathsf{ID}} = (\mathsf{ID}, D_0, D_1, D_2, \bar{D}_0, \bar{D}_1, \bar{D}_2)$, where $D_0 = g^\alpha (u^{\mathsf{ID}} h)^r R_3$, $D_1 = v^r R_3'$, $D_2 = g^r R_3''$, $\bar{D}_0 = g^\beta (u^{\mathsf{ID}} h)^{\bar{r}} \bar{R}_3$, $\bar{D}_1 = v^{\bar{r}} \bar{R}_3'$, $\bar{D}_2 = g^{\bar{r}} \bar{R}_3''$.

$\mathsf{Encrypt}_{ex}(\mathsf{PK}, \mathsf{ID} \in \mathbb{Z}_N, m \in \{0,1\})$: If $m = 1$, choose $s, t_4 \leftarrow \mathbb{Z}_N$ and compute $c_0 = W_{14}^s g_4^{t_4}$, $c_1 = (u^{\mathsf{ID}} v^{\mathsf{ID}'} h)^s g_4^{\mathsf{KDF}(e(g,g)^{\alpha s})}$, $K = e(g,g)^{\beta s}$, where $\mathsf{ID}' = \mathsf{H}(\mathsf{ID}, c_0)$, then output the ciphertext and the session key $(C, K) = ((c_0, c_1), K)$; otherwise (i.e., $m = 0$), choose $c_0, c_1 \leftarrow \mathsf{Sample}(\mathbb{G})$, and output the ciphertext $C = (c_0, c_1)$.

$\mathsf{Decrypt}_{ex}(\mathsf{PK}, \mathsf{SK}_{\mathsf{ID}} = (\mathsf{ID}, D_0, D_1, D_2, \bar{D}_0, \bar{D}_1, \bar{D}_2), C = (c_0, c_1))$: Compute $\mathsf{ID}' = \mathsf{H}(\mathsf{ID}, c_0)$ and $X = e(D_0 D_1^{\mathsf{ID}'}, c_0)/e(D_2, c_1)$. (One can view $(D_0 D_1^{\mathsf{ID}'}, D_2)$ as a private key associated to the 2-level identity $\widetilde{\mathsf{ID}} = (\mathsf{ID}, \mathsf{ID}')$.) Then, check whether $e(c_1/g_4^{\mathsf{KDF}(X)}, W_{14}) = e(c_0, u^{\mathsf{ID}} v^{\mathsf{ID}'} h)$. If not, set $m = 0$ and choose a session key $K \leftarrow \mathbb{G}_T$. Otherwise, set $m = 1$ and compute $K = e(\bar{D}_0 \bar{D}_1^{\mathsf{ID}'}, c_0)/e(\bar{D}_2, c_1)$. Output (m, K).

Correctness. Note that, if $C = (c_0, c_1)$ is an encryption of 1 under identity ID, then

$$X = e(D_0 D_1^{\mathsf{ID}'}, c_0)/e(D_2, c_1)$$
$$= e(g^\alpha (u^{\mathsf{ID}} v^{\mathsf{ID}'} h)^r, \ g^s)/e(g^r, \ (u^{\mathsf{ID}} v^{\mathsf{ID}'} h)^s) = e(g,g)^{\alpha s},$$
$$e(c_1/g_4^{\mathsf{KDF}(X)}, W_{14}) = e((u^{\mathsf{ID}} v^{\mathsf{ID}'} h)^s, W_{14})$$
$$= e(u^{\mathsf{ID}} v^{\mathsf{ID}'} h, W_{14}^s) = e(c_0, \ u^{\mathsf{ID}} v^{\mathsf{ID}'} h),$$
$$K = e(\bar{D}_0 \bar{D}_1^{\mathsf{ID}'}, c_0)/e(\bar{D}_2, c_1)$$
$$= e(g^\beta (u^{\mathsf{ID}} v^{\mathsf{ID}'} h)^{\bar{r}}, \ g^s)/e(g^{\bar{r}}, \ (u^{\mathsf{ID}} v^{\mathsf{ID}'} h)^s) = e(g,g)^{\beta s},$$

so decryption always succeeds. On the other hand, if $C = (c_0, c_1)$ is an encryption of 0 under identity ID, then $c_0, c_1 \in \mathbb{G}$ are chosen uniformly at random, thus $\Pr[e(c_1/g_4^{\mathsf{KDF}(X)}, W_{14}) = e(c_0, u^{\mathsf{ID}} v^{\mathsf{ID}'} h)] \leq \frac{1}{2^{2\kappa}}$ where κ is the security parameter. So the completeness error is $\frac{1}{2^{2\kappa}}$.

One-Sided Public Openability (1SPO). If $C = (c_0, c_1)$ is an encryption of 0 under identity ID, then c_0 and c_1 are both randomly distributed in $\mathbb{G}$. Since the group $\mathbb{G}$ is an efficiently samplable and explainable domain associated with Sample and Sample^{-1}, $\mathsf{POpen}(\mathsf{PK}, \mathsf{ID}, C = (c_0, c_1))$ can employ Sample^{-1} to open (c_0, c_1). More precisely, $(R_0, R_1) \leftarrow \mathsf{POpen}(\mathsf{PK}, \mathsf{ID}, (c_0, c_1))$, where $R_0 \leftarrow \mathsf{Sample}^{-1}(\mathbb{G}, c_0)$ and $R_1 \leftarrow \mathsf{Sample}^{-1}(\mathbb{G}, c_1)$.

Security. We now state the security theorem of our proposed extractable IBE scheme.

Theorem 2. *The above extractable 1SPO-IBE scheme is IND-ID-CCA secure.*

Proof. See the full version of this paper.

Acknowledgement. We are grateful to the anonymous reviewers for their helpful comments. The work of Junzuo Lai was supported by the National Natural Science Foundation of China (Nos. 61300226, 61272534, 61272453), the Research Fund for the Doctoral Program of Higher Education of China (No. 20134401120017), the Guangdong Provincial Natural Science Foundation (No. S2013040014826), and the Fundamental Research Funds for the Central Universities. The work of Shengli Liu was supported by the National Natural Science Foundation of China (No. 61170229, 61373153), the Specialized Research Fund for the Doctoral Program of Higher Education (No. 20110073110016), and the Scientic innovation projects of Shanghai Education Committee (No. 12ZZ021). The work of Jian Weng was supported by the National Science Foundation of China (Nos. 61272413, 61373158, 61133014, 61272415), the Fok Ying Tung Education Foundation (No. 131066), the Program for New Century Excellent Talents in University (No. NCET-12-0680), and the Research Fund for the Doctoral Program of Higher Education of China (No. 20134401110011). The work of Yunlei Zhao was supported by the National Basic Research Program of China (973 Program) (No. 2014CB340600), the National Natural Science Foundation of China (Nos. 61070248, 61332019, 61272012), and the Innovation Project of Shanghai Municipal Education Commission (No.12ZZ013).

References

1. Bellare, M., Dowsley, R., Waters, B., Yilek, S.: Standard security does not imply security against selective-opening. In: Pointcheval, D., Johansson, T. (eds.) EUROCRYPT 2012. LNCS, vol. 7237, pp. 645–662. Springer, Heidelberg (2012)
2. Bellare, M., Hofheinz, D., Yilek, S.: Possibility and impossibility results for encryption and commitment secure under selective opening. In: Joux, A. (ed.) EUROCRYPT 2009. LNCS, vol. 5479, pp. 1–35. Springer, Heidelberg (2009)
3. Bellare, M., Waters, B., Yilek, S.: Identity-based encryption secure against selective opening attack. In: Ishai, Y. (ed.) TCC 2011. LNCS, vol. 6597, pp. 235–252. Springer, Heidelberg (2011)
4. Bellare, M., Yilek, S.: Encryption schemes secure under selective opening attack. IACR Cryptology ePrint Archive, 2009:101 (2009)
5. Böhl, F., Hofheinz, D., Kraschewski, D.: On definitions of selective opening security. In: Fischlin, M., Buchmann, J., Manulis, M. (eds.) PKC 2012. LNCS, vol. 7293, pp. 522–539. Springer, Heidelberg (2012)
6. Boldyreva, A., Fehr, S., O'Neill, A.: On notions of security for deterministic encryption, and efficient constructions without random oracles. In: Wagner, D. (ed.) CRYPTO 2008. LNCS, vol. 5157, pp. 335–359. Springer, Heidelberg (2008)
7. Boneh, D., Canetti, R., Halevi, S., Katz, J.: Chosen-ciphertext security from identity-based encryption. SIAM J. Comput. 36(5), 1301–1328 (2007)
8. Boyen, X., Waters, B.: Anonymous hierarchical identity-based encryption (Without random oracles). In: Dwork, C. (ed.) CRYPTO 2006. LNCS, vol. 4117, pp. 290–307. Springer, Heidelberg (2006)
9. Canetti, R., Dwork, C., Naor, M., Ostrovsky, R.: Deniable encryption. In: Kaliski Jr., B.S. (ed.) CRYPTO 1997. LNCS, vol. 1294, pp. 90–104. Springer, Heidelberg (1997)
10. Canetti, R., Feige, U., Goldreich, O., Naor, M.: Adaptively secure multi-party computation. In: STOC, pp. 639–648 (1996)
11. De Caro, A., Iovino, V., Persiano, G.: Fully secure anonymous HIBE and secret-key anonymous IBE with short ciphertexts. In: Joye, M., Miyaji, A., Otsuka, A. (eds.) Pairing 2010. LNCS, vol. 6487, pp. 347–366. Springer, Heidelberg (2010)
12. Cramer, R., Shoup, V.: Design and analysis of practical public-key encryption schemes secure against adaptive chosen ciphertext attack. IACR Cryptology ePrint Archive, 2001:108 (2001)
13. Fehr, S., Hofheinz, D., Kiltz, E., Wee, H.: Encryption schemes secure against chosen-ciphertext selective opening attacks. In: Gilbert, H. (ed.) EUROCRYPT 2010. LNCS, vol. 6110, pp. 381–402. Springer, Heidelberg (2010)
14. Freeman, D.M., Goldreich, O., Kiltz, E., Rosen, A., Segev, G.: More constructions of lossy and correlation-secure trapdoor functions. In: Nguyen, P.Q., Pointcheval, D. (eds.) PKC 2010. LNCS, vol. 6056, pp. 279–295. Springer, Heidelberg (2010)
15. Hemenway, B., Libert, B., Ostrovsky, R., Vergnaud, D.: Lossy encryption: Constructions from general assumptions and efficient selective opening chosen ciphertext security. In: Lee, D.H., Wang, X. (eds.) ASIACRYPT 2011. LNCS, vol. 7073, pp. 70–88. Springer, Heidelberg (2011)
16. Hemenway, B., Ostrovsky, R.: Lossy trapdoor functions from smooth homomorphic hash proof systems. Electronic Colloquium on Computational Complexity (ECCC) 16, 127 (2009)
17. Hemenway, B., Ostrovsky, R.: Homomorphic encryption over cyclic groups implies chosen-ciphertext security. IACR Cryptology ePrint Archive, 2010:99 (2010)

18. Hofheinz, D.: Possibility and impossibility results for selective decommitments. IACR Cryptology ePrint Archive, 2008:168 (2008)
19. Hofheinz, D.: All-but-many lossy trapdoor functions. In: Pointcheval, D., Johansson, T. (eds.) EUROCRYPT 2012. LNCS, vol. 7237, pp. 209–227. Springer, Heidelberg (2012)
20. Huang, Z., Liu, S., Qin, B.: Sender equivocable encryption schemes secure against chosen-ciphertext attacks revisited. IACR Cryptology ePrint Archive, 2012:473 (2012)
21. Huang, Z., Liu, S., Qin, B.: Sender-equivocable encryption schemes secure against chosen-ciphertext attacks revisited. In: Kurosawa, K., Hanaoka, G. (eds.) PKC 2013. LNCS, vol. 7778, pp. 369–385. Springer, Heidelberg (2013)
22. Kiltz, E., Mohassel, P., O'Neill, A.: Adaptive trapdoor functions and chosen-ciphertext security. In: Gilbert, H. (ed.) EUROCRYPT 2010. LNCS, vol. 6110, pp. 673–692. Springer, Heidelberg (2010)
23. Lewko, A., Waters, B.: New techniques for dual system encryption and fully secure HIBE with short ciphertexts. In: Micciancio, D. (ed.) TCC 2010. LNCS, vol. 5978, pp. 455–479. Springer, Heidelberg (2010)
24. Myers, S., Shelat, A.: Bit encryption is complete. In: FOCS, pp. 607–616 (2009)
25. Peikert, C., Waters, B.: Lossy trapdoor functions and their applications. In: STOC, pp. 187–196 (2008)
26. Rosen, A., Segev, G.: Chosen-ciphertext security via correlated products. In: Reingold, O. (ed.) TCC 2009. LNCS, vol. 5444, pp. 419–436. Springer, Heidelberg (2009)
27. Waters, B.: Dual system encryption: Realizing fully secure IBE and HIBE under simple assumptions. In: Halevi, S. (ed.) CRYPTO 2009. LNCS, vol. 5677, pp. 619–636. Springer, Heidelberg (2009)

Key Derivation without Entropy Waste

Yevgeniy Dodis[1,*], Krzysztof Pietrzak[2,**], and Daniel Wichs[3,***]

[1] New York University
[2] IST Austria
[3] Northeastern University

Abstract. We revisit the classical problem of converting an imperfect source of randomness into a usable cryptographic key. Assume that we have some cryptographic application P that expects a uniformly random m-bit key R and ensures that the best attack (in some complexity class) against $P(R)$ has success probability at most δ. Our goal is to design a key-derivation function (KDF) h that converts any random source X of min-entropy k into a sufficiently "good" key $h(X)$, guaranteeing that $P(h(X))$ has comparable security δ' which is 'close' to δ.

Seeded randomness extractors provide a generic way to solve this problem for *all* applications P, with resulting security $\delta' = O(\delta)$, provided that we start with entropy $k \geq m + 2\log(1/\delta) - O(1)$. By a result of Radhakrishnan and Ta-Shma, this bound on k (called the "RT-bound") is also known to be tight in general. Unfortunately, in many situations the loss of $2\log(1/\delta)$ bits of entropy is unacceptable. This motivates the study KDFs with less entropy waste by placing some restrictions on the source X or the application P.

In this work we obtain the following new positive and negative results in this regard:

- Efficient samplability of the source X does not help beat the RT-bound for general applications. This resolves the SRT (samplable RT) conjecture of Dachman-Soled et al. [DGKM12] in the affirmative, and also shows that the existence of computationally-secure extractors beating the RT-bound implies the existence of one-way functions.
- We continue in the line of work initiated by Barak et al. [BDK+11] and construct new information-theoretic KDFs which beat the RT-bound for large but restricted classes of applications. Specifically, we design efficient KDFs that work for *all unpredictability applications* P (e.g., signatures, MACs, one-way functions, etc.) and can either: (1) extract *all* of the entropy $k = m$ with a very modest security loss $\delta' = O(\delta \cdot \log(1/\delta))$, or alternatively, (2) achieve essentially optimal security $\delta' = O(\delta)$ with a very modest entropy loss $k \geq m + \log\log(1/\delta)$. In comparison, the best prior results from [BDK+11] for this class of applications would only guarantee $\delta' = O(\sqrt{\delta})$ when $k = m$, and would need $k \geq m + \log(1/\delta)$ to get $\delta' = O(\delta)$.

* Research partially supported by gifts from VMware Labs and Google, and NSF grants 1319051, 1314568, 1065288, 1017471, 0845003.
** Research supported by ERC starting grant (259668-PSPC).
*** Research supported by NSF grant 1314722.

P.Q. Nguyen and E. Oswald (Eds.): EUROCRYPT 2014, LNCS 8441, pp. 93–110, 2014.

- The weaker bounds of [BDK+11] hold for a larger class of so-called "square-friendly" applications (which includes all unpredictability, but also some important indistinguishability, applications). Unfortunately, we show that these weaker bounds are tight for the larger class of applications.

- We abstract out a clean, information-theoretic notion of (k, δ, δ')-*unpredictability extractors*, which guarantee "induced" security δ' for any δ-secure unpredictability application P, and characterize the parameters achievable for such unpredictability extractors. Of independent interest, we also relate this notion to the previously-known notion of (min-entropy) *condensers*, and improve the state-of-the-art parameters for such condensers.

1 Introduction

Key Derivation is a fundamental cryptographic task arising in a wide variety of situations where a given application P was designed to work with a uniform m-bit key R, but in reality one only has a "weak" n-bit random source X. Examples of such sources include biometric data [DORS08, BDK+05], physical sources [BST03, BH05], secrets with partial leakage, and group elements from Diffie-Hellman key exchange [GKR04, Kra10], to name a few. We'd like to have a *Key Derivation Function* (KDF) $h : \{0,1\}^n \to \{0,1\}^m$ with the property that the derived key $h(X)$ can be safely used by P, even though the original security of P was only analyzed under the assumption that its key R is uniformly random.

Of course, good key derivation is generally impossible unless X has some amount of entropy k to begin with, where the "right" notion of entropy in this setting is *min-entropy*: a source X has min-entropy $\mathbf{H}_\infty(X) = k$ if for any $x \in \{0,1\}^n$ we must have $\Pr[X = x] \le 2^{-k}$. We call such a distribution X over n-bits strings an (n, k)-*source*, and generally wish to design a KDF h which "works" for all such (n, k)-sources X. More formally, assuming P was δ-secure (against some class of attackers) with the uniform key $R \equiv U_m$, we would like to conclude that P is still δ'-secure (against nearly the same class of attackers) when using $R = h(X)$ instead. The two most important parameters are: (1) ensuring that the new security δ' is "as close as possible" to the original security δ, and (2) allowing the source entropy k to be "as close as possible" to the application's key length m. Minimizing this threshold k is very important in many practical situations. For example, in the setting of biometrics and physical randomness, many natural sources are believed to have very limited entropy, while in the setting of Diffie-Hellman key exchange reducing the size of the Diffie-Hellman group (which is roughly 2^k) results in substantial efficiency improvements. Additionally, we prefer to achieve *information-theoretic* security for our KDFs (we discuss "computational KDFs" in Section 1.2), so that the derived key can be used for arbitrary (information-theoretic and computational) applications P.

This discussion leads us to the following central question of our work: *Can one find reasonable application scenarios where one can design a* **provably-secure,**

information-theoretic *KDF achieving "real security"* $\delta' \approx \delta$ *when* $k \approx m$?
More precisely, for a given (class of) application(s) P,

(A) *What is the best (provably) achievable security* δ' *(call it* δ^**) when* $k = m$?
(B) *What is the smallest (provable) entropy threshold* k *(call it* k^**) to achieve security* $\delta' = O(\delta)$?

Ideally, we would like to get $\delta^* = \delta$ and $k^* = m$, and the question is how close one can come to these "ideal" bounds. In this work we will provide several positive and negative answers to our main question, including a general way to *nearly achieve the above "ideal" for all unpredictability applications*. But first we turn to what is known in the theory of key derivation.

RANDOMNESS EXTRACTORS. In theory, the cleanest way to design a general, information-theoretically secure KDF is by using so called (strong) *randomness extractors* [NZ96]. Such a (k, ε)-extractor Ext has the property that the output distribution Ext(X) is ε-statistically close to the uniform distribution U_m, which means that using Ext(X) as a key will degrade the original security δ of *any* application P by at most ε: $\delta' \leq \delta + \varepsilon$. However, the sound use of randomness extractors comes with two important caveats. The first caveat comes from the fact that no deterministic extractor Ext can work for all (n, k)-sources [CG89] when $k < n$, which means that extractors must be probabilistic, or "seeded". This by itself is not a big limitation, since the extracted randomness Ext$(X; S)$ is ε-close to U_m even *conditioned on the seed* S, which means that the seed S can be reused and globally shared across many applications.[1] From our perspective, though, a more important limitation/caveat of randomness extractors comes from a non-trivial tradeoff between the min-entropy k and the security ε one can achieve to derive an m-bit key Ext$(X; S)$. The best randomness extractors, such as the one given by the famous Leftover Hash Lemma (LHL) [HILL99], can only achieve security $\varepsilon = \sqrt{2^{m-k}}$. This gives the following very general bound on δ' for *all* applications P:

$$\delta' \leq \delta_{\mathsf{ALL}} \overset{\text{def}}{=} \delta + \sqrt{2^{m-k}} \tag{1}$$

Translating this bound to answer our main questions (A) and (B) above, we see that $\delta^* = 1$ (no meaningful security is achieved when $k = m$) and min-entropy $k^* \geq m + 2\log(1/\delta) - O(1)$ is required to get $\delta' = O(\delta)$. For example, to derive a 128-bit key for a CBC-MAC with security $\delta \approx \delta' \approx 2^{-64}$, one needs $k \approx 256$ bits of min-entropy, and nothing is theoretically guaranteed when $k = 128$.

Of course, part of the reason why these provable bounds are "not too great" (compared both with the "ideal" bounds, as well as the "real" bounds we will

---

[1] However, it does come with an important assumption that the source distribution X must be independent of the seed S. Although this assumption could be problematic in some situations, such as leakage-resilient cryptography (and has led to some interesting research [TV00, CDH+00, KZ03, DRV12]), in many situations, such as the Diffie-Hellman key exchange or biometrics, the independence of the source and the seed could be naturally enforced/assumed.

achieve shortly) is their generality: extractors work for *all* (n, k)-sources X and *all* applications P. Unfortunately, Radhakrishnan and Ta-shma [RTS00] showed that in this level of generality nothing better is possible: any (k, ε)-extractor must have $k \geq m + 2 \log (1/\varepsilon)$ (we will refer to this as the "RT-bound"). This implies that for any candidate m-bit extractor Ext there exists some application P, some (possibly *inefficiently samplable*) source X of min-entropy k and some (possibly *exponential time*) attacker A, such that $A(S)$ can break P keyed by $R = \text{Ext}(X; S)$ with advantage $\sqrt{2^{m-k}}$.

Thus, there is hope that better results are possible if one restricts the type of applications P (e.g., unpredictability applications), sources X (e.g., efficiently samplable) or attackers A (e.g., polynomial-time) considered. We discuss such options below, stating what was known together with our new results.

1.1   Our Main Results

EFFICIENTLY SAMPLABLE SOURCES. One natural restriction is to require that the source X is efficiently sampleable. This restriction is known to be useful for relaxing the assumption that the source distribution X is independent of the seed S [TV00, DRV12], which was the first caveat in using randomness extractors. Unfortunately, it was not clear if efficient samplability of X helps with reducing the entropy loss $L = k - m$ below $2 \log (1/\varepsilon)$. In fact, Dachman-Soled et al. [DGKM12] conjectured that this is indeed not the case when Ext is also efficient, naming this conjecture the "SRT assumption" (where SRT stands for "samplable RT").

SRT Assumption [DGKM12]: *For any efficient extractor* Ext *with m-bit output there exists an efficiently samplable (polynomial in n) distribution X of min-entropy $k = m + 2 \log (1/\varepsilon) - O(1)$ and a (generally inefficient) distinguisher D which has at least an ε-advantage in distinguishing $(S, R = \text{Ext}(X; S))$ from $(S, R = U_m)$.*

As our first result, we show that the SRT assumption is indeed (unfortunately) true, even *without* restricting the extractor Ext to be efficient.

Theorem 1. *(Informal) The SRT assumption is true for any (possibly inefficient) extractor* Ext. *Thus, efficiently samplability does not help to reduce the entropy loss of extractors below $2 \log (1/\varepsilon)$.*

SQUARE-FRIENDLY APPLICATIONS. The next natural restriction is to limit the class of applications P in question. Perhaps, for some such applications, one can argue that the derived key $R = h_s(X)$ is still "good enough" for P despite *not* being statistically close to U_m (given s). This approach was recently pioneered by Barak et al [BDK+11], and then further extended and generalized by Dodis et al. [DRV12, DY13]. In these works the authors defined a special class of cryptographic applications, called *square-friendly*, where the pessimistic RT-bound can be provably improved. Intuitively, while any traditional application P demands that the expectation (over the uniform distribution $r \leftarrow U_m$)

of the attacker's advantage $f(r)$ on key r is at most δ, square-friendly applications additionally require that the expected value of $f(r)^2$ is also bounded by δ. The works of [BDK$^+$11, DY13] then showed that the class of square-friendly applications includes *all unpredictability applications* (signatures, MACs, one-way functions, etc.), and *some, but not all, indistinguishability applications* (including chosen plaintext attack secure encryption, weak pseudorandom functions and others). [2] Additionally, for all such square-friendly applications P, it was shown that universal (and thus also the stronger pairwise independent) hash functions $\{h_s\}$ yield the following improved bound on the security δ' of the derived key $R = h_s(X)$:

$$\delta' \leq \delta_{\mathsf{SQF}} \overset{\text{def}}{=} \delta + \sqrt{\delta \cdot 2^{m-k}} \qquad (2)$$

This provable (and still relatively general!) bound lies somewhere in between the "ideal" bounds and the fully generic bound (1): in particular, for the first time we get a meaningful security $\delta^* \approx \sqrt{\delta}$ when $k = m$ (giving non-trivial answer to Question (A)), or, alternatively, we get full security $\delta' = O(\delta)$ provided $k^* \geq m + \log(1/\delta)$ (giving much improved answer to Question (B) than the bound $k^* \geq k + 2\log(1/\delta)$ derived by using standard extractors). For example, to derive a 128-bit key for a CBC-MAC having ideal security $\delta = 2^{-64}$, we can either settle for much lower security $\delta' \approx 2^{-32}$ from entropy $k = 128$, or get full security $\delta' \approx 2^{-64}$ from entropy $k = 192$.

Given these non-trivial improvements, one can wonder if further improvements (for square-friendly applications) are still possible. As a simple (negative) result, we show that the bound in Equation (2) cannot be improved in general for *all* square-friendly applications. Interestingly, the proof of this result uses the proof of Theorem 1 to produce the desired source X for the counter-example. For space reasons, the proof of Theorem 2 below is only given in the full version [DPW13] of this paper.

Theorem 2. *(Informal) There exists a δ-square friendly application P with an m-bit key such that for any family $\mathcal{H} = \{h_s\}$ of m-bit key derivation functions there exists (even efficiently samplable) (n, k)-source X and a (generally inefficient) distinguisher D such that $D(S)$ has at least $\delta' = \Omega(\sqrt{\delta \cdot 2^{m-k}})$ advantage in breaking P with the derived key $R = h_S(X)$ (for random seed S).*

Hence, to improve the parameters in Equation (2) and still have information-theoretic security, we must place more restrictions on the class of applications P we consider.

UNPREDICTABILITY APPLICATIONS. This brings us to our main (positive) result: we get improved information-theoretic key derivation for *all unpredictability applications* (which includes MACs, signatures, one-way functions, identification schemes, etc.; see Footnote 2).

---

[2] Recall, in indistinguishability applications the goal of the attack is to win a game with probability noticeably greater than $1/2$; in contrast, for unpredictability applications the goal of the attacker is to win with only non-negligible probability.

Theorem 3. *(Main Result; Informal) Assume P is any unpredictability application which is δ-secure with a uniform m-bit key against some class of attackers $\mathcal{C}$. Then, there is an efficient family of hash functions $\mathcal{H} = \{h_s : \{0,1\}^n \to \{0,1\}^m\}$, such that for any (n,k)-source X, the application P with the derived key $R = h_S(X)$ (for random public seed S) is δ'-secure against class $\mathcal{C}$, where:*

$$\delta' = O\left(1 + \log\left(1/\delta\right) \cdot 2^{m-k}\right)\delta. \tag{3}$$

In particular, we get the following nearly optimal answers to Questions (A), (B):

- *With entropy $k = m$, we get security $\delta^* = (1 + \log(1/\delta))\delta$ (answering Question (A)).*
- *To get security $\delta' \leq 3\delta$, we only need entropy $k^* = m + \log\log(1/\delta) + 4$ (answering Question (B)).*

In fact, our basic KDF hash family $\mathcal{H}$ is simply a t-wise independent hash function where $t = O(\log(1/\delta))$. Hence, by using higher than pairwise independence (which was enough for weaker security given by Equations (1) and (2)), we get a largely improved entropy loss: $\log\log(1/\delta)$ instead of $\log(1/\delta)$.

As we can see, the *provable* bounds above nearly match the ideal bounds $\delta^* = \delta$ and $k^* = m$ and provide a vast improvement over what was known previously. For example, to derive a 128-bit key for a CBC-MAC having ideal security $\delta = 2^{-64}$ (so that $\log\log(1/\delta) = 6$), we can either have excellent security $\delta' \leq 2^{-57.9}$ starting with minimal entropy $k = 128$, or get essentially full security $\delta' \leq 2^{-62.4}$ with only slightly higher entropy $k = 138$. Thus, for the first time we obtained an efficient, *theoretically-sound* key derivation scheme which nearly matches "dream" parameters $k^* = m$ and $\delta^* = \delta$. Alternatively, as we discuss in Section 1.2, for the first time we can offer a provably-secure *alternative* to the existing practice of using cryptographic hash functions modeled as a random oracle for KDFs, and achieve nearly optimal parameters.

UNPREDICTABILITY EXTRACTORS AND CONDENSERS. To better understand the proof of Theorem 3, it is helpful to abstract the notion of an *unpredictability extractor* UExt which we define in this work. Recall, standard (k,ε)-extractors ε-fool any distinguisher $D(R, S)$ trying to distinguish $R = \mathsf{Ext}(X; S)$ from R being uniform. In contrast, when dealing with δ-secure unpredictability applications, we only care about "fooling" so called δ-distinguishers D: these are distinguishers s.t. $\Pr[D(U_m, S) = 1] \leq \delta$, which directly corresponds to the emulation of P's security experiment between the "actual attacker" A and the challenger $\mathcal{C}$. Thus, we define (k, δ, δ')-*unpredictability extractors* as having the property that $\Pr[D(\mathsf{UExt}(X; S), S) = 1] \leq \delta'$ for any δ-distinguisher D.[3] With this cleaner notion in mind, our main Theorem 3 can be equivalently restated as follows:

Theorem 4. *(Main Result; Restated) A family $\mathcal{H} = \{h_s : \{0,1\}^n \to \{0,1\}^m\}$ which is $O(\log(1/\delta))$-wise independent defines a $(k, \delta, O(1 + \log(1/\delta) \cdot 2^{m-k})\delta)$-unpredictability extractor $\mathsf{UExt}(x; s) = h_s(x)$.*

---

[3] This notion can also be viewed as "one-sided" slice extractors [RTS00]. Unlike this work, though, the authors of [RTS00] did not use slice extractors as an interesting primitive by itself, and did not offer any constructions of such extractors.

In turn, we observe that unpredictability extractors are closely connected to the related notion of a *randomness condenser* [RR99, RSW06]: such a (k, ℓ, ε)-condenser Cond : $\{0, 1\}^n \rightarrow \{0, 1\}^m$ has the property that the output distribution Cond$(X; S)$ is ε-close (even given the seed S) to some distribution Y s.t. the conditional min-entropy $\mathbf{H}_\infty(Y|S) \geq m - \ell$ whenever $\mathbf{H}_\infty(X) \geq k$. In particular, instead of requiring the output to be close to uniform, we require it to be close to having almost full entropy, with some small "gap" ℓ. While $\ell = 0$ gives back the definition of (k, ε)-extractors, permitting a small non-zero "entropy gap" ℓ has recently found important applications for key derivation [BDK+11, DRV12, DY13]. In particular, it is easy to see that a (k, ℓ, ε)-condenser is also a $(k, \delta, \varepsilon + \delta \cdot 2^\ell)$-unpredictability extractor. Thus, to show Theorem 4 it suffices to show that $O(\log(1/\delta))$-wise independent hashing gives a (k, ℓ, δ)-condenser, where $\ell \approx \log\log(1/\delta)$.

Theorem 5. *(Informal) A family* $\mathcal{H} = \{h_s : \{0, 1\}^n \rightarrow \{0, 1\}^m\}$ *of* $O(\log(1/\delta))$*-wise independent hash functions defines a* (k, ℓ, δ)*-condenser* Cond$(x; s) = h_s(x)$ *for either of the following settings:*

- No Entropy Loss: *min-entropy* $k = m$ *and entropy gap* $\ell = \log\log(1/\delta)$.
- Constant Entropy Gap: *min-entropy* $k = m + \log\log(1/\delta) + O(1)$ *and entropy gap* $\ell = 1$.

It is instructive to compare this result with the RT-bound for (k, δ)-extractors: to have no entropy gap $\ell = 0$ requires us to start with entropy $k \geq m + 2\log(1/\delta)$. However, already 1-bit entropy gap $\ell = 1$ allows us to get away with $k = m + \log\log(1/\delta)$, while further increasing the gap to $\ell = \log\log(1/\delta)$ results in no entropy loss $k = m$.

BALLS and BINS, MAX-LOAD AND BALANCED HASHING. Finally, to prove Theorem 5 (and, thus, Theorem 4 and Theorem 3) we further reduce the problem of condensers to a very simple balls-and-bins problem. Indeed, we can think of our (k, ℓ, δ)-condenser as a way to hash 2^k items (out of a universe of size 2^n) into 2^m bins, so that the *load* (number of items per bin) is not too much larger than the expected 2^{k-m} for "most" of the bins. More concretely, it boils down to analyzing a version of average-load: if we choose a random item (and a random hash function from the family) then the probability that the item lands in a bin with more than $2^\ell(2^{k-m})$ items should be at most ε. We use Chernoff-type bounds for limited independence [Sie89, BR94] to analyze this version of average load when the hash function is $O(\log 1/\delta)$-independent.

OPTIMIZING SEED LENGTH. The description length d of our $O(\log(1/\delta))$-wise independent KDF h_s is $d = O(n\log(1/\delta))$ bits, which is much larger than that needed by universal hashing for standard extractors. In the full version of this paper [DPW13], we show how to adapt the elegant "gradual increase of independence" technique of Celis et al. [CRSW11] to reduce the seed length to nearly linear: $d = O(n\log k)$ (e.g., for $k = 128$ and $\delta = 2^{-64}$ this reduces the seed length from $128n$ to roughly $7n$ bits). It is an interesting open problem if the seed length can be reduced even further (and we show non-constructively that the answer is positive).

1.2   Computational Extractors

So far we considered information-theoretic techniques for designing theoretically-sound KDFs. Of course, given the importance of the problem, it is also natural to see if better parameters can be obtained when we assume that the attacker A is *computationally bounded*. We restrict our attention to the study of *computational extractors* [DGH+04, Kra10, DGKM12] Ext, whose output $R = \text{Ext}(X; S)$ looks *pseudorandom* to D (given S) for any *efficiently samplable* (n, k)-source X, which would suffice for our KDF goals if very strong results were possible for such extractors.

Unfortunately, while not ruling out the usefulness of computational extractors, we point out the following three negative results: (1) even "heuristic" computational computational extractors do not appear to beat the information-theoretic bound $k^* \geq m$ (which we managed to nearly match for all unpredictability applications); (2) existing "provably-secure" computational extractors do not appear to offer any improvement to our information-theoretic KDFs, when dealing with the most challenging "low entropy regime" (when k is roughly equal to the security parameter); (3) even for "medium-to-high entropy regimes", computational extractors beating the RT-bound require one-way functions. We discuss these points in the full version [DPW13], here only briefly mentioning points (1) and (3).

HEURISTIC EXTRACTORS. In practice, one would typically use so called "cryptographic hash function" h, such as SHA or MD5, for key derivation (or as a computational extractor). As discussed in detail by [DGH+04, Kra10, DRV12], there are several important reasons for this choice. From the perspective of this work, we will focus on the arguably the most important such reason — the common belief that cryptographic hash functions achieve excellent security $\delta' \approx \delta$ already when $k \approx m$. This can be easily *justified in the random oracle model*; assuming the KDF h is a random oracle which can be evaluated on at most q points (where q is the upper bound of the attacker's running time), one can upper bound $\delta' \leq \delta + q/2^k$, where $q/2^k$ is the probability the attacker evaluates $h(X)$. In turn, for most natural computationally-secure applications, in time q the attacker can also test about q out of 2^m possible m-bit keys, and hence achieve advantage $q/2^m$. This means that the ideal security δ of P cannot be lower than $q/2^m$, implying $q \leq \delta \cdot 2^m$. Plugging this bound on q in the bound of $\delta' \leq \delta + q/2^k$ above, we get that using a random oracle (RO) as a computational extractor/KDF achieves real security

$$\delta' \leq \delta_{\text{RO}} \stackrel{\text{def}}{=} \delta + \delta \cdot 2^{m-k} \tag{4}$$

Although this heuristic bound is indeed quite amazing (e.g., $\delta' \leq 2\delta$ even when $k = m$, meaning that $\delta^* = 2\delta$ and $k^* = m$), and, unsurprisingly, beats our provably-secure, information-theoretic bounds, it still requires $k^* \geq m$. So we are not that far off, especially given our nearly matching bound for all unpredictability applications.[4]

BEATING RT-BOUND IMPLIES OWFS. As observed by [Kra10, DGKM12], for medium-to-high entropy regimes, computational assumptions help in "beating" the RT-bound $k \geq m + 2\log(1/\varepsilon)$ for any (k, ε)-secure extractor, as applying the PRG allows one to increase m essentially arbitrarily (while keeping the original min-entropy the same). Motivated by this, Dachman-Soled et al. [DGKM12] asked an interesting theoretical question if the existence of one-way functions (and, hence, PRGs [HILL99]) is *essential* for beating the RT-bound for unconditional extractors. They also managed to give an affirmative answer to this question *under the SRT assumption* mentioned earlier. Since we unconditionally prove the SRT assumption (see Theorem 1), we immediately get the following Corollary, removing the conditional clause from the result of [DGKM12]:

Theorem 6. *(Informal) If* Ext *is an efficient* (k, ε)-*computational extractor with an m-bit output, where $m > k - 2\log(1/\varepsilon) - O(1)$, then one-way functions (and, hence, PRGs) exist.*

2   Preliminaries

We recap some definitions and results from probability theory. Let X, Y be random variables with supports S_X, S_Y, respectively. We define their *statistical difference* as

$$\Delta(X, Y) = \frac{1}{2} \sum_{u \in S_X \cup S_Y} |\Pr[X = u] - \Pr[Y = u]|.$$

We write $X \approx_\varepsilon Y$ and say that X and Y are ε-statistically close to denote that $\Delta(X, Y) \leq \varepsilon$.

The *min-entropy* of a random variable X is $\mathbf{H}_\infty(X) \stackrel{\text{def}}{=} -\log(\max_x \Pr[X = x])$, and measures the "best guess" for X. The *conditional min-entropy* is defined by $\mathbf{H}_\infty(X|Y = y) \stackrel{\text{def}}{=} -\log(\max_x \Pr[X = x|Y = y])$. Following Dodis et al. [DORS08], we define the *average* conditional min-entropy:

$$\mathbf{H}_\infty(X|Y) \stackrel{\text{def}}{=} -\log\left(\mathop{\mathbb{E}}_{y \leftarrow Y} \left[\max_x \Pr[X = x|Y = y] \right] \right)$$

$$= -\log\left(\mathop{\mathbb{E}}_{y \leftarrow Y} \left[2^{-\mathbf{H}_\infty(X|Y=y)} \right] \right).$$

Above, and throughout the paper, all "log" terms are base 2, unless indicated otherwise. We say that a random variable X is an (n, k)-*source* if the support of X is $\{0, 1\}^n$ and the entropy of X is $\mathbf{H}_\infty(X) \geq k$.

---

[4] Also, unlike our bound in Equation (3), one cannot apply the heuristic bound from Equation (4) to derive a key for an *information-theoretically* secure MAC.

Lemma 1 (A Tail Inequality [BR94]). *Let $q \geq 4$ be an even integer. Suppose $X_1, \ldots, X_n$ are q-wise independent random variables taking values in $[0, 1]$. Let $X := X_1 + \cdots + X_n$ and define $\mu := \mathbf{E}[X]$ be the expectation of the sum. Then, for any $A > 0$, $\Pr[|X - \mu| \geq A] \leq 8 \left(\frac{q\mu + q^2}{A^2} \right)^{q/2}$. In particular, for any $\alpha > 0$ and $\mu > q$, we have $\Pr[X \geq (1 + \alpha)\mu] \leq 8 \left(\frac{2q}{\alpha^2 \mu} \right)^{q/2}$.*

3 Defining Extractors for Unpredictability Applications

We start by abstracting out the notion of general unpredictability applications (e.g., one-way functions, signatures, message authentication codes, soundness of an argument, etc.) as follows. The security of such all such primitives is abstractly defined via a security game P which requires that, for all attackers $\mathcal{A}$ (in some complexity class), $\Pr[P^{\mathcal{A}}(U) = 1] \leq \delta$ where $P^{\mathcal{A}}(U)$ denotes the execution of the game P with the attacker $\mathcal{A}$, where P uses the uniform randomness U.[5] For example, in the case of a message-authentication code (MAC), the value U is used as secret key for the MAC scheme and the game P is the standard "existential unforgeability against chosen-message attack game" for the given MAC. Next, we will assume that δ is some small (e.g., negligible) value, and ask the question if we can still use the primitive P if, instead of a uniformly random U, we only have some arbitrary (n, k)-source X?

To formally answer this question, we would like a function $\mathsf{UExt} : \{0, 1\}^n \times \{0, 1\}^d \rightarrow \{0, 1\}^m$ (seeded unpredictability extractor) such that, for all attackers $\mathcal{A}$ (in some complexity class), $\Pr[P^{\mathcal{A}(S)}(\mathsf{UExt}(X; S)) = 1] \leq \varepsilon$, where the seed S is chosen uniformly at random and given to the attacker, and ε is not much larger than δ. Since we do not wish to assume much about the application P or the attacker $\mathcal{A}$, we can roll them up into a unified adversarial "distinguisher" defined by $D(R, S) := P^{\mathcal{A}(S)}(R)$. By definition, if $R = U$ is random and independent of S, then $\Pr[D(U, S) = 1] = \Pr[P^{\mathcal{A}(S)}(U) = 1] \leq \delta$. On the other hand, we need to ensure that $\Pr[P^{\mathcal{A}(S)}(\mathsf{UExt}(X; S)) = 1] = \Pr[D(\mathsf{UExt}(X; S), S) = 1] \leq \varepsilon$ for some ε which is not much larger than δ. This motivates the following definition of unpredictability extractor which ensures that the above holds for *all* distinguishers D.

Definition 1 (UExtract). *We say that a function $D : \{0, 1\}^m \times \{0, 1\}^d \rightarrow \{0, 1\}$ is a δ-distinguisher if $\Pr[D(U, S) = 1] \leq \delta$ where (U, S) is uniform over $\{0, 1\}^m \times \{0, 1\}^d$. A function $\mathsf{UExt} : \{0, 1\}^n \times \{0, 1\}^d \rightarrow \{0, 1\}^m$ is a (k, δ, ε)-unpredictability extractor (UExtract) if for any (n, k)-source X and any δ-distinguisher D, we have $\Pr[D(\mathsf{UExt}(X; S), S) = 1] \leq \varepsilon$ where S is uniform over $\{0, 1\}^d$.*

---

[5] In contrast, for *indistinguishability* games we typically require that $\Pr[P^{\mathcal{A}}(U) = 1] \leq \frac{1}{2} + \delta$.

Notice that the above definition is essentially the same as that of standard extractors except that: (1) we require that the distinguisher has a "small" probability δ of outputting 1 on the uniform distribution, and (2) we only require a one-sided error that the probability of outputting 1 does not increase too much. A similar notion was also proposed by [RTS00] and called a "slice extractor".

Toward the goal of understanding unpredictability extractors, we show tight connections between the above definition and two seemingly unrelated notions. Firstly, we define "condensers for min-entropy" and show that the they yield "good" unpredictability extractors. Second, we define something called "balanced hash functions" and show that they yield good condensers, and therefore also good unpredictability extractors. Lastly, we show that unpredictability extractors also yield balanced hash functions, meaning that all three notions are essentially equivalent up to a small gap in parameters.

Definition 2 (Condenser). *A function* Cond $: \{0,1\}^n \times \{0,1\}^d \to \{0,1\}^m$ *is a* (k,ℓ,ε)-*condenser if for all* (n,k)-*sources* X, *and a uniformly random and independent seed* S *over* $\{0,1\}^d$, *the joint distribution* $(S, \text{Cond}(X;S))$ *is* ε-*statistically-close to some joint distribution* (S,Y) *such that, for all* $s \in \{0,1\}^d$, $\mathbf{H}_\infty(Y|S=s) \geq m - \ell$.

First, we show that condensers already give us unpredictability extractors. This is similar in spirit to a lemma of [DY13] which shows that, if we use a key with a small entropy gap for an unpredictability application, the security of the application is only reduced by at most a small amount. One difference that prevents us from using that lemma directly is that we need to explicitly include the seed of the condenser and the dependence between the condenser output and the seed.

Lemma 2 (Condenser $\Rightarrow$ UExtract). *Any* (k,ℓ,ε)-*condenser is a* (k,δ,ε^*)-*UExtract where* $\varepsilon^* = \varepsilon + 2^\ell \delta$.

Proof. Let Cond $: \{0,1\}^n \times \{0,1\}^d \to \{0,1\}^m$ be a (k,ℓ,ε)-condenser and let X be an (n,k)-source. Let S be uniform over $\{0,1\}^d$, so that, by definition, there is a joint distribution (S,Y) which has statistical distance at most ε from $(S, \text{Cond}(X;S))$ such that $\mathbf{H}_\infty(Y|S=s) \geq m - \ell$ for all $s \in \{0,1\}^d$. Therefore, for any δ-distinguisher D, we have

$$\Pr[D(\text{Cond}(X;S), S) = 1] \leq \varepsilon + \Pr[D(Y,S) = 1]$$
$$= \varepsilon + \sum_{y,s} \Pr[S=s]\Pr[Y=y|S=s]\Pr[D(y,s)=1]$$
$$\leq \varepsilon + \sum_{y,s} 2^{-d} 2^{-\mathbf{H}_\infty(Y|S=s)} \Pr[D(y,s)=1]$$
$$\leq \varepsilon + 2^\ell \sum_{y,s} 2^{-(m+d)} \Pr[D(y,s)=1] \leq \varepsilon + 2^\ell \delta.$$

Definition 3 (Balanced Hashing). *Let* $h := \{h_s : \{0,1\}^n \to \{0,1\}^m\}_{s \in \{0,1\}^d}$ *be a hash function family. For* $\mathcal{X} \subseteq \{0,1\}^n, s \in \{0,1\}^d, x \in \mathcal{X}$ *we define*

$\mathsf{Load}_{\mathcal{X}}(x, s) := |\{x' \in \mathcal{X} : h_s(x') = h_s(x)\}|$.[6] *We say that the family h is (k, t, ε)-balanced if for all $\mathcal{X} \subseteq \{0, 1\}^n$ of size $|\mathcal{X}| = 2^k$, we have*

$$\Pr\left[\mathsf{Load}_{\mathcal{X}}(X, S) > t2^{k-m}\right] \leq \varepsilon$$

where S, X are uniformly random and independent over $\{0, 1\}^d, \mathcal{X}$ respectively.

Lemma 3 (Balanced $\Rightarrow$ Condenser). *Let $\mathcal{H} := \{h_s : \{0, 1\}^n \to \{0, 1\}^m\}_{s \in \{0,1\}^d}$ be a (k, t, ε)-balanced hash function family. Then the function $\mathsf{Cond} : \{0, 1\}^n \times \{0, 1\}^d \to \{0, 1\}^m$ defined by $\mathsf{Cond}(x; s) = h_s(x)$ is a (k, ℓ, ε)-condenser for $\ell = \log(t)$.*

Proof. Without loss of generality, we can restrict ourselves to showing that Cond satisfies the condenser definition for every *flat source* X which is uniformly random over some subset $\mathcal{X} \subseteq \{0, 1\}^n$, $|\mathcal{X}| = 2^k$. Let us take such a source X over the set $\mathcal{X}$, and define a *modified* hash family $\tilde{h} = \{\tilde{h}_s : \mathcal{X} \to \{0, 1\}^m\}_{s \in \{0,1\}^d}$ which depends on $\mathcal{X}$ and essentially "re-balances" h on the set $\mathcal{X}$. In particular, for every pair (s, x) such that $\mathsf{Load}_{\mathcal{X}}^h(x, s) \leq t2^{k-m}$ we set $\tilde{h}_s(x) := h_s(x)$, and for all other pairs (s, x) we define $\tilde{h}_s(x)$ in such a way that $\mathsf{Load}_{\mathcal{X}}^{\tilde{h}}(x, s) \leq t2^{k-m}$ (the super-script is used to denote the hash function with respect to which we are computing the load). It is easy to see that this "re-balancing" is always possible. We use the re-balanced hash function $\tilde{h}$ to define a joint distribution (S, Y) by choosing S uniformly at random over $\{0, 1\}^d$, choosing X uniformly/independently over $\mathcal{X}$ and setting $Y = \tilde{h}_S(X)$. It's easy to check that the statistical distance between $(S, \mathsf{Cond}(X; S))$ and (S, Y) is at most $\Pr[h_S(X) \neq \tilde{h}_S(X)] \leq \Pr[\mathsf{Load}_{\mathcal{X}}^h(X, S) > t2^{k-m}] \leq \varepsilon$. Furthermore, for every $s \in \{0, 1\}^d$, we have:

$$\begin{aligned}
\mathbf{H}_\infty(Y|S = s) &= -\log(\max_y \Pr[Y = y|S = s]) \\
&= -\log(\max_y \Pr[X \in \tilde{h}_s^{-1}(y)]) \geq -\log(t2^{k-m}/2^k) = m - \log t.
\end{aligned}$$

Therefore Cond is a $(k, \ell = \log t, \varepsilon)$-condenser.

Lemma 4 (UExtract $\Rightarrow$ Balanced). *Let $\mathsf{UExt} : \{0, 1\}^n \times \{0, 1\}^d \to \{0, 1\}^m$ be a (k, δ, ε)-UExtractor for some, $\varepsilon > \delta > 0$. Then the hash family $\mathcal{H} = \{h_s : \{0, 1\}^n \to \{0, 1\}^m\}_{s \in \{0,1\}^d}$ defined by $h_s(x) = \mathsf{UExt}(x; s)$ is $(k, \varepsilon/\delta, \varepsilon)$-balanced.*

Proof. Let $t = \varepsilon/\delta$ and assume that $\mathcal{H}$ is *not* (k, t, ε)-balanced. Then there exists some set $\mathcal{X} \subseteq \{0, 1\}^n$, $|\mathcal{X}| = 2^k$ such that $\hat{\varepsilon} := \Pr[\mathsf{Load}_{\mathcal{X}}(X, S) > t2^{k-m}] > \varepsilon$ where X is uniform over $\mathcal{X}$ and S is uniform over $\{0, 1\}^d$. Let $\mathcal{X}_s \subseteq \mathcal{X}$ be defined by $\mathcal{X}_s := \{x \in \mathcal{X} : \mathsf{Load}_{\mathcal{X}}(x, s) > t2^{k-m}\}$ and let $\varepsilon_s \stackrel{\text{def}}{=} |\mathcal{X}_s|/2^k$. By definition $\hat{\varepsilon} = \sum_s 2^{-d}\varepsilon_s$. Define $\mathcal{Y}_s \subseteq \{0, 1\}^m$ via $\mathcal{Y}_s := h_s(\mathcal{X}_s)$. Now by definition, each $y \in \mathcal{Y}_s$ has at least $t2^{k-m}$ pre-images in $\mathcal{X}_s$ and therefore $\delta_s \stackrel{\text{def}}{=} |\mathcal{Y}_s|/2^m \leq |\mathcal{X}_s|/(t2^{k-m}2^m) \leq \varepsilon_s/t$ and $\delta := \sum_s 2^{-d}\delta_s \leq \hat{\varepsilon}/t$.

Define the distinguisher D via $D(y, s) = 1$ iff $y \in \mathcal{Y}_s$. Then D is a δ-distinguisher for $\delta \leq \hat{\varepsilon}/t \leq \varepsilon/t$ but $\Pr[D(h_S(X), S) = 1] = \hat{\varepsilon} \geq \varepsilon$. Therefore, UExt is not a $(k, \varepsilon/t, \varepsilon)$-UExtractor.

---

[6] Note that we allow $x' = x$ and so $\mathsf{Load}_{\mathcal{X}}(x, s) \geq 1$.

Summary. Taking all of the above lemmata together, we see that they are close to tight. In particular, for any $\varepsilon > \delta > 0$, we get:

$$(k, \delta, \varepsilon)\text{-UExt} \overset{Lem.4}{\Rightarrow} (k, \varepsilon/\delta, \varepsilon)\text{-Balanced} \overset{Lem.3}{\Rightarrow}$$

$$(k, \log(\varepsilon/\delta), \varepsilon)\text{-Condenser} \overset{Lem.2}{\Rightarrow} (k, \delta, 2\varepsilon)\text{-UExt}$$

4 Constructing Unpredictability Extractors

Given the connections established in the previous section, we have paved the road for constructing unpredictability extractors via balanced hash functions, which is a seemingly simpler property to analyze. Indeed, we will give relatively simple lemmas showing that "sufficiently independent" hash functions are balanced. This will lead to the following parameters (restating Theorem 3 from the introduction):

Theorem 7. *There exists an efficient (k, δ, ε)-unpredictability extractor* UExt $: \{0,1\}^n \times \{0,1\}^d \to \{0,1\}^m$ *for the following parameters:*

1. *When $k = m$ (no entropy loss), we get $\varepsilon = (1 + \log(1/\delta))\delta$.*
2. *When $k \geq m + \log\log 1/\delta + 4$, we get $\varepsilon = 3\delta$.*
3. *In general, $\varepsilon = O(1 + 2^{m-k}\log(1/\delta))\delta$.*

In all cases, the function UExt *is simply a $(\log(1/\delta) + O(1))$-wise independent hash function and the seed length is $d = O(n\log(1/\delta))$.*

Although these constructions may already be practical, the level of independence we will need is $O(\log 1/\delta)$, which will result in a large seed $O(n\log(1/\delta))$. We will show how to achieve similar parameters with a shorter seed $O(n\log k)$ in the full version of this paper [DPW13]. We now proceed to prove all of the parts of Theorem 7 by constructing "good" balanced hash functions and using our connections between balanced hashing and unpredictability extractors from the previous section.

4.1 Sufficient Independence Provides Balance

First we start with a simple case where the output m is equal to the entropy k.

Lemma 5. *Let $\mathcal{H} := \{h_s : \{0,1\}^n \to \{0,1\}^k\}_{s \in \{0,1\}^d}$ be $(t + 1)$-wise independent. Then it is (k, t, ε)-balanced where $\varepsilon \leq \left(\frac{e}{t}\right)^t$ and e is the base of the natural logarithm.*

Proof. Fix any set $\mathcal{X} \subseteq \{0,1\}^n$ of size $|\mathcal{X}| = 2^k$. Let X be uniform over $\mathcal{X}$ and S be uniform/independent over $\{0,1\}^d$. Then

$$\Pr[\mathsf{Load}_{\mathcal{X}}(X, S) > t] \leq \Pr[\,\exists \mathcal{C} \subseteq \mathcal{X}, |\mathcal{C}| = t \;\; \forall x' \in \mathcal{C} : h_S(x') = h_S(X) \wedge x' \neq X]$$

$$\leq \sum_{\mathcal{C} \subseteq \mathcal{X}, |\mathcal{C}| = t} \Pr[\forall x' \in \mathcal{C} \;:\; h_S(x') = h_S(X) \wedge x' \neq X]$$

$$\leq \binom{2^k}{t} 2^{-tk} \leq \left(\frac{e2^k}{t}\right)^t 2^{-tk} \leq \left(\frac{e}{t}\right)^t.$$

Corollary 1. *For any $0 < \varepsilon < 2^{-2e}$, any $\delta > 0$, a $(\lceil \log(1/\varepsilon)\rceil + 1)$-wise independent hash family $\mathcal{H} = \{h_s : \{0,1\}^n \to \{0,1\}^k\}_{s \in \{0,1\}^d}$ is:*

$$(k, \log(1/\varepsilon), \varepsilon)\text{-balanced}, \quad (k, \log\log(1/\varepsilon), \varepsilon)\text{-condenser}, \quad (k, \delta, \log(1/\varepsilon)\delta + \varepsilon)\text{-UExtractor}.$$

In particular, setting $\delta = \varepsilon$, it is a $(k, \delta, (1 + \log(1/\delta))\delta)$-UExtractor.

Proof. Set $t = \lceil \log(1/\varepsilon)\rceil$ in Lemma 5 and notice that $\left(\frac{e}{t}\right)^t \leq 2^{-t} \leq \varepsilon$ as long as $t \geq 2e$.

This establishes part (1) of Theorem 7. Next we look at a more general case where k may be larger than m. This also covers the case $k = m$ but gets a somewhat weaker bound. It also requires a more complex tail bound for q-wise independent variables.

Lemma 6. *Let $\mathcal{H} := \{h_s : \{0,1\}^n \to \{0,1\}^m\}_{s \in \{0,1\}^d}$ be $(q+1)$-wise independent for some even q. Then, for any $\alpha > 0$, it is $(k, 1+\alpha, \varepsilon)$-balanced where*

$$\varepsilon \leq 8 \left(\frac{q2^{k-m} + q^2}{(\alpha 2^{k-m} - 1)^2} \right)^{q/2}.$$

Proof. Let $\mathcal{X} \subseteq \{0,1\}^n$ be a set of size $|\mathcal{X}| = 2^k$, X be uniform over $\mathcal{X}$, and S be uniform/independent over $\{0,1\}^d$. Define the indicator random variables $C(x^*, x)$ to be 1 if $h_S(x) = h_S(x^*)$ and 0 otherwise. Then:

$$\Pr[\text{Load}_{\mathcal{X}}(X, S) > (1+\alpha)2^{k-m}]$$

$$= \sum_{x^* \in \mathcal{X}} \Pr[X = x^*] \Pr[\text{Load}_{\mathcal{X}}(x^*, S) > (1+\alpha)2^{k-m}]$$

$$= 2^{-k} \sum_{x^* \in \mathcal{X}} \Pr\left[\sum_{x \in \mathcal{X}\setminus\{x^*\}} C(x^*, x) + 1 > (1+\alpha)2^{k-m} \right]$$

$$\leq 8 \left(\frac{q2^{k-m} + q^2}{(\alpha 2^{k-m} - 1)^2} \right)^{q/2}$$

Where the last line follows from the tail inequality Lemma 1 with the random variables $\{C(x^*, x)\}_{x \in \mathcal{X}\setminus\{x^*\}}$ which are q-wise independent and have expected value $\mu = \mathbb{E}[\sum_{x \in \mathcal{X}\setminus\{x^*\}} C(x^*, x)] = (2^k - 1)2^{-m} \leq 2^{k-m}$, and by setting $A = (1+\alpha)2^{k-m} - 1 - \mu \geq \alpha 2^{k-m} - 1$; recall that $C(x^*, x^*)$ is always 1 and $C(x^*, x)$ for $x \neq x^*$ is 1 with probability 2^{-m}.

Corollary 2. *For any $0 < \varepsilon < 2^{-5}$, $k \geq m + \log\log(1/\varepsilon) + 4$, a $(\lceil \log(1/\varepsilon)\rceil + 6)$-wise independent hash function family $\mathcal{H} = \{h_s : \{0,1\}^n \to \{0,1\}^m\}_{s \in \{0,1\}^d}$ is:*

$$(k, 2, \varepsilon)\text{-balanced}, \quad (k, 1, \varepsilon)\text{-condenser}, \quad (k, \delta, 2\delta + \varepsilon)\text{-UExt for any } \delta > 0.$$

In particular, setting $\delta = \varepsilon$, it is a $(k, \delta, 3\delta)$-UExt.

Proof. Set $\alpha := 1$ and choose $q \in (\log(1/\varepsilon)+3, \log(1/\varepsilon)+5)$ to be an even integer. Notice that $2^{k-m} \geq 16\log(1/\varepsilon) \geq 8(\log(1/\varepsilon)+5) \geq 8q$ since $\log(1/\varepsilon) \geq 5$. Then we apply Lemma 6

$$8\left(\frac{q2^{k-m}+q^2}{(\alpha 2^{k-m}-1)^2}\right)^{q/2} = 8\left(\frac{q(1+q/2^{k-m})}{2^{k-m}(1-1/2^{k-m})^2}\right)^{q/2} \leq 8\left(\frac{2q}{2^{k-m}}\right)^{q/2} \leq \varepsilon.$$

The above corollary establishes part (2) of Theorem 7. The next corollary gives us a general bound which establishes part (3) of the theorem. Asymptotically it implies variants of Corollary 2 and Corollary 1, but with worse constants.

Corollary 3. *For any $\varepsilon > 0$ and $q := \lceil \log(1/\varepsilon) \rceil + 3$, a $(q+1)$-wise independent hash function family $\mathcal{H} = \{h_s : \{0,1\}^n \to \{0,1\}^m\}_{s \in \{0,1\}^d}$ is $(k, 1+\alpha, \varepsilon)$-balanced for*

$$\alpha = 4\sqrt{q2^{m-k}+(q2^{m-k})^2} = O(2^{m-k}\log(1/\varepsilon)+1).$$

By setting $\delta = \varepsilon$, a $(\log\frac{1}{\delta}+4)$-wise independent hash function is a $(k, \delta, O(1+2^{m-k}\log\frac{1}{\delta})\delta)$-UExtactor.

Proof. The first part follows from Lemma 6 by noting that

$$8\left(\frac{q2^{k-m}+q^2}{(\alpha 2^{k-m}-1)^2}\right)^{q/2} \leq 8\left(\frac{q2^{k-m}+q^2}{\frac{1}{4}(\alpha 2^{k-m})^2}\right)^{q/2} \leq 8\left(\frac{1}{4}\right)^{q/2} \leq \varepsilon.$$

For the second part, we can consider two cases. If $q2^{m-k} \leq 1$ then $\alpha \leq 4\sqrt{2}$ and we are done. Else, $\alpha \leq 4\sqrt{2}(q2^{m-k}) = 4\sqrt{2}(\log(1/\varepsilon)+3)2^{m-k}$.

4.2   Minimizing the Seed Length

In both of the above constructions (Corollary 1, Corollary 2), to get an (k, δ, ε)-UExtractor, we need a $O(\log(1/\varepsilon))$-wise independent hash function $h_s : \{0,1\}^n \to \{0,1\}^m$, which requires a seed-length $d = O(\log(1/\varepsilon) \cdot n)$. Since in many applications, we envision $\varepsilon \approx 2^{-k}$, this gives a seed $d = O(kn)$. We should contrast this with standard extractors constructed using universal hash functions (via the leftover-hash lemma), where the seed-length is $d = n$. We now show how to optimize the seed-length of UExtractors, first to $d = O(n \log k)$ and eventually to $d = O(k \log k)$. In the full version [DPW13] of this paper, we adapt the technique of Celis et al. [CRSW11] which shows how to construct hash functions with a small seed that achieve essentially optimal "max-load" (e.g., minimize the hash value with the most items inside it). We show that a lightly modified analysis can also be used to show that such hash functions are "balanced" with essentially optimal parameters.

4.3   A Probabilistic Method Bound

In the full version [DPW13] of this paper, we give a probabilistic method argument showing the existence of unpredictability extractors with very small seed length $d \approx \log(1/\delta) + \log(n - k)$ as stated in Theorem 8 below. In other words, unpredictability extractors with small entropy loss do not, in principle, require a larger seed than standard randomness extractors (with much larger entropy loss).

Theorem 8. *There exists a* (k, δ, ε)-*UExtract* UExt $: \{0,1\}^n \times \{0,1\}^d \to \{0,1\}^m$ *as long as either:*

$$\varepsilon \geq \max\{ \ 2e\delta \ , \ (n - k + 2)2^{-d} + \log(e/\delta)\delta 2^{m-k} \ \}$$
$$2e\delta \geq \varepsilon \geq \delta + 2\delta\sqrt{(1/\delta)(n - k + 2)2^{-d} + \log(e/\delta)2^{m-k}}$$

In particular, as long as the seed-length $d \geq \log(1/\delta) + \log(n - k + 2) + 3$ *we get:*

- *In general:* $\varepsilon = O(1 + \log(1/\delta)2^{m-k})\delta$.
- *When* $k = m$ *and* $\delta < 2^{-2e}$: $\varepsilon = (2 + \log(1/\delta))\delta$.
- *When* $k \geq m + \log\log(e/\delta) + 3$: $\varepsilon = 2\delta$.

5 SRT Lower-Bound: Samplability Doesn't Improve Entropy Loss

The 'SRT' conjecture of Dachman-Soled et al. [DGKM12] states that randomness extractors need to incur a $2 \log 1/\varepsilon$ entropy loss (difference between entropy and output length) even if we only require them to work for *efficiently samplable sources*. In the full version [DPW13] of this paper we prove this conjecture as stated in Theorem 9 below. In fact, we show that the conjecture holds even if the extractor itself is not required to be efficient.

The efficient source for which we show a counter-example is sampled via a 4-wise independent hash function. That is, we define the source $X = h_r(Z)$ where $Z \leftarrow \{0,1\}^k$ is chosen uniformly at random and $h_r : \{0,1\}^k \to \{0,1\}^n$ is chosen from some 4-wise independent hash function family. The choice of the seed r will need to be fixed non-uniformly; we show that for any "candidate extractor" Ext $: \{0,1\}^n \times \{0,1\}^d \to \{0,1\}^m$ there is some seed r such that the above efficiently sampleable (n, k)-source X makes the statistical distance between $(\text{Ext}(X; S), S)$ and the uniform distribution at least $\approx 2^{(m-k)/2}$.

Let Ext $: \{0,1\}^n \times \{0,1\}^d \to \{0,1\}^m$ be a candidate strong extractor, and let X be some random variable over $\{0,1\}^n$. Define the *distinguishability* of Ext on X via:

$$\text{Dist}(X) \stackrel{\text{def}}{=} \frac{1}{2} \sum_{s \in \{0,1\}^d, y \in \{0,1\}^m} |\Pr[S = s, \text{Ext}(X; s) = y] - \Pr[S = s, Y = y]|$$

$$= \frac{1}{2^{d+1}} \sum_{s \in \{0,1\}^d, y \in \{0,1\}^m} \left| \Pr[\text{Ext}(X, s) = y] - \frac{1}{2^m} \right|.$$

where S, Y are uniformly and independently distributed over $\{0,1\}^d, \{0,1\}^m$ respectively. Note that $\text{Dist}(X)$ is simply the statistical distance between $(S, \text{Ext}(X; S))$ and (S, U_m) where U_m is uniformly random m bit string.

Theorem 9. *For any (possibly inefficient) function* $\mathsf{Ext} : \{0,1\}^n \times \{0,1\}^d \to$ $\{0,1\}^m$, *any positive integer* $k \geq m+2$ *such that* $n > 3k - m + 14$, *there exists a distribution* X *with* $\mathbf{H}_\infty(X) \geq k$, *which is efficiently samplable by a* $\mathrm{poly}(n)$-*size circuit, such that* $\mathsf{Dist}(X) \geq 2^{(m-k)/2-8}$.

Alternatively, for any positive $k \geq m$ *such that* $n > k + \log(k) + 11$, *there exists some distribution* X *with* $\mathbf{H}_\infty(X) \geq k$, *which is efficiently samplable by a* $\mathrm{poly}(n)$-*size circuit such that* $\mathsf{Dist}(X) \geq 2^{(m-k-\log(k))/2-9}$.

Acknowledgements. We thank Hugo Krawczyk for many enlightening discussions about the topic of this work and for suggesting that we look at the 'SRT' conjecture, which lead to the results in Section 5.

References

[BDK+05] Boyen, X., Dodis, Y., Katz, J., Ostrovsky, R., Smith, A.: Secure remote authentication using biometric data. In: Cramer, R. (ed.) EUROCRYPT 2005. LNCS, vol. 3494, pp. 147–163. Springer, Heidelberg (2005)

[BDK+11] Barak, B., Dodis, Y., Krawczyk, H., Pereira, O., Pietrzak, K., Standaert, F.-X., Yu, Y.: Leftover hash lemma, revisited. In: Rogaway, P. (ed.) CRYPTO 2011. LNCS, vol. 6841, pp. 1–20. Springer, Heidelberg (2011)

[BH05] Barak, B., Halevi, S.: A model and architecture for pseudo-random generation with applications to /dev/random. In: Proceedings of the 12th ACM Conference on Computer and Communication Security, pp. 203–212 (2005)

[BR94] Bellare, M., Rompel, J.: Randomness-efficient oblivious sampling. In: 35th Annual Symposium on Foundations of Computer Science, pp. 276–287. IEEE (1994)

[BST03] Barak, B., Shaltiel, R., Tromer, E.: True random number generators secure in a changing environment. In: Walter, C.D., Koç, Ç.K., Paar, C. (eds.) CHES 2003. LNCS, vol. 2779, pp. 166–180. Springer, Heidelberg (2003)

[CDH+00] Canetti, R., Dodis, Y., Halevi, S., Kushilevitz, E., Sahai, A.: Exposure-resilient functions and all-or-nothing transforms. In: Preneel, B. (ed.) EUROCRYPT 2000. LNCS, vol. 1807, pp. 453–469. Springer, Heidelberg (2000)

[CG89] Chor, B., Goldreich, O.: On the power of two-point based sampling. Journal of Complexity 5, 96–106 (1989)

[CRSW11] Elisa Celis, L., Reingold, O., Segev, G., Wieder, U.: Balls and bins: Smaller hash families and faster evaluation. In: Ostrovsky, R. (ed.) FOCS, pp. 599–608. IEEE (2011)

[DGH+04] Dodis, Y., Gennaro, R., Håstad, J., Krawczyk, H., Rabin, T.: Randomness extraction and key derivation using the CBC, cascade and HMAC modes. In: Franklin, M. (ed.) CRYPTO 2004. LNCS, vol. 3152, pp. 494–510. Springer, Heidelberg (2004)

[DGKM12] Dachman-Soled, D., Gennaro, R., Krawczyk, H., Malkin, T.: Computational extractors and pseudorandomness. In: Cramer, R. (ed.) TCC 2012. LNCS, vol. 7194, pp. 383–403. Springer, Heidelberg (2012)

[DORS08] Dodis, Y., Ostrovsky, R., Reyzin, L., Smith, A.: Fuzzy extractors: How to generate strong keys from biometrics and other noisy data. SIAM Journal on Computing 38(1), 97–139 (2008)

[DPW13]   Dodis, Y., Pietrzak, K., Wichs, D.: Key derivation without entropy waste. Cryptology ePrint Archive, Report 2013/708 (2013), http://eprint.iacr.org/

[DRV12]   Dodis, Y., Ristenpart, T., Vadhan, S.: Randomness condensers for efficiently samplable, seed-dependent sources. In: Cramer, R. (ed.) TCC 2012. LNCS, vol. 7194, pp. 618–635. Springer, Heidelberg (2012)

[DY13]   Dodis, Y., Yu, Y.: Overcoming weak expectations. In: Sahai, A. (ed.) TCC 2013. LNCS, vol. 7785, pp. 1–22. Springer, Heidelberg (2013)

[GKR04]   Gennaro, R., Krawczyk, H., Rabin, T.: Secure hashed diffie-hellman over non-DDH groups. In: Cachin, C., Camenisch, J.L. (eds.) EUROCRYPT 2004. LNCS, vol. 3027, pp. 361–381. Springer, Heidelberg (2004)

[HILL99] Håstad, J., Impagliazzo, R., Levin, L.A., Luby, M.: Construction of pseudorandom generator from any one-way function. SIAM Journal on Computing 28(4), 1364–1396 (1999)

[Kra10]   Krawczyk, H.: Cryptographic Extraction and Key Derivation: The HKDF Scheme. In: Rabin, T. (ed.) CRYPTO 2010. LNCS, vol. 6223, pp. 631–648. Springer, Heidelberg (2010)

[KZ03]   Kamp, J., Zuckerman, D.: Deterministic extractors for bit-fixing sources and exposure-resilient cryptography. In: 44th Annual Symposium on Foundations of Computer Science, pp. 92–101. IEEE, Cambridge (2003)

[NZ96]   Nisan, N., Zuckerman, D.: Randomness is linear in space. Journal of Computer and System Sciences 52(1), 43–53 (1996)

[RR99]   Raz, R., Reingold, O.: On recycling the randomness of states in space bounded computation. In: Proceedings of the 31st ACM Symposium on the Theory of Computing, pp. 159–168 (1999)

[RSW06]   Reingold, O., Shaltiel, R., Wigderson, A.: Extracting randomness via repeated condensing. SIAM J. Comput. 35(5), 1185–1209 (2006)

[RTS00]   Radhakrishnan, J., Ta-Shma, A.: Bounds for dispersers, extractors, and depth-two superconcentrators. SIAM Journal on Computing 13(1), 2–24 (2000)

[Sie89]   Siegel, A.: On universal classes of fast high performance hash functions, their time-space tradeoff, and their applications (extended abstract). In: FOCS, pp. 20–25 (1989)

[TV00]   Trevisan, L., Vadhan, S.: Extracting randomness from samplable distributions. In: 41st Annual Symposium on Foundations of Computer Science, pp. 32–42. IEEE, Redondo Beach (2000)

Efficient Non-malleable Codes
and Key-Derivation for Poly-size
Tampering Circuits

Sebastian Faust[1], Pratyay Mukherjee[2,*],
Daniele Venturi[3], and Daniel Wichs[4,**]

[1] EPFL Switzerland
[2] Aarhus University, Denmark
[3] Sapienza University of Rome
[4] Northeastern University, USA

Abstract. Non-malleable codes, defined by Dziembowski, Pietrzak and Wichs (ICS '10), provide roughly the following guarantee: if a codeword c encoding some message x is tampered to $c' = f(c)$ such that $c' \neq c$, then the tampered message x' contained in c' reveals no information about x. Non-malleable codes have applications to immunizing cryptosystems against tampering attacks and related-key attacks.

One *cannot* have an *efficient* non-malleable code that protects against *all efficient* tampering functions f. However, in this work we show "the next best thing": for any polynomial bound s given a-priori, there is an efficient non-malleable code that protects against all tampering functions f computable by a circuit of size s. More generally, for any family of tampering functions $\mathcal{F}$ of size $|\mathcal{F}| \leq 2^s$, there is an efficient non-malleable code that protects against all $f \in \mathcal{F}$. The *rate* of our codes, defined as the ratio of message to codeword size, approaches 1. Our results are information-theoretic and our main proof technique relies on a careful probabilistic method argument using limited independence. As a result, we get an efficiently samplable family of efficient codes, such that a random member of the family is non-malleable with overwhelming probability. Alternatively, we can view the result as providing an efficient non-malleable code in the "common reference string" (CRS) model.

We also introduce a new notion of non-malleable key derivation, which uses randomness x to derive a secret key $y = h(x)$ in such a way that, even if x is tampered to a different value $x' = f(x)$, the derived key $y' = h(x')$ does not reveal any information about y. Our results for non-malleable key derivation are analogous to those for non-malleable codes.

As a useful tool in our analysis, we rely on the notion of "leakage-resilient storage" of Davì, Dziembowski and Venturi (SCN '10) and, as a result of independent interest, we also significantly improve on the parameters of such schemes.

* Research supported by a European Research Commission Starting Grant (no. 279447), the CTIC and CFEM research center.
** Research supported by NSF grant 1314722.

P.Q. Nguyen and E. Oswald (Eds.): EUROCRYPT 2014, LNCS 8441, pp. 111–128, 2014.

1   Introduction

Non-malleable codes were introduced by Dziembowski, Pietrzak and Wichs [18]. They provide meaningful guarantees on the integrity of an encoded message in the presence of tampering, even in settings where error-correction and error-detection may not be possible. Intuitively, a code (Enc, Dec) is non-malleable w.r.t. a family of tampering functions $\mathcal{F}$ if the message contained in a codeword modified via a function $f \in \mathcal{F}$ is either the original message, or a completely unrelated value. For example, it should not be possible to just flip 1 bit of the message by tampering the codeword via a function $f \in \mathcal{F}$. More formally, we consider an experiment Tamper_x^f in which a message x is (probabilistically) encoded to $c \leftarrow \mathsf{Enc}(x)$, the codeword is tampered to $c' = f(c)$ and, if $c' \neq c$, the experiment outputs the tampered message $x' = \mathsf{Dec}(c')$, else it outputs a special value same*. We say that the code is non-malleable w.r.t. some family of tampering functions $\mathcal{F}$ if, for every function $f \in \mathcal{F}$ and every messages x, the experiment Tamper_x^f reveals almost no information about x. More precisely, we say that the code is ε-non-malleable if for every pair of messages x, x' and every $f \in \mathcal{F}$, the distributions Tamper_x^f and $\mathsf{Tamper}_{x'}^f$ are statistically ε-close. The encoding/decoding functions are public and do not contain any secret keys. This makes the notion of non-malleable codes different from (but conceptually related to) the well-studied notions of non-malleability in cryptography, introduced by the seminal work of Dolev, Dwork and Naor [16].

Relation to Error Correction/Detection. Notice that non-malleability is a weaker guarantee than error correction/detection; the latter ensure that any change in the codeword can be corrected or at least detected by the decoding procedure, whereas the former does allow the message to be modified, but only to an unrelated value. However, when studying error correction/detection we usually restrict ourselves to limited forms of tampering which preserve some notion of distance (e.g., usually hamming distance) between the original and tampered codeword. (One exception is [12], which studies error-detection for more complex tampering.) For example, it is already impossible to achieve error correction/detection for the simple family of functions $\mathcal{F}_{const}$ which, for every constant c^*, includes a "constant" function f_{c^*} that maps all inputs to c^*. There is always some function in $\mathcal{F}_{const}$ that maps everything to a *valid* codeword c^*. In contrast, it is trivial to construct codes that are non-malleable w.r.t $\mathcal{F}_{const}$, as the output of a constant function is clearly independent of its input. The prior works on non-malleable codes, together with the results from this work, show that one can construct non-malleable codes for highly complex tampering-function families $\mathcal{F}$ for which error correctin/detection are unachievable.

Applications to Tamper-Resilience. The fact that non-malleable codes can be built for large and complex families of functions makes them particularly attractive as a mechanism for protecting memory against tampering attacks, known to be a serious threat for the security of cryptographic schemes [7,2,29,11].

As shown in [18], to protect a scheme with some secret state against memory-tampering, we simply encode the state via a non-malleable code and store the encoding in the memory instead of the original secret. One can show that if the code is non-malleable with respect to function family $\mathcal{F}$, the transformed system is secure against tampering attacks carried out by any function in $\mathcal{F}$. See [18] for a discussion of the application of non-malleable codes to tamper resilience.

Limitations and Possibility. It is *impossible* to have codes that are non-malleable for *all* possible tampering functions. For any coding scheme (Enc, Dec), there exists a tampering function $f_{bad}(c)$ that recovers $x = \mathsf{Dec}(c)$, creates x' by (e.g.,) flipping the first bit of x, and outputs a valid encoding c' of x'. Notice that if Enc, Dec are *efficient*, then the function f_{bad} is efficient as well. Thus, it is also impossible to have an *efficient* code which is non-malleable w.r.t all *efficient* functions. Prior works [26,10,17,1,9,19] (discussed shortly) constructed non-malleable codes for several rich and interesting function families. In all cases, the families are restricted through their *granularity* rather than their computational *complexity*. In particular, these works envision that the codeword is split into several (possibly just 2) components, each of which can only be tampered independently of the others. The tampering function therefore only operates on a "granular" rather than "global" view of the codeword.

1.1 Our Contribution

In this work, we are interested in designing non-malleable codes for large families of functions which are only restricted by their "computational complexity" rather than "granularity". As we saw, we cannot have a single efficient code that is non-malleable for all efficient tampering functions. However, we show the following positive result, which we view as the "next best thing":

Main Result: For any polynomial bound $s = s(n)$ in the codeword size n, and any tampering family $\mathcal{F}$ of size $|\mathcal{F}| \leq 2^s$, there is an efficient code of complexity $\mathsf{poly}(s, \log(1/\varepsilon))$ which is ε-non-malleable w.r.t. $\mathcal{F}$. In particular, $\mathcal{F}$ can be the family of all circuits of size at most s.

The code is secure in the information theoretic setting, and achieves *optimal rate* (message/codeword size) arbitrarily close to 1. It has a *simple* construction relying only on t-wise independent hashing.

The CRS Model. In more detail, if we fix some family $\mathcal{F}$ of tampering functions (e.g., circuits of bounded size), our result gives us a *family* of efficient codes, such that, with overwhelming probability, a random member of the family is non-malleable w.r.t $\mathcal{F}$. Each code in the family is indexed by some hash function h from a t-wise independent family of hash functions $\mathcal{H}$. This result already shows the *existence* of efficient non-malleable codes with some small *non-uniform advice* to indicate a "good" hash function h.

However, we can also efficiently sample a random member of the code family by sampling a random hash function h. Therefore, we find it most appealing to think of this result as providing a uniformly efficient *construction* of non-malleable code in the "common reference string (CRS)" model, where a random public string consisting of the hash function h is selected once and fixes the non-malleable code. We emphasize that, although the family $\mathcal{F}$ (e.g., circuits of bounded size) is fixed prior to the choice of the CRS, the attacker can choose the tampering function $f \in \mathcal{F}$ (e.g., a particular small circuit) adaptively depending on the choice of h.

We argue that it is unlikely that we can completely de-randomize our construction and come up with a fixed uniformly-efficient code which is non-malleable for all circuits of size (say) $s = O(n^2)$. In particular, this would require a circuit lower bound, showing that the function f_{bad} (described above) *cannot* be computed by a circuit of size $O(n^2)$.

Non-malleable Key-Derivation. As an additional contribution, we introduce a new primitive called *non-malleable key derivation*. Intuitively, a function $h : \{0,1\}^n \to \{0,1\}^k$ is a non-malleable key derivation for tampering-family $\mathcal{F}$ if it guarantees that for any tampering function $f \in \mathcal{F}$, if we sample uniform randomness $x \leftarrow \{0,1\}^n$, the "derived key" $y = h(x)$ is statistically close to uniform even given $y' = h(f(x))$ derived from "tampered" randomness $f(x) \neq x$. Our positive results for non-malleable key derivation are analogous to those for non-malleable codes. One difference is that the rate k/n is now at most $1/2$ rather than 1, and we show that this is optimal.

While we believe that non-malleable key derivation is an interesting notion on its own (e.g., it can be viewed as a dual version of non-malleable extractors [15]), we also show it has useful applications for tamper resilience. For instance, consider some cryptographic scheme G using a uniform key in $y \leftarrow \{0,1\}^k$. To protect G against tampering attacks, we can store a bigger key $x \leftarrow \{0,1\}^n$ on the device and temporarily derive $y = h(x)$ each time we want to execute G. In the full version of this paper [20], we show that this approach protects any cryptographic scheme with a uniform key against one-time tampering attacks. The main advantage of using a non-malleable key-derivation rather than non-malleable codes is that the key x stored in memory is simply a uniformly random string with no particular structure (in contrast, the codeword in a non-malleable code requires structure).

In the full version, we also show how to use non-malleable key derivation to build a tamper-resilient stream cipher. Our construction is based on a PRG $\mathsf{prg} : \{0,1\}^k \to \{0,1\}^{n+v}$ and a non-malleable key derivation function $h : \{0,1\}^n \to \{0,1\}^k$. For an initial key $s_0 \leftarrow \{0,1\}^n$, sampled uniformly at random, the output of the stream cipher at each round $i \in [q]$ is $(s_i, x_i) := \mathsf{prg}(h(s_{i-1}))$.

1.2   Our Techniques

Non-malleable Codes. Our construction of non-malleable codes is incredibly simple and relies on t-wise independent hashing, where t is proportional to $s = \log |\mathcal{F}|$. In particular, if h_1, h_2 are two such hash functions, we encode a message x into a codeword $c = (r, z, \sigma)$ where r is randomness, $z = x \oplus h_1(r)$

and $\sigma = h_2(r, z)$. The security analysis, on the other hand, requires two independently interesting components. Firstly, we rely on the notion of *leakage-resilient encodings*, proposed by Davì, Dziembowski and Venturi [14]. These provide a method to encode a secret in such a way that a limited form of leakage on the encoding does not reveal anything about the secret. One of our contributions is to significantly improve the parameters of the construction from [14] by using a fresh and more careful analysis, which gives us such schemes with an essentially optimal rate. Secondly, we analyze a simpler/weaker notion of *bounded* non-malleability, which intuitively guarantees that an adversary seeing the decoding of a tampered codeword can learn only a bounded amount of information on the encoded value. This notion of bounded non-malleability is significantly simpler to analyze than full non-malleability. Finally, we show how to carefully combine leakage-resilient encodings with bounded non-malleability to get our full construction of non-malleable codes. On a very high (and not entirely precise) level, we can think of h_1 above as providing "leakage resilience" and h_2 as providing "bounded non-malleability".

We stress that the fact that t has to be proportional to s is not an artefact of our proof. In fact, one can see that whenever the hash function has seed size s, there is a family of 2^s functions that breaks the construction with probability 1: For each seed, just have a new function that decodes with that seed and encodes a related value. This shows that the t has to be proportional to $\log |\mathcal{F}|$.

Non-malleable Key-Derivation. Our construction of non-malleable key-derivation functions is even simpler: a random t-wise independent hash function h already satisfies the definition with overwhelming probability, where t is proportional to $s = \log |\mathcal{F}|$. The analysis is again subtle and relies on a careful probabilistic method argument.

Similar to the case of non-malleable codes, the fact that t has to be proportional to s is necessary.

1.3   Related Works

Granular Tampering. Most of the earlier works on non-malleable codes focus on granular tampering models, where the tampering functions are restricted to act on individual components of the codeword independently. The original work of [18] gives efficient construction for bit-tampering (i.e., the adversary can tamper with each bit of the codeword independently of every other bit). Very recently, Cheraghchi and Guruswami [9] gave a construction with improved rate and better efficiency for the same family. Choi *et al.* [10] considered an extended tampering family, where the tampering function can be applied to a small (logarithmic in the security parameter) number of blocks independently.

Perhaps the least granular and most general such model is the so-called *split-state* model, where the encoding consists of two parts L (left) and R (right), and the adversary can tamper L and R *arbitrarily but independently*. Starting with the random oracle construction of [18], a few other constructions of non-malleable split-state codes have been proposed, both in the computational setting [26,19] and in the information theoretic setting [17,1,9]. Notice that the family $\mathcal{F}_{split}$ of all split-state tampering functions (without restricting efficiency), has doubly exponential size $2^{O(2^{n/2})}$ in the codeword size n, and therefore it is not covered by our results, which can efficiently handle at most singly-exponential-size families $2^{\mathsf{poly}(n)}$. On the other hand, the split-state model doesn't cover "computationally simple" functions, such as the function computing the XOR or the bit-wise inner-product of L, R. Therefore, although the works are technically orthogonal, we believe that looking at computational complexity may be more natural.

Global Tampering. The work of [18] gives an *existential* (inefficient) construction of non-malleable codes for doubly-exponential sized function families. More precisely, for any constant $0 < \alpha < 1$ and any family $\mathcal{F}$ of functions of size $|\mathcal{F}| \leq 2^{2^{\alpha n}}$ in the codeword size n, there exists an inefficient non-malleable code w.r.t. $\mathcal{F}$; indeed a completely random function gives such a code with high probability. The code is clearly not efficient, and this should be expected for such a broad result: the families $\mathcal{F}$ can include all circuits of size (e.g.,) $s(n) = 2^{n/2}$, which means that the efficiency of the code must exceed $O(2^{n/2})$. Unfortunately, there is no direct way to "scale down" the result in [18] so as to get an efficient construction for singly-exponential-size families. (One can view our work as providing such "scaled down" result.) Moreover, the analysis only yielded a rate of at most $(1 - \alpha)/3 < 1/3$, and it was previously not known if such codes can achieve a rate close to 1, even for "small" function families. We note that [18] also showed that the probabilistic method construction can yield efficient non-malleable codes for large function families in the *random-oracle model*. However, this only considers function families that don't have access to the random-oracle. For example, one cannot interpret this as giving any meaningful result for tampering-functions with bounded complexity.

Concurrent and Independent Work. In a concurrent and independent work, Cheraghchi and Guruswami [8] give two related results. Firstly, they improve the probabilistic method construction of [18] and show that, for families $\mathcal{F}$ of size $|\mathcal{F}| \leq 2^{2^{\alpha n}}$, there exist (inherently inefficient) non-malleable codes with rate $1 - \alpha$, which they also show to be optimal. This gives the first characterization of the rate of non-malleable codes. Secondly, similar to our results, they use limited independence to construct efficient non-malleable codes when restricted to tampering families $\mathcal{F}$ of size $|\mathcal{F}| \leq 2^{s(n)}$ for a polynomial $s(n)$. However, the construction of [8] is not "efficient" in the usual cryptographic sense: to get error-probability ε, the encoding and decoding procedures require complexity $\mathsf{poly}(1/\varepsilon)$. If we set ε to be negligible, as usually desired in cryptography, then the encoding/decoding procedures would require super-polynomial time. In contrast, the encoding/decoding procedures in our construction have efficiency $\mathsf{poly}(\log(1/\varepsilon))$, and therefore we can set ε to be negligible while maintaining polynomial-time encoding/decoding.

Other Approaches to Achieve Tamper Resilience. There is a vast body of literature that considers tampering attacks using other approaches besides non-malleable codes. See, e.g., [5,22,24,4,21,25,3,23,27,30,6,13]. The reader is referred to (e.g.,) [18] for a more detailed comparison between these approaches and non-malleable codes.

2 Preliminaries

Notation. We denote the set of first n natural numbers, i.e. $\{1, \ldots, n\}$, by $[n]$. Let X, Y be random variables with supports $S(X), S(Y)$, respectively. We define

$$\mathbf{SD}(X, Y) \overset{\text{def}}{=} \frac{1}{2} \sum_{s \in S(X) \cup S(Y)} |\Pr[X = s] - \Pr[Y = s]|$$

to be their *statistical distance*. We write $X \approx_\varepsilon Y$ and say that X and Y are ε-statistically close to denote that $\mathbf{SD}(X, Y) \leq \varepsilon$. We let U_n denote the uniform distribution over $\{0, 1\}^n$. We use the notation $x \leftarrow X$ to denote the process of sampling a value x according to the distribution X. If f is a randomized algorithm, we write $f(x; r)$ to denote the execution of f on input x with random coins r. We let $f(x)$ denote a random variable over the random coins.

2.1 Definitions of Non-malleable Codes

Definition 1 (Coding Scheme). *A (k, n)-coding scheme consists of two functions: a randomized encoding function* Enc $: \{0, 1\}^k \rightarrow \{0, 1\}^n$, *and deterministic decoding function* Dec $: \{0, 1\}^n \rightarrow \{0, 1\}^k \cup \{\bot\}$ *such that, for each $x \in \{0, 1\}^k$, $\Pr[\mathsf{Dec}(\mathsf{Enc}(x)) = x] = 1$.*

We now define non-malleability w.r.t. some family $\mathcal{F}$ of tampering functions. The work of [18] defines a default and a strong version of non-malleability. The main difference is that, in the default version, the tampered codeword $c' \neq c$ may still encode the original message x whereas the strong version ensures that any change to the codeword completely destroys the original message. We only define the strong version below. We then add an additional strengthening which we call *super* non-malleability.

Definition 2 (Strong Non-malleability [18]). *Let* (Enc, Dec) *be a (k, n)-coding scheme and $\mathcal{F}$ be a family of functions $f : \{0, 1\}^n \rightarrow \{0, 1\}^n$. We say that the scheme is $(\mathcal{F}, \varepsilon)$-non-malleable if for any $x_0, x_1 \in \{0, 1\}^k$ and any $f \in \mathcal{F}$, we have* $\mathsf{Tamper}_{x_0}^f \approx_\varepsilon \mathsf{Tamper}_{x_1}^f$ *where*

$$\mathsf{Tamper}_x^f \overset{\text{def}}{=} \left\{ \begin{array}{c} c \leftarrow \mathsf{Enc}(x), c' := f(c), x' = \mathsf{Dec}(c') \\ \textit{Output } \mathsf{same}^\star \textit{ if } c' = c, \textit{ and } x' \textit{ otherwise.} \end{array} \right\}. \tag{1}$$

For *super* non-malleable security (defined below), if the tampering manages to modify c to c' such that $c' \neq c$ and $\mathsf{Dec}(c') \neq \bot$, then we will even give the attacker the tampered codeword c' in *full* rather than just giving $x' = \mathsf{Dec}(c')$. We do not immediately see a concrete application of this strengthening, but it seems sufficiently interesting to define explicitly.

Definition 3 (Super Non-malleability). *Let* (Enc, Dec) *be a* (k, n)-*coding scheme and* $\mathcal{F}$ *be a family of functions* $f : \{0, 1\}^n \to \{0, 1\}^n$. *We say that the scheme is* $(\mathcal{F}, \varepsilon)$-*super non-malleable if for any* $x_0, x_1 \in \{0, 1\}^k$ *and any* $f \in \mathcal{F}$, *we have* $\mathsf{Tamper}_{x_0}^f \approx_\varepsilon \mathsf{Tamper}_{x_1}^f$ *where:*

$$\mathsf{Tamper}_x^f \stackrel{def}{=} \left\{ \begin{array}{c} c \leftarrow \mathsf{Enc}(x), c' := f(c) \\ Output\ \mathsf{same}^\star\ if\ c' = c,\ output \perp if\ \mathsf{Dec}(c') = \perp, \\ and\ else\ output\ c'. \end{array} \right\}. \quad (2)$$

3   Improved Leakage-Resilient Codes

We will rely on leakage-resilience as an important tool in our analysis. The following notion of leakage-resilient codes was defined by [14]. Informally, a code is leakage resilience w.r.t some leakage family $\mathcal{F}$ if, for any $f \in \mathcal{F}$, "leaking" $f(c)$ for a codeword c does not reveal anything about the encoded value.

Definition 4 (Leakage-Resilient Codes [14]). *Let* (LREnc, LRDec) *be a* (k, n)-*coding scheme. For a function family* $\mathcal{F}$, *we say that* (LREnc, LRDec) *is* $(\mathcal{F}, \varepsilon)$-*leakage-resilient, if for any* $f \in \mathcal{F}$ *and any* $x \in \{0, 1\}^k$ *we have* $\mathsf{SD}(f(\mathsf{LREnc}(x)), f(U_n)) \leq \varepsilon$.

The work of [14] gave a probabilistic method construction showing that such codes exist and can be efficient when the size of the leakage family $|\mathcal{F}|$ is singly-exponential. However, the rate k/n was at most some small constant ($< \frac{1}{4}$), even when the family size $|\mathcal{F}|$ and the leakage size ℓ are small. Here, we take the construction of [14] and give an improved analysis with improved parameters, showing that the rate can approach 1. In particular, the additive overhead of the code is very close to the leakage-amount ℓ, which is optimal. Our result and analysis are also related to the "high-moment crooked leftover hash lemma" of [28], although our construction is somewhat different, relying only on high-independence hash-functions rather than permutations.

Construction. Let $\mathcal{H}$ be a t-wise independent function family consisting of functions $h : \{0, 1\}^v \to \{0, 1\}^k$. For any $h \in \mathcal{H}$ we define the $(k, n = k + v)$-coding scheme (LREnc$_h$, LRDec$_h$) where: (1) LREnc$_h(x) := (r, h(r) \oplus x)$ for $r \leftarrow \{0, 1\}^v$; (2) LRDec$_h((r, z)) := z \oplus h(r)$.

Theorem 1. *Fix any function family* $\mathcal{F}$ *consisting of functions* $f : \{0, 1\}^n \to \{0, 1\}^\ell$. *With probability* $1 - \rho$ *over the choice of a random* $h \leftarrow \mathcal{H}$, *the coding scheme* (LREnc$_h$, LRDec$_h$) *is* $(\mathcal{F}, \varepsilon)$-*leakage-resilient as long as:*

$$t \geq \log |\mathcal{F}| + \ell + k + \log(1/\rho) + 3 \quad and \quad v \geq \ell + 2\log(1/\varepsilon) + \log(t) + 3.$$

For space reasons, the proof of Theorem 1 is deferred to the full version [20].

4   Non-malleable Codes

We now construct a non-malleable code for any family $\mathcal{F}$ of sufficiently small size. We will rely on leakage-resilience as an integral part of the analysis.

Construction. Let $\mathcal{H}_1$ be a family of hash functions $h_1 : \{0,1\}^{v_1} \to \{0,1\}^k$, and $\mathcal{H}_2$ be a family of hash functions $h_2 : \{0,1\}^{k+v_1} \to \{0,1\}^{v_2}$ such that $\mathcal{H}_1$ and $\mathcal{H}_2$ are both t-wise independent. For any $(h_1, h_2) \in \mathcal{H}_1 \times \mathcal{H}_2$, define $\mathsf{Enc}_{h_1,h_2}(x) = (r, z, \sigma)$ where $r \leftarrow \{0,1\}^{v_1}$ is random, $z := x \oplus h_1(r)$ and $\sigma := h_2(r, z)$. The codewords are of size $n := |(r, z, \sigma)| = k + v_1 + v_2$. Correspondingly define $\mathsf{Dec}((r, z, \sigma))$ which first checks $\sigma \stackrel{?}{=} h_2(r, z)$ and if this fails, outputs $\perp$, else outputs $z \oplus h_1(r)$. Notice that, we can think of (r, z) as being a leakage-resilient encoding of x; i.e., $(r, z) = \mathsf{LREnc}_{h_1}(x; r)$.

Theorem 2. *For any function family $\mathcal{F}$, the above construction (Enc_{h_1,h_2}, Dec_{h_1,h_2}) is an $(\mathcal{F}, \varepsilon)$-super non-malleable code with probability $1 - \rho$ over the choice of h_1, h_2 as long as:*

$$t \geq t^* \quad \text{for some} \quad t^* = O(\log|\mathcal{F}| + n + \log(1/\rho))$$
$$v_1 > v_1^* \quad \text{for some} \quad v_1^* = 3\log(1/\varepsilon) + 3\log(t^*) + O(1)$$
$$v_2 > v_1 + 3.$$

For example, in the above theorem, if we set $\rho = \varepsilon = 2^{-\lambda}$ for "security parameter" λ, and $|\mathcal{F}| = 2^{s(n)}$ for some polynomial $s(n) = n^{O(1)} \geq n \geq \lambda$, then we can set $t = O(s(n))$ and the message length $k := n - (v_1 + v_2) = n - O(\lambda + \log n)$. Therefore the rate of the code k/n is $1 - O(\lambda + \log n)/n$ which approaches 1 as n grows relative to λ.

4.1   Proof of Theorem 2

Useful Notions. For a coding scheme ($\mathsf{Enc}, \mathsf{Dec}$), we say that $c \in \{0,1\}^n$ is *valid* if $\mathsf{Dec}(c) \neq \perp$. For any function $f : \{0,1\}^n \to \{0,1\}^n$, we say that $c' \in \{0,1\}^n$ is δ-*heavy* for f if $\Pr[f(\mathsf{Enc}(U_k)) = c'] \geq \delta$. Define

$$H_f(\delta) = \{c' \in \{0,1\}^n : c' \text{ is } \delta\text{-heavy for } f\}.$$

Notice that $|H_f(\delta)| \leq 1/\delta$.

Definition 5 (Bounded-malleable). *We say that a coding scheme* ($\mathsf{Enc}, \mathsf{Dec}$) *is* $(\mathcal{F}, \delta, \tau)$-*bounded-malleable if for all $f \in \mathcal{F}, x \in \{0,1\}^k$ we have*

$$\Pr[c' \neq c \wedge c' \text{ is valid } \wedge c' \notin H_f(\delta) \mid c \leftarrow \mathsf{Enc}(x), c' = f(c)] \leq \tau,$$

where the probability is over the randomness of the encoding.

Intuition. The above definition says the following. Take any message $x \in \{0,1\}^k$, tampering function $f \in \mathcal{F}$ and do the following: choose $c \leftarrow \mathsf{Enc}(x)$, set $c' = f(c)$, and output: (1) $\mathsf{same}^\star$ if $c' = c$, (2) $\perp$ if c' is not valid, (3) c' otherwise. Then, with probability $1 - \tau$ the output of the above experiment takes on one of the values: $\{\mathsf{same}^\star, \perp\} \cup H_f(\delta)$. Therefore, the output of the above tampering experiment only leaks a bounded amount of information about c; in particular it leaks at most $\ell = \lceil \log(1/\delta + 2) \rceil$ bits. Furthermore the "leakage" on c is independent of the choice of the code, up to knowing which codewords are valid and which are δ-heavy. In particular, in our construction, the "leakage" only depends on the choice of h_2 but *not* on the choice of h_1. This will allow us to then rely on the fact that $\mathsf{LREnc}_{h_1}(x; r) = (r, h_1(r) \oplus x)$ is a leakage-resilient encoding of x to argue that the output of the above experiment is the same for x as for a uniformly random value. We formalize this intuition below.

From Bounded-Malleable to Non-malleable. For any "tampering function" family $\mathcal{F}$ consisting of functions $f : \{0,1\}^n \to \{0,1\}^n$, any $\delta > 0$, and any $h_2 \in \mathcal{H}_2$ we define the "leakage function" family $\mathcal{G} = \mathcal{G}(\mathcal{F}, h_2, \delta)$ which consists of the functions $g_f : \{0,1\}^{k+v_1} \to H_f(\delta) \cup \{\mathsf{same}^\star, \perp\}$ for each $f \in \mathcal{F}$. The functions are defined as follows:

- $g_f(c_1)$: Compute $\sigma = h_2(c_1)$. Let $c := (c_1, \sigma), c' = f(c)$. If c' is not valid output $\perp$. Else if $c' = c$ output $\mathsf{same}^\star$. Else if $c' \in H_f(\delta)$ output c'. Lastly, if none of the above cases holds, output $\perp$.

Notice that the notion of "δ-heavy" and the set $H_f(\delta)$ are completely specified by h_2 and do not depend on h_1. This is because the distribution $\mathsf{Enc}_{h_1,h_2}(U_k)$ is equivalent to $(U_{k+v_1}, h_2(U_{k+v_1}))$ and therefore c' is δ-heavy if and only if $\Pr[f(U_{k+v_1}, h_2(U_{k+v_1})) = c'] \geq \delta$. Therefore the family $\mathcal{G} = \mathcal{G}(\mathcal{F}, h_2, \delta)$ is fully specified by $\mathcal{F}, h_2, \delta$. Also notice that $|\mathcal{G}| = |\mathcal{F}|$ and that the output length of the functions g_f is given by $\ell = \lceil \log(|H_f(\delta)| + 2) \rceil \leq \lceil \log(1/\delta + 2) \rceil$.

Lemma 1. *Let $\mathcal{F}$ be any function family and let $\delta > 0$. Fix any h_1, h_2 such that $(\mathsf{Enc}_{h_1,h_2}, \mathsf{Dec}_{h_1,h_2})$ is $(\mathcal{F}, \delta, \varepsilon/4)$-bounded-malleable and $(\mathsf{LREnc}_{h_1}, \mathsf{LRDec}_{h_1})$ is $(\mathcal{G}(\mathcal{F}, h_2, \delta), \varepsilon/4)$-leakage-resilient, where the family $\mathcal{G} = \mathcal{G}(\mathcal{F}, h_2, \delta)$, with size $|\mathcal{G}| = |\mathcal{F}|$, is defined above, and the leakage amount is $\ell = \lceil \log(1/\delta + 2) \rceil$. Then $(\mathsf{Enc}_{h_1,h_2}, \mathsf{Dec}_{h_1,h_2})$ is $(\mathcal{F}, \varepsilon)$-non-malleable.*

Proof. For any $x_0, x_1 \in \{0,1\}^k$ and any $f \in \mathcal{F}$:

$$\mathsf{Tamper}_{x_0}^f = \left\{ \begin{array}{c} c \leftarrow \mathsf{Enc}_{h_1,h_2}(x_0), c' := f(c) \\ \text{Output} : \mathsf{same}^\star \text{ if } c' = c, \perp \text{ if } \mathsf{Dec}_{h_1,h_2}(c') = \perp, \\ c' \text{ otherwise.} \end{array} \right\}$$

$$\overset{\mathsf{stat}}{\approx}_{\varepsilon/4} \left\{ \begin{array}{c} c_1 \leftarrow \mathsf{LREnc}_{h_1}(x_0) \\ \text{Output} : g_f(c_1) \end{array} \right\} \tag{3}$$

$$\overset{\mathsf{stat}}{\approx}_{\varepsilon/4} \left\{ \begin{array}{c} c_1 \leftarrow \mathsf{LREnc}_{h_1}(U_k) \\ \text{Output} : g_f(c_1) \end{array} \right\} \tag{4}$$

$$\overset{\text{stat}}{\approx}_{\varepsilon/4} \left\{ \begin{array}{l} c_1 \leftarrow \mathsf{LREnc}_{h_1}(x_1) \\ \text{Output} \; : g_f(c_1) \end{array} \right\} \tag{5}$$

$$\overset{\text{stat}}{\approx}_{\varepsilon/4} \left\{ \begin{array}{c} c \leftarrow \mathsf{Enc}_{h_1,h_2}(x_1), c' := f(c) \\ \text{Output} \; : \mathsf{same}^\star \; \text{if} \; c' = c, \perp \; \text{if} \; \mathsf{Dec}_{h_1,h_2}(c') = \perp, \\ c' \; \text{otherwise.} \end{array} \right\} \tag{6}$$

$$= \mathsf{Tamper}^f_{x_1}$$

Eq. (3) and Eq. (6) follows as $(\mathsf{Enc}_{h_1,h_2}, \mathsf{Dec}_{h_1,h_2})$ is an $(\mathcal{F}, \delta, \varepsilon/4)$-bounded-malleable code, and Eq. (4) and Eq. (5) follow as the code $(\mathsf{LREnc}_{h_1}, \mathsf{LRDec}_{h_1})$ is $(\mathcal{G}(\mathcal{F}, \delta), \varepsilon/4)$-leakage-resilient.

We can use Theorem 1 to show that $(\mathsf{LREnc}_{h_1}, \mathsf{LRDec}_{h_1})$ is $(\mathcal{G}(\mathcal{F}, h_2, \delta), \varepsilon/4)$-leakage-resilient with overwhelming probability. Therefore, it remains to show that our construction is $(\mathcal{F}, \delta, \tau)$-bounded-malleable, which we do below.

Analysis of Bounded-Malleable Codes. We now show that the code $(\mathsf{Enc}_{h_1,h_2}, \mathsf{Dec}_{h_1,h_2})$ is bounded-malleable with overwhelming probability. As a very high-level intuition, if a tampering function f can often map valid codewords to other valid codewords (and many different ones), then it must guess the output of h_2 on many different inputs. If the family $\mathcal{F}$ is small enough, it is highly improbable that it would contain some such f. For more detailed intuition, we show that the following two properties hold for any message x and any function f with overwhelming probability: (1) there is at most some "small" set of q valid codewords c' that we can hit by tampering some encoding of x via f (2) for each such codeword c' which is not in δ-heavy, the probability of landing in c' after tampering an encoding of x cannot be higher than 2δ. This shows that the total probability of tampering an encoding of x and landing in a valid codeword which not δ-heavy is at most $2q\delta$, which is small. Property (1) roughly follows by showing that f would need to "predict" the output of h_2 on q different inputs, and property (2) follows by using "leakage-resilience" of h_1 to argue that we cannot distinguish an encoding of x from an encoding of a random message, for which the probability of landing in c' is at most δ.

Lemma 2. *For any function family $\mathcal{F}$, any $\delta > 0$, the code $(\mathsf{Enc}_{h_1,h_2}, \mathsf{Dec}_{h_1,h_2})$ is $(\mathcal{F}, \delta, \tau)$-bounded-malleable with probability $1 - \psi$ over the choice of h_1, h_2 as long as:*

$$\tau \geq 2(\log |\mathcal{F}| + k + \log(1/\psi) + 2)\delta$$
$$t \geq \log |\mathcal{F}| + n + k + \log(1/\psi) + 5$$
$$v_1 \geq 2\log(1/\delta) + \log(t) + 4 \quad and \quad v_2 \geq v_1 + 3.$$

Proof. Set $q := \lceil \log |\mathcal{F}| + k + \log(1/\psi) + 1 \rceil$. For any $f \in \mathcal{F}, x \in \{0,1\}^k$ define the events $E_1^{f,x}$ and $E_2^{f,x}$ over the random choice of h_1, h_2 as follows:

1. $E_1^{f,x}$ occurs if there exist at least q distinct values $c'_1, \ldots, c'_q \in \{0,1\}^n$ such that each c'_i is valid and $c'_i = f(c_i)$ for some $c_i \neq c'_i$ which encodes the message x (i.e., $c_i = \mathsf{Enc}_{h_1,h_2}(x; r_i)$ for some r_i).

2. $E_2^{f,x}$ occurs if there exists some $c' \in \{0,1\}^n \setminus H_f(\delta)$ such that

$$\Pr_{r \leftarrow \{0,1\}^{v_1}} [f(\mathsf{Enc}_{h_1,h_2}(x;r)) = c'] \geq 2\delta.$$

Let $E_1 = \bigvee_{f,x} E_1^{f,x}$, $E_2 = \bigvee_{f,x} E_2^{f,x}$ and $\mathrm{BAD} = E_1 \vee E_2$. Assume (h_1, h_2) are any hash functions for which the event BAD does *not* occur. Then, for every $f \in \mathcal{F}, x \in \{0,1\}^k$:

$$\Pr[f(C) \neq C \wedge f(C) \text{ is valid } \wedge f(C) \notin H_f(\delta)]$$
$$= \sum_{c': \, c' \text{valid and } c' \notin H_f(\delta)} \Pr[f(C) = c' \wedge C \neq c'] < 2q\delta \leq \tau, \tag{7}$$

where $C = \mathsf{Enc}_{h_1,h_2}(x; U_{v_1})$ is a random variable. Eq. (7) holds since (1) given that E_1 does not occur, there are fewer than q values c' that are valid and for which $\Pr[f(C) = c' \wedge C \neq c'] > 0$, and (2) given that E_2 does not occur, for any $c' \notin H_f(\delta)$, we also have $\Pr[f(C) = c' \wedge C \neq c'] \leq \Pr[f(C) = c'] < 2\delta$.

Therefore, if the event BAD does not occur, then the code is $(\mathcal{F}, \delta, \tau)$-bounded-malleable. This means:

$$\Pr_{h_1,h_2}[(\mathsf{Enc}_{h_1,h_2}, \mathsf{Dec}_{h_1,h_2}) \text{ is not } (\mathcal{F}, \delta, \tau)\text{-bounded-malleable}]$$

$$\leq \Pr[\mathrm{BAD}] \leq \Pr[E_1] + \Pr[E_2]$$

So it suffices to show that $\Pr[E_1]$ and $\Pr[E_2]$ are both bounded by $\psi/2$, which we do next.

Claim. $\Pr[E_1] \leq \psi/2$.

Proof. Fix some message $x \in \{0,1\}^k$ and some function $f \in \mathcal{F}$. Assume that the event $E_1^{f,x}$ occurs for some choice of hash functions (h_1, h_2). Then there must exist some values $\{r_1, \ldots, r_q\}$ such that: if we define $c_i := \mathsf{Enc}(x; r_i), c_i' := f(c_i)$ then $c_i' \neq c_i$, c_i' is valid, and $|\{c_1', \ldots, c_q'\}| = q$. The last condition also implies $|\{c_1, \ldots, c_q\}| = q$. However, it is possible that $c_i = c_j'$ for some $i \neq j$. We claim that we can find a subset of at least $s := \lceil q/3 \rceil$ of the indices such that the $2s$ values $\{c_{a_1}, \ldots, c_{a_s}, c_{a_1}', \ldots, c_{a_s}'\}$ are all distinct. To do so, notice that if we want to keep some index i corresponding to values c_i, c_i', we need to take out at most two indices j, k if $c_j' = c_i$ or $c_k = c_i'$.[1] To summarize, if $E_1^{f,x}$ occurs, then (by re-indexing) there is some set $R = \{r_1, \ldots, r_s\} \subseteq \{0,1\}^{v_1}$ of size $|R| = s$ satisfying the following two conditions:

(1) If we define $c_i := \mathsf{Enc}(x; r_i)$, $c_i' \neq c_i$ and c_i' is valid meaning that $c_i' = (r_i', z_i', \sigma_i')$ where $\sigma' = h_2(r', z')$.
(2) $|\{c_1, \ldots, c_s, c_1', \ldots, c_s'\}| = 2s$.

---

[1] In other words, if we take any set of tuples $\{(c_i, c_i')\}$ such that all the left components are distinct $c_i \neq c_j$ and all the right components are distinct $c_i' \neq c_j'$, but there may be common values $c_i = c_j'$, then there is a subset of at least $1/3$ of the tuples such that all left and right components in this subset are mutually distinct.

Therefore we have:

$$\Pr[E_1^{f,x}] \leq \Pr_{h_1,h_2}[\exists R \subseteq \{0,1\}^{v_1}, |R| = s, R \text{ satisfies } (1) \text{ and } (2)]$$

$$\leq \sum_R \Pr_{h_1,h_2}[R \text{ satisfies } (1) \text{ and } (2)]$$

$$\leq \sum_{R=\{r_1,\ldots,r_s\}} \max_{h_1,\sigma_1,\ldots,\sigma_s} \Pr_{h_2}\left[\forall i, c_i' \text{ valid} \begin{array}{|l} c_i := (r_i, z_i = h_1(r_i) \oplus x, \sigma_i), \\ c_i' := f(c_i), c_i' \neq c_i \\ |\{c_1, \ldots, c_s, c_1', \ldots, c_s'\}| = 2s \end{array}\right]$$

$$\leq \binom{2^{v_1}}{s} 2^{-sv_2} \leq \left(\frac{e2^{v_1}}{s}\right)^s 2^{-sv_2} \leq 2^{s(v_1-v_2)} \leq 2^{q(v_1-v_2)/3} \leq 2^{-q}, \tag{8}$$

where Eq. (8) follows from the fact that, even if we condition on any choice of the hash function h_1 which fixes $z_i = h_1(r_i) \oplus x$, and any choice of the s values $\sigma_i = h_2(r_i, z_i)$, which fixes $c_i := (r_i, z_i = h_1(r_i) \oplus x, \sigma_i), c_i' := f(c_i)$ such that $c_i' \neq c_i$ and $|\{c_1, \ldots, c_s, c_1', \ldots, c_s'\}| = 2s$, then the probability that $h_2(r_i', z_i') = \sigma_i'$ for all $i \in [s]$ is at most 2^{-sv_2}. Here we use the fact that $\mathcal{H}_2$ is t-wise independent where $t \geq q \geq 2s$. Now, we calculate

$$\Pr[E_1] \leq \sum_{f \in \mathcal{F}} \sum_{x \in \{0,1\}^k} \Pr[E_1^{f,x}] \leq |\mathcal{F}|2^{k-q} \leq \psi/2,$$

where the last inequality follows from the assumption, $q = \lceil \log |\mathcal{F}| + k + \log(1/\psi) + 1 \rceil$.

Claim. $\Pr[E_2] \leq \psi/2$.

Proof. For this proof, we will rely on the leakage-resilience property of the code $(\mathsf{LREnc}_{h_1}, \mathsf{LRDec}_{h_1})$ as shown in Theorem 1. First, let us write:

$$\Pr[E_2] = \Pr_{h_1,h_2}\left[\exists (f,x,c') \in \mathcal{F} \times \{0,1\}^k \times \{0,1\}^n \setminus H_f(\delta) : \right.$$

$$\left. \Pr[f(\mathsf{Enc}_{h_1,h_2}(x; U_{v_1})) = c'] \geq 2\delta\right]$$

$$\leq \Pr_{h_1,h_2}\left[\exists (f,x,c') \in \mathcal{F} \times \{0,1\}^k \times \{0,1\}^n \setminus H_f(\delta) : \right. \tag{9}$$

$$\left. \left| \begin{array}{l} \Pr[f(\mathsf{Enc}_{h_1,h_2}(x; U_{v_1})) = c'] \\ - \Pr[f(\mathsf{Enc}_{h_1,h_2}(U_k; U_{v_1})) = c'] \end{array} \right| \geq \delta \right]$$

since, for any $c' \notin H_f(\delta)$, we have $\Pr[f(\mathsf{Enc}_{h_1,h_2}(U_k; U_{v_1})) = c'] < \delta$ by definition. Notice that we can write $\mathsf{Enc}_{h_1,h_2}(x; r) = (c_1, c_2)$ where $c_1 = \mathsf{LREnc}_{h_1}(x; r)$, $c_2 = h_2(c_1)$. We will now rely on the leakage-resilience of the code $(\mathsf{LREnc}_{h_1}, \mathsf{LRDec}_{h_1})$ to bound the above probability by $\psi/2$. In fact, we show that the above holds even if we take the probability over h_1 only, for a worst-case choice of h_2.

Let us fix some choice of h_2 and define the family $\mathcal{G} = \mathcal{G}(h_2)$ of leakage-functions $\mathcal{G} = \{g_{f,c'} : \{0,1\}^{k+v_1} \to \{0,1\} \mid f \in \mathcal{F}, c' \in \{0,1\}^n\}$ with output size $\ell = 1$ bits as follows:

- $g_{f,c'}(c_1)$: Set $c = (c_1, c_2 = h_2(c_1))$. If $f(c) = c'$ output 1, else output 0.

Notice that the size of the family $\mathcal{G}$ is $2^n|\mathcal{F}|$ and the family does not depend on the choice of h_1. Therefore, continuing from inequality (9), we get:

$$\Pr[E_2] \leq \Pr_{h_1,h_2}\left[\exists (f,x,c') \in \mathcal{F} \times \{0,1\}^k \times \{0,1\}^n \setminus H_f(\delta) : \right.$$
$$\left. \begin{vmatrix} \Pr[f(\mathsf{Enc}_{h_1,h_2}(x; U_{v_1})) = c'] \\ - \Pr[f(\mathsf{Enc}_{h_1,h_2}(U_k; U_{v_1})) = c'] \end{vmatrix} \geq \delta \right]$$

$$\leq \max_{h_2} \Pr_{h_1}\left[\exists (g_{f,c'}, x) \in \mathcal{G}(h_2) \times \{0,1\}^k : \right.$$
$$\left. \begin{vmatrix} \Pr[g_{f,c'}(\mathsf{LREnc}_{h_1}(x; U_{v_1})) = 1] \\ - \Pr[g_{f,c'}(\mathsf{LREnc}_{h_1}(U_k; U_{v_1})) = 1] \end{vmatrix} \geq \delta \right]$$

$$= \max_{h_2} \Pr_{h_1}\left[\exists (g_{f,c'}, x) \in \mathcal{G}(h_2) \times \{0,1\}^k : \right.$$
$$\left. \begin{vmatrix} \Pr[g_{f,c'}(\mathsf{LREnc}_{h_1}(x; U_{v_1})) = 1] \\ - \Pr[g_{f,c'}(U_{k+v_1}) = 1] \end{vmatrix} \geq \delta \right]$$

$$\leq \max_{h_2} \Pr_{h_1}\left[(\mathsf{LREnc}_{h_1}, \mathsf{LRDec}_{h_1}) \text{ is not } (\mathcal{G}(h_2), \delta)\text{-Leakage-Resilient} \right]$$
$$\leq \psi/2,$$

where the last inequality follows from Theorem 1 by the choice of parameters.

Putting it All Together. Lemma 1 tells us that for any $\delta > 0$ and any function family $\mathcal{F}$:

$$\Pr[(\mathsf{Enc}_{h_1,h_2}, \mathsf{Dec}_{h_1,h_2}) \text{ is not } (\mathcal{F}, \varepsilon)\text{-super-non-malleable}]$$
$$\leq \Pr[(\mathsf{Enc}_{h_1,h_2}, \mathsf{Dec}_{h_1,h_2}) \text{ is not } (\mathcal{F}, \delta, \varepsilon/4)\text{-bounded-malleable}] \tag{10}$$
$$+ \Pr[(\mathsf{LREnc}_{h_1}, \mathsf{LRDec}_{h_1}) \text{ is not } (\mathcal{G}(\mathcal{F}, h_2, \delta), \varepsilon/4)\text{-leakage-resilient}], \tag{11}$$

where $\mathcal{G} = \mathcal{G}(\mathcal{F}, h_2, \delta)$ is of size $|\mathcal{G}| = |\mathcal{F}|$ and consists of function with output size $\ell = \lceil \log(1/\delta + 2) \rceil$.

Let us set $\delta := (\varepsilon/8)(\log|\mathcal{F}| + k + \log(1/\rho) + 3)^{-1}$. This ensures that the first requirement of Lemma 2 is satisfied with $\tau = \varepsilon/4$. We choose $t^* = O(\log|\mathcal{F}| + n + \log(1/\rho))$ such that $\log(1/\delta) \leq \log(1/\varepsilon) + \log(t^*) + O(1)$. Notice that the leakage amount of $\mathcal{G}$ is $\ell = \lceil \log(1/\delta + 2) \rceil \leq \log(1/\varepsilon) + \log(t^*) + O(1)$. With v_1, v_2 as in Theorem 2, we satisfy the remaining requirements of Lemma 2 (bounded-malleable codes) and Theorem 1 (leakage-resilient codes) to ensure that the probabilities (10), (11) are both bounded by $\rho/2$, which proves our theorem.

Experiment $\mathsf{Real}_h(f)$ vs. $\mathsf{Sim}_h(f)$

Experiment $\mathsf{Real}_h(f)$:
  Sample $x \leftarrow U_n$.
  If $f(x) = x$:
    Output $(h(x), \mathsf{same}^\star))$.
  Else
    Output $(h(x), h(f(x)))$.

Experiment $\mathsf{Sim}_h(f)$:
  Sample $x \leftarrow U_n; \, y \leftarrow U_k$
  If $f(x) = x$:
    Output $(y, \mathsf{same}^\star)$.
  Else
    Output $(y, h(f(x)))$.

Fig. 1. Experiments defining a non-malleable key derivation function h

5 Non-malleable Key-Derivation

In this section we introduce a new primitive, which we name non-malleable key derivation. Intuitively a function h is a non-malleable key derivation function if $h(x)$ is close to uniform even given the output of h applied to a related input $f(x)$, as long as $f(x) \neq x$.

Definition 6 (Non-malleable Key-Derivation). *Let $\mathcal{F}$ be any family of functions $f : \{0,1\}^n \to \{0,1\}^n$. We say that a function $h : \{0,1\}^n \to \{0,1\}^k$ is an $(\mathcal{F}, \varepsilon)$-non-malleable key derivation function if for every $f \in \mathcal{F}$ we have $\mathsf{SD}\big(\mathsf{Real}_h(f); \mathsf{Sim}_h(f)\big) \leq \varepsilon$ where $\mathsf{Real}_h(f)$ and $\mathsf{Sim}_h(f)$ denote the output distributions of the corresponding experiments described in Fig. 1.*

Note that the above definition can be interpreted as a dual version of the definition of non-malleable extractors [15].[2] The theorem below states that by sampling a function h from a set $\mathcal{H}$ of t-wise independent hash functions, we obtain a non-malleable key derivation function with overwhelming probability.

Theorem 3. *Let $\mathcal{H}$ be a $2t$-wise independent function family consisting of functions $h : \{0,1\}^n \to \{0,1\}^k$ and let $\mathcal{F}$ be some function family as above. Then with probability $1 - \rho$ over the choice of a random $h \leftarrow \mathcal{H}$, the function h is an $(\mathcal{F}, \varepsilon)$-non-malleable key-derivation function as long as:*

$$n \geq 2k + \log(1/\varepsilon) + \log(t) + 3 \quad \text{and} \quad t > \log(|\mathcal{F}|) + 2k + \log(1/\rho) + 5.$$

Proof. For any $h \in \mathcal{H}$ and $f \in \mathcal{F}$, define a function $h_f : \{0,1\}^n \to \{0,1\}^k \cup \mathsf{same}^\star$ such that if $f(x) = x$ then $h_f(x) = \mathsf{same}^\star$ otherwise $h_f(x) = h(f(x))$. Fix a function family $\mathcal{F}$. Now, taking probabilities (only) over the choice of h, let BAD be the event that h is not an $(\mathcal{F}, \varepsilon)$-non-malleable-key-derivation function. Then:

$$\Pr[\textsc{Bad}] = \Pr_{h \leftarrow \mathcal{H}}\left[\exists f \in \mathcal{F} \; : \quad \mathsf{SD}(\, \mathsf{Real}_h(f) \,, \, \mathsf{Sim}_h(f) \,) > \varepsilon\right]$$

---

[2] The duality comes from the fact that the output of a non-malleable extractor is close to uniform even given a certain number of outputs computed with related seeds (whereas for non-malleable key derivation the seed is unchanged but the input can be altered).

$$= \Pr_{h \leftarrow \mathcal{H}} \left[\exists f \in \mathcal{F} \ : \quad \mathbf{SD}(\, (h(X), h_f(X)) \, , \, (U_k, h_f(X)) \,) > \varepsilon \right]$$

$$\leq \sum_{f \in \mathcal{F}} \Pr_{h \leftarrow \mathcal{H}} \left[\sum_{y \in \{0,1\}^k} \sum_{y' \in \{0,1\}^k \cup \text{same}^*} \left| \Pr[h(X) = y \wedge h_f(X) = y'] \right. \right.$$
$$\left. \left. - \Pr[U_k = y \wedge h_f(X) = y'] \right| > 2\varepsilon \right]$$

$$\leq \sum_{f \in \mathcal{F}} \Pr_{h \leftarrow \mathcal{H}} \left[\exists \, y \in \{0,1\}^k, y' \in \{0,1\}^k \cup \text{same}^* \ : \right.$$
$$\left. \left| \begin{matrix} \Pr[h(X) = y \wedge h_f(X) = y'] \\ - \Pr[U_k = y \wedge h_f(X) = y'] \end{matrix} \right| > 2^{-2k}\varepsilon \right]$$

$$\leq \sum_{f \in \mathcal{F}} \sum_{y \in \{0,1\}^k} \sum_{y' \in \{0,1\}^k \cup \text{same}^*} \Pr_{h \leftarrow \mathcal{H}} \left[\left| \begin{matrix} \Pr[h(X) = y \wedge h_f(X) = y'] \\ -2^{-k} \Pr[h_f(X) = y'] \end{matrix} \right| > 2^{-2k}\varepsilon \right] \quad (12)$$

Fix f, y, y'. For every $x \in \{0,1\}^n$, define a random variable C_x over the choice of $h \leftarrow \mathcal{H}$, such that

$$C_x = \begin{cases} 1 - 2^{-k} & \text{if } h(x) = y \wedge h_f(x) = y' \\ -2^{-k} & \text{if } h(x) \neq y \wedge h_f(x) = y' \\ 0 & \text{otherwise.} \end{cases}$$

Notice that each C_x is 0 on expectation. However, the random variables C_x are not even pairwise independent.[3] In the full version of this paper [20], we prove the following lemma about the variables C_x.

Lemma 3. *There exists a partitioning of $\{0,1\}^n$ into four disjoint subsets $\{A_j\}_{j=1}^4$, such that for any $A > 0$ and for all $j = 1, \ldots, 4$:*

$$\Pr \left[\left| \sum_{x \in A_j} C_x \right| > A \right] < K_t \left(\frac{t}{A} \right)^t,$$

where $K_t \leq 8$.

Continuing from Eq. (12), we get:

$$\Pr_{h \leftarrow \mathcal{H}} \left[\left| \Pr[h(X) = y \wedge h_f(X) = y'] - 2^{-k} \Pr[h_f(X) = y'] \right| > 2^{-2k}\varepsilon \right]$$

$$= \Pr_{h \leftarrow \mathcal{H}} \left[\left| \sum_{x \in \{0,1\}^n} C_x \right| > 2^{n-2k}\varepsilon \right] \quad (13)$$

$$\leq \sum_{j=1}^{4} \Pr_{h \leftarrow \mathcal{H}} \left[\left| \sum_{x \in A_j} C_x \right| > 2^{n-2k-2}\varepsilon \right] < 4K_t \left(\frac{t}{2^{n-2k-2}\varepsilon} \right)^t. \quad (14)$$

Eq. (13) follows from the definitions of the variables C_x and Eq. (14) follows by applying Lemma 3 to the sum. Combining Eq. (12) and Eq. (14), we get $\Pr[\text{BAD}] < |\mathcal{F}| 2^{2k} \left[4K_t \left(\frac{t}{2^{n-2k-2}\varepsilon} \right)^t \right]$. In particular, it holds that $\Pr[\text{BAD}] \leq \rho$ as long as:

$$n \geq 2k + \log(1/\varepsilon) + \log(t) + 3 \quad \text{and} \quad t > \log(|\mathcal{F}|) + 2k + \log(1/\rho) + 5.$$

---

[3] For example if $f(x) = f(x')$ and $C_x = 0$ then $C_{x'} = 0$ as well.

Optimal Rate of Non-Malleable Key-Derivation. We can define the rate of a key derivation function $h : \{0,1\}^n \to \{0,1\}^k$ as the ratio k/n. Notice that our construction achieves rate arbitrary close to $1/2$. We claim that this is *optimal* for non-malleable key derivation. To see this, consider a tampering function $f : \{0,1\}^n \to \{0,1\}^n$ which is a permutation and never identity: $f(x) \neq x$. In this case the joint distribution $(h(X), h(f(X)))$ is ε-close to $(U_k, h(f(X)))$ which is ε-close to the distribution (U_k, U_k') consisting of $2k$ random bits. Since all of the randomness in $(h(X), h(f(X)))$ comes from X, this means that X must contain at least $2k$ bits of randomness, meaning that $n > 2k$.

Acknowledgements. We thank Ivan Damgård for useful discussions at the early stages of this research.

References

1. Aggarwal, D., Dodis, Y., Lovett, S.: Non-malleable codes from additive combinatorics. Electronic Colloquium on Computational Complexity (ECCC) 20, 81 (2013)
2. Anderson, R., Kuhn, M., England, U.S.A.: Tamper resistance — a cautionary note. In: Proceedings of the Second Usenix Workshop on Electronic Commerce, pp. 1–11 (1996)
3. Applebaum, B., Harnik, D., Ishai, Y.: Semantic security under related-key attacks and applications. In: ICS, pp. 45–60 (2011)
4. Bellare, M., Cash, D.: Pseudorandom functions and permutations provably secure against related-key attacks. In: Rabin, T. (ed.) CRYPTO 2010. LNCS, vol. 6223, pp. 666–684. Springer, Heidelberg (2010)
5. Bellare, M., Kohno, T.: A theoretical treatment of related-key attacks: RKA-PRPs, RKA-PRFs, and applications. In: Biham, E. (ed.) EUROCRYPT 2003. LNCS, vol. 2656, pp. 491–506. Springer, Heidelberg (2003)
6. Bellare, M., Paterson, K.G., Thomson, S.: RKA security beyond the linear barrier: IBE, encryption and signatures. In: Wang, X., Sako, K. (eds.) ASIACRYPT 2012. LNCS, vol. 7658, pp. 331–348. Springer, Heidelberg (2012)
7. Boneh, D., DeMillo, R.A., Lipton, R.J.: On the importance of eliminating errors in cryptographic computations. J. Cryptology 14(2), 101–119 (2001)
8. Cheraghchi, M., Guruswami, V.: Capacity of non-malleable codes. Electronic Colloquium on Computational Complexity (ECCC) 20, 118 (2013)
9. Cheraghchi, M., Guruswami, V.: Non-malleable coding against bit-wise and split-state tampering. IACR Cryptology ePrint Archive, 2013:565 (2013)
10. Choi, S.G., Kiayias, A., Malkin, T.: BiTR: Built-in tamper resilience. In: Lee, D.H., Wang, X. (eds.) ASIACRYPT 2011. LNCS, vol. 7073, pp. 740–758. Springer, Heidelberg (2011)
11. Coron, J.-S., Joux, A., Kizhvatov, I., Naccache, D., Paillier, P.: Fault attacks on rsa signatures with partially unknown messages. In: Clavier, C., Gaj, K. (eds.) CHES 2009. LNCS, vol. 5747, pp. 444–456. Springer, Heidelberg (2009)
12. Cramer, R., Dodis, Y., Fehr, S., Padró, C., Wichs, D.: Detection of algebraic manipulation with applications to robust secret sharing and fuzzy extractors. In: Smart, N.P. (ed.) EUROCRYPT 2008. LNCS, vol. 4965, pp. 471–488. Springer, Heidelberg (2008)

13. Damgård, I., Faust, S., Mukherjee, P., Venturi, D.: Bounded tamper resilience: How to go beyond the algebraic barrier. In: Sako, K., Sarkar, P. (eds.) ASIACRYPT 2013, Part II. LNCS, vol. 8270, pp. 140–160. Springer, Heidelberg (2013)
14. Davì, F., Dziembowski, S., Venturi, D.: Leakage-resilient storage. In: Garay, J.A., De Prisco, R. (eds.) SCN 2010. LNCS, vol. 6280, pp. 121–137. Springer, Heidelberg (2010)
15. Dodis, Y., Wichs, D.: Non-malleable extractors and symmetric key cryptography from weak secrets. In: STOC, pp. 601–610 (2009)
16. Dolev, D., Dwork, C., Naor, M.: Nonmalleable cryptography. SIAM J. Comput. 30(2), 391–437 (2000)
17. Dziembowski, S., Kazana, T., Obremski, M.: Non-malleable codes from two-source extractors. In: Canetti, R., Garay, J.A. (eds.) CRYPTO 2013, Part II. LNCS, vol. 8043, pp. 239–257. Springer, Heidelberg (2013)
18. Dziembowski, S., Pietrzak, K., Wichs, D.: Non-malleable codes. In: ICS, pp. 434–452 (2010)
19. Faust, S., Mukherjee, P., Nielsen, J.B., Venturi, D.: Continuous non-malleable codes. In: Lindell, Y. (ed.) TCC 2014. LNCS, vol. 8349, pp. 465–488. Springer, Heidelberg (2014)
20. Faust, S., Mukherjee, P., Venturi, D., Wichs, D.: Efficient non-malleable codes and key-derivation for poly-size tampering circuits. IACR Cryptology ePrint Archive, 2013:702 (2013)
21. Faust, S., Pietrzak, K., Venturi, D.: Tamper-proof circuits: How to trade leakage for tamper-resilience. In: Aceto, L., Henzinger, M., Sgall, J. (eds.) ICALP 2011, Part I. LNCS, vol. 6755, pp. 391–402. Springer, Heidelberg (2011)
22. Gennaro, R., Lysyanskaya, A., Malkin, T., Micali, S., Rabin, T.: Algorithmic tamper-proof (ATP) security: Theoretical foundations for security against hardware tampering. In: Naor, M. (ed.) TCC 2004. LNCS, vol. 2951, pp. 258–277. Springer, Heidelberg (2004)
23. Goyal, V., O'Neill, A., Rao, V.: Correlated-input secure hash functions. In: Ishai, Y. (ed.) TCC 2011. LNCS, vol. 6597, pp. 182–200. Springer, Heidelberg (2011)
24. Ishai, Y., Prabhakaran, M., Sahai, A., Wagner, D.: Private circuits II: Keeping secrets in tamperable circuits. In: Vaudenay, S. (ed.) EUROCRYPT 2006. LNCS, vol. 4004, pp. 308–327. Springer, Heidelberg (2006)
25. Kalai, Y.T., Kanukurthi, B., Sahai, A.: Cryptography with tamperable and leaky memory. In: Rogaway, P. (ed.) CRYPTO 2011. LNCS, vol. 6841, pp. 373–390. Springer, Heidelberg (2011)
26. Liu, F.-H., Lysyanskaya, A.: Tamper and leakage resilience in the split-state model. In: Safavi-Naini, R., Canetti, R. (eds.) CRYPTO 2012. LNCS, vol. 7417, pp. 517–532. Springer, Heidelberg (2012)
27. Pietrzak, K.: Subspace LWE. In: Cramer, R. (ed.) TCC 2012. LNCS, vol. 7194, pp. 548–563. Springer, Heidelberg (2012)
28. Raghunathan, A., Segev, G., Vadhan, S.: Deterministic public-key encryption for adaptively chosen plaintext distributions. In: Johansson, T., Nguyen, P.Q. (eds.) EUROCRYPT 2013. LNCS, vol. 7881, pp. 93–110. Springer, Heidelberg (2013)
29. Skorobogatov, S.P., Anderson, R.J.: Optical fault induction attacks. In: Kaliski Jr., B.S., Koç, Ç.K., Paar, C. (eds.) CHES 2002. LNCS, vol. 2523, pp. 2–12. Springer, Heidelberg (2003)
30. Wee, H.: Public key encryption against related key attacks. In: Fischlin, M., Buchmann, J., Manulis, M. (eds.) PKC 2012. LNCS, vol. 7293, pp. 262–279. Springer, Heidelberg (2012)

Revocable Quantum Timed-Release Encryption

Dominique Unruh

University of Tartu, Estonia

Abstract. Timed-release encryption is a kind of encryption scheme that a recipient can decrypt only after a specified amount of time T (assuming that we have a moderately precise estimate of his computing power). A *revocable* timed-release encryption is one where, before the time T is over, the sender can "give back" the timed-release encryption, provably loosing all access to the data. We show that revocable timed-release encryption without trusted parties is possible using quantum cryptography (while trivially impossible classically).

Along the way, we develop two proof techniques in the quantum random oracle model that we believe may have applications also for other protocols.

Finally, we also develop another new primitive, *unknown recipient encryption*, which allows us to send a message to an unknown/unspecified recipient over an insecure network in such a way that at most one recipient will get the message.

1 Introduction

We present and construct revocable timed-release encryption schemes (based on quantum cryptography). To explain what revocable timed-release encryption is, we first recall the notion of timed-release encryption (also known as a time-lock puzzle); we only consider the setting without trusted parties in this paper. A timed-release encryption (TRE) for time T is an algorithm that takes a message m and "encrypts" it in such a way that the message cannot be decrypted in time T but can be decrypted in time $T' > T$. (Here T' should be as close as possible to T, preferably off by only an additive offset.)

The crucial point here is that the recipient can open the encryption without any interaction with the sender. (E.g., [21] publishes a secret message that is supposed not to be openable before 2034.) Example use cases could be: messages for posterity [22]; data that should be provided to a recipient at a given time, even if the sender goes offline; A sells some information to B that should be revealed only later, but B wants to be sure that A cannot withdraw this information any more;[1] exchange of secrets where none of the parties should be able to abort depending on the data received by the other; fair contract signing [6]; electronic auctions [6]; mortgage payments [22]; concurrent zero-knowledge protocols [6]; etc.

Physically, one can imagine TRE as follows: The message m is put in a strongbox with a timer that opens automatically after time T'. The recipient cannot get the message in time T because the strongbox will not be open by then.

---

[1] In this case, zero-knowledge proofs could be used to show that the TRE indeed contains the right plaintext.

P.Q. Nguyen and E. Oswald (Eds.): EUROCRYPT 2014, LNCS 8441, pp. 129–146, 2014.

It turns out, however, that a physical TRE is more powerful than a digital one. Consider the following example setting: Person P goes to a meeting with a criminal organization. As a safe guard, he leaves compromising information m with his friend F, to be released if P does not resurface after one day. (WikiLeaks/Assange seems to have done something similar [19].) As P assumes F to be curious, P puts m in a physical TRE, to be opened only after one day. If P returns before the day is over, P asks the TRE back. If F hands the TRE over to P, P will be sure that F did not and will not read m. (Of course, F may refuse to hand back the TRE, but F cannot get m without P noticing.)

This works fine with physical TRE, but as soon as P uses a digital TRE, F can cheat. F just copies the TRE before handing it back and continues decrypting. After one day, F will have m, without P noticing.

So physical TREs are "revocable". The recipient can give back the encryption before the time T has passed. And the sender can check that this revocation was performed honestly. In the latter case, the sender will be sure that the recipient does not learn anything. Obviously, a digital TRE can never have that property, because it can be copied before revocation.

However, if we use quantum information in our TRE, things are different. Quantum information cannot, in general, be copied. So it is conceivable that a quantum TRE is revocable.

1.1 Example Applications

We sketch a few more possible applications of revocable TREs. Some of them are far beyond the reach of current technology (because they need reliable storage of quantum states for a long time). In some cases, however, TREs with very short time T are used, this might be within the reach of current technology. The applications are not worked out in detail (some are just first ideas), and we do not claim that they are necessarily the best options in their respective setting, but they illustrate that revocable TREs could be a versatile tool worth investigating further.

Deposits. A client has to provide a deposit for some service (e.g., car rental). The dealer should be able to cash in the deposit if the client does not return. Solution: The client produces a T-revocable TRE containing a signed transaction that empowers the dealer to withdraw the deposit. When the client returns the car within time T, the client can make sure the dealer did not keep the deposit.[2]

---

[2] One challenge: The client needs to convince the dealer that the TRE indeed contains a signature on a transaction. I.e., we need a way to prove that a TRE V contains a given value (and the running time of this proof should not depend on T). At least for our constructions (see below), this could be achieved as follows: The client produces a commitment c on the content of the classical inner TRE V_0 and proves that c contains the right content (using a SNARK [4] so that the verification time does not depend on T). Then client and dealer perform a quantum two-party computation [12] with inputs c, V, and opening information for c, and with dealer outputs V and b where b is a bit indicating whether the message in V satisfies P.

Such deposits might also be part of a cryptographic protocol where deposits are revoked or redeemed automatically depending on whether a party is caught cheating (to produce an incentive against cheating). In this case, the time T might well be in the range of seconds or minutes, which could be within the reach of near future quantum memory [15].

Data Retention with Verifiable Deletion. Various countries have laws requiring the retention of telecommunication data, but mandate the deletion of the data after a certain period (e.g., [14]). Using revocable TREs, clients could provide their data within revocable TREs (together with a proof of correctness, cf. footnote 2). At the end of the prescribed period, the TRE is revoked, unless it is needed for law-enforcement. This way, the clients can verify that their data is indeed erased from the storage.

Unknown Recipient Encryption. An extension of revocable TREs is "unknown recipient encryption" (URE) which allows a sender to encrypt a message m in such a way that any recipient but at most one recipient can decrypt it. That is, the sender can send a message to an unknown recipient, and that recipient can, after decrypting, be sure that only he got the message, even if the ciphertext was transferred over an insecure channel. Think, e.g., of a client connecting to a server in an anonymous fashion, e.g., through (a quantum variant of) TOR [11], and receiving some data m. Since the connection is anonymous and the client has thus no credentials to authenticate with the server, we cannot avoid that the data gets "stolen" by someone else. However, with unknown recipient encryption, it is possible to make sure that the client will detect if someone else got his data. This application shows that revocable TREs can be the basis for other unexpected cryptographic primitives. Again, the time T may be small in some applications, thus in the reach of the near future. We stress that URE is non-interactive, so this works even if no bidirectional communication is possible. It could be used for a cryptographic dead letter box where a "spy" deposits secret information, and the recipient can verify that no-one found it. Unknown recipient encryption is formalized in the full version [27].

A variant of this is "one-shot" quantum key distribution: Only a single message is sent from Alice to Bob, and as long as Bob receives that message within time T, he can be sure no-one else got the key. (This is easily implemented by encrypting the key with a URE.)

1.2 Our Contribution

Definitions. We give formal definitions of TREs and revocable TREs (Section 2). These definitions come in two flavors: T-hiding (no information is leaked before time T) and T-one-way (before time T, the plaintext cannot be guessed completely).)

One-Way Revocable TREs. Then we construct one-way revocable TREs (Section 3). Although one-wayness is too weak a property for almost all purposes, the construction and its proof are useful as a warm-up for the hiding

construction, and also useful on their own for the random oracle based constructions (see below). The construction itself is very simple: To encrypt a message
m, a quantum state $|\Psi\rangle$ is constructed that encodes m in a random BB84 basis
B.[3] Then B is encrypted in a (non-revocable) T-hiding TRE V_0. The resulting
TRE $(|\Psi\rangle, V_0)$ is sent to the recipient. Revocation is straightforward: the recipi-
ent sends $|\Psi\rangle$ back to the sender, who checks that $|\Psi\rangle$ still encodes m in basis B.
Intuitively, $|\Psi\rangle$ cannot be reliably copied without knowledge of basis B, hence
before time T the recipient cannot copy $|\Psi\rangle$ and thus looses access to $|\Psi\rangle$ and
thus to m upon revocation.

The proof of this fact is not as easy as one might think at the first glance ("use
the fact that B is unknown before time T, and then use that a state $|\Psi\rangle$ cannot
be cloned without knowledge of the basis") because information-theoretical and
complexity-theoretic reasoning need to be mixed carefully.

The resulting scheme even enjoys everlasting security (cf., e.g., [17,10,1,7,20]):
after successful revocation, the adversary cannot break the TRE even given
unlimited computation.

We hope that the ideas in the proof benefit not only the construction of
revocable TREs, but might also be useful in other contexts where it is necessary to prove uncloneability of quantum-data based on cryptographic and not
information-theoretical secrecy (quantum-money perhaps?).

Revocably Hiding TREs. The next step is to construct revocably *hiding*
TREs (Section 4). The construction described before is not hiding, because if
the adversary guesses a few bits of B correctly, he will learn some bits of m
while still passing revocation. A natural idea would be to use privacy amplification: the sender picks a universal hash function F and includes it in the TRE
V_0. The actual plaintext is XORed with $F(m)$ and transmitted. Surprisingly, we
cannot prove this construction secure, see the beginning of Section 4 for a discussion. Instead, we prove a construction that is based on CSS codes. The resulting
scheme uses the same technological assumptions as the one-way revocable one:
sending and measuring of individual qubits, quantum memory. Unfortunately,
the reduction in this case is not very efficient; as a consequence the underlying
non-revocable TRE needs to be exponentially hard, at least if we want to encrypt messages of superlogarithmic length. Notice that the random oracle based
solutions described below do not have this drawback.

Like the previous scheme, this scheme enjoys everlasting security.

Random Oracle Transformations. We develop two transformations of TREs
in the quantum random oracle model. The first transformation takes a revocably
one-way TRE and transforms it into a revocably hiding one (by sending $m \oplus H(k)$
and putting k into the revocably one-way TRE; Section 5.1). This gives a simpler
and more efficient alternative to the complex construction for revocably hiding
TREs described above, though at the cost of using the random-oracle model
and loosing everlasting security. The second transformation allows us to assume

---

[3] I.e., each bit of m is randomly encoded either in the computational or the diagonal
basis.

without loss of generality that the adversary performs no oracle queries before receiving the TRE, simplifying other security proof (Section 5.2).

For both transformations we prove general lemmas that allow us to use analogous transformations also on schemes unrelated to TREs (e.g., to make an encryption scheme semantically secure). We believe these to be of independent interest, because the quantum random oracle model is notoriously difficult to use, and many existing classical constructions are not known to work in the quantum case.

Classical TREs. Unfortunately, only very few constructions of classical TRE are known. Rivest, Shamir, and Wagner [22] present a construction based on RSA; it is obviously not secure in the quantum setting [23]. Other constructions are iterated hashing (to send m, we send $H(H(H(\ldots(r)\ldots)))\oplus m$) and preimage search (to decrypt, one needs to invert $H(k)$ where $k \in \{1,\ldots,T\}$); with suitable amplification this becomes a TRE [26]). Preimage search is not a good TRE because it breaks down if the adversary can compute in parallel. This leaves iterated hashing.[4] We prove that (a slight variation of) iterated hashing is hiding even against quantum adversaries and thus suitable for plugging into our constructions of revocable TREs (Section 5.3). (Note, however, that the hardness of iterated hashing could also be used as a very reasonable assumption on its own. The random oracle model is thus not strictly necessary here, it just provides additional justification for that assumption.)

We leave it as an open problem to identify more practical candidates for iterated hashing, perhaps following the ideas of [22] but not based on RSA or other quantum-easy problems.

For space reasons, details and full proofs are deferred to the full version [27] of this paper.

1.3 Preliminaries

For the necessary background in quantum computing, see, e.g., [18].

Let $\omega(x)$ denote the Hamming weight of x. By $[q + n]_q$ we denote the set of all size-q subsets of $\{1,\ldots,q+n\}$. I.e., $S \in [q+n]_q$ iff $S \subseteq \{1,\ldots,q+n\}$ and $|S| = q$. By $\oplus$ we mean bitwise XOR (or equivalently, addition in $GF(2)^n$). Given a linear code C, let $C^{\perp}$ be the dual code ($C^{\perp} := \{x : \forall y \in C.\ x, y \text{ orthogonal}\}$).

Let X, Y, Z denote the Pauli operators. Let $|\beta_{ij}\rangle$ denote the four Bell states, namely $|\beta_{00}\rangle := \frac{1}{\sqrt{2}}|00\rangle + \frac{1}{\sqrt{2}}|11\rangle$ and $|\beta_{fe}\rangle = (Z^f X^e \otimes I)|\beta_{00}\rangle = (I \otimes X^e Z^f)|\beta_{00}\rangle$. In slight abuse of notation, we call $|\beta_{00}\rangle$ an *EPR pair* (originally, [13] used

---

[4] Iterated hashing has the downside that producing the TRE takes as long as decrypting it. However, this long computation can be moved into a precomputation phase that is independent of the message m, making this TRE suitable at least for some applications. [16] present a sophisticated variant of iterated hashing that circumvents this problem; their construction, however, does not allow the sender to predict the recipient's output and is thus not suitable for sending a message into the future.

$|\beta_{11}\rangle$). And a state consisting of EPR pairs we call an *EPR state*. H denotes the Hadamard gate, and I_n the identity on $\mathbb{C}^{2^n}$ (short I if n is clear from the context). Let $|m\rangle_B$ denote $m \in \{0,1\}^n$ encoded in basis $B \in \{0,1\}^n$, where 0 stands for the computational and 1 for the diagonal basis.

Given an operator A and a bitstring $x \in \{0,1\}^n$, we write A^x for $A^{x_1} \otimes \cdots \otimes A^{x_n}$. E.g., $X^x|y\rangle = |x \oplus y\rangle$, and $H^B|x\rangle = |x\rangle_B$.

Given $f, e \in \{0,1\}^n$, we write $|\widetilde{fe}\rangle$ for $|\beta_{f_1 e_1}\rangle \otimes \cdots \otimes |\beta_{f_n e_n}\rangle$, except for the order of qubits: the first qubits of all EPR pairs, followed by the last qubits of all EPR pairs. In other words, $|\widetilde{0^n 0^n}\rangle = \sum_{x \in \{0,1\}^n} |w\rangle|w\rangle$ and $|\widetilde{fe}\rangle = (Z^f X^e \otimes I)|\widetilde{0^n 0^n}\rangle$.

Let $\|\cdot\|$ be the Euclidean norm (i.e., $\||\Psi\rangle\|^2 = |\langle\Psi|\Psi\rangle|$) and let $\|\|\cdot\|\|$ denote the corresponding operator norm (i.e., $\|\|A\|\| := \sup_{x \neq 0} \|Ax\|/\|x\|$).

By $\mathrm{TD}(\rho_1, \rho_2)$ we denote the trace distance between density operators ρ_1, ρ_2. We write short $\mathrm{TD}(|\Psi_1\rangle, |\Psi_2\rangle)$ for $\mathrm{TD}(|\Psi_1\rangle\langle\Psi_1|, |\Psi_2\rangle\langle\Psi_2|)$.

Whenever we speak about algorithms, we mean quantum algorithms. (In particular, adversaries are always assumed to be quantum.)

2   Defining Revocable TREs

A timed-release encryption (TRE) consists of: An encryption algorithm $\mathrm{TRE}(m)$ that returns a (possibly quantum) ciphertext V containing m. A decryption algorithm that computes m from V (without using any key). Possibly: a revocation algorithm in which the recipient gives back V to the sender and the sender performs some check on V. We have two basic security properties for TREs: T-hiding means that within time T, an adversary cannot learn anything about m, and T-one-way means that within time T, an adversary cannot guess m. (These basic security properties do not refer to the revocation algorithm.) For formal definitions of these basic properties, and a discussion on timing-models and definitions in related work, see the full version [27].

We now define the *revocable* hiding property. A TRE is revocably T-hiding if an adversary cannot both successfully pass the revocation protocol within time T and learn something about the message m contained in the TRE. When formalizing this, we have to be careful. A definition like: "conditioned on revocation succeeding, $p_0 := \Pr[\text{adversary outputs 1 given } \mathrm{TRE}(m_0)]$ and $p_1 := \Pr[\text{adversary outputs 1 given } \mathrm{TRE}(m_1)]$ are close ($|p_0 - p_1|$ is negligible)" does not work: if $\Pr[\text{revocation succeeds}]$ is very small, $|p_0 - p_1|$ can become large even if the adversary rarely succeeds in distinguishing. (Consider, e.g., an adversary that intentionally fails revocation except in the very rare case that he guesses an encryption key that allows to decrypt the TRE immediately.) Also, a definition like "$|p_0 - p_1| \cdot \Pr[\text{revocation succeeds}]$" is problematic: Does $\Pr[\text{revocation succeeds}]$ refer to an execution with $\mathrm{TRE}(m_0)$ or $\mathrm{TRE}(m_1)$?. Instead, we will require "$|p_0 - p_1|$ is negligible with $p_i := \Pr[\text{adversary outputs 1 and revocation succeeds given } \mathrm{TRE}(m_i)]$". This definition avoids the complications of a conditional probability and additionally implies as side effect that also $\Pr[\text{revocation succeeds given } \mathrm{TRE}(m_0)]$ and $\Pr[\text{revocation succeeds given } \mathrm{TRE}(m_1)]$ are close.

Definition 1 (Revocably hiding timed-release encryption). *Given a revocable timed-release encryption* TRE *with message space M, and an adversary (A_0, A_1, A_2) (that is assumed to be able to keep state between activations of A_0, A_1, A_2) consider the following game $G(b)$ for $b \in \{0, 1\}$:*

- $(m_0, m_1) \leftarrow A_0()$.
- $V \leftarrow \text{TRE}(m_b)$.
- *Run the revocation protocol of* TRE, *where the sender is honest, and the recipient is $A_1(V)$. Let ok be the output of the sender (i.e., ok $= 1$ if the sender accepts).*
- $b' \leftarrow A_2()$.

A timed-release encryption TRE *with message space M is T-revocably hiding, if for any adversary (A_0, A_1, A_2) where A_1 is sequential-polynomial-time and T-time and A_0, A_2 are sequential-polynomial-time, $\left| \Pr[b' = 1 \wedge ok = 1 : G(0)] - \Pr[b' = 1 \wedge ok = 1 : G(1)] \right|$ is negligible.*

Note that although revocably hiding seems to be a stronger property than hiding, we are not aware of any proof that a T-revocably hiding TRE is also T-hiding. (It might be that it is possible to extract the message m in time $\ll T$, but only at the cost of making a later revocation impossible. This would contradict T-hiding but not T-revocably hiding.) Therefore we always need to show that our revocable TREs are both T-hiding and T-revocably hiding.

Again, we define the weaker property of revocable one-wayness which only requires the adversary to guess the message m. We need this weaker property for intermediate constructions. Like for hiding, we stress that revocable one-wayness does not seem to imply one-wayness.

Definition 2 (Revocably one-way TRE). *Given a revocable timed-release encryption* TRE *with message space M, and an adversary (A_0, A_1, A_2) (that is assumed to be able to keep state between activations of A_0, A_1, A_2) consider the following game G:*

- *Run $A_0()$.*
- *Pick $m \xleftarrow{\$} M$, run $V \leftarrow \text{TRE}(m)$.*
- *Run the revocation protocol of* TRE, *where the sender is honest, and the recipient is $A_1(V)$. Let ok be the output of the sender (i.e., ok $= 1$ if the sender accepts).*
- $m' \leftarrow A_2()$.

A timed-release encryption TRE *with message space M is T-revocably one-way, if for any quantum adversary (A_0, A_1, A_2) where A_1 is sequential-polynomial-time and T-time and A_0, A_2 are sequential-polynomial-time, we have that $\Pr[m = m' \wedge ok = 1 : G]$ is negligible.*

3 Constructing Revocably One-Way TREs

In this section, we present our construction RTRE_{ow} for revocably one-way TREs. Although one-wayness is too weak a property, this serves as a warm-up for our considerably more involved revocably hiding TREs (Section 4), and also as a building block in our random-oracle based construction (Section 5.1).

The following protocol is like we sketched in the introduction, except that we added a one-time pad p. That one-time pad has no effect on the revocable one-wayness, but we introduce because it makes the protocol (non-revocably) hiding at little extra cost.

Definition 3 (Revocably one-way TRE $RTRE_{ow}$)

- *Let n be an integer.*
- *Let TRE_0 be a T-hiding TRE with message space $\{0,1\}^{2n}$.*

We construct a revocable TRE $RTRE_{ow}$ with message space $\{0,1\}^n$.

Encryption *of $m \in \{0,1\}^n$:*

- *Pick $p, B \xleftarrow{\$} \{0,1\}^n$.*
- *Construct the state $|\Psi\rangle := |m \oplus p\rangle_B$. (Recall that $|x\rangle_B$ is x encoded in basis B, see page 134.)*
- *Compute $V_0 \leftarrow TRE_0(B, p)$.*
- *Send V_0 and $|\Psi\rangle$.*

Decryption:

- *Decrypt V_0.*
- *Measure $|\Psi\rangle$ in basis B; call the outcome γ.*
- *Return $m := \gamma \oplus p$.*

Revocation:

- *The recipient sends $|\Psi\rangle$ back to the sender.*
- *The sender measures $|\Psi\rangle$ in basis B; call the outcome γ.*
- *If $\gamma = m \oplus p$, revocation succeeds (sender outputs 1).*

Naive Proof Approach. (In the following discussions, for clarity we omit all occurrences of the one-time pad p.) At a first glance, it seems the security of this protocol should be straightforward to prove: We know that without knowledge of the basis B, one cannot clone the state $|\Psi\rangle$, not even approximately.[5] We also know that until time T, the adversary does not know anything about B (since TRE_0 is T-hiding). Hence the adversary cannot reliably clone $|\Psi\rangle$ before time T. But the adversary would need to do so to pass revocation and still keep a state that allows him to measure m later (when he learns B).

Unfortunately, this argument is not sound. It would be correct if TRE_0 were implemented using a trusted third party (i.e., if B is sent to the adversary after time T).[6] However, the adversary has access to $V_0 = TRE_0(B)$ when trying to clone $|\Psi\rangle$. From the information-theoretical point of view, this is the same as having access to B. Thus the no-cloning theorem and its variants cannot be applied because they rely on the fact that B is *information-theoretically* hidden.

---

[5] This fact also underlies the security of BB84-style QKD protocols [3].

[6] Again, this is implicit in proofs for BB84-style QKD protocols: there the adversary gets a state $|\Psi\rangle = |m\rangle_B$ from Alice (key m encoded in a secret base B), which he has to give back to Bob unchanged (because otherwise Alice and Bob will detect tampering). And he wishes to, at the same time, keep information to later be able to compute the key m when given B.

One might want to save the argument in the following way: Although $V_0 = \mathrm{TRE}_0(B)$ information-theoretically contains B, it is indistinguishable from $\hat{V}_0 = \mathrm{TRE}_0(\hat{B})$ which does not contain B but an independently chosen $\hat{B}$. And if the adversary is given $\hat{V}_0$ instead of V_0, we can use information-theoretical arguments to show that he cannot learn m. But although this argument would work if TRE_0 were hiding against polynomial-time adversaries (e.g., if TRE_0 were a commitment scheme). But TRE_0 is only hiding for T-time adversaries! This only guarantees that all observable events that happen with V_0 *before time T* also happen with $\hat{V}_0$ *before time T* and vice versa. In particular, since with $\hat{V}_0$, the adversary cannot learn m before time T, he cannot learn m before time T with V_0. But although with $\hat{V}_0$, after successful revocation, the adversary provably cannot ever learn m, it might be possible that with V_0, he can learn m right after time T has passed.

Indeed, it is not obvious how to exclude that there is some "encrypted-cloning" procedure that, given $|\Psi\rangle = |m\rangle_B$ and $\mathrm{TRE}_0(B)$, without disturbing $|\Psi\rangle$, produces a state $|\Psi'\rangle$ that for a T-time distinguisher looks like a random state, but still $|\Psi'\rangle$ can be transformed into $|\Psi\rangle$ in time $\gg T$. Such an "encrypted-cloning" would be sufficient for breaking RTRE_{ow}. (Of course, it is a direct corollary from our security proof that such encrypted-cloning is impossible.)[7]

Proof Idea. As we have seen in the preceding discussion, we can prove that the property "the adversary cannot learn m ever" holds when sending $\hat{V}_0 = \mathrm{TRE}_0(\hat{B})$ for an independent $\hat{B}$ instead of $V_0 = \mathrm{TRE}_0(B)$. But we cannot prove that this property carries over to the V_0-setting because it cannot be tested in time T. Examples for properties that do carry over would be "the adversary cannot learn m in time T" or "revocation succeeds" or "when measured in basis B, the adversary's revocation-message does not yield outcome m". But we would like to have a property like "the entropy of m is large (or revocation fails)". That property cannot be tested in time T, so it does not carry over. Yet, we can use a trick to still guarantee that this property holds in the V_0-setting.

For this, we first modify the protocol in an (information-theoretically) indistinguishable way: Normally, we would pick m at random and send $|\Psi\rangle := |m\rangle_B$

---

[7] To illustrate that "encrypted-cloning" is not a far fetched idea, consider the following quite similar revocable TRE: Let $E_K(|\Psi\rangle)$ denote the quantum one-time pad encryption of $|\Psi\rangle \in \mathbb{C}^{2^n}$ using key $K \in \{0,1\}^{2n}$, i.e., $E_K(|\Psi\rangle) = Z^{K_1} X^{K_2} |\Psi\rangle$ with $K = K_1 \| K_2$ [2]. $\mathrm{RTRE}(m) := (E_K(|m\rangle_B), B, \mathrm{TRE}_0(K))$. For revocation, the sender sends $E_K(|m\rangle_B)$ back, and the recipient checks if it is the right state. Again, if K is unknown, it is not possible to clone $E_K(|m\rangle_B)$ as it is effectively a random state even given B. But we can break RTRE as follows:

The recipient measures $|\Phi\rangle := E_K(|m\rangle_B)$ in basis B. Using $XH = HZ$ and $ZH = HX$, we have $|\Phi\rangle = Z^{K_1} X^{K_2} H^B |m\rangle = H^B X^{K_1 * B} Z^{K_1 * \bar{B}} Z^{K_2 * B} X^{K_2 * \bar{B}} |m\rangle = \pm |m \oplus (K_2 * \bar{B}) \oplus (K_1 * B)\rangle_B$ where $*$ is the bit-wise product and $\bar{B}$ the complement of B. Thus the measurement of $|\Phi\rangle$ in basis B does not disturb $|\Phi\rangle$, and the recipient learns $m \oplus (K_1 * B) \oplus (K_2 * \bar{B})$. He can then send back the undisturbed state $|\Phi\rangle$ and pass revocation. After decrypting $\mathrm{TRE}_0(K)$, he can compute m, and reconstruct the state $|\Phi\rangle = E_K(|m\rangle_B)$ using known K, m, B. Thus he performed an "encrypted cloning" of $|\Phi\rangle$ *before* decrypting $\mathrm{TRE}_0(K)$.

to the adversary. Instead, we initialize two n-bit quantum registers X, Y with EPR pairs and send X to the adversary. The value m is computed by measuring Y in basis B. Now we can formulate a new property: "after revocation but before measuring m, XY are still EPR pairs (up to some errors) or revocation fails". This property can be shown to hold in the $\hat{V}_0$-setting using standard information-theoretical tools. And the property tested in time T, all we have to do is a measurement in the Bell basis. Thus the property also holds in the V_0-setting. And finally, due to the monogamy of entanglement ([9]; but we need a custom variant of it) we have that this property implies "the entropy of m is high (or revocation fails)".

We have still to be careful in the details, of course. E.g., the revocation check itself contains a measurement in basis B which would destroy the EPR state XY; this can be fixed by only measuring whether the revocation check would succeeds, without actually measuring m.

Theorem 1 (RTRE$_{ow}$ is revocably one-way). *Let δ_T^{ow} be the time to compute the following things: a measurement whether two n-qubit registers are equal in a given basis B, a measurement whether two n-qubit registers are in an EPR state up to $t := \sqrt{n}$ phase flips and t bit flips, and one NOT- and one AND-gate.*

Assume that the protocol parameter n is superlogarithmic.

The protocol RTRE$_{ow}$ from Definition 3 is $(T - \delta_T^{ow})$-revocably one-way, even if adversary A_2 is unlimited (i.e., after revocation, security holds information-theoretically).

A concrete security bound is derived in the full version [27].

Since revocable one-wayness does not imply (non-revocable) one-wayness, we additionally show the hiding property of RTRE$_{ow}$. Due to the presence of the one-time pad p, the proof is unsurprising.

4   Revocably Hiding TREs

We now turn to the problem of constructing revocably hiding TREs. The construction from the previous section is revocably one-way, but it is certainly not revocably hiding because the adversary might be lucky enough to guess a few bits of the basis B, measure the corresponding bits of the message m without modifying the state, and successfully pass revocation. So some bits of m will necessarily leak. The most natural approach for dealing with partial leakage (at least in the case of QKD) is to use privacy amplification. That is, we pick a function F from a suitable family of functions (say, universal hash functions with suitable parameters), and then to send m, we encrypt a random x using the revocably one-way TRE, and additionally transmit $F(x) \oplus m$. If x has sufficiently high min-entropy, $F(x)$ will look random, and thus $F(x) \oplus m$ will not leak anything about m. Additionally, we need to transmit F to the recipient, in a way that the adversary does not have access to it when measuring the quantum state. Thus, we have to include F in the classical TRE. So, altogether, we would send $(m \oplus F(x), \text{TRE}_0(B, f))$ and $|m\rangle_B$. In fact, this scheme might be secure, we do not have an attack. Yet, when it comes to proving its security, we face difficulties: In the proof of RTRE_{ow}, to use the hiding property of TRE_0, we identified a property that can be checked in time T, and that guarantees that m cannot be guessed. (Namely, we used that the registers XY contain EPR pairs up to some errors which implies that the adversary cannot predict the outcome m of measuring Y.) In the present case, we would need more. We need a property P that guarantees that $F(x)$ is indistinguishable from random given the adversary's state when x is the outcome of measuring Y. Note that here it is not sufficient to just use that x has high min-entropy and that F is a strong randomness extractor; at the point when we test the property P, F is already fixed and thus not random. Instead, we have to find a measurable property P' that guarantees: For the particular value F chosen in the game, $F(x)$ is indistinguishable from randomness. (And additionally, we need that P' holds with overwhelming probability when $\text{TRE}_0(B, f)$ is replaced by a fake TRE not containing B, f.) We were not able to identify such a property.[8]

Using CSS Codes. This discussion shows that, when we try to use privacy amplification, we encounter the challenge how to transmit the hash function F. Yet, in the context of QKD, there is a second approach for ensuring that the final key does not leak any information: Instead of first exchanging a raw key and then applying privacy amplification to it, Shor and Preskill [24] present a protocol where Alice and Bob first create shared EPR pairs with a low number of errors. In our language: Alice and Bob share a superposition of states $|\widetilde{fe}\rangle$ with $\omega(f), \omega(e) \leqslant t$. Then they use the fact that, roughly speaking, $|\widetilde{0^n 0^n}\rangle$ is an encoding of $|\widetilde{0^\ell 0^\ell}\rangle$ for some $\ell < n$ using a random CSS code correcting t bit/phase error. (Calderbank-Shor-Steane codes [8,25].) So if Alice and Bob apply error correction and decoding to $|\widetilde{fe}\rangle$, they get the state $|\widetilde{0^\ell 0^\ell}\rangle$. Then, if Alice and Bob measure that state, they get identical and uniformly distributed keys, and the adversary has no information. Furthermore, the resulting protocol can be seen to be equivalent to one that does not need quantum codes (and

---

[8] To illustrate the difficulty of identifying such a property: Call a function F s-good if $F(x)$ is uniformly random if all bits x_i with $s_i = 0$ are uniformly random (and independent). In other words, F tolerates leakage of the bits with $s_i = 1$. For suitable families of functions F, and for s with low Hamming weight, a random F will be s-good with high probability. Furthermore, when using a fake TRE_0, XY is in state $|\widetilde{fe}\rangle$ with $s := (f \vee e)$ of low Hamming weight with overwhelming probability after successful revocation (this we showed in the security proof for RTRE_{ow}). In this case, all bits of Y with $s_i = 0$ will be "untampered" and we expect that $F(x)$ is uniformly random for s-good F (when x is the outcome of measuring Y). So we are tempted to choose P' as: "XY is in a superposition of states $|\widetilde{fe}\rangle$ such that the chosen F is $(f \vee e)$-good". This property holds with overwhelming property using a fake TRE_0. But unfortunately, this fails to guarantee that $f(x)$ is random. E.g., if $F(ab) = a \oplus b$, then F is 10-good and 01-good. Thus a superposition of $|\widetilde{10\,00}\rangle$ and $|\widetilde{01\,00}\rangle$ satisfies property P' for that F. But $\frac{1}{\sqrt{2}}|\widetilde{10\,00}\rangle + \frac{1}{\sqrt{2}}|\widetilde{01\,00}\rangle = \frac{1}{\sqrt{2}}|0000\rangle - \frac{1}{\sqrt{2}}|1111\rangle$, so $x \in \{00, 11\}$ with probability 1 and thus $F(x) = 0$ always. So P' fails to guarantee that $F(x)$ is random.

thus quantum computers) but only transmits and measures individual qubits (BB84-style). It turns out that we can apply the same basic idea to revocably hiding TREs.

For understanding the following proof sketch, it is not necessary to understand details of CSS codes. It is only important to know that for any CSS code C, there is a family of disjoint codes $C_{u,v}$ such that $\bigcup_{u,v} C_{u,v}$ forms an orthonormal basis of $\mathbb{C}^{\{0,1\}^n}$.

Consider the following protocol (simplified):

Definition 4 (Simplified protocol RTRE'_{hid}). *Let C be a CSS code on $\{0,1\}^n$ that encodes plaintexts from a set $\{0,1\}^m$ and that corrects t phase and bit flips. Let q be a parameter.*

- **Encryption:** *Create $q+n$ EPR pairs in registers X,Y. Pick a set $Q = \{i_1,\ldots,i_q\} \in [q+n]_q$ of qubit pair indices and a basis $B \in \{0,1\}^q$, and designate the qubit pairs in XY selected by Q as "test bits" in basis B. (The remaining pairs in XY will be considered as an encoding of EPR pairs using C.) Send X together with the description of C and a hiding TRE $\mathrm{TRE}_0(Q)$ to the recipient.*

  The plaintext contained in the TRE is x where x results from: Consider the bits of Y that are not in Q as a codeword from one of the codes $C_{u,v}$. Measure what u,v are (this is possible since the $C_{u,v}$ are orthogonal). Decode the code word. Measure the result in the computational basis.

- **Decryption:** *Decrypt $\mathrm{TRE}_0(Q)$. Considering the bits of X that are not in Q as a codeword from $C_{u,v}$ and decode and measure as in the encryption.*

- **Revocation:** *Send back X. The sender measures the bit pairs from XY selected by Q using bases B, yielding r,r'. If $r = r'$, revocation succeeds.*

Note that this simplified protocol is a "randomized" TRE which does not allow us to encrypt an arbitrary message, but instead chooses the message x. The obvious approach to transform it to a normal TRE for encrypting a given message m is to send $m \oplus x$ in addition to the TRE. This is indeed what we do, but there are some difficulties that we discuss below.

Entanglement-Free Protocol. The protocol RTRE'_{hid} requires Alice to prepare EPR pairs and apply the decoding operation of CSS codes. While our protocol may not be feasible with current technology anyway due to the required quantum memory, we wish to reduce the technological requirements as much as possible. Fortunately, CSS codes have the nice property that decoding with subsequent measurement in the computational basis is equivalent to a sequence of individual qubit measurements. Using these properties, we can rewrite Alice so that she only sends and measures individual qubits in BB84 bases, and Bob stores and measures individual qubits in BB84 bases (i.e., like in RTRE_{ow}). See the final protocol description (Definition 5) below for details. In the full proof, this change means that we have to add further games in front of the sequence of games to rewrite the entanglement-free operations into EPR-pair based ones.

Early Key Revelation. One big problem remains: the security definition used for proving security of Definition 4 gives $m_b \oplus x$ to A_2, and not to A_1 as a natural definition of randomized TREs would do. (We call this *late key revelation*) The effect of this is that RTRE'_{hid} is only secure if the plaintext x is not used before time T. This limitation, of course, contradicts the purpose of TREs and needs to be removed. We need *early key revelation* where the adversary A_1 is given $m_b \oplus x$. As our proof needs the fact that x is picked only after A_1 runs, our solution is to reduce security with early key revelation to security with late key revelation. This is done by guessing what x will be when invoking A_1. If that guess turns out incorrect in the end, we abort the game. Unfortunately, this reduction multiplies the advantage of the adversary by a factor of $2^{|x|} = 2^{\ell}$; the effect is that our final protocol will need an underlying scheme TRE_0 with security exponential in ℓ.

We can now present the precise protocol and its security:

Definition 5 (The protocol)

- Let C_1, C_2 be a *CSS code with parameters* n, k_1, k_2, t. *(n is the bit length of the codes, k_1, k_2 refer to the parameters of the codes C_1, C_2, and t to the number of corrected errors.)*
- Let q be an integer.
- Let TRE_0 be a TRE with message space $\{0,1\}^q \times [q+n]_q \times C_1/C_2$. *(Recall, $[q+n]_q$ refers to q-size subsets of $\{1,\dots,q+n\}$, see page 133. C_1/C_2 denotes the quotient of codes.)*

We construct a revocable TRE RTRE_{hid} with message space C_1/C_2 *(isomorphic to $\{0,1\}^{\ell}$ with $\ell := k_1 - k_2$).*

We **encrypt** a message $m \in C_1/C_2$ as follows:
- *Pick uniformly* $B \in \{0,1\}^q$, $Q \in [q+n]_q$, $p \in C_1/C_2$. $u \in \{0,1\}^n/C_1$, $r \in \{0,1\}^q$, $x \in C_1/C_2$, $w \in C_2$.
- *Construct the state* $|\Psi\rangle := U_Q^{\dagger}(H^B \otimes I_n)(|r\rangle \otimes |x \oplus w \oplus u\rangle)$. *Here U_Q denotes the unitary that permutes the qubits in Q into the first half of the system. (I.e., $U_Q|x_1 \dots x_{q+n}\rangle = |x_{a_1} \dots x_{a_q} x_{b_1} \dots x_{b_n}\rangle$ with $Q =: \{a_1, \dots, a_q\}$ and $\{1, \dots, q+n\}\backslash Q =: \{b_1, \dots, b_n\}$; the relative order of the a_i and of the b_i does not matter.)*[9]
- *Compute* $V_0 \leftarrow \mathrm{TRE}_0(B, Q, r, p)$.
- *The TRE consists of* $(V_0, u, m \oplus x \oplus p)$ *and* $|\Psi\rangle$.

Decryption *is performed as follows:*
- *Decrypt V_0, this gives* B, Q, r, p.
- *Apply U_Q to $|\Psi\rangle$ and measure the last n qubits in the computational basis; call the outcome γ.*[10]
- *Return* $m := (\gamma \oplus u) \bmod C_2$.

The **revocation** *protocol is the following:*
- *The recipient sends $|\Psi\rangle$ back to the sender.*

---

[9] Notice that, since $U_Q^{\dagger}$ is just a reordering of qubits, and H^B is a sequence of Hadamards applied to a known basis state, the state $|\Psi\rangle$ can also directly be produced by encoding individual qubits in the computational or diagonal basis, which is technologically simpler.

[10] Since U_Q is just a reordering of qubits, this just corresponds to measuring a subset of the qubits in the computational basis.

- *The sender applies $(H^B \otimes I_n)U_Q$ to $|\Psi\rangle$ and measures the first q qubits, call the outcome r'.*[11]
- *If $r = r'$, revocation succeeds (sender outputs 1).*

Notice that in this protocol (and in contrast to the simplified description above), we have included B, r in the TRE V_0, even though they are not needed by the recipient. In fact, the protocol would still work (and be secure with almost unmodified proof) if we did not include these values. However, when constructing unknown recipient encryption, the inclusion of B, r will turn out to be useful.

Theorem 2 (RTRE$_{hid}$ is revocably hiding). *Let δ_T^{hid} be the time to compute the following things: q controlled Hadamard gates, applying an already computed permutation to $n + q$ qubits, a q-qubit measurement in the computational basis (called M_R in the proof), a comparison of two q-qubit strings, the error-correction/decoding operations U_{uv}^{EC}, U_{uv}^{dec} of the CSS code, a measurement whether two n-qubit registers are in the state $\sum_{x \in C_1/C_2} |x\rangle|x\rangle$ (called P_{C_1/C_2}^{EPR} in the proof), one AND-gate, and one NOT-gate.*

Assume that TRE_0 is T-hiding with $(2^{-2(k_1-k_2)} \cdot negligible)$-security.[12] *Assume that $tq/(q + n) - 4(k_1 - k_2) \ln 2$ is superlogarithmic.*

Then the TRE from Definition 5 is $(T - \delta_T^{hid})$-revocably hiding even if A_2 is unlimited (i.e., after revocation, security holds information-theoretically).

A concrete security bound is derived in the full version [27].

Those parameters can always be instantiated [27], leading to a revocable TRE for logarithmic length messages, and a TRE for arbitrary length messages if TRE_0 has exponential security. Furthermore, RTRE$_{hid}$ is also T-hiding.

5   TREs in the Random Oracle Model

We present constructions and transformations of TREs in the random oracle model. (We use the quantum random oracle that can be accessed in superposition, cf. [5].)

The results in this section will be formulated with respect to two different timing models. In the *sequential oracle-query timing model*, one oracle query is one time step. I.e., if we say an adversary runs in time T, this means he performs at most T random oracle queries. In the *parallel oracle-query timing model*, an arbitrary number of parallel oracle-queries can be performed in one time step. However, in time T, at most T oracle queries that depend on each other may be performed.[13] More formally, if the oracle is H, the adversary can query $H(x_1), \ldots, H(x_q)$ for arbitrarily large q and arbitrary $x_1, \ldots, x_n$ in each

---

[11] Since U_Q is just a reordering of the qubits, this is equivalent to measuring a subset of the qubits in the bases specified by B.

[12] I.e., in Definition 1, we require that the advantage is not only negligible, but actually $\leqslant 2^{-2(k_1-k_2)}\mu$ for some negligible μ.

[13] In [16], this is called "T levels of adaptivity".

time step. (Of course, if the adversary is additionally sequential-polynomial-time, then q will be polynomially bounded.)

Security in those timing models implies security in timing models that count actual (sequential/parallel) computation steps because in each step, at most one oracle call can be made.

5.1   One-Way to Hiding

In the previous section, we have seen how to construct revocably hiding TREs. However, the construction was relatively complex and came with an exponential security loss in the reduction. As an alternative, we present a transformation takes a TRE that is (revocably) one-way and transforms it into one that is (revocably) hiding in the random oracle model. The basic idea is straightforward: we encrypt a key k in a one-way TRE, and use $H(k)$ as a one-time-pad to encrypt the message:

Theorem 3 (Hiding TREs). *Let H be a random oracle and let* TRE *be a (revocable or non-revocable) TRE (not using H).*

Then the TRE TRE' *encrypts m as follows: Run $k \xleftarrow{\$} \{0,1\}^n$, $V' \leftarrow \text{TRE}(k)$, and then return $V := (V', m \oplus H(k))$. (Decryption is analogous, and revocation is unchanged from* TRE.*)*

Then, if TRE *is T-oneway and T-revocably one-way then* TRE' *is T-revocably hiding. And if* TRE *is T-oneway then* TRE' *is T-hiding. (The same holds "without offline-queries"; see Section 5.2 below.)*

This holds both for the parallel and the sequential oracle-query timing model.[14]

Notice that we assume that TRE does not access H. Otherwise simple counterexamples can be constructed. (E.g., TRE(k) could include $H(k)$ in the TRE V'.) However, TRE may access another random oracle, say G, and TRE' then uses both G and H.

In a classical setting, this theorem would be straightforward to prove (using lazy sampling of the random oracle). Yet, in the quantum setting, we need a new technique for dealing with this. We present a generic lemma for reducing hiding-style properties (semantic security) to a one-wayness-style properties (unpredictability) from which we can derive Theorem 3.

5.2   Precomputation

We will now develop a second transformation for TREs in the random oracle model. The security definition for TREs permit the adversary to run an arbitrary (sequential-polynomial-time) computation before receiving the TRE. In particular, we do not have a good upper bound on the number of oracle queries performed in this precomputation phase ("offline queries"). This can make proofs harder because even if the adversary runs in time T, this does not allow us to conclude that only T oracle queries will be performed. Our transformation will allow us to transform a TRE that is only secure when the adversary makes no offline queries (such as the one presented in Section 5.3 below) into a TRE that is secure without this restriction.

We call a TRE T-*hiding without offline-queries* if the hiding property holds for adversaries were A_0 makes no random oracle queries. Analogously we define T-*revocably hiding without offline-queries* and T-*one-way without offline-queries*.

To transform a TRE that is secure without offline-queries into a fully secure one, the idea is to make sure that the offline-queries are useless for the adversary. We do this by using only a part $H(a\|\cdot)$ of the random oracle where a is chosen randomly with the TRE. Intuitively, since during the offline-phase, the adversary does not know a, none of his offline-queries will be of the form $H(a\|\cdot)$, thus they are useless.

Theorem 4 (TREs with offline-queries). *Let G and H be random oracles and ℓ superlogarithmic. Let* TRE *be a revocable TRE using G. Let* TRE$'$ *be the result of replacing in* TRE *all oracle queries $G(x)$ by queries $H(a\|x)$, where a is chosen by the encryption algorithm of* TRE$'$ *and is included in the message send to the recipient.*

If TRE *is T-revocably hiding without offline-queries then* TRE$'$ *is T-revocably hiding (and analogously for T-hiding). This holds both for the parallel and the sequential oracle-query timing model.*[14]

To prove this, we develop a general lemma for this kind of transformations. (In the classical setting this is simple using the lazy sampling proof technique, but that is not available in the quantum setting.)

5.3 Iterated Hashing

In all constructions so far we assumed that we already have a (non-revocable) TRE. In the classical setting, only two constructions of TREs are known. The one from [22] can be broken by factoring, this leaves only repeated hashing as a candidate for the quantum setting. We prove that the following construction to be one-way without offline queries:

Definition 6 (Iterated hashing). *Let n and T be polynomially-bounded integers (depending on the security parameter), and assume that n is superlogarithmic. Let $H : \{0,1\}^n \to \{0,1\}^n$ denote the random oracle. The timed-release encryption* TRE$_{ih}$ *with message space $\{0,1\}^n$ encrypts m as $V := H^{T+1}(0^n) \oplus m$.*

We can prove that TRE$_{ih}$ is T-one-way *without* offline queries. TRE$_{ih}$ is obviously not one-way *with* offline queries, the adversary can precompute $H^{T+1}(0^n)$. Yet, using the random-oracle transformations from Theorems 3 and 4, we can transform it into a hiding TRE. This is plugged into RTRE$_{ow}$, to get a revocably one-way TRE, and using Theorem 3 again, we get a revocably hiding TRE in the random oracle model. (The resulting protocol is spelled out in the full version [27].)

---

[14] For other timing models, the reduction described in the proof may incur a overhead, leading to a smaller T for TRE$'$.

An alternative construction is to plug TRE_{ih} (after transforming it using Theorems 3 and 4) into $RTRE_{hid}$. This results in a more complex yet everlastingly secure scheme.

And finally, if we wish to avoid the random oracle model altogether, we can take as our basic assumption that a suitable variant of iterated hashing[15] is a hiding TRE, and get a revocably hiding, everlastingly secure TRE by plugging it into $RTRE_{hid}$.

Acknowledgements. Dominique Unruh was supported by the Estonian ICT program 2011-2015 (3.2.1201.13-0022), the European Union through the European Regional Development Fund through the sub-measure "Supporting the development of R&D of info and communication technology", by the European Social Fund's Doctoral Studies and Internationalisation Programme DoRa, by the Estonian Centre of Excellence in Computer Science, EXCS. We thank Sébastien Gambs for the suggesting the data retention application.

References

1. Alleaume, R., Bouda, J., Branciard, C., Debuisschert, T., Dianati, M., Gisin, N., Godfrey, M., Grangier, P., Langer, T., Leverrier, A., Lutkenhaus, N., Painchault, P., Peev, M., Poppe, A., Pornin, T., Rarity, J., Renner, R., Ribordy, G., Riguidel, M., Salvail, L., Shields, A., Weinfurter, H., Zeilinger, A.: Secoqc white paper on quantum key distribution and cryptography. arXiv:quant-ph/0701168v1 (2007)
2. Ambainis, A., Mosca, M., Tapp, A., Wolf, R.: Private quantum channels. In: FOCS 2000, pp. 547–553. IEEE (2000)
3. Bennett, C.H., Brassard, G.: Quantum cryptography: Public-key distribution and coin tossing. In: Proceedings of IEEE International Conference on Computers, Systems and Signal Processing 1984, pp. 175–179. IEEE Computer Society (1984)
4. Bitansky, N., Canetti, R., Chiesa, A., Tromer, E.: From extractable collision resistance to succinct non-interactive arguments of knowledge, and back again. In: ITCS 2012, pp. 326–349. ACM, New York (2012)
5. Boneh, D., Dagdelen, Ö., Fischlin, M., Lehmann, A., Schaffner, C., Zhandry, M.: Random oracles in a quantum world. In: Lee, D.H., Wang, X. (eds.) ASIACRYPT 2011. LNCS, vol. 7073, pp. 41–69. Springer, Heidelberg (2011)
6. Boneh, D., Naor, M.: Timed commitments. In: Bellare, M. (ed.) CRYPTO 2000. LNCS, vol. 1880, pp. 236–254. Springer, Heidelberg (2000)
7. Cachin, C., Maurer, U.: Unconditional security against memory-bounded adversaries. In: Kaliski Jr., B.S. (ed.) CRYPTO 1997. LNCS, vol. 1294, pp. 292–306. Springer, Heidelberg (1997)
8. Calderbank, A.R., Shor, P.W.: Good quantum error-correcting codes exist. Phys. Rev. A 54, 1098 (1996), http://arxiv.org/abs/quant-ph/9512032v2
9. Coffman, V., Kundu, J., Wootters, W.K.: Distributed entanglement. Phys. Rev. A 61, 052306 (2000)

---

[15] E.g., $(a, H^{T+2}(a) \oplus m)$ for random a. Or the protocol resulting from applying Theorems 3 and 4 to Definition 6. That this is a realistic assumption for suitable hash functions is confirmed by our analysis in the random oracle model.

10. Damgård, I., Fehr, S., Salvail, L., Schaffner, C.: Cryptography in the bounded quantum-storage model. In: FOCS 2005, pp. 449–458 (2005), Full version is arXiv:quant-ph/0508222v2
11. Dingledine, R., Mathewson, N., Syverson, P.: Tor: the second-generation onion router. In: USENIX 2004, SSYM 2004, p. 21. USENIX Association, Berkeley (2004)
12. Dupuis, F., Nielsen, J.B., Salvail, L.: Actively secure two-party evaluation of any quantum operation. In: Safavi-Naini, R., Canetti, R. (eds.) CRYPTO 2012. LNCS, vol. 7417, pp. 794–811. Springer, Heidelberg (2012)
13. Einstein, A., Podolsky, B., Rosen, N.: Can quantum-mechanical description of physical reality be considered complete? Phys. Rev. 47, 777–780 (1935)
14. European Parliament & Council. Directive 2006/24/ec, directive on the retention of data generated or processed in connection with the provision of publicly available electronic communications services or of public communications networks. Official Journal of the European Union L 105, 54–63 (2006), http://eur-lex.europa.eu/LexUriServ/LexUriServ.do?uri=OJ:L:2006:105:0054:0063:EN:PDF
15. Khodjasteh, K., Sastrawan, J., Hayes, D., Green, T.J., Biercuk, M.J., Viola, L.: Designing a practical high-fidelity long-time quantum memory. Nature Communications 4 (2013)
16. Mahmoody, M., Moran, T., Vadhan, S.: Time-lock puzzles in the random oracle model. In: Rogaway, P. (ed.) CRYPTO 2011. LNCS, vol. 6841, pp. 39–50. Springer, Heidelberg (2011)
17. Müller-Quade, J., Unruh, D. (January 2007), http://eprint.iacr.org/2006/422
18. Nielsen, M., Chuang, I.: Quantum Computation and Quantum Information, 10th anniversary edn. Cambridge University Press, Cambridge (2010)
19. Palmer, E.: Wikileaks backup plan could drop diplomatic bomb. CBS News (December 2010), http://www.cbsnews.com/stories/2010/12/02/eveningnews/main7111845.shtml
20. Rabin, M.O.: Hyper-encryption by virtual satellite. Science Center Research Lecture Series (December 2003), http://athome.harvard.edu/programs/hvs/
21. Rivest, R.: Description of the LCS35 time capsule crypto-puzzle (April 1999), http://people.csail.mit.edu/rivest/lcs35-puzzle-description.txt
22. Rivest, R.L., Shamir, A., Wagner, D.A.: Time-lock puzzles and timed-release crypto. Technical Report MIT/LCS/TR-684, Massachusetts Institute of Technology (February 1996), http://theory.lcs.mit.edu/~rivest/RivestShamirWagner-timelock.ps
23. Shor, P.W.: Algorithms for quantum computation: Discrete logarithms and factoring. In: 35th Annual Symposium on Foundations of Computer Science, Proceedings of FOCS 1994, pp. 124–134. IEEE Computer Society (1994)
24. Shor, P.W., Preskill, J.: Simple proof of security of the BB84 quantum key distribution protocol. Phys. Rev. Lett. 85, 441–444 (2000)
25. Steane, A.M.: Multiple particle interference and quantum error correction. Proc. R. Soc. London A 452, 2551–2576 (1996)
26. Unruh, D.: Protokollkomposition und Komplexität (Protocol Composition and Complexity). PhD thesis, Universität Karlsruhe (TH), Berlin (2006), http://www.cs.ut.ee/~unruh/publications/unruh07protokollkomposition.html (in German)
27. Unruh, D.: Revocable quantum timed-release encryption. IACR ePrint 2013/606 (2013) (full version of this paper)

Generic Universal Forgery Attack
on Iterative Hash-Based MACs

Thomas Peyrin and Lei Wang

Division of Mathematical Sciences, School of Physical and Mathematical Sciences,
Nanyang Technological University, Singapore
thomas.peyrin@gmail.com, wang.lei@ntu.edu.sg

Abstract. In this article, we study the security of iterative hash-based MACs, such as HMAC or NMAC, with regards to universal forgery attacks. Leveraging recent advances in the analysis of functional graphs built from the iteration of HMAC or NMAC, we exhibit the very first generic universal forgery attack against hash-based MACs. In particular, our work implies that the universal forgery resistance of an n-bit output HMAC construction is not 2^n queries as long believed by the community. The techniques we introduce extend the previous functional graphs-based attacks that only took in account the cycle structure or the collision probability: we show that one can extract much more meaningful secret information by also analyzing the distance of a node from the cycle of its component in the functional graph.

Keywords: HMAC, NMAC, hash function, universal forgery.

1 Introduction

A message authentication code (MAC) is a crucial symmetric-key cryptographic primitive, which provides both authenticity and integrity for messages. It takes a k-bit secret key K and an arbitrary long message M as inputs, and produces an n-bit tag. In the classical scenario, the sender sends both a message M and a tag $T = \text{MAC}(K, M)$ to the receiver, where the secret key K is shared between the sender and the receiver prior to the communication. Then, the receiver computes another tag value $T' = \text{MAC}(K, M)$ using her own key K, and matches T' to the received T. If a match occurs, the receiver is ensured that M was indeed sent by the sender and has not been tampered with by a third party.

There are several ways to build a MAC from other symmetric-key cryptographic primitives, but a very popular approach is to use a hash function. In particular, a well-known example is HMAC [2], designed by Bellare, Canetti and Krawczyk in 1996. HMAC has been internationally standardized by ANSI, IETF, ISO and NIST, and is widely implemented in various worldwide security protocols such as SSL, TLS, IPSec, etc.

Being cryptographic objects, MACs should satisfy various security requirements and the classical notions are key recovery resistance and unforgeability:

P.Q. Nguyen and E. Oswald (Eds.): EUROCRYPT 2014, LNCS 8441, pp. 147–164, 2014.

- *Key recovery resistance*: it should be practically infeasible for an adversary to recover the value of the secret key.

- *Unforgeability*: it should be practically infeasible for an adversary to generate a message and tag pair (M, T) such that T is a valid tag for M and such that M has not been queried to MAC previously by the adversary.

In the case of an ideal MAC, the attacker should not be able to recover the key in less than 2^k computations, nor to forge a valid MAC in less than 2^n computations. Depending on the control of the attacker over the message, one discriminates between two types of forgery attacks: existential forgery and universal forgery attack. In the former case, the attacker can fully choose the message M for which he will forge a valid tag T, while in the later case he will be challenged to a certain message M and must find the MAC tag value T for this particular message. In other words, universal forgery asks the attacker to be able to forge a valid MAC on any message, and as such is a much more powerful attack than existential forgery and would lead to much more damaging effects in practice. Yet, because this security notion is easier to break, most published attacks on MACs concern existential forgery.

Moreover, cryptographers have also proposed a few extra security notions with respect to distinguishing games such as distinguishing-R and distinguishing-H [12]. The goal of a distinguishing-R attack is to distinguish a MAC scheme from a monolithic random oracle, while the goal of a distinguishing-H attack is to distinguish hash function-based MACs (resp. block cipher and operating mode-based MACs) instantiated with either a known dedicated compression function (resp. a dedicated block cipher) or a random function (resp. a random block cipher). While these distinguishers provide better understanding of the security margin, the impact to the practical security of a MAC scheme would be rather limited.

Given the importance of HMAC in practice, it is only natural that many researchers have analyzed the security of this algorithm and of hash-based MACs in general. On one hand, cryptographers are devoted to find reduction-based security proofs to provide lower security bound. Usually a MAC based on a hash function with a l-bit internal state is proven secure up to the bound $O(2^{l/2})$. Examples include security proofs for HMAC, NMAC and Sandwich-MAC [2,1,25]. Namely, it is guaranteed that no generic attack succeeds with a complexity below the security bound $O(2^{l/2})$ (when $l \leq 2n$) in the single-key model.

On the other hand, cryptographers are also continuously searching for generic attacks to get upper security bound for hash-based MACs, since the gap between the $2^{l/2}$ lower bound and the best known generic attacks is still very large for several security properties. The cases of existential forgery and distinguishing-R attacks are tight: in [17], Preneel and van Oorschot proposed generic distinguishing-R and existential forgery attacks with a complexity of $O(2^{l/2})$ computations. Their methods are based on the generation of internal collisions which are detectable on the MAC output due to the length extension property of the inner iterated hash function (one can generate an existential forgery by simply looking for an internal collision in the hash chain and then, given any pair of messages using this internal collision as prefix, it is easy to forge the tag for one message by querying the other message to the tag oracle).

In [16] Peyrin *et al.* utilized the cycle property of HMAC in the related-key model to distinguish it from a random mapping and eventually described generic distinguishing-R attack with a complexity of only $O(2^{n/2})$ computations (note that these related-key attacks do not contradict the $O(2^{l/2})$ security proof which was provided in the single-key model only). A similar weakness was independently pointed out by Dodis *et al.* in the context of indifferentiabiity of HMAC [5]. One year after, leveraging the ideas of cycle detection in functional graphs from [16], Leurent *et al.* [14] showed that, contrary to the community belief, there exists a generic distinguishing-H attack requiring only $O(2^{l/2})$ computations on iterative hash-based MACs in the single-key model. All security bounds on iterative hash-based MACs are therefore tight, except the case of universal forgery for which the best generic attack still requires 2^n computations and it remains unknown exactly where the security lies between 2^n and $\min\{2^{l/2}, 2^n\}$ computations.

Besides generic attacks, cryptanalysts also evaluated MACs based on (standardized) dedicated hash functions, mainly by exploiting some weakness of the compression function [3,12,8,23,19,20,13,24,26,22,9]. The details of such attacks will be omitted in the rest of this article, since we deal with generic attacks irrespective to the specifications of the internal compression function.

Our Contribution. In this article, we describe the first generic universal forgery attack on iterative hash-based MACs, requiring less then 2^n computations. More precisely, our attack complexity is $O(\max(2^{l-s}, 2^{5l/6}, 2^s))$, where 2^s represents the block length of the challenge message. In other words, for reasonable message sizes, the complexity directly decreases along with an increase of s, up to a message size of $2^{l/6}$ where the complexity hits a plateau at $2^{5l/6}$ computations. Previously known attacks and proven bounds are summarized in Table 1 and we emphasize that this is the first generic universal forgery attack on HMAC in the single key model (except the trivial 2^n brute force attack). For example, a corollary to our work is that HMAC instantiated with the standardized hash function RIPEMD-160 [4] (or MD5 [21] and RIPEMD-128 [4]), which allows arbitrarily long input messages (this conditions is needed since even though the challenge message can have a small length, we will need to be able to query $2^{l/2}$-block long messages during the attack), only provides a $2^{133.3}$ (resp. $2^{106.7}$) computations security with regards to universal forgery attacks, while it was long believed that the full 2^{160} (resp. 2^{128}) was holding for this strong security property.

Moreover, our techniques are novel as they show that one can extract much more meaningful secret information than by just analyzing the cycle structure or the collision probability of the functional graphs of the MAC algorithm, as was done previously [16,14]. Indeed, the distance of a node from the cycle of its components in the functional graph is a very valuable information to know for an attacker, and we expect even more complex types of information to be exploitable by attackers against iterative hash-based MACs.

Table 1. We summarize the security state of HMAC (with $n \leq l \leq 2n$) including previous results and our universal forgery attacks. Notation max() is to choose the largest value.

security notion	single key setting		related-key setting
	provable security	generic attack	generic attack
Distinguishing-R	$O(2^{l/2})$ [2,1]	$O(2^{l/2})$ [17]	$O(2^{n/2})$ [16]
Distinguishing-H	$O(2^{l/2})$ [2,1]	$O(2^{l/2})$ [14]	$O(2^{n/2} + 2^{l-n})$ † [16]
Existential forgery	$O(2^{l/2})$ [2,1]	$O(2^{l/2})$ [17]	$O(2^{n/2} + 2^{l-n})$ † [16]
Universal forgery	$O(2^{l/2})$ [2,1]	previous: $O(2^n)$ new: $O(\max(2^{l-s}, 2^{5l/6}, 2^s))$ ‡	

†: the attacks have complexity advantage with $n < l < 2n$;
‡: 2^s is the blocks length of the challenge message. The attack has complexity advantage with $n \leq l < 6n/5$.

2   Description of NMAC and HMAC

A Hash Function. H maps arbitrarily long messages to an n-bit digest. It is usually built by iterating a fixed input length compression function f, which maps inputs of $l + b$ bits to outputs of l bits (note that $l \geq n$). In details, H first pads an input message M to be a multiple of b bits, then splits it into blocks of b bits $m_0 || m_1 || \cdots || m_{s-1}$, and calls the compression function f iteratively to process these blocks. Finally, H might use a finalization function g that maps l bits to n bits in order to produce the hash digest.

$$x_0 = IV \qquad x_{i+1} = f(x_i, m_i) \qquad \texttt{hashdigest} = g(x_s)$$

Each of the chaining variables x_i are l bits long, and IV (initial value) is a public constant.

NMAC algorithm [2] keys a hash function H by replacing the public IV with a secret key K, which is denoted as H_K. It then uses two l-bit secret keys K_{in} and K_{out} referred to as the inner and the outer keys respectively, and makes two calls to the hash function H. NMAC is simply defined to process an input message M as:

$$\text{NMAC}(K_{out}, K_{in}, M) = H_{K_{out}}(H_{K_{in}}(M)).$$

The keyed hash functions $H_{K_{in}}$ and $H_{K_{out}}$ are referred to as the inner and the outer hash functions respectively.

HMAC algorithm [2] is a single-key variant of NMAC, depicted in Figure 1. It derives K_{in} and K_{out} from the single secret key K as:

$$K_{in} = f(IV, K \oplus \texttt{ipad}) \qquad\qquad K_{out} = f(IV, K \oplus \texttt{opad})$$

where ipad and opad are two distinct public constants. HMAC is then simply defined to process an input message M as:

$$\text{HMAC}(K, M) = H(K \oplus \text{opad} \| H(K \oplus \text{ipad} \| M)))$$

where $\|$ denotes the concatenation operation. It is interesting to note that HMAC can use any key size. If the key K is shorter than b bits, then it is padded with 0 bits to reach the size b of an entire message block. Otherwise, if the key K is longer than b bits, then it is hashed and then padded with 0 bits: $K \leftarrow H(K) \| 0^{b-n}$.

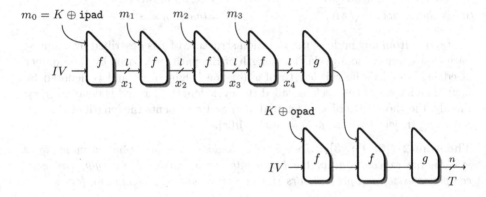

Fig. 1. HMAC with an iterated hash function with compression function f, and output function g

For simplicity, in the rest of this article we will describe the attacks based on the utilization of the HMAC algorithm. However, we emphasize that our methods apply similarly to hash-based MACs such as NMAC [2], Sandwich-MAC [25], etc.

3   Previous Functional-Graph-Based Attacks for HMAC

Our universal forgery attack is based on recent advances in hash-based MACs cryptanalysis [16,14] and in this section we quickly recall these methods and explain how we extend them. First of all, we need to introduce the notion of functional graph and the various properties that can be observed from it.

The functional graph $\mathcal{G}_f$ of a function $f : \{0,1\}^l \rightarrow \{0,1\}^l$ is simply the directed graph in which the vertices (or nodes) are all the values in $\{0,1\}^l$ and where the directed edges are the iterations of f (i.e. a directed edge from a vertex a to a vertex b exists iff $f(a) = b$). The functional graph of a function is composed of one or several components, each having its own internal cycle.

For a random function, the functional graph will possess several statistical properties that have been extensively studied. For example, it is to be noted that with high probability the functional graph of a random function will have a logarithmic number of components and among them there is one giant component that covers most of the nodes. In addition, this giant component will contain a giant tree in which are present about a third of the nodes of $\mathcal{G}_f$. Theorems 1 and 2 state these remarks in a more formal way.

Theorem 1 ([6, Th. 2]). *The expectations of the number of components, number of cyclic nodes (a node belonging to the cycle of its component), number of terminal nodes (a node without a preimage), and number of image nodes (a node with a preimage) in a random mapping of size N have the asymptotic forms, as $N \to \infty$:*

(i) #*Components:* $\frac{1}{2} \log N$ (iii) #*Terminal nodes:* $e^{-1} N$

(ii) #*Cyclic nodes:* $\sqrt{\pi N/2}$ (iv) #*Image nodes:* $(1 - e^{-1}) N$

Starting from any node x, the iteration structure of f is described by a simple path that connects to a cycle. The length of the path (measured by the number of edges) is called the tail length of x (or the height of x) and is denoted by $\lambda(x)$. The length of the cycle is called the cycle length of x and is denoted $\mu(x)$. Finally, the rho-length of x is denoted $\rho(x)$ and represents the length of the non repeating trajectory of x: $\rho(x) = \lambda(x) + \mu(x)$.

Theorem 2 ([6, Th. 3]). *Seen from a random node in a random mapping of size N, the expectations of the tail length, cycle length, rho length, tree size, component size, and predecessors size have the following asymptotic forms:*

(i) *Tail length* (λ): $\sqrt{\pi N/8}$ (iv) *Tree size:* $N/3$

(ii) *Cycle length* (μ): $\sqrt{\pi N/8}$ (v) *Component size:* $2N/3$

(iii) *Rho length* $(\rho = \lambda + \mu)$: $\sqrt{\pi N/2}$ (vi) *Predecessors size:* $\sqrt{\pi N/8}$

Moreover, the asymptotic expectations of the giant component and its giant tree have been provided in [7].

Theorem 3 ([7, VII.14]). *In a random mapping of size N, the largest tree and the largest component have expectations asymptotic, respectively, of $0.48 * N$ and $0.7582 * N$.*

Knowing all these statistical properties for the functional graph of a random function, Peyrin et al. [16] studied the successive iterations of HMAC with a fixed small message block for two related-keys K and $\bar{K} = K \oplus \mathtt{ipad} \oplus \mathtt{opad}$. Thanks to a small weakness of HMAC in the related-key setting, they observed that the two corresponding functional graphs are exactly the same (while ideally they should look like the functional graphs of two independent random functions) and this can be detected on the output of HMAC by measuring the cycle lengths. They used this property to derive generic distinguishing-R, distinguishing-H and existential forgery attacks in the related-key setting.

Later, Leurent et al. [14] extended the scope of cycle detection by providing a single-key utilization of this technique. Namely, they show how to craft two special long messages (mainly composed of identical message blocks), both following two separate cycle loops in the functional graph of the internal compression function. This trick allows the two messages to collide after the last processed message block, but also to have the same length (and thus the processing of the final padding block would not reintroduce differences). Such a collision can therefore be detected on the output of HMAC, and they use this special information leakage (information is leaked on the unknown internal compression function used) to derive a generic distinguishing-H attack in the single-key setting. They also provide another attack that can trade extra complexity cost for smaller message size, and in which the property scrutinized is the probability distribution of the collisions in the functional graph.

From a high-level perspective, these two previous works mainly considered as distinguishing properties the cycle nodes or the collisions distribution in a functional graph. In this article, we consider a functional graph property which seems not trivial to exploit: the height λ of a tail node, i.e. the distance of a node from the cycle of its component. While not trivial and likely to be costly, the potential outcome of analyzing such a property is that if one can extract this information leakage from the HMAC output, he would get direct information on a particular node of the computation. The attack can therefore be much sharper (the size of the cycle is not a powerful property as it represents a footprint equivalent for all the nodes of the component, while the height of a node is much more discriminating), and that is the reason why it eventually allows us to derive a generic universal forgery attack in the classical single-key setting.

4   General Description of the Universal Forgery Attack

Let $M_t = m_1 \| m_2 \| \ldots \| m_s$ be the target message to forge given by the challenger to the adversary (we start the counting from m_1 since the first message block m_0 to be processed by the inner hash function call is $m_0 = K \oplus \mathtt{ipad}$). In order to forge the tag value corresponding to this message, we will construct a different message M_t' which will collide with M_t in the inner hash function of HMAC, namely $H_{K_{in}}(M_t') = H_{K_{in}}(M_t)$, and this directly leads to colliding tags on the output of the HMAC: $T = H_{K_{out}}(H_{K_{in}}(M_t')) = H_{K_{out}}(H_{K_{in}}(M_t))$. Then, by simply querying the HMAC value T of M_t', we eventually forge a valid tag corresponding to M_t by outputting T.

Constructing such a message M_t' is in fact equivalent to finding a second preimage of M_t on the keyed hash function $H_{K_{in}}$. While second preimage attacks have been published on public iterative hash functions [11], unfortunately they cannot be applied to a keyed hash function as they depend on the knowledge of the intermediate hash values when processing M_t. However, in our situation the intermediate hash values for $H_{K_{in}}(M_t)$ are hidden since only the tag is given as output and since K_{in} is unknown to the adversary, and so he will not be able to guess them. We will overcome this issue by proposing a novel approach to recover some intermediate hash value x_i from the computation of $H_{K_{in}}(M_t)$. We stress that this is different from and much harder than previous so-called internal state recovery in [14], which recovers some internal state of a message completely chosen by the adversary himself. Note that once x_i is recovered, we get to know all the next intermediate hash values by simply computing $x_{i+1} = f(x_i, m_i), \ldots,$ $x_{s+1} = f(x_s, m_s)$ since H is an iterative hash function. Once these intermediate hash values are known, we can apply the previous second preimage attacks [11] in order to find M'_t.

In order to recover one value from the set of the intermediate chaining values $X = \{x_1, x_2, \ldots, x_{s+1}\}$ of $H_{K_{in}}(M)$, we choose offline $2^l/s$ values $Y = \{y_1, y_2, \ldots, y_{2^l/s}\}$, and one can see that with a good probability one element y_j of Y will collide with an element in X. We need to filter out this y_j value and this seems not easy since there is no previously published suitable property on the intermediate hash values of HMAC that the adversary can detect on the output.

One may consider using internal collisions, which are detectable by searching for colliding tags due to the length extension property: finding a message pair (m, m') for x_i such that $f(x_i, m) = f(x_i, m')$ by querying HMAC online and then using this pair to determine if $y_j = x_i$ holds by checking offline if $f(y_j, m) = f(y_j, m')$ holds. However, note that with this naive method only a single x_i can be tested at a time (since other $x_{i'}$ with $i' \neq i$ are very likely not to collide with the message pair (m, m')) and we will therefore have to repeat this procedure for each value of X independently. Thus, this attack fails as we would end up testing 2^l pairs and reaching a too high complexity.

Overall, it is essential to find a new property on the intermediate hash values of HMAC such that it can be detected by the adversary and such that it can be exploited to match a value of Y to all the values in X **simultaneously**. In our attack, we will use a novel property, yet unexploited: the height $\lambda(x_i)$ of each x_i of X in the functional graph of f_V, where f_V stands for the compression function with the message block fixed to a value V; $f_V(\cdot) = f(\cdot, V)$. In the rest of this article, without loss of generality, we will let V be the message block only composed of zero bits and we denote $f_{[0]}(\cdot) = f(\cdot, [0])$ the corresponding compression function.

4.1   The Height Property of a Node in a Functional Graph

In the functional graph of a random mapping on a finite set of size N, it is easy to see that each node x has a unique path connecting it with a cycle node, and we denoted the length of this path the **height** $\lambda(x)$ of x (or **tail length**). Obviously, for cycle nodes, we have $\lambda = 0$. The set of all nodes with the same height λ is usually called the λ-th **stratum** of the functional graph and we denote it as S_λ. Researchers have carried out extensive studies on the distribution of S_λ as $N \to \infty$. In particular, Harris proved that the mean value of S_0 is $\sqrt{\pi N/2}$ [10], which is consistent with Theorem 1 as the number of the cycle nodes. After that, Mutafchiev [15] proved the following theorem as an extension of Harris's result.

Theorem 4 ([15, Lemma 2]). *If $N \to \infty$ and $\lambda = o(\sqrt{N})$, the mean value of the λ-th stratum S_λ is $\sqrt{\pi N/2}$.*

Note that Mutafchiev's result is no longer true for $\lambda = O(\sqrt{N})$ and, for interested readers, we refer to [18] for the limit distribution of S_λ with $\lambda = O(\sqrt{N})$.

Interestingly, if the largest component is removed from the functional graph, then the remaining components also form a functional graph of a random mapping on a finite set of size $(1 - 0.7582) * N = 0.2418 * N$ (since Theorem 3 tells us that the largest component has an expected number of nodes of $0.7582 * N$). Thus we get the following corollary.

Corollary 1. *If $N \to \infty$ and $\lambda = o(\sqrt{N})$, the mean value of the λ-th stratum S_λ in the largest component is $0.64\sqrt{N} = \sqrt{\pi N/2} - \sqrt{\pi N * 0.2418/2}$.*

Now we move back to discuss about the height distribution in the functional graph $\mathcal{G}_{f_{[0]}}$ of $f_{[0]}$. From Corollary 1, we can deduce that if $l \to \infty$ and $\lambda = o(2^{l/2})$, the mean value of S_λ in the largest component of $f_{[0]}$ is $0.64 * 2^{l/2}$. In order to illustrate the notion of $\lambda = o(2^{l/2})$ more clearly, we rewrite the corollary into the following equivalent one.

Corollary 2. *Let $\delta(l)$ be any function such that $\delta(l) \to \infty$ as $l \to \infty$. There exists a positive value l_0 such that for any $l > l_0$, the mean value of λ-th stratum S_λ with $0 \leq \lambda \leq 2^{l/2}/\delta(l)$ in the largest component is $0.64 * 2^{l/2}$.*

Next, we will utilize Corollary 2 to prove the lower bound on the number of distinct height values of the intermediate chaining values in X, which we will use in order to evaluate the attack complexity. Denote the set of all the nodes with a height $\lambda \in [0, 2^{l/2}/\delta(l)]$ as N', which covers in total $0.64 * 2^l/\delta(l)$ nodes. Thus, a random node belongs to N' with a probability $0.64/\delta(l)$. Moreover, from Corollary 2, for a random node in N', its height is uniformly distributed in $[0, 2^{l/2}/\delta(l)]$. From these properties of N', we get that $0.64 * s/\delta(l)$ elements in X belong to N'. Moreover, there is no collision on the height among these elements with an overwhelming probability if $s \ll 2^{l/4}$ holds. Note that in our forgery attack, we will set s to be at most $2^{l/6}$ (see Section 5.1 for the details). Overall, the lower bound on the number of distinct height values in X is $0.64 * s/\delta(l)$. It is important and interesting to note that from Corollary 2, if l becomes very large, $\delta(l)$ will become negligible compared to exponential-order computations $2^{\Omega(l)}$, e.g., $\delta(l) = \log(l)$.

On the other hand, we performed experiments to evaluate the expected number of the distinct height values in X. More precisely, we used SHA-256 compression function for small values of l. We prepend 0^{256-l} to a l-bit value x, then compute $y=$SHA-256 $(0^{256-l} \| x)$, and finally output the l LSBs of y. With $l \leq 30$, we generated random pairs and checked if their heights collide or not in the functional graph of l-bit truncated SHA-256 compression function. The experimental results show that a pair of random values has a colliding height with a probability of around $2^{-l/2}$. Moreover, it is matched with a rough probability estimation as follows. Let x and x' be two randomly chosen l-bit values. Suppose x and x' have the same height, then it implies that after i iterations of $f_{[0]}$ (denoted as $f_{[0]}^i$), either one of the following two cases occurs. One is $f_{[0]}^i(x) = f_{[0]}^i(x')$, which has a probability of roughly 2^{-l} for each i conditioned on $f_{[0]}^{i-1}(x) \neq f_{[0]}^{i-1}(x')$. The other one is that $f_{[0]}^i(x) \neq f_{[0]}^i(x')$ and both $f_{[0]}^i(x)$

and $f_{[0]}^i(x')$ enter the component cycle simultaneously, which has a probability of roughly $(\sqrt{\pi/2}*2^{-l/2})^2 = \pi/2*2^{-l}$ for each i, since the number of cycle nodes is $\sqrt{\pi/2}*2^{l/2}$. Note that Theorem 2 proved the expected tail length is $\sqrt{\pi/8}*2^{l/2}$. Thus, if neither of the two cases occurs up to $\sqrt{\pi/8}*2^{l/2}$ iterations, we get that $f^i(x)$ and $f^{i'}(x')$ enter the component cycle with different i and i', namely x and x' have different heights. So the total probability of randomly chosen x and x' having the same height is at most $2^{-l}*\sqrt{\pi/8}*2^{l/2}+\pi/2*2^{-l}*\sqrt{\pi/8}*2^{l/2} \approx 2^{-l/2}$. Overall, we make a natural, conservative and confident conjecture as follows (note that s is at most $2^{l/6}$ in our attacks. See Section 5.1 for the details).

Conjecture 1. With $s \leq 2^{l/6}$, there is only a negligible probability that a collision exists among the heights of s random values in a functional graph of a l-bit random mapping.

In the rest of the paper, we will describe our attacks based on the Conjecture 1, namely the heights of the intermediate hash values in X are distinct. However, if only taking in account the proven lower bound $0.64 * s/\delta(l)$ of the number of the distinct heights in X, the number of offline nodes should be increased by $\delta(l)/0.64$ times, and the attack complexity is increased by a factor of $O(\delta(l))$. Note that $O(\delta(l))$ is negligible compared to $2^{O(l)}$, and thus it has very limited influence to the complexity for large l.

4.2   Deducing Online the Height of a Few Intermediate Hash Values

We now explain how to deduce the height $\lambda(x_i)$ of a node x_i in the functional graph $\mathcal{G}_{f_{[0]}}$ of $f_{[0]}$. We start by finding the cycle length of the largest component of $\mathcal{G}_{f_{[0]}}$, and we denote it by L. This can be done offline with a complexity of $O(2^{l/2})$ computations, as explained in [16]. Then, we ask for the MAC computation of two messages M_1 and M_2:

$$M_1 = m_1\|m_2\|\dots\|m_{i-1}\|[0]^{2^{l/2}+L}\|[1]\|[0]^{2^{l/2}}$$

$$M_2 = m_1\|m_2\|\dots\|m_{i-1}\|[0]^{2^{l/2}}\|[1]\|[0]^{2^{l/2}+L}$$

where $[0]^j$ represents j consecutive zero-bit message blocks, and we check if the two tags collide. It is important to note that if the intermediate hash value x_i is located in the largest component of $\mathcal{G}_{f_{[0]}}$ and has a height $\lambda(x_i)$ no larger than $2^{l/2}$, then the intermediate hash value after processing $m_1\|m_2\|\dots\|m_{i-1}\|[0]^{2^{l/2}}$ is in the cycle of the largest component. Also, the intermediate hash values after processing $m_1\|m_2\|\dots\|m_{i-1}\|[0]^{2^{l/2}}\|[1]$ and $m_1\|m_2\|\dots\|m_{i-1}\|[0]^{2^{l/2}+L}\|[1]$ will be equal (and we denote it by x) since in the latter we just make an extra cycle walk before processing the message block $[1]$. Under a similar reasoning, if x is also in the largest component[1] and has a height $\lambda(x)$ no larger than $2^{l/2}$, we get

---

[1] Since we processed a message block [1], different from [0], the last computation will not follow the functional graph $\mathcal{G}_{f_{[0]}}$ and we will be mapped to a random point in $\mathcal{G}_{f_{[0]}}$.

that the intermediate hash values after processing $m_1 \| m_2 \| \dots \| m_{i-1} \| [0]^{2^{l/2}+L} \|$ $[1] \| [0]^{2^{l/2}}$ and $m_1 \| m_2 \| \dots \| m_{i-1} \| [0]^{2^{l/2}} \| [1] \| [0]^{2^{l/2}+L}$ are equal. Moreover, since M_1 and M_2 have the same block length, we get a collision on the inner hash function, which directly extends to a collision on the output tag. From the functional graph properties of a random function given in Sections 3 and 4.1, a randomly chosen node will be located in the largest component of $\mathcal{G}_{f_{[0]}}$ with a probability of about 0.7582 and will have a height no larger than $2^{l/2}$ with a probability roughly 0.5. Thus, M_1 and M_2 will collide with a probability $(0.7582 * 0.5)^2 = 0.14$.

In order to recover the height $\lambda(x_i)$ of one node x_i in the functional graph $\mathcal{G}_{f_{[0]}}$ of $f_{[0]}$, we will test $\log(l)$ message pairs obtained from (M_1, M_2) by changing the block $[1]$ to other values. If (at least) one of these pairs collides, we can deduce that with overwhelming probability[2] x_i is in the largest component, and has a height $\lambda(x_i)$ of at most $2^{l/2}$. Otherwise, we give up on recovering the height $\lambda(x_i)$ of x_i, and move to find the height $\lambda(x_{i+1})$ of the next intermediate hash value x_{i+1}.

In the former situation, we can start to search for the exact node height $\lambda(x_i)$ of x_i in $\mathcal{G}_{f_{[0]}}$, and we will accomplish this task thanks to a **binary search**. Namely, we first check whether the intermediate hash value after processing $m_1 \| m_2 \| \dots \| m_{i-1} \| [0]^{2^{l/2}-1}$ is in the cycle or not (note that we now have $2^{l/2}-1$ $[0]$ blocks in the middle, instead of $2^{l/2}$ originally), and this can be done by asking for the MAC computation of two messages M_1^* and M_2^*

$$M_1^* = m_1 \| m_2 \| \dots \| m_{i-1} \| [0]^{2^{l/2}-1} \| [1] \| [0]^{2^{l/2}+L}$$
$$M_2^* = m_1 \| m_2 \| \dots \| m_{i-1} \| [0]^{2^{l/2}-1+L} \| [1] \| [0]^{2^{l/2}}$$

and by checking if their respective tags collide. After testing $\log(l)$ such pairs obtained from (M_1^*, M_2^*) by modifying the block $[1]$ to other values, if (at least) one pair collides, we can deduce that with overwhelming probability the intermediate hash value after processing $m_1 \| m_2 \| \dots \| m_{i-1} \| [0]^{2^{l/2}-1}$ is in the cycle, and the height $\lambda(x_i)$ of x_i is no larger than $2^{l/2}-1$. Otherwise, we deduce that $\lambda(x_i)$ lies between $2^{l/2-1}$ and $2^{l/2}$. Thus, the amount of possible height values for x_i are reduced by one half. We continue iterating this binary search procedure $\log_2(2^{l/2}) = l/2$ times, and we will eventually obtain the exact height value $\lambda(x_i)$ of x_i. By applying such a height recovery procedure, we get to know the height value for $0.38 * s$ values in X on average (one intermediate hash value x_i has probability 0.7582 to be located in the biggest component, and probability about $1/2$ to have a height not greater than $2^{l/2}$).

4.3   Deducing Offline the Height of Many Chosen Values

Before we start to retrieve a value x_i of X, we need to handle the set Y offline. When we choose values to build the set $Y = \{y_1, y_2, \dots, y_{2^l/s}\}$, we also have

---

[2] Since the probability that x_i is in the largest component and has a height $\lambda(x_i) \leq 2^{l/2}$ is constant, choosing $\log(l)$ messages will ensure that the success probability of this step is very close to one, see [14].

to compute their respective height in the functional graph of $f_{[0]}$. One may consider to use a trivial and random sampling, i.e. choosing random nodes first and then computing their height. Note that such a procedure is very expensive, since computing height for a random value requires around $2^{l/2}$ computations on average, which renders the total complexity of building Y beyond 2^l. We propose instead to use an offline sampling procedure as follows.

We first initialize Y as an empty set and we start by choosing a new and random value y_1, namely $y_1 \notin Y$. Then, we apply $f_{[0]}$ to update it successively; $y_{i+1} = f(y_i, [0])$, and memorize all the y_i's in the computation chain. The iteration terminates if y_{i+1} collides with a previous stored value $y \in Y$ whose height is already known (we denote it as λ), or if it collides with a previous node y_j $(1 \le j \le i)$ in the current chain, namely a new cycle is generated. In the former case, we naturally compute the height of nodes y_p $(1 \le p \le i)$ in the chain as $\lambda + i + 1 - p$, and store all of them in Y. For the latter case, we set the height of all the nodes from y_j to y_i as 0 (since they belong to the cycle of their own component), and we then compute the height of tail nodes y_p $(0 \le p < j)$ as $j - p$ and store all of them in Y.

Using this procedure, we can select $2^l/s$ values and obtain their height with a complexity of only $2^l/s$ computations. Moreover, from the functional graph properties of a random function given in Sections 3 and 4.1, we know that on average 38% values in Y are located in the largest components and have a height no larger than $2^{l/2}$.

Note that Y is not a set of random values. We do not know the distribution of height values of the elements in Y, which essentially makes Conjecture 1 be necessary for our attack. The detailed discussion follows in next section.

4.4   Exploiting the Height Information Leakage

At this point, the attacker built the sets X and Y and knows the height of almost all their elements (for X, only the heights of $0.38 * s$ elements are known). The next step is to recover one value in X (which are still unknown to the attacker) by matching between the elements in set X and the elements in set Y. However, for each x_i in X, we do not have to try to match every value in Y. Indeed, we just need to pay attention to a smaller subset of Y in which the elements have the same height value as x_i. Moreover, since the elements in the set X have distinct heights (see details in Section 4.1), these subsets of Y are all disjoint. Thus in total we need to match at most $2^l/s$ pairs, namely the size of Y. This point is precisely where the adversary will get a complexity advantage during his attack.

4.5   Attack Summary

Finally, let us wrap everything up and describe the universal forgery attack from the very beginning. The adversary is given a target message $M_t = m_1\|m_2\|\ldots\|m_s$

by the challenger, for which he has to forge a valid tag. He splits M_t into two parts $M_{t_1} \| M_{t_2}$:

$M_{t_1} = m_1 \| m_2 \| \ldots \| m_{s_1}$ will be used for the intermediate hash value recovery,

$M_{t_2} = m_{s_1+1} \| m_{s_1+2} \| \ldots \| m_s$ will be used in the second preimage attack.

During the online phase, the adversary applies the height recovery procedure from Section 4.2 for each x_i $(1 \leq i \leq s_1+1)$, and stores them in X. Moreover, he produces a filter (m, m') for each x_i such that $f(x_i, m) = f(x_i, m')$ holds. During the offline phase, the adversary chooses $2^l/s_1$ values following the sampling procedure from Section 4.3 and stores them in Y.

Then, he recovers the value of one of the x_i's by matching the sets X and Y: for each x_i, he checks if $f(y, m) = f(y, m')$ holds or not for all y's that have the same height as x_i in Y. If a collision is found, then y is equal to x_i with a good probability. Once one x_i $(1 \leq i \leq s_1+1)$ is recovered, the adversary gets to know the value of x_{s_1+1} by computing the iteration $x_{i+1} = f(x_i, m_{i+1}), \ldots, x_{s_1+1} = f(x_{s_1}, m_{s_1})$, which induces that the latter half of the inner hash function when processing M_t is equivalent to a public hash function by regarding x_{s_1+1} as the public IV. Thus, the adversary is able to apply previous second preimage attacks on public hash functions [11] to find a second preimage M'_{t_2} for M_{t_2}. In the end, the adversary queries $M_{t_1} \| M'_{t_2}$ to the MAC oracle and receives a tag value T. This tag T is also a valid tag for the challenge M_t and the universal forgery attack succeeds.

5 Full Procedure of the Universal Forgery Attack

In this section, we provide the entire procedure of this complex attack and we first recall the notations used. Let $M_t = m_1 \| m_2 \| \ldots \| m_s$ be the challenge message (we start the counting from m_1, since $m_0 = K \oplus \text{ipad}$ during the first compression function call of the inner hash call of HMAC) and we denote by $x_1, x_2, \ldots, x_{s+1}$ the successive intermediate hash values of $H_{K_{in}}(M_t)$ when processing M_t. During the attack, M_t is divided into $M_{t_1} \| M_{t_2}$, where M_{t_1} is $m_1 \| m_2 \| \ldots \| m_{s_1}$ and M_{t_2} is $m_{s_1+1} \| m_{s_1+2} \| \ldots \| m_s$. As an example, we will use the functional graph $\mathcal{G}_{f_{[0]}}$ of the hash compression function f when iterated with a fixed message block $[0]$ and we denote by L the cycle length of the largest component of $\mathcal{G}_{f_{[0]}}$.

Phase 1 (online). Recover the height of $x_1, x_2, \ldots,$ and x_{s_1+1} in $\mathcal{G}_{f_{[0]}}$ and store them in a set X. The procedure is detailed as below.

1. Initialize an index counter c as 1, and the set X as empty.
2. Query to the MAC oracle and receive the corresponding tag pairs of $\log(l)$ distinct message pairs $m_1 \| \ldots \| m_{c-1} \| [0]^{2^{l/2}+L} \| [i] \| [0]^{2^{l/2}}$ and $m_1 \| \ldots \| m_{c-1} \| [0]^{2^{l/2}} \| [i] \| [0]^{2^{l/2}+L}$, where $[i] \neq [0]$ and $[i]$s are distinct among pairs.
3. If there is no tag pair that collides, increment the index counter $c \leftarrow c + 1$ and if $c \leq s_1 + 1$ then go to step 2, otherwise terminate this phase. If there is (at least) one tag pair that collides, then just execute the following steps.

(a) Set two integer variables $z_1 = 0$ and $z_2 = 2^{l/2}$.

(b) Set $z = (z_1 + z_2)/2$. Query to the MAC oracle and receive the corresponding tag pairs of $\log(l)$ distinct message pairs $m_1 \| \ldots \| m_{c-1} \| [0]^{2^z + L} \| [i] \| [0]^{2^{l/2}}$ and $m_1 \| \ldots \| m_{c-1} \| [0]^{2^z} \| [i] \| [0]^{2^{l/2} + L}$, where $[i] \neq [0]$ and $[i]$s are distinct among pairs.

(c) If (at least) one tag pair collides, set $z_2 = z$. Otherwise, set $z_1 = z$.

(d) If $z_2 \neq z_1 + 1$ holds, go to step 3-b. Otherwise, set the height of x_c as $\lambda(x_c) = z_2$, store z_2 in position c in X and increment the index counter $c \leftarrow c+1$. If $c \leq s_1 + 1$ then go to step 2, otherwise terminate this phase.

Phase 2 (online). Generate a pair of one-block messages (m, m') for each $x_i \in X$, which is used as a filter in Phase 4. The procedure is detailed as below.

1. For all $x_i \in X$ do the following steps.
   (a) Select $2^{l/2}$ distinct one-block messages, append them to $m_1 \| \ldots \| m_{i-1}$, and send these newly formatted messages to the MAC oracle. Find the pairs $m_1 \| \ldots \| m_{i-1} \| m$ and $m_1 \| \ldots \| m_{i-1} \| m'$ that collides on the output of the MAC.
   (b) For all the found pairs (m, m'), choose another random one-block message m'', and query $m_1 \| \ldots \| m_{i-1} \| m \| m''$ and $m_1 \| \ldots \| m_{i-1} \| m' \| m''$ to the MAC oracle in order to check if their corresponding tags collide again or not. If none collide, go to step 1-a. Otherwise, store a colliding pair (m, m') as the filter for x_i in X and go to the next x_i in step 1.

Phase 3 (offline). Choose $2^l/s_1$ values with their height in $\mathcal{G}_{f_{[0]}}$, and store them in a set Y (sorted according to the height values). The procedure is detailed as below.

1. Initialize a counter c as 0 and the set Y as empty.

2. Choose a new random value y_1 such that $y_1 \notin Y$, and set the chain counter cc to 1.

3. Compute $y_{cc+1} = f_{[0]}(y_{cc})$

4. Check if y_{cc+1} matches a value y stored in Y. If it does, then set the height $\lambda(y_i)$ of y_i (with $1 \leq i \leq cc$) as $\lambda(y) + cc + 1 - i$ and store the $(y_i, \lambda(y_i))$ pairs (with $1 \leq i \leq cc$) in Y.

5. Check if y_{cc+1} matches a previously computed chain value y_i (with $1 \leq i \leq cc$). If it does, then set the height $\lambda(y_j)$ of all values y_j (with $i \leq j \leq cc$) as 0, and the height $\lambda(y_j)$ of y_j (with $1 \leq j < i - 1$) as $i - j$. Store the $(y_j, \lambda(y_j))$ pairs (with $1 \leq j \leq cc$) in Y.

6. If no match was found in step 4 or 5, then increment the chain counter $cc \leftarrow cc + 1$ and go to step 3. Otherwise, update the counter c by $c \leftarrow c + cc$ and if $c < 2^l/s_1$ then go to step 2, otherwise terminate this phase.

Phase 4 (offline). Recover one intermediate hash value x_i in set X. The procedure is detailed as below.

1. For all $x_i \in X$ do the following steps.
   (a) Get the height $\lambda(x_i)$ of x_i and its filter pair (m, m') from the set X. Get all the $(y, \lambda(y))$ pairs in set Y such that $\lambda(y) = \lambda(x_i)$.
   (b) For each y, we check if $f(y, m) = f(y, m')$ holds or not. If it holds for a y_j, then output y_j as the value of x_i and terminate this phase. If there is no such a y_j, then go to the next x_i in step 1.

Phase 5 (offline). Find a second preimage for the processing of M_{t_2} as the second message part of $H_{K_{in}}(M_t)$. The block length of M_{t_2} is denoted $s_2 = s - s_1$. The procedure is briefly described below. For the complete algorithm please refer to [11].

1. Compute the intermediate hash values $x_{s_1}, x_{s_1+1}, \ldots, x_s$ from the value x_i recovered at Phase 4, i.e. $x_{i+1} = f(x_i, m_i), \ldots, x_s = f(x_{s-1}, m_{s-1})$. Note that it is not necessary to compute until x_s.
2. Build a $[\log(s_2), s_2]$-expandable message starting from x_{s_1} to a value denoted as x. More precisely, for any integer i between $\log(s_2)$ and s_2, there is a message $m'_{s_1} \| m'_{s_1+1} \| \cdots \| m'_{s_1+i}$ from the expandable message such that it has i blocks and links from x_{s_1} to x:

$$x = f(\ldots f(f(x_{s_1}, m'_{s_1}), m'_{s_1+1}), \ldots, m'_{s_1+i}).$$

3. Choose $2^l/(s_2 - \log(s_2))$ random one-block messages m, compute $f(x, m)$, and check if this matches to an element of the intermediate hash values set $\{x_{s_1+\log(s_2)}, x_{s_1+1+\log(s_2)}, \ldots, x_s\}$.
4. If a match to x_i (with $s_1 + \log(s_2) \leq i \leq s$) is found, derive the $(i - s_1)$-block long message $m'_{s_1+1} \| m'_{s_1+2} \| \cdots \| m'_i$ from the expandable message, append the blocks $m_{i+1} \| m_{i+2} \| \cdots \| m_s$ to it to produce M'_{t_2}, namely $M'_{t_2} = m'_{s_1+1} \| m'_{s_1+2} \| \cdots \| m'_i \| m_{i+1} \| m_{i+2} \| \cdots \| m_s$.

Phase 6 (online). Forge a valid tag for the challenge M_t.

1. Query message $M'_t = M_{t_1} \| M'_{t_2}$ to the MAC oracle, and receive its tag T.
2. Output (M_t, T) where T is a valid tag for M_t.

5.1   Complexity and Success Probability Analysis

Complexity Analysis. We use a single compression function call as complexity unit. We evaluated the complexity of each phase as below.

Phase 1: $O(s_1 \cdot l \cdot \log(l) \cdot 2^{l/2})$ **Phase 2:** $s_1^2 \cdot 2^{l/2}$ **Phase 3:** $2^l/s_1$

Phase 4: $2^l/s_1$ **Phase 5:** $2^l/s_2$ **Phase 6:** s

The overall complexity of our generic universal forgery attack therefore depends on the block length s of the target message M_t:

- For the case $s \leq 2^{l/6}$, the overall complexity is dominated by Phase 3 and Phase 5. So we set $s_1 = s_2 = s/2$, and get the overall complexity of $O(2^l/s)$ computations.
- For the case $2^{l/6} < s \leq 2^{5l/6}$, the overall complexity is dominated by Phase 2. So we set $s_1 = 2^{l/6}$, and get the overall complexity of $O(2^{5l/6})$ computations.
- For the case $s > 2^{5l/6}$, the overall complexity is dominated by Phase 6. So we set $s_1 = 2^{l/6}$, and get the overall complexity of $O(s) = 2^{5l/6}$ computations.

Success Probability Analysis. First, note that we only need to pay attention to the phases that dominate the complexity, since the other phases can be repeated enough times to approach a success probability of 1. For the case $s \leq 2^{l/6}$, we note that Phase 3 always succeeds with probability 1 and the success probability of Phase 5 is 0.63. For the case $2^{l/6} < s \leq 2^{5l/6}$, the success probability of Phase 2 is approximately 1. For the case $s > 2^{5l/6}$, the success probability of Phase 6 is approximately 1 after previous phases were repeated enough times. Therefore, the overall success probability of our attack tends to 1 when repeating a constant time the corresponding complexity dominating phases.

5.2 Experimental Verification

For verification purposes, we have implemented the attack by using HMAC-SHA-256 on a desktop computer. Due to computational and memory limitations, we shortened the input/output bits of the SHA-256 compression function to 32 bits. In more details, we input a 32-bit value x to the compression function, and the compression function expands it to 256 bits by prepending 0 bits: $0^{224} \| x$. Then, the compression function also shortens its outputs by only outputting the 32 LSBs. Particularly for Phase 4, we paid attentions to the average number of pairs left after matching the heights between the elements in X and the elements in Y, since it is essential for the complexity advantages. The experiments results confirmed that the universal forgery attack works with the claimed complexity.

6   Conclusion

In this article, we presented the very first generic universal forgery attack against hash-based MACs, and we reduced the gap between the HMAC security proof and the best known attack for this crucial security property. We leave as an open problem if better attacks can be found to further reduce this gap. Our cryptanalysis method is new and uses the information leaked by the distance of a node from the cycle (its height) in the functional graph of the compression function with a fixed message block. We believe other graph properties, even more complex, might be exploitable and could perhaps further improve the generic complexity of universal forgery attacks against hash-based MACs.

References

1. Bellare, M.: New Proofs for NMAC and HMAC: Security Without Collision-Resistance. In: Dwork, C. (ed.) CRYPTO 2006. LNCS, vol. 4117, pp. 602–619. Springer, Heidelberg (2006)
2. Bellare, M., Canetti, R., Krawczyk, H.: Keying Hash Functions for Message Authentication. In: Koblitz, N. (ed.) CRYPTO 1996. LNCS, vol. 1109, pp. 1–15. Springer, Heidelberg (1996)
3. Contini, S., Yin, Y.L.: Forgery and Partial Key-Recovery Attacks on HMAC and NMAC Using Hash Collisions. In: Lai, X., Chen, K. (eds.) ASIACRYPT 2006. LNCS, vol. 4284, pp. 37–53. Springer, Heidelberg (2006)
4. Dobbertin, H., Bosselaers, A., Preneel, B.: RIPEMD-160: A Strengthened Version of RIPEMD. In: Gollmann, D. (ed.) FSE 1996. LNCS, vol. 1039, pp. 71–82. Springer, Heidelberg (1996)
5. Dodis, Y., Ristenpart, T., Steinberger, J., Tessaro, S.: To Hash or Not to Hash Again (In)Differentiability Results for H^2 and HMAC. In: Safavi-Naini, R., Canetti, R. (eds.) CRYPTO 2012. LNCS, vol. 7417, pp. 348–366. Springer, Heidelberg (2012)
6. Flajolet, P., Odlyzko, A.M.: Random Mapping Statistics. In: Quisquater, J.-J., Vandewalle, J. (eds.) EUROCRYPT 1989. LNCS, vol. 434, pp. 329–354. Springer, Heidelberg (1990)
7. Flajolet, P., Sedgewick, R.: Analytic Combinatorics. Cambridge University Press (2009)
8. Fouque, P.-A., Leurent, G., Nguyen, P.Q.: Full Key-Recovery Attacks on HMAC/NMAC-MD4 and NMAC-MD5. In: Menezes, A. (ed.) CRYPTO 2007. LNCS, vol. 4622, pp. 13–30. Springer, Heidelberg (2007)
9. Guo, J., Sasaki, Y., Wang, L., Wu, S.: Cryptanalysis of HMAC/NMAC-Whirlpool. In: Sako, K., Sarkar, P. (eds.) ASIACRYPT 2013, Part II. LNCS, vol. 8270, pp. 21–40. Springer, Heidelberg (2013)
10. Harris, B.: Probability Distributions Related to Random Mappings. Ann. Math. Statist. 31(4), 1045–1062 (1960)
11. Kelsey, J., Schneier, B.: Second Preimages on n-Bit Hash Functions for Much Less than 2^n Work. In: Cramer, R. (ed.) EUROCRYPT 2005. LNCS, vol. 3494, pp. 474–490. Springer, Heidelberg (2005)
12. Kim, J.-S., Biryukov, A., Preneel, B., Hong, S.H.: On the Security of HMAC and NMAC Based on HAVAL, MD4, MD5, SHA-0 and SHA-1 (Extended Abstract). In: De Prisco, R., Yung, M. (eds.) SCN 2006. LNCS, vol. 4116, pp. 242–256. Springer, Heidelberg (2006)
13. Lee, E., Chang, D., Kim, J.-S., Sung, J., Hong, S.H.: Second Preimage Attack on 3-Pass HAVAL and Partial Key-Recovery Attacks on HMAC/NMAC-3-Pass HAVAL. In: Nyberg, K. (ed.) FSE 2008. LNCS, vol. 5086, pp. 189–206. Springer, Heidelberg (2008)
14. Leurent, G., Peyrin, T., Wang, L.: New Generic Attacks Against Hash-based MACs. In: Sako, K., Sarkar, P. (eds.) ASIACRYPT 2013, Part II. LNCS, vol. 8270, pp. 1–20. Springer, Heidelberg (2013)
15. Mutafchiev, L.R.: The limit distribution of the number of nodes in low strata of a random mapping. Statistics & Probability Letters 7(3), 247–251 (1988)
16. Peyrin, T., Sasaki, Y., Wang, L.: Generic Related-Key Attacks for HMAC. In: Wang, X., Sako, K. (eds.) ASIACRYPT 2012. LNCS, vol. 7658, pp. 580–597. Springer, Heidelberg (2012)

17. Preneel, B., van Oorschot, P.C.: On the Security of Two MAC Algorithms. In: Maurer, U.M. (ed.) EUROCRYPT 1996. LNCS, vol. 1070, pp. 19–32. Springer, Heidelberg (1996)
18. Proskurin, G.V.: On the Distribution of the Number of Vertices in Strata of a Random Mapping. Theory Probab. Appl., 803–808 (1973)
19. Rechberger, C., Rijmen, V.: On authentication with hmac and non-random properties. In: Dietrich, S., Dhamija, R. (eds.) FC 2007 and USEC 2007. LNCS, vol. 4886, pp. 119–133. Springer, Heidelberg (2007)
20. Rechberger, C., Rijmen, V.: New Results on NMAC/HMAC when Instantiated with Popular Hash Functions. J. UCS 14(3), 347–376 (2008)
21. Rivest, R.L.: The md5 message-digest algorithm. RFC 1321 (Informational) (April 1992)
22. Sasaki, Y., Wang, L.: Improved Single-Key Distinguisher on HMAC-MD5 and Key Recovery Attacks on Sandwich-MAC-MD5. In: Selected Areas in Cryptography (2013)
23. Wang, L., Ohta, K., Kunihiro, N.: New Key-Recovery Attacks on HMAC/NMAC-MD4 and NMAC-MD5. In: Smart, N.P. (ed.) EUROCRYPT 2008. LNCS, vol. 4965, pp. 237–253. Springer, Heidelberg (2008)
24. Wang, X., Yu, H., Wang, W., Zhang, H., Zhan, T.: Cryptanalysis on HMAC/NMAC-MD5 and MD5-MAC. In: Joux, A. (ed.) EUROCRYPT 2009. LNCS, vol. 5479, pp. 121–133. Springer, Heidelberg (2009)
25. Yasuda, K.: "Sandwich" Is Indeed Secure: How to Authenticate a Message with Just One Hashing. In: Pieprzyk, J., Ghodosi, H., Dawson, E. (eds.) ACISP 2007. LNCS, vol. 4586, pp. 355–369. Springer, Heidelberg (2007)
26. Yu, H., Wang, X.: Full Key-Recovery Attack on the HMAC/NMAC Based on 3 and 4-Pass HAVAL. In: Bao, F., Li, H., Wang, G. (eds.) ISPEC 2009. LNCS, vol. 5451, pp. 285–297. Springer, Heidelberg (2009)

Links between Truncated Differential and Multidimensional Linear Properties of Block Ciphers and Underlying Attack Complexities

Céline Blondeau and Kaisa Nyberg

Department of Information and Computer Science,
Aalto University School of Science, Finland
{celine.blondeau, kaisa.nyberg}@aalto.fi

Abstract. The mere number of various apparently different statistical attacks on block ciphers has raised the question about their relationships which would allow to classify them and determine those that give essentially complementary information about the security of block ciphers. While mathematical links between some statistical attacks have been derived in the last couple of years, the important link between general truncated differential and multidimensional linear attacks has been missing. In this work we close this gap. The new link is then exploited to relate the complexities of chosen-plaintext and known-plaintext distinguishing attacks of differential and linear types, and further, to explore the relations between the key-recovery attacks. Our analysis shows that a statistical saturation attack is the same as a truncated differential attack, which allows us, for the first time, to provide a justifiable analysis of the complexity of the statistical saturation attack and discuss its validity on 24 rounds of the PRESENT block cipher. By studying the data, time and memory complexities of a multidimensional linear key-recovery attack and its relation with a truncated differential one, we also show that in most cases a known-plaintext attack can be transformed into a less costly chosen-plaintext attack. In particular, we show that there is a differential attack in the chosen-plaintext model on 26 rounds of PRESENT with less memory complexity than the best previous attack, which assumes known plaintext. The links between the statistical attacks discussed in this paper give further examples of attacks where the method used to sample the data required by the statistical test is more differentiating than the method used for finding the distinguishing property.

Keywords: statistical cryptanalysis, block cipher, chosen plaintext, known plaintext, differential cryptanalysis, truncated differential cryptanalysis, linear cryptanalysis, multidimensional linear cryptanalysis, statistical saturation, integral, zero-correlation, impossible differential.

1 Introduction

After the invention of the differential and linear cryptanalyses several extensions and related statistical cryptanalysis methods for block ciphers have been presented. The need for a common framework for statistical attacks that would facilitate their

P.Q. Nguyen and E. Oswald (Eds.): EUROCRYPT 2014, LNCS 8441, pp. 165–182, 2014.

comparison has been raised in the literature at least by Vaudenay [1] and Wagner [2], who also put forward such frameworks. While the former aims at providing provable security against all statistical attacks, the latter takes a high level view on the iterated Markov ciphers. In this paper, we propose a more pragmatic approach to show that, no matter whether we use a linear or differential characteristic to identify some non-random behavior, it can be exploited for a known-plaintext (KP) attack and a chosen-plaintext (CP) attack.

Previously, many mathematical relationships between statistical cryptanalysis methods have been established. They concern the computation of the main statistic of the cryptanalysis method under consideration. In [3], Leander studied relations between the statistical saturation (SS) attack [4] and the multidimensional linear (ML) cryptanalysis using the χ^2 statistical test [5]. In the former the strength of the distinguishing property is measured by the non-uniformity of the distribution of partial ciphertext values when part of the plaintext is fixed. In the latter, the non-uniformity of the joint distribution of plaintext parts and ciphertext parts is under consideration. Leander showed that the non-uniformities computed in the SS attack are on average equal to the non-uniformity of the distribution considered in the ML attack.

Later more links were established in [6] and also applied in practice. For example, an efficient zero-correlation (ZC) property was found on a variant of Skipjack. Using the mathematical link it was then transformed to an integral property to launch an efficient CP attack on 31 rounds of this cipher. The question arises, whether it would have been possible to use the ZC property directly. Or would it have consumed essentially more data, time, or memory to exploit the ZC property directly in this attack? The purpose of this paper is to give an exhaustive answer to such questions in the more general setting of truncated differential (TD) [7] and ML attacks.

Building on the link proposed by Chabaud and Vaudenay [8] and applied by Blondeau and Nyberg [9], we establish now a more general mathematical link between differential and linear statistical properties of block ciphers. This link provides a unified view on statistical distinguishers of block ciphers that measure the uniformity of a distribution of pairs of partial plaintext and ciphertext values and covers any TD and ML distinguishers. It allows for examination and comparison of the corresponding KP and CP distinguishing attacks and the related statistical models. In this paper, we will make a detailed comparison between the data, time and memory complexities of the CP TD and KP ML distinguishing attacks. Also the SS distinguisher will be considered and shown to be essentially identical to a TD distinguisher.

One of the main results given in this paper is that for any KP ML distinguishing attack there is a stronger CP TD distinguishing attack, where the strength is measured in terms of the data, time and memory complexities of the distinguishers. We will see that the main advantage of the CP TD distinguishers over the KP ML distinguishers is due to the better organisation of the chosen data and allows some data, time and memory savings. Overall, the results obtained in this paper show that the method used for finding the distinguishing property, differential or linear, may be quite irrelevant when performing the attack. We show cases where, for the same distinguisher, the data, time and memory complexities of the attack are essentially different depending on what kind of data sampling methods are used for the statistical test.

The knowledge of the relationships between the different distinguishers and their complexities will then be applied to the outstanding key-recovery attacks. In particular, we will compare the KP and CP scenarios and their effects on the complexities of the key-recovery attacks based on different but mathematically equivalent distinguishing properties of the cipher. The cost difference of using KP instead of CP can be quite small. When such a case occurs in practice, the cryptanalyst can choose whether to use KP data with small additional cost instead of CP data to perform the key-recovery attack.

The resistance of PRESENT [6] against TD attacks has been a longstanding open problem. Since the strong differentials of the Sbox diffuse faster than the strong linear approximations as the number of rounds increases, it has been very difficult to achieve accurate estimates of differential probabilities directly. In [9], linear approximations were used to evaluate some differential probabilities. While the obtained estimates were accurate, no differentials were found that would essentially improve the best known differential attack, which can break 19 rounds of PRESENT [9]. Using the results obtained in this paper, we convert the 24-round ML distinguisher of [10] to a TD distinguisher and use it to present a TD key-recovery attack on a 26-round reduced version of PRESENT. This attack which reach the same number of rounds than the KP ML attack of [10] illustrates than one can make use of linear properties to conduct a differential attack.

The rest of the paper is organized as follows. In Sect. 2, we present a general link between the TD and ML properties. In Sect. 3, we study the data, time and memory complexities of the CP TD, CP SS and KP ML distinguishing attacks, which depending on the parameters of the underlying properties suggest different time-memory tradeoffs. By showing that the SS attacks correspond to TD attacks, in Sect. 4, we provide improved complexity estimates of the SS attacks. Sect. 5 is dedicated to the link between the TD and ML key-recovery attack. We show how to convert a CP attack to a KP attack and analyze the cost of this conversion. On the other hand, we show the existence of a TD attack on 26 rounds of PRESENT, which requires less memory than the best known ML attack on PRESENT. In Sect. 6, we analyze other known statistical attacks on block cipher and discuss their relations. Sect. 7 summarizes the results on these different links.

2   Preliminaries

2.1   ML and TD Setting and Notation

In differential cryptanalysis [11], the attacker is interested in finding and exploiting non-uniformity in occurrences of plaintext and ciphertext differences.

Given a vectorial Boolean function $F : \mathbb{F}_2^n \to \mathbb{F}_2^n$, a differential is a pair (δ, Δ) where $\delta \in \mathbb{F}_2^n$ and $\Delta \in \mathbb{F}_2^n$ and its probability is defined as

$$\mathbf{P}[\delta \xrightarrow{F} \Delta] = 2^{-n} \#\{x \in \mathbb{F}_2^n \mid F(x) \oplus F(x \oplus \delta) = \Delta\}.$$

Linear cryptanalysis [12] uses a linear relation between bits from plaintexts, corresponding ciphertexts and encryption key. The strength of the linear relation is measured by its correlation. The correlation of a Boolean function $f : \mathbb{F}_2^n \to \mathbb{F}_2$ is defined as

$$\mathbf{cor}(f) = \mathbf{cor}(f(x)) = 2^{-n} \Big[\#\{x \in \mathbb{F}_2^n | f(x) = 0\} - \#\{x \in \mathbb{F}_2^n | f(x) = 1\} \Big],$$

where the quantity within brackets can be computed as the Walsh transform of f evaluated at zero, see e.g. [13].

In block ciphers, the data is usually represented as vectors in some basis over $\mathbb{F}_2$. For the purposes of our analysis, we also present the input and output data as vectors over $\mathbb{F}_2$. The selection of the basis we use is determined by the linear or differential properties of the cipher. Hence the basis we use may or may not be the same as used for the description of the cipher. The input and output spaces are divided into two orthogonal spaces as follows

$$F : \mathbb{F}_2^s \times \mathbb{F}_2^t \to \mathbb{F}_2^q \times \mathbb{F}_2^r : (x_s, x_t) \mapsto (y_q, y_r) = F(x_s, x_t), \text{where } s + t = q + r = n.$$

In this study, we focus on ML approximations composed of 2^s input masks $(a_s, 0) \in \mathbb{F}_2^s \times \{0\}$, and 2^q output masks $(b_q, 0) \in \mathbb{F}_2^q \times \{0\}$, which makes in total 2^{s+q} linear approximations over F. The correlation of a linear approximation determined by a mask pair $(a_s, 0), (b_q, 0)$ is then $\mathbf{cor}(a_s \cdot x_s + b_q \cdot y_q)$, where $x = (x_s, x_t) \in \mathbb{F}_2^s \times \mathbb{F}_2^t$ and $F(x_s, x_t) = (y_q, y_r) \in \mathbb{F}_2^q \times \mathbb{F}_2^r$.

The strength of the ML approximation $[(a_s, 0), (b_q, 0)]_{a_s \in \mathbb{F}_2^s, b_q \in \mathbb{F}_2^q}$ is measured by its capacity C defined as follows

$$C = \sum_{(a_s, b_q) \neq (0,0)} \mathbf{cor}^2(a_s \cdot x_s \oplus b_q \cdot y_q). \tag{1}$$

The capacity can also be computed as an L^2-distance between the probability distribution of the pairs (x_s, y_q) of partial plaintext and ciphertext values and the uniform distribution over $\mathbb{F}_2^s \times \mathbb{F}_2^q$. As we will show in this paper, this ML approximation is related to a certain TD. This TD is composed of 2^t input differences $(0, \delta_t) \in \{0\} \times \mathbb{F}_2^t$, and 2^r output differences $(0, \Delta_r) \in \{0\} \times \mathbb{F}_2^r$, which makes in total 2^{t+r} differentials over the cipher F. The probability of a differential determined by the input and output differences $(0, \delta_t)$ and $(0, \Delta_r)$ is then $\mathbf{P}[(0, \delta_t) \xrightarrow{F} (0, \Delta_r)] = 2^{-n} \#\{x \in \mathbb{F}_2^n \mid F(x) \oplus F(x \oplus (0, \delta_t)) = (0, \Delta_r)\}$.

Then the probability p of the TD $[(0, \delta_t), (0, \Delta_r)]_{\delta_t \in \mathbb{F}_2^t, \Delta_r \in \mathbb{F}_2^r}$ is defined as the average probability that the output difference is in the set $\{(0, \Delta_r) \mid \Delta_r \in \mathbb{F}_2^r\}$ taken over the input differences $(0, \delta_t)$, $\delta_t \in \mathbb{F}_2^t$, which are assumed to be equally likely. Hence

$$p = 2^{-t} \sum_{\delta_t \in \mathbb{F}_2^t, \Delta_r \in \mathbb{F}_2^r} P[(0, \delta_t) \xrightarrow{F} (0, \Delta_r)]. \tag{2}$$

Note that this definition of TD probability includes the zero input difference.

2.2   Mathematical Link

Chabaud and Vaudenay [8] provide a link between the differential probabilities and the squared correlations of linear approximations of vectorial Boolean functions. In the context of this paper, this one can be written as

$$\mathbf{P}[\delta \xrightarrow{F} \Delta] = 2^{-n} \sum_{a \in \mathbb{F}_2^n} \sum_{b \in \mathbb{F}_2^n} (-1)^{a \cdot \delta \oplus b \cdot \Delta} \mathbf{cor}^2 (a \cdot x \oplus b \cdot F(x)),$$

where $F : \mathbb{F}_2^n \to \mathbb{F}_2^n$ is a vectorial Boolean function. By applying this link to the splitted spaces defined above and summing up over all $\delta_t \in \mathbb{F}_2^t$ and $\Delta_r \in \mathbb{F}_2^r$, the following expression for the probability of a TD is given in [9].

Theorem 1 ([9]). *For all $\delta_s \in \mathbb{F}_2^s$ and $\Delta_q \in \mathbb{F}_2^q$ it holds that*

$$2^{-t} \sum_{\delta_t \in \mathbb{F}_2^t, \Delta_r \in \mathbb{F}_2^r} \mathbf{P}[(\delta_s, \delta_t) \xrightarrow{F} (\Delta_q, \Delta_r)] =$$

$$2^{-q} \sum_{a_s \in \mathbb{F}_2^s, b_q \in \mathbb{F}_2^q} (-1)^{a_s \cdot \delta_s \oplus b_q \cdot \Delta_q} \mathbf{cor}^2 ((a_s, 0) \cdot x \oplus (b_q, 0) \cdot F(x)).$$

In [9] this result was used in the case when $q = t$ and all the nontrivial correlations and differential probabilities are equal to zero, to provide a link between zero-correlation linear (ZC) cryptanalysis [14,6] and impossible differential (ID) cryptanalysis [15]. In this paper, we focus on the case where $\delta_s = 0$ and $\Delta_q = 0$, but no other assumptions are made about the correlations and differential probabilities. If $\delta_s = 0$ and $\Delta_q = 0$, then $a_s \cdot \delta_s \oplus b_q \cdot \Delta_q = 0$, $a_s \in \mathbb{F}_2^s$ and $b_q \in \mathbb{F}_2^q$. By using the notations of (1) and (2) we get the following corollary of Th. 1.

Corollary 1. *Let the TD probability p be defined as in (2) and the ML capacity C as in (1). Then*

$$p = 2^{-q}(C + 1). \tag{3}$$

In the ML context, we evaluate the non-uniformity of the distribution of partial plaintext and ciphertext pairs (x_s, y_q) in terms of the L^2-distance. By Cor. 1 this non-uniformity can be measured in terms of probability of coincidences in the observed values (x_s, y_q). As a special case of Cor. 1, we get the method of Index of Coincidence [16] over some binary alphabet by taking $s = 0$ and $q = n$. Notice that the link given in (3) holds for a block cipher with a fixed-key as well as on average over the keys.

Next we examine the different statistical models developed for ML and TD types of distinguishers and derive relationships between their data, time and memory complexities.

2.3   Complexity of an Attack

While the most powerful statistical attacks aim at recovering some information on the secret key, they are often derived from a distinguishing attack consisting of identifying if a cipher is drawn at random or not. Given some statistical distribution, the data complexity of an attack corresponds to the number of plaintexts necessary to successfully perform this distinguishing operation.

When the distinguishing attack is turned to a key-recovery attack, it is common to separate the process into a *distillation phase* consisting of the extraction of some statistics for all subkey candidates from the available data, an *analysis phase* consisting of the computation of the likelihood of each of the key candidates and a *search phase* for the exhaustive search of the corresponding master key from the list of kept candidates. In the following, we denote by K the set of key candidates.

Throughout this paper, to facilitate the comparison of attacks, we assume that the success probability of finding the key is fixed to 50%. For a key-recovery attack the probability of false positives determines the time complexity of the search phase. The notion of advantage a defined in [17] corresponds to a probability of false positives of 2^{-a}. For simplicity, in the statistical derivations of this paper, we denote by φ_a the quantity $\Phi^{-1}(1 - 2^{-a})$ where Φ is the cumulative function of the standard normal distribution $\mathcal{N}(0, 1)$.

3   Complexity of a Distinguishing Attack

Having established the link (3) between the ML and TD properties of a vector-valued Boolean function, we now examine the distinguishers derived from these properties for block ciphers and their complexities. We use the most commonly accepted statistical models for the distinguishing attacks. The major difference between the distinguishing attacks based on ML and TD is that the former is a KP attack and the latter a CP attack. In this section we analyze this difference in more detail and discuss how it affects the complexities of the distinguishing attacks.

3.1   ML Distinguishing Attacks

For ML attacks both LLR and χ^2 statistical tests have been used in the literature. In this paper, we restrict our analysis to the χ^2 test, which first, according to the results discussed in the following of this section seems to be in good accordance with the common statistical test for a TD distinguishing attack, and secondly, is more applied in practice since it does not require having accurate prediction of the distributions derived from the cipher data.

The data complexity of an ML attack has been studied in [5], and can be computed similarly than for a classical linear attack modelled in [17].

Proposition 1. *For a success probability of 50% and an advantage of a bits, the data complexity N^{ML} of an ML distinguishing attack using 2^{s+q} linear approximations with capacity C as defined in (1) is*

$$N^{ML} = \frac{2^{(s+q+1)/2}}{C} \varphi_a. \tag{4}$$

Given a set of 2^{s+q} linear approximations, the general algorithm presented in Alg. 1, for an ML distinguisher using the χ^2 statistical test requiring N plaintexts can be performed using 2^{q+s} simple operations[1].

Alg. 1. Multidimensional linear distinguisher

```
Set a counter D to 0
Create a table T of size 2^(q+s)
for N plaintexts do
    (y_q, y_r) = E((x_s, x_t))
    T[(x_s, y_q)]+ = 1
for all (x_s, y_q) do
    D+ = (T[(x_s, y_q)] − N/2^(q+s))^2
```

ML distinguishing attacks typically require 2^{s+q} counters, either for evaluating the correlations of the 2^{s+q} linear approximations or evaluating the distributions over the 2^{s+q} values. We observe that in the general ML setting it is possible that 2^{s+q} is larger than the data complexity N^{ML}, in which case the memory requirement can be reduced to N^{ML}. Then it is enough for such an algorithm to deal with a sorted list of maximum size N^{ML}. Using a binary search the time complexity of this KP ML distinguisher is $N^{ML} \log(N^{ML})$.

3.2   TD and SS Distinguishing Attacks

The probability of a TD as given in (2) is computed as an average probability over the input differences. By ordering the plaintexts into structures we can efficiently handle an evaluation of the TD probability for multiple input differences.

In the following, let us assume that all structures are of equal size, and let us denote by S the size of the structures and by M the number of structures used in the attack. Then the total amount of data N^{TD} used for the TD attack is equal to $M \cdot S$. For a further comparison with the complexity derived for the ML attack, we express the relation between the data complexity and the advantage of the TD attack using the framework of [17]. In the context where $p = 2^{-q} + 2^{-q}C$ is close to the uniform probability 2^{-q} ($C \ll 1$) this model is in accordance with the more general model presented in [18].

Proposition 2. *For a success probability of 50% and an advantage of a bits, the data complexity of a TD distinguishing attack using 2^t input differences and 2^r output differences with probability p as defined in (2) is*

$$N^{TD} = \frac{2^{-q+1}}{S \cdot (p - 2^{-q})^2} \cdot \varphi_a^2, \text{ where } S \leq 2^t. \tag{5}$$

Proof. According to the framework of [17], the number of pairs N_S required for such a TD distinguisher is $N_S = \frac{2^{-q}}{(p-2^{-q})^2} \varphi_a^2$. By using M structures of S

---

[1] In some cases this complexity can be reduced using a FFT.

plaintexts, we can generate $N_S = M \cdot (S-1)S/2$ pairs, which we obtain if the amount of available CP data is $N^{TD} = M \cdot S \approx 2N_S/S$.

Alg. 2. TD and SS distinguishers

Set a counter D to 0
for M values of $x_s \in \mathbb{F}_2^q$ **do**
Create a table T of size S
for S values of $x_t \in \mathbb{F}_2^t$ **do**
$(y_q, y_r) = E((x_s, x_t))$
$T[x_t] = y_q$
for all pairs (x_t, x_t') **do**
if $T[x_t] = T[x_t']$ **then**
$D+=1$

(2a) Generic TD distinguisher

Set a counter D (D') to 0
for M values of $x_s \in \mathbb{F}_2^q$ **do**
Initialize to 0 a table T of size 2^q
for S values of $x_t \in \mathbb{F}_2^t$ **do**
$(y_q, y_r) = E((x_s, x_t))$
$T[y_q]+=1$
for all $y_q \in \mathbb{F}_2^q$ **do**
$D+=T[y_q] \cdot (T[y_q]-1)/2$
$(D'+=T[y_q]^2)$

(2b) Improved TD distinguisher (SS distinguisher)

When in the context of TD cryptanalysis, the number of considered input differences t is relatively small, the cryptanalyst usually runs a distinguisher of the type given in Alg. 2a. Each structure is handled separately. To minimize the number of encryptions, the partial ciphertexts y_q are stored. The time complexity of the CP TD distinguisher represented in Alg. 2a corresponds to N^{TD} encryptions and $M \cdot S^2/2$ simple operations. The time taken by the comparison between all ciphertext pairs is then often considered as the limiting factor for the attack. We observe that by using the memory differently meaning that instead of storing all partial ciphertexts y_q, storing only their distribution, we can also reduce the time complexity. Indeed, if ℓ partial ciphertexts y_q are equal, then $\ell(\ell-1)/2$ ciphertext pairs have difference zero in these q bits. The TD distinguishing algorithm modified in this manner is presented in Alg. 2b. At a memory cost of 2^q counters, its time complexity is $M \cdot 2^q$ simple operations and N^{TD} encryptions.

The SS attack has been proposed by Collard and Standaert [4] and applied on the cipher PRESENT [19]. It exploits the non-uniformity of the distribution of the partial ciphertexts $y_q \in \mathbb{F}_2^q$ obtained by encryption of plaintexts (x_s, x_t) by keeping x_s fixed. The non-uniformity is measured using the L^2-distance. This is exactly what Alg. 2b computes using the score D'. By noticing that the score D of the TD distinguisher satisfies $D = \sum_M \sum_{y_q \mathbb{F}_2^q} T[y_q] \cdot (T[y_q]-1)/2 = D' - M \cdot S/2$, we conclude that the CP TD distinguisher as described in Alg. 2b is identical to the CP SS distinguisher of [4].

In 2011, Leander [3] observed a mathematical relation between the expected values of the SS score D' computed in Alg. 2b and the ML score D in Alg. 1. But this link has not been used for developing a statistical model for SS attacks. The statistical model developed in this paper, allows for the first time to derive accurate estimates of the data complexity for the last-rounds SS key-recovery attack on PRESENT proposed in [4]. This key recovery attack will be explained and analyzed in Sect. 4.

3.3 Comparison between ML and TD Distinguishers

Recalling Cor. 1 we can summarize the results from (4) and (5) and get the following relationship between the data complexities N^{ML} and N^{TD} of the ML distinguisher and the TD distinguisher.

Corollary 2. *Consider an ML distinguisher and a TD distinguisher based on the ML and TD properties defined in Sect. 2.1. Then*

$$N^{TD} = \frac{(N^{ML})^2}{S \cdot 2^s} = \frac{2^{q+1}}{S \cdot C^2} \cdot \varphi_a^2.$$

In Table 1, we summarize the complexities of the KP ML and CP TD distinguishers presented in this section. Given the splitted input and output spaces,

Table 1. Complexities of the ML and TD distinguishing algorithms

Alg.	Data	Time	Memory	Condition
ML, Alg. 1	N^{ML}	N^{ML}	2^{s+q}	$2^{s+q} < N^{ML}$
TD, Alg. 2a	N^{TD}	$N^{TD} + N^{TD}S$	$S(\leq 2^t)$	$N^{TD}S < 2^n$
TD, Alg. 2b	N^{TD}	$N^{TD} + M \cdot 2^q$	$\min(S, 2^q)$	-

$\mathbb{F}_2^n = \mathbb{F}_2^s \times \mathbb{F}_2^t = \mathbb{F}_2^q \times \mathbb{F}_2^r$, a TD distinguisher as presented in Alg. 2b is less memory demanding than a ML distinguisher as presented in Alg. 1. According to a commonly adopted practice in differential cryptanalysis, the structure size is maximized to minimize the time complexity. If $S = 2^t$ we obtain by Cor. 2 that

$$N^{TD} = 2^{-n}(N^{ML})^2.$$

This means that also the data and the time complexities of the TD distinguisher is smaller than the ones of the corresponding ML distinguisher.

   In the remaining sections of this paper, we focus on the TD and ML key-recovery attacks. In particular, we investigate whether a CP attack is always less costly than a KP attack, and extract links with other statistical key-recovery attacks on block ciphers.

4 TD and SS Key-Recovery Attacks

4.1 Last-Rounds TD and SS Key-Recovery Attack

For the results described in this section, we use the notation of Alg. 3. The s bits of the TD distinguisher on which the input difference is fixed to 0 is called a fixation. As suggested by [4], if the size of the fixation is small, we can increase the number of rounds of the distinguisher. Given the fixation on s bits, we denote by W_s the larger fixation after adding some rounds at the beginning of the distinguisher. By choosing structures such that the part w_s

of the plaintext $w = (w_s, w_t) \in W_s \times W_t$ is fixed we remain certain that the s-bits part x_s of $x = (x_s, x_t)$ is fixed and ensures zero difference in these bits between two plaintexts in a same structure. The space Z_q, described in Alg. 3 corresponds to the minimal space needed for checking the distribution of the q bits y_q after partial decryption of the ciphertexts $z = (z_q, z_r)$. The resulting CP TD last-rounds key-recovery attack is depicted in Alg. 3.

Alg. 3. Last-rounds CP TD and SS key-recovery attack

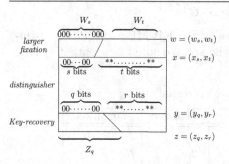

For all $|K|$ key candidates k, set a counter D_k to 0
for M values of $w_s \in W_s$ do
  Initialize a vector V of size $|Z_q|$ to 0
  for S values of $w_t \in W_t$ do
    $(z_q, z_r) = E((w_s, w_t))$
    $V[z_q]+ = 1$
for all key candidates k do
  Initialize a vector T of size 2^q to 0
  for all $z_q \in Z_q$ do
    Partially decrypt to obtain y_q from z_q
    $T[y_q]+ = V[z_q]$
  for all $y_q \in \mathbb{F}_2^q$ do
    $D_k+ = T[y_q] \cdot (T[y_q] - 1)/2$
Sort the counters D_k to obtain the most likely keys.

Implementing Alg. 3 requires storing $|K|+|Z_q|$ counters. This algorithm which runs in a time corresponding to $M \cdot S$ encryptions and $M \cdot |K| \cdot |Z_q|$ partial inversions requires $M \cdot S$ chosen plaintexts. Note that by increasing the size of the fixation, the size S of a structure is limited to $S \leq |W_t| \leq 2^t$. Then according to (5) the increasing data complexity constitutes a major limiting factor to this process which consists of adding rounds at the beginning of the distinguisher without guessing any key-bits on these rounds.

4.2 Using the Link between TD and SS Attacks to Analyze the SS Attack on 24 Rounds of PRESENT

From the complexity of the last-rounds TD key-recovery attack given in Alg. 3 and the relation between TD and SS described in Sect. 3.2 , we analyze in this section the SS key-recovery attack of [4] on 24 rounds of PRESENT.

When linking the statistic computed in the SS attack with the capacity of a ML approximation, Leander [3] also confirms that the capacity of the ML distinguisher can be estimated as suggested in [4] by multiplying by a factor close to 2^{-3} when adding a round to the distinguisher (see Fig. 1). In ML attacks the data complexity is inversely proportional to the capacity, and the same was assumed to hold for the SS distinguisher used in [4]. While the experiments of [20] confirm this hypothesis when the attack is limited to one structure, a gap was observed in [20] starting from rounds 18 (or 19). Next we present an explanation of this behavior based on the statistical model of the SS distinguisher we derived using the TD model.

From Cor. 2 we know that the number of samples of a TD attack so also of a SS attack is a multiple of $\frac{2^q}{C^2}$. As long as only one structure is used, with N plaintexts we can generate $N^2/2$ plaintext pairs and the data complexity is $N = \frac{2^{(q+1)/2}}{C}\varphi_a$. But when more than one structure is used the data complexity is proportional to the square of the inverse of the capacity: $N = \frac{2^{q+1}}{|W_t| \cdot C^2}\varphi_a^2$. This phenomenon is illustrated in Fig. 1. Given a distinguisher on r rounds, the data complexity computed from Cor. 2 of the SS attack on $r+3$ rounds, meaning with a fixation of $log(|W_s|) = 16$ bits, and on $r + 4$ rounds, meaning with a fixation of $log(|W_s|) = 32$ bits, is given in Fig. 1. In particular, the computed values on the right figure are, for the first time, in accordance with the experiments done in [20]. From Fig. 1, one can see that by fixing 32 bits only 21 rounds can be attacked. By fixing 16 bits, one can compute that an attack on 24 rounds will require more than the full codebook. From these observations, we conclude that the SS attack described in [4] only works for 23 rounds of PRESENT instead of 24 rounds as originally claimed.

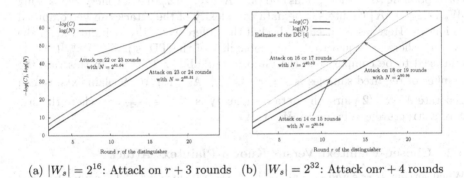

(a) $|W_s| = 2^{16}$: Attack on $r + 3$ rounds   (b) $|W_s| = 2^{32}$: Attack on $r + 4$ rounds

Fig. 1. Capacity C of the r-round ML of [4] as computed in [3] and data complexity N (computed using Cor. 2) of the underlined attacks on $r + r'$-rounds for $a = 8$

5   Comparison of TD and ML Key-Recovery Attacks

5.1   Partial Key-Recovery Attack on the First Rounds

In the previous section, we discussed the limitation of adding rounds at the beginning of the distinguisher without guessing any key-bits on these rounds. In this section, we develop a TD key-recovery attack which allow to find the key of the first rounds. For more generality and to illustrate some data, time and memory trade-offs, we assume that the aim is to guess only part of the possible key bits in the first rounds. In Alg. 4, we describe this TD key-recovery attack. From the fixation of s bits, we want to keep a fixation on s_0 bits, and we define a space W_{s_0} such that given a fixation on W_{s_0} after partial encryption we have a fixation on these s_0 bits. We then take advantage of the non-fixed $s_1 + t$ bits to

Alg. 4. First-rounds and last-rounds TD key-recovery attack

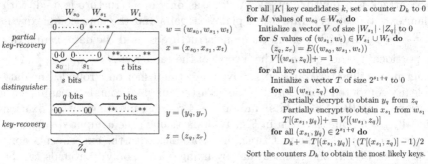

For all $|K|$ key candidates k, set a counter D_k to 0
for M values of $w_{s_0} \in W_{s_0}$ **do**
   Initialize a vector V of size $|W_{s_1}| \cdot |Z_q|$ to 0
   for S values of $(w_{s_1}, w_t) \in W_{s_1} \cup W_t$ **do**
      $(z_q, z_r) = E((w_{s_0}, w_{s_1}, w_t))$
      $V[(w_{s_1}, z_q)]+ = 1$
for all key candidates k **do**
   Initialize a vector T of size 2^{s_1+q} to 0
   for all (w_{s_1}, z_q) **do**
      Partially decrypt to obtain y_q from z_q
      Partially encrypt to obtain x_{s_1} from w_{s_1}
      $T[(x_{s_1}, y_q)]+ = V[(w_{s_1}, z_q)]$
   for all $(x_{s_1}, y_q) \in 2^{s_1+q}$ **do**
      $D_k+ = T[(x_{s_1}, y_q)] \cdot (T[(x_{s_1}, z_q)] - 1)/2$
Sort the counters D_k to obtain the most likely keys.

find some information on the first rounds subkey. In Alg. 4, the space $W_{s_1} \times W_t$ corresponds to the non-fixed bits of $w = (w_{s_0}, w_{s_1}, w_t)$.

The partial first rounds TD key-recovery attack of Alg. 4 can be done in a time corresponding to N encryptions and $|M| \cdot |K| \cdot |W_{s_1}| \cdot |Z_q|$ partial encryptions using $|W_{s_1}| \cdot |Z_q| + |K|$ counters. The data complexity of the attack can be computed as follows. Here, as we need to check if the difference in the s_1 input bits of the distinguishers are equal to 0, the probability of the TD is $p = 2^{-(s_1+q)}(C + 1)$ and need to be compared to the uniform probability $2^{-(s_1+q)}$. In this case the number of required samples is $N_S = \frac{2^{q+s_1}}{C^2}\varphi_a^2$. As with $M \cdot S$ plaintexts we can generate $M \cdot S^2/2$ pairs, the data complexity is $N = \frac{2^{q+s_1+1}}{S \cdot C^2}\varphi_a^2$, where the size S of a structure can be up to $|W_{s_1} \cup W_t|$.

5.2 Chosen-Plaintext Versus Known-Plaintext Attack

When setting $s_1 = s$ and $s_0 = 0$ in Alg. 4, we transform a CP TD attack to a KP TD attack. In this case with N plaintexts we can generate $N(N - 1)/2 \approx N^2/2$ pairs. As in the TD setting the uniform probability is equal to 2^{-q-s}, the number of required samples is $N_S = \frac{2^{q+s}}{C^2} \cdot \varphi_a^2$. The data complexity of a CP TD attack is then equal to the one of a KP ML key-recovery attack: $N^{TD} = N^{ML} = \frac{2^{(s+q+1)/2}}{C}\varphi_a$. The time and memory complexities are then also similar. While all KP attacks can be converted to a CP attack, by this result we show, that in some cases, we can also with small data, time and memory complexity overhead, convert a CP key-recovery attack to a KP one.

5.3 A Differential Attack on 26 Rounds of PRESENT

In [10], Cho proposed a KP ML attack on 26 rounds of PRESENT. This attack which is based on a combination of 9 ML approximations can be converted to a TD attack in the KP model as presented in the previous section. In this particular case the data complexity is $N^{TD} = N^{ML} = \frac{\sqrt{9 \cdot 2^{8+1}}}{C}\varphi_a$. The time and memory complexities of the TD key-recovery attack are similar to the ones of the ML key-recovery attack.

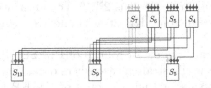

Fig. 2. Partial key recovery on the first round of PRESENT

More importantly, inspired by the KP attack of Cho [10] on PRESENT, we illustrate that, in many cases, when changing from the KP model to the CP model with only a partial key recovery on the first rounds data, time and memory complexities can be reduced.

In the KP ML attack of Cho, 16 bits of keys corresponding to the ones at the input of S_4, S_5, S_6, S_7 (see Fig. 2) are guessed for partial encryption on the first round. If we are in the CP model and we want to only guess part of these 16 key bits, we can specify that the input differences of some Sboxes are equal to 0. We assume that out of the 4 Sboxes S_4, S_5, S_6, S_7, the input of b of them are fixed (see Fig. 2). In this case, $|W_{s_0}| = 2^{4b}$ and we can use structure of size $|W_{s_1}| \cdot |W_t| = 2^{64-4b}$. The data complexity of the attack is then $N = \frac{9 \cdot 2^{4+(4-b)+1}}{2^{64-4b}C^2} \varphi_a^2$. In Fig. 3, we illustrate that depending of the size $|W_{s_0}|$ of the fixation, the data complexity of the key-recovery attack in the CP model can be smaller than in the KP model.

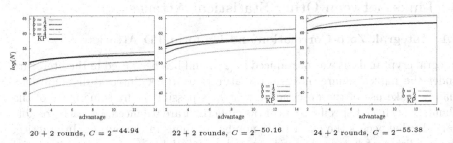

20 + 2 rounds, $C = 2^{-44.94}$ 22 + 2 rounds, $C = 2^{-50.16}$ 24 + 2 rounds, $C = 2^{-55.38}$

Fig. 3. Evolution of the data complexity of a CP key-recovery attack depending of the size of the fixation and comparison with a KP attack for different number of rounds of PRESENT

Given the same advantage, if the data complexity of the KP model is smaller than the one in the CP model, it is the same for the time complexity of the distillation phase. By storing only a vector of size $|Z_q| \cdot |W_{s_1}|$ instead of $|Z_q| \cdot |W_s|$, the memory complexity of the CP attack is always smaller than the one of the KP attack. Assuming a fixation of $4b$ bits and independent keys in the first and last rounds the time complexity of the distillation phase (Time$_1$ in Table 2) corresponds to $N \cdot 2^{-4b}$ partial encryptions and N encryptions. In the CP model 2^{33-4b} counters are necessary for the attack. The time complexity to recover the

80 bit master key (Time$_2$ in Table 2) is 2^{80-a}. For illustration, we compare in Table 2 the complexities of some KP attacks and CP attacks with $b = 1$ on PRESENT.

Out of the proposed attacks on 24 rounds of PRESENT, with complexities summarized in Table 2a we illustrate a case where data, time and memory complexities of the CP are smaller than the ones of the KP attacks. Out of the 26-round attacks summarized in Table 2b, we show that even when close to the full codebook, the proposed CP attack required less memory than the KP attack.

Table 2. Complexity of attacks on PRESENT for a success probability of 50%. Time$_1$: Complexity of the distillation phase. Time$_2$: Complexity of the search phase.

(a) Attacks on 24 rounds of PRESENT, with different complexities

Model	a	Data	Memory	Time$_1$	Time$_2$
CP	10	$2^{54.75}$	2^{29}	$2^{54.75}$	2^{70}
KP	5	$2^{57.14}$	2^{33}	$2^{57.14}$	2^{75}

(b) Attacks on 26 rounds of PRESENT, with same advantage

Model	a	Data	Memory	Time$_1$	Time$_2$
CP	4	$2^{63.16}$	2^{29}	$2^{63.16}$	2^{76}
KP	4	$2^{62.08}$	2^{33}	$2^{62.08}$	2^{76}

While it has always been assumed that the security of PRESENT in regards to differential cryptanalysis was always better than the one in regards to linear cryptanalysis, these examples illustrate the fact that we can build a CP TD attack on 26 rounds of PRESENT with less memory complexity than the best KP ML attack of [10] done with 2^{64} KP and in time 2^{72}.

6   Links between Other Statistical Attacks

6.1   Integral, Zero-Correlation and Uniform TD Attacks

Integral cryptanalysis was introduced in [21], and has been used in the literature under the names square, integral or saturation attack. Integral distinguishers mainly make use of the observation that it is possible to fix some parts of the plaintext such that specific parts of the ciphertext are balanced, i.e. each possible partial value occurs the exact same number of times in the output. In practice, the condition of balancedness is typically verified by summing up all partial ciphertexts. In [6], however, in the attack called as zero-correlation integral attack, the authors suggest to store the partial ciphertexts and to verify the proper balancedness condition.

ZC distinguishers [14,6] are built out of linear approximations with zero bias. In that case the expected capacity of the ML approximation is $C = 0$, and it has been shown in [6] that distinguishing from random can be successful only if no repetition of the plaintexts is allowed. In [6], the authors present a mathematical link between integral and ZC distinguishers. Using this link, the authors of [6] convert a ZC distinguisher on 30 rounds of Skipjack-BABABABA to an integral attack on 31 rounds.

By observing that the output distribution is balanced exactly when the counters $T[y_q]$ of Alg. 3 are all equal, we show that the integral attack is a TD attack where the TD probability of having zero difference in the q bits corresponds to the uniform probability $p = 2^{-q}$. If $q \neq t = n - s$, a ZC distinguisher gives a *uniform truncated differential* distinguisher where the attacker takes advantage of differences which occur uniformly for the cipher.

While the CP integral attack of [6] requires 2^{48} plaintexts and a memory of 2^{32} counters, the same attack on 31 rounds of Skipjack-BABABABA in the KP (without repetition) ZC model would have required roughly the same data and time complexities but a memory of 2^{48} counters. Indeed, the use of structures as in the TD case allows to reduce the memory complexity of the attack as described in Sect. 4.

6.2   Impossible Differential and ML Attacks

Impossible differential (ID) cryptanalysis [15] takes advantage of differentials that never occur. From (2), in the ID case we have $p = 2^{-t}$ and from the formula $p = 2^{-q}(C+1)$, we deduce that $C = 2^{q-t}-1$. This formula was used directly in [9] to show the equivalence between the ID distinguisher and the ZC distinguisher in the case where $t = q$. Nevertheless, in many concrete applications [15,22,23], t is small in comparison to n and q is close to n.

It is often assumed that the data complexity N^{ID} of an ID is of order of magnitude $N^{ID} = \mathcal{O}(2^{q-t})$. As the corresponding KP ML distinguisher will require a data complexity of $N^{ML} = \mathcal{O}(\frac{2^{(q+s)/2}}{2^{q-t}-1})$, we discuss in this section the limitations of converting a CP ID distinguisher to a KP ML one.

In practice, ID distinguisher are defined for small $r = n-q$ and $t = n-s$. From $C = 2^{q-t} - 1$, one can note that the ID property occurs only if $q \geq t$. In that case an ID distinguishing attack can be performed using 2^{q-t} plaintexts, in time 2^{q+t} by storing 2^t counters. On the other hand, a KP ML distinguishing attack would require to analyse a distribution of size $2^{(n+q-t)}$ using $2^{(n-q+t)/2}$ known plaintexts. Nevertheless, when the size of the ML distribution is much larger than the data requirement given by the statistical model, the data complexity needs to be adjusted to approximately to $2^{(n+q-t)/2}$ for the χ^2 test to give meaningful results.

While it is possible to find practical ID distinguishers [24] where the data complexity of the ML and ID distinguishers are similar, the time and memory complexity of the ML distinguisher constitutes a limiting factor for this transformation. Nevertheless as the data complexity of a TD or an ID attack is modified when it comes to a key-recovery on the first rounds, it remains an open question to see if we can transform a CP ID key-recovery attack to a KP ML one.

6.3   Classical Differential and Linear Cryptanalysis

As a special case, we see that any classical KP linear distinguishing attack ($s = q = 1$) can be seen as a CP TD distinguishing attack described in Alg. 2b. As summarized in Table 1, both distinguishing attacks have similar complexities. While a last-rounds key-recovery attack remain similar for the CP TD and the

KP ML attacks, due to the small fixation $s = 1$, a CP TD key-recovery attack on the first rounds will be equivalent to a KP one. This link has been used previously, although in an implicit manner, for the attack on Salsa and ChaCha [25], where a TD distinguisher with probability $1/2 + \varepsilon$ was extracted.

A transformation from the CP classical differential ($s = q = n - 1$) to a KP ML does not work in a similar way. While the classical differential distinguisher is memoryless, the ML one required huge memory as shown in Table 1. As in practical security considerations the data complexity typically is close to the full codebook, this KP ML distinguisher has also too high time complexity. A far comparison of the data complexity between these attacks will require more investigation since in that case this one can not be computed from (5).

7   Conclusion

In this paper, we have been investigating many statistical single-key key-recovery attacks on block ciphers both in the KP and CP models. We have shown that many of them are equivalent or that a data-time-memory tradeoffs allow for conversion from a CP to a KP attack. While as shown in Table 3, it is always possible to convert a last-round KP attack of linear type to a CP attack that requires less data, time and/or memory complexity, converting a CP attack to a KP attack is often less profitable. As illustrated by the key-recovery attacks on PRESENT in Sect. 5 on the first rounds, it is not always straightforward to make comparison between KP and CP key-recovery cryptanalysis methods.

The results and links presented in this paper allow to achieve a better understanding of the statistical models of a large number of statistical attacks. For instance, by showing the equivalence between the SS and TD attack, we have been able to compute the data requirement of the SS key-recovery attack.

The attacks are usually called after the method used to derive the distinguisher. For instance, the distinguishers for the differential-linear cryptanalysis are found by combining a truncated differential and a linear approximation. Nevertheless, the attack itself can be treated as a TD attack, see e.g. [26]. In this paper we also presented a concrete example of a distinguisher originally found as a linear property but now used to launch a CP differential attack. It has been a common belief that PRESENT was more secure against differential than linear cryptanalysis, since it is easy to derive linear properties, but practically impossible to compute the probabilities of differential trails. In this paper, we have shown how to derive from the known ML distinguisher a CP differential key-recovery attack on 26 rounds of PRESENT that uses less memory than the previously known KP attack.

We have focused on the most basic ML and TD attacks on block ciphers. We do not claim to have covered them all and many variants and refinements remain to be studied. More generally, it would be interesting to analyze our approach in more detail in the context of decorrelation theory [1] which provides a unified framework for all statistical attacks on block ciphers in the single-key model.

Table 3. Links between last-rounds key-recovery attacks

Linear context		Differential context
ML	$\xrightarrow{2^{s+q} \lessgtr 2^n}$	TD = Statistical Saturation
ML	$\xrightarrow{q>t \text{ and } C=2^{-t+q}-1}$	ID (TD with $p_* = 0$)
ZC (ML with $C = 0$)	$\xrightarrow{t>q}$	Integral (TD with $p = 2^{-q}$)
ZC (ML with $C = 0$)	$\xrightarrow{q=t}$	ID (TD with $p_* = 0$)
Linear (ML with $s = q = 1$)	$\longrightarrow$	TD

Acknowledgments. We wish to thank Gregor Leander for useful discussions. We also wish to thank the anonymous reviewers for helpful comments which help us to improve the quality of this paper.

References

1. Vaudenay, S.: Decorrelation: A Theory for Block Cipher Security. J. Cryptology 16, 249–286 (2003)
2. Wagner, D.: Towards a Unifying View of Block Cipher Cryptanalysis. In: Roy, B., Meier, W. (eds.) FSE 2004. LNCS, vol. 3017, pp. 16–33. Springer, Heidelberg (2004)
3. Leander, G.: On Linear Hulls, Statistical Saturation Attacks, PRESENT and a Cryptanalysis of PUFFIN. In: Paterson, K.G. (ed.) EUROCRYPT 2011. LNCS, vol. 6632, pp. 303–322. Springer, Heidelberg (2011)
4. Collard, B., Standaert, F.-X.: A Statistical Saturation Attack against the Block Cipher PRESENT. In: Fischlin, M. (ed.) CT-RSA 2009. LNCS, vol. 5473, pp. 195–210. Springer, Heidelberg (2009)
5. Hermelin, M., Cho, J.Y., Nyberg, K.: Multidimensional Extension of Matsui's Algorithm 2. In: Dunkelman, O. (ed.) FSE 2009. LNCS, vol. 5665, pp. 209–227. Springer, Heidelberg (2009)
6. Bogdanov, A., Leander, G., Nyberg, K., Wang, M.: Integral and Multidimensional Linear Distinguishers with Correlation Zero. In: Wang, X., Sako, K. (eds.) ASIACRYPT 2012. LNCS, vol. 7658, pp. 244–261. Springer, Heidelberg (2012)
7. Knudsen, L.R.: Truncated and Higher Order Differentials. In: Preneel, B. (ed.) FSE 1994. LNCS, vol. 1008, pp. 196–211. Springer, Heidelberg (1995)
8. Chabaud, F., Vaudenay, S.: Links Between Differential and Linear Cryptanalysis. In: De Santis, A. (ed.) EUROCRYPT 1994. LNCS, vol. 950, pp. 356–365. Springer, Heidelberg (1995)
9. Blondeau, C., Nyberg, K.: New Links between Differential and Linear Cryptanalysis. In: Johansson, T., Nguyen, P.Q. (eds.) EUROCRYPT 2013. LNCS, vol. 7881, pp. 388–404. Springer, Heidelberg (2013)
10. Cho, J.Y.: Linear Cryptanalysis of Reduced-Round PRESENT. In: Pieprzyk, J. (ed.) CT-RSA 2010. LNCS, vol. 5985, pp. 302–317. Springer, Heidelberg (2010)
11. Biham, E., Shamir, A.: Differential Cryptanalysis of DES-like Cryptosystems. In: Menezes, A., Vanstone, S.A. (eds.) CRYPTO 1990. LNCS, vol. 537, pp. 2–21. Springer, Heidelberg (1991)

12. Matsui, M.: Linear Cryptanalysis Method for DES Cipher. In: Helleseth, T. (ed.) EUROCRYPT 1993. LNCS, vol. 765, pp. 386–397. Springer, Heidelberg (1994)
13. Carlet, C.: Boolean Functions for Cryptography and Error Correcting. In: Crama, Y., Hammer, P.L. (eds.) Boolean Models and Methods in Mathematics, Computer Science, and Engineering, pp. 257–397. Cambridge University Press, Oxford (2010)
14. Bogdanov, A., Wang, M.: Zero Correlation Linear Cryptanalysis with Reduced Data Complexity. In: Canteaut, A. (ed.) FSE 2012. LNCS, vol. 7549, pp. 29–48. Springer, Heidelberg (2012)
15. Biham, E., Biryukov, A., Shamir, A.: Cryptanalysis of Skipjack Reduced to 31 Rounds Using Impossible Differentials. In: Stern, J. (ed.) EUROCRYPT 1999. LNCS, vol. 1592, pp. 12–23. Springer, Heidelberg (1999)
16. Friedman, W.F.: The index of coincidence and its applications in cryptology. Riverbank Laboratories. Department of Ciphers. Publ., 22, Geneva, Ill (1922)
17. Selçuk, A.A.: On Probability of Success in Linear and Differential Cryptanalysis. J. Cryptology 21, 131–147 (2008)
18. Blondeau, C., Gérard, B., Tillich, J.-P.: Accurate estimates of the data complexity and success probability for various cryptanalyses. Des. Codes Cryptography 59, 3–34 (2011)
19. Bogdanov, A., Knudsen, L.R., Leander, G., Paar, C., Poschmann, A., Robshaw, M.J.B., Seurin, Y., Vikkelsoe, C.: PRESENT: An Ultra-Lightweight Block Cipher. In: Paillier, P., Verbauwhede, I. (eds.) CHES 2007. LNCS, vol. 4727, pp. 450–466. Springer, Heidelberg (2007)
20. Kerckhof, S., Collard, B., Standaert, F.-X.: FPGA Implementation of a Statistical Saturation Attack against PRESENT. In: Nitaj, A., Pointcheval, D. (eds.) AFRICACRYPT 2011. LNCS, vol. 6737, pp. 100–116. Springer, Heidelberg (2011)
21. Daemen, J., Knudsen, L.R., Rijmen, V.: The Block Cipher Square. In: Biham, E. (ed.) FSE 1997. LNCS, vol. 1267, pp. 149–165. Springer, Heidelberg (1997)
22. Luo, Y., Lai, X., Wu, Z., Gong, G.: A Unified Method for Finding Impossible Differentials of Block Cipher Structures. Inf. Sci. 263, 211–220 (2014)
23. Chen, J., Wang, M., Preneel, B.: Impossible Differential Cryptanalysis of the Lightweight Block Ciphers TEA, XTEA and HIGHT. In: Mitrokotsa, A., Vaudenay, S. (eds.) AFRICACRYPT 2012. LNCS, vol. 7374, pp. 117–137. Springer, Heidelberg (2012)
24. Wu, S., Wang, M.: Automatic Search of Truncated Impossible Differentials for Word-Oriented Block Ciphers. In: Galbraith, S., Nandi, M. (eds.) INDOCRYPT 2012. LNCS, vol. 7668, pp. 283–302. Springer, Heidelberg (2012)
25. Aumasson, J.P., Fischer, S., Khazaei, S., Meier, W., Rechberger, C.: New Features of Latin Dances: Analysis of Salsa, ChaCha, and Rumba. In: Nyberg, K. (ed.) FSE 2008. LNCS, vol. 5086, pp. 470–488. Springer, Heidelberg (2008)
26. Blondeau, C., Leander, G., Nyberg, K.: Differential-Linear Cryptanalysis Revisited. In: Cid, C., Rechberger, C. (eds.) FSE 2014. Springer (to appear, 2014)

Faster Compact Diffie–Hellman:
Endomorphisms on the x-line

Craig Costello[1], Huseyin Hisil[2], and Benjamin Smith[3,4]

[1] Microsoft Research, Redmond, USA
craigco@microsoft.com
[2] Yasar University, Izmir, Turkey
huseyin.hisil@yasar.edu.tr
[3] INRIA (Équipe-projet GRACE), France
[4] LIX (Laboratoire d'Informatique), École polytechnique, France
smith@lix.polytechnique.fr

Abstract. We describe an implementation of fast elliptic curve scalar multiplication, optimized for Diffie–Hellman Key Exchange at the 128-bit security level. The algorithms are compact (using only x-coordinates), run in constant time with uniform execution patterns, and do not distinguish between the curve and its quadratic twist; they thus have a built-in measure of side-channel resistance. (For comparison, we also implement two faster but non-constant-time algorithms.) The core of our construction is a suite of two-dimensional differential addition chains driven by efficient endomorphism decompositions, built on curves selected from a family of $\mathbb{Q}$-curve reductions over $\mathbb{F}_{p^2}$ with $p = 2^{127} - 1$. We include state-of-the-art experimental results for twist-secure, constant-time, x-coordinate-only scalar multiplication.

Keywords: Elliptic curve cryptography, scalar multiplication, twist-secure, side channel attacks, endomorphism, Kummer variety, addition chains, Montgomery curve.

1 Introduction

In this paper, we discuss the design and implementation of state-of-the-art Elliptic Curve Diffie–Hellman key exchange (ECDH) primitives for security level of approximately 128 bits. The major priorities for our implementation are

1. **Compactness:** We target x-coordinate-only systems. These systems offer the advantages of shorter keys, simple and fast algorithms, and (when properly designed) the use of arbitrary x-values, not just legitimate x-coordinates of points on a curve (the "illegitimate" values are x-coordinates on the quadratic twist). For x-coordinate ECDH, the elliptic curve exists only to supply formulæ for scalar multiplications, and a hard elliptic curve discrete logarithm problem (ECDLP) to underwrite a hard computational Diffie–Hellman problem (CDHP) on x-coordinates. The users should not have to verify whether given values correspond to points on a curve, nor

P.Q. Nguyen and E. Oswald (Eds.): EUROCRYPT 2014, LNCS 8441, pp. 183–200, 2014.

should they have to compute any quantity that cannot be derived simply from x-coordinates alone. In particular, neither a user nor an algorithm should have to distinguish between the curve and its quadratic twist—and the curve must be chosen to be twist-secure.

2. **Fast, constant-time execution:** Every Diffie–Hellman key exchange is essentially comprised of four scalar multiplications,[1] so optimizing scalar multiplication $P \mapsto [m]P$ for varying P and m is a very high priority. At the same time, a minimum requirement for protecting against side-channel timing attacks is that every scalar multiplication $P \mapsto [m]P$ must be computed in constant time (and ideally with the same execution pattern), regardless of the values of m and P.

Our implementation targets a security level of approximately 128 bits (comparable with `Curve25519` [3], `secp256r1` [12], and `brainpoolP256t1` [11]). The reference system with respect to our desired properties is Bernstein's `Curve25519`, which is based on an efficient, uniform differential addition chain applied to a well-chosen pair of curve and twist presented as Montgomery models. These models not only provide highly efficient group operations, but they are optimized for x-coordinate-only operations, which (crucially) do not distinguish between the curve and its twist. Essentially, well-chosen Montgomery curves offer compactness straight out of the box.

Having chosen Montgomery curves as our platform, we must implement a fast, uniform, and constant-time scalar multiplication on their x-coordinates. To turbocharge our scalar multiplication, we apply a combination of efficiently computable pseudo-endomorphisms and two-dimensional differential addition chains. The use of efficient endomorphisms follows in the tradition of [21], [33], [16], and [15], but to the best of our knowledge, this work represents the first use of endomorphism scalar decompositions in the *pure* x-coordinate setting (that is, without additional input to the addition chain).

Our implementation is built on a curve-twist pair $(\mathcal{E}, \mathcal{E}')$ equipped with efficiently computable endomorphisms (ψ, ψ'). The family of $\mathbb{Q}$-curve reductions in [32] offer a combination of fast endomorphisms and compatibility with fast underlying field arithmetic. Crucially (and unlike earlier endomorphism constructions such as [16] and [15]), they also offer the possibility of twist-secure group orders over fast fields. One of these curves, with almost-prime order over a 254-bit field, forms the foundation of our construction (see §2). Any other curve from the same family over the same field could be used with only very minor modifications to the formulæ below and the source code for our implementations; we explain our specific curve choice in Appendix A. The endomorphisms ψ and ψ' induce efficient pseudo-endomorphisms ψ_x and ψ'_x on the x-line; we explain their construction and use in §3.

---

[1] We do not count the cost of authenticating keys, etc., here. In the *static* Diffie–Hellman protocol, two of the scalar multiplications can be computed in advance; in this fixed-base scenario (where P is constant but m varies) one can profit from extensive precomputations. For simplicity, in this work we concentrate on the *dynamic* case (where P and m are variable).

The key idea of this work is to replace conventional scalar multiplications $(m, x(P)) \mapsto x([m]P)$ with multiscalar multiexponentiations

$$((a, b), x(P)) \longmapsto x([a]P \oplus [b]\psi(P)) \text{ or } x([a]P \oplus [b]\psi'(P)) ,$$

where (a, b) is either a short multiscalar decomposition of a random full-length scalar m (that is, such that $[m]P = [a]P \oplus [b]\psi(P)$ or $[a]P \oplus [b]\psi'(P)$), or a random short multiscalar. The choice of ψ or ψ' formally depends on whether P is on $\mathcal{E}$ or $\mathcal{E}'$, but there is no difference between ψ and ψ' on the level of x-coordinates: they are implemented using exactly the same formulæ. Since every element of the base field is the x-coordinate of a point on $\mathcal{E}$ or $\mathcal{E}'$, we may view the transformation above as acting purely on field elements and not curve points.

From a practical point of view, the two crucial differences compared with conventional ECDH over a 254-bit field are

1. The use of 128-bit **multiscalars** (a, b) in $\mathbb{Z}^2$ in place of the 254-bit scalar m in $\mathbb{Z}$. We treat the geometry of multiscalars, the distribution of their corresponding scalar values, and the derivation of constant-bitlength scalar decompositions in §4.

2. The use of **two-dimensional differential addition chains** to compute $x([a]P \oplus [b]\psi(P))$ given only (a, b) and $x(P)$. We detail this process in §5.

We have implemented three different two-dimensional differential addition chains: one due to Montgomery [24] via Stam [34], one due to Bernstein [4], and one due to Azarderakhsh and Karabina [1]. We provide implementation details and timings for scalar multiplications based on each of our chains in §6. Each offers a different combination of speed, uniformity, and constant-time execution. The differential nature of these chains is essential in the x-coordinate setting, which prevents the effective use of the vector chains traditionally used in the endomorphism literature (such as [35]).

A Magma implementation is publicly available at

http://research.microsoft.com/en-us/downloads/ef32422a-af38-4c83-a033-a7aafbc1db55/

and a complete mixed-assembly-and-C implementation is publicly available (in eBATS [8] format) at

http://hhisil.yasar.edu.tr/files/hisil20140318compact.tar.gz .

2   The Curve

We begin by defining our curve-twist pair $(\mathcal{E}, \mathcal{E}')$. We work over

$$\mathbb{F}_{p^2} := \mathbb{F}_p(i) , \quad \text{where} \quad p := 2^{127} - 1 \quad \text{and} \quad i^2 = -1 .$$

We chose this Mersenne prime for its compatibility with a range of fast techniques for modular arithmetic, including Montgomery- and NIST-style approaches. We build efficient $\mathbb{F}_{p^2}$-arithmetic on top of the fast $\mathbb{F}_p$-arithmetic described in [10].

In what follows, it will be convenient to define the constants

$$u := 1466100457131508421 , \quad v := \tfrac{1}{2}(p-1) = 2^{126} - 1 , \quad w := \tfrac{1}{4}(p+1) = 2^{125} .$$

The Curve $\mathcal{E}$ and its Twist $\mathcal{E}'$. We define $\mathcal{E}$ to be the elliptic curve over $\mathbb{F}_{p^2}$ with affine Montgomery model

$$\mathcal{E}: y^2 = x(x^2 + Ax + 1) \,,$$

where

$$A = A_0 + A_1 \cdot i \quad \text{with} \quad \begin{cases} A_0 = 45116554344555875085017627593321485421 \,, \\ A_1 = 2415910908 \,. \end{cases}$$

The element $12/A$ is not a square in $\mathbb{F}_{p^2}$, so the curve over $\mathbb{F}_{p^2}$ defined by

$$\mathcal{E}': (12/A)y^2 = x(x^2 + Ax + 1)$$

is a model of the quadratic twist of $\mathcal{E}$. The twisting $\mathbb{F}_{p^4}$-isomorphism $\delta: \mathcal{E} \to \mathcal{E}'$ is defined by $\delta: (x, y) \mapsto (x, (A/12)^{1/2}y)$. The map $\delta_1: (x, y) \mapsto (x_W, y_W) = (\frac{12}{A}x + 4, \frac{12^2}{A^2}y)$ defines an $\mathbb{F}_{p^2}$-isomorphism between $\mathcal{E}'$ and the Weierstrass model

$$\mathcal{E}_{2,-1,s}: y_W^2 = x_W^3 + 2(9(1 + si) - 24)x_W - 8(9(1 + si) - 16)$$

of [32, Theorem 1] with

$$s = i(1 - 8/A^2) = 86878915556079486902897638486322141403 \,,$$

so $\mathcal{E}$ is a Montgomery model of the quadratic twist of $\mathcal{E}_{2,-1,s}$. (In the notation of [32, §5] we have $\mathcal{E} \cong \mathcal{E}'_{2,-1,s}$ and $\mathcal{E}' \cong \mathcal{E}_{2,-1,s}$.) These curves all have j-invariant

$$j(\mathcal{E}) = j(\mathcal{E}') = j(\mathcal{E}_{2,-1,s}) = 2^8 \frac{(A^2 - 3)^3}{A^2 - 4} = 2^6 \frac{(5 - 3si)^3(1 - si)}{(1 + s^2)^2} \,.$$

Group Structures. Using the SEA algorithm [28], we find that

$$\#\mathcal{E}(\mathbb{F}_{p^2}) = 4N \qquad \text{and} \qquad \#\mathcal{E}'(\mathbb{F}_{p^2}) = 8N'$$

where

$$N = v^2 + 2u^2 \qquad \text{and} \qquad N' = 2w^2 - u^2$$

are 252-bit and 251-bit primes, respectively. Looking closer, we see that

$$\mathcal{E}(\mathbb{F}_{p^2}) \cong (\mathbb{Z}/2\mathbb{Z})^2 \times \mathbb{Z}/N\mathbb{Z} \qquad \text{and} \qquad \mathcal{E}'(\mathbb{F}_{p^2}) \cong \mathbb{Z}/2\mathbb{Z} \times \mathbb{Z}/4\mathbb{Z} \times \mathbb{Z}/N'\mathbb{Z} \,.$$

Recall that every element of $\mathbb{F}_{p^2}$ is either the x-coordinate of two points in $\mathcal{E}(\mathbb{F}_{p^2})$, the x-coordinate of two points in $\mathcal{E}'(\mathbb{F}_{p^2})$, or the x-coordinate of one point of order two in both $\mathcal{E}(\mathbb{F}_{p^2})$ and $\mathcal{E}'(\mathbb{F}_{p^2})$. The x-coordinates of the points of exact order 2 in $\mathcal{E}(\mathbb{F}_{p^2})$ (and in $\mathcal{E}'(\mathbb{F}_{p^2})$) are 0 and $-\frac{1}{2}A \pm \frac{1}{2}\sqrt{A^2 - 4}$; the points of exact order 4 in $\mathcal{E}'(\mathbb{F}_{p^2})$ have x-coordinates ± 1. Either of the points with x-coordinate 2 will serve as a generator for the cryptographic subgroup $\mathcal{E}(\mathbb{F}_{p^2})[N]$; either of the points with x-coordinate $2 - i$ generate $\mathcal{E}'(\mathbb{F}_{p^2})[N']$.

Curve Points, x-Coordinates, and Random Bitstrings. Being Montgomery curves, both $\mathcal{E}$ and $\mathcal{E}'$ are compatible with the Elligator 2 construction [5, §5]. For our curves, [5, Theorem 5] defines efficiently invertible injective maps $\mathbb{F}_{p^2} \to \mathcal{E}(\mathbb{F}_{p^2})$ and $\mathbb{F}_{p^2} \to \mathcal{E}'(\mathbb{F}_{p^2})$. This allows points on $\mathcal{E}$ and/or $\mathcal{E}'$ to be encoded in such a way that they are indistinguishable from uniformly random 254-bit strings. Since we work with x-coordinates only in this article, a square root is saved when computing the injection (see [5, §5.5] for more details).

The ECDLP on $\mathcal{E}$ and $\mathcal{E}'$. Suppose we want to solve an instance of the DLP in $\mathcal{E}(\mathbb{F}_{p^2})$ or $\mathcal{E}'(\mathbb{F}_{p^2})$. Applying the Pohlig–Hellman–Silver reduction [25], we almost instantly reduce to the case of solving a DLP instance in either $\mathcal{E}(\mathbb{F}_{p^2})[N]$ or $\mathcal{E}'(\mathbb{F}_{p^2})[N']$. The best known approach to solving such a DLP instance is Pollard's rho algorithm [26], which (properly implemented) can solve DLP instances in $\mathcal{E}(\mathbb{F}_{p^2})[N]$ (resp. $\mathcal{E}'(\mathbb{F}_{p^2})[N']$) in around $\frac{1}{2}\sqrt{\pi N} \sim 2^{125.8}$ (resp. $\frac{1}{2}\sqrt{\pi N'} \sim 2^{125.3}$) group operations on average [9]. One might expect that working over $\mathbb{F}_{p^2}$ would imply a $\sqrt{2}$-factor speedup in the rho method by using Frobenius classes; but this seems not to be the case, since neither $\mathcal{E}$ nor $\mathcal{E}'$ is a subfield curve [36, §6].

The embedding degrees of $\mathcal{E}$ and $\mathcal{E}'$ with respect to N and N' are $\frac{1}{50}(N-1)$ and $\frac{1}{2}(N'-1)$, respectively, so ECDLP instances in $\mathcal{E}(\mathbb{F}_{p^2})[N]$ and $\mathcal{E}(\mathbb{F}_{p^2})[N']$ are not vulnerable to the Menezes–Okamoto–Vanstone [22] or Frey–Rück [14] attacks. The trace of $\mathcal{E}$ is $p^2 + 1 - 4N \neq \pm 1$, so neither $\mathcal{E}$ nor $\mathcal{E}'$ are amenable to the Smart–Satoh–Araki–Semaev attack [27], [29], [30].

While our curves are defined over a quadratic extension field, this does not seem to reduce the expected difficulty of the ECDLP when compared with elliptic curves over similar-sized prime fields. Taking the Weil restriction of $\mathcal{E}$ (or $\mathcal{E}'$) to $\mathbb{F}_p$ as in the Gaudry–Hess–Smart attack [18], for example, produces a simple abelian surface over $\mathbb{F}_p$; and the best known attacks on DLP instances on simple abelian surfaces over $\mathbb{F}_p$ offer no advantage over simply attacking the ECDLP on the original curve (see [31], [17], and [15, §9] for further discussion).

Superficially, $\mathcal{E}$ is what we would normally call twist-secure (in the sense of Bernstein [3] and Fouque–Réal–Lercier–Valette [13]), since its twist $\mathcal{E}'$ has a similar security level. Indeed, $\mathcal{E}$ (and the whole class of curves from which it was drawn) was designed with this notion of twist-security in mind. However, twist-security is more subtle in the context of endomorphism-based scalar decompositions; we will return to this subject in §4 below.

The Endomorphism Ring. Let $\pi_{\mathcal{E}}$ denote the Frobenius endomorphism of $\mathcal{E}$. The curve $\mathcal{E}$ is ordinary (its trace $t_{\mathcal{E}}$ is prime to p), so its endomorphism ring is an order in the quadratic field $K := \mathbb{Q}(\pi_{\mathcal{E}})$. (The endomorphism ring of an ordinary curve and its twist are always isomorphic, so what holds below for $\mathcal{E}$ also holds for $\mathcal{E}'$.) We will see below that $\mathcal{E}$ has an endomorphism ψ such that $\psi^2 = -[2]\pi_{\mathcal{E}}$. The discriminant of $\mathbb{Z}[\psi]$ is the fundamental discriminant

$$D_K = -8 \cdot 5 \cdot 397 \cdot 10528961 \cdot 6898209116497 \cdot 1150304667927101$$

of K, so $\mathbb{Z}[\psi]$ is the maximal order in K; hence, $\text{End}(\mathcal{E}) = \mathbb{Z}[\psi]$.

The `safecurves` specification [7] suggests that the discriminant of the CM field should have at least 100 bits; our $\mathcal{E}$ easily meets this requirement, since D_K has 130 bits. We note that well-chosen GLS curves can also have large CM field discriminants, but GLV curves have tiny CM field discriminants by construction: for example, the endomorphism ring of the curve `secp256k1` [12] (at the heart of the Bitcoin system) has discriminant -3.

`Brainpool` [11] requires the ideal class number of K to be larger than 10^6; this property is never satisfied by GLV curves, which have tiny class numbers (typically ≤ 2) by construction. But $\mathcal{E}$ easily meets this requirement: the class number of $\mathrm{End}(\mathcal{E})$ is

$$h(\mathrm{End}(\mathcal{E})) = h(D_K) = 2^7 \cdot 31 \cdot 37517 \cdot 146099 \cdot 505117 \sim 10^{19} \ .$$

3   Efficient Endomorphisms on $\mathcal{E}$, $\mathcal{E}'$, and the x-line

Theorem 1 of [32] defines an efficient endomorphism

$$\psi_{2,-1,s} : (x_W, y_W) \longmapsto \left(\frac{-x_W^p}{2} - \frac{9(1-si)}{x_W^p - 4} \ , \ \frac{y_W^p}{\sqrt{-2}} \left(\frac{-1}{2} + \frac{9(1-si)}{(x_W^p - 4)^2} \right) \right)$$

of degree $2p$ on the Weierstrass model $\mathcal{E}_{2,-1,s}$, with kernel $\langle (4,0) \rangle$. To avoid an ambiguity in the sign of the endomorphism, we must fix a choice of $\sqrt{-2}$ in $\mathbb{F}_{p^2}$. We choose the "small" root:

$$\sqrt{-2} := 2^{64} \cdot i \ . \tag{1}$$

Applying the isomorphisms δ and δ_1, we define efficient $\mathbb{F}_{p^2}$-endomorphisms

$$\psi := (\delta_1 \delta)^{-1} \psi_{2,-1,s} \delta_1 \delta \qquad \text{and} \qquad \psi' := \delta \psi \delta^{-1} = \delta_1^{-1} \psi_{2,-1,s} \delta_1$$

of degree $2p$ on $\mathcal{E}$ and $\mathcal{E}'$, respectively, each with kernel $\langle (0,0) \rangle$. More explicitly: if we let

$$n(x) := \tfrac{A^p}{A} \left(x^2 + Ax + 1 \right) \ , \quad d(x) := -2x \ , \quad s(x) := n(x)^p / d(x)^p \ ,$$

$$r(x) := \tfrac{A^p}{A} (x^2 - 1) \ , \quad \text{and} \quad m(x) := n'(x)d(x) - n(x)d'(x) \ ,$$

then ψ and ψ' are defined (using the same value of $\sqrt{-2}$ fixed in Eq. (1)) by

$$\psi : (x,y) \longmapsto \left(s(x) \ , \ \frac{-12^v}{A^v \sqrt{-2}} \frac{y^p m(x)^p}{d(x)^{2p}} \right)$$

and

$$\psi' : (x,y) \longmapsto \left(s(x) \ , \ \frac{-12^{2v} \sqrt{-2}}{A^{2v}} \frac{y^p r(x)^p}{d(x)^{2p}} \right) \ .$$

Actions of the Endomorphisms on Points. Theorem 1 of [32] tells us that

$$\psi^2 = -[2]\pi_{\mathcal{E}} \quad \text{and} \quad (\psi')^2 = [2]\pi_{\mathcal{E}'} , \tag{2}$$

where $\pi_{\mathcal{E}}$ and $\pi_{\mathcal{E}'}$ are the p^2-power Frobenius endomorphisms of $\mathcal{E}$ and $\mathcal{E}'$, respectively, and

$$P(\psi) = P(\psi') = 0 , \quad \text{where} \quad P(T) = T^2 - 4uT + 2p .$$

If we restrict to the cryptographic subgroup $\mathcal{E}(\mathbb{F}_{p^2})[N]$, then ψ must act as multiplication by an integer eigenvalue λ, which is one of the two roots of $P(T)$ modulo N. Similarly, ψ' acts on $\mathcal{E}'(\mathbb{F}_{p^2})[N']$ as multiplication by one of the roots λ' of $P(T)$ modulo N'. The correct eigenvalues are

$$\lambda \equiv -\frac{v}{u} \pmod{N} \quad \text{and} \quad \lambda' \equiv -\frac{2w}{u} \pmod{N'} .$$

Equation (2) implies that $\lambda^2 \equiv -2 \pmod{N}$ and $\lambda'^2 \equiv 2 \pmod{N'}$. (Note that choosing the other square root of -2 in Eq. (1) negates ψ, ψ', λ, λ', and u.)

To complete our picture of the action of ψ on $\mathcal{E}(\mathbb{F}_{p^2})$ and ψ' on $\mathcal{E}'(\mathbb{F}_{p^2})$, we describe its action on the points of order 2 and 4 listed above:

$$
\begin{aligned}
(0,0) &\longmapsto 0 &&\text{under } \psi \text{ and } \psi' , \\
\left(-\tfrac{1}{2}A \pm \tfrac{1}{2}\sqrt{A^2-4},0\right) &\longmapsto (0,0) &&\text{under } \psi \text{ and } \psi' , \\
\left(1, \pm\tfrac{1}{2}\sqrt{A(A+2)/3}\right) &\longmapsto \left(-\tfrac{1}{2}A - \tfrac{1}{2}\sqrt{A^2-4},0\right) &&\text{under } \psi' , \\
\left(-1, \pm\tfrac{1}{2}\sqrt{-A(A+2)/3}\right) &\longmapsto \left(-\tfrac{1}{2}A + \tfrac{1}{2}\sqrt{A^2-4},0\right) &&\text{under } \psi' .
\end{aligned}
$$

Pseudo-endomorphisms on the x-line. One advantage of the Montgomery model is that it allows a particularly efficient arithmetic using only the x-coordinate. Technically speaking, this corresponds to viewing the x-line $\mathbb{P}^1$ as the Kummer variety of $\mathcal{E}$: that is, $\mathbb{P}^1 \cong \mathcal{E}/\langle\pm1\rangle$.

The x-line is not a group: if P and Q are points on $\mathcal{E}$, then $x(P)$ and $x(Q)$ determine the pair $\{x(P \oplus Q), x(P \ominus Q)\}$, but not the individual elements $x(P \oplus Q)$ and $x(P \ominus Q)$. However, the x-line inherits part of the endomorphism structure of $\mathcal{E}$: every endomorphism ϕ of $\mathcal{E}$ induces a pseudo-endomorphism[2] $\phi_x : x \mapsto \phi_x(x)$ of $\mathbb{P}^1$, which determines ϕ up to sign; and if ϕ_1 and ϕ_2 are two endomorphisms of $\mathcal{E}$, then

$$(\phi_1)_x(\phi_2)_x = (\phi_2)_x(\phi_1)_x = (\phi_1\phi_2)_x = (\phi_2\phi_1)_x .$$

Montgomery's explicit formulæ for pseudo-doubling (DBL), pseudo-addition (ADD), combined pseudo-doubling and pseudo-addition (DBLADD) on $\mathbb{P}^1$ are available in [6]. In addition to these, we need expressions for both ψ_x and $(\psi\pm1)_x$ to initialise the addition chains in §5. Moving to projective coordinates: write

---

[2] "Pseudo-endomorphisms" are true endomorphisms of $\mathbb{P}^1$. We use the term pseudo-endomorphism to avoid confusion with endomorphisms of elliptic curves, and to reflect the use of terms like "pseudo-addition" for basic operations on the x-line.

$x = X/Z$ and $y = Y/Z$. Then the negation map on $\mathcal{E}$ is $[-1] : (X : Y : Z) \mapsto (X : -Y : Z)$, and the double cover $\mathcal{E} \to \mathcal{E}/\langle[\pm 1]\rangle \cong \mathbb{P}^1$ is $(X : Y : Z) \mapsto (X : Z)$. The pseudo-doubling on $\mathbb{P}^1$ is

$$[2]_x((X : Z)) = ((X + Z)^2(X - Z)^2 : (4XZ)\left((X - Z)^2 + \tfrac{A+2}{4} \cdot 4XZ\right)) . \quad (3)$$

Our endomorphism ψ induces the pseudo-endomorphism

$$\psi_x((X : Z)) = \left(A^p\left((X - Z)^2 - \tfrac{A+2}{2}(-2XZ)\right)^p : A(-2XZ)^p\right) .$$

Composing ψ_x with itself, we confirm that $\psi_x\psi_x = -[2]_x(\pi_\mathcal{E})_x$.

Proposition 1. *With the notation above, and with $\sqrt{-2}$ chosen as in Eq. (1),*

$$(\psi \pm 1)_x(x) = (\psi' \pm 1)_x(x)$$
$$= \frac{2s^2nd^{4p} - x(xn)^p m^{2p} A^{p-1}}{2s(x - s)^2 d^{4p} A^{p-1}} \mp \frac{m^p(xn)^{(p+1)/2}\sqrt{-2}}{A^{(p-1)/2}(x - s)^2 d^{2p}} . \quad (4)$$

Proof. If P and Q are points on a Montgomery curve $By^2 = x(x^2 + Ax + 1)$, then

$$x(P \pm Q) = \frac{B\left(x(P)y(Q) \mp x(Q)y(P)\right)^2}{x(P)x(Q)\left(x(P) - x(Q)\right)^2} .$$

Taking $P = (x, y)$ to be a generic point on $\mathcal{E}$ (where $B = 1$), setting $Q = \psi(P)$, and eliminating y using $y^2 = -\frac{A^p}{2A}dn$ yields the expression for $(\psi \pm 1)_x$ above. The same process for $\mathcal{E}'$ (with $B = \frac{12}{A}$), eliminating y with $\frac{12}{A}y^2 = -\frac{A^p}{2A}dn$, yields the same expression for $(\psi' \pm 1)_x$. $\square$

Deriving explicit formulæ to compute the pseudo-endomorphism images in Eq. (4) is straightforward. We omit these formulæ here for space considerations, but they can be found in our code online. If $P \in \mathcal{E}$, then on input of $x(P)$, the combined computation of the three projective elements $(X_{\lambda-1} : Z_{\lambda-1})$, $(X_\lambda : Z_\lambda)$, $(X_{\lambda+1} : Z_{\lambda+1})$, which respectively correspond to the three affine elements $x([\lambda-1]P)$, $x([\lambda]P)$, $x([\lambda+1]P)$, incurs 15 multiplications, 129 squarings and 10 additions in $\mathbb{F}_{p^2}$. The bottleneck of this computation is raising dn to the power of $(p + 1)/2 = 2^{126}$, which incurs 126 squarings. We note that squarings are significantly faster than multiplications in $\mathbb{F}_{p^2}$.

4 Scalar Decompositions

We want to evaluate scalar multiplications $[m]P$ as $[a]P \oplus [b]\psi(P)$, where

$$m \equiv a + b\lambda \pmod{N}$$

and the multiscalar (a, b) has a significantly shorter bitlength[3] than m. For our applications we impose two extra requirements on multiscalars (a, b), so as to add a measure of side-channel resistance:

---

[3] The bitlength of a scalar m is $\lceil \log_2 |m| \rceil$; the bitlength of a multiscalar (a, b) is $\lceil \log_2 \|(a, b)\|_\infty \rceil$.

1. both a and b must be **positive**, to avoid branching and to simplify our algorithms; and
2. the multiscalar (a, b) must have **constant bitlength** (independent of m as m varies over $\mathbb{Z}$), so that multiexponentiation can run in constant time.

In some protocols—notably Diffie–Hellman—we are not interested in the particular values of our random scalars, as long as those values remain secret. In this case, rather than starting with m in $\mathbb{Z}/N\mathbb{Z}$ (or $\mathbb{Z}/N'\mathbb{Z}$) and finding a short, positive, constant-bitlength decomposition of m, it would be easier to randomly sample some short, positive, constant-bitlength multiscalar (a, b) from scratch. The sample space must be chosen to ensure that the corresponding distribution of values $a + b\lambda$ in $\mathbb{Z}/N\mathbb{Z}$ does not make the discrete logarithm problem of finding $a + b\lambda$ appreciably easier than if we started with a random m.

Zero Decomposition Lattices. The problems of finding good decompositions and sampling good multiscalars are best addressed using the geometric structure of the spaces of decompositions for $\mathcal{E}$ and $\mathcal{E}'$. The multiscalars (a, b) such that $a + b\lambda \equiv 0 \pmod{N}$ or $a + b\lambda' \equiv 0 \pmod{N'}$ form lattices

$$\mathcal{L} = \langle (N, 0), (-\lambda, 1) \rangle \quad \text{and} \quad \mathcal{L}' = \langle (N', 0), (-\lambda', 1) \rangle \ ,$$

respectively, with $a + b\lambda \equiv c + d\lambda \pmod{N}$ if and only if $(a, b) - (c, d)$ is in $\mathcal{L}$ (similarly, $a + b\lambda' \equiv c + d\lambda' \pmod{N'}$ if and only if $(a, b) - (c, d)$ is in $\mathcal{L}'$).

The sets of decompositions of m for $\mathcal{E}(\mathbb{F}_p)[N]$ and $\mathcal{E}(\mathbb{F}_{p^2})[N']$ therefore form lattice cosets

$$(m, 0) + \mathcal{L} \quad \text{and} \quad (m, 0) + \mathcal{L}' \ ,$$

respectively, so we can compute short decompositions of m for $\mathcal{E}(\mathbb{F}_p)[N]$ (resp. $\mathcal{E}(\mathbb{F}_{p^2})[N']$) by subtracting vectors near $(m, 0)$ in $\mathcal{L}$ (resp. $\mathcal{L}'$) from $(m, 0)$. To find these vectors, we need $\| \cdot \|_\infty$-reduced[4] bases for $\mathcal{L}$ and $\mathcal{L}'$.

Proposition 2 (Definition of $\mathbf{e}_1, \mathbf{e}_2, \mathbf{e}'_1, \mathbf{e}'_2$). *Up to order and sign, the shortest possible bases for $\mathcal{L}$ and $\mathcal{L}'$ (with respect to $\| \cdot \|_\infty$) are given by*

$$\mathcal{L} = \langle\ \mathbf{e}_1 := (v, u)\ ,\ \mathbf{e}_2 := (-2u, v)\ \rangle \quad \text{and}$$
$$\mathcal{L}' = \langle\ \mathbf{e}'_1 := (u, w)\ ,\ \mathbf{e}'_2 := (2u - 2w, 2w - u)\ \rangle \ .$$

Proof. The proof of [32, Prop. 2] constructs sublattices

$$\langle \tilde{\mathbf{e}}_1 := -2(v, u), \tilde{\mathbf{e}}_2 := -2(2u, v) \rangle \subset \mathcal{L}$$

and

$$\langle \tilde{\mathbf{e}}'_1 := 2(2w, -u), \tilde{\mathbf{e}}'_2 := 4(u, w) \rangle \subset \mathcal{L}'$$

with $[\mathcal{L} : \langle \tilde{\mathbf{e}}_1, \tilde{\mathbf{e}}_2 \rangle] = 4$ and $[\mathcal{L}' : \langle \tilde{\mathbf{e}}'_1, \tilde{\mathbf{e}}'_2 \rangle] = 8$. We easily verify that $\mathbf{e}_1 = -\frac{1}{2}\tilde{\mathbf{e}}_2$ and $\mathbf{e}_2 = -\frac{1}{2}\tilde{\mathbf{e}}_1$ are both in $\mathcal{L}$; then, since $\langle \tilde{\mathbf{e}}_1, \tilde{\mathbf{e}}_2 \rangle$ has index 4 in $\langle \mathbf{e}_1, \mathbf{e}_2 \rangle$, we

---

[4] Reduced with respect to Kaib's generalized Gauss reduction algorithm [20] for $\| \cdot \|_\infty$.

must have $\mathcal{L} = \langle \mathbf{e}_1, \mathbf{e}_2 \rangle$. Similarly, both $\mathbf{e}_1' = \frac{1}{4}\tilde{\mathbf{e}}_2'$ and $\mathbf{e}_2' = \frac{1}{2}(\tilde{\mathbf{e}}_2' - \tilde{\mathbf{e}}_1')$ are in $\mathcal{L}'$, and thus form a basis for $\mathcal{L}'$. According to [20, Definition 3], an ordered lattice basis $[\mathbf{b}_1, \mathbf{b}_2]$ is $\|\cdot\|_\infty$-reduced if

$$\|\mathbf{b}_1\|_\infty \leq \|\mathbf{b}_2\|_\infty \leq \|\mathbf{b}_1 - \mathbf{b}_2\|_\infty \leq \|\mathbf{b}_1 + \mathbf{b}_2\|_\infty .$$

This holds for $[\mathbf{b}_1, \mathbf{b}_2] = [\mathbf{e}_2, -\mathbf{e}_1]$ and $[\mathbf{e}_1', \mathbf{e}_2']$, so $\|\mathbf{e}_2\|_\infty$ and $\|\mathbf{e}_1\|_\infty$ (resp. $\|\mathbf{e}_1'\|_\infty$ and $\|\mathbf{e}_2'\|_\infty$) are the successive minima of $\mathcal{L}$ (resp. $\mathcal{L}'$) by [20, Theorem 5].[5]   □

In view of Proposition 2, the fundamental parallelograms of $\mathcal{L}$ and $\mathcal{L}'$ are the regions of the (a, b)-plane defined by

$$\mathcal{A} := \left\{ (a, b) \in \mathbb{R}^2 \ : \ 0 \leq vb - ua < N, \ 0 \leq 2ub + va < N \right\} \text{ and}$$
$$\mathcal{A}' := \left\{ (a, b) \in \mathbb{R}^2 \ : \ 0 \leq ub - wa < N', \ 0 \leq (2u - 2w)b - (2w - u)a < N' \right\} ,$$

respectively. Every integer m has precisely one decomposition for $\mathcal{E}(\mathbb{F}_{p^2})[N]$ (resp. $\mathcal{E}'(\mathbb{F}_{p^2})[N']$) in any translate of $\mathcal{A}$ by $\mathcal{L}$ (resp. $\mathcal{A}'$ by $\mathcal{L}'$).

Short, Constant-Bitlength Scalar Decompositions. Returning to the problem of finding short decompositions of m: let (α, β) be the (unique) solution in $\mathbb{Q}^2$ to the system $\alpha \mathbf{e}_1 + \beta \mathbf{e}_2 = (m, 0)$. Since $\mathbf{e}_1, \mathbf{e}_2$ is reduced, the closest vector to $(m, 0)$ in $\mathcal{L}$ is one of the four vectors $\lfloor \alpha \rfloor \mathbf{e}_1 + \lfloor \beta \rfloor \mathbf{e}_2$, $\lfloor \alpha \rfloor \mathbf{e}_1 + \lceil \beta \rceil \mathbf{e}_2$, $\lceil \alpha \rceil \mathbf{e}_1 + \lfloor \beta \rfloor \mathbf{e}_2$, or $\lceil \alpha \rceil \mathbf{e}_1 + \lceil \beta \rceil \mathbf{e}_2$ by [20, Theorem 19]. Following Babai [2], we subtract $\lfloor \alpha \rfloor \mathbf{e}_1 + \lfloor \beta \rfloor \mathbf{e}_2$ from $(m, 0)$ to get a decomposition $(\tilde{a}, \tilde{b})$ of m; by the triangle inequality, $\|(\tilde{a}, \tilde{b})\|_\infty \leq \frac{1}{2}(\|\mathbf{e}_1\|_\infty + \|\mathbf{e}_2\|_\infty)$. This decomposition is approximately the shortest possible, in the sense that the true shortest decomposition is at most $\pm \mathbf{e}_1 \pm \mathbf{e}_2$ away. Observe that $\|\mathbf{e}_1\|_\infty = \|\mathbf{e}_2\|_\infty = 2^{126} - 1$, so $(\tilde{a}, \tilde{b})$ has bitlength at most 126.

However, $\tilde{a}$ or $\tilde{b}$ may be negative (violating the positivity requirement), or have fewer than 126 bits (violating the constant bitlength requirement). Indeed, $m \mapsto (\tilde{a}, \tilde{b})$ maps $\mathbb{Z}$ onto $(\mathcal{A} - \frac{1}{2}(\mathbf{e}_1 + \mathbf{e}_2)) \cap \mathbb{Z}^2$. This region of the (a, b)-plane, "centred" on $(0, 0)$, contains multiscalars of every bitlength between 0 and 126—and the majority of them have at least one negative component. We can achieve positivity and constant bitlength by adding a carefully chosen offset vector from $\mathcal{L}$, translating $(\mathcal{A} - \frac{1}{2}(\mathbf{e}_1 + \mathbf{e}_2)) \cap \mathbb{Z}^2$ into a region of the (a, b)-plane where every multiscalar is positive and has the same bitlength. Adding $3\mathbf{e}_1$ or $3\mathbf{e}_2$ ensures that the first or second component always has precisely 128 bits, respectively; but adding $3(\mathbf{e}_1 + \mathbf{e}_2)$ gives us a constant bitlength of 128 bits in both. Theorem 1 makes this all completely explicit.

Theorem 1. *Given an integer m, let (a, b) be the multiscalar defined by*

$$a := m + (3 - \lfloor \alpha \rceil) v - 2 (3 - \lfloor \beta \rceil) u \quad and \quad b := (3 - \lfloor \alpha \rceil) u + (3 - \lfloor \beta \rceil) v ,$$

---

[5] For the Euclidean norm, the bases $[\mathbf{e}_1, \mathbf{e}_2]$ and $[\mathbf{e}_1', 2\mathbf{e}_1' - \mathbf{e}_2']$ are $\|\cdot\|_2$-reduced, but $[\mathbf{e}_1', \mathbf{e}_2']$ is not.

where α and β are the rational numbers

$$\alpha := (v/N)m \quad and \quad \beta := -(u/N)m .$$

Then $2^{127} < a, b < 2^{128}$, and $m \equiv a + b\lambda \pmod{N}$. In particular, (a,b) is a positive decomposition of m, of bitlength exactly 128, for any m.

Proof. We have $m \equiv a + b\lambda \pmod{N}$ because $(a,b) = (\tilde{a}, \tilde{b}) + 3(\mathbf{e}_1 + \mathbf{e}_2) \equiv (m,0) \pmod{\mathcal{L}}$, where $(\tilde{a}, \tilde{b})$ is the translate of $(m,0)$ by the Babai roundoff $\lfloor\alpha\rceil\mathbf{e}_1 + \lfloor\beta\rceil\mathbf{e}_2$ described above. Now $(\tilde{a}, \tilde{b})$ lies in $\mathcal{A} - \frac{1}{2}(\mathbf{e}_1 + \mathbf{e}_2)$, so (a,b) lies in $\mathcal{A} + \frac{5}{2}(\mathbf{e}_1, \mathbf{e}_2)$; our claim on the bitlength of (a,b) follows because the four "corners" of this domain all have 128-bit components. $\square$

Random Multiscalars. As we remarked above, in a pure Diffie–Hellman implementation it is more convenient to simply sample random multiscalars than to decompose randomly sampled scalars. Proposition 3 shows that random multiscalars of at most 127 bits correspond to reasonably well-distributed values in $\mathbb{Z}/N\mathbb{Z}$ and in $\mathbb{Z}/N'\mathbb{Z}$, in the sense that none of the values occur more than one more or one fewer times than the average, and the exceptional values are in $O(\sqrt{N})$. Such multiscalars can be trivially turned into constant-bitlength positive 128-bit multiscalars—compatible with our implementation—by (for example) completing a pair of 127-bit strings with a 1 in the 128-th bit position of each component.

Proposition 3. *Let $\mathcal{B} = [0, p]^2$; we identify $\mathcal{B}$ with the set of all pairs of strings of 127 bits.*

1. *The map $\mathcal{B} \to \mathbb{Z}/N\mathbb{Z}$ defined by $(a, b) \mapsto a + b\lambda \pmod{N}$ is 4-to-1, except for $4(p - 6u + 4) \approx 4\sqrt{2N}$ values in $\mathbb{Z}/N\mathbb{Z}$ with 5 preimages in $\mathcal{B}$, and $8(u^2 - 3u + 2) \approx \frac{1}{5}\sqrt{N}$ values in $\mathbb{Z}/N\mathbb{Z}$ with only 3 preimages in $\mathcal{B}$.*
2. *The map $\mathcal{B} \to \mathbb{Z}/N'\mathbb{Z}$ defined by $(a, b) \mapsto a + b\lambda' \pmod{N'}$ is 8-to-1, except for $8u^2 \approx \frac{2}{7}\sqrt{N'}$ values with 9 preimages in $\mathcal{B}$.*

Proof (Sketch). For (1): the map $(a, b) \mapsto a + b\lambda \pmod{N}$ defines a bijection between each translate of $\mathcal{A} \cap \mathbb{Z}^2$ by $\mathcal{L}$ and $\mathbb{Z}/N\mathbb{Z}$. Hence, every m in $\mathbb{Z}/N\mathbb{Z}$ has a unique preimage (a_0, b_0) in $\mathcal{A} \cap \mathbb{Z}^2$, so it suffices to count $((a_0, b_0) + \mathcal{L}) \cap \mathcal{B}$ for each (a_0, b_0) in $\mathcal{A} \cap \mathbb{Z}^2$. Cover $\mathbb{Z}^2$ with translates of $\mathcal{A}$ by $\mathcal{L}$; the only points in $\mathbb{Z}^2$ that are on the boundaries of tiles are the points in $\mathcal{L}$. Dissecting $\mathcal{B}$ along the edges of translates of $\mathcal{A}$ and reassembling the pieces, we see that $8v - 24u + 20 < 4p$ multiscalars in $\mathcal{B}$ occur with multiplicity five, $8u^2 - 24u + 16 < p/9$ with multiplicity three, and every other multiscalar occurs with multiplicity four. There are therefore $4N + (8v - 24u + 20) - (8u^2 - 24u + 16) = (p+1)^2$ preimages in total, as expected. The proof of (2) is similar to (1), but counting $((a, b) + \mathcal{L}') \cap \mathcal{B}$ as (a, b) ranges over $\mathcal{A}'$. $\square$

Twist-Security with Endomorphisms. We saw in §2 that DLPs on $\mathcal{E}$ and its twist $\mathcal{E}'$ have essentially the same difficulty, while Proposition 3 shows that the real DLP instances presented to an adversary by 127-bit multiscalar multiplications are not biased into a significantly more attackable range. But there is an additional subtlety when we consider the fault attacks considered in [3] and [13]: If we try to compute $[m]P$ for P on $\mathcal{E}$, but an adversary sneaks in a point P' on the twist $\mathcal{E}'$ instead, then in the classical context the adversary can derive m after solving the discrete logarithm $[m \mod N']P'$ in $\mathcal{E}'(\mathbb{F}_{p^2})$. But in the endomorphism context, we compute $[m]P$ as $[a]P \oplus [b]\psi(P)$, and the attacker sees $[a+b\lambda']P'$, which is *not* $[m \mod N']P'$ (or even $[a+b\lambda \mod N']P'$); we should ensure that the values $(a + b\lambda' \mod N')$ are not concentrated in a small subset of $\mathbb{Z}/N'\mathbb{Z}$ when (a,b) is a decomposition for $\mathcal{E}(\mathbb{F}_{p^2})[N]$. This can be achieved by a similar argument to that of Proposition 3: the map $\mathbb{Z}/N\mathbb{Z} \to \mathbb{Z}/N'\mathbb{Z}$ defined by $m \mapsto (a,b) \mapsto a+b\lambda' \pmod{N'}$ is a good approximation of a 2-to-1 mapping.

5   Two-Dimensional Differential Addition Chains

Addition chains are used to compute scalar multiplications using a sequence of group operations (or pseudo-group operations). A *one-dimensional* addition chain computes $[m]P$ for a given integer m and point P; a *two-dimensional* addition chain computes $[a]P \oplus [b]Q$ for a given multiscalar (a,b) and points P and Q. In a *differential* addition chain, the computation of any ADD, $P \oplus Q$, is always preceded (at some earlier stage in the chain) by the computation of its associated difference $P \ominus Q$. The simplest differential addition chain is the original one-dimensional "Montgomery ladder" [23], which computes scalar multiplications $[m]P$ for a single exponent m and point P. Every ADD in the Montgomery ladder is in the form $[i]P \oplus [i+1]P$, so every associated difference is equal to P. Several two-dimensional differential addition chains have been proposed, targeting multiexponentiations in elliptic curves and other primitives; we suggest [4] and [34] for overviews.

In any two-dimensional differential chain computing $[a]P \oplus [b]Q$ for general P and Q, the input consists of the multiscalar (a,b) and the three points P, Q, and $P \ominus Q$. The initial difference $P \ominus Q$ (or equivalently, the initial sum $P \oplus Q$) is essential to kickstart the chain on P and Q, since otherwise (by definition) $P \oplus Q$ cannot appear in the chain. As we noted in §1, computing this initial difference is an inconvenient obstruction to pure x-coordinate multiexponentiations on general input: the pseudo-group operations ADD, DBL, and DBLADD can all be made to work on x-coordinates (the ADD and DBLADD operations make use of the associated differences available in a differential chain), but in general it is impossible to compute the initial difference $x(P \ominus Q)$ in terms of $x(P)$ and $x(Q)$.

For our application, we want to compute $x([a]P \oplus [b]\psi(P))$ given inputs (a,b) and $x(P)$. Crucially, we can compute $x(P \ominus \psi(P))$ as $(\psi - 1)_x(x(P))$ using Proposition 1; this allows us to compute $x([a]P \oplus [b]\psi(P))$ using two-dimensional differential addition chains with input (a,b), $x(P)$, $\psi_x(x(P))$, and $(\psi-1)_x(x(P))$.

We implemented one one-dimensional differential addition chain (LADDER) and three two-dimensional differential addition chains (PRAC, AK, and DJB). We briefly describe each chain, with its relative benefits and drawbacks, below.

(Montgomery) LADDER Chains. We implemented the full-length one-dimensional Montgomery ladder as a reference, to assess the speedup that our techniques offer over conventional scalar multiplication (It is also used as a subroutine within our two-dimensional PRAC chain). LADDER can be made constant-time by adding a suitable multiple of N to the input scalar.

(Two-dimensional) PRAC Chains. Montgomery [24] proposed a number of algorithms for generating differential addition chains that are often much shorter than his eponymous ladder. His one-dimensional "PRAC" routine contains an easily-implemented two-dimensional subroutine, which computes the double-exponentiation $[a]P \oplus [b]Q$ very efficiently. The downside for our purposes is that the chain is not *uniform*: different inputs (a, b) give rise to different execution patterns, rendering the routine vulnerable to a number of side-channel attacks. Our implementation of this chain follows Algorithm 3.25 of [34][6]: given a multiscalar (a, b) and points P, Q, and $P - Q$, this algorithm computes $d = \gcd(a, b)$ and $R = [\frac{a}{d}]P \oplus [\frac{b}{d}]Q$. To finish computing $[a]P \oplus [b]Q$, we write $d = 2^i e$ with $i \geq q$ and e odd, then compute $S = [2^i]R$ with i consecutive DBLs, before finally computing $[e]S$ with a one-dimensional LADDER chain[7].

AK Chains. Azarderakhsh and Karabina [1] recently constructed a two-dimensional differential addition chain which offers some middle ground in the trade-off between uniform execution and efficiency. While it is less efficient than PRAC, their chain has the advantage that all but one of the iterations consist of a single DBLADD; this uniformity may be enough to thwart some simple side-channel attacks. The single iteration which does *not* use a DBLADD requires a separate DBL and ADD, and this slightly slower step can appear at different stages of the algorithm. The location of this longer step could leak some information to a side-channel adversary under some circumstances, but we can protect against this by replacing all of the DBLADDs with separate DBL and ADDs, incurring a very minor performance penalty. A more serious drawback for this chain is its variable length: the total number of iterations depends on the input multiscalar. This destroys any hope of achieving a runtime that is independent of the input. Nevertheless, depending on the physical threat model, this chain may still be a suitable alternative. Our implementation of this chain follows Algorithm 1 in [1].

DJB Chains. Bernstein gives the fastest known two-dimensional differential chain that is both fixed length and uniform [4, §4]. This chain is slightly slower

---

[6] We implemented the binary version of Montgomery's two-dimensional PRAC chain, neglecting the ternary steps in [24, Table 4] (see also [34, Table 3.1]). Including these ternary steps could be significantly faster than our implementation, though it would require fast explicit formulæ for tripling on Montgomery curves.

[7] In practice d is very small, so there is little benefit in using a more complicated chain for this final step.

than the PRAC and AK chains, but it offers stronger resistance against many side-channel attacks.[8] If the multiscalar (a, b) has bitlength ℓ, then this chain requires precisely $\ell - 1$ iterations, each of which computes one ADD and one DBLADD. In our context, Theorem 1 allows us to fix the number of iterations at 127. The execution pattern of the multiexponentiation is therefore independent of the input, and will run in constant time.

Operation Counts. Table 1 profiles the number of high-level operations required by each of our addition chain implementations on $\mathcal{E}$. We used the decomposition in Theorem 1 to guarantee positive constant-bitlength multiscalars. In situations where side-channel resistance is not a priority, and the AK or PRAC chain is preferable, variable-length decompositions could be used: these would give lower operation counts and slightly faster average timings.

Table 1. Pseudo-group operation counts per scalar multiplication on the x-line for the 2-dimensional DJB, AK and PRAC chains (using endomorphism decompositions) and the 1-dimensional LADDER. The counts for LADDER and DJB are exact; those for PRAC and AK are averages, with corresponding standard deviations, over 10^6 random trials (random scalars and points). In addition to the operations listed here, each chain requires a final $\mathbb{F}_{p^2}$-inversion to convert the result into affine form.

chain	dim.	endomorphisms $\psi_x, (\psi \pm 1)_x$	#DBL av.	std. dev.	#ADD av.	std. dev.	#DBLADD av.	std. dev.
LADDER	1	—	1	—	—	—	253	—
DJB	2	affine	1	—	128	—	127	—
AK	2	affine	1	—	1	—	179.6	6.7
PRAC	2	projective	0.2	0.4	113.8	11.6	73.4	11.1

The LADDER and DJB chains offer some slightly faster high-level operations. In these chains, the "difference elements" fed into the ADDs are fixed; if these points are affine, then this saves one $\mathbb{F}_{p^2}$-multiplication for each ADD. In LADDER, the difference is always the affine $x(P)$, so these savings come for free. In DJB, the difference is always one of the four values $x(P)$, $\psi_x(x(P))$, or $(\psi \pm 1)_x(x(P))$, so a shared inversion is used to convert $\psi_x(x(P))$ and $(\psi \pm 1)_x(x(P))$ from projective to affine coordinates. While this costs one $\mathbb{F}_{p^2}$-inversion and six-$\mathbb{F}_{p^2}$ multiplications, it saves 253 $\mathbb{F}_{p^2}$-inversions inside the loop.

6   Timings

Table 2 lists cycle counts for our implementations run on an Intel Core i7-3520M (Ivy Bridge) processor at 2893.484 MHz with hyper-threading turned off, over-clocking ("turbo-boost") disabled, and all-but-one of the cores switched off in

---

[8] It would be interesting to implement our techniques with Bernstein's non-uniform two-dimensional *extended-gcd* differential addition chain [4], which can outperform PRAC (though it "takes more time to compute and is not easy to analyse").

Table 2. Performance timings for four different implementations of compact, x-coordinate-only scalar multiplications targeting the 128-bit security level. Timings are given for the one-dimensional Montgomery LADDER, as well as the two-dimensional chains (DJB, AK and PRAC) that benefit from the application of an endomorphism and subsequent short scalar decompositions.

addition chain	dimension	uniform?	constant time?	cycles
LADDER	1	✓	✓	159,000
DJB	2	✓	✓	148,000
AK	2	✓	✗	133,000
PRAC	2	✗	✗	109,000

BIOS. The implementations were compiled with gcc 4.6.3 with the -O2 flag set and tested on a 64-bit Linux environment. Cycles were counted using the SUPERCOP toolkit [8].

The most meaningful comparison that we can draw is with Bernstein's Curve25519 software. Like our software, Curve25519 works entirely on the x-line, from start to finish; using the uniform one-dimensional Montgomery ladder, it runs in constant time. Thus, fair performance comparisons can only be made between his implementation and the two of ours that are also both uniform and constant-time: LADDER and DJB. Benchmarked on our hardware with all settings as above, Curve25519 scalar multiplications ran in 182,000 cycles on average. Looking at Table 2, we see that using the one-dimensional LADDER on the x-line of $\mathcal{E}$ gives a factor 1.14 speed up over Curve25519, while combining an endomorphism with the two-dimensional DJB chain on the x-line of $\mathcal{E}$ gives a factor 1.23 speed up over Curve25519.

While there are several other implementations targeting the 128-bit security level that give faster performance numbers than ours, we reiterate that our aim was to push the boundary in the arena of x-coordinate-only implementations.

Hamburg [19] has also documented a fast software implementation employing x-coordinate-only Montgomery arithmetic. However, it is difficult to compare Hamburg's software with ours: his is not available to be benchmarked, and his figures were obtained on the Sandy Bridge architecture (and manually scaled back to compensate for turbo-boost being enabled). Nevertheless, Hamburg's own comparison with Curve25519 suggests that a fair comparison between our constant-time implementations and his would be close.

Acknowledgements. We thank Joppe W. Bos for independently benchmarking our code on his computer and for discussions on arithmetic modulo $p = 2^{127} - 1$.

References

1. Azarderakhsh, R., Karabina, K.: A new double point multiplication algorithm and its application to binary elliptic curves with endomorphisms. IEEE Trans. Comput. 99, 1 (2013) (preprints)

2. Babai, L.: On Lovász' lattice reduction and the nearest lattice point problem. Combinatorica 6(1), 1–13 (1986)
3. Bernstein, D.J.: Curve25519: New Diffie-Hellman speed records. In: Yung, M., Dodis, Y., Kiayias, A., Malkin, T. (eds.) PKC 2006. LNCS, vol. 3958, pp. 207–228. Springer, Heidelberg (2006)
4. Bernstein, D.J.: Differential addition chains (February 2006), http://cr.yp.to/ecdh/diffchain-20060219.pdf
5. Bernstein, D.J., Hamburg, M., Krasnova, A., Lange, T.: Elligator: elliptic-curve points indistinguishable from uniform random strings. In: Sadeghi, A.R., Gligor, V.D., Yung, M. (eds.) ACM Conference on Computer and Communications Security, pp. 967–980. ACM (2013)
6. Bernstein, D.J., Lange, T.: Explicit-formulas database, http://www.hyperelliptic.org/EFD/ (accessed October 10, 2013)
7. Bernstein, D.J., Lange, T.: SafeCurves: choosing safe curves for elliptic-curve cryptography, http://safecurves.cr.yp.to (accessed October 16, 2013)
8. Bernstein, D.J., Lange, T.: eBACS: ECRYPT Benchmarking of Cryptographic Systems, http://bench.cr.yp.to (accessed September 28, 2013)
9. Bernstein, D.J., Lange, T., Schwabe, P.: On the correct use of the negation map in the Pollard rho method. In: Catalano, D., Fazio, N., Gennaro, R., Nicolosi, A. (eds.) PKC 2011. LNCS, vol. 6571, pp. 128–146. Springer, Heidelberg (2011)
10. Bos, J.W., Costello, C., Hisil, H., Lauter, K.: Fast cryptography in genus 2. In: Johansson, T., Nguyen, P.Q. (eds.) EUROCRYPT 2013. LNCS, vol. 7881, pp. 194–210. Springer, Heidelberg (2013)
11. Brainpool: ECC Brainpool standard curves and curve generation (October 2005), http://www.ecc-brainpool.org/download/Domain-parameters.pdf
12. Certicom Research: Standards for Efficient Cryptography 2 (SEC 2) (January 2010), http://www.secg.org/collateral/sec2_final.pdf
13. Fouque, P.A., Lercier, R., Réal, D., Valette, F.: Fault attack on elliptic curve Montgomery ladder implementation. In: Breveglieri, L., Gueron, S., Koren, I., Naccache, D., Seifert, J.P. (eds.) FDTC, pp. 92–98. IEEE Computer Society (2008)
14. Frey, G., Müller, M., Rück, H.G.: The Tate pairing and the discrete logarithm applied to elliptic curve cryptosystems. IEEE Trans. Inform. Theory 45(5), 1717–1719 (1999)
15. Galbraith, S.D., Lin, X., Scott, M.: Endomorphisms for faster elliptic curve cryptography on a large class of curves. J. Cryptology 24(3), 446–469 (2011)
16. Gallant, R.P., Lambert, R.J., Vanstone, S.A.: Faster point multiplication on elliptic curves with efficient endomorphisms. In: Kilian, J. (ed.) CRYPTO 2001. LNCS, vol. 2139, pp. 190–200. Springer, Heidelberg (2001)
17. Gaudry, P.: Index calculus for abelian varieties of small dimension and the elliptic curve discrete logarithm problem. J. Symb. Comp. 44(12), 1690–1702 (2009)
18. Gaudry, P., Hess, F., Smart, N.P.: Constructive and destructive facets of Weil descent on elliptic curves. J. Cryptology 15(1), 19–46 (2002)
19. Hamburg, M.: Fast and compact elliptic-curve cryptography. Cryptology ePrint Archive, Report 2012/309 (2012), http://eprint.iacr.org/
20. Kaib, M.: The Gauß lattice basis reduction algorithm succeeds with any norm. In: Budach, L. (ed.) FCT 1991. LNCS, vol. 529, pp. 275–286. Springer, Heidelberg (1991)
21. Koblitz, N.: CM-curves with good cryptographic properties. In: Feigenbaum, J. (ed.) CRYPTO 1991. LNCS, vol. 576, pp. 279–287. Springer, Heidelberg (1992)
22. Menezes, A., Okamoto, T., Vanstone, S.A.: Reducing elliptic curve logarithms to logarithms in a finite field. IEEE Trans. Inform. Theory 39(5), 1639–1646 (1993)

23. Montgomery, P.L.: Speeding the Pollard and elliptic curve methods of factorization. Math. Comp. 48(177), 243–264 (1987)
24. Montgomery, P.L.: Evaluating recurrences of form $X_{m+n} = f(X_m, X_n, X_{m-n})$ via Lucas chains (1992), `ftp.cwi.nl/pub/pmontgom/lucas.ps.gz`
25. Pohlig, S.C., Hellman, M.E.: An improved algorithm for computing logarithms over GF(p) and its cryptographic significance. IEEE Trans. Inform. Theory 24(1), 106–110 (1978)
26. Pollard, J.M.: Monte Carlo methods for index computation (mod p). Math. Comp. 32(143), 918–924 (1978)
27. Satoh, T., Araki, K.: Fermat quotients and the polynomial time discrete log algorithm for anomalous elliptic curves. Comment. Math. Univ. St. Pauli 47(1), 81–92 (1998)
28. Schoof, R.: Counting points on elliptic curves over finite fields. J. Théor. Nombres Bordeaux 7(1), 219–254 (1995)
29. Semaev, I.: Evaluation of discrete logarithms in a group of p-torsion points of an elliptic curve in characteristic p. Math. Comp. 67(221), 353–356 (1998)
30. Smart, N.P.: The discrete logarithm problem on elliptic curves of trace one. J. Cryptology 12(3), 193–196 (1999)
31. Smart, N.P.: How secure are elliptic curves over composite extension fields? In: Pfitzmann, B. (ed.) EUROCRYPT 2001. LNCS, vol. 2045, pp. 30–39. Springer, Heidelberg (2001)
32. Smith, B.: Families of fast elliptic curves from Q-curves. In: Sako, K., Sarkar, P. (eds.) ASIACRYPT 2013, Part I. LNCS, vol. 8269, pp. 61–78. Springer, Heidelberg (2013)
33. Solinas, J.A.: An improved algorithm for arithmetic on a family of elliptic curves. In: Kaliski Jr., B.S. (ed.) CRYPTO 1997. LNCS, vol. 1294, pp. 357–371. Springer, Heidelberg (1997)
34. Stam, M.: Speeding up subgroup cryptosystems. Ph.D. thesis, Technische Universiteit Eindhoven (2003)
35. Straus, E.G.: Addition chains of vectors. Amer. Math. Monthly 71, 806–808 (1964)
36. Wiener, M.J., Zuccherato, R.J.: Faster attacks on elliptic curve cryptosystems. In: Tavares, S., Meijer, H. (eds.) SAC 1998. LNCS, vol. 1556, pp. 190–200. Springer, Heidelberg (1999)

A   How Was This Curve Chosen?

The curve-twist pair implemented in this paper was chosen from the family of degree-2 Q-curve reductions with efficient endomorphisms (over $\mathbb{F}_{p^2}$) described in [32]. These curves are equipped with efficient endomorphisms, and the arithmetic properties of the family are not incompatible with twist-security.

We fixed $p = 2^{127} - 1$, a Mersenne prime; this p facilitates very fast modular arithmetic. Next, we chose a tiny nonsquare to define $\mathbb{F}_{p^2} = \mathbb{F}_p(i)$ with $i^2 = -1$; this makes for slightly faster $\mathbb{F}_{p^2}$-arithmetic, and much simpler formulæ. The most secure group orders for a Montgomery curve-twist pair $(\mathcal{E}, \mathcal{E}')$ over $\mathbb{F}_{p^2}$ have the form $(\#\mathcal{E}, \#\mathcal{E}') = (4N, 8N')$ (or $(8N, 4N')$) with N and N' prime. The cofactor of 4 is forced by the existence of a Montgomery model, and then $p^2 \equiv 1 \pmod 8$ forces a cofactor of 8 on the twist.

The family in [32, §5] is parametrised by a free parameter s; each choice of s in $\mathbb{F}_p$ yields a curve over $\mathbb{F}_{p^2}$, each in a distinct $\overline{\mathbb{F}}_p$-isomorphism class. If the curve corresponding to s in $\mathbb{F}_p$ has a Montgomery model $\mathcal{E} : BY^2 = X(X^2 + AX + 1)$ over $\mathbb{F}_{p^2}$, then $8/A^2 = 1 + si$. If we write $A = A_0 + A_1 i$ with A_0 and A_1 in $\mathbb{F}_p$, then

$$A_0^4 + 2A_0^2 A_1^2 + A_1^4 + 8(A_1^2 - A_0^2) = 0 . \tag{5}$$

To optimise performance, we searched for parameter values s in $\mathbb{F}_p$ yielding Montgomery representations with "small" coefficients: that is, where A_0 and A_1 could be represented as small integers. But in view of Eq. (5), for any small value of A_1 there are at most four corresponding possibilities for A_0, none of which have any reason to be small (and vice versa). Given the number of curves to be searched to find a twist-secure pair, we could not expect to find a twist-secure curve with both A_0 and A_1 small. Our $\mathbb{F}_{p^2}$-arithmetic placed no preference on which of these two coefficients should be small, so we flipped a coin and restricted our search to s yielding A_1 with integer representations less than 2^{32} (occupying only one word on 32- and 64-bit platforms). The constant appearing in Montgomery's formulæ [23, p. 261] is $(A+2)/4$, so we also required the integer representation of A_1 to be congruent to 2 modulo 4.

Our search prioritised A_1 values whose integer representations had low signed Hamming weight, in the hope that multiplication by A_1 might be faster when computed via sequence of additions and shifts. We did not find any curve-twist pairs with optimal cofactors and A_1 of weight 1, 2, or 3, but we found ten such pairs with A_1 of weight 4. Three of these pairs had an A_1 of precisely 32 bits; the curve-twist pair in §2 corresponds to the *smallest* such A_1. Although the low signed Hamming weight of A_1 did not end up improving our implementation, the small size of A_1 yielded a minor but noticeable speedup.

The takeaway message is that the construction in [32, §5] is flexible enough to find a vast number of twist-secure curves over any quadratic extension field, to which all of the techniques in this paper can be directly applied (or easily adapted), regardless of how the parameter search is designed. Such curve-twist pairs can be readily found in a *verifiably random* manner, following, for instance, the method described in [11, §5].

Replacing a Random Oracle: Full Domain Hash from Indistinguishability Obfuscation

Susan Hohenberger[1,*], Amit Sahai[2,**], and Brent Waters[3,***]

[1] Johns Hopkins University, USA
susan@cs.jhu.edu
[2] UCLA, USA
sahai@cs.ucla.edu
[3] University of Texas at Austin, USA
bwaters@cs.utexas.edu

Abstract. Our main result gives a way to instantiate the random oracle with a concrete hash function in "full domain hash" applications. The term full domain hash was first proposed by Bellare and Rogaway [BR93, BR96] and referred to a signature scheme from any trapdoor permutation that was part of their seminal work introducing the random oracle heuristic. Over time the term full domain hash has (informally) encompassed a broader range of notable cryptographic schemes including the Boneh-Franklin [BF01] IBE scheme and Boneh-Lynn-Shacham (BLS) [BLS01] signatures. All of the above described schemes required a hash function that had to be modeled as a random oracle to prove security. Our work utilizes recent advances in indistinguishability obfuscation to construct specific hash functions for use in these schemes. We then prove security of the *original* cryptosystems when instantiated with our specific hash function.

Of particular interest, our work evades the impossibility results of Dodis, Oliveira, and Pietrzak [DOP05], who showed that there can be no black-box construction of hash functions that allow Full-Domain Hash

* Susan Hohenberger is supported in part by NSF CNS-1154035 and CNS-1228443; DARPA and the Air Force Research Laboratory under contract FA8750-11-2-0211, DARPA N11AP20006, the Office of Naval Research under contract N00014-11-1-0470, and a Microsoft Faculty Fellowship. Applying to all authors, the views expressed are those of the authors and do not reflect the official policy or position of DARPA, the NSF, or the U.S. Government.

** Amit Sahai is supported in part from a DARPA/ONR PROCEED award, NSF grants 1228984, 1136174, 1118096, and 1065276, a Xerox Faculty Research Award, a Google Faculty Research Award, an equipment grant from Intel, and an Okawa Foundation Research Grant. This material is based upon work supported by the Defense Advanced Research Projects Agency through the U.S. Office of Naval Research under Contract N00014-11- 1-0389.

*** Brent Waters is supported in part by NSF CNS-0915361 and CNS-0952692, CNS-1228599 DARPA through the U.S. Office of Naval Research under Contract N00014-11-1-0382, DARPA N11AP20006, Google Faculty Research award, the Alfred P. Sloan Fellowship, Microsoft Faculty Fellowship, and Packard Foundation Fellowship.

P.Q. Nguyen and E. Oswald (Eds.): EUROCRYPT 2014, LNCS 8441, pp. 201–220, 2014.
© International Association for Cryptologic Research 2014

Signatures to be based on trapdoor permutations, and its extension by
Dodis, Haitner, and Tentes [DHT12] to the RSA Full-Domain Hash Signatures. This indicates our techniques applying indistinguishability obfuscation may be useful for circumventing other black-box impossibility
proofs.

1   Introduction

Since Bellare and Rogaway [BR93] introduced the Random Oracle Model, a major effort in cryptography has been to understand when and if random oracles can
be instantiated with families of actual hash functions while maintaining security.
Over the years, we have seen real progress in this effort: Firstly we have seen the
discovery of alternative schemes that do not require random oracles but achieve
the same security properties as earlier schemes that do require random oracles.
For example, Cramer and Shoup [CS98] achieved efficient chosen ciphertext security from DDH hard groups. As another example Canetti, Halevi, and Katz
[CHK07] achieved secure IBE without random oracles, following the seminal
work of [BF01] giving IBE in the Random Oracle Model. More recently, we have
seen the discovery of schemes that not only work in the standard model without random oracles, but work in a manner very similar to the original schemes
that used random oracles (e.g. [HSW13, FHPS13] following schemes in the random oracle model [BF01, BLS01]). However, all of these schemes proven secure
without random oracles required *changing the underlying cryptographic scheme*
in addition to instantiating the random oracle with a concrete hash function.
Thus, despite these advances, the following basic question has remained open:

Can we instantiate the random oracle with an actual family of hash functions
for existing cryptographic schemes in the random oracle model, such as Full
Domain Hash signatures?

In other words, can we achieve security *without changing the underlying cryp-*
tographic scheme at all, but only by replacing the random oracle with a specific
family of hash functions? In this work, we give the first positive answer to this
question. We do this by leveraging the notion of indistinguishability obfuscation [BGI+01, BGI+12] that was recently achieved in the work of [GGH+13].

Our result is particularly interesting in light of negative results on the Random Oracle Model [CGH98, GK03, BBP04] which have called into question the
secure applicability of the Random Oracle Model. Our work is the first to show
natural examples of schemes that were originally invented with the Random Oracle Model in mind, that nevertheless remain secure when the random oracle is
specifically instantiated.

In particular, our work evades the impossibility result of Dodis, Oliveira, and
Pietrzak [DOP05], who showed that there can be no black-box construction of
hash functions that allow Full-Domain Hash Signatures to be based on trapdoor
permutations. Because we make use of obfuscation, our constructions are inherently non-black-box, and thus are not ruled out by this type of black-box impossibility result. This indicates that our techniques applying indistinguishability

obfuscation may be useful in the future for circumventing other such black-box impossibility proofs.

Our Result. Our main result gives a way to instantiate the random oracle with a concrete hash function in "full domain hash" (FDH) signatures. The FDH signature scheme was first proposed[1] in the original Bellare-Rogaway [BR93] paper as a way to build a signature scheme from any trapdoor permutation using the introduced random oracle heuristic. This work was very influential and formed the foundation for part of the PKCS#1 standard [KS98]. While the terminology of "full-domain hash" originally applied to the trapdoor permutation signature scheme of Bellare and Rogaway, over time it has (informally) encompassed a broader range of notable cryptographic schemes including the Boneh-Franklin [BF01] IBE scheme, the Cock's IBE scheme [Coc01], and Boneh-Lynn-Shacham (BLS) [BLS01] signatures. Although these schemes exist in different algebraic domains and have different aims, they share common construction and proof structures that uses random oracle programming in very similar ways.

Our work develops a methodology for replacing the programming of a random oracle in these construction using indistinguishable obfuscation in a novel manner. We begin by describing a scheme that replaces the RO hash function in the original Bellare-Rogaway trapdoor permutation (TDP) signature scheme. Our newly instantiated scheme is then proven to be selectively secure.

Let's begin by informally recalling the Bellare-Rogaway TDP-based FDH scheme. The signature setup algorithm generates a trapdoor permutation pair of functions $g_{\text{PK}}, g_{\text{SK}}^{-1}$. It chooses a hash function $H(\cdot)$ that maps from the message space to the domain (and co-domain) of the permutation. The permutation g_{PK} and hash function are published as the verification key and the inverse g_{SK}^{-1} is kept secret. To sign a message m, the signer computes $g_{\text{SK}}^{-1}(H(m))$. To verify a signature σ on message m, the verifier simply checks whether $g_{\text{PK}}(\sigma) \overset{?}{=} H(m)$.

The proof of the Bellare-Rogaway FDH system uses the random oracle heuristic to model $H(\cdot)$ as a programmable random oracle. Suppose a poly-time attacker makes at most Q_H oracle queries. One can create a reduction algorithm to the security of the trapdoor permutation as follows. For all but one of the (unique) queries of a message m to the oracle, the reduction algorithm chooses a random value t from the domain and outputs $g_{\text{PK}}(t)$ as the result of the query. For any of these messages, the reduction algorithm can easily generate a signature by outputting t. However, at one query point m^* it programs the output of the random oracle to be $z^* = g_{\text{PK}}(t^*)$ where z^* was given from the trapdoor permutation challenger. If the attacker forges at this message, then the forgery will be t^* which is immediately the solution for the trapdoor permutation inversion.

Our first result is creating a *replacement* hash function for the oracle $H(\cdot)$ and developing a security proof without relying on the random oracle heuristic. To keep with our original goals, our only modifications will be to $H(\cdot)$ and we

---

[1] The terminology "full-domain hash" was actually introduced by Bellare-Rogaway in 1996 [BR96]. They applied this label to the noted signature scheme of their earlier work.

will use the signature system construction as is, with no changes to the underlying trapdoor permutation family. The two main tools we use to build $H(\cdot)$ are an indistinguishability obfuscator [BGI+01, GGH+13] and a recently introduced primitive called constrained PRFs [BW13, BGI14, KPTZ13]. In short, a constrained PRF key is a secret key K that allows the evaluator to evaluate the a PRF at a limited set of points, while the rest will appear pseudorandom to him. For our results, we only need a simple form of constrained PRFs called "punctured PRFs" [SW13]. In this setting a private key will be associated with a polynomial set S, where a key $K(S)$ can evaluate the PRF $F(K, x)$ at all x except when $x \in S$. For our proofs we only ever need S to be a singleton set.

We now overview the hash function construction and how we prove it to be selectively secure. (One could use the usual complexity leveraging arguments to claim adaptive security, but we will address adaptive security in a direct way shortly.) To create the hash function the reduction algorithm first chooses a puncturable PRF key K (note this "master key" can evaluate the PRF at all points). Next, the hash function itself will be an obfuscation of the program which on input m computes $g_{\mathrm{PK}}(F(K, m))$. That is the program simply computes the PRF at point m and then applies the trapdoor permutation. We call this program Full Domain Hash. To prove security we will apply the "punctured programs" method of Sahai and Waters [SW13], where we surgically remove a key element of a program, but in a way that does not alter input/output functionality.

Our security proof is formed from a sequence of hybrids. In the first hybrid, we replace the obfuscation of the program Full Domain Hash with an obfuscation of an equivalent program called Full Domain Hash*. This program operates the same as the original except on input m^*, where m^* is the message the attacker selectively chose to attack (before seeing the verification key). At this point instead of computing $F(K, m^*)$ the program is simply hardwired to output a constant z^* to output where z^* is set to be $F(K, m^*)$. Since $z^* = F(K, m^*)$, the input/output behavior is identical. In addition, the program is not given the full PRF key K, but instead is given a punctured PRF key $K(\{m^*\})$. By the security of indistinguishable obfuscation the advantage of any poly-time attacker must be negligibly close between these hybrids. In the next hybrid experiment we replace z^* with a random value chosen from the domain/range of the permutation. The advantage between of this hybrid must also be close due to the constrained PRF security. Now we are finally in a position where we can reduce to the security of the trapdoor permutation. The reduction algorithm receives a TDP challenge z^* and hardcodes that in as the output of $H(m^*)$. It can use a signature on this to invert the challenge. At all other points it knows the punctured PRF key and can therefore compute valid signatures without knowing the inverse of the trapdoor permutation.

Our reduction actually shares some of the spirit of the original random oracle reduction, where a challenge is programmed in at one point and signatures are made by knowing the pre images at all others. A key aspect is that the obfuscation hides the fact that at a certain hybrid m^* is treated differently. If an attacker were able to see inside the obfuscation it could actually see the preimages and break the scheme. Another interesting aspect is that our proof does not leverage the fact that the function $g_{PK}(\cdot)$ is a permutation. It would go through equally well if we only assumed that it was an injective trapdoor function.

In our construction and proof, there is a hash function created as part of each public key. Taking things further, we might want to have *one* hash function built as a common reference string that could serve as part of many public keys. Creating similar results in this setting will require further work.

There is also a connection between the proof techniques we use and the proof technique for the selectively secure signature scheme of Sahai and Waters [SW13]. In the Sahai-Waters work, the verification key is an obfuscated program that evaluates the punctured PRF on a message and then outputs the evaluation of a one-way function on that. A signer signs by evaluating the punctured PRF on the message. In comparison, in our case, the hash function is the obfuscated program that evaluates the punctured PRF on a message and then outputs the evaluation of a trapdoor permutation on that. Here in contrast, the signing is done by applying the inverse permutation and the signer isn't necessarily "aware" of the punctured PRF.

Overcoming the Black-Box Impossibility. We now see more precisely why our work evades the impossibility result of Dodis, Oliveira, and Pietrzak [DOP05] and Dodis, Haitner, and Tentes [DHT12]. Our hash function is obfuscation of code that runs the underlying permutation. The obfuscation will intuitively hide the evaluation of this code. In particular, no attacker can tell if the trapdoor permutation was actually computed on an input or whether it was a special point where the output was hardcoded in. In the DOP negative result, they build an attack oracle that specifically leverages the black box access to the TDP to watch whenever it is called. It is interesting to see this very strong correlation between the negative result and how non-black box access to a primitive and indistinguishability obfuscation can combine to circumvent it.

Getting Adaptive Security. For our next result we show how to get adaptive (or standard) signature security without complexity leveraging for the case where the trapdoor permutation is the RSA function. The use of RSA as a trapdoor permutation candidate was suggested in Bellare-Rogaway'93 [BR93] and explicitly given in Bellare-Rogaway'96 [BR96]. The public parameters in their scheme are an RSA modulus $N = pq$ for hidden primes p, q and an RSA exponent e chosen such that $\gcd(\phi(N), e) = 1$. The secret key is the integer d where $d \cdot e = 1$ mod $\phi(N)$. A signature on message m is of the form $H(m)^d \mod N$ and one verifies a signature σ by checking if $H(m) \stackrel{?}{=} \sigma^e \mod N$.

We develop a different set of techniques that can leverage the particular structure of the RSA function. The first new ingredient is use of admissible hash functions first introduced in the context of Identity-Based Encryption by Boneh-Boyen [BB04a]. We use a simplification due to Freire et. al. [FHPS13]. At a high level the system is a pair of a hash function $h : \{0,1\}^{\ell(\lambda)} \to \{0,1\}^{n(\lambda)}$ that hashes from the message space to n bit strings and an efficient randomized algorithm AdmSample. The sampling algorithm takes in the security parameter as well as second parameter Q which intuitively corresponds to the number of signature queries an attacker makes. It outputs a string $u \in \{0, 1, \perp\}^n$. Informally, we say that the system is admissible if the following conditions hold. Consider any sequence of Q values $x_1, \ldots, x_Q$ and $x^* \neq x_i$. The event we consider is where the string $h(x_i)$ has a bit in common with u in at least one position, but $h(x^*)$ is different from u at all positions. (Note, if $u_j = \perp$ then it is different at position j from all bit strings.) If this event occurs with non-negligible probability, we say it is an admissible system. Intuitively, when used in a proof of a signature scheme, the admissible hash function is utilized to partition the message space into messages that can be signed in the query phase and those that can be used in the challenge phase. A sampled string u corresponds to a particular partition. When running a reduction, one hopes that the actual signature oracle queries and forgery message align with a partition, and the reduction aborts otherwise.

To build the hash function candidate, the setup first chooses a random $v \in \mathbb{Z}_N^*$ as well as exponents $a_{i,b}$ chosen randomly in $[0, \phi(N)]$, for all $i \in [1, n], b \in \{0, 1\}$. Next, it builds the hash function as an obfuscation of the program RSA Hash. The program will first compute $m' = h(m)$. Then, it computes and outputs $v^{\prod_{i \in [n]} a_{i,m_i'}}$.

Our proof proceeds in a few hybrid steps. In the first hybrid experiment the challenger creates a partition internally by calling AdmSample$(1^\lambda, Q) \to u$ for an attacker that makes at most $Q = Q(\lambda)$ queries. The game aborts and declares the attacker unsuccessful if any of the query messages or forgery message violates the partition. The property of admissible hashes states any attacker with non-negligible advantage in the real game will also have non-negligible advantage here. In the next hybrid, we change the way we sample the exponents $a_{i,b}$. One first chooses random $y_{i,b} \in [1, N]$. Then for when $u_i = b$ we set $c_{i,b} = e \cdot y_{i,b}$. If $u_i \neq b$ we set $c_{i,b} = e \cdot y_{i,b} + 1$. Note in the first case $c_{i,b}$ is a multiple of e and in the second case $e \nmid c_{i,b}$. The values $a_{i,b} = c_{i,b} \mod \phi(N)$. We show that this way of choosing a values is statistically close to the previous uniform way, because $\gcd(\phi(N), e) = 1$.

Next, we use an alternative program where we directly use the $c_{i,b}$ values in place of the $a_{i,b}$ values. Since the group $\mathbb{Z}_N^*$ is of order $\phi(N)$ we have that $v^{\prod_{i \in [n]} a_{i,m_i'}} = v^{\prod_{i \in [n]} c_{i,m_i'}}$ for all m'. Therefore the input/output behavior is the same between the two programs and we can argue the advantage in the hybrids for poly-time attackers must be close by indistinguishability obfuscation. This is the critical hybrid experiment in that it most radically departs from previous such proofs, by leveraging indistinguishability obfuscation. Observe that this hybrid experiment eliminates the need for the reduction to know $\phi(N)$, which is crucial to the reduction, since it uses $c_{i,b}$ values instead of $a_{i,b}$ values. However, if the values $c_{i,b}$ were completely visible to an attacker, they would be trivially distinguishable from the "true" uniform $a_{i,b}$ values. However, indistinguishability obfuscation guarantees that these values are hidden from the attacker, and that indeed the attacker cannot distinguish this hybrid from the previous one.

Finally, we show that any attacker that is successful in the last hybrid can be used to break the RSA assumption. For any signature query message m that respects the partition, the reduction will view $H(m)$ as v raised to some integer that is a multiple of e and taking the e-th root is then easy. Any forgery on m^* that respects the partition, the reduction will view $H(m^*)$ as v^z for some z where $\gcd(e, z) = 1$ and from this can derive $v^{1/e}$.

BLS Signatures and More. We extend our techniques to replacing the random oracle in the BLS [BLS01] signature scheme. In Section 5 we give a candidate that has a selective proof of security based on the computational Diffie-Hellman problem (along with indistinguishability obfuscation). In the full version [HSW14], we give an adaptive proof of security based on an assumption equivalent to the n-Diffie-Hellman inversion assumption. The high level structures of these are similar to the respective selective and adaptive construction and proof methods above. The lower level mechanisms are adapted to the context of bilinear groups. In Section 7, we sketch how the BLS ideas extend to the Boneh-Franklin IBE scheme.

1.1   Other Related Work

Early work on replacing random oracles for the problem of obfuscating point functions under entropy conditions began with the work of Canetti [Can97].

Recently, the work of Bellare, Hoang and Keelveedhi [BHK13] looked at a complementary question of identifying a definitional abstraction to replace the random oracle heuristic in several random oracle-based constructions. The abstraction is a notion of security called UCE (Universal Computational Extractor). The authors emphasize that a random oracle is *known* not to exist and "behaves like a random oracle" is not a rigorously defined property, whereas UCE is a well defined property of a hash function. They then show how several previous constructions proven secure in the random schemes can be proven secure if we assume the hash functions are UCE secure. One can then conjecture that standard cryptographic hash functions like SHA-256 may satisfy the UCE security notion. In contrast, our work is focused on providing *new* candidate constructions for hash functions, that allow for a security proof to work with the original constructions in the random oracle model. Interestingly, the work of [BHK13] does not encompass the case of Full Domain Hash signatures, arguably one of the most natural and well-studied constructions in the Random Oracle Model, that we address here.

Dodis, Haitner, and Tentes [DHT12] show how to give an FDH signature that is secure for at most q queries when the hash function grows with q.

2   Preliminaries

We define indistinguishability obfuscation, and variants of pseudo-random functions (PRFs) that we will make use of. All the variants of PRFs that we consider will be constructed from one-way functions.

2.1 Indistinguishability Obfuscation

The definition below is from [GGH+13]; there it is called a "family-indistinguishable obfuscator". They show that this notion follows immediately from their standard definition of indistinguishability obfuscator using a non-uniform argument.

Definition 1 (Indistinguishability Obfuscator ($i\mathcal{O}$)). *A uniform PPT machine $i\mathcal{O}$ is called an* indistinguishability obfuscator *for a circuit class $\{\mathcal{C}_\lambda\}$ if the following conditions are satisfied:*

- *For all security parameters $\lambda \in \mathbb{N}$, for all $C \in \mathcal{C}_\lambda$, for all inputs x, we have that*
$$\Pr[C'(x) = C(x) : C' \leftarrow i\mathcal{O}(\lambda, C)] = 1$$

- *For any (not necessarily uniform) PPT adversaries Samp, D, there exists a negligible function α such that the following holds: if $\Pr[\forall x, C_0(x) = C_1(x) : (C_0, C_1, \tau) \leftarrow Samp(1^\lambda)] > 1 - \alpha(\lambda)$, then we have:*

$$\left| \Pr\left[D(\tau, i\mathcal{O}(\lambda, C_0)) = 1 : (C_0, C_1, \tau) \leftarrow Samp(1^\lambda) \right] \right.$$
$$\left. - \Pr\left[D(\tau, i\mathcal{O}(\lambda, C_1)) = 1 : (C_0, C_1, \tau) \leftarrow Samp(1^\lambda) \right] \right| \le \alpha(\lambda)$$

In this paper, we will make use of such indistinguishability obfuscators for all polynomial-size circuits:

Definition 2 (Indistinguishability Obfuscator for $P/poly$). *A uniform PPT machine $i\mathcal{O}$ is called an* indistinguishability obfuscator *for $P/poly$ if the following holds: Let $\mathcal{C}_\lambda$ be the class of circuits of size at most λ. Then $i\mathcal{O}$ is an indistinguishability obfuscator for the class $\{\mathcal{C}_\lambda\}$.*

Such indistinguishability obfuscators for all polynomial-size circuits were constructed under novel algebraic hardness assumptions in [GGH+13].

2.2 Constrained PRFs

We first consider some simple types of constrained PRFs [BW13, BGI14, KPTZ13], where a PRF is only defined on a subset of the usual input space. We focus on *puncturable* PRFs, which are PRFs that can be defined on all bit strings of a certain length, except for any polynomial-size set of inputs:

Definition 3. *A puncturable family of PRFs F mapping is given by a triple of Turing Machines Key_F, Puncture_F, and Eval_F, and a pair of computable functions $n(\cdot)$ and $m(\cdot)$, satisfying the following conditions:*

- *[**Functionality preserved under puncturing**] For every PPT adversary A such that $A(1^\lambda)$ outputs a polynomial-size set $S \subseteq \{0,1\}^{n(\lambda)}$, then for all $x \in \{0,1\}^{n(\lambda)}$ where $x \notin S$, we have that:*

$$\Pr\left[\text{Eval}_F(K, x) = \text{Eval}_F(K_S, x) : K \leftarrow \text{Key}_F(1^\lambda), K_S = \text{Puncture}_F(K, S) \right] = 1$$

- *[Pseudorandom at punctured points]* For every PPT adversary (A_1, A_2) such that $A_1(1^\lambda)$ outputs a polynomial-size set $S \subseteq \{0,1\}^{n(\lambda)}$ and state τ, consider an experiment where $K \leftarrow \text{Key}_F(1^\lambda)$ and $K_S = \text{Puncture}_F(K, S)$. Then we have

$$\left| \Pr\left[A_2(\tau, K_S, S, \text{Eval}_F(K, S)) = 1\right] - \Pr\left[A_2(\tau, K_S, S, U_{m(\lambda) \cdot |S|}) = 1\right] \right| = negl(\lambda)$$

where $\text{Eval}_F(K, S)$ denotes the concatenation of $\text{Eval}_F(K, x_1)), \ldots, \text{Eval}_F (K, x_k))$ where $S = \{x_1, \ldots, x_k\}$ is the enumeration of the elements of S in lexicographic order, $negl(\cdot)$ is a negligible function, and U_ℓ denotes the uniform distribution over ℓ bits.

For ease of notation, we write $F(K, x)$ to represent $\text{Eval}_F(K, x)$. We also represent the punctured key $\text{Puncture}_F(K, S)$ by $K(S)$.

The GGM tree-based construction of PRFs [GGM84] from one-way functions are easily seen to yield puncturable PRFs, as observed by [BW13, BGI14, KPTZ13]. Thus we have:

Theorem 1. *[GGM84, BW13, BGI14, KPTZ13]* If one-way functions exist, then for all efficiently computable functions $n(\lambda)$ and $m(\lambda)$, there exists a puncturable PRF family that maps $n(\lambda)$ bits to $m(\lambda)$ bits.

2.3   RSA Assumption and Shamir's Lemma

We begin by recalling (one of the) standard versions of the RSA assumption [RSA78].

Assumption 1 (RSA). *Let λ be the security parameter. Let positive integer N be the product of two λ-bit, distinct odd primes p, q. Let e be a randomly chosen positive integer less than and relatively prime to $\phi(N) = (p-1)(q-1)$. Given (N, e) and a random $y \in \mathbb{Z}_N^*$, it is hard to compute x such that $x^e \equiv y \mod N$.*

We also make use of the following lemma due to Shamir.

Lemma 1 (Shamir [Sha83]). *Given $x, y \in \mathbb{Z}_N$ together with $a, b \in \mathbb{Z}$ such that $x^a = y^b \pmod{N}$ and $\gcd(a, b) = 1$, there is an efficient algorithm for computing $z \in \mathbb{Z}_N$ such that $z^a = y \pmod{N}$.*

2.4   Bilinear Groups and the CDH Assumption

Let $\mathbb{G}$ and $\mathbb{G}_T$ be groups of prime order p. A *bilinear map* is an efficient mapping $e : \mathbb{G} \times \mathbb{G} \to \mathbb{G}_T$ which is both: *(bilinear)* for all $g \in \mathbb{G}$ and $a, b \leftarrow \mathbb{Z}_p$, $e(g^a, g^b) = e(g, g)^{ab}$; and *(non-degenerate)* if g generates $\mathbb{G}$, then $e(g, g) \neq 1$.

Assumption 2 (Computational Diffie-Hellman). *Let g generate a group $\mathbb{G}$ of prime order $p \in \Theta(2^\lambda)$. For all p.p.t. adversaries $\mathcal{A}$, the following probability is negligible in λ:*

$$\Pr[a, b \leftarrow \mathbb{Z}_p; z \leftarrow \mathcal{A}(g, g^a, g^b) : z = g^{ab}].$$

2.5   The n-Diffie-Hellman Inversion Assumption

Our full version [HSW14] contains a construction of adaptively secure BLS signatures that makes use of the n-Diffie-Hellman Inversion assumption [BB04b]. This is a parameterized family of assumptions, where the number of group elements involved increases with n. (For our application, n will be dependent only on the security parameter.)

Assumption 3 (n-**Diffie-Hellman Inversion**). *Let h generate a group $\mathbb{G}$ of prime order $p \in \Theta(2^\lambda)$. For all p.p.t. adversaries $\mathcal{A}$, the following probability is negligible in λ:*

$$\Pr[b \leftarrow \mathbb{Z}_p; z \leftarrow \mathcal{A}(h, h^b, h^{b^2}, \dots, h^{b^n}) : z = g^{1/b}].$$

3   Full-Domain Hash Signatures (Selectively Secure)

In this section, we revisit the Bellare-Rogaway Full-Domain Hash (FDH) signature scheme [BR93, BR96], and show how to make it selectively secure in the standard model by instantiating the random oracle in a specific way. We stress that we do not modify the Bellare-Rogaway FDH signature scheme in any way; the only new aspect of our construction is our instantiation of the random oracle with a specific function whose description becomes part of the public key.

Recall that the Bellare-Rogaway FDH signature scheme required a trapdoor permutation family. Our method, in fact, not only applies to trapdoor permutation families, but indeed to any *injective* trapdoor function family. We prove the selective security of the FDH signature scheme based on the security of the indistinguishability obfusctor, the security of a puncturable PRF family, and the security of an injective trapdoor function family.

For simplicity of exposition, we assume that there is a polynomial $\ell(\lambda)$ which denotes the length of messages to be signed; we denote this message space by $\mathcal{M} = \{0,1\}^{\ell(\lambda)}$. More generally, a collision-resistant hash function may be used to hash messages to this size.

- Setup(1^λ) : The setup algorithm first runs TDFSetup(1^λ) and that produces a public index PK along with a trapdoor SK, yielding the map $g_{PK} : \{0,1\}^n \to \{0,1\}^w$ together with its inverse. Next, the setup algorithm chooses a puncturable PRF key K for F where $F(K, \cdot) : \{0,1\}^{\ell(\lambda)} \to \{0,1\}^n$. Then, it creates an obfuscation of the of the program Full Domain Hash Figure 1. The size of the program is padded to be the maximum of itself and the program Full Domain Hash* of Figure 2. We refer to the obfuscated program as the function $H : \{0,1\}^{\ell(\lambda)} \to \{0,1\}^w$, which acts as the random oracle type hash function in the Bellare-Rogaway scheme.

  The verification key VK consists of the trapdoor index PK as well as the hash function $H(\cdot)$. The secret key is the trapdoor SK as well as $H(\cdot)$.
- Sign(SK, $m \in \mathcal{M}$) : The signature algorithm outputs $\sigma = g_{SK}^{-1}(H(m)) \in \{0,1\}^n$.

Full Domain Hash

Constants: PRF key K, trapdoor function index PK.
Input: Message m.

   1. Output $g_{PK}(F(K, m))$.

Fig. 1. Full Domain Hash

Full Domain Hash*

Constants: Punctured PRF key $K(\{m^*\})$, $m^* \in \mathcal{M}$, $z^* \in \{0, 1\}^w$, trapdoor function index PK.
Input: Message m.

   1. If $m = m^*$ output z^* and exit.
   2. Else output $g_{PK}(F(K, m))$.

Fig. 2. Full Domain Hash*

- Verify(VK, m, σ) The verification algorithm tests if $g_{PK}(\sigma) \overset{?}{=} H(m)$ and outputs accept if and only if this holds.

Theorem 2. *If our obfuscation scheme is indistingishuably secure, F is a secure punctured PRF, and the injective trapdoor function is secure, then the above signature scheme is selectively secure.*

We describe a proof as a sequence of hybrid experiments where the first hybrid corresponds to the original signature security game. We prove that a poly-time attacker's advantage must be negligibly close between each successive one. Then, we show that any poly-time attacker in the final experiment that succeeds in forging with non-negligible probability can be used to invert the injective trapdoor function.

- Hyb_0 : In the first hybrid the following game is played:
  1. The attacker selectively gives the challenger the message m^*.
  2. The TDF index is chosen by the challenger running $\mathsf{TDFSetup}(1^\lambda)$.
  3. K is chosen as a key for the puncturable PRF.
  4. The hash function $H(\cdot)$ is created as an obfuscation of the program Full Domain Hash.
  5. The attacker queries the sign oracle a polynomial number of times on messages $m \neq m^*$. It receives back $g_{SK}^{-1}(H(m)) = F(K, m)$. (Note the equality holds since the function g_{PK} is injective.)
  6. The attacker sends a forgery σ^* and wins if Verify(VK, m^*, σ^*) = 1.
- Hyb_1 : Is the same as Hyb_0 except we let $z^* = g_{PK}(F(K, m^*))$ and let VK be the obfuscation of the program Verify Signature* of Figure 2.
- Hyb_2 : Is the same as Hyb_1 except $z^* = g_{PK}(t)$ for t chosen uniformly at random in $\{0, 1\}^n$.

The following three lemmas together yield our result in Theorem 2 that the full domain hash signature scheme in Section 3 is selectively secure.

Lemma 2. *If our obfuscation scheme is indistinguishability secure, then the advantage of a poly-time attacker in* Hyb_0 *is negligibly close to the advantage in* Hyb_1.

Proof. We prove this lemma by giving a reduction to the indistinguishability security of the obfuscator. To do so, we must build the two algorithms *Samp* and *D*.

$Samp(1^\lambda)$ behaves as follows: It invokes the adversary to obtain m^* and the adversary's state τ'. It runs $\mathsf{TDFSetup}(1^\lambda)$ to obtain PK and SK. It then chooses K as a key for the puncturable PRF. It sets $z^* = g_{\mathrm{PK}}(F(K, m^*))$. It sets $\tau = (m^*, \mathrm{PK}, \mathrm{SK}, K, \tau')$ and builds C_1 as the program for Full Domain Hash, and C_2 as the program for Full Domain Hash*.

Before describing D, we observe that by construction and the functionality preservation property of puncturable PRFs, the circuits C_1 and C_2 always behave identically on every input. Because of padding, both C_1 and C_2 have the same size. Thus, *Samp* satisfies the conditions needed for invoking the indistinguishability property of the obfuscator.

Now, we can describe the algorithm D, which takes as input τ as given above, and either the obfuscation of C_1, which is the program Full Domain Hash, or C_2, which is the program Full Domain Hash*. D creates the verification key for the signature scheme by combining PK with the obfuscated program as the hash function description. It then invokes the adversary on this verification key, and the adversary then makes requests for signatures on messages $m \neq m^*$. For each such message, D constructs the signatures $g_{\mathrm{SK}}^{-1}(H(m)) = F(K, m)$, through its knowledge of K within τ. Finally, the attacker sends a forgery σ^* and wins if $\mathsf{Verify}(m^*, \sigma^*) = 1$. If the attacker wins, D outputs 1.

By construction, if D receives an obfuscation of C_1, then the probability that D outputs 1 is exactly the probability of the adversary winning in hybrid Hyb_0. On the other hand, if D receives an obfuscation of C_2, then the probability that D outputs 1 is the probability of the adversary winning in hybrid Hyb_1.

The lemma follows.

Lemma 3. *If our confined PRF is secure, then the advantage of a poly-time attacker in* Hyb_1 *is negligibly close to the advantage in* Hyb_2.

Proof. We prove this lemma by giving a reduction to the pseudorandomness property at punctured points for punctured PRFs. To do so, we must build the algorithms A_1 and A_2.

$A_1(1^\lambda)$ simply invokes the adversary to obtain the challenge message m^* and state τ', and outputs the singleton set $S = \{m^*\}$ and $\tau = (1^\lambda, \tau')$.

A_2 obtains as input τ, the punctured key K_S, the singleton set $S = \{m^*\}$, and either a value $t^* = F(K, m^*)$ or a uniformly random value t^*. Then, A_2 invokes $\mathsf{TDFSetup}(1^\lambda)$ to obtain PK and SK. Now given t^*, it can compute $z^* = g_{\mathrm{PK}}(t^*)$. Note that this yields either the z^* value computed in hybrid Hyb_1

or in hybrid Hyb_2. Since it knows K_S, now A_2 can obfuscate the program Full Domain Hash*, and then execute the adversary and answer its signature queries using the punctured key K_S. Finally, A_2 outputs 1 if the adversary succeeds.

By construction, the pseudorandomness property for punctured PRFs implies the lemma.

Lemma 4. *If our injective trapdoor function is hard to invert, then the advantage of a poly-time attacker in* Hyb_2 *is negligible.*

Proof. We prove this lemma by giving a reduction to the one-wayness of the injective trapdoor function. To do so, we build an inverting algorithm Inv.

Inv takes as input a public index PK for an injective trapdoor function, and a target $z^* = g_{\mathrm{PK}}(t^*)$ for some (as yet unknown) random value t^*. The algorithm Inv then invokes the adversary to obtain m^*, and chooses a PRF key K and builds the punctured key $K(S)$ where $S = \{m^*\}$. It uses this key, together with PK and z^*, to obfuscate the program Full Domain Hash*. It can then execute the adversary, and use its knowledge of $K(S)$ to answer all adversary signing queries. The adversary then terminates with an attempted forgery σ^* on message m^*. By the definition of the program Full Domain Hash*, this forgery can only be valid if $g_{\mathrm{PK}}(\sigma^*) = z^*$, and because g_{PK} is injective, this can only happen if $\sigma^* = t^*$. Thus if the adversary is successful, Inv can output σ^* as a valid pre-image of z^*.

We observe that by construction of Inv, the probability of success of Inv is exactly the probability that the attacker succeeds in hybrid Hyb_2. The lemma follows.

4   Adaptively Secure RSA Full Domain Hash Signatures

We first overview what advantage indistinguishability obfuscation gives us in this situation: In several previous constructions of adaptively secure schemes in the plain model starting with the adaptively secure IBE scheme of [BB04a], a special hash function was chosen that allowed for a "partitioning" proof of security. In essence, for this to work, the hash function should have two "modes":

- In the "normal" mode, the hash function's parameters are typically just chosen at random, and it behaves like an ordinary hash function.
- In the "partitioning" mode, the hash function parameters are chosen according to a special distribution. This special distribution allows for the efficient computation of the inverse of the hash value for a large fraction of points, but it has the property that computing the inverse of the hash value at any other point is computationally hard.

It is crucial that the input/output functionality of the hash function should be identical in the two modes, and we will also use this property. However, in previous proofs (like [BB04a]), it was also critical that the hash function parameters in "partitioning" mode be information theoretically indistinguishable from the parameters in "normal" mode, and thus the partition should be hidden from the adversary even when given the hash function parameters. This restriction significantly limited the applicability of this technique, as it could only be applied with algebraic structures that allowed for such "pseudorandom" hash parameters. Thanks to indistinguishability obfuscation, however, we can avoid this restriction by obfuscating the hash function description. Thus, even if the natural hash function parameters in "partitioning" mode clearly reveal the partition and thus are distinguishable from normal parameters, because the resulting hash function is *functionally* identical to a hash function in "normal" mode, the obfuscated hash function *must* hide the partition, and this allows the proof of adaptive security to go through.

In describing our signature scheme, For simplicity of exposition, we assume that there is a polynomial $\ell(\lambda)$ which denotes the length of messages to be signed; we denote this message space by $\mathcal{M} = \{0,1\}^{\ell(\lambda)}$. More generally, a collision-resistant hash function may be used to hash messages to this size. Below, for any polynomial in λ, after the first mention of this polynomial, we will often suppress the dependence on λ for ease of notation. Thus, below often we will simply refer to the size of messages to be signed by ℓ.

Before describing our construction, we first recall a (simplified) description of the notion of *admissible* hash functions due to [BB04a]. Our definition is a slight variation of the simplified definition due to [FHPS13].

Definition 4. *Let ℓ, n and θ be efficiently computable univariate polynomials. We say that an efficiently computable function $h : \{0,1\}^{\ell(\lambda)} \to \{0,1\}^{n(\lambda)}$, and an efficient randomized algorithm* AdmSample, *is θ-admissible if the following condition holds:*

For any $u \in (\{0,1\} \cup \{\perp\})^n$, define $P_u : \{0,1\}^\ell \to \{0,1\}$ as follows: $P_u(x) = 0$ iff $\forall i : h(x)_i \neq u_i$, and otherwise (if $\exists i : h(x)_i = u_i$) we have $P_u(x) = 1$.

Then we require that for any efficiently computable polynomial $Q(\lambda)$, for all $x_1, \ldots, x_Q, z \in \{0,1\}^\ell$, where $z \notin \{x_i\}$, we have that

$$\Pr\left[P_u(x_1) = P_u(x_2) = \cdots = P_u(x_Q) = 1 \wedge P_u(z) = 0\right] \geq 1/\theta(Q)$$

where the probability is taken only over $u \leftarrow$ AdmSample$(1^\lambda, Q)$.

Theorem 3 (Admissible Function Families [BB04a], see also [FHPS13] for a simple proof). *For any efficiently computable polynomials ℓ, n, there exists an efficiently computable polynomial θ such that there exist $\theta-$admissible function families mapping ℓ bits to n bits.*

We leverage the structure of the RSA trapdoor permutation to prove adaptive security. The use of RSA as a candidate for a trapdoor permutation was first discussed in the original Bellare-Rogaway [BR93] paper, however, it was in [BR96] that Bellare and Rogaway gave an explicit full domain hash RSA construction. This construction formed the basis for part of the standard PKCS#1 [KS98].

- Setup(1^λ) : The setup algorithm first runs an RSA type setup. It chooses random primes p, q of λ bits each. We define $N = p \cdot q$ and $\phi(N) =$

$(p-1)(q-1)$. We let e be a random chosen integer between 1 and $\phi(N)$ such that $\gcd(\phi(N), e) = 1$. Next, it chooses integers $(a_{1,0}, a_{1,1}), \ldots, (a_{n,0}, a_{n,1})$ each uniformly at random from the range $[1, \phi(N)-1]$. In addition, it chooses a group element $v \in \mathbb{Z}_N^*$. It then creates an obfuscation of the of the program RSA Hash of Figure 3. The size of the program is padded to be the maximum of itself and the program RSA Hash* of Figure 4. We refer to the obfuscated program as the function $H(\cdot)$. This function $H(\cdot)$ will replace the random oracle in the RSA FDH scheme, but no other part of the scheme is modified. The verification key VK is the integers N, e and the hash function $H : \{0,1\}^{\ell(\lambda)} \to \mathbb{Z}_N^*$. The secret key is the integer d where $e \cdot d \equiv 1 \mod \phi(N)$.

- Sign(SK, $m \in \mathcal{M}$) : The signature algorithm outputs $\sigma = H(M)^d \mod N$.
- Verify(VK, m, σ) The verification algorithm tests if $\sigma^e \equiv H(m) \mod N$ and outputs accept if and only if this holds.

RSA Hash

Constants: RSA modulus N, integers $(a_{1,0}, a_{1,1}), \ldots, (a_{n,0}, a_{n,1})$ each in $[1, \phi(N) - 1]$, and $v \in \mathbb{Z}_N^*$.
Input: Message m.

1. Compute $m' = h(m)$.
2. Compute the integer $\pi(m') = \prod_{i \in [n]} a_{i,m_i'}$.
3. Output $v^{\pi(m')} \pmod{N}$.

Fig. 3. RSA Hash

RSA Hash*

Constants: RSA modulus N, integers $(c_{1,0}, c_{1,1}), \ldots, (c_{n,0}, c_{n,1})$ each chosen as in Hyb_2, and $v \in \mathbb{Z}_N^*$.
Input: Message m.

1. Compute $m' = h(m)$.
2. Compute the integer $\pi(m') = \prod_{i \in [n]} c_{i,m_i'}$.
3. Output $v^{\pi(m')} \pmod{N}$.

Fig. 4. RSA Hash*

Remark 1. For simplicity of exposition we describe computing the programs output by first computing a integer $\pi(m')$ as a product of n integers and then raising v to this mod N. In practice, it might be more efficient to incrementally raise an accumulated value to each $a_{i,m_i'}$.

Theorem 4. *If our obfuscation scheme is indistingishuably secure and the RSA assumption holds, the above signature scheme is existentially unforgeable against chosen message attacks.*

In the full version [HSW14], we describe a proof as a sequence of hybrid experiments where the first hybrid corresponds to the original signature security game. In the first hybrid step we do a "partitioning" of the message space. Consider a poly-time attacker that makes $Q = Q(\lambda)$ signature queries $m_1, \ldots, m_Q$ and attempts to forge on message $m^* \neq m_i$ for all i. Roughly, at the beginning of Hyb_1 the challenger will now (behind the scenes) partition the message space such that a large fraction of messages will fall into a "query" space and a much smaller, but still non-negligible fraction of messages will fall into the "challenge" space. Furthermore, in this new game the attacker is only considered to have won if he both forged a signature *and* all his signature queries $m_1, \ldots, m_n$ fall into the query space and m^* falls into the challenge space. We can show that if an attacker succeeds in the original security game (that does not have these additional restrictions on winning) with non-negligible advantage, then if will succeed in Hyb_1 with non-negligible advantage. Our system uses the Boneh-Boyen [BB04a] admissible hash function defined above, where if an attacker has advantage ϵ in Hyb_0, he will have advantage $\epsilon/\theta(Q)$ in Hyb_1. After the first proof step we prove that a poly-time attacker's advantage must be negligibly close between each successive hybrid experiment. We finally show that any poly-time attacker in the final experiment that succeeds with non-negligible probability can be used to break the RSA assumption.

5   Selectively Secure BLS Signatures

We now give a concrete construction for the hash function modeled as a random oracle in the Boneh-Lynn-Shacham (BLS) signature scheme. BLS signatures fall into a broad interpretation (see e.g., [Boy08]) of the full domain hash paradigm of Bellare and Rogaway. Below we give the BLS signature scheme with a concrete hash function built from an indistinguishability obfuscator. We prove the signature scheme selectively secure based on the computational Diffie-Hellman problem in bilinear groups and a indistinguishability obfuscator.

On a technical level this selective proof of security follows a very similar structure to that of our selectively secure scheme from trapdoor functions from Section 3. The main difference is that here we deal with the mechanics of an algebraic bilinear group instead of a trapdoor function. We present the scheme for simplicity in terms of a symmetric bilinear group, however, moving to asymmetric groups is straightforward. As in Section 3, we assume that there is a polynomial $\ell(\lambda)$ which denotes the length of messages to be signed; we denote this message space by $\mathcal{M} = \{0, 1\}^{\ell(\lambda)}$. More generally, a collision-resistant hash function may be used to hash messages to this size.

- Setup(1^λ) : The setup algorithm first runs the group generator on input 1^λ to produce a description of groups $\mathbb{G}, \mathbb{G}_T$ of prime order p along with generator $g \in \mathbb{G}$. These groups are related by a bilinear map $e : \mathbb{G} \times \mathbb{G} \to \mathbb{G}_T$. Next, it chooses a random exponent $a \in \mathbb{Z}_p$. Then, the setup algorithm chooses a puncturable PRF key K for F where $F(K, \cdot) : \{0, 1\}^{\ell(\lambda)} \to \mathbb{Z}_p$. Finally, it creates an obfuscation of the program BLS Selective Hash of Figure 5. The size of the program is padded to be the maximum of itself and the program BLS Selective Hash* of Figure 6. We refer to the obfuscated program as the function $H : \{0,1\}^{\ell} \to \mathbb{G}$, which acts as the random oracle type hash function in the BLS scheme.

The verification key VK consists of the group descriptions $\mathbb{G}, \mathbb{G}_T$, the order p, the generator g and $A = g^a$ as well as the hash function $H(\cdot)$. The secret key is $a \in \mathbb{Z}_p$ as well as $H(\cdot)$.

- Sign(SK, $m \in \mathcal{M}$) : The signature algorithm outputs $\sigma = H(M)^a \in \mathbb{G}$.
- Verify(VK, m, σ) The verification algorithm tests if $e(\sigma, g) \stackrel{?}{=} e(A, H(m))$ and outputs accept if and only if this holds.

BLS Selective Hash

Constants: PRF key K, group generator $g \in \mathbb{G}$.
Input: Message m.

   1. Output $g^{F(K,m)}$.

Fig. 5. BLS Selective Hash

BLS Selective Hash*

Constants: Punctured PRF key $K(\{m^*\})$, $m^* \in \mathcal{M}$, $z^* \in \mathbb{G}$ and group generator $g \in \mathbb{G}$.
Input: Message m.

   1. If $m = m^*$ output z^* and exit.
   2. Output $g^{F(K,m)}$.

Fig. 6. BLS Selective Hash*

Remark 2. The confined PRFs from [BW13] use the GGM tree and get PRFs in range $\{0,1\}^n$ for some n, whereas our PRFs need to hash to $\mathbb{Z}_p$. One can achieve a punctured PRF for the proper range by simply setting $n > 2\lg(p)$ and taking interpreting the GGM output as an integer that is then mod by p. This is sufficient since sampling an integer in $[0, 2^n - 1]$ and then reducing it mod p is statistically close to choosing an integer in $[0, p-1]$.

Theorem 5. *If our obfuscation scheme is indistingishability secure, F is a secure punctured PRF, and the computational Diffie-Hellman problem holds in bilinear groups, then the above signature scheme is selectively secure.*

In the full version [HSW14], we describe a proof as a sequence of hybrid experiments where the first hybrid corresponds to the original signature security game. We prove that a poly-time attacker's advantage must be negligibly close between each successive one. Then, we show that any poly-time attacker in the final experiment that succeeds in forging with non-negligible probability can be used to break the computational Diffie-Hellman assumption in bilinear groups.

6   Adaptively Secure BLS Signatures

In the full version [HSW14], we give a hash function for BLS signatures that can be used to prove adaptive (or standard) security. Our construction is identical to that given in Section 5 with the exception of how the setup creates the hash function. Our proof structure will follow in a similar path to that of our adaptively secure RSA full domain hash signatures in Section 4. In particular, we will again apply an admissible hash function to partition the message space in our proof. At the same time, there are important distinctions and corresponding challenges that arise in this setting as discussed in [HSW14]. Our proof of security relies on indistinguishability obfuscation and the Diffie-Hellman Inversion Assumption.

7   Extensions to Boneh-Franklin IBE and Aggregate Signatures

Boneh-Franklin IBE. We can adapt our techniques for proving security of BLS signatures to the Boneh-Franklin [BF01] Identity-Based Encryption system. BLS signatures directly correspond to IBE private keys in the BF scheme. The proof for the BF adapts with a few minor changes:

- For proving BF selectively secure we can use the Decisional Bilinear Diffie-Hellman assumption.
- The second random oracle in the BF IBE can be replaced with an extractor.
- For proving adaptive security we use the following assumption. Namely that given $g, g^s, g^a, g^{a^2}, \ldots, g^{a^n}$ it is hard to distinguish $e(g,g)^{a^{n+1}s}$ from a random group element in $\mathbb{G}_T$. We note this assumption is weaker than the decision Bilinear Diffie-Hellman Exponent assumption [BGW05].

BGLS Aggregate Signatures. Boneh, Gentry, Lynn and Shacham [BGLS03] showed that the BLS signatures are aggregateable by reduction to the BDH assumption. Later Bellare, Namprempre and Neven [BNN07] showed how an aggregate signature scheme could built directly from and reduced to the security of BLS signatures. Using their results we immediately get an aggregate signature scheme.

Acknowledgments. We thank Mihir Bellare for discussions relating to the origins and terminology of full domain hash signatures and other helpful discussions. We thank Dan Boneh for many helpful discussions and also for pointing out the equivalence of our assumption used for adaptive BLS case to the Diffie-Hellman

Inversion Assumption. We thank Dennis Hofheinz for clarifications on admissible hash functions and pointing us to the simplified version we used. Finally, we are grateful to the anonymous reviewers of Eurocrypt 2014 for their helpful comments.

References

[BB04a]   Boneh, D., Boyen, X.: Secure identity based encryption without random oracles. In: Franklin, M. (ed.) CRYPTO 2004. LNCS, vol. 3152, pp. 443–459. Springer, Heidelberg (2004)

[BB04b]   Boneh, D., Boyen, X.: Short signatures without random oracles. In: Cachin, C., Camenisch, J.L. (eds.) EUROCRYPT 2004. LNCS, vol. 3027, pp. 56–73. Springer, Heidelberg (2004)

[BBP04]   Bellare, M., Boldyreva, A., Palacio, A.: An uninstantiable random-oracle-model scheme for a hybrid-encryption problem. In: Cachin, C., Camenisch, J.L. (eds.) EUROCRYPT 2004. LNCS, vol. 3027, pp. 171–188. Springer, Heidelberg (2004)

[BF01]   Boneh, D., Franklin, M.: Identity-based encryption from the Weil pairing. In: Kilian, J. (ed.) CRYPTO 2001. LNCS, vol. 2139, pp. 213–229. Springer, Heidelberg (2001)

[BGI+01] Barak, B., Goldreich, O., Impagliazzo, R., Rudich, S., Sahai, A., Vadhan, S.P., Yang, K.: On the (im)possibility of obfuscating programs. In: Kilian, J. (ed.) CRYPTO 2001. LNCS, vol. 2139, pp. 1–18. Springer, Heidelberg (2001)

[BGI+12] Barak, B., Goldreich, O., Impagliazzo, R., Rudich, S., Sahai, A., Vadhan, S.P., Yang, K.: On the (im)possibility of obfuscating programs. J. ACM 59(2), 6 (2012)

[BGI14]   Boyle, E., Goldwasser, S., Ivan, I.: Functional signatures and pseudorandom functions. In: Krawczyk, H. (ed.) PKC 2014. LNCS, vol. 8383, pp. 501–519. Springer, Heidelberg (2014)

[BGLS03] Boneh, D., Gentry, C., Lynn, B., Shacham, H.: Aggregate and verifiably encrypted signatures from bilinear maps. In: Biham, E. (ed.) EUROCRYPT 2003. LNCS, vol. 2656, pp. 416–432. Springer, Heidelberg (2003)

[BGW05]   Boneh, D., Gentry, C., Waters, B.: Collusion resistant broadcast encryption with short ciphertexts and private keys. In: Shoup, V. (ed.) CRYPTO 2005. LNCS, vol. 3621, pp. 258–275. Springer, Heidelberg (2005)

[BHK13]   Bellare, M., Hoang, V.T., Keelveedhi, S.: Instantiating Random Oracles via UCEs. In: Canetti, R., Garay, J.A. (eds.) CRYPTO 2013, Part II. LNCS, vol. 8043, pp. 398–415. Springer, Heidelberg (2013)

[BLS01]   Boneh, D., Lynn, B., Shacham, H.: Short signatures from the Weil pairing. In: Boyd, C. (ed.) ASIACRYPT 2001. LNCS, vol. 2248, pp. 514–532. Springer, Heidelberg (2001)

[BNN07]   Bellare, M., Namprempre, C., Neven, G.: Unrestricted aggregate signatures. In: Arge, L., Cachin, C., Jurdziński, T., Tarlecki, A. (eds.) ICALP 2007. LNCS, vol. 4596, pp. 411–422. Springer, Heidelberg (2007)

[Boy08]   Boyen, X.: A tapestry of identity-based encryption: practical frameworks compared. IJACT 1(1), 3–21 (2008)

[BR93]   Bellare, M., Rogaway, P.: Random oracles are practical: A paradigm for designing efficient protocols. In: ACM Conference on Computer and Communications Security, pp. 62–73 (1993)

[BR96]   Bellare, M., Rogaway, P.: The exact security of digital signatures - how to sign with RSA and Rabin. In: Maurer, U.M. (ed.) EUROCRYPT 1996. LNCS, vol. 1070, pp. 399–416. Springer, Heidelberg (1996)

[BW13]   Boneh, D., Waters, B.: Constrained pseudorandom functions and their applications. In: Sako, K., Sarkar, P. (eds.) ASIACRYPT 2013, Part II. LNCS, vol. 8270, pp. 280–300. Springer, Heidelberg (2013)

[Can97]   Canetti, R.: Towards realizing random oracles: Hash functions that hide all partial information. In: Kaliski Jr., B.S. (ed.) CRYPTO 1997. LNCS, vol. 1294, pp. 455–469. Springer, Heidelberg (1997)

[CGH98]   Canetti, R., Goldreich, O., Halevi, S.: The random oracle methodology, revisited (preliminary version). In: STOC, pp. 209–218 (1998)

[CHK07]   Canetti, R., Halevi, S., Katz, J.: A forward-secure public-key encryption scheme. J. Cryptology 20(3), 265–294 (2007)

[Coc01]   Cocks, C.: An identity based encryption scheme based on quadratic residues. In: Honary, B. (ed.) Cryptography and Coding 2001. LNCS, vol. 2260, pp. 360–363. Springer, Heidelberg (2001)

[CS98]   Cramer, R., Shoup, V.: A practical public key cryptosystem provably secure against adaptive chosen ciphertext attack. In: Krawczyk, H. (ed.) CRYPTO 1998. LNCS, vol. 1462, pp. 13–25. Springer, Heidelberg (1998)

[DHT12]   Dodis, Y., Haitner, I., Tentes, A.: On the instantiability of hash-and-sign RSA signatures. In: Cramer, R. (ed.) TCC 2012. LNCS, vol. 7194, pp. 112–132. Springer, Heidelberg (2012)

[DOP05]   Dodis, Y., Oliveira, R., Pietrzak, K.: On the generic insecurity of the full domain hash. In: Shoup, V. (ed.) CRYPTO 2005. LNCS, vol. 3621, pp. 449–466. Springer, Heidelberg (2005)

[FHPS13]   Freire, E.S.V., Hofheinz, D., Paterson, K.G., Striecks, C.: Programmable hash functions in the multilinear setting. In: Canetti, R., Garay, J.A. (eds.) CRYPTO 2013, Part I. LNCS, vol. 8042, pp. 513–530. Springer, Heidelberg (2013)

[GGH+13]   Garg, S., Gentry, C., Halevi, S., Raykova, M., Sahai, A., Waters, B.: Candidate indistinguishability obfuscation and functional encryption for all circuits. In: FOCS (2013)

[GGM84]   Goldreich, O., Goldwasser, S., Micali, S.: How to construct random functions (extended abstract). In: FOCS, pp. 464–479 (1984)

[GK03]   Goldwasser, S., Kalai, Y.T.: On the (in)security of the Fiat-Shamir paradigm. In: FOCS, pp. 102–113 (2003)

[HSW13]   Hohenberger, S., Sahai, A., Waters, B.: Full domain hash from (leveled) multilinear maps and identity-based aggregate signatures. In: Canetti, R., Garay, J.A. (eds.) CRYPTO 2013, Part I. LNCS, vol. 8042, pp. 494–512. Springer, Heidelberg (2013)

[HSW14]   Hohenberger, S., Sahai, A., Waters, B.: Replacing a random oracle: Full domain hash from indistinguishability obfuscation. In: Eurocrypt (2014), Full version available at http://eprint.iacr.org/2013/509

[KPTZ13]   Kiayias, A., Papadopoulos, S., Triandopoulos, N., Zacharias, T.: Delegatable pseudorandom functions and applications. In: ACM Conference on Computer and Communications Security, pp. 669–684 (2013)

[KS98]   Kaliski, B., Staddon, J.: PKCS #1: RSA Cryptography Specifications Version 2.0 (1998)

[RSA78]   Rivest, R.L., Shamir, A., Adleman, L.M.: A method for obtaining digital signatures and public-key cryptosystems. Commun. ACM 21(2), 120–126 (1978)

[Sha83]   Shamir, A.: On the generation of cryptographically strong pseudorandom sequences. ACM Trans. Comput. Syst. 1(1), 38–44 (1983)

[SW13]   Sahai, A., Waters, B.: How to use indistinguishability obfuscation: Deniable encryption, and more. Cryptology ePrint Archive, Report 2013/454 (2013) (to appear in STOC, 2014), http://eprint.iacr.org/

Protecting Obfuscation
against Algebraic Attacks

Boaz Barak[1], Sanjam Garg[2,*], Yael Tauman Kalai[1],
Omer Paneth[3,**], and Amit Sahai[4,***]

[1] Microsoft Research
[2] IBM Research
[3] Boston University
[4] UCLA

Abstract. Recently, Garg, Gentry, Halevi, Raykova, Sahai, and Waters (FOCS 2013) constructed a general-purpose obfuscating compiler for $\mathbf{NC}^1$ circuits. We describe a simplified variant of this compiler, and prove that it is a virtual black box obfuscator in a generic multilinear map model. This improves on Brakerski and Rothblum (eprint 2013) who gave such a result under a strengthening of the Exponential Time Hypothesis. We remove this assumption, and thus resolve an open question of Garg et al. As shown by Garg et al., a compiler for $\mathbf{NC}^1$ circuits can be bootstrapped to a compiler for all polynomial-sized circuits under the learning with errors (LWE) hardness assumption.

Our result shows that there is a candidate obfuscator that cannot be broken by algebraic attacks, hence reducing the task of creating secure obfuscators in the plain model to obtaining sufficiently strong security guarantees on candidate instantiations of multilinear maps.

1 Introduction

The goal of general-purpose program obfuscation is to make an arbitrary computer program "unintelligible" while preserving its functionality. At least as

* Research conducted while at the IBM Research, T.J.Watson funded by NSF Grant No.1017660.
** Work done while the author was an intern at Microsoft Research New England. Supported by the Simons award for graduate students in theoretical computer science and an NSF Algorithmic foundations grant 1218461.
*** Work done in part while visiting Microsoft Research, New England. Research supported in part from a DARPA/ONR PROCEED award, NSF grants 1228984, 1136174, 1118096, and 1065276, a Xerox Faculty Research Award, a Google Faculty Research Award, an equipment grant from Intel, and an Okawa Foundation Research Grant. This material is based upon work supported by the Defense Advanced Research Projects Agency through the U.S. Office of Naval Research under Contract N00014-11-1-0389. The views expressed are those of the author and do not reflect the official policy or position of the Department of Defense, the National Science Foundation, or the U.S. Government.

P.Q. Nguyen and E. Oswald (Eds.): EUROCRYPT 2014, LNCS 8441, pp. 221–238, 2014.
© International Association for Cryptologic Research 2014

far back as the work of Diffie and Hellman in 1976 [7][1], researchers have contemplated applications of general-purpose obfuscation. The first mathematical definitions of obfuscation were given by Hada [11] and Barak, Goldreich, Impagliazzo, Rudich, Sahai, Vadhan, and Yang [2].[2] Barak et al. also enumerated several additional applications of general-purpose obfuscation, ranging from software intellectual property protection and removing random oracles, to eliminating software watermarks. However, until 2013, even heuristic constructions for general-purpose obfuscation were not known.

This changed with the work of Garg, Gentry, Halevi, Raykova, Sahai, and Waters in 2013 [9], which gave the first candidate construction for a general-purpose obfuscator. At the heart of their construction is an obfuscator for log-depth ($\mathbf{NC^1}$) circuits, building upon a simplified subset of the Approximate Multilinear Maps framework of Garg, Gentry, and Halevi [8] that they call Multilinear Jigsaw Puzzles. They proved that their construction achieves a notion called indistinguishability obfuscation (see below for further explanation), under a complex new intractability assumption. They then used fully homomorphic encryption to bootstrap this construction to work for all circuits, proving their transformation secure under the Learning with Error (LWE) assumption, a well-studied intractability assumption.

Our result— protecting against algebraic attacks. Given the importance of general-purpose obfuscation, it is imperative that we gain as much confidence as possible in candidates for general-purpose obfuscation. Potential attacks on the [9] obfuscator can be classified into two types— attacks on the underlying Multilinear Jigsaw Puzzle construction, and attacks on the obfuscation construction that treat the Multilinear Jigsaw Puzzle as an ideal black box. [8] gave some cryptanalytic evidence for the security of their Approximate Multilinear Maps candidate (this evidence immediately extends to Mathematical Jigsaw Puzzles, since it is a weaker primitive), and there is also an alternative candidate [6] for such maps. Our focus in this paper is to find out whether there exists a *purely algebraic* attack against the candidate obfuscation schemes, or whether any attack against the scheme must rely on some weakness of the underlying Multilinear Jigsaw Puzzle (i.e., some deviation of the implementation from the ideal model). Indeed, [9] pose the problem of proving that there exist no generic multilinear attacks against their core $\mathbf{NC^1}$ scheme as a major open problem in their work.[3]

---

[1] Diffie and Hellman suggested the use of general-purpose obfuscation to convert private-key cryptosystems to public-key cryptosystems.

[2] The work of [2] is best known for their constructions of "unobfuscatable" classes of functions $\{f_s\}$ that roughly have the property that given *any* circuit evaluating f_s, one can extract the secret s, yet given only *black-box* access to f_s, the secret s is hidden. We will discuss the implications of this for our setting below.

[3] [9] did rule out a certain subset of algebraic attacks which fall under a model they called the "generic colored matrix model". However, this model assumes that an adversary can only attack the schemes by performing a limited subset of matrix operations, and does not prove any security against an adversary that can perform algebraic operations on the individual entries of the matrices.

This problem was first addressed in the recent work of Brakerski and Rothblum [4], who constructed a variant of the [9] candidate obfuscator, and proved that it is an indistinguishability obfuscation against all generic multilinear attacks. They also proved that their obfuscator achieves the strongest definition of security for general-purpose obfuscation — Virtual Black Box (VBB) security — against all generic multilinear attacks, albeit under an unproven assumption they introduce as the Bounded Speedup Hypothesis, which strengthens the Exponential Time Hypothesis from computational complexity.[4]

In this work, we resolve the open problem of [9] completely, by removing the need for this additional assumption. More specifically, we describe a different (and arguably simpler) variant of the construction of [9], for which we can prove that it achieves Virtual Black Box security against all generic multilinear attacks, *with no further assumptions*. Our result gives evidence for the soundness of [9]'s approach for building obfuscators based on Multilinear Jigsaw Puzzles.

Notions of Security and attacks. In this work, we focus on arguing security against a large class of natural algebraic attacks, captured in the *generic multilinear* model. Intuitively speaking, the generic multilinear model imagines an exponential-size collection of "groups" $\{G_S\}$, where the subscript S denotes a subset $S \subseteq \{1, 2, \ldots, k\}$. Each of these groups is a separate copy of $\mathbb{Z}_p$, under addition, for some fixed large random prime p. The adversary is initially given some collection of elements from various groups. However, the only way that the adversary can process elements of these groups is through access to an oracle $\mathcal{M}$ that performs the following three operations[5]:

- **Addition:** $G_S \times G_S \to G_S$, defined in the natural way over $\mathbb{Z}_p$, for all $S \subset \{1, 2, \ldots, k\}$.
- **Negation:** $G_S \to G_S$, defined in the natural way over $\mathbb{Z}_p$, for all $S \subset \{1, 2, \ldots, k\}$.
- **Multiplication:** $G_S \times G_T \to G_{S \cup T}$, defined in the natural way over $\mathbb{Z}_p$, for all $S, T \subset \{1, 2, \ldots, k\}$, where $S \cap T = \emptyset$. Note that the constraint that $S \cap T = \emptyset$ intuitively captures why we call this a *multilinear* model.

These operations capture precisely the algebraic operations supported by the Multilinear Jigsaw Puzzles of [9].

With the algebraic attack model defined, the next step is to consider what security property we would like to achieve with respect to this attack model. We first recall two security notions for obfuscation – indistinguishability obfuscation

---

[4] Roughly speaking, the Bounded Speedup Hyptothesis says that there is some $\epsilon > 0$ such that for every subset $\mathcal{X}$ of $\{0, 1\}^n$, any circuit C that solves SAT on all inputs in $\mathcal{X}$ must have size at least $|\mathcal{X}|^\epsilon$. The Exponential Time Hypothesis is recovered by considering $\mathcal{X} = \{0, 1\}^n$. The exponent of the polynomial slowdown of the [4] simulator is a function of ϵ.

[5] In the technical exposition, we discuss how it is enforced that the adversary can *only* access the elements of the group via the oracles. For this intuitive exposition, we ask the reader to simply imagine that an algebraic adversary is defined to be limited in this way.

(iO) security and Virtual Black-Box (VBB) security – and state them both in comparable language, in the generic multilinear model. Below, we write "generic adversary" or "generic distinguisher" to refer to an algorithm that has access to the oracle $\mathcal{M}$ described above.

Indistinguishability obfuscation[6] requires that for every polynomial-time generic adversary, there exists an *computationally unbounded* simulator, such that for every circuit C, no polynomial-time generic distinguisher can distinguish the output of the adversary given the obfuscation of C as input, from the output of the simulator given oracle access to C, where the simulator can make an *unbounded* number of queries to C. Virtual Black-Box obfuscation[7] requires that for every polynomial-time generic adversary, there exists a *polynomial-time* simulator, such that for every circuit C, no polynomial-time generic distinguisher can distinguish the output of the adversary given the obfuscation of C as input, from the output of the simulator given oracle access to C, where the simulator can make a *polynomial* number of queries to C.

In our work, we focus on proving the Virtual Black-Box definition of security against generic attacks. We do so for several reasons:

- Our first, and most basic, reason is that Virtual Black-Box security is the strongest security notion of obfuscation we are aware of, and so proving VBB security against generic multilinear attacks is, mathematically speaking, the strongest result we could hope to prove. As we can see from the definitions above, the definition of security provided by the VBB definition is significantly stronger than the indistinguishability obfuscation definition. As such, it represents the natural end-goal for research on proving resilience to such algebraic attacks.

  This may seem surprising in light of the negative results of [2], who showed that there exist (contrived) families of "unobfuscatable" functions for which the VBB definition is impossible to achieve *in the plain model*. However, we stress that this result does not apply to security against generic multilinear attacks. Thus it does not present a barrier to the goal of proving VBB security against generic multilinear attacks.

- Given the existence of "unobfuscatable" function families, how can we interpret a result showing VBB security against generic attacks, in terms of the real-world applicability of obfuscation? One plausible interpretation is that it offers heuristic evidence that our obfuscation mechanism will offer strong security for "natural" functions, that do not have the self-referential properties of the [2] counter-examples. This is similar to the heuristic evidence

---

[6] The formulation of indistinguishability obfuscation sketched here was used, for example, in [9].

[7] We note that we are referring to a stronger definition of VBB obfuscation than the one given in [2], which limits the adversary to only outputting one bit. In our definition, the adversary can output arbitrary length strings. This stronger formulation of VBB security implies all other known meaningful security definitions for obfuscation, including natural definitions that are not known to be implied by the one-bit-output formulation of VBB security.

given by a proof in the Random Oracle Model. We stress, however, that our result cannot offer any specific theoretical guidance on *which* function families can be VBB-obfuscated in the plain model, and which cannot.

– Finally, our VBB result against generic attacks suggests that there is a significant gap between what security is *actually* achieved by our candidate in the plain model, and the best security *definitions* for obfuscation that we have in the plain model. This suggests a research program for studying relaxations of VBB obfuscation that could plausibly be achievable in the plain model. Indistinguishability Obfuscation is one such example, but other notions have been suggested in the literature, and it's quite possible we haven't yet found the "right" notion. For every such definition of obfuscation X, one can of course make the assumption that our candidate is "X secure" in the plain model, but in fact our VBB proof in the generic multilinear model shows that "X security" of our candidate will follow from a concrete intractability assumption on the Multilinear Jigsaw Puzzle implementation *that is unrelated to our specific obfuscation candidate* (see below for more details).

Remark 1.1 (Capturing a Generic Model by Meta-Assumptions). While a generic model allows us to precisely define and argue about large classes of algebraic attacks, it is unsatisfying because any such oracle model, by definition, cannot be achieved in the plain model. Thus, we would like to capture as much as we can of a generic model by means of what we would call a "Meta-Assumption." Intuitively, a Meta-Assumption specifies conditions under which the only attacks that are possible in the plain model with a specific instantiation of the oracle, are those that are possible in the oracle model itself – where the conditions that the Meta-Assumption imposes allow the assumption to be plausible. For example, one can consider the Decisional Diffie Hellman (DDH) assumption as a meta assumption on the instantiation of the group $\mathbb{Z}_q$ as a multiplicative subgroup of $\mathbb{Z}^*_{p=kq+1}$, stipulating that certain attacks that would be infeasible in the ideal setting, are also infeasible when working with the actual encoding of the group elements.

1.1   Our Techniques

The starting point for our construction is a simplified form of the construction of [9]. That work used the fact that one can express an $\mathbf{NC}^1$ computation as a *Branching Program*, which is a sequence of $2n$ permutations (or more generally, functions) $\{B_{i,\sigma}\}_{i\in[n],\sigma\in\{0,1\}}$. The program is evaluated on an input $x \in \{0,1\}^\ell$ by applying for $i = 1, \ldots, n$ the permutation $B_{i,x_{\mathsf{inp}(i)}}$ where inp is some map from $[n]$ to $[\ell]$ that says which input bit the branching program looks at the ith step. The output of the program is obtained based on the composition of all these permutations; that is, we have some permutation P_{accept} (without loss of generality, the identity) and say that the output is 1 if the composition is equal to P_{accept} and the output is 0 otherwise.[8] We can identify these permutations with matrices,

---

[8] Barrington's Theorem [3] shows that these permutations can be taken to have a finite domain (in fact, 5) but for our construction, a domain of $\mathsf{poly}(\ell)$ size is fine.

and so evaluating the program amounts to matrix multiplication. Matrix multiplication is an algebraic (and in fact multilinear) operation, that can be done in a group supporting multilinear maps. Thus a naive first attempt at obfuscation of an $\mathbf{NC}^1$ computation would be to encode all the elements of the matrices $\{B_{i,\sigma}\}_{i\in[n],\sigma\in\{0,1\}}$ in the multilinear maps setting (using disjoint subsets to encode elements of matrices that would be multiplied together, e.g., by encoding the elements of $B_{i,\sigma}$ in the group $G_{\{i\}}$). This would allow to run the computation on every $x \in \{0,1\}^\ell$. However, as an obfuscation it would be completely insecure, since it will also allow an adversary to perform tricks such as "mixing inputs" by starting the computation on a particular input x and then at some step switching to a different input x'. Even if it fixes some particular input $x \in \{0,1\}^\ell$, the adversary might learn not just the product of the n matrices $B_{1,x_{\mathrm{inp}(1)}}, \ldots, B_{n,x_{\mathrm{inp}(n)}}$ but also information about partial products. To protect against this latter attack, [9] used a trick of Kilian [12] where instead of the matrices $\{B_{i,\sigma}\}_{i\in[n],\sigma\in\{0,1\}}$ they published the matrices $\{B'_{i,\sigma} = R_{i-1}^{-1} B_{i,\sigma} R_i\}_{i\in[n],\sigma\in\{0,1\}}$ where R_0, R_n are the identity and $R_1, \ldots, R_{n-1}$ are random permutation matrices.[9] We follow the same approach. The crucial obstacle is that in our setting, because we need to supply a single program that works on *all* inputs $x \in \{0,1\}^\ell$, we need to reveal both the matrix $B_{i,0}$ and the matrix $B_{i,1}$, and will need to multiply them both with the same random matrix. Unfortunately, Kilian's trick does not guarantee security in such a setting. It also does not protect against the "mixed input" attack described above.

We deviate from the works [9, 4] in the way we handle the above issues. Specifically, the most important difference is that we employ specially designed set systems in our use of the generic multilinear model. Roughly speaking, in the original work of [9], the encoding of the elements of matrix $B'_{i,\sigma}$ was in the group $G_{\{i\}}$. In contrast, in our obfuscation, while the actual elements from $\mathbb{Z}_p$ that we use are very similar to those used in [9], these elements will live in groups G_S where the sets S will come from specially designed set systems. To illustrate this idea, consider the toy example where $\ell = 1$ and $n = 2$. That is, we have a single input bit $x \in \{0,1\}$ and 4 matrices $B'_{1,0}, B'_{1,1}, B'_{2,0}, B'_{2,1}$. We want to supply encodings that will allow computing the products $B'_{1,0}B'_{2,0}$ and $B'_{1,1}B'_{2,1}$, but not any of the "mixed products" such as $B'_{1,0}B'_{2,1}$ which corresponds to pretending the input bit is equal to 0 in the first step of the branching program, and equal to 1 in the second step. The idea is that our groups will be of the form $\{G_S\}$ where S is a subset of the universe $\{1,2,3\}$. We will encode the elements of $B_{1,0}$ in $G_{\{1,2\}}$, the elements of $B_{1,1}$ in $G_{\{1\}}$, the elements of $B_{2,0}$ in $G_{\{3\}}$, and the elements of $B_{2,1}$ in $G_{\{2,3\}}$. One can see that one can use our oracle to obtain an encoding of the two matrices corresponding to the "proper" products in $G_{\{1,2,3\}}$, but it is not possible to compute the "mixed product" since it would involved multiplying elements in G_S and G_T for non-disjoint S and T. This idea

---

[9] Instead of using R_0, R_{n+1} as the identity, [9] and us added some additional encoding of elements they called "bookends". We ignore this detail in this section's high level description. We also defer discussion of an additional trick of multiplying each element in $B'_{i,\sigma}$ by a scalar $\alpha_{i,\sigma}$.

can be easily extended to the case of larger ℓ and n, and can be used to rule out the mixed product attack.

However, the idea above still does not rule out "partial evaluation attacks", where the adversary might try to learn, for example, whether the first k steps of the branching program evaluate to the same permutation regardless of the value of the first bit of x. To do that we enhance our set system by creating interlocking sets that combine several copies of the straddling set systems above. Roughly speaking, these interlocking sets ensure that the adversary cannot create "interesting" combinations of the encoded elements, without in effect committing to a particular input $x \in \{0,1\}^{\ell}$. This prevents the adversary from creating polynomials that combine terms corresponding to a super-polynomial set of different inputs. In contrast, in the recent work of [4], this was accomplished by means of a reduction to the Bounded Speedup Hypothesis. In contrast, our generic proof does not use any assumptions except the properties of our set systems.

The second deviation in our construction from that of [9] is in our usage of the random scalar values $\{\alpha_{i,\sigma}\}_{i \in [n], \sigma \in \{0,1\}}$ that are used to multiply every element in the encoding of $B'_{i,\sigma}$. In [9] these random scalars $\alpha_{i,b}$ were used for two purposes: First, they were chosen with specific multiplicative constraints in order to prevent "input mixing" attacks as described above (a similar multiplicative bundling method was used by [4] as well). As noted above, we no longer need this use of the $\alpha_{i,b}$ values as this is handled by our set systems. The second purpose these values served was to provide a "per-input" randomization in polynomial terms created by the adversary. We continue the use of this role of the $\alpha_{i,b}$ values, leveraging this "per-input" randomization using a method of explicitly invoking Kilian's randomization technique. This is similar to (but arguably simpler than) the beautiful use of Kilian's randomization technique in the recent work of [4].

Additional Related Work. Our work deals with analyzing candidate general-purpose obfuscators in an idealized mathematical model (the generic multilinear model). There has also been recent work suggesting general-purpose obfuscators in idealized mathematical models which currently do not have candidate instantiations in the standard model: the work of [5] describes a general-purpose obfuscator for NC^1 in a generic group setting with a group $G = G_1 \times G_2 \times G_3 \times G_4$, where G_1 is a pseudo-free Abelian group, G_2 and G_3 are pseudo-free non-Abelian groups, and G_4 is a group supporting Barrington's theorem, such as S_5. In this generic setting, obfuscator described by [5] achieves Virtual Black-Box security. However, no candidate methods for heuristically implementing such a group G are known, and therefore, the work of [5] does not describe a candidate general-purpose obfuscator at this time, though this may change with future work[10].

We note that question of whether there exists any oracle with respect to which virtual black-box obfuscation for general circuits is possible is a trivial question: one can consider a universal oracle that (1) provides secure encryptions e_C for any circuit C to be obfuscated, and (2) given an encrypted circuit

---

[10] Indeed, one way to obtain a heuristic generic group G is by building it using a general-purpose obfuscator, but this would not be useful for the work of [5], since their goal is a general-purpose obfuscator.

e_C and an input x outputs $C(x)$. The only way we can see this "solution" as being interesting is if one considers implementing this oracle with trusted hardware. The work of Goyal *et al.* [10] shows that there exists an oracle that can be implemented with trusted hardware of size that is only a fixed polynomial in the security parameter, with respect to which virtual black-box obfuscation is possible. However, once again, the focus of our paper is to consider oracles that abstract the natural algebraic functionality underlying actual plain-model candidates for general-purpose obfuscation.

2   Preliminaries

In this section we define the notion of "virtual black-box" obfuscation in an idealized model, we recall the definition of branching programs and describe a *"dual-input"* variant of branching programs used in our construction.

2.1   "Virtual Black-Box" Obfuscation in an Idealized Model

Let $\mathcal{M}$ be some oracle. We define obfuscation in the $\mathcal{M}$-idealized model. In this model, both the obfuscator and the evaluator have access to the oracle $\mathcal{M}$. However, the function family that is being obfuscated does not have access to $\mathcal{M}$

Definition 2.1 ("Virtual Black-Box" Obfuscation in an $\mathcal{M}$-idealized model). *For a (possibly randomized) oracle $\mathcal{M}$, and a circuit class $\{\mathcal{C}_\ell\}_{\ell \in \mathbb{N}}$, we say that a uniform PPT oracle machine $\mathcal{O}$ is a "Virtual Black-Box" Obfuscator for $\{\mathcal{C}_\ell\}_{\ell \in \mathbb{N}}$ in the $\mathcal{M}$-idealized model, if the following conditions are satisfied:*

- *Functionality: For every $\ell \in \mathbb{N}$, every $C \in \mathcal{C}_\ell$, every input x to C, and for every possible coins for $\mathcal{M}$:*

$$\Pr[(\mathcal{O}^\mathcal{M}(C))(x) \neq C(x)] \leq negl(|C|) \ ,$$

  where the probability is over the coins of $\mathcal{O}$.
- *Polynomial Slowdown: there exist a polynomial p such that for every $\ell \in \mathbb{N}$ and every $C \in \mathcal{C}_\ell$, we have that $|\mathcal{O}^\mathcal{M}(C)| \leq p(|C|)$.*
- *Virtual Black-Box: for every PPT adversary $\mathcal{A}$ there exist a PPT simulator $\mathcal{S}$, and a negligible function μ such that for all PPT distinguishers D, for every $\ell \in \mathbb{N}$ and every $C \in \mathcal{C}_\ell$:*

$$\left| \Pr[D(\mathcal{A}^\mathcal{M}(\mathcal{O}^\mathcal{M}(C))) = 1] - \Pr[D(\mathcal{S}^C(1^{|C|})) = 1] \right| \leq \mu(|C|) \ ,$$

  where the probabilities are over the coins of $D, \mathcal{A}, \mathcal{S}, \mathcal{O}$ and $\mathcal{M}$

Remark 2.1. We note that the definition above is stronger than the definition of VBB obfuscation given in [2], in that it allows adversaries to output an unbounded number of bits.

Definition 2.2 ("Virtual Black-Box" Obfuscation for NC^1 in an $\mathcal{M}$-idealized model). *We say that $\mathcal{O}$ is a "Virtual Black-Box" Obfuscator for NC^1 in the $\mathcal{M}$-idealized model, if for every circuit class $\mathcal{C} = \{\mathcal{C}_\ell\}_{\ell \in \mathbb{N}}$ such that every circuit in $\mathcal{C}_\ell$ is of size $\mathsf{poly}(\ell)$ and of depth $O(\log(\ell))$, $\mathcal{O}$ is a "Virtual Black-Box" Obfuscator for $\mathcal{C}$ in the $\mathcal{M}$-idealized model.*

2.2 Branching Programs

The focus of this paper is on obfuscating *branching programs*, which are known to be powerful enough to simulate NC^1 circuits.

A branching program consists of a sequence of steps, where each step is defined by a pair of permutations. In each step the the program examines one input bit, and depending on its value the program chooses one of the permutations. The program outputs 1 if and only if the multiplications of the permutations chosen in all steps is the identity permutation.

Definition 2.3 (Oblivious Matrix Branching Program). *A branching program of width w and length n for ℓ-bit inputs is given by a permutation matrix $P_{\mathsf{reject}} \in \{0,1\}^{w \times w}$ such that $P_{\mathsf{reject}} \neq I_{w \times w}$, and by a sequence:*

$$BP = \left(\mathsf{inp}(i), B_{i,0}, B_{i,1}\right)_{i=1}^{n},$$

where each $B_{i,b}$ is a permutation matrix in $\{0,1\}^{w \times w}$, and $\mathsf{inp}(i) \in [\ell]$ is the input bit position examined in step i. The output of the branching program on input $x \in \{0,1\}^\ell$ is as follows:

$$BP(x) \overset{def}{=} \begin{cases} 1 & \text{if } \prod_{i=1}^{n} B_{i,x_{\mathsf{inp}(i)}} = I_{w \times w} \\ 0 & \text{if } \prod_{i=1}^{n} B_{i,x_{\mathsf{inp}(i)}} = P_{\mathsf{reject}} \\ \bot & \text{otherwise} \end{cases}$$

The branching program is said to be oblivious *if $\mathsf{inp} : [n] \to [\ell]$ is a fixed function, independent of the function being evaluated.*

Theorem 2.1 ([3]). *For any depth-d fan-in-2 boolean circuit C, there exists an oblivious branching program of width 5 and length at most 4^d that computes the same function as the circuit C.*

Remark 2.2. In our obfuscation construction we do not require that the branching program is of constant width. In particular we can use any reductions that result in a polynomial size branching program.

In our construction we will obfuscate a variant of branching programs that we call *dual-input* branching programs. Instead of reading one input bit in every step, a dual-input branching program inspects a pair of input bits and chooses a permutation based on the values of both bits.

Definition 2.4 (Dual-Input Branching Program) . *A* Oblivious dual-input *branching program of width w and length n for ℓ-bit inputs is given by a permutation matrix $P_{\text{reject}} \in \{0,1\}^{w \times w}$ such that $P_{\text{reject}} \neq I_{w \times w}$, and by a sequence*

$$\mathsf{BP} = \left(\mathsf{inp}_1(i), \mathsf{inp}_2(i), \{B_{i,b_1,b_2}\}_{b_1,b_2 \in \{0,1\}}\right)_{i=1}^{n},$$

where each B_{i,b_1,b_2} is a permutation matrix in $\{0,1\}^{w \times w}$, and $\mathsf{inp}_1(i), \mathsf{inp}_2(i) \in [\ell]$ are the positions of the input bits inspected in step i. The output of the branching program on input $x \in \{0,1\}^{\ell}$ is as follows:

$$\mathsf{BP}(x) \stackrel{\text{def}}{=} \begin{cases} 1 & \text{if } \prod_{i=1}^{n} B_{i,x_{\mathsf{inp}_1(i)},x_{\mathsf{inp}_2(i)}} = I_{w \times w} \\ 0 & \text{if } \prod_{i=1}^{n} B_{i,x_{\mathsf{inp}_1(i)},x_{\mathsf{inp}_2(i)}} = P_{\text{reject}} \\ \bot & \text{otherwise} \end{cases}$$

As before, the dual-input branching program is said to be oblivious if both $\mathsf{inp}_1 : [n] \to [\ell]$ and $\mathsf{inp}_2 : [n] \to [\ell]$ are fixed functions, independent of the function being evaluated.

Note that any branching program can be simulated by a dual-input branching program with the same width and length, since the dual-input branching program can always "ignore" one input bit in each pair. Moreover, note that any dual-input branching program can be simulated by a branching program with the same width and with length that is twice the length of the dual-input branching program.

3   Straddling Set System

In this section, we define the notion of a *straddling set system*, and prove combinatorial properties regarding this set system. This set system will be an ingredient in our construction, and the combinatorial properties that we establish will be used in our generic proof of security.

Definition 3.1. *A straddling set system with n entries is a collection of sets $\mathbb{S}_n = \{S_{i,b}, : i \in [n], b \in \{0,1\}\}$ over a universe U, such that*

$$\cup_{i \in [n]} S_{i,0} = \cup_{i \in [n]} S_{i,1} = U$$

and for every distinct non-empty sets $C, D \subseteq \mathbb{S}_n$ we have that if:

1. *(Disjoint Sets:) C contains only disjoint sets. D contains only disjoint sets.*
2. *(Collision:) $\cup_{S \in C} S = \cup_{S \in D} S$*

Then, it must be that $\exists\, b \in \{0,1\}$:

$$C = \{S_{j,b}\}_{j \in [n]} \quad, \quad D = \{S_{j,(1-b)}\}_{j \in [n]} .$$

Therefore, in a straddling set system, the only exact covers of the universe U are $\{S_{j,0}\}_{j \in [n]}$ and $\{S_{j,1}\}_{j \in [n]}$.

Construction 3.1. *Let* $\mathbb{S}_n = \{S_{i,b}, : i \in [n], b \in \{0,1\}\}$, *over the universe* $U = \{1, 2, \ldots, 2n - 1\}$, *where:*
$S_{1,0} = \{1\}$, $S_{2,0} = \{2,3\}$, $S_{3,0} = \{4,5\}$, ..., $S_{i,0} = \{2i - 2, 2i - 1\}$, ...,
$S_{n,0} = \{2n - 2, 2n - 1\}$; *and,*
$S_{1,1} = \{1,2\}$, $S_{2,1} = \{3,4\}$, ..., $S_{i,1} = \{2i - 1, 2i\}$, ..., $S_{n-1,1} = \{2n - 3, 2n - 2\}$, $S_{n,1} = \{2n - 1\}$.

The proof that Construction 3.1 satisfies the definition of a straddling set system is straightforward and is given in the full version of this work [1].

4 The Ideal Graded Encoding Model

In this section describe the ideal graded encoding model where all parties have access to an oracle $\mathcal{M}$, implementing an ideal graded encoding. The oracle $\mathcal{M}$ implements an idealized and simplified version of the graded encoding schemes from [8]. Roughly, $\mathcal{M}$ will maintain a list of *elements* and will allow a user to perform valid arithmetic operations over these elements. We start by defining the an algebra over elements.

Definition 4.1. *Given a ring R and a universe set U, an element is a pair (α, S) where $\alpha \in R$ is the* value *of the element and $S \subseteq U$ is the* index *of the element. Given an element e we denote by $\alpha(e)$ the value of the element, and we denote by $S(e)$ the index of the element. We also define the following binary operations over elements:*

- *For two elements e_1, e_2 such that $S(e_1) = S(e_2)$, we define $e_1 + e_2$ to be the element $(\alpha(e_1) + \alpha(e_2), S(e_1))$, and $e_1 - e_2$ to be the element $(\alpha(e_1) - \alpha(e_2), S(e_1))$.*
- *For two elements e_1, e_2 such that $S(e_1) \cap S(e_2) = \emptyset$, we define $e_1 \cdot e_2$ to be the element $(\alpha(e_1) \cdot \alpha(e_2), S(e_1) \cup S(e_2))$.*

Next we describe the oracle $\mathcal{M}$. $\mathcal{M}$ is a stateful oracle mapping elements to "generic" representations called *handles*. Given handles to elements, $\mathcal{M}$ allows the user to perform operations on the elements. $\mathcal{M}$ will implement the following interfaces:

Initialization. $\mathcal{M}$ will be initialized with a ring R, a universe set U, and a list L of initial elements. For every element $e \in L$, $\mathcal{M}$ generates a handle. We do not specify how the handles are generated, but only require that the value of the handles are independent of the elements being encoded, and that the handles are distinct (even if L contains the same element twice). $\mathcal{M}$ maintains a handle table where it saves the mapping from elements to handles. $\mathcal{M}$ outputs the handles generated for all the element in L. After $\mathcal{M}$ has been initialize, all subsequent calls to the initialization interfaces fail.

Algebraic operations. Given two input handles h_1, h_2 and an operation $\circ \in \{+, -, \cdot\}$, $\mathcal{M}$ first locates the relevant elements e_1, e_2 in the handle table. If any of the input handles does not appear in the handle table (that is, if the handle was not previously generated by $\mathcal{M}$) the call to $\mathcal{M}$ fails. If the expression $e_1 \circ e_2$ is undefined (i.e., $S(e_1) \neq S(e_2)$ for $\circ \in \{+, -\}$, or $S(e_1) \cap S(e_2) \neq \emptyset$ for $\circ \in \{\cdot\}$) the call fails. Otherwise, $\mathcal{M}$ generates a new handle for $e_1 \circ e_2$, saves this element and the new handle in the handle table, and returns the new handle.

Zero testing. Given an input handle h, $\mathcal{M}$ first locates the relevant element e in the handle table. If h does not appear in the handle table (that is, if h was not previously generated by $\mathcal{M}$) the call to $\mathcal{M}$ fails. If $S(e) \neq U$ the call fails. Otherwise, $\mathcal{M}$ returns 1 if $\alpha(e) = 0$, and returns 0 if $\alpha(e) \neq 0$.

5   Obfuscation in the Ideal Graded Encoding Model

In this section we describe our "virtual black-box" obfuscator $\mathcal{O}$ for $\mathbf{NC}^1$ in the ideal graded encoding model.

Input. The obfuscator $\mathcal{O}$ takes as input a circuit and transforms it into an oblivious dual-input branching program BP of width w and length n for ℓ-bit inputs:

$$BP = \left(\mathsf{inp}_1(i), \mathsf{inp}_2(i), \{B_{i,b_1,b_2}\}_{b_1,b_2 \in \{0,1\}}\right)_{i=1}^n.$$

Recall that each B_{i,b_1,b_2} is a permutation matrix in $\{0,1\}^{w \times w}$, and $\mathsf{inp}_1(i)$, $\mathsf{inp}_2(i) \in [\ell]$ are the positions of the input bits inspected in step i. Without loss of generality, we make the following assumptions on the structure of the brunching program BP:

- In every step BP inspects two different input bits; that is, for every step $i \in [n]$, we have $\mathsf{inp}_1(i) \neq \mathsf{inp}_2(i)$.
- Every pair of different input bits are inspected in some step of BP; that is, for every $j_1, j_2 \in [\ell]$ such that $j_1 \neq j_2$ there exists a step $i \in [n]$ such that $(\mathsf{inp}_1(i), \mathsf{inp}_2(i)) = (j_1, j_2)$.
- Every bit of the input is inspected by BP exactly ℓ' times. More precisely, for input bit $j \in [\ell]$, we denote by $\mathsf{ind}(j)$ the set of steps that inspect the j'th bit:

$$\mathsf{ind}(j) = \{i \in [n] : \mathsf{inp}_1(i) = j\} \cup \{i \in [n] : \mathsf{inp}_2(i) = j\} .$$

We assume that for every input bit $j \in [\ell]$, $|\mathsf{ind}(j)| = \ell'$. Note that in every step, the j'th input bit can be inspected at most once.

Randomizing. Next, the Obfuscator $\mathcal{O}$ "randomizes" the branching program BP as follows. First, $\mathcal{O}$ samples a prime p of length $\Theta(n)$. Then, $\mathcal{O}$ samples random and independent elements as follows:

- Non-zero scalars $\{\alpha_{i,b_1,b_2} \in \mathbb{Z}_p : i \in [n], b_1, b_2 \in \{0,1\}\}$.
- Pair of vectors $\mathbf{s}, \mathbf{t} \in \mathbb{Z}_p^w$.
- $n+1$ random full-rank matrices $R_0, R_1, \ldots, R_n \in \mathbb{Z}_p^{w \times w}$.

Finally, $\mathcal{O}$ computes the pair of vectors:

$$\tilde{\mathbf{s}} = \mathbf{s}^t \cdot R_0^{-1}, \quad \tilde{\mathbf{t}} = R_n \cdot \mathbf{t} \ ,$$

and for every $i \in [n]$ and $b_1, b_2 \in \{0,1\}$, $\mathcal{O}$ computes the matrix:

$$\hat{B}_{i,b_1,b_2} = R_{i-1} \cdot B_{i,b_1,b_2} \cdot R_i^{-1}.$$

Initialization. For every $j \in [\ell]$, let $\mathbb{S}^j$ be a straddling set system with ℓ' entries over a set U_j, such that the sets $U_1, \ldots, U_\ell$ are disjoint. Let $U = \bigcup_{j \in [\ell]} U_j$, and let B_s and B_t be sets such that U, B_s, B_t are disjoint. We associate the set system $\mathbb{S}^j$ with the j'th input bit. We index the elements of $\mathbb{S}^j$ by the steps of the branching program BP that inspect the j'th input. Namely,

$$\mathbb{S}^j = \left\{ S_{k,b}^j : k \in \mathsf{ind}(j), b \in \{0,1\} \right\}.$$

For every step $i \in [n]$ and bits $b_1, b_2 \in \{0,1\}$ we denote by $S(i, b_1, b_2)$ the union of pairs of sets that are indexed by i:

$$S(i, b_1, b_2) = S_{i,b_1}^{\mathsf{inp}_1(i)} \cup S_{i,b_2}^{\mathsf{inp}_2(i)} \ .$$

Note that by the way we defined the set $\mathsf{ind}(j)$ for input bit $j \in [\ell]$, and by the way the elements of $\mathbb{S}^j$ are indexed, indeed, $S_{i,b_1}^{\mathsf{inp}_1(i)} \in \mathbb{S}^{\mathsf{inp}_1(i)}$ and $S_{i,b_2}^{\mathsf{inp}_2(i)} \in \mathbb{S}^{\mathsf{inp}_2(i)}$.

$\mathcal{O}$ initializes the oracle $\mathcal{M}$ with the ring $\mathbb{Z}_p$, the universe set $U \cup B_s \cup B_t$ and with the following initial elements:

$$(\mathbf{s} \cdot \mathbf{t}, B_s \cup B_t),$$
$$\left\{ (\tilde{\mathbf{s}}[j], B_s), (\tilde{\mathbf{t}}[j], B_t) \right\}_{j \in [w]}$$
$$\left\{ (\alpha_{i,b_1,b_2}, S(i, b_1, b_2)) \right\}_{i \in [n], b_1, b_2 \in \{0,1\}}$$
$$\left\{ (\alpha_{i,b_1,b_2} \cdot \hat{B}_{i,b_1,b_2}[j,k], S(i, b_1, b_2)) \right\}_{i \in [n], b_1, b_2 \in \{0,1\}, j,k \in [w]}$$

$\mathcal{O}$ receives back a list of handles. We denote the handle to the element (α, S) by $[\alpha]_S$. For a matrix M, $[M]_S$ denotes a matrix of handles such that $[M]_S[j,k]$ is the handle to the element $(M[j,k], S)$. Using this notation, $\mathcal{O}$ receives back the following handles:

$$[\tilde{\mathbf{s}}]_{B_s}, \quad [\tilde{\mathbf{t}}]_{B_t}, \quad [\mathbf{s} \cdot \mathbf{t}]_{B_s \cup B_t},$$
$$\left\{ [\alpha_{i,b_1,b_2}]_{S(i,b_1,b_2)}, \quad \left[\alpha_{i,b_1,b_2} \cdot \hat{B}_{i,b_1,b_2}\right]_{S(i,b_1,b_2)} \right\}_{i \in [n], b_1, b_2 \in \{0,1\}}.$$

Output. The obfuscator $\mathcal{O}$ outputs a circuit $\mathcal{O}(\mathsf{BP})$ that has all the handles received from the Initialization stage hardcoded into it. Given access to the oracle $\mathcal{M}$, $\mathcal{O}(\mathsf{BP})$ can add and multiply handles.

Notation. Given two handles $[\alpha]_S$ and $[\beta]_S$, we let $[\alpha]_S + [\beta]_S$ denote the handle obtained from $\mathcal{M}$ upon sending an addition query with $[\alpha]_S$ and $[\beta]_S$. Similarly, given two handles $[\alpha_1]_{S_1}$ and $[\alpha_2]_{S_2}$ such that $S_1 \cap S_2 = \emptyset$, we denote by $[\alpha_1]_{S_1} \cdot [\alpha_2]_{S_2}$ the handle obtained from $\mathcal{M}$ upon sending a multiplication query with $[\alpha_1]_{S_1}$ and $[\alpha_2]_{S_2}$. Given two matrices of handles $[M_1]_{S_1}, [M_2]_{S_2}$, we define their matrix multiplication in the natural way, and denote it by $[M_1]_{S_1} \cdot [M_2]_{S_2}$.

For input $x \in \{0,1\}^\ell$ to $\mathcal{O}(\mathsf{BP})$, and for every $i \in [n]$ let $(b_1^i, b_2^i) = (x_{\mathsf{inp}_1(i)}, x_{\mathsf{inp}_2(i)})$. On input x, $\mathcal{O}(\mathsf{BP})$ obtains the following handles:

$$h = [\tilde{\mathbf{s}}]_{B_s} \cdot \prod_{i=1}^{n} \left[\alpha_{i,b_1^i,b_2^i} \cdot \tilde{B}_{i,b_1^i,b_2^i} \right]_{S(i,b_1^i,b_2^i)} \cdot [\tilde{\mathbf{t}}]_{B_t},$$

$$h' = [\mathbf{s} \cdot \mathbf{t}]_{B_s \cup B_t} \cdot \prod_{i=1}^{n} \left[\alpha_{i,b_1^i,b_2^i} \right]_{S(i,b_1^i,b_2^i)}$$

$\mathcal{O}(\mathsf{BP})$ uses the oracle $\mathcal{M}$ to subtract the handle h' from h and performs a zero test on the result. If the zero test outputs 1 then $\mathcal{O}(\mathsf{BP})$ outputs 1, and otherwise $\mathcal{O}(\mathsf{BP})$ outputs 0.

Correctness. By construction we have that as long as none of the calls to the oracle $\mathcal{M}$ fail, subtracting the handle h' from h results in a handle to 0 if and only if:

$$0 = \tilde{\mathbf{s}} \cdot \prod_{i=1}^{n} \alpha_{i,b_1^i,b_2^i} \cdot \tilde{B}_{i,b_1^i,b_2^i} \cdot \tilde{\mathbf{t}} - \mathbf{s} \cdot \mathbf{t} \cdot \prod_{i=1}^{n} \alpha_{i,b_1^i,b_2^i}$$

$$= \left(\tilde{\mathbf{s}} \cdot \prod_{i=1}^{n} \tilde{B}_{i,b_1^i,b_2^i} \cdot \tilde{\mathbf{t}} - \mathbf{s} \cdot \mathbf{t} \right) \cdot \prod_{i=1}^{n} \alpha_{i,b_1^i,b_2^i}$$

$$= \left(\mathbf{s}^t \cdot R_0^{-1} \cdot \prod_{i=1}^{n} \left(R_{i-1} \cdot B_{i,b_1,b_2} \cdot R_i^{-1} \right) \cdot R_n^{-1} \cdot \mathbf{t} - \mathbf{s} \cdot \mathbf{t} \right) \cdot \prod_{i=1}^{n} \alpha_{i,b_1^i,b_2^i}$$

$$= \mathbf{s}^t \cdot \left(\prod_{i=1}^{n} B_{i,b_1,b_2} - I_{w \times w} \right) \cdot \mathbf{t} \cdot \prod_{i=1}^{n} \alpha_{i,b_1^i,b_2^i}$$

From the definition of the branching program we have:

$$\mathsf{BP}(x) = 1 \Leftrightarrow \prod_{i=1}^{n} B_{i,b_1^i,b_2^i} = I_{w \times w}$$

Thus, if $\mathsf{BP}(x) = 1$ then $\mathcal{O}(\mathsf{BP})$ outputs 1 with probability 1. If $\mathsf{BP}(x) = 0$ then $\mathcal{O}(\mathsf{BP})$ outputs 1 with probability at most $1/p = \mathsf{negl}(n)$ over the choice of $\mathbf{s}$ and $\mathbf{t}$.

It is left to show that none of the calls to the oracle $\mathcal{M}$ fail. Note that when multiplying two matrices of handles $[M_1]_{S_1} \cdot [M_2]_{S_2}$, none of the addition or multiplication calls fail as long as $S_1 \cap S_2 = \emptyset$. Therefore, to show that none of the addition or multiplication calls to $\mathcal{M}$ fail, it is enough to show that following sets are disjoint:

$$B_s, B_t, S(1, b_1^1, b_2^1), \ldots, S(n, b_1^n, b_2^n) \ .$$

Their disjointness follows from the fact that $U_1, \ldots, U_\ell, B_s, B_t$ are disjoint, together with definition of $S(i, b_1^i, b_2^i)$ and with the fact that for every set system $\mathbb{S}^j$, for every distinct $i, i' \in \mathsf{ind}(j)$, and for every $b \in \{0, 1\}$, we have that $S_{i,b}^j \cap S_{i',b}^j = \emptyset$.

To show that the zero testing call to the oracle $\mathcal{M}$ does not fail we need to show that the index set of the elements corresponding to h and h' is the entire universe. Namely, we need to show that

$$\left(\bigcup_{i=1}^n S(i, b_1^i, b_2^i) \right) \cup B_s \cup B_t = U \cup B_s \cup B_t \ ,$$

which follows from the following equalities:

$$\bigcup_{i=1}^n S(i, b_1^i, b_2^i) = \bigcup_{i=1}^n S_{i,b_1^i}^{\mathsf{inp}_1(i)} \cup S_{i,b_2^i}^{\mathsf{inp}_2(i)} = \bigcup_{j=1}^\ell \bigcup_{k \in \mathsf{ind}(j)} S_{k,x_i}^j = \bigcup_{j=1}^\ell U_j = U \ .$$

6   Proof of VBB in the the Ideal Graded Encoding Model

In this section we prove that the obfuscator $\mathcal{O}$ described in Section 5 is a good VBB obfuscator for $\mathbf{NC}^1$ in the ideal graded encoding model.

Let $\mathcal{C} = \{\mathcal{C}_\ell\}_{\ell \in \mathbb{N}}$ be a circuit class such that every circuit in $\mathcal{C}_\ell$ is of size $\mathsf{poly}(\ell)$ and of depth $O(\log \ell)$. We assume WLOG that all circuits in $\mathcal{C}_\ell$ are of the same depth (otherwise the circuit can be padded). It follows from Theorem 2.1 that there exist polynomial functions n and w such that on input circuit $C \in \mathcal{C}_\ell$, the branching program BP computed by $\mathcal{O}$ is of size $n(|C|)$, width $w(|C|)$, and computes on $\ell(|C|)$-bit inputs.

In Section 5 we showed that $\mathcal{O}$ satisfies the functionality requirement where the probability of $\mathcal{O}$ computing the wrong output is negligible in n. Since n is a polynomial function of $|C|$ we get that the functionality error is negligible in $|C|$, as required. It is straightforward to verify that $\mathcal{O}$ also satisfies the polynomial slowdown property. In the rest of this section we prove that $\mathcal{O}$ satisfies the virtual black-box property.

The simulator. To prove that $\mathcal{O}$ satisfies the virtual black-box property, we construct a simulator Sim that is given $1^{|C|}$, the description of an adversary $\mathcal{A}$, and oracle access to the circuit C. Sim starts by emulating the obfuscation algorithm $\mathcal{O}$. Recall that $\mathcal{O}$ converts the circuit C into a branching program BP.

However, since Sim is not given C it cannot compute the matrices B_{i,b_1,b_2} in the description of BP (note that Sim can compute the input mapping functions $\mathsf{inp}_1, \mathsf{inp}_2$ since the branching program is oblivious). Without knowing the B matrices, Sim cannot simulate the list of initial elements to the oracle $\mathcal{M}$. Instead Sim initializes $\mathcal{M}$ with formal variables.

Concretely, we extend the definition of an element to allow for values that are formal variables, as opposed to ring elements. When performing an operation $\circ$ on elements e_1, e_2 that contain formal variables, the value of the resulting element $e_1 \circ e_2$ is just the formal arithmetic expression $\alpha(e_1) \circ \alpha(e_2)$ (assuming the indexes of the elements are such that the operation is defined). We represent formal expressions as arithmetic circuits, thereby guaranteeing that the representation size remains polynomial. We say that an element is *basic* if its value is an expression that contains no gates (i.e., its just a formal variable). We say that an element e' is a *sub-element* of an element e if e was generated from e' through a sequence of operations.

To emulate $\mathcal{O}$, Sim must also emulate the oracle $\mathcal{M}$ that $\mathcal{O}$ accesses. Sim can efficiently emulate all the interfaces of $\mathcal{M}$ except for the zero testing. The problem with simulating zero tests is that Sim cannot test if the value of a formal expression is 0. Note however that the emulation of $\mathcal{O}$ does not make any zero-test queries to $\mathcal{M}$ (zero-test queries are made only by the evaluator).

When Sim completes the emulation of $\mathcal{O}$ it obtains a simulated obfuscation $\tilde{\mathcal{O}}(C)$. Sim proceeds to emulate the execution of the adversary $\mathcal{A}$ on input $\tilde{\mathcal{O}}(C)$. When $\mathcal{A}$ makes an oracle call that is not a zero test, Sim emulates $\mathcal{M}$'s answer (note that emulation of the oracle $\mathcal{M}$ is stateful and will therefore use the same handle table to emulate both $\mathcal{O}$ and $\mathcal{A}$). Since the distribution of handles generated during the simulation and during the real execution are identical, and since the simulated obfuscation $\tilde{\mathcal{O}}(C)$ consists only of handles (as opposed to elements), we have that the simulation of the obfuscation $\tilde{\mathcal{O}}(C)$ and the simulation of $\mathcal{M}$'s answers to all the queries, except for zero-test queries, is perfect.

Simulating zero testing queries. In the rest of the proof we describe how the simulator correctly simulates zero-test queries made by $\mathcal{A}$. Simulating the zero-test queries is non-trivial since the handle being tested may correspond to a formal expression whose value is unknown to Sim. (The "real" value of the formal variables depend on the circuit C). Instead we show how Sim can efficiently simulate the zero-test queries given oracle access to the circuit C.

The high-level strategy for simulating zero-test queries is as follows. Given a handle to some element, Sim tests if the value of the element is zero in two parts. In the first part, Sim decomposes the element into a sum of polynomial number of "simpler" elements that we call *single-input elements*. Each single-input element has a value that depends on a subset of the formal variables that correspond to a *specific* input to the branching program. Namely, for every single-input element there exists $x \in \{0,1\}^{\ell}$ such that the value of the element only depends on the formal variables in the matrices $\tilde{B}_{i,b_1^i,b_2^i}$, where $b_1^i = x_{\mathsf{inp}_1(i)}$ and $b_2^i = x_{\mathsf{inp}_2(i)}$. The main difficulty in the first step is to prove that the number of single-input elements in the decomposition is polynomial.

In the second part, Sim simulates the value of every single-input element separately. The main idea in this step is to show that the value of a single-input element for input x can be simulated only given $C(x)$. To this end, we use Kilian's proof on randomized encoding of branching programs. Unfortunately, we cannot simulate all the single-input elements at once (given oracle access to C), since their values may not be independent; in particular, they all depend on the obfuscator's randomness. Instead, we show that it is enough to zero test every single-input element individually. More concretely, we show that from every single input element that the adversary can construct, it is possible to factor out a product of the α_{i,b_1^i,b_2^i} variables. We also show that every single-input element depends on a different set of the α_{i,b_1^i,b_2^i} variables. Since the values of the α variables are chosen at random by the obfuscation, it is unlikely that the adversary makes a query where the value of two single-input elements "cancel each other" and result in a zero. Therefore, with high probability an element is zero iff it decomposes into single-input element's that are all zero individually.

Decomposition to single-input elements. Next we show that every element can be decomposed into polynomial number of single-input elements. We start by introducing some notation.

For every element e we assign an *input-profile* $\mathsf{prof}(e) \in \{0, 1, *\}^\ell \cup \{\bot\}$. Intuitively, if we think of e as an intermediate element in the evaluation of the branching program on some input x, the input-profile $\mathsf{prof}(e)$ represents the partial information that can be inferred about x based on the formal variables that appear in the value of e. Formally, for every element e and for every $j \in [\ell]$, we say that the j'th bit of e's input-profile is *consistent* with the value $b \in \{0, 1\}$ if e has a basic sub-element e' such that $S(e') = S(i, b_1, b_2)$ and either $j = \mathsf{inp}_1(i)$ and $b_1 = b$, or $j = \mathsf{inp}_2(i)$ and $b_2 = b$.

For every $j \in [\ell]$ and for $b \in \{0, 1\}$ we set $\mathsf{prof}(e)_j = b$ if the j'th bit of e's input-profile is consistent with b but not with $1 - b$. If the j'th bit of e's input-profile is not consistent with either 0 or 1 then $\mathsf{prof}(e)_j = *$. If there exist $j \in [\ell]$ such that the j'th bit of e's input-profile is consistent with both 0 and 1, then $\mathsf{prof}(e) = \bot$. In this case we say that e is *not* a single-input element and that it's profile is invalid. If $\mathsf{prof}(e) \neq \bot$ then we say that e is a single-input element. We say that an input-profile is complete if it is in $\{0, 1\}^\ell$.

Next we describe an algorithm D used by Sim to decompose elements into single-input elements. Given an input element e, D outputs a set of single-input elements with distinct input-profiles such that $e = \sum_{s \in D(e)} s$, where the equality between the elements means that their values compute the same function (it does not mean that the arithmetic circuits that represent these values are identical). Note that the above requirement implies that for every $s \in D(e)$, $S(s) = S(e)$.

The decomposition algorithm D is defined recursively, as follows:

- If the input element e is basic, D outputs the singleton set $\{e\}$.
- If the input element e is of the form $e_1 + e_2$, D executes recursively and obtains the set $L = D(e_1) \cup D(e_2)$. If there exist elements $s_1, s_2 \in L$ with the same input-profile, D replaces the two elements with a single element $s_1 + s_2$. D repeats this process until all the input-profiles in L are distinct and outputs L.

– If the input element e is of the form $e_1 \cdot e_2$, D executes recursively and obtains the sets $L_1 = D(e_1), L_2 = D(e_2)$. For every $s_1 \in L_1$ and $s_2 \in L_2$, D adds the expression $s_1 \cdot s_2$ to the output set L. D then eliminates repeating input-profiles from L as described above, and outputs L.

The fact that in the above decomposition algorithm indeed $e = \sum_{s \in D(e)} s$, and that the input profiles are distinct follows from a straightforward induction. The usefulness of the above decomposition algorithm is captured by the following two claims:

Claim 6.1. *If $U \subseteq S(e)$ then all the elements in $D(e)$ are single-input elements. Namely, for every $s \in D(e)$ we have that $\mathsf{prof}(s) \neq \perp$.*

Claim 6.2. *D runs in polynomial time, and in particular, the number of elements in the output decomposition is polynomial.*

The proofs of Claims 6.1, 6.2 and the formal description of how to simulate zero tests appear in the full version of this work [1].

References

[1] Barak, B., Garg, S., Kalai, Y.T., Paneth, O., Sahai, A.: Protecting obfuscation against algebraic attacks. Cryptology ePrint Archive, Report 2013/631 (2013), http://eprint.iacr.org/

[2] Barak, B., Goldreich, O., Impagliazzo, R., Rudich, S., Sahai, A., Vadhan, S.P., Yang, K.: On the (im)possibility of obfuscating programs. IACR Cryptology ePrint Archive 2001, 69 (2001)

[3] Barrington, D.A.: Bounded-width polynomial-size branching programs recognize exactly those languages in nc_1. In: STOC (1986)

[4] Brakerski, Z., Rothblum, G.N.: Virtual black-box obfuscation for all circuits via generic graded encoding. Cryptology ePrint Archive, Report 2013/563 (2013), http://eprint.iacr.org/

[5] Canetti, R., Vaikuntanathan, V.: Obfuscating branching programs using black-box pseudo-free groups. Cryptology ePrint Archive (2013)

[6] Coron, J.-S., Lepoint, T., Tibouchi, M.: Practical multilinear maps over the integers. In: Canetti, R., Garay, J.A. (eds.) CRYPTO 2013, Part I. LNCS, vol. 8042, pp. 476–493. Springer, Heidelberg (2013)

[7] Diffie, W., Hellman, M.E.: Multiuser cryptographic techniques. In: AFIPS National Computer Conference, pp. 109–112 (1976)

[8] Garg, S., Gentry, C., Halevi, S.: Candidate multilinear maps from ideal lattices. In: Johansson, T., Nguyen, P.Q. (eds.) EUROCRYPT 2013. LNCS, vol. 7881, pp. 1–17. Springer, Heidelberg (2013)

[9] Garg, S., Gentry, C., Halevi, S., Raykova, M., Sahai, A., Waters, B.: Candidate indistinguishability obfuscation and functional encryption for all circuits. Cryptology ePrint Archive, Report 2013/451 (2013), http://eprint.iacr.org/

[10] Goyal, V., Ishai, Y., Sahai, A., Venkatesan, R., Wadia, A.: Founding cryptography on tamper-proof hardware tokens. In: Micciancio, D. (ed.) TCC 2010. LNCS, vol. 5978, pp. 308–326. Springer, Heidelberg (2010)

[11] Hada, S.: Zero-knowledge and code obfuscation. In: Okamoto, T. (ed.) ASIACRYPT 2000. LNCS, vol. 1976, pp. 443–457. Springer, Heidelberg (2000)

[12] Kilian, J.: Founding cryptography on oblivious transfer. In: Simon, J. (ed.) STOC, pp. 20–31. ACM (1988)

GGHLite: More Efficient Multilinear Maps from Ideal Lattices

Adeline Langlois[1], Damien Stehlé[1], and Ron Steinfeld[2]

[1] ENS de Lyon, Laboratoire LIP (U. Lyon, CNRS, ENS Lyon, INRIA, UCBL),
46 Allée d'Italie, 69364 Lyon Cedex 07, France
[2] Clayton School of Information Technology, Monash University, Clayton, Australia

Abstract. The GGH Graded Encoding Scheme [9], based on ideal lattices, is the first plausible approximation to a cryptographic multilinear map. Unfortunately, using the security analysis in [9], the scheme requires very large parameters to provide security for its underlying "encoding re-randomization" process. Our main contributions are to formalize, simplify and improve the efficiency and the security analysis of the re-randomization process in the GGH construction. This results in a new construction that we call GGHLite. In particular, we first lower the size of a standard deviation parameter of the re-randomization process of [9] from exponential to polynomial in the security parameter. This first improvement is obtained via a finer security analysis of the "drowning" step of re-randomization, in which we apply the *Rényi divergence* instead of the conventional *statistical distance* as a measure of distance between distributions. Our second improvement is to reduce the number of randomizers needed from $\Omega(n \log n)$ to 2, where n is the dimension of the underlying ideal lattices. These two contributions allow us to decrease the bit size of the public parameters from $O(\lambda^5 \log \lambda)$ for the GGH scheme to $O(\lambda \log^2 \lambda)$ in GGHLite, with respect to the security parameter λ (for a constant multilinearity parameter κ).

1 Introduction

Boneh and Silverberg [6] defined a *cryptographic κ-multilinear map* e as a map from $G_1 \times \ldots \times G_\kappa$ to G_T, all cyclic groups of order p, which enjoys three main properties: first, for any elements $g_i \in G_i$ for $i \le \kappa$, $j \le \kappa$ and $\alpha \in \mathbb{Z}_p$, we have $e(g_1, \ldots, \alpha \cdot g_j, \ldots, g_\kappa) = \alpha \cdot e(g_1, \ldots, g_\kappa)$; second, the map e is non-degenerate, i.e., if the g_i's are generators of their respective G_i's then $e(g_1, \ldots, g_\kappa)$ generates G_T; and third, there is no efficient algorithm to compute discrete logarithms in any of the G_i's. Bilinear maps ($\kappa = 2$) and multilinear maps have a lot of cryptographic applications, see [11,21,5] and [6,20,16,19], respectively. But unlike bilinear maps, built with pairings on elliptic curves, the construction of cryptographic multilinear maps was an open problem for several years. In [6], Boneh and Silverberg studied the interest of such maps, and gave two applications: multipartite Diffie-Hellman key exchange and very efficient broadcast encryption. But they conjectured that multilinear maps will probably "come from outside the realm of algebraic geometry." In 2013, Garg, Gentry

P.Q. Nguyen and E. Oswald (Eds.): EUROCRYPT 2014, LNCS 8441, pp. 239–256, 2014.

and Halevi [9] introduced the first "approximate" multilinear maps contruction, based on ideal lattices, and the powerful notion of *graded encoding scheme*. Based on their work, Coron, Lepoint and Tibouchi [7] recently described an alternative construction of graded encoding scheme.

We first give a high level description of the GGH graded encoding scheme [9]. If we come back to the definition of cryptographic multilinear maps, the authors of [9] notice that $\alpha \cdot g_i$ can be viewed as an "encoding" of the "plaintext" $\alpha \in \mathbb{Z}_q$. They consider the polynomial rings $R = \mathbb{Z}[x]/\langle x^n + 1\rangle$ and $R_q = R/qR$ (replacing the exponent space $\mathbb{Z}_p$). They generate a small secret $g \in R$ and let $\mathcal{I} = \langle g \rangle$ be the principal ideal over R generated by g. They also sample a uniform $z \in R_q$ which stays secret. The "plaintext" is an element of $R/\mathcal{I}$, and is encoded via a division by z in R_q: to encode a coset of $R/\mathcal{I}$, return $[c/z]_q$, where c is an arbitrary small coset representative. In practice, as g is hidden, they give another public parameter y, which is an encoding of 1, and the encoding of the coset is computed as $[e \cdot y]_q$, where e is a small coset representative (possibly different from c). But, as opposed to multilinear maps, their graded encoding scheme uses the notion of *encoding level*: the plaintext e is a level-0 encoding, the encoding $[c/z]_q$ is a level-1 encoding, and at level i, an encoding of $e + \mathcal{I}$ is given by $[c/z^i]_q = [e \cdot y^i]_q$. These encodings are both additively and multiplicatively homomorphic, up to a limited number of operations. More precisely, a product of i level-1 encodings is a level-i encoding. One can multiply any number of encodings up to κ, instead of exactly κ in multilinear maps (the parameter κ is called the multilinearity parameter).

The authors of [9] introduced new hardness assumptions: the Graded Decisional Diffie-Hellman (GDDH) and its computational variant (GCDH). These are natural analogues of the Diffie-Hellman problems from group-based cryptography. To ensure their hardness, and hence the security of the cryptographic constructions, the second main difference with multilinear maps is the randomization of the encodings. The principle is as follows: first some level-1 encodings of 0, called $\{x_j = [b_j/z]_q\}_{j \le m_r}$, are given as part of the public parameters; then, to randomize a level-1 encoding $u' = [e \cdot y]_q$, one outputs $u = [u' + \sum_j \rho_j x_j]_q = [c/z]_q$ with $c = c' + \sum_j \rho_j b_j$, where the ρ_j's are sampled from a discrete Gaussian distribution over $\mathbb{Z}$ with deviation parameter σ^*. Without this re-randomization, the encoding u' of e allows e to be efficiently recovered using $u = [u'y^{-1}]_q$. Adding the re-randomization step prevents this division attack, but the statistical properties of the distribution of the re-randomized encoding u remain correlated to some extent with the original encoding u' (for instance, the center of the distribution of c is c', since the distribution of $\sum_j \rho_j b_j$ is known to be centered at 0). This property may allow other attacks that exploit this correlation. The question arises as to how to set the re-randomization parameter σ^* in order to guarantee security against such potential "statistical correlation" attacks – the larger the re-randomization parameters the smaller the correlation, and heuristically the more resistant the scheme is to such attacks. But increasing σ^* impacts the efficiency of the scheme.

In [9], the authors use a "drowning step" to solve this problem. This technique, also called "smudging," was previously used in other applications [3,10,2,4]. Generally, "drowning" consists in hiding a secret vector $s \in \mathbb{Z}^n$ by adding a sufficiently large random noise $e \in \mathbb{Z}^n$ to it, so that the distribution of $s + e$ becomes "almost independent" of s. In all of the above applications, to achieve a security level 2^λ (where λ denotes the security parameter), the security analysis requires "almost independent" to be interpreted as "within statistical distance $2^{-\lambda}$ from a distribution that is independent of s." In turn, this requirement implies the need for "exponential drowning," i.e., the ratio $\gamma = \|e\|/\|s\|$ between the magnitude of the noise and the magnitude of secret needs to be $2^{\Omega(\lambda)}$. Exponential drowning imposes a severe penalty on the efficiency of these schemes, as their security is related to γ-approximation lattice problems, whose complexity decreases exponentially with $\log \gamma$. As a result, the schemes require a lattice dimension n at least quadratic in λ and key length at least cubic in λ. In summary, the GGH re-randomization step, necessary for its security, is also a primary factor in its inefficiency.

OUR CONTRIBUTIONS. First, we formalize the re-randomization security goal in the GGH construction, that is implicit in the work of [9]. A primary security goal of re-randomization is to guarantee security of the GDDH problem against statistical correlation attacks. Accordingly, we formulate a security goal that captures this security guarantee, by introducing a canonical variant of GDDH, called cGDDH. In this variant, the encodings of some elements are sampled from a canonical distribution whose statistical properties are independent of the encoded elements. Consequently, the canonical problems are by construction not subject to "statistical correlation" attacks. Our re-randomization security goal is formulated as the existence of an efficient computational reduction from the canonical problems to their corresponding non-canonical variants.

Our first main improvement to the GGH scheme relies on a new security analysis of the drowning step in the GGH re-randomization algorithm. We show that our re-randomization security goal can be satisfied *without* "exponential drowning," thus removing the main efficiency bottleneck. Namely, our analysis provides a re-randomization at security level 2^λ while allowing the use of a re-randomization deviation parameter σ^* that only drowns the norm of the randomness offset $r' \in \mathcal{I}$ (from the original encoding to be re-randomized) by a *polynomial* (or even constant) drowning ratio $\gamma = \lambda^{O(1)}$ (rather than $\gamma = 2^{\Omega(\lambda)}$, as needed in the analysis of [9]). However, our analysis only works for the search variant of the Graded Diffie-Hellman problem. Fortunately, we show that the two flagship applications of the GGH scheme – the N-party Key Agreement and the Attribute Based Encryption – can be modified to rely on this computational assumption (in the random oracle model).

Our second main improvement of the re-randomization process is to decrease m_r, the number of encodings of 0 needed, from $\Omega(n \log n)$ to 2. We achieve this result by presenting a new discrete Gaussian Leftover Hash Lemma (LHL) over algebraic rings. In [9], the authors apply the discrete Gaussian LHL from [1] to show that the distribution of the sum $\sum_{j \le m_r} \rho_j r_j$ is close to a discrete Gaussian on the ideal $\mathcal{I}$. Our improvement consists in sampling the randomizers ρ_j as elements of the full n-dimensional ring R, rather than just from $\mathbb{Z}$. Since each randomizer now has n times more entropy than before, one may hope to obtain a similar LHL result as in [1] while reducing m_r by a factor $\approx n$. However, as the designers of the GGH scheme notice in [9, Se. 6.4], the proof techniques from [1] do not seem to immediately carry over to our "algebraic ring" LHL setting. Our new LHL over rings resolves this problem.

These contributions allow us to decrease the bit size of the public parameters from $O(\kappa^3 \lambda^5 \log(\kappa\lambda))$ for the GGH scheme to $O(\kappa^2 \lambda \log^2(\kappa\lambda))$ for GGHLite, for security level 2^λ for the graded Diffie-Hellman problem.

TECHNICAL OVERVIEW. Our first main result is to reduce the size of the parameter σ^* in the re-randomization process. Technically, our improved analysis of drowning is obtained by using the *Rényi divergence* (RD) to replace the conventional statistical distance (SD) as a measure of distribution closeness. The RD was already exploited in a different context in [13, Claim 5.11], to show the hardness of Ring-LWE. Here, we use the RD to decrease the amount of drowning, by bounding the RD between a discrete Gaussian distribution and its offset. This suffices for relating the hardness of the search problems using these encoding distributions, even though the SD between the distributions is non-negligible. The technique does not seem to easily extend to the decision problems, as RD induces a multiplicative relationship between success probabilities, rather than an additive relationship as SD does.

Our second main result is a new LHL over the ring R. We now briefly explain this result and its proof. For a fixed $X = [x_1, x_2] \in R^2$, with each x_i sampled from $D_{R,s}$, our goal is to study the distribution $\widetilde{\mathcal{E}}_{X,s} = x_1 \cdot D_{R,s} + x_2 \cdot D_{R,s}$. In particular, we prove that $\widetilde{\mathcal{E}}_{X,s}$ is statistically close to $D_{\mathbb{Z}^n, sX^T}$. For this, we adapt the proof of the LHL in [1]: we follow a similar series of steps, but the proofs of these steps differ technically, as we exploit the ring structure.

We first show that $X \cdot R^2 = R$, except with some constant probability < 1. For this, we adapt a result from [23] on the probability that two Gaussian samples of R are coprime. Note that in contrast to the LHL over $\mathbb{Z}$ in [1], in our setting the probability that $X \cdot R^2 \neq R$ is non-negligible. This is unavoidable with the ring $R = \mathbb{Z}[x]/\langle x^n + 1 \rangle$, since each random element of R falls in the ideal $\langle x + 1 \rangle$ with probability $\approx 1/2$, both x_1 and x_2 (and hence the ideal they generate) get "stuck" in $\langle x + 1 \rangle$ with probability $\approx 1/4$. However, the probability of this bad event is bounded away from 1 by a constant and thus we only need a constant number of trials on average with random X's to obtain a good X by rejection.

Then, we define the orthogonal R-module $A_X = \{v \in R^2 : X \cdot v = 0\}$, and apply a directly adapted variant of [1, Le. 10] to show that if the parameter s is larger than the smoothing parameter $\eta_\varepsilon(A_X)$ (with A_X viewed as an integral lattice), then the SD between $\widetilde{\mathcal{E}}_{X,s}$ and the ellipsoidal Gaussian $D_{\mathbb{Z}^n, sX^T}$ is bounded by 2ε. We finally show that this condition on the smoothing parameter of A_X holds. For this, we observe that the Minkowski minima of the lattice A_X are equal, due to the R-module structure of A_X. This allows us to bound the last minimum from above using Minkowski's second theorem. A similar approach was previously used (e.g., in [12]) to bound the smoothing parameter of ideal lattices.

NOTATION. A function $f(\lambda)$ is said negligible if it is $\lambda^{-\omega(1)}$. For an integer q, we let $\mathbb{Z}_q$ denote the ring of integers modulo q. The notation $[\cdot]_q$ means that all operations within the square brackets are performed modulo q. We choose $n \geq 4$ as a power of 2, and let K and R respectively denote the polynomial ring $\mathbb{Q}[X]/\langle x^n + 1\rangle$ and $\mathbb{Z}[X]/\langle x^n+1\rangle$. The rings K and R are isomorphic to the cyclotomic field of order $2n$ and its ring of integers, respectively. For an integer q, we let R_q denote the ring $\mathbb{Z}_q[x]/\langle x^n+1\rangle \simeq R/qR$. For $z \in R$ we denote by $\mathrm{MSB}_\ell(z) \in \{0,1\}^{\ell \cdot n}$ the ℓ most-significant bits of each of the n coefficients of z. Vectors are denoted in bold. For $\boldsymbol{b} \in \mathbb{R}^d$ (resp. $g \in K$), we let $\|\boldsymbol{b}\|$ (resp. $\|g\|$) denote its Euclidean norm (resp. norm of its coefficient vector). The uniform distribution on finite set E is denoted by $U(E)$. The statistical distance (SD) between distributions D_1 and D_2 over a countable domain E is $\frac{1}{2}\sum_{x \in E} |D_1(x) - D_2(x)|$. For a function f over a countable domain E, we let $f(E) = \sum_{x \in E} f(x)$. Let $X \in \mathbb{R}^{m \times n}$ be a rank-n matrix and $U_X = \{\|X\boldsymbol{u}\| : \boldsymbol{u} \in \mathbb{R}^n, \|\boldsymbol{u}\| = 1\}$. The smallest (resp. largest) singular value of X is denoted by $\sigma_n(X) = \inf(U_X)$ (resp. $\sigma_1(X) = \sup(U_X)$).

REMARK. Due to lack of space, some contents have been postponed to the full version of this paper, available from the webpages of the authors.

2   Preliminaries

Lattices. We refer to [14,17] for introductions to the computational aspects of lattices. A d-dimensional *lattice* $\Lambda \subseteq \mathbb{R}^n$ is the set of all integer linear combinations $\sum_{i=1}^d x_i \boldsymbol{b}_i$ of some linearly independent vectors $\boldsymbol{b}_i \in \mathbb{R}^n$. The determinant $\det(\Lambda)$ is defined as $\sqrt{\det(B^T B)}$, where $B = (\boldsymbol{b}_i)_i$ is any such *basis* of Λ. For $i \leq d$, the ith minimum $\lambda_i(\Lambda)$ is the smallest r such that Λ contains i linearly independent vectors of norms $\leq r$.

Gaussian Distributions. For a rank-n matrix $S \in \mathbb{R}^{m \times n}$ and a vector $\boldsymbol{c} \in \mathbb{R}^n$, the *ellipsoid* Gaussian distribution with parameter S and center $\boldsymbol{c}$ is defined as: $\forall \boldsymbol{x} \in \mathbb{R}^n, \rho_{S,\boldsymbol{c}}(x) = \exp(-\pi(\boldsymbol{x} - \boldsymbol{c})^T(S^T S)^{-1}(\boldsymbol{x} - \boldsymbol{c}))$. Note that $\rho_{S,\boldsymbol{c}}(x) = \exp(-\pi\|(S^T)^\dagger(\boldsymbol{x}-\boldsymbol{c})\|)$, where $X^\dagger$ denotes the pseudo-inverse of X. The *ellipsoid* discrete Gaussian distribution over a coset $\Lambda + z$ of a lattice Λ, with parameter S and center $\boldsymbol{c}$ is defined as: $\forall \boldsymbol{x} \in \Lambda + z, D_{\Lambda+z,S,\boldsymbol{c}} = \rho_{S,\boldsymbol{c}}(\boldsymbol{x})/\rho_{S,\boldsymbol{c}}(\Lambda)$.

Smoothing Parameter. Introduced by [15], the *smoothing parameter* $\eta_\varepsilon(\Lambda)$ of an n-dimensional lattice Λ and a real $\varepsilon > 0$ is defined as the smallest s such that $\rho_{1/s}(\Lambda^* \setminus \{0\}) \leq \varepsilon$. We use the following properties.

Lemma 2.1 ([15, Le. 3.3]). *Let Λ be an n-dimensional lattice and $\varepsilon > 0$. Then* $\eta_\varepsilon(\Lambda) \leq \sqrt{\ln(2n(1 + 1/\varepsilon))/\pi} \cdot \lambda_n(\Lambda)$.

Lemma 2.2 ([1, Le. 3]). *For a rank-n lattice Λ, constant $0 < \varepsilon < 1$, vector $\boldsymbol{c}$ and matrix S with $\sigma_n(S) \geq \eta_\varepsilon(\Lambda)$, if $\boldsymbol{x}$ is sampled from $D_{\Lambda,S,\boldsymbol{c}}$ then $\|\boldsymbol{x}\| \leq \sigma_1(S)\sqrt{n}$, except with probability $\leq \frac{1+\varepsilon}{1-\varepsilon} \cdot 2^{-n}$.*

Algebraic Number Rings and Ideal Lattices. For $g, x \in R$, we let $[x]_g$ denote the reduction of x modulo the principal ideal $I = \langle g \rangle$ with respect to the $\mathbb{Z}$-basis $(g, x \cdot g, \ldots, x^{n-1} \cdot g)$, i.e., $[x]_g$ is the unique element of R in $\mathcal{P}_g = \{\sum_{i=0}^{n-1} c_i x^i g : c_i \in [-1/2, 1/2) \cap \mathbb{R}\}$ such that $x - [x]_g \in \langle g \rangle$. The set $\mathcal{P}_g \cap R$ is a set of unique representatives of the cosets of I in R, that make up the quotient ring R/I. To use our improved drowning lemma in Section 4, we need a lower bound on the last singular value $\sigma_n(\mathrm{rot}(b))$ of the matrix $\mathrm{rot}(b) \in \mathbb{Z}^{n \times n}$ corresponding to the map $x \mapsto b \cdot x$ over R, for a Gaussian distributed $b \hookleftarrow D_{I,\sigma}$. In the following, and in the rest of the paper, we abuse notation and write b for this matrix.

Lemma 2.3 (Adapted from [23, Le. 4.1]). *Let $R = \mathbb{Z}^n[x]/(x^n + 1)$ for n a power of 2. For any ideal $I \subseteq R$, $\delta \in (0, 1)$, $t \geq \sqrt{2\pi}$ and $\sigma \geq \frac{t}{\sqrt{2\pi}} \cdot \eta_\delta(I)$, we have:*

$$\Pr_{b \hookleftarrow D_{I,\sigma}}\left[\|b^{-1}\| \geq \frac{t}{\sigma\sqrt{n/2}}\right] \leq \Pr_{b \hookleftarrow D_{I,\sigma}}\left[\sigma_n(b) \leq \frac{\sigma\sqrt{n/2}}{t}\right] \leq \frac{1+\delta}{1-\delta}\frac{n\sqrt{2\pi e}}{t}.$$

3   GGH and Its Re-randomization Procedure

In this section, we recall the Garg et al. scheme from [9], and its related hard problems. We then discuss the re-randomization step of the scheme and explain what should be expected from it, in terms of security. This security requirement is unclear in [9] and [1]. We formulate it precisely. This will drive our re-randomization design in the following sections.

3.1   The GGH Scheme

We recall the GGH scheme in Figure 1. We present it here in a slightly more general form than [9]: we leave as a parameter the distribution χ_k of the re-randomization coefficients ρ_j for a level-k encoding (for any $k \leq \kappa$). In the original GGH scheme, we have $\chi_k = D_{\mathbb{Z}, \sigma_k^*}$ for some σ_k^*'s, i.e., the ρ_j's are integers sampled from a discrete Gaussian distribution. Looking ahead, in Section 5, we analyze a more efficient variant, in which $\chi_k = D_{R, \sigma_k^*}$, so that the ρ_j's belong to R.

The aim of isZero is to test whether the input $u = [c/z^\kappa]_q$ is a level-κ encoding of 0 or not, i.e., whether $c = g \cdot r$ for some $r \in R$. The following conditions ensure correctness of isZero, when $\chi_k = D_{\mathbb{Z}, \sigma_k^*}$ (for all $k \leq \kappa$): the first one implies that false negatives do not exist (if u is level-κ encoding of 0, then isZero(u) returns 1), whereas the second one implies that false positives occur with negligible probability.

$$q > \max((n\ell_{g^{-1}})^8, ((m_r + 1) \cdot n\sigma_1^*\sigma')^{8\kappa}) \tag{1}$$
$$q > (2n\sigma)^4. \tag{2}$$

The aim of ext is to extract a quantity from its input $u = [c/z^\kappa]_q$ that depends only on the encoded value $[c]_g$, but not on the randomizers. To avoid trivial solutions, one requires that this extracted value has min-entropy $\geq 2\lambda$ (if that is the

- **Instance generation** $\mathsf{InstGen}(1^\lambda, 1^\kappa)$: Given security parameter λ and multilinearity parameter κ, determine scheme parameters n, q, m_r, σ, σ', $\ell_{g^{-1}}$, ℓ, based on the scheme analysis. Then proceed as follows:
  - Sample $g \leftarrow D_{R,\sigma}$ until $\|g^{-1}\| \le \ell_{g^{-1}}$ and $\mathcal{I} = \langle g \rangle$ is a prime ideal. Define encoding domain $R_g = R/\langle g \rangle$.
  - Sample $z \leftarrow U(R_q)$.
  - Sample a level-1 encoding of 1: set $y = [a \cdot z^{-1}]_q$ with $a \leftarrow D_{1+I,\sigma'}$.
  - For $k \le \kappa$, sample m_r level-k encodings of 0: set $x_j^{(k)} = [b_j^{(k)} \cdot z^{-k}]_q$ with $b_j^{(k)} \leftarrow D_{I,\sigma'}$ for all $j \le m_r$.
    (Note that $a = 1 + gr_y$ and $b_j^{(k)} = gr_j^{(k)}$ for some $r_y, r_j^{(k)} \in R$.)
  - Sample $h \leftarrow D_{R,\sqrt{q}}$ and define the zero-testing parameter $p_{zt} = [\frac{h}{g} z^\kappa]_q \in R_q$.
  - Return public parameters $\mathrm{par} = (n, q, y, \{x_j^{(k)}\}_{j \le m_r, k \le \kappa})$ and p_{zt}.
- **Level-0 sampler** $\mathsf{samp}(\mathrm{par})$: Sample $e \leftarrow D_{R,\sigma'}$ and return e.
  (Note that $e = e_L + ge_H$ for some unique coset representative $e_L \in \mathcal{P}_g$, and some $e_H \in R$.)
- **Level-k encoding** $\mathsf{enc}_k(\mathrm{par}, e)$: Given level-0 encoding $e \in R$ and parameters par:
  - Encode e at level k: Compute $u' = [e \cdot y^k]_q$.
  - Re-randomize: Sample $\rho_j \leftarrow \chi_k$ for $j \le m_r$ and return $u = [u' + \sum_{j=1}^{m_r} \rho_j x_j^{(k)}]_q$.
    (Note that $u' = [c'/z^k]_q$ with $c' \in e_L + I$ and $u = [(c' + \sum_j \rho_j b_j^{(k)})/z^k]_q$.)
- **Adding encodings** add: Given level-k encodings $u_1 = [c_1/z^k]_q$ and $u_2 = [c_2/z^k]_q$:
  - Return $u = [u_1 + u_2]_q$, a level-k encoding of $[c_1 + c_2]_g$.
- **Multiplying encodings** mult: Given level-k_1 encoding $u_1 = [c_1/z^{k_1}]_q$ and a level-k_2 encoding $u_2 = [c_2/z^{k_2}]_q$:
  - Return $u = [u_1 \cdot u_2]_q$, a level-$(k_1 + k_2)$ encoding of $[c_1 \cdot c_2]_g$.
- **Zero testing at level κ** $\mathsf{isZero}(\mathrm{par}, p_{zt}, u)$: Given a level-$\kappa$ encoding $u = [c/z^\kappa]_q$, return 1 if $\|[p_{zt} u]_q\|_\infty < q^{3/4}$ and 0 else.
  (Note that $[p_{zt} \cdot u]_q = [hc/g]_q$.)
- **Extraction at level κ** $\mathsf{ext}(\mathrm{par}, p_{zt}, u)$: Given a level-$\kappa$ encoding $u = [c/z^\kappa]_q$, return $v = \mathrm{MSB}_\ell([p_{zt} \cdot u]_q)$.
  (Note that if $c = [c]_g + gr$ for some $r \in R$, then $v = \mathrm{MSB}_\ell(\frac{h}{g}([c]_g + gr)) = \mathrm{MSB}_\ell(\frac{h}{g}[c]_g + hr)$, which is equal to $\mathrm{MSB}_\ell(\frac{h}{g}[c]_g)$, with probability $1 - \lambda^{-\omega(1)}$.)

Fig. 1. The GGH graded encoding scheme

case, then one can obtain a uniform distribution on $\{0,1\}^\lambda$, using a strong randomness extractor). The following two inequalities guarantee these properties, when $\chi_k = D_{\mathbb{Z}, \sigma_k^*}$ (for all k). The first one implies that $\varepsilon_{ext} = \Pr[\mathsf{ext}(u) \ne \mathsf{ext}(u')]$ is negligible, when u and u' encode the same value $[c]_g$, whereas the second one provides large min-entropy.

$$1/4 \log q - \log(\frac{2n}{\varepsilon_{ext}}) \ge \ell \ge \log(\frac{n\sigma}{8}). \tag{3}$$

3.2 The GDDH, GCDH and Ext-GCDH Problems

The computational problems that are required to be hard for the GGH scheme depend on the application. Here we recall the definitions of the Graded Decisional and Computational Diffie-Hellman (GDDH and GCDH) problems from [9]. We introduce another natural variant that we call the Extraction Graded Computational Diffie-Hellman (Ext-GCDH), in which the goal is to compute the extracted string of a Diffie-Hellman encoding.

Definition 3.1 (GCDH/Ext-GCDH/GDDH). *The problems GCDH, Ext-GCDH and GDDH are defined as follows with respect to experiment of Figure 2:*[1]

- κ-***graded CDH problem (GCDH):*** *On inputs* par, p_{zt} *and the* u_i*'s of Step 2, output a level-*κ *encoding of* $\prod_{i \geq 0} e_i + \mathcal{I}$*, i.e.,* $w \in R_q$ *such that* $\|[p_{zt}(v_C - w)]_q\| \leq q^{3/4}$.
- ***Extraction*** κ-***graded CDH problem (Ext-GCDH):*** *On inputs* par, p_{zt} *and the* u_i*'s of Step 2, output the extracted string for a level-*κ *encoding of* $\prod_{i \geq 0} e_i + \mathcal{I}$*, i.e.,* $w = \text{ext}(\text{par}, p_{zt}, v_C) = MSB_\ell([p_{zt} \cdot v_C]_q)$.
- κ-***graded DDH problem (GDDH):*** *Distinguish between* v_D *and* v_R*, i.e., between the distributions* $\mathcal{D}_{DDH} = \{\text{par}, p_{zt}, (u_i)_{0 \leq i \leq \kappa}, v_D\}$ *and* $\mathcal{D}_R = \{\text{par}, p_{zt}, (u_i)_{0 \leq i \leq \kappa}, v_R\}$.

Given parameters $\lambda, n, q, m_r, \kappa, \sigma'$, proceed as follows:

1. Run $\text{InstGen}(1^n, 1^\kappa)$ to get
   $\text{par} = (n, q, y, \{x_j^{(k)}\}_{j,k})$ and p_{zt}.
2. For $i = 0, \ldots, \kappa$:
   - Sample $e_i \leftarrow D_{R,\sigma'}$, $f_i \leftarrow D_{R,\sigma'}$,
   - Set $u_i = [e_i \cdot y + \sum_j \rho_{ij} x_j]_q$
     with $\rho_{ij} \leftarrow \chi_1$ for all j.
3. Set $u^* = \left[\prod_{i=1}^\kappa u_i\right]_q$.
4. Set $v_C = [e_0 u^*]_q$.
5. Sample $\rho_j \leftarrow \chi_\kappa$ for all j,
   set $v_D = [e_0 u^* + \sum_j \rho_j x_j^{(\kappa)}]_q$.
6. Set $v_R = [f_0 u^* + \sum_j \rho_j x_j^{(\kappa)}]_q$.

Given parameters $\lambda, n, q, m_r, \kappa, (\sigma_k^*)_{k \leq \kappa}$, proceed as follows:

1. Run $\text{InstGen}(1^n, 1^\kappa)$ to get
   $\text{par} = (n, q, y, \{x_j^{(k)}\}_{j,k})$ and p_{zt}.
   Write $x_j^{(k)} = [b_j^{(k)} z^{-k}]_q$ and
   $B^{(k)} = [b_1^{(k)}, \cdots, b_{m_r}^{(k)}] \in \mathcal{I}^{m_r}$.
2. For $i = 0, \ldots, \kappa$:
   - Sample $e_i \leftarrow U(R_g)$, $f_i \leftarrow U(R_g)$,
   - Set $u_i = [c_i z^{-1}]_q \leftarrow D_{can}^{(1)}(e_i)$
     with $c_i \leftarrow D_{\mathcal{I}+e_i, \sigma_1^*(B^{(1)})^T}$.
3. Set $u^* = \left[\prod_{i=1}^\kappa u_i\right]_q$.
4. Set $v_C = [e_0 u^*]_q$.
5. Set $v_D = [c_D \cdot z^{-\kappa}]_q \leftarrow D_{can}^{(\kappa)}(\prod_{i=0}^\kappa e_i)$,
   with $c_D \leftarrow D_{\mathcal{I}+\prod_{i=0}^\kappa e_i, \sigma_\kappa^*(B^{(\kappa)})^T}$.
6. Set $v_R = [c_R z^{-\kappa}]_q \leftarrow D_{can}^{(\kappa)}(f_0 \prod_{i=1}^\kappa e_i)$,
   with $c_R \leftarrow D_{\mathcal{I}+f_0 \prod_{i=1}^\kappa e_i, \sigma_\kappa^*(B^{(\kappa)})^T}$.

Fig. 2. The GGH security experiment   **Fig. 3.** The canonical security experiment

---

[1] Note that we use a slightly different process from [9], by adding a re-randomization to the element v_D. Without it, there exists a "division attack" against GDDH.

Ext-GCDH is at least as hard as GDDH: given v_x with $x \in \{\text{DDH}, \text{R}\}$, use the Ext-GCDH oracle to compute $w = \text{ext}(\text{par}, p_{zt}, v_C)$. Nevertheless, we show (see full version) that it suffices for instantiating, in the random oracle model, at least some of the interesting applications of graded encoding schemes, at a higher efficiency than the instantiations of [9] based on GDDH.

3.3 The GGH Re-randomization Security Requirement

The encoding re-randomization step in the GGH scheme is necessary for the hardness of the problems above. In [9], Garg et al. imposed the informal requirement that the re-randomization process "erases" the structure of the input encoding, while preserving the encoded coset. In setting parameters, they interpreted this requirement in the following natural way.

Definition 3.2 (Strong re-randomization security requirement). *Let $u' = [c'/z^k]_q$, with $c' = e_L + gr'$ be a fixed level-k encoding of $e_L \in R_g$, and let $u = [u' + \sum_j \rho_j x_k^{(j)}]_q = [c/z^k]_q$ with $c = e_L + gr$ and $r = r' + \sum_j \rho_j r_j^{(k)}$ be the re-randomized encoding, with $\rho_j \hookleftarrow \chi_k$ for $j \leq m_r$. Let $D_u^{(k)}(e_L, r')$ denote the distribution of u (over the randomness of ρ_j's), parameterized by (e_L, r') and let $D_{\text{can}}^{(k)}(e_L)$ denote some canonical distribution, parameterized by e_L, that is independent of r'. Then we say that the* strong *re-randomization security requirement is satisfied at level k with respect to $D_{\text{can}}^{(k)}(e_L)$ and encoding norm $\gamma^{(k)}$ if $\Delta(D_u^{(k)}(e_L, r'), D_{\text{can}}^{(k)}(e_L)) \leq 2^{-\lambda}$ for any $u' = [c'/z^k]_q$ with $\|c'\| \leq \gamma^{(k)}$.*

The authors of [9] argued that with $\chi_k = D_{\mathbb{Z}, \sigma_k^*}$ (for $k \leq \kappa$) and a "drowning ratio" $\sigma_k^*/\|r'\|$ exponential in security parameter λ, the distribution $D_u^{(k)}(e_L, r')$ is within negligible statistical distance to the canonical distribution $D_{\text{can}}^{(k)}(e_L) = [D_{\mathcal{I}+e_L, \sigma_k^*(B^{(k)})^T} \cdot z^{-k}]_q$. This requirement may be stronger than needed. Accordingly, we now clarify the desired goal.

3.4 Our Security Goal: Canonical Assumptions

We formalize a re-randomization security goal to capture a security guarantee against "statistical correlation" attacks on GCDH/Ext-GCDH/GDDH. We define *canonical variants* cGCDH/Ext-cGCDH/cGDDH of GCDH/Ext-GCDH/GDDH, using Figure 3. The main difference with Figure 2 is that the encodings $u_i = [c_i/z]_q$ of the hidden elements e_i, are sampled from a canonical distribution $D_{\text{can}}^{(1)}(e_i)$, parameterized by e_i, whose statistical parameters are independent of the encoded coset e_i, so that it is "by construction" immune against statistical correlation attacks. In particular, in the canonical distribution $D_{\text{can}}^{(1)}(e_i)$ that we use, c_i is sampled from a discrete Gaussian distribution $D_{\mathcal{I}+e_i, \sigma_1^*(B^{(1)})^T}$ (over the choice of the randomization, for a fixed e_i), whose statistical parameters such as center (namely 0) and deviation matrix $\sigma_1^*(B^{(1)})^T$ are independent of e_i. The only dependence this distribution has on the encoded element e_i is via its support $\mathcal{I} + e_i$.

We believe the canonical problems are cleaner and more natural than the non-canonical variants, since they decouple the re-randomization aspect from the rest of the computational problem. As a further simplification, the canonical variants also have their level-0 elements e_i distributed uniformly on R_g (rather than as reductions mod $\mathcal{I}$ of Gaussian samples).

Definition 3.3 (cGCDH/Ext-cGCDH/cGDDH). *The canonical problems cGCDH, Ext-cGCDH and cGDDH are defined as follows with respect to the experiment of Figure 3 and canonical encoding distribution $D_{can}^{(k)}(e)$ (parameterized by encoding level k and encoded element e):*

- **cGCDH:** *On inputs* par, p_{zt} *and the* u_i*'s, output* $w \in R_q$ *such that* $\|[p_{zt}(v_C - w)]_q\| \leq q^{3/4}$.
- **Ext-cGCDH:** *On inputs* par, p_{zt} *and the* u_i*'s, output:* $w = \text{ext}(\text{par}, p_{zt}, v_C) = MSB_\ell([p_{zt} \cdot v_C]_q)$.
- **cGDDH:** *Distinguish between* $\mathcal{D}_{DDH} = \{\text{par}, p_{zt}, (u_i)_{0 \leq i \leq \kappa}, v_D\}$ *and* $\mathcal{D}_R = \{\text{par}, p_{zt}, (u_i)_{0 \leq i \leq \kappa}, v_R\}$.

REMARK. One could consider alternative definitions of natural canonical encoding distributions besides the one we adopt here (see full paper for examples for which our results also apply).

Given the canonical problems on whose hardness we wish to rely, our security goal for re-randomization with respect to the GCDH (resp. Ext-GCDH/GDDH) problems can now be easily formulated: hardness of the latter should be implied by hardness of the former.

Definition 3.4 (Re-randomization security goal). *We say that the re-randomization security goal is satisfied with respect to GCDH (resp. Ext-GCDH/GDDH) if any adversary against GCDH (resp. Ext-GCDH/ GDDH) with run-time $T = O(2^\lambda)$ and advantage $\varepsilon = \Omega(2^{-\lambda})$ can be used to construct an adversary against cGCDH (resp. Ext-cGCDH/cGDDH) with run-time $T' = \text{poly}(T, \lambda)$ and advantage $\varepsilon' = \Omega(\text{poly}(\varepsilon, \lambda))$.*

4 Polynomial Drowning via Rényi Divergence

In this section, we present our first result towards our improvement of the GGH scheme re-randomization. It shows that one may reduce the re-randomization "drowning" ratio $\sigma_k^*/\|r'\|$ from exponential to polynomial in the security parameter λ. Although the SD between the re-randomized encoding distribution D_1 (essentially a discrete Gaussian with an added offset vector r') and the desired canonical encoding distribution D_2 (a discrete Gaussian without an added offset vector) is then non-negligible, we show that these encoding distributions are still sufficiently close with respect to an alternative closeness measure to the SD, in the sense that switching between them preserves the success probability of any search problem adversary receiving these encodings as input, up to a small multiplicative constant. This allows us to show that our re-randomization goal is satisfied for the search problems GCDH and Ext-GCDH.

Technically, the closeness measure we study is the *Rényi divergence* $R(D_1 \| D_2)$ between the distributions D_1 and D_2, defined as the expected value of $D_1(r)/D_2(r)$ over the randomness of r sampled from D_1 (for brevity we will call $R(D_1 \| D_2)$ the RD between D_1 and D_2). Intuitively, the RD is an alternative to SD as measure of distribution closeness, where we replace the *difference* between the distributions in SD, by the *ratio* of the distributions in RD. Accordingly, one may hope RD to have analogous properties to SD, where addition in the property of SD is replaced by multiplication in the analogous property of RD. Remarkably, this holds true in some sense, and we explore some of this below. In particular, a very important property of the SD is that for any two distributions D_1, D_2 on space X, and any event $E \subseteq X$, we have $D_1(E) \geq D_2(E) - \Delta(D_1, D_2)$. Lyubashevsky et al. [13] observed an analogous property of the RD that follows roughly the above intuition: $D_1(E) \geq D_2(E)^2 / R(D_1 \| D_2)$. The latter property implies that as long as $R(D_1 \| D_2)$ is bounded as $\mathrm{poly}(\lambda)$, any event of non-negligible probability $D_2(E)$ under D_2 will also have non-negligible probability $D_1(E)$ under D_1. We show that for our offset discrete Gaussian distributions D_1, D_2 above, we have $R(D_1 \| D_2) = O(\mathrm{poly}(\lambda))$, if $\sigma_k^* / \|r'\| = \Omega(\mathrm{poly}(\lambda))$, as required for our re-randomization security goal.

The Rényi divergence (RD) and its properties. We review the RD [18,8] and some of its properties. For convenience, our definition of the RD is the exponential of the usual definition used in information theory [8], and coincides with a discrete version of the quantity R defined for continuous density functions in [13, Claim 5.11].

For any two discrete probability distributions P and Q such that $\mathrm{Supp}(P) \subseteq \mathrm{Supp}(Q)$ over a domain X and $\alpha > 1$, we define the Rényi Divergence of orders α and ∞ by

$$R_\alpha(P \| Q) = \left(\sum_{x \in X} \frac{P(x)^\alpha}{Q(x)^{\alpha-1}} \right)^{\frac{1}{\alpha-1}} \quad \text{and} \quad R_\infty(P \| Q) = \max_{x \in X} \frac{P(x)}{Q(x)},$$

with the convention that the fraction is zero when both numerator and denominator are zero. A convenient choice for computations (as also used in [13]) is $\alpha = 2$, in which case we omit α. Note that $R_\alpha(P \| Q)^{\alpha-1} = \sum_x P(x) \cdot (P(x)/Q(x))^{\alpha-1} \leq R_\infty(P \| Q)^{\alpha-1}$. We list several properties of the RD that can be considered the multiplicative analogues of those of the SD. The following lemma is proven in the full version.

Lemma 4.1. *Let* P_1, P_2, P_3 *and* Q_1, Q_2, Q_3 *denote discrete distributions on a domain* X *and let* $\alpha \in (1, \infty]$. *Then the following properties hold:*

- **Log. Positivity:** $R_\alpha(P_1 \| Q_1) \geq R_\alpha(P_1 \| P_1) = 1$.
- **Data Processing Inequality:** $R_\alpha(P_1^f \| Q_1^f) \leq R_\alpha(P_1 \| Q_1)$ *for any function* f, *where* P_1^f *(resp.* Q_1^f*) denotes the distribution of* $f(y)$ *induced by sampling* $y \hookleftarrow P_1$ *(resp.* $y \hookleftarrow Q_1$*).*
- **Multiplicativity:** *Let* P *and* Q *denote any two distributions of a pair of random variables* (Y_1, Y_2) *on* $X \times X$. *For* $i \in \{1, 2\}$, *assume* P_i *(resp.* Q_i*) is the marginal distribution of* Y_i *under* P *(resp.* Q*), and let* $P_{2|1}(\cdot|y_1)$ *(resp.*

$Q_{2|1}(\cdot|y_1))$ denote the conditional distribution of Y_2 given that $Y_1 = y_1$. Then we have:

- $R_\alpha(P\|Q) = R_\alpha(P_1\|Q_1) \cdot R_\alpha(P_2\|Q_2)$ if Y_1 and Y_2 are independent.
- $R_\alpha(P\|Q) \le R_\infty(P_1\|Q_1) \cdot \max_{y_1 \in X} R_\alpha(P_{2|1}(\cdot|y_1)\|Q_{2|1}(\cdot|y_1))$.

- **Weak Triangle Inequality:** We have:

$$R_\alpha(P_1\|P_3) \le \begin{cases} R_\alpha(P_1\|P_2) \cdot R_\infty(P_2\|P_3), \\ R_\infty(P_1\|P_2)^{\frac{\alpha}{\alpha-1}} \cdot R_\alpha(P_2\|P_3). \end{cases}$$

- R_∞ **Triangle Inequality:** If $R_\infty(P_1\|P_2)$ and $R_\infty(P_2\|P_3)$ are defined, then $R_\infty(P_1\|P_3) \le R_\infty(P_1\|P_2) \cdot R_\infty(P_2\|P_3)$.
- **Probability Preservation:** Let $A \subseteq X$ be an arbitrary event. Then $Q_1(A) \ge P_1(A)^{\frac{\alpha}{\alpha-1}}/R_\alpha(P_1\|Q_1)$.

We note that the RD does not satisfy the (multiplicative) triangle inequality $R(P_1\|P_3) \le R(P_1\|P_2) \cdot R(P_2\|P_3)$ in general (see [8]), but a weaker inequality holds if one of the pairs of distributions has a bounded R_∞ divergence, as shown above. We also observe that R_∞ *does* satisfy the triangle inequality.

For our re-randomization application, we are interested in the RD between two discrete Gaussians with the same deviation matrix S, that differ by some fixed offset vector d. The following result (proved in the full version) shows that their RD is $O(1)$ if $\sigma_n(S)/\|d\| = \Omega(1)$.

Lemma 4.2. *For any n-dimensional lattice Λ in $\mathbb{R}^n$ and matrix S, let P be the distribution $D_{\Lambda,S,w}$ and Q be the distribution $D_{\Lambda,S,z}$ for some fixed $w, z \in \mathbb{R}^n$. If $w, z \in \Lambda$, let $\varepsilon = 0$. Otherwise, fix $\varepsilon \in (0,1)$ and assume that $\sigma_n(S) \ge \eta_\varepsilon(\Lambda)$. Then $R(P\|Q) \le \left(\frac{1+\varepsilon}{1-\varepsilon}\right)^2 \cdot \exp\left(2\pi\|w-z\|^2/\sigma_n(S)^2\right)$.*

5   A Discrete Gaussian Leftover Hash Lemma over R

In this section, we present our second main result for improving the GGH scheme re-randomization algorithm. Recall that the GGH algorithm re-randomizes a level-k encoding u' into $u = [u' + \sum_{j=1}^{m_r} \rho_j x_j^{(k)}]_q$, where the ρ_j's are sampled from $\chi_1 = D_{\mathbb{Z},\sigma_1^*}$ and $x_j^{(k)} = [b_j^{(k)}/z^k]_q = [gr_j^{(k)}/z^k]_q$. To show that the distribution of $\sum_{j=1}^{m_r} \rho_j b_j^{(k)}$ is close to a discrete Gaussian over $\mathcal{I}$, they then apply the discrete Gaussian LHL from [1, Th. 3], using $m_r = \Omega(n \log n)$ fixed elements $b_j^{(k)} \in \mathcal{I}$ that are published obliviously as randomizers "inside" the public zero-encodings $x_j^{(k)}$. We show that it suffices to sample 2 randomizers as elements of the full n-dimensional ring R, rather than just from $\mathbb{Z}$, i.e., we set $\chi_1 = D_{R,\sigma_1^*}$. Our proof follows the same high-level steps as the proof of [1, Th. 3], but differs technically, as explained in the introduction.

For a fixed $X = (x_1, x_2) \in R^2$, we define the distribution $\widetilde{\mathcal{E}}_{X,s} = x_1 D_{R,s} + x_2 D_{R,s}$ as the distribution induced by sampling $\boldsymbol{u} = (u_1, u_2) \in R^2$ from a discrete spherical Gaussian with parameter s, and outputting $y = x_1 u_1 + x_2 u_2$. We prove the following result on $\widetilde{\mathcal{E}}_{X,s}$.

Theorem 5.1. *Let* $R = \mathbb{Z}[x]/\langle x^n + 1 \rangle$ *with* n *a power of* 2 *and* $\mathcal{I} = \langle g \rangle \subseteq R$, *for some* $g \in R$. *Fix* $\varepsilon \in (0, 1/3)$, $X = (x_1, x_2) \in \mathcal{I}^2$ *and* $s > 0$ *satisfying the conditions*

- **Column span:** $X \cdot R^2 = \mathcal{I}$.
- **Smoothing:** $s \geq \max(\|g^{-1}x_1\|_\infty, \|g^{-1}x_2\|_\infty) \cdot n \cdot \sqrt{\frac{2}{\pi} \log(2n(1 + 1/\varepsilon))}$.

Then, for all $x \in \mathcal{I}$ *we have* $\widetilde{\mathcal{E}}_{X,s}(x) \in [\frac{1-\varepsilon}{1+\varepsilon}, 1] \cdot D_{\mathcal{I}, sX^T}(x)$. *In particular, we have* $\Delta(\widetilde{\mathcal{E}}_{X,s}, D_{\mathcal{I}, sX^T}) \leq 2\varepsilon$. *Finally, if* $s \cdot \sigma_n(g^{-1}) \geq 7n^{1.5} \ln^{1.5}(n)$,[2] $x_1, x_2 \hookleftarrow D_{\mathcal{I}, s}$ *and* n *grows to infinity, then the first condition holds with probability* $\Omega(1)$.

We prove this result for $g = 1$, and then we generalize to general g. First, we consider the column span condition.

Lemma 5.2 (Adapted from [23, Le. 4.2 and Le. 4.4]). *Let* $S \in \mathbb{R}^{n \times n}$, *and* $\sigma_n(S) \geq 7n^{1.5} \ln^{1.5}(n)$. *For* n *going to infinity, we have* $\Pr_{x_1, x_2 \hookleftarrow D_{R,S}}[X \cdot R^2 = R] \geq \Omega(1)$.

Let $A_X \subseteq \{(v_1, v_2) \in R^2 : x_1 v_1 + x_2 v_2 = 0\}$ be the 1-dimensional R-module of vectors orthogonal to X. We view A_X as an n-dimensional lattice in $\mathbb{Z}^{2n}$, via the polynomial-to-coefficient-vector mapping.

Lemma 5.3 (Adapted from [1, Le. 10]). *Fix* X *such that* $X \cdot R^2 = R$ *and* A_X *as above. If* $s \geq \eta_\varepsilon(A_X)$, *then* $\widetilde{\mathcal{E}}_{X,s}(z) \in [\frac{1-\varepsilon}{1+\varepsilon}, 1] \cdot D_{\mathbb{Z}^n, sX^T}(z)$ *for any* $z \in R$.

We now study the quantity $\eta_\varepsilon(A_X)$. First, we show that all successive Minkowski minima of A_X are equal. This property is inherited from the "equal minima property" of ideal lattices in R.

Lemma 5.4. *Let* X *and* A_X *be as above. Then* $\lambda_1(A_X) = \cdots = \lambda_n(A_X)$.

Lemma 5.5. *Let* X *and* A_X *be as above. Let* $s \geq \max(\|x_1\|_\infty, \|x_2\|_\infty)$. *Then we have:* $\eta_\varepsilon(A_X) \leq sn \cdot \sqrt{\frac{2}{\pi} \log(2n(1 + 1/\varepsilon))}$.

Combining the above lemmas, we get Theorem 5.1 for $g = 1$. The general case is proved as follows. The injective map $y \mapsto g \cdot y$ on R takes the distribution $\widetilde{\mathcal{E}}_{\overline{X},s}$ with $\overline{X} = g^{-1} \cdot X$ to the distribution $\widetilde{\mathcal{E}}_{X,s}$, while it takes $D_{R, s\overline{X}^T}$ to $D_{\mathcal{I}, sX^T}$, with $I = \langle g \rangle$. The conditions $X \cdot R^2 = \mathcal{I}$ and $\overline{X} \cdot R^2 = R$ are equivalent. The smoothing condition is satisfied for $\overline{X}$ by the choice of s. Thus we can apply Theorem 5.1 with $g = 1$ to $\widetilde{\mathcal{E}}_{\overline{X},s}$, and conclude by applying the mapping M_g to get the general case of Theorem 5.1. For the very last statement of Theorem 5.1, it suffices to observe that $D_{\mathcal{I}, s} = g \cdot D_{R, s(g^{-1})^T}$.[3] $\square$

---

[2] By abuse of notation, we identify $g^{-1} \in K$ with the linear map over $\mathbb{Q}^n$ obtained by applying the polynomial-to-coefficient-vector mapping to the map $r \mapsto g^{-1}r$.

[3] With the same abuse of notation as in the previous footnote, for the term $(g^{-1})^T$.

6   Our Improved GGH Grading Scheme: GGHLite

We are now ready to describe our simpler and more efficient variant of the GGH grading scheme, that we call GGHLite. The scheme is summarized in Figure 4. The modifications from the original GGH scheme consist in:

- Using $m_r = 2$ re-randomization elements x_1, x_2 in the public key, sampling the randomizers ρ_1, ρ_2 from a discrete Gaussian D_{R,σ_1^*} over the whole ring R (rather than from $\mathbb{Z}$), applying our algebraic ring variant of the LHL from Section 5.
- Saving an exponential factor $\approx 2^\lambda$ in the re-randomization parameter σ_1^* by applying the RD bounds from Section 4.

In terms of re-randomization security requirement, we relax the strong SD-based requirement on the original GGH scheme to the following weaker RD-based requirement on GGHLite.

Definition 6.1 (Weak re-randomization security requirement). *Using the notations of Definition 3.2, we say that the* weak *re-randomization security requirement is satisfied at level k with respect to $D_{\mathrm{can}}^{(k)}(e_L)$ and encoding norm $\gamma^{(k)}$ if $R(D_u^{(k)}(e_L, r') \| D_{\mathrm{can}}^{(k)}(e_L)) = O(\mathrm{poly}(\lambda))$ for any $u' = [c'/z^k]_q$ such that $\|c'\| \le \gamma^{(k)}$.*

We summarize GGHLite in Figure 4, which only shows the algorithms differing from those in the GGH scheme of Figure 1.

- **Instance generation** $\mathsf{InstGen}(1^\lambda, 1^\kappa)$: Given security parameter λ and multilinearity parameter κ, determine scheme parameters $n, q, m_r = 2, \sigma, \sigma', \ell_{g^{-1}}, \ell_b, \ell$, based on the scheme analysis. Then proceed as follows:
  - Sample $g \hookleftarrow D_{R,\sigma}$ until $\|g^{-1}\| \le \ell_{g^{-1}}$ and $\mathcal{I} = \langle g \rangle$ is a prime ideal.
  - Sample $z \hookleftarrow U(R_q)$.
  - Sample a level-1 encoding of 1: $y = [a \cdot z^{-1}]_q$ with $a \hookleftarrow D_{1+I,\sigma'}$.
  - For $k \le \kappa$:
    * Sample $B^{(k)} = (b_1^{(k)}, b_2^{(k)})$ from $(D_{I,\sigma'})^2$. If $\langle b_1^{(k)}, b_2^{(k)} \rangle \ne \mathcal{I}$, or $\sigma_n(\mathrm{rot}(B^{(k)})) < \ell_b$, then re-sample.
    * Define level-k encodings of 0: $x_1^{(k)} = [b_1^{(k)} \cdot z^{-k}]_q$, $x_2^{(k)} = [b_2^{(k)} \cdot z^{-k}]_q$.
  - Sample $h \hookleftarrow D_{R,\sqrt{q}}$ and define the zero-testing parameter $p_{zt} = [\frac{h}{g} z^\kappa]_q \in R_q$.
  - Return public parameters $\mathrm{par} = (n, q, y, \{(x_1^{(k)}, x_2^{(k)})\}_{k \le \kappa})$ and p_{zt}.
- **Level-k encoding** $\mathsf{enc}_k(\mathrm{par}, e)$: Given level-0 encoding $e \in R$ and parameters par:
  - Encode e at level k: Compute $u' = [e \cdot y^k]_q$.
  - Return $u = [(u' + \rho_1 \cdot x_1^{(k)} + \rho_2 \cdot x_2^{(k)})]_q$, with $\rho_1, \rho_2 \hookleftarrow D_{R,\sigma_k^*}$.

Fig. 4. The new algorithms of our GGHLite scheme

Choice of σ, $\ell_{g^{-1}}$ *and* σ', ℓ_b. The upper bound $\ell_{g^{-1}}$ on $\|g^{-1}\|$ in the rejection test of InstGen can be chosen as small as possible while keeping the rejection probability p_g bounded from 1. According to Lemma 2.3 with $t = 2\sqrt{2\pi e}np_g^{-1}$ and $\delta = 1/3$, one can choose

$$\ell_{g^{-1}} = 4\sqrt{\pi e n}/(p_g\sigma) \text{ and } \sigma \geq 2n\sqrt{e\ln(8n)/\pi}/p_g, \tag{4}$$

to achieve $p_g < 1$. Note that the same choices apply to the GGH scheme: here we have a rigorous bound on p_g instead of the heuristic arguments for estimating in $\|g^{-1}\|$ in [9]; however, as in [9], we do not have a rigorous bound on the probability that $\mathcal{I}$ is prime conditioned on this choice.

Let p_b be the rejection probability for the lower bound ℓ_b on $\sigma_n(B^{(k)})$ in the rejection test of InstGen. To keep p_b away from 1, we use that $\sigma_n(B^{(k)})^2 = \min_{u \in K, \|u\|=1} \sum_{i=1,2} \|u \cdot b_i^{(k)}\|^2 \geq \sum_{i=1,2} \sigma_n(b_i^{(k)})^2$. Applying Lemma 2.3 with $t = 2\sqrt{2\pi e}np_b^{-1}$ and $\delta = 1/3$, we get that $\sigma_n(b_i^{(k)}) > \frac{p_b}{8\sqrt{\pi e n}} \cdot \sigma'$, except with probability $\leq p_b$ for $i \in \{1,2\}$ if $\sigma' \geq \frac{t}{\sqrt{2\pi}}\eta_{1/3}(\mathcal{I})$, where $\eta_{1/3}(\mathcal{I}) \leq \sqrt{\ln(8n)/\pi} \cdot \|g\|$ by Lemma 2.1. Therefore, we can choose

$$\ell_b = \frac{p_b}{2\sqrt{\pi e n}} \cdot \sigma' \text{ and } \sigma' \geq 2n^{1.5}\sigma\sqrt{e\ln(8n)/\pi}/p_b. \tag{5}$$

Zero-testing and extraction correctness. The correctness conditions for zero-testing and correctness remain the same as conditions (2), (3) for the original GGH scheme. The only modification needed is for condition (1), because in GGHLite, $m_r = 2$ and $\rho_j \in R$ so $\|\rho_j b_j^{(1)}\| \leq \sqrt{n}\|\rho_j\|\|b_j^{(1)}\|$. Accordingly, condition (1) is replaced by:

$$q > \max\left((n\ell_{g^{-1}})^8, (3 \cdot n^{1.5}\sigma^*\sigma')^{8\kappa}\right). \tag{6}$$

Security. We state our improved re-randomization security reduction for GGHLite, that works with much smaller parameters than GGH. To our knowledge, it is the first security proof in which the RD is used to replace the SD in a sequence of games, using the RD properties from Section 4 to combine the bounds on changes between games. This allows us to gain the benefits of RD over SD, for both the drowning and smoothing aspects. Namely, with $\varepsilon_d, \varepsilon_\rho, \varepsilon_e$ in Theorem 6.2 set as large as $O(\log \lambda/\kappa)$, our weak security requirement of Definition 6.1 is satisfied (the RD between real and canonical encoding distributions is bounded by the quantity $R = \text{poly}(\lambda)$ in Theorem 6.2), and our re-randomization goal for Ext-GCDH is achieved (whereas the strong requirement of Definition 3.2 is not satisfied).

Theorem 6.2 (Security of GGHLite). *Let* $\varepsilon_d, \varepsilon_\rho, \varepsilon_e \in (0, 1/2)$ *and* $\kappa \leq 2^n$. *Suppose that the following conditions are satisfied for* GGHLite:

– **LHL Smoothing:**

$$\sigma_1^* \geq n^{1.5} \cdot \ell_{g^{-1}} \cdot \sigma \cdot \sqrt{2\log(4n \cdot \varepsilon_\rho^{-1})/\pi}. \tag{7}$$

– **Offset "Drowning:"**

$$\sigma_1^* \geq n^{1.5} \cdot (\sigma')^2 \cdot \sqrt{2\pi\varepsilon_d^{-1}}/\ell_b. \tag{8}$$

– samp **Uniformity Smoothing:**

$$\sigma' \geq \sigma \cdot \sqrt{n \ln(4n \cdot \varepsilon_e^{-1})/\pi}. \tag{9}$$

Then, if A is an adversary against the (non-canonical) Ext-GCDH problem for GGHLite *with run-time T and advantage ε, then A is also an adversary against the canonical problem Ext-cGCDH for* GGHLite *with $T' = T$ and advantage*

$$\varepsilon' \geq (\varepsilon - O(\kappa \cdot 2^{-n}))^2 / R \text{ with } R = 2^{O(\kappa \cdot (\varepsilon_d + \varepsilon_\rho + \varepsilon_e + 2^{-n}))}. \tag{10}$$

In particular, there exist ε_d, ε_e, ε_ρ bounded as $O(\log \lambda/\kappa)$ such that the re-randomization security goal in Definition 3.4 is satisfied by GGHLite *with respect to problem Ext-GCDH.*

7 Parameter Settings

In Table 1, we summarize asymptotic parameters for GGHLite to achieve 2^λ security for the underlying Ext-GCDH problem, assuming the hardness of the canonical Ext-cGCDH problem, and to satisfy the zero-testing/extraction correctness conditions with error probability $\lambda^{-\omega(1)}$. For simplicity, we assume that $\kappa = \omega(1)$. For comparison, we also show the corresponding parameters for GGH. The "Condition" column lists the conditions that determine the corresponding parameter in the case of GGHLite. For security of the canonical Ext-cGCDH problem, we assume (as in [9]) that the best attack is the one described in [9, Se. 6.3.3], whose complexity is dominated by the cost of solving γ-SVP (the

Table 1. Asymptotic parameters

Parameter	GGHLite	GGH[9]	Condition
m_r	2	$\Omega(n \log n)$	LHL: Th. 5.1
σ	$O(n \log n)$	$O(n \log n)$	Eq. (4)
$\ell_{g^{-1}}$	$O(1/\sqrt{n \log n})$	$O(1/\sqrt{n \log n})$	Eq. (4)
$\varepsilon_d, \varepsilon_e, \varepsilon_\rho$	$O(\kappa^{-1})$	$O(2^{-\lambda}\kappa^{-1})$	Eq. (10)
σ'	$\widetilde{O}(n^{2.5})$	$\widetilde{O}(n^{1.5}\sqrt{\lambda})$	Eq. (5)
σ_1^*	$\widetilde{O}(n^{4.5}\sqrt{\log \kappa})$	$\widetilde{O}(2^\lambda n^{4.5}(\lambda + \log \kappa))$	Drown: Eq. (8)
ε_{ext}	$O(\lambda^{-\omega(1)})$	$O(\lambda^{-\omega(1)})$	
q	$\widetilde{O}((n^{8.5}\sqrt{\log \kappa})^{8\kappa})$	$\widetilde{O}((2^\lambda n^8 \lambda^{1.5})^{8\kappa})$	Corr.: Eq. (6)
n	$O(\kappa\lambda \log \lambda)$	$O(\kappa\lambda^2)$	SVP: Eq. (11)
$|\text{enc}|$	$O(\kappa^2\lambda \log^2(\kappa\lambda))$	$O(\kappa^2\lambda^3)$	$O(n \log q)$
$|\text{par}|$	$O(\kappa^3\lambda \log^2(\kappa\lambda))$	$O(\kappa^3\lambda^5 \log(\kappa\lambda))$	$O(m_r\kappa n \log q)$

Shortest lattice Vector Problem with approximation factor γ) for the lattice $\mathcal{I}$, with γ set at $\approx q^{3/8}$ to get a sufficiently short multiple of g. By the lattice reduction "rule of thumb," to make this cost 2^λ, we need to set

$$n = \Omega(\lambda \log q). \tag{11}$$

When $\kappa = \text{poly}(\log \lambda)$, the dimension n, encoding length $|\text{enc}|$ and public parameters length $|\text{par}|$ in our scheme GGHLite are all asymptotically close to optimal, namely quasi-linear in the security parameter λ, versus quadratic (resp. cubic and quintic) in λ for GGH [9]. Thus we expect GGHLite's public parameters and encodings to be orders of magnitudes shorter than GGH for typical $\lambda \approx 100$.

Acknowledgments. We thank Vadim Lyubashevsky for useful discussions. This work has been supported in part by ERC Starting Grant ERC-2013-StG-335086-LATTAC, an Australian Research Fellowship (ARF) from the Australian Research Council (ARC), and ARC Discovery Grants DP0987734 and DP110100628.

References

1. Agrawal, S., Gentry, C., Halevi, S., Sahai, A.: Discrete gaussian leftover hash lemma over infinite domains. In: Sako, K., Sarkar, P. (eds.) ASIACRYPT 2013, Part I. LNCS, vol. 8269, pp. 97–116. Springer, Heidelberg (2013)
2. Alperin-Sheriff, J., Peikert, C.: Circular and KDM security for identity-based encryption. In: Fischlin, M., Buchmann, J., Manulis, M. (eds.) PKC 2012. LNCS, vol. 7293, pp. 334–352. Springer, Heidelberg (2012)
3. Asharov, G., Jain, A., López-Alt, A., Tromer, E., Vaikuntanathan, V., Wichs, D.: Multiparty computation with low communication, computation and interaction via threshold FHE. In: Pointcheval, D., Johansson, T. (eds.) EUROCRYPT 2012. LNCS, vol. 7237, pp. 483–501. Springer, Heidelberg (2012)
4. Banerjee, A., Peikert, C., Rosen, A.: Pseudorandom functions and lattices. In: Pointcheval, D., Johansson, T. (eds.) EUROCRYPT 2012. LNCS, vol. 7237, pp. 719–737. Springer, Heidelberg (2012)
5. Boneh, D., Franklin, M.K.: Identity-based encryption from the Weil pairing. SIAM J. Comput. 32(3), 586–615 (2003)
6. Boneh, D., Silverberg, A.: Applications of multilinear forms to cryptography. Contemporary Mathematics 324, 71–90 (2003)
7. Coron, J.-S., Lepoint, T., Tibouchi, M.: Practical multilinear maps over the integers. In: Canetti, R., Garay, J.A. (eds.) CRYPTO 2013, Part I. LNCS, vol. 8042, pp. 476–493. Springer, Heidelberg (2013)
8. van Erven, T., Harremoës, P.: Rényi divergence and Kullback-Leibler divergence. CoRR, abs/1206.2459 (2012)
9. Garg, S., Gentry, C., Halevi, S.: Candidate multilinear maps from ideal lattices. In: Johansson, T., Nguyen, P.Q. (eds.) EUROCRYPT 2013. LNCS, vol. 7881, pp. 1–17. Springer, Heidelberg (2013)
10. Gentry, C.: Fully homomorphic encryption using ideal lattices. In: Proc. of STOC, pp. 169–178. ACM (2009)
11. Joux, A.: A one round protocol for tripartite Diffie-Hellman. In: Bosma, W. (ed.) ANTS-IV 2000. LNCS, vol. 1838, pp. 385–394. Springer, Heidelberg (2000)

12. Lyubashevsky, V., Micciancio, D.: Generalized compact knapsacks are collision resistant. In: Bugliesi, M., Preneel, B., Sassone, V., Wegener, I. (eds.) ICALP 2006, Part II. LNCS, vol. 4052, pp. 144–155. Springer, Heidelberg (2006)

13. Lyubashevsky, V., Peikert, C., Regev, O.: On ideal lattices and learning with errors over rings. J. ACM 60(6), 43 (2013)

14. Micciancio, D., Goldwasser, S.: Complexity of lattice problems: a cryptographic perspective. Kluwer Academic Press (2002)

15. Micciancio, D., Regev, O.: Worst-case to average-case reductions based on Gaussian measures. SIAM J. Comput 37(1), 267–302 (2007)

16. Papamanthou, C., Tamassia, R., Triandopoulos, N.: Optimal authenticated data structures with multilinear forms. In: Joye, M., Miyaji, A., Otsuka, A. (eds.) Pairing 2010. LNCS, vol. 6487, pp. 246–264. Springer, Heidelberg (2010)

17. Regev, O.: Lecture notes of lattices in computer science, taught at the Computer Science Tel Aviv University, http://www.cims.nyu.edu/~regev/

18. Rényi, A.: On measures of entropy and information. In: Proc. of the Fourth Berkeley Symposium on Math. Statistics and Probability, vol. 1, pp. 547–561 (1961)

19. Rothblum, R.D.: On the circular security of bit-encryption. In: Sahai, A. (ed.) TCC 2013. LNCS, vol. 7785, pp. 579–598. Springer, Heidelberg (2013)

20. Rückert, M., Schröder, D.: Aggregate and verifiably encrypted signatures from multilinear maps without random oracles. In: Park, J.H., Chen, H.-H., Atiquzzaman, M., Lee, C., Kim, T.-h., Yeo, S.-S. (eds.) ISA 2009. LNCS, vol. 5576, pp. 750–759. Springer, Heidelberg (2009)

21. Sakai, R., Ohgishi, K., Kasahara, M.: Cryptosystems based on pairing. In: SCIS (2000)

22. Stehlé, D., Steinfeld, R.: Making NTRU as secure as worst-case problems over ideal. lattices. In: Paterson, K.G. (ed.) EUROCRYPT 2011. LNCS, vol. 6632, pp. 27–47. Springer, Heidelberg (2011)

23. Stehlé, D., Steinfeld, R.: Making NTRUEncrypt and NTRUSign as secure standard worst-case problems over ideal lattices, Full version of [22] (2013), http://perso.ens-lyon.fr/damien.stehle/NTRU.html

Reconsidering Generic Composition

Chanathip Namprempre[1], Phillip Rogaway[2], and Thomas Shrimpton[3]

[1] Dept. of Electrical and Computer Engineering, Thammasat University, Thailand
[2] Dept. of Computer Science, University of California, Davis, USA
[3] Dept. of Computer Science, Portland State University, Portland, USA

Abstract. In the context of authenticated encryption (AE), *generic composition* has referred to the construction of an AE scheme by gluing together a conventional (privacy-only) encryption scheme and a MAC. Since the work of Bellare and Namprempre (2000) and then Krawczyk (2001), the conventional wisdom has become that there are three forms of generic composition, with Encrypt-then-MAC the only one that generically works. However, many caveats to this understanding have surfaced over the years. Here we explore this issue further, showing how this understanding oversimplifies the situation because it ignores the results' sensitivity to definitional choices. When encryption is formalized differently, making it either IV-based or nonce-based, rather than probabilistic, and when the AE goal is likewise changed to take in a nonce, qualitatively different results emerge. We explore these alternatives versions of the generic-composition story. We also evidence the overreaching understanding of prior generic-composition results by pointing out that the Encrypt-then-MAC mechanism of ISO 19772 is completely wrong.

Keywords: authenticated encryption, generic composition, IV-based encryption, nonce-based encryption.

1 Introduction

SPECIFICITY OF GC RESULTS. We revisit the problem of creating an authenticated encryption (AE) scheme by generic composition (GC). This well-known problem was first articulated and studied in a paper by Bellare and Namprempre [4, 5] (henceforth BN). A review of discourse surrounding BN makes clear that, to its readers, the paper's message was that

1. there are **three ways** to glue together a (privacy-only) encryption scheme and a MAC, well summarized by the names Encrypt-and-MAC, Encrypt-then-MAC, and MAC-then-Encrypt;
2. but of these three ways, only **Encrypt-then-MAC** works well: it alone will always be secure when the underlying primitives are sound.

While BN does of course contain such results, we claim that the understanding articulated above is nonetheless off-base, for it makes no reference to the *type* of schemes from which one starts, nor the *type* of scheme one aims to build.

P.Q. Nguyen and E. Oswald (Eds.): EUROCRYPT 2014, LNCS 8441, pp. 257–274, 2014.

type	$\mathcal{E}$ takes	$\mathcal{D}$ takes	summary of basic security requirement
pE	K, M	K, C	privacy: ind = (ciphertexts $\approx \mathcal{E}_K$(rand-bits))
pAE	K, M	K, C	privacy + auth: ind, plus adv can't forge ciphertexts
ivE	K, IV, M	K, IV, C	privacy: $(IV_i \parallel C_i) \approx$ rand-bits
nE	K, N, M	K, N, C	privacy: ind\$ = (ciphertexts $\approx$ rand-bits)
nAE	K, N, A, M	K, N, A, C	privacy + auth: ind\$ + adv can't forge ciphertexts

Fig. 1. Types of AE schemes. The first column gives the name we will use for this type of symmetric encryption scheme. The second and third columns specify the inputs to encryption $\mathcal{E}$ and decryption $\mathcal{D}$: the key K, plaintext M, ciphertext C, initialization vector IV, nonce N, and associated data A. The final column gives a brief description of the main security definition we will use.

The omission is untenable because GC results turn out to depend crucially on these choices—and multiple alternatives are as reasonable as those selected by BN.

TYPES OF ENCRYPTION SCHEMES. What are these definitional choices allegedly so important for GC? See Fig. 1. To begin, in schemes for **probabilistic encryption** (pE), the encryption algorithm is provided a key and plaintext, and, by a process that employs internal coins, it generates a ciphertext [3, 13]. The plaintext must be recoverable from (just) the ciphertext and key. Syntactically, a **probabilistic authenticated-encryption** (pAE) scheme is the same as a pE scheme. But a pAE scheme should also detect *forged* ciphertexts [4–6].

BN focuses on turning a pE scheme and a MAC into a pAE scheme. But conventional, standardized encryption schemes—modes like CBC or CTR [12, 9]—are not really pE schemes, for in lieu of internally generated random coins they use an externally provided IV (initialization vector). Let us call such schemes **IV-based encryption** (ivE). When security is proven for such schemes [3, 1] the IV is selected uniformly at random, and then, for definitional purposes, prepended to the ciphertext. But the standards do not insist that the IV be uniform, nor do they consider it to be part of the ciphertext [12, 9, 14]. In practice, IVs are frequently non-random or communicated out-of-band. In effect, theorists have considered the pE scheme canonically induced by an ivE scheme—but the two objects are not the same thing.

A scheme for **nonce-based encryption** (nE) is syntactically similar to an ivE scheme. Again there is an externally provided value, like the IV, but now referred to as a *nonce* ("number used once"). Security for nE is expected to hold as long as the nonce is not repeated [20]. One expects ease-of-correct-use advantages over ivE, insofar as it should be easier for a user to successfully provide a non-repeating value than a random IV. Standard ivE schemes that are secure when the IV is random (eg, CBC or CTR) are not secure in the nE sense: they are easily attacked if the IV is merely a nonce.

Finally, a scheme for **nonce-based authenticated-encryption** (nAE) is like an nE scheme but the decrypting party should reject illegitimate ciphertexts.

Standardized AE methods—modes like CCM, GCM, and OCB [10, 11, 15]—are secure as nAE schemes. Following standard practice, nAE schemes are further assumed to include *associated data* (AD). This string, provided to the encryption and decryption algorithms, is authenticated but not encrypted [19]. For practical utility of AE, the AD turns out to be crucial.

CONTRIBUTIONS. This paper explores how GC results turn on the basic definitional distinctions named above. Consider the GC scheme of ISO 19772 [15]. The scheme is in the Encrypt-then-MAC tradition, and the standard appeals to BN to support this choice [15, p. 15]. Yet the ISO scheme is wrong. (It is currently being revised in response to our critique [17].) The root problem, we maintain, is that the standard attends to none of the distinctions just described. To apply BN's Encrypt-then-MAC result to a scheme like CBC one would need to select its IV uniformly at random, prepend this to the ciphertext, then take the MAC over this string. But the ISO standard does none of this; the IV is not required to be random, and the scope of the MAC doesn't include it. This makes the scheme trivial to break. A discussion of the ISO scheme appears in Section 6.

One might view the ISO problem as just a document's failure to make clear that which cryptographers know quite well. We see it differently—as symptomatic of an overreaching understanding of BN. For years we have observed, in papers and talks, that people say, and believe, that "Encrypt-then-MAC works well, while MAC-then-Encrypt does not." But this claim should be understood as a specific fact about pE + MAC → pAE conversion. Viewed as a general, definitionally-robust statement about AE, the claim is without foundation.

A modern view of AE should entail a multiplicity of starting points and ending points. Yet not all starting points, or ending points, are equal. The ISO 19772 attack suggests that ivE makes a good starting point for GC; after all, the aim of GC is to support *generic* use of off-the-shelf primitives, and ivE nicely formalizes what is found on that shelf. Similarly, the nAE goal has proven to be the desired-in-practice ending point. We thus explore ivE+MAC → nAE conversion. We start off by assuming that the MAC can authenticate tuples of strings (a vecMAC). We then consider a universe of 160 candidate schemes, the A-schemes. Eight of these are *favored*: they are always secure when their underlying primitives are sound, and with good bounds. See Fig. 2. One A-scheme is *transitional*: it has an inferior established bound. Three A-schemes are *elusive*: for them, we have been unable to generically establish security or insecurity. The remaining 148 A-schemes are meaningless or wrong. Next we show how to realize any of the favored A-scheme using a conventional string-input MAC (a strMAC). The resulting B-schemes are shown in Fig. 3.

Two of the schemes given are already known. Scheme A4 is SIV [21] (apart from the fact that the latter permits vector-valued AD, a natural extension that we ignore), while B1 is EAX [7] (or the generalization of it called EAX2). Our treatment places these modes within a generic-composition framework. In the process, the correctness proof of each mode is actually simplified.

To ensure that we did not overlook any correct schemes, we initially used a computer to identify those with trivial attacks. We were left to deal with the

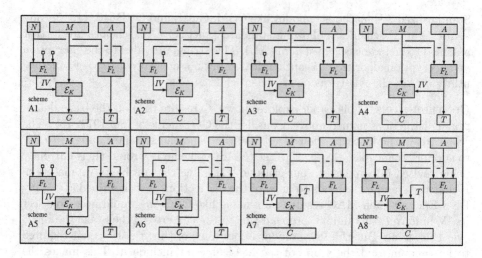

Fig. 2. The eight "favored" A-schemes. These convert an ivE scheme $\mathcal{E}$ and a vecMAC F into an nAE scheme. The IV is $F_L(N\,[,A]\,[,M])$ and the tag T is either $T = F_L(N, A, M)$ or $T = F_L(N, A, C)$. For this diagram we assume $F^{\mathrm{iv}} = F^{\mathrm{tag}} = F$.

more modest number of remaining schemes. The computer-assisted work was eventually rendered unnecessary by conventional proofs.

We also look at the construction of nAE schemes from an nE scheme and a MAC [19, 20]. While nE schemes are not what practice directly provides—no more than pE schemes are—they are trivial to construct from an ivE scheme, and they mesh well with the nAE target. For this nE + MAC $\rightarrow$ nAE problem we identify 20 candidate schemes, which we call N-schemes. Three of them turn out to be secure, all with tight bounds. The security of one scheme we cannot resolve. The other 16 N-schemes are insecure.

TIDY ENCRYPTION.   Our formalization of ivE, nE, and nAE schemes includes a syntactic requirement, *tidiness*, that, when combined with the usual correctness requirement, demands that encryption and decryption be inverses of each other. (For an ivE scheme, correctness says that $\mathcal{E}_K(IV, M) = C \neq \perp$ implies that $\mathcal{D}_K(IV, C) = M$, while tidiness says that $\mathcal{D}_K(IV, C) = M \neq \perp$ implies that $\mathcal{E}_K(IV, M) = C$.) In the context of deterministic symmetric encryption, we regard *sloppy* schemes—those that are not tidy—as perilous in practice, and needlessly degenerate. Tidiness, we feel, is what one should expect from deterministic encryption.

Were sloppy nE and ivE schemes allowed, the generic composition story would shift again: only schemes A5 and A6, B5 and B6, and N2 would be generically secure. The sensitivity of GC to the sloppy/tidy distinction is another manifestation of the sensitivity of GC results to definitional choices. The conventional wisdom, that Encrypt-then-MAC is the only safe GC method, is arguably an artifact of having considered only pE + MAC $\rightarrow$ pAE conversions and admitting sloppy schemes.

A PREEMPTIVE WARNING AGAINST MISINTERPRETATION.   A body of results (eg, [22, 8]) have shown traditional MAC-then-Encrypt (MtE) schemes to be difficult to use properly in practice. Although some of our secure schemes can be viewed as being in the style of MtE, the results of this paper **should not** be interpreted as providing blanket support for MtE schemes. We urge extreme caution when applying *any* generic composition result from the literature, as implementers and standardizing bodies must insure that the underlying encryption and MAC primitives are of the type assumed by the result, and that they are composed in exactly the way the security result demands. Experience has demonstrated this area to be fraught with instantiation and usage difficulties.

Relatedly, we point out that our AE notions of security follow tradition in assuming that decryption failures return a *single kind of error message*, regardless of the cause. Hence implementations of our GC methods should insure, to the maximum extent possible, that this requirement is met.

FINAL INTRODUCTORY REMARKS.   Nothing in this paper should be understood as suggesting that there is anything wrong with BN. If that paper has been misconstrued, it was not for a lack of clarity. Our definitions and results are complementary.

We recently received a note from Bellare and Tackmann [2] pointing out that for the original nE definition of Rogaway [19], neither Encrypt-and-MAC nor MAC-then-Encrypt work for nE + MAC → nAE conversion, contradicting a (therefore buggy) theorem statement [19, Th. 7]. We had previously noticed the need to outlaw sloppy or length-increasing nE schemes to get these results to go through.

A full version of the present paper is available [18]. It contains the proofs we have had to omit.

2   Definitions

This section provides key definitions. Some aspects are standard, but others (particularly tidiness, schemes recognizing their own domains, and identifying encryption schemes by their encryption algorithms) are not.

KINDS OF ENCRYPTION SCHEME.   A scheme for **nonce-based AE** (nAE) is a triple $\Pi = (\mathcal{K}, \mathcal{E}, \mathcal{D})$. The key space $\mathcal{K}$ is a finite nonempty set. Sampling from it is denoted $K \twoheadleftarrow \mathcal{K}$. Encryption algorithm $\mathcal{E}$ is deterministic and takes a four-tuple of strings K, N, A, M to a value $C \leftarrow \mathcal{E}_K^{N,A}(M)$ that is either a string or the symbol $\perp$ ("invalid"). We require the existence of sets $\mathcal{N}$, $\mathcal{A}$, and $\mathcal{M}$, the nonce space, associated-data space (AD space), and message space, such that $\mathcal{E}_K^{N,A}(M) \neq \perp$ iff $(K, N, A, M) \in \mathcal{K} \times \mathcal{N} \times \mathcal{A} \times \mathcal{M}$. We require that $\mathcal{M}$ contains two or more strings; that if $\mathcal{M}$ contains a string of length m it contains all strings of length m, and the same for $\mathcal{A}$; and that when $\mathcal{E}_K(N, A, M)$ is a string its length $\ell(|N|, |A|, |M|)$ depends only on $|N|$, $|A|$, and $|M|$. Decryption algorithm $\mathcal{D}$ is deterministic and takes a four-tuple of strings K, N, A, C to a value M that is

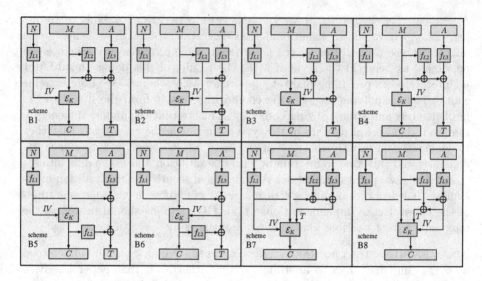

Fig. 3. The eight B-schemes corresponding to the favored A-schemes. Each converts an ivE scheme $\mathcal{E}$ and a strMAC f to an nAE scheme. The methods instantiate the vecMAC with a strMAC using the "XOR3" construction.

either a string in $\mathcal{M}$ or the symbol $\perp$. We require that $\mathcal{E}$ and $\mathcal{D}$ be inverses of one another, implying:

(*Correctness*)   if $\mathcal{E}_K^{N,A}(M) = C \neq \perp$ then $\mathcal{D}_K^{N,A}(C) = M$, and

(*Tidiness*)   if $\mathcal{D}_K^{N,A}(C) = M \neq \perp$ then $\mathcal{E}_K^{N,A}(M) = C$.

Algorithm $\mathcal{D}$ is said to *reject* ciphertext C if $\mathcal{D}_K^{N,A}(C) = \perp$ and to *accept* it otherwise. Our security notion for a nAE scheme is given in Fig. 4. The definition measures how well an adversary can distinguish an encryption-oracle / decryption-oracle pair from a corresponding pair of oracles that return random bits and $\perp$. Here and later, queries that would allow trivial wins are disallowed.

The syntax changes little when we are not expecting authenticity: schemes for **IV-based encryption** (ivE) and **nonce-based encryption** (nE) have the syntax above except for omitting all mention of AD. Security is specified in Fig. 4. For ivE, the nonce N and nonce space $\mathcal{N}$ are renamed IV and $\mathcal{IV}$. With each query M the oracle selects a random IV and returns it alongside the ciphertext. For nE, the adversary provides a plaintext and a non-repeating nonce with each encryption query.

A scheme for **probabilistic encryption** (pE) or **probabilistic AE** (pAE) is a triple $\Pi = (\mathcal{K}, \mathcal{E}, \mathcal{D})$. Key space $\mathcal{K}$ is a finite nonempty set. Encryption algorithm $\mathcal{E}$ is probabilistic and maps a pair of strings K, M to a value $C \twoheadleftarrow \mathcal{E}_K(M)$ that is either a string or the symbol $\perp$ ("invalid"). We require the existence of a set $\mathcal{M}$, the message space, such that $\mathcal{E}_K(M) \neq \perp$ iff $(K, M) \in \mathcal{K} \times \mathcal{M}$. We assume that $\mathcal{M}$ contains two or more strings and if $\mathcal{M}$ contains a string of length m then it contains all strings of length m. We demand that when $\mathcal{E}_K(M)$ is a string, its length $\ell(|M|)$ depends only on $|M|$. Decryption function $\mathcal{D}$ is deterministic and maps a pair of strings K, C to a value $M \leftarrow \mathcal{D}_K(C)$ that is either a string or the symbol $\perp$. We require *correctness*: if $\mathcal{E}_K(M) = C$ then $\mathcal{D}_K(C) = M$. Algorithm $\mathcal{D}$ *rejects* ciphertext C if $\mathcal{D}_K(C) = \perp$ and *accepts* it otherwise. Representative security definitions for pE and pAE schemes are given in Fig. 4. For pE the adversary aims to distinguish an encryption oracle from an oracle that returns an appropriate number of random bits. For pAE the adversary also gets a decryption oracle or an oracle that always returns $\perp$.

TIDINESS. In a pE or pAE scheme, what happens if the decryption algorithm $\mathcal{D}_K$ is fed an *illegitimate* ciphertext—a string C that is not the encryption of any string M under the key K? We didn't require $\mathcal{D}$ to reject, and perhaps it wouldn't make sense to, as a party has no realistic way to know, in general, if an alleged plaintext M for C would encrypt to it. But the situation is different for an ivE, nE, or nAE, as the decrypting party can easily check if a candidate plaintext M really does encrypt to a provided ciphertext C. And, in practice, this re-encryption never needs to be done: for real-world schemes, the natural decryption algorithm rejects illegitimate ciphertexts. Philosophically, once encryption and decryption become deterministic, one would expect them to be inverses of one another, as with a blockcipher.

An nE scheme is *sloppy* if it satisfies everything but the tidiness condition. Might a "real world" nE scheme be sloppy? The only case we know is when removal of padding is done wrong. Define $\mathcal{E}_K^{IV}(M) = \mathrm{CBC}_K^{IV}(M10^p)$, meaning CBC encryption over some n-bit blockcipher, with $p \geq 0$ the least number such that n divides $|M10^p|$. Let $\mathcal{D}_K^{IV}(C) = \perp$ if $|C|$ is not a positive multiple of n, and, otherwise, CBC-decrypt C to get M', strip away all trailing 0-bits, then strip any trailing 1-bit, then return what remains. Then any ciphertexts that CBC-decrypts to a string of zero-bits will give a plaintext of ε, which never encrypts to what we started from. So the method is sloppy. But it *should* be considered wrong: the intermediate plaintext M' was supposed to end in 10^p, for some $p \in [0..n-1]$, and if it did not, then $\perp$ should be returned. One is asking for trouble by silently accepting an improperly padded string.

COMPACT NOMENCLATURE. We formalized encryption schemes—all kinds—as tuples $\Pi = (\mathcal{K}, \mathcal{E}, \mathcal{D})$. But tidiness means we don't need to specify decryption: given $\mathcal{E}$ one *must* have $\mathcal{D}_K(IV, C) = M$ if there is a (necessarily unique) $M \in \{0,1\}^*$ such that $\mathcal{E}_K(IV, M) = C$, and $\mathcal{D}_K(IV, C) = \perp$ otherwise. While there may still be reasons for writing down a decryption algorithm (eg, to demonstrate efficient computability), its not needed for well-definedness. We thus identify an ivE/nE/nAE scheme $\Pi = (\mathcal{K}, \mathcal{E}, \mathcal{D})$ by its encryption algorithm, writing $\mathcal{E}: \mathcal{K} \times \mathcal{IV} \times \mathcal{M} \rightarrow \{0,1\}^*$ for an ivE scheme, $\mathcal{E}: \mathcal{K} \times \mathcal{N} \times \mathcal{M} \rightarrow \{0,1\}^*$ for an nE scheme, and $\mathcal{E}: \mathcal{K} \times \mathcal{N} \times \mathcal{A} \times \mathcal{M} \rightarrow \{0,1\}^*$ for an nAE scheme.

MACs. A message authentication code (MAC) is a deterministic algorithm F that takes in a key K and a value X and outputs either an n-bit string T or the symbol $\perp$. The *domain* of F is the set $\mathcal{X}$ such that $F_K(X) \neq \perp$ (we forbid this to depend on K). We write $F: \mathcal{K} \times \mathcal{X} \rightarrow \{0,1\}^n$ for a MAC with domain $\mathcal{X}$.

$\mathbf{Adv}_{\Pi}^{\mathrm{pE}}(\mathcal{A}) = \Pr[\mathcal{A}^{\mathcal{E}(\cdot)} \Rightarrow 1] - \Pr[\mathcal{A}^{\$(\cdot)} \Rightarrow 1]$ where $\Pi = (\mathcal{K}, \mathcal{E}, \mathcal{D})$ is a pE scheme; $K \twoheadleftarrow \mathcal{K}$ at the beginning of each game; $\mathcal{E}(M)$ returns $C \twoheadleftarrow \mathcal{E}_K(M)$; and $\$(M)$ computes $C \twoheadleftarrow \mathcal{E}_K(M)$, returns $\bot$ if $C = \bot$, and otherwise returns $|C|$ random bits.

$\mathbf{Adv}_{\Pi}^{\mathrm{pAE}}(\mathcal{A}) = \Pr[\mathcal{A}^{\mathcal{E}(\cdot),\, \mathcal{D}(\cdot)} \Rightarrow 1] - \Pr[\mathcal{A}^{\$(\cdot),\, \bot(\cdot)} \Rightarrow 1]$ where $\Pi = (\mathcal{K}, \mathcal{E}, \mathcal{D})$ is a pAE scheme; $K \twoheadleftarrow \mathcal{K}$ at the beginning of each game; $\mathcal{E}(M)$ returns $C \twoheadleftarrow \mathcal{E}_K(M)$ and $\mathcal{D}(C)$ returns $\mathcal{D}_K(M)$; $\$(M)$ computes $C \twoheadleftarrow \mathcal{E}_K(M)$ and returns $\bot$ if $C = \bot$ and $|C|$ random bits otherwise; $\bot(M)$ returns $\bot$; and $\mathcal{A}$ may not make a decryption (=right) query C if C was returned by a prior encryption (=left) query.

$\mathbf{Adv}_{\Pi}^{\mathrm{ivE}}(\mathcal{A}) = \Pr[\mathcal{A}^{\mathcal{E}(\cdot)} \Rightarrow 1] - \Pr[\mathcal{A}^{\$(\cdot)} \Rightarrow 1]$ where $\Pi = (\mathcal{K}, \mathcal{E}, \mathcal{D})$ is an ivE scheme; $K \twoheadleftarrow \mathcal{K}$ at the beginning of each game; $\mathcal{E}(M)$ selects $IV \twoheadleftarrow \mathcal{IV}$ and returns $IV \parallel \mathcal{E}_K(IV, M)$; and $\$(M)$ selects $IV \twoheadleftarrow \mathcal{IV}$, computes $C = \mathcal{E}_K(IV, M)$, returns $\bot$ if $C = \bot$, and otherwise returns $|IV \parallel C|$ random bits.

$\mathbf{Adv}_{\Pi}^{\mathrm{nE}}(\mathcal{A}) = \Pr[\mathcal{A}^{\mathcal{E}(\cdot, \cdot)} \Rightarrow 1] - \Pr[\mathcal{A}^{\$(\cdot, \cdot)} \Rightarrow 1]$ where $\Pi = (\mathcal{K}, \mathcal{E}, \mathcal{D})$ is a nE scheme; $K \twoheadleftarrow \mathcal{K}$ at the beginning of each game; $\mathcal{E}(N, M)$ returns $\mathcal{E}_K(N, M)$; $\$(N, M)$ computes $C \twoheadleftarrow \mathcal{E}_K(N, M)$, returns $\bot$ if $C = \bot$, and otherwise returns $|C|$ random bits; and $\mathcal{A}$ may not repeat the first component of an oracle query.

$\mathbf{Adv}_{\Pi}^{\mathrm{nAE}}(\mathcal{A}) = \Pr[\mathcal{A}^{\mathcal{E}(\cdot, \cdot, \cdot),\, \mathcal{D}(\cdot, \cdot, \cdot)} \Rightarrow 1] - \Pr[\mathcal{A}^{\$(\cdot, \cdot, \cdot),\, \bot(\cdot, \cdot, \cdot)} \Rightarrow 1]$ where $\Pi = (\mathcal{K}, \mathcal{E}, \mathcal{D})$ is an nAE scheme; $K \twoheadleftarrow \mathcal{K}$ at the beginning of each game; $\mathcal{E}(N, A, M)$ returns $\mathcal{E}_K(N, A, M)$ and $\mathcal{D}(N, A, C)$ returns $\mathcal{D}_K(N, A, C)$; and $\$(N, A, M)$ computes $C \twoheadleftarrow \mathcal{E}_K(N, A, M)$, returns $\bot$ if $C = \bot$, and $|C|$ random bits otherwise, and $\bot(N, A, M)$ returns $\bot$; and $\mathcal{A}$ may not repeat the first component of an encryption (=left) query, nor make a decryption (=right) query (N, A, C) after C was obtained from a prior encryption (=left) query (N, A, M).

Fig. 4. Definitions for encryption: probabilistic encryption (pE), probabilistic authenticated encryption (pAE), iv-based encryption (ivE), nonce-based encryption (nE), and nonce-based AE (nAE). For consistency, we give ind\$-style notions throughout.

Security of F is defined by $\mathbf{Adv}_F^{\mathrm{prf}}(\mathcal{A}) = \Pr[\mathcal{A}^F \Rightarrow 1] - \Pr[\mathcal{A}^{\rho} \Rightarrow 1]$. The game on the left selects $K \twoheadleftarrow \mathcal{K}$ and then provides the adversary an oracle for $F_K(\cdot)$. The game on the right selects a uniformly random function ρ from $\mathcal{X}$ to $\{0, 1\}^n$ and provides the adversary an oracle for it. With either oracle, queries outside $\mathcal{X}$ return $\bot$. A *string-input* MAC (strMAC) (the conventional setting) has domain $\mathcal{X} \subseteq \{0, 1\}^*$. A *vector-input* MAC (vecMAC) has a domain $\mathcal{X}$ with one or more component, and not necessarily strings.

INFECTIOUSNESS OF $\bot$. Encryption schemes and MACs return $\bot$ when applied to a point outside their domain. To specify algorithms without having tedious checks for this, we establish the convention that all functions return $\bot$ if any input is $\bot$. For example, if $T = \bot$ then $\mathcal{C} = C \parallel T$ is $\bot$; and if $IV = \bot$ then $C = \mathcal{E}_K(IV, M)$ is $\bot$.

3   AE from IV-Based Encryption and a vecMAC

We study a family of nAE constructions that combine an ivE encryption scheme and a MAC. The former is assumed to provide ind\$-style privacy when the IV is chosen uniformly and prepended to the ciphertext (ivE-security). The latter comes in two varieties, a vector-input MAC (vecMAC) and a string-input MAC (strMAC). This section assumes a vecMAC; the next section extends the treatment to a strMAC. Using a vecMAC provides a clean starting point for situations where one would like to authenticate a collection of typed values, like a nonce, AD, and plaintext. It is also a convenient waypoint for getting to $\text{ivE} + \text{strMAC} \rightarrow \text{nAE}$.

CANDIDATE SCHEMES. We define a set of candidate schemes, the A-schemes, to make an nAE scheme out of an ivE scheme $\mathcal{E}\colon \mathcal{K} \times \{0,1\}^\eta \times \mathcal{M} \rightarrow \{0,1\}^*$, a vecMAC $F^{\text{iv}}\colon \mathcal{L} \times \mathcal{X}^{\text{iv}} \rightarrow \{0,1\}^\eta$, and a vecMAC $F^{\text{tag}}\colon \mathcal{L} \times \mathcal{X}^{\text{tag}} \rightarrow \{0,1\}^\tau$. Our constructions come in three types.

- **Type A_1 schemes.** The nAE scheme $\mathcal{E} = A_1.\text{bbbbbb}[\mathcal{E}, F^{\text{iv}}, F^{\text{tag}}]$ defines $\mathcal{E}_{KL}^{N,A}(M) = C \parallel T$ where $IV = F_L^{\text{iv}}(N \mid \sqcup, A \mid \sqcup, M \mid \sqcup)$, $C = \mathcal{E}_K(IV, M)$, and $T = F_L^{\text{tag}}(N \mid \sqcup, A \mid \sqcup, M \mid \sqcup)$. The notation $X \mid \sqcup$ means that the value is either the binary string X (the value is *present*) or the distinguished symbol $\sqcup$ (it is *absent*). The binary string bbbbbb $\in \{0,1\}^6$ specifies the chosen inputs to F^{iv} and F^{tag}, with 1 for present and 0 for absent, and ordered as above. For example, scheme $A_1.100111[\mathcal{E}, F^{\text{iv}}, F^{\text{tag}}]$ sets $IV = F_L^{\text{iv}}(N, \sqcup, \sqcup)$ and $T = F_L^{\text{tag}}(N, A, M)$.

- **Type A_2 schemes.** The nAE scheme $\mathcal{E} = A_2.\text{bbbbbb}[\mathcal{E}, F^{\text{iv}}, F^{\text{tag}}]$ defines $\mathcal{E}_{KL}^{N,A}(M) = C \parallel T$ where $IV = F_L^{\text{iv}}(N \mid \sqcup, A \mid \sqcup, M \mid \sqcup)$, $C = \mathcal{E}_K(IV, M)$, and $T = F_L^{\text{tag}}(N \mid \sqcup, A \mid \sqcup, C)$. Notation is as above. In particular, bbbbbb remains a 6-bit string, but its final bit is fixed: it's always 1. (Nothing new would be included by allowing $\sqcup$ in place of C, since that's covered as a type A_1 scheme.)

- **Type A_3 schemes.** The nAE scheme $\mathcal{E} = A_3.\text{bbbbbb}[\mathcal{E}, F^{\text{iv}}, F^{\text{tag}}]$ defines $\mathcal{E}_{KL}^{N,A}(M) = C$ where $IV = F_L^{\text{iv}}(N \mid \sqcup, A \mid \sqcup, M \mid \sqcup)$, $T = F_L^{\text{tag}}(N \mid \sqcup, A \mid \sqcup, M \mid \sqcup)$, and $C = \mathcal{E}_K(IV, M \parallel T)$.

According to our conventions, the formulas above return $\mathcal{E}_{KL}^{N,A}(M) = \bot$ if the calculation of IV, C, or T returns $\bot$. This happens when points are outside of the domain $\mathcal{E}$, F^{iv}, or F^{tag}.

Many of the "schemes" named above are not valid schemes: while there are a total of $2^6 + 2^5 + 2^6 = 160$ candidates, many will fail to satisfy the syntax of an nAE schemes. A candidate scheme might be invalid for all $(\mathcal{E}, F^{\text{iv}}, F^{\text{tag}})$, or it might be valid for some $(\mathcal{E}, F^{\text{iv}}, F^{\text{tag}})$ but not for others. We are only interested in candidate schemes $\mathcal{E}$ with parameters $(\mathcal{E}, F^{\text{iv}}, F^{\text{tag}})$ that are *compatible*—ones where the specified composition does indeed satisfy the syntax of an nAE scheme. For example, with $A_1.001111$ (where $IV = F_L^{\text{iv}}(\sqcup, \sqcup, M)$ and $T = F_L^{\text{tag}}(N, A, M)$) there will never be a way to decrypt. And even for a scheme like $A_1.100111$ (where $IV = F_L^{\text{iv}}(N, \sqcup, \sqcup)$ and $T = F_L^{\text{tag}}(N, A, M)$), still we need for the domains to properly mesh. If they do not, the (non-)scheme is excluded from study.

Type A_1 and type A_2 schemes are *outer-tag* schemes, as T falls outside of what's encrypted by $\mathcal{E}$. Type A_3 schemes are *inner-tag* schemes, as T lies inside the scope of what's encrypted by $\mathcal{E}$. This distinction seems as compelling as the A_1, A_2, A_3 distinction that corresponds to E&M, EtM, and MtE style composition.

It is a *thesis* that our enumeration of A-schemes includes all natural ways to make an nAE scheme from an ivE scheme and a vecMAC. More specifically, the schemes are designed to exhaust all possibilities that employ one call to the ivE, two calls to the MAC, and one concatenation involving a MAC-produced tag.

UNDERLYING PRF. It is unintuitive why, in the context of GC, we should use a common key L for components F^{iv} and F^{tag}. The choice enhances generality and uniformity of treatment: the two MACs have the *option* of employing non-overlapping portions of the key L (supporting key separation), but they are not obliged to do so (enabling a significant, additional scheme).

Yet common keying has drawbacks. When MACs F_L^0, F_L^1 are queried on disjoint sets $\mathcal{X}_0, \mathcal{X}_1$ the pair need not resemble random functions ρ^0, ρ^1. To overcome this, retaining the generality and potential key-concision we seek, we assume that any (F^{iv}, F^{tag}) used to instantiate an A-scheme $\mathcal{E} = A_i.\text{bbbbbb}[\mathcal{E}, F^{iv}, F^{tag}]$ can be derived from an underlying PRF $F: \mathcal{L} \times \mathcal{X} \to \{0,1\}^n$ by either

$$F_L^{iv}(\mathbf{x}) = F_L(\mathbf{x})[1 \mathbin{..} \eta] \quad \text{and} \quad F_L^{tag}(\mathbf{x}) = F_L(\mathbf{x})[1 \mathbin{..} \tau], \quad \text{or} \tag{1}$$

$$F_L^{iv}(\mathbf{x}) = F_L(iv, \mathbf{x})[1 \mathbin{..} \eta] \quad \text{and} \quad F_L^{tag}(\mathbf{x}) = F_L(tag, \mathbf{x})[1 \mathbin{..} \tau], \tag{2}$$

$$\text{for distinct constants iv and tag,}$$

where $n \geq \max\{\eta, \tau\}$. In words, F^{iv} and F^{tag} must spring from an underlying PRF F, either with or without domain separation. The approach encompass all schemes that would arise by assuming independent keys for F^{iv} and F^{tag}, plus all schemes that arise by using a singly-keyed PRF for both of these MACs.

SUMMARY OF SECURITY RESULTS. We identify nine provably secure A-schemes, nicknamed A1–A9. See Fig. 5. When one selects an ivE-scheme $\mathcal{E}$ and a MAC F that induces F^{iv} and F^{tag} so as to get a valid nAE scheme (which can always be done in these cases), these nine compositional methods are secure, assuming $\mathcal{E}$ is ivE-secure and F is PRF secure. The concrete bounds proven for A1–A8 are tight. The bound for A9 is inferior, due to the (somewhat curious) presence of ivE-advantage (i.e., privacy) term appearing in the authenticity bound. Additionally, the absence of the nonce N in the computation of F^{tag} prohibits its generic realization (by the construction we will give) from a conventional, string-input MAC. For these reasons we consider A1–A8 "better" than A9 and call them *favored*; A9 is termed *transitional*. The favored schemes are exactly those A-schemes for which the IV depends on (at least) the nonce N, while the tag T depends on everything: $T = F_L^{tag}(N, A, M)$ or $T = F_L(N, A, C)$.

Also shown in Fig. 5 are three *elusive* schemes, A10, A11 and A12, whose status remains open. That they provide privacy (in the nE-sense) follows from the ivE-security of the underlying encryption scheme. But we have been unable to prove that these schemes provide authenticity under the same assumptions used for A1–A9. Nor have we been able to construct a counterexample to demonstrate that those assumptions do not suffice. (We have spent a considerable effort on both possibilities.) It may seem surprising that the security status of schemes

A10, A11, and A12 remains open. Indeed we initially thought that these schemes would admit (more-or-less) straightforward proofs or counterexamples, like other GC schemes. In the full version [18], we discuss the technical challenges encountered, and also prove that A10, A11, and A12 do provide authenticity under an additional security assumption, what we call the *knowledge-of-tags* assumption.

All A-schemes other than A1–A12 are insecure. In the full version of this paper we exhibit an attack on each of them [18]. We must do so in a systematic manner, of course, there being 148 such schemes.

FOR-FREE DOMAIN-SEPARATION. It's important to notice that for all secure and potentially secure A-schemes except A4, the *pattern* of arguments fed to F^{iv} and F^{tag} (ie, which arguments are present and which are absent) are distinct. In particular, the domain-of-application for these MACs are intrinsically separated: no vector $\mathbf{x}$ that might be fed to one MAC could ever be fed to the other. So, in all of these cases, there is no loss of generality to drop the domain-separation constants of equation (2). As for A4, the only natural way to achieve validity—for plaintexts to be recoverable from ciphertexts—is for $F_K^{iv}(\mathbf{x}) = F_K^{tag}(\mathbf{x}) = F_K(\mathbf{x})$. Our subsequent analysis assumes this for A4. In short, our security analysis establishes that there is no loss of generality to assume no domain separation, equation (1), for all secure A-schemes.

THEOREMS. We are now ready to state our results about the security of the A-schemes. For the proofs of Theorems 1 and 2, see the full version [18]. The characterization leaves a small "hole" (schemes A10, A11, and A12); see the full version [18] for discussion and results about those three schemes. For compactness, our theorem statements are somewhat qualitative. But the proofs give a quantitative analysis of the reductions and concrete bounds.

Theorem 1 (Security of A1–A9). Fix a compositional method $An \in \{A1, \ldots, A9\}$ and let $\mathcal{E} : \mathcal{K} \times \{0,1\}^{\eta} \times \mathcal{M} \to \{0,1\}^*$ be an ivE-scheme. Fix integers $1 \le \eta, \tau \le r$ and let $F: \mathcal{L} \times \mathcal{X} \to \{0,1\}^r$ be a vecMAC from which $F^{iv}: \mathcal{L} \times \mathcal{X}^{iv} \to \{0,1\}^{\eta}$ and $F^{tag}: \mathcal{L} \times \mathcal{X}^{tag} \to \{0,1\}^{\tau}$ are derived. Let the resulting nAE-scheme be denoted $\mathcal{E} = An[\mathcal{E}, F^{iv}, F^{tag}]$. Then there are blackbox reductions, explicitly given and analyzed in the proof of this theorem, that transform an adversary breaking the nAE-security of $\mathcal{E}$ into adversaries breaking the ivE-security of $\mathcal{E}$, the PRF-security of F^{iv}, and the PRF-security of F^{tag}. For schemes A1–A8, the reductions are tight.

Theorem 2 (Insecurity of A-schemes other than A1–A12). Fix an A-compositional method other than A1–A12 and integers $1 \le \eta, \tau \le r$. Then there is an ivE-secure encryption scheme $\mathcal{E}: \mathcal{K} \times \{0,1\}^{\eta} \times \mathcal{M} \to \{0,1\}^*$ and a vecMAC $F^{iv}: \mathcal{L} \times \mathcal{X}^{iv} \to \{0,1\}^{\eta}$ and $F^{tag}: \mathcal{L} \times \mathcal{X}^{tag} \to \{0,1\}^{\tau}$, derived from a a PRF-secure $F: \mathcal{L} \times \mathcal{X} \to \{0,1\}^r$, such that the resulting nAE-scheme is completely insecure. The claim holds under standard, scheme-dependent cryptographic assumptions stated in the proof.

An	Scheme	IV	Tag	Sec	Comments
A1	$A_1.100111$	$F_L^{iv}(N,\sqcup,\sqcup)$	$F_L^{tag}(N,A,M)$	yes	(Favored) C and T computable in parallel.
A2	$A_1.110111$	$F_L^{iv}(N,A,\sqcup)$	$F_L^{tag}(N,A,M)$	yes	(Favored) C and T computable in parallel.
A3	$A_1.101111$	$F_L^{iv}(N,\sqcup,M)$	$F_L^{tag}(N,A,M)$	yes	(Favored) Assume IV recoverable. Untruncatable.
A4	$A_1.111111$	$F_L^{iv}(N,A,M)$	$F_L^{tag}(N,A,M)$	yes	(Favored) Assume $F^{iv}=F^{tag}$. Untruncatable. Nonce-reuse secure.
A5	$A_2.100111$	$F_L^{iv}(N,\sqcup,\sqcup)$	$F_L^{tag}(N,A,C)$	yes	(Favored) Decrypt can validate T first, compute M and T in parallel.
A6	$A_2.110111$	$F_L^{iv}(N,A,\sqcup)$	$F_L^{tag}(N,A,C)$	yes	(Favored) Decrypt can validate T first, compute M and T in parallel.
A7	$A_3.100111$	$F_L^{iv}(N,\sqcup,\sqcup)$	$F_L^{tag}(N,A,M)$	yes	(Favored) Untruncatable.
A8	$A_3.110111$	$F_L^{iv}(N,A,\sqcup)$	$F_L^{tag}(N,A,M)$	yes	(Favored) Untruncatable.
A9	$A_3.110101$	$F_L^{iv}(N,A,\sqcup)$	$F_L^{tag}(N,\sqcup,M)$	yes	(Transitional)Weaker bound.Untruncatable.
A10	$A_3.110011$	$F_L^{iv}(N,A,\sqcup)$	$F_L^{tag}(\sqcup,A,M)$	??	(Elusive) Security unresolved.
A11	$A_3.110001$	$F_L^{iv}(N,A,\sqcup)$	$F_L^{tag}(\sqcup,\sqcup,M)$	??	(Elusive) Security unresolved.
A12	$A_3.100011$	$F_L^{iv}(N,\sqcup,\sqcup)$	$F_L^{tag}(\sqcup,A,M)$	??	(Elusive) Security unresolved.
—	all others	—	—	no	Counterexamples given.

Fig. 5. Security of A-schemes: ivE+vecMAC $\to$ nAE. The first column gives a nickname for the scheme. The next column gives the full name. The next two columns (formally redundant) serve as a reminder for how IV and T are determined. A "yes" in the "Sec" column means that we give a proof of security assuming ivE and PRF security for the primitives. A "no" means that we give a counterexample to such a proof existing. A "??" means that we have been unable to find a proof or counterexample. Comments include notes on security and efficiency. "Untruncatable" means that the tag T cannot be truncated. Favored schemes were earlier pictured in Fig. 2.

4 AE from IV-Based Encryption and a strMAC

We turn our attention to achieving nAE from an ivE scheme and a conventional, string-input MAC. In place of our vector-input MAC we will call a string-input MAC multiple times, xoring the results.

There are two basic approaches to this enterprise. The first is to mimic the process already carried out in Section 3. One begins by identifying all candidate "B-schemes" *de novo*: methods that combine one call to an ivE scheme and three calls to a MAC algorithm, one for each of N, A, and either M or $C = \mathcal{E}_K(IV, M)$. The generated ciphertext is either $C \parallel T$ (outer-MAC schemes) or $C = \mathcal{E}_K(IV, M \parallel T)$ (inner-MAC schemes), where T is the xor of computed MAC values. Each MAC is computed using a different key, one of $L1$, $L2$, or $L3$. For each candidate scheme, one seeks either a proof of security (under the ivE and PRF assumptions) or a counter-example. Carrying out this treatment leads to a taxonomy paralleling that discovered for A-schemes.

A second approach is to leverage our ivE + vecMAC results, instantiating the secure schemes using a strMAC. On the downside, this does not give rise to a secure/insecure classification of all schemes cut from a common cloth. On the upside, it is simpler, and with it we identify a set of schemes desirable for a high-level reason: an abstraction boundary that lets us cleanly understand *why* security holds. Namely, it holds because the subject scheme is an instantiation of a scheme already known to be secure.

In the rest of this section, we follow the second approach, identifying nine secure ivE + strMAC $\rightarrow$ nAE schemes corresponding to A1–A9 (eight of them preferred, owing to the better bound). Scheme A10, by nature of its structure, does not admit the same generic strMAC instantiation that suffices for A1–A9. We drop it from consideration.

FROM STRMAC TO VECMAC. We recall that schemes A1–A9 can be regarded as depending on an ivE scheme $\mathcal{E}$ and a vecMAC $F \colon \mathcal{L} \times (\mathcal{N} \times (\mathcal{A} \cup \{\sqcup\}) \times (\mathcal{M} \cup \{\sqcup\})) \rightarrow \{0,1\}^r$ from which functions F^{iv} and F^{tag} are defined. Here, we give a method to transform a strMAC $f \colon \mathcal{L} \times \mathcal{X} \rightarrow \{0,1\}^r$ into a vecMAC $F \colon \mathcal{L}^3 \times (\mathcal{X} \times (\mathcal{X} \cup \{\sqcup\}) \times (\mathcal{X} \cup \{\sqcup\})) \rightarrow \{0,1\}^r$, in order to instantiate A1–A9. We do this via the *three-xor construction*, defined by

$$F_{L1,L2,L3}(N, A, M) = f'_{L1}(N) \oplus f'_{L2}(A) \oplus f'_{L3}(M) \quad \text{where}$$
$$f'_L(X) = \begin{cases} f_L(X) & \text{if } X \in \{0,1\}^*, \text{ and} \\ 0^n & \text{if } X = \sqcup \end{cases} \tag{3}$$

We write the construction $F = \mathrm{XOR3}[f]$. Now the three-xor construction certainly does not work, *in general*, to transform a PRF with domain $\mathcal{X}$ to one with domain $\mathcal{X} \times (\mathcal{X} \cup \{\sqcup\}) \times (\mathcal{X} \cup \{\sqcup\})$; for example, an adversary that obtains, by queries, $Y_0 = F_{L1,L2,L3}(N, \sqcup, \sqcup)$ and $Y_1 = F_{L1,L2,L3}(N, \sqcup, M)$ and $Y_2 = F_{L1,L2,L3}(N, A, \sqcup)$ and $Y_3 = F_{L1,L2,L3}(N, A, M)$ can trivially distinguish if F is given by the xor-construction or is uniform: in the former case, $Y_3 = Y_0 \oplus Y_1 \oplus Y_2$. All the same, that the xor construction works well in the context of realizing any of schemes A1–A9.

For $k \geq 1$ a number, define a sequence of queries $(N_1, \cdots), \ldots, (N_q, \cdots)$ as *at-most-k-repeating* if no value N occurs as a first query coordinate more than k times. An adversary *at-most-k-repeats* if the sequence of queries it asks is at-most-k-repeating, regardless of query responses.

Our observation is that, if f is a good PRF, then $\mathrm{XOR3}[f]$ is a good PRF when restricted to at-most-2-repeats adversaries. We omit the proof.

Lemma 1 (XOR3 construction). Fix $r \geq 1$, let $f \colon \mathcal{L} \times \mathcal{X} \rightarrow \{0,1\}^r$, and let $F = \mathrm{XOR3}[f]$. There is an explicitly given blackbox reduction $\mathcal{B}$ with the following property: for any at-most-2-repeats adversary $\mathcal{A}_F$ there is an adversary $\mathcal{A}_f = \mathcal{B}(\mathcal{A}_F)$ such that $\mathbf{Adv}_f^{\mathrm{prf}}(\mathcal{A}_f) \geq \mathbf{Adv}_F^{\mathrm{prf}}(\mathcal{A}_F)$. Adversary $\mathcal{A}_f$ makes at most three times the number of queries as $\mathcal{A}_F$, the total length μ of those queries is unchanged, and the running time of $\mathcal{A}_f$ is essentially unchanged as well.

To apply Lemma 1 we use the characterization of nAE security that allows the adversary only a single decryption query [21]. This notion is equivalent to our nAE notion of security (which gives the adversary an arbitrary number of decryption queries) apart from a multiplicative degradation in the security bound by a

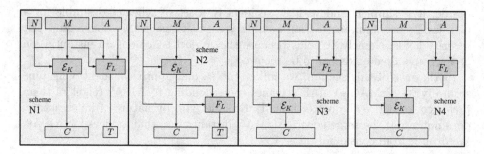

Fig. 6. Three correct N-schemes (left) and an elusive one (right). The methods achieve nE + vecMAC → nAE conversion. Application of the XOR3 construction to N1, N2, and N3 will result in three corresponding schemes that achieve nE + strMAC → nAE conversion. A second application of the XOR3 construction will recover the ivE + strMAC → nAE constructions B1, B5, and B7.

factor of q_d, the number of decryption queries. But for the 1-decryption game, the sequence of adversarial queries is at-most-2-repeating (no repetitions among encryption queries; then a single nonce-repetition for the decryption query). As a result, there is no significant loss in using XOR3[f] to instantiate a vecMAC F

We conclude that the underlying MAC F of all favored A-scheme, and also A9, can be realized by the XOR3 construction. There is a quantitative loss of q_d, which is due to the "weaker" definition for nAE security; we have not determined if this loss is artifactual or necessary. In Fig. 3 we draw the eight B schemes obtained by applying the XOR3 construction to the corresponding A-schemes. Methods B1 and B4 essentially coincide with EAX and SIV [7, 21], neither of which was viewed as an instance of a framework like that described here.

COLLAPSING THE PRF KEYS. For simplicity, we defined the XOR3 construction as using three different keys. But of course we can realize f_{L1}, f_{L2}, f_{L3} by, for example, $f_{L1}(X) = f_L(\mathsf{c1} \,\|\, X)$, $f_{L2}(X) = f_L(\mathsf{c2} \,\|\, X)$, and $f_{L3}(X) = f_L(\mathsf{c3} \,\|\, X)$, for distinct, equal-length constants $\mathsf{c1}, \mathsf{c2}, \mathsf{c3}$.

5   AE from Nonce-Based Encryption and a MAC

We study nAE constructions obtained by generically combining an nE encryption scheme and a MAC. The nE scheme from which we start is assumed to provide ind\$-style privacy when the nonce is never repeated (nE-security), while the MAC can be either a strMAC or a vecMAC. We focus on the latter, as the XOR3 construction can again be used to convert to to a secure nE + strMAC scheme. Our treatment follows, but abbreviates, that of Section 3, as the current setting is substantially simpler.

CANDIDATE SCHEMES. We define schemes, the N-schemes, to make an nAE scheme from an nE scheme $\mathcal{E} : \mathcal{K} \times \{0,1\}^\eta \times \mathcal{M} \to \{0,1\}^*$ and a vecMAC $F : \mathcal{L} \times \mathcal{X} \to \{0,1\}^\tau$. Our constructions come in three types.

Nn	Scheme	Tag	Sec	Comments
N1	N_1.111	$F_L(N, A, M)$	yes	(Favored) Encrypt can compute C, T in parallel
N2	N_2.111	$F_L(N, A, M)$	yes	(Favored) Decrypt can validate T first, compute M, T in parallel
N3	N_3.111	$F_L(N, A, M)$	yes	(Favored) Untruncatable.
N4	N_3.011	$F_L(\sqcup, A, M)$	??	(Elusive) Security unresolved. Tag untruncatable.
—	others	—	no	Counterexamples given.

Fig. 7. Security of N-schemes: nE+vecMAC $\rightarrow$ nAE

- **Type N_1 schemes.** The nAE scheme $\mathcal{E} = N_1.\text{bbb}[\mathcal{E}, F]$ defines $\mathcal{E}_{KL}^{N,A}(M) = C \parallel T$ where $C = \mathcal{E}_K(N, M)$ and $T = F_L(N \mid \sqcup, A \mid \sqcup, M \mid \sqcup)$.
- **Type N_2 schemes.** The nAE scheme $\mathcal{E} = N_2.\text{bbb}[\mathcal{E}, F]$ defines $\mathcal{E}_{KL}^{N,A}(M) = C \parallel T$ where $C = \mathcal{E}_K(N, M)$ and $T = F_L(N \mid \sqcup, A \mid \sqcup, C)$. We again take bbb $\in \{0,1\}^3$, but the third bit must be one.
- **Type N_3 schemes.** The nAE scheme $\mathcal{E} = N_3.\text{bbb}[\mathcal{E}, F]$ defines $\mathcal{E}_{KL}^{N,A}(M) = C$ where $T = F_L(N \mid \sqcup, A \mid \sqcup, M \mid \sqcup)$ and $C = \mathcal{E}_K(N, M \parallel T)$.

As before, the formulas return $\mathcal{E}_{KL}^{N,A}(M) = \perp$ if the calculation of C or T returns $\perp$.

There are a total of $2^3 + 2^2 + 2^3 = 20$ candidate schemes, but many fail to satisfy the syntax of an nAE scheme. We are only interested in candidate methods that are valid nAE schemes.

SECURITY RESULTS. We identify three provably secure schemes, nicknamed N1, N2, and N3. See Fig. 6 and 7. The methods are secure when $\mathcal{E}$ is nE-secure and F is PRF-secure. For all three schemes, the concrete bounds are tight. Also shown in Fig. 5 is a scheme N4 whose status remains open. Similar to the elusive A-schemes, N4 provides privacy (in the nE-sense), as follows from the nE-security of the underlying encryption scheme. But we have been unable to prove that N4 provides authenticity (under the same assumptions used for N1–N3); nor have we been able to construct a counterexample to demonstrate that the nE and PRF assumptions do not suffice. The technical difficulties are similar to those encountered in the attempts to deal with A11 and A12. As for N-schemes other than N1–N4, all 16 are insecure; we exhibit attacks in [18].

THEOREMS. We now state our results about the security of the N-schemes. For proofs, see the full version. These proofs leave a small "hole," which is scheme N4. For compactness, our theorem statements are again somewhat qualitative. But the proofs are not. They provide explicit reductions and quantitative analyses.

Theorem 3 (Security of N1–N3). Fix a compositional method $Nn \in \{N1, N2, N3\}$ and integer $\tau \geq 1$. Fix an nE-scheme $\mathcal{E}: \mathcal{K} \times \{0,1\}^\eta \times \mathcal{M} \rightarrow \{0,1\}^*$ and a vecMAC $F: \mathcal{L} \times \mathcal{X} \rightarrow \{0,1\}^\tau$ that results in a valid nAE scheme $\mathcal{E} = Nn[\mathcal{E}, F]$. Then there are blackbox reductions, explicitly given and analyzed in the proof of this theorem, that transform an adversary breaking the nAE-security of $\mathcal{E}$ to adversaries breaking the nE-security of $\mathcal{E}$ and the PRF-security of F. The reductions are tight.

A claim that N2 and N3 correctly accomplish nE + vecMAC → nAE conversion appears in earlier work by Rogaway [19, 20]. As pointed out by Bellare and Tackmann [2], the claim there was wrong for N3, as Rogaway's definitions had permitted sloppy schemes. This would make a counterexample for N3 (and also for N1) straightforward.

6   The ISO-Standard for Generic Composition

In this section we consider the Encrypt-then-MAC (EtM) mechanism of the ISO 19772 standard [15, Section 10]. We explore what went wrong, and why.

THE PROBLEM.   The EtM method of ISO 19772 (mechanism 5; henceforth isoEtM) combines a conventional encryption mode $\mathcal{E}$ and a MAC f.[1] For the former the standard allows CBC, CFB, OFB, or CTR—any ISO 10116 [14] scheme except ECB. For the MAC, f, the standard permits any of the algorithms of ISO 9797 [16]. These are variants of the CBC MAC. The latest edition of the standard names six CBC MAC variants, but the actual number is greater, as there are multiple possibilities for padding and key-separation.

The standard describes isoEtM encryption in just nine lines of text. After choosing an appropriate "starting variable" (SV) S for encryption mode $\mathcal{E}$, we're told to encrypt plaintext D to ciphertext $C = C' \parallel T$ by setting $C' = \mathcal{E}_{K_1}(D)$ and $T = f_{K_2}(C')$. In describing what "appropriate" means for S, the standard asserts that [t]his variable shall be distinct for every message to be protected during the lifetime of a key, and must be made available to the recipient of the message [15, p. 14]. It continues: Further possible requirements for S are described in the appropriate clauses of ISO 10116. The document levies no requirements on SV, but an annex says that a randomly chosen statistically unique SV is recommended [14, Annex B].

We aren't certain what this last phrase means, but suppose it to urge the use of uniformly random bits. But that possibility runs contrary to the requirement that SV not repeat. One is left to wonder if the SV is a nonce, a random value, or something else. But even if one insists that SV be uniformly random, still we have the biggest problem: ISO 10116 makes clear that the SV it is not a part of the ciphertext C' one gets from applying the encryption mode $\mathcal{E}$. The SV is separate from the ciphertext, communicated out-of-band. The result is that isoEtM never provides authenticity for SV, which leads to trivial attacks. See Fig. 8. For example, let the adversary ask for the encryption of any message, obtaining a ciphertext $C = C' \parallel T$ and its associated SV S. Then a valid forgery is C itself, along with any SV S' other than S. Attacks like this break not only the AE property, but also weaker aims, like nonmalleability.

Overall, it is unclear if isoEtM aims to provide pAE, nAE (without AD), or something else. But the omission of the SV from the scope of the MAC renders the method incorrect no matter what. There is no clear message space for the scheme, as padding is implicit and out of scope. It is unclear what one is

---

[1] This section mostly follows naming conventions of the ISO standard, rather than the names used elsewhere in this paper.

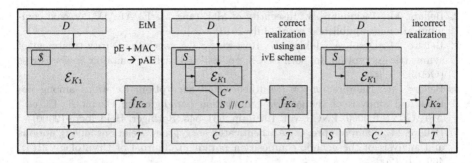

Fig. 8. Possible provenance of the ISO 19772 error. *Left*: The EtM method of BN, employing a probabilistic encryption algorithm $\mathcal{E}$ and a MAC f. The final ciphertext is $\mathcal{C} = C \parallel T$. *Middle*: A correct instantiation of EtM using an IV-based encryption scheme. With each encryption a random S is generated and embedded in C. The final ciphertext is $\mathcal{C} = C \parallel T$. *Right*: Mechanism 5 of ISO 19772. We can consider the final ciphertext as $\mathcal{C} = S \parallel C \parallel T$, but the string S is never MACed.

supposed to do, on decryption, when padding problems arise. As for the MACs themselves, some ISO 9797 schemes are insecure when message lengths vary, a problem inherited by the enclosing AE scheme.

DIAGNOSIS. ISO 19772 standardized five additional AE schemes, and we notice no problems with any of them. (A minor bug in the definition of GCM was pointed out by others, and is currently being corrected[17].) Why did the committee have bigger problems with (the conceptually simpler) GC?

When Bellare and Namprempre formalized Encrypt-then-MAC they assumed probabilistic encryption as the starting point. This is what any theory-trained cryptographer would have done at that time. But pE has remained a theorists' conceptualization: it is not an abstraction boundary widely understood by practitioners, realized by standards, embodied in APIs, or explained in popular books. Using this starting point within a standard is unlike building a scheme from a blockcipher, a primitive that *is* widely understood by practitioners, realized by standards, embodied in APIs, and explained in popular books. Given the difference between pE and actual, standardized encryption schemes, and given GC's sensitivity to definitional and algorithmic adjustments, it seems, in retrospect, a setting for which people are likely to err.

Acknowledgments. Thanks to Yusi (James) Zhang for identifying an error in a proof that formerly resulted in scheme A10 being classified as transitional instead of elusive. Thanks to the NSF, who sponsored Rogaway's work under NSF grants CNS 0904380, CNS 1228828, and CNS 1314885, and Shrimpton's work under NSF grants CNS 0845610 and CNS 1319061.

References

1. Alkassar, A., Geraldy, A., Pfitzmann, B., Sadeghi, A.-R.: Optimized self-synchronizing mode of operation. In: Matsui, M. (ed.) FSE 2001. LNCS, vol. 2355, pp. 78–91. Springer, Heidelberg (2002)

2. Bellare, M., Tackmann, B.: Insecurity of MtE (and M&E) AEAD. Personal communications (unpublished note) (July 2013)
3. Bellare, M., Desai, A., Jokipii, E., Rogaway, P.: A concrete security treatment of symmetric encryption. In: 38th FOCS, pp. 394–403. IEEE Computer Society Press (October 1997)
4. Bellare, M., Namprempre, C.: Authenticated encryption: Relations among notions and analysis of the generic composition paradigm. In: Okamoto, T. (ed.) ASIACRYPT 2000. LNCS, vol. 1976, pp. 531–545. Springer, Heidelberg (2000)
5. Bellare, M., Namprempre, C.: Authenticated encryption: Relations among notions and analysis of the generic composition paradigm. Journal of Cryptology 21(4), 469–491 (2008)
6. Bellare, M., Rogaway, P.: Encode-then-encipher encryption: How to exploit nonces or redundancy in plaintexts for efficient cryptography. In: Okamoto, T. (ed.) ASIACRYPT 2000. LNCS, vol. 1976, pp. 317–330. Springer, Heidelberg (2000)
7. Bellare, M., Rogaway, P., Wagner, D.: The EAX mode of operation. In: Roy, B., Meier, W. (eds.) FSE 2004. LNCS, vol. 3017, pp. 389–407. Springer, Heidelberg (2004)
8. Canvel, B., Hiltgen, A.P., Vaudenay, S., Vuagnoux, M.: Password interception in a SSL/TLS channel. In: Boneh, D. (ed.) CRYPTO 2003. LNCS, vol. 2729, pp. 583–599. Springer, Heidelberg (2003)
9. Dworkin, M.: Recommendation for block cipher modes of operation: Methods and techniques. NIST Special Publication 800-38B (December 2001)
10. Dworkin, M.: Recommendation for block cipher modes of operation: The CCM mode for authentication and confidentiality. NIST Special Publication 800-38C (May 2004)
11. Dworkin, M.: Recommendation for block cipher modes of operation: Galois/counter mode (GCM) and GMAC. NIST Special Publication 800-38D (November 2007)
12. FIPS Publication 81. DES modes of operation. National Institute of Standards and Technology. U.S. Department of Commerce (December 1980)
13. Goldwasser, S., Micali, S.: Probabilistic encryption. Journal of Computer and System Sciences 28(2), 270–299 (1984)
14. ISO/IEC 10116. Information technology — Security techniques — Modes of operation of an n-bit cipher, 3rd edn. (2006)
15. ISO/IEC 19772. Information technology — Security techniques — Authenticated encryption, 1st edn. (2009)
16. ISO/IEC 9797-1. Information technology — Security techniques — Message Authentication Codes (MACs) — Part 1: Mechanisms using a block cipher (2011)
17. Mitchell, C.: Personal communications (August 2011)
18. Namprempre, C., Rogaway, P., Shrimpton, T.: Reconsidering generic composition. Cryptology ePrint Archive, Report 2014/206 (2014) (full version of this paper)
19. Rogaway, P.: Authenticated-encryption with associated-data. In: Atluri, V. (ed.) ACM CCS 2002, pp. 98–107. ACM Press (November 2002)
20. Rogaway, P.: Nonce-based symmetric encryption. In: Roy, B., Meier, W. (eds.) FSE 2004. LNCS, vol. 3017, pp. 348–359. Springer, Heidelberg (2004)
21. Rogaway, P., Shrimpton, T.: A provable-security treatment of the key-wrap problem. In: Vaudenay, S. (ed.) EUROCRYPT 2006. LNCS, vol. 4004, pp. 373–390. Springer, Heidelberg (2006)
22. Vaudenay, S.: Security flaws induced by CBC padding — applications to SSL, IPSEC, WTLS. In: Knudsen, L.R. (ed.) EUROCRYPT 2002. LNCS, vol. 2332, pp. 534–545. Springer, Heidelberg (2002)

Parallelizable Rate-1 Authenticated Encryption from Pseudorandom Functions*

Kazuhiko Minematsu

NEC Corporation, Japan
k-minematsu@ah.jp.nec.com

Abstract. This paper proposes a new scheme for authenticated encryption (AE) which is typically realized as a blockcipher mode of operation. The proposed scheme has attractive features for fast and compact operation. When it is realized with a blockcipher, it requires one blockcipher call to process one input block (i.e. rate-1), and uses the encryption function of the blockcipher for both encryption and decryption. Moreover, the scheme enables one-pass, parallel operation under two-block partition. The proposed scheme thus attains similar characteristics as the seminal OCB mode, without using the inverse blockcipher. The key idea of our proposal is a novel usage of two-round Feistel permutation, where the round functions are derived from the theory of tweakable blockcipher. We also provide basic software results, and describe some ideas on using a non-invertible primitive, such as a keyed hash function.

Keywords: Authenticated Encryption, Blockcipher Mode, Pseudorandom Function, OCB.

1 Introduction

Authenticated Encryption. Authenticated encryption, AE for short, is a method to simultaneously provide message confidentiality and integrity (authentication) using a symmetric-key cryptographic function. Although a secure AE function can be basically obtained by an adequate composition of secure encryption and message authentication [10, 23], this requires at least two independent keys, and the composition methods in practice (say, AES + HMAC in TLS) frequently deviate from what proved to be secure [31]. Considering this situation, there have been numerous efforts devoted to efficient, one-key constructions. Among many approaches to AE, blockcipher mode of operation is one of the most popular ones. We have CCM [2], GCM [3], EAX [11], OCB [24, 33, 35] and the predecessors [18, 22], and CCFB [27], to name a few. We have some standards, such as NIST SP 800-38C (CCM) and 38D (GCM), and ISO/IEC 19772 [4].

This paper presents a new AE mode using a blockcipher, or more generally, a pseudorandom function (PRF). Our proposal has a number of desirable features

---

* A corresponding ePrint report is available at http://eprint.iacr.org/2013/628

P.Q. Nguyen and E. Oswald (Eds.): EUROCRYPT 2014, LNCS 8441, pp. 275–292, 2014.

for fast and compact operations. Specifically, when the underlying n-bit block-cipher is E_K (where K denotes the key), the properties of our proposal can be summarized as follows.

- The key is one blockcipher key, K.
- Encryption and decryption can be done by the encryption function of E_K.
- For s-bit input, the number of E_K calls is $\lceil s/n \rceil + 2$, i.e., rate-1 processing, for both encryption and decryption.
- On-line, one-pass, and parallel encryption and decryption, under two-block partition.
- Provable security up to about $2^{n/2}$ input blocks, based on the assumption that E_K is a pseudorandom function (PRF) or a pseudorandom permutation (PRP).

These features are realized with a novel usage of two-round Feistel permutation, where internal round functions are PRFs with input masking. From this we call our proposal OTR, for Offset Two-round. Table 1 provides a summary of properties of popular AE modes and ours, which shows that OTR attains similar characteristics as the seminal OCB mode, without using the inverse blockcipher. The proposed scheme generates input masks to E_K using $\mathrm{GF}(2^n)$ constant multiplications. This technique is called GF doubling [33], which is a quite popular tool for mode design. However, our core idea is rather generic and thus allows other masking methods. We also remark that Liting et al.'s iFeed mode [39] has similar properties to ours, without introducing 2-block partition. However, its decryption is inherently serial, and it seems that a formal security proof has not been presented so far. In return for these attractive features, one potential drawback of OTR is that it inherently needs two-block partition (though the message itself can be of any length in bits), which implies more state memories required than that of OCB. The parallelizability of our scheme is up to the half of the message blocks, while OCB has full parallelizability, up to the number of message blocks. On-line processing capability is restrictive as it needs buffering of consecutive two input blocks.

We also warn that the security is proved for the standard nonce-respecting adversary [34], i.e. the encryption never processes duplicate nonces (or initial vectors), see Section 2.2. Some recent proposals have a provable security under nonce-reusing adversary, or even security without nonce (called on-line encryption) [5,17]. However we do not claim any security guarantee for such adversaries.

Benefits of Inverse-Freeness. The use of blockcipher inversion, as in OCB, has mainly two drawbacks, as discussed by Iwata and Yasuda [21]. The first is efficiency. The integration of encryption and decryption functions increases size, e.g. footprint of hardware, or memory of software (See Section 6). Moreover, some ciphers have unequal speed for enc/dec. For AES, decryption is slower than encryption on some, typically constrained, platforms. For example, an AES implementation on Atmel AVR by Osvik et al. [30] has about 45% slower decryption than encryption. This property is the initial design choice [15], in preference of encryption-only mode, e.g., CTR, OFB, and CFB. IDEA is another

Table 1. A comparison of AE modes. Calls denotes the number of calls for m-block message and a-block header and one-block nonce, without constants.

Mode	Calls	On-line	Parallel	Primitive
CCM [2]	$a + 2m$	no	no	E
GCM [3]	m [E] and $a + m$ [Mul]	yes	yes	$E, \mathrm{Mul}^\dagger$
EAX [11]	$a + 2m$	yes	no	E
OCB [24,33,35]	$a + m$	yes	yes	E, E^{-1}
CCFB [27]	$a + cm$ for some $1 < c^\ddagger$	yes	no	E
OTR	$a + m$	yes[¶]	yes	E

[†] $GF(2^n)$ multiplication
[‡] Security degrades as c approaches 1
[¶] two-block partition

example, where decryption is exceptionally slower than encryption on microcontrollers [32]. The uneven performance figures of blockcipher enc/dec functions is undesirable in practice, when the mode uses both functions.

The second is security. Usually the security of a mode using both enc/dec functions of a blockcipher, denoted by E and E^{-1}, needs (E, E^{-1}) to be a strong pseudorandom permutation (Strong PRP or SPRP). This holds true for the original security proofs of all versions of OCB [24,33,35], though a recent work of Aoki and Yasuda [7] showed a relaxation on the security condition for OCB without tag truncation. In contrast, when the mode uses only E, the security assumption is relaxed to PRP or PRF.

In addition, the inverse-freeness allows instantiations using non-blockcipher primitives, such as a hash function. Some basic ideas on this direction are explained in Section 7.4.

Hardware Assistance. We remark that some software platforms have hardware-assisted blockcipher, most notably AES instructions called AESNI in Intel and AMD CPUs. AESNI enables the same performance for AES encryption and decryption. Therefore, when our proposal uses AESNI, the performance would be roughly similar to that of OCB-AES with AESNI, though the increased number of states may degrade the result. We have other SW platforms where hardware AES is available but decryption is slower (e.g., [19]). Basically, the value of our proposal is *not* to provide the fastest operation on modern CPUs, instead, to increase the availability of OCB-like performance for various platforms, using single algorithm.

2 Preliminaries

2.1 Basic Notations

Let $\mathbb{N} = \{1, 2, \ldots, \}$, and let $\{0,1\}^*$ be the set of all finite-length binary strings, including the empty string ε. The bit length of a binary string X is denoted by $|X|$, and let $|X|_a \stackrel{\text{def}}{=} \max\{\lceil |X|/a\rceil, 1\}$. Here, if $X = \varepsilon$ we have $|X|_a = 1$ for any $a \geq 1$ and $|X| = 0$. A concatenation of $X, Y \in \{0, 1\}^*$ is written as $X\|Y$ or simply XY. A sequence of a zeros is denoted by 0^a. For $k \geq 1$, we denote $\bigcup_{i=1}^{k} \{0, 1\}^i$ by $\{0, 1\}^{\leq k}$. For $X \in \{0, 1\}^*$, let $(X[1], \ldots, X[x]) \xleftarrow{n} X$ denote the n-bit block partitioning of X, i.e., $X[1]\|X[2]\| \ldots \|X[x] = X$ where $x = |X|_n$, and $|X[i]| = n$ for $i < x$ and $|X[x]| \leq n$. If $X = \varepsilon$ the parsing with any $n \geq 1$ makes $x = 1$, $X[1] = \varepsilon$. The sequence of first c bits of $X \in \{0, 1\}^*$ is denoted by $\mathtt{msb}_c(X)$. We have $\mathtt{msb}_0(X) = \varepsilon$ for any X.

For a finite set $\mathcal{X}$, if X is uniformly chosen from $\mathcal{X}$ we write $X \xleftarrow{\$} \mathcal{X}$. We assume $X \oplus Y$ is ε if X or Y is ε. For a binary string X with $0 \leq |X| \leq n$, $\underline{X}$ denotes the padding written as $X\|1\|0^{n-|X|-1}$. When $|X| = n$, $\underline{X}$ denotes X.

For keyed function $F : \mathcal{K} \times \mathcal{X} \to \mathcal{Y}$ with key $K \in \mathcal{K}$, we may simply write $F_K : \mathcal{X} \to \mathcal{Y}$ if key space is obvious, or even write as F if being keyed with K is obvious. If $E_K : \mathcal{X} \to \mathcal{X}$ is a keyed permutation, or a blockcipher, E_K is a permutation over $\mathcal{X}$ for every $K \in \mathcal{K}$. Its inverse is denoted by E_K^{-1}. A keyed function may have an additional parameter called tweak, in the sense of Liskov, Rivest and Wagner [25]. It is called a tweakable keyed function and written as $\widetilde{F} : \mathcal{K} \times \mathcal{T} \times \mathcal{X} \to \mathcal{Y}$ or $\widetilde{F}_K : \mathcal{T} \times \mathcal{X} \to \mathcal{Y}$, where $\mathcal{T}$ denotes the space of tweaks. Instead of writing $\widetilde{F}_K(T, X)$, we may write as $\widetilde{F}_K^{\langle T \rangle}(X)$. A tweakable keyed permutation, or a tweakable blockcipher (TBC), is defined analogously by requiring that every combination of (T, K) produces a permutation over $\mathcal{X}$.

Galois Field. An n-bit string X may be viewed as an element of $\mathrm{GF}(2^n)$ by taking X as a coefficient vector of a polynomial in $\mathrm{GF}(2^n)$. We write $2X$ to denote the multiplication of 2 and X over $\mathrm{GF}(2^n)$, where 2 denotes the generator of the field $\mathrm{GF}(2^n)$. This operation is called *doubling*. We also write $3X$ and $4X$ to denote $2X \oplus X$ and $2(2X)$. The doubling is efficiently implemented by one-bit shift with conditional XOR of a constant, and frequently used as a tool to build efficient blockcipher modes, e.g. [11, 20, 33].

2.2   Random Function and Pseudorandom Function

Let $\mathrm{Func}(n, m)$ be the set of all functions $\{0, 1\}^n \to \{0, 1\}^m$. In addition, let $\mathrm{Perm}(n)$ be the set of all permutations over $\{0, 1\}^n$. A uniform random function (URF) having n-bit input and m-bit output is uniformly distributed over $\mathrm{Func}(n, m)$. It is denoted by $\mathsf{R} \xleftarrow{\$} \mathrm{Func}(n, m)$. An n-bit uniform random permutation (URP), denoted by P, is similarly defined as $\mathsf{P} \xleftarrow{\$} \mathrm{Perm}(n)$.

We also define tweakable URF and URP. Let $\mathcal{T}$ be a set of tweak and $\mathrm{Func}^{\mathcal{T}}(n, m)$ be a set of functions $\mathcal{T} \times \{0, 1\}^n \to \{0, 1\}^m$. A tweakable URF with tweak $T \in \mathcal{T}$, and n-bit input, m-bit output is written as $\widetilde{\mathsf{R}} \xleftarrow{\$} \mathrm{Func}^{\mathcal{T}}(n, m)$. Note that if $\mathcal{T} = \{0, 1\}^t$, $\mathrm{Func}^{\mathcal{T}}(n, m)$ has the same cardinality as $\mathrm{Func}(n+t, m)$, hence $\widetilde{\mathsf{R}}$ is simply realized with URF of $(n + t)$-bit input. In addition, let $\mathrm{Perm}^{\mathcal{T}}(n)$ be a set of functions $\mathcal{T} \times \{0, 1\}^n \to \{0, 1\}^n$ such that, for any $f \in \mathrm{Perm}^{\mathcal{T}}(n)$ and $t \in \mathcal{T}$, $f(t, *)$ is a permutation. A tweakable n-bit URP with tweak $T \in \mathcal{T}$ is defined as $\widetilde{\mathsf{P}} \xleftarrow{\$} \mathrm{Perm}^{\mathcal{T}}(n)$. We also define a URF having variable input length

(VIL), denoted by $\mathsf{R}^\infty : \{0,1\}^* \to \{0,1\}^n$. This can be realized by stateful lazy sampling.

PRF. For c oracles, $O_1, O_2, \ldots, O_c$, we write $\mathcal{A}^{O_1,O_2,\ldots,O_c}$ to represent the adversary $\mathcal{A}$ accessing these c oracles in an arbitrarily order. If O and O' are oracles having the same input and output domains, we say they are compatible. Let $F_K : \{0,1\}^n \to \{0,1\}^m$ and $G_{K'} : \{0,1\}^n \to \{0,1\}^m$ be two compatible keyed functions, with $K \in \mathcal{K}$ and $K' \in \mathcal{K}'$ (key spaces are not necessarily the same). Let $\mathcal{A}$ be an adversary trying distinguish them using chosen-plaintext queries. Then the advantage of $\mathcal{A}$ is defined as

$$\mathrm{Adv}^{\mathrm{cpa}}_{F_K,G_{K'}}(\mathcal{A}) \stackrel{\text{def}}{=} \Pr[K \stackrel{\$}{\leftarrow} \mathcal{K} : \mathcal{A}^{F_K} \Rightarrow 1] - \Pr[K' \stackrel{\$}{\leftarrow} \mathcal{K}' : \mathcal{A}^{G_{K'}} \Rightarrow 1].$$

The above definition can be naturally extended to the case when $G_{K'}$ is a URF, $\mathsf{R} \stackrel{\$}{\leftarrow} \mathrm{Func}(n, m)$. We have

$$\mathrm{Adv}^{\mathrm{prf}}_{F_K}(\mathcal{A}) \stackrel{\text{def}}{=} \mathrm{Adv}^{\mathrm{cpa}}_{F_K,\mathsf{R}}(\mathcal{A}).$$

If F_K is a VIL function we define $\mathrm{Adv}^{\mathrm{prf}}_{F_K}(\mathcal{A})$ as $\mathrm{Adv}^{\mathrm{cpa}}_{F_K,\mathsf{R}^\infty}(\mathcal{A})$. Similarly, for tweakable keyed function $\widetilde{F}_K : \mathcal{T} \times \{0,1\}^n \to \{0,1\}^m$ and $\widetilde{\mathsf{R}} \stackrel{\$}{\leftarrow} \mathrm{Func}^{\mathcal{T}}(n, m)$, we have

$$\mathrm{Adv}^{\mathrm{prf}}_{\widetilde{F}_K}(\mathcal{A}) \stackrel{\text{def}}{=} \mathrm{Adv}^{\mathrm{cpa}}_{\widetilde{F}_K,\widetilde{\mathsf{R}}}(\mathcal{A}).$$

We stress that $\mathcal{A}$ in the above is allowed to choose tweaks, arbitrarily and adaptively. By convention we say F_K is a pseudorandom function (PRF) if $\mathrm{Adv}^{\mathrm{prf}}_{F_K}(\mathcal{A})$ is small (though the formal definition requires F_K to be a function family). Similarly we say F_K is a pseudorandom permutation (PRP) if $\mathrm{Adv}^{\mathrm{prp}}_{F_K}(\mathcal{A}) = \mathrm{Adv}^{\mathrm{cpa}}_{F_K,\mathsf{P}}(\mathcal{A})$ is small and F_K is invertible. A VIL-PRF is defined in a similar way.

2.3   Definition of Authenticated Encryption

Following [11, 34], we define nonce-based AE, or more formally, AE with assosiated data, called AEAD. We then introduce two security notions, privacy and authenticity, to model AE security.

Definition. Let $\mathsf{AE}[\tau]$ be an AE having τ-bit tag, where the encryption and decryption algorithms are $\mathsf{AE}\text{-}\mathcal{E}_\tau$ and $\mathsf{AE}\text{-}\mathcal{D}_\tau$. They are keyed functions. Besides the key, the input to $\mathsf{AE}\text{-}\mathcal{E}_\tau$ consists of a nonce $N \in \mathcal{N}_{ae}$, a header (or associated data) $A \in \mathcal{A}_{ae}$, and a plaintext $M \in \mathcal{M}_{ae}$. The output consists of $C \in \mathcal{M}_{ae}$ and $T \in \{0,1\}^\tau$, where $|C| = |M|$. The tuple (N, A, C, T) will be sent to the receiver. The decryption function is denoted by $\mathsf{AE}\text{-}\mathcal{D}_\tau$. It takes $(N, A, C, T) \in \mathcal{N}_{ae} \times \mathcal{A}_{ae} \times \mathcal{M}_{ae} \times \{0,1\}^\tau$, and outputs a plaintext M with $|M| = |C|$ if input is determined as valid, or error symbol $\perp$ if determined as invalid.

Security. A PRIV-adversary $\mathcal{A}$ against $\mathsf{AE}[\tau]$ accesses $\mathsf{AE}\text{-}\mathcal{E}_\tau$, where the i-th query consists of nonce N_i, header A_i, and plaintext M_i. We define $\mathcal{A}$'s parameter list to be (q, σ_A, σ_M), where q denotes the number of queries, and

$\sigma_A \stackrel{\text{def}}{=} \sum_{i=1}^{q} |A_i|_n$ and $\sigma_M \stackrel{\text{def}}{=} \sum_{i=1}^{q} |M_i|_n$. We assume $\mathcal{A}$ is nonce-respecting, i.e., all N_is are distinct. We also define random-bit oracle, \$, which takes $(N, A, M) \in \mathcal{N}_{ae} \times \mathcal{A}_{ae} \times \mathcal{M}_{ae}$ and returns $(C, T) \stackrel{\$}{\leftarrow} \{0,1\}^{|M|} \times \{0,1\}^{\tau}$. The privacy notion for $\mathcal{A}$ is defined as

$$\text{Adv}_{\text{AE}[\tau]}^{\text{priv}}(\mathcal{A}) \stackrel{\text{def}}{=} \Pr[K \stackrel{\$}{\leftarrow} \mathcal{K} : \mathcal{A}^{\text{AE-}\mathcal{E}_\tau} \Rightarrow 1] - \Pr[\mathcal{A}^\$ \Rightarrow 1]. \tag{1}$$

An AUTH-adversary $\mathcal{A}$ against $\text{AE}[\tau]$ accesses $\text{AE-}\mathcal{E}_\tau$ and $\text{AE-}\mathcal{D}_\tau$, using q encryption queries and q_v decryption queries. Let $(N_1, A_1, M_1), \ldots, (N_q, A_q, M_q)$ and $(N'_1, A'_1, C'_1, T'_1), \ldots, (N'_{q_v}, A'_{q_v}, C'_{q_v}, T'_{q_v})$ be all the encryption and decryption queries made by $\mathcal{A}$. We define $\mathcal{A}$'s parameter list to be $(q, q_v, \sigma_A, \sigma_M, \sigma_{A'}, \sigma_{C'})$, where $\sigma_{A'} \stackrel{\text{def}}{=} \sum_{i=1}^{q_v} |A'_i|_n$ and $\sigma_{C'} \stackrel{\text{def}}{=} \sum_{i=1}^{q_v} |C'_i|_n$, in addition to σ_A and σ_M. The authenticity notion for the AUTH-adversary $\mathcal{A}$ is defined as

$$\text{Adv}_{\text{AE}[\tau]}^{\text{auth}}(\mathcal{A}) \stackrel{\text{def}}{=} \Pr[K \stackrel{\$}{\leftarrow} \mathcal{K} : \mathcal{A}^{\text{AE-}\mathcal{E}_\tau, \text{AE-}\mathcal{D}_\tau} \text{ forges }], \tag{2}$$

where $\mathcal{A}$ forges if $\text{AE-}\mathcal{D}_\tau$ returns a bit string (other than $\perp$) for a decryption query (N'_i, A'_i, C'_i, T'_i) for some $1 \leq i \leq q_v$ such that $(N'_i, A'_i, C'_i, T'_i) \neq (N_j, A_j, C_j, T_j)$ for all $1 \leq j \leq q$. We assume AUTH-adversary $\mathcal{A}$ is always nonce-respecting with respect to encryption queries; using the same N for encryption and decryption queries is allowed, and the same N can be repeated within decryption queries, i.e. N_i is different from N_j for any $j \neq i$ but N'_i may be equal to N_j or $N'_{i'}$ for some j and $i' \neq i$.

Moreover, when F_K and $G_{K'}$ are compatible with $\text{AE-}\mathcal{E}_\tau$, let $\text{Adv}_{F,G}^{\text{cpa-nr}}(\mathcal{A})$ be the same function as $\text{Adv}_{F,G}^{\text{cpa}}(\mathcal{A})$ but $\mathcal{A}$ is restricted to be nonce-respecting. Note that $\text{Adv}_{\text{AE}[\tau]}^{\text{priv}}(\mathcal{A}) = \text{Adv}_{\text{AE-}\mathcal{E}_\tau, \$}^{\text{cpa-nr}}(\mathcal{A})$ holds for any nonce-respecting $\mathcal{A}$. Let $\mathbf{F} = (F_K^e, F_K^d)$ and $\mathbf{G} = (G_{K'}^e, G_{K'}^d)$ be the pairs of encryption and decryption functions that are compatible with $(\text{AE-}\mathcal{E}_\tau, \text{AE-}\mathcal{D}_\tau)$. We define

$$\text{Adv}_{\mathbf{F},\mathbf{G}}^{\text{cca-nr}}(\mathcal{A}) \stackrel{\text{def}}{=} \Pr[K \stackrel{\$}{\leftarrow} \mathcal{K} : \mathcal{A}^{F_K^e, F_K^d} \Rightarrow 1] - \Pr[K' \stackrel{\$}{\leftarrow} \mathcal{K}' : \mathcal{A}^{G_{K'}^e, G_{K'}^d} \Rightarrow 1], \tag{3}$$

where $\mathcal{A}$ is assumed to be nonce-respecting for encryption queries. Then we have

$$\text{Adv}_{\text{AE}[\tau]}^{\text{auth}}(\mathcal{A}) \leq \text{Adv}_{\text{AE}[\tau], \text{AE}'[\tau]}^{\text{cca-nr}}(\mathcal{A}) + \text{Adv}_{\text{AE}'[\tau]}^{\text{auth}}(\mathcal{A}) \tag{4}$$

for any AE scheme $\text{AE}'[\tau]$ and any AUTH-adversary $\mathcal{A}$.

3   Specification of OTR

We present an AE scheme based on an $E_K : \{0,1\}^n \to \{0,1\}^n$, which is denoted by $\text{OTR}[E, \tau]$, where $\tau \in \{1, \ldots, n\}$ denotes the length of tag. The encryption function and decryption function of $\text{OTR}[E, \tau]$ are denoted by $\text{OTR-}\mathcal{E}_{E,\tau}$ and $\text{OTR-}\mathcal{D}_{E,\tau}$. Here $\text{OTR-}\mathcal{E}_{E,\tau}$ ($\text{OTR-}\mathcal{D}_{E,\tau}$) has the same interface as $\text{AE-}\mathcal{E}_\tau$ ($\text{AE-}\mathcal{D}_\tau$) of Section 2.3, with nonce space $\mathcal{N}_{ae} = \{0,1\}^{\leq n-1} \setminus \{\varepsilon\}$, header space $\mathcal{A}_{ae} = \{0,1\}^*$, message space $\mathcal{M}_{ae} = \{0,1\}^*$, and tag space $\{0,1\}^\tau$. The functions $\text{OTR-}\mathcal{E}_{E,\tau}$ and $\text{OTR-}\mathcal{D}_{E,\tau}$ are further decomposed into the encryption and decryption cores, EF_E, DF_E, and the authentication core, AF_E. Figs. 1 and 2 depict the scheme. As shown by Fig. 2, OTR consists of two-round Feistel permutations using a blockcipher taking a distinct input mask in each round. To authenticate the plaintext a check sum is computed for the right part of two-round Feistel (namely the even plaintext blocks), and the tag is derived from encrypting the check sum with an input mask. The overall structure has a similarity to OCB, and the function AF_E is a variant of PMAC [33].

4   Security Bounds

We provide the security bounds of OTR. Here we assume the underlying blockcipher is an n-bit URP, P. The bounds when the underlying blockcipher is a PRP are easily derived from our bounds, using a standard technique, thus omitted.

Theorem 1. *Fix* $\tau \in \{1, \ldots, n\}$. *For any PRIV-adversary* $\mathcal{A}$ *with parameter* (q, σ_A, σ_M),

$$\mathrm{Adv}^{\mathrm{priv}}_{\mathrm{OTR}[\mathsf{P}, \tau]}(\mathcal{A}) \leq \frac{6\sigma_{\mathrm{priv}}^2}{2^n}$$

holds for $\sigma_{\mathrm{priv}} = q + \sigma_A + \sigma_M$.

Theorem 2. *Fix* $\tau \in \{1, \ldots, n\}$. *For any AUTH-adversary* $\mathcal{A}$ *with parameter* $(q, q_v, \sigma_A, \sigma_M, \sigma_{A'}, \sigma_{C'})$,

$$\mathrm{Adv}^{\mathrm{auth}}_{\mathrm{OTR}[\mathsf{P}, \tau]}(\mathcal{A}) \leq \frac{6\sigma_{\mathrm{auth}}^2}{2^n} + \frac{q_v}{2^\tau}$$

holds for $\sigma_{\mathrm{auth}} = q + q_v + \sigma_A + \sigma_M + \sigma_{A'} + \sigma_{C'}$.

5   Proofs of Theorems 1 and 2

Overview. For the limited space we here explain the basic proof steps of Theorems 1 and 2, with some intuitions. Full proofs will appear at the full version of this paper. The proofs consist of two steps, where in the first step we interpret OTR as a mode of TBC and in the second step we prove the indistinguishability between the tweakable URF and the TBC used in OTR. This structure is essentially the same as OCB proofs, as well as many other schemes based on TBC.

First Step: TBC-Based Design. In the first step, we define an AE scheme denoted by $\mathbb{OTR}'[\tau]$. It is compatible with $\mathrm{OTR}[E, \tau]$ and uses a tweakable n-bit URF, $\widetilde{\mathsf{R}} : \mathcal{T} \times \{0,1\}^n \to \{0,1\}^n$, and an independent VIL-URF, $\mathsf{R}^\infty : \{0,1\}^* \to \{0,1\}^n$, Here, tweak $T \in \mathcal{T}$ is written as $T = (x, i, \omega) \in \mathcal{N}_{ae} \times \mathbb{N} \times \Omega$, where $\Omega \overset{\mathrm{def}}{=} \{\mathsf{f}, \mathsf{s}, \mathsf{a}_1, \mathsf{a}_2, \mathsf{b}_1, \mathsf{b}_2, \mathsf{h}, \mathsf{g}_1, \mathsf{g}_2\}$. The values $\mathsf{h}, \mathsf{g}_1, \mathsf{g}_2$ will not be used until the next step. Here $\mathbb{OTR}'[\tau]$ consists of encryption core $\mathbb{OTR}'\text{-}\mathcal{E}_\tau$ and decryption core $\mathbb{OTR}'\text{-}\mathcal{D}_\tau$. The definition of $\mathbb{OTR}'$ is in Fig. 3. Counterparts to EF and DF are denoted by $\mathbb{EF}$ and $\mathbb{DF}$, also shown in Fig. 3. The bounds of $\mathbb{OTR}'$ are in the following theorem. The proof of Theorem 3 will be given in the full version.

Algorithm OTR-$\mathcal{E}_{E,\tau}(N,A,M)$	**Algorithm** OTR-$\mathcal{D}_{E,\tau}(N,A,C,T)$
1. $(C,TE) \leftarrow \mathrm{EF}_E(N,M)$	1. $(M,TE) \leftarrow \mathrm{DF}_E(N,C)$
2. **if** $A \neq \varepsilon$ **then** $TA \leftarrow \mathrm{AF}_E(A)$	2. **if** $A \neq \varepsilon$ **then** $TA \leftarrow \mathrm{AF}_E(A)$
3. **else** $TA \leftarrow 0^n$	3. **else** $TA \leftarrow 0^n$
4. $T \leftarrow \mathrm{msb}_\tau(TE \oplus TA)$	4. $\widehat{T} \leftarrow \mathrm{msb}_\tau(TE \oplus TA)$
5. **return** (C,T)	5. **if** $\widehat{T} = T$ **return** M
	6. **else return** $\perp$

Algorithm EF$_E(N,M)$	**Algorithm** DF$_E(N,C)$
1. $\Sigma \leftarrow 0^n$	1. $\Sigma \leftarrow 0^n$
2. $\delta \leftarrow E(\underline{N}),\ L \leftarrow 4\delta$	2. $\delta \leftarrow E(\underline{N}),\ L \leftarrow 4\delta$
3. $(M[1],\ldots,M[m]) \xleftarrow{n} M$	3. $(C[1],\ldots,C[m]) \xleftarrow{n} C$
4. **for** $i = 1$ **to** $\lceil m/2 \rceil - 1$ **do**	4. **for** $i = 1$ **to** $\lceil m/2 \rceil - 1$ **do**
5. $C[2i-1] \leftarrow E(L \oplus M[2i-1]) \oplus M[2i]$	5. $M[2i-1] \leftarrow E(L \oplus \delta \oplus C[2i-1]) \oplus C[2i]$
6. $C[2i] \leftarrow E(L \oplus \delta \oplus C[2i-1]) \oplus M[2i-1]$	6. $M[2i] \leftarrow E(L \oplus M[2i-1]) \oplus C[2i-1]$
7. $\Sigma \leftarrow \Sigma \oplus M[2i]$	7. $\Sigma \leftarrow \Sigma \oplus M[2i]$
8. $L \leftarrow 2L$	8. $L \leftarrow 2L$
9. **if** m **is even**	9. **if** m **is even**
10. $L^* \leftarrow L \oplus \delta$	10. $L^* \leftarrow L \oplus \delta$
11. $Z \leftarrow E(L \oplus M[m-1])$	11. $M[m-1] \leftarrow E(L^* \oplus C[m]) \oplus C[m-1]$
12. $C[m] \leftarrow \mathrm{msb}_{|M[m]|}(Z) \oplus M[m]$	12. $Z \leftarrow E(L \oplus M[m-1])$
13. $C[m-1] \leftarrow E(L^* \oplus C[m]) \oplus M[m-1]$	13. $M[m] \leftarrow \mathrm{msb}_{|C[m]|}(Z) \oplus C[m]$
14. $\Sigma \leftarrow \Sigma \oplus Z \oplus \underline{C[m]}$	14. $\Sigma \leftarrow \Sigma \oplus Z \oplus \underline{C[m]}$
15. **if** m **is odd**	15. **if** m **is odd**
16. $L^* \leftarrow L$	16. $L^* \leftarrow L$
17. $C[m] \leftarrow \mathrm{msb}_{|M[m]|}(E(L^*)) \oplus M[m]$	17. $M[m] \leftarrow \mathrm{msb}_{|C[m]|}(E(L^*)) \oplus C[m]$
18. $\Sigma \leftarrow \Sigma \oplus \underline{M[m]}$	18. $\Sigma \leftarrow \Sigma \oplus \underline{M[m]}$
19. **if** $|M[m]| \neq n$ **then** $TE \leftarrow E(3L^* \oplus \Sigma)$	19. **if** $|C[m]| \neq n$ **then** $TE \leftarrow E(3L^* \oplus \Sigma)$
20. **else** $TE \leftarrow E(3L^* \oplus \delta \oplus \Sigma)$	20. **else** $TE \leftarrow E(3L^* \oplus \delta \oplus \Sigma)$
21. $C \leftarrow (C[1],\ldots,C[m])$	21. $M \leftarrow (M[1],\ldots,M[m])$
22. **return** (C,TE)	22. **return** (M,TE)

Algorithm AF$_E(A)$
1. $\Xi \leftarrow 0^n$
2. $\gamma \leftarrow E(0^n),\ Q \leftarrow 4\gamma$
3. $(A[1],\ldots,A[a]) \xleftarrow{n} A$
4. **for** $i = 1$ **to** $a-1$ **do**
5. $\Xi \leftarrow \Xi \oplus E(Q \oplus A[i])$
6. $Q \leftarrow 2Q$
7. $\Xi \leftarrow \Xi \oplus \underline{A[a]}$
8. **if** $|A[a]| \neq n$ **then** $TA \leftarrow E(Q \oplus \gamma \oplus \Xi)$
9. **else** $TA \leftarrow E(Q \oplus 2\gamma \oplus \Xi)$
10. **return** TA

Fig. 1. The encryption and decryption algorithms of OTR with n-bit blockcipher E. Tag size is $0 < \tau \leq n$, and $\underline{X}$ denotes the 10^* padding of X (See Section 2.1).

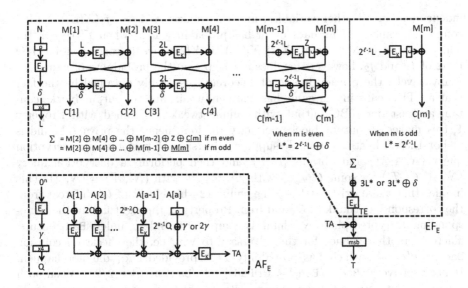

Fig. 2. Encryption of OTR. The p box denotes the 10^* padding of input X ($\underline{X}$), and the c box denotes the msb_i function.

Theorem 3. *Fix* $\tau \in \{1,\ldots,n\}$. *For any PRIV-adversary* $\mathcal{A}$,

$$\mathrm{Adv}^{\mathrm{priv}}_{\mathrm{OTR}'[\tau]}(\mathcal{A}) = 0.$$

Moreover, for any AUTH-adversary $\mathcal{A}$ *using* q *encryption queries and* q_v *decryption queries,*

$$\mathrm{Adv}^{\mathrm{auth}}_{\mathrm{OTR}'[\tau]}(\mathcal{A}) \leq \frac{2q_v}{2^n} + \frac{q_v}{2^\tau}.$$

Proof Intuition. To understand Theorem 3, there are two important properties of a two-round Feistel permutation, denoted by $\phi_{f_1,f_2} : \{0,1\}^{2n} \to \{0,1\}^{2n}$. Here $\phi_{f_1,f_2}(X[1], X[2]) = (Y[1], Y[2])$ where $Y[1] = f_1(X[1]) \oplus X[2]$ and $Y[2] = f_2(Y[1]) \oplus X[1]$ and f_1 and f_2 are independent n-bit URFs. Then we have the followings.

Property 1. For any $(X[1], X[2]) \in \{0,1\}^{2n}$, $\phi_{f_1,f_2}(X[1], X[2])$ is uniformly random.

Property 2. Let $(Y[1], Y[2]) = \phi_{f_1,f_2}(X[1], X[2])$, and let $(Y'[1], Y'[2])$ be a function of $(X[1], X[2], Y[1], Y[2])$ satisfying $(Y'[1], Y'[2]) \neq (Y[1], Y[2])$. Then $X'[2]$, where $(X'[1], X'[2]) = \phi^{-1}_{f_1,f_2}(Y'[1], Y'[2])$, is uniform unless the event $\mathrm{Bad}_1 : X[1] = X'[1]$ occurs, which has the probability at most $1/2^n$.

Property 1 is simple because f_1 and f_2 are independent and the output of ϕ consists of those of f_1 and f_2. Property 2 needs some cares. It holds because if $X[1] \neq X'[1] = f_2(Y'[1]) \oplus Y'[2]$, $f_1(X'[1])$ is distributed uniformly random, independent of all other variables, and this makes $X'[2] = f_1(X'[1]) \oplus Y'[1]$ completely random. The Bad_1 event has probability $1/2^n$ when $Y'[1] \neq Y'[1]$, and otherwise 0. Note that $(X[1], X[2], Y[1], Y[2])$ reveals corresponding I/O pairs of f_1 and f_2, however this does not help gain the probability of Bad_1.

Intuitively, the privacy bound of Theorem 3 is simply obtained by the fact that all TBC calls in the game has distinct tweaks and all output blocks contain at least one TBC output with unique tweak. Combined with Property 1, this makes all output blocks perfectly random, hence the privacy bound is 0. For the authenticity bound, suppose adversary $\mathcal{A}$ performs an encryption query (N, A, M) and obtains (C, T), and then performs a decryption query (N', A', C', T') for some $C \neq C'$ with $|C| = |C'|$, with $(N', A') = (N, A)$. This implies that there exists at least one chunk ($2n$-bit block) of C' different from the corresponding chunk in C, and from Property 2, the right half of the corresponding decrypted plaintext chunk is completely random, unless Bad_1 occurs. There is another chance for the adversary to win, i.e. the checksum collision $\mathsf{Bad}_2 : \Sigma' = \Sigma$, which has probability $1/2^n$ provided Bad_1 did not happen. Hence we have $\Pr[\mathsf{Bad}_1 \cup \mathsf{Bad}_2] \leq \Pr[\mathsf{Bad}_1] + \Pr[\mathsf{Bad}_2|\overline{\mathsf{Bad}_1}] \leq 2/2^n$. When both events did not happen (i.e. given $\overline{\mathsf{Bad}_1 \cup \mathsf{Bad}_2}$), the final chance is to successfully guess the tag, where the probability is clearly bounded by $1/2^\tau$ because different checksums yield independent tags. Hence the authenticity bound is $2/2^n + 1/2^\tau$ for any $\mathcal{A}$ using $q_v = 1$ decryption query (of course we need to consider the existence of other encryption queries and many other cases for (N', A', C', T') as well, however the above bound holds for all cases). Finally we use a well-known result of Bellare, Goldreich and Mityagin [9] to obtain $2q_v/2^n + q_v/2^\tau$ for any $q_v \geq 1$.

Second Step: Analysis of TBC. In the bottom of Fig. 3 we define a TBC, $\widetilde{G}[\mathsf{P}]^{\langle N,i,\omega \rangle}(X)$, where (N, i, ω) is a tweak. It uses an n-bit URP P. We remark that $\widetilde{G}[\mathsf{P}]$ slightly abuse N as it allows $N = 0^n$. Hence the tweak space is $\mathcal{T}' = \{\mathcal{N}_{ae} \cup \{0^n\}\} \times \mathbb{N} \times \Omega$. For tweaks that do not appear in Fig. 3, we let them as undefined. Let $\widetilde{\mathsf{R}}$ be a tweakable URF compatible with $\widetilde{G}[\mathsf{P}]$. Then we have the following proposition and lemma.

Proposition 1. *If* $\mathrm{EF}_{\widetilde{\mathsf{R}}}$ *(*$\mathrm{DF}_{\widetilde{\mathsf{R}}}$*) uses* $\widetilde{G}[\mathsf{P}]$ *instead of* $\widetilde{\mathsf{R}}$*, we obtain* EF_P *(*DF_P*).*

Lemma 1. *For any* $\mathcal{A}$ *with* q *queries,* $\mathrm{Adv}^{\mathrm{cpa}}_{\widetilde{G}[\mathsf{P}],\widetilde{\mathsf{R}}}(\mathcal{A}) \leq 5q^2/2^n$.

Fig. 3 shows a function $\mathbb{AF}_{\widetilde{\mathsf{R}}} : \{0,1\}^* \to \{0,1\}^n$. The internal $\widetilde{\mathsf{R}}$ is a tweakable URF compatible with $\widetilde{G}[\mathsf{P}]$. It is again easy to observe that if $\mathbb{AF}_{\widetilde{\mathsf{R}}}$ uses $\widetilde{G}[\mathsf{P}]$ instead of $\widetilde{\mathsf{R}}$, we obtain AF_P. We provide the security bound for $\mathbb{AF}_{\widetilde{\mathsf{R}}}$, which is as follows.

Lemma 2. *For any* $\mathcal{A}$ *with* σ *input blocks, we have* $\mathrm{Adv}^{\mathrm{prf}}_{\mathbb{AF}_{\widetilde{\mathsf{R}}}}(\mathcal{A}) \leq \sigma^2/2^{n+1}$.

The proofs of Lemmas 1 and 2 are almost the same as XE mode and (a part of) PMAC proofs [33] and will be given in the full version.

Algorithm $\mathbb{OTR}'\text{-}\mathcal{E}_\tau(N, A, M)$	**Algorithm** $\mathbb{OTR}'\text{-}\mathcal{D}_\tau(N, A, C, T)$
1. $(C, TE) \leftarrow \mathbb{EF}_{\widetilde{\mathsf{R}}}(N, M)$	1. $(M, TE) \leftarrow \mathbb{DF}_{\widetilde{\mathsf{R}}}(N, C)$
2. **if** $A \neq \varepsilon$ **then** $TA \leftarrow \mathsf{R}^\infty(A)$	2. **if** $A \neq \varepsilon$ **then** $TA \leftarrow \mathsf{R}^\infty(A)$
3. **else** $TA \leftarrow 0^n$	3. **else** $TA \leftarrow 0^n$
4. $T \leftarrow \mathtt{msb}_\tau(TE \oplus TA)$	4. $\widehat{T} \leftarrow \mathtt{msb}_\tau(TE \oplus TA)$
5. **return** (C, T)	5. **if** $\widehat{T} = T$ **return** M
	6. **else return** $\perp$

Algorithm $\mathbb{OTR}\text{-}\mathcal{E}_\tau(N, A, M)$	**Algorithm** $\mathbb{OTR}\text{-}\mathcal{D}_\tau(N, A, C, T)$
1. $(C, TE) \leftarrow \mathbb{EF}_{\widetilde{\mathsf{R}}}(N, M)$	1. $(M, TE) \leftarrow \mathbb{DF}_{\widetilde{\mathsf{R}}}(N, C)$
2. **if** $A \neq \varepsilon$ **then** $TA \leftarrow \mathbb{AF}_{\widetilde{\mathsf{R}}}(A)$	2. **if** $A \neq \varepsilon$ **then** $TA \leftarrow \mathbb{AF}_{\widetilde{\mathsf{R}}}(A)$
3. **else** $TA \leftarrow 0^n$	3. **else** $TA \leftarrow 0^n$
4. $T \leftarrow \mathtt{msb}_\tau(TE \oplus TA)$	4. $\widehat{T} \leftarrow \mathtt{msb}_\tau(TE \oplus TA)$
5. **return** (C, T)	5. **if** $\widehat{T} = T$ **return** M
	6. **else return** $\perp$

Algorithm $\mathbb{EF}_{\widetilde{\mathsf{R}}}(N, M)$	**Algorithm** $\mathbb{DF}_{\widetilde{\mathsf{R}}}(N, C)$
1. $\Sigma \leftarrow 0^n$	1. $\Sigma \leftarrow 0^n$
2. $(M[1], \ldots, M[m]) \xleftarrow{n} M$	2. $(C[1], \ldots, C[m]) \xleftarrow{n} C$
3. $\ell \leftarrow \lceil m/2 \rceil$	3. $\ell \leftarrow \lceil m/2 \rceil$
4. **for** $i = 1$ **to** $\ell - 1$ **do**	4. **for** $i = 1$ **to** $\ell - 1$ **do**
5. $\quad C[2i - 1] \leftarrow \widetilde{\mathsf{R}}^{\langle N, i, t \rangle}(M[2i - 1]) \oplus M[2i]$	5. $\quad M[2i - 1] \leftarrow \widetilde{\mathsf{R}}^{\langle N, i, s \rangle}(C[2i - 1]) \oplus C[2i]$
6. $\quad C[2i] \leftarrow \widetilde{\mathsf{R}}^{\langle N, i, s \rangle}(C[2i - 1]) \oplus M[2i - 1]$	6. $\quad M[2i] \leftarrow \widetilde{\mathsf{R}}^{\langle N, i, t \rangle}(M[2i - 1]) \oplus C[2i - 1]$
7. $\quad \Sigma \leftarrow \Sigma \oplus M[2i]$	7. $\quad \Sigma \leftarrow \Sigma \oplus M[2i]$
8. **if** m **is even**	8. **if** m **is even**
9. $\quad Z \leftarrow \widetilde{\mathsf{R}}^{\langle N, \ell, t \rangle}(M[m - 1])$	9. $\quad M[m - 1] \leftarrow \widetilde{\mathsf{R}}^{\langle N, \ell, s \rangle}(C[m]) \oplus C[m - 1]$
10. $\quad C[m] \leftarrow \mathtt{msb}_{|M[m]|}(Z) \oplus M[m]$	10. $\quad Z \leftarrow \widetilde{\mathsf{R}}^{\langle N, \ell, t \rangle}(M[m - 1])$
11. $\quad C[m - 1] \leftarrow \widetilde{\mathsf{R}}^{\langle N, \ell, s \rangle}(C[m]) \oplus M[m - 1]$	11. $\quad M[m] \leftarrow \mathtt{msb}_{|C[m]|}(Z) \oplus C[m]$
12. $\quad \Sigma \leftarrow \Sigma \oplus Z \oplus C[m]$	12. $\quad \Sigma \leftarrow \Sigma \oplus Z \oplus C[m]$
13. $\quad$ **if** $|M[m]| \neq n$	13. $\quad$ **if** $|M[m]| \neq n$
14. $\quad\quad$ **then** $TE \leftarrow \widetilde{\mathsf{R}}^{\langle N, \ell, \mathtt{a}_1 \rangle}(\Sigma)$	14. $\quad\quad$ **then** $TE \leftarrow \widetilde{\mathsf{R}}^{\langle N, \ell, \mathtt{a}_1 \rangle}(\Sigma)$
15. $\quad\quad$ **else** $TE \leftarrow \widetilde{\mathsf{R}}^{\langle N, \ell, \mathtt{a}_2 \rangle}(\Sigma)$	15. $\quad\quad$ **else** $TE \leftarrow \widetilde{\mathsf{R}}^{\langle N, \ell, \mathtt{a}_2 \rangle}(\Sigma)$
16. **if** m **is odd**	16. **if** m **is odd**
17. $\quad C[m] \leftarrow \mathtt{msb}_{|M[m]|}(\widetilde{\mathsf{R}}^{\langle N, \ell, t \rangle}(0^n)) \oplus M[m]$	17. $\quad M[m] \leftarrow \mathtt{msb}_{|C[m]|}(\widetilde{\mathsf{R}}^{\langle N, \ell, t \rangle}(0^n)) \oplus C[m]$
18. $\quad \Sigma \leftarrow \Sigma \oplus M[m]$	18. $\quad \Sigma \leftarrow \Sigma \oplus M[m]$
19. $\quad$ **if** $|M[m]| \neq n$	19. $\quad$ **if** $|C[m]| \neq n$
20. $\quad\quad$ **then** $TE \leftarrow \widetilde{\mathsf{R}}^{\langle N, \ell, \mathtt{b}_1 \rangle}(\Sigma)$	20. $\quad\quad$ **then** $TE \leftarrow \widetilde{\mathsf{R}}^{\langle N, \ell, \mathtt{b}_1 \rangle}(\Sigma)$
21. $\quad\quad$ **else** $TE \leftarrow \widetilde{\mathsf{R}}^{\langle N, \ell, \mathtt{b}_2 \rangle}(\Sigma)$	21. $\quad\quad$ **else** $TE \leftarrow \widetilde{\mathsf{R}}^{\langle N, \ell, \mathtt{b}_2 \rangle}(\Sigma)$
22. $C \leftarrow (C[1], \ldots, C[m])$	22. $M \leftarrow (M[1], \ldots, M[m])$
23. **return** (C, TE)	23. **return** (M, TE)

Algorithm $\mathbb{AF}_{\widetilde{\mathsf{R}}}(A)$	**Algorithm** $\widetilde{G}[\mathsf{P}]^{\langle N, i, \omega \rangle}(X)$
1. $\Xi \leftarrow 0^n$	1. **Preprocessing:** $\gamma \leftarrow \mathsf{P}(0^n)$, $Q \leftarrow 4\gamma$
2. $(A[1], \ldots, A[a]) \xleftarrow{n} A$	2. **if** $N \neq 0^n$ **then** $\delta \leftarrow \mathsf{P}(\underline{N})$, $L \leftarrow 4\delta$
3. **for** $i = 1$ **to** $a - 1$ **do**	3. **switch** ω
4. $\quad \Xi \leftarrow \Xi \oplus \widetilde{\mathsf{R}}^{\langle 0^n, i, \mathtt{h} \rangle}(A[i])$	4. $\quad$ **Case** $\mathtt{f}$: $\Delta \leftarrow 2^{i-1}L$
5. $\quad \Xi \leftarrow \Xi \oplus A[a]$	5. $\quad$ **Case** $\mathtt{s}$: $\Delta \leftarrow 2^{i-1}L \oplus \delta$
	6. $\quad$ **Case** $\mathtt{a}_1$: $\Delta \leftarrow 3(2^{i-1}L \oplus \delta)$
6. **if** $|A[a]| \neq n$ **then** $TA \leftarrow \widetilde{\mathsf{R}}^{\langle 0^n, a, \mathtt{g}_1 \rangle}(\Xi)$	7. $\quad$ **Case** $\mathtt{a}_2$: $\Delta \leftarrow 3(2^{i-1}L \oplus \delta) \oplus \delta$
7. **else** $TA \leftarrow \widetilde{\mathsf{R}}^{\langle 0^n, a, \mathtt{g}_2 \rangle}(\Xi)$	8. $\quad$ **Case** $\mathtt{b}_1$: $\Delta \leftarrow 2^{i-1}3L$
8. **return** TA	9. $\quad$ **Case** $\mathtt{b}_2$: $\Delta \leftarrow 2^{i-1}3L \oplus \delta$
	10. **else switch** ω
	11. $\quad$ **Case** $\mathtt{h}$: $\Delta \leftarrow 2^{i-1}Q$
	12. $\quad$ **Case** $\mathtt{g}_1$: $\Delta \leftarrow 2^{i-1}Q \oplus \gamma$
	13. $\quad$ **Case** $\mathtt{g}_2$: $\Delta \leftarrow 2^{i-1}Q \oplus 2\gamma$
	14. $Y \leftarrow \mathsf{P}(\Delta \oplus X)$
	15. **return** Y

Fig. 3. The components of $\mathbb{OTR}'[\tau]$ and $\mathbb{OTR}[\tau]$. An exception is $\widetilde{G}[\mathsf{P}]$, which is a tweakable PRP implicitly used by $\mathrm{OTR}[\mathsf{P}, \tau]$.

Deriving Bounds. Let $\mathbb{OTR}[\tau]$ be an AE consisting of $\mathbb{EF}_{\widetilde{\mathsf{R}}}$, $\mathbb{DF}_{\widetilde{\mathsf{R}}}$, and $\mathbb{AF}_{\widetilde{\mathsf{R}}}$ shown in Fig. 3. For privacy notion, there exist adversaries $\mathcal{B}$ against $\mathbb{AF}_{\widetilde{\mathsf{R}}}$ with σ_A input blocks, and $\mathcal{C}$ against $\widetilde{G}[P]$ with σ_{priv} queries, satisfying

$$\mathrm{Adv}^{\text{priv}}_{\mathbb{OTR}[P,\tau]}(\mathcal{A}) \leq \mathrm{Adv}^{\text{cpa-nr}}_{\mathbb{OTR}[P,\tau],\mathbb{OTR}[\tau]}(\mathcal{A}) + \mathrm{Adv}^{\text{cpa-nr}}_{\mathbb{OTR}[\tau],\mathbb{OTR}'[\tau]}(\mathcal{A}) + \mathrm{Adv}^{\text{cpa-nr}}_{\mathbb{OTR}'[\tau],\$}(\mathcal{A}) \tag{5}$$

$$\leq \mathrm{Adv}^{\text{cpa-nr}}_{\mathbb{OTR}[P,\tau],\mathbb{OTR}[\tau]}(\mathcal{A}) + \mathrm{Adv}^{\text{cpa}}_{\mathbb{AF}_{\widetilde{\mathsf{R}}},\mathsf{R}\infty}(\mathcal{B}) + \mathrm{Adv}^{\text{cpa-nr}}_{\mathbb{OTR}'[\tau],\$}(\mathcal{A}) \tag{6}$$

$$\leq \mathrm{Adv}^{\text{cpa}}_{\widetilde{G}[P],\widetilde{\mathsf{R}}}(\mathcal{C}) + \frac{\sigma_A^2}{2^{n+1}} \tag{7}$$

$$\leq \frac{5\sigma_{\text{priv}}^2}{2^n} + \frac{\sigma_A^2}{2^{n+1}} \tag{8}$$

$$\leq \frac{6\sigma_{\text{priv}}^2}{2^n}. \tag{9}$$

where the third inequality follows from Proposition 1, Lemma 2, and Theorem 3, and the fourth inequality follows from Lemma 1. Similarly, for authenticity notion, there exist $\mathcal{B}$ against $\mathbb{AF}_{\widetilde{\mathsf{R}}}$ with $\sigma_A + \sigma_{A'}$ input blocks, and $\mathcal{C}$ against $\widetilde{G}[P]$ with σ_{auth} queries, satisfying

$$\mathrm{Adv}^{\text{auth}}_{\mathbb{OTR}[P,\tau]}(\mathcal{A}) \leq \mathrm{Adv}^{\text{cca-nr}}_{\mathbb{OTR}[P,\tau],\mathbb{OTR}'[\tau]}(\mathcal{A}) + \mathrm{Adv}^{\text{auth}}_{\mathbb{OTR}'[\tau]}(\mathcal{A}) \tag{10}$$

$$\leq \mathrm{Adv}^{\text{cca-nr}}_{\mathbb{OTR}[P,\tau],\mathbb{OTR}[\tau]}(\mathcal{A}) + \mathrm{Adv}^{\text{cca-nr}}_{\mathbb{OTR}[\tau],\mathbb{OTR}'[\tau]}(\mathcal{A}) + \mathrm{Adv}^{\text{auth}}_{\mathbb{OTR}'[\tau]}(\mathcal{A}) \tag{11}$$

$$\leq \mathrm{Adv}^{\text{cca-nr}}_{\mathbb{OTR}[P,\tau],\mathbb{OTR}[\tau]}(\mathcal{A}) + \mathrm{Adv}^{\text{cpa}}_{\mathbb{AF}_{\widetilde{\mathsf{R}}},\mathsf{R}\infty}(\mathcal{B}) + \mathrm{Adv}^{\text{auth}}_{\mathbb{OTR}'[\tau]}(\mathcal{A}) \tag{12}$$

$$\leq \mathrm{Adv}^{\text{cpa}}_{\widetilde{G}[P],\widetilde{\mathsf{R}}}(\mathcal{C}) + \frac{(\sigma_A + \sigma_{A'})^2}{2^{n+1}} + \frac{2q_v}{2^n} + \frac{q_v}{2^\tau} \tag{13}$$

$$\leq \frac{5\sigma_{\text{auth}}^2}{2^n} + \frac{(\sigma_A + \sigma_{A'})^2}{2^{n+1}} + \frac{2\sigma_{A'}}{2^n} + \frac{q_v}{2^\tau} \tag{14}$$

$$\leq \frac{6\sigma_{\text{auth}}^2}{2^n} + \frac{q_v}{2^\tau}, \tag{15}$$

where the fourth inequality follows from Proposition 1, Lemma 2, and Theorem 3, and the fifth inequality follows from Lemma 1. This concludes the proof.

6 Experimental Results on Software

We implemented OTR on software. The purpose of this implementation is not to provide a fast code, but to see the effect of inverse-freeness in an experimental environment. We wrote a reference-like AES C code that takes byte arrays and uses 4Kbyte tables for combined S-box and Mixcolumn lookup, so-called T-tables. AES decryption of our code is slightly slower than encryption (see Table 2). We then wrote pure C code of OTR using the above AES code. All components, e.g. XOR of blocks and GF doubling, are byte-wise codes. For comparison we also wrote a C code of OCB2 [33] in the same manner, which is similar to a reference code by Krovetz [1].

We ran both codes on an x86 PC (Core i7 3770, Ivy bridge, 3.4GHz) with 64-bit Windows 7. We used Visual C++ 2012 (VC12) to obtain 32-bit and 64-bit executables and used GCC 4.7.1 for 32-bit executables, with option -O2. We measured speed for 4Kbyte messages and one-block header. We also tested the same code on an ARM board (Cortex-A8 1GHz) using GCC 4.7.3 with -O2 option. Their speed figures in cycles per byte[1] are shown in the upper part of Table 2. For both OTR and OCB2, we can observe a noticeable slowdown from raw AES, however, OTR still receives the benefit of faster AES encryption. Another metric is the size, which is shown in the lower part of Table 2. For OTR we can remove the inverse T-tables and inverse S-box from AES code, as they are not needed for AES encryption, resulting in smaller AES objects.

We also measured the performance of these codes when AES is implemented using AESNI (on the Core i7 machine, using VC12). We simply substituted T-table AES with single-block AES routine using AESNI. In addition, two common functions to OCB2 and OTR, namely XOR of two 16-byte blocks and GF doubling, are substituted with SIMD intrinsic codes. Other byte-wise functions are unchanged. On our machine single-block AES ran at around 4.5 to 5.5 cycles per byte, for both encryption and decryption. Table 3 shows the results. It looks interesting, in that, although we did not write a parallel AESNI routine, we could observe the obvious effect of AESNI parallelism via compiler. Notably, both OTR and OCB2 achieved about 2 cycles per byte for 4K data, and OCB2 is slight faster as expected. We think further optimization of OTR as well as OCB2 would be possible if we use parallel AES routine with a careful register handling.

These experiments, though quite naive, imply OTR's good performance under multiple platforms with a simple code. Of course, optimized implementations for various platforms are interesting future topics.

7   Remarks

7.1   Remove Inverse from OCB

The abstract structure of OTR has a similarity to OCB, however, removing inverse is not a trivial task. Roughly, in OCB, each plaintext block is given to the ECB mode of an n-bit TBC $\widetilde{E}_K$ [25], namely $C[i] = \widetilde{E}_K^{\langle T \rangle}(M[i])$, where tweak T consists of nonce N and other parameters, based on a blockcipher E_K. The OCB decryption uses the inversion of TBC, $\widetilde{E}_K^{-1}$, and the security proof requires that $\widetilde{E}_K$ is a tweakable SPRP, i.e. $(\widetilde{E}_K, \widetilde{E}_K^{-1})$ and $(\widetilde{P}, \widetilde{P}^{-1})$ are hard to distinguish when $\widetilde{P} \xleftarrow{\$} \mathrm{Perm}^{\mathcal{T}}(n)$. Since $\widetilde{E}_K^{-1}$ needs a computation of E_K^{-1}, a natural way to remove E_K^{-1} from OCB is to compose $\widetilde{E}_K$ from a PRP or a PRF. For example we can do this by using a $2n$-bit 4-round Feistel cipher as $\widetilde{E}_K$, based on an n-bit PRF, F_K. Then, the resulting mode (of F_K) is inverse-free and provably secure,

---

[1] As we were unable to use cycle counter in the ARM device, the measurement of ARM was based on a timer.

Table 2. Reference implementation results of OTR and OCB2. (Upper) Speed in cycles per byte. (Lower) Object size in Kbyte.

	x86			ARM
Algorithm	VC12(32-bit)	VC12(64-bit)	gcc 4.7.1(32-bit)	gcc 4.7.3
OTR Enc	27.59	18.94	22.02	69.88
OTR Dec	27.56	18.99	22.2	69.78
OCB2 Enc	27.38	19.93	22.69	71.22
OCB2 Dec	30.86	25.43	34.29	76.16
AES Enc	18.29	12.98	15.9	54.38
AES Dec	22.28	18.36	26.64	58.14

	x86			ARM
Object	VC12(32-bit)	VC12(64-bit)	gcc 4.7.1(32-bit)	gcc 4.7.3
OTR.o	19.9	21.3	5.4	5.9
OCB2.o	20.5	21.7	4.6	5.3
AES_Enc.o	20.2	20.7	6.7	7.1
AES_EncDec.o	45.4	46.2	17.3	17.9
OTR Total	40.1	42.0	12.1	13.0
OCB2 Total	65.9	67.9	21.9	23.2

Table 3. Performance of codes with single-block AES routine using AES-NI. Data x denotes the plaintext length in bytes, and a/b denotes a (b) cycles per byte in 32-bit (64-bit) VC12 compilation.

Data (byte)	128	512	1024	2048	4096
OTR Enc	6.01/5.43	3.32/3.16	2.85/2.74	2.66/2.51	2.49/2.40
OTR Dec	7.22/5.60	3.81/3.15	3.06/2.72	2.79/2.51	2.59/2.39
OCB2 Enc	6.39/5.60	3.26/2.76	2.81/2.26	2.53/2.02	2.37/1.90
OCB2 Dec	6.36/5.86	3.04/2.80	2.59/2.26	2.28/2.03	2.11/1.91

since 4-round Feistel cipher is an SPRP, as shown by Luby and Rackoff [26] (it is easy to turn a SPRP into a tweakable SPRP). However, we then need four F_K calls per two blocks, i.e. the rate is degraded to two. Considering this, the two-round Feistel is seemingly a bad choice, since it even fails to provide a (tweakable) PRP. As explained in Section 5, the crucial observation is that, the encryption of two-round Feistel in OTR is invoked only once for each tweak, and that the authenticity needs only an n-bit unpredictable value in the decryption, rather than $2n$ bits. Two-round Feistel fulfills these requirements, which makes OTR provably secure.

7.2   Design Rationale for Masking

We remark that using the same mask for the two round functions, i.e. using $2^i L$ for the first and second rounds of a two-round Feistel, does not work. This is because Property 2 of Section 5 does not hold anymore since the two-round Feistel becomes an involution. Once you query $(X[1], X[2])$ and receive $(Y[1], Y[2]) = \phi_{f_1, f_2}(X[1], X[2])$, you know $X'[2] = Y[2]$ always holds (where $(X'[1], X'[2]) = \phi_{f_1, f_2}^{-1}(Y'[1], Y'[2]))$, when $(Y'[1], Y'[2]) = (X[1], X[2])$. This implies that the adversary can control the checksum value in the decryption, hence breaks authenticity.

We also remark that the masks for EF_E depend on N, hence do not allow precomputation. In contrast the latest OCB3 allows mask precomputation by using $E_K(0^n)$ [24]. The reason is that we want our scheme not to generate $E_K(0^n)$ for header-less usage (i.e. when A is always empty). As a result our scheme has a rather similar structure as OCB2 and an AEAD mode based on OCB2, called AEM [33]. Recent studies reported that the doubling is not too slow [6], hence we employ on-the-fly doubling as a practical masking option.

7.3   Comparison with Other Inverse-Free Modes

Section 6 only considers a comparison with OCB. Here we provide a basic comparison with other modes, in particular those not using the blockcipher inverse. Table 1 shows examples of such inverse-free modes. Among them, CCM, GCM, and EAX are rate-2, assuming the speed of field multiplication in GCM is comparable with blockcipher encryption. At least in theory, OTR is faster for sufficiently long messages for its rate-1 computation. For CCFB, the rate c is a variable satisfying $1 < c$ and $c \approx 1$ is impractical for weak security guarantee[2]. For memory consumption, all inverse-free modes including OTR have a similar profile, as long as the blockcipher encryption is the dominant factor. An exception is GCM since field multiplication usually needs large memories. At the same time, a potential disadvantage of OTR is the complexity introduced by the two-round Feistel, such as a limited on-line/parallel capability, and a slight complex design compared with simple designs reusing existing modes like CTR, CFB, and CMAC.

7.4   Other Instantiations

As the core idea of our proposal is general, it allows various instantiations, by seeing $\mathbb{OTR}$ or $\mathbb{OTR}'$ as a prototype. What we need is just to instantiate $\tilde{R}$ accepting n-bit input and tweak (N, i, ω), and producing n-bit output. While we employ GF doubling, one can use a different masking scheme, such as Gray code [24,35], or word-oriented LFSR [14,24,38], or bit-rotation of a special prime length [28]. Moreover, we can use non-invertible cryptographic primitives, typically a Hash-based PRF such as HMAC, or a permutation of Keccak [12] with Even-Mansour conversion [16] for implementing a keyed permutation. In the latter case the resulting scheme does not need an inversion of the permutation, which is different from the permutation-based OCB described at [29], and there is no output loss like "capacity" bits of SpongeWrap [13]. In these settings, it is

---

[2] More formally, the security bound is roughly $\sigma^2/2^{n/c}$ for privacy and $(\sigma^2/2^{n/c} + 1/2^{n(1-(1/c))})$ for authenticity, with single decryption query and σ total blocks.

possible that the underlying primitive accepts longer input than output. Then a simple tweaking method by tweak prepending can be an option. For example we take SipHash [8], which is a VIL-PRF with 64-bit output. A SipHash-based scheme would be obtained by replacing $\widetilde{\mathsf{R}}^{\langle N,i,\omega\rangle}(*)$ of $\mathbb{OTR}'$ (Fig. 3) with $\text{SipHash}_K(N\|i\|\omega\|*)$, and replacing $\mathsf{R}^\infty(*)$ with $\text{SipHash}_K(0^n\|0\|\mathbf{h}\|*)$, accompanied with an appropriate input encoding. As SipHash has an iterative structure, a caching of an internal value allows efficient computation of $\text{SipHash}_K(N\|i\|\omega\|X)$ from $\text{SipHash}_K(N\|i'\|\omega'\|X')$. We remark that this scheme has roughly 64-bit security. The proof is trivial from Theorem 3, combined with the assumption that SipHash is a VIL-PRF.

8   Concluding Remarks

We have presented an authenticated encryption scheme using a PRF. This scheme enables rate-1, on-line, and parallel processing for both encryption and decryption. The core idea of our proposal is to use two-round Feistel with input masking, combined with a message check sum. As a concrete instantiation we provide a blockcipher mode, called OTR, entirely based on a blockcipher encryption function, which may be seen as an "inverse-free" version of OCB. Our proposal has a higher complexity than OCB outside the blockcipher, hence it will not outperform OCB when the blockcipher enc/dec functions are natively supported and equally fast (say CPU with AESNI), despite the relaxed security assumption. Still, our proposal would be useful for various other environments where the use of blockcipher inverse imposes a non-negligible cost, or simply when the available crypto function is not invertible.

Acknowledgments. The author would like to thank anonymous reviewers for careful reading and invaluable suggestions, which greatly improved the presentation of the paper. The author also would like to thank Tetsu Iwata for fruitful discussions, and Sumio Morioka and Tomoyasu Suzaki for useful comments on implementation aspects.

References

1. Reference C code of OCB2,
   http://www.cs.ucdavis.edu/~rogaway/ocb/code-2.0.htm/
2. Recommendation for Block Cipher Modes of Operation: The CCM Mode for Authentication and Confidentiality. NIST Special Publication of 800-38C (2004), National Institute of Standards and Technology
3. Recommendation for Block Cipher Modes of Operation: Galois/Counter Mode (GCM) and GMAC. NIST Special Publication 800-38D (2007), national Institute of Standards and Technology
4. Information Technology - Security techniques - Authenticated encryption, ISO/IEC 19772:2009. International Standard ISO/IEC 19772 (2009)

5. Andreeva, E., Bogdanov, A., Luykx, A., Mennink, B., Tischhauser, E., Yasuda, K.: Parallelizable and Authenticated Online Ciphers. In: Sako, K., Sarkar, P. (eds.) ASIACRYPT 2013, Part I. LNCS, vol. 8269, pp. 424–443. Springer, Heidelberg (2013)

6. Aoki, K., Iwata, T., Yasuda, K.: How Fast Can a Two-Pass Mode Go? A Parallel Deterministic Authenticated Encryption Mode for AES-NI. DIAC 2012: Directions in Authenticated Ciphers (2012), http://hyperelliptic.org/DIAC/

7. Aoki, K., Yasuda, K.: The Security of the OCB Mode of Operation without the SPRP Assumption. In: Susilo, Reyhanitabar (eds.) [37], pp. 202–220

8. Aumasson, J.P., Bernstein, D.J.: SipHash: A Fast Short-Input PRF. In: Galbraith, S., Nandi, M. (eds.) INDOCRYPT 2012. LNCS, vol. 7668, pp. 489–508. Springer, Heidelberg (2012)

9. Bellare, M., Goldreich, O., Mityagin, A.: The Power of Verification Queries in Message Authentication and Authenticated Encryption. Cryptology ePrint Archive, Report 2004/309 (2004), http://eprint.iacr.org/

10. Bellare, M., Namprempre, C.: Authenticated Encryption: Relations among Notions and Analysis of the Generic Composition Paradigm. In: Okamoto, T. (ed.) ASIACRYPT 2000. LNCS, vol. 1976, pp. 531–545. Springer, Heidelberg (2000)

11. Bellare, M., Rogaway, P., Wagner, D.: The EAX Mode of Operation. In: Roy, Meier (eds.) [36], pp. 389–407

12. Bertoni, G., Daemen, J., Peeters, M., Assche, G.V.: The Keccak SHA-3 submission (January 2011), http://keccak.noekeon.org/

13. Bertoni, G., Daemen, J., Peeters, M., Van Assche, G.: Duplexing the Sponge: Single-Pass Authenticated Encryption and Other Applications. In: Miri, A., Vaudenay, S. (eds.) SAC 2011. LNCS, vol. 7118, pp. 320–337. Springer, Heidelberg (2012)

14. Chakraborty, D., Sarkar, P.: A general construction of tweakable block ciphers and different modes of operations. IEEE Transactions on Information Theory 54(5), 1991–2006 (2008)

15. Daemen, J., Rijmen, V.: AES Proposal: Rijndael (1999)

16. Even, S., Mansour, Y.: A Construction of a Cipher From a Single Pseudorandom Permutation. In: Matsumoto, T., Imai, H., Rivest, R.L. (eds.) ASIACRYPT 1991. LNCS, vol. 739, pp. 210–224. Springer, Heidelberg (1993)

17. Fleischmann, E., Forler, C., Lucks, S.: McOE: A Family of Almost Foolproof On-Line Authenticated Encryption Schemes. In: Canteaut, A. (ed.) FSE 2012. LNCS, vol. 7549, pp. 196–215. Springer, Heidelberg (2012)

18. Gligor, V.D., Donescu, P.: Fast Encryption and Authentication: XCBC Encryption and XECB Authentication Modes. In: Matsui, M. (ed.) FSE 2001. LNCS, vol. 2355, pp. 92–108. Springer, Heidelberg (2002)

19. Gouvêa, C.P.L., López, J.: High Speed Implementation of Authenticated Encryption for the MSP430X Microcontroller. In: Hevia, A., Neven, G. (eds.) LatinCrypt 2012. LNCS, vol. 7533, pp. 288–304. Springer, Heidelberg (2012)

20. Iwata, T., Kurosawa, K.: OMAC: One-Key CBC MAC. In: Johansson, T. (ed.) FSE 2003. LNCS, vol. 2887, pp. 129–153. Springer, Heidelberg (2003)

21. Iwata, T., Yasuda, K.: BTM: A Single-Key, Inverse-Cipher-Free Mode for Deterministic Authenticated Encryption. In: Jacobson Jr., M.J., Rijmen, V., Safavi-Naini, R. (eds.) SAC 2009. LNCS, vol. 5867, pp. 313–330. Springer, Heidelberg (2009)

22. Jutla, C.S.: Encryption Modes with Almost Free Message Integrity. In: Pfitzmann, B. (ed.) EUROCRYPT 2001. LNCS, vol. 2045, pp. 529–544. Springer, Heidelberg (2001)

292   K. Minematsu

23. Krawczyk, H.: The Order of Encryption and Authentication for Protecting Communications (or: How Secure Is SSL?). In: Kilian, J. (ed.) CRYPTO 2001. LNCS, vol. 2139, pp. 310–331. Springer, Heidelberg (2001)
24. Krovetz, T., Rogaway, P.: The Software Performance of Authenticated-Encryption Modes. In: Joux, A. (ed.) FSE 2011. LNCS, vol. 6733, pp. 306–327. Springer, Heidelberg (2011)
25. Liskov, M., Rivest, R.L., Wagner, D.: Tweakable Block Ciphers. In: Yung, M. (ed.) CRYPTO 2002. LNCS, vol. 2442, pp. 31–46. Springer, Heidelberg (2002)
26. Luby, M., Rackoff, C.: How to Construct Pseudorandom Permutations from Pseudorandom Functions. SIAM J. Comput. 17(2), 373–386 (1988)
27. Lucks, S.: Two-Pass Authenticated Encryption Faster Than Generic Composition. In: Gilbert, H., Handschuh, H. (eds.) FSE 2005. LNCS, vol. 3557, pp. 284–298. Springer, Heidelberg (2005)
28. Minematsu, K.: A Short Universal Hash Function from Bit Rotation, and Applications to Blockcipher Modes. In: Susilo, Reyhanitabar (eds.) [37], pp. 221–238
29. Namprempre, C., Rogaway, P., Shrimpton, T.: Reconsidering Generic Composition. DIAC 2013: Directions in Authenticated Ciphers (2013), http://2013.diac.cr.yp.to/
30. Osvik, D.A., Bos, J.W., Stefan, D., Canright, D.: Fast Software AES Encryption. In: Hong, S., Iwata, T. (eds.) FSE 2010. LNCS, vol. 6147, pp. 75–93. Springer, Heidelberg (2010)
31. Paterson, K.: Authenticated Encryption in TLS. DIAC 2013: Directions in Authenticated Ciphers (2013), http://2013.diac.cr.yp.to/
32. Rinne, S.: Performance Analysis of Contemporary Light-Weight Cryptographic Algorithms on a Smart Card Microcontroller. SPEED – Software Performance Enhancement for Encryption and Decryption (2007), http://www.hyperelliptic.org/SPEED/start07.html
33. Rogaway, P.: Efficient Instantiations of Tweakable Blockciphers and Refinements to Modes OCB and PMAC. In: Lee, P.J. (ed.) ASIACRYPT 2004. LNCS, vol. 3329, pp. 16–31. Springer, Heidelberg (2004)
34. Rogaway, P.: Nonce-Based Symmetric Encryption. In: Roy, Meier (eds.) [36], pp. 348–359
35. Rogaway, P., Bellare, M., Black, J.: OCB: A block-cipher mode of operation for efficient authenticated encryption. ACM Trans. Inf. Syst. Secur. 6(3), 365–403 (2003)
36. Roy, B., Meier, W. (eds.): FSE 2004. LNCS, vol. 3017. Springer, Heidelberg (2004)
37. Susilo, W., Reyhanitabar, R. (eds.): ProvSec 2013. LNCS, vol. 8209. Springer, Heidelberg (2013)
38. Zeng, G., Han, W., He, K.: High Efficiency Feedback Shift Register: σ-LFSR. Cryptology ePrint Archive, Report 2007/114 (2007), http://eprint.iacr.org/
39. Zhang, L., Han, S., Wu, W., Wang, P.: iFeed: the Input-Feed AE Modes. In: Rump Session of FSE 2013 (2013), slides from http://fse.2013.rump.cr.yp.to/

Honey Encryption:
Security Beyond the Brute-Force Bound

Ari Juels* and Thomas Ristenpart

University of Wisconsin–Madison
ajuels@gmail.com,
rist@cs.wisc.edu

Abstract. We introduce *honey encryption* (HE), a simple, general approach to encrypting messages using low min-entropy keys such as passwords. HE is designed to produce a ciphertext which, when decrypted with any of a number of *incorrect* keys, yields plausible-looking but bogus plaintexts called *honey messages*. A key benefit of HE is that it provides security in cases where too little entropy is available to withstand brute-force attacks that try every key; in this sense, HE provides security beyond conventional brute-force bounds. HE can also provide a hedge against partial disclosure of high min-entropy keys.

HE significantly improves security in a number of practical settings. To showcase this improvement, we build concrete HE schemes for password-based encryption of RSA secret keys and credit card numbers. The key challenges are development of appropriate instances of a new type of randomized message encoding scheme called a *distribution-transforming encoder* (DTE), and analyses of the expected maximum loading of bins in various kinds of balls-and-bins games.

1 Introduction

Many real-world systems rely for encryption on low-entropy or weak secrets, most commonly user-chosen passwords. Password-based encryption (PBE), however, has a fundamental limitation: users routinely pick poor passwords. Existing PBE mechanisms attempt to strengthen bad passwords via salting, which slows attacks against multiple users, and iterated application of one-way functions, which slows decryption and thus attacks by a constant factor c (e.g., $c = 10,000$). Recent results [6] prove that for conventional PBE schemes (e.g., [32]), work q suffices to crack a single ciphertext with probability $q/c2^\mu$ for passwords selected from a distribution with min-entropy μ. This *brute-force bound* is the best possible for in-use schemes.

Unfortunately empirical studies show this level of security to frequently be insufficient. A recent study [12] reports $\mu < 7$ for passwords observed in a real-world population of 69+ million users. (1.08% of users chose the same password.) For any slowdown c small enough to support timely decryption in normal use, the security offered by conventional PBE is clearly too small to prevent message-recovery (MR) attacks.

We explore a new approach to PBE that provides security beyond the brute-force bound. The idea is to build schemes for which attackers are *unable to succeed in message recovery even after trying every possible password / key*. We formalize this approach by way of a new cryptographic primitive called *honey encryption* (HE).

---

* Independent researcher.

P.Q. Nguyen and E. Oswald (Eds.): EUROCRYPT 2014, LNCS 8441, pp. 293–310, 2014.

We provide a framework for realizing HE schemes and show scenarios useful in practice in which even computationally unbounded attackers can provably recover an HE-encrypted plaintext with probability at most $2^{-\mu} + \epsilon$ for negligible ϵ. Since there exists a trivial, fast attack that succeeds with probability $2^{-\mu}$ (guess the most probable password), we thus demonstrate that HE can yield optimal security.

While HE is particularly useful for password-based encryption (PBE), we emphasize that "password" here is meant very loosely. HE is applicable to *any* distribution of low min-entropy keys, including passwords, PINs, biometrically extracted keys, etc. It can also serve usefully as a hedge against partial compromise of high min-entropy keys.

Background. Stepping back, let us review briefly how brute-force message-recovery attacks work. Given an encryption $C = \mathsf{enc}(K, M)$ of message M, where K and M are drawn from known distributions, an attacker's goal is to recover M. The attacker decrypts C under as many candidate keys as she can, yielding messages $M_1, \ldots, M_q$. Should one of the candidate keys be correct (i.e., K is from a low-entropy distribution), M is guaranteed to appear in this list, and at this stage the attacker wins with probability equal to her ability to pick out M from the q candidates. Conventional PBE schemes make this easy in almost all settings. For example, if M is a 16-digit credit card number encoded via ASCII and the PBE scheme acts like an ideal cipher, the probability that any $M_i \neq M$ is a valid ASCII encoding of a 16-digit string is negligible, at $(10/256)^{16} < 2^{-74}$. An attacker can thus reject incorrect messages and recover M with overwhelming probability. In fact, cryptographers generally ignore the problem of identifying valid plaintexts and assume conservatively that if M appears in the list, the attacker wins.

Prior theoretical frameworks for analyzing PBE schemes have focused on showing strong security bounds for sufficiently unpredictable keys. Bellare, Ristenpart, and Tessaro [6] prove of PKCS#5 PBE schemes that no attacker can break semantic security (learn partial information about plaintexts) with probability greater than $q/(c2^{\mu})$; here, c is the time to perform a single decryption, μ is the min-entropy of the distribution of the keys, and negligible terms are ignored. As mentioned above, though, when $\mu = 7$, such a result provides unsatisfying security guarantees, and the formalisms and proof techniques of [6] cannot offer better results. It may seem that this is the best one can do and that providing security beyond this "brute-force barrier" remains out of reach.

Perhaps unintuitively (at least to the authors of the present paper), the bounds above are actually *not* tight for all settings, as they do not take into account the distribution of the challenge message M. Should M be a uniformly chosen bit-string of length longer than μ, for instance, then the best possible message recovery attack would appear to work with probability at most $1/2^{\mu}$. This is because for typical PBE schemes an attacker will have a hard time, in practice, distinguishing the result of $\mathsf{dec}(K, C)$ for any K from a uniform bit string. Said another way, the candidate messages $M_1, \ldots, M_q$ would all appear to be equally valid as plaintexts. Thus an adversary would seem to maximize her probability of message recovery simply by decrypting C using the key with the highest probability, which is at most $1/2^{\mu}$.

Previously proposed security tools have exploited exactly this intuition for special cases. Hoover and Kausik [26] consider the problem of encrypting a (uniformly-chosen) RSA or DSA secret exponent for authenticating a user to a remote system. Only the remote system holds the associated public key. To hedge against compromise of the user's machine, they suggest encrypting the secret exponent under a PIN (a short decimal-string password). They informally argue that brute-force decryption yields valid-looking exponents, and that an attacker can at best use each candidate exponent in a brute-force online attack against the remote system. Their work led to a commercially deployed system [29]. Other systems similarly seek to foil offline brute-force attacks, but mainly by means of hiding valid authentication credentials in an *explicitly stored list* of plausible-looking fake ones (often called "decoys" or "honeywords") [10,28]. Similarly, detection of system breaches using "honeytokens," such as fake credit-card numbers, is a common industry practice [38].

Honey Encryption (HE). Inspired by such decoy systems, we set out to build HE schemes that provide security beyond the brute-force barrier. These schemes yield candidate messages during brute-force attacks that are indistinguishable from valid ones. We refer to the incorrect plaintext candidates in HE as *honey messages*, following the long established role of this sweet substance in computer security terminology.

We provide a formal treatment of HE. Functionally, an HE scheme is exactly like a PBE scheme: it takes arbitrary strings as passwords and uses them to perform randomized encryption of a message. We ask that HE schemes simultaneously target two security goals: message recovery (MR) security, as parameterized by a distribution over messages, and the more (multi-instance) semantic-security style goals of [6]. As we noted, the latter can only be achieved up to the brute-force barrier, and is thus meaningful only for high min-entropy keys; our HR schemes achieve the goals of [6] using standard techniques. The bulk of our efforts in this paper will be on MR security, where we target security better than $q/c2^\mu$. Our schemes will, in fact, achieve security bounds close to $1/2^\mu$ for unbounded attackers when messages are sufficiently unpredictable.

HE schemes can also produce compact ciphertexts (unlike explicitly stored decoys). While lengths vary by construction and message distribution, we are able to give schemes for which the HE ciphertext for M can be as small as a constant multiple (e.g., 2) of the length of a conventional PBE ciphertext on M.

Framework for HE Schemes. We provide a general methodology for building HE schemes. Its cornerstone is a new kind of (randomized) message encoding that we call a *distribution-transforming encoder (DTE)*. A DTE is designed with an estimate of the message distribution p_m in mind, making it conceptually similar to arithmetic/Huffman coding [19]. The message space for a DTE is exactly the support of p_m (messages with non-zero probability). Encoding a message sampled from p_m yields a "seed" value distributed (approximately) uniformly. It is often convenient for seeds to be binary strings. A DTE must have an efficient decoder that, given a seed, obtains the corresponding message. Applying the decoder to a uniformly sampled seed produces a message distributed (approximately) under p_m. A good (secure) DTE is such that no attacker can distinguish with significant probability between these two distributions: (1) a pair (M, S) generated by selecting M from p_m and encoding it to obtain seed S, and (2) a pair (M, S) generated by selecting a seed S uniformly at random and decoding it to obtain message M. Building DTEs is non-trivial in many cases, for example when p_m is non-uniform.

Encrypting a message M under HE involves a two-step procedure that we call *DTE-then-encrypt*. First, the DTE is applied to M to obtain a seed S. Second, the seed S is encrypted under a conventional encryption scheme enc using the key K, yielding an HE ciphertext C. This conventional encryption scheme enc must have message space equal to the seed space and all ciphertexts must decrypt under any key to a valid seed. Typical PBE schemes operating on bitstrings provide all of this (but authenticated encryption schemes do not). Appropriate care must be taken, however, to craft a DTE whose outputs require no padding (e.g., for CBC-mode encryption).

We prove a general theorem (Theorem 2) that upper bounds the MR security of any DTE-then-encrypt scheme by the DTE's security and a scheme-specific value that we call the expected maximum load. Informally, the expected maximum load measures the worst-case ability of an unbounded attacker to output the right message; we relate it to the expected maximum load of a bin in a kind of balls-and-bins game. Analyzing an HE scheme built with our approach (and a good DTE) therefore reduces to analyzing the balls-and-bins game that arises for the particular key and message distribution. Assuming the random oracle model or ideal cipher model for the underlying conventional encryption scheme enables us to assume balls are thrown independently in these games. (We conjecture that k-wise independent hashing, and thus k-wise independent ball placement, may achieve strong security in many cases as well.)

A DTE is designed using an estimate of the target message distribution p_m. If the DTE is only approximately right, we can nevertheless prove message-recovery security far beyond the brute-force-barrier. If the DTE is bad, i.e., based on a poor estimate of p_m, we fall back to normal security (up to the brute-force barrier), at least provably achieving the semantic security goals in [6]. This means we never do worse than prior PBE schemes, and, in particular, attackers must always first perform the work of offline brute-force attacks before HE security becomes relevant.

HE Instantiations. We offer as examples several concrete instantiations of our general DTE-then-encrypt construction. We build HE schemes that work for RSA secret keys by crafting a DTE for uniformly chosen pairs of prime numbers. This enables us to apply HE to RSA secret keys as used by common tools such as OpenSSL, and improves on the non-standard selection of RSA secret exponents in Hoover and Kausik [26]. Interestingly, simple encoding strategies here fail. For example, encoding the secret keys directly as binary integers (in the appropriate range) would enable an attacker to rule out candidate messages resulting from decryption by running primality tests. Indeed, the DTE we design has decode (essentially) implement a prime number generation algorithm. (This approach slows down decryption significantly, but as noted above, in PBE settings slow decryption can be advantageous.)

We also build HE schemes for password-based encryption of credit card numbers, their associated Card Verification Values (CVVs), and (user-selected) PINs. Encryption of PINs requires a DTE that handles a non-uniform distribution over messages, as empirical studies show a heavy user bias in PIN selection [8]. The resulting analysis consequently involves a balls-and-bins game with non-uniform bin capacities, a somewhat unusual setup in the literature.

In each of the cases above we are able to prove close to optimal MR security.

Limitations of HE. The security guarantees offered by HE come with some strings attached. First, HE security does not hold when the adversary has side information about the target message. As a concrete example, the RSA secret key HE scheme provides strong MR guarantees only when the attacker does not know the public key associated with the encrypted secret key. Thus the HE cannot effectively protect normal HTTPS certificate keys. (The intended application for this HE scheme is client authorization, where the public key is stored only at the remote server, a typical setting for SSH users. See, e.g., [26].) Second, because decryption of an HE ciphertext under a wrong key produces fake but valid-looking messages, typos in passwords might confuse legitimate users in some settings. We address this issue of "typo-safety" in Section 7. Third and finally, we assume in our HE analyses that the key and message distributions are independent. If they are correlated, an attacker may be able to identify a correct message by comparing it with the decryption key that produced it. Similarly, encrypting two correlated messages under the same key may enable an adversary to identify correct messages. (Encrypting independent messages under the same key is fine.) We emphasize, however, that should any of these assumptions fail, HE security falls back to normal PBE security: there is never any harm in using HE.

Full Version. Due to page constraints, this abstract omits proofs and some other content. Refer to the full version of the paper for the omitted material [27].

2 Related Work

Our HE schemes provide a form of information-theoretic encryption, as their MR security does not rely on any computational hardness assumption. Information-theoretic encryption schemes, starting with the one-time pad [36], have seen extensive study. Most closely related is entropic security [21, 35], where the idea is to exploit high-entropy messages to perform encryption that leaks no predicate on the plaintext even against unbounded attackers (and hence beyond the brute-force bound). Their goal was to enable use of uniform, smaller (than one-time pads) keys yet achieve information-theoretic security. HE similarly exploits the entropy of messages, but also provides useful bounds (by targeting MR security) even when the combined entropy of messages and keys is insufficient to achieve entropic security. See also the discussion in the full version.

Deterministic [2, 4, 11] and hedged [3, 34] public-key encryption rely on entropy in messages to offset having no or only poor randomness during encryption. HE similarly exploits adversarial uncertainty about messages in the case that keys are poor; HE can be viewed as "hedging" against poor keys (passwords) as opposed to poor randomness.

In natural applications of HE, the message space $\mathcal{M}$ must encompass messages of special format, rather than just bitstrings. In this sense, HE is related to format-preserving encryption (FPE) [5], although HE is randomized and has no preservation requirement (our ciphertexts are unstructured bit strings). An implication of our approach, however, is that some FPE constructions (e.g., for credit-card encryption) can be shown to achieve HE-like security guarantees when message distributions are uniform. HE is also conceptually related to collisionful hashing [9], the idea of creating password hashes for which it is relatively easy to find inverses and thus hard to identify the original, correct password (as opposed to identifying a correct message).

Under (non-interactive) non-committing encryption [17, 31], a ciphertext can be "opened" to an arbitrary message under a suitably selected key. (For example, a one-time pad is non-committing.) HE has a different requirement, namely that decrypting a fixed ciphertext under different keys yields independent-looking samples of the message space. Note that unlike non-committing encryption [31], HE is achievable in the non-programmable random oracle model. Deniable encryption [16] also allows ciphertexts to be opened to chosen messages; HE schemes do not in general offer deniability.

Canetti, Halevi, and Steiner [18] propose a protocol in which a password specifies a subset of CAPTCHAs that must be solved to decrypt a credential store. Their scheme creates ambiguity around where human effort can be most effectively invested, rather than around the correctness of the contents of the credential store, as HE would.

Perhaps most closely related to HE is a rich literature on deception and decoys in computer security. Honeypots, fake computer systems intended to attract and study attacks, are a stock-in-trade of computer security research [37]. Researchers have proposed honeytokens [20, 38], which are data objects whose use signals a compromise, and honeywords [28], a system that uses passwords as honeytokens. Additional proposals include false documents [14], false network traffic [13], and many variants.

The Kamouflage system [10] is particularly relevant. It conceals a true password vault encrypted under a true master password among N bogus vaults encrypted under bogus master passwords. Kamouflage requires $O(N)$ storage. With a suitable DTE, HE can in principle achieve similar functionality and security with $O(1)$ storage. Kamouflage and related systems require the construction of plausible decoys. This problem has seen study specifically for password protection in, e.g., [10, 28], but to the best of our knowledge, we are the first to formalize it with the concept of DTEs.

3   HE Overview

HE Schemes. An HE scheme has syntax and semantics equivalent to that of a symmetric encryption scheme. Encryption maps a key and message to a ciphertext and, in our schemes, is randomized. Decryption recovers messages from ciphertexts. The departure from conventional symmetric encryption schemes will be in how HE decryption behaves when one uses the wrong key in attempting to decrypt a ciphertext. Instead of giving rise to some error, decryption will emit a plaintext that "looks" plausible.

Formally, let $\mathcal{K}$ and $\mathcal{M}$ be sets, the key space and message space. For generality, we assume that $\mathcal{K}$ consists of variable-length bit strings. (This supports, in particular, varying length passwords.) An HE scheme $\mathsf{HE} = (\mathsf{HEnc}, \mathsf{HDec})$ is a a pair of algorithms. Encryption HEnc takes input a key $K \in \mathcal{K}$, message $M \in \mathcal{M}$, some uniform random bits, and outputs a ciphertext C. We write this as $C \leftarrow_\$ \mathsf{HEnc}_K(M)$, where $\leftarrow_\$$ denotes that HEnc may use some number of uniform random bits. Decryption HDec takes as input a key $K \in \mathcal{K}$, ciphertext C, and outputs a message $M \in \mathcal{M}$. Decryption, always deterministic, is written as $M \leftarrow \mathsf{HDec}_K(C)$.

We require that decryption succeeds: Formally, $\Pr[\mathsf{HDec}_K(\mathsf{HEnc}_K(M)) = M] = 1$ for all $K \in \mathcal{K}$ and $M \in \mathcal{M}$, where the event is defined over the randomness in HEnc.

We will write $\mathsf{SE} = (\mathsf{enc}, \mathsf{dec})$ to denote a conventional symmetric encryption scheme, but note that the syntax and semantics match those of an HE scheme.

Message and Key Distributions. We denote a distribution on set S by a map $p \colon S \to [0, 1]$ and require that $\sum_{s \in S} p(s) = 1$. The min-entropy of a distribution is defined to be

$-\log \max_{s \in S} p(s)$. Sampling according to such a distribution is written $s \leftarrow_p S$, and we assume all sampling is efficient. We use p_m to denote a message distribution over $\mathcal{M}$ and p_k for a key distribution over $\mathcal{K}$. Thus sampling according to these distributions is denoted $M \leftarrow_{p_m} \mathcal{M}$ and $K \leftarrow_{p_k} \mathcal{K}$. Note that we assume that draws from p_m and p_k are independent, which is not always the case but will be in our example applications; see Section 7. Whether HE schemes can provide security for any kind of dependent distributions is an interesting question for future work.

Message Recovery Security. To formalize our security goals, we use the notion of security against message recovery attacks. Normally, one aims that, given the encryption of a message, the probability of any adversary recovering the correct message is negligible. But this is only possible when both messages and keys have high entropy, and here we may have neither. Nevertheless, we can measure the message recovery advantage of any adversary concretely, and will do so to show (say) that attackers cannot achieve advantage better than $1/2^\mu$ where μ is the min-entropy of the key distribution p_k.

Formally, we define the MR security game as shown in Figure 1 and define advantage for an adversary $\mathcal{A}$ against a scheme HE by $\mathbf{Adv}_{\mathsf{HE},p_m,p_k}^{\mathrm{mr}}(\mathcal{A}) = \Pr[\mathrm{MR}_{\mathsf{HE},p_m,p_k}^{\mathcal{A}} \Rightarrow \mathsf{true}]$. When working in the random oracle (RO) model, the MR game additionally has a procedure implementing a random function that $\mathcal{A}$ may query. For our schemes, we allow $\mathcal{A}$ to run for an unbounded amount of time and make an unbounded number of queries to the RO. For simplicity we assume p_m and p_k are independent of the RO.

$$\begin{array}{|l|}
\hline
\mathrm{MR}_{\mathsf{HE},p_m,p_k}^{\mathcal{A}} \\
\hline
K^* \leftarrow_{p_k} \mathcal{K} \\
M^* \leftarrow_{p_m} \mathcal{M} \\
C^* \leftarrow_{\$} \mathsf{HEnc}(K^*, M^*) \\
M \leftarrow_{\$} \mathcal{A}(C^*) \\
\text{return } M = M^* \\
\hline
\end{array}$$

Fig. 1. Game defining MR security

Semantic Security. In the case that keys are sufficiently unpredictable and adversaries are computationally bounded, our HE schemes will achieve semantic security [24]. Our schemes will therefore never provide worse confidentiality than conventional encryption, and in particular the MR advantage in this case equals the min-entropy of the message distribution p_m plus the (assumed) negligible semantic security term. When combined with a suitable password-based key-derivation function [32], our schemes will also achieve the multi-instance security guarantees often desired for password-based encryption [6]. Note that the results in [6] still hold only for attackers that cannot exhaust the min-entropy of the key space.

In the full version we discuss why existing or naïve approaches, e.g., conventional encryption or hiding a true plaintext in a list of fake ones, aren't satisfactory HE schemes.

4 Distribution-Transforming Encoders

We introduce a new type of message encoding scheme that we refer to as a *distribution-transforming encoder* (DTE). Formally, it is a pair $\mathsf{DTE} = (\mathsf{encode}, \mathsf{decode})$ of algorithms. The usually randomized algorithm encode takes as input a message $M \in \mathcal{M}$ and outputs a value in a set $\mathcal{S}$. We call the range $\mathcal{S}$ the *seed space* for reasons that will become clear in a moment. The deterministic algorithm decode takes as input a value $S \in \mathcal{S}$ and outputs a message $M \in \mathcal{M}$. We call a DTE scheme *correct* if for any $M \in \mathcal{M}$, $\Pr[\mathsf{decode}(\mathsf{encode}(M)) = M] = 1$.

A DTE encodes a priori knowledge of the message distribution p_m. One goal in constructing a DTE is that **decode** applied to uniform points provides sampling close to that of a target distribution p_m. For a given DTE (that will later always be clear from context), we define p_d to be the distribution over $\mathcal{M}$ defined by

$$p_d(M) = \Pr\left[\, M' = M \;:\; U \leftarrow\!\!{}_\$\, S \;;\; M' \leftarrow \mathsf{decode}(S) \,\right] .$$

We will often refer to p_d as the DTE distribution. Intuitively, in a good or secure DTE, the distributions p_m and p_d are "close."

Formally, we define this notion of DTE security or goodness, as follows. Let $\mathcal{A}$ be an adversary attempting to distinguish between the two games shown in Figure 2. We define advantage of an adversary $\mathcal{A}$ for a message distribution p_m and encoding scheme DTE = (encode, decode) by

$$\mathbf{Adv}^{\mathrm{dte}}_{\mathsf{DTE},p_m}(\mathcal{A}) = \left| \Pr\left[\, \mathsf{SAMP1}^{\mathcal{A}}_{\mathsf{DTE},p_m} \Rightarrow 1 \,\right] - \Pr\left[\, \mathsf{SAMP0}^{\mathcal{A}}_{\mathsf{DTE}} \Rightarrow 1 \,\right] \right| .$$

While we focus mostly on adversaries with unbounded running times, we note that these measures can capture computationally-good DTEs as well. A perfectly secure DTE is a scheme for which the indistinguishability advantage is zero for even unbounded adversaries. In the full version we explore another way of measuring DTE goodness that, while more complex, sometimes provides slightly better bounds.

Inverse Sampling DTE. We first build a general purpose DTE using inverse sampling, a common technique for converting uniform random variables into ones from some other distribution. Let F_m be the cumulative distribution function (CDF) associated with a known message distribution p_m according to some ordering of $\mathcal{M} =$

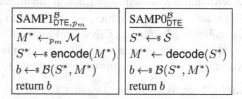

Fig. 2. Games defining DTE goodness

$\{M_1, \ldots, M_{|\mathcal{M}|}\}$. Define $F_m(M_0) = 0$. Let the seed space be $S = [0,1)$. Inverse sampling picks a value according to p_m by selecting $S \leftarrow\!\!{}_\$\, [0,1)$; it outputs M_i such that $F_m(M_{i-1}) \leq S < F_m(M_i)$. This amounts to computing the inverse CDF $M = F_m^{-1}(S) = \min_i\{F_m(M_i) > S\}$. The associated DTE scheme IS-DTE = (is-encode, is-decode) encodes by picking uniformly from the range $[F_m(M_{i-1}), F_m(M_i))$ for input message M_i, and decodes by computing $F_m^{-1}(S)$.

All that remains is to fix a suitably granular representation of the reals between $[0,1)$. The representation error gives an upper bound on the DTE security of the scheme. We defer the details and analysis to the full version. Encoding and decoding each work in time $\mathcal{O}(\log |\mathcal{M}|)$ using a tables of size $\mathcal{O}(|\mathcal{M}|)$, though its performance can easily be improved for many special cases (e.g., uniform distributions).

DTEs for RSA Secret Keys. We turn to building a DTE for RSA secret keys. A popular key generation algorithm generates an RSA key of bit-length 2ℓ via rejection sampling of random values $p, q \in [2^{\ell-1}, 2^\ell)$. The rejection criterion for either p or q is failure of a Miller-Rabin primality test [30, 33]; the resulting distribution of primes is (essentially) uniform over the range. The private exponent is computed as $d = e^{-1} \bmod (p-1)(q-1)$ for some fixed e (typically 65537), yielding secret key (N, d) and public key (N, e). Usually, the key p, q is stored with some ancillary values (not efficiently recoverable from d) to speed up exponentiation via the Chinese Remainder Theorem. Since for fixed e, the pair p, q fully defines the secret key, we now focus on building DTEs that take as input primes $p, q \in [2^{\ell-1}, 2^{\ell})$ for some ℓ and aim to match the message distribution p_m that is uniformly distributed over the primes in $[2^{\ell-1}, 2^{\ell})$.

One strawman approach is just to encode the input p, q as a pair of $(\ell - 2)$-bit strings (the leading '1' bit left implicit), but this gives a poor DTE. The prime number theorem indicates that an ℓ-bit integer will be prime with probability about $1/\ell$; thus an adversary $\mathcal{A}$ that applies primality tests to a candidate plaintext has a (very high) DTE advantage of about $1 - 1/\ell^2$.

We can instead adapt the rejection-sampling approach to prime generation itself as a DTE, RSA-REJ-DTE $=$ (rsa-rej-encode, rsa-rej-decode), which works as follows. Encoding (rsa-rej-encode) takes a pair of primes (p, q), constructs a vector of t bitstrings selected uniformly at random from the range $[2^{\ell-1}, 2^{\ell})$, replaces the first (resp. second) prime integer in the list by p (resp. q), and outputs the modified vector of t integers (each encoded using $\ell - 2$ bits). (If there's one prime and it's not the last integer in the vector, then that prime is replaced by p and the last integer is replaced by q. Should there be no primes in the vector, or one prime in the last position, then the last two integers in the vector are replaced by (p, q).) Decoding (rsa-rej-decode) takes as input a vector of the t integers, and outputs its first two primes. If there do not exist two primes, then it outputs some (hard-coded) fixed primes.[1] For simplicity, we assume a perfect primality testing algorithm; it is not hard to generalize to probabilistic ones.[2] We obtain the following security bound.

Theorem 1. *Let* p_m *be uniform over primes in* $[2^{\ell-1}, 2^{\ell})$ *for some* $\ell \geq 2$ *and let RSA-REJ-DTE be the scheme described above. Then* $\mathbf{Adv}^{\mathrm{dte}}_{\mathit{RSA\text{-}REJ\text{-}DTE}, p_m}(\mathcal{A}) \leq (1 - 1/(3\ell))^{t-1}$ *for any adversary* $\mathcal{A}$.

This scheme is simple, but a small adversarial advantage does translate into a large encoding. For example with $\ell = 1024$ (2048-bit RSA), in order to achieve a bound of $\mathbf{Adv}^{\mathrm{dte}}_{\mathsf{RSA\text{-}REJ\text{-}DTE}, p_m}(\mathcal{A}) < 10^{-5}$ requires $t \geq 35,361$, resulting in an encoding of about 4.5 megabytes. (Assuming keys of low entropy, 10^{-5} is small enough to contribute insignificantly to security bounds on the order of those in Section 7.) It may be tempting to try to save on space by treating S as a seed for a pseudorandom generator (PRG) that is then used to generate the t values during decoding. Encoding, though, would then need to identify seed values that map to particular messages (prime pairs), effectively inverting the PRG, which is infeasible.

Some RSA key generators do not use rejection-sampling, but instead use the classic algorithm that picks a random integer in $[2^{\ell-1}, 2^{\ell})$ and increments it by two until a prime is found (c.f., [15,25]). In this case, a DTE can be constructed (see the full version for details) that requires only $2(\ell - 2)$-bit seeds, and so is space-optimal. Other, more

---

[1] We could also output bottom, but would then need to permit errors in decoding and HE decryption.

[2] Doing so would also require our definition of DTE correctness to allow errors.

$\mathsf{HEnc}^H(K, M)$	$\mathsf{HDec}^H(K, (R, C_2))$
$S \leftarrow_\$ \mathsf{encode}(M)$	$S \leftarrow C_2 \oplus H(R, K)$
$R \leftarrow_\$ \{0,1\}^n$	$M \leftarrow \mathsf{decode}(S)$
$C_2 \leftarrow_\$ H(R, K) \oplus S$	return M
return (R, C_2)	

Fig. 3. A particularly simple instantiation of DTE-then-Encrypt using a hash-function H to implement the symmetric encryption

randomness-efficient rejection-sampling techniques [23] may also be used to obtain smaller encodings.

In some special settings it may be possible to hook existing key-generation software, extract the PRG key / seed κ used for the initial generation of an RSA key pair, and apply HE directly to κ. A good DTE (and thus HE scheme) can then be constructed trivially, as κ is just a short (e.g., 256-bit) uniformly random bitstring.

5   DTE-Then-Encrypt Constructions

We now present a general construction for HE schemes for a target distribution p_m. Intuitively, the goal of any HE scheme is to ensure that the plaintext resulting from decrypting a ciphertext string under a key is indistinguishable from freshly sampling a plaintext according to p_m. Let $\mathsf{DTE} = (\mathsf{encode}, \mathsf{decode})$ be a DTE scheme whose outputs are in the space $\mathcal{S} = \{0,1\}^s$. Let $\mathsf{SE} = (\mathsf{enc}, \mathsf{dec})$ be a conventional symmetric encryption scheme with message space $\mathcal{S}$ and some ciphertext space $\mathcal{C}$.

Then DTE-then-Encrypt $\mathsf{HE}[\mathsf{DTE}, \mathsf{SE}] = (\mathsf{HEnc}, \mathsf{HDec})$ applies the DTE encoding first, and then performs encryption under the key. Decryption works in the natural way. It is easy to see that the resulting scheme is secure in the sense of semantic security (when keys are drawn from a large enough space) should SE enjoy the same property.

We fix a simple instantiation using a hash function $H : \{0,1\}^n \times \mathcal{K} \to \mathcal{S}$ to perform symmetric encryption, see Figure 3. It is denoted as $\mathsf{HE}[\mathsf{DTE}, H]$. Of course, one should apply a password-based key-derivation function to K first, as per [32]; we omit this for simplicity.

To analyze security, we use the following approach. First we establish a general theorem (Theorem 2) that uses the goodness of the DTE scheme to move to a setting where, intuitively, the attacker's best bet is to output the message M that maximizes the probability (over choice of key) of M being the result of decrypting a random challenge ciphertext. The attacker wins, then, with exactly the sum of the probabilities of the keys that map the ciphertext to that message. Second, we define a weighted balls-and-bins game with non-uniform bin sizes in a way that makes the expected load of the maximally loaded bin at the end of the game exactly the winning probability of the attacker. We can then analyze these balls-and-bins games for various message and key distributions combinations (in the random oracle model). We put all of this together to derive bounds for some concrete applications in Section 7, but emphasize that the results here provide a general framework for analyzing HE constructions.

Applying DTE Goodness. Let $\mathcal{K}_{M,C} = \{K : K \in \mathcal{K} \wedge M = \mathsf{HDec}(K,C)\}$ be the set of keys that decrypt a specific ciphertext to a specific message and (overloading notation slightly) let $p_k(\mathcal{K}_{M,C}) = \sum_{K \in \mathcal{K}_{M,C}} p_k(K)$ be the aggregate probability of selecting a key that falls in any such set. Then for any $C \in \mathcal{C}$ we define $L_{\mathsf{HE},p_k}(C) = \max_M p_k(\mathcal{K}_{M,C})$. Let L_{HE,p_k} represent the random variable $L_{\mathsf{HE},p_k}(C)$ defined over C uniformly chosen from $\mathcal{C}$ and any coins used to define HDec. (For example in the hash-based scheme, we take this over the coins used to define H when modeled as a random oracle.) We will later show, for specific message/key distributions and using balls-and-bins-style arguments, bounds on $\mathrm{E}\,[\,L_{\mathsf{HE},p_k}\,]$. We call this value the expected maximum load, following the terminology from the balls-and-bins literature.

For the following theorem we require from SE only that encrypting uniform messages gives uniform ciphertexts. More precisely, that $S \leftarrow_{\$} \mathcal{S}$; $C \leftarrow_{\$} \mathsf{enc}(K, S)$ and $C \leftarrow_{\$} \mathcal{C}$; $S \leftarrow \mathsf{dec}(K, C)$ define identical distributions for any key $K \in \mathcal{K}$. This is true for many conventional schemes, including the hash-based scheme used in Figure 3, CTR mode over a block-cipher, and CBC-mode over a block cipher (assuming the DTE is designed so that $\mathcal{S}$ includes only bit strings of length a multiple of the block size). The proof of the following theorem is given in the full version.

Theorem 2. *Fix distributions p_m, p_k, an encoding scheme DTE for p_m, and a symmetric encryption scheme* $\mathsf{SE} = (\mathsf{enc}, \mathsf{dec})$. *Let $\mathcal{A}$ be an MR adversary. Then we give a specific adversary $\mathcal{B}$ in the proof such that* $\mathbf{Adv}^{\mathrm{mr}}_{\mathsf{HE},p_m,p_k}(\mathcal{A}) \leq \mathbf{Adv}^{\mathrm{dte}}_{\mathsf{DTE},p_m}(\mathcal{B}) + \mathrm{E}\,[\,L_{\mathsf{HE},p_k}\,]$. *Adversary $\mathcal{B}$ runs in time that of $\mathcal{A}$ plus the time of one* enc *operation.*

The Balls-and-Bins Interpretation. What remains is to bound $\mathrm{E}\,[\,L_{\mathsf{HE},p_k}\,]$. To do so, we use the following equivalent description of the probability space as a type of balls-and-bins game. Uniformly pick a ciphertext $C \leftarrow_{\$} \mathcal{C}$. Each ball represents one key K and has weight equal to $p_k(K)$. We let $a = |\mathcal{K}|$ be the number of balls. Each bin represents a message M and $b = |\mathcal{M}|$ is the number of bins.[3] A ball is placed in a particular bin should C decrypt under K to the message labeling that bin. Then L_{HE,p_k} as defined above is exactly the random variable defined as the maximum, over bins, sum of weights of all balls thrown into that bin. In this balls-and-bins game the balls are weighted, the bins have varying capacities, and the (in)dependence of ball throws depends on the details of the symmetric encryption scheme used.

To derive bounds, then, we must analyze the expected maximum load for various balls-and-bins games. For brevity in the following sections we focus on the hash-based HE scheme shown in Figure 3. By modeling H as a random oracle,[4] we get that all the ball throws are independent. At this stage we can also abstract away the details of the DTE, instead focusing on the distribution p_d defined over $\mathcal{M}$. The balls-and-bins game is now completely characterized by p_k and p_d, and we define the random variable L_{p_k,p_d} as the load of the maximally loaded bin at the end of the balls-and-bins game that throws $|\mathcal{K}|$ balls with weights described by p_k independently into $|\mathcal{M}|$ bins, choosing a bin according to p_d. The following lemma formalizes this transition.

---

[3] Convention is to have m balls and n bins, but we use a balls and b bins to avoid confusion since m connotes messages.

[4] Technically speaking we only require the non-programmable random oracle [22, 31].

Lemma 1. *Consider HE[DTE, H] for H modeled as a RO and DTE having distribution p_d. For any key distribution p_k, $E[L_{HE,p_k}] \leq E[L_{p_k,p_d}]$.*

We give similar lemmas for block-cipher based modes (in the ideal cipher model) in the full version. Thus we can interchange the hash-based symmetric encryption scheme for other ones in the final results of Section 7 with essentially the same security bounds.

6   Balls-and-Bins Analyses

In this section we derive bounds for various types of balls-and-bins games, as motivated and used for the example applications of HE in the next section. These cases are by no means exhaustive; they illustrate the power of our general HE analysis framework. Treating p_k and p_d as vectors, we can write their dimension as $|p_k| = a$ and $|p_d| = b$.

In the special case of $a = b$ and both p_k and p_d uniform, the balls-and-bins game becomes the standard one. One can use the classic proof to show that $E[L_{p_k,p_d}] \leq \frac{1}{b} + \frac{3\ln b}{b\ln\ln b}$. HE schemes for real applications, however, are unlikely to coincide with this special case, and so we seek other bounds.

Majorization. To analyze more general settings, we exploit a result due to Berenrink, Friedetzky, Hu, and Martin [7] that builds on a technique called "majorization" earlier used for the balls-and-bins setting by Azar, Broder, Karlin, and Upfal [1].

Distributions such as p_k and p_d can be viewed as vectors of appropriate dimension over $\mathbb{R}$. We assume below that vector components are in decreasing order, e.g. that $p_k(i) \geq p_k(j)$ for $i < j$. Let m be a number and $p_k, p'_k \in \mathbb{R}^a$. Then p'_k *majorizes* p_k, denoted $p'_k \succ p_k$, if $\sum_{i=1}^{a} p'_k[i] = \sum_{i=1}^{a} p_k[i]$ and $\sum_{i=1}^{j} p'_k[i] \geq \sum_{i=1}^{j} p_k[i]$ for all $1 \leq j \leq a$.

Majorization intuitively states that p'_k is more "concentrated" than p_k: a prefix of any length of p'_k has cumulative weight at least as large as the cumulative weight of the same-length prefix of p_k. We have the following theorem from [7, Cor. 3.5], slightly recast to use our terminology. We also extend our definition of load to include the i highest loaded bins: let $L^i_{p_k,p_d}$ be the random variable which is the total weight in the i highest-loaded bins at the end of the balls-and-bins game.

Theorem 3 (BFHM08). *Let p_k, p'_k, p_d be distributions. If $p'_k \succ p_k$, then $E[L^i_{p'_k,p_d}] \geq E[L^i_{p_k,p_d}]$ for all $i \in [1, b]$.*

Consider the case $i = 1$, which corresponds to the expected maximum bin loads for the two key distributions. As a concrete example, let $p_k = (1/2, 1/4, 1/4)$, $p'_k = (1/2, 1/2, 0)$. Then $p'_k \succ p_k$ and thus $E[L(p'_k, p_d)] \geq E[L(p_k, p_d)]$ because "fusion" of the two 1/4-weight balls into one ball biases the expected maximum load upwards.

Our results will use majorization to shift from a setting with non-uniform key distribution p_k having max-weight w to a setting with uniform key distribution with weight $\lceil 1/w \rceil$.

Non-uniform Key Distributions. We turn now to giving a bound for the case that p_k has maximum weight w (meaning $p_k(M) \leq w$ for all M) and p_d is uniform. In our examples in the next section we have that $a \ll b$, and so we focus on results for this case. We start with the following lemma (whose proof is given in the full version).

Lemma 2. *Suppose p_k has maximum weight w and p_d is such that $b = ca$ for some positive integer c. Then for any positive integer $s > 2e/c$, where e is Euler's constant, it holds that*

$$\mathrm{E}\left[L_{p_k,p_d}\right] \leq w \left((s-1) + 2 \left(\frac{a^2}{c^{s-1}} \right) \left(\frac{e}{s} \right)^s \right).$$

For cases in which $b = \mathcal{O}(a^2)$, a convenient, somewhat tighter bound on $\mathrm{E}\left[L_{p_k,p_d}\right]$ is possible. We observe that in many cases of interest, the term $r(c,b)$ in the bound below will be negligible. Proof of this next lemma is given in the full version.

Lemma 3. *Suppose p_k has maximum weight w and p_d is such that $b = ca^2$ for some positive integer c. Then $\mathrm{E}\left[L_{p_k,p_d}\right] \leq w \left[1 + \frac{1}{2c} + r(c,b)\right]$, where e is Euler's constant and $r(c,b) = \left(\frac{e}{27c^2}\right)\left(1 - \frac{e}{cb}\right)^{-1}$.*

Non-uniform Balls-and-Bins. To support our examples in the next section, we also consider the case of non-uniform p_d. Proof of this lemma is given in the full version.

Lemma 4. *Let $L_\mathcal{B}$ denote the maximum load yielded by throwing a balls (of weight 1) into a set $\mathcal{B}$ of b bins of non-uniform capacity at most $0 \leq \gamma \leq 3 - \sqrt{5}$. Let $L_{\mathcal{B}^*}$ denote the maximum load yielded by throwing $a^* = 3a$ balls (of weight 1) into a set $\mathcal{B}^*$ of $b^* = \lfloor 2/\gamma \rfloor$ bins of uniform capacity. Then $\mathrm{E}[L_\mathcal{B}] \leq \mathrm{E}[L_{\mathcal{B}^*}]$.*

7   Example Applications, Bounds, and Deployment Considerations

We now draw together the results of the previous sections into some concrete examples involving honey encryption of RSA secret keys and credit card data. For concreteness, we assume password-based encryption of these secrets, although our proven results are much more general. Appealing again to Bonneau's Yahoo! study [12] in which the most common password was selected by $1.08\% \approx 1/100$ of users, we assume for simplicity that the maximum-weight password / key is selected with probability $w = 1/100$. (At this level of entropy, prior security results for PBE schemes are not very useful.)

7.1   HE for Credit Card Numbers, PINs, and CVVs

We first consider application of HE to credit card numbers. For convenience, we evaluate HE as applied to a single value, e.g., one credit-card number. Recall, though, that HE security is unaffected by simultaneous encryption of multiple, independent messages drawn from the same distribution. So our security bounds in principle apply equally well to encryption of a vault or repository of multiple credit-card numbers.

A (Mastercard or Visa) credit card number, known technically as a Primary Account Number (PAN), consists of sixteen decimal digits. Although structures vary somewhat, commonly nine digits constitute the cardholder's account number, and may be regarded as selected uniformly at random upon issuance. One digit is a (mod 10) checksum (known as the Luhn formula). A useful result then is the following theorem, whose proof is given in the full version.

Theorem 4. *Consider HE[IS-DTE, H] with H modeled as a RO and IS-DTE using an ℓ-bit representation. Let p_m be a uniform distribution over b messages and p_k be a key-distribution with maximum weight w. Let $\alpha = \lceil 1/w \rceil$. Then for any adversary $\mathcal{A}$,*
$$\mathbf{Adv}^{mr}_{HE,p_m,p_k}(\mathcal{A}) \le w(1+\delta) + \frac{1+\alpha}{2^\ell} \text{ where } \delta = \frac{\alpha^2}{2b} + \frac{e\alpha^4}{27b^2}\left(1 - \frac{e\alpha^2}{b^2}\right)^{-1}.$$

For many cases of interest, $b \gg \alpha^2$, and thus δ will be small. We can also set ℓ appropriately to make $(1+\alpha)/2^\ell$ negligible. Theorem 4 then yields a simple and useful bound, as for our next two examples.

As cardholder account numbers are uniformly selected nine-digit values, they induce a uniform distribution over a space of $b = 10^9$ messages. Given $w = 1/100$, then, $\alpha^2/b = 10^{-5}$ and so $\delta \approx 0$. The upper bound on MR advantage is $w = 1/100$. This bound is essentially tight, as there exists an adversary $\mathcal{A}$ achieving advantage $w = \frac{1}{100}$. Namely, the adversary that decrypts the challenge ciphertext with the most probable key and then outputs the resulting message. This adversary has advantage at least w.

Finally, consider encrypting both 5-digits of the credit-card / debit-card account number (the last 4 digits still considered public) along with the user's PIN number. (Credit card PINs are used for cash withdrawals and to authorize debit-card transactions.) A detailed examination of a corpus of 3.4 million user-selected PINs is given in [8], and gives in particular a CDF that can be used to define an inverse sampling DTE. The most common user-selected PIN is '1234'; it has an observed frequency of 10.713%. Thus, PINs have very little minimum entropy (roughly 3 bits). Combining a PIN with a five-digit effective account number induces a *non-uniform* message space, with maximum message probability $\gamma = 1.0713 \times 10^{-6}$. Consequently, Theorem 4 is not applicable to this example.

A variant of the proof of Theorem 4, however, that makes use of Lemma 4 for non-uniform bin sizes, establishes the following corollary.

Corollary 1. *Consider HE[IS-DTE, H] with H modeled as a RO and IS-DTE using an ℓ-bit representation. Let p_m be a non-uniform distribution with maximum message probability $\gamma \le 3 - \sqrt{5}$, and p_k be a key-distribution with maximum weight w. Let $\alpha = \lceil 1/w \rceil$. Then for any adversary $\mathcal{A}$, $\mathbf{Adv}^{mr}_{HE,p_m,p_k}(\mathcal{A}) \le w(1+\delta) + \frac{(1+\alpha)}{2^\ell}$ where $\delta = \frac{\overline{\alpha}^2}{2\overline{b}} + \frac{e\overline{\alpha}^4}{27\overline{b}^2}\left(1 - \frac{e\overline{\alpha}^2}{\overline{b}^2}\right)^{-1}$ and $\overline{\alpha} = \lceil 3/w \rceil$ and $\overline{b} = \lfloor 2/\gamma \rfloor$.*

Corollary 1 yields a bound defined by the expected maximum load of a balls-and-bins experiment with 300 balls (of weight $w = 1/100$) and $\lfloor 2/\gamma \rfloor = 1,866,890$ uniform-capacity bins, with $c = \overline{\alpha}^2/\overline{b} = 1/20.74$. The final MR bound is therefore about 1.02%. This is slightly better than the bound of the previous example (at 1.05%). It shows, significantly, that Corollary 1 is tight enough to give improved bounds despite the scant minimum entropy in a PIN.

Credit cards often have an associated three- or four-digit *card verification value*, a secret used to conduct transactions. In the full version, we investigate the case of applying HE to such small messages.

7.2 HE for RSA Secret Keys

We now show how to apply HE to RSA secret keys using the DTE introduced for this purpose in Section 4.

In some settings, RSA is used without making a user's public key readily available to attackers. A common example is RSA-based client authentication to authorize access to a remote service using HTTPS or SSH. The client stores an RSA secret / private key and registers the corresponding public key with the remote service.

Practitioners recommend encrypting the client's secret key under a password to provide defense-in-depth should the client's system be passively compromised.[5] With password-based encryption, though, an attacker can mount an offline brute-force attack against the encrypted secret key. Use of straightforward unauthenticated encryption wouldn't help here: as the secret key is usually stored as a pair of primes p and q (to facilitate use of the Chinese Remainder Theorem), an attacker can quickly test the correctness of a candidate secret key by applying a primality test to its factors. Similarly, given the passwords used in practice (e.g., for $w = 1/100$), key-hardening mechanisms (e.g., iterative hashing) do not provide an effective slowdown against brute-force attack. Cracking a password-encrypted RSA secret key remains fairly easy.

HE is an attractive option in this setting. To build an HE scheme for 2ℓ-bit RSA secret keys we can use the DTE from Section 4. We have the following theorem.

Theorem 5. *Consider* HE[RSA-REJ-DTE, H] *with* RSA-REJ-DTE *the 2ℓ-bit RSA DTE using seed space vectors of size t and H modeled as a RO. Let p_m be uniform over primes in $[2^{-\ell-1}, 2^\ell)$ and let p_k be a key-distribution with maximum weight w. Let $\alpha = \lceil 1/w \rceil$. Then for any adversary $\mathcal{A}$ it holds that*

$$\mathbf{Adv}^{mr}_{HE, p_m, p_k}(\mathcal{A}) \le w(1 + \delta) + (1 + \alpha)\left(1 - \frac{1}{3\ell}\right)^{t-1}$$

where $\delta = \frac{\alpha^2}{2\lceil 2^{\ell-1}/\ell \rceil} + \left(\frac{e\alpha^4}{27\lceil 2^{\ell-1}/\ell \rceil^2}\right) \cdot \left(1 - \frac{e\alpha^2}{\lceil 2^{\ell-1}/\ell \rceil^2}\right)^{-1}$.

The proof is much like that of Theorem 4 (the full version): apply Theorem 2; plug in the advantage upper bound for the RSA rejection sampling DTE (Theorem 1); apply Lemma 1 to get independent ball tosses; majorize to get uniform-weighted balls (Theorem 3); apply a union bound to move from p_d back to uniform bin selection; and then finally apply the balls-and-bins analysis for uniform bins (Lemma 3).

The term δ is small when $-\log w \ll \ell$. For example, with $\ell = 1024$ and $w = 1/100$ and setting $t = 35,393$, we have that $\delta \approx 0$ and the overall MR advantage is upper bounded by 1.1%. The ciphertext size will still be somewhat large, at about 4.5 megabytes; one might use instead the DTEs discussed in the full version for which similar MR bounds can be derived yet ciphertext size ends up short.

---

[5] Obviously an active attacker can sniff the keyboard or otherwise capture the secret key. We also are ignoring the role of network attackers that may also gain access to transcripts dependent on the true secret key. See [26] for discussion.

7.3 Deployment Considerations

A number of considerations and design options arise in the implementation and use of HE. Here we briefly mention a couple involving the use of checksums.

Typo-Safety. Decryption of an HE ciphertext C^* under an incorrect password / key K yields a fake but valid-looking message M. This is good for security, but can be bad for usability if a fake plaintext appears valid to a legitimate user.

One possible remedy, proposed in [28], is the use of error-detecting codes or checksums, such as those for ISBN book codes. For example, a checksum on the password / key K^* might be stored with the ciphertext C^*. Such checksums would reduce the size of the key space $\mathcal{K}$ and cause some security degradation, and thus require careful construction and application. Another option in some cases is online verification of plaintexts. For example, if a credit-card number is rejected by an online service after decryption, the user might be prompted to re-enter her password.

Honeytokens without Explicit Sharing. In [10], it is suggested that fake passwords / honeytokens be shared explicitly between password vault applications and service providers. Application of error-correcting codes to plaintexts in HE can create *honeytokens without explicit sharing*. As a naïve example (and crude error-correcting code), an HE scheme for credit-card numbers might explicitly store the first two digits of the credit-card account number. If a service provider then receives an invalid credit-card number in which these digits are correct, it gains evidence of a decryption attempt on the HE ciphertext by an adversary. This approach degrades security slightly by reducing the message space, and must be applied with care. But it offers an interesting way of coupling HE security with online security checks.

8   Conclusion

Low-entropy secrets such as passwords are likely to persist in computer systems for many years. Their use in encryption leaves resources vulnerable to offline attack. Honey encryption can offer valuable additional protection in such scenarios. HE yields plausible looking plaintexts under decryption with invalid keys (passwords), so that offline decryption attempts alone are insufficient to discover the correct plaintext. HE also offers a gracefully degrading hedge against partial disclosure of high min-entropy keys, and, by simultaneously meeting standard PBE security notions should keys be high entropy, HE never provides worse security than existing PBE schemes.

We showed applications in which HE security upper bounds are equal to an adversary's conditional knowledge of the key distribution, i.e., they min-entropy of keys. These settings have message space entropy greater than the entropy of keys, but our framework can also be used to analyze other settings.

A key challenge for HE—as with all schemes involving decoys—is the generation of plausible honey messages through good DTE construction. We have described good DTEs for several natural problems. For the case where plaintexts consist of passwords, e.g., password vaults, the relationship between password-cracking and DTE construction mentioned above deserves further exploration. DTEs offer an intriguing way of potentially repurposing improvements in cracking technology to achieve improvements in encryption security by way of HE.

More generally, for human-generated messages (password vaults, e-mail, etc.), estimation of message distributions via DTEs is interesting as a natural language processing problem. Similarly, the reduction of security bounds in HE to the expected maximum load for balls-and-bins problems offers an interesting connection with combinatorics. The concrete bounds we present can undoubtedly be tightened for a variety of cases. Finally, a natural question to pursue is what kinds of HE bounds can be realized in the standard model via, e.g., k-wise independent hashing.

Acknowledgements. The authors thank the anonymous reviewers, as well as Daniel Wichs and Mihir Bellare, for their insightful comments.

References

1. Azar, Y., Broder, A., Karlin, A., Upfal, E.: Balanced allocations. SIAM Journal on Computing 29(1), 180–200 (1999)
2. Bellare, M., Boldyreva, A., O'Neill, A.: Deterministic and efficiently searchable encryption. In: Menezes, A. (ed.) CRYPTO 2007. LNCS, vol. 4622, pp. 535–552. Springer, Heidelberg (2007)
3. Bellare, M., Brakerski, Z., Naor, M., Ristenpart, T., Segev, G., Shacham, H., Yilek, S.: Hedged public-key encryption: How to protect against bad randomness. In: Matsui, M. (ed.) ASIACRYPT 2009. LNCS, vol. 5912, pp. 232–249. Springer, Heidelberg (2009)
4. Bellare, M., Fischlin, M., O'Neill, A., Ristenpart, T.: Deterministic encryption: Definitional equivalences and constructions without random oracles. In: Wagner, D. (ed.) CRYPTO 2008. LNCS, vol. 5157, pp. 360–378. Springer, Heidelberg (2008)
5. Bellare, M., Ristenpart, T., Rogaway, P., Stegers, T.: Format-preserving encryption. In: Selected Areas in Cryptography, pp. 295–312 (2009)
6. Bellare, M., Ristenpart, T., Tessaro, S.: Multi-instance security and its application to password-based cryptography. In: Safavi-Naini, R., Canetti, R. (eds.) CRYPTO 2012. LNCS, vol. 7417, pp. 312–329. Springer, Heidelberg (2012)
7. Berenbrink, P., Friedetzky, T., Hu, Z., Martin, R.: On weighted balls-into-bins games. Theoretical Computer Science 409(3), 511–520 (2008)
8. Berry, N.: PIN analysis. DataGenetics blog (2012)
9. Berson, T.A., Gong, L., Lomas, T.M.A.: Secure, keyed, and collisionful hash functions. Technical Report SRI-CSL-94-08. SRI International Laboratory (1993) (revised September 2, 1994)
10. Bojinov, H., Bursztein, E., Boyen, X., Boneh, D.: Kamouflage: loss-resistant password management. In: Gritzalis, D., Preneel, B., Theoharidou, M. (eds.) ESORICS 2010. LNCS, vol. 6345, pp. 286–302. Springer, Heidelberg (2010)
11. Boldyreva, A., Fehr, S., O'Neill, A.: On notions of security for deterministic encryption, and efficient constructions without random oracles. In: Wagner, D. (ed.) CRYPTO 2008. LNCS, vol. 5157, pp. 335–359. Springer, Heidelberg (2008)
12. Bonneau, J.: The science of guessing: analyzing an anonymized corpus of 70 million passwords. In: IEEE Symposium on Security and Privacy, pp. 538–552. IEEE (2012)
13. Bowen, B.M., Kemerlis, V.P., Prabhu, P., Keromytis, A.D., Stolfo, S.J.: Automating the injection of believable decoys to detect snooping. In: WiSec, pp. 81–86. ACM (2010)
14. Bowen, B.M., Hershkop, S., Keromytis, A.D., Stolfo, S.J.: Baiting Inside Attackers Using Decoy Documents, pp. 51–70 (2009)

15. Brandt, J., Damgård, I.B.: On generation of probable primes by incremental search. In: Brickell, E.F. (ed.) CRYPTO 1992. LNCS, vol. 740, pp. 358–370. Springer, Heidelberg (1993)

16. Canetti, R., Dwork, C., Naor, M., Ostrovsky, R.: Deniable encryption. In: Kaliski Jr., B.S. (ed.) CRYPTO 1997. LNCS, vol. 1294, pp. 90–104. Springer, Heidelberg (1997)

17. Canetti, R., Friege, U., Goldreich, O., Naor, M.: Adaptively secure multi-party computation (1996)

18. Canetti, R., Halevi, S., Steiner, M.: Hardness amplification of weakly verifiable puzzles. In: Kilian, J. (ed.) TCC 2005. LNCS, vol. 3378, pp. 17–33. Springer, Heidelberg (2005)

19. Cormen, T.H., Leiserson, C.E., Rivest, R.L., Stein, C.: Introduction to Algorithms, 3rd edn., pp. 428–436. MIT Press (2009)

20. Paes de Barros, A.: IDS mailing list, "RES: Protocol anomaly detection IDS – honeypots" (February 2003), http://seclists.org/focus-ids/2003/Feb/95

21. Dodis, Y., Smith, A.: Entropic security and the encryption of high entropy messages. In: Kilian, J. (ed.) TCC 2005. LNCS, vol. 3378, pp. 556–577. Springer, Heidelberg (2005)

22. Fischlin, M., Lehmann, A., Ristenpart, T., Shrimpton, T., Stam, M., Tessaro, S.: Random oracles with(out) programmability. In: Abe, M. (ed.) ASIACRYPT 2010. LNCS, vol. 6477, pp. 303–320. Springer, Heidelberg (2010)

23. Fouque, P.A., Tibouchi, M.: Close to uniform prime number generation with fewer random bits. Cryptology ePrint Archive, Report 2011/481 (2011), http://eprint.iacr.org/

24. Goldwasser, S., Micali, S.: Probabilistic encryption. Journal of Computer and System Sciences 28(2), 270–299 (1984)

25. Gordon, J.A.: Strong primes are easy to find. In: Beth, T., Cot, N., Ingemarsson, I. (eds.) EUROCRYPT 1984. LNCS, vol. 209, pp. 216–223. Springer, Heidelberg (1985)

26. Hoover, D.N., Kausik, B.N.: Software smart cards via cryptographic camouflage. In: IEEE Symposium on Security and Privacy, pp. 208–215. IEEE (1999)

27. Juels, A., Ristenpart, T.: Honey encryption: Beyond the brute-force barrier (full version) (2014), http://pages.cs.wisc.edu/~rist/papers/honeyenc.html

28. Juels, A., Rivest, R.: Honeywords: Making password-cracking detectable. In: ACM Conference on Computer and Communications Security, CCS 2013, pp. 145–160. ACM (2013)

29. Kausik, B.: Method and apparatus for cryptographically camouflaged cryptographic key. U.S. Patent 6, 170, 058 (2001)

30. Miller, G.: Riemann's hypothesis and tests for primality. Journal of Computer and System Sciences 13(3), 300–317 (1976)

31. Nielsen, J.B.: Separating random oracle proofs from complexity theoretic proofs: The non-committing encryption case. In: Yung, M. (ed.) CRYPTO 2002. LNCS, vol. 2442, pp. 111–126. Springer, Heidelberg (2002)

32. PKCS #5: Password-based cryptography standard (rfc 2898). RSA Data Security, Inc., Version 2.0. (September 2000)

33. Rabin, M.: Probabilistic algorithms. Algorithms and Complexity 21 (1976)

34. Ristenpart, T., Yilek, S.: When good randomness goes bad: Virtual machine reset vulnerabilities and hedging deployed cryptography. In: NDSS (2010)

35. Russell, A., Wang, H.: How to fool an unbounded adversary with a short key. In: Knudsen, L.R. (ed.) EUROCRYPT 2002. LNCS, vol. 2332, pp. 133–148. Springer, Heidelberg (2002)

36. Shannon, C.E.: Communication theory of secrecy systems. Bell System Technical Journal 28(4), 656–715 (1948)

37. Spitzner, L.: Honeypots: Tracking Hackers. Addison-Wesley Longman Publishing Co., Inc., Boston (2002)

38. Spitzner, L.: Honeytokens: The other honeypot. Symantec Security Focus (July 2003)

Sometimes-Recurse Shuffle

Almost-Random Permutations
in Logarithmic Expected Time

Ben Morris[1] and Phillip Rogaway[2]

[1] Dept. of Mathematics, University of California, Davis, USA
[2] Dept. of Computer Science, University of California, Davis, USA

Abstract. We describe a security-preserving construction of a random permutation of domain size N from a random function, the construction tolerating adversaries asking all N plaintexts, yet employing just $\Theta(\lg N)$ calls, on average, to the one-bit-output random function. The approach is based on card shuffling. The basic idea is to use the *sometimes-recurse* transformation: lightly shuffle the deck (with some other shuffle), cut the deck, and then recursively shuffle one of the two halves. Our work builds on a recent paper of Ristenpart and Yilek.

Keywords: Card shuffling, format-preserving encryption, PRF-to-PRP conversion, mix-and-cut shuffle, pseudorandom permutations, sometimes-recurse shuffle, swap-or-not shuffle.

1 Introduction

FORMAT-PRESERVING ENCRYPTION. Suppose you are given a blockcipher, say AES, and want to use it to efficiently construct a cipher on a smaller domain, say the set of $N = 10^{16}$ sixteen-digit credit card numbers. You could, for example, use AES as the round function for several rounds of a Feistel network, the approach taken by emerging standards [1, 7]. But information-theoretic security will vanish by the time the adversary asks $\sqrt{N}$ queries, which is a problem on small-sized domains. (It is a problem from the point of view of having a satisfying provable-security claim; likely it is not a problem with respect to their being a feasible attack.) Alternatively, you could precompute a random permutation on N points, but spending $\Omega(N)$ time in computation will become undesirable before $\sqrt{N}$ adversarial queries becomes infeasible.

This paper provides a new solution to this problem of *format-preserving encryption*, where we aim to build ciphers with an arbitrary finite domain [3, 4, 8, 5], frequently $[N] = \{0, 1, \ldots, N-1\}$ for some N. Our solution lets you encipher a sixteen-digit credit card with about 1000 expected AES calls, getting an essentially ideal provable-security claim. (One thousand AES calls comes to about 80K clock cycles, or 25 μsec, on a recent Intel processor.) In particular, the adversary can ask any number of queries—including all N of them—and its advantage in distinguishing the constructed cipher from a random permutation

P.Q. Nguyen and E. Oswald (Eds.): EUROCRYPT 2014, LNCS 8441, pp. 311–326, 2014.
© International Association for Cryptologic Research 2014

will be insignificantly more than its ability to break the underlying primitive (in our example, AES) with a like number of queries.

Cast in more general language, this paper is about constructing ciphers—meaning information theoretic or complexity theoretic PRPs—on an arbitrary domain $[N]$, starting from a PRF. (If starting from AES, only a single bit of each 128-bit output will be used. A random permutation on 128 bits that gets truncated to a single bit is extremely close to a random function [2].) As in other recent work [14, 11, 9], our ideas are motivated by card shuffling and its cryptographic interpretation. This connection was first observed by Naor [15, p. 62], [17, p. 17], who explained that when a card shuffle is *oblivious*—meaning that you can trace the trajectory of a card without attending to the trajectories of *other* cards in the deck—then it determines a computationally plausible cipher. We will move back and forth between the language of encryption and that of card shuffling: a PRP/cipher is a shuffle; a plaintext x encrypts to ciphertext y if the card initially at position x ends up at position y; the PRP's key is the randomness underlying the shuffle.

THE SWAP-OR-NOT AND MIX-AND-CUT SHUFFLES. Hoang, Morris, and Rogaway describe an oblivious shuffle well-suited for enciphering on a small domain [11]. In the binary-string setting ($N = 2^n$), round i of their *swap-or-not* shuffle employs a random string $K_i \in \{0,1\}^n$ and replaces X by $K_i \oplus X$ if $F(i, \hat{X}) = 1$, where F is a random function to bits and $\hat{X} = \max(X, X \oplus K_i)$. If $F(i, \hat{X}) = 0$, then X is left alone. After all rounds are complete, the final value of input X is the result of the shuffle. The authors show that $O(\lg N)$ rounds suffice to get a cipher that will look uniform to an adversary that makes $q < (1 - \epsilon)N$ queries. But as q approaches N, one would need more and more rounds and, eventually, one gets a non-result.

Ristenpart and Yilek were looking for practical ways to tolerate adversaries asking all $q = N$ queries, a goal they called *full* security. Assume again that we want to shuffle $N = 2^n$ cards. Then Ristenpart and Yilek's *Icicle* construction first mixes the cards using some given (we'll call it the *inner*) shuffle. Then they cut the deck into two piles and recursively shuffle each. The authors explain that if the inner shuffle is a good *pseudorandom separator* (PRS), then the constructed shuffle will achieve full security. A shuffle is a good PRS if, after shuffling, the (unordered) *set* of cards ending up in each of the two piles is indistinguishable from a uniform partitioning of the cards into two equal-sized sets.

Ristenpart and Yilek apply the Icicle construction to the swap-or-not shuffle, a combination they call *mix-and-cut*. The combination achieves full security in $\Theta(\lg^2 N)$ rounds. When the underlying round function is realized by an AES call, mix-and-cut constructs a cipher on N points, achieving full security, with $\Theta(\lg^2 N)$ AES calls. While full security is directly achieved by other oblivious shuffles [9, 13, 18], mix-and-cut would seem to be much faster.

CONTRIBUTIONS. We reconceptualize what is going on in Ristenpart and Yilek's mix-and-cut. Instead of thinking of the underlying transformation as turning a PRS into a PRP, we think of it as turning a mediocre PRP into a better one.

If the inner shuffle is good enough to mix half the cards—in the inverse shuffle, any $N/2$ cards end up in almost uniform positions—then the constructed shuffle will achieve full security.

After this shift in viewpoint, we make a simple change to mix-and-cut that dramatically improves its speed. As before, one begins by applying the inner shuffle to the N cards. Then one splits the deck and recursively shuffles *one* (rather than both) of the two halves. Using swap-or-not (SN) for the inner shuffle we now get a PRP over $[N]$ enjoying full security and computable in $\Theta(\lg N)$ expected time. We call the SN-based construction SR, for *sometimes-recurse*. The underlying transformation we call **SR** (in bold font).

Our definitions and results apply to an arbitrary domain size N (it need not be a power of two). We emphasize that the adversary may query *all* points in the domain. We give numerical examples to illustrate that the improvement over mix-and-cut is large. We also explain why, with SR, having the running time depend on the key and plaintext does *not* give rise to side-channel attacks. Finally, we explain how to cheaply tweak [12] the construction, degrading neither the run-time nor the security bound compared to the untweaked counterpart. (Ristenpart and Yilek likewise support tweaks [16], but their quantitative bounds give up more, and each round key needs to depend on the tweak.)

ADDITIONAL RELATED WORK. Granboulan and Pornin [9] also give a shuffle achieving full security, and Ristenpart and Yilek's paper [16] can likewise be seen as building on it, reconceptualizing their work as the application of the Icicle construction to a particular PRS. But the chosen PRS is computationally expensive to realize, involving extensive use of arbitrary-precision floating-point arithmetic to do approximate sampling from a hypergeometric distribution. The mix-and-cut and sometimes-recurse shuffles are much more practical.

For realistic domain sizes N, both mix-and-cut and sometimes-recurse are also much faster than the method of Stefanov and Shi [18], which spends $\tilde{\Theta}(N)$ time to preprocess the key into a table of size $\tilde{\Theta}(\sqrt{N})$ that supports $\tilde{\Theta}(\sqrt{N})$-time evaluation of the constructed cipher.

2 Preliminaries

SHUFFLES AS FORMAL OBJECTS. A shuffle SH_N on $N \geq 1$ cards is a distribution on permutations of $[N]$. We are only interested in distributions that can be described by efficient probabilistic algorithms, so one can alternatively consider a shuffle SH_N on N cards to be a probabilistic algorithm that bijectively maps each $x \in [N]$ to a value $\mathrm{SH}_N(x) \in [N]$. The algorithm may be thought of as keyed, the key coinciding with the algorithm's coins. A shuffle SH (now on an arbitrary number of cards) is a family of shuffles on N cards, one for each number $N \geq 1$. One can regard SH as taking two arguments, with $\mathrm{SH}_N(x) \in [N]$ being the image of $x \in [N]$ under the random permutation on $[N]$. If we write $\mathrm{SH}(x)$ for some shuffle SH we mean $\mathrm{SH}_N(x)$ for some understood N.

As suggested already, we may refer to points $x \in [N]$ as *cards*. We then think of $\mathrm{SH}_N(x)$ as the location that card x landed at following the shuffle of these N cards. Locations are indexed 0 to $N - 1$. We think of 0 as the leftmost position and $N - 1$ as the rightmost position. If we shuffle a deck with an even number N of cards, the lefthand pile would be positions $\{0, \ldots, N/2 - 1\}$ and the righthand pile would be positions $\{N/2, \ldots, N - 1\}$. The card that landed at position $y \in [N]$ is card $\mathrm{SH}_N^{-1}(y)$.

We are interested in operators that transform one shuffle into another. Such an operator **OP** takes a shuffle SH and produces a shuffle $\mathrm{SH}' = \mathbf{OP}[\mathrm{SH}]$. The definition of $\mathrm{SH}'_N(x)$ may depend on $\mathrm{SH}_{N'}(x')$ values with $N' \neq N$.

PROBABILITY. For distributions μ and ν on a finite set V, define the total variation distance

$$\|\mu - \nu\| = \tfrac{1}{2} \sum_{x \in V} |\mu(x) - \nu(x)|.$$

If $V_1, \ldots, V_k$ are finite sets and τ is a probability distribution on $V_1 \times \cdots \times V_k$, then for l with $0 \leq l \leq k - 1$ define

$$\tau(\cdot \mid x_1, \ldots, x_l) = \mathbf{P}(X_{l+1} = \cdot \mid X_1 = x_1, \ldots, X_l = x_l),$$

where $(X_1, \ldots, X_k) \sim \tau$.

Lemma 1. *Let $V_1, \ldots, V_n$ be finite sets and let μ and ν be probability distributions on $V_1 \times \cdots \times V_n$. Suppose that $(Z_1, \ldots, Z_n) \sim \mu$. Then*

$$\|\mu - \nu\| \leq \sum_{l=0}^{n-1} \mathbf{E}\left(\|\mu(\cdot \mid Z_1, \ldots, Z_l) - \nu(\cdot \mid Z_1, \ldots, Z_l)\|\right).$$

We defer the proof of Lemma 1 to Appendix A. The lemma immediately gives us the following.

Corollary 2. *Suppose that for every l with $1 \leq l \leq n$ there is an $\epsilon_l > 0$ such that for any $z_1, z_2, \ldots, z_l$ we have $\|\mu(\cdot \mid z_1, \ldots, z_l) - \nu(\cdot \mid z_1, \ldots, z_l)\| \leq \epsilon_l$. Then $\|\mu - \nu\| \leq \epsilon_1 + \cdots + \epsilon_n$.*

Let us explain part of the utility of this fact. Consider a random permutation π on $\{0, 1, \ldots, N-1\}$, which we view as a random ordering of cards arranged from left to right. Suppose $N_1, \ldots, N_n$ are positive integers with $N_1 + N_2 + \cdots + N_n = N$. Let Z_1 be the configuration of cards in the rightmost N_1 positions, let Z_2 be the configuration of cards in the N_2 positions to the immediate left of these, and so on. Applying Corollary 2 to $(Z_1, \ldots, Z_n)$ shows that if the distribution of the rightmost N_1 cards is within ϵ_1 of uniform, and regardless of the values of these cards the conditional distribution of the N_2 cards to their immediate left is within ϵ_2 of uniform, and so on, then the whole deck is within distance $\epsilon = \epsilon_1 + \epsilon_2 + \cdots + \epsilon_n$ of a uniform random permutation.

3   Mix-and-Cut Shuffle

This section reviews and reframes the prior work of Ristenpart and Yilek [16].

The mix-and-cut transformation can be described recursively as follows. Assume we want to shuffle $N = 2^n$ cards. If $N = 1$ then we are done; a single card is already shuffled. Otherwise, to mix-and-cut shuffle $N \geq 2$ cards,

1. shuffle the N cards using some other, inner shuffle; and then
2. cut the deck into two halves (that is, the cards in positions $0, \ldots, \frac{N}{2} - 1$ and the cards in positions $\frac{N}{2}, \ldots, N - 1$) and, recursively, shuffle each half.

The method can be seen as an operator, **MC**, that maps a shuffle SH on a power-of-two number of cards to a shuffle SH$'$ = **MC**[SH] on the same number of cards. A sufficient condition for SH$'$ to achieve full security is for SH to *lightly shuffle* the deck. Informally, to lightly shuffle the deck means that if one identifies some $N/2$ positions of the deck, then the cards that land in these positions should be nearly uniform, that is, like $N/2$ samples without replacement from the N cards. More formally, we say that SH ε-*lightly shuffles* if for any $N/2$ positions the distribution of the *unordered set* of cards in those positions is within distance ε of a uniform random subset of cards of size $N/2$. Note that if the shuffle SH is swap-or-not (SN) then it is equivalent to ask that SH itself send $N/2$ cards to something ε-close to uniform, as SN is identical in its forward and backward direction, up to the naming of keys.

Let's consider the speed of **MC** with SN as the underlying shuffle, a combination we'll write as MC = **MC**[SN]. First some preliminaries. For a round-parameterized shuffle SH that approaches the uniform distribution, let $\tau_q^r(N)$ be the induced distribution after r rounds on some q distinct cards $(x_1, \ldots, x_q) \in [N]^q$ from a deck of size N, and let $\pi_q(N)$ be the distribution of q samples, without replacement, from $[N]$. Let $\Delta_{\mathrm{SH}}(N, q, r) = \|\tau_q^r(N) - \pi_q(N)\|$ be the total variation distance between these two distributions. Hoang, Morris, and Rogaway show that, for the swap-or-not shuffle, SN,

$$\Delta_{\mathrm{SN}}(N, q, r) \leq \frac{2N^{3/2}}{r+2} \left(\frac{q+N}{2N} \right)^{r/2+1} = \Delta_{\mathrm{SN}}^{\mathrm{ub}}(N, q, r). \tag{1}$$

Assuming even N, setting $q = N/2$ in this equation gives

$$\Delta_{\mathrm{SN}}(N, N/2, r) \leq N^{3/2} \left(\frac{3}{4} \right)^{r/2}$$

and so $\Delta_{\mathrm{SN}}(N, N/2, r) \leq \varepsilon$ if

$$\frac{3}{2} \lg N + \frac{r}{2} \lg(3/4) \leq \lg \varepsilon,$$

which occurs if

$$\begin{aligned}
r &\geq \frac{\lg \varepsilon - (3/2) \lg N}{(1/2) \lg(3/4)} \\
&\geq 7.23 \lg N - 4.82 \lg \varepsilon \tag{2} \\
&\in \Theta(\lg N - \lg \varepsilon).
\end{aligned}$$

Let SH be a round-based shuffle approaching the uniform distribution and let $T_{\mathrm{SH}}(N, q, \varepsilon)$ be the minimum number r such that $\Delta_{\mathrm{SH}}(N, q, r) \leq \varepsilon$. Let $T_{\mathrm{SH}}(N, \varepsilon) = T_{\mathrm{SH}}(N, N, \varepsilon)$ be the time to mix all the cards to within ε. For $\mathrm{MC} = \mathbf{MC}[\mathrm{SN}]$ to mix all $N = 2^n$ cards to within ε it will suffice if we arrange that each invocation of SN mixes half the cards to within ε/n. Assuming this strategy, the total number of needed rounds will be

$$T_{\mathrm{MC}}(2^n, \varepsilon) \leq \sum_{\ell=1}^{n} T_{\mathrm{SN}}(2^\ell, 2^{\ell-1}, \varepsilon/n)$$

$$\leq \sum_{\ell=1}^{n} \left(7.23\,\ell - 4.82\,\lg(\varepsilon/n) \right) \qquad \text{(from (2))}$$

$$\leq 14.46\,n^2 + 4.82\,n \lg n - 4.82\,n \lg \varepsilon$$

$$\in \Theta(\lg^2 N - \lg N \lg \varepsilon)$$

Interpreting, the MC construction can encipher n-bit strings, getting to within any fixed total variation distance ε of uniform, by using $\Theta(n)$ stages of $\Theta(n)$ rounds, so $\Theta(n^2)$ total rounds. The round functions here are assumed uniform and independent. Replacing them by a complexity-theoretic PRF, we are converting a PRF into a PRP on domain $\{0,1\}^n$ with $\Theta(n^2)$ calls, achieving tight provable security and no limit on the number of adversarial queries.

4 Sometimes-Recurse Shuffle

The SN shuffle has a stronger mixing property than light shuffling: namely, the SN shuffle randomizes the *sequence* of cards in any $N/2$ positions of the deck (as made precise by equation (1)). Therefore, after shuffling the deck with SN and cutting it in half, there is no need to recurse on one of the two halves. Either pile can be declared finished and in the next stage we recursively shuffle only the other pile. Assuming that the first stage brings the distribution of the cards in the rightmost $N/2$ positions to within distance ϵ_1 of uniform, and the next stage brings the conditional distribution of the cards in the prior $N/4$ positions to within distance ϵ_2 of uniform, and so on, the final permutation is with distance $\epsilon_1 + \cdots + \epsilon_n$ of a uniform random permutation, where n is the number of stages. This follows by the remark that immediately followed Corollary 2.

POWER-OF-TWO DOMAINS. The *sometimes-recurse* (**SR**) transform can thus be described as follows. Assume for now that want to shuffle $N = 2^n$ cards. (We will generalize afterward.) If $N = 1$ then we are done; a single card is already shuffled. Otherwise, to **SR** shuffle $N \geq 2$ cards,

1. shuffle the N cards using some other, inner shuffle; and then
2. cut the deck into two halves and, recursively, shuffle the first half.

The method can be seen as an operator, **SR**, that maps a shuffle SH on any power-of-two cards to a shuffle $\mathrm{SH}' = \mathbf{SR}[\mathrm{SH}]$ on any power-of-two cards.

Recasting the method into more cryptographic language, suppose you are given a variable-input-length PRP $E: \mathcal{K} \times \{0,1\}^* \to \{0,1\}^*$. Write $E_K(\cdot)$ for $E(K, \cdot)$. Each $E_K(\cdot)$ is a length-preserving permutation. We construct from E a PRP $E' = \mathbf{SR}[E]$ as follows. First, assert that $E'_K(\epsilon) = \epsilon$, where ϵ is the empty string. Otherwise, let $E'_K(X) = Y$ if $Y = E_K(X) = 1 \parallel Y'$ begins with a 1-bit, and let $E'_K(X) = 0 \parallel E_K(Y')$ if $Y = E_K(X) = 0 \parallel Y'$ begins with a 0-bit.

THE **SR** TRANSFORMATION. The description above assumes a power-of-two number of cards and an even cut of the deck. The first assumption runs contrary to our intended applications, and dropping this assumption necessitates dropping the second assumption as well. Here then is the **SR** transform stated more broadly. Assume an inner shuffle, SH, that can mix an arbitrary number of cards. Let $p: \mathbb{N} \to \mathbb{N}$, the *split*, be a function with $1 \le p(N) < N$. We'll sometimes write p_N for $p(N)$. We construct a shuffle SH$' = \mathbf{SR}_p[\text{SH}]$. Namely, if $N = 1$, we are done; a single card is shuffled. Otherwise,

1. shuffle the N cards using the inner shuffle, SH; and then
2. cut the deck into a first pile having p_N cards and a second pile having $q_N = N - p_N$ cards. Recursively, shuffle the first pile.

INITIAL AND GENERATED N-VALUES. A potential point of confusión is that, above, the name "N" effectively has two different meanings: it is used for both the *initial* N, call it N_0, that specifies the domain $[N_0]$ on which we seek to encipher; and it is used as a generic name for any of the N-values that can arise in recursive calls that begin with the initial N. These are the *generated* N-values, a set of numbers $\mathcal{G}_p(N_0) = \mathcal{G}(N_0)$. Note that we count the initial N among the generated N-values $\mathcal{G}_g(N_0)$. As an example, if the initial N is $N_0 = 10^{16}$ and $p_N = \lfloor N/2 \rfloor$, then there are 54 generated N-values, which are $\mathcal{G}_p(10^{16}) = \{10^{16}, 10^{16}/2, 10^{16}/4, \ldots, 71, 35, 17, 8, 4, 2, 1\}$. In general, $\mathcal{G}_p(N_0)$ is the set $\{N_0, N_1, \ldots, N_n\}$ where $N_i = p(N_{i-1})$ and $N_n = 1$. We call n the number of *stages*.

THE TRANSFORMATION WORKS. Let $q: \mathbb{N} \to \mathbb{N}$ and let $\varepsilon: \mathbb{N} \to [0,1]$ be functions, $1 \le q(N) \le N$. We may write $q(N)$ and ε_N for $q(N)$ and $\varepsilon(N)$. Let SH be a shuffle that can mix any number of cards. We say that SH is (q, ε)-*good* if for all $N \in \mathbb{N}$, for any distinct $y_1, \ldots, y_{q(N)} \in [N]$, the total-variation distance between $(\text{SH}^{-1}(y_1), \ldots, \text{SH}^{-1}(y_{q(N)}))$ and the uniform distribution on $q(N)$ distinct points from $[N]$ is at most $\varepsilon(N)$. A shuffle is ε-*good* if it is (q, ε)-good for $q(N) = N$. We have the following:

Theorem 3. *Let* $p, q: \mathbb{N} \to \mathbb{N}$ *and* $\varepsilon: \mathbb{N} \to [0,1]$ *be functions,* $p(N) + q(N) = N$, *and fix* $N_0 \in \mathbb{N}$. *Suppose that* SH *is a* (q, ε)-*good shuffle. Then* $\mathbf{SR}_p[\text{SH}]$ *is a* δ-*good shuffle where* $\delta = \sum_{N \in \mathcal{G}_g(N_0)} \varepsilon_N$.

Proof. Consider the indicated shuffle π on domain $[N_0]$. Enumerate the elements of $\mathcal{G}_p(N_0)$ as $\{N_0, N_1, \ldots, N_n\}$ where $N_0 > N_1 > \cdots > N_n$. The first stage of the shuffle brings the distribution of the rightmost q_{N_0} cards to within a distance

```
10   procedure E_{KF}^N(X)                                    //invariant: X ∈ [N]
11   if N = 1 then return X                          //a single card is already shuffled

20   for i ← 1 to t_N do                                      //SN, for t_N-rounds
21       X' ← K_i − X (mod N)                          //X' is the "partner" of X
22       X̂ ← max(X, X')                             //canonical name for {X, X'}
23       if F(i, X̂) = 1 then X ← X'                     //maybe swap X and X'

30   if X < p_N then return E_{KF}^{p_N}(X)          //recursively shuffle the first pile
31   if X ≥ p_N then return X                          //but second pile is done
```

Fig. 1. Construction SR = **SR**[SN]. The method enciphers on $[N_0]$ (the initial value of N), each stage (recursive invocation) employing t_N-rounds of SN (lines 20–23). The split values, p_N, are a second parameter on which SR depends. The randomness for SN is determined by $F\colon \mathbb{N} \times \mathbb{N} \to \{0, 1\}$ and $K\colon \mathbb{N} \to \mathbb{N}$.

ε_{N_0} of uniform. Regardless of the values of these cards the second stage brings the conditional distribution of the preceding q_{N_1} cards to within distance ε_{N_1} of uniform, and so on. Therefore, applying Corollary 2 (as explained in the argument immediately following the statement of Corollary 2) shows that the final permutation is within δ of a uniform random permutation, where $\delta = \varepsilon_{N_0} + \varepsilon_{N_1} + \cdots + \varepsilon_{N_n}$. □

USING SN AS THE INNER SHUFFLE. We'll write SR (no bold) for **SR**[SN], the sometimes-recurse transformation applied to the swap-or-not shuffle. The algorithm is shown in Fig. 1, now written out in the manner of a cipher, where the trajectory of a single card X is followed. Of course SN = SN_t depends on the round count and **SR** = **SR**$_p$ depends on the split, so SR = $SR_{t,p}$ depends on both. The canonical choice for the split p_N is $p_N = \lfloor N/2 \rfloor$; when no mention of p_N is made, this is assumed. There is no default for the round counts t_N; we must select these values with care.

We proceed to analyze SR, for the canonical split, with the help of Proposition 3 and equation (2). We aim to shuffle N cards to within a target distance ε. Assume we run each stage (that is, each SN shuffle) with t_N adequate to achieve error ε/n for any half, rounded up, of the cards. When N is a power of 2, the expected total number of rounds to encipher a point will then be

$$\mathbf{E}[T_{\text{SR}}(N, \varepsilon)] \leq T_{\text{SN}}(N, \tfrac{N}{2}, \tfrac{\varepsilon}{\lg N}) + \frac{T_{\text{SN}}(\tfrac{N}{2}, \tfrac{N}{4}, \tfrac{\varepsilon}{\lg N})}{2} + \frac{T_{\text{SN}}(\tfrac{N}{4}, \tfrac{N}{8}, \tfrac{\varepsilon}{\lg N})}{4} + \cdots$$

$$\leq 2(7.23 \lg N + 4.82 \lg \lg N - 4.82 \log \varepsilon) \qquad \text{from (2)}$$

For arbitrary N (not necessarily a power of two), simply replace N by $2N$ in the equation just given to get an upper bound. This is valid because the sequence of generated N-values for N_0 are bounded above by the sequence of generated

N-values for N_0' the next higher power of two, and, additionally, the bound $\Delta_{\mathrm{SN}}^{\mathrm{ub}}(N, N/2, r)$ is increasing in N. Thus, for any N,

$$\mathbf{E}[T_{\mathrm{SR}}(N, \varepsilon)] \leq 14.46 \lg N + 4.82 \lg \lg 2N - 4.82 \lg \varepsilon + 14.46 \qquad (3)$$
$$\in \Theta(\lg N - \lg \varepsilon)$$

The worst-case number of rounds is similarly bounded. We summarize the result as follows.

Theorem 4. *For any $N \geq 1$ and $\varepsilon \in (0,1)$, the SR construction enciphers points on $[N]$ in $\Theta(\lg N - \lg \varepsilon)$ expected rounds and $\Theta(\lg^2 - \lg N \lg \varepsilon)$ rounds in the worst case. No adversary can distinguish the construction from a uniform permutation on $[N]$ with advantage exceeding ε. This assumes uniformly random round keys and round functions for SN, appropriate round counts t_N, and the canonical split.*

As a numerical example, equation (3) gives $\mathbf{E}[T_{\mathrm{SR}}(10^{16}, 10^{-10})] \leq 1159$. In the next section we will do better than this—but not by much—by doing calculations directly from equation (1) and by partitioning the error ε so as to give a larger portion to earlier (that is, larger) generated N.

5   Parameter Optimization

ROUND COUNTS. Let us continue to assume the canonical split of $p_N = \lfloor N/2 \rfloor$ and look at the optimization of round counts t_N under this assumption.

In speaking below of the number p of nontrivial stages of SR, we only count generated N-values with $N \geq 3$. This is because we will always select $t_2 = 1$, as this choice already contributes zero error, and the degenerate SR stage with $N = 1$ contributes no error and needs no t_1 value (let $t_1 = 0$). Corresponding to this convention for counting the number of nontrivial stages, we let $\mathcal{G}'(N_0) = \mathcal{G}(N_0) \setminus \{1, 2\}$ be the generated N-values when starting with N_0 but excluding $N = 1$ and $N = 2$.

Given an initial N_0 and a target ε, we consider two strategies for computing the round counts t_N for $N \in \mathcal{G}'(N_0)$. Both use the upper bound $\Delta_{\mathrm{SN}}^{\mathrm{ub}}(N, q, r) = (2N^{3/2}/(r+2)) \cdot ((q+N)/(2N))^{r/2+1}$ on $\Delta_{\mathrm{SN}}(N, q, r)$ given by equation (1).

1. *Split the error equally.* Let $n = |\mathcal{G}'(N_0)| \approx \lg N_0$ be the number of nontrivial stages. For each $N \in \mathcal{G}'(N_0)$ let t_N be smallest number r for which $\Delta_{\mathrm{SN}}^{\mathrm{ub}}(N, \lceil N/2 \rceil, r) \leq \varepsilon/n$. This will result in rounds counts t_N that diminish with diminishing N, each stage contributing about the same portion to the error.
2. *Constant round count.* Let r_0 be the smallest number r for which the sum $\sum_{N \in \mathcal{G}'(N_0)} \Delta_{\mathrm{SN}}^{\mathrm{ub}}(N, \lceil N/2 \rceil, r) < \varepsilon$, and let $t_N = r_0$ for all $N \in \mathcal{G}'(N_0)$. This will result in stages that contribute a diminishing amount to the error.

The table of Fig. 2 illustrates the expected and worst-case number of rounds that result from these two strategies if we encipher on a domain of $N_0 = 10^d$

d	2	4	6	8	10	12	14	15	16	18	20	30
min-1	187	239	289	337	386	435	483	507	531	580	628	869
mean-1	359	464	563	660	758	856	952	1000	1048	1145	1242	1723
max-1	1110	2442	4411	6402	8885	11842	14790	16639	18239	22158	26069	51453
min-2	218	225	272	318	365	413	460	484	507	555	602	840
mean-2	427	450	544	636	730	826	920	968	1014	1110	1204	1680
max-2	1308	2701	5168	7951	11681	16107	20701	23716	26365	32745	39131	83160

Fig. 2. Speed of SR shuffle. Minimum, mean (rounded to nearest integer), and maximum number of rounds to SR-encipher a d-digit decimal string with error $\varepsilon \le 10^{-10}$ and round counts t_N selected by strategy 1 or strategy 2, as marked. The split is $p_N = \lfloor N/2 \rfloor$. Round-counts for MC always coincide with the max-labeled rows.

points and cap the error at $\varepsilon = 10^{-10}$. The pronounced differences between mean and max round counts (a factor exceeding 17 when $n = 16$) coincides with the saving of SR over MC. In contrast, there is only a modest difference in mean round-counts between the two round-count selection strategies.

In numerical experiments, more complex strategies for determining the round counts did not work better.

NON-EQUAL SPLITS. Besides the split of $p_N = \lfloor N/2 \rfloor$, we considered splits of $p_N = \lfloor \alpha N \rfloor$ for $\alpha \in (0, 1)$. For example, if the input is a decimal string then a selection of $\alpha = 0.1$ corresponds to using SN until a 90% fraction of the cards are (almost) properly distributed, at which point there would be only a 10% chance of needing to recurse. When a recursive call is made, it would be on a string of length one digit less than before. But splits this uneven turn out to be inefficient; see Fig. 3. On the other hand, when the split $p_N = \lfloor \alpha N \rfloor$ has α close to 1/2, the expected number of rounds is not very sensitive to α; again see the figure. Small α make each SN stage slower, but there will be fewer of them; large α make each SN stage faster, but there will be more.

Given the similar mean round counts for strategies 1 and 2, the similar mean round counts all α near 1/2, the implementation simplicity of dividing by 2, and the better maximum rounds counts of strategy 1, the choice of strategy 1 and $\alpha = 1/2$ seems best.

6   Incorporating Tweaks

The possibly-small domain for FPE makes it important, in applications, to have the constructed cipher be *tweaked*: an additional argument T, the tweak, names the desired permutation in a family of keyed permutations [12]. In the reference experiment that defines security one asks for indistinguishability (complexity theoretic or information theoretic) from a family of tweak-indexed, uniformly random permutations, each tweak naming an independent permutation from

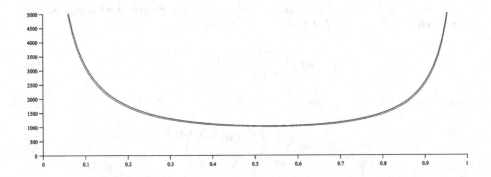

Fig. 3. Selecting the split. Expected number of rounds (the y-coordinate) to encipher $N = 10^{16}$ points using SR and a split of $p_N = \lfloor \alpha N \rfloor$ for various α (the x-axis). The total variation distance is capped at $\varepsilon = 10^{-10}$. The top (blue) curve is with round counts t_N determined by for strategy 1; the bottom (red) curve for strategy 2. In both cases the smallest expected number of rounds occurs with a non-canonical split: 1048 rounds ($\alpha = 0.5$) reduced to 1043 rounds ($\alpha = 0.53$) for strategy 1; and 1014 rounds ($\alpha = 0.5$) reduced to 1010 rounds ($\alpha = 0.52$) for strategy 2.

the collection. As an example of a tweak's use, in the context of enciphering a credit card number, one might encipher only the middle six digits, using the first six and last four digits as the tweak.

The obvious way to incorporate a tweak in SR is to make the round constants K_i (line 21 of Fig. 1) depend on it, and to make the round functions $F(i, \hat{X})$ (line 23 of Fig. 1) depend on it. Note, however, that an inefficiency emerges when the former is done: if there is a large space of possible tweaks, it will no longer be possible to precompute the round constants K_i. In addition, we do not want to get a security bound that gives up a factor corresponding to the number of tweaks used, which would be a potentially major loss in quantitative security.

As it turns out, neither price need be paid. In particular, it is fine to leave the round constants independent of the tweak T, and, even when doing so, there need be no quantitative security loss in the bound from making this change. What we call tweaked-SR, then, is identical to Fig. 1 except that the tweak T is added to the scope of F at line 23.

To establish security for this scheme, obtaining the same bounds as before, we go back to the swap-or-not shuffle and show that, in that context, if the round constants are left untweaked but the round function is tweaked, then equation (1) continues to hold. The result is as follows.

Theorem 5. *Fix $q_1, \ldots, q_l$ with $\sum_{i=1}^{l} q_i = q$. Let $X_t^1, X_t^2, \ldots, X_t^l$ be SN shuffles on G driven by the same round constants $K_1, \ldots, K_r$, but independent round functions. Let $X_t = (X_t^1, \ldots, X_t^l)$. For i with $1 \leq i \leq l$, let π^i be the uniform distribution on q_i samples without replacement from G, and let*

$\pi = \pi^1 \times \pi^2 \cdots \times \pi^l$. *That is, π is the distribution of l independent samples, one each from $\pi^1, \pi^2, \ldots, \pi^l$. Let τ be the distribution of X_r. Then*

$$\|\tau - \pi\| \le \frac{2N^{3/2}}{r+2} \left(\frac{q+N}{2N}\right)^{r/2+1}. \tag{4}$$

Proof. Let

$$\Delta(j) = \sum_{m=0}^{j-1} \frac{\sqrt{N}}{2} \left(\frac{m+N}{2N}\right)^{r/2}.$$

We show that

$$\|\tau - \pi\| \le \Delta(q)$$

from which (4) follows by way of

$$\|\tau - \pi\| \le \sum_{m=0}^{q-1} \frac{\sqrt{N}}{2} \left(\frac{m+N}{2N}\right)^{r/2}$$

$$\le N^{3/2} \int_0^{q/2N} (1/2 + x)^{r/2} \, dx$$

$$\le \frac{2N^{3/2}}{r+2} \left(\frac{q+N}{2N}\right)^{r/2+1}.$$

For random variables $W_1, W_2, \ldots, W_j$, we write $\tau^i(\cdot \mid W_1, W_2, \ldots, W_j)$ for the conditional distribution of X_r^i given $W_1, W_2, \ldots, W_j$. Then Lemma 1 implies that

$$\|\tau - \pi\| \le \sum_{i=1}^l \mathbf{E}\left(\|\tau^i(\cdot \mid X_r^1, \ldots, X_r^{i-1}) - \pi^i\|\right). \tag{5}$$

We claim that

$$\mathbf{E}\left(\|\tau^i(\cdot \mid X_r^1, \ldots, X_r^{i-1}) - \pi^i\|\right) \le \Delta(q_i). \tag{6}$$

For distributions μ and ν the total variation distance $\|\mu - \nu\|$ is half the L^1-norm of $\mu - \nu$. Since the L^1-norm is convex, to verify the claim it is enough to show that

$$\mathbf{E}\left(\|\tau^i(\cdot \mid X_r^1, \ldots, X_r^{i-1}, K_1, \ldots, K_r) - \pi^i\|\right) \le \Delta(q_i).$$

But the X_r^i are conditionally independent given $K_1, K_2, \ldots, K_r$, so

$$\tau^i(\cdot \mid X_r^1, \ldots, X_r^{i-1}, K_1, \ldots, K_r) = \tau^i(\cdot \mid K_1, \ldots, K_r).$$

Thus it remains to show that

$$\mathbf{E}\left(\|\tau^i(\cdot \mid K_1, \ldots, K_r) - \pi^i\|\right) \le \Delta(q_i) = \sum_{m=0}^{q_i-1} \frac{\sqrt{N}}{2} \left(\frac{m+N}{2N}\right)^{r/2},$$

but this inequality is shown on page 8 of [11]. This verifies (6), and combining
this with (5) gives

$$\|\tau - \pi\| \leq \sum_{i=1}^{l} \Delta(q_i)$$
$$\leq \Delta(q),$$

where the second inequality holds because the summands in the definition of
$\Delta(j)$ are increasing. This completes the proof.   □

Theorem 5 plays the same role in establishing the security for tweaked-SR as
equation (1) played for establishing the security of the basic version. The values
in the table of Fig. 2, for example, apply equally well to the tweakable-SR.

We comment that in the the tweakable version of SR, the round constants do
depend on the generated N-values. This dependency can also be eliminated, but
we do not pursue this for now.

7 Absence of Timing Attacks

With SR (and, more generally, with **SR**), the total number of rounds t^* used to
encipher a plaintext $X \in [N_0]$ to a ciphertext $Y \in [N_0]$ will depend on X and
the key $\mathbf{K} = KF$. This suggests that an adversary's acquiring t^*, perhaps by
measuring the running time of the algorithm, could be damaging. But this is not
the case—not in the typical setting, where the adversary knows the ciphertext—
for, knowing Y, one can determine the corresponding t^* value.

It is easiest to describe this when $N_0 = 2^n$ is a power of two, whence the
generated N-values are $2^n, 2^{n-1}, \ldots, 4, 2, 1$. Let $t'_0, t'_1, \ldots, t'_{n-2}, t'_{n-1}, t'_n$ be the
corresponding round counts (the last two values are 1 and 0, respectively). Let
$t^*_j = \sum_{i \leq j} t'_i$ be the cumulative round counts: the total number of SN rounds if
we run for $j + 1$ stages. Then t^* is simply t^*_ℓ where ℓ is the number of leading 0-
bits in the n-bit binary representation of Y. The adversary holding a ciphertext
of $Y = 0^z 1 Z$, knows that it was produced using $t^* = t^*_z$ rounds of SN. Ciphertext
0^n is the slowest to produce, needing t^*_n rounds.

The observation generalizes when N_0 is not a power of 2: the set $[N_0]$ is
partitioned into easily-calculated intervals and the number of SN rounds that a
ciphertext Y was subjected to is determined by the interval containing it.

8 Discussion

ALTERNATIVE DESCRIPTION. It is easy to eliminate the tail recursion of Fig. 1;
no stack is needed. This and other changes are made to the alternative description of tweaked-SR given in Fig. 4. While the algorithm looks rather different
from before, it is equivalent.

WHICH PILE TO RECURSE ON? The convention that **SR** recurses on the first
(left) pile of cards, rather than on the second (right) pile of cards, simplifies

```
50   procedure E_{KF}^{T,N_0}(X)              //Encipher X ∈ [N_0] with tweak T, key KF
51   N ← N_0                                  //initial-N
52   for j ← 0 to ∞ do                        //for each stage, until we return
53     for i ← 1 to t_N do        //SN, for as many rounds as needed for this stage
54       X' ← K_i − X (mod N)                 //X' is the partner of X
55       X̂ ← max(X, X')                       //canonical name for {X, X'}
56       if F(i, X̂, T) = 1 then X ← X'        //maybe swap X and X'
57     if X ≥ ⌊N/2⌋ then return X             //right pile is done
58     N ← ⌊N/2⌋                              //left pile is new domain to shuffle
```

Fig. 4. Alternative description of the tweaked construction. We eliminate the recursion and assume the canonical split. The values t_N again parameterize the algorithm, influencing the mechanism's speed and the quality of enciphering.

bookkeeping: in this way, we will always be following a card $X \in [N]$ for decreasing values of N. Had we recursed on the second pile we would be following a card $X \in [N_0−N+1 .. N_0−1]$ for decreasing values of N. Concretely, the code in Figures 1 and 4 would become more complex with the recurse-right convention.

MULTIPLE CONCURRENT DOMAINS. Our assumption has been that the domain for the constructed cipher is $[N_0]$ for some N_0. As with variable-input-length (VIL) PRFs, it makes sense to seek security against adversaries that can simultaneously encipher points from any number of domains $\{[N_0] : N_0 \in \mathcal{N}\}$, as previously formalized [3]. This can be handled by having the round-function and round-keys depend on the description of the domain N_0. Once again it seems unnecessary to reflect the N_0 dependency in the round-keys. To prove the conjecture will take a generalization of Theorem 5.

OPEN QUESTION. The outstanding open question in this domain is whether there is an oblivious shuffle on N cards where a card can be tracked through the shuffle in *worst-case* $\Theta(\lg N)$-time. Equivalently, can we do information-theoretic PRF to PRP conversion with $\Theta(\lg N)$ calls, always, to a constant-output-length PRF?

Acknowledgments. This work was made possible by Tom Ristenpart and Scott Yilek generously sharing an early draft of their work [16]. Thanks also to Tom and Scott for their comments and interaction. Thanks to Terence Spies and Voltage Security, whose interest in FPE has motivated this line of work. Our work was supported under NSF grants CNS-0904380, CNS-1228828 and DMS-1007739.

References

1. Accredited Standards Committee X9, Incorporated (ANSI X9): X9.124: Symmetric Key Cryptography for the Financial Services Industry — Format Preserving Encryption (2011) (manuscript)

2. Bellare, M., Impagliazzo, R.: A Tool for Obtaining Tighter Security Analyses of Pseudorandom Function Based Constructions, with Applications to PRP to PRF Conversion. ePrint report 1999/024 (1999)
3. Bellare, M., Ristenpart, T., Rogaway, P., Stegers, T.: Format-Preserving Encryption. In: Jacobson Jr., M.J., Rijmen, V., Safavi-Naini, R. (eds.) SAC 2009. LNCS, vol. 5867, pp. 295–312. Springer, Heidelberg (2009)
4. Black, J.A., Rogaway, P.: Ciphers with Arbitrary Finite Domains. In: Preneel, B. (ed.) CT-RSA 2002. LNCS, vol. 2271, pp. 114–130. Springer, Heidelberg (2002)
5. Brightwell, M., Smith, H.: Using Datatype-preserving Encryption to Enhance Data Warehouse Security. In: 20th National Information Systems Security Conference Proceedings (NISSC), pp. 141–149 (1997)
6. Did, user profile http://math.stackexchange.com/users/6179/did: Total Variation Inequality for the Product Measure. Mathematics Stack Exchange, http://math.stackexchange.com/q/72322 (2011) (last visited June 2, 2014)
7. Dworkin, M.: NIST Special Publication 800-38G: Draft. Recommendation for Block Cipher Modes of Operation: Methods for Format-Preserving Encryption (July 2013)
8. FIPS 74: Guidelines for Implementing and Using the NBS Data Encryption Standard. U.S. National Bureau of Standards, U.S. Dept. of Commerce (1981)
9. Granboulan, L., Pornin, T.: Perfect Block Ciphers with Small Blocks. In: Biryukov, A. (ed.) FSE 2007. LNCS, vol. 4593, pp. 452–465. Springer, Heidelberg (2007)
10. Håstad, J.: The Square Lattice Shuffle. Random Structures and Algorithms 29(4), 466–474 (2006)
11. Hoang, V.T., Morris, B., Rogaway, P.: An Enciphering Scheme Based on a Card Shuffle. In: Safavi-Naini, R., Canetti, R. (eds.) CRYPTO 2012. LNCS, vol. 7417, pp. 1–13. Springer, Heidelberg (2012)
12. Liskov, M., Rivest, R., Wagner, D.: Tweakable Block Ciphers. J. of Cryptology 24(3), 588–613 (2011)
13. Morris, B.: The Mixing Time of the Thorp Shuffle. SIAM J. on Computing 38(2), 484–504 (2008)
14. Morris, B., Rogaway, P., Stegers, T.: How to Encipher Messages on a Small Domain: Deterministic Encryption and the Thorp Shuffle. In: Halevi, S. (ed.) CRYPTO 2009. LNCS, vol. 5677, pp. 286–302. Springer, Heidelberg (2009)
15. Naor, M., Reingold, O.: On the Construction of Pseudo-Random Permutations: Luby-Rackoff Revisited. J. of Cryptology 12(1), 29–66 (1999)
16. Ristenpart, T., Yilek, S.: The Mix-and-Cut Shuffle: Small-Domain Encryption Secure against N Queries. In: Canetti, R., Garay, J.A. (eds.) CRYPTO 2013, Part I. LNCS, vol. 8042, pp. 392–409. Springer, Heidelberg (2013)
17. Rudich, S.: Limits on the Provable Consequences of One-Way Functions. Ph.D. Thesis, UC Berkeley (1989)
18. Stefanov, E., Shi, E.: FastPRP: Fast Pseudo-Random Permutations for Small Domains. Cryptology ePrint Report 2012/254 (2012)
19. Thorp, E.: Nonrandom Shuffling with Applications to the Game of Faro. J. of the American Statistical Association 68, 842–847 (1973)

A   Proof of Lemma 1

We follow the approach outlined in [6] for bounding the total variation distance between two product measures. Define $V = V_1 \times V_2 \times \cdots \times V_n$. Note that

$$2 \|\mu - \nu\| = \sum_{x \in V} |\mu(x) - \nu(x)| \tag{7}$$

$$= \sum_{x \in V} |\mu_1(x)\mu_2(x) \cdots \mu_n(x) - \nu_1(x)\nu_2(x) \cdots \nu_n(x)|, \tag{8}$$

where, for j with $1 \leq j \leq n$, we define $\mu_j(x)$ to be $\mu(x_j \mid x_1, \ldots, x_{j-1})$, with a similar definition for $\nu_j(x)$. For $x \in V$, define $s_j(x)$ as

$$\mu_1(x)\mu_2(x) \cdots \mu_j(x)\nu_{j+1}(x) \cdots \nu_n(x).$$

Then

$$s_0(x) = \nu_1(x)\nu_2(x) \cdots \nu_n(x) \text{ and}$$
$$s_n(x) = \mu_1(x)\mu_2(x) \cdots \mu_n(x),$$

and hence by the triangle inequality the quantity (8) is at most

$$\sum_{x \in V} \sum_{j=0}^{n-1} \left| s_{j+1}(x) - s_j(x) \right| \tag{9}$$

$$= \sum_{l=0}^{n-1} \sum_{x \in V} \left| \mu_{l+1}(x) - \nu_{l+1}(x) \right| \mu_1(x)\mu_2(x) \cdots \mu_l(x)\nu_{l+2}(x) \cdots \nu_n(x). \tag{10}$$

If we sum the terms over all $x \in V$ whose first l components are $x_1, x_2, \ldots, x_l$ we get

$$\mu(x_1, x_2, \ldots, x_l) \sum_{v \in V_{l+1}} \left| \mu(v \mid x_1, x_2, \ldots, x_l) - \nu_l(v \mid x_1, x_2, \ldots, x_l) \right|$$

$$= 2\, \mu(x_1, x_2, \ldots, x_l) \, \|\mu(\cdot \mid x_1, \ldots, x_l) - \nu(\cdot \mid x_1, \ldots, x_l)\|.$$

Summing this over $x_1, \ldots, x_l$ gives

$$2\, \mathbf{E}\Big(\|\mu(\cdot \mid Z_1, \ldots, Z_l) - \nu(\cdot \mid Z_1, \ldots, Z_l)\| \Big)$$

where $(Z_1, \ldots, Z_n) \sim \mu$, and now summing this over l proves the lemma.

Tight Security Bounds
for Key-Alternating Ciphers

Shan Chen and John Steinberger[*]

Institute for Interdisciplinary Information Sciences, Tsinghua University, Beijing
{dragoncs16,jpsteinb}@gmail.com

Abstract. A t-round *key-alternating cipher* (also called *iterated Even-Mansour cipher*) can be viewed as an abstraction of AES. It defines a cipher E from t fixed public permutations $P_1, \ldots, P_t : \{0,1\}^n \rightarrow \{0,1\}^n$ and a key $k = k_0 \| \cdots \| k_t \in \{0,1\}^{n(t+1)}$ by setting $E_k(x) = k_t \oplus P_t(k_{t-1} \oplus P_{t-1}(\cdots k_1 \oplus P_1(k_0 \oplus x) \cdots))$. The indistinguishability of E_k from a truly random permutation by an adversary who also has oracle access to the (public) random permutations $P_1, \ldots, P_t$ was investigated in 1997 by Even and Mansour for $t = 1$ and for higher values of t in a series of recent papers. For $t = 1$, Even and Mansour proved indistinguishability security up to $2^{n/2}$ queries, which is tight. Much later Bogdanov et al. (2011) conjectured that security should be $2^{\frac{t}{t+1}n}$ queries for general t, which matches an easy distinguishing attack (so security cannot be more). A number of partial results have been obtained supporting this conjecture, besides Even and Mansour's original result for $t = 1$: Bogdanov et al. proved security of $2^{\frac{2}{3}n}$ for $t \geq 2$, Steinberger (2012) proved security of $2^{\frac{3}{4}n}$ for $t \geq 3$, and Lampe, Patarin and Seurin (2012) proved security of $2^{\frac{t}{t+2}n}$ for all even values of t, thus "barely" falling short of the desired $2^{\frac{t}{t+1}n}$.

Our contribution in this work is to prove the long-sought-for security bound of $2^{\frac{t}{t+1}n}$, up to a constant multiplicative factor depending on t. Our method is essentially an application of Patarin's H-coefficient technique.

1 Introduction

Given t permutations $P_1, \ldots, P_t : \{0,1\}^n \rightarrow \{0,1\}^n$ the t-round *key-alternating cipher* based on $P_1, \ldots, P_t$ is a blockcipher $E : \{0,1\}^{(t+1)n} \times \{0,1\}^n \rightarrow \{0,1\}^n$ of keyspace $\{0,1\}^{(t+1)n}$ and message space $\{0,1\}^n$, where for a key $k = k_0 \| k_1 \| \cdots \| k_t \in \{0,1\}^{(t+1)n}$ and a message $x \in \{0,1\}^n$ we set

$$E(k, x) = k_t \oplus P_t(k_{t-1} \oplus P_{t-1}(\cdots P_1(k_0 \oplus x) \cdots)). \qquad (1)$$

(See Figure 1.) Plainly, $E(k, \cdot)$ is a permutation of $\{0,1\}^n$ for each fixed $k \in \{0,1\}^{(t+1)n}$; we let $E^{-1}(k, \cdot)$ denote the inverse permutation. The P_i's are called

[*] Supported by National Basic Research Program of China Grant 2011CBA00300, 2011CBA00301, the National Natural Science Foundation of China Grant 61033001, 61361136003, and by the China Ministry of Education grant number 20121088050.

P.Q. Nguyen and E. Oswald (Eds.): EUROCRYPT 2014, LNCS 8441, pp. 327–350, 2014.
© International Association for Cryptologic Research 2014

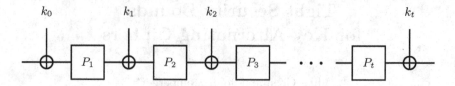

Fig. 1. A t-round key alternating cipher

the *round permutations* of E and t is the *number of rounds* of E. Thus t and the permutations $P_1, \ldots, P_t$ are parameters determining E.

Key-alternating ciphers were first proposed (for values of t greater than 1) by the designers of AES [5,6], the Advanced Encryption Standard. Indeed, AES-128 itself can be viewed as a particular instantiation of the key-alternating cipher paradigm in which the round permutations $P_1, \ldots, P_t$ equal a single permutation P (the Rijndael round function, in this case), in which $t = 10$, and in which only a subset of the $\{0,1\}^{(t+1)n} = \{0,1\}^{11n}$ possible keys are used (more precisely, the $11n$ bits of key are derived pseudorandomly from a seed of n bits, making the key space $\{0,1\}^n = \{0,1\}^{128}$). However, for $t = 1$ the design was proposed much earlier by Even and Mansour as a means of constructing a blockcipher from a fixed permutation [7]. Indeed, key-alternating ciphers also go by the name of *iterated Even-Mansour ciphers*.

Even and Mansour accompanied their proposal with "provable security" guarantees by showing that, for $t = 1$, an adversary needs roughly $2^{n/2}$ queries to distinguish $E(k, \cdot)$ for a random key k (k being hidden from the adversary) from a true random permutation, in a model where the adversary is given oracle access to $E(k, \cdot)$, $E^{-1}(k, \cdot)$ as well as to P_1, P_1^{-1}, where P_1 is modeled as a random permutation (in the dummy world, the adversary is given oracle access to two independent random permutations and their inverses). Their bound was matched by Daemen [4], who showed a $2^{n/2}$-query distinguishing attack for $t = 1$.

For $t > 1$, we can generalize the Even-Mansour indistinguishability experiment by giving the adversary oracle access to $P_1, \ldots, P_t$ and their inverses and to $E(k, \cdot)$, $E^{-1}(k, \cdot)$ in the real world (for a randomly chosen, hidden $k \in \{0,1\}^{(t+1)n}$), and to a tuple of $t + 1$ independent random permutations and their inverses in the "ideal" or "dummy" world (see Figure 2). In this case, Daemen's attack can be easily generalized to an attack of query complexity $2^{\frac{t}{t+1}n}$, as pointed out by Bogdanov et al. [2], but the security analysis of Even and Mansour could not be easily generalized to match this bound.

Bogdanov et al. did show, though, security of $2^{\frac{2}{3}n}$ for $t \geq 2$ (modulo lower-order terms), which is tight for $t = 2$ as it matches the $2^{\frac{t}{t+1}n}$-query attack. Later Steinberger [19] improved this bound to $2^{\frac{3}{4}n}$ queries for $t \geq 3$ by modifying technical aspects of Bogdanov et al.'s analysis. Orthogonally and simultaneously, Lampe, Patarin and Seurin [13] used coupling-based techniques to show security of $2^{\frac{t}{t+1}n}$ queries for nonadaptive adversaries and security $2^{\frac{t}{t+2}n}$ for adaptive adversaries (and even values of t). While the bound $2^{\frac{t}{t+2}n}$ might seem "almost" sharp, we note that

$$2^{\frac{t}{t+2}n} = 2^{\frac{(t/2)}{(t/2)+1}n}$$

is actually the conjectured adaptive security for $t/2$ rounds. Indeed, Lampe et al. basically show that an adaptive adversary attacking the t-round construction has no more advantage than a nonadapative adversary attacking $t/2$ rounds (this reduction follows upon work of Maurer et al. [16,17]). Seen this way, Lampe et al.'s result appears less sharp. The issue is not only qualitative since their bound only improves on Steinberger's for $t \geq 8$.

OUR RESULTS. In this paper we finally prove security of $2^{\frac{t}{t+1}n}$ queries for key-alternating ciphers, which has been the conjectured security since the paper of Bogdanov et al., and which is provably tight by the attack in the same paper. More precisely, we show that an adaptive adversary making at most q queries to each of its oracles has distinguishing advantage bounded by $O(1)q^{t+1}/N^t + O(1)$, where $N = 2^n$ and the two $O(1)$ terms depend on t. (See Section 2 for a formal statement.)

Our techniques are (maybe disappointingly) not as conceptually novel as those of [19] or [13], as we simply apply Patarin's H-coefficient technique. The crucial step is lower bounding the probability of a certain event, namely of the event that q input-output values become linked when t partially defined composed permutations (whose composition so far poses no contradiction to the linking of said q input-output pairs) are randomly extended. The surprising aspect of these computations is that various "second-order" factors (that one might otherwise expect to not matter) actually need to be taken into account. Informally, this can be ascribed to the fact that the values of q under consideration are far beyond birthday.

Besides shedding some light on the structural and probabilistic aspects of key-alternating ciphers in the ideal permutation model, we also hope this paper will serve as a useful additional tutorial on (or introduction to) Patarin's H-coefficient technique, which still seems to suffer from a lack of exposure.

We note that [13] also uses H-coefficient-based techniques and, indeed, our approach is much more closely inspired by that of [13] than by [2,19].

PAPER ORGANIZATION. Definitions relating to key-alternating ciphers as well as a formal statement of our main result are given in Section 2. An overview of the H-coefficient technique is given in Section 3. The proof of the main theorem is given in Section 4, while a key lemma is proved in the paper's full version [3].

EXTENSIONS. As we note in the proof, our main result holds even if the subkeys $k_0, \ldots, k_t$ are only t-wise independent instead of $(t + 1)$-wise independent. This is particularly interesting for $t = 1$. Along different lines, and as pointed out to us by Jooyoung Lee, our result also implies tight security bounds for the "XOR-cascade" cipher introduced by Gaži and Tessaro [9,10] via a reduction by Peter Gaži [10,11].

2   Definitions and Main Result

A t-round key-alternating cipher E has keyspace $\{0,1\}^{(t+1)n}$ and message space $\{0,1\}^n$. We refer back to equation (1) for the definition of $E(k,x)$ (which implicitly depends on the choice of round permutations $P_1, \ldots, P_t$). We note that $E^{-1}(k,y)$ has an analoguous formula in which $P_t^{-1}, \ldots, P_1^{-1}$ are called. We write E_k for the permutation $E(k, \cdot)$.

We work in the ideal permutation model. For our purposes, the PRP security of a t-round key-alternating cipher E against a distinguisher (or "adversary") D is defined as

$$\mathbf{Adv}_{E,t}^{\mathrm{PRP}}(D) = \Pr[k = k_0 \cdots k_t \longleftarrow \{0,1\}^{(t+1)n}; D^{E_k, P_1, \ldots, P_t} = 1] - \Pr[D^{Q, P_1, \ldots, P_t} = 1] \tag{2}$$

where in each experiment $Q, P_1, \ldots, P_t$ are independent uniform random permutations, where D^A denotes that D has oracle access to A and A^{-1} (since all oracles are permutations), and where $k = k_0 \cdots k_t$ is selected uniformly at random (and hidden from D). See Figure 2. We further define

$$\mathbf{Adv}_{E,t}^{\mathrm{PRP}}(q_e, q) = \max_D \mathbf{Adv}_{E,t}^{\mathrm{PRP}}(D)$$

where the maximum is taken over all distinguishers D that make at most q_e queries to their first oracle and at most q queries to each of their other oracles. (The notation $\mathbf{Adv}_{E,t}^{\mathrm{PRP}}(\cdot)$ is thus overloaded.) Accounting for cipher queries and permutation queries separately has the main advantage of clarifying "which q is which" in the security bound. We also note that, besides t, n is a parameter on which E (and hence $\mathbf{Adv}_{E,t}^{\mathrm{PRP}}(q)$) depends.

(As an aside, we note the above indistinguishability experiment differs from the recently popular framework of *indifferentiability* by, among others, the presence of a secret key and the absence of a simulator; the similarity, on the other

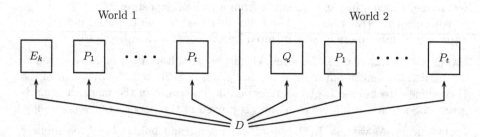

Fig. 2. The two worlds for the Even-Mansour security experiment. In World 1 the distinguisher D has oracle access to random permutations $P_1, \ldots, P_t$ and the key-alternating cipher E_k (cf. Eq. (1)) for a random key k. In World 2, D has oracle access to $t + 1$ independent random permutations. In either world D also has oracle access to the inverse of each permutation.

hand, is that the adversary can query the internal components of the structure. The end goal of the security proof is also different, since we simply prove PRP-security (with tight bounds) whereas indifferentiability aims to prove something much stronger, but, typically, with much inferior bounds. See [1, 14] for indifferentiability results on key-alternating ciphers.)

Our main result is the following:

Theorem 1. *Let $N = 2^n$ and let $q \leq N/3$, $t \geq 1$. Then for any constant $C > 0$,*

$$\mathbf{Adv}_{E,t}^{\mathrm{PRP}}(q_e, q) \leq \frac{q_e q^t}{N^t} \cdot Ct^2(6C)^t + (t+1)^2 \frac{1}{C}.$$

The presence of the adjustable constant C in Theorem 1 is typical of security proofs that involve a threshold-based "bad event". The constant corresponds to the bad event's (adjustable) threshold. Some terms in the security bound grow with C, others decrease with C, and for every q_e, q, t and N there is an optimal C. Choosing

$$C = \left(\frac{(t+1)N^t}{6^t t^2 q_e q^t} \right)^{1/(t+2)}$$

(which happens to be the analytical optimum) and using a little algebra yields the following, more readable corollary for the case $q = q_e$:

Corollary 1. *Let $N = 2^n$, $q \leq N/3$, $t \geq 1$. Then*

$$\mathbf{Adv}_{E,t}^{\mathrm{PRP}}(q, q) \leq (t+1)^2(t+2) \left(\frac{6tq}{N^{t/(t+1)}} \right)^{(t+1)/(t+2)}. \tag{3}$$

Security therefore holds up to about $q \approx N^{\frac{t}{t+1}}/6t^4$, with "security exponent" $(t+1)/(t+2)$. Since t is typically viewed as a constant the polynomial factor $6t^4$ is not bothersome from the asymptotic point of view even though, obviously, such a factor considerably waters down the security bound for concrete parameters like $t = 10$, $n = 128$. We also note that if we fix q and N and let $t \to \infty$ then (3) becomes worse and worse (i.e., closer to 1 and eventually greater than 1) for sufficiently large t. This apparent security degradation is obviously an artefact of our bound, since a straightforward reduction shows that security can only increase with t.

3   The H-Coefficient Technique in a Nutshell

In this section we give a quick high-level outline of Patarin's H-coefficient technique. This tutorial takes a broader view than Patarin's own [18], but [18] mentions refinements for nonadaptive adversaries and "plaintext only" attacks that we don't touch upon here. We emphasize that the material in this section is "informal by design".

The general setting is that of a q-query information-theoretic distinguisher D interacting with one of two oracles, the "real world" oracle or the "ideal world" oracle. (Each oracle might consist of several interfaces for D to query.) By such interaction, D creates a transcript, which is a list of queries made and answers returned. We can assume without loss of generality[1] that D is deterministic, and makes its final decision as a (deterministic) function of the transcript obtained.

Denoting X the probability distribution on transcripts induced by the real world and denoting Y the probability distribution on transcripts induced by the ideal world (for some fixed deterministic distinguisher D) then D's distinguishing advantage (cf. (2)) is easily seen to be upper bounded by

$$\Delta(X, Y) := \frac{1}{2} \sum_{\tau \in \mathcal{T}} |\Pr[X = \tau] - \Pr[Y = \tau]|$$

(the so-called *statistical distance* or *total variation distance* between X and Y) where $\mathcal{T}$ denotes the set of possible transcripts.

The technique's central idea is to use the fact that

$$\Delta(X, Y) = 1 - E_{\tau \sim Y} \left[\min(1, \Pr[X = \tau] / \Pr[Y = \tau]) \right] \qquad (4)$$

in order to upper bound $\Delta(X, Y)$. Here $E_{\tau \sim Y}[Z(\tau)]$ is the expectation of the random variable $Z(\tau)$ when τ is sampled according to Y, and one assumes $\min(1, \Pr[X = \tau] / \Pr[Y = \tau]) = 1$ if $\Pr[Y = \tau] = 0$. For completeness we record the easy proof of (4):

$$\Delta(X, Y) = \sum_{\tau \in \mathcal{T} : \Pr[Y=\tau] > \Pr[X=\tau]} (\Pr[Y = \tau] - \Pr[X = \tau])$$

$$= \sum_{\tau \in \mathcal{T} : \Pr[Y=\tau] > \Pr[X=\tau]} \Pr[Y = \tau](1 - \Pr[X = \tau] / \Pr[Y = \tau])$$

$$= \sum_{\tau \in \mathcal{T}} \Pr[Y = \tau](1 - \min(1, \Pr[X = \tau] / \Pr[Y = \tau]))$$

$$= 1 - E_{\tau \sim Y} \left[\min(1, \Pr[X = \tau] / \Pr[Y = \tau]) \right].$$

Thus, by (4), upper bounding the distinguisher's advantage reduces to lower bounding the expectation

$$E_{\tau \sim Y} \left[\min(1, \Pr[X = \tau] / \Pr[Y = \tau]) \right]. \qquad (5)$$

Typically, some transcripts are better than others, in the sense that for some transcripts τ the ratio

$$\Pr[X = \tau] / \Pr[Y = \tau]$$

might be quite small (when we would rather the ratio be near 1), but these "bad" transcripts occur with small probability. A typical proof classifies the set $\mathcal{T}$ of possible transcripts into a finite number of combinatorially distinct classes $\mathcal{T}_1, \ldots, \mathcal{T}_k$ and exhibits values $\varepsilon_1, \ldots, \varepsilon_k \geq 0$ such that

$$\tau \in \mathcal{T}_i \implies \Pr[X = \tau] / \Pr[Y = \tau] \geq 1 - \varepsilon_i. \qquad (6)$$

---

[1] See Appendix A.

Then

$$E_{\tau \sim Y}\left[\min(1, \Pr[X = \tau]/\Pr[Y = \tau])\right] \geq \sum_{i=1}^{k} \Pr[Y \in \mathcal{T}_i](1 - \varepsilon_i)$$

and, by (4),

$$\Delta(X, Y) \leq \sum_{i=1}^{k} \Pr[Y \in \mathcal{T}_i]\varepsilon_i.$$

The "ideal world" random variable Y often has a very simple distribution, making the probabilities $\Pr[Y \in \mathcal{T}_i]$ easy to compute. On the other hand, proving the lower bounds (6) for $i = 1 \ldots k$ can be difficult, and we rediscuss this issue below.

Many proofs (including ours) have $k = 2$, with $\mathcal{T}_1$ consisting of the set of "good" transcripts and $\mathcal{T}_2$ consisting of the set of "bad" transcripts (i.e., those with small value of $\Pr[X = \tau]/\Pr[Y = \tau]$); then ε_1 is small and ε_2 is large, while (hopefully) $\Pr[Y \in \mathcal{T}_1]$ is large and $\Pr[Y \in \mathcal{T}_2]$ is small, and

$$\Delta(X, Y) \leq \Pr[Y \in \mathcal{T}_1]\varepsilon_1 + \Pr[Y \in \mathcal{T}_2]\varepsilon_2 \leq \varepsilon_1 + \Pr[Y \in \mathcal{T}_2].$$

The final upper bound on $\Delta(X, Y)$, in this case, can thus be verbalized as "one minus the probability ratio of good transcripts [i.e., ε_1], plus the probability of a transcript being bad" (the latter probability being computed with respect to the distribution Y). This is the form taken by our own bound.

LOWER BOUNDING THE RATIO $\Pr[X = \tau]/\Pr[Y = \tau]$. The random variables X and Y are, formally, defined on underlying probability spaces that contain respectively all the coins needed for the real and ideal world experiments. To be more illustrative, in the case of the key-alternating cipher distinguishability experiment X's underlying probability space consists of all possible $(t + 1)$-tuples of the form $(k, P_1, \ldots, P_t)$ where $k \in \{0, 1\}^{(t+1)n}$ and where each P_i is a permutation of $\{0, 1\}^n$, while Y's underlying probability space is all $(t + 1)$-tuples of the form $(Q, P_1, \ldots, P_t)$ where Q as well as each P_i is a permutation of $\{0, 1\}^n$. (In either case the measure is uniform, and for simplicity we also assume uniform—and hence finite—probability spaces in our discussion here.) For the following, we write Ω_X, Ω_Y for the probability spaces on which respectively X and Y are defined. We note that each ω in Ω_X or Ω_Y can be viewed as an oracle for D to interact with, thus we may use phrases such as "D runs with oracle ω", etc. To summarize, X and Y are, formally, functions $X : \Omega_X \to \mathcal{T}$, $Y : \Omega_Y \to \mathcal{T}$, where $X(\omega)$ is the transcript obtained by running D with oracle $\omega \in \Omega_X$, and where $Y(\omega)$ is the transcript obtained by running D oracle $\omega \in \Omega_Y$.

There is usually an obvious notion of "compatibility" between a transcript τ and an element $\omega \in \Omega_X$ or $\omega \in \Omega_Y$. For example, in the case of key-alternating ciphers, if τ contains a query to P_1 and nothing else, the ω's in Ω_X that are compatible with τ will be exactly those where the P_1-coordinate of ω agrees with the query in τ; there are $2^{(t+1)n} \cdot (2^n - 1)! \cdot (2^n!)^{t-1}$ such "compatible" ω's in Ω_X. For the same transcript, there would be $(2^n - 1)! \cdot (2^n!)^t$ compatible ω's in Ω_Y. We write $\mathsf{comp}_X(\tau)$ for the set of ω's in Ω_X compatible with a transcript τ, and we define $\mathsf{comp}_Y(\tau)$ likewise with respect to Ω_Y.

We note that the statement "ω is compatible with τ" is actually not equivalent to the statement "running D with oracle ω produces τ". Indeed, some τ's may never be produced by D at all; e.g., if a transcript τ contains more than q queries, or if it contains queries to P_1 when D is a distinguisher that never queries P_1, etc, then τ is never produced by D (i.e., $\Pr[X = \tau] = \Pr[Y = \tau] = 0$), but this does not prevent $\mathsf{comp}_X(\tau)$, $\mathsf{comp}_Y(\tau)$ from being well-defined.

A central insight of the H-coefficient technique (but which is usually taken for granted and used without mention) is that when τ is a possible transcript of D at all (i.e., if either $\Pr[X = \tau] > 0$ or $\Pr[Y = \tau] > 0$) then

$$\Pr[X = \tau] = \frac{|\mathsf{comp}_X(\tau)|}{|\Omega_X|} \quad \text{and} \quad \Pr[Y = \tau] = \frac{|\mathsf{comp}_Y(\tau)|}{|\Omega_Y|}. \qquad (7)$$

These equalities, argued below, might seem obvious (or not) but one should note they carry some counterintuitive consequences. Firstly:

(c1) The order in which queries appear in a transcript τ does not affect the probability of τ occuring; only the set of queries appearing in τ matters.

(This because the sets $\mathsf{comp}_X(\tau)$, $\mathsf{comp}_Y(\tau)$ are unaffected by the order with which queries appear in τ.) Along the same lines, one has:

(c2) If two different (deterministic) distinguishers can obtain a transcript τ each with nonzero probability, these distinguishers will obtain τ with equal probability. Moreover, by (c1), this holds even if the transcript carries no information about the order in which queries are made.

(This because the right-hand sides in (7) are distinguisher-independent.) Thus, if D_1 and D_2 are two adaptive, deterministic distinguishers that can arrive (by a potentially completely different query order) at transcripts τ_1 and τ_2 that contain the same *set* of queries, then D_1 has the same probability of obtaining τ_1 as D_2 has of obtaining τ_2, with this equality holding separately both in the real and ideal worlds. While very basic, the order-independence property *(c1)* and distinguisher-independence property *(c2)* of deterministic distinguishers seem not to have been highlighted anywhere before[2].

We now informally argue (7), focusing on the first equality (the X-world) for concreteness. Firstly, executing D with an $\omega \in \Omega_X$, $\omega \notin \mathsf{comp}_X(\tau)$ can obviously not produce τ as a transcript, since ω is not compatible with τ. It therefore suffices to show that running D on an oracle $\omega \in \mathsf{comp}_X(\tau)$ produces

---

[2] A bit of thought reveals that *(c1)*, *(c2)* hold for any experiment involving *stateless* oracles. More precisely, the oracle's answer is a deterministic function of a random tape sampled at the beginning of the experiment.

the transcript τ. For this, we know by assumption that there exists[3] an $\omega' \in \Omega_X \cup \Omega_Y$ such that running D on oracle ω' produces τ. However, one can show by induction on the number of queries made by D that the computations D^ω and $D^{\omega'}$ will not "diverge", since every time D makes a query to ω' this query appears in τ and, hence, because $\omega \in \mathsf{comp}_X(\tau)$, will be answered the same by ω (also recall that D is deterministic). Hence D^ω will produce the same transcript as $D^{\omega'}$, i.e., τ.

By (7), the ratio $\Pr[X = \tau]/\Pr[Y = \tau]$ is equal to

$$\frac{\Pr_{\Omega_X}[\omega \in \mathsf{comp}_X(\tau)]}{\Pr_{\Omega_Y}[\omega \in \mathsf{comp}_Y(\tau)]}. \tag{8}$$

Here $\Pr_{\Omega_X}[\omega \in \mathsf{comp}_X(\tau)] = |\mathsf{comp}_X(\tau)|/|\Omega_X|$, $\Pr_{\Omega_Y}[\omega \in \mathsf{comp}_Y(\tau)] = |\mathsf{comp}_Y(\tau)|/|\Omega_Y|$ are different notations[4] for the ratios appearing in (7).

Looking at (8) it is possible to wonder whether anything substantial has been gained so far, or whether notations are simply being shuffled around; after all, $\Pr[X = \tau]$ and $\Pr_{\Omega_X}[\omega \in \mathsf{comp}_X(\tau)]$ are "obviously the same thing"[5] (and the same for Y). However the probability $\Pr_{\Omega_X}[\omega \in \mathsf{comp}_X(\tau)]$ offers a considerable conceptual advantage over the probability $\Pr[X = \tau]$, as $\Pr_{\Omega_X}[\omega \in \mathsf{comp}_X(\tau)]$ refers to an experiment with a non-adaptive flavor (a transcript τ is fixed, and a uniform random element of Ω_X is drawn—what is the probability of compatibility?) while the probability $\Pr[X = \tau]$ refers, by definition, to the adaptive interaction of D with its oracle, which is much messier to think about. Indeed, *(c1)* and *(c2)* already show that adaptivity is in a sense "thrown out" when (7) is applied.

4   Proof of Theorem 1

We make the standard simplifying assumption that the distinguisher D is deterministic. For simplicity, moreover, we assume that D makes exactly q_e queries to its first oracle and exactly q queries to each of its other oracles. This is without loss of generality.

We refer to the case where D has an oracle tuple of the type $(E_k, P_1, \ldots, P_t)$ as the "real world" and to the case when D has an oracle tuple of the type $(Q, P_1, \ldots, P_t)$ as the "ideal world". For convenience, we will be generous with the distinguisher in the following way: at the end of the experiment (when the distinguisher has made its $(t+1)q$ queries, but before the distinguisher outputs its

---

[3] Here ω' could also lie outside $\Omega_X \cup \Omega_Y$; the argument goes through as long as there exists *some* oracle leading to the transcript τ.

[4] In fact, replacing $|\mathsf{comp}_X(\tau)|/|\Omega_X|$ and $|\mathsf{comp}_X(\tau)|/|\Omega_X|$ by respectively $\Pr_{\Omega_X}[\omega \in \mathsf{comp}_X(\tau)]$ and $\Pr_{\Omega_Y}[\omega \in \mathsf{comp}_Y(\tau)]$ in (7) gives a more general formulation of these identities, for cases where the probability distributions on Ω_X, Ω_Y are not uniform. We prefer the fractions $|\mathsf{comp}_X(\tau)|/|\Omega_X|$, $|\mathsf{comp}_X(\tau)|/|\Omega_X|$ because these expressions seem more concrete.

[5] In fact, as already pointed out, $\Pr[X = \tau]$ and $\Pr_{\Omega_X}[\omega \in \mathsf{comp}_X(\tau)]$ are *not* the same thing for τ's outside the range of D.

decision) we reveal the key $k = k_0 k_1 \cdots k_t$ to the distinguisher in the real world, while in the ideal world we sample a dummy key $k' = k_0' k_1' \cdots k_t'$ and reveal this dummy key to the distinguisher. A distinguisher playing this "enhanced" game is obviously at no disadvantage, since it can disregard the key if it wants.

For the remainder of the proof we consider a fixed distinguisher D conforming to the conventions above. We can summarize D's interaction with its oracles by a transcript consisting of a sequence of tuples of the form (i, σ, x, y) where $i \in \{0, \ldots, t\}$, $\sigma \in \{+, -\}$ and $x, y \in \{0, 1\}^n$, plus the key value k at the end of the transcript. If $\sigma = +$ such a tuple denotes that D made the query $P_i(x)$ obtaining answer y, or if $\sigma = -$ that D made the query $P_i^{-1}(y)$ obtaining answer x, and D's interaction with its oracles (as well as D's final output bit) can be uniquely reconstructed from such a sequence of tuples. In fact, we can (and shall) encode the transcript as an *unordered set* of *directionless* tuples of the form (i, x, y) (plus the key value k). Indeed, given that D is deterministic, D's interaction can still be reconstructed from such a transcript. (Consider that D always makes the same first query, since it is deterministic; we can look up the answer to this query in the transcript, deduce the second query made by D again since D is deterministic, and so on.) All in all, therefore, the transcript can be encoded as a tuple $(k, p_0, p_1, \ldots, p_t)$ where $k \in \{0, 1\}^{(t+1)n}$ is the key (real or dummy) and where p_i, $i \geq 1$, is a table containing q pairs (x, y), where each such pair either indicates a query $P_i(x) = y$ or a query $P_i^{-1}(y) = x$ (which it is can be deduced from the transcript), and where p_0 similarly contains the q_e input-output pairs queried to the cipher. One can also view p_i as a bipartite graph with shores $\{0, 1\}^n$ and containing q (resp. q_e, in the case of p_0) disjoint edges.

We let $\mathcal{T}$ denote the set of all possible transcripts, i.e., the set of all tuples of the form $(k, p_0, \ldots, p_t)$ as described above. We note that some elements of $\mathcal{T}$—in fact, most elements—may never be obtained by D. For example, if D's first query is $P_1(0^n)$ then (this first query never varies and) any transcript obtained by D contains a pair of the form $(0^n, y)$ in the table p_1, for some $y \in \{0, 1\}^n$.

Let $\mathcal{P}$ be the set of all permutations of $\{0, 1\}^n$; thus $|\mathcal{P}| = (2^n)!$. Let $\mathcal{P}^t = \mathcal{P} \times \cdots \times \mathcal{P}$ be the t-fold direct product of $\mathcal{P}$. Let $\Omega_X = \{0, 1\}^{(t+1)n} \times \mathcal{P}^t$ and let $\Omega_Y = \{0, 1\}^{(t+1)n} \times \mathcal{P}^{t+1}$. In the obvious way, elements of Ω_X can be viewed as real world oracles for D while elements of Ω_Y can be viewed as "ideal world" oracles for D. (We note that Ω_Y is slightly different from the Ω_Y appearing in the discussion of Section 3, due to our convention of giving away the key as part of the transcript.) We write $X(\omega)$ for the transcript obtained by running D with oracle $\omega \in \Omega_X$, and $Y(\omega)$ for the transcript obtained by running D with oracle $\omega \in \Omega_Y$. By endowing Ω_X, Ω_Y with the uniform probability distribution, X and Y become random variables of range $\mathcal{T}$, whose distributions are exactly those obtained by running D in the real and ideal worlds respectively.

Since D's output is a deterministic function of the transcript, D's distinguishing advantage is upper bounded by $\Delta(X, Y)$. In order to upper bound $\Delta(X, Y)$ we make use of the equality

$$\Delta(X, Y) = 1 - E_{\tau \sim Y}\left[\min(1, \Pr[X = \tau] / \Pr[Y = \tau])\right]$$

mentioned in Section 3. More precisely, we will identify a set $\mathcal{T}_1 \subseteq \mathcal{T}$ of "good" query transcripts, and a set $\mathcal{T}_2 \subseteq \mathcal{T}$ of "bad" transcripts, such that $\mathcal{T}$ is the disjoint union of $\mathcal{T}_1$ and $\mathcal{T}_2$. Then, as shown in Section 3,

$$\Delta(X, Y) \leq \varepsilon_1 + \Pr[Y \in \mathcal{T}_2] \tag{9}$$

where ε_1 is a number such that

$$\frac{\Pr[X = \tau]}{\Pr[Y = \tau]} \geq 1 - \varepsilon_1$$

for all $\tau \in \mathcal{T}_1$ such that $\Pr[Y = \tau] > 0$. Theorem 1 will follow by showing that

$$\Pr[Y \in \mathcal{T}_2] \leq (t+1)^2 \frac{1}{C} \quad \text{and} \quad \tau \in \mathcal{T}_1 \implies \frac{\Pr[X = \tau]}{\Pr[Y = \tau]} \geq 1 - \varepsilon_1 \tag{10}$$

where C is a constant appearing in the definition of a "bad" transcript, and where $\varepsilon_1 = q_e \left(\frac{q}{N}\right)^t C t^2 (6C)^t$ is the first term appearing in the bound of Theorem 1. For the remainder of the proof we assume that $C q_e q^t < N^t$. This is without loss of generality since Theorem 1 is vacuous otherwise.

BAD TRANSCRIPTS. Let $\tau = (k, p_0, p_1, \ldots, p_t) \in \mathcal{T}$ be a transcript. We associate to τ a graph $G(\tau)$, dubbed the *round graph*, that encodes the information contained in k as well as in $p_1, \ldots, p_t$ (but that ignores p_0). $G(\tau)$ has $2(t+1) \cdot 2^n$ vertices, grouped into "shores" of size 2^n each, with each shore being identified with a copy $\{0, 1\}^n$. We index the $2(t+1)$ shores as 0^-, 0^+, 1^-, 1^+, $\ldots$, t^-, t^+. Vertex y in shore i^- is connected to vertex $y \oplus k_i$ in shore i^+ by an edge, and these are the only edges between shores i^- and i^+. Moreover, for each $(x, y) \in p_i$, $1 \leq i \leq t$, we connect vertex x in shore $(i-1)^+$ to vertex y in shore i^-. Thus $G(\tau)$ consists of $(t+1)$ full bipartite matchings (one per subkey) alternately glued with q-edge partial matchings (one for each p_i, $1 \leq i \leq t$). Since $G(\tau)$ encodes all the information in k, $p_1, \ldots, p_t$, we can also write a transcript τ in the form $\tau = (p_0, G)$ where $G = G(\tau)$.

Obviously, the presence of the full bipartite graphs corresponding to the subkeys $k_0, \ldots, k_t$ within $G(\tau)$ is not topologically interesting. Call an edge of $G(\tau)$ a "key edge" if the edge joins the shores i^-, i^+ for some $i \in \{0, \ldots, t\}$. We then define the *contracted round graph* $\tilde{G}(\tau)$ obtained from $G(\tau)$ by contracting all key edges; thus $\tilde{G}(\tau)$ has only $t + 1$ shores; moreover, when an edge $(y, y \oplus k_i)$ between shores i^-, i^+ of $G(\tau)$ is contracted, the resulting vertex of $\tilde{G}(\tau)$ is given label y if $0 \leq i \leq t-1$, and is given label $y \oplus k_i$ if $i = t$. (The labeling of vertices of $\tilde{G}(\tau)$ is somewhat unimportant and arbitrary, but we adopt the above convention so that vertices in shores 0^- and t^+ of $G(\tau)$ keep their original labels in $\tilde{G}(\tau)$. The latter ensures compatibility between these vertex labels and triples in p_0.) We note that a transcript τ is not determined by the pair $(p_0, \tilde{G}(\tau))$ (the key material being unrecoverable from the latter pair) but, as we will see, $\Pr[X = \tau]$ is determined by $(p_0, \tilde{G}(\tau))$.

An edge between shores $(i-1)$ and i of $\tilde{G}(\tau)$ is called an *i-edge*. (Each i-edge arises from an entry in p_i.) We write $Z_{ij}(\tilde{G}(\tau))$ for the set of (necessarily edge-disjoint) paths that exists between shores i and j of $\tilde{G}(\tau)$. We write $Z_{ij}^-(\tilde{G}(\tau))$,

$Z_{ij}^+(\tilde{G}(\tau))$ for vertices of paths in $Z_{ij}(\tilde{G}(\tau))$ that are respectively in shores i and j of $\tilde{G}(\tau)$. We write $p_0^- = \{x : (x,y) \in p_0\}$ and $p_0^+ = \{y : (x,y) \in p_0\}$ be the projection of p_0 to its first and second coordinates respectively.

We say a transcript τ is *bad* if there exist $0 \le i < j \le t$ such that

$$|Z_{ij}(\tilde{G}(\tau))| > \frac{Cq^{j-i}}{N^{j-i-1}} \tag{11}$$

or if there exists $0 \le i \le j \le t$ such that

$$|\{(x,y) \in p_0 : x \in Z_{0,i}^-(\tilde{G}(\tau)) \wedge y \in Z_{j,t}^+(\tilde{G}(\tau))\}| > \frac{Cq_e q^{i+t-j}}{N^{i+t-j}}. \tag{12}$$

To motivate this definition we note that q^{j-i}/N^{j-i-1} is exactly the expected number of paths from shore i to shore j in the ideal world, whereas, likewise, $q_e q^{i+t-j}/N^{i+t-j}$ is the expected number of paths from shore j to shore i that "wrap around" through an edge in p_0 (though such edges are not encoded in $\tilde{G}(\tau)$ and, hence, such "wrap around" paths don't physically exist in $\tilde{G}(\tau)$). The set of bad transcripts is denoted $\mathcal{T}_2$ and we let $\mathcal{T}_1 = \mathcal{T} \backslash \mathcal{T}_2$. Transcripts in $\mathcal{T}_1$ are called *good*.

The easy, Markov-inequality-based proof that $\Pr[Y \in \mathcal{T}_2] \le (t+1)^2 \frac{1}{C}$ can be found in this paper's full version [3].

LOWER BOUNDING $\Pr[X = \tau]/\Pr[Y = \tau]$ FOR $\tau \in \mathcal{T}_1$. An element $\omega = (k, P_1, \ldots, P_t) \in \Omega_x$ is *compatible* with a transcript $\tau = (k^*, p_0, \ldots, p_t)$ if $k = k^*$, if $P_i(x) = y$ for every $(x,y) \in p_i$, $1 \le i \le t$, and if $E_k(x) = y$ for every $(x,y) \in p_0$, where E_k stands for the Even-Mansour cipher instantiated with permutations $P_1, \ldots, P_t$ (and key k). We write $\mathsf{comp}_X(\tau)$ for the set of w's in Ω_X that are compatible with τ.

Analogously, an $w = (k, P_0, P_1, \ldots, P_t) \in \Omega_Y$ is compatible with τ if the same conditions as above are respected, but replacing the constraint $E_k(x) = y$ with $P_0(x) = y$ for $(x,y) \in p_0$. We write $\mathsf{comp}_Y(\tau)$ for the set of w's in Ω_Y that are compatible with τ.

We also say $\omega = (k, P_1, \ldots, P_t)$ is *partially compatible* with $\tau = (k^*, p_0, p_1, \ldots, p_t)$ if $k = k^*$ and if $P_i(x) = y$ for all $(x,y) \in p_i$, $1 \le i \le t$. (Thus, the requirement that p_0 agrees with E_k is dropped for partial compatibility.) Likewise $\omega \in \Omega_Y$ is *partially compatible* with τ if (exactly as above) $k = k^*$ and $P_i(x) = y$ for all $(x,y) \in p_i$, $1 \le i \le t$. (Thus, the requirement that p_0 agrees with P_0 is dropped.) We write $\mathsf{comp}'_X(\tau)$, $\mathsf{comp}'_Y(\tau)$ for the set of w's in, respectively, Ω_X or Ω_Y that are partially compatible with τ. Note that

$$\frac{|\mathsf{comp}'_X(\tau)|}{|\Omega_X|} = \frac{|\mathsf{comp}'_Y(\tau)|}{|\Omega_Y|} = \frac{1}{N^{t+1}} \cdot \prod_{i=1}^{t} \frac{(N - |p_i|)!}{N!} \tag{13}$$

for any transcript $\tau = (k, p_0, p_1, \ldots, p_t)$, where $|p_i|$ denotes the number of pairs in p_i.

We say that a transcript $\tau \in \mathcal{T}$ is *attainable* if $\Pr[Y = \tau] > 0$. (Note that $\Pr[X = \tau] > 0 \implies \Pr[Y = \tau] > 0$.) In other words, a transcript is attainable if there exists an $\omega \in \Omega_Y$ such that D^ω produces the transcript τ.

It is necessary and sufficient to lower bound $\Pr[X = \tau]/\Pr[Y = \tau]$ for attainable transcripts $\tau \in \mathcal{T}_1$. By (7) and (13),

$$\frac{\Pr[X = \tau]}{\Pr[Y = \tau]} = \frac{|\mathsf{comp}_X(\tau)|}{|\mathsf{comp}'_X(\tau)|} \bigg/ \frac{|\mathsf{comp}_Y(\tau)|}{|\mathsf{comp}'_Y(\tau)|} \tag{14}$$

for τ such that $\Pr[Y = \tau] > 0$. (We emphasize that both equalities in (7) hold as long as D produces τ as a transcript on *some* oracle in $\Omega_X \cup \Omega_Y$.) For the remainder of the argument we fix an arbitrary transcript $\tau = (k, p_0, p_1, \ldots, p_t) \in \mathcal{T}_1$. We aim to lower bound the right-hand side fraction in (14).

For random permutations $P_1, \ldots, P_t$ and partial permutations $p_1, \ldots, p_t$, let $P_i \downarrow p_i$ denote the event that P_i extends p_i, i.e., that $P_i(x) = y$ for all $(x, y) \in p_i$; then it is easy to see that

$$\frac{|\mathsf{comp}_X(\tau)|}{|\mathsf{comp}'_X(\tau)|} = \Pr\left[E_k \downarrow p_0 \mid k, P_1 \downarrow p_1, \ldots, P_t \downarrow p_k\right] \tag{15}$$

where the underlying probability space is the choice of the uniform random permutations $P_1, \ldots, P_t$ (the notation conditions on τ's key k only to emphasize that k is not randomly chosen) and where $E_k \downarrow p_0$ is the event that $E_k(x) = y$ for all $(x, y) \in p_0$, where E_k is the Even-Mansour cipher with key k and permutations $P_1, \ldots, P_t$. Similarly,

$$\frac{|\mathsf{comp}_Y(\tau)|}{|\mathsf{comp}'_Y(\tau)|} = \Pr\left[P_0 \downarrow p_0 \mid k, P_1 \downarrow p_1, \ldots, P_t \downarrow p_k\right]$$

where the underlying probability space is the uniform random choice of $P_0, P_1, \ldots, P_t$. In the latter conditional probability, however, the event $P_0 \downarrow p_0$ is independent of the conditioned premise, so

$$\frac{|\mathsf{comp}_Y(\tau)|}{|\mathsf{comp}'_Y(\tau)|} = \Pr\left[P_0 \downarrow p_0\right] = \prod_{\ell=0}^{q_e-1} \frac{1}{N - \ell}. \tag{16}$$

To facilitate the computation of the conditional probability that appears in (15), let (in accordance with the definition of the graph $\tilde{G}(\tau)$ above) $\tilde{p}_i$ be defined by

$$(x, y) \in \tilde{p}_i \iff (x \oplus k_{i-1}, y) \in p_i$$

for $1 \leq i \leq t - 1$, and by

$$(x, y) \in \tilde{p}_i \iff (x \oplus k_{i-1}, y \oplus k_i) \in p_i$$

for $i = t$. Thus $\tilde{p}_1, \ldots, \tilde{p}_t$ are the t edge sets of the graph $\tilde{G}(\tau)$, i.e., $\tilde{p}_i$ is the set of edges between shores $i - 1$ and i of $\tilde{G}(\tau)$. By elementary considerations, one has

$$\Pr\left[E_k \downarrow p_0 \mid k, P_1 \downarrow p_1, \ldots, P_t \downarrow p_k\right] = \Pr\left[E_0 \downarrow p_0 \mid P_1 \downarrow \tilde{p}_1, \ldots, P_t \downarrow \tilde{p}_k\right] \tag{17}$$

where E_0 denotes the Even-Mansour cipher instantiated with key $0^{(t+1)n}$, and where the probability is taken (on either side) over the choice of the uniform random permutations $P_1, \ldots, P_t$. We will therefore focus on the right-hand side probability in (17).

We say shore i of $\tilde{G}(\tau)$ is "to the left" of shore j if $i < j$. We also view paths in $\tilde{G}(\tau)$ as oriented from left to right: the path "starts" at the leftmost vertex and "ends" at the rightmost vertex.

Let $(x_1, y_1), \ldots, (x_{q_e}, y_{q_e})$ be the q_e edges in p_0. We write $\mathsf{R}(x_\ell)$ for the rightmost vertex in the path of $\tilde{G}(\tau)$ starting at x_ℓ, and $\mathsf{L}(y_\ell)$ for the leftmost vertex in the path of $\tilde{G}(\tau)$ ending at y_ℓ. (More often than not, x_ℓ and y_ℓ are not adjacent to any edges of $\tilde{G}(\tau)$, in which case $\mathsf{R}(x_\ell) = x_\ell$, $\mathsf{L}(y_\ell) = y_\ell$.) We write the index of the shore containing vertex v as $\mathsf{Sh}(v)$. (Thus $\mathsf{Sh}(v) \in \{0, 1, \ldots, t\}$.) Because τ is good, and because we are assuming $Cq_e(q/N)^t < 1$, $\mathsf{Sh}(\mathsf{R}(x_\ell)) < \mathsf{Sh}(\mathsf{L}(y_\ell))$ for $1 \leq \ell \leq q_e$.

A vertex in shore $i \geq 1$ is *left-free* if it is not adjacent to a vertex in shore $i - 1$. A vertex in shore $i \leq t - 1$ is *right-free* if it is not adjacent to a vertex in shore $i + 1$.

To compute the conditional probability

$$\Pr\left[E_0 \downarrow p_0 \,\middle|\, P_1 \downarrow \tilde{p}_1, \ldots, P_t \downarrow \tilde{p}_t\right]$$

we imagine the following experiment in q_e stages. Let $G_0 = \tilde{G}(\tau)$. At the ℓ-th stage, G_ℓ is inductively defined from $G_{\ell-1}$. Let $\tilde{p}_i^\ell$ be the edges between shore $i - 1$ and i of G_ℓ. Initially, $G_\ell = G_{\ell-1}$. Then, as long as $\mathsf{R}(x_\ell)$ is not in shore t, a value y is chosen uniformly at random from the set of left-free vertices in shore $\mathsf{Sh}(\mathsf{R}(x_\ell)) + 1$, and the edge $(\mathsf{R}(x_\ell), y)$ is added to $\tilde{p}_{\mathsf{Sh}(\mathsf{R}(x_\ell))+1}^\ell$. G_ℓ is the result obtained when $\mathsf{R}(x_\ell)$ reaches shore t. Thus, G_ℓ has at most t more edges than $G_{\ell-1}$.

Since the permutations $P_1, \ldots, P_t$ are uniformly random and independently chosen, it is easy to see that

$$\Pr\left[E_0 \downarrow p_0 \,\middle|\, P_1 \downarrow \tilde{p}_1, \ldots, P_t \downarrow \tilde{p}_t\right] = \Pr\left[G_{q_e} \downarrow p_0\right]$$

for the random graph G_{q_e} defined in the process above, where the notation $G_{q_e} \downarrow p_0$ is a shorthand to indicate that vertices x_ℓ and y_ℓ are connected by a path in G_{q_e} for $1 \leq \ell \leq q_e$. Moreover, writing $x_\ell \to y_\ell$ for the event that x_ℓ and y_ℓ are connected by a path in G_ℓ (and thus in G_{q_e}), and writing $G_\ell \downarrow p_0$ for the event $x_j \to y_j$ for $1 \leq j \leq \ell$, we finally find

$$\frac{|\mathsf{comp}_X(\tau)|}{|\mathsf{comp}'_X(\tau)|} = \prod_{\ell=0}^{q_e-1} \Pr[x_{\ell+1} \to y_{\ell+1} \mid G_\ell \downarrow p_0]. \tag{18}$$

This formula should be compared with (16). Indeed, (16) and (18) imply that

$$\frac{|\mathsf{comp}_X(\tau)|}{|\mathsf{comp}'_X(\tau)|} \,\middle/\, \frac{|\mathsf{comp}_Y(\tau)|}{|\mathsf{comp}'_Y(\tau)|} = \prod_{\ell=0}^{q_e-1} \frac{\Pr[x_{\ell+1} \to y_{\ell+1} \mid G_\ell \downarrow p_0]}{1/(N-\ell)} \tag{19}$$

which suggests that to lower bound $\Pr[X = \tau]/\Pr[Y = \tau]$ one should compare $\Pr[x_{\ell+1} \to y_{\ell+1} | G_\ell \downarrow p_0]$ and $1/(N - \ell)$. (More specifically, give a lower bound for the former that is not much less than the latter.)

SOME PRELIMINARY QUANTITATIVE INTUITION FOR (19). At this stage we "pause" the proof to give some quantitative intuition about the product that appears in (19). The lower bounding of this product, indeed, is the heart of our proof. While discussing intuition we will make the simplifying assumption that $\mathsf{Sh}(\mathsf{R}(x_\ell)) = 0$, $\mathsf{Sh}(\mathsf{L}(y_\ell)) = t$ for all $1 \leq \ell \leq q_e$ (which, as it turns out, still captures the most interesting features of the problem).

As a warm-up we can consider the case $t = 1$. In this case, firstly, the "simplifying assumption" $\mathsf{Sh}(\mathsf{R}(x_\ell)) = 0$, $\mathsf{Sh}(\mathsf{L}(y_\ell)) = 1$ actually holds with probability 1 for all $\tau \in \mathcal{T}_1$, by the second bad event in the definition of a bad transcript (i.e., (12)), and by our wlog assumption that

$$1 > Cq_e(q/N)^t = Cq_e q/N. \tag{20}$$

(In more detail, the right-hand side of (12) is $Cq_e q/N$ for $i = j = 0$ or $i = j = 1$. Thus, if there exists an $(x_\ell, y_\ell) \in p_0$ such that either $\mathsf{R}(x_\ell) = 1$ or $\mathsf{L}(y_\ell) = 0$, then $\tau \in \mathcal{T}_2$.) Next (still for $t = 1$) it can be directly observed that

$$\Pr\left[x_{\ell+1} \to y_{\ell+1} | G_\ell \downarrow p_0\right] = \frac{1}{N - q - \ell}$$

since $\tilde{p}_1 = \tilde{p}_1^0$ contains q edges and since ℓ additional edges have been drawn by the time $G_{\ell+1}$ is constructed. In fact, the ratio $1/(N - q - \ell)$ is *greater* than $1/(N - \ell)$, which means that in this case the product (19) is also greater than 1, and one can therefore use $\varepsilon_1 = 0$. I.e., for $t = 1$ the distinguisher's advantage is upper bounded by

$$\varepsilon_1 + \Pr[Y \in \mathcal{T}_2] \leq 0 + \Pr[Y \in \mathcal{T}_2] \leq \frac{2q_e q}{N}$$

where the last inequality is obtained by direct inspection of the event $\tau \in \mathcal{T}_2$ for $t = 1$. (For $t = 1$, the only thing that can cause a transcript to be bad is if $p_0^- \oplus k_0 \cap p_1^- \neq \emptyset$ or if $p_0^+ \oplus k_1 \cap p_1^+ \neq \emptyset$.) Note that even while $\Pr[X = \tau]/\Pr[Y = \tau] \geq 1$ for all $\tau \in \mathcal{T}_1$ such that $\Pr[Y = \tau] > 0$, one has $\Pr[X = \tau]/\Pr[Y \in \tau] = 0$ for most $\tau \in \mathcal{T}_2$ such that $\Pr[Y = \tau] > 0$. This is why ε_1 can attain zero.

In passing, note we have proved the $(2q_e q/N)$-security of the key-alternating cipher for $t = 1$, which exactly recovers Even and Mansour's original result for $t = 1$. The difference is that the H-coefficient technique "mechanizes" the bound-proving, to a certain extent. (Even and Mansour's proof [7] is more complicated, though it pursues the same basic idea. See also Kilian and Rogaway's paper on DESX [12] for a nice game-based take on this argument.)

Given these auspicious beginnings for $t = 1$ one might feel inclined to optimism and to conjecture, say, that the product (19) is *always* greater than 1 for good transcripts. However, these hopes are quickly dashed by the case $t = 2$. We do an example. For this example, assume that $\tilde{p}_1$ and $\tilde{p}_2$ are disjoint, i.e., no edge in $\tilde{p}_1$ touches an edge in $\tilde{p}_2$. (Thus $G_0 = \tilde{G}(\tau)$ contains no paths of length 2.) The example will be clearer if we start by examining the case $\tilde{p}_1 = \emptyset$ (i.e., when there are *no* edges between shore 0 and shore 1). Then one can compute that[6]

$$\Pr[x_1 \to y_1] = \left(1 - \frac{|\tilde{p}_2|}{N}\right)\frac{1}{N - |\tilde{p}_2|} = \left(\frac{N - |\tilde{p}_2|}{N}\right)\frac{1}{N - |\tilde{p}_2|} = \frac{1}{N}$$

and more generally, one similarly computes

$$\Pr[x_{\ell+1} \to y_{\ell+1}|G_\ell \downarrow p_0] = \left(1 - \frac{|\tilde{p}_2|}{N - \ell}\right)\frac{1}{N - \ell - |\tilde{p}_2|} = \frac{1}{N - \ell}. \tag{21}$$

for all $0 \le \ell \le q_e - 1$, since the vertex sampled in shore 1 to which $x_{\ell+1}$ is connected is sampled uniformly from a set of size $N - \ell$, and similarly the new vertex sampled in shore 2 (if such vertex is sampled) comes uniformly from a set of size $N - \ell - |\tilde{p}_2|$. So far, so good: (21) is exactly the same probability as in the ideal case.

Now we remove the assumption $\tilde{p}_1 = \emptyset$, but keep the assumption that $\tilde{p}_1$ and $\tilde{p}_2$ are disjoint. In this case, one has

$$\Pr[x_1 \to y_1] = \left(1 - \frac{|\tilde{p}_2|}{N - |\tilde{p}_1|}\right)\frac{1}{N - |\tilde{p}_2|} = \left(\frac{N - 2q}{N - q}\right)\frac{1}{N - q} = \frac{N - 2q}{(N - q)^2}.$$

As our interest is to compare this quantity to $1/N$, we further massage this expression by writing

$$\frac{N - 2q}{(N - q)^2} = \frac{1}{N} - \frac{1}{N} + \frac{N - 2q}{(N - q)^2} = \frac{1}{N} - \frac{(N - q)^2}{N(N - q)^2} + \frac{N(N - 2q)}{N(N - q)^2} = \frac{1}{N} - \frac{q^2}{N(N - q)^2}.$$

More generally, one finds that

$$\Pr[x_{\ell+1} \to y_{\ell+1}|G_\ell \downarrow p_0] = \left(1 - \frac{|\tilde{p}_2|}{N - \ell - |\tilde{p}_1|}\right)\frac{1}{N - \ell - |\tilde{p}_2|} = \frac{1}{N - \ell} - \frac{q^2}{(N - \ell)(N - \ell - q)^2} \tag{22}$$

as can be seen by substituting N by $N - \ell$ everywhere in the first computation. Thus the probability $\Pr[x_{\ell+1} \to y_{\ell+1}|G_\ell \downarrow p_0]$ is now slightly *lower* than $1/(N - \ell)$, which rules out the optimistic conjecture above. As for the value of the product (19) one finds, by (22),

$$\prod_{\ell=0}^{q_e-1}\left(1 - \frac{q^2}{(N - \ell - q)^2}\right) \ge \left(1 - \frac{q^2}{(N - 2q)^2}\right)^{q_e} \ge 1 - \frac{q_e q^2}{(N - 2q)^2}.$$

---

[6] In more detail: when we travel from x_1 to y_1, the sampling process first chooses a random endpoint in shore 1 to attach x_1 to, and this endpoint has probability $|\tilde{p}_2|/N$ of "hitting" an edge in $\tilde{p}_2$ (in which case we have no hope of reaching y_1). If we don't hit an edge in $\tilde{p}_2$, there is further chance $1/(N - |\tilde{p}_2|)$ that we reach y_1, since the vertex in shore 2 is sampled uniformly at random from a set of size $N - |\tilde{p}_2|$.

This is acceptably close to 1 (i.e., taking $\varepsilon_1 = q_e q^2 / (N - 2q)^2$ is acceptably close to zero) as long as $q_e q^2 \ll N^2$. We are (coincidentally or not, since the assumption $q_e q^2 \ll N^2$ has already been used to upper bound $\Pr[\tau \in \mathcal{T}_2]$) "bumping into" the security bound for $t = 2$. Thus, the approach still works for $t = 2$, but this time the approach "barely" works!

In fact, the simplifying assumption that $\tilde{p}_1$ and $\tilde{p}_2$ are disjoint can easily be removed since, as is not hard to see, having $\tilde{p}_1$ and $\tilde{p}_2$ disjoint is actually the worst case possible[7] for $t = 2$.

Moreover, the initial simplifying assumption that $\mathsf{R}(x_\ell) = 0$, $\mathsf{L}(y_\ell) = 2$ for all ℓ is also easy to remove for $t = 2$, because $\Pr[x_{\ell+1} \to y_{\ell+1} | G_\ell \downarrow p_0]$ actually increases to $1/(N - q - \ell)$ (cf. the case $t = 1$) when either[8] $\mathsf{R}(x_\ell) = 1$ or $\mathsf{L}(y_\ell) = 1$. Thus, the above computations essentially prove security of $q_e q^2 / N^2$ for $t \geq 2$ (indeed, security is easily seen to "transfer upwards" from smaller to larger values of t), which is the main result of Bogdanov et al. [2]. The proof sketched above is arguably simpler than Bogdanov et al.'s, though. (Also, Bogdanov et al. seem to forget that if the only goal is to prove security of $q_e q^2 / N^2$ for $t \geq 2$ it suffices to restrict oneself to the case $t = 2$. Their general approach, however, can be pushed slightly further to cover the case $t = 3$, as shown by Steinberger [19].)

We now consider the case $t = 3$. Already, doing an exact probability computation for the conditional probability $\Pr[x_{\ell+1} \to y_{\ell+1} | G_\ell \downarrow p_0]$ (as done in (22) for $t = 2$) promises to be quite tedious for $t = 3$, so we can look at doing back-of-the-envelope estimates instead. The simplest estimate is to lower bound the probability of $x_{\ell+1}$ reaching $y_{\ell+1}$ by upper bounding the probability that the path being constructed meets a pre-existing edge in either shore 1 or shore 2, viz.,

$$\Pr[x_{\ell+1} \to y_{\ell+1} | G_\ell \downarrow p_0] \geq \left(1 - \frac{2q}{N - \ell - q}\right) \frac{1}{N - \ell - q} \tag{23}$$

where $2q/(N - \ell - q)$ is a (crude) upper bound on the probability that the path touches a pre-existing edge in either shore 1 or shore 2, and where $1/(N - \ell - q)$ is the probability of reaching $y_{\ell+1}$ if the path reaches a right-free vertex in shore 2. However, (23) is *worse* than (22), so we are heading at best for security of $\varepsilon_1 \approx q_e q^2 / N^2$ if we use this estimate. One can argue that $2q/(N - \ell - q)$ can be replaced by $q/(N - \ell - q)$ in (23) (because: if we hit an edge in $\tilde{p}_2$ that is not adjacent to an edge in $\tilde{p}_3$ this only helps us, and if we hit an edge in $\tilde{p}_2$ that is adjacent to an edge in $\tilde{p}_3$ this can be "billed" to the corresponding edge in $\tilde{p}_3$) but even so we are headed towards a security of $q_e q^2 / N^2$, by comparison with

---

[7] On the other hand, we cannot count on $\tilde{p}_1$ and $\tilde{p}_2$ having some small intersection in order to possibly repair our optimistic conjecture. Indeed, the distinguisher could make sure that $\tilde{p}_1$ and $\tilde{p}_2$ are almost certainly disjoint. For example, the distinguisher could make q P_2-queries with values that start with $n/3$ 0's, and also make q P_1^{-1}-queries with values that start with $n/3$ 0's. Then $\tilde{p}_1$ and $\tilde{p}_2$ are disjoint unless the first $n/3$ bits of the key are 0, which occurs with negligible probability.

[8] Note that one always has $\mathsf{R}(x_\ell) < \mathsf{L}(y_\ell)$ by the definition of $\mathcal{T}_2$ and by the wlog assumption $C q_e q^t < N^t$.

(22). In fact, we can reflect that any approach that doesn't somehow seriously take into account the presence of three rounds is doomed to fail, because the computation for $t = 2$ is actually tight (cf. footnote 7), and thus cannot be tweaked to give security better than $q_e q^2/N^2$.

As it turns out, the "exact but tedious" probability computation that we shied from above does deliver a bound that implies the desired security of $q_e q^3/N^3$, even while back-of-the-envelope estimates indicate a security bound of $q_e q^2/N^2$. Intuitively, the gain that occurs is due to the fact that when the path hits an edge of $\tilde{p}_2$ not connected to an edge of $\tilde{p}_3$—and at most $Cq^2/N \ll q$ edges in $\tilde{p}_2$ are adjacent to edges in $\tilde{p}_3$, by definition of $\mathcal{T}_2$—this is actually better than not hitting any edge at all at shore 1, because it *guarantees* we won't hit an edge in $\tilde{p}_3$. While this intuition is easy to see, it is somewhat harder to believe such a small "second-order" effect would make a crucial difference in the final security bound. Yet, this is exactly so. In fact, given the "completeness" of the H-coefficient method it makes sense to have faith that the exact probability computation (if doable) will deliver security $q_e q^3/N^3$. (Though in reality even this is not a given: by giving away the key at the end of each transcript we have been more generous to the adversary than those who devised the security conjecture of $q_e q^t/N^t$, so it's possible to conceive that it's the "key's fault" if the security is (apparently) topping off at $q_e q^2/N^2$ (as opposed to the fault of our lossy estimates). Note that even if we have the correct intuition, and we believe it isn't the "key's fault" and that the approach is theoretically sound, we are still up against the problem of actually doing the computations in a such way that the desired security gain becomes apparent, and isn't lost in a sea of fractions.)

Before proceeding with the exact-but-tedious computation for $t = 3$ it will be useful if we first estimate what kind of lower bound is actually needed for $\Pr[x_{\ell+1} \to y_{\ell+1}|G_\ell \downarrow p_0]$ in order to reach overall security $\approx q_e q^t/N^t$. Writing

$$\Pr[x_{\ell+1} \to y_{\ell+1}|G_\ell \downarrow p_0] = \frac{1}{N-\ell} + z_t$$

where z_t is an "error term" whose magnitude will determine ε_1, we find that

$$\prod_{\ell=0}^{q_e-1} \frac{\Pr[x_{\ell+1} \to y_{\ell+1}|G_\ell \downarrow p_0]}{1/(N-\ell)} = \prod_{\ell=0}^{q_e-1}(1-(N-\ell)z_t) \geq (1-N|z_t|)^{q_e} \geq 1 - Nq_e|z_t|.$$

Thus we will have $\varepsilon_1 \approx Nq_e|z_t|$ and so we need need $Nq_e|z_t| \ll 1$ in order for ε_1 to be small. Having

$$|z_t| = q^t/N^{t+1} \tag{24}$$

gives us precisely this under the assumption $q_e q^t/N^t \ll 1$.

DETAILS ON THE CASE $t = 3$. Let U_{ij} be the set of paths from shore i to shore j in $G(\tau)$, $0 \leq i < j \leq 3$, such that the vertex of the path in shore i is left-free (i.e., is the head of the path), but where the vertex in shore j may or may not be right-free. The U_{ij}'s are therefore "half-open" paths. Note $|U_{ij}| \leq |Z_{ij}| \leq Cq^{j-1}/N^{j-i-1}$ by definition of $\mathcal{T}_2$. For notational consistency with Lemma 1 below we rename $\tilde{p}_i$ as E_i for $i = 1, 2, 3$. Thus $|E_i| = q$ and E_i is the set of edges between shores $(i-1)$ and i of $\tilde{G}(\tau)$. Moreover, one can note that $E_i = \bigcup_{0 \leq j < i} U_{ji}$ for all i, with the latter being a disjoint union.

We start by computing $\Pr[x_1 \rightarrow y_1]$, from which the general case $\Pr[x_{\ell+1} \rightarrow y_{\ell+1} | G_\ell \downarrow p_0]$ will be easy to deduce. We view the underlying probability space as the selection of three vertices u_1, u_2 and u_3 from shores 1, 2 and 3 of $\tilde{G}(\tau)$ respectively, such that u_i is selected independently and uniformly at random from the set of left-free vertices in shore i. This defines a path $w_0 := x_1, w_1 := u_1$, w_2, w_3 where w_2 equals u_2 if u_1 is right-free and equals the other endpoint of the edge adjacent to u_1 otherwise, and where w_3 equals u_3 if w_2 is right-free, otherwise equals the vertex in shore 3 adjacent to w_2. Then $\Pr[x_1 \rightarrow y_1]$ is equal to the probability that $w_3 = y_1$.

Since y_1 is left-free we have

$$w_3 = y_1 \iff (u_3 = y_1) \wedge \neg(w_1 \in U_{13} \vee w_2 \in U_{23}).$$

(The event $\neg(w_1 \in U_{13} \vee w_2 \in U_{23})$ coincides with the event that w_2 is right-free.) Note the event $u_3 = y_1$ is independent from the event $\neg(w_1 \in U_{13} \vee w_2 \in U_{23})$, and also that the events $w_1 \in U_{13}$ and $w_2 \in U_{23}$ are disjoint. Moreover,

$$w_2 \in U_{23} \iff (u_2 \in U_{23}) \wedge \neg(w_1 \in U_{12})$$

since the vertices in shore 2 of U_{23} are left-free. By independence of u_1 and u_2, thus,

$$
\begin{aligned}
\Pr[w_2 \in U_{23}] &= \Pr[u_2 \in U_{23}] \cdot (1 - \Pr[w_1 \in U_{12}]) \\
&= \frac{|U_{23}|}{N - |E_2|}\left(1 - \frac{|U_{12}|}{N - |E_1|}\right) \\
&= \frac{|U_{23}|}{N - |E_2|} - \frac{|U_{12}||U_{23}|}{(N - |E_1|)(N - |E_2|)}.
\end{aligned}
$$

Thus

$$
\begin{aligned}
\Pr[w_3 = y_1] &= \Pr[u_3 = y_1](1 - \Pr[w_1 \in U_{13}] - \Pr[w_2 \in U_{23}]) \\
&= \frac{1}{N - |E_3|}\left(1 - \frac{|U_{13}|}{N - |E_1|} - \frac{|U_{23}|}{N - |E_2|} + \frac{|U_{12}||U_{23}|}{(N - |E_1|)(N - |E_2|)}\right) \\
&= \frac{1}{N - |E_3|} - \frac{|U_{13}|}{(N - |E_1|)(N - |E_3|)} - \frac{|U_{23}|}{(N - |E_2|)(N - |E_3|)} \\
&\quad + \frac{|U_{12}||U_{23}|}{(N - |E_1|)(N - |E_2|)(N - |E_3|)}.
\end{aligned}
$$

(Note that none of the terms above are as small as $\approx q^3/N^4$ (cf. (24)), even with the approximation $\frac{1}{N-|E_i|} \approx \frac{1}{N}$, so none of the terms above can (yet) be folded into the error term.) Adding and subtracting the "ideal" probability $\frac{1}{N}$ to $\frac{1}{N-|E_3|}$ gives

$$\frac{1}{N} - \frac{1}{N} + \frac{1}{N - |E_3|} = \frac{1}{N} + \frac{|E_3|}{N(N - |E_3|)} = \frac{1}{N} + \frac{|U_{03}| + |U_{13}| + |U_{23}|}{N(N - |E_3|)}$$

(Here $\frac{|U_{03}|}{N(N-|E_3|)}$ is basically the same order of magnitude as q^3/N^4, given that $|U_{03}| \leq |Z_{03}| \leq Cq^3/N^2$. So we can leave this term alone.) Next,

$$\frac{|U_{13}|}{N(N-|E_3|)} - \frac{|U_{13}|}{(N-|E_1|)(N-|E_3|)} = -\frac{|E_1||U_{13}|}{N(N-|E_1|)(N-|E_3|)} = -\frac{|U_{01}||U_{13}|}{N(N-|E_1|)(N-|E_3|)}$$

(same order of magnitude as q^3/N^4, given that $|U_{13}| \leq Cq^2/N$), and

$$\frac{|U_{23}|}{N(N-|E_3|)} - \frac{|U_{23}|}{(N-|E_2|)(N-|E_3|)} = -\frac{|E_2||U_{13}|}{N(N-|E_2|)(N-|E_3|)}$$
$$= -\frac{|U_{02}||U_{13}|}{N(N-|E_2|)(N-|E_3|)} - \frac{|U_{12}||U_{23}|}{N(N-|E_2|)(N-|E_3|)}$$

where only $\frac{|U_{02}||U_{13}|}{N(N-|E_2|)(N-|E_3|)}$ is small enough to fit inside the error term. But then, of course, we lastly compute that

$$-\frac{|U_{12}||U_{23}|}{N(N-|E_2|)(N-|E_3|)} + \frac{|U_{12}||U_{23}|}{(N-|E_1|)(N-|E_2|)(N-|E_3|)}$$
$$= \frac{|E_1||U_{12}||U_{23}|}{N(N-|E_1|)(N-|E_2|)(N-|E_3|)}$$
$$= \frac{|U_{01}||U_{12}||U_{23}|}{N(N-|E_1|)(N-|E_2|)(N-|E_3|)}$$

which is small enough to fit inside the error term. Collecting the leftovers after the various cancellations above, thus, we find

$$\Pr[w_3 = y_1] = \frac{1}{N} + \frac{|U_{03}|}{N(N-|E_3|)} - \frac{|U_{01}||U_{13}|}{N(N-|E_1|)(N-|E_3|)}$$
$$- \frac{|U_{02}||U_{13}|}{N(N-|E_1|)(N-|E_3|)} + \frac{|U_{01}||U_{12}||U_{23}|}{N(N-|E_1|)(N-|E_2|)(N-|E_3|)} \quad (25)$$

where all the terms except $\frac{1}{N}$ are "error-term small". Moreover, when we compute $\Pr[x_{\ell+1} \to y_{\ell+1}|G_\ell \downarrow p_0]$ for $\ell \geq 1$ we can discard the ℓ completed paths from shore 0 to shore 3 linking the vertex pairs $(x_1, y_1), \ldots, (x_\ell, y_\ell)$, and thus reduce to the case $\ell + 1 = 1$ with N replaced by $N - \ell$. I.e., the expression for $\Pr[x_{\ell+1} \to y_{\ell+1}|G_\ell \downarrow p_0]$ will be identical to (25) except with N replaced by $N - \ell$ throughout.

From here the proof for $t = 3$ can be finished without many suprises. The crux of the proof is indeed the very simple idea of adding and subtracting $\frac{1}{N}$ from the probability, and of letting cancellations occur. This approach is purely algebraic. When we carry out the same process for an arbitrary value of t (see the proof of Lemma 1 in the full version of this paper [3]) we adopt a more combinatorial approach that recasts the algebraic manipulations as manipulations of events, which seems more satisfying because it gives the algebraic cancellations a concrete probabilistic interpretation. We note that doing so requires enlarging the probability space beyond its original confines. Indeed, for example, the original probability space for $t = 3$ has no event that occurs with probability $\frac{1}{N}$ even while factors of $\frac{1}{N}$ are ubiquitous in the final expression.

UPSHOT. The lemma below essentially generalizes the computation for $t = 3$ to arbitrary t. In this lemma U_{ij} stands for the set of paths from shore i to shore j of G_ℓ such that the vertex in shore i is left-free but where, as before, the vertex in shore j may or may not be right-free.

Lemma 1. *We have, under the notations described above,*

$$\Pr[x_{\ell+1} \to y_{\ell+1} \,|\, G_\ell \downarrow p_0] = \frac{1}{N-\ell} - \frac{1}{N-\ell} \sum_{\sigma \in \mathfrak{S}_\ell} (-1)^{|\sigma|} \prod_{j=1}^{|\sigma|} \frac{|U_{i_j i_{j-1}}|}{N - |E_{i_j}|}$$

for each ℓ, $0 \le \ell \le q_e - 1$, where $\mathfrak{S}_\ell$ is the set of all sequences $\sigma = (i_0, \ldots, i_s)$ with $\mathsf{R}(x_{\ell+1}) = i_0 < \ldots < i_s = \mathsf{L}(y_{\ell+1})$, and where $|\sigma| = s$.

The proof of this lemma is given in the paper's full version [3].

FINISHING THE PROOF OF THEOREM 1. We now apply Lemma 1 to lower bounding the product (19). For $1 \le r \le t$, let

$$\mathcal{L}_r = \{\ell : \mathsf{L}(y_\ell) - \mathsf{R}(x_\ell) = r\} \subseteq \{1, \ldots, q_e\}$$

where (we recall) the elements of p_0 are $(x_1, y_1), \ldots, (x_{q_e}, y_{q_e})$. By the definition of $\mathcal{T}_2$, $\mathcal{L}_1, \ldots, \mathcal{L}_t$ cover $\{1, \ldots, q_e\}$ (i.e., there is no ℓ with $\mathsf{R}(x_\ell) \ge \mathsf{L}(y_\ell)$). Note that $|U_{ij}| \le Cq^{j-i}/N^{j-i-1}$ (by the definition of $\mathcal{T}_2$) for $0 \le i < j \le t$, and $|E_i| \le q$ for $1 \le i \le r$. Thus for $\ell+1 \in \mathcal{L}_r$ we obtain, by Lemma 1,

$$\Pr[x_{\ell+1} \to y_{\ell+1} | G_\ell \downarrow p_0] = \frac{1}{N-\ell} - \frac{1}{N-\ell} \sum_{\sigma \in \mathfrak{S}_\ell} (-1)^{|\sigma|} \prod_{h=1}^{|\sigma|} \frac{|U_{i_{h-1} i_h}|}{N - \ell - |E_{i_h}|}$$

$$\ge \frac{1}{N-\ell} - \frac{1}{N-\ell} \sum_{\sigma \in \mathfrak{S}_\ell} \prod_{h=1}^{|\sigma|} \frac{Cq^{i_h - i_{h-1}}/N^{i_h - i_{h-1} - 1}}{N - \ell - q}$$

$$= \frac{1}{N-\ell} - \frac{1}{N-\ell} 2^{r-1} \left(\frac{q}{N}\right)^r \left(\frac{CN}{N-\ell-q}\right)^{|\sigma|}$$

$$\ge \frac{1}{N-\ell} - \frac{1}{N-\ell} \left(\frac{2q}{N}\right)^r \left(\frac{CN}{N-2q}\right)^r$$

$$\ge \frac{1}{N-\ell} - \frac{1}{N-\ell} \left(\frac{6Cq}{N}\right)^r.$$

Moreover $|\mathcal{L}_r| \leq t \cdot \frac{Cq_e q^{t-r}}{N^{t-r}}$ by the definition of $\mathcal{T}_2$, so

$$\prod_{\ell+1 \in \mathcal{L}_r} \frac{\Pr[x_{\ell+1} \to y_{\ell+1} | G_\ell \downarrow p_0]}{1/(N-\ell)} \geq \prod_{\ell+1 \in \mathcal{L}_r} \left(1 - \left(\frac{6Cq}{N}\right)^r\right)$$

$$\geq 1 - \frac{Ctq_e q^{t-r}}{N^{t-r}} \left(\frac{6Cq}{N}\right)^r$$

$$= 1 - \frac{Ctq_e q^t}{N^t}(6C)^r$$

Thus

$$\prod_{\ell=0}^{q_e-1} \frac{\Pr[x_{\ell+1} \to y_{\ell+1} | G_\ell \downarrow p_0]}{1/(N-\ell)} \geq 1 - \sum_{r=1}^{t} \frac{Ctq_e q^t}{N^t}(6C)^r$$

$$\geq 1 - \frac{q_e q^t}{N^t} Ct^2 (6C)^t.$$

This means

$$\frac{\Pr[X = \tau]}{\Pr[Y = \tau]} \geq 1 - \varepsilon_1$$

for $\varepsilon_1 = \frac{q_e q^t}{N^t} Ct^2 (6C)^t$, for all $\tau \in \mathcal{T}_1$ such that $\Pr[Y = \tau] > 0$. Together with the fact that $\Pr[Y \in \mathcal{T}_2] \leq (t+1)^2 \frac{1}{C}$ this concludes the proof of Theorem 1 by (9).

Acknowledgments. The authors would like to thank Jooyoung Lee, Rodolphe Lampe and Yannick Seurin for helpful conversations.

References

1. Andreeva, E., Bogdanov, A., Dodis, Y., Mennink, B., Steinberger, J.: Indifferentiability of Key-Alternating Ciphers
2. Bogdanov, A., Knudsen, L.R., Leander, G., Standaert, F.-X., Steinberger, J., Tischhauser, E.: Key-Alternating Ciphers in a Provable Setting: Encryption Using a Small Number of Public Permutations. In: Pointcheval, D., Johansson, T. (eds.) EUROCRYPT 2012. LNCS, vol. 7237, pp. 45–62. Springer, Heidelberg (2012)
3. Chen, S., Steinberger, J.: Tight Security Bounds for Key-Alternating Ciphers. IACR eprint, http://eprint.iacr.org/2013/222.pdf (full version of this paper)
4. Daemen, J.: Limitations of the Even-Mansour Construction. In: Matsumoto, T., Imai, H., Rivest, R.L. (eds.) ASIACRYPT 1991. LNCS, vol. 739, pp. 495–498. Springer, Heidelberg (1993)
5. Daemen, J., Rijmen, V.: The Design of Rijndael. Springer (2002)
6. Daemen, J., Rijmen, V.: The Wide Trail Design Strategy. In: Honary, B. (ed.) Cryptography and Coding 2001. LNCS, vol. 2260, pp. 222–238. Springer, Heidelberg (2001)
7. Even, S., Mansour, Y.: A Construction of a Cipher From a Single Pseudorandom Permutation. In: Matsumoto, T., Imai, H., Rivest, R.L. (eds.) ASIACRYPT 1991. LNCS, vol. 739, pp. 210–224. Springer, Heidelberg (1993)

8. Even, S., Mansour, Y.: A Construction of a Cipher from a Single Pseudorandom Permutation. J. Cryptology 10(3), 151–162 (1997)
9. Gaži, P., Tessaro, S.: Efficient and optimally secure key-length extension for block ciphers via randomized cascading. In: Pointcheval, D., Johansson, T. (eds.) EUROCRYPT 2012. LNCS, vol. 7237, pp. 63–80. Springer, Heidelberg (2012)
10. Gaži, P.: Plain versus Randomized Cascading-Based Key-Length Extension for Block Ciphers. In: Canetti, R., Garay, J.A. (eds.) CRYPTO 2013, Part I. LNCS, vol. 8042, pp. 551–570. Springer, Heidelberg (2013)
11. Gaži, P.: Plain versus Randomized Cascading-Based Key-Length Extension for Block Ciphers. In: Canetti, R., Garay, J.A. (eds.) CRYPTO 2013, Part I. LNCS, vol. 8042, pp. 551–570. Springer, Heidelberg (2013), http://eprint.iacr.org/2013/019.pdf
12. Kilian, J., Rogaway, P.: How to protect DES against exhaustive key search (an analysis of DESX). Journal of Cryptology 14(1), 17–35 (2001)
13. Lampe, R., Patarin, J., Seurin, Y.: An Asymptotically Tight Security Analysis of the Iterated Even-Mansour Cipher. In: Wang, X., Sako, K. (eds.) ASIACRYPT 2012. LNCS, vol. 7658, pp. 278–295. Springer, Heidelberg (2012)
14. Lampe, R., Seurin, Y.: How to Construct an Ideal Cipher from a Small Set of Public Permutations. In: Sako, K., Sarkar, P. (eds.) ASIACRYPT 2013, Part I. LNCS, vol. 8269, pp. 444–463. Springer, Heidelberg (2013)
15. Luby, M., Rackoff, C.: How to Construct Pseudorandom Permutations from Pseudorandom Functions. SIAM J. Comput. 17(2), 373–386 (1988)
16. Maurer, U.M., Pietrzak, K.: Composition of Random Systems: When Two Weak Make One Strong. In: Naor, M. (ed.) TCC 2004. LNCS, vol. 2951, pp. 410–427. Springer, Heidelberg (2004)
17. Maurer, U.M., Pietrzak, K., Renner, R.S.: Indistinguishability Amplification. In: Menezes, A. (ed.) CRYPTO 2007. LNCS, vol. 4622, pp. 130–149. Springer, Heidelberg (2007)
18. Patarin, J.: The "Coefficients H" Technique. In: Avanzi, R.M., Keliher, L., Sica, F. (eds.) SAC 2008. LNCS, vol. 5381, pp. 328–345. Springer, Heidelberg (2009)
19. Steinberger, J.: Improved Security Bounds for Key-Alternating Ciphers via Hellinger Distance, http://eprint.iacr.org/2012/481.pdf

A   Derandomizing an Information-Theoretic Distinguisher

The fact that an information-theoretic distinguisher can be derandomized is seldom proved, though admittedly simple. For a change and for the sake of completeness we include a proof here.

Let D be an information-theoretic distinguisher, which we view as a deterministic function taking an *oracle* input ω and a *random string* input r, and producing one bit of output. Formally D is a function

$$D : \Omega \times \mathcal{R} \rightarrow \{0, 1\}$$

where Ω is the set of possible oracles and where $\mathcal{R}$ is the set of possible random strings. The fact that an "oracle" is an object for D to "interact" with according to certain rules doesn't matter here. All that matters that D defines a deterministic function from $\Omega \times \mathcal{R}$ to $\{0, 1\}$.

Let r be an arbitrary random variable of range $\mathcal{R}$ and let ω_X, ω_Y be two random variables of range Ω, where ω_X is distributed according to the distribution of real-world oracles and ω_Y is distributed according to the distribution of ideal-world oracles, and where r is independent from ω_X, ω_Y. By definition D's advantage (with respect to source of randomness r) is

$$\Delta_D := \Pr_{\omega_X, r}[D(\omega_X, r) = 1] - \Pr_{\omega_Y, r}[D(\omega_Y, r) = 1] \tag{26}$$

which can also be written

$$\Delta_D = \Delta(D(\omega_X, r), D(\omega_Y, r)) \tag{27}$$

where, on the right, we have the statistical distance of the random variables $D(\omega_X, r)$, $D(\omega_Y, r)$ of range $\{0, 1\}$. Note that the right-hand side of (26) can be written

$$\mathbb{E}_r[\mathbb{E}_{\omega_X}[D(\omega_X, r)]] - \mathbb{E}_r[\mathbb{E}_{\omega_Y}[D(\omega_Y, r)]]$$

since D is $\{0, 1\}$-valued, and where $\mathbb{E}$ denotes expectation. By linearity of expectation, then,

$$\Delta_D = \mathbb{E}_r[\mathbb{E}_{\omega_X}[D(\omega_X, r)] - \mathbb{E}_{\omega_Y}[D(\omega_Y, r)]]$$

and so there must exist some $r_0 \in \mathcal{R}$ such that

$$\Delta_D \leq \mathbb{E}_{\omega_X}[D(\omega_X, r_0)] - \mathbb{E}_{\omega_Y}[D(\omega_Y, r_0)]$$
$$= \Pr_{\omega_X}[D(\omega_X, r_0) = 1] - \Pr_{\omega_Y}[D(\omega_Y, r_0) = 1]$$

so that D's random string can be fixed to r_0 without harming D's advantage. (The fact that r is independent from ω_X, ω_Y is used to condition on $r = r_0$ without affecting the distribution of ω_X, ω_Y.) Alternatively, one can use (27) together with the more general fact that

$$\Delta(f(X, Z), f(Y, Z)) \leq \mathbb{E}_Z[\Delta(f(X, Z), f(Y, Z))] := \sum_z \Pr[Z = z]\Delta(f(X, z), f(Y, z)) \tag{28}$$

for any random variables X, Y, Z such that Z is independent from X and Y, for any function f. But to be complete (28) would require its own proof.

The Locality of Searchable Symmetric Encryption

David Cash[1] and Stefano Tessaro[2]

[1] Department of Computer Science, Rutgers University, Piscataway, NJ 08855, USA
david.cash@cs.rutgers.edu
[2] Department of Computer Science, University of California, Santa Barbara
tessaro@cs.ucsb.edu

Abstract. This paper proves a lower bound on the trade-off between server storage size and the locality of memory accesses in searchable symmetric encryption (SSE). Namely, when encrypting an index of N identifier/keyword pairs, the encrypted index must have size $\omega(N)$ *or* the scheme must perform searching with $\omega(1)$ non-contiguous reads to memory *or* the scheme must read many more bits than is necessary to compute the results. Recent implementations have shown that non-locality of server memory accesses create a throughput-bottleneck on very large databases. Our lower bound shows that this is due to the security notion and not a defect of the constructions. An upper bound is also given in the form of a new SSE construction with an $O(N \log N)$ size encrypted index that performs $O(\log N)$ reads during a search.

Keywords: Symmetric Encryption, Lower Bound.

1 Introduction

Searchable symmetric encryption (SSE) [24,15,13] enables a client to encrypt an index of record/keyword pairs and later issue tokens allowing an untrusted server to retrieve the (identifiers of) all records matching a keyword. SSE aims to hide statistics about the index to the greatest extent possible while maintaining practical efficiency for large indexes like email repositories or United States census data. These schemes employ only fast symmetric primitives and recent implementations [10] have shown that, in contrast to most applications of advanced cryptography, cryptographic processing like encryption is not the bottleneck for scaling. Instead, lower-level issues dealing with memory layouts required by the schemes are the limiting factor for large indexes.

This work studies how the security definitions for SSE inherently hamper scaling for large indexes. It proves an unconditional lower bound on the trade-off between server storage space and the *spatial locality* of its accesses to the encrypted index during a search. At a high level, the bound says that, for an index with N pairs, any secure SSE must either pad the encrypted index to an impractical (super-linear, $\omega(N)$) size *or* perform searching in a very non-local way (with $\omega(1)$ contiguous accesses or by reading far more bits than is

P.Q. Nguyen and E. Oswald (Eds.): EUROCRYPT 2014, LNCS 8441, pp. 351–368, 2014.

necessary). Either of these options is likely to incur a large slow-down over a properly designed plaintext searching system with an $O(N)$-size index that can search with $O(1)$ contiguous accesses.

The issue of locality in SSE surfaced in recent works [13,10] where implementations showed that the non-local use of external storage was a main bottleneck preventing scaling to large indexes. The only works with a highly local access pattern generated very large (roughly $O(N^2)$) encrypted databases that also prevented scaling. This paper explains this dichotomy of padding versus spatial locality by proving it is an unavoidable consequence of the SSE security definition. As more cryptographic applications are developed for securely outsourcing large amounts of data (while maintaining either authenticity or secrecy), lower-level issues like locality may become more relevant. While in some contexts (like secure multiparty computation) it is clear that the entire input must be touched during computation, this work appears to be the first to study of the effect of security on locality in detail.

The lower bound suggests the question of a matching upper bound. We give a new scheme with an $O(N \log N)$ size encrypted index and $O(\log N)$ locality via a different padding strategy, which compares to a scheme with a $O(N^2)$ size encrypted index and $O(1)$ locality.[1] This scheme may not be competitive with prior highly-optimized implementations, but it serves as intermediate point in the trade-off curve implied by the lower bound. The interesting question of closing the gap is left open.

Scheme	Leakage	EDB Size	Locality	Read Efficiency
CGKO'06-1 [13]	m, N	$O(N+m)$	$O(t_w)$	$O(1)$
CGKO'06-2 [13]	$M \cdot n$	$O(Mn)$	$O(t_w)$	$O(1)$
CK'10 [12]	m, n, M	$O(Mn)$	$O(1)$	$O(1)$
LSDHJ'10 [25]	m, n	$O(mn)$	$O(t_w)$	$O(1)$
KO'12 [20]	n, M	$O(Mn)$	$O(t_w)$	$O(1)$
KPR'12 [19]	m, N	$O(N+m)$	$O(t_w)$	$O(1)$
KP'13 [18]	m, n	$O(mn)$	$O(t_w \log n)$	$O(n \log n)$
CJJKRS'13 [10]	N	$O(N)$	$O(t_w)$	$O(1)$
This paper: Scheme	N	$O(N \log N)$	$O(\log N)$	$O(1)$
This paper: Lower Bound	Any from above	$\omega(N)$	$O(1)$	$O(1)$

Fig. 1. Comparison of some SSE schemes. Legend: Leakage is leakage from EDB only, and all schemes also leak search results and access pattern. n = total # of unique identifiers, $N = \sum_w |\mathsf{DB}(w)|$, m = total # of unique keywords, $M = \max_w |\mathsf{DB}(w)|$, $t_w = |\mathsf{DB}(w)|$ for the query w. For [12] we mean the scheme in Section 5.2 of the full version there. The lower bound is achieved with $\alpha = 0$ in Theorem 8. If a scheme support updates or more advanced searches then we consider a simplified static version for keyword searching as formalized in Section 2. Differences in security (simulation versus indistinguishability, adaptivity) are ignored here but explain why some schemes appear to be strictly worse than others.

---

[1] There are various ways to achieve a smaller index (see Figure 1), but these will achieve a slightly different notion of security.

SSE AND LOCALITY. Let us describe the issue in more detail, starting with SSE and its security goals. An input to an SSE scheme, denoted DB, is essentially an index associating with each keyword w a set of identifiers (bit strings) $DB(w) = \{id_1, \cdots, id_{t_w}\}$, where the number t_w can vary. "Searching" means retrieving those identifiers, given w. An SSE scheme is a system for storing and retrieving these sets while hiding statistics about the identifier sets matching un-searched keywords such as their number, size, the size of their intersections, and so on. Security is formally parameterized with a leakage function $\mathcal{L}$ that describes an upper bound on what a server learns. One example of good leakage is $N = \sum_w |DB(w)|$, along with the identifier sets $DB(w)$ for each keyword that is searched for. Other statistics like $\max_w |DB(w)|$ and the number of unique keywords are also usually considered acceptable leakage. In any case, the defined leakage is *all* the server should learn, so plaintext keywords, identifiers, and anything else other than the output of $\mathcal{L}$ must be hidden.

A scheme of Curtmola et al. [13] forms the basis for most subsequent SSE schemes. This scheme leaks only N and the number of unique keywords by placing all N of the identifier/keyword pairs in random order into a large array (along with some auxiliary tables) and enabling retrieval with encrypted linked lists that could be opened for the server. Searching for w requires walking through $|DB(w)|$ pseudorandom locations in this large array. When the array is stored on disk, it means that each retrieved pair requires a disk read at a random location. Since each identifier is on the order of several bytes but the disk block size is now often 4KB, this searching will sacrifice throughput and latency compared to a plaintext search system which can store the identifiers together in sectors, and moreover in contiguous sectors which can be read together more efficiently without additional seeking. Naive modifications, like packing several identifiers from a single $DB(w)$ set into one sector, render the scheme insecure for the leakage function they consider.

One work [12] addressed locality by enlarging the index to $\omega(N)$ size. This scheme pads every set $DB(w)$ to size $\max_w |DB(w)|$ and then store these padded sets in the own contiguous rows. For very large indexes (with billions of pairs as in [10]), even doubling the plaintext size may be unreasonable, so these works do not appear to scale for realistic datasets where the padding will be large.

RESULTS. In the sections that follow a precise model is given for measuring and comparing the memory usage of SSE schemes. The parameters of locality, read-efficiency, and read disjointness are defined and discussed in relation to lower bounds. Briefly, *locality* is the number of non-contiguous memory accesses made by the server, *read-efficiency* is the number of bits read beyond the minimum necessary, and a scheme has α-*overlapping reads* if reads for different searches overlap in at most α bits. In Figure 1 we compare the leakage, locality, and read efficiency of prior SSE constructions. (For read efficiency, the number listed is a multiplicative factor over the binary encoding of the identifiers matching the query.)

This paper's primary results are summarized below. For the following two theorems, let $\mathcal{L}$ be any of the leakage functions in Figure 1 (or any function efficiently computable from them). Below we write BinEnc(DB) to mean an encoding on DB as a binary string formed by concatening the lists of identifiers matching each keyword. See Sections 2 and 3 for definitions.

Theorem 1. *If Π is an $\mathcal{L}$-IND-secure SSE scheme with locality r as well as α-overlapping reads, then Π has $\omega\left(\frac{|\mathsf{BinEnc(DB)}|}{r\cdot(\alpha+2)}\right)$ server storage.*

We remark that a very weak read efficiency requirement is implicit in the condition on overlapping reads, and all existing schemes have highly non-overlapping reads.

Theorem 2. *Assuming one-way functions exist, there exists an $\mathcal{L}$-IND-secure SSE scheme with locality $O(\log N)$, $O(1)$ read efficiency and $O(N \log N)$ storage.*

The bulk of the paper is spent proving the first theorem. We now start with an intuitive sketch of how one might prove a weak lower bound. See Section 4 for a detailed sketch of the actual proof, which is more complicated.

LOWER BOUND APPROACH. Intuitively, if a scheme is very local, then after some searching the server can look at what is *not* read after several searches and infer statistics about what has not been opened. In particular, if one of the sets DB(w) is very large, then good locality means there is a very large region of the encrypted index that will not be touched by other searches, and the server will notice that this happens after several searches with small number of results.

The lower bound develops this intuition, but requires further ideas to achieve a lower bound of $\omega(N)$ on the server storage. For now let us sketch how one shows the server must approximately double the size of a plaintext index if it is to be *perfectly* local and read-efficient, meaning it processes a search by reading exactly the required number of bits from a single contiguous section of EDB, and moreover that the reads for all searches are disjoint. This seems highly restrictive, but later will we be able to weaken all of these assumptions to realistic versions.

Now suppose we have a perfectly local SSE scheme. Consider two index inputs, DB_0 and DB_1, where DB_0 consists of N keywords each matching a single unique document and DB_1 consists of 2 keywords matching a single unique document and a third keyword matching $N-2$ documents. If two random keywords matching single documents are searched for then the server learns which locations of the encrypted index are read in order to respond. If DB_0 was encrypted, then pigeon-hole argument shows that with constant probability, there is no remaining contiguous interval large enough to contain the bits that would be read for the third keyword (it is here that we use an assumed bound on the server storage). This is diagrammed in the top part of Figure 2, where when the red regions are read there is no longer space between them for a larger interval. This is in contrast to the case when DB_1 is encrypted, because after observing the two small reads, a perfectly local scheme there will always be a contiguous unread region large enough to hold the $N-2$ identifiers for the third keyword.

The full lower bound is an extension of this idea to consider a family of indexes with result sets of several sizes. Later it is argued that the technique above is limited to showing a factor 2 overhead in server storage, and that the complexity of the main attack seems necessary. We also address several extensions, such as when the server does not perform a single contiguous read but up to $O(1)$ reads, the leakage function parameter varies, and the reads are allowed to partially overlap.

RELATED WORK ON SECURE SEARCHING. Following the initial work of [24] that suggested searchable encryption, Curtmola et al. [13] formalized the version of SSE that we consider in this paper. Subsequently SSE schemes were given with different efficiency properties [15,11,12], support for data updates [19,18], authenticity [20] and support more advanced searches [10]. These improvements are rthogonal to the lower bound, which applies to these schemes when used for basic (non-dynamic, non-authenticated) SSE.

The problem of searching on encrypted data can be addressed in several ways using generic multiparty computation protocols, oblivious RAM schemes [16] or fully homomorphic encryption [14]. These approaches achieve slightly levels of functionality and different notions of security, meaning that the lower bound does not seem to apply. Order-preserving encryption [6,7] takes a different approach to searching that achieves high efficiency for rich queries but is less secure than SSE. Implementations that use order-preserving encryption, notably CryptDB [22], inherit these properties. Our lower bound does not apply to them.

There is also a line of work on searching on *public-key* ciphertexts. Public-key encryption with keyword search [9,17,1,2] In these schemes and subsequent work, the server performing the search by testing each encrypted record individually, resulting in a scheme that is trivial from the point of view of the lower bound. The line of work on deterministic public-key encryption [4,8,5] enables fast searching but achieves different, weaker security meaning our lower bound does not apply.

RELATED WORK ON LOCALITY. Algorithmic performance with data stored on disk has been studied extensively in *external memory models* (c.f. [26,23,3]). These models usually consider block-oriented devices with varying degrees of precision (e.g., including modeling parallelism, drive geometry, memory hierarchies, caching, locality of blocks, etc.). Typically one measures the external memory efficiency of an algorithm by counting the number of blocks it accesses, and a wide array of techniques have been developed to optimize disk utilization at the algorithmic level.

Interestingly, matching lower and upper bounds are known for many natural problems like, e.g., dictionary retrieval, sorting, range searching – see, e.g., Chapter 6 of [26]. Our lower bound is fundamentally different from these results. There, one can give an information theoretic argument that a certain number of disk accesses are necessary in the worst case, with a flavor similar to the classic $O(n \log n)$ comparison-based sorting lower bound. Our lower bound, however, will proceed by showing that any SSE scheme that meets a certain level of efficiency will be *insecure* (rather than *incorrect* as in traditional external memory lower bounds). That is, our lower bound comes in the form of an attack. Due to the nature of our lower bound we opt for an extremely simplified version of locality and leave its adaptation to fine-grained external memory models to future work.

We are not aware of any prior similar lower bounds on cryptographic primitives, other than the folklore observation that security forces many primitives to touch every bit their inputs (e.g., homomorphic encryption [14], multiparty computation).

ORGANIZATION. Preliminaries and definitions are recalled in Section 2. New definitions relating to locality are given and discussed in Section 3. The lower bound is stated and proved in Section 4, and the upper bound is in Section 5.

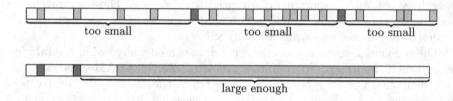

Fig. 2. Intuition for a basic lower bound

2 Preliminaries

Throughout this paper the security parameter is denoted λ and all algorithms (and adversaries) are assumed to run in time polynomial in λ. We write $[n]$ for the set $\{1, \ldots, n\}$. For a vector $\mathbf{v}$ we write $|\mathbf{v}|$ for the dimension (length) of $\mathbf{v}$ and for $i \in [|\mathbf{v}|]$ we write $\mathbf{v}[i]$ for the i-th component of $\mathbf{v}$. For a bitstring s, we write $s[a, b]$ for the substring starting with the bit in position a and ending in position b.

DATABASES AND SSE SCHEMES. An index (or database) $\mathsf{DB} = (\mathrm{id}_i, \mathsf{W}_i)_{i=1}^n$ is a list of identifier/keyword-set pairs, where each $\mathrm{id}_i \in \{0,1\}^\lambda$ and each W_i is a set of bitstrings. When the DB under consideration is clear, we will write $\mathsf{W} = \bigcup_{i=1}^n \mathsf{W}_i$. For a keyword $w \in \mathsf{W}$, we write $\mathsf{DB}(w)$ for $\{\mathrm{id}_i : w \in \mathsf{W}_i\}$. We will always use $N = \sum_{w \in \mathsf{W}} |\mathsf{DB}(w)| = \sum_{i=1}^n |\mathsf{W}_i|$ to mean the total number of keyword/identifier pairs in DB, n to mean the number of unique identifiers, and $m = |\mathsf{W}|$ to mean the number of unique keywords.

A *searchable symmetric encryption (SSE) scheme* Π consists of algorithms (KeyGen, EDBSetup, TokGen, Search) that satisfy the following syntax. The key generation algorithm KeyGen takes as input the security parameter and outputs a key K. The algorithm EDBSetup takes as input a key K and a database DB and outputs an encrypted database EDB. The token generation protocol takes as input a string w and key K and outputs a token τ. Finally, the searching algorithm Search takes as input τ and EDB and outputs as set L of results.

We note that formalization of an SSE scheme does not model the storage of actual document payloads, but only of metadata encoded in a keyword index. This simplifies the definition and makes it modular, but some care must be taken when combining an SSE scheme with a document storage scheme (see e.g. [13] for an example of how to store the payloads).

An SSE scheme is *correct* if the natural usage returns the correct results for the keyword being searched (i.e., $DB(w)$), except with negligible probability. Formally, for every database DB, consider an experiment where $K \xleftarrow{\$} \mathsf{KeyGen}(1^\lambda)$ and EDB $\xleftarrow{\$} \mathsf{EDBSetup}(K, DB)$ are initially sampled. Then, an attacker learns EDB and can issue adaptive queries w_i, which are answered by first generating a token $\tau_i \leftarrow \mathsf{TokGen}(K, w_i)$ and then returning it together with $S_i \leftarrow \mathsf{Search}(\tau_i, EDB)$ to the attacker. The scheme is *correct* if for all polynomial-time attackers, $S_i = DB(w_i)$ for all i, except with negligible probability.

We say that the scheme Π has *server storage* $s(N, \lambda)$ if on input a database DB with N keyword/identifier pairs and a key $K \xleftarrow{\$} \mathsf{KeyGen}(1^\lambda)$, EDBSetup outputs EDB such that $|EDB| = s(N, \lambda)$, where $|EDB|$ is the bit-length of EDB.

SECURITY. We recall the non-adaptive indistinguishability-based version of security from [13] which will be considered in the lower bound.

Definition 3. *Let* $\Pi = (\mathsf{KeyGen}, \mathsf{EDBSetup}, \mathsf{TokGen}, \mathsf{Search})$ *be an SSE scheme and let* $\mathcal{L}$ *be a leakage function and* $\mathcal{A}$ *be an adversary. For* $b \in \{0, 1\}$ *we define the game* $\text{IND-SSE}^b_{\Pi, \mathcal{L}, \mathcal{A}}(\lambda)$ *as follows: The adversary chooses* $DB_0, DB_1, \mathbf{w}$. *The game runs* $K \xleftarrow{\$} \mathsf{KeyGen}(1^\lambda)$, EDB $\xleftarrow{\$} \mathsf{EDBSetup}(K, DB_b)$ *and* $\mathbf{t}[i] \leftarrow \mathsf{TokGen}(K, \mathbf{w}[i])$ *for each* $i \in [|\mathbf{w}|]$. *It gives* $(EDB, \mathbf{t})$ *to* $\mathcal{A}$, *which outputs a bit* $\hat{b}$. *Finally, if* $\mathcal{L}(DB_0, \mathbf{w}) \neq \mathcal{L}(DB_1, \mathbf{w})$, *the game outputs* $\perp$ *and otherwise it outputs* $\hat{b}$.

We define the $\mathcal{L}$*-IND advantage of* $\mathcal{A}$ *to be*

$$\mathbf{Adv}^{\text{ind-sse}}_{\Pi, \mathcal{L}, \mathcal{A}}(\lambda) = |\Pr[\text{IND-SSE}^0_{\Pi, \mathcal{L}, \mathcal{A}}(\lambda) = 1] - \Pr[\text{IND-SSE}^1_{\Pi, \mathcal{L}, \mathcal{A}}(\lambda) = 1]|,$$

and we say that Π *is* $\mathcal{L}$*-IND-secure if* $\mathbf{Adv}^{\text{ind-sse}}_{\Pi, \mathcal{L}, \mathcal{A}}(\lambda)$ *is negligible for every* $\mathcal{A}$.

Our construction will achieve the stronger (adaptive, simulation-based) definition from [13], which we recall here. (A non-adaptive version is such that in both games $\mathcal{A}$ must choose all of its queries beforehand.)

Definition 4. *Let* $\Pi = (\mathsf{KeyGen}, \mathsf{EDBSetup}, \mathsf{TokGen}, \mathsf{Search})$ *be an SSE scheme and let* $\mathcal{L}$ *be a leakage function. For algorithms* $\mathcal{A}$ *and* $\mathcal{S}$, *we define the two games* $\text{SIM-SSE}^0_{\Pi, \mathcal{L}, \mathcal{A}}(\lambda)$ *and* $\text{SIM-SSE}^1_{\Pi, \mathcal{L}, \mathcal{A}, \mathcal{S}}(\lambda)$ *as follows:*

$\text{SIM-SSE}^0_{\Pi, \mathcal{L}, \mathcal{A}}(\lambda)$: $\mathcal{A}(1^\lambda)$ *chooses* $DB, \mathbf{w}$. *The game then runs* $(K, EDB) \leftarrow \mathsf{EDBSetup}(DB)$ *and* $\mathbf{t}[i] \leftarrow \mathsf{TokGen}(K, \mathbf{w}[i])$ *for each* $i \in [|\mathbf{w}|]$. *It gives* $EDB, \mathbf{t}$ *to* $\mathcal{A}$, *which eventually returns a bit that the game uses as its own output.*

$\text{SIM-SSE}^1_{\Pi, \mathcal{L}, \mathcal{A}, \mathcal{S}}(\lambda)$: $\mathcal{A}(1^\lambda)$ *chooses* $DB, \mathbf{w}$. *The game then runs* $(EDB, \mathbf{t}) \leftarrow \mathcal{S}(\mathcal{L}(DB, \mathbf{w}))$ *and gives* $EDB, \mathbf{t}$ *to* $\mathcal{A}$, *which eventually returns a bit that the game uses as its own output.*

We define the $\mathcal{L}$*-SIM-advantage of* $\mathcal{A}$ *and* $\mathcal{S}$ *to be*

$$\mathbf{Adv}^{\text{sim-sse}}_{\Pi, \mathcal{L}, \mathcal{A}, \mathcal{S}}(\lambda) = |\Pr[\text{SIM-SSE}^0_{\Pi, \mathcal{L}, \mathcal{A}}(\lambda) = 1] - \Pr[\text{SIM-SSE}^1_{\Pi, \mathcal{L}, \mathcal{A}, \mathcal{S}}(\lambda) = 1]|,$$

and we say that Π *is* $\mathcal{L}$*-SIM-secure if for all adversaries* $\mathcal{A}$ *there exists an algorithm* $\mathcal{S}$ *such that* $\mathbf{Adv}^{\text{sim-sse}}_{\Pi, \mathcal{L}, \mathcal{A}, \mathcal{S}}(\lambda)$ *is negligible.*

LEAKAGE FUNCTIONS. Below we will consider two leakage functions $\mathcal{L}_{\min}$ and $\mathcal{L}_{\max}$. The first is called the *size minimal leakage function*,[2] which is defined as follows: $\mathcal{L}_{\min}(\mathsf{DB}, \mathbf{w})$ outputs $N = \sum_{w \in \mathsf{W}} |\mathsf{DB}(w)|$ and the sets $(\mathsf{DB}(\mathbf{w}[1]), \ldots, \mathsf{DB}(\mathbf{w}[\|\mathbf{w}\|]))$. The second is called the *maximal leakage function* which outputs (N, n, m, M) as well as $(\mathsf{DB}(\mathbf{w}[1]), \ldots, \mathsf{DB}(\mathbf{w}[\|\mathbf{w}\|]))$, where N is defined as before, n is the number of unique identifiers in DB, $m = |\mathsf{W}|$ (the number of unique keywords), and $M = \max_w |\mathsf{DB}(w)|$. It is of course possible to consider "more" leakage, but this is more than any existing scheme leaks, meaning out lower bound will apply to all of them.

3   Read Efficiency and Locality Metrics for SSE Schemes

This section introduces the notions of locality and read efficiency of SSE schemes.

READ PATTERNS. First, we observe that the searching procedure of any SSE scheme can be decomposed into a sequence of *contiguous* reads from the encrypted database. To formalize this point of view, fix an SSE scheme Π, an EDB output by EDBSetup and a token τ output by TokGen. Viewing EDB as a bitstring of length M, we may express the computation of $\mathsf{Search}(\tau, \mathsf{EDB})$ as follows: It starts by computing an interval $[a_1, b_1]$ that depends only on τ. It then computes another interval $[a_2, b_2]$ that depends only on τ and $\mathsf{EDB}[a_1, b_1]$, and continues computing intervals to read based on τ and all previously read intervals from EDB. We write $\mathsf{RdPat}(\tau, \mathsf{EDB})$ for these intervals. In the following, denote as $\mathsf{BinEnc}(\mathsf{DB}(w))$ the binary *representation* of $\mathsf{DB}(w)$, i.e., the concatenation of all identifiers represented as bit strings, and $\mathsf{BinEnc}(\mathsf{DB})$ to be the concatenation of all the $\mathsf{BinEnc}(\mathsf{DB}(w))$ for each w in the database. Under our assumption that all identifiers are in $\{0, 1\}^\lambda$, we have $|\mathsf{BinEnc}(\mathsf{DB})| = \lambda |\mathsf{DB}(w)|$ and $\mathsf{BinEnc}(\mathsf{DB}) = \lambda N$.

LOCALITY OF AN SSE SCHEME. We put forward the notion of locality of an SSE scheme, capturing the fact that every read pattern consists of at most a bounded number of intervals.

Definition 5 (Locality). *An SSE scheme Π is r-local (or has locality r) if for any λ, DB, and $w \in \mathsf{W}$, we have that $\mathsf{RdPat}(\tau, \mathsf{EDB})$ consists of at most r intervals with probability 1 when EDB, τ are computed as $K \xleftarrow{\$} \mathsf{KeyGen}(1^\lambda)$, $\mathsf{EDB} \xleftarrow{\$} \mathsf{EDBSetup}(K, \mathsf{DB})$, $\tau \leftarrow \mathsf{TokGen}(K, w)$. If $r = 1$, we say Π has perfect locality.*

In particular, the value r can depend both on the security parameter λ *and* the index size $|\mathsf{DB}|$.

READ EFFICIENCY. The notion of locality alone is not very meaningful. Of course, we can just make every scheme perfectly local by reading the whole EDB. This is why the notion of locality is directly tied to the notion of *read efficiency*, which measures the overall size of the portion read by a search operation.

---

[2] It appears to be impossible to define a true "minimal" amount of leakage, as we could consider a leakage function that leaks only some upper bound on N.

Definition 6 (Read Efficiency). *An SSE scheme Π is c-read efficient (or has read efficiency c) if for any λ,* DB *and* $w \in$ W*, we have that* $\mathsf{RdPat}(\tau, \mathsf{EDB})$ *consists of intervals of total length at most* $c \cdot |\mathsf{BinEnc}(\mathsf{DB}(w))|$ *bits.*

We allow c to depend on the security parameter here.

READ DISJOINTNESS. The above definition of read efficiency is very general. In particular, for sufficiently large c, it allows multiple queries to read *exactly* the same bits. Our lower bound below will apply to a more restricted class of r-local schemes which read sufficiently many new bits. We feel this class is natural, and moreover it contains all prior constructions.

Definition 7 (Overlapping reads). *An SSE scheme Π has α-overlapping reads if for all λ and all* DB*, the read pattern induced by the search of each keyword in* DB *has an overlap of at most α with the read patterns induced by the searches of all previous keywords (with probability 1 over the computation of $K \leftarrow \mathsf{KeyGen}(1^\lambda)$,* EDB $\leftarrow \mathsf{EDBSetup}(K, \mathsf{DB})$*, and the computation of the tokens). When $\alpha = 0$ we say Π has disjoint reads.*

In general, the value α is independent of N, but may additionally depend on λ or possibly on the number of words |W| in order for example to take into account a common portion of EDB which can be read at every search operation. Typically, a scheme will read some metadata like hash table entries and then perform reads to retrieve the actual results. (Of course we make no assumption on what computation the scheme actually does, beyond being of the form above.)

4 Lower Bound

In this section we sketch our proof that a secure SSE scheme cannot simultaneously achieve $O(1)$ locality and $O(|\mathsf{BinEnc}(\mathsf{DB})|)$ server storage. Concretely, we are going to prove the following theorem, where $\mathcal{L}_{\max}$ was defined at the end of Section 2 and the locality metrics were defined in the previous section.

Theorem 8. *If Π is an $\mathcal{L}_{\max}$-IND-secure SSE scheme with locality r as well as α-overlapping reads, then Π has $\omega\left(\frac{|\mathsf{BinEnc}(\mathsf{DB})|}{r \cdot (\alpha+2)}\right)$ server storage.*

We note that we consider $\mathcal{L}_{\max}$ for the lower bound as this strengthens the result by considering schemes that are "very leaky." In the theorem statement, we assume that α does not depend on N, but may additionally depend on λ or possibly on the number of words |W|.

The proof is rather long and will not fit in this version of the paper (a full proof was submitted and will appear in the full version). Instead, we provide a sketch of the proof approach and its implementation.

PROOF APPROACH. We will first sketch our lower bound with a few simplifications. First, we assume the SSE scheme is has perfect locality and read efficiency, meaning the server always performs exactly one contiguous read for exactly

$|\mathsf{BinEnc}(\mathsf{DB}(w))| = \lambda \cdot |\mathsf{DB}(w)|$ bits from EDB when searching for a word w, the minimum required for the response. Second, we assume all reads are perfectly disjoint. Third, we consider the lower bound leakage against SSE schemes achieving security with leakage function $\mathcal{L}_{\min}$ instead of $\mathcal{L}_{\max}$ (thus making the result easier). It turns out that this case encompasses most of the technical difficulties for the general result, which we derive afterwards.

The principle behind the attack extends the idea sketched in Section 1. The adversary will choose two indexes $\mathsf{DB}_0, \mathsf{DB}_1$ of the same size in a careful way so that DB_1 has keywords that match a large number of documents while DB_0 does not. Then it will query for tokens for several keywords matching relatively small numbers of documents. Using the tokens, it will compute the read pattern of the server when searching for those keywords, and then look at the *unread* portions of EDB. Since we are assuming perfect locality, if DB_1 was encrypted, there must be large regions that go untouched by any query. On the other hand, we will show that this is sometimes not the case if DB_0 is encrypted, allowing the adversary to distinguish.

To describe the proof it will be useful to introduce a compact notation for the *shape* of a DB input.

Definition 9. *We write*

$$\mathsf{DB} \leftarrow (n_1 \times s_1;\ n_2 \times s_2;\ \ldots\ ;\ n_t \times s_t)$$

when $\mathsf{DB} = (\mathsf{id}_i, \mathsf{W}_i)$ *has shape* $(n_1 \times s_1;\ n_2 \times s_2;\ \ldots\ ;\ n_t \times s_t)$*, which means that it satisfies the following:*

- *DB has a keyword set* W *of size* $\sum_{j=1}^t n_j$ *comprised of* λ*-bit strings.*
- *For each* $j \in [t]$*, there are* n_j *keywords* $w \in \mathsf{W}$ *such that* $|\mathsf{DB}(w)| = s_j$*.*
- *For all* $w \neq w'$*, the sets* $\mathsf{DB}(w)$ *and* $\mathsf{DB}(w')$ *are disjoint.*

Our attack sketched in the introduction corresponded to picking indexes $\mathsf{DB}_0, \mathsf{DB}_1$ with shapes $\mathsf{DB}_0 \leftarrow (N \times 1)$ and $\mathsf{DB}_1 \leftarrow (1 \times 1\,; 1 \times N - 2)$, meaning that DB_0 consists of N "singletons" and DB_1 consists of two singletons and one large set of results. It is possible to formalize that attack and show that a secure perfectly local SSE scheme must produce an EDB that is at least twice as large as the bit representation of DB, but as we observe at the end of this section, any attack that uses indexes with such simple shapes will not be able to prove a better lower bound.

We now proceed to extend that attack. Let Π be perfectly local scheme with server storage $k\lambda N$ for some constant $k \geq 1$. Our attack against the security Π will select two random inputs $\mathsf{DB}_0, \mathsf{DB}_1$ with shapes

$$\mathsf{DB}_0 \leftarrow (n_1 \times \varepsilon_1 N;\ n_2 \times \varepsilon_2 N;\ \ldots\ ;\ n_{k-1} \times \varepsilon_{k-1} N;\ \hat{n}_k \times \varepsilon_k N) \tag{1}$$

$$\mathsf{DB}_1 \leftarrow (n_1 \times \varepsilon_1 N;\ n_2 \times \varepsilon_2 N;\ \ldots\ ;\ n_{k-1} \times \varepsilon_{k-1} N;\ n_k \times \varepsilon_k N;\ \hat{n}_{k+1} \times \varepsilon_{k+1} N) \tag{2}$$

where $n_1 > n_2 > \cdots > n_k > 1$ and $\varepsilon_1 < \varepsilon_2 < \ldots < \varepsilon_k < \varepsilon_{k+1} < 1$ are appropriately chosen constants. Intuitively, DB_0 consists only of many small result sets

$\mathsf{DB}_0(w)$ while DB_1 consists of many small result sets and some relatively large sets of $\varepsilon_{k+1}N$ keywords.

The attack will query for tokens for all $\sum_{i=1}^{k} n_i$ keywords matching $\varepsilon_i N$ documents with $i \in [k]$. It then calculates the read patterns of the server. Since Π is perfectly local, the reads are for $\varepsilon_i \lambda N$ bit intervals respectively, and moreover they are all disjoint. Thus if DB_1 is encrypted, then the perfect locality of Π means there must exist an interval of $\varepsilon_{k+1} \lambda N$ bits in EDB that was not touched by the observed reads (actually, there will be at least $\hat{n}_{k+1}$ such intervals) – These are where the large result sets are stored (note that the adversary does not query for the keyword corresponding to any of large sets, but only notices the presence of a suspiciously large untouched interval). However, as we will show, if DB_0 was encrypted then the security of Π will mean there is a noticeable probability that there is no such interval remaining untouched. We stress that this will be due to the (forced) distribution of the reads, and not simply because there is no room, as the same number of bits is read when either DB_0 or DB_1 in encrypted.

Proving the latter claim on DB_0 is the main technical part of the proof. Intuitively, it holds because security forces the small intervals (say of size $\varepsilon_i \lambda N$) to be located in random-looking locations which do not leave large gaps (say of size $\varepsilon_{i+1} \lambda N$) between them too often, which implies that large intervals cannot fit between them while remaining disjoint, effectively "killing" that space for large intervals.

We will show that, for a specific choice of the constants, that for each $i = 1, \ldots, k$, the queried sets of size $\varepsilon_i \lambda N$ will each kill at least λN bits of the EDB from storing any larger intervals (in particular, intervals of size $\varepsilon_j \lambda N$ for $j > i$) with constant probability. Since we have k different read pattern sets each killing λN bits from storing anything larger with constant probability, we get that $k \lambda N$ bits are killed with constant probability. But this means the entire EDB has been killed with constant probability (here we use that k is a constant), and when that happens the adversary can conclude that DB_0 was encrypted – If DB_1 had been encrypted this would happen with probability 0.

We now discuss how to show that queries for a constant number of sets of size $\varepsilon_i N$ will kill λN bits (which is much larger than the actual number of bits read by the server during its perfectly-local searching). To prove this we will consider a sequence of adversaries $\mathcal{A}_1, \mathcal{A}_2, \ldots, \mathcal{A}_k$ - the purpose of $\mathcal{A}_i$ is to show that the sets of size $\varepsilon_i N$ kill enough space with constant probability, assuming that the smaller sets each do so. The first adversary $\mathcal{A}_1$ is the simplest to describe, and resembles our original attack from the Introduction. Adversary $\mathcal{A}_1$ draws $\mathsf{DB}_0, \mathsf{DB}_1$ of size N with shapes

$$\mathsf{DB}_0 \leftarrow (\hat{n}_1 \times \varepsilon_1 N) \tag{3}$$

$$\mathsf{DB}_1 \leftarrow (n_1 \times \varepsilon_1 N; \; \hat{n}_2 \times \varepsilon_2 N), \tag{4}$$

where $n_1 < \hat{n}_1 = \varepsilon_1^{-1}$ and $\varepsilon_1 < \varepsilon_2$ are constants. It populates the two databases with a consistent set of keywords, meaning that the n_1 keywords matching $\varepsilon_1 N$ documents DB_1 are a random subset of the $\hat{n}_1$ such keywords in DB_0.

Intuitively, DB_0 has a large number of keywords matching $\varepsilon_1 N$ documents each, and searching for each keyword induces a read by the server for a disjoint interval $\lambda \varepsilon_1 N$ bits. Thus searching for a random subset of $n_1 < \hat{n}_1$ of those keywords will reveal the location of a random subset of the disjoint intervals. In DB_1, however, there are only n_1 of these keywords, but we can show that security forces their distributions to be as they are in DB_0.

Specifically, we have $\mathcal{A}_1$ query for the n_1 keywords matching $\varepsilon_1 N$ documents in either database, and then it computes their read patterns. If DB_0 was encrypted, then the intervals read by the server are chosen randomly from amongst $\hat{n}_1$ intervals of that size. We show (unconditionally) with good probability there is a lot of space (about λN bits) in EDB where intervals of size $\varepsilon_2 N$ or larger cannot fit after the n_1 intervals have been read. This happens because, for randomly chosen intervals, the gap between them cannot be larger than $\varepsilon_2 N$ too often. Thus the larger intervals must go elsewhere in EDB. And since the scheme is secure, DB_1 must also exhibit this behavior (despite the read intervals not being chosen from a larger set of intervals). In fact, this shows that when any database contains n_1 keywords with εN results each, then the resulting reads for those keywords must be laid out in a way that eliminates a large amount of space for larger intervals even though the actual bits read for them is very small, namely $n_1 \varepsilon_1 \lambda N \ll \hat{n}_1 \varepsilon_1 \lambda N$.

We then iterate this approach; The next adversary $\mathcal{A}_2$ queries DB_0, DB_1 with shapes

$$DB_0 \leftarrow (n_1 \times \varepsilon_1 N;\ \hat{n}_2 \times \varepsilon_2 N) \tag{5}$$

$$DB_1 \leftarrow (n_1 \times \varepsilon_1 N;\ n_2 \times \varepsilon_2 N;\ \hat{n}_3 \times \varepsilon_3 N). \tag{6}$$

(So DB_0 now has the shape that $\mathcal{A}_1$ chose for DB_1.) The adversary $\mathcal{A}_2$ then queries for tokens for all n_1 keywords matching $\varepsilon_1 N$ documents, and then a random subset of the $\hat{n}_2$ keywords matching $\varepsilon_2 N$ documents in DB_1. (As before these databases are made with consistent keywords and identifiers.) We show that when DB_0 is encrypted, conditioned on the read intervals of size $\varepsilon_1 \lambda N$ disallowing λN bits for larger intervals, a random subset of intervals of size $\varepsilon_2 \lambda N$ will disallow about another λN bits for larger intervals. Security again forces this is to be true when DB_1 is encrypted despite not being forced statistically. The result is that with constant probability about $2\lambda N$ bits of EDB can no longer accommodate larger intervals.

By considering the sequence of $\mathcal{A}_1, \ldots, \mathcal{A}_k$ of adversaries and applying this reasoning k times, we have that the entire database has been disallowed by a relatively small number of small reads intervals with good probability, and then we can finish the proof as sketched above.

EXTENSIONS TO MORE GENERAL LOCALITY. The argument above worked for *perfect* locality, meaning the server search algorithm for keyword w worked with a single, contiguous read from EDB for exactly $\lambda \cdot |DB(w)|$ bits that is disjoint from the read for any other search. It is easy to extend the lower bound to when the server works with $r = O(1)$ contiguous reads that total exactly $\lambda \cdot |DB(w)|$ bits and are disjoint from all other reads by observing that one of the r reads must have size at least $\lambda \cdot |DB(w)|/r$ contiguous bits, and then adjusting the parameters of the above argument to ensure that intervals of that size can be be disallowed with good probability by the final adversary.

Other relaxations will be given. For instance, to adaptive the attack to work with leakage function $\mathcal{L}_{max}$, we need to additionally arrange for the submitted databases to always have the same number of documents, keywords, maximum size result set $DB(w)$. This only introduces minor technicalities.

WOULD A SIMPLER ATTACK WORK? It is fair to ask if the complexity of this attack is necessary, and specifically if an attack like $\mathcal{A}_1$, which only queries for keyword with $|DB(w)|$ equal to two possible sizes (either $\varepsilon_1 N$ or $\varepsilon_2 N$) could give the lower bound and avoid the iterative argument.

While it is always possible in principle to simplify proofs, we *can* argue that no such simple adversary could prove a lower bound better than $M \geq 2\lambda N$ by observing read patterns alone. This is because an SSE scheme, knowing that it will only be queried for keywords with two different sizes $|DB(w)|$, could have EDB reserve λN bits for the first size, and another λN bits for the second size. Then it could simply store sets $DB(w)$ of the first size in random order first half of EDB with padding, then the sets $DB(w)$ with the second size in the second half.

This reasoning generalizes to show that any attack proving $M \geq k\lambda N$ must query keywords with $|DB(w)|$ having at least $k + 1$ different sizes, as our attack does.

5   A Positive Result: SSE with Logarithmic Locality

In the previous section, we have seen that any scheme with *constant* locality produces encrypted index of size $\omega(N)$. To complement this result, we provide a new scheme with logarithmic locality, at the cost of an asymptotically larger encrypted index of size roughly $N \log N$. At the same time, our scheme is going to *only* leak the database size N, i.e., it is going to be $\mathcal{L}_{min}$-secure. None of the previous SSE schemes achieved such locality level without additional leakage or a larger worst-case blow-up of the encrypted database.

HASH TABLES. The scheme below relies on *hash tables*. Concretely, a hash table *implementation* consists of a pair of algorithms (HTCreate, HTGet). The function HTCreate takes as input a list $L = \{(l_i, d_i)\}_{1 \leq i \leq k}$ of pairs (l_i, d_i) of strings, where $l_i \in \{0,1\}^\ell$ is the *label* and $d_i \in \{0,1\}^r$ is the *data*, and outputs the *hash table* HT. After running HT $\leftarrow$ HTCreate(L), we have that HTGet(HT, l) returns d if and only if $(l, d) \in L$, and returns $\perp$ otherwise.

There exist hash-table implementations (for example, via variants of cuckoo hashing [21]) with the following properties: The overall size of HT is $O(k(r + \ell) + \log^2 k)$, and the algorithm HTGet needs to read from the hash table HT a constant number (e.g. two) of blocks of ℓ contiguous bits, as well as one r-bit block, when searching for a label $l = l_i$. Moreover, HT does not depend on the ordering of the list L.

DESCRIPTION OF THE SCHEME. We now proceed to specify our new SSE scheme $\Pi = (\mathsf{KeyGen}, \mathsf{EDBSetup}, \mathsf{TokGen}, \mathsf{Search})$ with logarithmic locality. It relies on two keyed functions F and F', where $F : \mathcal{K} \times \{0,1\}^* \to \mathcal{K} \times \mathcal{K}'$ and $F' : \mathcal{K} \times \mathbb{N} \to \{0,1\}^\ell$ (both later to be assumed as pseudorandom). Moreover, it uses a symmetric encryption scheme $(\mathcal{E}, \mathcal{D})$ with key space $\mathcal{K}'$ and m-bit ciphertexts. In particular, we are going to use the latter scheme to encrypt document identifiers and we are going to assume that all identifiers are in the message space of the scheme $(\mathcal{E}, \mathcal{D})$ and their encryption results in ciphertext of *exactly* length s.

The four algorithms of Π now operate as follows:

Key Generation. Algorithm KeyGen simply generates a key $K \xleftarrow{\$} \mathcal{K}$ for F.

Setup. Assume that we are given DB with size $N = 2^t$ for some $t \geq 1$, and for every word $w \in \mathsf{W}$, we use the notation $\mathsf{DB}(w) = \{\mathrm{id}_1, \ldots, \mathrm{id}_{n_w}\}$ to denote its n_w associated identifiers. We also need to consider the binary expansion $n_w = \sum_{i=0}^{t-1} n_{w,i} \cdot 2^i$. (If N is not a power of two, we need to pad DB to satisfy this by adding some dummy keyword-identifier pairs.)

Algorithm $\mathsf{EDBSetup}$, on input DB and K, proceeds as follows: It initially sets up t empty lists $L_0, L_1, \ldots, L_{t-1}$. For every word $w \in \mathsf{W}$, it then computes two derived keys $F_K(w) = (K_{w,0}, K_{w,1})$ and sets $c = 0$. Subsequently, for all $i = 0, \ldots, t-1$, if $n_{w,i} = 1$, we define the ℓ-bit label $l = F'_{K_{w,0}}(i)$ and the $(2^i \cdot s)$-bit data

$$d = \mathcal{E}(K_{w,1}, \mathrm{id}_c) \parallel \ldots \parallel \mathcal{E}(K_{w,1}, \mathrm{id}_{c+2^i}) ,$$

increase c by 2^i, and add (l, d) to L_i. Once done with the iteration, for all $i = 0, \ldots, t-1$, we first add pairs (l, d) to L_i until it contains *exactly* 2^{t-i} elements, where l is a random label and d is a random $(2^i \cdot s)$-bit string, and then compute $\mathsf{HT}_i \leftarrow \mathsf{HTCreate}(L_i)$. The final output is

$$\mathsf{EDB} = \mathsf{HT}_0 \parallel \mathsf{HT}_1 \parallel \ldots \parallel \mathsf{HT}_{t-1} .$$

Token Generation. Algorithm TokGen, on inputs K and w, computes and outputs the two derived keys $(K_{w,0}, K_{w,1}) \leftarrow F_K(w)$.

Search. The search algorithm Search, on input $\mathsf{EDB} = \mathsf{HT}_0 \parallel \mathsf{HT}_1 \parallel \ldots \parallel \mathsf{HT}_{t-1}$ and (K_0, K_1), initially defines an empty response set $R = \emptyset$. Then, for all $i = 0, \ldots, t-1$, it computes $l \leftarrow F'_{K_0}(i)$ and $d \leftarrow \mathsf{HTGet}(\mathsf{HT}_i, l)$. If $d = C_1 \parallel \ldots \parallel C_{2^i} \neq \perp$, it adds $\mathcal{D}(K_1, C_1), \ldots, \mathcal{D}(K_1, C_{2^i})$ to the response set R. At the end, it outputs R.

CORRECTNESS, COMPLEXITY AND LOCALITY. Correctness of the SSE scheme Π holds with high probability assuming pseudorandomness of F and F' – we dispense with a formal analysis.

Assume now that we use the space- and lookup-efficient hash-table implementation mentioned above. Note first that every L_i is going to always contain 2^{t-i} elements consisting of a pair (l, d) where $|l| = \ell$ and $|d| = 2^i \cdot s$. Indeed, we cannot add more than 2^{t-i} pairs (before possibly filling up L_i) because each such pair is associated with 2^i keyword-identifier pairs, and overall there are $N = 2^t$ such pairs. For this reason, the size of HT_i is going to be $O(N(\ell+s)+\log(N)^2)$, and thus the overall size of EDB is

$$|\mathsf{EDB}| = O(N\log N \cdot (\ell+s) + \log(N)^3) .$$

As for locality, by the property of the hash tables, we are going to read $O(1)$ blocks of consecutive values for every $i = 0,\ldots,t-1$, thus obtaining locality $O(\log N)$. Also, read efficiency is constant.

SECURITY. We turn to the security of the SSE scheme Π. We start with non-adaptive security, and below discuss the changes necessary in order to prove adaptive security in the random-oracle model. Here, we are going to prove that the scheme achieves the strong notion $\mathcal{L}_{\min}$-SIM-security. Recall that we say that $(\mathcal{E},\mathcal{D})$ has *pseudorandom ciphertexts* if no polynomial-time attacker can decide whether a given oracle is behaving as $\mathcal{E}_K(\cdot)$ for random secret key K or whether it is returning a fresh random string upon each invocation, except with negligible advantage.

Theorem 10 (Non-adaptive Security of Π.). *The above SSE-scheme Π is $\mathcal{L}_{\min}$-SIM-secure against non-adaptive attacks if F and F' are pseudorandom functions and $(\mathcal{E},\mathcal{D})$ has pseudorandom ciphertexts.*

Proof. Recall that in a non-adaptive attack, the attacker $\mathcal{A}$ first commits to keyword queries $\mathbf{w}$ and a database DB. We also recall that in the real experiment $\text{SIM-SSE}^0{}_{\Pi,\mathcal{L}_{\min},\mathcal{A}}(\lambda)$, KeyGen is run, resulting in a key K, and then EDBSetup is run, producing the encrypted database EDB. The attacker $\mathcal{A}$ is then given EDB, together with the search tokens $(K_{\mathbf{w}[i],0}, K_{\mathbf{w}[i],1}) = F_K(\mathbf{w}[i])$ for $i \in [|\mathbf{w}|]$. In contrast, in the ideal experiment $\text{SIM-SSE}^1{}_{\Pi,\mathcal{L}_{\min},\mathcal{A},\mathcal{S}}(\lambda)$, the simulator $\mathcal{S}$ initially only obtains $N = |\mathsf{DB}|$ and $\mathsf{DB}(\mathbf{w}[i])$ for $i \in [|\mathbf{w}|]$, and needs to output EDB' as well as search tokens $(K'_{\mathbf{w}[i],0}, K'_{\mathbf{w}[i],1})$ such that

$$\Pr[\text{SIM-SSE}^0{}_{\Pi,\mathcal{L}_{\min},\mathcal{A}}(\lambda) \Rightarrow 1] - \Pr[\text{SIM-SSE}^1{}_{\Pi,\mathcal{L}_{\min},\mathcal{A},\mathcal{S}}(\lambda) \Rightarrow 1] = \text{negl}(\lambda) .$$

Concretely, the simulator $\mathcal{S}$ operates as follows, assuming $N = 2^t$. First, it creates random and independent tokens $(K_{\mathbf{w}[i],0}, K_{\mathbf{w}[i],1})$ for $i \in [|\mathbf{w}|]$ and initializes empty sets $L_0,\ldots,L_{t-1}$. For every $i \in [|\mathbf{w}|]$, it then does the following, with $\mathsf{DB}(\mathbf{w}[i]) = \{\text{id}_1,\ldots,\text{id}_{n_w}\}$ and $n_{\mathbf{w}[i]} = \sum_{j=0}^{t-1} n_{\mathbf{w}[i],j} \cdot 2^j$. It sets $c = 0$, and for every $j = 0,\ldots t-1$, if $n_{\mathbf{w}[i],j} = 1$, it computes

$$d = \mathcal{E}(K_{\mathbf{w}[i],1},\text{id}_c) \| \ldots \| \mathcal{E}(K_{\mathbf{w}[i],1},\text{id}_{c+2^j}) ,$$

adds $(F_{K_{\mathbf{w}[i],0}}(j), d)$ to L_j, and increases c by 2^j. Once done with the iteration, for all $j = 0,\ldots,t-1$, the simulator adds pairs (l,d) to L_j until it contains *exactly* 2^{t-j} elements (where l is a random ℓ-bit label and d is a random $(2^j \cdot s)$-bit string) and computes $\mathsf{HT}_j \leftarrow \mathsf{HTCreate}(L_j)$. The final output is $\mathsf{EDB}' = \mathsf{HT}_0 \| \mathsf{HT}_1 \| \ldots \| \mathsf{HT}_{t-1}$, together with the tokens $(K_{\mathbf{w}[i],0}, K_{\mathbf{w}[i],1})$ for $i \in [|\mathbf{w}|]$.

The proof now proceeds via a hybrid argument. The first hybrid experiment H_0 behaves the real-world experiment, in particular returning the distribution

[EDB, $\{(K_{\mathbf{w}[i],0}, K_{\mathbf{w}[i],1})\}_{i \in [\|\mathbf{w}\|]}]$ to $\mathcal{A}$. In the second hybrid, the function F_K is replaced by a truly random function when running EDBSetup and when producing the tokens $(K_{\mathbf{w}[i],0}, K_{\mathbf{w}[i],1})$ given to $\mathcal{A}$, i.e., every search token is replaced with a truly-random key pair. It is easy to see that $\Pr[H_0 \Rightarrow 0] - \Pr[H_1 \Rightarrow 1] = \mathrm{negl}(\lambda)$ by the pseudorandomness of F.

For the next hybrid H_2, when running EDBSetup, we are going to replace $F'_{K_{\mathbf{w}[i],0}}$ with an independent random function for every $i \in [\|\mathbf{w}\|]$. In particular, this means that every label l of a pair (l, d) added to L_j when processing the key-word w in EDBSetup is independent and uniform. Similarly to the above, $\Pr[H_1 \Rightarrow 0] - \Pr[H_2 \Rightarrow 1] = \mathrm{negl}(\lambda)$ by the pseudorandomness of F'.

Finally, in H_3, for all $i \in [\|\mathbf{w}\|]$, we replace every data-block d containing encryptions of identifiers in $\mathsf{DB}(\mathbf{w}[i])$ produced in EDBSetup with a randomly chosen string of the appropriate length. It is not hard to see that H_3 behaves exactly as $\mathrm{SIM\text{-}SSE}^1_{\Pi, \mathcal{L}_{\min}, \mathcal{A}, \mathcal{S}}$, and moreover, $\Pr[H_2 \Rightarrow 0] - \Pr[H_3 \Rightarrow 1] = \mathrm{negl}(\lambda)$ by the pseudorandomness of $(\mathcal{E}, \mathcal{D})$.   □

ADAPTIVE SECURITY. We additionally propose an efficient instantiation of the above scheme which is actively secure *in the random oracle model*. Note that, in this case, the security notion allows the simulator to *program* the random oracle.

Concretely, we instantiate $(\mathcal{E}, \mathcal{D})$ with the scheme encrypting M under secret key K as $\mathcal{E}_K(M) = R \| (H(K \| R) \oplus M)$, where R is a random λ-bit string, and H is a hash function with output length equal the message length, to be modeled as a random oracle in the proof. (As above, the total ciphertext length is denoted as s.) Moreover, we also instantiate F' using the same hash function H, letting $F'(K_{w,0}, i) = H(K_{w,0} \| \langle i \rangle)$, where $\langle i \rangle$ is a binary encoding of the integer $i \in \mathbb{N}$.

In the proof, the simulator $\mathcal{S}$ handles the random oracle queries, setting $H(x)$ to a random value whenever handling a query on input $x \in \{0,1\}^*$. Moreover, when the attacker chooses an index DB, $\mathcal{S}$ is given $N = 2^t$ and for all $i = 0, 1, \ldots, t-1$, adds 2^{t-i} pairs (l, d) to the set L_i, where l is a random ℓ-bit label and d is a random $(2^i \cdot s)$-bit string. It then generates EDB as the concatenation of the hash table created from $L_0, \ldots, L_{t-1}$, and hands EDB over to the attacker. (Still, $\mathcal{S}$ keeps $L_0, L_1, \ldots, L_{t-1}$ as its state.)

Later, upon each query w from the attacker, the simulator learns $\mathsf{DB}(w) = \{\mathrm{id}_1, \ldots, \mathrm{id}_{n_w}\}$, where $n_w = \sum_{i=0}^{t-1} n_{w,i} \cdot 2^i$. In this case, it generates random $K_{w,0}$ and $K_{w,1}$ as the corresponding token. Moreover, it sets $c = 0$, and for every $i = 0, 1, \ldots, t-1$, if $n_{w,i} = 1$, the simulator picks a random pair $(l, d) \in L_i$ where $d = R_1 \| C_1 \| \ldots \| R_{2^i} \| C_{2^i}$, removes (l, d) from L_i, and *programs* the random oracle so that

$$H(K_{w,0} \| \langle i \rangle) = l, \qquad H(K_{w,1} \| R_j) \oplus C_j = \mathrm{id}_{c+j} \text{ for all } j = 1, \ldots, 2^i,$$

and adds 2^i to c. If the programming cannot succeed (because the corresponding values are already set for H), the simulator aborts.

We omit a formal analysis that the above is a good simulation strategy, as it follows from standard techniques. Overall, we obtain the following theorem.

Theorem 11 (Adaptive Security of Π.). *The above hash-based instantiation of the SSE-scheme Π is $\mathcal{L}_{\min}$-SIM-secure in the random oracle model if F is a pseudorandom function.*

Acknowledgments. Part of this work was done when the second author was with MIT CSAIL, partially supported by NSF Contract CCF-1018064. Moreover, this material is based on research sponsored by DARPA under agreement number FA8750-11-2-0225. The U.S. Government is authorized to reproduce and distribute reprints for Governmental purposes notwithstanding any copyright notation thereon. The views and conclusions contained herein are those of the authors and should not be interpreted as necessarily representing the official policies or endorsements, either expressed or implied, of DARPA or the U.S. Government.

References

1. Abdalla, M., Bellare, M., Catalano, D., Kiltz, E., Kohno, T., Lange, T., Malone-Lee, J., Neven, G., Paillier, P., Shi, H.: Searchable encryption revisited: Consistency properties, relation to anonymous IBE, and extensions. In: Shoup, V. (ed.) CRYPTO 2005. LNCS, vol. 3621, pp. 205–222. Springer, Heidelberg (2005)

2. Abdalla, M., Bellare, M., Catalano, D., Kiltz, E., Kohno, T., Lange, T., Malone-Lee, J., Neven, G., Paillier, P., Shi, H.: Searchable encryption revisited: Consistency properties, relation to anonymous IBE, and extensions. Journal of Cryptology 21(3), 350–391 (2008)

3. Barve, R.D., Shriver, E.A.M., Gibbons, P.B., Hillyer, B., Matias, Y., Vitter, J.S.: Modeling and optimizing i/o throughput of multiple disks on a bus. In: SIGMETRICS, pp. 83–92 (1999)

4. Bellare, M., Boldyreva, A., O'Neill, A.: Deterministic and efficiently searchable encryption. In: Menezes, A. (ed.) CRYPTO 2007. LNCS, vol. 4622, pp. 535–552. Springer, Heidelberg (2007)

5. Bellare, M., Fischlin, M., O'Neill, A., Ristenpart, T.: Deterministic encryption: Definitional equivalences and constructions without random oracles. In: Wagner, D. (ed.) CRYPTO 2008. LNCS, vol. 5157, pp. 360–378. Springer, Heidelberg (2008)

6. Boldyreva, A., Chenette, N., Lee, Y., O'Neill, A.: Order-preserving symmetric encryption. In: Joux, A. (ed.) EUROCRYPT 2009. LNCS, vol. 5479, pp. 224–241. Springer, Heidelberg (2009)

7. Boldyreva, A., Chenette, N., O'Neill, A.: Order-preserving encryption revisited: Improved security analysis and alternative solutions. In: Rogaway, P. (ed.) CRYPTO 2011. LNCS, vol. 6841, pp. 578–595. Springer, Heidelberg (2011)

8. Boldyreva, A., Fehr, S., O'Neill, A.: On notions of security for deterministic encryption, and efficient constructions without random oracles. In: Wagner, D. (ed.) CRYPTO 2008. LNCS, vol. 5157, pp. 335–359. Springer, Heidelberg (2008)

9. Boneh, D., Di Crescenzo, G., Ostrovsky, R., Persiano, G.: Public key encryption with keyword search. In: Cachin, C., Camenisch, J.L. (eds.) EUROCRYPT 2004. LNCS, vol. 3027, pp. 506–522. Springer, Heidelberg (2004)

10. Cash, D., Jarecki, S., Jutla, C., Krawczyk, H., Roşu, M.-C., Steiner, M.: Highly-scalable searchable symmetric encryption with support for boolean queries. In: Canetti, R., Garay, J.A. (eds.) CRYPTO 2013, Part I. LNCS, vol. 8042, pp. 353–373. Springer, Heidelberg (2013), http://eprint.iacr.org/2013/169

11. Chang, Y.-C., Mitzenmacher, M.: Privacy preserving keyword searches on remote encrypted data. In: Ioannidis, J., Keromytis, A.D., Yung, M. (eds.) ACNS 2005. LNCS, vol. 3531, pp. 442–455. Springer, Heidelberg (2005)

12. Chase, M., Kamara, S.: Structured encryption and controlled disclosure. In: Abe, M. (ed.) ASIACRYPT 2010. LNCS, vol. 6477, pp. 577–594. Springer, Heidelberg (2010)

13. Curtmola, R., Garay, J.A., Kamara, S., Ostrovsky, R.: Searchable symmetric encryption: improved definitions and efficient constructions. In: Juels, A., Wright, R.N., Vimercati, S. (eds.) ACM CCS 2006, pp. 79–88. ACM Press (October / November 2006)

14. Gentry, C.: Fully homomorphic encryption using ideal lattices. In: Mitzenmacher, M. (ed.) 41st ACM STOC, pp. 169–178. ACM Press (May/June 2009)

15. Goh, E.-J.: Secure indexes. Cryptology ePrint Archive, Report 2003/216 (2003), http://eprint.iacr.org/

16. Goldreich, O., Ostrovsky, R.: Software protection and simulation on oblivious RAMs. Journal of the ACM 43(3), 431–473 (1996)

17. Golle, P., Staddon, J., Waters, B.: Secure conjunctive keyword search over encrypted data. In: Jakobsson, M., Yung, M., Zhou, J. (eds.) ACNS 2004. LNCS, vol. 3089, pp. 31–45. Springer, Heidelberg (2004)

18. Kamara, S., Papamanthou, C.: Parallel and dynamic searchable symmetric encryption. In: Sadeghi, A.-R. (ed.) FC 2013. LNCS, vol. 7859, pp. 258–274. Springer, Heidelberg (2013)

19. Kamara, S., Papamanthou, C., Roeder, T.: Dynamic searchable symmetric encryption. In: ACM CCS 2012, pp. 965–976. ACM Press (2012)

20. Kurosawa, K., Ohtaki, Y.: UC-secure searchable symmetric encryption. In: Keromytis, A.D. (ed.) FC 2012. LNCS, vol. 7397, pp. 285–298. Springer, Heidelberg (2012)

21. Pagh, R., Rodler, F.F.: Cuckoo hashing. J. Algorithms 51(2), 122–144 (2004)

22. Popa, R.A., Redfield, C.M.S., Zeldovich, N., Balakrishnan, H.: Cryptdb: protecting confidentiality with encrypted query processing. In: SOSP, pp. 85–100 (2011)

23. Ruemmler, C., Wilkes, J.: An introduction to disk drive modeling. IEEE Computer 27(3), 17–28 (1994)

24. Song, D.X., Wagner, D., Perrig, A.: Practical techniques for searches on encrypted data. In: 2000 IEEE Symposium on Security and Privacy, pp. 44–55. IEEE Computer Society Press (May 2000)

25. van Liesdonk, P., Sedghi, S., Doumen, J., Hartel, P., Jonker, W.: Computationally efficient searchable symmetric encryption. In: Jonker, W., Petković, M. (eds.) SDM 2010. LNCS, vol. 6358, pp. 87–100. Springer, Heidelberg (2010)

26. Vitter, J.S.: Algorithms and data structures for external memory. Foundations and Trends in Theoretical Computer Science 2(4), 305–474 (2006)

A Bound for Multiparty Secret Key Agreement and Implications for a Problem of Secure Computing

Himanshu Tyagi[1] and Shun Watanabe[2]

[1] Information Theory and Applications (ITA) Center,
University of California, San Diego, La Jolla, CA 92093, USA
htyagi@eng.ucsd.edu

[2] Department of Information Science and Intelligent Systems,
University of Tokushima, Tokushima 770-8506, Japan, and Institute for Systems
Research, University of Maryland, College Park, MD 20742, USA
shun-wata@is.tokushima-u.ac.jp

Abstract. We consider secret key agreement by multiple parties observing correlated data and communicating interactively over an insecure communication channel. Our main contribution is a *single-shot* upper bound on the length of the secret keys that can be generated, without making any assumptions on the distribution of the underlying data. Heuristically, we bound the secret key length in terms of "how far" is the joint distribution of the initial observations of the parties and the eavesdropper from a distribution that renders the observations of the parties conditionally independent across some partition, when conditioned on the eavesdropper's side information. The closeness of the two distributions is measured in terms of the exponent of the probability of error of type II for a binary hypothesis testing problem, thus bringing out a structural connection between secret key agreement and binary hypothesis testing. When the underlying data consists of an independent and identically distributed sequence, an application of our bound recovers several known upper bounds for the asymptotic rate of a secret key that can be generated, without requiring the agreement error probability or the security index to vanish to 0 asymptotically.

Also, we consider the following problem of secure function computation with trusted parties: Multiple parties observing correlated data seek to compute a function of their collective data. To this end, they communicate interactively over an insecure communication channel. It is required that the value of the function be concealed from an eavesdropper with access to the communication. When is such a secure computation of a given function feasible? Using the aforementioned upper bound, we derive a necessary condition for the existence of a communication protocol that allows the parties to reliably recover the value of a given function, while keeping this value concealed from an eavesdropper with access to (only) the communication.

Keywords: secret key agreement, single shot bound, secure computing.

P.Q. Nguyen and E. Oswald (Eds.): EUROCRYPT 2014, LNCS 8441, pp. 369–386, 2014.

1   Introduction

A uniformly distributed random string that is shared by legitimate parties and remains concealed from eavesdroppers is a cherished resource in cryptography. It can be used to authenticate or secure the communication between the parties, or as a password granting access to one or more members of a group. It was pointed out first by Bennett, Brassard, and Robert [3] that parties observing correlated data and with access to an authenticated, error-free, albeit insecure, communication channel can harness the correlation in their observations to share a (almost) uniform random string that is concealed from an eavesdropper observing the communication as well as some correlated side information. Such a shared random string, termed a *secret key* (SK), is secure in the sense of *information theoretic security*, without making any assumptions on the computation capabilities of the eavesdropper.[1]

For two parties, the problem of SK agreement from correlated observations is well-studied. The problem was introduced by Maurer [20] and Ahlswede and Csiszár [1], who considered the case where the correlated observations of the two parties are long sequences, generated by an *independent and identically distributed* (IID) random process. However, in certain applications it is of interest to consider observations arising from a single realization of correlated *random variables* (RVs).[2] For instance, in applications such as biometric and hardware authentication (cf. [23,14]), the correlated observations consist of different versions of the biometric and hardware signatures, respectively, recorded at the registration and the authentication stages. To this end, Renner and Wolf [27] derived bounds on the length of a SK that can be generated by two parties observing a single realization of correlated RVs, using one-side communication.

The problem of SK agreement with multiple parties, for the IID setup, was introduced in [13] (also, see [7] for an early formulation). In this work, we consider the SK agreement problem for multiple parties observing a single realization of correlated RVs.

Our main contributions are summarized below.

1.1   Main Contributions

We derive a single-shot upper bound on the length of SKs that can be generated by multiple parties observing correlated data, using interactive public communication. Unlike the single-shot upper bound in [27], which is restricted to two parties with one-way communication, we allow arbitrary interactive communication between multiple parties.[3] Asymptotically our bound is tight – its

---

[1] While the SK is information theoretically secure, the security of the cryptographic protocols using it might be based on computation complexity.

[2] This model is sometimes referred to as the *single-shot* model to distinguish it from the IID case.

[3] A comparison between a restriction of our bound to one-way communication and the bound in [27] is unavailable, since the latter involves auxiliary RVs and therefore, is difficult to evaluate.

application to the IID case recovers some previously known (tight) bounds on the asymptotic SK rates. In fact, we strengthen the previously known asymptotic results since we do not require the probability of error in SK agreement or the security index to be asymptotically 0.[4]

For the heuristic idea underlying our upper bound, consider the two party case when the eavesdropper observes only the communication between the legitimate parties (no side-information). Clearly, if the observations of the legitimate parties are independent, a SK cannot be generated. We upper bound the length of SKs that can be generated in terms of "how far" is the joint distribution of the observations of the parties and from a distribution that renders their observations independent. Specifically, for this special case, we show

$$S_\epsilon\left(X_1, X_2\right) \leq -\log \beta_{\epsilon+\eta}\left(\mathsf{P}_{X_1 X_2}, \mathsf{P}_{X_1} \times \mathsf{P}_{X_2}\right) + 2\log(1/\eta),$$

where $S_\epsilon\left(X_1, X_2\right)$ is the maximum length of a SK (for a given security index ϵ). Here the distance between $\mathsf{P}_{X_1 X_2}$ and $\mathsf{P}_{X_1} \times \mathsf{P}_{X_2}$ is measured by β_ϵ, which is the optimal probability of error of type II for testing the null hypothesis $\mathsf{P}_{X_1 X_2}$ with the alternative $\mathsf{P}_{X_1} \times \mathsf{P}_{X_2}$, given that the probability of error of type I is smaller than ϵ. Similarly, in the general case, our main result in Theorem 1 bounds the secret key length in terms of the distance between the joint distribution of the observations of the parties and the eavesdropper and a distribution that renders the observations of the parties conditionally independent across some partition, when conditioned on the eavesdropper's side information.

Our approach brings out a structural connection between SK agreement and binary hypothesis testing. This is in the spirit of [24], where a connection between channel coding and binary hypothesis testing was used to establish an upper bound on the rate of good channel codes (see, also, [35,16]). Also, our upper bound is reminiscent of the *measure of entanglement* for a quantum state proposed in [34], namely the minimum distance between the density matrix of the state and that of a disentangled state. This measure of entanglement was shown to be an upper bound on the entanglement of distillation in [34], where the latter is the largest proportion of maximally entangled states that can be distilled using a purification process [4].

As an application, we relate our result to the following problem of *secure function computation with trusted parties* introduced in [33] (for an early version of the problem, see [22]): Multiple parties observing correlated data seek to compute a function of their collective data. To this end, they communicate interactively over a public communication channel, which is assumed to be authenticated and error-free. It is required that the value of the function be concealed from an eavesdropper with access to the communication. When is such a secure computation of a given function feasible?[5] Using our aforementioned upper bound, we derive a necessary condition for the existence of a communication protocol that allows

---

[4] Such bounds that do not require the probability of error to vanish to 0 are called *strong converse* bounds [12].

[5] In contrast to the traditional definition of secure computing [37], the legitimate parties are trusted and allowed to get any information about each other's data.

the parties to reliably recover the value of a given function, while keeping this value concealed from an eavesdropper with access to (only) the communication.

1.2   Outline of Paper

The next section contains formal descriptions of our model, the allowed interactive communication, and a SK, along with a definition of the SK capacity. Also, we review some basic notions in binary hypothesis testing that will be used in this paper. Our main result is Theorem 1 in Section 3; implications of this main result are presented as corollaries. In Section 4, we show that our new upper bound is asymptotically tight and leads to a strong converse for the SK capacity. Implications for the secure computing problem with trusted parties, along with illustrative examples, are given in Section 5. The final section contains a discussion of our results.

1.3   Notations

For brevity, we use abbreviations SK, RV, and IID for secret key, random variable, and independent and identically distributed, respectively; a plural form will be indicated by appending an 's' to the abbreviation. The RVs are denoted by capital letters and the corresponding range sets are denoted by calligraphic letters. The distribution of a RV U is given by P_U. The set of all parties $\{1, ..., m\}$ is denoted by $\mathcal{M}$. For a collection of RVs $\{U_1, .., U_m\}$ and a subset A of $\mathcal{M}$, U_A denotes the RVs $\{U_i, i \in A\}$. For a RV U, U^n denotes n IID repetitions of the RV U. Similarly, P^n denotes the distribution corresponding to the n IID repetitions generated from P. All logarithms in this paper are to the base 2.

2   Preliminaries

We consider the problem of SK agreement using interactive public communication by m (trusted) parties. The ith party observes a discrete RV X_i taking values in a finite set $\mathcal{X}_i$, $1 \le i \le m$.[6] Upon making these observations, the parties communicate interactively over a public communication channel that is accessible by an eavesdropper, who additionally observes a RV Z such that the RVs $(X_{\mathcal{M}}, Z)$ have a distribution $P_{X_{\mathcal{M}}Z}$. We assume that the communication is error-free and each party receives the communication from every other party. Furthermore, we assume that the public communication is authenticated and the eavesdropper cannot tamper with it. Specifically, the communication is sent over r rounds of interaction. In the jth round of communication, $1 \le j \le r$, the ith party sends F_{ij}, which is a function of its observation X_i, a *locally generated* randomness[7] U_i and the previously observed communication

$$F_{11}, ..., F_{m1}, F_{12}, ..., F_{m2}, ..., F_{1j}, ..., F_{(i-1)j}.$$

---

[6] Our main theorem remains valid for RVs taking countably many values.

[7] The RVs $U_1, ..., U_m$ are mutually independent and independent jointly of $(X_{\mathcal{M}}, Z)$.

The overall interactive communication $F_{11}, ..., F_{m1}, ..., F_{1r}, ..., F_{mr}$ is denoted by $\mathbf{F}$.

Using the interactive communication $\mathbf{F}$ and their local observations, the parties agree on a SK. In the next section, we formally explain this notion.

2.1 Secret Keys

A SK is a collection of RVs $K_1, ..., K_m$, where the ith party gets K_i, that agree with probability close to 1 and are concealed, in effect, from an eavesdropper. Formally, the ith party computes a function K_i of $(U_i, X_i, \mathbf{F})$. Traditionally, the RVs $K_1, ..., K_m$ with a common range $\mathcal{K}$ constitute an (ϵ, δ)-SK if the following two conditions are satisfied (for alternative definitions of secrecy, see [20,11,13])

$$P(K_1 = \cdots = K_m) \geq 1 - \epsilon, \tag{1}$$

$$\frac{1}{2} \|P_{K_1 \mathbf{F} Z} - P_{\text{unif}} \times P_{\mathbf{F} Z}\| \leq \delta, \tag{2}$$

where $\| \cdot \|$ is the variational distance and P_{unif} is the uniform distribution on $\mathcal{K}$. The first condition above represents the reliable *recovery* of the SK and the second condition guarantees *security*. In this work, we use the following alternative definition of a SK, which conveniently combines the recoverability and the security conditions (cf. [25]): The RVs $K_1, ..., K_m$ above constitute an ϵ-SK with common range $\mathcal{K}$ if

$$\frac{1}{2} \left\| P_{K_{\mathcal{M}} \mathbf{F} Z} - P_{\text{unif}}^{(\mathcal{M})} \times P_{\mathbf{F} Z} \right\| \leq \epsilon, \tag{3}$$

where

$$P_{\text{unif}}^{(\mathcal{M})}(k_{\mathcal{M}}) = \frac{\mathbb{1}(k_1 = \cdots = k_m)}{|\mathcal{K}|}.$$

In fact, the two definitions above are closely related.

Proposition 1. *Given $0 \leq \epsilon, \delta \leq 1$, if $K_{\mathcal{M}}$ constitute an (ϵ, δ)-SK under (1) and (2), then they constitute an $(\epsilon + \delta)$-SK under (3).*

Conversely, if $K_{\mathcal{M}}$ constitute an ϵ-SK under (3), then they constitute an (ϵ, ϵ)-SK under (1) and (2).

Note that a SK generation protocol that satisfies (3) *universally composable-emulates* an ideal SK generation protocol (see [6] for a definition).[8] Therefore, by the composition theorem in [6], the complex cryptographic protocols using such SKs instead of perfect SKs are secure.[9]

We are interested in characterizing the maximum length $\log |\mathcal{K}|$ of an ϵ-SK.

---

[8] The emulation is with emulation slack ϵ, for an environment of unbounded computational complexity.

[9] A perfect SK refers to unbiased shared bits that are independent of eavesdropper's observations.

Definition 1. *Given* $0 \leq \epsilon < 1$, *denote by* $S_\epsilon(X_1, ..., X_m \mid Z)$ *the maximum length* $\log |\mathcal{K}|$ *of an* ϵ-*SK* $K_\mathcal{M}$ *with common range* $\mathcal{K}$.

Next, we define the concept of SK capacity [20,1,13].

Definition 2. *Given* $0 < \epsilon < 1$, *the* ϵ-*SK capacity* $C(\epsilon)$ *is defined as follows:*

$$C(\epsilon) := \liminf_{n \to \infty} \frac{1}{n} S_\epsilon(X_1^n, ..., X_m^n \mid Z^n),$$

where the RVs $\{X_{\mathcal{M}t}, Z_t\}$ are IID for $1 \leq t \leq n$, with a common distribution $P_{X_\mathcal{M}Z}$.

The SK capacity C is defined as the limit

$$C := \lim_{\epsilon \to 0} C(\epsilon).$$

For the case when the eavesdropper does not observe any side information, i.e., $Z = constant$, the SK capacity for two parties was characterized by Maurer [20] and Ahlswede and Csiszár [1]. Later, the SK capacity for a multiterminal model, with $Z =$ constant was characterized by Csiszár and Narayan [13]. The general problem of characterizing the SK capacity for arbitrary Z remains open. Several upper bounds for SK capacity are known [20,1,21,26,13,15], which are tight for special cases.

In this paper, we present a single-shot upper bound on $S_\epsilon(X_1, ..., X_m \mid Z)$. As a consequence, we obtain an upper bound on $C(\epsilon)$. In fact, for the case $Z=$ constant, this upper bound coincides with C, thus establishing that

$$C = C(\epsilon), \quad \forall 0 < \epsilon < 1.$$

This is a strengthening of the result in [32], where a *strong converse* was established for (ϵ, δ_n)-SKs under (1) and (2), with $\delta_n \to 0$ as $n \to 0$.

Our upper bound is based on relating the SK agreement problem to a binary hypothesis testing problem; in the next section we review some basic concepts in hypothesis testing that will be used.

2.2   Hypothesis Testing

Consider a binary hypothesis testing problem with null hypothesis P and alternative hypothesis Q, where P and Q are distributions on the same alphabet $\mathcal{X}$. Upon observing a value $x \in \mathcal{X}$, the observer needs to decide if the value was generated by the distribution P or the distribution Q. To this end, the observer applies a stochastic test T, which is a conditional distribution on $\{0, 1\}$ given an observation $x \in \mathcal{X}$. When $x \in \mathcal{X}$ is observed, the test T chooses the null hypothesis with probability $T(0|x)$ and the alternative hypothesis with probability $T(1|x) = 1 - T(0|x)$. For $0 \leq \epsilon < 1$, denote by $\beta_\epsilon(P, Q)$ the infimum of the probability of error of type II given that the probability of error of type I is less than ϵ, i.e.,

$$\beta_\epsilon(\mathrm{P}, \mathrm{Q}) := \inf_{\mathrm{T}:\mathrm{P}[\mathrm{T}]\geq 1-\epsilon} \mathrm{Q}[\mathrm{T}], \tag{4}$$

where

$$\mathrm{P}[\mathrm{T}] = \sum_x \mathrm{P}(x)\mathrm{T}(0|x),$$

$$\mathrm{Q}[\mathrm{T}] = \sum_x \mathrm{Q}(x)\mathrm{T}(0|x).$$

We close this section by noting two important properties of the quantity $\beta_\epsilon(\mathrm{P}, \mathrm{Q})$.

1. **Data Processing Inequality.** Let W be a stochastic mapping from $\mathcal{X}$ to $\mathcal{Y}$, i.e., for each $x \in \mathcal{X}$, $\mathrm{W}(\cdot \mid x)$ is a distribution on $\mathcal{Y}$. Then, with $\mathrm{PW}(y) = \sum_x \mathrm{P}(x)\mathrm{W}(y|x)$ and $\mathrm{QW}(y) = \sum_x \mathrm{Q}(x)\mathrm{W}(y|x)$, we have

$$\beta_\epsilon(\mathrm{P}, \mathrm{Q}) \leq \beta_\epsilon(\mathrm{PW}, \mathrm{QW}). \tag{5}$$

   In other words, if we add extra noise to the observations, then β_ϵ can only increase.

2. **Stein's Lemma.** (cf. [19, Theorem 3.3]) For every $0 < \epsilon < 1$, we have

$$\lim_{n\to\infty} -\frac{1}{n} \log \beta_\epsilon(\mathrm{P}^n, \mathrm{Q}^n) = D(\mathrm{P}\|\mathrm{Q}), \tag{6}$$

where $D(\mathrm{P}\|\mathrm{Q})$ is the Kullback-Leibler divergence given by

$$D(\mathrm{P}\|\mathrm{Q}) = \sum_{x\in\mathcal{X}} \mathrm{P}(x) \log \frac{\mathrm{P}(x)}{\mathrm{Q}(x)},$$

with the convention $0 \log(0/0) = 0$.

3   Main Result: Upper Bound on the Length of a Multiparty Secret Key

In this section, we present a new methodology for proving converse results for the multiparty SK agreement problem. Our main result is an upper bound on the length $\log |\mathcal{K}|$ of a SK generated by multiple parties, using interactive public communication.

Consider a (nontrivial) partition $\pi = \{\pi_1, ..., \pi_l\}$ of the set $\mathcal{M}$. Heuristically, if the underlying distribution of the observations $\mathrm{P}_{X_\mathcal{M}Z}$ is such that $X_\mathcal{M}$ are conditionally independent across the partition π given Z, the length of a SK that can be generated is 0. Our approach is to bound the length of a generated SK in terms of "how far" is the distribution $\mathrm{P}_{X_\mathcal{M}Z}$ from another distribution $\mathrm{Q}^\pi_{X_\mathcal{M}Z}$ that renders $X_\mathcal{M}$ conditionally independent across the partition π given Z – the closeness of the two distributions is measured by $\beta_\epsilon\big(\mathrm{P}_{X_\mathcal{M}Z}, \mathrm{Q}^\pi_{X_\mathcal{M}Z}\big)$.

Specifically, for a partition π with $|\pi| \geq 2$ parts, let $\mathcal{Q}(\pi)$ be the set of all distributions $\mathrm{Q}^\pi_{X_\mathcal{M}Z}$ that factorize as follows:

$$\mathrm{Q}^\pi_{X_\mathcal{M}|Z}(x_1, \ldots, x_m|z) = \prod_{i=1}^{|\pi|} \mathrm{Q}^\pi_{X_{\pi_i}|Z}(x_{\pi_i}|z). \tag{7}$$

Our main result is given below.

Theorem 1 (Single-Shot Converse). *Given* $0 \le \epsilon < 1$, $0 < \eta < 1 - \epsilon$, *and a partition* π *of* $\mathcal{M}$. *It holds that*

$$S_\epsilon(X_1, ..., X_m \mid Z) \le \frac{1}{|\pi| - 1}\left[-\log \beta_{\epsilon+\eta}(P_{X_{\mathcal{M}}Z}, Q^\pi_{X_{\mathcal{M}}Z}) + |\pi| \log(1/\eta) \right] \quad (8)$$

for all $Q^\pi_{X_{\mathcal{M}}Z} \in \mathcal{Q}(\pi)$.

To prove Theorem 1, we first relate the SK length to the exponent of the probability of error of type II in a binary hypothesis testing problem where an observer of $(K_{\mathcal{M}}, \mathbf{F}, Z)$ seeks to find out if the underlying distribution was $P_{X_{\mathcal{M}}Z}$ or $Q^\pi_{X_{\mathcal{M}}Z}$. This result is stated next.

Lemma 1. *For an* ϵ-*SK* $K_{\mathcal{M}}$ *with a common range* $\mathcal{K}$ *generated using an interactive communication* $\mathbf{F}$, *let* $W_{K_{\mathcal{M}}\mathbf{F}|X_{\mathcal{M}}Z}$ *be the resulting conditional distribution on* $(K_{\mathcal{M}}, \mathbf{F})$ *given* $(X_{\mathcal{M}}, Z)$. *Then, for every* $0 < \eta < 1 - \epsilon$ *and every* $Q^\pi_{X_{\mathcal{M}}Z} \in \mathcal{Q}(\pi)$, *we have*

$$\log |\mathcal{K}| \le \frac{1}{|\pi| - 1}\left[-\log \beta_{\epsilon+\eta}(P_{K_{\mathcal{M}}\mathbf{F}Z}, Q^\pi_{K_{\mathcal{M}}\mathbf{F}Z}) + |\pi| \log(1/\eta) \right], \quad (9)$$

where $P_{K_{\mathcal{M}}\mathbf{F}Z}$ *is the marginal of* $(K_{\mathcal{M}}, \mathbf{F}, Z)$ *for the joint distribution*

$$P_{K_{\mathcal{M}}\mathbf{F}X_{\mathcal{M}}Z} = W_{K_{\mathcal{M}}\mathbf{F}|X_{\mathcal{M}}Z} P_{X_{\mathcal{M}}Z},$$

and $Q^\pi_{K_{\mathcal{M}}\mathbf{F}Z}$ *is the corresponding marginal for the joint distribution*

$$Q^\pi_{K_{\mathcal{M}}\mathbf{F}X_{\mathcal{M}}Z} = W_{K_{\mathcal{M}}\mathbf{F}|X_{\mathcal{M}}Z} Q^\pi_{X_{\mathcal{M}}Z}.$$

Also, we need the following basic property of interactive communication which was pointed out in [32].

Lemma 2. *Given* $Q^\pi_{X_{\mathcal{M}}Z} \in \mathcal{Q}(\pi)$ *and an interactive communication* $\mathbf{F}$, *the following holds:*

$$Q^\pi_{X_{\mathcal{M}}|\mathbf{F}Z}(x_{\mathcal{M}}|\mathbf{f}, z) = \prod_{i=1}^{|\pi|} Q^\pi_{X_{\pi_i}|\mathbf{F}Z}(x_{\pi_i}|\mathbf{f}, z),$$

i.e., conditionally independent observations remain so when conditioned additionally on an interactive communication.

Proof of Lemma 1. We establish (9) by constructing a test for the hypothesis testing problem with null hypothesis $P = P_{K_{\mathcal{M}}\mathbf{F}Z}$ and alternative hypothesis $Q = Q^\pi_{K_{\mathcal{M}}\mathbf{F}Z}$. Specifically, we use a deterministic test[10] with the following acceptance region (for the null hypothesis)[11]:

$$\mathcal{A} := \left\{ (k_{\mathcal{M}}, \mathbf{f}, z) : \log \frac{P^{(\mathcal{M})}_{\text{unif}}(k_{\mathcal{M}})}{Q^\pi_{K_{\mathcal{M}}|\mathbf{F}Z}(k_{\mathcal{M}}|\mathbf{f}, z)} \ge \lambda_\pi \right\},$$

---

[10] In fact, we use a simple threshold test on the log-likelihood ratio but with $P^{(\mathcal{M})}_{\text{unif}} \times P_{\mathbf{F}Z}$ in place of $P_{K_{\mathcal{M}}\mathbf{F}Z}$, since the two distributions are close to each other by the security condition (3).

[11] The values $(k_{\mathcal{M}}, \mathbf{f}, z)$ with $Q^\pi_{K_{\mathcal{M}}|\mathbf{F}Z}(k_{\mathcal{M}}|\mathbf{f}, z) = 0$ are included in $\mathcal{A}$.

where
$$\lambda_\pi = (|\pi| - 1) \log |\mathcal{K}| - |\pi| \log(1/\eta).$$

For this test, the probability of error of type II is bounded above as

$$
\begin{aligned}
Q_{K_\mathcal{M}FZ}^\pi(\mathcal{A}) &= \sum_{\mathbf{f},z} Q_{\mathbf{F}Z}^\pi(\mathbf{f},z) \sum_{\substack{k_\mathcal{M}: \\ (k_\mathcal{M},\mathbf{f},z)\in\mathcal{A}}} Q_{K_\mathcal{M}|\mathbf{F}Z}^\pi(k_\mathcal{M}|\mathbf{f},z) \\
&\leq 2^{-\lambda_\pi} \sum_{\mathbf{f},z} Q_{\mathbf{F}Z}^\pi(\mathbf{f},z) \sum_{k_\mathcal{M}} P_{\text{unif}}^{(\mathcal{M})}(k_\mathcal{M}) \\
&= |\mathcal{K}|^{1-|\pi|} \eta^{-|\pi|}.
\end{aligned}
\tag{10}
$$

On the other hand, the probability of error of type I is bounded above as

$$
\begin{aligned}
P_{K_\mathcal{M}FZ}(\mathcal{A}^c) &\leq \frac{1}{2} \left\| P_{K_\mathcal{M}FZ} - P_{\text{unif}}^{(\mathcal{M})} \times P_{\mathbf{F}Z} \right\| + P_{\text{unif}}^{(\mathcal{M})} \times P_{ZF}(\mathcal{A}^c) \\
&\leq \epsilon + P_{\text{unif}}^{(\mathcal{M})} \times P_{\mathbf{F}Z}(\mathcal{A}^c),
\end{aligned}
\tag{11}
$$

where the first inequality follows from the definition of variational distance, and the second is a consequence of the security condition (3) satisfied by the ϵ-SK $K_\mathcal{M}$. The second term above can be expressed as follows:

$$
\begin{aligned}
P_{\text{unif}}^{(\mathcal{M})} \times P_{\mathbf{F}Z}(\mathcal{A}^c) &= \sum_{\mathbf{f},z} P_{\mathbf{F}Z}(\mathbf{f},z) \frac{1}{|\mathcal{K}|} \sum_k \mathbb{1}\left((\mathbf{k},\mathbf{f},z)\in\mathcal{A}^c\right) \\
&= \sum_{\mathbf{f},z} P_{\mathbf{F}Z}(\mathbf{f},z) \frac{1}{|\mathcal{K}|} \sum_k \mathbb{1}\left(Q_{K_\mathcal{M}|\mathbf{F}Z}^\pi(\mathbf{k}|\mathbf{f},z)|\mathcal{K}|^{|\pi|}\eta^{|\pi|} > 1\right),
\end{aligned}
\tag{12}
$$

where $\mathbf{k} = (k,\dots,k)$. The inner sum can be further upper bounded as

$$
\begin{aligned}
\sum_k \mathbb{1}\left(Q_{K_\mathcal{M}|\mathbf{F}Z}^\pi(\mathbf{k}|\mathbf{f},z)|\mathcal{K}|^{|\pi|}\eta^{|\pi|} > 1\right) &\leq \sum_k \left(Q_{K_\mathcal{M}|\mathbf{F}Z}^\pi(\mathbf{k}|\mathbf{f},z)|\mathcal{K}|^{|\pi|}\eta^{|\pi|}\right)^{\frac{1}{|\pi|}} \\
&= |\mathcal{K}|\eta \sum_k Q_{K_\mathcal{M}|\mathbf{F}Z}^\pi(\mathbf{k}|\mathbf{f},z)^{\frac{1}{|\pi|}} \\
&= |\mathcal{K}|\eta \sum_k \prod_{i=1}^{|\pi|} Q_{K_{\pi_i}|\mathbf{F}Z}^\pi(\mathbf{k}|\mathbf{f},z)^{\frac{1}{|\pi|}},
\end{aligned}
\tag{13}
$$

where the previous equality uses Lemma 2 and the fact that given $\mathbf{F}$, K_{π_i} is a function of (X_{π_i}, U_{π_i}). Next, an application of Hölder's inequality to the sum on the right-side of (13) yields

$$
\begin{aligned}
\sum_k \prod_{i=1}^{|\pi|} Q_{K_{\pi_i}|\mathbf{F}Z}^\pi(\mathbf{k}|\mathbf{f},z)^{\frac{1}{|\pi|}} &\leq \prod_{i=1}^{|\pi|} \left(\sum_k Q_{K_{\pi_i}|\mathbf{F}Z}^\pi(\mathbf{k}|\mathbf{f},z)\right)^{\frac{1}{|\pi|}} \\
&\leq \prod_{i=1}^{|\pi|} \left(\sum_{k_\pi} Q_{K_{\pi_i}|\mathbf{F}Z}^\pi(k_{\pi_i}|\mathbf{f},z)\right)^{\frac{1}{|\pi|}} \\
&= 1.
\end{aligned}
\tag{14}
$$

Upon combining (12)-(14) we obtain

$$P_{\text{unif}}^{(\mathcal{M})} \times P_{\mathbf{F}Z}(\mathcal{A}^c) \leq \eta,$$

which along with (11) gives

$$P_{K_{\mathcal{M}}\mathbf{F}Z}(\mathcal{A}^c) \leq \epsilon + \eta. \tag{15}$$

It follows from (15) and (10) that

$$\beta_{\epsilon+\eta}\big(P_{K_{\mathcal{M}}\mathbf{F}Z}, Q_{K_{\mathcal{M}}\mathbf{F}Z}^\pi\big) \leq |\mathcal{K}|^{1-|\pi|}\eta^{-|\pi|},$$

which completes the proof. □

Proof of Theorem 1. Using the data processing inequality (5) with $P = P_{X_{\mathcal{M}}Z}$, $Q = Q_{X_{\mathcal{M}}Z}^\pi$, and $W = W_{K_{\mathcal{M}}\mathbf{F}|X_{\mathcal{M}}Z}$, we get

$$\beta_{\epsilon+\eta}\big(P_{X_{\mathcal{M}}Z}, Q_{X_{\mathcal{M}}Z}^\pi\big) \leq \beta_{\epsilon+\eta}\big(P_{K_{\mathcal{M}}\mathbf{F}Z}, Q_{K_{\mathcal{M}}\mathbf{F}Z}^\pi\big),$$

which along with Lemma 1 gives Theorem 1. □

We close this section with a simple extension of the bound of Theorem 1. Consider a RV $\overline{Z}$ such that $X_{\mathcal{M}} - Z - \overline{Z}$ is a Markov chain. Then, $S_\epsilon(X_1, ..., X_m \mid Z)$ cannot decrease if the eavesdropper observes $\overline{Z}$ instead of Z, i.e.,

$$S_\epsilon(X_1, ..., X_m \mid Z) \leq S_\epsilon(X_1, ..., X_m \mid \overline{Z}).$$

This observation and Theorem 1 give the following result.

Corollary 1. *Given $0 \leq \epsilon < 1$, $0 < \eta < 1 - \epsilon$, a partition π of $\mathcal{M}$ and a RV $\overline{Z}$ such that $X_{\mathcal{M}} - Z - \overline{Z}$ is a Markov chain. It holds that*

$$S_\epsilon(X_1, ..., X_m \mid Z) \leq \frac{1}{|\pi| - 1}\Big[-\log \beta_{\epsilon+\eta}\big(P_{X_{\mathcal{M}}\overline{Z}}, Q_{X_{\mathcal{M}}\overline{Z}}^\pi\big) + |\pi|\log(1/\eta)\Big],$$

for all $Q_{X_{\mathcal{M}}\overline{Z}}^\pi$ satisfying $Q_{X_{\mathcal{M}}|\overline{Z}}^\pi = \prod_{i=1}^{|\pi|} Q_{X_{\pi_i}|\overline{Z}}^\pi.$

4 Asymptotic Tightness of the Upper Bound

In this section, we show that our upper bound on $S_\epsilon(X_1, ..., X_m \mid Z)$ in Theorem 1 is asymptotically tight. Moreover, it extends some previously known upper bounds on C to upper bounds on $C(\epsilon)$, for all $0 < \epsilon < 1$.

First, consider the case where the eavesdropper gets no side information, i.e., $Z = $ constant. With this simplification, the SK capacity C for multiple parties was characterized by Csiszár and Narayan [13]. Furthermore, they introduced the remarkable expression on the right-side of (16) below as an upper bound for C, and showed its tightness for $m = 2, 3$. Later, the tightness of the upper bound for arbitrary m was shown in [9]; we summarize these developments in the result below.

Theorem 2. *[13,9] The SK capacity C for the case when eavesdropper's side information $Z = $ constant is given by*

$$C = \min_{\pi} \frac{1}{|\pi| - 1} D\left(P_{X_{\mathcal{M}}} \middle\| \prod_{i=1}^{|\pi|} P_{X_{\pi_i}}\right), \tag{16}$$

where the min is over all partitions π of $\mathcal{M}$.

This generalized the classic result of Maurer [20] and Ahlswede and Csiszár [1], which established that for two parties, $C = D(P_{X_1 X_2} \| P_{X_1} \times P_{X_2})$, which is the same as Shannon's mutual information between X_1 and X_2.

The converse part of Theorem 2 relied critically on the fact that $\epsilon \to 0$ as $n \to 0$. Below we strengthen the converse and show that the upper bound for SK rates implied by Theorem 2 holds even when ϵ is fixed. Specifically, for $0 < \epsilon < 1$ and $Z = $ constant, an application of Theorem 1 to the IID rvs $X_{\mathcal{M}}^n$, with $Q_{X_{\mathcal{M}}^n}^{\pi} = \prod_{i=1}^{|\pi|} P_{X_{\pi_i}}^n$, yields

$$S_{\epsilon}(X_1^n, ..., X_m^n) \leq \frac{1}{|\pi| - 1} \left[-\log \beta_{\epsilon + \eta}\left(P_{X_{\mathcal{M}}}^n, \prod_{i=1}^{|\pi|} P_{X_{\pi_i}}^n\right) + |\pi| \log(1/\eta) \right],$$

where $\eta < 1 - \epsilon$. Therefore, using Stein's Lemma (see (6)) we get

$$C(\epsilon) \leq \frac{1}{|\pi| - 1} \liminf_{n \to \infty} -\frac{1}{n} \log \beta_{\epsilon + \eta}\left(P_{X_{\mathcal{M}}}^n, \prod_{i=1}^{|\pi|} P_{X_{\pi_i}}^n\right)$$

$$= \frac{1}{|\pi| - 1} D\left(P_{X_{\mathcal{M}}} \middle\| \prod_{i=1}^{|\pi|} P_{X_{\pi_i}}\right).$$

Thus, we have established the following *strong converse* for the SK capacity when $Z = $ constant.

Corollary 2 (Strong Converse). *For every $0 < \epsilon < 1$, the ϵ-SK capacity when $Z = $ constant is given by*

$$C(\epsilon) = C = \min_{\pi} \frac{1}{|\pi| - 1} D\left(P_{X_{\mathcal{M}}} \middle\| \prod_{i=1}^{|\pi|} P_{X_{\pi_i}}\right).$$

Next, we consider the general case for two parties, where the eavesdropper's side information Z may not be constant. Applying Corollary 1 with

$$Q_{X_1^n X_2^n \overline{Z}^n}^{\pi} = P_{X_1|\overline{Z}}^n P_{X_2|\overline{Z}}^n P_{\overline{Z}}^n$$

and following the steps above, we get the *intrinsic conditional information* bound of [21], without requiring the ϵ to vanish to 0.[12]

---

[12] This bound is a stepping stone for other, often tighter, bounds [26,15].

Corollary 3. *For every $0 < \epsilon < 1$, the ϵ-SK capacity for two parties ($m = 2$) is bounded above as[13]*

$$C(\epsilon) \leq \min_{\mathsf{P}_{\bar{Z}|Z}} I(X_1 \wedge X_2 | \bar{Z}).$$

5   Implications for Secure Computing with Trusted Parties

In this section, we present a connection of our result to a problem of secure function computation with trusted parties, where the parties seek to compute a function of their observations using a communication that does not reveal the value of the function by itself (without the observations at the terminals). This is in contrast to the traditional definition of secure computing [37] where the communication is secure but the parties are required not to get any more information than the computed function value. This problem was introduced in [33] where a matching necessary and sufficient condition was given for the feasibility of secure computing in the asymptotic case with IID observations. Here, using Theorem 1, we derive a necessary condition for the feasibility of such secure computing for general observations (not necessarily IID).

5.1   Problem Formulation

Consider $m \geq 2$ parties observing RVs $X_1, ..., X_m$ taking values in finite sets $\mathcal{X}_1, ..., \mathcal{X}_m$, respectively. Upon making these observations, the parties communicate interactively in order to *securely compute* a function $g : \mathcal{X}_1 \times ... \times \mathcal{X}_m \to \mathcal{G}$ in the following sense: The ith party forms an estimate $G_{(i)}$ of the function based on its observation X_i, local randomization U_i and interactive communication $\mathbf{F}$, i.e., $G_{(i)} = G_{(i)}(U_i, X_i, \mathbf{F})$. For $0 \leq \epsilon, \delta < 1$, a function g is (ϵ, δ)-*securely computable* if there exists a protocol satisfying

$$\mathsf{P}\left(G = G_{(1)} = ... = G_{(m)}\right) \geq 1 - \epsilon, \tag{17}$$

$$\frac{1}{2} \left\| \mathsf{P}_{G\mathbf{F}} - \mathsf{P}_G \times \mathsf{P}_\mathbf{F} \right\| \leq \delta, \tag{18}$$

where $G = g(X_{\mathcal{M}})$. The first condition captures the reliability of computation and the second condition ensures the security of the protocol. Heuristically, for security we require that an observer of (only) $\mathbf{F}$ must not get to know the computed value of the function. We seek to characterize the (ϵ, δ)-securely computable functions g.

In [33], an asymptotic version of this problem was addressed. The parties observe $X_1^n, ..., X_m^n$ and seek to compute $G_t = g(X_{1t}, ..., X_{mt})$ for each $t \in \{1, ..., n\}$; consequently, the RVs $\{G_t, 1 \leq t \leq n\}$ are IID. A function g is securely computable if the parties can form estimates $G_{(1)}^{(n)}, ..., G_{(m)}^{(n)}$ such that

$$\mathsf{P}\left(G^n = G_{(1)}^{(n)} = ... = G_{(m)}^{(n)}\right) \geq 1 - \epsilon_n, \quad \tfrac{1}{2}\left\|\mathsf{P}_{G^n\mathbf{F}} - \mathsf{P}_{G^n} \times \mathsf{P}_{\mathbf{F}Z}\right\| \leq \epsilon_n,$$

---

[13] The min instead of inf is justified by the support lemma [12] (see also [10]).

where $\lim_{n\to\infty} \epsilon_n = 0$. The following characterization of securely computable functions g is known.

Theorem 3. *[33] For the asymptotic case described above, a function g is securely computable if $H(G) < C$, where $H(G)$ is the entropy of the RV $G = g(X_1, ..., X_m)$ and C is the SK capacity.*

Conversely, if a function g is securely computable, then $H(G) \le C$.

Heuristically, the necessary condition above follows upon observing that if the parties can securely compute the function g, then they can extract a SK of rate $H(G)$ from RVs G^n. Therefore, $H(G)$ must be necessarily less than the maximum rate of a SK that can be generated, namely the SK capacity C.

In the next section, this heuristic is applied to obtain a necessary condition for a function g to be (ϵ, δ)-securely computable for general observations.

5.2 A Necessary Condition for Functions to Be Securely Computable

We present a necessary condition for a function g to be (ϵ, δ)-securely computable. The following definition is required.

Definition 3. *Denote by $\mathcal{P}(\mathcal{X})$ the set $\{P : P(x) \ge 0 \ \forall x, \ and \ \sum_x P(x) \le 1\}$. For $P_X \in \mathcal{P}(\mathcal{X})$, the min-entropy of P_X is given by*

$$H_{\min}(P_X) = -\log \max_x P_X(x).$$

The ϵ-smooth min-entropy of P_X (cf. [5,25,27]) is defined as

$$H_{\min}^{\epsilon}(P_X) := \max_{\substack{P \in \mathcal{P}(\mathcal{X}): \\ \frac{1}{2}\|P_X - P\| \le \epsilon}} H_{\min}(P).$$

Corollary 4. *For $0 \le \epsilon, \delta < 1$ with $\epsilon + \delta < 1$, if a function g is (ϵ, δ)-securely computable, then*

$$H_{\min}^{\xi}(P_G) \le \frac{1}{|\pi| - 1}\left[-\log \beta_\mu\left(P_{X_{\mathcal{M}}Z}, Q_{X_{\mathcal{M}}Z}^\pi\right) + |\pi| \log(1/\eta)\right] + 2\log(1/2\zeta) + 1,$$

$$\forall Q_{X_{\mathcal{M}}Z}^\pi \in \mathcal{Q}(\pi), \quad (19)$$

for every $\mu := \epsilon + \delta + 2\xi + \zeta + \eta$ with $\xi, \zeta, \eta > 0$ such that $\mu < 1$, and for every partition π of $\mathcal{M}$.

The proof of Corollary 4 is based on extracting an ϵ-SK from the RV G that the parties share. We need the following version of the *Leftover-Hash Lemma*, which is a significant extension of the original result of Impagliazzo-Levin-Luby in [17] (see, also, [2]).

Lemma 3. *(cf. [25,27]) For $0 \leq \epsilon < 1$ and a RV X taking values in $\mathcal{X}$, there exists[14] $K : \mathcal{X} \to \mathcal{K}$ such that the RV $K = K(X)$ satisfies*

$$\frac{1}{2} \|P_K - P_{\text{unif}}\| \leq 2\epsilon + \frac{1}{2}\sqrt{|\mathcal{K}|2^{-H_{\min}^\epsilon(P_X)}}, \tag{20}$$

where P_{unif} is the uniform distribution on $\mathcal{K}$.

Proof of Corollary 4. Lemma 3 with $X = G$ and condition (18) imply that there exists $K = K(G)$ with

$$\frac{1}{2} \|P_{K(G)\mathbf{F}} - P_{\text{unif}} \times P_{\mathbf{F}}\|$$

$$\leq \frac{1}{2} \|P_{K(G)\mathbf{F}} - P_{K(G)} \times P_{\mathbf{F}}\| + \frac{1}{2} \|P_{K(G)} \times P_{\mathbf{F}} - P_{\text{unif}} \times P_{\mathbf{F}}\|$$

$$\leq \frac{1}{2} \|P_{G\mathbf{F}} - P_G \times P_{\mathbf{F}}\| + \frac{1}{2} \|P_{K(G)} - P_{\text{unif}}\|$$

$$\leq \delta + 2\xi + \frac{1}{2}\sqrt{|\mathcal{K}|2^{-H_{\min}^\xi(P_G)}}.$$

Thus, in the view of Proposition 1, for $|\mathcal{K}| = \lfloor 2^{H_{\min}^\xi(P_G)}4\zeta^2 \rfloor$, the RV K constitutes[15] an $(\epsilon + \delta + 2\xi + \zeta)$-SK. An application of Theorem 1 gives (19). $\square$

5.3 Illustrative Examples

Example 1. (**Computing functions of independent observations using a perfect SK**). Suppose the ith party observes U_i, where the RVs $U_1, ..., U_m$ are mutually independent. Furthermore, all parties share a κ-bit perfect SK K which is independent of $U_{\mathcal{M}}$. How many bits κ are required to (ϵ, δ)-securely compute a function $g(U_1, ..., U_m)$?

Note that the data observed by the ith party is given by $X_i = (U_i, K)$. A simple calculation shows that for every partition π of $\mathcal{M}$,

$$\beta_\epsilon \left(P_{X_{\mathcal{M}}}, \prod_{i=1}^{|\pi|} P_{X_{\pi_i}} \right) \geq (1 - \epsilon)\kappa^{1 - |\pi|},$$

and therefore, by Corollary 4 a necessary condition for g to be (ϵ, δ)-securely computable is

$$H_{\min}^\xi(P_G) \leq \kappa + \frac{1}{|\pi| - 1} \left(|\pi| \log(1/\eta) + \log(1/(1 - \mu)) \right) + 2\log(1/2\zeta) + 1, \tag{21}$$

for every $\xi, \zeta, \eta > 0$ satisfying $\mu = \epsilon + \delta + 2\xi + \zeta + \eta < 1$.

---

[14] A randomly chosen function from a 2-universal hash family suffices.
[15] Strictly speaking, the estimates $K_1, ..., K_m$ of K formed by different parties constitute the $(\epsilon + \delta + 2\xi + \zeta)$-SK in the sense of (3).

For the special case when $U_i = B_i^n$, a sequence of independent, unbiased bits, and

$$g\left(B_1^n, ..., B_m^n\right) = B_{11} \oplus ... \oplus B_{m1}, ..., B_{1n} \oplus ... \oplus B_{mn},$$

i.e., the parties seek to compute the (element-wise) parities of the bit sequences, it holds that $H_{\min}^\xi(\mathrm{P}_G) \geq n$. Therefore, (ϵ, δ)-secure computing is feasible only if $n \leq \kappa + O(1)$. We remark that this necessary condition is also (almost) sufficient. Indeed, if $n \leq \kappa$, all but the mth party can reveal all their bits $B_1^n, ..., B_{m-1}^n$ and the mth party can send back $B_1^n \oplus ... \oplus B_m^n \oplus K_n$, where K_n denotes any n out of κ bits of K. Clearly, this results in a secure computation of g.

Example 2. **(Secure transmission).** Two parties sharing a κ-bit perfect SK K seek to exchange a message M securely.[16] To this end, they communicate interactively using a communication $\mathbf{F}$, and based on this communication the second party forms an estimate $\hat{M}$ of the first party's message M. This protocol accomplishes (ϵ, δ)-secure transmission if

$$\mathrm{P}\left(M = \hat{M}\right) \geq 1 - \epsilon, \quad \tfrac{1}{2} \|\mathrm{P}_{MF} - \mathrm{P}_M \times \mathrm{P}_\mathbf{F}\| \leq \delta.$$

The classic result of Shannon [30] implies that $(0,0)$-secure transmission is feasible only if κ is at least $\log \|M\|$, where $\|M\|$ denotes the size of the message space.[17] But, can we relax this constraint for $\epsilon, \delta > 0$? In this example, we will give a necessary condition for the feasibility of (ϵ, δ)-secure transmission by relating it to the previous example.

Specifically, let the observations of the two parties consist of $X_1 = (M, K)$, $X_2 = K$. Then, (ϵ, δ)-secure transmission of M is tantamount to securely computing the function $g(X_1, X_2) = M$. Therefore, using (21), (ϵ, δ)-secure transmission of M is feasible only if

$$H_{\min}^\xi(\mathrm{P}_M) \leq \kappa + 2\log(1/\eta) + \log(1/(1 - \mu)) + 2\log(1/2\zeta) + 1, \qquad (22)$$

for every $\xi, \zeta, \eta > 0$ satisfying $\mu = \epsilon + \delta + 2\xi + \zeta + \eta < 1$.

Condition (22) brings out a trade-off between κ and $\epsilon + \delta$ (cf. [18, Problems 2.12 and 2.13]). For an illustration, consider a message M consisting of a RV Y taking values in a set $\mathcal{Y} = \{0,1\}^n \cup \{0,1\}^{2n}$ and with the following distribution:

$$\mathrm{P}_Y(y) = \begin{cases} \frac{1}{2} \cdot \frac{1}{2^n} & y \in \{0,1\}^n \\ \frac{1}{2} \cdot \frac{1}{2^{2n}} & y \in \{0,1\}^{2n} \end{cases}.$$

For $\epsilon + \delta = 0$, we know that secure transmission will require κ to be more than the *worst-case message length* $2n$. But perhaps by allowing $\epsilon + \delta$ to be greater than 0, we can make do with fewer SK bits; for instance, perhaps κ equal to $H(M) = (3/2)n + 1$ will suffice (note that the *average message length* equals $(3/2)n$). The necessary condition above says that this is not possible if

---

[16] A message M is a RV with known distribution P_M.

[17] This is a slight generalization of Shannon's original result; see [18, Theorem 2.7] for a proof.

$\epsilon + \delta < 1/2$. Indeed, since $H_{\min}^{\xi}(P_Y) \geq 2n$ for $\xi = 1/4$, we get from (22) that the message $M = Y$ can be (ϵ, δ)-securely transmitted only if $2n \leq \kappa + O(1)$, where the constant depends on ϵ and δ.

6   Discussion

The evaluation of the upper bound in Theorem 1 relies on the computation of $\beta_\epsilon(P, Q)$. The latter is given by a linear program (see (4)), solving which has a polynomial complexity in the size of the observation space. Also, weaker bounds than (8) can be obtained by using upper bounds on $- \log \beta_\epsilon(P, Q)$; the following is easy to show:

$$- \log \beta_\epsilon(P, Q) \leq \inf_\gamma \gamma - \log \left(P \left(\log \frac{P(X)}{Q(X)} \leq \gamma \right) - \epsilon \right).$$

In particular, using $\gamma = D_\alpha(P, Q) + \frac{1}{1-\alpha} \log(1 - \epsilon - \epsilon')$, where $D_\alpha(P, Q)$ is the Rényi's divergence of order $\alpha > 1$ [29] given by

$$D_\alpha(P, Q) = \frac{1}{\alpha - 1} \log \sum_{x \in \mathcal{X}} P(x)^\alpha Q(x)^{1-\alpha},$$

it can be shown that

$$- \log \beta_\epsilon(P, Q) \leq D_\alpha(P, Q) + \frac{1}{1 - \alpha} \log(1 - \epsilon - \epsilon') - \log(\epsilon').$$

In general, this bound is not tight, but it can lead to an upper bound on SK length that is easier to evaluate than the original bound (8) and can also be used to prove Stein's lemma (see (6)). Tighter bounds are available when P and Q correspond to IID RVs or a Markov chain [36].

Finally, we remark that we did not present any general protocols for multiparty SK agreement or for secure function computation with trusted parties. For the SK agreement problem, it is possible to mimic the approach in [20,1,13,27] to obtain protocols that first use communication for *information reconciliation* and then extract SKs using *privacy amplification*. The challenge in the multiparty setup is to identify the appropriate *information to be reconciled*. The task is perhaps even more daunting for the secure function computation with trusted parties where, at the outset, the communication must be selected to be almost independent of the computed function value. A sufficient condition for the existence of such communication can be derived based on the approach in [8] (cf. [28]). Specifically, the sufficient condition will guarantee the existence of random (noninteractive) communication that is almost independent of the function value and at the same time allows each party to recover the collective data of all the parties. But it is unclear if the resulting sufficient condition matches the necessary condition in Corollary 4. In particular, we cannot verify or contradict the following intriguing observations made in [13] and [33] (see, also, [31]), respectively:

1. A largest rate SK can be generated by recovering the collective data of all the parties $X_{\mathcal{M}}^n$, locally, at each party.[18]
2. Every securely computable function can be computed by first recovering the entire data at each terminal, using a communication that does not give away the value of g.

Examining if these asymptotic principles hold in the general single-shot setting is an interesting future research direction.

Acknowledgment. The authors would like to thank Prakash Narayan for helpful comments and discussions. Also, thanks are due to Jonathan Katz for comments that helped us to improve the presentation.

References

1. Ahlswede, R., Csiszár, I.: Common randomness in information theory and cryptography–part i: Secret sharing. IEEE Trans. Inf. Theory 39(4), 1121–1132 (1993)
2. Bennett, C.H., Brassard, G., Crépeau, C., Maurer, U.M.: Generalized privacy amplification. IEEE Trans. Inf. Theory 41(6), 1915–1923 (1995)
3. Bennett, C.H., Brassard, G., Robert, J.M.: Privacy amplification by public discussion. SIAM J. Comput. 17(2), 210–229 (1988)
4. Bennett, C.H., DiVincenzo, D.P., Smolin, J.A., Wootters, W.K.: Mixed-state entanglement and quantum error correction. Phys. Rev. A 54, 3824–3851 (1996)
5. Cachin, C.: Smooth entropy and Rényi entropy. In: Fumy, W. (ed.) EUROCRYPT 1997. LNCS, vol. 1233, pp. 193–208. Springer, Heidelberg (1997)
6. Canetti, R.: Universally composable security: a new paradigm for cryptographic protocols. Proc. Annual Symposium on Foundations of Computer Science (also, see Cryptology ePrint Archive, Report 2000/067), 136–145 (2001)
7. Cerf, N., Massar, S., Schneider, S.: Multipartite classical and quantum secrecy monotones. Physical Review A 66(4), 042309 (2002)
8. Chan, C.: Agreement of a restricted secret key. In: Proc. IEEE International Symposium on Information Theory, pp. 1782–1786 (July 2012)
9. Chan, C., Zheng, L.: Mutual dependence for secret key agreement. In: Proc. Annual Conference on Information Sciences and Systems (CISS) (2010)
10. Christandl, M., Renner, R., Wolf, S.: A property of the intrinsic mutual information. In: Proc. IEEE International Symposium on Information Theory, p. 258 (June 2003)
11. Csiszár, I.: Almost independence and secrecy capacity. Prob. Pered. Inform. 32(1), 48–57 (1996)
12. Csiszár, I., Körner, J.: Information theory: Coding theorems for discrete memoryless channels, 2nd edn. Cambridge University Press (2011)
13. Csiszár, I., Narayan, P.: Secrecy capacities for multiple terminals. IEEE Trans. Inf. Theory 50(12), 3047–3061 (2004)
14. Dodis, Y., Ostrovsky, R., Reyzin, L., Smith, A.: Fuzzy extractors: How to generate strong keys from biometrics and other noisy data. SIAM Journal on Computing 38(1), 97–139 (2008)

---

[18] Recovering $X_{\mathcal{M}}^n$ at a party is referred to as the party attaining *omniscience* [13].

15. Gohari, A.A., Anantharam, V.: Information-theoretic key agreement of multiple terminals part i. IEEE Trans. Inf. Theory 56(8), 3973–3996 (2010)
16. Hayashi, M., Nagaoka, H.: General formulas for capacity of classical-quantum channels. IEEE Trans. Inf. Theory 49(7), 1753–1768 (2003)
17. Impagliazzo, R., Levin, L.A., Luby, M.: Pseudo-random generation from one-way functions. In: Proc. Annual Symposium on Theory of Computing, pp. 12–24 (1989)
18. Katz, J., Lindell, Y.: Introduction to Modern Cryptography. Chapman & Hall/CRC (2007)
19. Kullback, S.: Information Theory and Statistics. Dover Publications (1968)
20. Maurer, U.M.: Secret key agreement by public discussion from common information. IEEE Trans. Inf. Theory 39(3), 733–742 (1993)
21. Maurer, U.M., Wolf, S.: Unconditionally secure key agreement and the intrinsic conditional information. IEEE Trans. Inf. Theory 45(2), 499–514 (1999)
22. Orlitsky, A., Gamal, A.E.: Communication with secrecy constraints. In: STOC, pp. 217–224 (1984)
23. Pappu, R.S.: Physical one-way functions. Ph. D. Dissertation, Massachussetts Institute of Technology (2001)
24. Polyanskiy, Y., Poor, H.V., Verdú, S.: Channel coding rate in the finite blocklength regime. IEEE Trans. Inf. Theory 56(5), 2307–2359 (2010)
25. Renner, R.: Security of quantum key distribution. Ph. D. Dissertation, ETH Zurich (2005)
26. Renner, R., Wolf, S.: New bounds in secret-key agreement: The gap between formation and secrecy extraction. In: Biham, E. (ed.) EUROCRYPT 2003. LNCS, vol. 2656, pp. 562–577. Springer, Heidelberg (2003)
27. Renner, R., Wolf, S.: Simple and tight bounds for information reconciliation and privacy amplification. In: Roy, B. (ed.) ASIACRYPT 2005. LNCS, vol. 3788, pp. 199–216. Springer, Heidelberg (2005)
28. Renner, R., Wolf, S., Wullschleger, J.: Trade-offs in information-theoretic multi-party one-way key agreement. In: Desmedt, Y. (ed.) ICITS 2007. LNCS, vol. 4883, pp. 65–75. Springer, Heidelberg (2009)
29. Rényi, A.: On measures of entropy and information. In: Proc. Fourth Berkeley Symposium on Mathematics Statistics and Probability, vol. 1, pp. 547–561. Univ. of Calif. Press (1961)
30. Shannon, C.E.: Communication theory of secrecy systems. Bell System Technical Journal 28, 656–715 (1949)
31. Tyagi, H.: Common randomness principles of secrecy. Ph. D. Dissertation, Univeristy of Maryland, College Park (2013)
32. Tyagi, H., Narayan, P.: How many queries will resolve common randomness? IEEE Trans. Inf. Theory 59(9), 5363–5378 (2013)
33. Tyagi, H., Narayan, P., Gupta, P.: When is a function securely computable? IEEE Trans. Inf. Theory 57(10), 6337–6350 (2011)
34. Vedral, V., Plenio, M.B.: Entanglement measures and purification procedures. Phys. Rev. A 57, 1619–1633 (1998)
35. Wang, L., Renner, R.: One-shot classical-quantum capacity and hypothesis testing. Phys. Rev. Lett. 108(20), 200501 (2012)
36. Watanabe, S., Hayashi, M.: Finite-length analysis on tail probability and simple hypothesis testing for Markov chain. arXiv:1401.3801
37. Yao, A.C.: Protocols for secure computations. In: Proc. Annual Symposium on Foundations of Computer Science, pp. 160–164 (1982)

Non-Interactive Secure Computation
Based on Cut-and-Choose

Arash Afshar[1], Payman Mohassel[1], Benny Pinkas[2,*], and Ben Riva[2,3,**]

[1] University of Calgary, Canada
[2] Bar-Ilan University, Israel
[3] Tel Aviv University, Israel

Abstract. In recent years, secure two-party computation (2PC) has been demonstrated to be feasible in practice. However, all efficient general-computation 2PC protocols require multiple rounds of interaction between the two players. This property restricts 2PC to be only relevant to scenarios where both players can be simultaneously online, and where communication latency is not an issue.

This work considers the model of 2PC with a *single* round of interaction, called *Non-Interactive Secure Computation (NISC)*. In addition to the non-interaction property, we also consider a flavor of NISC that allows reusing the first message for many different 2PC invocations, possibly with different players acting as the player who sends the second message, similar to a public-key encryption where a single public-key can be used to encrypt many different messages.

We present a NISC protocol that is based on the cut-and-choose paradigm of Lindell and Pinkas (Eurocrypt 2007). This protocol achieves concrete efficiency similar to that of best multi-round 2PC protocols based on the cut-and-choose paradigm. The protocol requires only t garbled circuits for achieving cheating probability of 2^{-t}, similar to the recent result of Lindell (Crypto 2013), but only needs a single round of interaction.

To validate the efficiency of our protocol, we provide a prototype implementation of it and show experiments that confirm its competitiveness with that of the best multi-round 2PC protocols. This is the *first* prototype implementation of an efficient NISC protocol.

In addition to our NISC protocol, we introduce a new encoding technique that significantly reduces communication in the NISC setting. We further show how our NISC protocol can be improved in the multi-round setting, resulting in a highly efficient constant-round 2PC that is also suitable for pipelined implementation.

1 Introduction

Secure two-party computation (2PC) is a very powerful tool that allows two participants to compute any function of their private inputs without revealing

* Supported by the Israeli Ministry of Science and Technology (grant 3-9094).
** Supported by the Check Point Institute for Information Security and an ISF grant 20006317.

P.Q. Nguyen and E. Oswald (Eds.): EUROCRYPT 2014, LNCS 8441, pp. 387–404, 2014.

any information about the inputs except for the value of the function. Furthermore, if the execution of the 2PC protocol is completed, it is guaranteed that its output is the correct output. In this work, unless said otherwise, we only discuss 2PC protocols that are secure even against malicious (aka active) participants, who might arbitrarily deviate from the protocol that they should be executing. The investigation of secure two-party protocols began with the seminal work of Yao [Yao86] that showed the feasibility of this concept. In recent years it was shown that the theoretical framework of secure two-party computation can be efficiently implemented and can be run in reasonable time, even under the strongest security guarantees (see, e.g. [PSSW09, SS11, NNOB12, KSS12]).

Non-Interactive Secure Computation (NISC). A major drawback of many 2PC protocols is that they require several rounds of interaction (e.g., [LP07, LP11] with a constant number of rounds, or [NNOB12] with a number of rounds that depends on the function). This paper focuses on efficient constructions of protocols for non-interactive secure computation (NISC) that run in a single round of interaction.

We consider three flavors of NISC. In the first, which we refer to by *One-Sender NISC (OS-NISC)*, there are only two parties, a receiver and a sender. The receiver sends the first message, the sender replies with the second message, and then the receiver outputs the result of the computation. This is essentially a 2PC protocol with the additional restriction of having only one round of interaction. (Following [IKO$^+$11], throughout this work we refer to the party that sends the first message and receives the final output as the *receiver* or as P_1, and refer to the party that sends the second message as the *sender* or P_2.)

The second flavor of NISC, which we call *Multi-Sender NISC (MS-NISC)*, is an extension of OS-NISC where the first message can be used for running secure computation with many different senders. I.e., the receiver broadcasts its first (single) message; each party that wants to participate in a secure computation with the receiver sends a message back to the receiver; then, after receiving second messages from several (possibly different) senders, the receiver outputs the results of its computation with all thee senders (or uses these output values in other protocols). We stress that each sender does not trust other senders, nor the receiver, and wishes to maintain privacy of its input even if everyone else colludes.

A limitation of MS-NISC is that the receiver has to aggregate and output all the secure computation results together. The last flavor of NISC, which we call *Adaptive MS-NISC*, does not have this limitation. Adaptive MS-NISC is essentially like MS-NISC, except that the receiver outputs each of the secure computation results as soon as it gets it (thus, allowing the adversary, who might control some senders, to pick its next inputs based on those results).

In this work we focus on the first two flavors, and only briefly discuss the third flavor where relevant.

Why NISC? Let us begin with a motivating example. Suppose that there is a known algorithm that receives the DNA data of two individuals and decides whether they are related. People would like to use this algorithm to find family relatives, but on the other hand they are not willing to publish their DNA data (which can, e.g., predict their chances of being affected by different diseases). A possible solution is to use a secure computation that implements the algorithm and is run between any pair of people who suspect that they might be related. A multi-round protocol for secure computation requires the participants to coordinate a time where they can both participate in the protocol, and run a secure computation application that exchanges multiple rounds of communication with the application run by the other party. A solution using NISC is much simpler and eliminates the synchronization problem: each interested person can publish, say on his Facebook wall, his first message in the protocol, secretly encoding his DNA data. Those who are interested in finding out whether they are related to that person can send back the second message of the protocol. This message can be sent using Facebook or similar services, or even by email. Then, once in a while, the first person can run the computation with all those who answered him, and find out with whom he is related.

In the previous example, NISC was preferable since a multi-round protocol would have required the parties to synchronize the times in which they participate in the protocol (or incur long delays until the other party is online and sends the next message of the protocol). In general, requiring multiple rounds of interaction is also very limiting in scenarios in which each round of communication is very expensive and/or is slow. E.g., if the communication is done using physical means, for example encoded as a QR code on a brochure sent by snail-mail, or if the other party is a satellite that passes for only a short period above the receiver.

Previous NISC Protocols. A NISC protocol (for all three flavors) for general computation can be constructed from Yao's garbled circuit, non-interactive zero-knowledge proofs (NIZK), and fully-secure one-round oblivious transfer (OT): P_1, who is the evaluator of the circuit, sends the first message of the OT protocol. P_2, who is the circuit constructor, returns a garbled circuit, the second message of the OT protocol, and a NIZK proof that its message is correct. (See, for example, [CCKM00, HK07] for such protocols.) Unfortunately, the NIZK proof in this case requires a *non black-box* use of cryptographic primitives (namely, it must prove the correctness of each encryption in each gate of the circuit).

Efficient NISC protocols that do not require such non black-box constructions are presented in [IKO+11] based on the MPC-in-the-head technique of [IPS08]. The complexity of the OS-NISC protocol of [IKO+11] is $|C| \cdot \mathrm{poly}(\log(|C|), \log(t)) + \mathrm{depth}(C) \cdot \mathrm{poly}(\log(|C|), t)$ invocations of a Pseudo-Random Generator (PRG), where C is a boolean circuit that computes the function of interest, and t is a statistical security parameter. (Another protocol presented in that work uses only $\mathcal{O}(|C|)$ PRG invocations, but is based on a relaxed security notion.) [IKO+11] also shows an adaptive MS-NISC protocol for a bounded number of corrupted senders. The complexity of that protocol is $\mathcal{O}((t+Q)|C|)$ PRG invocations, where Q is the bound on the number of corrupted senders.

Although the protocols in [IKO+11] are very efficient asymptotically, their practicality is unclear and left as an open question in [IKO+11]. For instance, the protocols combine several techniques that are very efficient asymptotically, such as scalable MPC and using expanders in a non black-box way, each of which contributes large constant factors to the concrete complexity.

Cut and Choose Based 2PC. A very efficient approach for constructing 2PC with security against malicious parties is based on the *cut-and-choose* paradigm. (We refer here to protocols that use cut-and-choose for checking garbled circuits, as in [LP07], and not to protocols that use cut-and-choose in a different way, such as the protocols in [IKO+11].) [MF06, LP07, LP11, SS11, MR13, Lin13, SS13] give constructions that use this paradigm and require $\mathcal{O}(t|C|)$ PRG invocations, and some additional overhead that does not depend on $|C|$. Indeed, for a fixed circuit, this asymptotic overhead is larger than that of [IKO+11], which requires only a poly-logarithmic number of PRG calls per gate of the circuit. However, the concrete constants in the cut-and-choose based protocols are rather small (whereas for [IKO+11] the constants seem fairly large, e.g., the $\mathsf{poly}(\log(|C|))$ factor) making the cut and choose approach of high practical interest as shown in several implementations (e.g., [PSSW09, SS11, KSS12]). However, all current cut-and-choose based 2PC constructions require more than one round of interaction.

1.1 Our Contributions

In this paper, we take a major step beyond feasibility results for NISC. Our main contribution is a new OS-NISC/MS-NISC protocol that we believe to be conceptually simpler than previous NISC protocols, and extremely practical. The complexity of this protocol is similar or better than those of the best multi-round 2PC protocols based on cut-and-choose. We also describe an implementation and evaluation of our NISC protocol, that demonstrate its practicality.

We now discuss our contributions in more detail.

Revisiting the NISC Setting. In Section 3 we formalize the informal description of the MS-NISC model by using the ideal/real-model paradigm, defining an ideal functionality that receives an input from the receiver and inputs from many other senders, and returns to the receiver the outputs of the different evaluations.

Intuitively, one would expect that any OS-NISC protocol can also be a MS-NISC protocol with soundness that decreases at most polynomially in the number of senders. In the full version of this paper we show that this intuition is false by describing an attack on the technique of [LP07] for protecting against selective-OT attacks, which results in an exponential (in the number of senders) decrease in the soundness of the protocol.[1]

Our Protocols. As discussed earlier, the cut-and-choose technique requires several rounds of interaction since the player who generates the garbled circuits must first send them, and only then see the "cut" and send the circuit openings.

---

[1] We note that in the OS-NISC protocol of [IKO+11], a variant of the [LP07] technique is used for protecting against the selective-OT attack. As far as we can tell, our "attack" can be applied to that construction as well, if used for MS-NISC.

We introduce techniques that allow us to *squash this interaction to a single round* in the common random string model (CRS). Until recently, all cut-and-choose based 2PC protocols (e.g., [LP07, LP11, SS11] required at least $\sim 3t$ garbled circuits for achieving soundness of 2^{-t} (ignoring computational soundness). These techniques are sufficient to turn such protocols into NISCs that also use roughly $3t$ garbled circuits.

Reducing the Number of Circuits. Lindell [Lin13] recently introduced a cut-and-choose based 2PC that requires only t garbled circuits for the same soundness, reducing the number of garbled circuits by (at least) a factor of three. However, this protocol is inherently interactive since it executes two 2PC protocols, one after the other, where the second 2PC is used to recover from potential cheating, with no obvious way of making the protocol non-interactive. We show a new approach that allows working non-interactively with only t garbled circuits (for soundness 2^{-t}). We believe that our approach has significance also in the multi-round setting with several advantages over the techniques of [Lin13] such as (1) suitability for pipelining; and (2) an (arguably) conceptually simpler description.

Section 1.2 provides a high-level description of the protocol. This protocol is secure under the DDH assumption in the CRS model. We believe that this protocol is easier to understand than previous NISC protocols, and because of that, more approachable for people from outside the crypto community. Hopefully, NISC could gain interest as a model for practical protocols and applications.

We remark that we achieve only the OS-NISC/MS-NISC security notions. The same first message *can* be used for many executions of secure computation with many different senders. The only restriction to achieve adaptive MS-NISC is that once the receiver's outputs are revealed to the other parties, the receiver must refresh its first message, which requires computing only t OT queries.

In the full version of this paper we describe how the efficiency of the protocol can be improved if one permits more than one round of interaction. The resulting 2PC protocol requires only t garbled circuits (for statistical security of 2^{-t}), $\mathcal{O}(tn_1)$ symmetric-key operations, and $\mathcal{O}(tn_2 + t^2)$ exponentiations, where n_i is P_i's input length (and ignoring a small number of seed-OTs).

Reducing Communication. In addition to the main protocol, we show how to reduce communication significantly using a new non-interactive adaptation of the method of Goyal et al. [GMS08] to the NISC environment (Section 5). This method, based on the usage of erasure codes (specifically, of polynomials), reduces the communication size to be only slightly higher than the communication required for sending the garbled circuits that are evaluated (as opposed to sending also the garbled circuits that are checked). For example, for soundness 2^{-40}, this protocol requires using 44 garbled circuits, and communicating only 19 garbled circuits.

Implementation and Experiments. We describe a prototype implementation of our main protocol, implemented in C for a Linux environment. It is the *first* working implementation (that we are aware of) of a NISC protocol, and it allows using our protocol in all the scenarios described above. Additionally, this is also the first working implementation (that we are aware of) of a 2PC protocol that uses only t garbled circuits for security of 2^{-t}.

We evaluate the prototype with a circuit that computes an AES encryption and a circuit that computes SHA256. The resulting performance is significantly better than that of previous cut-and-choose based protocols. For example, a maliciously secure computation of AES circuit requires about 7 seconds , where the time needed for generating the first message is very small (e.g., much less than a second).

1.2   High Level Description of the Protocol

Step One: Squashing Cut-and-Choose 2PC to One Round. The starting point for the protocol is the most straightforward approach based on the cut-and-choose method with $3t$ garbled circuits. (The constant 3 is chosen for simplifying the description. The exact constants are analysed in [LP11, SS11].) The receiver's first message in this case is an OT query of its input using a two-message OT protocol (e.g., [PVW08]). Namely, if the receiver has n_1 input bits it sends the corresponding n_1 OT queries. The sender garbles $3t$ circuits $gc_1, \ldots, gc_{3t}$ and sends back a message that includes: (1) The $3t$ garbled circuits; (2) The OT answers for the receiver's query, using the input-wire labels that were used for garbling the receiver's inputs; (3) The input-wire labels that correspond to the sender's own input. The receiver is now able to retrieve the labels of its input-wires and evaluate the $3t$ garbled circuits by itself. It then takes the majority result to be its output. This protocol is obviously insufficient. There are three issues that need to be verified: (1) Were the garbled circuits garbled correctly? (2) Did the sender use the right input-wire labels in the OT? (i.e., consistent with the garbled circuits) (3) Was the sender's input consistent in all $3t$ circuits? The goal of our work is to present non-interactive and efficient solutions for these issues.

The standard solution for the first issue, of verifying the garbled circuits, is the cut-and-choose method [LP07] where the sender proves that a random subset of $c \cdot 3t$ circuits (where c is fixed and publicly known, e.g. $c = 1/2$, or $c = 3/5$ to optimize the success probability) were garbled correctly by revealing the randomness that was used to garble them. Normally, the cut-and-choose method requires more than one round of interaction. We solve this problem by using OT in the following way (similar to the technique used in [KSS12, KMR12] for the different purpose of reducing latency). The protocol includes additional $3t$ OTs, denoted as the *circuit-OTs*. In each of these OTs the receiver can choose to either check or evaluate the corresponding circuit: The receiver chooses a random subset of circuits of size $c \cdot 3t$ that it wants to check, and for each of these circuit it sends an OT query for the 1-bit. For the rest of the circuits it sends an OT query for the 0-bit. The sender picks $3t$ keys $seed_1, \ldots, seed_{3t}$ for a pseudo-random function (PRF) and uses key $seed_i$ to generate all the randomness needed for garbling gc_i. The sender also picks additional $3t$ keys $k_1, \ldots, k_{3t}$, and encrypts, under the key k_i, the labels of the sender's input-wires for circuit gc_i. Now, the sender answers the circuit-OT queries using the $3t$ pairs

$(k_i, seed_i)$ as inputs. Observe that if the receiver wants to check gc_i it learns the PRF key $seed_i$ that allows to reconstruct that circuit (using the same circuit construction algorithm used by the sender), but it is not able to decrypt the sender's input-wires labels. If the receiver wishes to evaluate circuit gc_i it learns the key k_i that enables to decrypt the input-wires labels of that circuit, but not the seed $seed_i$. In that case the receiver is able to evaluate the circuit but not to check it. Of course, the sender does not know which circuits are chosen to be checked, due to the security of the OT protocol.

As for the second issue, how to check that the sender uses consistent labels in the OTs for the receiver's input wires, we modify a technique of [KS06, SS11] to work in the NISC setting. Instead of using a regular OT protocol, we work with an OT in which the second OT message *commits* the sender to specific inputs. (I.e., given the second OT message, the sender cannot later claim that it used different inputs than the ones it actually used.) In practice, the highly efficient OT of [PVW08] is sufficient for our purpose. Since we have only one round of interaction, we require that all the randomness used for the second message of the OT queries for circuit gc_i, is also derived from the PRF key $seed_i$. In case the receiver does not ask to check gc_i, this OT is as secure as a regular OT by the security of the PRF. If the receiver chose to check gc_i, it learns $seed_i$, and since it knows both the input labels of the circuit and the randomness that should have been used in the OT it is able to recompute the second OT message by itself and compare it with the message sent by the receiver. If there is a difference, the receiver aborts, since this means that the sender tried to cheat in the OT for gc_i.

For the third issue, i.e. the consistency of the sender's inputs, we modify a technique of [MF06] for the NISC setting. We use a commitment scheme that allows proving, very efficiently, that two commitments are commitments to the same value. (Pedersen's commitment [Ped92] or an ElGamal based commitment suffice.) Instead of using random labels for the sender's input-wires, the sender uses commitments to zero as labels for the 0-bit inputs and commitments to one as labels for 1-bit inputs. In an interactive setting the sender decommits all input-wire labels of the checked circuits and proves that it used correct commitments.

In order to execute the protocol in a single round of interaction, we require that the randomness used for the commitments for the input wires of circuit gc_i is also generated using the seed $seed_i$. This allows the receiver to regenerate the commitments by itself in case it chose to check gc_i. In addition, the sender sends what we call *input commitments*, which are a set of commitments of its actual input bits that is not part of any garbled circuit. The protocol includes commitment equality proofs which prove that each input value in an evaluated circuit is equal to the value committed in the corresponding input commitment. (These proofs are secure since the input commitments are never decommitted, as opposed to the other commitments which are opened in checked circuits). The sender encrypts the commitment equality proofs using k_i in order to hide them from the receiver in the checked circuits. (Otherwise, the receiver could determine the sender's input.)

Note that so far our protocol requires $3t$ garbled circuits and relies on the cut-and-choose guarantee that the majority of the evaluated garbled circuits are correct.

Before we discuss how to reduce the number of garbled circuits, we note that although our protocol is not vulnerable to selective-OT attacks, namely attacks where the sender sets incorrect inputs in the OTs used by the receiver to learn its input labels, we still require the receiver to refresh its first message in case its outputs are revealed to the sender (or are used in other protocols, which can potentially leak them). Technically, this happens since a corrupted sender can use an invalid seed for garbled circuit gc_1, and valid circuits otherwise. This sender could then learn the receiver's first input bit in the circuit-OTs, based on whether the receiver aborted its execution with this sender. In the adaptive MS-NISC setting, this attack could be repeated by several corrupted senders, letting the adversary learn secret information about other bits of the cut-and-choose challenge. As a result, soundness is gone, since the adversary could set the input of the last sender based on the bits of the cut-and-choose challenge. In order to mitigate this attack, we require the receiver to refresh its first message once its outputs are revealed. Note, however, that some information about the receiver's choices in the circuit-OTs is indeed revealed even if the receiver does refresh its first message. However, these bits are revealed only *after* the execution of the protocol, thus do not undermine security. (In fact, in most cut-and-choose 2PC protocols the challenge is always public. E.g., [LP11, SS11].)

Step Two: Reducing the Number of Garbled Circuits. Assume for simplicity that the circuit the players use has only one output wire, and that the sender has only one input bit. We use the protocol from the previous section, but with only t garbled circuits, and let P_1 pick a random subset of them for verification (instead of a constant fraction c, as described above). Obviously, if all evaluated circuits output the same bit, then this bit is the correct output with probability $1 - 2^{-t}$ (since in order to cheat, the sender must guess *all* the checked circuits and *all* the evaluated ones). However, if some of the evaluated circuits output different bits, then the receiver knows that the sender is trying to cheat and needs to determine the right output. Following [Lin13], we would like to provide the receiver in this case with a "trapdoor" that allows it to recover the sender's input in case the sender behaves maliciously (but, of course, not in case it behaves honestly). Then, the receiver can simply use the sender's input in order to compute the function by itself, and output the correct result.

As described earlier, the sender's input-wire labels are commitments to their actual values. Let $\mathsf{EGCommit}(h; b, r) = (g^r, h^r g^b)$ be an ElGamal based commitment for a bit b, given a group $\mathcal{G}$ in which DDH is hard, and a generator g. This is a perfectly-binding commitment, even if the party that commits knows $\log_g(h)$. However, knowing $\log_g(h)$ allows "decrypting" g^b, which otherwise is hidden because of the DDH assumption.

In the protocol, the sender picks w, sends $h = g^w$ to the receiver, and sets the labels of its input wire in gc_i to be $\mathsf{EGCommit}(h; 0, r_{i,0})$ and $\mathsf{EGCommit}(h; 1, r_{i,1})$. Next, the sender picks at random w_0, w_1 such that $w = w_0 + w_1$, and sends

$h_0 = g^{w_0}$ and $h_1 = g^{w_1}$. (P_1 verifies that $h = h_0 \cdot h_1$.) For gc_i, the sender sends *output recovery commitments* $h_0 g^{l_{i,0}}$ and $h_1 g^{l_{i,1}}$, where $l_{i,0}, l_{i,1}$ are chosen at random.[2] Then, it sets the output wire labels of this circuit to be $l_{i,0}$ and $l_{i,1}$, corresponding to 0 and 1, respectively.

As part of the cut-and-choose stage, if the receiver chooses to check gc_i, then it learns $seed_i$ and can recover the output wire labels and verify both the input-wire labels and the output recovery commitments. However, if the receiver chooses to evaluate gc_i, then the sender also sends it the values $w_0 + l_{i,0}$ and $w_1 + l_{i,1}$. (These values are sent encrypted under k_i, so the receiver only gets them in case it chose to evaluate gc_i.) The receiver verifies that these values are consistent with the output recovery commitments by computing g to the power of these two values (if this verification fails then the receiver aborts). In addition, the receiver checks that the $l_{i,b}$ it received from the evaluation of gc_i is a valid decommitment of $h_0 g^{l_{i,b}}$. If this check pass, the receiver marks gc_i as a *semi-trusted* circuit. (Note that the probability of marking no circuit as semi-trusted is 2^{-t}, as it requires the sender to guess the set of evaluated circuits.)

After the receiver evaluates all the circuits chosen for evaluation, it is left with either a single output from all semi-trusted circuits, or with two outputs from at least two semi-trusted circuits. In the first case, since with probability 2^{-t} there is at least one good evaluated garbled circuit, that single output is the correct one. In case there are two different outputs, the receiver initiates the *cheating recovery process*: Say that gc_i's output is 0 and $gc_{i'}$'s output is 1 (and both are semi-trusted). From evaluating gc_i, the receiver learns $l_{i,0}$, and from the sender's message, it learns $w_0 + l_{i,0}$. Thus, it can recover w_0. Similarly, from $gc_{i'}$ it recovers w_1. Having $w = w_0 + w_1$ allows the receiver to decrypt the input-commitments, and recover the sender's input as needed. Note that in case the sender is honest, the receiver would get the same output from all evaluated circuits, and thus would learn only one of w_0 and w_1.

When there are more than one output wire, different w_0, w_1 are chosen for each output wire, thus the receiver learns one value from each pair. See Section 4 for a detailed description of the protocol.

2 Preliminaries: Notations and Primitives

Let $\mathsf{Hash}(\cdot)$ be a collision resistant hash function, $\mathsf{REHash}(\cdot)$ be a collision-resistant hash function that is a suitable randomness extractor (e.g., see [DGH+04]), $\mathsf{Commit}(\cdot)$ be a commitment scheme, and let $\mathsf{Enc}(k, m)$ be the symmetric encryption of message m under key k.

Garbled Circuits. Our protocol is based on the garbled circuit protocol of Yao [Yao86] and can work with any garbling scheme (see [LP09, BHR12] and the full version of this paper more details). We only require that the labels of the output-wires reveal the actual outputs of the circuit (but still consist of

---

[2] Clearly, since P_2 knows w_0, w_1, $h_0 g^{l_{i,0}}$ does not bind P_2 to h_0. Rather, it binds P_2 to $w_0 + l_{i,0}$.

random strings). We use the notation $\mathsf{label}(gc, j, b)$ to denote the label of wire j corresponding to bit value b in the garbled circuit

Commitments with Efficient Proof-of-Equality and Trapdoor. We use a commitment scheme that allows one to efficiently prove that two commitments are for the same bit, without revealing any information about the committed bit. Also, we require the commitment scheme to have a "trapdoor" that allows extracting the committed value.

A commitment that satisfies our requirement can be based on ElGamal. Given finite group $\mathcal{G}$ and a generator g, the committer picks a random element $h \in \mathcal{G}$, and sends $\mathsf{EGCommit}(h, m, r) = (g^r, h^r g^m)$. This commitment is computationally-hiding (under the DDH assumption) and perfectly-binding. Given $\mathsf{EGCommit}(h, m, r)$ and $\mathsf{EGCommit}(h, m, r')$, the commiter can prove equality by giving $r - r'$. Last, given the "trapdoor" $\log_g(h)$, one can decrypt the commitment, $\mathsf{EGCommit}(h, m, r)$, and recover m.

Batch Committing-OT. Batch committing-OT protocol is an OT protocol where the sender has two tuples of inputs $[K_1^0, K_2^0, \ldots, K_t^0]$, $[K_1^1, K_2^1, \ldots, K_t^1]$. The receiver has a bit b and wishes to learn the tuple $[K_1^b, K_2^b, \ldots, K_t^b]$.

We use a variant of the batch committing-OT protocol of [SS11] (which is based on the highly efficient one-round, UC-secure OT of [PVW08]). The protocol is secure under the DDH assumption. Let $\mathcal{G}$ be a group of prime order p in which the DDH assumption is assumed to hold, and let (g_0, g_1, h_0, h_1) be a common reference string (CRS) where g_0, g_1, h_0, h_1 are random elements in $\mathcal{G}$. The receiver picks $r \in \mathbb{Z}_p$ at random and sends $g = (g_b)^r, h = (h_b)^r$ to the sender. For $i = 1 \ldots t$ and $b' \in \{0, 1\}$, the sender picks at random $r_{i,b'}, s_{i,b'} \in \mathbb{Z}_p$ and sends $X_{i,b'} = g_{b'}^{r_{i,b'}} h_{b'}^{s_{i,b'}}$ and $Y_{i,b'} = g^{r_{i,b'}} h^{s_{i,b'}} K_i^{b'}$. For $i = 1 \ldots t$, the receiver retrieves $K_i^b = Y_{i,b}/X_{i,b}^r$.

After executing the above protocol, if the receiver asks the sender to reveal both its inputs K_i^0, K_i^1 for some i, the sender returns the values $K_i^0, K_i^1, r_{i,0}, s_{i,0}, r_{i,1}, s_{i,1}$ and the receiver verifies that the values $X_{i,0}, Y_{i,0}, X_{i,1}, Y_{i,1}$ that it received were properly constructed using these values.

For simplicity and generality, in our NISC protocols we denote by $\mathsf{COT}_1(b)$ the first message that is sent (from the receiver to the sender) in an invocation of the committing-OT protocol for the receiver's input bit b, and similarly denote the second message (that is sent from the sender to the receiver) by $\mathsf{COT}_2([K_1^0, K_2^0, \ldots, K_t^0], [K_1^1, K_2^1, \ldots, K_t^1], \mathsf{COT}_1(b))$.

In the full version of this paper we give further details about the security of this protocol, and discuss the CRS in case there are many invocations of MS-NISC with different senders.

3   The NISC Model

The OS-NISC notion is essentially like 2PC with one round of interaction, thus the security definition is exactly as for multi-round 2PC (e.g., [Gol04]), with the additional restriction on the number of rounds in the real execution.

For defining MS-NISC, we use the ideal/real paradigm (in the standalone setting), and use the ideal functionality from Figure 1. See the full version of this paper for a formal definition. Throughout this work we assume that senders cannot see or tamper with other senders' messages to avoid malleability concerns. In the full version of this paper we discuss how to correctly encrypt those messages if this is not the case. (Note that in many applications there is only one sender and then malleability is not an issue. E.g., if the sender is a satellite that sends messages periodically. In this case there is only one sender that sends many messages, and no malleability issues occur.)

Assume that $f(\bot, \cdot) = f(\cdot, \bot) = \bot$.

- Initialize a list L of pairs of strings.
- Upon receiving a message (input, x) from P_1, store x and continue as following:
  - Upon receiving a message (input, y) from P_i, insert the pair (P_i, y) to L. If P_1 is corrupted, send $(P_i, f(x, y))$ to the adversary. Else, send (messageReceived, P_i) to P_1.
  - Upon receiving a message (getOutputs) from P_1, send $\left(\left\{ (P_i, f(x, y)) \right\}_{(P_i, y) \in L} \right)$ to P_1, and halt.

Fig. 1. MS-NISC functionality $\mathcal{F}$

4   An OS-NISC/MS-NISC Protocol

The protocol is in the CRS (common reference string) model, which is a necessary requirement for the one-round OT protocol that we use [PVW08]. (Unlike other results that are presented in the OT-hybrid model, we use this specific OT protocol which is currently the most efficient fully-secure, simulation-proven OT. We preferred to use a concrete instantiation of OT in order to be able to use a committing variant of OT, in which the OT sender is committed to its OT inputs after it sends its OT message. Still, our techniques can be used with any committing-OT protocol that is proved secure using simulation and that can be executed concurrently without sacrificing security.) Since the nature of NISC is mostly for indirect communication (e.g, using a Facebook wall), we favor a solution that has a minimal communication overhead.

For high level description of the protocol, we refer the reader to Section 1.2. The detailed protocol is described in Figures 2-4. Its concrete efficiency analysis and proof of the following theorem are in the full version of this paper.

Theorem 1. *Assume that the Decisional Diffie-Hellman problem is hard in the group $\mathcal{G}$ and that* PRF, REHash, Commit *and* Enc *are secure. Then, the protocol of Figures 2-4 is a multi-sender non-interactive secure computation for any function $f : \{0,1\}^{n_1} \times \{0,1\}^{n_2} \to \{0,1\}^m$ computable in polynomial time. The complexity of the protocol is $\mathcal{O}(t(n_1 + n_2 + m))$ expensive operations and $\mathcal{O}(t(n_1 + n_2 + m + |C|))$ inexpensive operations.*

The protocol is described for a single sender. When there are more senders (or one with several inputs), each sender executes the steps that are described below for P_2.

Preliminaries: As defined in Section 2, we denote by $\mathsf{COT}_1()$ the first message sent in an invocation of the committing-OT protocol, and denote the second message of that protocol as $\mathsf{COT}_2()$. Also, denote by $\mathsf{EGCommit}(h; b, r)$ the ElGamal commitment (which supports an efficient proof-of-equality) to bit b. Let $\mathcal{G}$ be a group of size p with generator g.

Inputs: P_1 has input x and P_2 has input y. Let $f : \{0,1\}^{n_1} \times \{0,1\}^{n_2} \to \{0,1\}^m$ be the function of interest and let $C(x,y)$ be a circuit that computes f. The input wires of P_1 and P_2 are denoted by the sets $\mathrm{IN}_c(1)$ and $\mathrm{IN}_c(2)$, respectively. The output wires are denoted by the set OUT_c.

P_1's message:

- Picks a random t-bit string where t_i denotes the i-th bit of this string. We define T such that $i \in T$ if and only if $t_i = 1$.
- For all circuits $i \in [t]$ publishes $\mathsf{COT}_1(t_i)$. Denote these as the *circuit-OT* queries.
- For all inputs $j \in \mathrm{IN}_c(1)$ publishes $\mathsf{COT}_1(x_j)$, where x_j is P_1's input bit for the j-th input wire. Denote these as the *input-OT* queries.

Fig. 2. The OS-NISC/MS-NISC Protocol: Preliminaries and P_1's message

5   Reducing the Communication Overhead

Goyal et al. [GMS08] suggest a method that significantly reduces the communication overhead of 2PC protocols based on cut-and-choose. In their protocol, as in ours, P_2 picks a different seed for each garbled circuit and uses a pseudorandom function, keyed with that seed, to generate all the randomness needed for garbling that circuit. P_2 does not send the circuits to P_1 but only "commits" to them by sending the hash of each circuit. Then, when P_2 is asked to open a subset of the circuits, it sends to P_1 the seeds used for constructing these circuits, as well as the actual garbled tables of the evaluated circuits. P_1 uses the seeds to reconstruct the checked circuits and verify that they agree with the desired functionality and with the hashes that were sent in the initial step (the hashes are computed with a collision resistant hash function $\mathsf{Hash}(\cdot)$ and therefore prevent a circuit from being changed after its hash is received).

Trying to apply this modification in the NISC setting encounters a major obstacle: In order for P_2 to send only the gates of the evaluated circuits, it must learn, based on P_1's first message, which circuits are evaluated. Since P_2 learns this information before it sends any message to P_1, it is able to set its evaluated and checked circuits in a way that fools P_1's checks.

When Communication Is through a Third-Party Service. A simple solution can be based on the observation that in many applications of NISC the communication channel is actually implemented through a third-party service, e.g., a Facebook wall. In those cases, P_2 could upload *all* circuits to the service, along with their hash values. Then, P_1 downloads only the circuits for evaluation and the hashes of all circuits. Assuming that the service hides from P_2 which

Non-Interactive Secure Computation Based on Cut-and-Choose   399

- Picks $w \in_R \mathbb{Z}_p$ and sends $h = g^w$. Here, w would be the "trapdoor" to P_2's inputs.
- Sends $\mathsf{EGCommit}(h; y_j, r_j)$, for all $j \in \mathrm{IN}_c(2)$, where y_j is its input bit for input-wire j, and r_j is chosen randomly. We call these the *input-commitments*.
- Sends $h_{j,0} = g^{w_{j,0}}$ and $h_{j,1} = g^{w_{j,1}}$, where $w_{j,0} \in_R \mathbb{Z}_p$ and $w_{j,1} = w - w_{j,0}$, for all output wires $j \in \mathrm{OUT}_c$. We call these the *output-commitments*.
  For all $i \in [t]$,
  Generate garbled circuit:
    - Picks a random value $seed_i$.
    - Computes $u_{i,j,b} = \mathsf{EGCommit}(h; b, r_{i,j,b})$ for all $j \in \mathrm{IN}_c(2)$ and $b \in \{0,1\}$, where $r_{i,j,b} = \mathsf{PRF}_{seed_i}(\text{``}EGCommitment\text{''} \circ j \circ b)$.
    - Sends the garbled circuit gc_i, which is generated using a pseudo-random function PRF_{seed_i} in the following way:
      * For all $j \in \mathrm{IN}_c(2)$ and $b \in \{0,1\}$, let $\mathsf{label}(gc_i, j, b) = \mathsf{REHash}(u_{i,j,b})$. Namely, the label for bit b of the jth wire is associated with the value of $\mathsf{EGCommit}(h; b, \cdot)$ computed with randomness that is the output of a PRF keyed by $seed_i$. Note that given $u_{i,j,b}$, P_1 can compute $\mathsf{REHash}(u_{i,j,b})$ by itself and get the corresponding label.
      * The garbled circuit is constructed in a standard way, where all other labels in the circuit are generated by a PRF keyed by $seed_i$. (E.g., the 0-label of wire j is $\mathsf{PRF}_{seed_i}(\text{``}label\text{''} \circ j \circ 0)$.)
    - Sends the set of commitments $\{[\mathsf{Commit}(u_{i,j,\pi_{i,j}}), \mathsf{Commit}(u_{i,j,1-\pi_{i,j}})] \mid \pi_{i,j} \in_R \{0,1\}\}_{j \in \mathrm{IN}_c(2)}$. The randomness of the commitments is derived from a PRF keyed by $seed_i$ as well. Denote by $du_{i,j,b}$ the decommitment of $u_{i,j,b}$.
  Preparing and sending the cheating recovery box:
  Sends the cheating recovery box, for all output wires $j \in \mathrm{OUT}_c$, which includes:
    - Two *output recovery commitments* $h_{j,0} g^{K_{i,j,0}}, h_{j,1} g^{K_{i,j,1}}$, where $K_{i,j,0}, K_{i,j,1} \in_R \mathbb{Z}_p$.
    - Two encryptions $\mathsf{Enc}(\mathsf{label}(gc_i, j, 0), K_{i,j,0}), \mathsf{Enc}(\mathsf{label}(gc_i, j, 1), K_{i,j,1})$. (Note that given $\mathsf{label}(gc_i, j, b)$, one can recompute $h_{j,0} g^{K_{i,j,b}}$.)
  Preparing and sending proofs of consistency:
    - Let $inputs_i$ be the set $\{u_{i,j,y_j}, du_{i,j,y_j}\}_{j \in \mathrm{IN}_c(2)}$, and let $inputsEquality_i$ be the set $\{r_j - r_{i,j,y_j}\}_{j \in \mathrm{IN}_c(2)}$ (namely, P_2's input labels and their proof of equality with the input-commitments).
    - Let $outputDecom_i$ be the set $\{([w_{j,0} + K_{i,j,0}], [w_{j,1} + K_{i,j,1}])\}_{j \in \mathrm{OUT}_c}$ (namely, the discrete logarithms of $h_{j,0} g^{K_{i,j,0}}$ and $h_{j,0} g^{K_{i,j,1}}$).
    - Picks a random key k_i and sends the encryption $\mathsf{Enc}(k_i, inputs_i \circ inputsEquality_i \circ outputDecom_i)$.
  Sending the garbled values of P_1's inputs:
  Let $inp\text{-}q_j$ be the input-OT query for input-wire j of P_1. P_2 sends the OT answer, which includes the garbled values of either the 0 or 1 labels for the corresponding input wire. Namely, it sends the value $\mathsf{COT}_2([\mathsf{label}(gc_1, j, 0), \ldots, \mathsf{label}(gc_t, j, 0)], [\mathsf{label}(gc_1, j, 1), \ldots, \mathsf{label}(gc_t, j, 1)], inp\text{-}q_j)$. Moreover, we require that all the randomness used in the OT for the answers of the i-th circuit is generated from PRF_{seed_i}. (E.g., set $r_{i,1}$ of the j-th wire of the i-th circuit to be $\mathsf{PRF}_{seed_i}(\text{``}OT\text{''} \circ 1 \circ \text{``}r\text{''} \circ i \circ j)$.)
  Circuits cut-and-choose:
  Let $circ\text{-}q_i$ be the circuit-OT query for circuit i, P_2 sends $\mathsf{COT}_2([k_i], [seed_i], circ\text{-}q_i)$. Namely P_1 receives $seed_i$ if it asked to open this circuit, and k_i if it is about to evaluate the circuit.

Fig. 3. The OS-NISC/MS-NISC Protocol: P_2's response

After receiving responses from all senders, P_1 processes all of them together and outputs a vector of outputs. For each response it does the following:

- Decrypts all OT answers.
- Verifies that $h_{j,0} \cdot h_{j,1} = h$ for all $j \in \text{OUT}_c$.
- For all opened circuits $i \in T$, checks that $seed_i$ indeed correctly generates gc_i (with its commitments), and the answers of the input-OT queries. (Otherwise, it aborts processing this response.) It also checks the cheating recovery boxes and aborts if there is a problem.
- For all circuits $i \in [t] \setminus T$, decrypts $\text{inputs}_i, \text{inputsEquality}_i, \text{outputDecom}_i$.
  - Checks that inputs_i and inputsEquality_i are consistent with the input-commitments. (I.e., checks that $u_{i,j,y_j} \cdot (g^{r_i - r_{i,j,y_j}}, h^{r_i - r_{i,j,y_j}}) = \text{EGCommit}(h; y_j, r_j)$). Also, verifies the decommitments du_{i,j,y_j}. (Otherwise, it aborts.)
  - Checks that outputDecom_i are correct discrete-logs of the elements of the set $\left\{ h_{j,b} g^{K_{i,j,b}} \right\}_{j \in \text{OUT}_c, b \in \{0,1\}}$. (Otherwise, it aborts.)
  - Evaluates circuit gc_i. Say that it learns the labels $\{l_{i,j}\}_{j \in \text{OUT}_c}$. P_1 tries to use these labels to decrypt the corresponding encryptions $\text{Enc}(\text{label}(gc_i, j, b), K_{i,j,b})$ from the cheating recovery box. Then, it checks if the result is a correct "decommitment" of the output recovery commitment $h_{j,b} g^{K_{i,j,b}}$ (where the b values are the actual output bits it received from gc_i). If all these steps pass correctly for all output wires, we say that circuit gc_i is *semi-trusted*.
- If the outputs of all semi-trusted circuits are the same, P_1 outputs that output. Otherwise,
  - Let $gc_i, gc_{i'}$ be two semi-trusted circuits that have different output in the jth output wire, and let $l_{i,j}$ and $l_{i',j}$ be their output labels. From one of $l_{i,j}$ and $l_{i',j}$, P_1 learns $w_{j,0}$ and from the other value it learns $w_{j,1}$ (since it learns $K_{i,j,b}, K_{i',j,1-b}$ from the cheating recovery boxes, and $w_{j,b} + K_{i,j,b}, w_{j,1-b} + K_{i',j,1-b}$ from $\text{outputDecom}_i, \text{outputDecom}_{i'}$).
  - P_1 computes $w = w_{j,0} + w_{j,1}$ and decrypts P_2's input-commitments. Let y be the decrypted value of P_2's input.
  - P_1 outputs $f(x, y)$.

Fig. 4. The OS-NISC/MS-NISC Protocol: P_1's computation

circuits were actually downloaded by P_1, the result is secure, and the communication of P_1 and of the service (but not of P_2) depends only on the number of evaluated circuits.

A More General Solution. We describe a solution that does not depend on any third party. The solution requires that the number of evaluated circuits is known to P_2 (e.g., for soundness 2^{-40} the players can use 44 circuits and evaluate 19 of them. Communication would roughly be the size of 19 garbled circuits.)

The protocol is based on the usage of erasure codes, and in particular of polynomials. Say that P_2 garbles t circuits and that P_1 evaluates ct of them for some known constant $c < 1$. Also, let b be some convenient block length and denote the number of blocks in the description of a garbled circuit by l. P_2 garbles the t circuits, and then computes l polynomials $p_1(\cdot), p_2(\cdot), \ldots, p_l(\cdot)$

such that $p_j(i)$ equals to the j-th block of garbled circuit gc_i. The degree of each polynomial is $t-1$. Then, for each polynomial p_i, P_2 sends to P_1 ct values, $\langle p_i(t+1), p_i(t+2), \ldots, p_i(t+ct) \rangle$. It also sends to P_1 hashes of all garbled circuits. P_1 then picks the $(1-c)t$ circuits that it wishes to check, and receives from P_2 the PRF seeds that were used for generating them. Using these seeds, P_1 reconstructs the checked garbled circuits, checks that they agree with the hash values and validates their structure. Afterwards, P_1 uses polynomial interpolation to recover the polynomials $p_1(\cdot), p_2(\cdot), \ldots, p_l(\cdot)$. Using these polynomials it retrieves the garbled circuits that it chose to evaluate, verifies that they agree with the hash values that P_1 has sent, and continues with the protocol.

The main advantage of this technique is that it enables to reduce communication even without knowing P_1's challenge. The overall communication overhead of this method is as the size of the ct evaluated circuits, which matches the communication overhead of [GMS08], but allows us to use this technique in the NISC setting. The proof of security of the resulting protocol is almost identical to the proof of Theorem 1 (except that the hash is also checked by the simulator) and therefore omitted.

6   Evaluation

Prototype Implementation. Our prototype consists of several modules which communicate through files (for making the protocol suitable for asynchronous communication mechanisms like e-mail). It does not use the communication reduction techniques of Section 5. The prototype makes use of several libraries, namely RELIC-Toolkit [AG], JustGarble [BHKR13], and OpenSSL [OPE]. Relic-toolkit is chosen for its fast and efficient implementation of elliptic curve operations and is used to implement our OT and ElGamal based commitments. We use the binary curve B-251, which (roughly) provides 124-bit security. (Computing a single elliptic curve multiplication, which corresponds to a single exponentiation in our protocol, costs about 120,103 CPU cycles for a fixed base and 217,378 cycles for a general base.) JustGarble is chosen for its fast implementation of garbling and evaluating circuits. ([BHKR13] advocates using fixed-key AES as a cryptographic permutation, and its implementation takes advantage of the AES-NI instruction set.) We modified JustGarble to read the circuit format of [TS], and read/write garbled circuits from/to a file (and not only the circuit structure). Lastly, we use the AES implementation from OpenSSL, to realize a PRF.

The Setup. To evaluate our prototype we used two circuits, one for AES with non-expanded key (with 8,492 non-XOR gates and 25,124 XOR gates) and one for SHA256 (with 194,083 non-XOR gates and 42,029 XOR gates). The circuits were taken from [TS] (and slightly modified). In both circuits, each party has a 128 bit input value. The output of the AES circuit is 128 bit long, while SHA256 has a 256 bit output.

The experiments were run on a virtual Linux machine with a 64bit, i7-4650U CPU @ 1.70GHz and 5.4GB of RAM. (For a more accurate comparison, our code utilizes only a single core of the CPU. The average CPU frequency during the experiments was about 2.3GHz.) We measured clock cycles of each module of the system using the RDTSC instruction, and used the clock_gettime() system function to calculate the running time. Each experiment was run 10 times and the average run time was calculated in both cycles and seconds.

Performance. The experiments were done with statistical security parameter $t = 40$ and label length of 128 bits. Garbling was performed with the Free-XOR [KS08] and Garbled Row Reduction [PSSW09] techniques. (We also tested the protocol without those techniques. The results were slower by at most 10%.)

See Figure 5 for the running times of the main parts of our prototype. (Recall that when interacting with more than one sender, the receiver P_1 has to generate the first message only once. Then, for each sender, its running time will be similar to the time it takes it to process the sender's response in the single sender scenario that we examined.) The values represented in Figure 5 contain all operations, including I/O handling.

Observe that as the circuit size grows, the I/O portion becomes significant. For example, for the AES circuit, where every garbled circuit was stored in a 3 MB file, the total I/O time for the protocol is 0.53 seconds, whereas for the SHA256 circuit, where each circuit is stored in a 31 MB file, the total I/O time is 4.89 seconds. (For AES the I/O time was about 8% of the total time, whereas for SHA256 it was around 38% of the total time. This is expected since both functions have inputs of the same size, while the SHA256 circuit is much bigger.) The costs of garbling and evaluation of a garbled circuit are quite small (e.g., garbling takes less than 100 million cycles for the SHA256 circuit). The more significant overhead comes from I/O operations and the exponentiations done in the protocol.

In addition, we ran the experiment for AES with t=80 and got, as expected, that the costs are roughly twice those of the experiment with t=40. (Specifically, with t=80, it takes P_1 78 million cycles to compute its message, 16,518 million cycles for P_2 to compute its response, and 12,870 million cycles for P_1 to compute the output).

Module or part name	#Cycles	Time	#Cycles	Time
	AES circuit		SHA256 circuit	
Init	42	0.02	44	0.02
P_1's message	71	0.03	73	0.03
P_2's response	8216	3.55	17651	7.59
P_1's computation	6452	2.79	11771	5.10
Cheating recovery	0.7	< 0.01	0.7	< 0.01
Total time	-	6.39	-	12.74
I/O time	-	0.53	-	4.89

Fig. 5. Running times for the prototype with statistical security parameter $t = 40$ and label length $= 128$. Time is in seconds and cycles are measured in millions of cycles. Running times include file operations.

Due to lack of space, a comparison with previous multi-round 2PC implementations appears in the full version of this paper. We note here that although there is no standard benchmark for comparing 2PC implementations, it is clear that our NISC implementation is competitive with the best known interactive implementations.

Acknowledgements. The fourth author would like to thank Ran Canetti for helpful comments about this work, and to Yuval Ishai for introducing him to the work of [IKO+11]. We thank an anonymous EUROCRYPT reviewer for suggesting a simplification of the cheating-recovery commitments.

References

[AG]   Aranha, D.F., Gouvêa, C.P.L.: RELIC is an Efficient LIbrary for Cryptography, http://code.google.com/p/relic-toolkit/

[BHKR13]   Bellare, M., Hoang, V.T., Keelveedhi, S., Rogaway, P.: Efficient garbling from a fixed-key blockcipher. In: IEEE S&P (2013)

[BHR12]   Bellare, M., Hoang, V.T., Rogaway, P.: Foundations of garbled circuits. In: CCS, pp. 784–796. ACM (2012)

[CCKM00]   Cachin, C., Camenisch, J.L., Kilian, J., Müller, J.: One-round secure computation and secure autonomous mobile agents. In: Welzl, E., Montanari, U., Rolim, J.D.P. (eds.) ICALP 2000. LNCS, vol. 1853, pp. 512–523. Springer, Heidelberg (2000)

[DGH+04]   Dodis, Y., Gennaro, R., Håstad, J., Krawczyk, H., Rabin, T.: Randomness extraction and key derivation using the cbc, cascade and hmac modes. In: Franklin, M. (ed.) CRYPTO 2004. LNCS, vol. 3152, pp. 494–510. Springer, Heidelberg (2004)

[GMS08]   Goyal, V., Mohassel, P., Smith, A.: Efficient two party and multi party computation against covert adversaries. In: Smart, N.P. (ed.) EUROCRYPT 2008. LNCS, vol. 4965, pp. 289–306. Springer, Heidelberg (2008)

[Gol04]   Goldreich, O.: Foundations of Cryptography: vol. 2, Basic Applications. Cambridge University Press, New York (2004)

[HK07]   Horvitz, O., Katz, J.: Universally-composable two-party computation in two rounds. In: Menezes, A. (ed.) CRYPTO 2007. LNCS, vol. 4622, pp. 111–129. Springer, Heidelberg (2007)

[IKO+11]   Ishai, Y., Kushilevitz, E., Ostrovsky, R., Prabhakaran, M., Sahai, A.: Efficient non-interactive secure computation. In: Paterson, K.G. (ed.) EUROCRYPT 2011. LNCS, vol. 6632, pp. 406–425. Springer, Heidelberg (2011)

[IPS08]   Ishai, Y., Prabhakaran, M., Sahai, A.: Founding cryptography on oblivious transfer – efficiently. In: Wagner, D. (ed.) CRYPTO 2008. LNCS, vol. 5157, pp. 572–591. Springer, Heidelberg (2008)

[KMR12]   Kamara, S., Mohassel, P., Riva, B.: Salus: a system for server-aided secure function evaluation. In: CCS, pp. 797–808. ACM (2012)

[KS06]   Kiraz, M.S., Schoenmakers, B.: A protocol issue for the malicious case of yaos garbled circuit construction. In: Proceedings of 27th Symposium on Information Theory in the Benelux, pp. 283–290 (2006)

[KS08]   Kolesnikov, V., Schneider, T.: Improved garbled circuit: Free XOR gates and applications. In: Aceto, L., Damgård, I., Goldberg, L.A., Halldórsson, M.M., Ingólfsdóttir, A., Walukiewicz, I. (eds.) ICALP 2008, Part II. LNCS, vol. 5126, pp. 486–498. Springer, Heidelberg (2008)

[KSS12]   Kreuter, B., Shelat, A., Shen, C.-H.: Billion-gate secure computation with malicious adversaries. In: USENIX Security, p. 14 (2012)

[Lin13]   Lindell, Y.: Fast cut-and-choose based protocols for malicious and covert adversaries. In: Canetti, R., Garay, J.A. (eds.) CRYPTO 2013, Part II. LNCS, vol. 8043, pp. 1–17. Springer, Heidelberg (2013)

[LP07]   Lindell, Y., Pinkas, B.: An efficient protocol for secure two-party computation in the presence of malicious adversaries. In: Naor, M. (ed.) EUROCRYPT 2007. LNCS, vol. 4515, pp. 52–78. Springer, Heidelberg (2007)

[LP09]   Lindell, Y., Pinkas, B.: A proof of security of Yao's protocol for two-party computation. J. Cryptol. 22(2), 161–188 (2009)

[LP11]   Lindell, Y., Pinkas, B.: Secure two-party computation via cut-and-choose oblivious transfer. In: Ishai, Y. (ed.) TCC 2011. LNCS, vol. 6597, pp. 329–346. Springer, Heidelberg (2011)

[MF06]   Mohassel, P., Franklin, M.K.: Efficiency tradeoffs for malicious two-party computation. In: Yung, M., Dodis, Y., Kiayias, A., Malkin, T. (eds.) PKC 2006. LNCS, vol. 3958, pp. 458–473. Springer, Heidelberg (2006)

[MR13]   Mohassel, P., Riva, B.: Garbled circuits checking garbled circuits: More efficient and secure two-party computation. In: Canetti, R., Garay, J.A. (eds.) CRYPTO 2013, Part II. LNCS, vol. 8043, pp. 36–53. Springer, Heidelberg (2013)

[NNOB12]   Nielsen, J.B., Nordholt, P.S., Orlandi, C., Burra, S.S.: A new approach to practical active-secure two-party computation. In: Safavi-Naini, R., Canetti, R. (eds.) CRYPTO 2012. LNCS, vol. 7417, pp. 681–700. Springer, Heidelberg (2012)

[OPE]   OpenSSL: The open source toolkit for SSL/TLS, http://www.openssl.org

[Ped92]   Pedersen, T.P.: Non-interactive and information-theoretic secure verifiable secret sharing. In: Feigenbaum, J. (ed.) CRYPTO 1991. LNCS, vol. 576, pp. 129–140. Springer, Heidelberg (1992)

[PSSW09]   Pinkas, B., Schneider, T., Smart, N.P., Williams, S.C.: Secure two-party computation is practical. In: Matsui, M. (ed.) ASIACRYPT 2009. LNCS, vol. 5912, pp. 250–267. Springer, Heidelberg (2009)

[PVW08]   Peikert, C., Vaikuntanathan, V., Waters, B.: A framework for efficient and composable oblivious transfer. In: Wagner, D. (ed.) CRYPTO 2008. LNCS, vol. 5157, pp. 554–571. Springer, Heidelberg (2008)

[SS11]   Shelat, A., Shen, C.-H.: Two-output secure computation with malicious adversaries. In: Paterson, K.G. (ed.) EUROCRYPT 2011. LNCS, vol. 6632, pp. 386–405. Springer, Heidelberg (2011)

[SS13]   Shelat, A., Shen, C.-H.: Fast two-party secure computation with minimal assumptions. In: CCS, pp. 523–534. ACM (2013)

[TS]   Tillich, S., Smart, N.: Circuits of Basic Functions Suitable For MPC and FHE, http://www.cs.bris.ac.uk/Research/CryptographySecurity/MPC/

[Yao86]   Yao, A.C.-C.: How to generate and exchange secrets. In: SFCS, pp. 162–167. IEEE Computer Society (1986)

Garbled RAM Revisited

Craig Gentry[1], Shai Halevi[1], Steve Lu[2], Rafail Ostrovsky[2],
Mariana Raykova[3,*], and Daniel Wichs[4,**]

[1] IBM Research
[2] UCLA
[3] SRI
[4] Northeastern University

Abstract. The notion of *garbled random-access machines* (garbled RAMs) was introduced by Lu and Ostrovsky (Eurocrypt 2013). It can be seen as an analogue of Yao's garbled circuits, that allows a user to garble a RAM program directly, without performing the expensive step of converting it into a circuit. In particular, the size of the garbled program and the time it takes to create and evaluate it are only proportional to its running time on a RAM rather than its circuit size. Lu and Ostrovsky gave a candidate construction of this primitive based on pseudo-random functions (PRFs).

The starting point of this work is pointing out a subtle circularity hardness assumption in the Lu-Ostrovsky construction. Specifically, the construction requires a complex "circular" security assumption on the underlying Yao garbled circuits and PRFs. We then proceed to abstract, simplify and generalize the main ideas behind the Lu-Ostrovsky construction, and show two alternatives constructions that overcome the circularity of assumptions. Our first construction breaks the circularity by replacing the PRF-based encryption in the Lu-Ostrovsky construction by *identity-based encryption (IBE)*. The result retains the same asymptotic performance characteristics of the original Lu-Ostrovsky construction, namely overhead of $O(\mathsf{poly}(\kappa)\mathsf{polylog}(n))$ (with κ the security parameter and n the data size). Our second construction breaks the circularity assuming only the existence of one way functions, but with overhead $O(\mathsf{poly}(\kappa)n^\varepsilon)$ for any constant $\varepsilon > 0$. This construction works by adaptively "revoking" the PRFs at selected points, and using a delicate recursion argument to get successively better performance characteristics. It remains as an interesting open problem to achieve an overhead of $\mathsf{poly}(\kappa)\mathsf{polylog}(n)$ assuming only the existence of one-way functions.

1 Introduction

Garbled Circuits. Since their introduction by Yao [19], garbled circuits have found countless applications in cryptography, most notably for secure computation. On a basic level, garbled circuits allow a user to convert a circuit C into

---

* Research conducted in part while at IBM Research.
** Research conducted in part while visiting IBM Research.

P.Q. Nguyen and E. Oswald (Eds.): EUROCRYPT 2014, LNCS 8441, pp. 405–422, 2014.
ⓒ International Association for Cryptologic Research 2014

a garbled version $\tilde{C}$ and an input x into a garbled version $\tilde{x}$, so that $\tilde{C}$ can be evaluated on $\tilde{x}$ to reveal the output $C(x)$, but nothing else is revealed. As with most secure computation protocols, this technique crucially works at the level of "circuits" and the first step toward using it is to convert a desired program into a circuit representation.

Circuits vs. RAMs. Converting a program into a circuit often presents a major source of inefficiency. We naturally think of programs in the the *random-access machine* (RAM) model of computation. It is known that a RAM with run-time T can be converted into a Turing Machine with run-time $O(T^3)$ which can in turn be converted into the circuit of size $O(T^3 \log T)$ [8,16]. This is a significant amount of overhead. Perhaps an even more striking efficiency loss occurs in the setting of "big data", where the data is given in random-access memory. In this case, efficient programs can run in time which is sub-linear in the size of the data (e.g., binary search), but converting any such a program into a circuit representation incurs a cost which is (at the very least) linear in the size of the data. This exponential gap can mean the difference between an efficient Internet search and having to read the entire Internet!

Garbled RAMs. Motivated by the above considerations, Lu and Ostrovsky [14] proposed the notion of a *garbled RAM*, whose goal is to garble a RAM program directly without first converting it into a circuit. In particular, the size of the garbled program as well as the evaluation time should only be proportional to the running-time of the program on a RAM (up to poly-logarithmic factors), rather than the size of its circuit representation.

In more detail, we will use the notation $P^D(x)$ to denote the execution of some program P with random-access memory initially containing some data D and a "short" input x (e.g., P could be some complex query over a database D with search-terms x). A garbled RAM scheme can be used to garble the data D into $\tilde{D}$, the program P into $\tilde{P}$, and the input x into $\tilde{x}$ in such a way that $\tilde{P}, \tilde{D}, \tilde{x}$ reveals $P^D(x)$, but nothing else is revealed. Furthermore, the size of the garbled data $\tilde{D}$ is only proportional to that of D, the size of $\tilde{x}$ is only proportional to that of x, and the size and evaluation-time of the garbled program $\tilde{P}$ are only proportional to the run-time of $P^D(x)$ on a RAM.

Lu and Ostrovsky proposed a construction of garbled RAMs, relying on a clever use of Yao garbled circuits and oblivious RAM (ORAM), and using for security only pseudo-random functions (PRFs) (which can be constructed from any one-way function).

A Circularity Problem. It turns out that the Lu-Ostrovsky construction has a subtle yet difficult-to-overcome issue that prevents a proof of security from going through, in that it requires a complex "circular" use of Yao garbled circuits and PRF-based encryption. To understand the issue, recall that Yao garbled circuits assign two labels for each wire, corresponding to bits $0, 1$, and security relies heavily on the evaluator only learning one of these two labels. The Lu-Ostrovsky construction provides encryptions of *both* labels of an input wire w, under some secret-key K, and this secret key K is also hard-coded into the description of the circuit itself. This introduces the following circularity: to use the security of the encryption scheme we must rely on the security of the garbled circuit to hide the key K, but to use the security of the garbled circuit we must rely on the security of the encryption scheme so that the attacker cannot learn *both* wire labels. We emphasize that we do not have a concrete attack on the construction of Lu and Ostrovsky, and it may even seem reasonable to conjecture its security when instantiated with real-world primitives (e.g., AES). Unfortunately, we don't see much hope for proving the security of the scheme under standard assumptions. One could draw an analogy to other "subtle" difficulties in cryptography such as circular security [5,17], selective-opening security [4,2], or adaptively-chosen inputs of garbled circuits [3], where it may be reasonable to assume that standard constructions are secure (and it's a challenge to come up with insecure counterexamples), but it doesn't seem that one can prove security of standard constructions under standard assumptions.

Our Results. In this work we abstracts, simplifies, and generalizes the main ideas behind the Lu-Ostrovsky construction, and give two solutions to the circularity problem. Our first construction essentially replaces the PRF-based encryption in the construction from [14] by *identity-based encryption* (IBE). This breaks the circularity since we only need to embed in the circuit the public key of the IBE, not the secret key. This scheme can be proved secure under the security of the underlying IBE (and garbled circuits), and its overhead is only $\mathsf{poly}(\kappa)\mathsf{polylog}(n)$, where κ is the security parameter and n is the size of the data. (The overhead is measured as the evaluation time of a garbled programs vs. the original program.) This construction is described in detail in [9].

In the second construction, we break the circularity using *revocable PRFs* that enables adaptive revocation of the ability to compute the PRF on certain values.[1] Namely, from a PRF key K and a subset X of the domain, we can construct a weaker key K_X that enables the computation of $F_K(\cdot)$ on all the domain *except for* X, and the values $F_K(x)$ for $x \in X$ are pseudo-random even given K_X. Importantly for our application, we also need successive revocation, i.e. from K_X and some X' we should be able to to generate $K_{X \cup X'}$. Such revocable PRFs can be constructed based on the Goldreich-Goldwasser-Micali [10] PRF, where the size of the key K_X is at most $\kappa \cdot |X| \log N$ (with κ the security parameter and N the domain size).

We use revocable PRFs to break the circularity as follows: whenever we use some $F_K(x)$ in the encryption of the label values on the input wire w, we make sure to embed in the circuit itself not the original key K but rather the weaker key K_X (with $x \in X$), so the encryption remain secure even if K_X is known. A naive use of this technique yields a trivial scheme with overhead $\mathsf{poly}(\kappa) \cdot n$, which is no better than using circuits. However we show how to periodically refresh the keys to reduce the overhead to roughly $\mathsf{poly}(\kappa)\sqrt{n}$, and then use a

---

[1] This notion is similar to punctured PRFs [18], delegatable PRFs [13], functional PRFs [7], and constrained PRFs [6], see more details in Definition 3.

recursive strategy to reduce it further to $\mathsf{poly}(\kappa) \cdot min(t, n^\varepsilon)$ for any constant $\varepsilon > 0$ (where n is the data size and t is the running time). This construction is described in detail in [15].

Reusable/Persistent Data. We also carefully define and prove the security of an important use-case of garbled RAMs, where the garbled memory data can be reused across multiple program executions. If a program updates some location in memory, these changes will persist for future program executions and cannot be "rolled back" by the adversarial evaluator. For example, consider a client that garbles some huge database D and outsources the garbled version $\tilde{D}$ to a remote server. Later, the client can sequentially garble arbitrary database queries so as to allow the server to execute exactly the garbled query on the garbled database but not learn anything else. If the query updates some values in the database, these changes will persist for the future. The running time of the client and server per database query is only proportional to the RAM run-time of the query.[2] Prior to garbled RAMs, this could be done using oblivious RAM (ORAM) but would have required numerous rounds of interaction between the client and the server per database query. With garbled RAMs, the solution becomes non-interactive. This use-case was already envisioned by Lu and Ostrovsky [14], but we proceed to define and analyze it formally.

Worst-Case versus Per-Instance Running Time, Universal Programs, and Output Privacy. As was noted in the CRYPTO 2013 work of Goldwasser et al. [11], the power of secure computation on Turing Machines and RAM programs over that of circuits is that for algorithms with very different worst-case and average-case running times, the circuit must be of worst-case size. Randomized algorithms such as Las Vegas algorithms or even heuristically good-on-average programs would benefit greatly if the online running time of the secure computation ran in time proportional to that particular instance. In our solution, though we have an upper bound T on the number of execution steps of the algorithm which affects the offline time and space, the online evaluation can have a CPU step output "halt" in the clear when the program has halted and the evaluator will then only run in time depending on this particular input.

In order to further mask the program, one can consider a T time-bounded universal program u_T, which takes as input the code of a program π and an input for that program. One can also provide an auxiliary mask so that the output of P is blinded by this value (such a modification has appeared in the literature, see, e.g. [1]).

Organization. We describe our notations for RAM computation and define garbled RAM in Section 2. We then give a high-level description of the Lu-Ostrovsky

---

[2] In contrast to schemes for *outsourcing* computation, the client here does not save on work, but only saves on storage. In particular, only the garbled data $\tilde{D}$ is reusable, but the garbled program $\tilde{P}$ can still only be evaluated on a single garbled input $\tilde{x}$; the client must garble a fresh program for each execution, which requires time proportional to that of the execution.

construction in Section 3, along with an explanation of the "circularity" issue. In Section 4 we present our IBE-based solution, and in Section 5 we describe our solution based on one-way functions.

2   RAM Computation and Garbled RAM

Notation for RAM Computation. Consider a program P that has random-access to a memory of size n, which may initially contain some data $D \in \{0,1\}^n$, and a "short" input x. [3] We use the notation $P^D(x)$ to denote the execution of such program. The program can read/write to various locations in memory throughout the execution. We will also consider the case where several different programs are executed sequentially and the memory persists between executions. We denote this process as $(y_1, \ldots, y_\ell) = (P_1(x_1), \ldots, P_\ell(x_\ell))^D$ to indicate that first $P_1^D(x_1)$ is executed, resulting in some memory contents D_1 and output y_1, then $P_2^{D_1}(x_2)$ is executed resulting in some memory contents D_2 and output y_2 etc. As a useful example to keep in mind throughout this work, imagine that D is a huge database and the programs P_i are database queries that can read and possibly write to the database and are parameterized by some values x_i.

CPU-Step Circuit. A useful representation of a RAM program P is through a small *CPU-Step Circuit* which executes a single CPU step:

$$C_{\mathsf{CPU}}^P(\mathsf{state}, b^{\mathsf{read}}) = (\mathsf{state}', i^{\mathsf{read}}, i^{\mathsf{write}}, b^{\mathsf{write}})$$

This circuit takes as input the current CPU state and a bit b^{read} residing in the the last read memory location. It outputs an updated state', the next location to read $i^{\mathsf{read}} \in [n]$, a location to write to $i^{\mathsf{write}} \in [n] \cup \{\bot\}$ (where $\bot$ values are ignored), a bit b^{write} to write into that location.

The computation $P^D(x)$ starts in the initial state $\mathsf{state}_1 = x$, corresponding to the "short input" and by convention we will set the initial read bit to $b_1^{\mathsf{read}} := 0$. In each step j, the computation proceeds by running $C_{\mathsf{CPU}}^P(\mathsf{state}_j, b_j^{\mathsf{read}}) = (\mathsf{state}_{j+1}, i^{\mathsf{read}}, i^{\mathsf{write}}, b^{\mathsf{write}})$. We first read the requested location i^{read} by setting $b_{j+1}^{\mathsf{read}} := D[i^{\mathsf{read}}]$ and, if $i^{\mathsf{write}} \neq \bot$, we write to the location by setting $D[i^{\mathsf{write}}] := b^{\mathsf{write}}$. The value $y = \mathsf{state}$ output by the last CPU step serves as the output of the computation.

We say that a program P has **read-only** memory access, if it never overwrites any values in memory. In particular, using the above notation, the outputs of C_{CPU}^P always set $i^{\mathsf{write}} = \bot$.

2.1   Defining Garbled RAM

We consider a setting where the memory data D is garbled once, and then many different garbled programs can be executed sequentially with the memory

---

[3] In general, the distinction between what to include in the program P, the memory data D and the short input x can be somewhat arbitrary.

changes persisting from one execution to the next. We stress that each garbled program $\tilde{P}_i$ can only be executed on a *single* garbled input $\tilde{x}_i$. In other words, although the garbled data is reusable and allows for the execution of many programs, the garbled programs are *not* reusable. The programs can only be executed in the specified order and are not "interchangeable". Therefore, they cannot be garbled completely independently. In our case, we will assume that the garbling procedure of each program P_i gets t^{init} which is the total number of CPU steps executed so far by $P_1, \ldots, P_{i-1}$ and t^{cur} which is the number of CPU steps to be executed by P_i.

Syntax and Efficiency. A *garbled RAM* scheme consists of four procedures: (GData, GProg, GInput, GEval) with the following syntax:

- $\tilde{D} \leftarrow$ GData(D, k) : Takes memory data $D \in \{0, 1\}^n$ and a key k. Outputs the garbled data $\tilde{D}$.

- $(\tilde{P}, k^{in}) \leftarrow$ GProg$(P, k, n, t^{init}, t^{cur})$: Takes a key k and a description of a RAM program P with memory-size n and run-time consisting of t^{cur} CPU steps. In the case of garbling multiple programs, we also provide t^{init} indicating the cumulative number of CPU steps executed by all of the previous programs. Outputs a garbled program $\tilde{P}$ and an input-garbling-key k^{in}.

- $\tilde{x} \leftarrow$ GInput(x, k^{in}): Takes an input x and input-garbling-key k^{in} and outputs a garbled-input $\tilde{x}$.

- $y =$ GEval$^{\tilde{D}}(\tilde{P}, \tilde{x})$: Takes a garbled program $\tilde{P}$, garbled input $\tilde{x}$ and garbled memory data $\tilde{D}$ and computes the output $y = P^D(x)$. We model GEval itself as a RAM program that can read and write to arbitrary locations of its memory initially containing $\tilde{D}$.

We require that the run-time of GData be $O(n \cdot \mathsf{poly}(\kappa))$, which also serves as an upper bound on the size of $\tilde{D}$, and also require that the run-time of GInput should be $|x| \cdot \mathsf{poly}(\kappa)$. We also wish to minimize the run-time of GProg and GEval, preferably as low as $\mathsf{poly}(\kappa)\mathsf{polylog}(n) \cdot (|P| + t^{cur})$ for GProg and $\mathsf{poly}(\kappa)\mathsf{polylog}(n) \cdot t^{cur}$ for GEval (but not all our constructions achieve polylogarithmic overhead in n).

Correctness and Security. To define the correctness and security requirements of garbled RAMs, let $P_1, \ldots, P_\ell$ be any sequence of programs with polynomially-bounded run-times $t_1, \ldots, t_\ell$. Let $D \in \{0, 1\}^n$ be any initial memory data, let $x_1, \ldots, x_\ell$ be inputs and $(y_1, \ldots, y_\ell) = (P_1(x_1), \ldots, P_\ell(x_\ell))^D$ be the outputs given by the sequential execution of the programs. Consider the following experiment: choose a key $k \leftarrow \{0, 1\}^\kappa$, $\tilde{D} \leftarrow$ GData(D, k) and for $i = 1, \ldots, \ell$:

$$(\tilde{P}_i, k_i^{in}) \leftarrow \mathsf{GProg}\left(P_i, n, t_i^{init}, t_i, k\right), \tilde{x}_i \leftarrow \mathsf{GInput}(x_i, k_i^{in})$$

where $t_i^{init} := \sum_{j=1}^{i-1} t_i$ denotes the run-time of all programs prior to P_i. Let

$$(y_1', \ldots, y_\ell') = (\mathsf{GEval}(\tilde{P}_1, \tilde{x}_1), \ldots, \mathsf{GEval}(\tilde{P}_\ell, \tilde{x}_\ell))^{\tilde{D}},$$

denotes the output of evaluating the garbled programs sequentially over the garbled memory. We require that the following properties hold:

- **Correctness:** We require that $\Pr[y_1' = y_1, \ldots, y_\ell' = y_\ell] = 1$ in the above experiment.
- **Security:** we require that there exists a universal simulator Sim such that:

$$(\tilde{D}, \tilde{P}_1, \ldots, \tilde{P}_\ell, \tilde{x}_1, \ldots, \tilde{x}_\ell) \overset{comp}{\approx} \mathsf{Sim}(1^\kappa, \{P_i, t_i, y_i\}_{i=1}^\ell, n).$$

Our security definition is non-adaptive: the data/programs/inputs are all chosen ahead of time. This makes our definitions/analysis simpler and also matches the standard definitions for our building blocks such as ORAM. However, there does not seem to be any inherent hurdle to allowing each subsequent program/input (P_i, x_i) to be chosen adaptively after seeing $\tilde{D}, (\tilde{P}_1, \tilde{x}_1), \ldots, (\tilde{P}_{i-1}, \tilde{x}_{i-1})$.

Security with Unprotected Memory Access (UMA). We also consider a weaker security notion, which we call security with *unprotected memory access* (UMA). In this variant, the attacker may learn the initial contents of the memory D, as well as the complete memory-access pattern throughout the computation including the locations being read/written and their contents. In particular, we let $\mathsf{MemAccess} = \{(i_j^{\mathsf{read}}, i_j^{\mathsf{write}}, b_j^{\mathsf{write}}) : j = 1, \ldots, t\}$ correspond to the outputs of the CPU-step circuits during the execution of $P^D(x)$. For security with unprotected memory access, we give the simulator the additional values $(D, \mathsf{MemAccess})$. Using the notation from above, we require:

$$(\tilde{D}, \tilde{P}_1, \ldots, \tilde{P}_\ell, \tilde{x}_1, \ldots, \tilde{x}_\ell) \overset{comp}{\approx} \mathsf{Sim}(1^\kappa, \{P_i, t_i, y_i\}_{i=1}^\ell, D, \mathsf{MemAccess}, n).$$

In the long version [9], we show a general transformation that converts any garbled RAM scheme with UMA security into one with full security by encrypting the memory contents and applying oblivious RAM to hide the access pattern. Therefore, it is useful to focus on achieving just UMA security.

3   The Original Lu-Ostrovsky Construction

We now describe the main ideas behind the Lu-Ostrovsky construction from Eurocrypt 2013 [14] (but we use a substantially different exposition). In this extended abstract we only consider security with unprotected memory access (UMA), which completely abstracts out the use of oblivious RAM. Moreover, for ease of exposition, we begin by describing a solution for the case of "read-only" computation, which never writes to memory. Many of the main ideas, as well as the circularity problem, are already present in this simple case.

3.1   Garbling Read-Only Programs

Garbled Data. The garbled data $\tilde{D}$ consists of n secret keys for some symmetric-key encryption scheme. For each bit $i \in [n]$ of the original data D, the garbled data $\tilde{D}$ contains a secret key sk_i. The secret keys are chosen pseudo-randomly using a pseudo-random function (PRF) family F_k via $\mathsf{sk}_i = F_k(i, D[i])$. Note that, given k, there are two possible values $\mathsf{sk}_{(i,0)} = F_k(i,0)$ and $\mathsf{sk}_{(i,1)} = F_k(i,1)$ that can reside in $\tilde{D}[i]$ depending on the bit $D[i]$ of the original data, and we set $\tilde{D}[i] = \mathsf{sk}_{(i,D[i])}$.

Garbled Program (Overview). The garbled program P consists of t garbled copies of an "augmented" CPU-step circuit $C_{\mathsf{CPU+}}^P$, which we describe shortly. Recall that the basic CPU-step circuit takes as input the current CPU state and the last read bit $(\mathsf{state}, b^{\mathsf{read}})$ and outputs $(\mathsf{state}', i^{\mathsf{read}})$ containing the updated state and the next read location – we can ignore the other outputs $i^{\mathsf{write}}, b^{\mathsf{write}}$ since we are considering read-only computation.

We can garble copy j of the CPU-step circuit so that the labels for the output wires corresponding to the output state' match the labels of the input wires corresponding to the input state in the next copy $j + 1$ of the circuit. This allows the garbled state to securely travel from one garbled CPU-step circuit to the next. Each garbled copy j of the CPU-step circuit can also output the read location $i = i^{\mathsf{read}}$ in the clear. The question becomes, how can the evaluator incorporate the data from memory into the computation? In particular, let $\mathsf{lbl}_0^{(\mathsf{read},j+1)}, \mathsf{lbl}_1^{(\mathsf{read},j+1)}$ be the labels of the input wires corresponding to the bit b^{read} in garbled copy $j + 1$ of the circuit. We need to ensure that the evaluator who knows $\mathsf{sk}_{(i,b)} = F_k(i,b)$ can learn $\mathsf{lbl}_b^{(\mathsf{read},j+1)}$ but learns nothing about the other label. Unfortunately, the labels $\mathsf{lbl}_b^{(\mathsf{read},j+1)}$ need to be created at "compile time" when the garbled program is created, and therefore cannot depend on the location $i = i^{\mathsf{read}}$ which is only known at "run time" when the garbled program is being evaluated. Therefore the labels $\mathsf{lbl}_b^{(\mathsf{read},j+1)}$ cannot depend on the keys $\mathsf{sk}_{(i,b)}$ since i is not known.

Lu and Ostrovsky propose a clever solution to the above problem. We *augment* the CPU-step circuit so that the jth copy of the circuit outputs a *translation mapping* $\mathsf{translate}$ which allows the evaluator to translate between the keys $\mathsf{sk}_{(i,b)}$ contained in the garbled memory and the labels $\mathsf{lbl}_b^{(\mathsf{read},j+1)}$ of the read-bit in the next circuit. The translation mapping is computed by the jth CPU circuit at *run-time* and therefore can depend on the memory location $i = i^{\mathsf{read}}$ being requested in that step. The translation mapping computed by circuit j consists of two ciphertexts $\mathsf{translate} = (\mathsf{ct}_0, \mathsf{ct}_1)$ where ct_b is an encryption of the label $\mathsf{lbl}_b^{(\mathsf{read},j+1)}$ under the secret key $\mathsf{sk}_{(i,b)} = F_k(i,b)$.[4] In order to compute this encryption, the augmented CPU-step circuits contain the PRF key k as a *hard-coded value*.

Garbled Program (Technical). In more detail, we define an augmented CPU-step circuit $C_{\mathsf{CPU+}}^P$ which gets as input $(\mathsf{state}, b^{\mathsf{read}})$ and outputs $(\mathsf{state}', i^{\mathsf{read}},$

---

[4] Since we are only aiming for UMA security, we can reveal the bit b and therefore do not need to permute the ciphertexts.

translate). It contains some hard-coded parameters $(k, r_0, r_1, \mathsf{lbl}_0^{(\mathsf{read})}, \mathsf{lbl}_1^{(\mathsf{read})})$ and performs the following computation:

- $(\mathsf{state}', i^{\mathsf{read}}) = C_{\mathsf{CPU}}^P(\mathsf{state}, b^{\mathsf{read}})$ are the outputs of the basic CPU-step circuit.
- translate $= (\mathsf{ct}_0, \mathsf{ct}_1)$ consists of two ciphertexts, computed as follows. For $b \in \{0, 1\}$, first compute $\mathsf{sk}_{(i,b)} := F_k(i, b)$ for $i = i^{\mathsf{read}}$. Then set $c_b = \mathsf{Enc}_{\mathsf{sk}_{(i,b)}}(\mathsf{lbl}_b^{(\mathsf{read})}; r_b)$ where Enc is a symmetric key encryption and r_b is the encryption randomness.

The garbled program $\tilde{P}$ consists of t garbled copies of this augmented CPU-step circuit $\tilde{C}_{\mathsf{CPU+}}^P(j)$. We start garbling from the end $j = t$. Each garbled circuit $\tilde{C}_{\mathsf{CPU+}}^P(j)$ outputs the values i^{read}, translate in the clear and the updated state' is garbled with the same labels as the input state in the next circuit $\tilde{C}_{\mathsf{CPU+}}^P(j + 1)$; the last circuit outputs state' in the clear as the output of the computation. Each garbled circuit $\tilde{C}_{\mathsf{CPU+}}^P(j)$ contains hard-coded values $(k, r_0^{(j)}, r_1^{(j)}, \mathsf{lbl}_0^{(\mathsf{read}, j+1)}, \mathsf{lbl}_1^{(\mathsf{read}, j+1)})$ which are used to compute the translation mapping translate as described above. The key k is the PRF key which was used to garbled the memory data. The values $r_0^{(j)}, r_1^{(j)}$ are fresh encryption random coins, and $\mathsf{lbl}_0^{(\mathsf{read}, j+1)}, \mathsf{lbl}_1^{(\mathsf{read}, j+1)}$ are the labels of the input-wire for the bit b^{read} in the garbled circuit $\tilde{C}_{\mathsf{CPU+}}^P(j + 1)$.

Garbled Input and Evaluation. The garbled input $\tilde{x}$ consists of the wire-labels for the value $\mathsf{state}_1 = x$ for the garbled circuit $\tilde{C}_{\mathsf{CPU+}}^P(j = 1)$. The evaluator simply evaluates the garbled augmented CPU-step circuits one by one starting from $j = 1$. It can evaluate the first circuit using only $\tilde{x}$, and gets out a garbled output state_2 along with the values $(i^{\mathsf{read}}, \text{translate} = (c_0, c_1))$ in the clear. The evaluator looks up the secret key $\mathsf{sk} := \tilde{D}[i^{\mathsf{read}}]$ and attempts to use it to decrypt c_0 and c_1 to recover a label $\mathsf{lbl}^{(\mathsf{read}, j=2)}$. The evaluator then evaluates the second garbled circuit $\tilde{C}_{\mathsf{CPU+}}^P(j = 2)$ using the garbled input state_2 and the wire-label $\mathsf{lbl}^{(\mathsf{read}, j=2)}$ for the wire corresponding to the bit b^{read}. This process continues until the last circuit $j = t$ which outputs state' in the clear as the output of the computation.

3.2   Circularity in the Security Analysis

There is good intuition that the above construction *should* be secure. In particular, the evaluator only gets one label per wire of the first garbled circuit $\tilde{C}_{\mathsf{CPU+}}^P(j = 1)$ and therefore does not learn anything beyond its outputs $i = i^{\mathsf{read}}$, translate (in the clear) and the garbled value state_2 which can be used as an input to the second circuit. Now, assume that the memory-data contains (say) the bit $D[i] = 0$ and so the evaluator can get $\mathsf{sk}^{(i,0)}$ from the garbled memory $\tilde{D}$. Using the translation map translate $= (\mathsf{ct}_0, \mathsf{ct}_1)$, the evaluator can use this to recover the label $\mathsf{lbl}_0^{\mathsf{read}}$ corresponding to the read-bit $b^{\mathsf{read}} = 0$ of the next circuit $j = 2$. We need to argue that the evaluator does not learn anything about the "other" label: $\mathsf{lbl}_1^{\mathsf{read}}$. Intuitively, the above should hold since the evaluator does not have the secret key $\mathsf{sk}_{(i,1)} = F_k(i,1)$ needed to decrypt ct_1. Unfortunately, in attempting to make the above intuition formal, we uncover a complex circularity:

1. In order to argue that the evaluator does not learn anything about the "other" label $\mathsf{lbl}_1^{\mathsf{read}}$, we need to rely on the security of the ciphertext ct_1.

2. In order to rely on the security of the ciphertext ct_1 we need to argue that the attacker does not learn the decryption key $\mathsf{sk}_{(i,1)} = F_k(i,1)$, which requires us to argue that the attacker does not learn the PRF key k. However, the PRF key k is contained as a hard-coded value of the second garbled circuit $\tilde{C}_{\mathsf{CPU+}}^P (j = 2)$ and all future circuits as well. Therefore, to argue that the attacker does not learn k we need to (at the very least) rely on the security of the second garbled circuit.

3. In order to use the security of the second garbled circuit $\tilde{C}_{\mathsf{CPU+}}^P (j = 2)$, we need to argue that the evaluator only gets one label per wire, and in particular, we need to argue the the evaluator does not have the "other" label $\mathsf{lbl}_1^{\mathsf{read}}$. But this is what we wanted to prove in the first place!

We note that the above can be seen as a complex circularity problem involving the PRF, the encryption scheme and the garbled circuit. In particular, the PRF key k is used to encrypt both labels for some input-wire in the garbled circuit, but k is also a hard-coded in the garbled circuit. Therefore we cannot rely on the security of the garbled circuit unless we argue that k stays hidden, but we cannot argue that k stays hidden without relying on the security of the garbled circuit. Notice that this circularity problem comes up even if the evaluator didn't get the garbled data $\tilde{D}$ at all.

The problem is even more complex than described above since the key k is hard-coded in many other garbled circuits and the outputs of these circuits depend on k but do not reveal k directly. Therefore, the circularity problem is not "contained" to a single circuit. We do not know of any "simple" circular-security assumption that one could make on the circuit-garbling scheme, the PRF, and/or the encryption scheme that would allow us to prove security, other than simply assuming that the full construction is secure.

3.3   Writing to Memory

We now describe the main ideas behind how to handle "writes" in the Lu-Ostrovsky construction. Although the circularity problem remains in this solution, it will be useful to see the ideas as they will guide us in our fixes. We again note that our exposition here is substantially different from [14].

Predictably Timed Writes. Below we describe how to incorporate a limited form of writing to memory, which we call *predictably timed writes* (ptWrites). On a high level, this means that whenever we want to *read* some location i in memory, it is easy to figure out the time (i.e., CPU step) j in which that location was last *written* to, given only the current state of the computation and without reading any other values in memory. In the long version [9] we describe how to upgrade a solution for ptWrites to one that allows arbitrary writes. We give a formal definition of ptWrites below:

Definition 1 (Predictably Timed Writes (ptWrites)). *A program execution* $P^D(x)$ *has predictably timed writes (ptWrites) if there exists a poly-size circuit* WriteTime *such that the following holds for every CPU step* $j = 1, \ldots, t$. *Let the inputs/outputs of the jth CPU step be* $C^P_{\mathsf{CPU}}(\mathsf{state}_j, b^{\mathsf{read}}_j) = (\mathsf{state}_{j+1}, i^{\mathsf{read}}_j, i^{\mathsf{write}}_j, b^{\mathsf{write}}_j)$. *Then,* $u = \mathsf{WriteTime}(j, \mathsf{state}_j, i^{\mathsf{read}}_j)$ *is the largest value of* $u < j$ *such that the CPU step* u *wrote to location* i^{read}_j; *i.e.,* $i^{\mathsf{write}}_u = i^{\mathsf{read}}_j$. *We also define a ptWrites property for a sequence of program executions* $(P_1(x_1), \ldots, P_\ell(x_\ell))^D$ *if the above property holds for each CPU step in the sequence.*

Garbling programs with ptWrites. At any point in time, the garbled memory data $\tilde{D}$ maintained by the honest evaluator should consist of secret keys of the form $\mathsf{sk}_{(j,i,b)} = F_k(j, i, b)$ for each location $i \in [n]$, where the additional value j will denote a "time step" in which the location i was last written to, and b denotes the current bit in that location. Initially, for each location $i \in [n]$, we set $\tilde{D}[i] = \mathsf{sk}_{(0,i,D[i])}$ using the time period $j = 0$. Then, to read from a location i with last-write-time u, the CPU circuit encrypts the wire-label for bit b under some key which depends on (u, i, b), and to write a bit b to location i in time-step j the CPU circuit gives out some key which depends on (j, i, b).

In more detail, to write a bit b to memory location i^{write} in time step u, the augmented CPU circuit now simply computes a secret key $\mathsf{sk}_{(u,i,b)} = F_k(u, i, b)$, using the hard-coded PRF key k, and outputs $\mathsf{sk}_{(u,i,b)}$ in the clear. The honest evaluator will place this new key in to garbled memory by setting $\tilde{D}[i] := \mathsf{sk}_{(u,i,b)}$, and can "forget" the previous key in location i.

To read from location i^{read}, in time step j we now need to make sure that the evaluator can *only* use latest key (corresponding to the most recently written bit), and cannot use some outdated key (corresponding to an old value in that location). To do so, the augmented CPU circuit computes the last write time for the location i^{read} by calling $u = \mathsf{WriteTime}(j, \mathsf{state}_j, i^{\mathsf{read}})$ and then prepares the translation mapping $\mathsf{translate} = (c_0, c_1)$ as before, but with respect to the keys for time step u by encrypting the ciphertext c_0, c_1 under the secret key $\mathsf{sk}_{(u,i,0)} = F_k(u, i, 0), \mathsf{sk}_{(u,i,1)} = F_k(u, i, 1)$ respectively.

4 Our Solution Using IBE

We now outline our modifications to the Lu-Ostrovsky solution so as to remove the circular use of garbled circuits, using identity-based encryption. See the long version [9] for a full description. As above, we begin by describing our fix for read-only computation and then describe how to handle ptWrites.

4.1   A Read-Only Construction

The initial idea is to simply replace the symmetric-key encryption scheme with a public-key one. Each garbled circuit will have a hard-coded public-key which allows it to create ciphertexts translate $= (\mathsf{ct}_0, \mathsf{ct}_1)$, but does not provide enough information to "break" the security of these ciphertexts. Unfortunately, standard public-key encryption does not suffice and we will need to rely on *identity-based encryption* (IBE). Indeed, we can already think of the Lu-Ostrovsky construction outlined above as implicitly using a "symmetric-key" IBE where the master secret key k is needed to encrypt. In particular, we can think of the garbled memory data as consisting of "identity secret keys" $sk_{(i,b)}$ for identities of the form $(i, b) \in [n] \times \{0, 1\}$ depending on the data bit $b = D[i]$. The translation information consists of an encryption of the label $\mathsf{lbl}_0^{\mathsf{read}}$ for identity $(i, 0)$ and an encryption of $\mathsf{lbl}_1^{\mathsf{read}}$ for identity $(i, 1)$. We can view the Lu-Ostrovsky scheme as using a symmetric-key IBE scheme constructed from a PRF $F_k(\cdot)$ and a standard encryption scheme, where the encryption of a message msg for identity id is computed as $\mathsf{Enc}_{F_k(\mathsf{id})}(\mathsf{msg})$. We now simply replace this with a public-key IBE. In particular, we modify the augmented CPU-step circuit so that it now contains a hard-coded master public key MPK for an IBE scheme (instead of a PRF key k) and it now creates the translation map translate $= (c_0, c_1)$ by setting $c_b = \mathsf{Enc}_{\mathsf{MPK}}(\mathsf{id} = (i, b), \mathsf{msg} = \mathsf{lbl}_b^{(\mathsf{read})})$ to be an encryption of the message $\mathsf{lbl}_b^{\mathsf{read}}$ for identity (i, b).

Overview of Security Proof. The above scheme already removes the circularity problem and yields a secure construction for read-only computation with unprotected memory-access (UMA) security. In particular, we can now rely on the semantic-security of the IBE ciphertexts created by a garbled circuit j without needing to argue about the security of future garbled circuits $j + 1, j + 2, \ldots$ since they do not contain any secret information about the IBE scheme.

4.2   Writing to Memory

We present the solution for a predictably timed writes (ptWrites), cf. Definition 1. To handle writes, we now want the garbled data to consist of secret keys for identities of the form $\mathsf{id} = (j, i, b)$ where $i \in [n]$ is the location in the data, j is a time step when that location was last written to, and $b \in \{0, 1\}$ is the bit that was written to location i in time j. The honest evaluator only needs to keep the the most recent secret key for each location i. When the computation needs to read from location i, it computes the last time step j when this location was written to, then creates the translation mapping by encrypting ciphertexts for the two identities (j, i, b) for $b = 0, 1$.

When the computation needs to write a bit b to location i in time period j, the corresponding garbled circuit should output a secret key for the identity (j, i, b). Unfortunately, a naive implementation would require the garbled circuits to include the master secret key MSK of the IBE in order to compute these secret keys, and this would re-introduce the same circularity problem that we are trying to avoid! Instead we use a solution similar to hierarchical IBE (HIBE), as we describe next.

Timed IBE. To avoid circularity, we introduce a primitive that we call a *timed IBE* (TIBE) scheme. Such a scheme roughly lets us create "time-period keys" TSK_j for arbitrary time periods $j \geq 0$ such that TSK_j can be used to create identity-secret-keys $\mathsf{sk}_{(j,v)}$ for arbitrary v, but cannot break the security of any other identities with $j' \neq j$.[5] TIBEs as described above can be easily constructed from 2-level HIBE by thinking of the identities (j, v) as being of the form $j.v$ where the time-period j is the top level of the hierarchy and v is the lower level; the time-period key TSK_j would just be a secret key for the identity j. We note, however, that for our purposes we can use a slightly weaker version of TIBEs where we only give out limited number of keys, and these can be constructed from any selectively-secure IBE scheme.

Definition 2 (Timed IBE (TIBE)). *A TIBE scheme Consists of 5 PPT algorithms* MasterGen, TimeGen, KeyGen, Enc, Dec *with the syntax:*

- $(\mathsf{MPK}, \mathsf{MSK}) \leftarrow \mathsf{MasterGen}(1^\kappa)$: *generates master public/secret keys* MPK, MSK.
- $\mathsf{TSK}_j \leftarrow \mathsf{TimeGen}(\mathsf{MSK}, j)$: *Generates a key for time-period* $j \in \mathbb{N}$.
- $\mathsf{sk}_{(j,v)} \leftarrow \mathsf{KeyGen}(\mathsf{TSK}_j, (j, v))$: *creates a secret key for the identity* (j, v).
- $\mathsf{ct} \leftarrow \mathsf{Enc}_{\mathsf{MPK}}((j, v), \mathsf{msg})$ *encrypts* msg *for the identity* (j, v).
- $\mathsf{msg} = \mathsf{Dec}_{\mathsf{sk}_{(j,v)}}(\mathsf{ct})$: *decrypts* ct *for identity* (j, v) *using the secret key* $\mathsf{sk}_{(j,v)}$.

The scheme should satisfy the following properties:
Correctness: *For any* id $= (j, v)$, *and any* msg $\in \{0, 1\}^*$ *it holds that:*

$$\Pr\left[\mathsf{Dec}_{\mathsf{sk}}(\mathsf{ct}) = \mathsf{msg} \;\middle|\; \begin{array}{l} (\mathsf{MPK}, \mathsf{MSK}) \leftarrow \mathsf{MasterGen}(1^\kappa), \mathsf{TSK}_j \leftarrow \mathsf{TimeGen}(\mathsf{MSK}, j), \\ \mathsf{sk} \leftarrow \mathsf{KeyGen}(\mathsf{TSK}_j, (j, v)), \mathsf{ct} \leftarrow \mathsf{Enc}_{\mathsf{MPK}}((j, v), \mathsf{msg}) \end{array}\right] = 1.$$

Security: *Consider the following game between an attacker $\mathcal{A}$ and a challenger.*

- *The attacker $\mathcal{A}(1^\kappa)$ chooses target identity* id$^* = (j^*, v^*)$ *and bound* $t \geq j^*$ *(given in unary). The attacker also chooses a set of identities* $S = S_0 \cup S_{>0}$ *with* id$^* \notin S$ *such that: (I) S_0 contains arbitrary identities of the form* $(0, v)$, *(II) $S_{>0}$ contains exactly one identity (j, v) for each period* $j \in \{1, \ldots, j^*\}$. *Lastly, the adversary chooses messages* $\mathsf{msg}_0, \mathsf{msg}_1 \in \{0, 1\}^*$ *of equal size* $|\mathsf{msg}_0| = |\mathsf{msg}_1|$.
- *The challenger chooses* $(\mathsf{MPK}, \mathsf{MSK}) \leftarrow \mathsf{MasterGen}(1^\kappa)$, *and* $\mathsf{TSK}_j \leftarrow \mathsf{TimeGen}(\mathsf{MSK}, j)$ *for* $j = 0, \ldots, t$. *For each* id $= (j, v) \in S$ *it chooses* $\mathsf{sk}_{\mathsf{id}} \leftarrow \mathsf{KeyGen}(\mathsf{TSK}_j, \mathsf{id})$. *Lastly, the challenger chooses a challenge bit* $b \leftarrow \{0, 1\}$ *and sets* $\mathsf{ct} \leftarrow \mathsf{Enc}_{\mathsf{MPK}}(\mathsf{id}^*, \mathsf{msg}_b)$. *The challenger gives the attacker:*

$$\mathsf{MPK} \;, \quad \overline{\mathsf{TSK}} = \{\mathsf{TSK}_j\}_{j^* < j \leq t} \;, \quad \overline{\mathsf{sk}} = \{(\mathsf{id}, \mathsf{sk}_{\mathsf{id}})\}_{\mathsf{id} \in S} \;, \quad \mathsf{ct}.$$

- *The attacker outputs a bit* $\hat{b} \in \{0, 1\}$.

---

[5] In our use of TIBE, we will always set $v = (i, b)$ for some $i \in [n], b \in \{0, 1\}$.

The scheme is secure if, for all PPT $\mathcal{A}$, we have $|\Pr[b = \hat{b}] - \frac{1}{2}| \leq \mathsf{negl}(\kappa)$ in the above game.

In the full version [9], we show how to construct a TIBE scheme from *any* secure IBE scheme.

Solution Using TIBE. Using a TIBE scheme, we can solve the problem of writes. For each location $i \in [n]$ the honest evaluator will always have a secret key for identity $\mathsf{id} = (j, i, b)$ where j is the last-write-time for location i and $b \in \{0, 1\}$ is its value. Initially, the garbled data consists of secret keys for the time period $j = 0$. Each augmented-CPU-step-circuit in time period $j > 0$ will contain a hard-coded time-period key TSK_j and the master-public-key MPK. This allows each CPU step j to read an arbitrary location $i \in [n]$ with last-write time $u < j$ by encrypting the translation ciphertexts $\mathsf{translate} = (\mathsf{ct}_0, \mathsf{ct}_1)$ under MPK to the identities (u, i, b) for $b = 0, 1$. Each such CPU step j can also write a bit b to an arbitrary location i by creating a secret key $\mathsf{sk}_{\mathsf{id}}$ for the identity $\mathsf{id} = (j, i, b)$ using TSK_j. Notice that we create at most one such secret-key for each time period $j > 0$. This solution does not suffer from a circularity problem, since the ciphertexts created by CPU step j for an identity (u, i, b) must have $u < j$, and therefore we can rely on semantic security even given the hard-coded values $\mathsf{TSK}_{j+1}, \ldots, \mathsf{TSK}_t$ in all future garbled circuits.

5   Our Solution Using One-Way Functions

The main problem that arises in the circularity is that there is only one PRF key, and that this key when embedded in any future time step is able to decode anything the circuit does in the current time step. The intuitive way to circumvent this is to iteratively weaken the PRF key. In order to do so, we introduce the following notion of revocable PRFs.

5.1   Revocable PRFs

We define the notion of (adaptively) revocable PRFs and we explain how it differs from existing notions such as [6,7,13,18]. The idea is that we can revoke values from the key so that the PRF cannot be evaluated on these values, and given an already-revoked key, one can further revoke new values.

Definition 3. *A revocable PRF is a PRF F equipped with an additional revoke algorithm* Rev. *The keys for this PRF are of the form k_X where X is a subset of the domain (which is the revoked values), and we identify "fresh keys" with $k_\emptyset$. The revoke algorithm takes as input a key k_X and another subset Y, and output $k_{X \cup Y}$, satisfying the following properties:*

Correctness: $F_{k_{X \cup Y}}(x) = F_{k_X}(x)$ *if $x \notin X \cup Y$, and $F_{k_{X \cup Y}}(x) = \perp$ otherwise.*
Pseudorandomness: *Given any set of keys $\{k_{Y_1}, \ldots, k_{Y_m}\}$, $F_k(x)$ is pseudorandom for all $x \notin \bigcap_i Y_i$.*

Note that this definition appears similar to constrained PRFs [6]; however, we do not require that the revoked set to be hidden in any way, and we allow successive revocation of more and more values starting from an initial fresh key.

Revocable PRFs can be constructed based on the GGM construction [10], as we now sketch. Recall that GGM PRF is built out of a length-doubling PRG G. It can be thought of as filling the nodes of a complete binary tree with pseudo-random values: The PRF key is placed in the root, and then the values in all other nodes are computed by taking any node with value s and putting in its two children the two halves of the pseudo-random value $G(s)$. An input to the PRF specifies a leaf in the tree, and the corresponding output is the pseudo-random value in that leaf. To revoke a single leaf x, we simply replace the root value with the values of all the siblings of nods on the path to the revoked leaf. Clearly we can still compute the PRF on every input $y \neq x$, but the value of x is now pseudo-random even given the weaker key. More generally, let $X = \{x_1, x_2, \ldots, x_s\}$ be a set of s leaves that we want to revoke, the key k_X will contain siblings of nodes on the paths to all these x_i's, except these nodes that are themselves ancestors of some x_i. This key consists of at most $s \log N$ values, where N is the number of leaves in the tree.

5.2   Overview of the Second Construction

Step 1, read-once programs. We begin by describing a naive construction that solves the circularity issue by using revocable PRFs. Starting from a RAM program with ptWrites, we convert it to a "read-once" program (i.e. no location is read more than once before it is overwritten) by introducing a local cache in which the CPU keeps every value that it gets from memory. Of course this transformation comes with a steep performance price, as the CPU state after t steps grows to size roughly $\min(n, t)$.

Once we have a read-once program, we can use revocable PRFs to break the circularity in the original Lu-Ostrovsky construction as follows: instead of having the PRF key hard-wired in the augmented CPU-step circuit, we now let it be part of the input. In particular the circuit will get some key K_X as part of the input, compute the next address i to read from memory (if any), and will prepare the translation mapping table translate by evaluating $F_{K_X}(u, i, 0)$ and $F_{K_X}(u, i, 1)$, then revoke the two points $(u, i, 0)$ and $(u, i, 1)$, and pass to the next CPU-step function the PRF key $K_{X'}$ for $X' = X \cup \{(i, 0), (i, 1)\}$. Since this is a read-once program, then no future CPU step ever needs to evaluate the PRF at these points. Writing remains unchanged, and does not interfere with the PRF because all revocations only happened to CPU-steps in the past, and in the proof we can still plant the PRF challenge in the un-written bit $F_{K_X}(u, i, 1 - b)$.

This solves the circularity problem since the encryption in translate is secure even given all future keys K'_x. Moreover, the size of the augmented CPU step is not much larger than that of the original CPU step since the keys K_X only grow to size roughly $\kappa \cdot \min(n, t) \cdot \log n$. The naive construction would just garble all of these enhanced CPU steps, which entails time complexity of $\text{poly}(\kappa) \cdot \min(n, t) \cdot t \log n$ for both GProg and GEval. This solution, although secure, is not much better than just converting the original RAM program to a circuit and garbling that circuit (i.e. the generic t^3 transformation). We do obtain some *amortized* savings in the case of running multiple programs on persistent memory (e.g. repeated binary search).

We mention that instead of "read-once", we can consider a weakened version that allows for some bounded number of reads before a location is overwritten. In such a case, there exists a transformation (via ORAM, see [15]) from an arbitrary RAM program to one that satisfies ptWrites and poly-logarithmic bounded reads, *without a cache*. In order for GRAM to handle multiple reads to the same location, we can simply apply repetition and have multiple, independent PRFs. Unfortunately, even though this removes the cache, the bottleneck remains in the growth of the keys K_X. Only when combined with a more efficient revocable PRF scheme will this result in lower overhead. Instead, we propose the following approach.

Step 2, refreshing the memory. To reduce the complexity, we introduce a periodic memory-refresh operation which is designed to rein-in the growth in the (augmented) CPU-step functions: Namely, we refresh the entire memory and its representation every f steps, for some parameter $f < n$ to be determined later. In more detail, after every f CPU steps we introduce an special refresh circuit that (a) empties the cache, and (b) re-garbles the memory using a freshly chosen PRF key. The complexity of each such refresh step is $\mathsf{poly}(k) \cdot n$, and there is no need to hard-wire in it any PRF keys (since we can instead just hard-wire all the $O(n)$ PRF values that it needs, rather than computing them.)

The advantage of using these refresh steps is that now the augmented CPU steps only grow up to size at most $O(\kappa \cdot f \log n)$, and although each refresh step is expensive we only have t/f such steps. Hence the overall complexity is bounded by $\mathsf{poly}(\kappa) \cdot (t/f \cdot n + t \cdot f \log n)$. Setting $f = \sqrt{n/\log n}$ thus yields overall complexity $\mathsf{poly}(\kappa) \cdot t \cdot \sqrt{n \log n}$ for performing t steps, so we get overhead of $\mathsf{poly}(\kappa)\sqrt{n \log n}$.

Step 3, a recursive construction. To further reduce the overhead, we notice that instead of garbling the augmented CPU steps as circuits (which incurs complexity $s \cdot \mathsf{poly}(\kappa)$ for a size-s step), we can instead view these steps as RAM programs and apply the same RAM-garbling procedure recursively to these programs. Each augmented CPU state grows to $O(\kappa \cdot f \log n)$, and can be implemented as a RAM program of that size, but running in time $\tilde{O}(\kappa \log f \log n)$ by using appropriate data structures. This allows us to balance the refresh time with the cost of executing each of the t emulated steps as a recurrence relation. There are additional details required when applying this recursion. Since every level of the recursion induces a factor of κ, we must choose f so that the savings overcome this factor and while preserving polynomial complexity. Also, if we treat each step as an independent GRAM, the cost of running GData on the size-f cache would negate all savings. We must amortize this cost by treating the steps as running on the same persistent "mini-GRAM" memory. This requires a careful formalization of our recursion in terms of a composition theorem that states that a small, secure

GRAM can be bootstrapped into a larger one via treating CPU internals as persistent memory. In the long version [15] we give the details and show that for any constant $\varepsilon > 0$ we can choose the parameter f and the number of recursion levels to get overhead of $\mathsf{poly}(\kappa)n^\varepsilon$.

6 Conclusions

We conclude with two important open problems. Firstly, it would be interesting to give a garbled RAM scheme based only on the existence of one-way functions with poly-logarithmic overhead. Secondly, the work of Goldwasser et al. recently constructed the first *reusable* garbling schemes for *circuits* and *Turing machines* [12,11] where the garbled circuit/TM can be executed on multiple inputs. It would be interesting to analogously construct a reusable garbled RAM where the garbled program can be evaluated on many different "short" inputs.

Acknowledgments. The first two authors were supported in part by the Intelligence Advanced Research Projects Activity (IARPA) via Department of Interior National Business Center (DoI/NBC) contract number D11PC20202. The U.S. Government is authorized to reproduce and distribute reprints for Governmental purposes notwithstanding any copyright annotation thereon. Disclaimer: The views and conclusions contained herein are those of the authors and should not be interpreted as necessarily representing the official policies or endorsements, either expressed or implied, of IARPA, DoI/NBC, or the U.S. Government.

The third author was supported in part by NSF grants CCF-0916574; IIS-1065276; CCF-1016540; CNS-1118126; CNS-1136174.

The fourth author was supported in part by NSF grants CCF-0916574; IIS-1065276; CCF-1016540; CNS-1118126; CNS-1136174; US-Israel BSF grant 2008411, OKAWA Foundation Research Award, IBM Faculty Research Award, Xerox Faculty Research Award, B. John Garrick Foundation Award, Teradata Research Award, and Lockheed-Martin Corporation Research Award. This material is also based upon work supported by the Defense Advanced Research Projects Agency through the U.S. Office of Naval Research under Contract N00014-11-1-0392. The views expressed are those of the author and do not reflect the official policy or position of the Department of Defense or the U.S. Government.

The sixth author was supported in part by NSF grant 1347350.

References

1. Applebaum, B., Ishai, Y., Kushilevitz, E.: From secrecy to soundness: Efficient verification via secure computation. In: Abramsky, S., Gavoille, C., Kirchner, C., Meyer auf der Heide, F., Spirakis, P.G. (eds.) ICALP 2010. LNCS, vol. 6198, pp. 152–163. Springer, Heidelberg (2010)
2. Bellare, M., Dowsley, R., Waters, B., Yilek, S.: Standard security does not imply security against selective-opening. In: Pointcheval, D., Johansson, T. (eds.) EUROCRYPT 2012. LNCS, vol. 7237, pp. 645–662. Springer, Heidelberg (2012)

3. Bellare, M., Hoang, V.T., Rogaway, P.: Adaptively secure garbling with applications to one-time programs and secure outsourcing. In: Wang, X., Sako, K. (eds.) ASIACRYPT 2012. LNCS, vol. 7658, pp. 134–153. Springer, Heidelberg (2012)
4. Bellare, M., Hofheinz, D., Yilek, S.: Possibility and impossibility results for encryption and commitment secure under selective opening. In: Joux, A. (ed.) EUROCRYPT 2009. LNCS, vol. 5479, pp. 1–35. Springer, Heidelberg (2009)
5. Black, J., Rogaway, P., Shrimpton, T.: Encryption-scheme security in the presence of key-dependent messages. In: Nyberg, K., Heys, H.M. (eds.) SAC 2002. LNCS, vol. 2595, pp. 62–75. Springer, Heidelberg (2003)
6. Boneh, D., Waters, B.: Constrained pseudorandom functions and their applications. In: Sako, K., Sarkar, P. (eds.) ASIACRYPT 2013, Part II. LNCS, vol. 8270, pp. 280–300. Springer, Heidelberg (2013)
7. Boyle, E., Goldwasser, S., Ivan, I.: Functional signatures and pseudorandom functions. IACR Cryptology ePrint Archive, 2013:401 (2013)
8. Cook, S.A., Reckhow, R.A.: Time bounded random access machines. J. Comput. Syst. Sci. 7(4), 354–375 (1973)
9. Gentry, C., Halevi, S., Raykova, M., Wichs, D.: Garbled RAM revisited, part I. Cryptology ePrint Archive, Report 2014/082 (2014), http://eprint.iacr.org/
10. Goldreich, O., Goldwasser, S., Micali, S.: How to construct random functions (extended abstract). In: FOCS, pp. 464–479. IEEE Computer Society (1984)
11. Goldwasser, S., Kalai, Y.T., Popa, R.A., Vaikuntanathan, V., Zeldovich, N.: How to run turing machines on encrypted data. In: Canetti, R., Garay, J.A. (eds.) CRYPTO 2013, Part II. LNCS, vol. 8043, pp. 536–553. Springer, Heidelberg (2013)
12. Goldwasser, S., Kalai, Y.T., Popa, R.A., Vaikuntanathan, V., Zeldovich, N.: Reusable garbled circuits and succinct functional encryption. In: Boneh, D., Roughgarden, T., Feigenbaum, J. (eds.) STOC, pp. 555–564. ACM (2013)
13. Kiayias, A., Papadopoulos, S., Triandopoulos, N., Zacharias, T.: Delegatable pseudorandom functions and applications. In: Sadeghi, A.-R., Gligor, V.D., Yung, M. (eds.) ACM Conference on Computer and Communications Security, pp. 669–684. ACM (2013)
14. Lu, S., Ostrovsky, R.: How to garble RAM programs? In: Johansson, T., Nguyen, P.Q. (eds.) EUROCRYPT 2013. LNCS, vol. 7881, pp. 719–734. Springer, Heidelberg (2013)
15. Lu, S., Ostrovsky, R.: Garbled RAM revisited, part II. Cryptology ePrint Archive, Report 2014/083 (2014), http://eprint.iacr.org/
16. Pippenger, N., Fischer, M.J.: Relations among complexity measures. J. ACM 26(2), 361–381 (1979)
17. Rothblum, R.D.: On the circular security of bit-encryption. In: Sahai, A. (ed.) TCC 2013. LNCS, vol. 7785, pp. 579–598. Springer, Heidelberg (2013)
18. Sahai, A., Waters, B.: How to use indistinguishability obfuscation: Deniable encryption, and more. IACR Cryptology ePrint Archive, 2013:454 (2013)
19. Yao, A.C.-C.: Protocols for secure computations (extended abstract). In: FOCS, pp. 160–164 (1982)

Unifying Leakage Models: From Probing Attacks to Noisy Leakage[*]

Alexandre Duc[1,**], Stefan Dziembowski[2,3,***], and Sebastian Faust[1,†]

[1] Ecole Polytechnique Fédérale de Lausanne, 1015 Lausanne, Switzerland
[2] University of Warsaw, Poland
[3] Sapienza University of Rome, Italy

Abstract. A recent trend in cryptography is to formally show the leakage resilience of cryptographic implementations in a given leakage model. A realistic model is to assume that leakages are sufficiently noisy, following real-world observations. While the noisy leakage assumption has first been studied in the seminal work of Chari et al. (CRYPTO 99), the recent work of Prouff and Rivain (Eurocrypt 2013) provides the first analysis of a full masking scheme under a physically motivated noise model. Unfortunately, the security analysis of Prouff and Rivain has three important shortcomings: (1) it requires leak-free gates, (2) it considers a restricted adversarial model (random message attacks), and (3) the security proof has limited application for cryptographic settings. In this work, we provide an alternative security proof in the same noisy model that overcomes these three challenges. We achieve this goal by a new reduction from noisy leakage to the important theoretical model of probing adversaries (Ishai et al – CRYPTO 2003). Our work can be viewed as a next step of closing the gap between theory and practice in leakage resilient cryptography: while our security proofs heavily rely on concepts of theoretical cryptography, we solve problems in practically motivated leakage models.

1 Introduction

Physical side-channel attacks that exploit leakage emitting from devices are an important threat for cryptographic implementations. Prominent sources of such physical leakages include the running time of an implementation [17], its power consumption [18] or electromagnetic radiation emitting from it [26]. A large body of recent applied and theoretical research attempts to incorporate the information an adversary obtains from the leakage into the security analysis and develops countermeasures to defeat common side-channel attacks [4,14,20,1,9,31,30].

---

[*] This paper is an extended abstract of [7].

[**] Supported by a grant of the Swiss National Science Foundation, 200021_143899/1.

[***] Received founding from the European Research Council under the European Union's Seventh Framework Programme (FP7/2007-2013) / ERC Grant agreement number 207908.

[†] Received funding from the Marie Curie IEF/FP7 project GAPS, grant number: 626467.

P.Q. Nguyen and E. Oswald (Eds.): EUROCRYPT 2014, LNCS 8441, pp. 423–440, 2014.

While there is still a large gap between what theoretical models can achieve and what side-channel information is measured in practice, some recent important works propose models that better go align with the perspective of cryptographic engineering [29,24,30]. Our work follows this line of research by analyzing the security of a common countermeasure – the so-called masking countermeasure – in the model of Prouff and Rivain [24]. Our analysis works by showing that security in certain theoretical leakage models implies security in the model of [24], and hence may be seen as a first attempt to *unify* the large class of different leakage models used in recent results.

The masking countermeasure. A large body of work on cryptographic engineering has developed countermeasures to defeat side-channel attacks (see, e.g., [19] for an overview). While many countermeasures are specifically tailored to protect particular cryptographic implementations (e.g., key updates or shielded hardware), a method that generically works for most cryptographic schemes is *masking* [13,2,23,31]. The basic idea of a masking scheme is to secret share all sensitive information, including the secret key and all intermediate values that depend on it, thereby making the leakage independent of the secret data. The most prominent masking scheme is the Boolean masking: a bit b is encoded by a random bit string $(b_1, \ldots, b_n)$ such that $b = b_1 \oplus \ldots \oplus b_n$. The main difficulty in designing masking schemes is to develop masked operations, which securely compute on encoded data and ensure that *all* intermediate values are protected.

Masking against noisy leakages. Besides the fact that masking can be used to protect arbitrary computation, it has the advantage that it can be analyzed in formal security models. The first work that formally studies the soundness of masking in the presence of leakage is the seminal work of Chari et al. [4]. The authors consider a model where each share b_i of an encoding is perturbed by Gaussian noise and show that the number of noisy samples needed to recover the encoded secret bit b grows exponential with the number of shares. As stated in [4], this model matches real-world physical leakages that inherently are noisy. Moreover, many practical solutions exist to amplify leakage noise (see for instance the works of [6,5,19]).

One limitation of the security analysis given in [4] is the fact that it does not consider leakage emitting from masked computation. This shortcoming has been addressed in the recent important work of Prouff and Rivain [24], who extend at Eurocrypt 2013 the noisy leakage model of Chari et al. [4] to also include leakage from the masked operations. Specifically, they show that a variant of the construction of Ishai et al. [14] is secure even when there is noisy leakage from all the intermediate values that are produced during the computation. The authors of [24] also generalize the noisy leakage model of Chari et al. [4] to a wider range of leakage functions instead of considering only the Gaussian one. While clearly noisy leakage is closer to physical leakage occurring in real world, the security analysis of [24] has a number of shortcomings which puts strong limitations in which settings the masking countermeasure can be used and achieves the proved security statements. In particular, like earlier works on leakage resilient cryptography [8,10] the security analysis of Prouff and Rivain relies on so-called *leak-free* gates. Moreover, security is shown in a restricted adversarial model that assumes that plaintexts are chosen uniformly during an attack and the adversary does not exploit joint information from the leakages and, e.g., the ciphertext. We discuss these shortcomings in more detail in the next section.

1.1 The Work of Prouff and Rivain [25]

Prouff and Rivain [25] analyze the security of a block-cipher implementation that is masked with an additive masking scheme working over a finite field $\mathbb{F}$. More precisely, let t be the security parameter then a secret $s \in \mathbb{F}$ is represented by an encoding $(X_1, \ldots, X_t)$ such that each $X_i \leftarrow \mathbb{F}$ is uniformly random subject to $s = X_1 \oplus \ldots \oplus X_t$. As discussed above the main difficulty in designing secure masking schemes is to devise masked operations that work on masked values. To this end, Prouff and Rivain use the original scheme of Ishai et al. [14] augmented with some techniques from [3,27] to work over larger fields and to obtain a more efficient implementation. The masked operations are built out of several smaller components. First, a leak-free operation that refreshes encodings, i.e., it takes as input an encoding $(X_1, \ldots, X_t)$ of a secret s and outputs a freshly and independently chosen encoding of the same value. Second, a number of leaky elementary operations that work on a constant number of field elements. For each of these elementary operations the adversary is given leakage $f(X)$, where X are the inputs of the operation and f is a noisy function. Clearly, the noise-level has to be high enough so that given $f(X)$ the values of X is not completely revealed. To this end, the authors introduce the notion of a *bias*, which informally says that the statistical distance between the distribution of X and the conditional distribution $X|f(X)$ is bounded by some parameter.

While noisy leakages are certainly a step in the right direction to model physical leakage, we detail below some of the limitations of the security analysis of Prouff and Rivain [24]:

1. *Leak-free components:* The assumption of leak-free computation has been used in earlier works on leakage resilient computation [10,8]. It is a strong assumption on the physical hardware and, as stated in [24], an important limitation of the current proof approach. The leak-free component of [24] is a simple operation that takes as input an encoding and refreshes it. While the computation of this operation is supposed to be completely shielded against leakage, the inputs and the outputs of this computation may leak. Notice that the leak-free component of [24] depends on the computation that is carried out in the circuit by takeing inputs. In particular, this means that the computation of the leak-free component depends on secret information, which makes it harder to protect in practice and is different from earlier works that use leak-free components [10,8].

2. *Random message attacks:* The security analysis is given only for random message attacks. In particular, it is assumed that every masked secret is a

uniformly random value. This is in contrast to most works in cryptography, which usually consider at least a chosen message attack. When applied to a block-cipher, their proof implies that the adversary has only access to the *leakage* of the system without knowing which plaintext was used nor which ciphertext was obtained. Hence, the proof does not cover chosen plaintext or chosen ciphertext attacks. However, it is true that it is not clear how chosen message attacks change the picture in standard DPA attacks [32].

3. *Mutual-information-based security statement:* The final statement of Theorem 4 in [24] only gives a bound on the mutual information of the key and the leakages from the cipher. In particular, this does not include information that an adversary may learn from exploiting joint information from the leakages and plaintext/ciphertext pairs. Notice that the use of mutual information gets particularly problematic under continuous leakage attacks, since multiple plaintext/ciphertext pairs information theoretically completely reveal the secret key. The standard security notion used, e.g., in Ishai et al. is simulation-based and covers such subtleties when dealing with Shannon information theory.

4. *Strong noise requirements:* The amount of noise that is needed depends on the number of shares and on the size of the field which might be a bit unnatural. Moreover, the noise is independently sampled for each of the elementary operation that have constant size.

1.2 Our Contribution

We show in this work how to eliminate limitations 1-3 by a simple and elegant simulation-based argument and a reduction to the so-called t-probing adversarial setting [14] (that in this paper we call the *t-threshold-probing model* to emphasize the difference between this model and the *random*-probing model defined later.). The t-threshold-probing model considers an adversary that can learn the value of t intermediate values that are produced during the computation and is often considered as a good approximation for modelling higher-order attacks. We notice that limitation 4 from above is what enables our security analysis. The fact that the noise is independent for each elementary operation allows us to formally prove security under an *identical* noise model as [24], but using a simpler and improved analysis. In particular, we are able to show that the original construction of Ishai et al. satisfies the standard simulation-based security notion under noisy leakages without relying on any leak-free components. We emphasize that our techniques are very different (and much simpler) than the recent breakthrough result of Goldwasser and Rothblum [12] who show how to eliminate leak-free gates in the bounded leakage model. We will further discuss related works in Section 1.3.

Our proof considers three different leakage models and shows connections between them. One may view our work as a first attempt to "reduce" the number of different leakage models, which is in contrast to many earlier works that introduced new leakage settings. Eventually, we are able to reduce the security in the noisy leakage model to the security in the t -threshold-probing model.

This shows that, for the particular choice of parameters given in [24], security in the t-threshold-probing model implies security in the noisy leakage model. This goes align with the common approach of showing security against t-order attacks, which usually requires to prove security in the t–threshold-probing model. Moreover, it shows that the original construction of Ishai et al. that has been used in many works on masking (including the work of Prouff and Rivain) is indeed a sound approach for protecting against side-channel leakages when assuming that they are sufficiently noisy. We give some more details on our techniques below.

From noisy leakages to random probes. As a first step in our security proof we show that we can simulate any adversary in the noisy leakage model of Prouff and Rivain with an adversary in a simpler noise model that we name a *random probing adversary* and is similar to a model introduced in [14]. In this model, an adversary recovers an intermediate value with probability ϵ and obtains a special symbol $\perp$ with probability $1 - \epsilon$. This reduction shows that this model is worth studiying, although from the engineering perspective it may seem unnatural.

From random probes to the t-threshold-probing model. We show how to go from the random probing adversary setting to the more standard t-threshold-probing adversary of Ishai et al. in [14]. This step is rather easy as due to the independency of the noise we can apply Chernoff's bound almost immediately. One technical difficulty is that the work of Prouff and Rivain considers joint noisy leakage from elementary operations, while the standard t-threshold-probing setting only talks about leakage from wires. Notice, however, that the elementary operations of [24] only depend on two inputs and, hence, it is not hard to extend the result of Ishai et al. to consider "gate probing adversary" by tolerating a loss in the parameters. Finally, our analysis enables us to show security of the masking based countermeasure without the limitations 1-3 discussed above.

Leakage resilient circuits with simulation-based security. In our security analysis we use the the framework of leakage resilient circuits introduced in the seminal work of Ishai et al. [14]. A circuit compiler takes as input the description of a cryptographic scheme C with secret key K, e.g., a circuit that describes a block cipher, and outputs a transformed circuit C' and corresponding key K'. The circuit $C'[K']$ shall implement the same functionality as C running with key K, but additionally is resilient to certain well-defined classes of leakage. Notice that while the framework of [14] talks about circuits the same approach applies to software implementations, and we only follow this notation to abstract our description.

Moreover, our work uses the well-established simulation paradigm to state the security guarantees we achieve. Intuitively, simulation-based security says that whatever attack an adversary can carry out when knowing the leakage, he can also run (with similar success probability) by just having black-box access to C. In contrast to the approach based on Shannon information theory our analysis includes attacks that exploit joint information from the leakage and plaintext/ciphertext pairs. It seems impossible to us to incorporate the plaintext/ciphertext pairs into an analysis based on Shannon information theory. To see this, consider a block-cipher execution, where, clearly, when given a couple of plaintext/ciphertext pairs, the secret key is information theoretically revealed.[1] The authors of [24] are well aware of this problem and explicitly exclude such joint information. A consequence of the simulation-based security analysis is that we require an additional mild assumption on the noise – namely, that it is efficiently computable (see Section 3.1 for more details). While this is a standard assumption made in most works on leakage resilient cryptography, we emphasize that we can easily drop the assumption of efficiently computable noise (and hence considering the same noise model as [24]), when we only want to achieve the weaker security notion considered in [24]. Notice that in this case we are still able to eliminate the limitations 1 & 2 mentioned above.

1.3　Related Work

Masking & leakage resilient circuits. A large body of work has proposed various masking schemes and studies their security in different security models (see, e.g., [13,2,23,31,27]). The already mentioned t-threshold-probing model has been considered in the work of Rivain and Prouff [27], who show how to extend the work of Ishai et al. to larger fields and propose efficiency improvements. In [25] it was shown that techniques from multiparty computation can be used to show security in the t-threshold-probing model. The work of Standaert et al. [31] studies masking schemes using the information theoretic framework of [29] by considering the Hamming weight model. Many other works analyze the security of the masking countermeasure and we refer the reader for further details to [24].

With the emerge of leakage resilient cryptography [20,1,9] several works have proposed new security models and alternative masking schemes. The main difference between these new security models and the t-threshold-probing model is that they consider *joint leakages* from large parts of the computation. The work of Faust et al. [10] extends the security analysis of Ishai et al. beyond the t-threshold-probing model by considering leakages that can be described by low-depth circuits (so-called AC^0 leakages). Faust et al. use leak-free component that have been eliminated by Rohtblum in [28] using computational assumptions. The recent work of Miles and Viola [21] proposes a new circuit transformation using alternating groups and shows security with respect to AC^0 and TC^0 leakages.

Another line of work considers circuits that are provably secure in the so-called continuous bounded leakage model [15,11,8,12]. In this model, the adversary is allowed to learn arbitrary information from the computation of the circuit as

---

[1] More concretely: imagine an adversary that attacks a block-cipher implementation E_K, where K is the secret key. Then just by launching a known-plaintext attack he can obtain several pairs $V = (M_0, E_K(M_0)), (M_1, E_K(M_1)), \ldots$. Clearly a small number of such pairs is usually enough to determine K *information-theoretically*. Hence it makes no sense to require that "K is information-theoretically hidden given V and the side-channel leakage."

long as the amount of information is bounded. The proposed schemes rely additionally on the assumption of "only computation leaks information" of Micali and Reyzin [20].

Noisy leakage models. The work of Faust et al. [10] also considers circuit compilers for noisy models. Specifically, they propose a construction with security in the binomial noise model, where each value on a wire is flipped independently with probability $p \in (0, 1/2)$. In contrast to the work of [24] and our work the noise model is restricted to binomial noise, but the noise rate is significantly better (constant instead of linear noise). Similar to [24] the work of Faust et al. also uses leak-free components. Besides these works on masking schemes, several works consider noisy leakages for concrete cryptographic schemes [9,22,16]. Typically, the noise model considered in these works is significantly stronger than the noise model that is considered for masking schemes. In particular, no strong assumption about the independency of the noise is made.

2   Preliminaries

We start with some standard definitions and lemmas about the statistical distance. If $\mathcal{A}$ is a set then $U \leftarrow \mathcal{A}$ denotes a random variable sampled uniformly from $\mathcal{A}$. Recall that if A and B are random variables over the same set $\mathcal{A}$ then the *statistical distance between A and B* is denoted as $\Delta(A; B)$, and defined as $\Delta(A; B) = \frac{1}{2} \sum_{a \in \mathcal{A}} |\mathbb{P}(A = a) - \mathbb{P}(B = a)| = \sum_{a \in \mathcal{A}} \max\{0, \mathbb{P}(A = a) - \mathbb{P}(B = a)\}$. If $\mathcal{X}, \mathcal{Y}$ are some events then by $\Delta((A|\mathcal{X}) ; (B|\mathcal{Y}))$ we will mean the distance between variables A' and B', distributed according to the conditional distributions $P_{A|\mathcal{X}}$ and $P_{B|\mathcal{Y}}$. If $\mathcal{X}$ is an event of probability 1 then we also write $\Delta(A ; (B|\mathcal{Y}))$ instead of $\Delta((A|\mathcal{X}) ; (B|\mathcal{Y}))$. If C is a random variable then by $\Delta(A ; (B|C))$ we mean $\sum \mathbb{P}(C = c) \cdot \Delta(A ; (B|(C = c)))$.

   If A, B, and C are random variables then $\Delta((B; C) \mid A)$ denotes $\Delta((BA); (CA))$. It is easy to see that it is equal to $\sum_a \mathbb{P}(A = a) \cdot \Delta((B|A = a) ; (C|A = a))$. If $\Delta(A; B) \leq \epsilon$ then we say that A and B are *ϵ-close*. The "$\overset{d}{=}$" symbol denotes the equality of distributions, i.e., $A \overset{d}{=} B$ if and only if $\Delta(A; B) = 0$. We also have the following lemma, whose proof appears in the full version.

Lemma 1. *Let A, B be two random variables. Let B' be a variable distributed identically to B but independent from A. We have $\Delta(A; (A|B)) = \Delta((B; B') \mid A)$.*

3   Noise from Set Elements

We start with describing the basic framework for reasoning about the noise from elements of a finite set $\mathcal{X}$. Later, in Section 4, we will consider the leakage from the vectors over $\mathcal{X}$, and then, in Section 5, from the entire computation. The reason why we can smoothly use the analysis from Section 3.1 in the later sections is that, as in the work of Prouff and Rivain, we require that the noise is independent for all elementary operations. By elementary operations, [24] considers the basic underlying operations over the underlying field $\mathcal{X}$ used in a masked implementation. In this work, we consider the same setting and type of underlying operations (in fact, notice that our construction is identical to theirs – except that we eliminate the leak-free gates and prove a stronger statement). Notice that instead of talking about elementary operations, we consider the more standard term of "gates" that was used in the work of Ishai et al. [14].

3.1   Modeling Noise

Let us start with a discussion defining what it means that a randomized function $Noise : \mathcal{X} \to \mathcal{Y}$ is "noisy". We will assume that $\mathcal{X}$ is finite and rather small: typical choices for $\mathcal{X}$ would be GF(2) (the "Boolean case"), or GF(2^8), if we want to deal with the AES circuit. The set $\mathcal{Y}$ corresponds to the set of all possible noise measurements and may be infinite, except when we require the "efficient simulation" (we discuss it further at the end of this section). As already informally described in Section 1.1 our basic definition is as follows: we say that the function $Noise$ is δ-noisy if

$$\delta = \Delta(X; (X | Noise(X))). \tag{1}$$

Of course for (1) to be well-defined we need to specify the distribution of X. The idea to define noisy functions by comparing the distributions of X and "X conditioned on $Noise(X)$" comes from [24], where it is argued that the most natural choice for X is a random variable distributed uniformly over $\mathcal{X}$. We also adopt this convention and assume that $X \leftarrow \mathcal{X}$. We would like to stress, however, that in our proofs we will apply $Noise$ to inputs $\hat{X}$ that are not necessarily uniform and in this case the value of $\Delta(\hat{X}; (\hat{X} | Noise(\hat{X}))$ may obviously be some non-trivial function of δ. Of course if $X \leftarrow \mathcal{X}$ and $X' \leftarrow \mathcal{X}$ then $Noise(X')$ is distributed identically to $Noise(X)$, and hence, by Lemma 1, Eq. (1) is equivalent to:

$$\delta = \Delta((Noise(X); Noise(X')) \mid X), \tag{2}$$

where X and X' are uniform over $\mathcal{X}$. Note that at the beginning this definition may be a bit counter-intuitive, as *smaller* δ means *more* noise: in particular we achieve "full noise" if $\delta = 0$, and "no noise" if $\delta \approx 1$. Let us compare this definition with the definition of [24]. In a nutshell: the definition of [24] is similar to ours, the only difference being that instead of the statistical distance Δ in [24] the authors use a distance based on the Euclidean norm. More precisely, they start with defining d as: $\mathrm{d}(X; Y) := \sqrt{\sum_{x \in \mathcal{X}} (\mathbb{P}(X = x) - \mathbb{P}(Y = y))^2}$, and using this notion they define β as:

$$\beta(X | Noise(X)) := \sum_{y \in \mathcal{Y}} \mathbb{P}(Noise(X) = y) \cdot \mathrm{d}(X \; ; \; (X | Noise(X) = y))$$

(where X is uniform). In the terminology of [24] a function $Noise$ is "δ-noisy" if $\delta = \beta(X | Noise(X))$. Observe that the right hand side of our noise definition in Eq. (1) can be rewritten as: $\sum_{b \in \mathcal{Y}} \mathbb{P}\left(Noise(X) = y\right) \cdot \Delta(X \; ; \; (X|Noise(X) = y))$,hence the only difference between their approach and ours is that we use Δ where they use the distance d. The authors do not explain why they choose this particular measure. We believe that our choice to use the standard definition of statistical distance Δ is more natural in this setting, since, unlike the "d" distance, it has been used in hundreds of cryptographic papers in the past. The popularity of the Δ distance comes from the fact that it corresponds to an intuitive concept of the "indistinguishability of distributions" — it is well-known, and simple to verify, that $\Delta(X;Y) \leq \delta$ if and only if no adversary can distinguish between X and Y with advantage better than δ.[2] Hence, e.g., (2) can be interpreted as:

> δ is the maximum probability, over all adversaries $\mathcal{A}$, that $\mathcal{A}$ distinguishes between the noise from a uniform X that is *known to him*, and a uniform X' that is *unknown to him*.

It is unclear to us if a d distance has a similar interpretation. We emphasize, however, that the choice whether to use Δ or β is not too important, as the following inequality hold (c.f. [24]):

$$\frac{1}{2} \cdot \beta(X|Noise(X)) \leq \Delta(X; (X|Noise(X))) \leq \frac{\sqrt{|\mathcal{X}|}}{2} \cdot \beta(X|Noise(X)). \quad (3)$$

Hence, we decide to stick to the "Δ distance" in this paper. However, to allow for comparison between our work and the one of [24] we will at the end of the paper present our results also in terms of the β measure (this translation will be straightforward, thanks to the inequalities in (3)).In [24] (cf. Theorem 4) the result is stated in form of Shannon information theory. While such an information theoretic approach may be useful in certain settings [29], we follow the more "traditional" approach and provide an efficient simulation argument. As discussed in the introduction, this also covers a setting where the adversary exploits joint information of the leakage and, e.g., the plaintext/ciphertext pairs. We emphasize, however, that our results can easily be expressed in the information theoretic language as shown in the full version of the paper.

The Issue of "Efficient Simulation". To achieve the strong simulation-based security notion, we need an additional requirement on the leakage, namely, that the leakage can efficiently be "simulated" – which typically requires that the noise function is efficiently computable. In fact, for our proofs to go through we actually need something slightly stronger, namely that *Noise is efficiently decidable* by which we mean that (a) there exists a randomized poly-time algorithm that computes it, and (b) the set $\mathcal{Y}$ is finite and for every x and y the value of $\mathbb{P}\left(Noise(x) = y\right)$ is computable in polynomial time. While (b) may look like a strong assumption we note that in practice for most "natural" noise functions (like the Gaussian noise with a known parameter, measured with a very good, but finite, precision) it is easily satisfiable.

---

[2] This formally means that for every $\mathcal{A}$ we have $|\mathbb{P}\left(\mathcal{A}(X) = 1\right) - \mathbb{P}\left(\mathcal{A}(Y) = 1\right)| \leq \delta$.

Recall that the results of [24] are stated without taking into consideration the issue of the "efficient simulation". Hence, if one wants to compare our results with [24] then one can simply drop the efficient decidability assumption on the noise. To keep our presentation concise and clean, also in this case the results will be presented in a form "for every adversary $\mathcal{A}$ there exists an (inefficient) simulator $\mathcal{S}$". Here the "inefficient simulator" can be an arbitrary machine, capable, e.g., of sampling elements from *any* probability distributions.

3.2   Simulating Noise by ϵ-Identity Functions

Lemma 2 below is our main technical tool. Informally, it states that every δ-noisy function $Noise : \mathcal{X} \to \mathcal{Y}$ can be represented as a composition $Noise' \circ \varphi$ of efficiently computable randomized functions $Noise'$ and φ, where φ is a "$\delta \cdot |\mathcal{X}|$-identity function", defined in Definition 1 below.

Definition 1. *A randomized function* $\varphi : \mathcal{X} \to \mathcal{X} \cup \{\bot\}$ *is an ϵ-identity if for every x we have that either $\varphi(x) = x$ or $\varphi(x) = \bot$ and $\mathbb{P}(\varphi(x) \neq \bot) = \epsilon$.*

This will allow us to reduce the "noisy attacks" to the "random probing attacks", where the adversary learns each wire (or a gate, see Section 5.5) of the circuit with probability ϵ. Observe also, that thanks to the assumed independence of noise, the events that the adversary learns each element are independent, which, in turn, will allow us to use the Chernoff bound to prove that with a good probability the number of wires that the adversary learns is small.

Lemma 2. *Let $Noise : \mathcal{X} \to \mathcal{Y}$ be a δ-noisy function. Then there exist $\epsilon \leq \delta \cdot |\mathcal{X}|$ and a randomized function $Noise' : \mathcal{X} \cup \{\bot\} \to \mathcal{X}$ such that for every $x \in \mathcal{X}$ we have*

$$Noise(x) \stackrel{d}{=} Noise'(\varphi(x)), \tag{4}$$

where $\varphi : \mathcal{X} \to \mathcal{X} \cup \{\bot\}$ is the ϵ-identity function. Moreover, if $Noise$ is efficiently decidable then $Noise'(\varphi(x))$ is computable in time that is expected polynomial in $|\mathcal{X}|$.

The proof appears in the full version of the paper.

4   Leakage from Vectors

In this section we describe the leakage models relevant to this paper. We start with describing the models abstractly, by considering leakage from an arbitrary sequence $(x_1, \ldots, x_\ell) \in \mathcal{X}^\ell$, where $\mathcal{X}$ is some finite set and ℓ is a parameter. The adversary $\mathcal{A}$ will be able to obtain some partial information about $(x_1, \ldots, x_\ell)$ via the games described below. Note that we do not specify the computational power of $\mathcal{A}$, as the definitions below make sense for both computationally-bounded or infinitely powerful $\mathcal{A}$.

Noisy Model. For $\delta \geq 0$ a δ-*noisy adversary on* $\mathcal{X}^\ell$ is a machine $\mathcal{A}$ that plays the following game against an oracle that knows $(x_1, \ldots, x_\ell) \in \mathcal{X}^\ell$:

1. $\mathcal{A}$ specifies a sequence $\{Noise_i : \mathcal{X} \to \mathcal{Y}\}_{i=1}^\ell$ of noisy functions such that every $Noise_i$ is δ_i'-noisy, for some $\delta_i' \leq \delta$ and mutually independent noises.
2. $\mathcal{A}$ receives $Noise_1(x_1), \ldots, Noise_\ell(x_\ell)$ and outputs some value $out_\mathcal{A}$ $(x_1, \ldots, x_\ell)$.

If $\mathcal{A}$ works in polynomial time and the noise functions specified by $\mathcal{A}$ are efficiently decidable then we say that $\mathcal{A}$ *is poly-time-noisy.*

Random Probing Model. For $\epsilon \leq 0$ a ϵ-*random-probing adversary on* $\mathcal{X}^\ell$ is a machine $\mathcal{A}$ that plays the following game against an oracle that knows $(x_1, \ldots, x_\ell) \in \mathcal{X}^\ell$:

1. $\mathcal{A}$ specifies a sequence $(\epsilon_1, \ldots, \epsilon_\ell)$ such that each $\epsilon_i \leq \epsilon$.
2. $\mathcal{A}$ receives $\varphi_1(x_1), \ldots, \varphi_\ell(x_\ell)$ and outputs some value $out_\mathcal{A}(x_1, \ldots, x_\ell)$, where each φ_i is the ϵ_i-identity function with mutually independent randomness.

A similar model was introduced in the work of Ishai, Sahai and Wagner [14] to obtain circuit compilers with linear blow-up in the size.

Threshold Probing Model. For $t = 0, \ldots, \ell$ a t-*treshold-probing adversary on* $\mathcal{X}^\ell$ is a machine $\mathcal{A}$ that plays the following game against an oracle that knows $(x_1, \ldots, x_\ell) \in \mathcal{X}^\ell$:

1. $\mathcal{A}$ specifies a set $\mathcal{I} = \{i_1, \ldots, i_{|\mathcal{I}|}\} \subseteq \{1, \ldots, \ell\}$ of cardinality at most t,
2. $\mathcal{A}$ receives $(x_{i_1}, \ldots, x_{i_{|\mathcal{I}|}})$ and outputs some value $out_\mathcal{A}(x_1, \ldots, x_\ell)$.

4.1 Simulating the Noisy Adversary by a Random-Probing Adversary

The following lemma shows that every δ-noisy adversary can be simulated by a $\delta \cdot |\mathcal{X}|$-random probing adversary.

Lemma 3. *Let* $\mathcal{A}$ *be a* δ-*noisy adversary on* $\mathcal{X}^\ell$. *Then there exists a* $\delta \cdot |\mathcal{X}|$-*random-probing adversary* $\mathcal{S}$ *on* $\mathcal{X}^\ell$ *such that for every* $(x_1, \ldots, x_\ell)$ *we have*

$$out_\mathcal{A}(x_1, \ldots, x_\ell) \overset{d}{=} out_\mathcal{S}(x_1, \ldots, x_\ell). \tag{5}$$

Moreover, if $\mathcal{A}$ *is poly-time-noisy, then* $\mathcal{S}$ *works in time polynomial in* $|\mathcal{X}|$.

Intuitively, this lemma easily follows from Lemma 2 applied independently to each element of $(x_1, \ldots, x_\ell)$. The formal proof appears in the full version.

4.2 Simulating the Random-Probing Adversary

In this section we show how to simulate every δ-random probing adversary by a threshold adversary. This simulation, unlike the one in Section 4 will not be perfect in the sense that the distribution output by the simulator will be identical to the distribution of the original adversary only when conditioned on some event that happens with a large probability. We start with the following lemma, whose proof, which is a straightforward application of the Chernoff bound, appears in the full version.

Lemma 4. *Let $\mathcal{A}$ be an ϵ-random-probing adversary on $\mathcal{X}^\ell$. Then there exists a $(2\epsilon\ell - 1)$-threshold-probing adversary $\mathcal{S}$ on $\mathcal{X}^\ell$ operating in time linear in the working time of $\mathcal{A}$ such that for every $(x_1, \ldots, x_\ell)$ we have*

$$\Delta(out_{\mathcal{A}}(x_1, \ldots, x_\ell) \; ; \; out_{\mathcal{S}}(x_1, \ldots, x_\ell) \mid out_{\mathcal{S}}(x_1, \ldots, x_\ell) \neq \bot) = 0, \quad (6)$$

where

$$\mathbb{P}\left(out_{\mathcal{S}}(x_1, \ldots, x_\ell) = \bot\right) \leq \exp\left(-\frac{\epsilon\ell}{3}\right). \quad (7)$$

The following corollary, whose proof is given in the full version, combines Lemma 3 and 4 together, and will be useful in the sequel.

Corollary 1. *Let $d, \ell \in \mathbb{N}$ with $\ell > d$ and let $\mathcal{A}$ be a $d/(4\ell \cdot |\mathcal{X}|)$-noisy adversary on $\mathcal{X}^\ell$. Then there exists an $(d/2 - 1)$-threshold-probing adversary $\mathcal{S}$ such that*

$$\Delta(out_{\mathcal{A}}(x_1, \ldots, x_\ell) \; ; \; out_{\mathcal{S}}(x_1, \ldots, x_\ell) \mid out_{\mathcal{S}}(x_1, \ldots, x_\ell) \neq \bot) = 0 \quad (8)$$

and $\mathbb{P}(out_{\mathcal{S}}(x_1, \ldots, x_\ell) = \bot) \leq \exp(-d/12)$. Moreover, if $\mathcal{A}$ is poly-time-noisy then $\mathcal{S}$ works in time polynomial $\ell \cdot |\mathcal{X}|$.

5   Leakage from Computation

In this section we address the main topic of this paper, which is the noise-resilience of cryptographic computations. Our main model will be the model of arithmetic circuits over a finite field. First, in Section 5.1 we present our security definitions, and then, in Section 5.2 we describe a secure "compiler" that transforms any cryptographic scheme secure in the "black-box" model into one secure against the noisy leakage (it is essentially identical to the transformation of [14] later extended in [27]). Finally, in the last section we present our security results.

5.1   Definitions

A *(stateful arithmetic) circuit* Γ *over a field* $\mathbb{F}$ is a directed graph whose nodes are called *gates*. Each gate γ can be of one of the following types: an *input gate* γ^{inp} of fan-in zero, an *output gate* γ^{out} of fan-out zero, a *random gate* γ^{rand} of fan-in zero, a *multiplication gate* $\gamma^\times$ of fan-in 2, an *addition gate* γ^+ of fan-in 2, a *subtraction gate* γ^- of fan-in 2, a *constant gate* γ^{const}, and a *memory gate* γ^{mem} of fan-in 1. Following [14] we assume that the fan-out of every gate is at most 3. The only cycles that are allowed in Γ must contain exactly 1 memory gate. The *size* $|\Gamma|$ *of the circuit* Γ is defined to be the total number of its gates. The numbers of input gates, output gates and memory gates will be denoted $|\Gamma.inp|$, $|\Gamma.out|$, and $|\Gamma.mem|$, respectively.

The computation of Γ is performed in several "rounds" numbered $1, 2, \ldots$. In each of them the circuit will take some input, produce an output and update the memory state. Initially, the memory gates of Γ are preloaded with some initial "state" $k_0 \in \mathbb{F}^{|\Gamma.mem|}$. At the beginning of the ith round the input gates are loaded with elements of some vector $a_i \in \mathbb{F}^{|\Gamma.inp|}$ called the *input for the ith round*. The computation of Γ in the ith round depends on a_i and on the memory state k_{i-1}. It proceeds in a straightforward way: if all the input wires of a given gate are known then the value on its output wire can be computed naturally: if γ is a multiplication gate with input wires carrying values a and b, then its output wire will carry the value $a \cdot b$ (where "$\cdot$" is the multiplication operation in $\mathbb{F}$), and the addition and the subtraction gates are handled analogously. We assume that the random gates produce a fresh random field element in each round. The *output of the ith round* is read-off from the output gates and denoted $b_i \in \mathbb{F}^{|\Gamma.out|}$. The *state after the ith round* is contained in the memory gates and denoted k_i. For $k \in \mathbb{F}^{|\Gamma.mem|}$ and a sequence of inputs $(a_1, \ldots, a_m)$ (where each $a_i \in \mathbb{F}^{|\Gamma.inp|}$) let $\Gamma(k, a_1, \ldots, a_m)$ denote the sequence $(B_1, \ldots, B_m)$ where each B_i is the output of Γ with $k_0 = k$ and inputs $a_1, \ldots, a_m$ in rounds $1, 2, \ldots$. Observe that, since Γ is randomized, hence $\Gamma(k, a_1, \ldots, a_m)$ is a random variable.

A *black-box circuit adversary* $\mathcal{A}$ is a machine that adaptively interacts with a circuit Γ via the input and output interface. Then $out\left(\mathcal{A} \overset{bb}{\leftrightarrows} \Gamma(k)\right)$ denotes the output of $\mathcal{A}$ after interacting with Γ whose initial memory state is $k_0 = k$. A *δ-noisy circuit adversary* $\mathcal{A}$ is an adversary that has the following additional ability: after each ith round $\mathcal{A}$ gets some partial information about the internal state of the computation via the noisy leakage functions. More precisely: let $(X_1, \ldots, X_\ell)$ be the random variable denoting the values on the wires of $\Gamma(k)$ in the ith round. Then $\mathcal{A}$ plays the role of a δ-noisy adversary in a game against $(X_1, \ldots, X_\ell)$ (c.f. Section 4), namely: he choses a sequence $\{Noise_i : \mathbb{F} \to \mathcal{Y}\}_{i=1}^{\ell}$ of functions such that every $Noise_i$ is δ_i-noisy for some $\delta_i \leq \delta$ and he receives $Noise_1(X_1), \ldots, Noise_\ell(X_\ell)$. Let $out\left(\mathcal{A} \overset{noisy}{\leftrightarrows} \Gamma(k)\right)$ denote the output of such an $\mathcal{A}$ after interacting with Γ whose initial memory state is $k_0 = k$.

We can also replace, in the above definition, the "δ-noisy adversary" with the "ϵ-random probing adversary". In this case, after each ith round $\mathcal{A}$ choses a sequence $(\epsilon_1, \ldots, \epsilon_\ell)$ such that each $\epsilon_i \leq \epsilon$ and he learns $\varphi_1(X_1), \ldots, \varphi_\ell(X_\ell)$, where each φ_i is the ϵ_i-identity function. Let $out\left(\mathcal{A} \overset{rnd}{\leftrightarrows} \Gamma(k)\right)$ denote the output of such $\mathcal{A}$ after interacting with Γ whose initial memory state is $k_0 = k$.

Analogously we can replace the "δ-noisy adversary" with the "t-threshold probing adversary" obtaining an adversary that after each ith round $\mathcal{A}$ learns t elements of $(X_1), \ldots, \varphi_\ell(X_\ell)$. Let $out\left(\mathcal{A} \overset{thr}{\leftrightarrows} \Gamma(k)\right)$ denote the output of such $\mathcal{A}$ after interacting with Γ whose initial memory state is $k_0 = k$.

Definition 2. *Consider two stateful circuits Γ and Γ' (over some field $\mathbb{F}$) and a randomized encoding function Enc. We say that Γ' is a (δ, ξ)-noise resilient* implementation of a circuit Γ w.r.t. *Enc if the following holds for every* $k \in \mathbb{F}^{|\Gamma.inp|}$:

1. *the input-output behavior of* $\Gamma(k)$ *and* $\Gamma'(Enc(k))$ *is identical, i.e.: for every sequence of inputs* $a_1, \ldots, a_m$ *and outputs* $b_1, \ldots, b_m$ *we have*

$$\mathbb{P}\left(\Gamma(k, a_1, \ldots, a_m) = (b_1, \ldots, b_m)\right) = \mathbb{P}\left(\Gamma'(Enc(k), a_1, \ldots, a_m) = (b_1, \ldots, b_m)\right)$$

   and

2. *for every* δ-*noisy circuit adversary* $\mathcal{A}$ *there exists a black-box circuit adversary* $\mathcal{S}$ *such that*

$$\Delta\left(out\left(\mathcal{S} \overset{bb}{\leftrightarrows} \Gamma(k)\right) \; ; \; out\left(\mathcal{A} \overset{noisy}{\leftrightarrows} \Gamma'(Enc(k))\right)\right) \leq \xi. \tag{9}$$

The definition of Γ' *being a* (ϵ, ξ)-*random-probing resilient implementation of a circuit* Γ *is identical to the one above, except that Point 2 is replaced with:*

2'. *for every* ϵ-*random-probing circuit adversary* $\mathcal{A}$ *there exists a black-box circuit adversary* $\mathcal{S}$ *such that*

$$\Delta\left(out\left(\mathcal{S} \overset{bb}{\leftrightarrows} \Gamma(k)\right) \; ; \; out\left(\mathcal{A} \overset{rnd}{\leftrightarrows} \Gamma'(Enc(k))\right)\right) \leq \xi.$$

The definition of Γ' *being a* (t, ξ)-*threshold-probing resilient implementation of a circuit* Γ *is identical to the one above, except that Point 2 is replaced with:*

2". *for every* t-*threshold-probing circuit adversary* $\mathcal{A}$ *there exists a black-box circuit adversary* $\mathcal{S}$ *such that*

$$\Delta\left(out\left(\mathcal{S} \overset{bb}{\leftrightarrows} \Gamma(k)\right) \; ; \; out\left(\mathcal{A} \overset{thr}{\leftrightarrows} \Gamma'(Enc(k))\right)\right) \leq \xi.$$

In all cases above we will say that Γ' *is a an implementation* Γ *with efficient simulation if the simulator* $\mathcal{S}$ *works in time polynomial in* $\Gamma' \cdot |\mathbb{F}|$ *as long as* $\mathcal{A}$ *is poly-time and the noise functions specified by* $\mathcal{A}$ *are efficiently decidable.*

5.2   The Implementation

In the full version of the paper, we describe in details the circuit compiler of [14] which was generalized to larger fields in [27]. Due to space constraints, we just recall it here in few sentences. The encoding function is defined as: $Enc_+(x) := (X_1, \ldots, X_d)$, where $X_1, \ldots, X_d$ are uniform such that $X_1 + \cdots + X_d = x$. At a high level, each wire w in the original circuit Γ is represented by a *wire bundle* in Γ', consisting of d wires $\vec{w} = (w_1, \ldots, w_d)$, that carry an *encoding* of w. The gates in C are replaced gate-by-gate with so-called *gadgets*, computing on encoded values. Addition and subtraction are performed wire-wise. For multiplication, for input $\vec{a}$ and $\vec{b}$, the circuit Γ' generates, for every $1 \leq i < j \leq d$, a random field element $z_{i,j}$ (this is done using the random gates in Γ'). Then, for every $1 \leq j < i \leq d$ it computes $z_{i,j} := a_i b_j + a_j b_i - z_{j,i}$, and finally he computes each output c_i (for $i = 1, \ldots, d$) as $c_i := a_i b_i + \sum_{i \neq j} z_{i,j}$.

   This multiplication gadget turns out to a be useful as a building block for "refreshing" of the encoding.

5.3   Security in the Probing Model [14]

In [14] it is shown that the compiler from the pervious section is secure against probing attacks in which the adversary can probe at most $\lfloor (d-1)/2 \rfloor$ wires in each round.[3] This parameter may be a bit disappointing as the number of probes that the adversary needs to break the security does not grow with the size of the circuit. This assumption may seem particularity unrealistic for large circuits Γ. Fortunately, [14] also shows a small modification of the construction from Section 5.2 that is resilient to a larger number of probes, provided that the number of probes from each gadget is bounded. Before we present it let us argue why the original construction is not secure against such attacks. To this end, assume that our circuit Γ has a long sequence of wires $a_1, \ldots, a_m$, where each a_i (for $i > 1$) is the result of adding to a_{i-1} (using an addition gate) a 0 constant (that was generated using a γ_0^{const} gate). It is easy to see that in the circuit Γ' all the wire bundles $\overrightarrow{a_1}, \ldots, \overrightarrow{a_m}$ (where each $\overrightarrow{a_i}$ corresponds to a_i) will be identical. Hence, the adversary that probes even a single wire in each addition gadget in Γ' will learn the encoding of a_1 completely as long as $m \geq d$. Fortunately one can deal with this problem by "refreshing" the encoding after each subtraction and addition gate exactly in the same way as done before, i.e. by using the *Refresh* sub-gadget.

Lemma 5 ([14]). *Let Γ be an arbitrary stateful arithmetic circuit over some field $\mathbb{F}$. Let Γ' be the circuit that results from the procedure described above. Then Γ' is a $(\lfloor (d-1)/2 \rfloor \cdot |\Gamma|, 0)$-threshold-probing resilient implementation of a circuit Γ (with efficient simulation), provided that the adversary does not probe each gadget more than $\lfloor (d-1)/2 \rfloor$ times in each round.*

We notice that [14] also contains a second transformation with blow-up $\tilde{O}(d|\Gamma|)$. It may be possible that this transformation can provide better noise parameters as is achieved by Theorem 2. However, due to the hidden parameters in the $\tilde{O}$-notation we do not get a straightforward improvement of our result. In particular, using this transformation the size of the transformed circuit depends also on an additional statistical security parameter, which will affect the tolerated noise level.

5.4   Resilience to Noisy Leakage from the Wires

We now show that the construction from Section 5.3 is secure against the noisy leakage. More precisely, we show the following.

Theorem 1. *Let Γ be an arbitrary stateful arithmetic circuit over some field $\mathbb{F}$. Let Γ' be the circuit that results from the procedure described in Section 5.3. Then Γ' is a $(\delta, |\Gamma| \cdot \exp(-d/12))$-noise-resilient implementation of Γ (with efficient simulation), where $\delta := ((28d + 16)|\mathbb{F}|)^{-1} = O(1/(d \cdot |\mathbb{F}|))$.*

This lemma is proven by combining Corollary 1 that reduces the noisy adversary to the probing adversary, with Lemma 5 that shows that the construction from Section 5.3 is secure against probing. The full proof appears in the full version.

---

[3] Strictly speaking the proof of [14] considers only the case when $\mathbb{F} = \mathrm{GF}(2)$. It was observed in [27] that it can be extended to any finite field, as the only properties of $\mathrm{GF}(2)$ that are used in the proof are the field axioms.

5.5   Resilience to Noisy Leakage from the Gates

The model of Prouff and Rivain is actually slightly different than the one considered in the previous section. The difference is that they assume that the noise is generated by the *gates*, not by the *wires*. This can be formalized by assuming that each noise function *Noise* is applied to the "contents of a gate". We do not need to specify exactly what we mean by this. It is enough to observe that the contents of each gate γ can be described by at most 2 field elements: obviously if γ is a random gate, output gate, or memory gate then its entire state in a given round can be described by one field element, and if γ is an operation gate then it can be described by two field elements that correspond to γ's input. Hence, without loss of generality we can assume that the noise function is defined over the domain $\mathbb{F} \times \mathbb{F}$.

Formally, we define a *δ-gate-noisy circuit adversary* $\mathcal{A}$ as a machine that, besides of having black box access to a circuit $\Gamma(k)$, can, after each ith round, get some partial information about the internal state of the computation via the δ-noisy leakage functions applied to the gates (in a model described above). Let $out\left(\mathcal{A} \overset{g\text{-}noisy}{\leftrightarrows} \Gamma(k)\right)$ denote the output of such $\mathcal{A}$ after interacting with Γ whose initial memory state is $k_0 = k$.

We can accordingly modify the definition of noise-resilient circuit implementations (cf. Definition 2). We say that Γ' is a *(δ, ξ)-input-gate-noise resilient implementation of a circuit* Γ *w.r.t. Enc* if for every k and every δ-noisy circuit adversary $\mathcal{A}$ described above there exists a black-box circuit adversary $\mathcal{S}$ working in time polynomial in $\Gamma' \cdot |\mathbb{F}|$ such that

$$\Delta\left(out\left(\mathcal{S} \overset{bb}{\leftrightarrows} \Gamma(k)\right) ; out\left(\mathcal{A} \overset{g\text{-}noisy}{\leftrightarrows} \Gamma'(Enc(k))\right)\right) \leq \xi. \tag{10}$$

It turns out that the transformation from Section 5.3 also works in this model, although with different parameters. More precisely we have the following theorem, whose proof is given in the full version.[4]

Theorem 2. *Let Γ be an arbitrary stateful arithmetic circuit over some field $\mathbb{F}$. Let Γ' be the circuit that results from the procedure described in Section 5.3. Then Γ' is a $(\delta, |\Gamma| \cdot \exp(-d/24))$-noise-resilient implementation of Γ (with efficient simulation), where $\delta := \left((28d + 16) \cdot |\mathbb{F}|^2\right)^{-1} = O(1/(d \cdot |\mathbb{F}|^2))$.*

In the full version of the paper, we compare our noise parameters with the parameters of [24] and we show that they are roughly identical.

---

[4] Note that our result holds only when the number of shares is large. For small values of d (e.g., $d = 2, 3, 4$) like those considered in [31], our result does not give meaningful bounds. This is similar to the work of Prouff and Rivain [24] and it is an interesting open research question to develop security models that work for small security parameters.

References

1. Akavia, A., Goldwasser, S., Vaikuntanathan, V.: Simultaneous Hardcore Bits and Cryptography against Memory Attacks. In: Reingold, O. (ed.) TCC 2009. LNCS, vol. 5444, pp. 474–495. Springer, Heidelberg (2009)
2. Blömer, J., Guajardo, J., Krummel, V.: Provably Secure Masking of AES. In: Handschuh, H., Hasan, M.A. (eds.) SAC 2004. LNCS, vol. 3357, pp. 69–83. Springer, Heidelberg (2004)
3. Carlet, C., Goubin, L., Prouff, E., Quisquater, M., Rivain, M.: Higher-Order Masking Schemes for S-Boxes. In: Canteaut, A. (ed.) FSE 2012. LNCS, vol. 7549, pp. 366–384. Springer, Heidelberg (2012)
4. Chari, S., Jutla, C.S., Rao, J.R., Rohatgi, P.: Towards Sound Approaches to Counteract Power-Analysis Attacks. In: Wiener, M. (ed.) CRYPTO 1999. LNCS, vol. 1666, pp. 398–412. Springer, Heidelberg (1999)
5. Clavier, C., Coron, J.-S., Dabbous, N.: Differential Power Analysis in the Presence of Hardware Countermeasures. In: Paar, C., Koç, Ç.K. (eds.) CHES 2000. LNCS, vol. 1965, pp. 252–263. Springer, Heidelberg (2000)
6. Coron, J.-S., Kizhvatov, I.: Analysis and Improvement of the Random Delay Countermeasure of CHES 2009. In: Mangard, S., Standaert, F.-X. (eds.) CHES 2010. LNCS, vol. 6225, pp. 95–109. Springer, Heidelberg (2010)
7. Duc, A., Dziembowski, S., Faust, S.: Unifying Leakage Models: from Probing Attacks to Noisy Leakage. Cryptology ePrint Archive, Report 2014/079 (2014), http://eprint.iacr.org/
8. Dziembowski, S., Faust, S.: Leakage-Resilient Circuits without Computational Assumptions. In: Cramer, R. (ed.) TCC 2012. LNCS, vol. 7194, pp. 230–247. Springer, Heidelberg (2012)
9. Dziembowski, S., Pietrzak, K.: Leakage-Resilient Cryptography. In: FOCS, pp. 293–302 (2008)
10. Faust, S., Rabin, T., Reyzin, L., Tromer, E., Vaikuntanathan, V.: Protecting Circuits from Leakage: the Computationally-Bounded and Noisy Cases. In: Gilbert, H. (ed.) EUROCRYPT 2010. LNCS, vol. 6110, pp. 135–156. Springer, Heidelberg (2010)
11. Goldwasser, S., Rothblum, G.N.: Securing computation against continuous leakage. In: Rabin, T. (ed.) CRYPTO 2010. LNCS, vol. 6223, pp. 59–79. Springer, Heidelberg (2010)
12. Goldwasser, S., Rothblum, G.N.: How to Compute in the Presence of Leakage. In: FOCS, pp. 31–40 (2012)
13. Goubin, L., Patarin, J.: DES and Differential Power Analysis (The "Duplication" Method). In: Koç, Ç.K., Paar, C. (eds.) CHES 1999. LNCS, vol. 1717, pp. 158–172. Springer, Heidelberg (1999)
14. Ishai, Y., Sahai, A., Wagner, D.: Private Circuits: Securing Hardware against Probing Attacks. In: Boneh, D. (ed.) CRYPTO 2003. LNCS, vol. 2729, pp. 463–481. Springer, Heidelberg (2003)
15. Juma, A., Vahlis, Y.: Protecting Cryptographic Keys against Continual Leakage. In: Rabin, T. (ed.) CRYPTO 2010. LNCS, vol. 6223, pp. 41–58. Springer, Heidelberg (2010)
16. Katz, J., Vaikuntanathan, V.: Signature Schemes with Bounded Leakage Resilience. In: Matsui, M. (ed.) ASIACRYPT 2009. LNCS, vol. 5912, pp. 703–720. Springer, Heidelberg (2009)
17. Kocher, P.C.: Timing attacks on implementations of Diffie-Hellman, RSA, DSS, and other systems. In: Koblitz, N. (ed.) CRYPTO 1996. LNCS, vol. 1109, pp. 104–113. Springer, Heidelberg (1996)

18. Kocher, P.C., Jaffe, J., Jun, B.: Differential Power Analysis. In: Wiener, M. (ed.) CRYPTO 1999. LNCS, vol. 1666, pp. 388–397. Springer, Heidelberg (1999)
19. Mangard, S., Oswald, E., Popp, T.: Power Analysis Attacks: Revealing the Secrets of Smart Cards (Advances in Information Security). Springer-Verlag New York, Inc., Secaucus (2007)
20. Micali, S., Reyzin, L.: Physically Observable Cryptography (Extended Abstract). In: Naor, M. (ed.) TCC 2004. LNCS, vol. 2951, pp. 278–296. Springer, Heidelberg (2004)
21. Miles, E., Viola, E.: Shielding circuits with groups. In: STOC, pp. 251–260 (2013)
22. Naor, M., Segev, G.: Public-key cryptosystems resilient to key leakage. In: Halevi, S. (ed.) CRYPTO 2009. LNCS, vol. 5677, pp. 18–35. Springer, Heidelberg (2009)
23. Oswald, E., Mangard, S., Pramstaller, N., Rijmen, V.: A Side-Channel Analysis Resistant Description of the AES S-Box. In: Gilbert, H., Handschuh, H. (eds.) FSE 2005. LNCS, vol. 3557, pp. 413–423. Springer, Heidelberg (2005)
24. Prouff, E., Rivain, M.: Masking against Side-Channel Attacks: A Formal Security Proof. In: Johansson, T., Nguyen, P.Q. (eds.) EUROCRYPT 2013. LNCS, vol. 7881, pp. 142–159. Springer, Heidelberg (2013)
25. Prouff, E., Roche, T.: Higher-Order Glitches Free Implementation of the AES Using Secure Multi-party Computation Protocols. In: Preneel, B., Takagi, T. (eds.) CHES 2011. LNCS, vol. 6917, pp. 63–78. Springer, Heidelberg (2011)
26. Quisquater, J.-J., Samyde, D.: ElectroMagnetic Analysis (EMA): Measures and Counter-Measures for Smart Cards. In: Attali, S., Jensen, T. (eds.) E-smart 2001. LNCS, vol. 2140, pp. 200–210. Springer, Heidelberg (2001)
27. Rivain, M., Prouff, E.: Provably Secure Higher-Order Masking of AES. In: Mangard, S., Standaert, F.-X. (eds.) CHES 2010. LNCS, vol. 6225, pp. 413–427. Springer, Heidelberg (2010)
28. Rothblum, G.N.: How to Compute under $\mathcal{AC}^0$ Leakage without Secure Hardware. In: Safavi-Naini, R., Canetti, R. (eds.) CRYPTO 2012. LNCS, vol. 7417, pp. 552–569. Springer, Heidelberg (2012)
29. Standaert, F.-X., Malkin, T.G., Yung, M.: A Unified Framework for the Analysis of Side-Channel Key Recovery Attacks. In: Joux, A. (ed.) EUROCRYPT 2009. LNCS, vol. 5479, pp. 443–461. Springer, Heidelberg (2009)
30. Standaert, F.-X., Pereira, O., Yu, Y.: Leakage-Resilient Symmetric Cryptography under Empirically Verifiable Assumptions. In: Canetti, R., Garay, J.A. (eds.) CRYPTO 2013, Part I. LNCS, vol. 8042, pp. 335–352. Springer, Heidelberg (2013)
31. Standaert, F.-X., Veyrat-Charvillon, N., Oswald, E., Gierlichs, B., Medwed, M., Kasper, M., Mangard, S.: The World Is Not Enough: Another Look on Second-Order DPA. In: Abe, M. (ed.) ASIACRYPT 2010. LNCS, vol. 6477, pp. 112–129. Springer, Heidelberg (2010)
32. Veyrat-Charvillon, N., Standaert, F.-X.: Adaptive Chosen-Message Side-Channel Attacks. In: Zhou, J., Yung, M. (eds.) ACNS 2010. LNCS, vol. 6123, pp. 186–199. Springer, Heidelberg (2010)

Higher Order Masking of Look-Up Tables

Jean-Sébastien Coron

University of Luxembourg, Luxembourg
jean-sebastien.coron@uni.lu

Abstract. We describe a new algorithm for masking look-up tables of block-ciphers at any order, as a countermeasure against side-channel attacks. Our technique is a generalization of the classical randomized table countermeasure against first-order attacks. We prove the security of our new algorithm against t-th order attacks in the usual Ishai-Sahai-Wagner model from Crypto 2003; we also improve the bound on the number of shares from $n \geq 4t+1$ to $n \geq 2t+1$ for an adversary who can adaptively move its probes between successive executions.

Our algorithm has the same time complexity $\mathcal{O}(n^2)$ as the Rivain-Prouff algorithm for AES, and its extension by Carlet et al. to any look-up table. In practice for AES our algorithm is less efficient than Rivain-Prouff, which can take advantage of the special algebraic structure of the AES Sbox; however for DES our algorithm performs slightly better.

1 Introduction

Side-Channel Attacks. An implementation of a cryptographic algorithm on some concrete device, such as a PC or a smart-card, can leak additional information to an attacker through the device power consumption or electro-magnetic emanations, enabling efficient key-recovery attacks. One of the most powerful attack is the Differential Power Analysis (DPA) [KJJ99]; it consists in recovering the secret-key by performing a statistical analysis of the power consumption of the electronic device, for several executions of a cryptographic algorithm. Another powerful class of attack are template attacks [CRR02]; a template is a precise model for the noise and expected signal for all possible values of part of the key; the attack is then carried out iteratively to recover successive parts of the key.

Random Masking. A well-known countermeasure against side-channel attacks consists in masking all internal variables with a random r, as first suggested in [CJRR99]. Any internal variable x is first masked by computing $x' = x \oplus r$, and the masked variable x' and the mask r are then processed separately. An attacker trying to analyze the power consumption at a single point will obtain only random values; therefore, the implementation will be secure against first-order DPA. However, a first-order masking can be broken in practice by a second-order side channel attack, in which the attacker combines information from two leakage points [Mes00]; however such attack usually requires a larger

P.Q. Nguyen and E. Oswald (Eds.): EUROCRYPT 2014, LNCS 8441, pp. 441–458, 2014.

number of power consumption curves, which can be unfeasible in practice if the number of executions is limited (for example, by using a counter). For AES many countermeasures based on random masking have been described, see for example [HOM06].

More generally, one can split any variable x into n boolean shares by letting $x = x_1 \oplus \cdots \oplus x_n$ as in a secret-sharing scheme [Sha79]. The shares x_i must then be processed separately without leaking information about the original variable x. Most block-ciphers (such as AES or DES) alternate several rounds, each containing one linear transformation (or more), and a non-linear transformation. A linear function $y = f(x)$ is easy to compute when x is shared as $x = x_1 \oplus \cdots \oplus x_n$, as it suffices to compute $y_i = f(x_i)$ separately for every i. However securely computing a non-linear function $y = S(x)$ with shares is more difficult and is the subject of this paper.

The Ishai-Sahai-Wagner Private Circuit. The theoretical study of securing circuits against an adversary who can probe its wires was initiated by Ishai, Sahai and Wagner in [ISW03]. The goal is to protect a cryptographic implementation against side-channel attacks in a provable way. The authors consider an adversary who can probe at most t wires of the circuit. They showed how to transform any boolean circuit C of size $|C|$ into a circuit of size $\mathcal{O}(|C| \cdot t^2)$ that is perfectly secure against such adversary.

The Ishai-Sahai-Wagner (ISW) model is relevant even in the context of power attacks. Namely the number of probes in the circuit corresponds to the attack order in a high-order DPA. More precisely, if a circuit is perfectly secure against t probes, then combining t power consumption points as in a t-th order DPA will reveal no information to the adversary. To obtain useful information about the key the adversary will have to perform an attack of order at least $t + 1$. The soundness of higher-order masking in the context of power attacks was first demonstrated by Chari et al. in [CJRR99], who showed that in a realistic leakage model the number of acquisitions to recover the key grows exponentially with the number of shares. Their analysis was recently extended by Prouff and Rivain in [PR13]. The authors proved that the information obtained by observing the *entire* leakage of an execution (instead of the leakage of the n shares of a given variable) can be made negligible in the masking order. This shows that the number of shares n is a sound security parameter for protecting an implementation against side-channel attacks.

To protect against an adversary with at most t probes, the ISW approach consists in secret-sharing every variable x into n shares x_i where $n = 2t + 1$, that is $x = x_1 \oplus x_2 \oplus \cdots \oplus x_n$ where $x_2, \ldots, x_n$ are uniformly and independently distributed bits. An adversary probing at most $n - 1$ variables clearly does not learn any information about x. Processing a NOT gate is straightforward since $\bar{x} = \bar{x}_1 \oplus x_2 \oplus \cdots \oplus x_n$; therefore it suffices to invert the first share x_1. To process an AND gate $z = xy$, one writes:

$$z = xy = \left(\bigoplus_{i=1}^{n} x_i \right) \cdot \left(\bigoplus_{i=1}^{n} y_i \right) = \bigoplus_{1 \leq i,j \leq n} x_i y_j \tag{1}$$

and the cross-products $x_i y_j$ are processed and recombined without leaking information about the original inputs x and y. More precisely for each $1 \leq i < j \leq n$ one generates random bits $r_{i,j}$ and computes $r_{j,i} = (r_{i,j} \oplus x_i y_j) \oplus x_j y_i$; the n shares z_i of $z = xy$ are then computed as $z_i = x_i y_i \oplus \bigoplus_{j \neq i} r_{i,j}$. Since there are n^2 such cross-products, every AND gate of the circuit is expanded to $\mathcal{O}(n^2) = \mathcal{O}(t^2)$ new gates in the circuit.

The authors also describe a very convenient framework for proving the security against any set of t probes. Namely proving the security of a countermeasure against first-order attacks ($t = 1$) is usually straightforward, as it suffices to check that every internal variable has the uniform distribution (or at least a distribution independent from the secret-key). Such approach can be extended to second-order attacks by considering pairs of internal variables (as in [RDP08]); however it becomes clearly unfeasible for larger values of t, as the number of t-uples to consider would grow exponentially with t. Alternatively the ISW framework is simulation based: the authors prove the security of their construction against a adversary with at most t probes by showing that any set of t probes can be perfectly simulated without the knowledge of the original input variables (such as x, y in the AND gate $z = xy$). In [ISW03] this is done by iteratively generating a subset I of indices of the input shares that are sufficient to simulate the t probes; then if $|I| < n$ the corresponding input shares can be perfectly simulated without knowing the original input variable, simply by generating independently and uniformly distributed bits. In the ISW construction every probe adds at most two indices in I, so we get $|I| \leq 2t$ and therefore $n \geq 2t + 1$ is sufficient to achieve perfect secrecy against a t-limited adversary. A nice property of the ISW framework is that the technique easily extends from a single gate to the full circuit: it suffices to maintain a global subset of indices I that is iteratively constructed from the t probes as in a single gate.

The Rivain-Prouff Countermeasure. The Rivain-Prouff countermeasure [RP10] was the first provably secure higher-order masking scheme for the AES block-cipher. Namely, all previous masking schemes were secure against first-order or second-order attacks only. The classical randomized table countermeasure [CJRR99] is secure against first-order attacks only. The Schramm and Paar countermeasure [SP06] was designed to be secure at any order n, but an attack of order 3 was shown in [CPR07]. An alternative countermeasure based on table recomputation and provably secure against second-order attacks was described in [RDP08], but no extension to any order is known. The Rivain-Prouff countermeasure was therefore the first masking scheme for AES secure for any order $t \geq 3$.

The Rivain-Prouff countermeasure is an adaptation of the previous ISW construction to software implementations, working in the AES finite field $\mathbb{F}_{2^8}$ instead of $\mathbb{F}_2$. Namely the non-linear part of the AES Sbox can be written as $S(x) = x^{254}$ over $\mathbb{F}_{2^8}$, and as shown in [RP10] such monomial can be evaluated with only 4 non-linear multiplications (and a few linear squarings). These 4 multiplications can be evaluated with n-shared input using the previous technique based on Equation (1), by working over the field $\mathbb{F}_{2^8}$ instead of $\mathbb{F}_2$. In order to achieve resistance against an attack of order t, the Rivain-Prouff algorithm also requires $n \geq 2t + 1$ shares.

The Rivain-Prouff countermeasure was later extended by Carlet et al. to any look-up table [CGP+12]. Namely using Lagrange interpolation any Sbox with k-bit input can be written as a polynomial

$$S(x) = \sum_{i=0}^{2^k-1} \alpha_i \cdot x^i$$

over $\mathbb{F}_{2^k}$, for constant coefficients $\alpha_i \in \mathbb{F}_{2^k}$. The polynomial can then be evaluated with n-shared multiplications as in the Rivain-Prouff countermeasure. The authors of [CGP+12] describe two techniques for optimizing the evaluation of $S(x)$ by minimizing the number of non-linear multiplications: the cyclotomic method and the parity-split method; the later method is asymptotically faster and requires $\mathcal{O}(2^{k/2})$ multiplications. Therefore the Carlet et al. countermeasure with n shares has time complexity $\mathcal{O}(2^{k/2} \cdot n^2)$, where $n \geq 2t + 1$ to ensure resistance against t-th order attacks.

Extending the Randomized Table Countermeasure. Our new countermeasure is completely different from the Rivain-Prouff countermeasure and its extension by Carlet et al.. Namely it is essentially based on table recomputations and does not use multiplications over $\mathbb{F}_{2^k}$. To illustrate our technique we start with the classical randomized table countermeasure, secure against first order attacks only, as first suggested in [CJRR99]. The Sbox table $S(u)$ with k-bit input is first randomized in RAM by letting

$$T(u) = S(u \oplus r) \oplus s$$

for all $u \in \{0,1\}^k$, where $r \in \{0,1\}^k$ is the input mask and $s \in \{0,1\}^k$ is the output mask.[1] To evaluate $S(x)$ from the masked value $x' = x \oplus r$, it suffices to compute $y' = T(x')$, as we get $y' = T(x') = S(x' \oplus r) \oplus s = S(x) \oplus s$; this shows that y' is indeed a masked value for $S(x)$. In other words the randomized table countermeasure consists in first re-computing in RAM a temporary table with inputs shifted by r and with masked outputs, so that later it can be evaluated on a masked value $x' = x \oplus r$ to obtain a masked output.

A natural generalization at any order n would be as follows: given as input $x = x_1 \oplus \cdots \oplus x_n$ we would start with a randomized table with inputs shifted by x_1 only, and with $n-1$ output masks; then we would incrementally shift the full table by x_2 and so on until x_{n-1}, at which point the table could be evaluated at x_n. More precisely one would initially define the randomized table

$$T(u) = S(u \oplus x_1) \oplus s_2 \oplus \cdots \oplus s_n$$

where $s_2, \ldots, s_n$ are the output masks, and then progressively shift the randomized table by letting $T(u) \leftarrow T(u \oplus x_i)$ for all u, iteratively from x_2 until x_{n-1}.

---

[1] One can also take $s = r$. For simplicity we first assume that the Sbox has both k-bit input and k-bit output.

Eventually the table would have all its inputs shifted by $x_1 \oplus \cdots \oplus x_{n-1}$, so as previously one could evaluate $y' = T(x_n)$ and obtain $S(x)$ masked by $s_2, \ldots, s_n$.

What we have described above is essentially the Schramm and Paar countermeasure [SP06]. However as shown in [CPR07] this is insecure. Namely consider the table $T(u)$ after the last shift by x_{n-1}; at this point we have $T(u) = S(u \oplus x_1 \oplus \cdots \oplus x_{n-1}) \oplus s_2 \oplus \cdots \oplus s_n$ for all u. Now assume that we can probe $T(0)$ and $T(1)$; we can then compute $T(0) \oplus T(1) = S(x_1 \oplus \cdots \oplus x_{n-1}) \oplus S(1 \oplus x_1 \oplus \cdots \oplus x_{n-1})$, which only depends on $x_1 \oplus \cdots \oplus x_{n-1}$; therefore it suffices to additionally probe x_n to leak information about $x = x_1 \oplus \cdots \oplus x_{n-1} \oplus x_n$; this gives an attack of order 3 only for any value of n; therefore the countermeasure can only be secure against second-order attacks.

The main issue with the previous countermeasure is that the *same* masks $s_2, \ldots, s_n$ were used to mask all the $S(u)$ entries, so one can exclusive-or any two lines of the randomized table and remove all the output masks. A natural fix is to use *different* masks for every line $S(u)$ of the table, so one would write initially:

$$T(u) = S(u \oplus x_1) \oplus s_{u,2} \oplus \cdots \oplus s_{u,n}$$

for all $u \in \{0,1\}^k$, and as previously one would iteratively shift the table by $x_2, \ldots, x_{n-1}$, and also the masks $s_{u,i}$ separately for each i. The previous attack is thwarted because the lines of $S(u)$ are now masked with different set of masks. Eventually one would read $T(x_n)$, which would give $S(x)$ masked by $s_{x_n,2}, \ldots, s_{x_n,n}$.

Our Table-Recomputation Countermeasure. Our new countermeasure is based on using independent masks as above, with additionally a refresh of the masks between every successive shifts of the input. Since the above output masks $s_{u,j}$ are now different for all lines u of the table, we actually have a set of n randomized tables, as opposed to a single randomized table in the original Schramm and Paar countermeasure. Perhaps more conveniently one can view every line u of our randomized table as a n-dimensional vector of elements in $\{0,1\}^k$, and write for all inputs $u \in \{0,1\}^k$:

$$T(u) = (s_{u,1}, s_{u,2}, \ldots, s_{u,n})$$

where initially each vector $T(u)$ is a n-boolean sharing of the value $S(u \oplus x_1)$. The vectors $T(u)$ of our randomized table are then progressively shifted for all $u \in \{0,1\}^k$, first by x_2 and so on until x_{n-1}, as in the original Schramm and Paar countermeasure. Eventually the evaluation of $T(x_n)$ gives a vector of n output shares that corresponds to $S(x)$.

To refresh the masks between successive shifts we can generate a random n-sharing of 0, that is $a_1, \ldots, a_n \in \{0,1\}^k$ such that $a_1 \oplus \cdots \oplus a_n = 0$ and we xor the vector $T(u)$ with $(a_1, \ldots, a_n)$, independently for every u. More concretely one can use the RefreshMasks procedure from [RP10], which consists given $y = y_1 \oplus y_2 \oplus \cdots \oplus y_n$ in xoring both y_1 and y_i with $tmp \leftarrow \{0,1\}^k$, iteratively from $i = 2$ to n. In summary our new countermeasure is essentially the Schramm and Paar countermeasure with independent output masks for every line of the

Sbox table, and with mask refreshing after every shift of the table; we provide a full description in Section 3.1.[2]

We show that our new countermeasure is secure against any attack of order t in the ISW model, with at least $n = 2t + 1$ shares. The proof works as follows. Assume that there are at most $n - 3$ probes; then it must be the case that at least one of the $n - 2$ shifts of the table by x_i and subsequent mask refreshings are not probed at all. Since the corresponding mask refreshings are not probed, we can perfectly simulate any subset of $n - 1$ shares at the output of those mask refreshings. Therefore we can perfectly simulate all the internal variables up to the x_{i-1} shift by knowing $x_1, \ldots, x_{i-1}$, and any subset of $n - 1$ shares after the x_i shift by knowing $x_{i+1}, \ldots, x_n$. Since the knowledge of x_i is not needed in the simulation, the full simulation can be performed without knowing the original input x, which proves the security of our countermeasure.[3]

Note that it does not matter how the mask refreshing is performed; the only required property is that after a (non-probed) mask refreshing any subset of $n - 1$ shares among the n shares have independent and uniform distribution; such property is clearly satisfied by the RefreshMasks procedure from [RP10] recalled above. We stress that in the argument above only the mask refreshings corresponding to one of the x_i shift are assumed to be non-probed (which must be the case because of the limited number of probes), and that all the remaining mask refreshings can be freely probed by the adversary, and correctly simulated.

The previous argument only applies when the Sbox evaluation is considered in isolation. When combined with other operations (in particular Xor gates), we must actually apply the same technique (with the I subset) as in [ISW03], and we obtain the same bound $n \geq 2t + 1$ for the number of shares, as in the Rivain-Prouff countermeasure.

Asymptotic Complexities. With respect to the number n of shares, our new countermeasure has the same time complexity $\mathcal{O}(n^2)$ as the Rivain-Prouff and Carlet *et al.* countermeasures. However for a k-bit input table, our basic countermeasure has complexity $\mathcal{O}(2^k \cdot n^2)$ whereas the Carlet *et al.* countermeasure has complexity $\mathcal{O}(2^{k/2} \cdot n^2)$, which is better for large k.

In Section 3.3 we describe a variant of our countermeasure for processors with large register size, with the same time complexity $\mathcal{O}(2^{k/2} \cdot n^2)$ as the Carlet *et al.* countermeasure, using a similar approach as in [RDP08]. Our variant consists in packing multiple Sbox outputs into a single register, and performing the table

---

[2] The mask refreshing is necessary to prevent a different attack. Assume that we probe the first component of $T(0)$ for the initial configuration of the table $T(u)$, and we again probe the first component of $T(0)$ when the table $T(u)$ has eventually been shifted by $x_2 \oplus \cdots \oplus x_{n-1}$. If $x_2 \oplus \cdots \oplus x_{n-1} = 0$ then without mask refreshing those two probed values must be the same; this leaks information about $x_2 \oplus \cdots \oplus x_{n-1}$, and therefore it suffices to additionally probe x_1 and x_n to have an attack of order 4 for any n.

[3] The previous argument could be extended to the optimal number of probes $n - 1$ by considering the initial sharing of $S(u \oplus x_1)$ and by adding a final mask refreshing after the evaluation of $T(x_n)$, as actually done in Section 3.1.

recomputations at the register level first. For example for DES we can pack 8 output 4-bit nibbles into a single 32-bit register; in that case the running time is divided by a factor 8. We stress that our variant does *not* consist in putting multiple shares of the same variable into a single register, as reading such register would reveal many shares at once, and thereby decrease the number of probes t required to break the countermeasure.

Note that our countermeasure has memory complexity $\mathcal{O}(n)$, instead of $\mathcal{O}(n^2)$ for the Rivain-Prouff countermeasure as described in [RP10]. However we show in the full version of this paper [Cor13a] that the memory complexity of the Rivain-Prouff countermeasure can be reduced to $\mathcal{O}(n)$, simply by computing the variables in a different order; this extends to the Carlet *et al.* countermeasure. We summarize in Table 1 the complexity of the two countermeasures.

Table 1. Time, memory, and number of random bits used, for a k-bit input table masked with n shares and secure against any attack at order t, with $2t + 1 \leq n$

Countermeasure	Time	Memory	Randomness
Carlet *et al.* [CGP+12]	$\mathcal{O}(2^{k/2} \cdot n^2)$	$\mathcal{O}(2^{k/2} \cdot n)$	$\mathcal{O}(k2^{k/2} \cdot n^2)$
Table Recomputation	$\mathcal{O}(2^k \cdot n^2)$	$\mathcal{O}(2^k \cdot n)$	$\mathcal{O}(k2^k \cdot n^2)$
Table Recomputation (large register)	$\mathcal{O}(2^{k/2} \cdot n^2)$	$\mathcal{O}(2^k \cdot n)$	$\mathcal{O}(k2^k \cdot n^2)$

Protecting a Full Block-Cipher. We show how to integrate our countermeasure into the protection of a full block-cipher against t-th order attacks. We consider two models of security. In the *restricted* model, the adversary always probes the same t intermediate variables for different executions of the block-cipher. In the *full* model the adversary can change the position of its probes adaptively between successive executions; this is essentially the ISW model for stateful circuits.

The restricted model is relevant in practice because in a t-th order DPA attack, the statistical analysis is performed on a fixed set of t intermediate variables for all executions. In both models the key is initially provided in shared form as input, with n shares. In the full model it is necessary to re-randomize the shares of the key between executions, since otherwise the adversary could recover the key by moving its probes between successive executions; obviously this re-randomization of shares must also be secure against a t-th order attack.

We show that $n \geq 2t + 1$ is sufficient to achieve security against t-th order attacks in both models. In particular, this improves the bound $n \geq 4t + 1$ from [ISW03] for stateful circuits.[4] We get an improved bound because for every execution we use both an initial re-randomization of the key shares (before they are used to evaluate the block-cipher) and a final re-randomization of the key shares (before they are given as input to the next execution), whereas in [ISW03] only a final re-randomization was used. With the same technique we can obtain

---

[4] In [ISW03] the bounds are $n \geq 2t + 1$ for stateless circuits and $n \geq 4t + 1$ for stateful circuits.

the same improved bound in the full model for the Rivain-Prouff countermeasure and its extension by Carlet *et al.*.

Note that in the full model the bound $n \geq 2t + 1$ is actually optimal. Namely as noted in [ISW03] the adversary can probe t of the key shares at the end of one execution and then another t of the key shares at the beginning of the next execution, hence a total of $2t$ key shares of the same n-sharing of the secret-key. Hence $n \geq 2t + 1$ shares are necessary.[5]

Practical Implementation. Finally we have performed a practical implementation of our new countermeasure for both AES and DES, using a 32-bit architecture so that we could apply our large register variant. For comparison we have also implemented the Rivain-Prouff countermeasure for AES and the Carlet *et al.* countermeasure for DES; for the latter we have used the technique from [RV13], in which the evaluation of a DES Sbox requires only 7 non-linear multiplications. We summarize the result of our practical implementations in Section 5. We obtain that in practice for AES our algorithm is less efficient than Rivain-Prouff, which can take advantage of the special algebraic structure of the AES Sbox; however for DES our algorithm performs slightly better. Our implementation is publicly available [Cor13b].

2 Definitions

In this section we first recall the Ishai-Sahai-Wagner (ISW) framework [ISW03] for proving the resistance of circuits against probing attacks. In [RP10] Rivain and Prouff describe an adaptation of the ISW model for software implementations. We follow the same approach and describe two security models: a restricted model in which the adversary always probes the same t intermediate variables (which is essentially the model considered in [RP10]), and a full model in which the t probes can be changed adaptively between executions (which is essentially the ISW model for stateful circuits).

2.1 The Ishai-Sahai-Wagner Framework

Privacy for Stateless Circuits. A *stateless* circuit over $\mathbb{F}_2$ is a directed acyclic graph whose sources are labeled with the input variables, sinks are labeled with output variables, and internal vertices stand for function gates. A stateless circuit can be *randomized*, if it additionally contains *random gates*; every such gate has no input, and its only output at each invocation of the circuit is a uniform random bit.

A *t-limited adversary* can probe up to t wires in the circuit, and has unlimited computational power. A stateless circuit C is called (perfectly) secure against such adversary, if the distribution of the probes can be efficiently and perfectly simulated, without access to the internal wires of C. For stateless circuits one

---

[5] At least this holds for the shares of the secret-key. It could be that $n = t + 1$ shares are sufficient for the other variables.

assumes that the inputs and outputs of the circuit must remain private. For example in a block-cipher the input key must remain private. To prevent the adversary for learning the inputs and outputs one uses an *input encoder* I and an *output decoder* O, whose internal wires cannot be probed. Additionally, the inputs of I and the outputs of O are also assumed to be protected against probing. However, the outputs of I and the inputs to O can be probed. Finally the *t-private stateless transformer* (T, I, O) maps a stateless circuit C into a (randomized) stateless circuit C', such that C' is secure against the t-limited adversary, and $O \circ C' \circ I$ has the same input-output functionality as C.

The ISW Construction. As recalled in introduction in [ISW03] the authors showed how to transform any boolean circuit C of size $|C|$ into a circuit of size $\mathcal{O}(|C| \cdot t^2)$ that is perfectly secure against a t-limited adversary. The approach in [ISW03] consists in secret-sharing every variable x into n shares x_i where $n = 2t + 1$, that is $x = x_1 \oplus x_2 \oplus \cdots \oplus x_n$ where $x_2, \ldots, x_n$ are uniformly and independently distributed bits. The authors prove the security of their construction against a t-limited adversary by showing that any set of t probes can be perfectly simulated without knowing the internal wires of the circuit, for $n \geq 2t + 1$.

Extension to Stateful Circuits. The ISW model and construction can be extended to stateful circuits, that is a circuit containing memory cells. In the stateful model the inputs and outputs are known to the attacker and one does not use the input encoder I and output decoder O. For a block-cipher the secret key sk would be originally incorporated in a shared form sk_i inside the memory cells of the circuit; the key shares sk_i would be re-randomized after each invocation of the circuit. The authors show that for stateful circuits $n \geq 4t + 1$ shares are sufficient for security against a t-limited adversary; we refer to [ISW03] for more details.

2.2   Security Model for Software Implementations

In [RP10] Rivain and Prouff describe an adaptation of the ISW model for software implementations of encryption algorithms. They consider a *randomized encryption algorithm* $\mathcal{E}$ taking as input a plaintext m and a randomly shared secret-key sk and outputting a ciphertext c, with additional access to a random number generator. More precisely the secret-key sk is assumed to be split into n shares $sk_1, \ldots, sk_n$ such that $sk = sk_1 \oplus \cdots \oplus sk_n$ and any $(n-1)$-uple of sk_i's is uniformly and independently distributed. Instead of considering the internal wires of a circuit, they consider the intermediate variables of the software implementation. This approach seems well suited for proving the security of our countermeasure; in principle one could write our countermeasure with randomized table as a stateful circuit and work in the ISW model for stateful circuits, but that would be less convenient.

In the following we describe two different models of security. In the *restricted* model the adversary provides a message m as input and receives $c = \mathcal{E}_{sk}(m)$ as output. The adversary can run $\mathcal{E}_{sk}$ several times, but she always obtain the same set of t intermediate variables that she can freely choose before the first execution. In the *full* model, the adversary can adaptively change the set of t intermediate variables between executions. In both models the shares sk_i of the secret-key sk are initially incorporated in the memory cells of the block-cipher implementation. We say that a randomized encryption algorithm is secure against t-th order attack (in the restricted or full model) if the distribution of any t intermediate variables can be perfectly simulated without the knowledge of the secret-key sk. This implies that anything an adversary $\mathcal{A}$ can do from the knowledge of t intermediate variables, another adversary $\mathcal{A}'$ can do the same without the knowledge of those t intermediate variables. Note that since $\mathcal{A}$ initially provides the message m and receives the ciphertext c, we can consider that both m and c are public and given to the simulator.

Note that in the full model it is necessary to re-randomize in memory the shares sk_i of the key, since otherwise the adversary could recover sk by moving its probes between successive executions; obviously this re-randomization of shares must also be secure against a t-th order attack.

3   Our New Algorithm

3.1   Description

In this section we describe our new algorithm for computing $y = S(x)$ where

$$S : \{0,1\}^k \to \{0,1\}^{k'}$$

is a look-up table with k-bit input and k'-bit output. Our new algorithm takes as input $x_1, \ldots, x_n$ such that $x = x_1 \oplus \cdots \oplus x_n$ and must output $y_1, \ldots, y_n$ such that $y = S(x) = y_1 \oplus \cdots \oplus y_n$, without leaking information about x. Our algorithm uses two temporary tables T and T' in RAM; both have k-bit input and a vector of n elements of k'-bit as output, namely

$$T, T' : \{0,1\}^k \to (\{0,1\}^{k'})^n$$

Given a vector $\boldsymbol{v} = (v_1, \ldots, v_n)$ of n elements, we write $\oplus(\boldsymbol{v}) = v_1 \oplus \cdots \oplus v_n$. We denote by $T(u)[j]$ and $T'(u)[j]$ the j-th component of the vectors $T(u)$ and $T'(u)$ respectively, for $1 \le j \le n$. In practice the two tables can be implemented as 2-dimensional arrays of elements in $\{0,1\}^{k'}$. We use the same RefreshMasks procedure as in [RP10].

Correctness. It is easy to verify the correctness of Algorithm 1. We proceed by induction. Assume that at Line 4 for index i we have for all inputs $u \in \{0,1\}^k$:

$$\oplus(T(u)) = S(u \oplus x_1 \oplus \cdots \oplus x_{i-1}) \tag{2}$$

The assumption clearly holds for $i = 0$, since initially we have $\oplus(T(u)) = S(u)$ for all inputs $u \in \{0,1\}^k$. Assuming that (2) holds for index i at Line 4, after the shifts performed at Line 6 we have for all inputs $u \in \{0,1\}^k$,

$$\oplus(T'(u)) = \oplus(T(u \oplus x_i)) = S((u \oplus x_i) \oplus x_1 \oplus \cdots \oplus x_{i-1}) = S(u \oplus x_1 \oplus \cdots \oplus x_i)$$

Algorithm 1. Masked computation of $y = S(x)$

Input: $x_1, \ldots, x_n$ such that $x = x_1 \oplus \cdots \oplus x_n$
Output: $y_1, \ldots, y_n$ such that $y = S(x) = y_1 \oplus \cdots \oplus y_n$
1: **for all** $u \in \{0,1\}^k$ **do**
2:    $T(u) \leftarrow (S(u), 0, \ldots, 0) \in (\{0,1\}^{k'})^n$ $\triangleright \oplus(T(u)) = S(u)$
3: **end for**
4: **for** $i = 1$ **to** $n - 1$ **do**
5:    **for all** $u \in \{0,1\}^k$ **do**
6:       **for** $j = 1$ **to** n **do** $T'(u)[j] \leftarrow T(u \oplus x_i)[j]$ $\triangleright T'(u) \leftarrow T(u \oplus x_i)$
7:    **end for**
8:    **for all** $u \in \{0,1\}^k$ **do**
9:       $T(u) \leftarrow \mathsf{RefreshMasks}(T'(u))$ $\triangleright \oplus(T(u)) = S(u \oplus x_1 \oplus \cdots \oplus x_i)$
10:    **end for**
11: **end for** $\triangleright \oplus(T(u)) = S(u \oplus x_1 \oplus \cdots \oplus x_{n-1})$ for all $u \in \{0,1\}^k$.
12: $(y_1, \ldots, y_n) \leftarrow \mathsf{RefreshMasks}(T(x_n))$ $\triangleright \oplus(T(x_n)) = S(x)$
13: **return** $y_1, \ldots, y_n$

Algorithm 2. RefreshMasks

Input: $z_1, \ldots, z_n$ such that $z = z_1 \oplus \cdots \oplus z_n$
Output: $z_1, \ldots, z_n$ such that $z = z_1 \oplus \cdots \oplus z_n$
1: **for** $j = 2$ **to** n **do**
2:    $tmp \leftarrow \{0,1\}^{k'}$
3:    $z_1 \leftarrow z_1 \oplus tmp$
4:    $z_j \leftarrow z_j \oplus tmp$
5: **end for**
6: **return** $z_1, \ldots, z_n$

---

and therefore the assumption holds at Step $i + 1$. At the end of the loop we have therefore

$$\oplus(T(u)) = S(u \oplus x_1 \oplus \cdots \oplus x_{n-1})$$

for all $u \in \{0,1\}^k$, and then $\oplus(T(x_n)) = S(x_n \oplus x_1 \oplus \cdots \oplus x_{n-1}) = S(x)$ which gives $y_1 \oplus \cdots \oplus y_n = S(x)$ as required. This proves the correctness of Algorithm 1.

Remark 1. A NAND gate can be implemented as a 2-bit input, 1-bit output look-up table; therefore Algorithm 1 can be used to protect any circuit, with the same complexity $\mathcal{O}(n^2)$ in the number of shares n as the ISW construction.

3.2 Security Proof

The following Lemma proves the security of our countermeasure against t-th order attacks, for any t such that $2t + 1 \leq n$. The proof is done in the ISW model [ISW03]. Namely we show that from any given set of t probed intermediate variables, one can define a set $I \subset [1, n]$ with $|I| < n$ such that the knowledge of the input indices $x_{|I} := (x_i)_{i \in I}$ is sufficient to perfectly simulate those t intermediate variables. Then since $|I| < n$ those input shares can be perfectly simulated without knowing the original input variable, simply by generating independently and uniformly distributed variables.

Lemma 1. *Let $(x_i)_{1 \le i \le n}$ be the input shares of Algorithm 1 and let t be such that $2t < n$. For any set of t intermediate variables, there exists a subset $I \subset [1, n]$ of indices such that $|I| \le 2t < n$ and the distribution of those t variables can be perfectly simulated from the shares $x_{|I}$. The output shares $y_{|I}$ can also be perfectly simulated from $x_{|I}$.*

Proof. Given a set of t intermediate variables $v_1, \ldots, v_t$ probed by the adversary, we construct a subset $I \subset [1, n]$ of indices such that the distribution of those t variables can be perfectly simulated from $x_{|I}$. We call *Part i* the computation performed within the main for loop for index i for $1 \le i \le n-1$, that is from Line 5 to Line 10 of Algorithm 1; similarly we call *Part n* the computation performed at Line 12. We do not consider the intermediate variables from Line 2, as they can be perfectly simulated without the knowledge of x.

The proof intuition is as follows. Every intermediate variable v_h is identified by its "line" index i corresponding to the Part in which it appears, with $1 \le i \le n$, and by its "column" index j corresponding to the j-th component of the vector in which it appears; for any such intermediate variable v_h both indices i and j are added to the subset I (except for x_i and the tmp variables within RefreshMasks for which only i is added). The crucial observation is the following: if $i \notin I$, then no intermediate variable was probed within Part i of Algorithm 1; in particular the tmp variables within the corresponding RefreshMasks were not probed. Therefore we can perfectly simulate the outputs of the RefreshMasks function which have "column" index $j \in I$, by generating uniform and independent elements in $\{0, 1\}^{k'}$, as long as $|I| < n$. This means that for $i \notin I$ we can perfectly simulate all variables $T(u)[j]$ for $j \in I$ in Line 9. Considering now Part i for which $i \in I$, since we know x_i we can still perfectly simulate all intermediate variables with "column" index $j \in I$ (including also the tmp variables within RefreshMasks), which includes by definition of I all the intermediates variables v_h. Therefore all intermediate variables v_h can be perfectly simulated as long as $|I| < n$, which gives the condition $2t < n$.

Formally the procedure for constructing the set I is as follows:

1. We start with $I = \emptyset$.
2. For any intermediate variable v_h:
   (a) If $v_h = x_i$ or $v_h = u \oplus x_i$ at Line 6, then add i to I.
   (b) If $v_h = T(u \oplus x_i)[j]$ or $v_h = T'(u)[j]$ at Line 6 in Part i, then add both i and j to I.
   (c) If $v_h = T'(u)[j]$ or $v_h = T(u)[j]$ at Line 9 in Part i, then add both i and j to I.
   (d) If $v_h = tmp$ for any tmp within RefreshMasks in Part i (either at Line 9 or 12), then add i to I.
   (e) If $v_h = x_n$ at Line 12, then add n to I.
   (f) If $v_h = T(x_n)[j]$ or $v_h = y_j$ at Line 12, then add both n and j to I.

This terminates the description of the procedure for constructing the set I. Since any intermediate variable v_h adds at most two indices in I, we must have $|I| \leq 2t < n$.

We now show how to complete a perfect simulation of all intermediate variables v_h using only the values $x_{|I}$. We proceed by induction. Assume that at the beginning of Part i we can perfectly simulate all variables $T(u)[j]$ for all $j \in I$ and all $u \in \{0,1\}^k$. This holds for $i = 1$ since initially we have $T(u) = (S(u), 0, \ldots, 0)$ which does not depend on x.

We distinguish two cases. If $i \notin I$ then no tmp variable within the RefreshMasks in Part i has been probed. Therefore we can perfectly simulate all intermediate variables $T(u)[j]$ for $j \in I$ at the output of RefreshMasks at Line 9, or similarly all y_j for $j \in I$ at the output of RefreshMasks at Line 12 when $i = n$, as long as $|I| < n$. Formally this can be proven as follows. Let j^* be such that $j^* \notin I$. Since the internal variables of the RefreshMasks are not probed, we can redefine RefreshMasks where the randoms tmp are accumulated inside z_{j^*} instead of z_1. Since $j^* \notin I$ we have that z_{j^*} is never used in the computation of any variable v_h, and therefore every variables z_j for $j \in I$ is masked by a random tmp which is used only once. Therefore at the output of RefreshMasks the variables $T(u)[j]$ for $j \in I$ can be perfectly simulated for all $u \in \{0,1\}^k$, simply by generating uniform and independent values.

If $i \in I$ then knowing x_i we can perfectly simulate all intermediate variables with column index $j \in I$ in Part i. Namely our induction hypothesis states that at the beginning of Part i the variables $T(u)[j]$ for all $j \in J$ can already be perfectly simulated. Knowing x_i we can therefore propagate the simulation for all variables with column index j and perfectly simulate $T(u \oplus x_i)[j]$, $T'(u)[j]$ and the resulting $T(u)[j]$ at Line 9, and similarly the variables y_j at Line 12 if $i = n$; in particular the tmp variables within RefreshMasks are simulated exactly as in the RefreshMasks procedure.

Since in both cases we can perfectly simulate all intermediate variables $T(u)[j]$ for $j \in I$ at the end of Part i, the induction hypothesis holds for $i + 1$; therefore it holds for all $1 \leq i \leq n$. From the reasoning above we can therefore simulate all intermediate variables in Part i with column index j such that $i, j \in I$; by definition of I this includes all intermediate variables v_h, and all output shares $y_{|I}$; this proves Lemma 1. □

Remark 2. Although $n \geq 2t + 1$ shares are required for the security proof, our countermeasure seems heuristically secure with $n \geq t + 1$ shares only in the restricted model.

3.3 A Variant for Processors with Large Registers

With respect to the number n of shares, our new countermeasure has the same time complexity $\mathcal{O}(n^2)$ as the Rivain-Prouff and Carlet *et al.* countermeasures. However for a k-bit input table, our algorithm has complexity $\mathcal{O}(2^k \cdot n^2)$ whereas the Carlet *et al.* countermeasure has complexity $\mathcal{O}(2^{k/2} \cdot n^2)$ only.

In this section we describe a variant of our countermeasure with the same complexity as Carlet *et al.*, but for processors with large enough register size

ω bits, using a similar approach as in [RDP08, Section 3.3]. We assume that a read/write operation on such register takes unit time. As previously the goal is to compute $y = S(x)$ where

$$S : \{0,1\}^k \to \{0,1\}^{k'}$$

is a look-up table with k-bit input and k'-bit output.

Under the variant the k'-bit outputs of S are first packed into register words of $\omega = \ell \cdot k'$ bits, where ℓ is assumed to be a power of two. For example, for a DES Sbox with $k = 6$ input bits and $k' = 4$ output bits, on a $\omega = 32$ bits architecture we can pack $\ell = 8$ output 4-bit nibbles into a 32-bit word. Formally, we define a new Sbox S' with k_1-bit input and $\omega = \ell \cdot k'$ bits output with

$$S'(a) = S(a \| 0^{k_2}) \| \cdots \| S(a \| 1^{k_2})$$

for all $a \in \{0,1\}^{k_1}$, where $k = k_1 + k_2$ and $k_2 = \log_2 \ell$. To compute $S(x)$ for $x \in \{0,1\}^k$, we proceed in two steps:

1. Write $x = a\|b$ for $a \in \{0,1\}^{k_1}$ and $b \in \{0,1\}^{k_2}$, and compute $z = S'(a) = S(a\|0^{k_2})\| \cdots \|S(a\|1^{k_2})$
2. Viewing z as a k_2-bit input and k'-bit output table, compute $y = z(b) = S(x)$.

We must show how to compute $y = S(x)$ with the two steps above when the input x is shared with n shares x_i. In the first step we proceed as in Algorithm 1, except that the new table S' has a k_1-bit input instead of a k-bit input, and $\omega = \ell \cdot k'$-bit output instead of k'-bit output. Note that the table S' contains $2^{k_1} = 2^{k-k_2} = 2^k/\ell$ elements instead of 2^k for the original S. Since we assume that a read/write operation on a ω-bit register takes unit time, the complexity of the first step is now $\mathcal{O}(2^k/\ell \cdot n^2)$. Note that S and S' take the same amount of memory in RAM; in the first step of our countermeasure we can achieve a speed-up by a factor ℓ because we are moving ℓ blocks of k' bits at a time inside registers of size $\omega = \ell \cdot k'$ bits.

The second step requires a slight modification of Algorithm 1. Namely we must view the output z from Step 1 as a look-up table with k_2-bit input and k'-bit output. However this output z is now obtained in shared form, namely we get shares $z_1, \ldots, z_n$ such that $z = z_1 \oplus \cdots \oplus z_n$, whereas in Algorithm 1 the look-up table $S(x)$ is a public table. This is not a problem, as we can simply keep this table in shared form when initializing the $T(u)$ table at Line 2 of Algorithm 1. More precisely in the second step we can initialize the table $T(u)$ with:

$$T(u) = (z_1(u), \ldots, z_n(u)) \in (\{0,1\}^{k'})^n$$

for all $u \in \{0,1\}^{k_2}$, and we still have $\oplus(T(u)) = z(u)$ for all u as required. The rest of Algorithm 1 is the same. Since the second step uses a table of size $2^{k_2} = \ell$ elements, its complexity is $\mathcal{O}(\ell \cdot n^2)$.

The full complexity of our variant countermeasure is therefore $\mathcal{O}((2^k/\ell + \ell) \cdot n^2)$. This is minimized for $\ell = 2^{k/2}$. If we have large enough register size ω so that we can take $\ell = \omega/k' = 2^{k/2}$, then the complexity of our variant countermeasure becomes $\mathcal{O}(2^{k/2} \cdot n^2)$, the same complexity as the Carlet *et al.* countermeasure.[6]

The following Lemma shows that our variant countermeasure achieves the same level of security as Algorithm 1; the proof is essentially the same as the proof of Lemma 1 and is therefore omitted.

Lemma 2. *Let $(x_i)_{1 \le i \le n}$ be the input shares of the above countermeasure for large register size, and let t be such that $2t < n$. For any set of t intermediate variables, there exists a subset $I \subset [1, n]$ of indices such that $|I| \le 2t < n$ and the distribution of those t variables can be perfectly simulated from the x_i's with $i \in I$. The output shares $y_{|I}$ can also be perfectly simulated from $x_{|I}$.*

4   Higher Order Masking of a Full Block-Cipher

In this section we show how to integrate our countermeasure into a full block-cipher. We consider a block-cipher with the following operations: Xor operation $z = x \oplus y$, linear (or affine) transform $y = f(x)$, and look-up table $y = S(x)$. This covers both AES and DES block-ciphers. We show how to apply high-order masking to these operations, in order to protect a full block-cipher against t-th order attacks.[7]

Xor Operation. We consider a Xor operation $z = x \oplus y$. Taking as input the shares x_i and y_i such that $x = x_1 \oplus \cdots \oplus x_n$ and $y = y_1 \oplus \cdots \oplus y_n$, it suffices to compute the shares $z_i = x_i \oplus y_i$.

Linear Operation. We consider a linear operation $y = f(x)$. Taking as input the shares x_i such that $x = x_1 \oplus \cdots \oplus x_n$, it suffices to compute the shares $y_i = f(x_i)$ separately.

Table Look-Up. A table look-up $y = S(x)$ is computed using our previous Algorithm 1.

Input Encoding. Given x as input, we first encode x as $x_1 = x$ and $x_i = 0$ for $2 \le i \le n$. Secondly we let $(x_1, \ldots, x_n) \leftarrow \mathsf{RefreshMasks}(x_1, \ldots, x_n)$.

Output Decoding. Given $y_1, \ldots, y_n$ as input, we compute $y = y_1 \oplus \cdots \oplus y_n$ using Algorithm 3 below.

Key Shares Refreshing. As mentioned in Section 2.2 we must re-randomize the key shares between successive executions of the block-cipher in order to achieve security in the full model. Using Algorithm 4 below we perform both an initial Key Shares Refreshing (before the shares sk_i are used to evaluate the block-cipher), and a final Key Shares Refreshing (before the key shares sk_i are stored for the next execution).[8]

---

[6] Note that for DES with 32-bit registers we can take the optimum $\ell = 2^{6/2} = 8$. However for AES the optimum $\ell = 2^{8/2} = 16$ would require 128-bit registers.

[7] Xor is a linear operation, so one could consider the linear operation $y = f(x)$ only, but it seems more convenient to consider the Xor operation separately.

[8] Note that for both algorithms 3 and 4 the RefreshMasks procedure must be applied with the *tmp* randoms generated with the appropriate bit-size (instead of k').

Algorithm 3. Shares recombination

Input: $y_1, \ldots, y_n$
Output: y such that $y = y_1 \oplus \cdots \oplus y_n$
1: **for** $i = 1$ **to** n **do** $(y_1, \ldots, y_n) \leftarrow \mathsf{RefreshMasks}(y_1, \ldots, y_n)$
2: $c \leftarrow y_1$
3: **for** $i = 2$ **to** n **do** $c \leftarrow c \oplus y_i$
4: **return** c

Algorithm 4. Key Shares Refreshing

Input: $sk_1, \ldots, sk_n$ such that $sk = sk_1 \oplus \cdots \oplus sk_n$
Output: $sk_1, \ldots, sk_n$ such that $sk = sk_1 \oplus \cdots \oplus sk_n$
1: **for** $i = 1$ **to** n **do** $(sk_1, \ldots, sk_n) \leftarrow \mathsf{RefreshMasks}(sk_1, \ldots, sk_n)$
2: **return** $sk_1, \ldots, sk_n$

This terminates the description of our randomized encryption algorithm. The following theorem proves the security of the randomized encryption scheme defined above in the full model, under the condition $n \geq 2t + 1$; we give the proof in the full version of this paper [Cor13a]. This improves the bound $n \geq 4t + 1$ from [ISW03] for stateful circuits. We stress that any set of t intermediate variables can be probed by the adversary, including variables in the input encoding, output decoding, and key shares refreshing; that is, no operation is assumed to be leak-free.

Theorem 1. *The randomized encryption scheme defined above achieves t-th order security in the full model for $n \geq 2t + 1$.*

Remark 3. The input encoding operation need not be randomized by Refresh-Masks; this is because the input x is public and given to the simulator, who can therefore perfectly simulate the initial shares $x_{|I}$ for any subset $I \subset [1, n]$. Moreover in the restricted model the key shares refreshing is not necessary. In practice we can keep both operations as their time complexity is only $\mathcal{O}(n)$ and $\mathcal{O}(n^2)$ respectively.

Remark 4. We stress that the secret key sk must be initially provided with randomized shares, since sk is secret and not given to the simulator; in other words it would be insecure for the randomized block-cipher to receive sk as input and perform the initial input encoding on sk by himself.

Remark 5. In the output decoding operation we perform a series of n mask refreshing before computing y. This is to enable a correct simulation of the intermediate variables c at Line 3 in case they are probed by the adversary.

5   Practical Implementation

We have performed a practical implementation of our new countermeasure for both AES and DES, using a 32-bit architecture so that we could apply our large register variant. More precisely we could pack $\ell = 4$ output bytes for AES, and $\ell = 8$ output 4-bit nibbles for DES. For comparison we have also implemented the Rivain-Prouff countermeasure [RP10] for AES and the Carlet *et al.* countermeasure [CGP+12] for DES; for the latter we have used the technique from [RV13], in which the evaluation of a DES Sbox requires only 7 non-linear multiplications. The performances of our implementations are summarized in Table 2. We use the bound $n = 2t + 1$ for the full model of security (which implies security in the restricted model).

Table 2. Comparison of secure AES and DES implementations, for the Rivain-Prouff (RP) countermeasure, and our Table Recomputation (TR) countermeasure. The implementation was done in C on a MacBook Air running on a 1.86 GHz Intel processor. We denote the number of calls to the random number generator (times 10^3), the required memory in bytes (only for the Sbox computation part), the total running time in ms, and the Penalty Factor (PF) compared the the unmasked implementation.

	t	n	Rand	Mem	Time	PF
AES					0.0018	1
AES, RP	1	3	2.1	20	0.092	50
AES, TR	1	3	44	1579	0.80	439
AES, RP	2	5	6.8	30	0.18	96
AES, TR	2	5	176	2615	2.2	1205
AES, RP	3	7	14	40	0.31	171
AES, TR	3	7	394	3651	4.4	2411
AES, RP	4	9	24	50	0.51	276
AES, TR	4	9	700	4687	7.3	4003

	t	n	Rand	Mem	Time	PF
DES					0.010	1
DES, RP	1	3	2.8	72	0.47	47
DES, TR	1	3	8.5	423	0.31	31
DES, RP	2	5	9.2	118	0.78	79
DES, TR	2	5	33	691	0.59	59
DES, RP	3	7	19	164	1.3	129
DES, TR	3	7	75	959	0.90	91
DES, RP	4	9	33	210	1.9	189
DES, TR	4	9	133	1227	1.4	142

We obtain that in practice for AES our algorithm is an order of magnitude less efficient than Rivain-Prouff, which can take advantage of the special algebraic structure of the AES Sbox; however for DES our algorithm performs slightly better than the Carlet *et al.* countermeasure. Note that this holds for a 32-bit architecture; on a 8-bit architecture the comparison could be less favorable. The source code of our implementations is publicly available [Cor13b].

One could think that because of the large penalty factors the countermeasures above are unpractical. However in some applications the block-cipher evaluation can be only a small fraction of the full protocol (for example in a challenge-response authentication protocol), and in that case a penalty factor of say 100 for a single block-cipher evaluation may be acceptable.

Acknowledgments. We would like to thank the Eurocrypt 2014 referees for their helpful comments.

References

CGP⁺12. Carlet, C., Goubin, L., Prouff, E., Quisquater, M., Rivain, M.: Higher-order masking schemes for s-boxes. In: Canteaut, A. (ed.) FSE 2012. LNCS, vol. 7549, pp. 366–384. Springer, Heidelberg (2012)

CJRR99. Chari, S., Jutla, C.S., Rao, J.R., Rohatgi, P.: Towards sound approaches to counteract power-analysis attacks. In: Wiener, M. (ed.) CRYPTO 1999. LNCS, vol. 1666, pp. 398–412. Springer, Heidelberg (1999)

Cor13a. Coron, J.-S.: Higher order masking of look-up tables. Cryptology ePrint Archive, Report 2013/700. Full version of this paper (2013), http://eprint.iacr.org/

Cor13b. Coron, J.-S.: Implementation of higher-order countermeasures (2013), https://github.com/coron/htable/

CPR07. Coron, J.-S., Prouff, E., Rivain, M.: Side channel cryptanalysis of a higher order masking scheme. In: Paillier, P., Verbauwhede, I. (eds.) CHES 2007. LNCS, vol. 4727, pp. 28–44. Springer, Heidelberg (2007)

CRR02. Chari, S., Rao, J.R., Rohatgi, P.: Template attacks. In: Kaliski Jr., B.S., Koç, Ç.K., Paar, C. (eds.) CHES 2002. LNCS, vol. 2523, pp. 13–28. Springer, Heidelberg (2003)

HOM06. Herbst, C., Oswald, E., Mangard, S.: An AES smart card implementation resistant to power analysis attacks. In: Zhou, J., Yung, M., Bao, F. (eds.) ACNS 2006. LNCS, vol. 3989, pp. 239–252. Springer, Heidelberg (2006)

ISW03. Ishai, Y., Sahai, A., Wagner, D.: Private circuits: Securing hardware against probing attacks. In: Boneh, D. (ed.) CRYPTO 2003. LNCS, vol. 2729, pp. 463–481. Springer, Heidelberg (2003)

KJJ99. Kocher, P.C., Jaffe, J., Jun, B.: Differential power analysis. In: Wiener, M. (ed.) CRYPTO 1999. LNCS, vol. 1666, pp. 388–397. Springer, Heidelberg (1999)

Mes00. Messerges, T.S.: Using second-order power analysis to attack dpa resistant software. In: Paar, C., Koç, Ç.K. (eds.) CHES 2000. LNCS, vol. 1965, pp. 238–251. Springer, Heidelberg (2000)

PR13. Prouff, E., Rivain, M.: Masking against side-channel attacks: A formal security proof. In: Johansson, T., Nguyen, P.Q. (eds.) EUROCRYPT 2013. LNCS, vol. 7881, pp. 142–159. Springer, Heidelberg (2013)

RDP08. Rivain, M., Dottax, E., Prouff, E.: Block ciphers implementations provably secure against second order side channel analysis. In: Nyberg, K. (ed.) FSE 2008. LNCS, vol. 5086, pp. 127–143. Springer, Heidelberg (2008)

RP10. Rivain, M., Prouff, E.: Provably secure higher-order masking of AES. In: Mangard, S., Standaert, F.-X. (eds.) CHES 2010. LNCS, vol. 6225, pp. 413–427. Springer, Heidelberg (2010)

RV13. Roy, A., Vivek, S.: Analysis and improvement of the generic higher-order masking scheme of FSE 2012. In: Bertoni, G., Coron, J.-S. (eds.) CHES 2013. LNCS, vol. 8086, pp. 417–434. Springer, Heidelberg (2013)

Sha79. Shamir, A.: How to share a secret. Commun. ACM 22(11), 612–613 (1979)

SP06. Schramm, K., Paar, C.: Higher order masking of the AES. In: Pointcheval, D. (ed.) CT-RSA 2006. LNCS, vol. 3860, pp. 208–225. Springer, Heidelberg (2006)

How to Certify the Leakage of a Chip?

François Durvaux[1], François-Xavier Standaert[1],
and Nicolas Veyrat-Charvillon[2]

[1] UCL Crypto Group, Université catholique de Louvain
Place du Levant 3, B-1348, Louvain-la-Neuve, Belgium
[2] CNRS IRISA, INRIA Centre Rennes - Bretagne Atlantique, University Rennes 1
6 rue Kerampont, CS 80518, 22305 Lannion cedex, France

Abstract. Evaluating side-channel attacks and countermeasures requires determining the amount of information leaked by a target device. For this purpose, information extraction procedures published so far essentially combine a *"leakage model"* with a *"distinguisher"*. Fair evaluations ideally require exploiting a perfect leakage model (i.e. exactly corresponding to the true leakage distribution) with a Bayesian distinguisher. But since such perfect models are generally unknown, density estimation techniques have to be used to approximate the leakage distribution. This raises the fundamental problem that all security evaluations are potentially biased by both estimation and assumption errors. Hence, the best that we can hope is to be aware of these errors. In this paper, we provide and implement methodological tools to solve this issue. Namely, we show how sound statistical techniques allow both quantifying the leakage of a chip, and certifying that the amount of information extracted is close to the maximum value that would be obtained with a perfect model.

1 Introduction

Side-channel attacks aim to extract secret information from cryptographic implementations. For this purpose, they essentially compare key-dependent leakage models with actual measurements. As a result, models that accurately describe the target implementation are beneficial to the attack's efficiency.

In practice, this problem of model accuracy is directly reflected in the various distinguishers that have been published in the literature. Taking prominent examples, non-profiled Correlation Power Analysis (CPA) usually takes advantage of an a-priori (e.g. Hamming weight) leakage model [3]. By contrast, profiled Template Attacks (TA) take advantage of an offline learning phase in order to estimate the leakage model [5]. But even in the latter case, the profiling method is frequently based on some assumptions on the leakage distribution (e.g. that the noise is Gaussian). Furthermore, the model estimation can also be bounded by practical constraints (e.g. in terms of number of measurements available in the learning phase). Following these observations, the question *"how good is my leakage model?"* has become a central one in the analysis of side-channel attacks. In other words, whenever trying to quantify the security of an implementation, the goal is to reflect the actual target - not the evaluators' assumptions. Therefore, the main challenge for the evaluator is to avoid being biased by an incorrect

P.Q. Nguyen and E. Oswald (Eds.): EUROCRYPT 2014, LNCS 8441, pp. 459–476, 2014.

model, possibly leading to a false sense of security (i.e. an insecure cryptographic implementation that would look secure in front of one particular adversary).

More formally, the relation between accurate leakage models and fair security analyses is also central in evaluation frameworks such as proposed at Eurocrypt 2009 [18]. In particular, this previous work established that the leakage of an implementation (or the quality of a measurement setup) can be quantified by measuring the Mutual Information (MI) between the secret cryptographic keys manipulated by a device and the actual leakage produced by this device. Unfortunately, the design of unbiased and non-parametric estimators for the MI is a notoriously hard problem. Yet, since the goal of side-channel attacks is to use the "best available" models in order to recover information, a solution is to estimate the MI based on these models. This idea has been precised by Renauld et al. with the notion of Perceived Information (PI) - that is nothing else than an estimation of the MI biased by the side-channel adversary's model [15]. Intuitively, the MI captures the worst-case security level of an implementation, as it corresponds to an (hypothetical) adversary who can perfectly profile the leakage Probability Density Function (PDF). By contrast, the PI captures its practical counterpart, where actual estimation procedures are used to profile the PDF.

Our Contribution. The previous formal tools provide a sound basis for discussing the evaluation question *"how good is my leakage model?"*. The answer to this question actually corresponds to the difference between the MI and the PI. Nevertheless, we remain with the problem that the MI is generally unknown (just as the actual leakage PDF), which makes it impossible to compute this difference directly. Interestingly, we show in this paper that it is possible to perform sound(er) security analyses, where the approximations used by the side-channel evaluators are quantified, and their impact on security is kept under control.

In this context, we start with the preliminary observation that understanding these fair evaluation issues requires to clearly distinguish between estimation errors and assumption errors, leading to three main contributions. First, we show how cross–validation can be used in order to precisely gauge the convergence of an estimated model. Doing so, we put forward that certain evaluation metrics (e.g. Pearson's correlation or PI) are better suited for this purpose. Second, we propose a method for measuring assumption errors in side-channel attacks, taking advantage of the distance sampling technique introduced in [20]. We argue that it allows detecting imperfect hypotheses without any knowledge of the true leakage distribution[1]! Third, we combine these tools in order to determine the probability that a model error is due to estimation or assumption issues. We then discuss the (im)possibility to precisely (and generally) bound the resulting information loss. We also provide pragmatic guidelines for physical security evaluators. For illustration, we apply these contributions to actual measurements obtained from an AES implementation in an embedded microcontroller. As a

---

[1] By contrast, the direct solution for quantifying the PI/MI distance would be to compute a statistical (e.g. Kullback-Leibler) distance between the adversary's model and the actual leakages. But it requires knowing the true leakage distribution.

result and for the first time, we are able to certify that the leakage of a chip (i.e. its worst-case security level) is close to the one we are able to extract.

These results have implications for the certification of any cryptographic product against side-channel attacks - as they provide solutions to guarantee that the evaluation made by laboratories is based in sound assumptions. They could also be used to improve the comparison of measurement setups such as envisioned by the DPA contest v3 [6]. Namely, this contest suggests comparing the quality of side-channel measurements with a CPA based on an a-priori leakage model. But this implies that the best traces are those that best comply with this a-priori, independent of their true informativeness. Using the PI to compare the setups would already allow each participant to choose his leakage assumptions. And using the cross–validation and distance sampling techniques described in this work would allow determining how relevant these assumptions are.

Notations. We use capital letters for random variables, small caps for their realizations, sans serif fonts for functions and calligraphic letters for sets.

2 Background

2.1 Measurement Setups

Our experiments are based on measurements of an AES Furious implementation[2] run by an 8-bit Atmel AVR (AtMega 644p) microcontroller at a 20 MHz clock frequency. Since the goal of this paper is to analyze leakage informativeness and model imperfections, we compared traces from three different setups. First, we considered two types of "power-like" measurements. For this purpose, we monitored the voltage variations across both a 22 Ω resistor and a 2 μH inductance introduced in the supply circuit of our target chip. Second, we captured the electromagnetic radiation of our target implementation, using a Rohde & Schwarz (RS H 400-1) probe - with up to 3 GHz bandwidth - and a 20 dB low-noise amplifier. Measurements were taken without depackaging the chip, hence providing no localization capabilities. Acquisitions were performed using a Tektronix TDS 7104 oscilloscope running at 625 MHz and providing 8-bit samples. In practice, our evaluations focused on the leakage of the first AES master key byte (but would apply identically to any other enumerable target). Leakage traces were produced according to the following procedure. Let x and s be our target input plaintext byte and subkey, and $y = x \oplus s$. For each of the 256 values of y, we generated 1000 encryption traces, where the rest of the plaintext and key was random (i.e. we generated 256 000 traces in total, with plaintexts of the shape $p = x||r_1||\ldots||r_{15}$, keys of the shape $k = s||r_{16}||\ldots||r_{30}$, and the r_i's denoting uniformly random bytes). In order to reduce the memory cost of our evaluations, we only stored the leakage corresponding to the 2 first AES rounds (as the dependencies in our target byte $y = x \oplus s$ typically vanish after the first round, because of the strong diffusion properties of the AES). In the following,

---

[2] Available at http://point-at-infinity.org/avraes/

we will denote the 1000 encryption traces obtained from a plaintext p including the target byte x under a key k including the subkey s as: $\mathsf{AES}_{k_s}(p_x) \rightsquigarrow l_y^i$ (with $i \in [1; 1000]$). Furthermore, we will refer to the traces produced with the resistor, inductance and EM probe as $l_y^{r,i}$, $l_y^{l,i}$ and $l_y^{em,i}$. Eventually, whenever accessing the points of these traces, we will use the notation $l_y^i(j)$ (with $j \in [1; 10\,000]$, typically). These subscripts and superscripts will omitted when not necessary.

2.2 Evaluation Metrics

In this subsection, we recall a few evaluation metrics that have been introduced in previous works on side-channel attacks and countermeasures.

Correlation Coefficient (non-profiled). In view of the popularity of the CPA distinguisher in the literature, a natural candidate evaluation metric is Pearson's correlation coefficient. In a non-profiled setting, an a-priori (e.g. Hamming weight) model is used for computing the metric. The evaluator then estimates the correlation between his measured leakages and the modeled leakages of a target intermediate value. In our AES example and targeting an S-box output, it would lead to $\hat{\rho}(L_Y, \mathsf{model}(\mathsf{Sbox}(Y)))$, where the "hat" notation is used to denote the estimation of a statistic. In practice, this estimation is performed by sampling (i.e. measuring) N_t "test" traces from the leakage distribution L_Y. In the following, we will denote the set of these N_t test traces as $\mathcal{L}_Y^t$.

Correlation Coefficient (profiled). In order to avoid possible biases due to an incorrect a-priori choice of leakage model, a natural solution is to extend the previous proposal to a profiled setting. In this case, the evaluator will start by building a model from N_p "profiling" traces. We denoted this step as $\mathsf{model}_\rho \leftarrow \mathcal{L}_Y^p$ (with $\mathcal{L}_Y^p \perp\!\!\!\perp \mathcal{L}_Y^t$). In practice, it is easily obtained by computing the sample mean values of the leakage points corresponding to the target intermediate values.

Signal-to-Noise Ratio (SNR). Yet another solution put forward by Mangard is to compute the SNR of the measurements [13], defined as:

$$\hat{\mathsf{SNR}} = \frac{\hat{\mathsf{var}}_y(\hat{\mathsf{E}}_i(L_y^i))}{\hat{\mathsf{E}}_y(\hat{\mathsf{var}}_i(L_y^i))},$$

where $\hat{\mathsf{E}}$ and $\hat{\mathsf{var}}$ denote the sample mean and variance of the leakage variable, that are estimated from the N_t traces in $\mathcal{L}_Y^t$ (like the correlation coefficient).

Perceived Information. Eventually, as mentioned in introduction the PI can be used for evaluating the leakage of a cryptographic implementation. Its sample definition (that is most useful in evaluations of actual devices) is given by:

$$\hat{\mathsf{PI}}(S; X, L) = \mathsf{H}[S] - \sum_{s \in \mathcal{S}} \Pr[s] \sum_{x \in \mathcal{X}} \Pr[x] \sum_{l_y^i \in \mathcal{L}_Y^t} \Pr_{\mathsf{chip}}[l_y^i | s, x] . \log_2 \hat{\Pr}_{\mathsf{model}}[s | x, l_y^i],$$

where $\hat{\Pr}_{\mathsf{model}} \leftarrow \mathcal{L}_Y^p$. As already observed in several works, the sum over s is redundant whenever the target operations used in the attack follows a group operation (which is typically the case of a block cipher key addition).

Under the assumption that the model is properly estimated, it is shown in [12] that the three latter metrics are essentially equivalent in the context of standard univariate side-channel attacks (i.e. exploiting a single leakage point $l_y^i(j)$ at a time). By contrast, only the PI naturally extends to multivariate attacks [19]. It can be interpreted as the amount of information leakage that will be exploited by an adversary using an estimated model. So just as the MI is a good predictor for the success rate of an ideal TA exploiting the perfect model $\Pr_{\text{chip}}$, the PI is a good predictor for the success rate of an actual TA exploiting the "best available" model $\hat{\Pr}_{\text{model}}$ obtained through the profiling of a target device.

2.3   PDF Estimation Methods

Computing metrics such as the PI defined in the previous section requires one to build a probabilistic leakage model $\hat{\Pr}_{\text{model}}$ for the leakage behavior of the device. We now describe a few techniques that can be applied for this purpose.

Gaussian Templates. The seminal TA in [5] relies on an approximation of the leakages using a set of normal distributions. That is, it assumes that each intermediate computation generates samples according to a Gaussian distribution. In our typical scenario where the targets follow a key addition, we consequently use: $\hat{\Pr}_{\text{model}}[l_y|s,x] \approx \hat{\Pr}_{\text{model}}[l_y|s \oplus x] \sim \mathcal{N}(\mu_y, \sigma_y^2)$. This approach simply requires estimating the sample means and variances for each value of $y = x \oplus s$ (and mean vectors / covariance matrices in case of multivariate attacks).

Regression-Based Models. To reduce the data complexity of the profiling, an alternative approach proposed by Schindler et al. is to exploit Linear Regression (LR) [16]. In this case, a stochastic model $\hat{\theta}(y)$ is used to approximate the leakage function and built from a linear basis $\mathbf{g}(y) = \{\mathbf{g}_0(y), ..., \mathbf{g}_{B-1}(y)\}$ chosen by the adversary/evaluator (usually $\mathbf{g}_i(y)$ are monomials in the bits of y). Evaluating $\theta(\hat{y})$ boils down to estimating the coefficients α_i such that the vector $\hat{\theta}(y) = \sum_j \alpha_j \mathbf{g}_j(y)$ is a least-square approximation of the measured leakages L_y. In general, an interesting feature of such models is that they allow trading profiling efforts for online attack complexity, by adapting the basis $\mathbf{g}(y)$. That is, a simpler model with fewer parameters will converge for smaller values of N_p, but a more complex model can potentially approximate the real leakage function more accurately. Compared to Gaussian templates, another feature of this approach is that only a single variance (or covariance matrix) is estimated for capturing the noise (i.e. it relies on an assumption of homoscedastic errors).

Histograms and Kernels. See appendix A.

3   Estimation Errors and Cross–Validation

Estimating the PI from a leaking implementation essentially holds in two steps. First, a model has to be estimated from a set of profiling traces $\mathcal{L}_Y^p$: $\hat{\Pr}_{\text{model}} \leftarrow \mathcal{L}_Y^p$. Second, a set of test traces $\mathcal{L}_Y^t$ is used to estimate the perceived information, corresponding to *actual* leakage samples of the device (i.e. following the true distribution $\Pr_{\text{chip}}[l_y^i | s, x]$). As a result, two main model errors can arise. First, the number of traces in the profiling set may be too low to estimate the model properly. This corresponds to the estimation errors that we analyze in this section. Second, the model $\hat{\Pr}_{\text{model}}$ may not be able to predict the distribution of samples in the test set, even after intensive profiling. This corresponds to the assumption errors that will be analyzed in the next section. In both cases, such model errors will be reflected by a divergence between the PI and MI.

In order to verify that estimations in a security evaluation are sufficiently accurate, the standard solution is to exploit cross–validation. In general, this technique allows gauging how well a predictive (here leakage) model performs in practice [10]. In the rest of the paper, we use 10-fold cross–validations for illustration (which is commonly used in the literature [9]). What this means is that the set of acquired traces $\mathcal{L}_Y$ is first split into ten (non overlapping) sets $\mathcal{L}_Y^{(i)}$ of approximately the same size. Let us define the profiling sets $\mathcal{L}_Y^{p,(j)} = \bigcup_{i \neq j} \mathcal{L}_Y^{(i)}$ and the test sets $\mathcal{L}_Y^{t,(j)} = \mathcal{L}_Y \setminus \mathcal{L}_Y^{p,(j)}$. The sample PI is then repeatedly computed ten times for $1 \leq j \leq 10$ as follows. First, we build a model from a profiling set: $\hat{\Pr}_{\text{model}}^{(j)} \leftarrow \mathcal{L}_Y^{p,(j)}$. Then we estimate $\hat{\text{PI}}^{(j)}(S; X, L)$ with the associated test set $\mathcal{L}_Y^{t,(j)}$. Cross–validation protects us from obtaining too large PI values due to over-fitting, since the test computations are always performed with an independent data set. Finally, the 10 outputs can be averaged to get an unbiased estimate, and their spread characterizes the accuracy of the result[3].

3.1   Experimental Results

As a starting point, we represented illustrative traces corresponding to our three measurement setups in Appendix B, Figure 8, 9, 10. The figures further contain the SNRs and correlation coefficients of a CPA using Hamming weight leakage model and targeting the S-box output. While insufficient for fair security evaluations as stated below, these metrics are interesting preliminary steps, since they indicate the parts of the traces where useful information lies. In the following, we extract a number of illustrative figures from meaningful samples.

From a methodological point of view, the impact of cross–validation is best represented with the box plot of Figure 1: it contains the PI of point 2605 in the resistor-based traces, estimated with Gaussian templates and a stochastic model using a 17-element linear basis for the bits of the S-box input and output. This point is the most informative one in our experiments (across all measurements and estimation procedures we tried). Results show that the PI estimated with Gaussian templates is higher - hence suggesting that the basis used in our regression-based profiling was not fully reflective of the chip activity for this sample. More importantly, we observe that the estimation converges quickly (as

---

[3] Cross–validation can also apply to profiled CPA, by building models $\text{model}_\rho \leftarrow \mathcal{L}_Y^{p,(j)}$, and testing them with the remaining $\mathcal{L}_Y^{t,(j)}$ traces. By contrast, it does not apply to the SNR for which the computation does not include an a posteriori testing phase. We focus on the PI because of its possible extension to multivariate statistics.

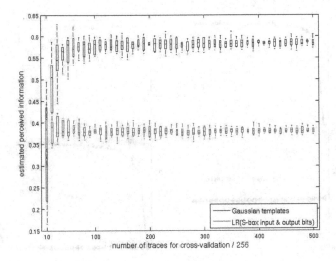

Fig. 1. Perceived information estimated from Gaussian templates and LR-based models, with cross–validation (target point 2605 from the resistor-based measurements)

the spread of our 10 PI estimates decreases quickly with the number of traces). As expected, this convergence is faster for regression-based profiling, reflecting the smaller number of parameters to estimate in this case. Note that we also performed this cross–validation for the Kernel-based PDF estimation described in Appendix A (see Appendix B, Figure 11 for the results). Both the expected value of the PI and its spread suggest that these two density estimation techniques provide equally satisfying results in our implementation context.

A natural next step is to analyze the quantity of information given by alternative leakage points. An example is given in Figure 2 (where we only plot the expected value of the PI). The left part of the figure corresponds exactly to the most informative point of Figure 1. The right part of the figure is computed with a later sample (time 4978) that (we assumed) corresponds to the computation of the S-box output. Interestingly, we observe that while this second point is less informative, it is more accurately explained by a stochastic model using the S-box output bits as a basis, hence confirming our expectations. Eventually, we also investigated the additional information gathered when performing multivariate attacks in Appendix B, Figure 12. For this purpose, we considered both a couple of points (2605 and 4978) coming from the same setup in the left part of the figure, and a single point (2605) coming from two different setups in the right part of the figure. This experiment clearly suggests that combining information from different operations leads to more PI than combining information from different setups. It naturally fits with the intuition that two different block cipher operations (corresponding to different intermediate values) lead to more information leakage (i.e. less correlation) than the same operation measured with two different (yet similar) measurement setups. Many variations of such evaluations are possible (for more samples, estimation procedures, ...). For simplicity,

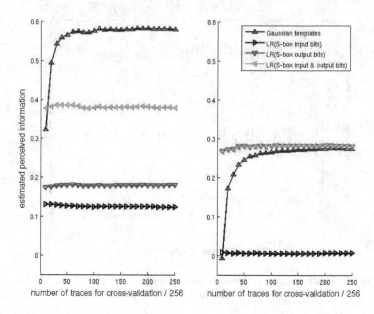

Fig. 2. PI for different PDF estimation techniques and two leakage (resistor-based) points. Left: most informative one (2605), right: other point of interest (4978).

we will limit our discussion to the previous examples, and use them to further discuss the critical question of assumption errors in the next section.

4   Assumption Errors and Distance Sampling

Looking at Figures 1 and 2, we can conclude that our estimation of the PI is reasonably accurate and that Gaussian templates are able to extract a given amount of information from the measurements. Nevertheless, such pictures still do not provide any clue about the closeness between our estimated PI and the (true, unknown) MI. As previously mentioned in introduction, evaluating the deviation between the PI and MI is generally hard. In theory, the standard approach for evaluating such a deviation would be to compute a statistical (e.g. Kullback-Leibler) distance $\hat{D}_{KL}(\hat{Pr}_{model}, Pr_{chip})$. But this requires knowing the (unknown) distribution Pr_{chip}, leading to an obvious chicken and egg problem.

Since standard probabilistic distances cannot be computed, an alternative solution that we will apply is to confront the test samples output by the device with estimated samples produced with the evaluator's model. In order to check their coherence, we essentially need a goodness-of-fit test. While several such tests exist in the literature for unidimensional distributions (e.g. Kolmogorov–Smirnov [4] or Cramér–von–Mises [1]), much fewer solutions exist that generalize to multivariate statistics. Since we additionally need a test that applies to any distribution, possibly dealing with correlated leakage points, a natural proposal is to exploit statistics based on spacings (or interpoint distance) [14].

The basic idea of such a test is to reduce the dimensionality of the problem by comparing the distributions of distances between pairs of points, consequently simplifying it into a one-dimensional goodness-of-fit test again. It exploits the fact that two multidimensional distributions $\mathcal{F}$ and $\mathcal{G}$ are equal if and only if the variables $\mathbf{X} \sim \mathcal{F}$ and $\mathbf{Y} \sim \mathcal{G}$ generate identical distributions for the distances $D(\mathbf{X_1}, \mathbf{X_2})$, $D(\mathbf{Y_1}, \mathbf{Y_2})$ and $D(\mathbf{X_3}, \mathbf{Y_3})$ [2,11]. In our evaluation context, we can simply check if the distance between pairs of simulated samples (generated with a profiled model) and the distance between simulated and actual samples behave differently. If the model estimated during the profiling phase of a side-channel attack is accurate, then the distance distributions should be close. Otherwise, there will be a discrepancy that the test will be able to detect, as we now detail.

The first step of our test for the detection of incorrect assumptions is to compute the simulated distance cumulative distribution as follows:

$$f_{\text{sim}}(d, s, x) = \Pr\left[L_y^1 - L_y^2 \leq d \,\middle|\, L_y^1, L_y^2 \sim \hat{\Pr}_{\text{model}}[L_y|s, x]\right].$$

Since the evaluator has an analytical expression for $\hat{\Pr}_{\text{model}}$, this cumulative distribution is easily obtained. Next, we compute the sampled distance cumulative distribution from the test sample set $\mathcal{L}_Y^t$ as follows:

$$\hat{g}_{N_t}(d, s, x) = \Pr\left[l_y^i - l_y^j \leq d \,\middle|\, \{l_y^i\}_{1 \leq i \leq N_t} \sim \hat{\Pr}_{\text{model}}[L_y|s, x], \{l_y^j\}_{1 \leq j \leq N_t} = \mathcal{L}_Y^t\right].$$

Eventually, we need to detect how similar f_{sim} and g_{N_t} are, which is made easy since these cumulative distributions are now univariate. Hence, we can compute the distance between them by estimating the Cramér–von–Mises divergence:

$$\hat{\text{CvM}}(f_{\text{sim}}, \hat{g}_{N_t}) = \int_{-\infty}^{\infty} [f_{\text{sim}}(x) - \hat{g}_{N_t}(x)]^2 \, dx.$$

As the number of samples in the estimation increases, this divergence should gradually tend towards zero provided the model assumptions are correct.

4.1 Experimental Results

As in the previous section, we applied cross–validation in order to compute the Cramér–von–Mises divergence between the distance distributions. That is, for each of the 256 target intermediate values, we generated 10 different estimates $\hat{g}_{N_t}^{(j)}(d, s, x)$ and computed $\hat{\text{CvM}}^{(j)}(f_{\text{sim}}, \hat{g}_{N_t})$ from them. An exemplary evaluation is given in Figure 3 for the same leakage point and estimation methods as in Figure 1. For simplicity, we plotted a picture containing the 256 (average) estimates at once[4]. It shows that Gaussian templates better converge towards a small divergence of the distance distributions. It is also noticeable that regression-based models lead to more outliers, corresponding to values y for which the leakage L_y is better approximated. Figure 4 additionally provides the

---

[4] It is also possible to investigate the quality of the model for any given $y = x \oplus s$.

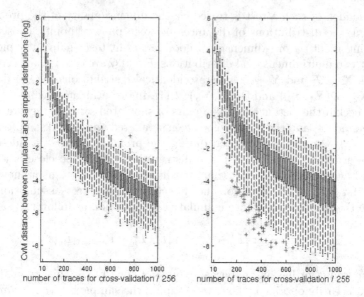

Fig. 3. Cramér–von–Mises divergence between simulated and sampled distributions, with cross–validation (target point 2605 from the resistor-based measurements). Left: Gaussian templates, right: LR-based estimation (S-box input and output bits).

quantiles of the Cramér–von–Mises divergence for both univariate and bivariate distributions (i.e. corresponding to the PIs in Appendix B, Figure 12). Interestingly, we observe that the better accuracy of Gaussian templates compared to regression-based models decreases when considering the second leakage point. This perfectly fits the intuition that we add a dimension that is better explained by a linear basis (as it corresponds to the right point in Figure 2). Note that any incorrect assumption would eventually lead the CvM divergence to saturate.

5 Estimation vs. Assumption Errors

From an evaluator's point of view, assumption errors are naturally the most damaging (since estimation errors can be made arbitrarily small by measuring more). In this respect, an important problem that we answer in this section is to determine whether a model error comes from estimation or assumption issues. For this purpose, the first statistic we need to evaluate is the *sampled* simulated distance cumulative distribution (for a given number of test traces N_t). This is the estimated counterpart of the distribution f_{sim} defined in Section 4:

$$\hat{f}_{\text{sim}}^{N_t}(d, s, x) = \Pr\left[l_y^i - l_y^j \leq d \,\Big|\, \{l_y^i, l_y^j\}_{1 \leq i \neq j \leq N_t} \sim \hat{\Pr}_{\text{model}}[L_y|s, x]\right].$$

From this definition, our main interest is to know, for a given divergence between f_{sim} and $\hat{f}_{\text{sim}}^{N_t}$, what is the probability that this divergence would be

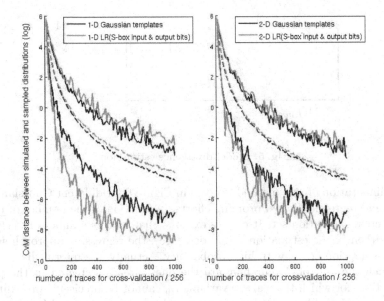

Fig. 4. Median, min and max of the CvM divergence btw. simulated and sampled distributions for Gaussian templates and LR-based models (resistor-based measurements). Left: univariate attack (sample 2605), right: bivariate attack (samples 2605 and 4978).

observed for the chosen amount of test traces N_t. This probability is directly given by the following cumulative divergence distribution:

$$\hat{\text{Div}}_{N_t}(x) = \Pr\left[\hat{\text{CvM}}(f_{\text{sim}}, \hat{f}_{\text{sim}}^{N_t}) \leq x\right].$$

How to exploit this distribution is then illustrated in Figure 5. For each model $\hat{\Pr}_{\text{model}}^{(j)}$ estimated during cross–validation, we build the corresponding $\hat{\text{Div}}_{N_t}^{(j)}$'s (i.e. the cumulative distributions in the figure). The cross–validation additionally provides (for each cumulative distribution) a value for $\hat{\text{CvM}}^{(j)}(f_{\text{sim}}, \hat{g}_{N_t})$ estimated from the actual leakage samples in the test set: they correspond to the small circles below the X axis in the figure. Eventually, we just derive:

$$\hat{\text{Div}}_{N_t}^{(j)}\left(\hat{\text{CvM}}^{(j)}(f_{\text{sim}}, \hat{g}_{N_t})\right).$$

Computing this statistic is simply obtained by projecting the circles towards the Y axis in the figure. Large values indicate that there is a small probability that the observed samples follow the simulated distributions. More precisely, they correspond to large p-values when testing the hypothesis that the estimated model is incorrect. Thanks to cross–validation, we can obtain 10 such values, leading to answers laid on a $[0; 1]$ interval, indicating the accuracy of each estimated model. Values grouped towards the top of the interval indicate that the assumptions used to estimate these models are likely incorrect.

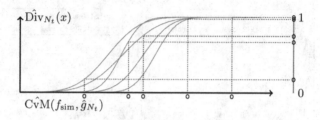

Fig. 5. Model divergence estimation

An illustration of this method is given in Figure 6 for different Gaussian templates and regression-based profiling efforts, in function of the number of traces in the cross–validation set. It clearly exhibits that as this number of traces increases (hence, the estimation errors decrease), the regression approach suffers from assumption errors with high probability. Actually, the intermediate values for which these errors occur first are the ones already detected in the previous section, for which the leakage variable L_y cannot be precisely approximated given our choice of basis. By contrast, no such errors are detected for the Gaussian templates (up to the amount of traces measured in our experiments). This process can be further systematized to all intermediate values, as in Figure 7. It allows an evaluator to determine the number of measurements necessary for the assumption errors to become significant in front of estimation ones.

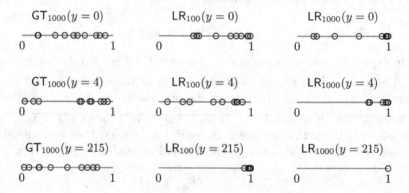

Fig. 6. Probability of assumption errors (p-values) for Gaussian templates (GT) and regression-based models (LR) corresponding to different target intermediate values y, in function of N_t (in subscript). Resistor-based measurements, sample 2605.

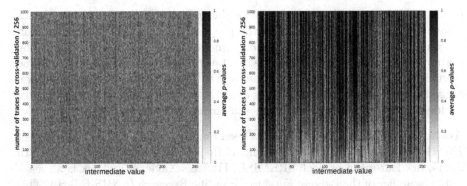

Fig. 7. Probability of assumption errors for Gaussian templates (left) and regression-based models with a 17-element basis (right) corresponding to all the target intermediate values y, in function of N_t. Resistor-based measurements, sample 2605.

6 Pragmatic Evaluation Guidelines and Conclusions

Interestingly, most assumptions will eventually be detected as incorrect when the number of traces in a side-channel evaluation increases[5]. As detailed in introduction, it directly raises the question whether the information loss due to such assumption errors can be bounded? Intuitively, the "threshold" value for which they are detected by our test provides a measure of their "amplitude" (since errors that are detected earlier should be larger in some sense). In the long version of this paper [7], we discuss whether this intuition can be exploited quantitatively and answer negatively. In this section, we conclude by arguing that our results still lead to qualitatively interesting outcomes, and describe how they can be exploited in the fair evaluation of side-channel attacks.

In this respect, first note that the maximum number of measurements in an evaluation is usually determined by practical constraints (i.e. how much time is allowed for the evaluation). Given this limit, estimation and assumption errors can be analyzed separately, leading to quantified results such as in Figures 1 and 3. These steps allow ensuring that the statistical evaluation has converged. Next, one should always test the hypothesis that the leakage model is incorrect, as described in Section 5. Depending on whether assumption errors are detected "early" or "late", the evaluator should be able to decide whether more refined PDF estimation techniques should be incorporated in his analyses. As discussed in [7], Section 6, the precise definition of "early" and "late" is hard to formalize in terms of information loss. Yet, later is always better and such a process will at least guarantee that if no such errors are detected *given some measurement capabilities*, an improved model will not lead to significantly improved attacks

---

[5] Non-parametric PDF estimation methods (e.g. as described in Appendix A) could be viewed as an exception to this fact, assuming that the sets of profiling traces $\mathcal{L}_Y^p$ and test traces $\mathcal{L}_Y^t$ come from the same distribution. Yet, this assumption may turn out to be contradicted in practice because of technological mismatches [8,15], in which case the detection of assumption errors remains critical even with such tools.

(since the evaluator will essentially not be able to distinguish the models with this amount of measurements). That is, the proposed methodology can provide an answer to the pragmatic question: "for an amount of measurements performed by a laboratory, is it worth spending time to refine the leakage model exploited in the evaluation?". In other words, it can be used to guarantee that the security level suggested by a side-channel analysis is close to the worst-case, and this guarantee is indeed conditional to number of measurement available for this purpose.

Acknowledgements. This work has been funded in parts by the ERC project 280141 (acronym CRASH), the Walloon Region MIPSs project and the 7th framework European project PREMISE. François-Xavier Standaert is an associate researcher of the Belgian Fund for Scientific Research (FNRS-F.R.S.). This work has been supported in part by the PAVOIS project (ANR 12 BS02 002 01).

References

1. Anderson, T.W.: On the distribution of the two-sample Cramer-von Mises criterion. The Annals of Mathematical Statistics 33(3), 1148–1159 (1962)
2. Bartoszynski, R., Pearl, D.K., Lawrence, J.: A multidimensional goodness-of-fit test based on interpoint distances. Journal of the American Statistical Association 92(438), 577–586 (1997)
3. Brier, E., Clavier, C., Olivier, F.: Correlation power analysis with a leakage model. In: Joye, M., Quisquater, J.-J. (eds.) CHES 2004. LNCS, vol. 3156, pp. 16–29. Springer, Heidelberg (2004)
4. Chakravarti, Laha, Roy: Handbook of methods of applied statistics, vol. I, pp. 392–394. John Wiley and Sons (1967)
5. Chari, S., Rao, J.R., Rohatgi, P.: Template Attacks. In: Kaliski Jr., B.S., Koç, Ç.K., Paar, C. (eds.) CHES 2002. LNCS, vol. 2523, pp. 13–28. Springer, Heidelberg (2003)
6. DPA Contest, http://www.dpacontest.org/v3/index.php (2012)
7. Durvaux, F., Standaert, F.-X., Veyrat-Charvillon, N.: How to certify the leakage of a chip? Cryptology ePrint Archive, Report 2013/706 (2013), http://eprint.iacr.org/
8. Elaabid, M.A., Guilley, S.: Portability of templates. J. Cryptographic Engineering 2(1), 63–74 (2012)
9. Geisser, S.: Predictive inference, vol. 55. Chapman & Hall/CRC (1993)
10. Hastie, T., Tibshirani, R., Friedman, J.: The elements of statistical learning. Springer Series in Statistics. Springer New York Inc., New York (2001)
11. Maa, J.-F., Pearl, D.K., Bartoszynski, R.: Reducing multidimensional two-sample data to one-dimensional interpoint comparisons. The Annals of Statistics 24(3), 1069–1074 (1996)
12. Mangard, S., Oswald, E., Standaert, F.-X.: One for all – all for one: Unifying standard differential power analysis attacks. IET Information Security 5(2), 100–110 (2011)
13. Mangard, S.: Hardware countermeasures against DPA? A statistical analysis of their effectiveness. In: Okamoto, T. (ed.) CT-RSA 2004. LNCS, vol. 2964, pp. 222–235. Springer, Heidelberg (2004)
14. Pyke, R.: Spacings revisited. In: Proceedings of the Sixth Berkeley Symposium on Mathematical Statistics and Probability, Univ. California, Berkeley, Calif. Theory of Statistics, vol. I, pp. 417–427. Univ. California Press (1970/1971)

15. Renauld, M., Standaert, F.-X., Veyrat-Charvillon, N., Kamel, D., Flandre, D.: A formal study of power variability issues and side-channel attacks for nanoscale devices. In: Paterson, K.G. (ed.) EUROCRYPT 2011. LNCS, vol. 6632, pp. 109–128. Springer, Heidelberg (2011)
16. Schindler, W., Lemke, K., Paar, C.: A stochastic model for differential side channel cryptanalysis. In: Rao, J.R., Sunar, B. (eds.) CHES 2005. LNCS, vol. 3659, pp. 30–46. Springer, Heidelberg (2005)
17. Silverman, B.W.: Density estimation for statistics and data analysis. Monographs on Statistics and Applied Probability. Taylor & Francis (1986)
18. Standaert, F.-X., Malkin, T.G., Yung, M.: A unified framework for the analysis of side-channel key recovery attacks. In: Joux, A. (ed.) EUROCRYPT 2009. LNCS, vol. 5479, pp. 443–461. Springer, Heidelberg (2009)
19. Standaert, F.-X., Veyrat-Charvillon, N., Oswald, E., Gierlichs, B., Medwed, M., Kasper, M., Mangard, S.: The world is not enough: Another look on second-order DPA. In: Abe, M. (ed.) ASIACRYPT 2010. LNCS, vol. 6477, pp. 112–129. Springer, Heidelberg (2010)
20. Veyrat-Charvillon, N., Standaert, F.-X.: Generic side-channel distinguishers: Improvements and limitations. In: Rogaway, P. (ed.) CRYPTO 2011. LNCS, vol. 6841, pp. 354–372. Springer, Heidelberg (2011)

A   Histograms and Kernels

The estimation methods of Section 2.3 make the assumption that the non-deterministic part of the leakage behaves according to a normal distribution. This may not always be correct, in which case one needs to use other techniques. For illustration, we considered two non-parametric solutions for density estimation, namely histograms and kernels. These allow one to finely characterize the non-deterministic part of the leakage. First, *histogram* estimation performs a partition of the samples by grouping them into bins. More precisely, each bin contains the samples of which the value falls into a certain range. The respective ranges of the bins have equal width and form a partition of the range between the extreme values of the samples. Using this method, one approximates a probability by dividing the number of samples that fall within a bin by the total number of samples. The optimal choice for the bin width h is an issue in statistical theory, as different bin sizes can have great impact on the estimation. In our case, we were able to tune this bin width according to the sensitivity of the oscilloscope. Second, *kernel* density estimation is a generalization of histograms. Instead of bundling samples together in bins, it adds (for each observed sample) a small kernel centered on the value of the leakage to the estimated PDF. The resulting estimation is a sum of small "bumps" that is much smoother than the corresponding histogram, which can be desirable when estimating a continuous distribution. In such cases it usually provides faster convergence towards the true distribution. Similarly to histograms, the most important parameter is the bandwidth h. In our case, we used the modified rule of thumb estimator in [17].

B   Additional Figures

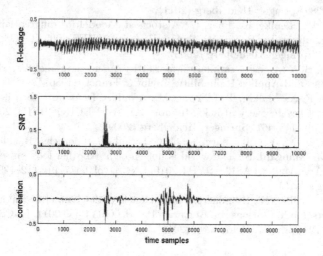

Fig. 8. Resistor-based measurements

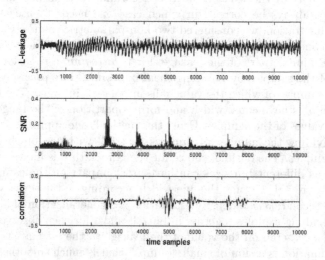

Fig. 9. Inductance-based measurements

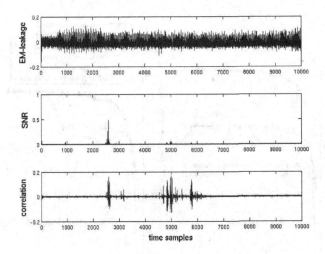

Fig. 10. Electromagnetic measurements

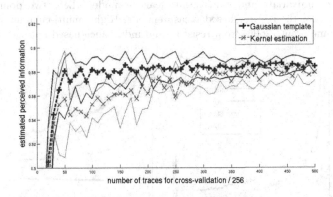

Fig. 11. Perceived information quantiles estimated from Gaussian templates and Kernels, with cross–validation (target point 2605 from the resistor-based measurements)

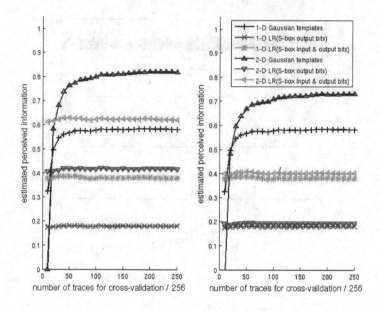

Fig. 12. PI for univariate and multivariate leakage models. Left: two points (2605, 4978) coming from the resistor-based measurements. Right: multi-channel attack exploiting the same point (2605) from resistor- and inductance-based measurements.

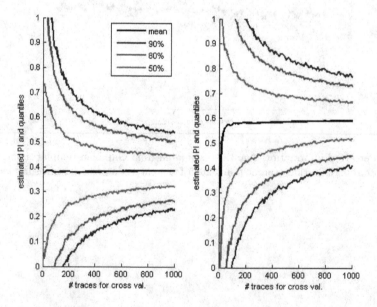

Fig. 13. Resistor-based measurements, sample 2605. Quantiles for the PI estimates obtained from the LR-based profiling (left) and Gaussian templates in Figure 1.

Efficient Round Optimal Blind Signatures

Sanjam Garg[1,*] and Divya Gupta[2]

[1] IBM T. J. Watson
sanjamg@cs.ucla.edu
[2] UCLA
divyag@cs.ucla.edu

Abstract. Known constructions of blind signature schemes suffer from at least one of the following limitations: (1) rely on parties having access to a common reference string or a random oracle, (2) are not round-optimal, or (3) are prohibitively expensive.

In this work, we construct the *first* blind-signature scheme that does not suffer from any of these limitations. In other words, besides being round optimal and having a standard model proof of security, our scheme is very efficient. Specifically, in our scheme, one signature is of size 6.5 KB and the communication complexity of the signing protocol is roughly 100 KB. An amortized variant of our scheme has communication complexity less that 1 KB.

1 Introduction

Blind signatures, introduced by Chaum [10], allow users to obtain signatures on messages of their choice without revealing the messages itself to the signer. Additionally, the blind signature scheme should satisfy unforgeability, i.e. no user can produce additional signatures on messages without interacting with the signer. Blind signatures have widespread applications such as e-cash, e-voting, and anonymous credentials.

Even after 30 years of research, and with 50+ candidate schemes in the literature, the state of the art is not completely satisfactory. Essentially, all schemes in the literature can be partitioned into two categories – (1) the schemes that rely on a random oracle or a setup, or (2) the schemes which are round inefficient. Examples of constructions argued to be secure using the random oracle methodology [7] include [26,27,25,1,5,8] and using a setup such as a shared random string include [4,3,11,13,21,23,22]. On the other hand, essentially all schemes that avoid the use of the random oracle methodology or a setup [20,9,23,19] are not round optimal.

The only scheme that does not fall in the above two categories is the recent construction of Garg et al. [16]. Unfortunately, this scheme is prohibitively expensive. For example, the communication complexity of this protocol is a

---

* Research conducted while at the IBM Research, T.J.Watson funded by NSF Grant No.1017660.

P.Q. Nguyen and E. Oswald (Eds.): EUROCRYPT 2014, LNCS 8441, pp. 477–495, 2014.

Table 1. Comparing the Efficiency of Different Round Optimal Blind Signature Schemes. κ is the security parameter of the scheme. $\epsilon > 1$ is an appropriate constant. The concrete parameters above correspond to the setting for 80 bits of security.

Scheme	Communication Complexity		Signature Size	
	Asymptotic	Concrete	Asymptotic	Concrete
Garg et al. [16]	poly(κ)		small[2]	
DLIN (This work)	$O(\kappa^{1+\epsilon})$	100.6KB	$O(\kappa^{\epsilon})$	6.5KB
Amortized (This work)	$O(\kappa^{\epsilon})$	836 Bytes	$O(\kappa^{\epsilon})$	6.5KB
q-SFP (This work)	$O(\kappa^{1+\epsilon})$	100.2KB	$O(\kappa^{\epsilon})$	3.2KB
Amortized (This work)	$O(\kappa^{\epsilon})$	472 bytes	$O(\kappa^{\epsilon})$	3.2KB

large polynomial in the security parameter[1]. In this work, we ask the following question:

Can we construct a very efficient round optimal blind signature scheme without relying on a random oracle or a setup?

1.1   Our Results

We construct the *first* blind signature scheme that avoids all of the above limitations, namely it is very efficient, round optimal and does not rely on a random oracle or a setup. We obtain parameters for our scheme by using the concept of work factors from [14,6]. A summary of the results is highlighted in Table 1.

- **Standard Setting:** We assume the sub-exponential hardness of Decisional Linear (DLIN) Assumption and a variant of the discrete-log assumption. Then our signature scheme has one signature of size 6.5 KB and the communication complexity of signing protocol roughly 100 KB.
- **Amortized Setting:** A number of applications require a user to obtain multiple signatures from the same signer. In such a setting, for our scheme almost all of the communication costs can be avoided. More specifically an amortized variant of our scheme has communication cost roughly 100 KB when obtaining the first signature. However, for every subsequent signature obtained the communication cost is less that 1 KB.
- **Stronger assumption:** Assuming a stronger assumption, sub-exponentially hard q-Simultaneous Flexible Pairing Assumption (SFP) from [3], we can improve the size of a signature and the amortized communication complexity of our signing protocol by roughly a factor of 2.

---

[1] To give an estimate on how big this polynomial is, we instantiate the proofs being given in their construction with Dwork-Naor Zaps using Kilian-Petrank NIZKs and get communication complexity of at least $O(\kappa^9)$ bits. One can also use asymptotically more efficient ZAPs instantiated with PCP based Groth NIZKs with ultimate proof size being $O(\kappa^5 \text{poly} \log(\kappa))$. Note that polylog($\kappa$) factor is quite large and for reasonable security parameters proof size would be comparable to $O(\kappa^7)$.

[2] This scheme uses general MPC techniques and can be instantiated using arbitrary signature scheme and thus has small signatures.

Qualitative Improvements. [16] uses *complexity leveraging* to obtain *standard model* round optimal blind signature scheme, and it is the use of these techniques which makes this scheme so inefficient. However, unfortunately, impossibility results of Fischlin et al. [12] and Pass [24] roughly indicate that the use of these techniques is essential for getting round optimal scheme in the standard model. Nonetheless, in this work, we introduce new techniques to *reduce* and *optimize* the use of complex leveraging, and thereby obtain a significantly more efficient scheme.

- **Reducing the use of complexity leveraging.** The technique of complexity leveraging works by creating a gap between the power of an adversarial entity and the reduction proving security. However, many a times this gap needs to be created multiple times in a layered fashion leading to larger parameters. The previous scheme of Garg et al. [16] needed to create this gap twice. However, in our scheme, we only need to create this gap once and this allows us to get smaller parameters.
- **Optimizing the use of complexity leveraging.** Complexity leveraging techniques (particularly for our application) inherently make non-black-box use of the underlying primitives. [16] in their construction end up rolling out the cryptographic primitive and viewing it as circuit. This leads to prohibitively inefficient schemes. We also make non-black-box use of the underlying primitive but avoid viewing it as a circuit. Instead, we cast it directly as a set of very structured equations which fit the framework of Groth-Sahai proofs, drastically improving the communication complexity of our protocol.

The techniques developed here are very general and we believe that they should be applicable to other settings. We leave this exploration for future work.

1.2   Technical Difficulties and New Ideas

Now we will describe the key ideas behind our scheme. We assume some familiarity with Groth-Sahai proofs. Lets us start by reminding the reader that GS proofs come in two modes – the hiding mode and the binding mode. In hiding mode, proofs reveal nothing about the witness used in the generation of a proof, and in binding mode, no fake proof exists.

Starting Point. The starting point for our construction is to use a blind signature scheme in the common reference string (CRS) model and remove the need for the CRS by letting the signer generate it. Of course this is problematic because a malicious signer can generate the CRS dishonestly (e.g. in a way such that it knows the trapdoors associated with the CRS) and use that to break the blindness property of the scheme. We solve this problem by using a special blind signature scheme for which blindness is statistical as long as the CRS is sampled from a certain "honest" distribution. In this setting, it is enough for the signer to prove that the CRS is sampled from the "honest" distribution. Looking ahead, this "honest" distribution is actually the CRS distribution for GS proofs in the hiding mode. However, we are faced with the following three issues.

Issue 1) First, in order to ensure blindness, the signer needs to prove to the user that the CRS was indeed sampled from the "honest" distribution.

Issue 2) Secondly, for proving unforgeability we will need that the reduction playing as the signer can "simulate" this proof. In other words, we need that the proof does not leak anything to the user.

Issue 3) The third issue is more subtle and arises as an interleaving of the first two issues. Specifically, the reduction for arguing unforgeability should be able to "extract" the messages on which the signatures are being issued and simulate the view of the attacking user. In other words, this extraction and simulation process should go unnoticed in the view of the attacking user. However, if a cheating signer could replicate the same behavior then this would go unnoticed as well. Hence, we certainly need to rule this out.

Before we describe our attempts to solve these issues, we note that for [16], this proof is the main reason for inefficiency.

Attempt at Using Range Proofs. As mentioned before, complexity leveraging makes non-black-box use of primitives essential making schemes prohibitively inefficient. In order to solve this issue we need to identify a problem such that: (1) the problem can be algebraically stated in groups of prime order p and has an efficient Groth-Sahai proof, (2) but solving the problem should be much easier than solving discrete log in the group of order p. The first property of the problem ensures efficiency of the proof. The second property as we will see later will be essential in making the complexity leveraging argument. We start by using a simple problem of solving discrete-log when the domain is restricted to some subspace. In particular, the problem we consider is: Given $C = g^c$ such that $c < q$ (where $q << p$), one needs to find c. We then show that it satisfies both the above properties. In particular, we will show that this problem can be cast in the language of efficient Groth-Sahai proofs thus satisfying the first requirement. Secondly, improvement in the brute-force attack when the sample space is restricted to $c < q$ is easy to see.

For the protocol, our idea is that user sends the value g^c for $c < q$ to the signer. Further instead of having the signer prove that the CRS was sampled honestly we have him prove that either the CRS was honestly generated or that it is aware of c. This immediately solves our problems 1 and 2 from above. We know that a cheating signer will not be able to recover c and hence will not be able to cheat. At the same time we can have the reduction for unforgeability extract c and thereby generate simulated proofs.

However our solution to issues 1 and 2 has created a 4th issue. A cheating user may cheat by generating g^c such that $c \geq q$. Next, we will show how issues 3 and 4 can be solved.

Solving Issue 3. Very interestingly we can resolve issue 3 by requiring that the signer generates the proof above under the CRS he had sampled for the underling blind signature scheme. This is very counter-intuitive as we are requiring the signer to generate a proof under a CRS that it generates on its own. The key idea is based on the observation that all we need is that the signer generates the

CRS from the hiding distribution for Groth-Sahai proofs. If this CRS is indeed hiding then the whole exercise of having a proof is redundant. On the other hand, if this CRS is actually generated dishonestly from the binding distribution then the signer is only hurting itself as it will not be able to generate his proof. [3]

Solving Issue 4. Recall that the 4th issue was that the user might generate g^c in a way such that $c > q$. We solve this problem by having the user provide a Groth-Sahai proof that the value c used is less that q. A question is under what CRS should this proof be give such that this proof does not leak c to the signer? Of course, we can not use the CRS that the signer generated for the underlying scheme. Our key observation here again is that we need to worry about this proof only if the original CRS has been generated maliciously, or in other words, if this CRS is binding. Recall that a binding CRS for Groth-Sahai proofs is a DLIN tuple. Our key idea here is that if $(g, g_1, g_2, h_1, h_2, h)$ is a DLIN tuple then its shift $(g, g_1, g_2, h_1, h_2, h \cdot g)$ can not be a DLIN tuple and hence the user can give his proof under this shifted CRS.[4]

2   Blind Signatures and Their Security

In this section we will recall the notion of blind signatures and define their security. Parts of this section have been taken verbatim from [16].

Definition 1. *A* blind signature scheme BS *consists of PPT algorithms* Gen, Vrfy *along with interactive PPT algorithms* S, U *such that for any* $\lambda \in \mathbb{N}$:

- Gen(1^λ) *generates a key pair* (sk, vk).
- *The joint execution of* $S(sk)$ *and* $U(vk, m)$, *where* $m \in \{0,1\}^\lambda$, *generates an output* σ *for the user and no output for the signer. We write this as* $(\perp, \sigma) \leftarrow \langle S(sk), U(vk, m) \rangle$.
- *Algorithm* Vrfy(vk, m, σ) *outputs a bit* b.

We require completeness *i.e., for any* $m \in \{0,1\}^\lambda$, *and for* $(sk, vk) \leftarrow$ Gen(1^λ), *and* σ *output by* U *in the joint execution of* $S(sk)$ *and* $U(vk, m)$, *it holds that* Vrfy$(vk, m, \sigma) = 1$ *with overwhelming probability in* $\lambda \in \mathbb{N}$.

Blind signatures must satisfy unforgeability and blindness [20,28].

Definition 2. *A blind signature scheme* BS $=$ (Gen, S, U, Vrfy) *is* unforgeable *if for any PPT algorithm* U^* *the probability that experiment* Unforge$_{U^*}^{BS}(\lambda)$ *defined in Figure 1 evaluates to 1 is negligible in* λ.

Blindness says that it should be infeasible for any malicious signer S^* to decide which of two messages m_0 and m_1 has been signed first in two executions with

---

[3] In the final construction (Figure 2), the signer will prove under the CRS he had sampled that it is aware of c. An honest signer who generates a hiding CRS will be able to simulate this proof successfully.

[4] A similar idea was also used by [17] to get perfectly sound NIWI in the standard model using statistically sound NIZKs.

Experiment Unforge$_{\mathcal{U}^*}^{\mathsf{BS}}(\lambda)$
  $(sk, vk) \leftarrow \mathsf{Gen}(1^\lambda)$
  $((m_1^*, \sigma_1^*), \ldots, (m_{k+1}^*, \sigma_{k+1}^*)) \leftarrow \mathcal{U}^{*\langle \mathcal{S}(sk), \cdot \rangle^\infty}(vk)$
  Return 1 iff
    $m_i^* \neq m_j^*$ for all i, j with $i \neq j$, and
    $\mathsf{Vrfy}(vk, m_i^*, \sigma_i^*) = 1$ for all $i \in [k+1]$, and
    at most k interactions with $\mathcal{S}(sk)$
    were completed.

Experiment Unblind$_{\mathcal{S}^*}^{\mathsf{BS}}(\lambda)$
  $(vk, m_0, m_1, \mathsf{st_{find}}) \leftarrow \mathcal{S}^*(\mathsf{find}, 1^\lambda)$
  $b \leftarrow \{0, 1\}$
  $\mathsf{st_{issue}} \leftarrow \mathcal{S}^{*\langle \cdot, \mathcal{U}(vk, m_b) \rangle^1, \langle \cdot, \mathcal{U}(vk, m_{\bar{b}}) \rangle^1}(\mathsf{issue}, \mathsf{st_{find}})$
    and let $\sigma_b, \sigma_{\bar{b}}$ denote the
      (possibly undefined) local outputs
    of $\mathcal{U}(vk, m_b)$ and $\mathcal{U}(vk, m_{\bar{b}})$ resp..
  set $(\sigma_0, \sigma_1) = (\perp, \perp)$ if $\sigma_0 = \perp$ or $\sigma_1 = \perp$
  $b^* \leftarrow \mathcal{S}^*(\mathsf{guess}, \sigma_0, \sigma_1, \mathsf{st_{issue}})$
  return 1 iff $b = b^*$.

Fig. 1. Security games of blind signatures

an honest user $\mathcal{U}$. We define the advantage of $\mathcal{S}^*$ in blindness game with respect to the experiment $\mathsf{Unblind}_{\mathcal{S}^*}^{\mathsf{BS}}(\lambda)$ as

$$\mathsf{Adv}_{\mathcal{S}^*,\mathsf{BS}}^{\mathsf{Unblind}}(\lambda) = \left| 2 \cdot \Pr[\mathsf{Unblind}_{\mathcal{S}^*}^{\mathsf{BS}}(\lambda) = 1] - 1 \right|$$

Definition 3. *A blind signature scheme* $\mathsf{BS} = (\mathsf{Gen}, \mathcal{S}, \mathcal{U}, \mathsf{Vrfy})$ *satisfies blindness if the advantage function* $\mathsf{Adv}_{\mathcal{S}^*,\mathsf{BS}}^{\mathsf{Unblind}}$ *is negligible for any* $\mathcal{S}^*$ *(working in modes* find, issue, *and* guess*) running in time* $poly(\lambda)$.

A blind signature scheme is secure if it is unforgeable and blind.

3   Preliminaries

In this section, we recall and define basic notation and primitives used briefly. For a detailed description of primitives, see full version [15]. Let λ denote the security parameter. We call a function *negligible* in λ if it is asymptotically smaller than any inverse polynomial.

Commitment Scheme on Groups. We describe a perfectly binding commitment scheme based on the decisional linear (DLIN) assumption with the special property that both the message space and the commitment comprise only of group elements. Let $(p, \mathbb{G}, \mathbb{G}_T, g, e)$ be a prime order bilinear pairing group. Then the function $\mathsf{Com}_{\mathbb{G}}(\cdot)$ generates a commitment to an element $m \in \mathbb{G}$ by first sampling $g_1, g_2 \xleftarrow{\$} \mathbb{G}$, $x, y \xleftarrow{\$} \mathbb{Z}_p$ and then outputting $(g, g_1, g_2, g_1^x, g_2^y, m \cdot g^{x+y})$.

Structure-Preserving Signatures. A signature scheme $(\mathsf{SPGen}, \mathsf{SPSign}, \mathsf{SPVerify})$ is said to be a *structure preserving signature scheme* over a prime order bilinear group $(p, \mathbb{G}, \mathbb{G}_T, g, e)$, if public keys, signatures and messages to be signed are vectors of group elements and verification only evaluates pairing product equations. Structure preserving signature schemes that sign a vector of group elements are known under different assumptions [17,3,2]. The first feasibility result was given by Groth [17]. This scheme is inefficient as the signature size grows linearly with the number of group elements in the message to be signed and the constants are quite big. In our scheme, we will use constant size structure preserving signatures [3,2]. Both of these results have been summarized in

Table 2. Efficiency of Structure Preserving Schemes

Scheme	$|msg|$	$|gk| + |vk|$	$|\sigma|$	#(PPE)	Assumption
AHO10	k	$2k + 12$	7	2	q-SFP
ACDKNO12	k	$2k + 25$	17	9	DLIN

the table given below. The size of different parameters are in terms of number of group elements.

When k is a constant, a public key as well as a signature generated consist of a constant number of group elements only. Hence, these schemes are highly efficient for constant size messages. From the security of these schemes, it follows that under assumptions which are hard to break in time T·poly(λ), these schemes are secure against existential forgery under chosen message attack for adversaries running in time T·poly(λ). More precisely, these schemes are T-eu-cma-secure under hardness of T-q-SFP and T-DLIN, respectively.

3.1 Two-CRS Non-interactive Zero-Knowledge Proofs

In this section, we will define a special notion of NIZK proofs that work in the setting with two common reference strings.

Let R be an efficiently computable binary relation. For pairs $(x, w) \in R$ we call x the statement and w the witness. Let L be the language consisting of statements in R. A *Two-CRS* non-interactive proof system for a relation R consists of three common reference string (CRS) generation algorithms K_B, Shift and Shift^{-1}, a prover algorithm $\mathcal{P}$ and a verification algorithm $\mathcal{V}$. We require that all these algorithms be efficient, i.e. polynomial time. The CRS generation algorithm K_B takes the security parameter 1^λ as input and produces a common reference string crs along with an extraction key τ. Both Shift and Shift^{-1} are deterministic algorithms. They take as input a string crs and output another string crs′. The prover algorithm $\mathcal{P}$ takes as input (crs, x, w) and produces a proof π. The verification algorithm $\mathcal{V}$ takes as input (crs, x, π) and outputs 1 or 0. We require that:

CRS Indistinguishability. For all PPT adversaries $\mathcal{A}$,

$$\mathsf{Adv}_{\mathcal{A}}^{\mathsf{CRS-distinguish}}(1^\lambda) =$$

$$2 \cdot \Pr\left[b = b' \left| \begin{array}{l} (\mathsf{crs}, \tau) \leftarrow K_B(1^\lambda); \mathsf{crs}' \leftarrow \mathsf{Shift}(\mathsf{crs}); \mathsf{crs}'' \leftarrow \mathsf{Shift}^{-1}(\mathsf{crs}) \\ b \xleftarrow{\$} \{0, 1\}; \text{ if } b = 0, (\mathsf{crs}_1, \mathsf{crs}_2) := (\mathsf{crs}, \mathsf{crs}') \\ \text{else } (\mathsf{crs}_1, \mathsf{crs}_2) := (\mathsf{crs}'', \mathsf{crs}) \\ b' \leftarrow \mathcal{A}(\mathsf{crs}_1, \mathsf{crs}_2) \end{array} \right. \right] - 1 .$$

We say that a Two-CRS NIZK system has CRS indistinguishability if for all PPT adversaries $\mathcal{A}$, $\mathsf{Adv}_{\mathcal{A}}^{\mathsf{CRS-distinguish}}$ is negligible in λ.

Perfect Completeness. Completeness requires that an honest prover with a valid witness can always make an honest verifier output 1. For $K \in \{K_B, \mathsf{Shift} \circ K_B, \mathsf{Shift}^{-1} \circ K_B\}$, where $\circ$ is the the composition of functions, we require that for all x, w such that $(x, w) \in R$:

$$\Pr\left[\mathcal{V}(\mathsf{crs}, x, \pi) = 1 \mid \mathsf{crs} \leftarrow K(1^\lambda); \pi \leftarrow \mathcal{P}(\mathsf{crs}, x, w)\right] = 1.$$

Perfect Knowledge Extraction. We require that there exists a probabilistic polynomial time knowledge extractor $\mathcal{E}$ such that for every $(\mathsf{crs}, \tau) \leftarrow K_B(1^\lambda)$, x and purported proof π such that $\mathcal{V}(\mathsf{crs}, x, \pi) = 1$ then we have

$$\Pr\left[(x, w) \in R \mid w := \mathcal{E}(\mathsf{crs}, \tau, x, \pi)\right] = 1.$$

Note that since perfect knowledge extraction implies the existence of a witness for the statement being proven, it implies *perfect soundness*.

Perfect Zero-Knowledge. A proof system is zero-knowledge if the proofs do not reveal any information about the witnesses. We require that there exists a polynomial time simulator $\mathcal{S}$ such that for all $(\mathsf{crs}, \tau) \leftarrow K_B(1^\lambda), \mathsf{crs}' := \mathsf{Shift}(\mathsf{crs})$ (or, $\mathsf{crs}' := \mathsf{Shift}^{-1}(\mathsf{crs})$) we have that for all $x \in L$ the distributions $\mathcal{P}(\mathsf{crs}', x, w)$ and $\mathcal{S}(\mathsf{crs}', \tau, x)$ are identical.

Efficient Realization of Two-CRS NIZKs Based on Groth-Sahai Proofs. Groth-Sahai proofs [18] can be used to give efficient Two-CRS NIZKs (under the DLIN assumption) for special languages, namely pairing product equations, multi-scalar multiplication equations, and quadratic equations (described below) in the setting of symmetric bilinear groups. We also show that the range equations also fit this framework. For details, refer to the full version [15].

- **Pairing Product Equation.** A pairing product equation (PPE) over the variables $X_1, \ldots X_n \in \mathbb{G}$ is an equation of the form[5]

$$\prod_{i=1}^{n} e(\mathcal{A}_i, X_i) \cdot \prod_{i=1, j \geq i}^{n,n} e(X_i, X_j)^{\gamma_{i,j}} = 1,$$

determined by constants $\mathcal{A}_i \in \mathbb{G}$ and $\gamma_{i,j} \in \mathbb{Z}_p$.

- **Multiscalar Multiplication Equation.** A multiscalar multiplication equation over the variables $X_1, \ldots X_n \in \mathbb{G}$ and $y_1, y_2, \ldots, y_m \in \{0, 1\}$ is of the form

$$\prod_{j=1}^{m} \mathcal{A}_j^{y_j} \cdot \prod_{i=1}^{n} X_i^{b_i} \cdot \prod_{i=1}^{n} \prod_{j=1}^{m} X_i^{\gamma_{i,j} y_j} = \mathcal{T},$$

determined by constants $\mathcal{A}_j \in \mathbb{G}$, $b_i, \gamma_{i,j} \in \mathbb{Z}_p$, and $\mathcal{T} \in \mathbb{G}$.

---

[5] General form of PPE can have any $\mathcal{T} \in \mathbb{G}_T$ on the R.H.S. Since GS NIZKs are only known for PPE having 1 on the R.H.S., we use only such equations in our construction.

- **Quadratic Equation.** A quadratic equation in $\mathbb{Z}_p$ over variables $y_1, y_2, \ldots,$ $y_n \in \{0,1\}$ is of the form

$$\sum_{i=1}^{n} a_i y_i + \sum_{i=1, j \geq i}^{n,n} \gamma_{i,j} y_i y_j = t,$$

  determined by constants $a_i \in \mathbb{Z}_p$, $\gamma_{i,j} \in \mathbb{Z}_p$, and $t \in \mathbb{Z}_p$.
- **Range Equation.** The range equation over the variable $c \in \mathbb{Z}_p$ is of the form.

$$\exists c \ : \ g^c = C \bigwedge c < q,$$

  determined by constants $C \in \mathbb{G}$ and $q < p$. We note that the range equation is not explicitly a part of the Groth-Sahai framework but is implied by it.

Remark 1. We note that for the first three kinds of equations, under the above mentioned realization of Two-CRS NIZKs, the proof size grows only linearly with the number of variables and the number of equations. This follows directly from the GS proofs as explained in the full version [15].

Remark 2. As shown in the full version [15], a range equation can be expressed as one multiscalar multiplication equation and $\log_2 q$ quadratic equations over $\log_2 q$ variables in $\mathbb{Z}_p$.

4   Blind Signature Scheme: Construction

We begin by giving an informal description of the scheme. In our scheme, we will use a bilinear group $\mathbb{G}$ of prime order p, a structure preserving signature scheme for signing vectors of elements in this group, Two-CRS NIZKs, and commitment scheme $\mathsf{Com}_\mathbb{G}$.

During the key generation phase, the signer generates the verification key vk and the secret key sk for the blind signature scheme as follows. vk consists of a verification key vk_{SP} for the structure preserving signature scheme, two CRSes, crs_1 and crs_2 under Two-CRS NIZK proof system, and a parameter $q = p^\epsilon$ for some constant $\epsilon \in (0,1)$. crs_1 is sampled from K_B and crs_2 is set to be the shifted crs_1, i.e. $\mathrm{crs}_2 \leftarrow \mathsf{Shift}(\mathrm{crs}_1)$. sk consists of the signing key sk_{SP} corresponding to vk_{SP} and the extraction key τ for crs_1.

Next, the two round blind signature scheme proceeds as follows: In the first round, the user generates its message as follows: It begins by checking whether crs_2 equals $\mathsf{Shift}(\mathrm{crs}_1)$. It aborts, if this is not the case. Next, it blinds its message m by generating a commitment m_{blind} using $\mathsf{Com}_\mathbb{G}$ under randomness r. Then, it samples a random $c < q$ and sets $C = g^c$. Finally, it generates a proof π under crs_1 for the NP-statement Φ: $\exists c \mid g^c = C \bigwedge c < q$. It sends $(m_{\mathsf{blind}}, C, \pi)$ as the first round message to the signer.

In the second round, the signer generates its message as follows: It begins by checking if the proof π is valid under crs_1. It aborts, if this is not the case. Next, it extracts the witness c from the proof π using extraction key τ. Then it

Recalling from Section 3, let $(\mathsf{SPGen}, \mathsf{SPSign}, \mathsf{SPVerify})$ be an existentially unforgeable structure preserving signature scheme, $(K_B, \mathsf{Shift}, \mathsf{Shift}^{-1}, \mathcal{P}, \mathcal{V})$ be a Two-CRS NIZK proof system and $\mathsf{Com}_{\mathbb{G}}$ be a group based commitment scheme. And let $0 < \epsilon < 1$ be an appropriate (specified later) constant parameter.

Key Generation Gen: On input 1^λ, choose an appropriate bilinear group $(p, \mathbb{G}, \mathbb{G}_T, g, e)^a$ and proceed as follows:

- Sample a key pair for the structure preserving signature scheme $(\mathsf{sk}_{\mathsf{SP}}, \mathsf{vk}_{\mathsf{SP}}) \leftarrow \mathsf{SPGen}(1^\lambda)$.
- Sample a CRS $(\mathrm{crs}_1, \tau) \leftarrow K_B(1^\lambda)$ and generate its shift $\mathrm{crs}_2 \leftarrow \mathsf{Shift}(\mathrm{crs}_1)$.
- Output the verification-key for the blind signature scheme as $vk = (\mathsf{vk}_{\mathsf{SP}}, \mathrm{crs}_1, \mathrm{crs}_2, q = p^\epsilon)$ and the secret-key as $sk = (\mathsf{sk}_{\mathsf{SP}}, \tau)$.

Signing Protocol: The user $\mathcal{U}$ with input $m \in \mathbb{G}, \mathsf{vk}_{\mathsf{SP}}$ and the signer $\mathcal{S}$ with input $\mathsf{sk}_{\mathsf{SP}}$ proceed as follows.

- **Round 1:** The user $\mathcal{U}$ generates its first message as follows:
  - Abort if $\mathrm{crs}_2 \neq \mathsf{Shift}(\mathrm{crs}_1)$.
  - Sample $m_{\mathsf{blind}} \leftarrow \mathsf{Com}_{\mathbb{G}}(m; r)$.
  - Samples a uniformly random c such that $c < q$ and sets $C := g^c$. Next sample a proof $\pi \leftarrow \mathcal{P}(\mathrm{crs}_1, \Phi, c)$ where Φ is the NP-statement:
  $$\exists\, c \mid g^c = C \bigwedge c < q. \tag{1}$$
  - Send $(m_{\mathsf{blind}}, C, \pi)$ to the signer.
- **Round 2:** $\mathcal{S}$ generates the second round message as:
  - If $\mathcal{V}(\mathrm{crs}_1, \Phi, \pi) \neq 1$ then abort, otherwise obtain $c := \mathcal{E}(\mathrm{crs}_1, \tau, \Phi, \pi)$ and sample a proof $\pi' \leftarrow \mathcal{P}(\mathrm{crs}_2, \Phi, c)$.
  - Sample a signature $\sigma_{\mathsf{SP}} := \mathsf{SPSign}(\mathsf{sk}_{\mathsf{SP}}, m_{\mathsf{blind}})$.
  - Send $(\pi', \sigma_{\mathsf{SP}})$ to the user $\mathcal{U}$.
- **Signature Generation:** $\mathcal{U}$ aborts if $\mathcal{V}(\mathrm{crs}_2, \Phi, \pi') \neq 1$. $\mathcal{U}$ also aborts if $\mathsf{SPVerify}(\mathsf{vk}_{\mathsf{SP}}, m_{\mathsf{blind}}, \sigma_{\mathsf{SP}}) \neq 1$ and otherwise outputs $\sigma \leftarrow \mathcal{P}(\mathrm{crs}_2, \Psi, (m_{\mathsf{blind}}, r, \sigma_{\mathsf{SP}}))$ where Ψ is the NP-statement:

$$\exists\, (m_{\mathsf{blind}}, r, \sigma_{\mathsf{SP}}) \mid m_{\mathsf{blind}} = \mathsf{Com}_{\mathbb{G}}(m; r) \bigwedge \mathsf{SPVerify}(\mathsf{vk}_{\mathsf{SP}}, m_{\mathsf{blind}}, \sigma_{\mathsf{SP}}) = 1 \tag{2}$$

Signature Verification Vrfy: For input a claimed signature σ on message m, output $\mathcal{V}(\mathrm{crs}_2, \Psi, \sigma)$.

---

^{a} All algorithms take this bilinear group as an implicit input.

Fig. 2. Blind Signature Scheme

generates a fresh proof π' for the statement Φ under crs_2. Finally, it generates a signature σ_{SP} on m_{blind} using signing key $\mathsf{sk}_{\mathsf{SP}}$. It sends $(\pi', \sigma_{\mathsf{SP}})$ as the second round message to the user.

On receiving the above message from the user, it computes the signature on m as follows: User aborts if π' is not a valid proof under crs_2. It then checks if σ_{SP} is a valid signature on m_{blind} under vk_{SP}. It aborts if this is not the case. Otherwise, it outputs σ as the proof under crs_2 of the NP-statement Ψ: $\exists\ (m_{blind}, r, \sigma_{SP})\ \mid\ m_{blind} = \mathsf{Com}_\mathbb{G}(m; r) \bigwedge \mathsf{SPVerify}(vk_{SP}, m_{blind}, \sigma_{SP}) = 1$. In other words, the user proves that there exists $(m_{blind}, r, \sigma_{SP})$ such that m_{blind} is the commitment of m using randomness r under commitment scheme $\mathsf{Com}_\mathbb{G}$ and σ_{SP} is a valid signature on m_{blind}.

To verify a signature σ on message m, check whether σ is a valid proof for the statement Ψ under crs_2.

Formal Description. Let $\mathsf{SPSig} = (\mathsf{SPGen}, \mathsf{SPSign}, \mathsf{SPVerify})$ be any structure preserving signature scheme which is existentially unforgeable, $(K_B, \mathsf{Shift}, \mathsf{Shift}^{-1}, \mathcal{P}, \mathcal{V})$ be a Two-CRS NIZK proof system, $\mathsf{Com}_\mathbb{G}$ be the DLIN based commitment scheme for elements in $\mathbb{G}$ (Section 3). Formal description of the blind signature scheme $(\mathsf{Gen}, \mathcal{S}, \mathcal{U}, \mathsf{Vrfy})$ is given in Figure 2.

5 Proof of Unforgeability

Let $\mathbf{T}_{\mathbb{G},q}^{dlog}$ be the time it takes to break the discrete log problem in $\mathbb{G}$ when exponents are chosen from $\mathbb{Z}_q$.

Theorem 1. *For any PPT malicious user $\mathcal{U}^*$ for the unforgeability game against the blind signature scheme given in Section 4 the following holds:*

$$\mathsf{Adv}_{\mathcal{U}^*, \mathsf{BS}}^{\mathsf{Unforge}}(\lambda) \leq \mathsf{Adv}_{\mathcal{B}}^{\mathsf{CRS-distinguish}}(\lambda) + \mathsf{Adv}_{\widehat{\mathcal{U}}^*, \mathsf{SPSig}}^{\mathsf{Unforge}}(\lambda),$$

where $\mathcal{B}$ is an adversary against the CRS indistinguishability property of the two-CRS NIZK proof system such that $\mathbf{T}(\mathcal{B}) = k \cdot \mathbf{T}_{\mathbb{G},q}^{dlog} + \mathbf{T}(\mathcal{U}^*) + poly(\lambda)$ and $\widehat{\mathcal{U}}^*$ is the adversary against the unforgeability of the underlying structure preserving signature scheme SPSig such that $\mathbf{T}(\widehat{\mathcal{U}}^*) = k \cdot \mathbf{T}_{\mathbb{G},q}^{dlog} + \mathbf{T}(\mathcal{U}^*) + poly(\lambda)$. Also, $\mathcal{U}^*$ and $\widehat{\mathcal{U}}^*$ make at most k signing queries.

If we use GS proof system based Two-CRS NIZKs in our construction, the above theorem immediately implies the following corollary:

Corollary 1. *For any PPT malicious user $\mathcal{U}^*$ for the unforgeability game against the blind signature scheme given in Section 4 the following holds:*

$$\mathsf{Adv}_{\mathcal{U}^*, \mathsf{BS}}^{\mathsf{Unforge}}(\lambda) \leq 2 \cdot \mathsf{Adv}_{\mathcal{B}, \mathbb{G}}^{dlin}(\lambda) + \mathsf{Adv}_{\widehat{\mathcal{U}}^*, \mathsf{SPSig}}^{\mathsf{Unforge}}(\lambda),$$

where $\mathcal{B}$ is an adversary against the DLIN assumption in $\mathbb{G}$ such that $\mathbf{T}(\mathcal{B}) = k \cdot \mathbf{T}_{\mathbb{G},q}^{dlog} + \mathbf{T}(\mathcal{U}^*) + poly(\lambda)$ and $\widehat{\mathcal{U}}^*$ is the adversary against the unforgeability of the underlying structure preserving signature scheme SPSig such that $\mathbf{T}(\widehat{\mathcal{U}}^*) = k \cdot \mathbf{T}_{\mathbb{G},q}^{dlog} + \mathbf{T}(\mathcal{U}^*) + poly(\lambda)$. Also, $\mathcal{U}^*$ and $\widehat{\mathcal{U}}^*$ make at most k signing queries.

Following is a corollary of the above theorem:

Theorem 2. *Assume that $\mathbf{T}_{\mathbb{G},q}^{dlog}$-DLIN holds in $\mathbb{G}$ and SPSig is $\mathbf{T}_{\mathbb{G},q}^{dlog}$-eu-cma-unforgeable. Then the blind signature scheme in Section 4 is unforgeable.*

Proof. (of Theorem 1) Let $\mathcal{U}^*$ be any PPT malicious user then we will prove our theorem by considering a sequence of games starting with the unforgeabilty game from Definition 2 (see Section 2).

- $Game_0$: This is the challenger-adversary game between the challenger following the honest signer $\mathcal{S}$ specification and the malicious user $\mathcal{U}^*$. More specifically, the game starts with the challenger generating a key pair (sk, vk). The challenger then sends vk to $\mathcal{U}^*$. At this point the challenger (playing as the honest signer) and $\mathcal{U}^*$ proceed by interacting in k executions of the signing protocol. Note that the challenger knows the secret key sk and uses it to participate as the signer in the executions of the signing protocol. Finally $\mathcal{U}^*$ outputs $k + 1$ message/signature pairs (m_i, σ_i). $\mathcal{U}^*$ is said to win if all the messages are distinct and all signatures verify under vk.

- $Game_1$: Recall that in the second round of the signing protocol the challenger (acting as the signer) obtains the secret value c using the extraction algorithm $\mathcal{E}$. $Game_1$ is same as the $Game_0$ except that in each of the k instances of the signing protocol, instead of extracting the secret c using the extraction algorithm, the challenger obtains c by evaluating the discrete log of C assuming that it is less than q. (The challenger aborts if no values less than q is a valid dlog of C.)

  Note that since crs_1 is sampled from K_B, proofs under crs_1 are perfectly sound. This implies that the value c that challenger extracts by solving discrete log is exactly the same as the one that challenger would have extracted using the extraction algorithm in $Game_0$.

  Note that the views of the malicious user $\mathcal{U}^*$ in games $Game_0$ and $Game_1$ are identical.

  It also follows from the perfect soundness of the two-CRS NIZK proof system that the challenger in $Game_1$ runs in time $k \cdot \mathbf{T}_{\mathbb{G},q}^{dlog} + poly(\lambda)$, where $\mathbf{T}_{\mathbb{G},q}^{dlog}$ is the time it takes to break discrete log problem in $\mathbb{G}$ when the exponent is chosen from $\mathbb{Z}_q$.

- $Game_2$: $Game_2$ is same as $Game_1$ except that the challenger generates the CRSes differently. Instead of generating the CRSes by first sampling $(crs_1, \tau) \leftarrow K_B(1^\lambda)$ and then generating its shift $crs_2 \leftarrow \mathsf{Shift}(crs_1)$, it reverses the order in which the CRSes are generated. This reverses the security properties of proofs under the two CRSes. More specifically the challenger first samples $(crs_2, \tau) \leftarrow K_B(1^\lambda)$ and then sets $crs_1 := \mathsf{Shift}^{-1}(crs_2)$. Note that now we get perfect zero-knowledge for crs_1 and perfect soundness for crs_2.

  Indistinguishability of $Game_1$ and $Game_2$ follows from the CRS-Indistinguishability property of the two-CRS NIZK proof system. More precisely, the success probability of $\mathcal{U}^*$ can change by at most $\mathsf{Adv}_\mathcal{B}^{CRS-distinguish}$, where $\mathcal{B}$ is an adversary against the CRS indistinguishability property of the two-CRS NIZK proof system such that $\mathbf{T}(\mathcal{B}) = k \cdot \mathbf{T}_{\mathbb{G},q}^{dlog} + \mathbf{T}(\mathcal{U}^*) + poly(\lambda)$.

Now we will show how $\mathcal{U}^*$ who wins in $Game_2$ can be used to construct a malicious user $\widehat{\mathcal{U}^*}$ that winning the existential unforgeability game of the underlying structure preserving signature scheme.

$\widehat{\mathcal{U}}^*$ starts by obtaining the verification key vk_{SP} from the challenger of the structure preserving signature scheme $(SPGen, SPSign, SPVerify)$. Furthermore, it samples $(crs_2, \tau) \leftarrow K_B(1^\lambda)$, sets $crs_1 := Shift^{-1}(crs_2)$ and invokes $\mathcal{U}^*$ with $(vk_{SP}, crs_1, crs_2, q)$ as input. At this point, the user $\mathcal{U}^*$ expects to interact in k instances of the signing protocol. In each of these executions, it provides its challenger (the adversary $\widehat{\mathcal{U}}^*$ in our case) with its first round message (m_{blind}, C, π). Our adversary $\widehat{\mathcal{U}}^*$ obtains c by solving the discrete log problem (aborting if $c \geq q$) and uses the extracted value to generate the response proof π'. Additionally, it obtains the signature σ_{SP} on m_{blind} from the signing oracle and passes (π', σ_{SP}) to $\mathcal{U}^*$. After k such executions, $\mathcal{U}^*$ returns $k+1$ pairs (m_j, σ_j). Note that each σ_j given by $\mathcal{U}^*$ is a proof of knowledge of $(m_{blind,j}, r_j, \sigma_{SP,j})$ under crs_2. Furthermore, since $\widehat{\mathcal{U}}^*$ generates crs_2 in the binding setting, therefore τ can be used to extract $(m_{blind,j}, r_j, \sigma_{SP,j})$ for each j by invoking $\mathcal{E}(crs_2, \tau, \Psi, \sigma_j)$. Since all messages m_j are distinct and $Com_{\mathbb{G}}$ is perfectly binding, all $m_{blind,j}$ will also be distinct. Since all $m_{blind,j}$ are distinct there exists at least one m_{blind,j^*} among these that $\widehat{\mathcal{U}}^*$ never queried its challenger. $\widehat{\mathcal{U}}^*$ outputs $(m_{blind,j^*}, \sigma_{SP,j^*})$ as its output.

Hence, the advantage of $\mathcal{U}^*$ in producing a valid forgery in $Game_3$ is at most the advantage of $\widehat{\mathcal{U}}^*$ in producing a valid forgery against the underlying structure preserving signature scheme, i.e. $Adv_{\mathcal{U}^*, BS, Game_3}^{Unforge} \leq Adv_{\widehat{\mathcal{U}}^*, SPSig}^{Unforge}(\lambda)$, where $\widehat{\mathcal{U}}^*$ runs in time $k \cdot \mathbf{T}_{\mathbb{G},q}^{dlog} + \mathbf{T}(\mathcal{U}^*) + poly(\lambda)$.

6   Proof of Blindness

Theorem 3. *For any PPT malicious signer $\mathcal{S}^*$ for the blindness game against the blind signature scheme given in Section 4, which successfully completes the blindness game, the following holds*

$$Adv_{\mathcal{S}^*, BS}^{Unblind}(\lambda) < 2 \cdot Adv_{\mathcal{A}, Com_{\mathbb{G}}}^{hid} + Adv_{\mathcal{B}, \mathbb{G}, q}^{dlog}$$

where $\mathcal{A}$ is an adversary against the non-uniform hiding property of $Com_{\mathbb{G}}$ such that $\mathbf{T}(\mathcal{A}) = \mathbf{T}(\mathcal{S}^*) + poly(\lambda)$ and $\mathcal{B}$ is an adversary against the non-uniform discrete log problem in $\mathbb{G}$ when exponents are chosen uniformly randomly in $\mathbb{Z}_q$ such that $\mathbf{T}(\mathcal{B}) = \mathbf{T}(\mathcal{S}^*) + poly(\lambda)$.

Since the hiding property of the $Com_{\mathbb{G}}$ holds under the DLIN assumption in $\mathbb{G}$, the above theorem immediately implies the following corollary.

Corollary 2. *For any PPT malicious signer $\mathcal{S}^*$ for the blindness game against the blind signature scheme given in Section 4, which successfully completes the blindness game, the following holds*

$$Adv_{\mathcal{S}^*, BS}^{Unblind}(\lambda) < 4 \cdot Adv_{\mathcal{C}, \mathbb{G}}^{DLIN} + Adv_{\mathcal{B}, \mathbb{G}, q}^{dlog}$$

where $\mathcal{C}$ is an adversary against the non-uniform DLIN assumption in $\mathbb{G}$ such that $\mathbf{T}(\mathcal{C}) = \mathbf{T}(\mathcal{S}^*) + poly(\lambda)$ and $\mathcal{B}$ is an adversary against the non-uniform *discrete log problem in* $\mathbb{G}$ *when exponents are chosen uniformly randomly in* $\mathbb{Z}_q$ *such that* $\mathbf{T}(\mathcal{B}) = \mathbf{T}(\mathcal{S}^*) + poly(\lambda)$.

Following is a corollary of the above.

Theorem 4. *Assume that non-uniform DLIN assumption holds in* $\mathbb{G}$ *and the non-uniform discrete log assumption holds in* $\mathbb{G}$ *even when the exponents are chosen uniformly randomly from* $\mathbb{Z}_q$. *Then the blind signature scheme from Section 4 is blind.*

Proof. (of Theorem 3) Let $\mathcal{S}^*$ be any PPT malicious signer then we will prove our theorem by considering a sequence of games starting with the blindness game from Definition 3 (see Section 2).

- Game_0: This is a challenger-adversary game between the challenger following the honest user strategy and the malicious signer $\mathcal{S}^*$. The malicious signer $\mathcal{S}^*$ has full control over the scheduling of instances of the user in an arbitrary order. Since our scheme is only two round, we can fix it to be the worst case ordering. Since $\mathcal{S}^*$ does not receive any response to the message it sends to the user, we can assume that $\mathcal{S}^*$ first gathers all the incoming messages from the user and then sends its responses. Thus, without loss of generality, the Game_0 proceeds as follows: $\mathcal{S}^*$ first outputs the public key vk and the challenge messages m_0, m_1. $\mathcal{S}^*$ then expects the two incoming blinded messages $m_{blind,0}$ and $m_{blind,1}$ from the user corresponding to m_b, m_{1-b} for a random bit b. After receiving both the messages, $\mathcal{S}^*$ outputs its responses to the challenger. Our challenger at this point outputs the signature on (m_0, m_1) generated in the two protocol executions. Finally the malicious signer $\mathcal{S}^*$ outputs a bit b' and its advantage $\mathsf{Adv}_{\mathcal{S}^*,\mathsf{BS}}^{\mathsf{Unblind}}$ is equal to $|2 \cdot \Pr[b = b'] - 1|$.
- Game_1: Same as Game_0 except the following: The challenger after receiving the public key vk, figures out whether crs_2 is in the range of K_B or not. The challenger may execute in unbounded time when figuring this out; storing the extraction key τ for later use. Now it proceeds as follows:
  - crs_2 is in the range of K_B: In this case, our challenger proceeds just as in Game_0, except that if the first instance of the signing protocol completes successfully then our challenger outputs DL-Abort.
  - crs_2 is not in the range of K_B: Proceed as in Game_0.

  Note that conditioned on the fact that DL-Abort does not happen, we have that Game_0 and Game_1 are identical. Next we will show that the probability of DL-Abort happening is bounded by $\mathsf{Adv}_{\mathcal{B},\mathbb{G},q}^{\mathsf{dlog}}$.

Lemma 1. *The probability of DL-Abort happening is bounded by* $\mathsf{Adv}_{\mathcal{B},\mathbb{G},q}^{\mathsf{dlog}}$, *with* $\mathbf{T}(\mathcal{B}) = \mathbf{T}(\mathcal{S}^*) + poly(\lambda)$, $\mathcal{B}$ *is an adversary against the non-uniform discrete log problem in* $\mathbb{G}$ *when exponents are chosen uniformly randomly in* $\mathbb{Z}_q$.

Proof. We will show that an $\mathcal{S}^*$ that can make our challenger output DL-Abort can be used to construct an adversary $\mathcal{B}$ that breaks the non-uniform discrete log problem in $\mathbb{G}$ when the exponent is restricted to $< q$.

Constructing the adversary $\mathcal{B}$. Given this cheating signer $\mathcal{S}^*$, there exists random coins for $\mathcal{S}^*$ such that our challenger in Game-1 outputs DL-Abort. We will hard-code the random coins of $\mathcal{S}^*$ such that our challenger outputs DL-Abort with maximum probability. Note that we are in the case when crs_2 is binding and hence crs_1 is hiding. Next, our adversary $\mathcal{B}$ or the challenger of the blindness game on receiving this public key vk will run in unbounded time to compute the extraction key τ for crs_2. Thus, the adversary $\mathcal{B}$ we constructed is a non-uniform adversary with auxiliary input as the random coins of $\mathcal{S}^*$ (specified above) and the extraction key τ corresponding to vk. Our adversary $\mathcal{B}$ obtains as input D (such that $D = g^d$ with $d < q$) and it wins if it outputs d. On receiving D, $\mathcal{B}$ proceeds as the challenger does in Game_1 except that it sets $C := D$ instead of choosing a fresh value for C. Also, invoking perfect zero-knowledge property of crs_1, $\mathcal{B}$ generates π as $\mathcal{S}(crs_1, \tau, \Phi)$, where $\mathcal{S}$ is the zero-knowledge simulator. At this point $\mathcal{S}^*$ must output a proof π' such that $\mathcal{V}(crs_2, \Phi, \pi') = 1$ for the challenger in Game_1 to output DL-Abort. On obtaining the proof π', $\mathcal{B}$ outputs $\mathcal{E}(crs_2, \tau, \Phi, \pi')$ as the discrete log of D. By perfect extraction under crs_2, the extracted value will be the discrete log of D.

Note that after receiving the challenge D, $\mathcal{B}$ runs in polynomial time. Thus, the probability of DL-Abort when we fix the worst case random coins of $\mathcal{S}^*$ (as described above) is bounded by $\mathsf{Adv}^{dlog}_{\mathcal{B},\mathbb{G},q}$. Hence, it holds that the probability of DL-Abort in Game_1 is bounded by $\mathsf{Adv}^{dlog}_{\mathcal{B},\mathbb{G},q}$.

- Game_2: Game_2 is identical to Game_1 except for the following modifications. Instead of generating the final signatures honestly, the challenger simulates them. More specifically, instead of generating the signatures as $\mathcal{P}(crs_2, \Psi, (m_{\mathsf{blind}}, r, \sigma_{\mathsf{SP}}))$, in Game_2 the challenger generates signatures as $\mathcal{S}(crs_2, \tau, \Psi)$. Game_2 and Game_1 are perfectly indistinguishable based on the non-uniform perfect zero-knowledge property of the two-CRS NIZK proof system.
- Game_3: Now, we modify Game_2 and remove all dependencies on the input messages m_0 and m_1. That is, we let the user algorithm compute the blinded message $m_{\mathsf{blind},0}$ as $\mathsf{Com}_{\mathbb{G}}(0)$ instead of $\mathsf{Com}_{\mathbb{G}}(m_b)$. We proceed similarly for m_{1-b}.

  The indistinguishability between Game_3 and Game_2 follows from the non-uniform computational hiding property of the commitment scheme $\mathsf{Com}_{\mathbb{G}}$.

In Game_3 the entire transcript is independent of the message: $\mathsf{Adv}^{\mathsf{Unblind}}_{\mathcal{S}^*, \mathsf{BS}, \mathrm{Game}_3} = 0$.

7 Concrete Efficiency

In this section we will compute the communication complexity and the size of the final blind signature for our scheme. First we need to compute the group size p and number q which will give us the desired level of security. For this we will calculate the work factors for different adversaries as discussed below.

WORK FACTORS. These have been used in [14,6] to calculate concrete parameters. This text has been taken verbatim from [6]. For any adversary running in time $\mathbf{T}(\mathcal{A})$ and gaining advantage ϵ, we define the *work factor* of $\mathcal{A}$ to be $\mathbf{WF}(\mathcal{A}) \leq \mathbf{T}(A)/\epsilon$. The ratio of $\mathcal{A}$'s running time to its advantage provides a measure of efficiency of the adversary. Generally speaking, to resist an adversary with work factor $\mathbf{WF}(\mathcal{A})$, a scheme should have its security parameter (bits of security) be $\kappa \geq \log \mathbf{WF}(\mathcal{A})$. Note that for a particular ϵ, this means a run time of $\mathbf{T}(A) \leq \epsilon 2^\kappa$.

Similar to [14,6], in the discussion that follows we will assume that Pollard Rho's algorithm for finding discrete logs in $\mathbb{G}$ is the best known attack[6] against DLIN in group $\mathbb{G}$ of prime order p. The work factor of Pollard's algorithm is

$$\mathbf{WF}(\mathcal{P}) = \frac{T(\mathcal{P})}{\epsilon_p} = \frac{0.88}{e} \sqrt{p} \frac{\log^2(p)}{10^3}$$

For security we require that the work factor of any adversary $\mathcal{A}$ against DLIN is at most the work factor of Pollard's algorithm, i.e. $\mathbf{WF}(\mathcal{A}) \leq \mathbf{WF}(\mathcal{P})$.

Parameters. In the full version [15], we calculate the values of p and q using the work factors for adversaries against the blindness game and unforgeability game. We summarize the parameters obtained in Table 3.

Table 3. Suggested parameters, where k is the number of signature queries and the adversary is allowed to run in time $t \cdot T_R$ where T_R is the time taken by the reduction.

k	t	$\log q$	$\log |\mathbb{G}|$
2^{20}	2^{30}	155	291
2^{20}	2^{40}	155	311
2^{30}	2^{30}	155	331
2^{30}	2^{40}	155	351

7.1   Efficiency

Verification Key Size. In our blind signature scheme, the verification key is $vk = (\text{vk}_{\mathsf{SP}}, \text{crs}_1, \text{crs}_2, q = p^\epsilon)$, where vk_{SP} is the verification key of the structure preserving signature scheme in $\mathbb{G}$ and crs_1 and crs_2 are two CRSes for Two-CRS NIZK. Furthermore, as can be seen in Table 2, to sign k group elements, vk_{SP} has $2k + 25$ group elements. Since in our case $k = 6$, there are 37 group elements in vk_{SP}. In GS proof system, we need 6 group elements in $\mathbb{G}$ to represent crs_1 and crs_2. Hence, the size of the verification key for our scheme is 43 group elements. Taking the number of bits to represent a group element as 291 bits, we get the key size to be 1.6KB.

Signature Size. The final signature is a Groth-Sahai [18] proof of knowledge in $\mathbb{G}$ using crs_2 as the common reference string. Under the DLIN assumption, the proof size is three group elements for each variable and nine group elements for each pairing product equation (see Figure 2 in [18]) that is proved. The variables

---

[6] If there is a faster attack against discrete log or DLIN problem for prime order groups, it can be used to obtain the parameters for our blind signature scheme.

are $m_{blind}, \sigma_{\mathsf{SP}}, r$. By $\mathsf{Com}_{\mathbb{G}}$, m_{blind} has six group elements and in order to prove $m_{blind} = \mathsf{Com}_{\mathbb{G}}(m; r)$, we will have two additional variables (which capture the randomness r used in commitment) and three pairing product equations in total. Furthermore, as can be seen in Table 2, σ_{SP} has 17 group elements and nine pairing product equations in verification algorithm. Hence, the size of the final blind signature will be 183 group elements in $\mathbb{G}$. Taking the number of bits to represent a group element as 291 bits, we get the signature size to be 6.5KB.

Communication Complexity. We begin by computing the communication complexity of the user step by step as follows:

- $\mathcal{U}$ computes a commitment m_{blind} in $\mathbb{G}$ which consists of six group elements.
- It computes a range proof π for an NP-statement which consists of $\log_2 q$ quadratic equations and one multiscalar multiplication equation over $\log_2 q$ variables in $\mathbb{Z}_p$ (Remark 2). In GS proof system, each quadratic equations adds six group elements, multiscalar multiplication equation adds nine group elements and each variable in $\mathbb{Z}_p$ adds three group elements to the proof ([18], Figure 2). Using this, π consists of $9 \log_2 q + 9$ group elements of $\mathbb{G}$.

Now we compute the communication complexity of signer as follows:

- It computes σ_{SP} consisting of 17 elements in $\mathbb{G}$ as explained above.
- It also computes a range proof π' for the same NP-statement as the user. As above, π' consists of $9 \log_2 q + 9$ group elements of $\mathbb{G}$.

Hence, the overall communication complexity of our blind signature protocol is $18 \log_2 q + 41$ elements in $\mathbb{G}$. Taking $\log_2 q$ as 155 and $\log_2 p$ as 291, the communication complexity is 100.56KB.

Acknowledgements. We thank Jens Groth for useful discussions relating to this work. We also thank the anonymous reviewers of EUROCRYPT 2014 for their insightful comments and an observation that helped improve the communication complexity of our signing protocol from 200 KB to 100 KB.

References

1. Abe, M.: A secure three-move blind signature scheme for polynomially many signatures. In: Pfitzmann, B. (ed.) EUROCRYPT 2001. LNCS, vol. 2045, pp. 136–151. Springer, Heidelberg (2001)
2. Abe, M., Chase, M., David, B., Kohlweiss, M., Nishimaki, R., Ohkubo, M.: Constant-size structure-preserving signatures: Generic constructions and simple assumptions. In: Wang, X., Sako, K. (eds.) ASIACRYPT 2012. LNCS, vol. 7658, pp. 4–24. Springer, Heidelberg (2012)
3. Abe, M., Haralambiev, K., Ohkubo, M.: Signing on elements in bilinear groups for modular protocol design. IACR ePrint 2010/133 (2010)
4. Abe, M., Ohkubo, M.: A framework for universally composable non-committing blind signatures. In: Matsui, M. (ed.) ASIACRYPT 2009. LNCS, vol. 5912, pp. 435–450. Springer, Heidelberg (2009)

5. Bellare, M., Namprempre, C., Pointcheval, D., Semanko, M.: The power of rsa inversion oracles and the security of chaum's rsa-based blind signature scheme. In: Syverson, P.F. (ed.) FC 2001. LNCS, vol. 2339, pp. 309–328. Springer, Heidelberg (2002)

6. Bellare, M., Ristenpart, T.: Simulation without the artificial abort: Simplified proof and improved concrete security for waters' ibe scheme. In: Joux, A. (ed.) EUROCRYPT 2009. LNCS, vol. 5479, pp. 407–424. Springer, Heidelberg (2009)

7. Bellare, M., Rogaway, P.: Optimal asymmetric encryption. In: De Santis, A. (ed.) EUROCRYPT 1994. LNCS, vol. 950, pp. 92–111. Springer, Heidelberg (1995)

8. Boldyreva, A.: Threshold signatures, multisignatures and blind signatures based on the gap-diffie-hellman-group signature scheme. In: Desmedt, Y.G. (ed.) PKC 2003. LNCS, vol. 2567, pp. 31–46. Springer, Heidelberg (2002)

9. Camenisch, J.L., Koprowski, M., Warinschi, B.: Efficient blind signatures without random oracles. In: Blundo, C., Cimato, S. (eds.) SCN 2004. LNCS, vol. 3352, pp. 134–148. Springer, Heidelberg (2005)

10. Chaum, D.: Blind signatures for untraceable payments. In: CRYPTO, pp. 199–203 (1982)

11. Fischlin, M.: Round-optimal composable blind signatures in the common reference string model. In: Dwork, C. (ed.) CRYPTO 2006. LNCS, vol. 4117, pp. 60–77. Springer, Heidelberg (2006)

12. Fischlin, M., Schröder, D.: On the impossibility of three-move blind signature schemes. In: Gilbert, H. (ed.) EUROCRYPT 2010. LNCS, vol. 6110, pp. 197–215. Springer, Heidelberg (2010)

13. Fuchsbauer, G.: Automorphic signatures in bilinear groups and an application to round-optimal blind signatures. IACR ePrint 2009/320 (2009)

14. Galindo, D.: The exact security of pairing based encryption and signature schemes. In: Based on a talk at Workshop on Provable Security, INRIA, Paris (2004), http://www.dgalindo.es/galindoEcrypt.pdf

15. Garg, S., Gupta, D.: Efficient round optimal blind signatures. Cryptology ePrint Archive, Report 2014/081 (2014), http://eprint.iacr.org/

16. Garg, S., Rao, V., Sahai, A., Schröder, D., Unruh, D.: Round optimal blind signatures. In: Rogaway, P. (ed.) CRYPTO 2011. LNCS, vol. 6841, pp. 630–648. Springer, Heidelberg (2011)

17. Groth, J.: Simulation-sound nizk proofs for a practical language and constant size group signatures. In: Lai, X., Chen, K. (eds.) ASIACRYPT 2006. LNCS, vol. 4284, pp. 444–459. Springer, Heidelberg (2006)

18. Groth, J., Sahai, A.: Efficient non-interactive proof systems for bilinear groups. In: Smart, N.P. (ed.) EUROCRYPT 2008. LNCS, vol. 4965, pp. 415–432. Springer, Heidelberg (2008)

19. Hazay, C., Katz, J., Koo, C.-Y., Lindell, Y.: Concurrently-secure blind signatures without random oracles or setup assumptions. In: Vadhan, S.P. (ed.) TCC 2007. LNCS, vol. 4392, pp. 323–341. Springer, Heidelberg (2007)

20. Juels, A., Luby, M., Ostrovsky, R.: Security of blind digital signatures (extended abstract). In: Kaliski Jr., B.S. (ed.) CRYPTO 1997. LNCS, vol. 1294, pp. 150–164. Springer, Heidelberg (1997)

21. Kiayias, A., Zhou, H.-S.: Concurrent blind signatures without random oracles. In: De Prisco, R., Yung, M. (eds.) SCN 2006. LNCS, vol. 4116, pp. 49–62. Springer, Heidelberg (2006)

22. Meiklejohn, S., Shacham, H., Freeman, D.M.: Limitations on transformations from composite-order to prime-order groups: The case of round-optimal blind signatures. In: Abe, M. (ed.) ASIACRYPT 2010. LNCS, vol. 6477, pp. 519–538. Springer, Heidelberg (2010)
23. Okamoto, T.: Efficient blind and partially blind signatures without random oracles. In: Halevi, S., Rabin, T. (eds.) TCC 2006. LNCS, vol. 3876, pp. 80–99. Springer, Heidelberg (2006)
24. Pass, R.: Limits of provable security from standard assumptions. In: STOC, pp. 109–118 (2011)
25. Pointcheval, D.: Strengthened security for blind signatures. In: Nyberg, K. (ed.) EUROCRYPT 1998. LNCS, vol. 1403, pp. 391–405. Springer, Heidelberg (1998)
26. Pointcheval, D., Stern, J.: Provably secure blind signature schemes. In: Kim, K.-C., Matsumoto, T. (eds.) ASIACRYPT 1996. LNCS, vol. 1163, pp. 252–265. Springer, Heidelberg (1996)
27. Pointcheval, D., Stern, J.: Security proofs for signature schemes. In: Maurer, U.M. (ed.) EUROCRYPT 1996. LNCS, vol. 1070, pp. 387–398. Springer, Heidelberg (1996)
28. Pointcheval, D., Stern, J.: Security arguments for digital signatures and blind signatures. Journal of Cryptology 13(3), 361–396 (2000)

Key-Versatile Signatures and Applications: RKA, KDM and Joint Enc/Sig

Mihir Bellare[1], Sarah Meiklejohn[2], and Susan Thomson[3]

[1] Department of Computer Science & Engineering,
University of California San Diego
`mihir@eng.ucsd.edu, cseweb.ucsd.edu/~mihir/`
[2] Department of Computer Science & Engineering,
University of California San Diego
`smeiklej@eng.ucsd.edu, cseweb.ucsd.edu/~smeiklejohn/`
[3] Department of Computer Science, University of Bristol
`susan.thomson@bristol.ac.uk, sthomson.co.uk`

Abstract. This paper introduces key-versatile signatures. Key-versatile signatures allow us to sign with keys already in use for another purpose, without changing the keys and without impacting the security of the original purpose. This allows us to obtain advances across a collection of challenging domains including joint Enc/Sig, security against related-key attack (RKA) and security for key-dependent messages (KDM). Specifically we can (1) Add signing capability to existing encryption capability with zero overhead in the size of the public key (2) Obtain RKA-secure signatures from any RKA-secure one-way function, yielding new RKA-secure signature schemes (3) Add integrity to encryption while maintaining KDM-security.

1 Introduction

One of the recommended principles of sound cryptographic design is key separation, meaning that keys used for one purpose (e.g. encryption) should not be used for another purpose (e.g. signing). The reason is that, even if the individual uses are secure, the joint usage could be insecure [39]. This paper shows, to the contrary, that there are important applications where key reuse is not only desirable but crucial to maintain security, and that when done "right" it works. We offer key-versatile signatures as a general tool to enable signing with existing keys already in use for another purpose, without adding key material and while maintaining security of both the new and the old usage of the keys. Our applications include: (1) adding signing capability to existing encryption capability with zero overhead in the size of the public key (2) obtaining RKA-secure signatures from RKA-secure one-way functions (3) adding integrity to encryption while preserving KDM security.

CLOSER LOOK. Key-versatility refers to the ability to take an arbitrary one-way function F and return a signature scheme where the secret signing key is a random domain point x for F and the public verification key is its image

P.Q. Nguyen and E. Oswald (Eds.): EUROCRYPT 2014, LNCS 8441, pp. 496–513, 2014.
© International Association for Cryptologic Research 2014

$y = F(x)$. By requiring strong simulatability and key-extractability security conditions [33] from these "F-keyed" signatures, and then defining F based on keys already existing for another purpose, we will be able to add signing capability while maintaining existing keys and security.

The most compelling motivation comes from security against related-key attack (RKA) and security for key-dependent messages (KDM), technically challenging areas where solutions create, and depend on, very specific key structures. We would like to expand the set of primitives for which we can provide these forms of security. Rather than start from scratch, we would like to leverage the existing, hard-won advances in these areas by modular design, transforming a primitive **X** into a primitive **Y** while preserving RKA or KDM security. Since security is relative to a set of functions (either key or message deriving) on the space of keys, the transform must preserve the existing keys. Key-versatile signatures will thus allow us to create new RKA and KDM secure primitives in a modular way.

We warn that our results are theoretical feasibility ones. They demonstrate that certain practical goals can in principle be reached, but the solutions are not efficient. Below we begin with a more direct application of key versatile signatures to Joint Enc/Sig and then go on to our RKA and KDM results.

JOINING SIGNATURES TO ENCRYPTION WITH ZERO PUBLIC-KEY OVERHEAD. Suppose Alice has keys (sk_e, pk_e) for a public-key encryption scheme and wants to also have signing capability. Certainly, she could pick new and separate keys (sk_s, pk_s) enabling her to use her favorite signature scheme. However, it means that Alice's public key, now $pk = (pk_e, pk_s)$, has doubled in size. Practitioners ask if one can do better. We want a joint encryption and signature (JES) scheme [49,57], where there is a single key-pair (sk, pk) used for both encryption and signing. We aim to minimize the public-key overhead, (loosely) defined as the size of pk minus the size of the public key pk_e of the underlying encryption scheme.

Haber and Pinkas [49] initiated an investigation of JES. They note that the key re-use requires defining and achieving new notions of security particular to JES: signatures should remain unforgeable even in the presence of a decryption oracle, and encryption should retain IND-CCA privacy even in the presence of a signing oracle. In the random oracle model [17], *specific* IND-CCA-secure public-key encryption schemes have been presented where signing can be added with no public-key overhead [49,34,53]. In the standard model, encryption schemes have been presented that allow signing with a public-key overhead lower than that of the "Cartesian product" solution of just adding a separate signing key [49,57], with the best results, from [57], using IBE or combining encryption and signature schemes of [27,23].

All these results, however, pertain to *specific* encryption schemes. We step back to ask a general theoretical question. Namely, suppose we are given an *arbitrary* IND-CCA-secure public-key encryption scheme. We wish to add signing capability to form a JES scheme. How low can the public-key overhead go? The (perhaps surprising) answer we provide is that we can achieve a public-key overhead of *zero*. The public key for our JES scheme remains *exactly* that of the given encryption scheme, meaning we add signing capability without changing the public key. (Zero public-key overhead has a particular advantage besides space savings, namely that, in adding signing, no new certificates are needed. This makes key management significantly easier for the potentially large number of entities already using Alice's public key. This advantage is absent if the public key is at all modified.) We emphasize again that this is for *any* starting encryption scheme.

To do this, we let F be the function that maps the secret key of the given encryption scheme to the public key. (Not all encryption schemes will directly derive the public key as a deterministic function of the secret key, although many, including Cramer-Shoup [35], do. However, we can modify any encryption scheme to have this property, *without changing the public key*, by using the coins of the key-generation algorithm as the secret key.) The assumed security of the encryption scheme means this function is one-way. Now, we simply use an F-keyed signature scheme, with the keys remaining those of the encryption scheme. No new keys are introduced. We need however to ensure that the joint use of the keys does not result in bad interactions that make either the encryption or the signature insecure. This amounts to showing that the JES security conditions, namely that encryption remains secure even given a signing oracle and signing remains secure even given a decryption oracle, are met. This will follow from the simulatability and key-extractability requirements we impose on our F-keyed signatures. See Section 4.

NEW RKA-SECURE SIGNATURES. In a related-key attack (RKA) [52,18,13,9] an adversary can modify a stored secret key and observe outcomes of the cryptographic primitive under the modified key. Such attacks may be mounted by tampering [25,19,44], so RKA security improves resistance to side-channel attacks. Achieving proven security against RKAs, however, is broadly recognized as very challenging. This has lead several authors [45,9] to suggest that we "bootstrap," building higher-level Φ-RKA-secure primitives from lower-level Φ-RKA-secure primitives. (As per the framework of [13,9], security is parameterized by the class of functions Φ that the adversary is allowed to apply to the key. Security is never possible for the class of all functions [13], so we seek results for specific Φ.) In this vein, [9] show how to build Φ-RKA signatures from Φ-RKA PRFs. Building Φ-RKA PRFs remains difficult, however, and we really have only one construction [8]. This has lead to direct (non-bootstrapping) constructions of Φ-RKA signatures for classes Φ of polynomials over certain specific pairing groups [16].

We return to bootstrapping and provide a much stronger result, building Φ-RKA signatures from Φ-RKA one-way functions rather than from Φ-RKA PRFs. (For a one-way function, the input is the "key." In attempting to recover x from $F(x)$, the adversary may also obtain $F(x')$ where x' is created by applying to x some modification function from Φ. The definition is from [45].) The difference is significant because building Φ-RKA one-way functions under standard assumptions is easy. Adapting the key-malleability technique of [8], we show that many natural one-way functions are Φ-RKA secure *assuming nothing more than their standard one-wayness*. In particular this is true for discrete exponentiation over an arbitrary group and for the one-way functions underlying the LWE and LPN problems. In this way we obtain Φ-RKA signatures for many new and natural classes Φ.

The central challenge in our bootstrapping is to preserve the keyspace, meaning that the space of secret keys of the constructed signature scheme must be the domain of the given Φ-RKA one-way function F. (Without this, it is not even meaningful to talk of preserving Φ-RKA security, let alone to show that it happens.) This is exactly what an F-keyed signature scheme allows us to do. The proof that Φ-RKA security is preserved exploits strong features built into our definitions of simulatability and key-extractability for F-keyed signatures, in particular that these conditions hold even under secret keys selected by the adversary. See Section 5.

KDM-SECURE STORAGE. Over the last few years we have seen a large number of sophisticated schemes to address the (challenging) problem of encryption of key-dependent data (e.g., [21,26,5,4,30,31,20,7,55,3,28,29,12,42,51]). The most touted application is secure outsourced storage, where Alice's decryption key, or some function thereof, is in a file she is encrypting and uploading to the cloud. But in this setting integrity is just as important as privacy. To this end, we would like to add signatures, thus enabling the server, based on Alice's public key, to validate her uploads, and enabling Alice herself to validate her downloads, all *while preserving KDM security*.

What emerges is a new goal that we call KDM-secure (encrypted and authenticated) storage. In Section 6 we formalize the corresponding primitive, providing both syntax and notions of security for key-dependent messages. Briefly, Alice uses a secret key sk to turn her message M into an encrypted and authenticated "data" object that she stores on the server. The server is able to check integrity based on Alice's public key. When Alice retrieves data, she can check integrity and decrypt based on her secret key. Security requires both privacy and integrity even when M depends on sk. (As we explain in more depth below, this goal is different from signcryption [62], authenticated public-key encryption [2] and authenticated symmetric encryption [15,58], even in the absence of KDM considerations.)

A natural approach to achieve our goal is for Alice to encrypt under a symmetric, KDM-secure scheme and sign the ciphertexts under a conventional signature scheme. But it is not clear how to prove the resulting storage scheme is KDM-secure. The difficulty is that sk would include the signing key in addition to the encryption (and decryption) key K, so that messages depend on both these keys while the KDM security of the encryption only covers messages depending on K. We could attempt to start from scratch and design a secure storage scheme meeting our notions. But key-versatile signatures offer a simpler and more modular solution. Briefly, we take a KDM-secure *public-key* encryption scheme and let F be the one-way function that maps a secret key to a public key. Alice holds (only) a secret key sk and the server holds $pk = F(sk)$. To upload M, Alice re-computes pk from sk, encrypts M under it using the KDM scheme, and signs the ciphertext with an F-keyed signature scheme using the *same* key sk. The server verifies signatures under pk.

In Section 6 we present in full the construction outlined above, and prove that it meets our notion of KDM security. The crux, as for our RKA-secure constructions, is that adding signing capability without changing the keys puts us in a position to exploit the assumed KDM security of the underlying encryption scheme. The strong simulatability and key-extractability properties of our signatures do the rest. We note that as an added bonus, we assume only CPA KDM security of the base encryption scheme, yet our storage scheme achieves CCA KDM security.

GETTING F-KEYED SIGNATURES. In Section 3 we define F-keyed signature schemes and show how to construct them for arbitrary one-way F. This enables us to realize the above applications.

Our simulatability condition, adapting [33,1,32], asks for a trapdoor allowing the creation of simulated signatures given only the message and public key, even when the secret key underlying this public key is adversarially chosen. Our key-extractability condition, adapting [33], asks that, using the same trapdoor, one can extract from a valid signature the corresponding secret key, even when the public key is adversarially chosen. Theorem 1, showing these conditions imply not just standard but strong unforgeability, functions not just as a sanity check but as a way to introduce, in a simple form, a proof template that we will extend for our applications.

Our construction of an F-keyed signature scheme is a minor adaptation of a NIZK-based signature scheme of Dodis, Haralambiev, López-Alt and Wichs (DHLW) [40]. While DHLW [40] prove leakage-resilience of their scheme, we prove simulatability and key-extractability. The underlying SE NIZKs are a variant of simulation-sound extractable NIZKs [36,47,48] introduced by [40] under the name tSE NIZKs and shown by [40,50] to be achievable for all of **NP** under standard assumptions.

DISCUSSION AND RELATED WORK. F-keyed signatures can be viewed as a special case of signatures of knowledge as introduced by Chase and Lysyanskaya [33]. The main novelty of our work is in the notion of key-versatility, namely that F-keyed signatures can add signing capability without changing keys, and the ensuing applications to Joint Enc/Sig, RKA and KDM. In particular our work shows that signatures of knowledge have applications beyond those envisaged in [33].

The first NIZK-based signature scheme was that of [10]. It achieved only unforgeability. Simulatability and extractability were achieved in [33] using dense cryptosystems [38,37] and simulation-sound NIZKs [60,36]. The DHLW construction we use can be viewed as a simplification and strengthening made possible by the significant advances in NIZK technology since then.

F-keyed signatures, and, more generally, signatures of knowledge [33] can be seen as a signing analogue of Witness encryption [43,11], and we might have named them Witness Signatures. GGSW [43] show how witness encryption allows encryption with a flexible choice of keys, just as we show that F-keyed signatures allow signing with a flexible choice of keys.

Signcryption [62], authenticated public-key encryption [2], JES [49,57] and our secure storage goal all have in common that both encryption and signature are involved. However, in signcryption and authenticated public-key encryption, there are two parties and thus two sets of keys, Alice encrypting under Bob's public key and signing under her own secret key. In JES and secure storage, there is one set of keys, namely Alice's. Thus for signcryption and authenticated public-key encryption, the question of using the same keys for the two purposes, which is at the core of our goals and methods, does not arise. Self-signcryption [41] is however similar to secure storage, minus the key-dependent message aspect. Authenticated symmetric encryption [15,58] also involves both encryption and authentication, but under a shared key, while JES and secure storage involve public keys. KDM-secure authenticated symmetric encryption was studied in [12,6].

KDM-secure signatures were studied in [56], who show limitations on the security achievable. Our secure storage scheme bypasses these limitations by signing ciphertexts rather than plaintexts and by avoiding KDM-secure signatures altogether: we use F-keyed signatures and are making no standalone claims or assumptions regarding their KDM security. Combining KDM encryption and KDM signatures would not give us KDM-secure storage because the keys for the two primitives would be different and we want joint KDM security.

Secure storage is an amalgam of symmetric and asymmetric cryptography, encryption being of the former kind and authentication of the latter. With secure storage, we are directly modeling a goal of practical interest rather than trying to create a general-purpose tool like many of the other works just mentioned. The difference between JES and secure storage is that in the former, arbitrary messages may be signed, while in the latter only ciphertexts may be signed. The difference is crucial for KDM security, which for JES would inherit the limitations of KDM-secure signatures just mentioned, but is not so limited for secure storage.

2   Notation

The empty string is denoted by ε. If x is a (binary) string then $|x|$ is its length. If S is a finite set then $|S|$ denotes its size and $s \leftarrow_{\$} S$ denotes picking an element uniformly from S and assigning it to s. We denote by $\lambda \in \mathbb{N}$ the security parameter and by 1^{λ} its unary representation. Algorithms are randomized unless otherwise indicated. "PT" stands for "polynomial time," whether for randomized algorithms or deterministic. By $y \leftarrow A(x_1, \ldots ; R)$, we denote the operation of running algorithm A on inputs $x_1, \ldots$ and coins R and letting y denote the output. By $y \leftarrow_{\$} A(x_1, \ldots)$, we denote the operation of letting $y \leftarrow A(x_1, \ldots ; R)$ for random R. We denote by $[A(x_1, \ldots)]$ the set of points that have positive probability of being output by A on inputs $x_1, \ldots$. Adversaries are algorithms.

We use games in definitions of security and in proofs. A game G (e.g. Fig. 1) has a MAIN procedure whose output (what it returns) is the output of the game.

We let $\Pr[G]$ denote the probability that this output is the boolean true. The boolean flag bad, if used in a game, is assumed initialized to false.

3   Key-Versatile Signatures

We define F-keyed signature schemes, for F a family of functions rather than the single function F used for simplicity in Section 1. The requirement is that the secret key sk is an input for an instance fp of the family and the public key $pk = \mathsf{F.Ev}(1^\lambda, fp, sk)$ is the corresponding image under this instance, the instance fp itself specified in public parameters. We intend to use these schemes to add authenticity in a setting where keys (sk, pk) may already be in use for another purpose (such as encryption). We need to ensure that signing will neither lessen the security of the existing usage of the keys nor have its own security be lessened by it. To ensure this strong form of composability, we define simulatability and key-extractability requirements for our F-keyed schemes. The fact that the keys will already be in use for another purpose also means that we do not have the luxury of picking the family F, but must work with an arbitrary family emerging from another setting. The only assumption we will make on F is thus that it is one-way. (This is necessary, else security is clearly impossible.) With the definitions in place, we go on to indicate how to build F-keyed signature schemes for arbitrary, one-way F.

We clarify that being F-keyed under an F assumed to be one-way does not mean that security (simulatability and key-extractability) of the signature scheme is based *solely* on the assumption that F is one-way. The additional assumption is a SE-secure NIZK. (But this itself can be built under standard assumptions.) It is possible to build a signature scheme that is unforgeable assuming only that a given F is one-way [59], but this scheme will not be F-keyed relative to the same F underlying its security, and it will not be simulatable or key-extractable.

SIGNATURE SCHEMES. A signature scheme DS specifies the following PT algorithms: via $pp \leftarrow_\$ \mathsf{DS.Pg}(1^\lambda)$ one generates public parameters pp common to all users; via $(sk, pk) \leftarrow_\$ \mathsf{DS.Kg}(1^\lambda, pp)$ a user can generate a secret signing key sk and corresponding public verification key pk; via $\sigma \leftarrow_\$ \mathsf{DS.Sig}(1^\lambda, pp, sk, M)$ the signer can generate a signature σ on a message $M \in \{0,1\}^*$; via $d \leftarrow \mathsf{DS.Ver}(1^\lambda, pp, pk, M, \sigma)$ a verifier can deterministically produce a decision $d \in \{\mathsf{true}, \mathsf{false}\}$ regarding whether σ is a valid signature of M under pk. Correctness requires that $\mathsf{DS.Ver}(1^\lambda, pp, pk, M, \mathsf{DS.Sig}(1^\lambda, pp, sk, M)) = \mathsf{true}$ for all $\lambda \in \mathbb{N}$, all $pp \in [\mathsf{DS.Pg}(1^\lambda)]$, all $(sk, pk) \in [\mathsf{DS.Kg}(1^\lambda, pp)]$, and all M.

FUNCTION FAMILIES. A function family F specifies the following. Via $fp \leftarrow_\$ \mathsf{F.Pg}(1^\lambda)$ one can in PT generate a description fp of a function $\mathsf{F.Ev}(1^\lambda, fp, \cdot)$: $\mathsf{F.Dom}(1^\lambda, fp) \to \mathsf{F.Rng}(1^\lambda, fp)$. We assume that membership of x in the non-empty domain $\mathsf{F.Dom}(1^\lambda, fp)$ can be tested in time polynomial in $1^\lambda, fp, x$ and one can in time polynomial in $1^\lambda, fp$ sample a point $x \leftarrow_\$ \mathsf{F.Dom}(1^\lambda, fp)$ from the domain $\mathsf{F.Dom}(1^\lambda, fp)$. The deterministic evaluation algorithm F.Ev is PT. The range is defined by $\mathsf{F.Rng}(1^\lambda, fp) = \{ \mathsf{F.Ev}(1^\lambda, fp, x) : x \in \mathsf{F.Dom}(1^\lambda, fp) \}$.

MAIN $\mathrm{SIM}_{\mathsf{DS},\mathsf{F}}^{A}(\lambda)$	MAIN $\mathrm{EXT}_{\mathsf{DS},\mathsf{F}}^{A}(\lambda)$
$b \leftarrow_{\$} \{0,1\}$	$fp \leftarrow_{\$} \mathsf{F.Pg}(1^{\lambda})$
$(fp, ap_1) \leftarrow_{\$} \mathsf{DS.Pg}(1^{\lambda})$	$Q \leftarrow \emptyset$; $(ap, std, xtd) \leftarrow_{\$} \mathsf{DS.SimPg}(1^{\lambda})$
$pp_1 \leftarrow (fp, ap_1)$	$pp \leftarrow (fp, ap)$
$(ap_0, std, xtd) \leftarrow_{\$} \mathsf{DS.SimPg}(1^{\lambda})$	$(pk, M, \sigma) \leftarrow_{\$} A^{\mathrm{SIGN}}(1^{\lambda}, pp)$
$pp_0 \leftarrow (fp, ap_0)$	If $pk \notin \mathsf{F.Rng}(1^{\lambda}, fp)$ then Ret false
$b' \leftarrow_{\$} A^{\mathrm{SIGN}}(1^{\lambda}, pp_b)$; Ret $(b = b')$	If not $\mathsf{DS.Ver}(1^{\lambda}, pp, pk, M, \sigma)$ then
	Ret false
$\mathrm{SIGN}(sk, M)$	If $(pk, M, \sigma) \in Q$ then Ret false
If $sk \notin \mathsf{F.Dom}(1^{\lambda}, fp)$ then Ret $\perp$	$sk \leftarrow_{\$} \mathsf{DS.Ext}(1^{\lambda}, pp, xtd, pk, M, \sigma)$
$pk \leftarrow \mathsf{F.Ev}(1^{\lambda}, fp, sk)$	Ret $(\mathsf{F.Ev}(1^{\lambda}, fp, sk) \neq pk)$
If $b = 1$ then $\sigma \leftarrow_{\$} \mathsf{DS.Sig}(1^{\lambda}, pp_1, sk, M)$	$\mathrm{SIGN}(sk, M)$
Else $\sigma \leftarrow_{\$} \mathsf{DS.SimSig}(1^{\lambda}, pp_0, std, pk, M)$	If $sk \notin \mathsf{F.Dom}(1^{\lambda}, fp)$ then Ret $\perp$
Ret σ	$pk \leftarrow \mathsf{F.Ev}(1^{\lambda}, fp, sk)$
	$\sigma \leftarrow_{\$} \mathsf{DS.SimSig}(1^{\lambda}, pp, std, pk, M)$
	$Q \leftarrow Q \cup \{(pk, M, \sigma)\}$; Ret σ

Fig. 1. Games defining security of F-keyed signature scheme DS. Left: Game defining simulatability. Right: Game defining key-extractability.

Testing membership in the range is not required to be PT. (But is in many examples.) We say that F is one-way or F is a OWF if $\mathbf{Adv}_{\mathsf{F},I}^{\mathrm{ow}}(\cdot)$ is negligible for all PT I, where $\mathbf{Adv}_{\mathsf{F},I}^{\mathrm{ow}}(\lambda) = \Pr[\mathsf{F.Ev}(1^{\lambda}, fp, x') = y]$ under the experiment $fp \leftarrow_{\$} \mathsf{F.Pg}(1^{\lambda})$; $x \leftarrow_{\$} \mathsf{F.Dom}(1^{\lambda}, fp)$; $y \leftarrow \mathsf{F.Ev}(1^{\lambda}, fp, x)$; $x' \leftarrow_{\$} I(1^{\lambda}, fp, y)$.

F-KEYED SIGNATURE SCHEMES. Let F be a function family. We say that a signature scheme DS is F-*keyed* if the following are true:

- Parameter compatibility: Parameters pp for DS are a pair $pp = (fp, ap)$ consisting of parameters fp for F and auxiliary parameters ap, these independently generated. Formally, there is a PT *auxiliary parameter generation* algorithm APg such that $\mathsf{DS.Pg}(1^{\lambda})$ picks $fp \leftarrow_{\$} \mathsf{F.Pg}(1^{\lambda})$; $ap \leftarrow_{\$} \mathsf{APg}(1^{\lambda})$ and returns (fp, ap).

- Key compatibility: The signing key sk is a random point in the domain of F.Ev and the verifying key pk its image under F.Ev. Formally, $\mathsf{DS.Kg}(1^{\lambda}, (fp, ap))$ picks $sk \leftarrow_{\$} \mathsf{F.Dom}(1^{\lambda}, fp)$, lets $pk \leftarrow \mathsf{F.Ev}(1^{\lambda}, fp, sk)$ and returns (sk, pk). (DS.Kg ignores the auxiliary parameters ap, meaning the keys do not depend on it.)

SECURITY OF F-KEYED SIGNATURE SCHEMES. We require two (strong) security properties of an F-keyed signature scheme DS:

- Simulatable: Under simulated auxiliary parameters and an associated simulation trapdoor std, a simulator, given $pk = \mathsf{F.Ev}(1^{\lambda}, fp, sk)$ and M, can produce a signature σ indistinguishable from the real one produced under sk, when not just M, *but even the secret key sk*, is adaptively chosen by the adversary. Formally, DS is *simulatable* if it specifies additional PT algorithms DS.SimPg (the auxiliary parameter simulator) and DS.SimSig (the signature simulator) such that $\mathbf{Adv}^{sim}_{DS,F,A}(\cdot)$ is negligible for every PT adversary A, where $\mathbf{Adv}^{sim}_{DS,F,A}(\lambda) = 2\Pr[\mathrm{SIM}^A_{DS,F}(\lambda)] - 1$ and game SIM is specified on the left-hand side of Fig. 1.

- Key-extractable: Under the same simulated auxiliary parameters and an associated extraction trapdoor xtd, an extractor can extract from any valid forgery relative to pk an underlying secret key sk, even when *pk is chosen by the adversary* and the adversary can adaptively obtain simulated signatures *under secret keys of its choice*. Formally, DS is *key-extractable* if it specifies another PT algorithm DS.Ext (the extractor) such that $\mathbf{Adv}^{ext}_{DS,F,A}(\cdot)$ is negligible for every PT adversary A, where $\mathbf{Adv}^{ext}_{DS,F,A}(\lambda) = \Pr[\mathrm{EXT}^A_{DS,F}(\lambda)]$ and game EXT is specified on the right-hand side of Fig. 1.

The EXT game includes a possibly non-PT test of membership in the range of the family, but we will ensure that adversaries (who must remain PT) do not perform this test. Our definition of simulatability follows [33,1,32]. Those definitions were for general signatures, not F-keyed ones, and one difference is that our simulator can set only the auxiliary parameters, not the full parameters, meaning it does not set fp.

SIM+EXT IMPLIES UNFORGEABILITY. The simulatability and key-extractability notions we have defined may seem quite unrelated to the standard unforgeability requirement for signature schemes [46]. As a warm-up towards applying these new conditions, we show that in fact they imply not just the standard unforgeability but strong unforgeability, under the minimal assumption that F is one-way. In [14] we recall the definition of strong unforgeability and formally prove the following:

Theorem 1. *Let* DS *be an* F-*keyed signature scheme that is simulatable and key-extractable. If* F *is one-way then* DS *is strongly unforgeable.*

CONSTRUCTION. A *key-versatile signing schema* is a transform **KvS** that given an arbitrary family of functions F returns an F-keyed signature scheme DS = **KvS**[F]. We want the constructed signature scheme to be simulatable and key-extractable. We now show that this is possible with the aid of appropriate NIZK systems which are themselves known to be possible under standard assumptions.

Theorem 2. *Assume there exist SE NIZK systems for all of* **NP**. *Then there is a key-versatile signing schema* **KvS** *such that if* F *is any family of functions then the signature scheme* DS = **KvS**[F] *is simulatable and key-extractable.*

In [14] we recall the definition of a SE (Simulation Extractable) NIZK system. SE was called tSE in [40] and is a variant of NIZK-security notions from [47,36,60]. We then specify the construction and prove it has the claimed properties. Here we sketch the construction and its history.

The scheme is simple. We define the relation $R((1^\lambda, fp, pk, M), sk)$ to return true iff $F.Ev(1^\lambda, fp, sk) = pk$. A signature of M under sk is then a SE-secure NIZK proof for this relation in which the witness is sk and the instance (input) is $(1^\lambda, fp, pk, M)$. The interesting aspect of this construction is that it at first sounds blatantly insecure, since the relation R ignores the message M. Does this not mean that a signature is independent of the message, in which case an adversary could violate unforgeability by requesting a signature σ of a message M under pk and then outputting (M', σ) as a forgery for some $M' \neq M$? What prevents this is the strength of the SE notion of NIZKs. The message M is present in the instance $(1^\lambda, fp, pk, M)$, even if it is ignored by the relation; the proof in turn depends on the instance, making the signature depend on M.

A similar construction of signatures was given in [40] starting from a leakage-resilient hard relation rather than (as in our case) a relation arising from a one-way function. Our construction could be considered a special case of theirs, with the added difference that they use labeled NIZKs with the message as the label while we avoid labels and put the message in the input. The claims established about the construction are however different, with [40] establishing leakage resilience and unforgeability of the signature and our work showing simulatability and key-extractability.

4   JES with No Public-Key Overhead

Let PKE be an arbitrary IND-CCA-secure public-key encryption scheme. Alice has already established a key-pair (sk_e, pk_e) for this scheme, allowing anyone to send her ciphertexts computed under pk_e that she can decrypt under sk_e. She wants now to add signature capability. This is easily done. She can create a key-pair (sk_s, pk_s) for her favorite signature scheme and sign an arbitrary message M under sk_s, verification being possible given pk_s. The difficulty is that her public key is now $pk = (pk_e, pk_s)$. It is not just larger but will require a new certificate. The question we ask is whether we can add signing capability in a way that is more parsimonious with regard to public key size. Technically, we seek a joint encryption and signature (JES) scheme where Alice has a single key-pair (sk, pk), with sk used to decrypt and sign, and pk used to encrypt and verify, each usage secure in the face of the other, and we want pk smaller than that of the trivial solution $pk = (pk_e, pk_s)$. Perhaps surprisingly, we show how to construct a JES scheme with pk-overhead zero, meaning pk is unchanged, remaining pk_e. Previous standard model JES schemes had been able to reduce the pk-overhead only for *specific* starting encryption schemes [49,57] while our result says the overhead can be zero regardless of the starting encryption scheme.

JES SCHEMES. A joint encryption and signature (JES) scheme JES specifies the following PT algorithms: via $jp \leftarrow_\$ JES.Pg(1^\lambda)$ one generates public parameters jp common to all users; via $(sk, pk) \leftarrow_\$ JES.Kg(1^\lambda, jp)$ a user can generate a secret (signing and decryption) key sk and corresponding public (verification and encryption) key pk; via $\sigma \leftarrow_\$ JES.Sig(1^\lambda, jp, sk, M)$ the user can generate a signature σ on a message $M \in \{0,1\}^*$; via $d \leftarrow JES.Ver(1^\lambda, jp, pk, M, \sigma)$

MAIN $\mathrm{IND}^A_{\mathsf{JES}}(\lambda)$	MAIN $\mathrm{SUF}^A_{\mathsf{JES}}(\lambda)$
$b \leftarrow_\$ \{0,1\}$; $C^* \leftarrow \perp$; $jp \leftarrow_\$ \mathsf{JES.Pg}(1^\lambda)$	$Q \leftarrow \emptyset$
$(pk, sk) \leftarrow_\$ \mathsf{JES.Kg}(1^\lambda, jp)$	$jp \leftarrow_\$ \mathsf{JES.Pg}(1^\lambda)$
$b' \leftarrow_\$ A^{\mathrm{DEC},\mathrm{SIGN},\mathrm{LR}}(1^\lambda, jp, pk)$	$(pk, sk) \leftarrow_\$ \mathsf{JES.Kg}(1^\lambda, jp)$
Ret $(b = b')$	$(M, \sigma) \leftarrow A^{\mathrm{SIGN},\mathrm{DEC}}(1^\lambda, jp, pk)$
	Ret $(\mathsf{JES.Ver}(1^\lambda, jp, pk, M, \sigma) \wedge (M,\sigma) \notin Q)$
proc $\mathrm{DEC}(C)$	
If $(C = C^*)$ then Ret $\perp$	proc $\mathrm{SIGN}(M)$
Else Ret $M \leftarrow \mathsf{JES.Dec}(1^\lambda, jp, sk, C)$	$\sigma \leftarrow_\$ \mathsf{JES.Sig}(1^\lambda, jp, sk, M)$
	$Q \leftarrow Q \cup \{(M, \sigma)\}$; Ret σ
proc $\mathrm{SIGN}(M)$	
Ret $\sigma \leftarrow_\$ \mathsf{JES.Sig}(1^\lambda, jp, sk, M)$	proc $\mathrm{DEC}(C)$
	Ret $M \leftarrow \mathsf{JES.Dec}(1^\lambda, jp, sk, C)$
proc $\mathrm{LR}(M_0, M_1)$	
If $(|M_0| \neq |M_1|)$ then Ret $\perp$	
Else Ret $C^* \leftarrow_\$ \mathsf{JES.Enc}(1^\lambda, jp, pk, M_b)$	

Fig. 2. Games defining security of joint encryption and signature scheme JES. Left: Game IND defining privacy against chosen-ciphertext attack in the presence of a signing oracle. Right: Game SUF defining strong unforgeability in the presence of a decryption oracle.

a verifier can deterministically produce a decision $d \in \{\mathsf{true}, \mathsf{false}\}$ regarding whether σ is a valid signature of M under pk; via $C \leftarrow_\$ \mathsf{JES.Enc}(1^\lambda, jp, pk, M)$ anyone can generate a ciphertext C encrypting message M under pk; via $M \leftarrow \mathsf{JES.Dec}(1^\lambda, jp, sk, C)$ the user can deterministically decrypt ciphertext C to get a value $M \in \{0,1\}^* \cup \{\perp\}$. Correctness requires that $\mathsf{JES.Ver}(1^\lambda, jp, pk, M, \mathsf{JES.Sig}(1^\lambda, jp, sk, M)) = \mathsf{true}$ and that $\mathsf{JES.Dec}(1^\lambda, jp, sk, \mathsf{JES.Enc}(1^\lambda, jp, pk, M)) = M$ for all $\lambda \in \mathbb{N}$, all $jp \in [\mathsf{JES.Pg}(1^\lambda)]$, all $(sk, pk) \in [\mathsf{JES.Kg}(1^\lambda, jp)]$, and all $M \in \{0,1\}^*$. We say that JES is IND-secure if $\mathbf{Adv}^{\mathrm{ind}}_{\mathsf{JES},A}(\cdot)$ is negligible for all PT adversaries A, where $\mathbf{Adv}^{\mathrm{ind}}_{\mathsf{JES},A}(\lambda) = 2\Pr[\mathrm{IND}^A_{\mathsf{JES}}(\lambda)] - 1$ and game IND is on the left-hand side of Fig. 2. Here the adversary is allowed only one query to LR. This represents privacy under chosen-ciphertext attack in the presence of a signing oracle. We say that JES is SUF-secure if $\mathbf{Adv}^{\mathrm{suf}}_{\mathsf{JES},A}(\cdot)$ is negligible for all PT adversaries A, where $\mathbf{Adv}^{\mathrm{suf}}_{\mathsf{JES},A}(\lambda) = \Pr[\mathrm{SUF}^A_{\mathsf{JES}}(\lambda)]$ and game SUF is on the right-hand side of Fig. 2. This represents (strong) unforgeability of the signature in the presence of a decryption oracle. These definitions are from [49,57].

THE BASE PKE SCHEME. We are given a public-key encryption scheme PKE, specifying the following PT algorithms: via $fp \leftarrow_\$ \mathsf{PKE.Pg}(1^\lambda)$ one generates public parameters; via $(sk, pk) \leftarrow_\$ \mathsf{PKE.Kg}(1^\lambda, fp)$ a user generates a decryption key sk and encryption key pk; via $C \leftarrow_\$ \mathsf{PKE.Enc}(1^\lambda, fp, pk, M)$ anyone can generate a ciphertext C encrypting a message M under pk; and via $M \leftarrow \mathsf{PKE.Dec}(1^\lambda, fp, sk, C)$ a user can deterministically decrypt a ciphertext C to get a value $M \in \{0,1\}^* \cup \{\perp\}$. Correctness requires that $\mathsf{PKE.Dec}(1^\lambda, fp, sk, \mathsf{PKE.Enc}(1^\lambda, fp, pk, M)) = M$ for all $\lambda \in \mathbb{N}$, all $fp \in [\mathsf{PKE.Pg}(1^\lambda)]$, all $(sk, pk) \in [\mathsf{PKE.Kg}(1^\lambda, fp)]$, and all $M \in \{0,1\}^*$. We assume that PKE meets the usual notion of IND-CCA security.

Let us say that PKE is *canonical* if the operation $(sk, pk) \leftarrow_{\$} \mathsf{PKE.Kg}(1^\lambda, fp)$ picks sk at random from a finite, non-empty set we denote $\mathsf{PKE.SK}(1^\lambda, fp)$, and then applies to $(1^\lambda, fp, sk)$ a PT deterministic *public-key derivation function* we denote $\mathsf{PKE.PK}$ to get pk. Canonicity may seem like an extra assumption, but isn't. First, many (most) schemes are already canonical. This is true for the Cramer-Shoup scheme [35], the Kurosawa-Desmedt scheme [54] and for schemes obtained via the BCHK transform [24] applied to the identity-based encryption schemes of Boneh-Boyen [22] or Waters [61]. Second, if by chance a scheme is not canonical, we can modify it be so. Crucially (for our purposes), the modification *does not change the public key.* (But it might change the secret key.) Briefly, the modification, which is standard, is to use the random coins of the key generation algorithm as the secret key.

CONSTRUCTION. Given canonical PKE as above, we construct a JES scheme JES. The first step is to construct from PKE a function family F as follows: let $\mathsf{F.Pg} = \mathsf{PKE.Pg}$, so the parameters of F are the same those of PKE; let $\mathsf{F.Dom} = \mathsf{PKE.SK}$, so the domain of F is the space of secret keys of PKE; and let $\mathsf{F.Ev} = \mathsf{PKE.PK}$, so the function defined by fp maps a secret key to a corresponding public key. Now let DS be an F-keyed signature scheme that is simulatable and key-extractable. (We can obtain DS via Theorem 2.) Now we define our JES scheme JES. Let $\mathsf{JES.Pg} = \mathsf{DS.Pg}$, so parameters for JES have the form $jp = (fp, ap)$, where fp are parameters for F, which by definition of F are also parameters for PKE. Let $\mathsf{JES.Kg} = \mathsf{DS.Kg}$. (Keys are those of PKE which are also those of DS.) Let $\mathsf{JES.Sig} = \mathsf{DS.Sig}$ and $\mathsf{JES.Ver} = \mathsf{DS.Ver}$, so the signing and verifying algorithms of the joint scheme JES are inherited from the signature scheme DS. Let $\mathsf{JES.Enc}(1^\lambda, (fp, ap), pk, M)$ return $\mathsf{PKE.Enc}(1^\lambda, fp, pk, M)$ and let $\mathsf{JES.Dec}(1^\lambda, (fp, ap), sk, C)$ return $\mathsf{PKE.Dec}(1^\lambda, fp, sk, C)$, so the encryption and decryption algorithms of the joint scheme JES are inherited from the PKE scheme PKE. Note that the public key of the joint scheme JES is exactly that of PKE, so there is zero public-key overhead. The following says that JES is both IND and SUF secure. The proof is in [14].

Theorem 3. *Let* PKE *be a canonical public-key encryption scheme. Let* F *be defined from it as above. Let* DS *be an* F-*keyed signature scheme, and let* JES *be the corresponding joint encryption and signature scheme constructed above. Assume* PKE *is IND-CCA secure. Assume* DS *is simulatable and key-extractable. Then (1)* JES *is IND secure, and (2)* JES *is SUF secure.*

MAIN $\text{RKAOWF}_{F,\Phi}^A(\lambda)$	MAIN $\text{RKASIG}_{DS,F,\Phi}^A(\lambda)$
$fp \leftarrow_{\$} \text{F.Pg}(1^\lambda)$	$Q \leftarrow \emptyset \,;\, (fp, ap) \leftarrow_{\$} \text{DS.Pg}(1^\lambda) \,;\, pp \leftarrow (fp, ap)$
$x \leftarrow_{\$} \text{F.Dom}(1^\lambda, fp)$	$(sk, pk) \leftarrow_{\$} \text{DS.Kg}(1^\lambda, pp)$
$y \leftarrow \text{F.Ev}(1^\lambda, fp, x)$	$(M, \sigma) \leftarrow_{\$} A^{\text{SIGN}}(1^\lambda, pp, pk)$
$x' \leftarrow_{\$} A^{\text{EVAL}}(1^\lambda, fp, y)$	Ret $(\text{DS.Ver}(1^\lambda, pp, pk, M, \sigma) \wedge (pk, M, \sigma) \notin Q)$
Ret $(\text{F.Ev}(1^\lambda, fp, x') = y)$	$\text{SIGN}(\phi, M)$
$\text{EVAL}(\phi)$	$sk' \leftarrow \Phi(1^\lambda, fp, \phi, sk) \,;\, pk' \leftarrow \text{F.Ev}(1^\lambda, fp, sk')$
$x' \leftarrow \Phi(1^\lambda, fp, \phi, x)$	$\sigma \leftarrow_{\$} \text{DS.Sig}(1^\lambda, pp, sk', M) \,;\, Q \leftarrow Q \cup \{(pk', M, \sigma)\}$
$y' \leftarrow \text{F.Ev}(1^\lambda, fp, x')$	Ret σ'
Ret y'	

Fig. 3. Games defining Φ-RKA security of a function family F (left) and an F-keyed signature scheme DS (right)

5   RKA-Secure Signatures from RKA-Secure OWFs

RKA security is notoriously hard to provably achieve. Recognizing this, several authors [45,9] have suggested a bootstrapping approach in which we build higher-level RKA-secure primitives from lower-level RKA-secure primitives. In this vein, a construction of RKA-secure signatures from RKA-secure PRFs was given in [9]. We improve on this via a construction of RKA-secure signatures from RKA-secure one-way functions. The benefit is that (as we will show) many popular OWFs are already RKA secure and we immediately get new RKA-secure signatures.

RKA SECURITY. Let F be a function family. A class of RKD (related-key deriving) functions Φ for F is a PT-computable function that specifies for each $\lambda \in \mathbb{N}$, each $fp \in [\text{F.Pg}(1^\lambda)]$ and each $\phi \in \{0,1\}^*$ a map $\Phi(1^\lambda, fp, \phi, \cdot) : \text{F.Dom}(1^\lambda, fp) \to \text{F.Dom}(1^\lambda, fp)$ called the RKD function described by ϕ. We say that F is Φ-RKA secure if $\mathbf{Adv}_{F,A,\Phi}^{\text{rka}}(\cdot)$ is negligible for every PT adversary A, where $\mathbf{Adv}_{F,A,\Phi}^{\text{rka}}(\lambda) = \Pr[\text{RKAOWF}_{F,\Phi}^A(\lambda)]$ and game RKAOWF is on the left-hand side of Fig. 3. The definition is from [45].

Let DS be an F-keyed signature scheme and let Φ be as above. We say that DS is Φ-RKA secure if $\mathbf{Adv}_{DS,F,A,\Phi}^{\text{rka}}(\cdot)$ is negligible for every PT adversary A, where $\mathbf{Adv}_{DS,F,A,\Phi}^{\text{rka}}(\lambda) = \Pr[\text{RKASIG}_{DS,F,\Phi}^A(\lambda)]$ and game RKASIG is on the right-hand side of Fig. 3. The definition is from [9].

CONSTRUCTION. Suppose we are given a Φ-RKA-secure OWF F and want to build a Φ-RKA-secure signature scheme. For the question to even make sense, RKD functions specified by Φ must apply to the secret signing key. Thus, the secret key needs to be an input for the OWF and the public key needs to be the image of the secret key under the OWF. The main technical difficulty is, given F, finding a signature scheme with this property. But this is exactly what a key-versatile signing schema gives us. The following says that if the signature scheme produced by this schema is simulatable and key-extractable then it inherits the Φ-RKA security of the OWF. The proof is in [14].

Theorem 4. *Let* DS *be an* F*-keyed signature scheme that is simulatable and key-extractable. Let* Φ *be a class of RKD functions. If* F *is* Φ*-RKA secure then* DS *is also* Φ*-RKA secure.*

FINDING Φ-RKA OWFs. Theorem 4 motivates finding Φ-RKA-secure function families F. The merit of our approach is that there are many such families. To enable systematically identifying them, we adapt the definition of key-malleable PRFs of [8] to OWFs. We say that a function family F is Φ-*key-malleable* if there is a PT algorithm M, called a Φ-key-simulator, such that $M(1^\lambda, fp, \phi,$ F.Ev$(1^\lambda, fp, x)) =$ F.Ev$(1^\lambda, fp, \Phi(1^\lambda, fp, \phi, x))$ for all $\lambda \in \mathbb{N}$, all $fp \in$ [F.Pg(1^λ)], all $\phi \in \{0,1\}^*$ and all $x \in$ F.Dom$(1^\lambda, fp)$. The proof of the following is in [14].

Proposition 5. *Let* F *be a function family and* Φ *a class of RKD functions. If* F *is* Φ*-key-malleable and one-way then* F *is* Φ*-RKA secure.*

Previous uses of key-malleability [8,16] for RKA security required additional conditions on the primitives, such as key-fingerprints in the first case and some form of collision-resistance in the second. For OWFs, it is considerably easier, key-malleability alone sufficing. In [14] we show how to leverage Proposition 5 to show Φ-RKA-security for three popular one-way functions, namely discrete exponentiation in a cyclic group, RSA, and the LWE one-way function, thence obtaining, via Theorem 4, Φ-RKA-secure signature schemes.

6   KDM-Secure Storage

Services like Dropbox, Google Drive and Amazon S3 offer outsourced storage. Users see obvious benefits but equally obvious security concerns. We would like to secure this storage, even when messages (files needing to be stored) depend on the keys securing them. If privacy is the only concern, existing KDM-secure encryption schemes (e.g., [21,26,5,4,30,31,20,7,55,3,28,29,12,42,51]) will do the job. However, integrity is just as much of a concern, and adding it without losing KDM security is challenging. This is because conventional ways of adding integrity introduce new keys and create new ways for messages to depend on keys. Key-versatile signing, by leaving the keys unchanged, will provide a solution.

In [14], we begin by formalizing our goal of encrypted and authenticated outsourced storage secure for key-dependent messages. In our syntax, the user encrypts and authenticates under her secret key, and then verifies and decrypts under the same secret key, with the public key utilized by the server for verification. Our requirement for KDM security has two components: IND for privacy and SUF for integrity. With the definitions in hand, we take a base KDM-secure encryption scheme and show how, via a key-versatile signature, to obtain storage schemes meeting our goal. Our resulting storage schemes will achieve KDM security with respect to the same class of message-deriving functions Φ as the underlying encryption scheme. Also, we will assume only CPA KDM security of the base scheme, yet achieve CCA KDM privacy for the constructed storage scheme. Interestingly, our solution uses a *public-key* base encryption scheme, even though the privacy component of the goal is symmetric and nobody but the user will encrypt. This allows us to start with KDM privacy under keys permitting signatures through key-versatile signing. This represents a novel application for public-key KDM-secure encryption. We refer the reader to [14] for details.

Acknowledgments. Bellare was supported in part by NSF grants CNS-0904380, CCF-0915675, CNS-1116800 and CNS-1228890. Meiklejohn was supported in part by NSF grant CNS-1237264. Part of this work was done while Thomson was at Royal Holloway, University of London supported in part by EPSRC Leadership Fellowship EP/H005455/1.

References

1. Abe, M., Fuchsbauer, G., Groth, J., Haralambiev, K., Ohkubo, M.: Structure-preserving signatures and commitments to group elements. In: Rabin, T. (ed.) CRYPTO 2010. LNCS, vol. 6223, pp. 209–236. Springer, Heidelberg (2010)
2. An, J.H., Dodis, Y., Rabin, T.: On the security of joint signature and encryption. In: Knudsen, L.R. (ed.) EUROCRYPT 2002. LNCS, vol. 2332, pp. 83–107. Springer, Heidelberg (2002)
3. Applebaum, B.: Key-dependent message security: Generic amplification and completeness. In: Paterson, K.G. (ed.) EUROCRYPT 2011. LNCS, vol. 6632, pp. 527–546. Springer, Heidelberg (2011)
4. Applebaum, B., Cash, D., Peikert, C., Sahai, A.: Fast cryptographic primitives and circular-secure encryption based on hard learning problems. In: Halevi, S. (ed.) CRYPTO 2009. LNCS, vol. 5677, pp. 595–618. Springer, Heidelberg (2009)
5. Backes, M., Dürmuth, M., Unruh, D.: OAEP is secure under key-dependent messages. In: Pieprzyk, J. (ed.) ASIACRYPT 2008. LNCS, vol. 5350, pp. 506–523. Springer, Heidelberg (2008)
6. Backes, M., Pfitzmann, B., Scedrov, A.: Key-dependent message security under active attacks - brsim/uc-soundness of dolev-yao-style encryption with key cycles. Journal of Computer Security 16(5), 497–530 (2008)
7. Barak, B., Haitner, I., Hofheinz, D., Ishai, Y.: Bounded key-dependent message security. In: Gilbert, H. (ed.) EUROCRYPT 2010. LNCS, vol. 6110, pp. 423–444. Springer, Heidelberg (2010)
8. Bellare, M., Cash, D.: Pseudorandom functions and permutations provably secure against related-key attacks. In: Rabin, T. (ed.) CRYPTO 2010. LNCS, vol. 6223, pp. 666–684. Springer, Heidelberg (2010)
9. Bellare, M., Cash, D., Miller, R.: Cryptography secure against related-key attacks and tampering. In: Lee, D.H., Wang, X. (eds.) ASIACRYPT 2011. LNCS, vol. 7073, pp. 486–503. Springer, Heidelberg (2011)
10. Bellare, M., Goldwasser, S.: New paradigms for digital signatures and message authentication based on non-interactive zero knowledge proofs. In: Brassard, G. (ed.) CRYPTO 1989. LNCS, vol. 435, pp. 194–211. Springer, Heidelberg (1990)
11. Bellare, M., Hoang, V.T.: Adaptive witness encryption and asymmetric password-based cryptography. Cryptology ePrint Archive, Report 2013/704 (2013)
12. Bellare, M., Keelveedhi, S.: Authenticated and misuse-resistant encryption of key-dependent data. In: Rogaway, P. (ed.) CRYPTO 2011. LNCS, vol. 6841, pp. 610–629. Springer, Heidelberg (2011)

13. Bellare, M., Kohno, T.: A theoretical treatment of related-key attacks: RKA-PRPs, RKA-PRFs, and applications. In: Biham, E. (ed.) EUROCRYPT 2003. LNCS, vol. 2656, pp. 491–506. Springer, Heidelberg (2003)

14. Bellare, M., Meiklejohn, S., Thomson, S.: Key-versatile signatures and applications: RKA, KDM and joint Enc/Sig. Cryptology ePrint Archive, Report 2013/326, Full version of this abstract (2013)

15. Bellare, M., Namprempre, C.: Authenticated encryption: Relations among notions and analysis of the generic composition paradigm. Journal of Cryptology 21(4), 469–491 (2008)

16. Bellare, M., Paterson, K.G., Thomson, S.: RKA security beyond the linear barrier: IBE, encryption and signatures. In: Wang, X., Sako, K. (eds.) ASIACRYPT 2012. LNCS, vol. 7658, pp. 331–348. Springer, Heidelberg (2012)

17. Bellare, M., Rogaway, P.: Random oracles are practical: A paradigm for designing efficient protocols. In: Ashby, V. (ed.) ACM CCS 1993, pp. 62–73. ACM Press (November 1993)

18. Biham, E.: New types of cryptanalytic attacks using related keys (extended abstract). In: Helleseth, T. (ed.) EUROCRYPT 1993. LNCS, vol. 765, pp. 398–409. Springer, Heidelberg (1994)

19. Biham, E., Shamir, A.: Differential fault analysis of secret key cryptosystems. In: Kaliski Jr., B.S. (ed.) CRYPTO 1997. LNCS, vol. 1294, pp. 513–525. Springer, Heidelberg (1997)

20. Bitansky, N., Canetti, R.: On strong simulation and composable point obfuscation. In: Rabin, T. (ed.) CRYPTO 2010. LNCS, vol. 6223, pp. 520–537. Springer, Heidelberg (2010)

21. Black, J., Rogaway, P., Shrimpton, T.: Encryption-scheme security in the presence of key-dependent messages. In: Nyberg, K., Heys, H.M. (eds.) SAC 2002. LNCS, vol. 2595, pp. 62–75. Springer, Heidelberg (2003)

22. Boneh, D., Boyen, X.: Efficient selective-ID secure identity based encryption without random oracles. In: Cachin, C., Camenisch, J.L. (eds.) EUROCRYPT 2004. LNCS, vol. 3027, pp. 223–238. Springer, Heidelberg (2004)

23. Boneh, D., Boyen, X.: Short signatures without random oracles. In: Cachin, C., Camenisch, J.L. (eds.) EUROCRYPT 2004. LNCS, vol. 3027, pp. 56–73. Springer, Heidelberg (2004)

24. Boneh, D., Canetti, R., Halevi, S., Katz, J.: Chosen-ciphertext security from identity-based encryption. SIAM Journal on Computing 36(5), 1301–1328 (2007)

25. Boneh, D., DeMillo, R.A., Lipton, R.J.: On the importance of checking cryptographic protocols for faults (extended abstract). In: Fumy, W. (ed.) EUROCRYPT 1997. LNCS, vol. 1233, pp. 37–51. Springer, Heidelberg (1997)

26. Boneh, D., Halevi, S., Hamburg, M., Ostrovsky, R.: Circular-secure encryption from decision diffie-hellman. In: Wagner, D. (ed.) CRYPTO 2008. LNCS, vol. 5157, pp. 108–125. Springer, Heidelberg (2008)

27. Boyen, X., Mei, Q., Waters, B.: Direct chosen ciphertext security from identity-based techniques. In: Atluri, V., Meadows, C., Juels, A. (eds.) ACM CCS 2005, pp. 320–329. ACM Press (November 2005)

28. Brakerski, Z., Goldwasser, S., Kalai, Y.T.: Black-box circular-secure encryption beyond affine functions. In: Ishai, Y. (ed.) TCC 2011. LNCS, vol. 6597, pp. 201–218. Springer, Heidelberg (2011)

29. Brakerski, Z., Vaikuntanathan, V.: Fully homomorphic encryption from ring-LWE and security for key dependent messages. In: Rogaway, P. (ed.) CRYPTO 2011. LNCS, vol. 6841, pp. 505–524. Springer, Heidelberg (2011)

30. Camenisch, J., Chandran, N., Shoup, V.: A public key encryption scheme secure against key dependent chosen plaintext and adaptive chosen ciphertext attacks. In: Joux, A. (ed.) EUROCRYPT 2009. LNCS, vol. 5479, pp. 351–368. Springer, Heidelberg (2009)
31. Canetti, R., Tauman Kalai, Y., Varia, M., Wichs, D.: On symmetric encryption and point obfuscation. In: Micciancio, D. (ed.) TCC 2010. LNCS, vol. 5978, pp. 52–71. Springer, Heidelberg (2010)
32. Chase, M., Kohlweiss, M., Lysyanskaya, A., Meiklejohn, S.: Malleable signatures: Complex unary transformations and delegatable anonymous credentials. Cryptology ePrint Archive, Report 2013/179 (2013)
33. Chase, M., Lysyanskaya, A.: On signatures of knowledge. In: Dwork, C. (ed.) CRYPTO 2006. LNCS, vol. 4117, pp. 78–96. Springer, Heidelberg (2006)
34. Coron, J.-S., Joye, M., Naccache, D., Paillier, P.: Universal padding schemes for RSA. In: Yung, M. (ed.) CRYPTO 2002. LNCS, vol. 2442, pp. 226–241. Springer, Heidelberg (2002)
35. Cramer, R., Shoup, V.: Design and analysis of practical public-key encryption schemes secure against adaptive chosen ciphertext attack. SIAM Journal on Computing 33(1), 167–226 (2003)
36. De Santis, A., Di Crescenzo, G., Ostrovsky, R., Persiano, G., Sahai, A.: Robust non-interactive zero knowledge. In: Kilian, J. (ed.) CRYPTO 2001. LNCS, vol. 2139, pp. 566–598. Springer, Heidelberg (2001)
37. De Santis, A., Di Crescenzo, G., Persiano, G.: Necessary and sufficient assumptions for non-interactive zero-knowledge proofs of knowledge for all np relations. In: Welzl, E., Montanari, U., Rolim, J.D.P. (eds.) ICALP 2000. LNCS, vol. 1853, pp. 451–462. Springer, Heidelberg (2000)
38. De Santis, A., Persiano, G.: Zero-knowledge proofs of knowledge without interaction. In: Proceedings of the 33rd Annual Symposium on Foundations of Computer Science, pp. 427–436. IEEE (1992)
39. Degabriele, J.P., Lehmann, A., Paterson, K.G., Smart, N.P., Strefler, M.: On the joint security of encryption and signature in EMV. In: Dunkelman, O. (ed.) CT-RSA 2012. LNCS, vol. 7178, pp. 116–135. Springer, Heidelberg (2012)
40. Dodis, Y., Haralambiev, K., López-Alt, A., Wichs, D.: Efficient public-key cryptography in the presence of key leakage. In: Abe, M. (ed.) ASIACRYPT 2010. LNCS, vol. 6477, pp. 613–631. Springer, Heidelberg (2010)
41. Fan, J., Zheng, Y., Tang, X.: A single key pair is adequate for the zheng signcryption. In: Parampalli, U., Hawkes, P. (eds.) ACISP 2011. LNCS, vol. 6812, pp. 371–388. Springer, Heidelberg (2011)
42. Galindo, D., Herranz, J., Villar, J.: Identity-based encryption with master key-dependent message security and leakage-resilience. In: Foresti, S., Yung, M., Martinelli, F. (eds.) ESORICS 2012. LNCS, vol. 7459, pp. 627–642. Springer, Heidelberg (2012)
43. Garg, S., Gentry, C., Sahai, A., Waters, B.: Witness encryption and its applications. In: Proceedings of the 45th annual ACM Symposium on Symposium on theory of Computing, pp. 467–476. ACM (2013)
44. Gennaro, R., Lysyanskaya, A., Malkin, T., Micali, S., Rabin, T.: Algorithmic tamper-proof (ATP) security: Theoretical foundations for security against hardware tampering. In: Naor, M. (ed.) TCC 2004. LNCS, vol. 2951, pp. 258–277. Springer, Heidelberg (2004)
45. Goldenberg, D., Liskov, M.: On related-secret pseudorandomness. In: Micciancio, D. (ed.) TCC 2010. LNCS, vol. 5978, pp. 255–272. Springer, Heidelberg (2010)

46. Goldwasser, S., Micali, S., Rivest, R.L.: A digital signature scheme secure against adaptive chosen-message attacks. SIAM Journal on Computing 17(2), 281–308 (1988)
47. Groth, J.: Simulation-sound NIZK proofs for a practical language and constant size group signatures. In: Lai, X., Chen, K. (eds.) ASIACRYPT 2006. LNCS, vol. 4284, pp. 444–459. Springer, Heidelberg (2006)
48. Groth, J., Ostrovsky, R.: Cryptography in the multi-string model. In: Menezes, A. (ed.) CRYPTO 2007. LNCS, vol. 4622, pp. 323–341. Springer, Heidelberg (2007)
49. Haber, S., Pinkas, B.: Securely combining public-key cryptosystems. In: ACM CCS 2001, pp. 215–224. ACM Press (November 2001)
50. Haralambiev, K.: Efficient Cryptographic Primitives for Non-Interactive Zero-Knowledge Proofs and Applications. PhD thesis, New York University (May 2011)
51. Hofheinz, D.: Circular chosen-ciphertext security with compact ciphertexts. In: Johansson, T., Nguyen, P.Q. (eds.) EUROCRYPT 2013. LNCS, vol. 7881, pp. 520–536. Springer, Heidelberg (2013)
52. Knudsen, L.R.: Cryptanalysis of LOKI91. In: Zheng, Y., Seberry, J. (eds.) AUSCRYPT 1992. LNCS, vol. 718, pp. 196–208. Springer, Heidelberg (1993)
53. Komano, Y., Ohta, K.: Efficient universal padding techniques for multiplicative trapdoor one-way permutation. In: Boneh, D. (ed.) CRYPTO 2003. LNCS, vol. 2729, pp. 366–382. Springer, Heidelberg (2003)
54. Kurosawa, K., Desmedt, Y.G.: A new paradigm of hybrid encryption scheme. In: Franklin, M. (ed.) CRYPTO 2004. LNCS, vol. 3152, pp. 426–442. Springer, Heidelberg (2004)
55. Malkin, T., Teranishi, I., Yung, M.: Efficient circuit-size independent public key encryption with KDM security. In: Paterson, K.G. (ed.) EUROCRYPT 2011. LNCS, vol. 6632, pp. 507–526. Springer, Heidelberg (2011)
56. Muñiz, M.G., Steinwandt, R.: Security of signature schemes in the presence of key-dependent messages. Tatra Mt. Math. Publ. 47, 15–29 (2010)
57. Paterson, K.G., Schuldt, J.C.N., Stam, M., Thomson, S.: On the joint security of encryption and signature, revisited. In: Lee, D.H., Wang, X. (eds.) ASIACRYPT 2011. LNCS, vol. 7073, pp. 161–178. Springer, Heidelberg (2011)
58. Rogaway, P.: Authenticated-encryption with associated-data. In: Atluri, V. (ed.) ACM CCS 2002, pp. 98–107. ACM Press (November 2002)
59. Rompel, J.: One-way functions are necessary and sufficient for secure signatures. In: 22nd ACM STOC, pp. 387–394. ACM Press (May 1990)
60. Sahai, A.: Non-malleable non-interactive zero knowledge and adaptive chosen-ciphertext security. In: 40th FOCS, pp. 543–553. IEEE Computer Society Press (October 1999)
61. Waters, B.: Efficient identity-based encryption without random oracles. In: Cramer, R. (ed.) EUROCRYPT 2005. LNCS, vol. 3494, pp. 114–127. Springer, Heidelberg (2005)
62. Zheng, Y.: Digital signcryption or how to achieve cost(signature & encryption) << cost(signature) + cost(encryption). In: Kaliski Jr., B.S. (ed.) CRYPTO 1997. LNCS, vol. 1294, pp. 165–179. Springer, Heidelberg (1997)

Non-malleability from Malleability: Simulation-Sound Quasi-Adaptive NIZK Proofs and CCA2-Secure Encryption from Homomorphic Signatures

Benoît Libert[1], Thomas Peters[2,*], Marc Joye[1], and Moti Yung[3]

[1] Technicolor
[2] Université catholique de Louvain, Crypto Group
[3] Google Inc. and Columbia University

Abstract. Verifiability is central to building protocols and systems with integrity. Initially, efficient methods employed the Fiat-Shamir heuristics. Since 2008, the Groth-Sahai techniques have been the most efficient in constructing non-interactive witness indistinguishable and zero-knowledge proofs for algebraic relations in the standard model. For the important task of proving membership in linear subspaces, Jutla and Roy (Asiacrypt 2013) gave significantly more efficient proofs in the quasi-adaptive setting (QA-NIZK). For membership of the row space of a $t \times n$ matrix, their QA-NIZK proofs save $\Omega(t)$ group elements compared to Groth-Sahai. Here, we give QA-NIZK proofs made of a *constant* number group elements – regardless of the number of equations or the number of variables – and additionally prove them *unbounded* simulation-sound. Unlike previous unbounded simulation-sound Groth-Sahai-based proofs, our construction does not involve quadratic pairing product equations and does not rely on a chosen-ciphertext-secure encryption scheme. Instead, we build on structure-preserving signatures with homomorphic properties. We apply our methods to design new and improved CCA2-secure encryption schemes. In particular, we build the first efficient threshold CCA-secure keyed-homomorphic encryption scheme (*i.e.*, where homomorphic operations can only be carried out using a dedicated evaluation key) with publicly verifiable ciphertexts.

1   Introduction

Non-interactive zero-knowledge proofs [6] play a fundamental role in the design of numerous cryptographic protocols. Unfortunately, until breakthrough results in the last decade [19–21], it was not known how to construct them efficiently without appealing to the random oracle methodology [5]. Groth and Sahai [21] described very efficient non-interactive witness indistinguishable (NIWI) and zero-knowledge (NIZK) proof systems for algebraic relations in groups equipped with a bilinear map. For these specific languages, the methodology of [21] does

---

* This author was supported by the CAMUS Walloon Region Project.

P.Q. Nguyen and E. Oswald (Eds.): EUROCRYPT 2014, LNCS 8441, pp. 514–532, 2014.

not require any proof of circuit satisfiability but rather leverages the properties of homomorphic commitments in bilinear groups. As a result, the length of each proof only depends on the number of equations and the number of variables.

While dramatically more efficient than general NIZK proofs, the GS techniques remain significantly more expensive than non-interactive proofs obtained from the Fiat-Shamir heuristic [18] in the random oracle model [5]: for example, proving that t variables satisfy a system of n linear equations demands $O(t + n)$ group elements where Σ-protocols allow for $O(t)$-size proofs. In addition, GS proofs are known to be malleable which, although useful in certain applications [3, 11], is undesirable when NIZK proofs serve as building blocks for non-malleable protocols. To construct chosen-ciphertext-secure encryption schemes [35], for example, the Naor-Yung/Sahai [31, 36] paradigm requires NIZK proofs satisfying a property called *simulation-soundness* [36]: informally, this property captures the inability of the adversary to prove false statements, even after having observed simulated proofs for possibly false statements of its choice.

Groth-Sahai proofs can be made simulation-sound using ideas suggested in [20, 9, 22]. However, even when starting from a linear equation, these techniques involve proofs for quadratic equations, which results in longer proofs. One-time simulation-soundness (*i.e.*, where the adversary only sees one simulated proof) is more economical to achieve as shown in [25, 26]. Jutla and Roy suggested a more efficient way to achieve a form of one-time simulation-soundness [23].

Quasi-Adaptive NIZK Proofs. For languages consisting of linear subspaces of a vector space, Jutla and Roy [24] recently showed how to significantly improve upon the efficiency of the GS paradigm in the *quasi-adaptive* setting. In quasi-adaptive NIZK proofs (QA-NIZK) for a class of languages $\{\mathcal{L}_\rho\}$ parametrized by ρ, the common reference string (CRS) is allowed to depend on the particular language $\mathcal{L}_\rho$ of which membership must be proved. At the same time, a single simulator should be effective for the whole class of languages $\{\mathcal{L}_\rho\}$. As pointed out in [24], QA-NIZK proofs are sufficient for many applications of Groth-Sahai proofs. In this setting, Jutla and Roy [24] gave very efficient QA-NIZK proofs of membership in linear subspaces. If $\mathbf{A} \in \mathbb{Z}_p^{t \times n}$ is a matrix or rank $t < n$, in order to prove membership of the language $\mathcal{L} = \{v \in \mathbb{G}^n \mid \exists x \in \mathbb{Z}_p^t \text{ s.t. } v = g^{x \cdot \mathbf{A}}\}$, the Jutla-Roy proofs only take $O(n - t)$ group elements – instead of $O(n + t)$ in [21] – at the expense of settling for computational soundness. While highly efficient in the case $t \approx n$, these proofs remain of linear size in n and may result in long proofs when $t \ll n$, as is the case in, *e.g.*, certain applications of the Naor-Yung paradigm [9]. In the general case, we are still lacking a method for building proofs of size $O(t)$ – at least without relying on non-falsifiable assumptions [30] – which contrasts with the situation in the random oracle model.

The problem is even harder if we aim for simulation-soundness. While the Jutla-Roy solutions [24] nicely interact with their one-time simulation-sound proofs [23], they do not seem to readily extend into unbounded simulation-sound (USS) proofs (where the adversary can see an arbitrary number of simulated proofs before outputting a proof of its own) while retaining the same efficiency. For this reason, although they can be applied in specific cases like [9], we cannot always use them in a modular way to build IND-CCA2-secure encryption schemes when security definitions involve many challenge ciphertexts.

Our Contributions. Recently [27], it was observed that structure-preserving signatures (SPS) [2, 1] with homomorphic properties have unexpected applications in the design of non-malleable structure-preserving commitments. Here, we greatly extend their range of applications and demonstrate that they can surprisingly be used (albeit non-generically) in the design of strongly non-malleable primitives like simulation-sound proofs and CCA2-secure cryptosystems.

Concretely, we describe unbounded simulation-sound QA-NIZK proofs of *constant-size* for linear subspaces. The length of a proof does not depend on the number of equations or the number of variables, but only on the underlying assumption. Like those of [24], our proofs are computationally sound under standard assumptions. Somewhat surprisingly, they are even asymptotically shorter than random-oracle-based proofs derived from Σ-protocols.

Moreover, our construction provides *unbounded* simulation-soundness. Under the Decision Linear assumption [7], we obtain QA-NIZK arguments consisting of 15 group elements and a one-time signature with its verification key. As it turns out, it is also the first unbounded simulation-sound proof system that does not involve quadratic pairing product equations or a CCA2-secure encryption scheme. Efficiency comparisons show that we only need 20 group elements per proof where the best USS extension [9] of Groth-Sahai costs $6t + 2n + 52$ group elements. Under the k-linear assumption, the proof length becomes $O(k^2)$ and thus avoids any dependency on the subspace dimension. Our proof system builds on the linearly homomorphic structure-preserving signatures of Libert, Peters, Joye and Yung [27], which allow signing vectors of group elements without knowing their discrete logarithms.

For applications, like CCA2 security [31, 36], where only one-time simulation-soundness is needed, we further optimize our proof system and obtain a relatively simulation-sound QA-NIZK proof system, as defined in [23], with constant-size proofs. Under the DLIN assumption (resp. the k-linear assumption), we achieve relative simulation-soundness with only 4 (resp. $k + 2$) group elements!

As a first application of our USS proofs, we build a chosen-ciphertext-secure keyed-homomorphic system with threshold decryption. Keyed-homomorphic encryption is a primitive, suggested by Emura *et al.* [16], where homomorphic ciphertext manipulations are only possible to a party holding a devoted evaluation key SK_h which, by itself, does not enable decryption. The scheme should provide IND-CCA2 security when the evaluation key is unavailable to the adversary and remain IND-CCA1 secure when SK_h is exposed. Other approaches to reconcile homomorphism and non-malleability were taken in [32–34, 8, 11] but they inevitably satisfy weaker security notions than adaptive chosen-ciphertext security [35]. The results of [16] showed that CCA2-security does not rule out homomorphicity when the capability to compute over encrypted data is restricted.

Emura *et al.* [16] gave chosen-ciphertext-secure keyed-homomorphic schemes based on hash proof systems [13]. However, these do not readily enable threshold decryption – as would be desirable in voting protocols – since valid ciphertexts are not publicly recognizable, which makes it harder to prove CCA security in the threshold setting. Moreover, these solutions are not known to satisfy the strongest security definition of [16]. The reason is that this definition seemingly requires a form of unbounded simulation-soundness. Our QA-NIZK proofs fulfill this requirement and provide an efficient CCA2-secure threshold keyed-homomorphic system where ciphertexts are 65% shorter than in instantiations of the same high-level idea using previous simulation-sound proofs.

Using our relatively simulation-sound QA-NIZK proofs, we build new adaptively secure non-interactive threshold cryptosystems [14, 15] with CCA2 security and improved efficiency. The constructions of [26] were improved by Escala *et al.* [17]. So far, the most efficient solution is obtained from the Jutla-Roy results [23, 24] via relatively sound proofs [23]. Using our relatively sound QA-NIZK proofs, we shorten ciphertexts by $\Theta(k)$ elements under the k-linear assumption.

Our Techniques. In our unbounded simulation-sound proofs, each QA-NIZK proof can be seen as a Groth-Sahai NIWI proof of knowledge of a one-time linearly homomorphic signature on the vector that allegedly belongs to the linear subspace. Here, the NIWI proof is generated for a Groth-Sahai CRS that depends on the verification key of a one-time signature (following an idea of Malkin *et al.* [29] which extends Waters' techniques [38]), the private key of which is used to sign the entire proof so as to prevent re-randomizations. The reason why it provides unbounded simulation-soundness is that, with non-negligible probability, the CRS is perfectly hiding on all simulated proofs and extractable in the adversarially-generated fake proof. Hence, if the adversary manages to prove membership of a vector outside the linear subspace, the reduction is able to extract a homomorphic signature that it would not have been able to compute itself, thereby breaking the DLIN assumption. At a high level, the system can be seen as a two-tier proof system made of a non-malleable proof of knowledge of a malleable proof of membership.

In our optimized relatively-sound proofs, we adapt ideas of Jutla and Roy [23] and combine the one-time linearly homomorphic signature of [27] with a smooth-projective hash function [13].

Our threshold keyed-homomorphic scheme combines a hash proof system and a publicly verifiable USS proof that the ciphertext is well-formed. The keyed-homomorphic property is achieved by using the simulation trapdoor of the proof system as an evaluation key SK_h, allowing the evaluator to generate proofs without the witnesses. As implicitly done in [16] using hash proof systems, the simulation trapdoor is used in the scheme and not only in the security proof.

2   Background and Definitions

2.1   Quasi-Adaptive NIZK Proofs

Quasi-Adaptive NIZK (QA-NIZK) proofs are NIZK proofs where the CRS is allowed to depend on the specific language for which proofs have to be generated. The CRS is divided into a fixed part Γ, produced by an algorithm K_0, and a language-dependent part ψ. However, there should be a single simulator for the entire class of languages.

Let λ be a security parameter. For public parameters Γ produced by K_0, let $\mathcal{D}_\Gamma$ be a probability distribution over a set of relations $\mathcal{R} = \{R_\rho\}$ parametrized by a string ρ with an associated language $\mathcal{L}_\rho = \{x \mid \exists w : R_\rho(x, w) = 1\}$.

We consider proof systems where the prover and the verifier both take a label lbl as additional input. For example, this label can be the message-carrying part of an Elgamal-like encryption. Formally, a tuple of algorithms (K_0, K_1, P, V) is a QA-NIZK proof system for $\mathcal{R}$ if there exists a PPT simulator (S_1, S_2) such that, for any PPT adversaries $\mathcal{A}_1, \mathcal{A}_2$ and $\mathcal{A}_3$, we have the following properties:

Quasi-Adaptive Completeness:

$$\Pr[\Gamma \leftarrow K_0(\lambda); \; \rho \leftarrow \mathcal{D}_\Gamma; \; \psi \leftarrow K_1(\Gamma, \rho); \; (x, w, \mathsf{lbl}) \leftarrow \mathcal{A}_1(\Gamma, \psi, \rho);$$
$$\pi \leftarrow P(\psi, x, w, \mathsf{lbl}) : V(\psi, x, \pi, \mathsf{lbl}) = 1 \text{ if } R_\rho(x, w) = 1] = 1.$$

Quasi-Adaptive Soundness:

$$\Pr[\Gamma \leftarrow K_0(\lambda); \; \rho \leftarrow \mathcal{D}_\Gamma; \; \psi \leftarrow K_1(\Gamma, \rho); \; (x, \pi, \mathsf{lbl}) \leftarrow \mathcal{A}_2(\Gamma, \psi, \rho) :$$
$$V(\psi, x, \pi, \mathsf{lbl}) = 1 \; \wedge \; \neg(\exists w : R_\rho(x, w) = 1)] \in \mathsf{negl}(\lambda).$$

Quasi-Adaptive Zero-Knowledge:

$$\Pr[\Gamma \leftarrow K_0(\lambda); \; \rho \leftarrow \mathcal{D}_\Gamma; \; \psi \leftarrow K_1(\Gamma, \rho) : \; \mathcal{A}_3^{P(\psi, \cdot, \cdot, \cdot)}(\Gamma, \psi, \rho) = 1] \approx$$
$$\Pr[\Gamma \leftarrow K_0(\lambda); \; \rho \leftarrow \mathcal{D}_\Gamma; \; (\psi, \tau_{sim}) \leftarrow S_1(\Gamma, \rho) : \; \mathcal{A}_3^{S(\psi, \tau_{sim}, \cdot, \cdot, \cdot)}(\Gamma, \psi, \rho) = 1],$$

where
- $P(\psi, ., ., .)$ emulates the actual prover. It takes as input (x, w) and lbl and outputs a proof π if $(x, w) \in R_\rho$. Otherwise, it outputs $\perp$.
- $S(\psi, \tau_{sim}, ., ., .)$ is an oracle that takes as input (x, w) and lbl. It outputs a simulated proof $S_2(\psi, \tau_{sim}, x, \mathsf{lbl})$ if $(x, w) \in R_\rho$ and $\perp$ if $(x, w) \notin R_\rho$.

We assume that the CRS ψ contains an encoding of ρ, which is thus available to V. The definition of Quasi-Adaptive Zero-Knowledge requires a single simulator for the entire family of relations $\mathcal{R}$.

2.2 Simulation-Soundness and Relative Soundness

It is often useful to have a property called *simulation-soundness*, which requires that the adversary be unable to prove false statements even after having seen simulated proofs for possibly false statements.

Unbounded Simulation-Soundness: For any PPT adversary $\mathcal{A}_4$,

$$\Pr[\; \Gamma \leftarrow K_0(\lambda); \; \rho \leftarrow \mathcal{D}_\Gamma; \; (\psi, \tau_{sim}) \leftarrow S_1(\Gamma, \rho);$$
$$(x, \pi, \mathsf{lbl}) \leftarrow \mathcal{A}_4^{S_2(\psi, \tau_{sim}, \cdot, \cdot)}(\Gamma, \psi, \rho) \; : \; V(\psi, x, \pi, \mathsf{lbl}) = 1$$
$$\wedge \; \neg(\exists w : R_\rho(x, w) = 1) \; \wedge \; (x, \pi, \mathsf{lbl}) \notin Q] \in \mathsf{negl}(\lambda),$$

where the adversary is allowed unbounded access to an oracle $S_2(\psi, \tau, ., .)$ that takes as input statement-label pairs (x, lbl) (where x may be outside $\mathcal{L}_\rho$) and outputs simulated proofs $\pi \leftarrow S_2(\psi, \tau_{sim}, x, \mathsf{lbl})$ before updating the set $Q = Q \cup \{(x, \pi, \mathsf{lbl})\}$, which is initially empty.

In the weaker notion of one-time simulation-soundness, only one query to the S_2 oracle is allowed.

In some applications, one may settle for a weaker notion, called *relative soundness* by Jutla and Roy [23], which allows for more efficient proofs, especially in the single-theorem case. Informally, relatively sound proof systems involve both a public verifier *and* a private verification algorithm, which has access to a trapdoor. For hard languages, the two verifiers should almost always agree on any adversarially-created proof. Moreover, the private verifier should not accept a non-trivial proof for a false statement, even if the adversary has already seen proofs for false statements.

A labeled single-theorem relatively sound QA-NIZK proof system is comprised of a quasi-adaptive labeled proof system $(\mathsf{K}_0, \mathsf{K}_1, \mathsf{P}, \mathsf{V})$ along with an efficient private verifier W and an efficient simulator $(\mathsf{S}_1, \mathsf{S}_2)$. Moreover, the following properties should hold for any PPT adversaries $(\mathcal{A}_1, \mathcal{A}_2, \mathcal{A}_3, \mathcal{A}_4)$.

Quasi Adaptive Relative Single-Theorem Zero-Knowledge:

$$\Pr[\Gamma \leftarrow \mathsf{K}_0(\lambda); \; \rho \leftarrow D_\Gamma; \; \psi \leftarrow \mathsf{K}_1(\Gamma, \rho); \; (x, w, \mathsf{lbl}, s) \leftarrow$$
$$\mathcal{A}_1^{\mathsf{V}(\psi, \cdot, \cdot)}(\Gamma, \psi, \rho); \pi \leftarrow \mathsf{P}(\psi, \rho, x, w, \mathsf{lbl}) : \mathcal{A}_2^{\mathsf{V}(\psi, \cdot, \cdot)}(\pi, s) = 1]$$
$$\approx \Pr[\Gamma \leftarrow \mathsf{K}_0(\lambda); \; \rho \leftarrow D_\Gamma; \; (\psi, \tau) \leftarrow \mathsf{S}_1(\Gamma, \rho); \; (x, w, \mathsf{lbl}, s) \leftarrow$$
$$\mathcal{A}_1^{\mathsf{W}(\psi, \tau, \cdot, \cdot)}(\Gamma, \psi, \rho); \pi \leftarrow \mathsf{S}_2(\psi, \rho, \tau, x, \mathsf{lbl}) : \mathcal{A}_2^{\mathsf{W}(\psi, \tau, \cdot, \cdot)}(\pi, s) = 1],$$

Here, $\mathcal{A}_1$ is restricted to choosing (x, w) such that $R_\rho(x, w) = 1$.

Quasi Adaptive Relative Single-Theorem Simulation-Soundness:

$$\Pr[\Gamma \leftarrow \mathsf{K}_0(\lambda); \; \rho \leftarrow D_\Gamma; \; (\psi, \tau) \leftarrow \mathsf{S}_1(\Gamma, \rho); \; (x, \mathsf{lbl}, s) \leftarrow \mathcal{A}_3^{\mathsf{W}(\psi, \tau, \cdot, \cdot)}(\Gamma, \psi, \rho);$$
$$\pi \leftarrow \mathsf{S}_2(\psi, \rho, \tau, x, \mathsf{lbl}) : (x', \mathsf{lbl}', \pi') \leftarrow \mathcal{A}_4^{\mathsf{W}(\psi, \tau, \cdot, \cdot)}(s, \pi) : (x, \pi, \mathsf{lbl}) \neq (x', \pi', \mathsf{lbl}')$$
$$\wedge \; \nexists w' \text{ s.t. } R_\rho(x', w') = 1 \; \wedge \; \mathsf{W}(\psi, \tau, x', \mathsf{lbl}', \pi') = 1] \in \mathsf{negl}(\lambda)$$

2.3   Definitions for Threshold Keyed-Homomorphic Encryption

A (t, N)-threshold keyed-homomorphic encryption scheme consists of the following algorithms.

Keygen(λ, t, N): inputs a security parameter λ and integers $t, N \in \mathsf{poly}(\lambda)$ (with $1 \leq t \leq N$), where N is the number of decryption servers and $t \leq N$ is the decryption threshold. It outputs a public key PK, a homomorphic evaluation key SK_h, a vector of private key shares $\mathbf{SK}_d = (SK_{d,1}, \ldots, SK_{d,N})$ and a vector of verification keys $\mathbf{VK} = (VK_1, \ldots, VK_N)$. For each i, the decryption server i is given the share $(i, SK_{d,i})$. The verification key VK_i will be used to check the validity of decryption shares generated using $SK_{d,i}$.

Encrypt(PK, M): takes a input a public key PK and a plaintext M. It outputs a ciphertext C.

Ciphertext-Verify(PK, C): takes as input a public key PK and a ciphertext C. It outputs 1 if C is deemed valid w.r.t. PK and 0 otherwise.

Share-Decrypt$(PK, i, SK_{d,i}, C)$: on input of a public key PK, a ciphertext C and a private-key share $(i, SK_{d,i})$, this (possibly randomized) algorithm outputs a special symbol $(i, \perp)$ if **Ciphertext-Verify**$(PK, C) = 0$. Otherwise, it outputs a decryption share $\mu_i = (i, \hat{\mu}_i)$.

Share-Verify(PK, VK_i, C, μ_i): takes in PK, the verification key VK_i, a ciphertext C and a purported decryption share $\mu_i = (i, \hat{\mu}_i)$. It outputs either 1 or 0. In the former case, μ_i is said to be a *valid* decryption share. We adopt the convention that $(i, \perp)$ is an invalid decryption share.

Combine$(PK, \mathbf{VK}, C, \{\mu_i\}_{i \in S})$: takes as input $(PK, \mathbf{VK}, C)$ and a t-subset $S \subset \{1, \ldots, N\}$ with decryption shares $\{\mu_i\}_{i \in S}$. It outputs either a plaintext M or $\perp$ if $\{\mu_i\}_{i \in S}$ contains invalid shares.

Eval$(PK, SK_h, C^{(1)}, C^{(2)})$: takes as input PK, the evaluation key SK_h and ciphertexts $C^{(1)}$, $C^{(2)}$. If **Ciphertext-Verify**$(PK, C^{(j)}) = 0$ for some $j \in \{1, 2\}$, the algorithm returns $\perp$. Otherwise, it conducts a binary homomorphic operation over $C^{(1)}$ and $C^{(2)}$ and outputs a ciphertext C.

The above syntax assumes a trusted dealer. It generalizes that of ordinary threshold cryptosystems. By setting $SK_h = \varepsilon$ and discarding the evaluation algorithm, we obtain a classical threshold system.

Definition 1. *A threshold keyed-homomorphic public-key cryptosystem is secure against chosen-ciphertext attacks (or KH-CCA secure) if no PPT adversary has noticeable advantage in this game:*

1. *The challenger runs* **Keygen**(λ) *to obtain a public key PK, vectors* $\mathbf{SK}_d$ *and* $\mathbf{VK}$ *and a homomorphic evaluation key SK_h. It gives PK and* $\mathbf{VK}$ *to the adversary $\mathcal{A}$ and keeps $(SK_h, \mathbf{SK}_d)$ to itself. In addition, the challenge initializes a set $\mathcal{D} \leftarrow \emptyset$, which is initially empty.*

2. *On multiple occasions, $\mathcal{A}$ adaptively invokes the following oracles:*
   - *Corruption query: at any time, $\mathcal{A}$ may decide to corrupt a decryption server. To this end, it specifies an index $i \in \{1, \ldots, N\}$ and obtains the private key share $SK_{d,i}$.*
   - *Evaluation query: $\mathcal{A}$ can invoke the evaluation oracle* Eval$(SK_h, .)$ *on a pair $(C^{(1)}, C^{(2)})$ of ciphertexts of its choice. If there exists $j \in \{1, 2\}$ such that* **Ciphertext-Verify**$(PK, C^{(j)}) = 0$, *return $\perp$. Otherwise, the oracle* Eval$(SK_h, .)$ *computes $C \leftarrow$* **Eval**$(SK_h, C^{(1)}, C^{(2)})$ *and returns C. In addition, if $C^{(1)} \in \mathcal{D}$ or $C^{(2)} \in \mathcal{D}$, it sets $\mathcal{D} \leftarrow \mathcal{D} \cup \{C\}$.*
   - *Reveal query: at any time, $\mathcal{A}$ may also decide to corrupt the evaluator by invoking the* RevHK *oracle on a unique occasion. The oracle responds by returning SK_h.*
   - *Partial decryption query: $\mathcal{A}$ can also choose arbitrary ciphertexts C and indexes $i \in \{1, \ldots, n\}$. If* **Ciphertext-Verify**$(PK, C) = 0$ *or if $C \in \mathcal{D}$, the oracle returns $\perp$. Otherwise, the oracle returns the decryption share $\mu_i \leftarrow$* **Share-Decrypt**$(PK, i, SK_{d,i}, C)$.*

3. *The adversary $\mathcal{A}$ chooses two equal-length messages M_0, M_1 and obtains $C^* = \mathbf{Encrypt}(PK, M_\beta)$ for some random bit $\beta \xleftarrow{R} \{0, 1\}$. In addition, the challenger sets $\mathcal{D} \leftarrow \mathcal{D} \cup \{C^*\}$.*

4. *$\mathcal{A}$ makes further queries as in step 2 with some restrictions. Namely, $\mathcal{A}$ cannot corrupt more than $t-1$ servers throughout the entire game. Moreover, if $\mathcal{A}$ chooses to obtain SK_h (via the RevHK oracle) at some point, no more post-challenge decryption query is allowed beyond that point.*

5. *$\mathcal{A}$ outputs a bit β' and is deemed successful if $\beta' = \beta$. As usual, $\mathcal{A}$'s advantage is measured as the distance $\mathbf{Adv}(\mathcal{A}) = |\Pr[\beta' = \beta] - \frac{1}{2}|$.*

Note that, even if $\mathcal{A}$ chooses to obtain SK_h immediately after having seen the public key PK, it still has access to the decryption oracle *before* the challenge phase. In other words, the scheme should remain IND-CCA1 if $\mathcal{A}$ is given PK and SK_h at the outset of the game. After the challenge phase, decryption queries are allowed until the moment when the adversary obtains SK_h.

In [16], Emura *et al.* suggested a weaker definition where the adversary is not allowed to query the evaluation oracle on derivatives of the challenge ciphertext. As a consequence, the set $\mathcal{D}$ is always the singleton $\{C^*\}$ after step 3. In this paper, we will stick to the stronger definition.

2.4 Hardness Assumptions

We will use symmetric bilinear maps $e : \mathbb{G} \times \mathbb{G} \to \mathbb{G}_T$ over groups of prime order p, but extensions to the asymmetric setting $e : \mathbb{G} \times \hat{\mathbb{G}} \to \mathbb{G}_T$ are possible.

Definition 2 ([7]). *The **Decision Linear Problem** (DLIN) in $\mathbb{G}$, is to distinguish the distributions $(g^a, g^b, g^{ac}, g^{bd}, g^{c+d})$ and $(g^a, g^b, g^{ac}, g^{bd}, g^z)$, where $a, b, c, d \xleftarrow{R} \mathbb{Z}_p, z \xleftarrow{R} \mathbb{Z}_p$.*

We sometimes use the Simultaneous Double Pairing (SDP) assumption, which is weaker than DLIN. As noted in [10], any algorithm solving SDP immediately yields a DLIN distinguisher.

Definition 3. *The **Simultaneous Double Pairing** problem (SDP) in $(\mathbb{G}, \mathbb{G}_T)$ is, given group elements $(g_z, g_r, h_z, h_u) \in \mathbb{G}^4$, to find a non-trivial triple $(z, r, u) \in \mathbb{G}^3 \setminus \{(1_\mathbb{G}, 1_\mathbb{G}, 1_\mathbb{G})\}$ such that $e(g_z, z) \cdot e(g_r, r) = 1_{\mathbb{G}_T}$ and $e(h_z, z) \cdot e(h_u, u) = 1_{\mathbb{G}_T}$.*

2.5 Linearly Homomorphic Structure-Preserving Signatures

Linearly homomorphic SPS schemes are homomorphic signatures where messages and signatures live in the domain group $\mathbb{G}$ (see [27] for syntactic definitions) of a bilinear map. Libert *et al.* [27] described the following one-time construction and proved its security under the SDP assumption. By "one-time", we mean that only one linear subspace can be signed using a given key pair.

Keygen(λ, n): given a security parameter λ and the dimension $n \in \mathbb{N}$ of vectors to be signed, choose bilinear group $(\mathbb{G}, \mathbb{G}_T)$ of prime order $p > 2^\lambda$. Choose $g_z, g_r, h_z, h_u \xleftarrow{R} \mathbb{G}$. Then, for $i = 1$ to n, pick $\chi_i, \gamma_i, \delta_i \xleftarrow{R} \mathbb{Z}_p$ and compute $g_i = g_z{}^{\chi_i} g_r{}^{\gamma_i}$ and $h_i = h_z{}^{\chi_i} h_u{}^{\delta_i}$. The private key is $\mathsf{sk} = \{(\chi_i, \gamma_i, \delta_i)\}_{i=1}^n$ while the public key is $\mathsf{pk} = (g_z, g_r, h_z, h_u, \{(g_i, h_i)\}_{i=1}^n)$.

Sign($\mathsf{sk}, (M_1, \ldots, M_n)$): to sign $(M_1, \ldots, M_n) \in \mathbb{G}^n$ using $\mathsf{sk} = \{(\chi_i, \gamma_i, \delta_i)\}_{i=1}^n$, return $(z, r, u) = \left(\prod_{i=1}^n M_i^{-\chi_i}, \prod_{i=1}^n M_i^{-\gamma_i}, \prod_{i=1}^n M_i^{-\delta_i}\right) \in \mathbb{G}^3$.

SignDerive($\mathsf{pk}, \{(\omega_i, \sigma^{(i)})\}_{i=1}^\ell$): given a public key pk and ℓ tuples $(\omega_i, \sigma^{(i)})$, where $\omega_i \in \mathbb{Z}_p$ for each i, parse $\sigma^{(i)}$ as $\sigma^{(i)} = (z_i, r_i, u_i) \in \mathbb{G}^3$ for $i = 1$ to ℓ. Then, compute and return $\sigma = (z, r, u) = \left(\prod_{i=1}^\ell z_i^{\omega_i}, \prod_{i=1}^\ell r_i^{\omega_i}, \prod_{i=1}^\ell u_i^{\omega_i}\right)$.

Verify($\mathsf{pk}, \sigma, (M_1, \ldots, M_n)$): given a signature $\sigma = (z, r, u) \in \mathbb{G}^3$ and a vector $(M_1, \ldots, M_n)$, return 1 if and only if $(M_1, \ldots, M_n) \neq (1_{\mathbb{G}}, \ldots, 1_{\mathbb{G}})$ and (z, r, u) satisfy the equalities $1_{\mathbb{G}_T} = e(g_z, z) \cdot e(g_r, r) \cdot \prod_{i=1}^n e(g_i, M_i)$ and $1_{\mathbb{G}_T} = e(h_z, z) \cdot e(h_u, u) \cdot \prod_{i=1}^n e(h_i, M_i)$.

One particularity of this scheme is that, even if the private key is available, it is difficult to find two distinct signatures on the same vector if the SDP assumption holds: by dividing out the two signatures, one obtains the solution of an SDP instance (g_z, g_r, h_z, h_u) contained in the public key.

Two constructions of full-fledged (as opposed to one-time) linearly homomorphic SPS were given in [27]. One of these will serve as a basis for our proof system. In these constructions, all algorithms additionally input a tag which identifies the dataset that vectors belongs to. Importantly, only vectors associated with the same tag can be homomorphically combined.

3   Unbounded Simulation-Sound Quasi-Adaptive NIZK Arguments

In the following, vectors are always considered as row vectors unless stated otherwise. If $\mathbf{A} \in \mathbb{Z}_p^{t \times n}$ is a matrix, we denote by $g^{\mathbf{A}} \in \mathbb{G}^{t \times n}$ the matrix obtained by exponentiating g using the entries of $\mathbf{A}$.

We consider public parameters $\Gamma = (\mathbb{G}, \mathbb{G}_T, g)$ consisting of bilinear groups $(\mathbb{G}, \mathbb{G}_T)$ with a generator $g \in \mathbb{G}$. Like [24], we will consider languages $\mathcal{L}_\rho = \{g^{\boldsymbol{x} \cdot \mathbf{A}} \in \mathbb{G}^n \mid \boldsymbol{x} \in \mathbb{Z}_p^t\}$ that are parametrized by $\rho = g^{\mathbf{A}} \in \mathbb{G}^{t \times n}$, where $\mathbf{A} \in \mathbb{Z}_q^{t \times n}$ is a $t \times n$ matrix of rank $t < n$.

As in [24], we assume that the distribution $\mathcal{D}_\Gamma$ is efficiently samplable: there exists a PPT algorithm which outputs a pair $(\rho, \mathbf{A})$ describing a relation R_ρ and its associated language $\mathcal{L}_\rho$ according to $\mathcal{D}_\Gamma$. One example of such a distribution is obtained by picking a uniform matrix $\mathbf{A} \xleftarrow{R} \mathbb{Z}_p^{t \times n}$ – which has full rank with overwhelming probability – and setting $\rho = g^{\mathbf{A}}$.

Our construction builds on the homomorphic signature recalled in Section 2.5. Specifically, the language-dependent CRS ψ contains one-time linearly homomorphic signatures on the rows of the matrix $\rho \in \mathbb{G}^{t \times n}$. For each vector $\boldsymbol{v} \in \mathcal{L}_\rho$, the prover can use the witness $\boldsymbol{x} \in \mathbb{Z}_p^t$ to derive and prove knowledge of a one-time homomorphic signature (z, r, u) on $\boldsymbol{v}$. This signature (z, r, u) is already a

QA-NIZK proof of membership but it is not simulation-sound. To acquire this property, we follow [29] and generate a NIWI proof of knowledge of (z, r, u) for a Groth-Sahai CRS that depends on the verification key of an ordinary one-time signature. The latter's private key is used to sign the NIWI proof so as to prevent unwanted proof manipulations. Using the private key of the homomorphic one-time signature as a trapdoor, the simulator is also able to create proofs for vectors $\boldsymbol{v} \notin \mathcal{L}_\rho$. Due to the use of perfectly NIWI proofs, these fake proofs do not leak any more information about the simulation key than the CRS does. At the same time, the CRS can be prepared in such a way that, with non-negligible probability, it becomes perfectly binding on an adversarially-generated proof, which allows extracting a non-trivial signature on a vector $\boldsymbol{v} \notin \mathcal{L}_\rho$.

Like [24], our quasi-adaptive NIZK proof system $(\mathsf{K}_0, \mathsf{K}_1, \mathsf{P}, \mathsf{V})$ is a split CRS construction in that K_1 can be divided into two algorithms $(\mathsf{K}_{10}, \mathsf{K}_{11})$. The first one K_{10} outputs some state information s and a first CRS $\mathbf{CRS}_2$ which is only used by the verifier and does not depend on the language $\mathcal{L}_\rho$. The second part K_{11} of K_1 inputs the state information s and the output of Γ of K_0 and outputs $\mathbf{CRS}_1$ which is only used by the prover. The construction goes as follows.

$\mathsf{K}_0(\lambda)$: choose groups $(\mathbb{G}, \mathbb{G}_T)$ of prime order $p > 2^\lambda$ with $g \xleftarrow{R} \mathbb{G}$. Then, output
$$\Gamma = (\mathbb{G}, \mathbb{G}_T, g)$$

The dimensions (t, n) of the matrix $\mathbf{A} \in \mathbb{Z}_p^{t \times n}$ can be either fixed or part of the language, so that t, n can be given as input to the CRS generation algorithm K_1.

$\mathsf{K}_1(\Gamma, \rho)$: parse Γ as $(\mathbb{G}, \mathbb{G}_T, g)$ and ρ as a matrix $\rho = (G_{i,j})_{1 \leq i \leq t, \ 1 \leq j \leq n} \in \mathbb{G}^{t \times n}$.

1. Generate a key pair $(\mathsf{pk}_{ots}, \mathsf{sk}_{ots})$ for the homomorphic signature of Section 2.5 in order to sign vectors of $\mathbb{G}^n$ and incorporate a set of Groth-Sahai common reference strings in the public key pk_{ots}. In details:

   a. Choose $g_z, g_r, h_z, h_u \xleftarrow{R} \mathbb{G}$. For $i = 1$ to n, pick $\chi_i, \gamma_i, \delta_i \xleftarrow{R} \mathbb{Z}_p$ and compute $g_i = g_z{}^{\chi_i} g_r{}^{\gamma_i}$ and $h_i = h_z{}^{\chi_i} h_u{}^{\delta_i}$.

   b. Generate $L + 1$ Groth-Sahai CRSes, for some $L \in \mathsf{poly}(\lambda)$. To this end, choose $f_1, f_2 \xleftarrow{R} \mathbb{G}$ and define vectors $\boldsymbol{f}_1 = (f_1, 1, g) \in \mathbb{G}^3$, $\boldsymbol{f}_2 = (1, f_2, g) \in \mathbb{G}^3$. Then, pick $\boldsymbol{f}_{3,i} \xleftarrow{R} \mathbb{G}^3$ for $i = 0$ to L.

   Let $\mathsf{sk}_{ots} = \{(\chi_i, \gamma_i, \delta_i)\}_{i=1}^n$ be the private key and the public key is
   $$\mathsf{pk}_{ots} = \Big(g_z, \ g_r, \ h_z, \ h_u, \ \{(g_i, h_i)\}_{i=1}^n, \ \mathbf{f} = (\boldsymbol{f}_1, \boldsymbol{f}_2, \{\boldsymbol{f}_{3,i}\}_{i=0}^L) \Big).$$

2. Use sk_{ots} to generate one-time homomorphic signatures $\{(z_i, r_i, u_i)\}_{i=1}^t$ on the rows $\boldsymbol{\rho}_i = (G_{i1}, \ldots, G_{in}) \in \mathbb{G}^n$ of ρ. These are obtained as $(z_i, r_i, u_i) = \big(\prod_{j=1}^n G_{i,j}^{-\chi_j}, \prod_{j=1}^n G_{i,j}^{-\gamma_j}, \prod_{j=1}^n G_{i,j}^{-\delta_j} \big)$ for all $i \in \{1, \ldots, t\}$.

3. Choose a strongly unforgeable one-time signature $\Sigma = (\mathcal{G}, \mathcal{S}, \mathcal{V})$ with verification keys consisting of L-bit strings.

4. The CRS $\psi = (\mathbf{CRS}_1, \mathbf{CRS}_2)$ consists of two parts which are defined as
   $$\mathbf{CRS}_1 = \Big(\rho, \ \mathsf{pk}_{ots}, \ \{(z_i, r_i, u_i)\}_{i=1}^t, \ \Sigma \Big), \qquad \mathbf{CRS}_2 = \Big(\mathsf{pk}_{ots}, \ \Sigma \Big),$$

   while the simulation trapdoor τ_{sim} is $\mathsf{sk}_{ots} = \{(\chi_i, \gamma_i, \delta_i)\}_{i=1}^n$.

$\mathsf{P}(\Gamma, \psi, \boldsymbol{v}, x, \mathsf{lbl})$: given $\boldsymbol{v} \in \mathbb{G}^n$ and a witness $\boldsymbol{x} = (x_1, \ldots, x_t) \in \mathbb{Z}_p^t$ such that $\boldsymbol{v} = g^{\boldsymbol{x} \cdot \mathbf{A}}$, generate a one-time signature key pair $(\mathsf{SVK}, \mathsf{SSK}) \leftarrow \mathcal{G}(\lambda)$.

1. Using $\{(z_j, r_j, u_j)\}_{j=1}^t$, derive a one-time linearly homomorphic signature (z, r, u) on $\boldsymbol{v}$. Namely, set $z = \prod_{i=1}^t z_i^{x_i}$, $r = \prod_{i=1}^t r_i^{x_i}$ and $u = \prod_{i=1}^t u_i^{x_i}$.

2. Using $\mathsf{SVK} \in \{0,1\}^L$, define the vector $\boldsymbol{f}_{\mathsf{SVK}} = \boldsymbol{f}_{3,0} \cdot \prod_{i=1}^L \boldsymbol{f}_{3,i}^{\mathsf{SVK}[i]}$ and assemble a Groth-Sahai CRS $\mathsf{f}_{\mathsf{SVK}} = (\boldsymbol{f}_1, \boldsymbol{f}_2, \boldsymbol{f}_{\mathsf{SVK}})$. Using $\mathsf{f}_{\mathsf{SVK}}$, generate commitments $\boldsymbol{C}_z, \boldsymbol{C}_r, \boldsymbol{C}_u$ to the components of (z, r, u) along with NIWI proofs $(\boldsymbol{\pi}_1, \boldsymbol{\pi}_2)$ that (z, r, u) is a valid homomorphic signature for $\boldsymbol{v}$. Let $(\boldsymbol{C}_z, \boldsymbol{C}_r, \boldsymbol{C}_u, \boldsymbol{\pi}_1, \boldsymbol{\pi}_2) \in \mathbb{G}^{15}$ be the resulting commitments and proofs.

3. Generate $\sigma = \mathcal{S}(\mathsf{SSK}, (\boldsymbol{v}, \boldsymbol{C}_z, \boldsymbol{C}_r, \boldsymbol{C}_u, \boldsymbol{\pi}_1, \boldsymbol{\pi}_2, \mathsf{lbl}))$ and output

$$\pi = (\mathsf{SVK}, \boldsymbol{C}_z, \boldsymbol{C}_r, \boldsymbol{C}_u, \boldsymbol{\pi}_1, \boldsymbol{\pi}_2, \sigma) \tag{1}$$

$\mathsf{V}(\Gamma, \psi, \boldsymbol{v}, \pi, \mathsf{lbl})$: parse π as per (1). Return 1 if (i) $(\boldsymbol{C}_z, \boldsymbol{C}_r, \boldsymbol{C}_u, \boldsymbol{\pi}_1, \boldsymbol{\pi}_2)$ forms a valid NIWI proof for the Groth-Sahai CRS $\mathsf{f}_{\mathsf{SVK}} = (\boldsymbol{f}_1, \boldsymbol{f}_2, \boldsymbol{f}_{\mathsf{SVK}})$; (ii) $\mathcal{V}(\mathsf{SVK}, (\boldsymbol{v}, \boldsymbol{C}_z, \boldsymbol{C}_r, \boldsymbol{C}_u, \boldsymbol{\pi}_1, \boldsymbol{\pi}_2, \mathsf{lbl}), \sigma) = 1$. If either condition fails to hold, return 0.

In order to simulate a proof for a given vector $\boldsymbol{v} \in \mathbb{G}^n$, the simulator uses $\tau_{sim} = \mathsf{sk}_{ots}$ to generate a fresh one-time homomorphic signature on $\boldsymbol{v} \in \mathbb{G}^n$ and proceeds as in steps 2-3 of algorithm P.

The proof π only consists of 15 group elements and a one-time pair (SVK, σ). Remarkably, its length does not depend on the number of equations n or the number of variables t. In comparison, Groth-Sahai proofs already require $3t + 2n$ group elements in their basic form and become even more expensive when it comes to achieve unbounded simulation-soundness. The Jutla-Roy techniques [24] reduce the proof length to $2(n-t)$ elements – which only competes with our proofs when $t \approx n$ – but it is unclear how to extend them to get unbounded simulation-soundness without affecting their efficiency. Our CRS consists of $O(t + n + L)$ group elements against $O(t(n - t))$ in [24].

Interestingly, the above scheme even outperforms Fiat-Shamir-like proofs derived from Σ-protocols which would give $O(t)$-size proofs here. The construction readily extends to rely on the k-linear assumption for $k > 2$. In this case, the proof comprises $(k + 1)(2k + 1)$ elements and its size thus only depends on k.

The verification algorithm only involves *linear* pairing product equations whereas all known unbounded simulation-sound extensions of GS proofs require either quadratic equations or a linearization step involving extra variables.

We finally remark that, if we give up the simulation-soundness property, the proof length drops to $k + 1$ group elements under the k-linear assumption.

Theorem 1. *The scheme is an unbounded simulation-sound QA-NIZK proof system if the DLIN assumption holds in $\mathbb{G}$ and Σ is strongly unforgeable.* (The proof is given in the full version of the paper [28]).

We note that the above construction is not tightly secure as the gap between the simulation-soundness adversary's advantage and the probability to break the DLIN assumption depends on the number of simulated proofs obtained by the adversary. For applications like tightly secure public-key encryption [22], it would be interesting to modify the proof system to obtain tight security.

4   Single-Theorem Relatively Sound Quasi-Adaptive NIZK Arguments

In applications where single-theorem relatively sound NIZK proofs suffice, we can further improve the efficiency. Under the k-linear assumption, the proof length reduces from $O(k^2)$ elements to $O(k)$ elements. Under the DLIN assumption, each proof fits within 4 elements and only costs $2n + 6$ pairings to verify. In comparison, the verifier needs $2(n - t)(t + 2)$ pairing evaluations in [24].

As in [23], we achieve relative soundness using smooth projective hash functions [13]. To this end, we encode the matrix $\rho \in \mathbb{G}^{t \times n}$ as a $2t \times (2n + 1)$ matrix.

$\mathsf{K}_0(\lambda)$: choose groups $(\mathbb{G}, \mathbb{G}_T)$ of prime order $p > 2^\lambda$ with $g \xleftarrow{R} \mathbb{G}$. Then, output $\Gamma = (\mathbb{G}, \mathbb{G}_T, g)$.

Again, the dimensions of $\mathbf{A} \in \mathbb{Z}_p^{t \times n}$ can be either fixed or part of $\mathcal{L}_\rho$, so that t, n can be given as input to the CRS generation algorithm K_1.

$\mathsf{K}_1(\Gamma, \rho)$: parse Γ as $(\mathbb{G}, \mathbb{G}_T, g)$ and ρ as $\rho = \left(G_{ij}\right)_{1 \leq i \leq t,\ 1 \leq j \leq n} \in \mathbb{G}^{t \times n}$.

1. Choose vectors $\boldsymbol{d} = (d_1, \ldots, d_n) \xleftarrow{R} \mathbb{Z}_p^n$ and $\boldsymbol{e} = (e_1, \ldots, e_n) \xleftarrow{R} \mathbb{Z}_p^n$. Define $\boldsymbol{W} = (W_1, \ldots, W_t) = g^{\mathbf{A} \cdot \boldsymbol{d}^\top} \in \mathbb{G}^t$ and $\boldsymbol{Y} = (Y_1, \ldots, Y_t) = g^{\mathbf{A} \cdot \boldsymbol{e}^\top} \in \mathbb{G}^t$, which will be used to define a projective hash function.

2. Generate a key pair for the one-time homomorphic signature of Section 2.5 in order to sign vectors in $\mathbb{G}^{2n+1}$. Let $\mathsf{sk}_{ots} = \{(\chi_i, \gamma_i, \delta_i)\}_{i=1}^{2n+1}$ be the private key and let $\mathsf{pk}_{ots} = \left((\mathbb{G}, \mathbb{G}_T), g_z, g_r, h_z, h_u, \{(g_i, h_i)\}_{i=1}^{2n+1}\right)$ be the corresponding public key.

3. Use sk_{ots} to generate one-time homomorphic signatures $\{(z_i, r_i, u_i)\}_{i=1}^{2t}$ on the independent vectors below, which are obtained from the rows of the matrix $\rho = \left(G_{i,j}\right)_{1 \leq i \leq t,\ 1 \leq j \leq n}$.

$$\boldsymbol{H}_{2i-1} = (G_{i,1}, \ldots, G_{i,n}, Y_i,\ 1,\quad \ldots\quad ,1\ ) \in \mathbb{G}^{2n+1} \qquad i \in \{1, \ldots, t\}$$
$$\boldsymbol{H}_{2i} = (1,\quad \ldots\quad ,1\ , W_i, G_{i,1}, \ldots, G_{i,n}) \in \mathbb{G}^{2n+1}$$

4. Choose a collision-resistant hash function $H : \{0,1\}^* \to \mathbb{Z}_p$.
5. The CRS $\psi = (\mathbf{CRS}_1, \mathbf{CRS}_2)$ consists of a first part $\mathbf{CRS}_1$ that is only used by the prover and a second part $\mathbf{CRS}_2$ which is only used by the verifier. These are defined as $\mathbf{CRS}_2 = \left(\mathsf{pk}_{ots}, \boldsymbol{W}, \boldsymbol{Y}, H\right)$ and

$$\mathbf{CRS}_1 = \left(\rho,\ \mathsf{pk}_{ots}, \boldsymbol{W}, \boldsymbol{Y}, \{(z_i, r_i, u_i)\}_{i=1}^{2t}, H\right).$$

The simulation trapdoor τ_{sim} is sk_{ots} and the private verification trapdoor is $\tau_v = \{\boldsymbol{d}, \boldsymbol{e}\}$.

$P(\Gamma, \psi, \boldsymbol{v}, \boldsymbol{x}, \mathsf{lbl})$: given $\boldsymbol{v} \in \mathbb{G}^n$, a witness $\boldsymbol{x} = (x_1, \ldots, x_t) \in \mathbb{Z}_p^t$ such that $\boldsymbol{v} = g^{\boldsymbol{x} \cdot \mathbf{A}}$ and a label lbl, compute $\alpha = H(\rho, \boldsymbol{v}, \mathsf{lbl}) \in \mathbb{Z}_p$. Then, using $\{(z_i, r_i, u_i)\}_{i=1}^{2t}$, derive a one-time homomorphic signature (z, r, u) on the vector $\tilde{\boldsymbol{v}} = (v_1, \ldots, v_n, \pi_0, v_1^\alpha, \ldots, v_n^\alpha) \in \mathbb{G}^{2n+1}$, where $\pi_0 = \prod_{i=1}^t (W_i^\alpha Y_i)^{x_i}$. Namely, output $\pi = (z, r, u, \pi_0) \in \mathbb{G}^4$, where $z = \prod_{i=1}^t (z_{2i-1} \cdot z_{2i}^\alpha)^{x_i}$, $r = \prod_{i=1}^t (r_{2i-1} \cdot r_{2i}^\alpha)^{x_i}$, $u = \prod_{i=1}^t (u_{2i-1} \cdot u_{2i}^\alpha)^{x_i}$ and $\pi_0 = \prod_{i=1}^t (W_i^\alpha Y_i)^{x_i}$.

$V(\Gamma, \psi, \boldsymbol{v}, \pi, \mathsf{lbl})$: parse $\boldsymbol{v}$ as $(v_1, \ldots, v_n) \in \mathbb{G}^n$ and π as $(z, r, u, \pi_0) \in \mathbb{G}^4$. Compute $\alpha = H(\rho, \boldsymbol{v}, \mathsf{lbl})$ and return 1 if and only if (z, r, u) is a valid signature on $\tilde{\boldsymbol{v}} = (v_1, \ldots, v_n, \pi_0, v_1^\alpha, \ldots, v_n^\alpha) \in \mathbb{G}^{2n+1}$. Namely, it should satisfy the equalities $1_{\mathbb{G}_T} = e(g_z, z) \cdot e(g_r, r) \cdot \prod_{i=1}^n e(g_i \cdot g_{i+n+1}^\alpha, v_i) \cdot e(g_{n+1}, \pi_0)$ and $1_{\mathbb{G}_T} = e(h_z, z) \cdot e(h_u, u) \cdot \prod_{i=1}^n e(h_i \cdot h_{i+n+1}^\alpha, v_i) \cdot e(h_{n+1}, \pi_0)$.

$W(\Gamma, \psi, \tau_v, \boldsymbol{v}, \pi, \mathsf{lbl})$: given $\boldsymbol{v} = (v_1, \ldots, v_n) \in \mathbb{G}^n$, parse π as $(z, r, u, \pi_0) \in \mathbb{G}^4$ and τ_v as $\{\boldsymbol{d}, \boldsymbol{e}\}$, with $\boldsymbol{d} = (d_1, \ldots, d_n) \in \mathbb{Z}_p^n$ and $\boldsymbol{e} = (e_1, \ldots, e_n) \in \mathbb{Z}_p^n$. Compute $\alpha = H(\rho, \boldsymbol{v}, \mathsf{lbl}) \in \mathbb{Z}_p$ and return 0 if the public verification test V fails. Otherwise, return 1 if $\pi_0 = \prod_{j=1}^n v_j^{e_j + \alpha d_j}$ and 0 otherwise.

We note that, while the proving algorithm is deterministic, each statement has many valid proofs. However, finding two valid proofs for the same statement is computationally hard, as will be shown in the proof of Theorem 2.

The scheme readily extends to rest on the k-linear assumption with $k > 2$. In this case, the proof requires $k + 2$ group elements – whereas combining the techniques of [23, 24] demands $k(n + 1 - t)$ elements per proof – and a CRS of size $O(k(n + t))$. We prove the following result in the full version of the paper.

Theorem 2. *The above proof system is a relatively sound QA-NIZK proof system if the SDP assumption holds in $(\mathbb{G}, \mathbb{G}_T)$ and if H is a collision-resistant hash function.*

As an application, we describe a new adaptively secure CCA2-secure non-interactive threshold cryptosystem based on the DLIN assumption in the full version of the paper. Under the k-linear assumption, the scheme provides ciphertexts that are $\Theta(k)$ group elements shorter than in previous such constructions. Under the DLIN assumption, ciphertexts consist of 8 elements of $\mathbb{G}$, which spares one group element w.r.t. the best previous variants [23, 24] of Cramer-Shoup with publicly verifiable ciphertexts.

5 An Efficient Threshold Keyed-Homomorphic KH-CCA-Secure Encryption Scheme from the DLIN Assumption

The use of linearly homomorphic signatures as publicly verifiable proofs of ciphertext validity in the Cramer-Shoup paradigm [12, 13] was suggested in [27]. However, the latter work only discusses non-adaptive (*i.e.*, CCA1) attacks. In the CCA2 case, a natural idea is to proceed as in our unbounded simulation-sound proof system and use the verification key of a one-time signature as the tag of a homomorphic signature: since cross-tag homomorphic operations are disallowed, the one-time signature will prevent illegal ciphertext manipulations after the challenge phase. To obtain the desired keyed-homomorphic property, we use the simulation trapdoor of a simulation-sound proof system as the homomorphic evaluation key. This approach was already used by Emura *et al.* [16] in the context of designated verifier proofs. Here, publicly verifiable proofs are obtained from a homomorphic signature scheme of which the private key serves as an evaluation key: anyone equipped with this key can multiply two ciphertexts (or, more precisely, their built-in homomorphic components), generate a new tag and sign the resulting ciphertext using the private key of the homomorphic signature. Moreover, we can leverage the fact that the latter private key is always available to the reduction in the security proof of the homomorphic signature [27]. In the game of Definition 1, the simulator can thus hand over the evaluation key SK_h to the adversary upon request.

Emura *et al.* [16] gave constructions of KH-CCA secure schemes based on hash proof systems [13]. However, these constructions are only known to provide a relaxed flavor of KH-CCA security where evaluation queries should not involve derivatives of the challenge ciphertext. The reason is that 2-universal hash proof systems [13] only provide a form of one-time simulation soundness whereas the model of Definition 1 seemingly requires unbounded simulation-soundness. Indeed, when the evaluation oracle is queried on input of a derivative of the challenge ciphertext in the security proof, the homomorphic operation may result in a ciphertext containing a vector outside the language $\mathcal{L}_\rho$. Since the oracle has to simulate a proof for this vector, each homomorphic evaluation can carry a proof for a potentially false statement. In some sense, each output of the evaluation oracle can be seen as yet another challenge ciphertext. In this setting, our efficient unbounded simulation-sound QA-NIZK proof system comes in handy.

It remains to make sure that CCA1 security is always preserved, should the adversary obtain the evaluation key SK_h at the outset of the game. To this end, we include a second derived one-time homomorphic signature (Z, R, U) in the ciphertext without including its private key in SK_h.

Keygen(λ, t, N): Choose bilinear groups $(\mathbb{G}, \mathbb{G}_T)$ of prime order $p > 2^\lambda$.

1. Pick $f, g, h \xleftarrow{R} \mathbb{G}$, $x_0, x_1, x_2 \xleftarrow{R} \mathbb{Z}_p$ and set $X_1 = f^{x_1} g^{x_0}$, $X_2 = h^{x_2} g^{x_0}$. Then, define $\boldsymbol{f} = (f, 1, g) \in \mathbb{G}^3$ and $\boldsymbol{h} = (1, h, g) \in \mathbb{G}^3$.

2. Pick random polynomials $P_1[Z], P_2[Z], P[Z] \in \mathbb{Z}_p[Z]$ of degree $t - 1$ such that $P_1(0) = x_1$, $P_2(0) = x_2$ and $P(0) = x_0$. For each $i \in \{1, \ldots, N\}$, compute $VK_i = (Y_{i,1}, Y_{i,2})$ where $Y_{i,1} = f^{P_1(i)} g^{P(i)}$ and $Y_{i,2} = h^{P_2(i)} g^{P(i)}$.

3. Choose $f_{r,1}, f_{r,2} \xleftarrow{R} \mathbb{G}$ and define $\boldsymbol{f}_{r,1} = (f_{r,1}, 1, g)$, $\boldsymbol{f}_{r,2} = (1, f_{r,2}, g)$ and $\boldsymbol{f}_{r,3} = \boldsymbol{f}_{r,1}^{\phi_1} \cdot \boldsymbol{f}_{r,2}^{\phi_2} \cdot (1, 1, g)^{-1}$, where $\phi_1, \phi_2 \xleftarrow{R} \mathbb{Z}_p$. These vectors will be used as a Groth-Sahai CRS for the generation of NIZK proofs showing the validity of decryption shares.

4. Choose a strongly unforgeable one-time signature $\Sigma = (\mathcal{G}, \mathcal{S}, \mathcal{V})$ with verification keys consisting of L-bit strings, for some $L \in \mathsf{poly}(\lambda)$.

5. Generate a key pair for the one-time homomorphic signature of Section 2.5 with $n = 3$. Let $\mathsf{pk}_{ot} = (G_z, G_r, H_z, H_u, \{(G_i, H_i)\}_{i=1}^3)$ be the public key and let $\mathsf{sk}_{ot} = \{(\varphi_i, \vartheta_i, \varpi_i)\}_{i=1}^3$ be the corresponding private key.

6. Generate one-time homomorphic signatures $\{(Z_j, R_j, U_j)\}_{j=1,2}$ on the vectors $\boldsymbol{f} = (f, 1, g)$ and $\boldsymbol{h} = (1, h, g)$ and erase sk_{ot}.

7. Generate another linearly homomorphic key pair $(\mathsf{pk}, \mathsf{sk})$ with $n = 3$. The public key pk is augmented so as to contain a set of Groth-Sahai CRSes as in step 1 of the proof system in Section 3. Let $\mathsf{sk} = \{(\chi_i, \gamma_i, \delta_i)\}_{i=1}^3$ be the private key for which the corresponding public key is

$$\mathsf{pk} = \Big(\ g_z, \ g_r, \ h_z, \ h_u, \ \{(g_i, h_i)\}_{i=1}^3, \ \mathbf{f} = (\boldsymbol{f}_1, \boldsymbol{f}_2, \{\boldsymbol{f}_{3,i}\}_{i=0}^L) \ \Big).$$

8. Use sk to generate one-time homomorphic signatures $\{(z_j, r_j, u_j)\}_{j=1,2}$ on the independent vectors $\boldsymbol{f} = (f, 1, g) \in \mathbb{G}^3$ and $\boldsymbol{h} = (1, h, g) \in \mathbb{G}^3$.

9. The public key is defined to be

$$PK = \Big(\ g, \ \boldsymbol{f}, \ \boldsymbol{h}, \ \boldsymbol{f}_{r,1}, \ \boldsymbol{f}_{r,2}, \ \boldsymbol{f}_{r,3}, \ X_1, \ X_2,$$
$$\mathsf{pk}_{ot}, \ \mathsf{pk}, \ \{(Z_j, R_j, U_j)\}_{j=1}^2, \ \{(z_j, r_j, u_j)\}_{j=1}^2 \Big).$$

The evaluation key is $SK_h = \mathsf{sk} = \{(\chi_i, \gamma_i, \delta_i)\}_{i=1}^3$ while the i-th decryption key share is defined to be $SK_{d,i} = (P_1(i), P_2(i), P(i))$. The vector of verification keys is defined as $\mathbf{VK} = (VK_1, \ldots, VK_N)$, where $VK_i = (Y_{i,1}, Y_{i,2})$ for $i = 1$ to N.

Encrypt(M, PK): to encrypt $M \in \mathbb{G}$, generate a one-time signature key pair $(\mathsf{SVK}, \mathsf{SSK}) \leftarrow \mathcal{G}(\lambda)$.

1. Set $(C_0, C_1, C_2, C_3) = (M \cdot X_1^{\theta_1} \cdot X_2^{\theta_2}, f^{\theta_1}, h^{\theta_2}, g^{\theta_1 + \theta_2})$, with $\theta_1, \theta_2 \overset{R}{\leftarrow} \mathbb{Z}_p$.

2. Compute a first homomorphic signature (Z, R, U) on $(C_1, C_2, C_3) \in \mathbb{G}^3$. Namely, compute $Z = Z_1^{\theta_1} \cdot Z_2^{\theta_2}$, $R = R_1^{\theta_1} \cdot R_2^{\theta_2}$ and $U = U_1^{\theta_1} \cdot U_2^{\theta_2}$.

3. Using $\{(z_j, r_j, u_j)\}_{j=1,2}$, derive another homomorphic signature (z, r, u) on (C_1, C_2, C_3). Namely, compute $(z, r, u) = (z_1^{\theta_1} \cdot z_2^{\theta_2}, r_1^{\theta_1} \cdot r_2^{\theta_2}, u_1^{\theta_1} \cdot u_2^{\theta_2})$.

4. Using $\mathsf{SVK} \in \{0,1\}^L$, define the vector $\boldsymbol{f}_{\mathsf{SVK}} = \boldsymbol{f}_{3,0} \cdot \prod_{i=1}^L \boldsymbol{f}_{3,i}^{\mathsf{SVK}[i]}$ and assemble a Groth-Sahai CRS $\mathsf{f}_{\mathsf{SVK}} = (\boldsymbol{f}_1, \boldsymbol{f}_2, \boldsymbol{f}_{\mathsf{SVK}})$. Using $\mathsf{f}_{\mathsf{SVK}}$, generate commitments $\boldsymbol{C}_z, \boldsymbol{C}_r, \boldsymbol{C}_u$ to the components of $(z, r, u) \in \mathbb{G}^3$ along with proofs $(\boldsymbol{\pi}_1, \boldsymbol{\pi}_2)$ as in step 2 of the proving algorithm of Section 3. Let $(\boldsymbol{C}_z, \boldsymbol{C}_r, \boldsymbol{C}_u, \boldsymbol{\pi}_1, \boldsymbol{\pi}_2) \in \mathbb{G}^{15}$ be the resulting NIWI proof.

5. Generate $\sigma = \mathcal{S}(\mathsf{SSK}, (C_0, C_1, C_2, C_3, Z, R, U, \boldsymbol{C}_z, \boldsymbol{C}_r, \boldsymbol{C}_u, \boldsymbol{\pi}_1, \boldsymbol{\pi}_2))$ and output

$$C = (\mathsf{SVK}, C_0, C_1, C_2, C_3, Z, R, U, \boldsymbol{C}_z, \boldsymbol{C}_r, \boldsymbol{C}_u, \boldsymbol{\pi}_1, \boldsymbol{\pi}_2, \sigma) \qquad (2)$$

Ciphertext-Verify(PK, C): parse C as in (2). Return 1 if and only if: (i) $\mathcal{V}(\mathsf{SVK}, (C_0, C_1, C_2, C_3, Z, R, U, \boldsymbol{C}_z, \boldsymbol{C}_r, \boldsymbol{C}_u, \boldsymbol{\pi}_1, \boldsymbol{\pi}_2), \sigma) = 1$; (ii) (Z, R, U) is a valid homomorphic signature on (C_1, C_2, C_3); (iii) $(\boldsymbol{C}_z, \boldsymbol{C}_r, \boldsymbol{C}_u, \boldsymbol{\pi}_1, \boldsymbol{\pi}_2) \in \mathbb{G}^{15}$ is a valid proof w.r.t. the CRS $(\boldsymbol{f}_1, \boldsymbol{f}_2, \boldsymbol{f}_{\mathsf{SVK}})$ that committed (z, r, u) form a valid homomorphic signature for the vector $(C_1, C_2, C_3) \in \mathbb{G}^3$. Here, we define $\boldsymbol{f}_{\mathsf{SVK}} = \boldsymbol{f}_{3,0} \cdot \prod_{i=1}^L \boldsymbol{f}_{3,i}^{\mathsf{SVK}[i]}$.

Share-Decrypt$(PK, i, SK_{d,i}, C)$: on inputs $SK_{d,i} = (P_1(i), P_2(i), P(i)) \in \mathbb{Z}_p^3$ and C, return $(i, \perp)$ if **Ciphertext-Verify**$(PK, C) = 0$. Otherwise, compute $\hat{\mu}_i = (\nu_i, C_{P_1}, C_{P_2}, C_P, \pi_{\mu_i})$ which consists of a partial decryption $\nu_i = C_1^{P_1(i)} \cdot C_2^{P_2(i)} \cdot C_3^{P(i)}$ as well as commitments C_{P_1}, C_{P_2}, C_P to exponents $P_1(i), P_2(i), P(i) \in \mathbb{Z}_p$ and a proof π_{ν_i} that these satisfy the equations

$$\nu_i = C_1^{P_1(i)} \cdot C_2^{P_2(i)} \cdot C_3^{P(i)}, \qquad Y_{i,1} = f^{P_1(i)} g^{P(i)}, \qquad Y_{i,2} = h^{P_2(i)} g^{P(i)}.$$

The commitments C_{P_1}, C_{P_2}, C_P and the proof π_{ν_i} are generated using the CRS $(\boldsymbol{f}_{r,1}, \boldsymbol{f}_{r,2}, \boldsymbol{f}_{r,3})$. Then, return $\mu_i = (i, \hat{\mu}_i)$.

Share-Verify$(PK, VK_i, C, (i, \hat{\mu}_i))$: parse C as in (2) and VK_i as $(Y_{i,1}, Y_{i,2})$. If $\hat{\mu}_i = \perp$ or $\hat{\mu}_i$ cannot be parsed as $(\nu_i, C_{P_1}, C_{P_2}, C_P, \pi_{\mu_i})$, return 0. Otherwise, return 1 if and only if π_{μ_i} is valid.

Combine$(PK, \mathbf{VK}, C, \{(i, \hat{\mu}_i)\}_{i \in S})$: for each index $i \in S$, parse the share $\hat{\mu}_i$ as $(\nu_i, C_{P_1}, C_{P_2}, C_P, \pi_{\mu_i})$ and return $\perp$ if **Share-Verify**$(PK, C, (i, \hat{\mu}_i)) = 0$. Otherwise, compute $\nu = \prod_{i \in S} \nu_i^{\Delta_{i,S}(0)} = C_1^{x_1} \cdot C_2^{x_2} \cdot C_3^{x_0} = X_1^{\theta_1} \cdot X_2^{\theta_2}$ and output $M = C_0 / \nu$.

Eval$(PK, SK_h, C^{(1)}, C^{(2)})$: parse SK_h as $\{(\chi_i, \gamma_i, \delta_i)\}_{i=1}^3$. For each $j \in \{1, 2\}$, parse $C^{(j)}$ as

$$(\mathsf{SVK}^{(j)}, C_0^{(j)}, C_1^{(j)}, C_2^{(j)}, C_3^{(j)}, Z^{(j)}, R^{(j)}, U^{(j)}, \boldsymbol{C}_z^{(j)}, \boldsymbol{C}_r^{(j)}, \boldsymbol{C}_u^{(j)}, \pi_1^{(j)}, \pi_2^{(j)}, \sigma^{(j)})$$

and return $\perp$ if either $C^{(1)}$ or $C^{(2)}$ is invalid. Otherwise,

1. Compute $C_0 = \prod_{j=1}^2 C_0^{(j)}$, $C_1 = \prod_{j=1}^2 C_1^{(j)}$, $C_2 = \prod_{j=1}^2 C_2^{(j)}$ and $C_3 = \prod_{j=1}^2 C_3^{(j)}$ as well as $Z = \prod_{j=1}^2 Z^{(j)}$, $R = \prod_{j=1}^2 R^{(j)}$ and $U = \prod_{j=1}^2 U^{(j)}$.
2. Generate a new one-time signature key pair $(\mathsf{SVK}, \mathsf{SSK}) \leftarrow \mathcal{G}(\lambda)$. Using $SK_h = \{(\chi_i, \gamma_i, \delta_i)\}_{i=1}^3$, generate proof elements $\boldsymbol{C}_z, \boldsymbol{C}_r, \boldsymbol{C}_u, \pi_1, \pi_2$ on the vector (C_1, C_2, C_3) using the simulator of the proof system in Section 3 with the one-time verification key SVK.
3. Return $C = (\mathsf{SVK}, C_0, C_1, C_2, C_3, Z, R, U, \boldsymbol{C}_z, \boldsymbol{C}_r, \boldsymbol{C}_u, \pi_1, \pi_2, \sigma)$ where $\sigma = \mathcal{S}(\mathsf{SSK}, (C_0, C_1, C_2, C_3, Z, R, U, \boldsymbol{C}_z, \boldsymbol{C}_r, \boldsymbol{C}_u, \pi_1, \pi_2))$.

In the full version of the paper [28], we prove the KH-CCA security of the scheme assuming that Σ is a strongly unforgeable one-time signature and that the DLIN assumption holds in $\mathbb{G}$.

In some applications, it may be desirable to add an extra randomization step to the evaluation algorithm in order to make sure that derived ciphertexts will be indistinguishable from freshly generated encryption (similarly to [33]). It is straightforward to modify the scheme to obtain this property.

If the scheme is instantiated using Groth's one-time signature [20], the ciphertext consists of 25 elements of $\mathbb{G}$ and two elements of $\mathbb{Z}_p$. It is interesting to compare the above system with an instantiation of the same design principle using the best known Groth-Sahai-based unbounded simulation-sound proof [9][Appendix A.2], which requires 65 group elements in this specific case. With this proof system, we end up with 77 group elements per ciphertexts under the

DLIN assumption (assuming that an element of $\mathbb{Z}_p$ has the same length as the representation of a group element). The above realization thus saves 50 group elements and compresses ciphertexts to 35% of their original length.

References

1. Abe, M., Fuchsbauer, G., Groth, J., Haralambiev, K., Ohkubo, M.: Structure-Preserving Signatures and Commitments to Group Elements. In: Rabin, T. (ed.) CRYPTO 2010. LNCS, vol. 6223, pp. 209–236. Springer, Heidelberg (2010)
2. Abe, M., Haralambiev, K., Ohkubo, M.: Signing on Elements in Bilinear Groups for Modular Protocol Design. In: Cryptology ePrint Archive: Report 2010/133 (2010)
3. Belenkiy, M., Camenisch, J., Chase, M., Kohlweiss, M., Lysyanskaya, A., Shacham, H.: Randomizable Proofs and Delegatable Anonymous Credentials. In: Halevi, S. (ed.) CRYPTO 2009. LNCS, vol. 5677, pp. 108–125. Springer, Heidelberg (2009)
4. Bellare, M., Ristenpart, T.: Simulation without the Artificial Abort: Simplified Proof and Improved Concrete Security for Waters' IBE Scheme. In: Joux, A. (ed.) EUROCRYPT 2009. LNCS, vol. 5479, pp. 407–424. Springer, Heidelberg (2009)
5. Bellare, M., Rogaway, P.: Random oracles are practical: A paradigm for designing efficient protocols. In: ACM CCS, pp. 62–73 (1993)
6. Blum, M., Feldman, P., Micali, S.: Non-Interactive Zero-Knowledge and Its Applications. In: STOC 1988, pp. 103–112 (1988)
7. Boneh, D., Boyen, X., Shacham, H.: Short group signatures. In: Franklin, M. (ed.) CRYPTO 2004. LNCS, vol. 3152, pp. 41–55. Springer, Heidelberg (2004)
8. Boneh, D., Segev, G., Waters, B.: Targeted malleability: homomorphic encryption for restricted computations. In: ITCS 2012, pp. 350–366 (2012)
9. Camenisch, J., Chandran, N., Shoup, V.: A public key encryption scheme secure against key dependent chosen plaintext and adaptive chosen ciphertext attacks. In: Joux, A. (ed.) EUROCRYPT 2009. LNCS, vol. 5479, pp. 351–368. Springer, Heidelberg (2009)
10. Cathalo, J., Libert, B., Yung, M.: Group Encryption: Non-Interactive Realization in the Standard Model. In: Matsui, M. (ed.) ASIACRYPT 2009. LNCS, vol. 5912, pp. 179–196. Springer, Heidelberg (2009)
11. Chase, M., Kohlweiss, M., Lysyanskaya, A., Meiklejohn, S.: Malleable Proof Systems and Applications. In: Pointcheval, D., Johansson, T. (eds.) EUROCRYPT 2012. LNCS, vol. 7237, pp. 281–300. Springer, Heidelberg (2012)
12. Cramer, R., Shoup, V.: A practical public key cryptosystem provably secure against adaptive chosen ciphertext attack. In: Krawczyk, H. (ed.) CRYPTO 1998. LNCS, vol. 1462, pp. 13–25. Springer, Heidelberg (1998)
13. Cramer, R., Shoup, V.: Universal Hash Proofs and a Paradigm for Adaptive Chosen Ciphertext Secure Public-Key Encryption. In: Knudsen, L.R. (ed.) EUROCRYPT 2002. LNCS, vol. 2332, pp. 45–64. Springer, Heidelberg (2002)
14. Desmedt, Y.: Society and Group Oriented Cryptography: A New Concept. In: Pomerance, C. (ed.) CRYPTO 1987. LNCS, vol. 293, pp. 120–127. Springer, Heidelberg (1988)
15. Desmedt, Y., Frankel, Y.: Threshold Cryptosystems. In: Brassard, G. (ed.) CRYPTO 1989. LNCS, vol. 435, pp. 307–315. Springer, Heidelberg (1990)
16. Emura, K., Hanaoka, G., Ohtake, G., Matsuda, T., Yamada, S.: Chosen Ciphertext Secure Keyed-Homomorphic Public-Key Encryption. In: Kurosawa, K., Hanaoka, G. (eds.) PKC 2013. LNCS, vol. 7778, pp. 32–50. Springer, Heidelberg (2013)

17. Escala, A., Herold, G., Kiltz, E., Ràfols, C., Villar, J.: An Algebraic Framework for Diffie-Hellman Assumptions. In: Canetti, R., Garay, J.A. (eds.) CRYPTO 2013, Part II. LNCS, vol. 8043, pp. 129–147. Springer, Heidelberg (2013)

18. Fiat, A., Shamir, A.: How to prove yourself: Practical solutions to identification and signature problems. In: Odlyzko, A.M. (ed.) CRYPTO 1986. LNCS, vol. 263, pp. 186–194. Springer, Heidelberg (1987)

19. Groth, J., Ostrovsky, R., Sahai, A.: Perfect non-interactive zero knowledge for NP. In: Vaudenay, S. (ed.) EUROCRYPT 2006. LNCS, vol. 4004, pp. 339–358. Springer, Heidelberg (2006)

20. Groth, J.: Simulation-sound NIZK proofs for a practical language and constant size group signatures. In: Lai, X., Chen, K. (eds.) ASIACRYPT 2006. LNCS, vol. 4284, pp. 444–459. Springer, Heidelberg (2006)

21. Groth, J., Sahai, A.: Efficient non-interactive proof systems for bilinear groups. In: Smart, N.P. (ed.) EUROCRYPT 2008. LNCS, vol. 4965, pp. 415–432. Springer, Heidelberg (2008)

22. Hofheinz, D., Jager, T.: Tightly Secure Signatures and Public-Key Encryption. In: Safavi-Naini, R., Canetti, R. (eds.) CRYPTO 2012. LNCS, vol. 7417, pp. 590–607. Springer, Heidelberg (2012)

23. Jutla, C., Roy, A.: Relatively-Sound NIZKs and Password-Based Key-Exchange. In: Fischlin, M., Buchmann, J., Manulis, M. (eds.) PKC 2012. LNCS, vol. 7293, pp. 485–503. Springer, Heidelberg (2012)

24. Jutla, C., Roy, A.: Shorter Quasi-Adaptive NIZK Proofs for Linear Subspaces. In: Sako, K., Sarkar, P. (eds.) ASIACRYPT 2013, Part I. LNCS, vol. 8269, pp. 1–20. Springer, Heidelberg (2013)

25. Katz, J., Vaikuntanathan, V.: Round-Optimal Password-Based Authenticated Key Exchange. In: Ishai, Y. (ed.) TCC 2011. LNCS, vol. 6597, pp. 293–310. Springer, Heidelberg (2011)

26. Libert, B., Yung, M.: Non-Interactive CCA2-Secure Threshold Cryptosystems with Adaptive Security: New Framework and Constructions. In: Cramer, R. (ed.) TCC 2012. LNCS, vol. 7194, pp. 75–93. Springer, Heidelberg (2012)

27. Libert, B., Peters, T., Joye, M., Yung, M.: Linearly Homomorphic Structure-Preserving Signatures and their Applications. In: Canetti, R., Garay, J.A. (eds.) CRYPTO 2013, Part II. LNCS, vol. 8043, pp. 289–307. Springer, Heidelberg (2013)

28. Libert, B., Peters, T., Joye, M., Yung, M.: Non-Malleability from Malleability: Simulation-Sound Quasi-Adaptive NIZK Proofs and CCA2-Secure Encryption from Homomorphic Signatures. In: Cryptology ePrint Archive: Report 2013/691

29. Malkin, T., Teranishi, I., Vahlis, Y., Yung, M.: Signatures resilient to continual leakage on memory and computation. In: Ishai, Y. (ed.) TCC 2011. LNCS, vol. 6597, pp. 89–106. Springer, Heidelberg (2011)

30. Naor, M.: On cryptographic assumptions and challenges. In: Boneh, D. (ed.) CRYPTO 2003. LNCS, vol. 2729, pp. 96–109. Springer, Heidelberg (2003)

31. Naor, M., Yung, M.: Public-key cryptosystems provably secure against chosen ciphertext attacks. In: STOC 1990, pp. 427–437 (1990)

32. Prabhakaran, M., Rosulek, M.: Rerandomizable RCCA Encryption. In: Menezes, A. (ed.) CRYPTO 2007. LNCS, vol. 4622, pp. 517–534. Springer, Heidelberg (2007)

33. Prabhakaran, M., Rosulek, M.: Homomorphic Encryption with CCA Security. In: Aceto, L., Damgård, I., Goldberg, L.A., Halldórsson, M.M., Ingólfsdóttir, A., Walukiewicz, I. (eds.) ICALP 2008, Part II. LNCS, vol. 5126, pp. 667–678. Springer, Heidelberg (2008)

34. Prabhakaran, M., Rosulek, M.: Towards Robust Computation on Encrypted Data. In: Pieprzyk, J. (ed.) ASIACRYPT 2008. LNCS, vol. 5350, pp. 216–233. Springer, Heidelberg (2008)
35. Rackoff, C., Simon, D.: Non-Interactive Zero-Knowledge Proof of Knowledge and Chosen Ciphertext Attack. In: Feigenbaum, J. (ed.) CRYPTO 1991. LNCS, vol. 576, pp. 433–444. Springer, Heidelberg (1992)
36. Sahai, A.: Non-Malleable Non-Interactive Zero Knowledge and Adaptive Chosen-Ciphertext Security. In: FOCS 1999, pp. 543–553 (1999)
37. Shoup, V., Gennaro, R.: Securing Threshold Cryptosystems against Chosen Ciphertext Attack. In: Nyberg, K. (ed.) EUROCRYPT 1998. LNCS, vol. 1403, pp. 1–16. Springer, Heidelberg (1998)
38. Waters, B.: Efficient Identity-Based Encryption Without Random Oracles. In: Cramer, R. (ed.) EUROCRYPT 2005. LNCS, vol. 3494, pp. 114–127. Springer, Heidelberg (2005)

Fully Key-Homomorphic Encryption, Arithmetic Circuit ABE and Compact Garbled Circuits*

Dan Boneh[1], Craig Gentry[2], Sergey Gorbunov[3,**], Shai Halevi[2],
Valeria Nikolaenko[1], Gil Segev[4,***], Vinod Vaikuntanathan[3],
and Dhinakaran Vinayagamurthy[5]

[1] Stanford University, Stanford, CA, USA
{dabo, valerini}@cs.stanford.edu
[2] IBM Research, Yorktown, NY, USA
cbgentry@us.ibm.com, shaih@alum.mit.edu
[3] MIT, Cambridge, MA, USA
sergeyg@mit.edu, vinodv@csail.mit.edu
[4] Hebrew University, Jerusalem, Israel
segev@cs.huji.ac.il.
[5] University of Toronto, Toronto, Ontario, Canada
dhinakaran5@cs.toronto.edu

Abstract. We construct the first (key-policy) attribute-based encryption (ABE) system with short secret keys: the size of keys in our system depends only on the depth of the policy circuit, not its size. Our constructions extend naturally to arithmetic circuits with arbitrary fan-in gates thereby further reducing the circuit depth. Building on this ABE system we obtain the first reusable circuit garbling scheme that produces garbled circuits whose size is the same as the original circuit *plus* an additive $\mathsf{poly}(\lambda, d)$ bits, where λ is the security parameter and d is the circuit depth. All previous constructions incurred a *multiplicative* $\mathsf{poly}(\lambda)$ blowup.

We construct our ABE using a new mechanism we call *fully key-homomorphic encryption*, a public-key system that lets anyone translate a ciphertext encrypted under a public-key $\mathbf{x}$ into a ciphertext encrypted under the public-key $(f(\mathbf{x}), f)$ of the same plaintext, for any efficiently computable f. We show that this mechanism gives an ABE with short keys. Security of our construction relies on the subexponential hardness of the learning with errors problem.

We also present a second (key-policy) ABE, using multilinear maps, with short ciphertexts: an encryption to an attribute vector $\mathbf{x}$ is the size of $\mathbf{x}$ plus $\mathsf{poly}(\lambda, d)$ additional bits. This gives a reusable circuit garbling scheme where the garbled input is short.

---

* This paper is the result of merging two works [GGH+] and [BNS].

** This work was partially done while the author was visiting IBM T. J. Watson.

*** This work was partially done while the author was visiting Stanford University.

P.Q. Nguyen and E. Oswald (Eds.): EUROCRYPT 2014, LNCS 8441, pp. 533–556, 2014.

1   Introduction

(Key-policy) attribute-based encryption [SW05, GPSW06] is a public-key encryption mechanism where every secret key sk_f is associated with some function $f : \mathcal{X} \rightarrow \mathcal{Y}$ and an encryption of a message μ is labeled with a public attribute vector $\mathbf{x} \in \mathcal{X}$. The encryption of μ can be decrypted using sk_f only if $f(\mathbf{x}) = 0 \in \mathcal{Y}$. Intuitively, the security requirement is collusion resistance: a coalition of users learns nothing about the plaintext message μ if none of their individual keys are authorized to decrypt the ciphertext.

Attribute-based encryption (ABE) is a powerful generalization of identity-based encryption [Sha84, BF03, Coc01] and fuzzy IBE [SW05, ABV+12] and is a special case of functional encryption [BSW11]. It is used as a building-block in applications that demand complex access control to encrypted data [PTMW06], in designing protocols for verifiably outsourcing computations [PRV12], and for single-use functional encryption [GKP+13b]. Here we focus on key-policy ABE where the access policy is embedded in the secret key. The dual notion called ciphertext-policy ABE can be realized from this using universal circuits, as explained in [GPSW06, GGH+13c].

The past few years have seen much progress in constructing secure and efficient ABE schemes from different assumptions and for different settings. The first constructions [GPSW06, LOS+10, OT10, LW12, Wat12, Boy13, HW13] apply to predicates computable by Boolean formulas which are a subclass of logspace computations. More recently, important progress has been made on constructions for the set of all polynomial-size circuits: Gorbunov, Vaikuntanathan, and Wee [GVW13] gave a construction from the Learning With Errors (LWE) problem and Garg, Gentry, Halevi, Sahai, and Waters [GGH+13c] gave a construction using multilinear maps. In both constructions the policy functions are represented as Boolean circuits composed of fan-in 2 gates and the secret key size is proportional to the *size* of the circuit.

Our Results. We present two new key-policy ABE systems. Our first system, which is the centerpiece of this paper, is an ABE based on the learning with errors problem [Reg05] that supports functions f represented as arithmetic circuits with large fan-in gates. It has secret keys whose size is proportional to *depth* of the circuit for f, not its size. Secret keys in previous ABE constructions contained an element (such as a matrix) for every gate or wire in the circuit. In our scheme the secret key is a single matrix corresponding only to the final output wire from the circuit. We prove *selective* security of the system and observe that by a standard complexity leveraging argument (as in [BB11]) the system can be made adaptively secure.

Theorem 1.1 (Informal). *Let λ be the security parameter. Assuming subexponential LWE, there is an ABE scheme for the class of functions with depth-d circuits where the size of the secret key for a circuit C is $\mathsf{poly}(\lambda, d)$.*

Our second ABE system, based on multilinear maps ([BS02],[GGH13a]), optimizes the ciphertext size rather than the secret key size. The construction here relies on a generalization of broadcast encryption [FN93, BGW05, BW13] and the attribute-based encryption scheme of [GGH+13c]. Previously, ABE schemes with short ciphertexts were known only for the class of Boolean formulas [ALdP11].

Theorem 1.2 (Informal). *Let λ be the security parameter. Assuming that d-level multilinear maps exist, there is an ABE scheme for the class of functions with depth-d circuits where the size of the encryption of an attribute vector $\mathbf{x}$ is $|\mathbf{x}| + \mathsf{poly}(\lambda, d)$.*

Our ABE schemes result in a number of applications and have many desirable features, which we describe next.

Applications to reusable garbled circuits. Over the years, garbled circuits and variants have found many uses: in two party [Yao86] and multi-party secure protocols [BMR90], one-time programs [GKR08], verifiable computation [GGP10], homomorphic computations [GHV10] and many others. Classical circuit garbling schemes produced single-use garbled circuits which could only be used in conjunction with one garbled input. Goldwasser et al. [GKP+13b] recently showed the first fully reusable circuit garbling schemes and used them to construct token-based program obfuscation schemes and k-time programs [GKP+13b].

Most known constructions of both single-use and reusable garbled circuits proceed by garbling each gate to produce a garbled truth table, resulting in a *multiplicative* size blowup of $\mathsf{poly}(\lambda)$. A fundamental question regarding garbling schemes is: *How small can the garbled circuit be?*

There are three exceptions to the gate-by-gate garbling method that we are aware of. The first is the "free XOR" optimization for *single-use* garbling schemes introduced by Kolesnikov and Schneider [KS08] where one produces garbled tables only for the AND gates in the circuit C. This still results in a multiplicative $\mathsf{poly}(\lambda)$ overhead but proportional to the number of AND gates (as opposed to the total number of gates). Secondly, Lu and Ostrovsky [LO13] recently showed a *single-use* garbling scheme for RAM programs, where the size of the garbled program grows as $\mathsf{poly}(\lambda)$ times its running time. Finally, Goldwasser et al. [GKP+13a] show how to (reusably) garble non-uniform Turing machines under a non-standard and non-falsifiable assumption and incurring a multiplicative $\mathsf{poly}(\lambda)$ overhead in the size of the non-uniformity of the machine. In short, all known garbling schemes (even in the single-use setting) suffer from a multiplicative overhead of $\mathsf{poly}(\lambda)$ in the circuit size or the running time.

Using our first ABE scheme (based on LWE) in conjunction with the techniques of Goldwasser et al. [GKP+13b], we obtain the first reusable garbled circuits whose size is $|C| + \mathsf{poly}(\lambda, d)$. For large and shallow circuits, such as those that arise from database lookup, search and some machine learning applications, this gives significant bandwidth savings over previous methods (even in the single use setting).

Theorem 1.3 (Informal). *Assuming subexponential LWE, there is a reusable circuit garbling scheme that garbles a depth-d circuit C into a circuit $\hat{C}$ such that $|\hat{C}| = |C| + \mathsf{poly}(\lambda, d)$, and garbles an input x into an encoded input $\hat{x}$ such that $|\hat{x}| = |x| \cdot \mathsf{poly}(\lambda, d)$.*

We next ask if we can obtain short garbled inputs of size $|\hat{\mathbf{x}}| = |\mathbf{x}| + \text{poly}(\lambda, d)$, analogous to what we achieved for the garbled circuit. In a beautiful recent work, Applebaum, Ishai, Kushilevitz and Waters [AIKW13] showed constructions of *single-use* garbled circuits with short garbled inputs of size $|\hat{\mathbf{x}}| = |\mathbf{x}| + \text{poly}(\lambda)$. We remark that while their garbled inputs are short, their garbled circuits still incur a multiplicative $\text{poly}(\lambda)$ overhead.

Using our second ABE scheme (based on multilinear maps) in conjunction with the techniques of Goldwasser et al. [GKP+13b], we obtain the first reusable garbling scheme with garbled inputs of size $|\mathbf{x}| + \text{poly}(\lambda, d)$.

Theorem 1.4 (Informal). *Assuming subexponential LWE and the existence of d-level multilinear maps, there is a reusable circuit garbling scheme that garbles a depth-d circuit C into a circuit $\hat{C}$ such that $|\hat{C}| = |C| \cdot \text{poly}(\lambda, d)$, and garbles an input $\mathbf{x}$ into an encoded input $\hat{x}$ such that $|\hat{\mathbf{x}}| = |\mathbf{x}| + \text{poly}(\lambda, d)$.*

A natural open question is to construct a scheme which produces both short garbled circuits and short garbled inputs. We focus on describing the ABE schemes in the rest of the paper and postpone the details of the garbling scheme to the full version.

ABE for arithmetic circuits. For a prime q, our first ABE system (based on LWE) directly handles arithmetic circuits with weighted addition and multiplication gates over $\mathbb{Z}_q$, namely gates of the form

$$g_+(x_1, \ldots, x_k) = \alpha_1 x_1 + \ldots + \alpha_k x_k \quad \text{and} \quad g_\times(x_1, \ldots, x_k) = \alpha \cdot x_1 \cdots x_k$$

where the weights α_i can be arbitrary elements in $\mathbb{Z}_q$. Previous ABE constructions worked with Boolean circuits.

Addition gates g_+ take arbitrary inputs $x_1, \ldots, x_k \in \mathbb{Z}_q$. However, for multiplication gates $g_\times$, we require that the inputs are somewhat smaller than q, namely in the range $[-p, p]$ for some $p < q$. (In fact, our construction allows for one of the inputs to $g_\times$ to be arbitrarily large in $\mathbb{Z}_q$). Hence, while $f : \mathbb{Z}_q^\ell \to \mathbb{Z}_q$ can be an arbitrary polynomial-size arithmetic circuit, decryption will succeed only for attribute vectors $\mathbf{x}$ for which $f(\mathbf{x}) = 0$ and the inputs to all multiplication gates in the circuit are in $[-p, p]$. We discuss the relation between p and q at the end of the section.

We can in turn apply our arithmetic ABE construction to Boolean circuits with large fan-in resulting in potentially large savings over constructions restricted to fan-in two gates. An AND gate can be implemented as $\wedge(x_1, \ldots, x_k) = x_1 \cdots x_k$ and an OR gate as $\vee(x_1, \ldots, x_k) = 1 - (1 - x_1) \cdots (1 - x_k)$. In this setting, the inputs to the gates g_+ and $g_\times$ are naturally small, namely in $\{0, 1\}$. Thus, unbounded fan-in allows us to consider circuits with smaller size and depth, and results in smaller overall parameters.

ABE with key delegation. Our first ABE system also supports key delegation. That is, using the master secret key, user Alice can be given a secret key sk_f for a function f that lets her decrypt whenever the attribute vector $\mathbf{x}$ satisfies

$f(\mathbf{x}) = 0$. In our system, for any function g, Alice can then issue a delegated secret key $\mathsf{sk}_{f \wedge g}$ to Bob that lets Bob decrypt if and only if the attribute vector $\mathbf{x}$ satisfies $f(\mathbf{x}) = g(\mathbf{x}) = 0$. Bob can further delegate to Charlie, and so on. The size of the secret key increases quadratically with the number of delegations.

We note that Gorbunov et al. [GVW13] showed that their ABE system for Boolean circuits supports a somewhat restricted form of delegation. Specifically, they demonstrated that using a secret key sk_f for a function f, and a secret key sk_g for a function g, it is possible to issue a secret key $\mathsf{sk}_{f \wedge g}$ for the function $f \wedge g$. In this light, our work resolves the naturally arising open problem of providing full delegation capabilities (i.e., issuing $\mathsf{sk}_{f \wedge g}$ using only sk_f). We postpone a detailed description of the key delegation capabilities to the full version.

Other Features. In the full version, we state several other extensions of our constructions, namely an Attribute-Based Fully Homomorphic Encryption scheme as well as a method of outsourcing decryption in our ABE scheme.

1.1 Building an ABE for Arithmetic Circuits with Short Keys

Key-homomorphic public-key encryption. We obtain our ABE by constructing a public-key encryption scheme that supports computations on public keys. Basic public keys in our system are vectors $\mathbf{x}$ in $\mathbb{Z}_q^\ell$ for some ℓ. Now, let $\mathbf{x}$ be a tuple in $\mathbb{Z}_q^\ell$ and let $f : \mathbb{Z}_q^\ell \to \mathbb{Z}_q$ be a function represented as a polynomial-size arithmetic circuit. Key-homomorphism means that:

> anyone can transform an encryption under key $\mathbf{x}$ into an encryption under key $f(\mathbf{x})$.

More precisely, suppose $\mathbf{c}$ is an encryption of message μ under public-key $\mathbf{x} \in \mathbb{Z}_q^\ell$. There is a public algorithm $\mathsf{Eval}_{\mathsf{ct}}(f, \mathbf{x}, \mathbf{c}) \longrightarrow \mathbf{c}_f$ that outputs a ciphertext $\mathbf{c}_f$ that is an encryption of μ under the public-key $f(\mathbf{x}) \in \mathbb{Z}_q$. In our constructions $\mathsf{Eval}_{\mathsf{ct}}$ is deterministic and its running time is proportional to the size of the arithmetic circuit for f.

If we give user Alice the secret-key for the public-key $0 \in \mathbb{Z}_q$ then Alice can use $\mathsf{Eval}_{\mathsf{ct}}$ to decrypt $\mathbf{c}$ whenever $f(\mathbf{x}) = 0$, as required for ABE. Unfortunately, this ABE is completely insecure! This is because the secret key is not bound to the function f: Alice could decrypt any ciphertext encrypted under $\mathbf{x}$ by simply finding some function g such that $g(\mathbf{x}) = 0$.

To construct a secure ABE we slightly extend the basic key-homomorphism idea. A base encryption public-key is a tuple $\mathbf{x} \in \mathbb{Z}_q^\ell$ as before, however $\mathsf{Eval}_{\mathsf{ct}}$ produces ciphertexts encrypted under the public key $(f(\mathbf{x}), \langle f \rangle)$ where $f(\mathbf{x}) \in \mathbb{Z}_q$ and $\langle f \rangle$ is an encoding of the circuit computing f. Transforming a ciphertext $\mathbf{c}$ from the public key $\mathbf{x}$ to $(f(\mathbf{x}), \langle f \rangle)$ is done using algorithm $\mathsf{Eval}_{\mathsf{ct}}(f, \mathbf{x}, \mathbf{c}) \longrightarrow \mathbf{c}_f$ as before. To simplify the notation we write a public-key $(y, \langle f \rangle)$ as simply (y, f). The precise syntax and security requirements for key-homomorphic public-key encryption are provided in Section 3.

To build an ABE we simply publish the parameters of the key-homomorphic PKE system. A message μ is encrypted with attribute vector $\mathbf{x} = (x_1, \ldots, x_\ell) \in$

$\mathbb{Z}_q^{\ell}$ that serves as the public key. Let $\mathbf{c}$ be the resulting ciphertext. Given an arithmetic circuit f, the key-homomorphic property lets anyone transform $\mathbf{c}$ into an encryption of μ under key $(f(\mathbf{x}), f)$. The point is that now the secret key for the function f can simply be the decryption key for the public-key $(0, f)$. This key enables the decryption of $\mathbf{c}$ when $f(\mathbf{x}) = 0$ as follows: the decryptor first uses $\mathsf{Eval}_{\mathsf{ct}}(f, \mathbf{x}, \mathbf{c}) \longrightarrow \mathbf{c}_f$ to transform the ciphertext to the public key $(f(\mathbf{x}), f)$. It can then decrypt $\mathbf{c}_f$ using the decryption key it was given whenever $f(\mathbf{x}) = 0$. We show that this results in a secure ABE.

A construction from learning with errors. Fix some $n \in \mathbb{Z}^+$, prime q, and $m = \Theta(n \log q)$. Let $\mathbf{A}$, $\mathbf{G}$ and $\mathbf{B}_1, \dots, \mathbf{B}_{\ell}$ be matrices in $\mathbb{Z}_q^{n \times m}$ that will be part of the system parameters. To encrypt a message μ under the public key $\mathbf{x} = (x_1, \dots, x_{\ell}) \in \mathbb{Z}_q^{\ell}$ we use a variant of dual Regev encryption [Reg05, GPV08] using the following matrix as the public key:

$$(\mathbf{A} \mid x_1\mathbf{G} + \mathbf{B}_1 \mid \cdots \mid x_{\ell}\mathbf{G} + \mathbf{B}_{\ell}) \in \mathbb{Z}_q^{n \times (\ell+1)m} \qquad (1)$$

We obtain a ciphertext $\mathbf{c}_{\mathbf{x}}$. We note that this encryption algorithm is the same as encryption in the hierarchical IBE system of [ABB10] and encryption in the predicate encryption for inner-products of [AFV11].

We show that, remarkably, this system is key-homomorphic: given a function $f : \mathbb{Z}_q^{\ell} \to \mathbb{Z}_q$ computed by a poly-size arithmetic circuit, anyone can transform the ciphertext $\mathbf{c}_{\mathbf{x}}$ into a dual Regev encryption for the public-key matrix

$$(\mathbf{A} \mid f(\mathbf{x}) \cdot \mathbf{G} + \mathbf{B}_f) \in \mathbb{Z}_q^{n \times 2m}$$

where the matrix $\mathbf{B}_f \in \mathbb{Z}_q^{n \times m}$ serves as the encoding of the circuit for the function f. This $\mathbf{B}_f$ is uniquely determined by f and $\mathbf{B}_1, \dots, \mathbf{B}_{\ell}$. The work needed to compute $\mathbf{B}_f$ is proportional to the size of the arithmetic circuit for f.

To illustrate the idea, assume that we have the ciphertext under the public key (x, y): $\mathbf{c}_{\mathbf{x}} = (\mathbf{c}_0 \mid \mathbf{c}_x \mid \mathbf{c}_y)$. Here $\mathbf{c}_0 = \mathbf{A}^T\mathbf{s} + \mathbf{e}$, $\mathbf{c}_x = (x\mathbf{G} + \mathbf{B}_1)^T\mathbf{s} + \mathbf{e}_1$ and $\mathbf{c}_y = (y\mathbf{G} + \mathbf{B}_2)^T\mathbf{s} + \mathbf{e}_2$. To compute the ciphertext under the public key $(x + y, \mathbf{B}_+)$ one takes the sum of the ciphertexts $\mathbf{c}_x$ and $\mathbf{c}_y$. The result is the encryption under the matrix

$$(x + y)\mathbf{G} + (\mathbf{B}_1 + \mathbf{B}_2) \in \mathbb{Z}_q^{n \times m}$$

where $\mathbf{B}_+ = \mathbf{B}_1 + \mathbf{B}_2$. One of the main contributions of this work is a novel method of multiplying the public keys. Together with addition, described above, this gives full key-homomorphism. To construct the ciphertext under the public key $(xy, \mathbf{B}_{\times})$, we first compute a small-norm matrix $\mathbf{R} \in \mathbb{Z}_q^{m \times m}$, s.t. $\mathbf{GR} = -\mathbf{B}_1$. With this in mind we compute

$$\mathbf{R}^T\mathbf{c}_y = \mathbf{R}^T \cdot \left[(y\mathbf{G} + \mathbf{B}_2)^T\mathbf{s} + \mathbf{e}_2\right] \approx (-y\mathbf{B}_1 + \mathbf{B}_2\mathbf{R})^T s, \quad \text{and}$$

$$y \cdot \mathbf{c}_x = y\left[(x\mathbf{G} + \mathbf{B}_1)^T\mathbf{s} + \mathbf{e}_1\right] \approx (xy\mathbf{G} + y\mathbf{B}_1)^T\mathbf{s}$$

Adding the two expressions above gives us

$$(xy\mathbf{G} + \mathbf{B}_2\mathbf{R})^T\mathbf{s} + \mathbf{noise}$$

which is a ciphertext under the public key $(xy, \mathbf{B}_\times)$ where $\mathbf{B}_\times = \mathbf{B}_2\mathbf{R}$. Note that performing this operation requires that we know y. This is reason why this method gives an ABE and not (private index) predicate encryption. In Section 4.1 we show how to generalize this mechanism to arithmetic circuits with arbitrary fan-in gates.

As explained above, this key-homomorphism gives us an ABE for arithmetic circuits: the public parameters contain random matrices $\mathbf{B}_1, \ldots, \mathbf{B}_\ell \in \mathbb{Z}_q^{n \times m}$ and encryption to an attribute vector $\mathbf{x}$ in $\mathbb{Z}_q^\ell$ is done using dual Regev encryption to the matrix (1). A decryption key sk_f for an arithmetic circuit $f : \mathbb{Z}_q^\ell \to \mathbb{Z}_q$ is a decryption key for the public-key matrix $(\mathbf{A} \mid 0 \cdot \mathbf{G} + \mathbf{B}_f) = (\mathbf{A}|\mathbf{B}_f)$. This key enables decryption whenever $f(\mathbf{x}) = 0$. The key sk_f can be easily generated using a short basis for the lattice $\Lambda_q^\perp(\mathbf{A})$ which serves as the master secret key.

We prove selective security from the learning with errors problem (LWE) by using another homomorphic property of the system implemented in an algorithm called $\mathsf{Eval}_{\mathsf{sim}}$. Using $\mathsf{Eval}_{\mathsf{sim}}$ the simulator responds to the adversary's private key queries and then solves the given LWE challenge.

Parameters and performance. Applying algorithm $\mathsf{Eval}_{\mathsf{ct}}(f, \mathbf{x}, \mathbf{c})$ to a ciphertext $\mathbf{c}$ increases the magnitude of the noise in the ciphertext by a factor that depends on the depth of the circuit for f. A k-way addition gate (g_+) increases the norm of the noise by a factor of $O(km)$. A k-way multiplication gate $(g_\times)$ where all (but one) of the inputs are in $[-p, p]$ increases the norm of the noise by a factor of $O(p^{k-1}m)$. Therefore, if the circuit for f has depth d, the noise in $\mathbf{c}$ grows in the worst case by a factor of $O((p^{k-1}m)^d)$. Note that the weights α_i used in the gates g_+ and $g_\times$ have no effect on the amount of noise added.

For decryption to work correctly the modulus q should be slightly larger than the noise in the ciphertext. Hence, we need q on the order of $\Omega(B \cdot (p^{k-1}m)^d)$ where B is the maximum magnitude of the noise added to the ciphertext during encryption. For security we rely on the hardness of the learning with errors (LWE) problem, which requires that the ratio q/B is not too large. In particular, the underlying problem is believed to be hard even when q/B is $2^{(n^\epsilon)}$ for some fixed $0 < \epsilon < 1/2$. In our settings $q/B = \Omega((p^{k-1}m)^d)$. Then to support circuits of depth $t(\lambda)$ for some polynomial $t(\cdot)$ we choose n such that $n \geq t(\lambda)^{(1/\epsilon)} \cdot (2\log_2 n + k \log p)^{1/\epsilon}$, set $q = 2^{(n^\epsilon)}$, $m = \Theta(n \log q)$, and the LWE noise bound to $B = O(n)$. This ensures correctness of decryption and hardness of LWE since we have $\Omega((p^k m)^{t(\lambda)}) < q \leq 2^{(n^\epsilon)}$, as required. The ABE system of [GVW13] uses similar parameters due to a similar growth in noise as a function of circuit depth.

Secret key size. A decryption key in our system is a single $2m \times m$ low-norm matrix, namely the trapdoor for the matrix $(\mathbf{A}|\mathbf{B}_f)$. Since $m = \Theta(n \log q)$ and $\log_2 q$ grows linearly with the circuit depth d, the overall secret key size grows as $O(d^2)$ with the depth. In previous ABE systems for circuits [GVW13, GGH+13c] secret keys grew as $O(d^2 s)$ where s is the number of boolean gates or wires in the circuit.

Other related work. Predicate encryption [BW07, KSW08] provides a stronger privacy guarantee than ABE by additionally hiding the attribute vector **x**. Predicate encryption systems for inner product functionalities can be built from bilinear maps [KSW08] and LWE [AFV11]. More recently, Garg et al. [GGH⁺13b] constructed functional encryption (which implies predicate encryption) for all polynomial-size functionalities using indistinguishability obfuscation.

The encryption algorithm in our system is similar to that in the hierarchical-IBE of Agrawal, Boneh, and Boyen [ABB10]. We show that this system is key-homomorphic for polynomial-size arithmetic circuits which gives us an ABE for such circuits. The first hint of the key homomorphic properties of the [ABB10] system was presented by Agrawal, Freeman, and Vaikuntanathan [AFV11] who showed that the system is key-homomorphic with respect to low-weight linear transformations and used this fact to construct a (private index) predicate encryption system for inner-products. To handle high-weight linear transformations [AFV11] used bit decomposition to represent the large weights as bits. This expands the ciphertext by a factor of $\log_2 q$, but adds more functionality to the system. Our ABE, when presented with a circuit containing only linear gates (i.e. only g_+ gates), also provides a predicate encryption system for inner products in the same security model as [AFV11], but can handle high-weight linear transformations directly, without bit decomposition, thereby obtaining shorter ciphertexts and public-keys.

A completely different approach to building circuit ABE was presented by Garg, Gentry, Sahai, and Waters [GGSW13] who showed that a general primitive they named *witness encryption* implies circuit ABE when combined with witness indistinguishable proofs.

2   Preliminaries

2.1   Attribute-Based Encryption

An attribute-based encryption (ABE) scheme for a class of functions $\mathcal{F}_\lambda = \{f : \mathcal{X}_\lambda \to \mathcal{Y}_\lambda\}$ is a quadruple $\Pi = (\mathsf{Setup}, \mathsf{Keygen}, \mathsf{Enc}, \mathsf{Dec})$ of probabilistic polynomial-time algorithms. Setup takes a unary representation of the security parameter λ and outputs public parameters mpk and a master secret key msk; $\mathsf{Keygen}(\mathsf{msk}, f \in \mathcal{F}_\lambda)$ output a decryption key sk_f; $\mathsf{Enc}(\mathsf{mpk}, x \in \mathcal{X}_\lambda, \mu)$ outputs a ciphertext **c**, the encryption of message μ labeled with attribute vector x; $\mathsf{Dec}(\mathsf{sk}_f, \mathbf{c})$ outputs a message μ or the special symbol $\perp$. (When clear from the context, we drop the subscript λ from $\mathcal{X}_\lambda$, $\mathcal{Y}_\lambda$ and $\mathcal{F}_\lambda$.)

Correctness. We require that for every circuit $f \in \mathcal{F}$, attribute vector $x \in \mathcal{X}$ where $f(x) = 0$, and message μ, it holds that $\mathsf{Dec}(\mathsf{sk}_f, \mathbf{c}) = \mu$ with an overwhelming probability over the choice of $(\mathsf{mpk}, \mathsf{msk}) \leftarrow \mathsf{Setup}(\lambda)$, $\mathbf{c} \leftarrow \mathsf{Enc}(\mathsf{mpk}, x, \mu)$, and $\mathsf{sk}_f \leftarrow \mathsf{Keygen}(\mathsf{msk}, f)$.

Security. We refer the reader to the full version of this paper or [GPSW06] for the definition of selective and full security of the ABE scheme.

2.2 Background on Lattices

Lattices. Let q, n, m be positive integers. For a matrix $\mathbf{A} \in \mathbb{Z}_q^{n \times m}$ we let $\Lambda_q^{\perp}(\mathbf{A})$ denote the lattice $\{\mathbf{x} \in \mathbb{Z}^m \; : \; \mathbf{A}\mathbf{x} = 0 \text{ in } \mathbb{Z}_q\}$. More generally, for $\mathbf{u} \in \mathbb{Z}_q^n$ we let $\Lambda_q^{\mathbf{u}}(\mathbf{A})$ denote the coset $\{\mathbf{x} \in \mathbb{Z}^m \; : \; \mathbf{A}\mathbf{x} = \mathbf{u} \text{ in } \mathbb{Z}_q\}$.

We note the following elementary fact: if the columns of $\mathbf{T_A} \in \mathbb{Z}^{m \times m}$ are a basis of the lattice $\Lambda_q^{\perp}(\mathbf{A})$, then they are also a basis for the lattice $\Lambda_q^{\perp}(x\mathbf{A})$ for any nonzero $x \in \mathbb{Z}_q$.

Learning with errors (LWE) [Reg05]. Fix integers n, m, a prime integer q and a noise distribution χ over $\mathbb{Z}$. The (n, m, q, χ)-LWE problem is to distinguish the following two distributions:

$$(\mathbf{A}, \; \mathbf{A}^\mathsf{T}\mathbf{s} + \mathbf{e}) \qquad \text{and} \qquad (\mathbf{A}, \mathbf{u})$$

where $\mathbf{A} \leftarrow \mathbb{Z}_q^{n \times m}$, $\mathbf{s} \leftarrow \mathbb{Z}_q^n$, $\mathbf{e} \leftarrow \chi^m$, $\mathbf{u} \leftarrow \mathbb{Z}_q^m$ are independently sampled. Throughout the paper we always set $m = \Theta(n \log q)$ and simply refer to the (n, q, χ)-LWE problem.

We say that a noise distribution χ is B-bounded if its support is in $[-B, B]$. For any fixed $d > 0$ and sufficiently large q, Regev [Reg05] (through a quantum reduction) and Peikert [Pei09] (through a classical reduction) show that taking χ as a certain q/n^d-bounded distribution, the (n, q, χ)-LWE problem is as hard as approximating the worst-case GapSVP to $n^{O(d)}$ factors, which is believed to be intractable. More generally, let $\chi_{\max} < q$ be the bound on the noise distribution. The difficulty of the LWE problem is measured by the ratio $q/\chi_{\max}$. This ratio is always bigger than 1 and the smaller it is the harder the problem. The problem appears to remain hard even when $q/\chi_{\max} < 2^{n^\epsilon}$ for some fixed $\epsilon \in (0, 1/2)$.

Matrix norms. For a vector $\mathbf{u}$ we let $\|\mathbf{u}\|$ denote its ℓ_2 norm. For a matrix $\mathbf{R} \in \mathbb{Z}^{k \times m}$, let $\tilde{\mathbf{R}}$ be the result of applying Gram-Schmidt (GS) orthogonalization to the columns of $\mathbf{R}$. We define three matrix norms:

- $\|\mathbf{R}\|$ denotes the ℓ_2 length of the longest column of $\mathbf{R}$.
- $\|\mathbf{R}\|_{\text{GS}} = \|\tilde{\mathbf{R}}\|$ where $\tilde{\mathbf{R}}$ is the GS orthogonalization of $\mathbf{R}$.
- $\|\mathbf{R}\|_2$ is the operator norm of $\mathbf{R}$ defined as $\|\mathbf{R}\|_2 = \sup_{\|\mathbf{x}\|=1} \|\mathbf{R}\mathbf{x}\|$.

Note that $\|\mathbf{R}\|_{\text{GS}} \le \|\mathbf{R}\| \le \|\mathbf{R}\|_2 \le \sqrt{k}\|\mathbf{R}\|$ and that $\|\mathbf{R} \cdot \mathbf{S}\|_2 \le \|\mathbf{R}\|_2 \cdot \|\mathbf{S}\|_2$.

Trapdoor generators. The following lemma states properties of algorithms for generating short basis of lattices.

Lemma 2.1. *Let $n, m, q > 0$ be integers with q prime. There are polynomial time algorithms with the properties below:*

- TrapGen$(1^n, 1^m, q) \longrightarrow (\mathbf{A}, \mathbf{T_A})$ *([Ajt99, AP09, MP12]): a randomized algorithm that, when $m = \Theta(n \log q)$, outputs a full-rank matrix $\mathbf{A} \in \mathbb{Z}_q^{n \times m}$ and basis $\mathbf{T_A} \in \mathbb{Z}^{m \times m}$ for $\Lambda_q^{\perp}(\mathbf{A})$ such that $\mathbf{A}$ is negl(n)-close to uniform and $\|\mathbf{T}\|_{\text{GS}} = O(\sqrt{n \log q})$, with all but negligible probability in n.*

- ExtendRight($\mathbf{A}, \mathbf{T_A}, \mathbf{B}$) $\longrightarrow \mathbf{T_{(A|B)}}$ ([CHKP10]): *a deterministic algorithm that given full-rank matrices* $\mathbf{A}, \mathbf{B} \in \mathbb{Z}_q^{n \times m}$ *and a basis* $\mathbf{T_A}$ *of* $\Lambda_q^\perp(\mathbf{A})$ *outputs a basis* $\mathbf{T_{(A|B)}}$ *of* $\Lambda_q^\perp(\mathbf{A|B})$ *such that* $\|\mathbf{T_A}\|_{\mathrm{GS}} = \|\mathbf{T_{(A|B)}}\|_{\mathrm{GS}}$.
- ExtendLeft($\mathbf{A}, \mathbf{G}, \mathbf{T_G}, \mathbf{S}$) $\longrightarrow \mathbf{T_H}$ *where* $\mathbf{H} = (\mathbf{A} \mid \mathbf{G} + \mathbf{AS})$ ([ABB10]): *a deterministic algorithm that given full-rank matrices* $\mathbf{A}, \mathbf{G} \in \mathbb{Z}_q^{n \times m}$ *and a basis* $\mathbf{T_G}$ *of* $\Lambda_q^\perp(\mathbf{G})$ *outputs a basis* $\mathbf{T_H}$ *of* $\Lambda_q^\perp(\mathbf{H})$ *such that* $\|\mathbf{T_H}\|_{\mathrm{GS}} \leq \|\mathbf{T_G}\|_{\mathrm{GS}} \cdot (1 + \|\mathbf{S}\|_2)$.
- BD($\mathbf{A}$) $\longrightarrow \mathbf{R}$ *where* $m = n\lceil \log q \rceil$: *a deterministic algorithm that takes in a matrix* $\mathbf{A} \in \mathbb{Z}_q^{n \times m}$ *and outputs a matrix* $\mathbf{R} \in \mathbb{Z}_q^{m \times m}$, *where each element* $a \in \mathbb{Z}_q$ *that belongs to the matrix* $\mathbf{A}$ *gets transformed into a column vector* $\mathbf{r} \in \mathbb{Z}_q^{\lceil \log q \rceil}$, $\mathbf{r} = [a_0, ..., a_{\lceil \log q \rceil - 1}]^T$. *Here* a_i *is the i-th bit of the binary decomposition of a ordered from LSB to MSB. For any matrix* $\mathbf{A} \in \mathbb{Z}_q^{n \times m}$, *matrix* $\mathbf{R} = \mathsf{BD}(\mathbf{A})$ *has the norm* $\|\mathbf{R}\|_2 \leq m$ *and* $\|\mathbf{R}^T\|_2 \leq m$.
- *For* $m = n\lceil \log q \rceil$ *there is a fixed full-rank matrix* $\mathbf{G} \in \mathbb{Z}_q^{n \times m}$ *s.t. the lattice* $\Lambda_q^\perp(\mathbf{G})$ *has a publicly known basis* $\mathbf{T_G} \in \mathbb{Z}^{m \times m}$ *with* $\|\mathbf{T_G}\|_{\mathrm{GS}} \leq \sqrt{5}$. *The matrix* $\mathbf{G}$ *is such that for any matrix* $\mathbf{A} \in \mathbb{Z}_q^{n \times m}$, $\mathbf{G} \cdot \mathsf{BD}(\mathbf{A}) = \mathbf{A}$.

To simplify the notation we will always assume that the matrix $\mathbf{R}$ from part 4 and matrix $\mathbf{G}$ from part 5 of Lemma 2.1 has the same width m as the matrix $\mathbf{A}$ output by algorithm TrapGen from part 1 of the lemma. We do so without loss of generality since $\mathbf{R}$ (and $\mathbf{G}$) can always be extended to the size of $\mathbf{A}$ by adding zero columns on the right of $\mathbf{R}$ (and $\mathbf{G}$).

Discrete Gaussians. Regev [Reg05] defined a natural distribution on $\Lambda_q^{\mathbf{u}}(\mathbf{A})$ called a *discrete Gaussian* parameterized by a scalar $\sigma > 0$. We use $\mathcal{D}_\sigma(\Lambda_q^{\mathbf{u}}(\mathbf{A}))$ to denote this distribution. For a random matrix $\mathbf{A} \in \mathbb{Z}_q^{n \times m}$ and $\sigma = \tilde{\Omega}(\sqrt{n})$, a vector $\mathbf{x}$ sampled from $\mathcal{D}_\sigma(\Lambda_q^{\mathbf{u}}(\mathbf{A}))$ has ℓ_2 norm less than $\sigma\sqrt{m}$ with probability at least $1 - \mathrm{negl}(m)$.

For a matrix $\mathbf{U} = (\mathbf{u}_1 | \cdots | \mathbf{u}_k) \in \mathbb{Z}_q^{n \times k}$ we let $\mathcal{D}_\sigma(\Lambda_q^{\mathbf{U}}(\mathbf{A}))$ be a distribution on matrices in $\mathbb{Z}^{m \times k}$ where the i-th column is sampled from $\mathcal{D}_\sigma(\Lambda_q^{\mathbf{u}_i}(\mathbf{A}))$ independently for $i = 1, \ldots, k$. Clearly if $\mathbf{R}$ is sampled from $\mathcal{D}_\sigma(\Lambda_q^{\mathbf{U}}(\mathbf{A}))$ then $\mathbf{AR} = \mathbf{U}$ in $\mathbb{Z}_q$.

Solving $\mathbf{AX} = \mathbf{U}$. We review algorithms for finding a low-norm matrix $\mathbf{X} \in \mathbb{Z}^{m \times k}$ such that $\mathbf{AX} = \mathbf{U}$.

Lemma 2.2. *Let* $\mathbf{A} \in \mathbb{Z}_q^{n \times m}$ *and* $\mathbf{T_A} \in \mathbb{Z}^{m \times m}$ *be a basis for* $\Lambda_q^\perp(\mathbf{A})$. *Let* $\mathbf{U} \in \mathbb{Z}_q^{n \times k}$. *There are polynomial time algorithms that output* $\mathbf{X} \in \mathbb{Z}^{m \times k}$ *satisfying* $\mathbf{AX} = \mathbf{U}$ *with the properties below:*

- SampleD($\mathbf{A}, \mathbf{T_A}, \mathbf{U}, \sigma$) $\longrightarrow \mathbf{X}$ ([GPV08]): *a randomized algorithm that, when* $\sigma = \|\mathbf{T_A}\|_{\mathrm{GS}} \cdot \omega(\sqrt{\log m})$, *outputs a random sample* $\mathbf{X}$ *from a distribution that is statistically close to* $\mathcal{D}_\sigma(\Lambda_q^{\mathbf{U}}(\mathbf{A}))$.
- RandBasis($\mathbf{A}, \mathbf{T_A}, \sigma$) $\longrightarrow \mathbf{T}'_A$ ([CHKP10]): *a randomized algorithm that, when* $\sigma = \|\mathbf{T_A}\|_{\mathrm{GS}} \cdot \omega(\sqrt{\log m})$, *outputs a basis* $\mathbf{T}'_A$ *of* $\Lambda_q^\perp(\mathbf{A})$ *sampled from a distribution that is statistically close to* $(\mathcal{D}_\sigma(\Lambda_q^\perp(\mathbf{A})))^m$. *Note that* $\|\mathbf{T}'_A\|_{\mathrm{GS}} < \sigma\sqrt{m}$ *with all but negligible probability.*

3   Fully Key-Homomorphic PKE (FKHE)

Our new ABE constructions are a direct application of fully key-homomorphic public-key encryption (FKHE), a notion that we introduce. Such systems are public-key encryption schemes that are homomorphic with respect to the public encryption key. We begin by precisely defining FKHE and then show that a key-policy ABE with short keys arises naturally from such a system.

Let $\{\mathcal{X}_\lambda\}_{\lambda \in \mathbb{N}}$ and $\{\mathcal{Y}_\lambda\}_{\lambda \in \mathbb{N}}$ be sequences of finite sets. Let $\{\mathcal{F}_\lambda\}_{\lambda \in \mathbb{N}}$ be a sequence of sets of functions, namely $\mathcal{F}_\lambda = \{f : \mathcal{X}_\lambda^\ell \to \mathcal{Y}_\lambda\}$ for some $\ell > 0$. Public keys in an FKHE scheme are pairs $(x, f) \in \mathcal{Y}_\lambda \times \mathcal{F}_\lambda$. We call x the "value" and f the associated function. All such pairs are valid public keys. We also allow tuples $\mathbf{x} \in \mathcal{X}_\lambda^\ell$ to function as public keys. To simplify the notation we often drop the subscript λ and simply refer to sets $\mathcal{X}$, $\mathcal{Y}$ and $\mathcal{F}$.

In our constructions we set $\mathcal{X} = \mathbb{Z}_q$ for some q and let $\mathcal{F}$ be the set of ℓ-variate functions on $\mathbb{Z}_q$ computable by polynomial size arithmetic circuits.

Now, an FKHE scheme for the family of functions $\mathcal{F}$ consists of five PPT algorithms:

- $\mathsf{Setup}_{\mathrm{FKHE}}(1^\lambda) \to (\mathsf{mpk}_{\mathrm{FKHE}}, \mathsf{msk}_{\mathrm{FKHE}})$: outputs a master secret key $\mathsf{msk}_{\mathrm{FKHE}}$ and public parameters $\mathsf{mpk}_{\mathrm{FKHE}}$.
- $\mathsf{KeyGen}_{\mathrm{FKHE}}(\mathsf{msk}_{\mathrm{FKHE}}, (y, f)) \to \mathsf{sk}_{y,f}$: outputs a decryption key for the public key $(y, f) \in \mathcal{Y} \times \mathcal{F}$.
- $\mathsf{E}_{\mathrm{FKHE}}(\mathsf{mpk}_{\mathrm{FKHE}}, \mathbf{x} \in \mathcal{X}^\ell, \mu) \longrightarrow \mathbf{c_x}$: encrypts message μ under the public key $\mathbf{x}$.
- Eval : a *deterministic* algorithm that implements key-homomorphism. Let $\mathbf{c}$ be an encryption of message μ under public key $\mathbf{x} \in \mathcal{X}^\ell$. For a function $f : \mathcal{X}^\ell \to \mathcal{Y} \in \mathcal{F}$ the algorithm does:

$$\mathsf{Eval}(f, \mathbf{x}, \mathbf{c}) \longrightarrow \mathbf{c}_f$$

  where if $y = f(x_1, \dots, x_\ell)$ then $\mathbf{c}_f$ is an encryption of message μ under public-key (y, f).
- $\mathsf{D}_{\mathrm{FKHE}}(\mathsf{sk}_{y,f}, \mathbf{c})$: decrypts a ciphertext $\mathbf{c}$ with key $\mathsf{sk}_{y,f}$. If $\mathbf{c}$ is an encryption of μ under public key (x, g) then decryption succeeds only when $x = y$ and f and g are identical arithmetic circuits.

Algorithm Eval captures the key-homomorphic property of the system: ciphertext $\mathbf{c}$ encrypted with key $\mathbf{x} = (x_1, \dots, x_\ell)$ is transformed to a ciphertext $\mathbf{c}_f$ encrypted under key $(f(x_1, \dots, x_\ell), f)$.

Correctness. The key-homomorphic property is stated formally in the following requirement: For all $(\mathsf{mpk}_{\mathrm{FKHE}}, \mathsf{msk}_{\mathrm{FKHE}})$ output by Setup, all messages μ, all $f \in \mathcal{F}$, and $\mathbf{x} = (x_1, \dots, x_\ell) \in \mathcal{X}^\ell$:

If $\quad \mathbf{c} \leftarrow \mathsf{E}_{\mathrm{FKHE}}(\mathsf{mpk}_{\mathrm{FKHE}}, \mathbf{x} \in \mathcal{X}^\ell, \mu), \quad y = f(x_1, \dots, x_\ell),$

$\qquad \mathbf{c}_f = \mathsf{Eval}(f, \mathbf{x}, \mathbf{c}), \quad \mathsf{sk} \leftarrow \mathsf{KeyGen}_{\mathrm{FKHE}}(\mathsf{msk}_{\mathrm{FKHE}}, (y, f))$

Then $\mathsf{D}_{\mathrm{FKHE}}(\mathsf{sk}, \mathbf{c}_f) = \mu$.

An ABE from a FKHE. A FKHE for a family of functions $\mathcal{F} = \{f : \mathcal{X}^\ell \to \mathcal{Y}\}$ immediately gives a key-policy ABE. Attribute vectors for the ABE are ℓ-tuples over $\mathcal{X}$ and the supported key-policies are functions in $\mathcal{F}$. The ABE system works as follows:

- Setup$(1^\lambda, \ell)$: Run Setup$_{\mathsf{FKHE}}(1^\lambda)$ to get public parameters mpk and master secret msk. These function as the ABE public parameters and master secret.
- Keygen(msk, f) : Output $\mathsf{sk}_f \leftarrow \mathsf{KeyGen}_{\mathsf{FKHE}}(\mathsf{msk}_{\mathsf{FKHE}}, (0, f))$.
  Jumping ahead, we remark that in our FKHE instantiation (in Section 4), the number of bits needed to encode the function f in sk_f depends only on the depth of the circuit computing f, not its size. Therefore, the size of sk_f depends only on the depth complexity of f.
- Enc$(\mathsf{mpk}, \mathbf{x} \in \mathcal{X}^\ell, \mu)$: output $(\mathbf{x}, \mathbf{c})$ where $\mathbf{c} \leftarrow \mathsf{E}_{\mathsf{FKHE}}(\mathsf{mpk}_{\mathsf{FKHE}}, \mathbf{x}, \mu)$.
- Dec$(\mathsf{sk}_f, (\mathbf{x}, \mathbf{c}))$: if $f(\mathbf{x}) = 0$ set $\mathbf{c}_f = \mathsf{Eval}(f, \mathbf{x}, \mathbf{c})$ and output the decrypted answer $\mathsf{D}_{\mathsf{FKHE}}(\mathsf{sk}_f, \mathbf{c}_f)$.
  Note that c_f is the encryption of the plaintext under the public key $(f(\mathbf{x}), f)$. Since sk_f is the decryption key for the public key $(0, f)$, decryption will succeed whenever $f(\mathbf{x}) = 0$ as required.

The security of FKHE systems. Security for a fully key-homomorphic encryption system is defined so as to make the ABE system above secure. More precisely, we define security as follows.

Definition 3.1 (Selectively-secure FKHE). *A fully key homomorphic encryption scheme* $\Pi = (\mathsf{Setup}_{\mathsf{FKHE}}, \mathsf{KeyGen}_{\mathsf{FKHE}}, \mathsf{E}_{\mathsf{FKHE}}, \mathsf{Eval})$ *for a class of functions* $\mathcal{F}_\lambda = \{f : \mathcal{X}_\lambda^{\ell(\lambda)} \to \mathcal{Y}_\lambda\}$ *is selectively secure if for all p.p.t. adversaries* $\mathcal{A}$ *where* $\mathcal{A} = (\mathcal{A}_1, \mathcal{A}_2, \mathcal{A}_3)$, *there is a negligible function* $\nu(\lambda)$ *such that*

$$\mathbf{Adv}_{\Pi, \mathcal{A}}^{FKHE}(\lambda) \stackrel{\text{def}}{=} \left| \Pr\left[EXP_{FKHE, \Pi, \mathcal{A}}^{(0)}(\lambda) = 1 \right] - \Pr\left[EXP_{FKHE, \Pi, \mathcal{A}}^{(1)}(\lambda) = 1 \right] \right| \leq \nu(\lambda),$$

where for each $b \in \{0, 1\}$ *and* $\lambda \in \mathbb{N}$ *the experiment* $EXP_{FKHE, \Pi, \mathcal{A}}^{(b)}(\lambda)$ *is defined as:*

1. $(\mathbf{x}^* \in \mathcal{X}_\lambda^{\ell(\lambda)}, \; state_1) \leftarrow \mathcal{A}_1(\lambda)$
2. $(\mathsf{mpk}_{\mathsf{FKHE}}, \mathsf{msk}_{\mathsf{FKHE}}) \leftarrow \mathsf{Setup}_{\mathsf{FKHE}}(\lambda)$
3. $(\mu_0, \mu_1, state_2) \leftarrow \mathcal{A}_2^{\mathsf{KG}_{\mathsf{KH}}(\mathsf{msk}_{\mathsf{FKHE}}, x^*, \cdot, \cdot)}(\mathsf{mpk}_{\mathsf{FKHE}}, \; state_1)$
4. $\mathbf{c}^* \leftarrow \mathsf{E}_{\mathsf{FKHE}}(\mathsf{mpk}_{\mathsf{FKHE}}, \mathbf{x}^*, \mu_b)$
5. $b' \leftarrow \mathcal{A}_3^{\mathsf{KG}_{\mathsf{KH}}(\mathsf{msk}_{\mathsf{FKHE}}, x^*, \cdot, \cdot)}(\mathbf{c}^*, state_2)$ // $\mathcal{A}$ outputs a guess b' for b
6. *output* $b' \in \{0, 1\}$

where $\mathsf{KG}_{\mathsf{KH}}(\mathsf{msk}_{\mathsf{FKHE}}, x^*, y, f)$ *is an oracle that on input* $f \in \mathcal{F}$ *and* $y \in \mathcal{Y}_\lambda$, *returns* $\perp$ *whenever* $f(\mathbf{x}^*) = y$, *and otherwise returns* $\mathsf{KeyGen}_{\mathsf{FKHE}}(\mathsf{msk}_{\mathsf{FKHE}}, (y, f))$.

With Definition 3.1 the following theorem is now immediate.

Theorem 3.2. *The ABE system above is selectively secure provided the underlying FKHE is selectively secure.*

4   An FKHE for Arithmetic Circuits from LWE

We now turn to building an FKHE for arithmetic circuits from the learning with errors (LWE) problem. Our construction follows the key-homomorphism paradigm outlined in the introduction.

For integers n and $q = q(n)$ let $m = \Theta(n \log q)$. Let $\mathbf{G} \in \mathbb{Z}_q^{n \times m}$ be the fixed matrix from Lemma 2.1 (part 5). For $x \in \mathbb{Z}_q$, $\mathbf{B} \in \mathbb{Z}_q^{n \times m}$, $\mathbf{s} \in \mathbb{Z}_q^n$, and $\delta > 0$ define the set

$$E_{\mathbf{s},\delta}(x, \mathbf{B}) = \left\{ (x\mathbf{G} + \mathbf{B})^\mathsf{T}\mathbf{s} + \mathbf{e} \in \mathbb{Z}_q^m \text{ where } \|\mathbf{e}\| < \delta \right\}$$

For now we will assume the existence of three efficient *deterministic* algorithms $\mathsf{Eval}_{pk}, \mathsf{Eval}_{ct}, \mathsf{Eval}_{sim}$ that implement the key-homomorphic features of the scheme and are at the heart of the construction. We present them in the next section. These three algorithms must satisfy the following properties with respect to some family of functions $\mathcal{F} = \{f : (\mathbb{Z}_q)^\ell \to \mathbb{Z}_q\}$ and a function $\alpha_{\mathcal{F}} : \mathbb{Z} \to \mathbb{Z}$.

- $\mathsf{Eval}_{pk}(f \in \mathcal{F}, \ \vec{\mathbf{B}} \in (\mathbb{Z}_q^{n \times m})^\ell) \longrightarrow \mathbf{B}_f \in \mathbb{Z}_q^{n \times m}$.
- $\mathsf{Eval}_{ct}(f \in \mathcal{F}, \ ((x_i, \mathbf{B}_i, \mathbf{c}_i))_{i=1}^\ell) \longrightarrow \mathbf{c}_f \in \mathbb{Z}_q^m$.   Here $x_i \in \mathbb{Z}_q$, $\mathbf{B}_i \in \mathbb{Z}_q^{n \times m}$ and $\mathbf{c}_i \in E_{\mathbf{s},\delta}(x_i, \mathbf{B}_i)$ for some $\mathbf{s} \in \mathbb{Z}_q^n$ and $\delta > 0$. Note that the same $\mathbf{s}$ is used for all $\mathbf{c}_i$. The output $\mathbf{c}_f$ must satisfy

$$\mathbf{c}_f \in E_{\mathbf{s},\Delta}(f(\mathbf{x}), \mathbf{B}_f) \quad \text{where} \quad \mathbf{B}_f = \mathsf{Eval}_{pk}(f, (\mathbf{B}_1, \dots, \mathbf{B}_\ell))$$

and $\mathbf{x} = (x_1, \dots, x_\ell)$. We further require that $\Delta < \delta \cdot \alpha_{\mathcal{F}}(n)$ for some function $\alpha_{\mathcal{F}}(n)$ that measures the increase in the noise magnitude in $\mathbf{c}_f$ compared to the input ciphertexts.

  This algorithm captures the key-homomorphic property: it translates ciphertexts encrypted under public-keys $\{x_i\}_{i=1}^\ell$ into a ciphertext $\mathbf{c}_f$ encrypted under public-key $(f(\mathbf{x}), f)$.

- $\mathsf{Eval}_{sim}(f \in \mathcal{F}, \ ((x_i^*, \mathbf{S}_i))_{i=1}^\ell, \ \mathbf{A}) \longrightarrow \mathbf{S}_f \in \mathbb{Z}_q^{m \times m}$.   Here $x_i^* \in \mathbb{Z}_q$ and $\mathbf{S}_i \in \mathbb{Z}_q^{m \times m}$. With $\mathbf{x}^* = (x_1^*, \dots, x_n^*)$, the output $\mathbf{S}_f$ satisfies

$$\mathbf{A}\mathbf{S}_f - f(\mathbf{x}^*)\mathbf{G} = \mathbf{B}_f \quad \text{where} \quad \mathbf{B}_f = \mathsf{Eval}_{pk}(f, (\mathbf{A}\mathbf{S}_1 - x_1^*\mathbf{G}, \dots, \mathbf{A}\mathbf{S}_\ell - x_\ell^*\mathbf{G})).$$

We further require that for all $f \in \mathcal{F}$, if $\mathbf{S}_1, \dots, \mathbf{S}_\ell$ are random matrices in $\{\pm 1\}^{m \times m}$ then $\|\mathbf{S}_f\|_2 < \alpha_{\mathcal{F}}(n)$ with all but negligible probability.

Definition 4.1. *The deterministic algorithms* $(\mathsf{Eval}_{pk}, \mathsf{Eval}_{ct}, \mathsf{Eval}_{sim})$ *are* $\alpha_{\mathcal{F}}$-FKHE *enabling for some family of functions* $\mathcal{F} = \{f : (\mathbb{Z}_q)^\ell \to \mathbb{Z}_q\}$ *if there are functions* $q = q(n)$ *and* $\alpha_{\mathcal{F}} = \alpha_{\mathcal{F}}(n)$ *for which the properties above are satisfied.*

We want $\alpha_{\mathcal{F}}$-FKHE enabling algorithms for a large function family $\mathcal{F}$ and the smallest possible $\alpha_{\mathcal{F}}$. In the next section we build these algorithms for polynomial-size arithmetic circuits. The function $\alpha_{\mathcal{F}}(n)$ will depend on the depth of circuits in the family.

The FKHE system. Given FKHE-enabling algorithms $(\mathsf{Eval}_{\mathrm{pk}}, \mathsf{Eval}_{\mathrm{ct}}, \mathsf{Eval}_{\mathrm{sim}})$ for a family of functions $\mathcal{F} = \{f : (\mathbb{Z}_q)^\ell \to \mathbb{Z}_q\}$ we build an FKHE for the same family of functions $\mathcal{F}$. We prove selective security based on the learning with errors problem.

- Parameters : Choose n and $q = q(n)$ as needed for $(\mathsf{Eval}_{\mathrm{pk}}, \mathsf{Eval}_{\mathrm{ct}}, \mathsf{Eval}_{\mathrm{sim}})$ to be $\alpha_{\mathcal{F}}$-*FKHE enabling* for the function family $\mathcal{F}$. In addition, let χ be a $\chi_{\max}$-bounded noise distribution for which the (n, q, χ)-LWE problem is hard as discussed in Appendix 2.2. As usual, we set $m = \Theta(n \log q)$.

  Set $\sigma = \omega(\alpha_{\mathcal{F}} \cdot \sqrt{\log m})$. We instantiate these parameters concretely in the next section.
  For correctness of the scheme we require that $\alpha_{\mathcal{F}}^2 \cdot m < \frac{1}{12} \cdot (q/\chi_{\max})$ and $\alpha_{\mathcal{F}} > \sqrt{n \log m}$.

- $\mathsf{Setup}_{\mathrm{FKHE}}(1^\lambda) \to (\mathsf{mpk}_{\mathrm{FKHE}}, \mathsf{msk}_{\mathrm{FKHE}})$: Run algorithm $\mathsf{TrapGen}(1^n, 1^m, q)$ from Lemma 2.1 (part 1) to generate $(\mathbf{A}, \mathbf{T_A})$ where $\mathbf{A}$ is a uniform full-rank matrix in $\mathbb{Z}_q^{n \times m}$.
  Choose random matrices $\mathbf{D}, \mathbf{B}_1, \ldots, \mathbf{B}_\ell \in \mathbb{Z}_q^{n \times m}$ and output a master secret key $\mathsf{msk}_{\mathrm{FKHE}}$ and public parameters $\mathsf{mpk}_{\mathrm{FKHE}}$:

$$\mathsf{mpk}_{\mathrm{FKHE}} = (\mathbf{A}, \mathbf{D}, \mathbf{B}_1, \ldots, \mathbf{B}_\ell) \quad ; \quad \mathsf{msk}_{\mathrm{FKHE}} = (\mathbf{T_A})$$

- $\mathsf{KeyGen}_{\mathrm{FKHE}}(\mathsf{msk}_{\mathrm{FKHE}}, (y, f)) \to \mathsf{sk}_{y,f}$: Let $\mathbf{B}_f = \mathsf{Eval}_{\mathrm{pk}}(f, (\mathbf{B}_1, \ldots, \mathbf{B}_\ell))$. Output $\mathsf{sk}_{y,f} := \mathbf{R}_f$ where $\mathbf{R}_f$ is a low-norm matrix in $\mathbb{Z}^{2m \times m}$ sampled from the discrete Gaussian distribution $\mathcal{D}_\sigma(\Lambda_q^{\mathbf{D}}(\mathbf{A}|y\mathbf{G} + \mathbf{B}_f))$ so that $(\mathbf{A}|y\mathbf{G} + \mathbf{B}_f) \cdot \mathbf{R}_f = \mathbf{D}$.
  To construct $\mathbf{R}_f$ build the basis $\mathbf{T_F}$ for $\mathbf{F} = (\mathbf{A}|y\mathbf{G} + \mathbf{B}_f) \in \mathbb{Z}_q^{n \times 2m}$ as $\mathbf{T_F} \leftarrow \mathsf{ExtendRight}(\mathbf{A}, \mathbf{T_A}, y\mathbf{G} + \mathbf{B}_f)$ from Lemma 2.1 (part 2).
  Then run $\mathbf{R}_f \leftarrow \mathsf{SampleD}(\mathbf{F}, \mathbf{T_F}, \mathbf{D}, \sigma)$. Here σ is sufficiently large for algorithm $\mathsf{SampleD}$ (Lemma 2.2 part 2) since $\sigma = \|\mathbf{T_F}\|_{\mathrm{GS}} \cdot \omega(\sqrt{\log m})$. where $\|\mathbf{T_F}\|_{\mathrm{GS}} = \|\mathbf{T_A}\|_{\mathrm{GS}} = O(\sqrt{n \log q})$.
  Note that the secret key $\mathsf{sk}_{y,f}$ is always in $\mathbb{Z}^{2m \times m}$ independent of the complexity of the function f. We assume $\mathsf{sk}_{y,f}$ also implicitly includes $\mathsf{mpk}_{\mathrm{FKHE}}$.

- $\mathsf{E}_{\mathrm{FKHE}}(\mathsf{mpk}_{\mathrm{FKHE}}, \mathbf{x} \in \mathcal{X}^\ell, \mu) \longrightarrow \mathbf{c_x}$: Choose a random n dimensional vector $\mathbf{s} \leftarrow \mathbb{Z}_q^n$ and error vectors $\mathbf{e}_0, \mathbf{e}_1 \leftarrow \chi^m$. Choose ℓ uniformly random matrices $\mathbf{S}_i \leftarrow \{\pm 1\}^{m \times m}$ for $i \in [\ell]$.
  Set $\mathbf{H} \in \mathbb{Z}_q^{n \times (\ell+1)m}$ and $\mathbf{e} \in \mathbb{Z}_q^{(\ell+1)m}$ as

$$\mathbf{H} = (\mathbf{A} \mid x_1 \mathbf{G} + \mathbf{B}_1 \mid \cdots \mid x_\ell \mathbf{G} + \mathbf{B}_\ell) \quad \in \mathbb{Z}_q^{n \times (\ell+1)m}$$

$$\mathbf{e} = (\mathbf{I}_m | \mathbf{S}_1 | \ldots | \mathbf{S}_\ell)^{\mathsf{T}} \cdot \mathbf{e}_0 \quad \in \mathbb{Z}_q^{(\ell+1)m}$$

Let $\mathbf{c_x} = (\mathbf{H}^T \mathbf{s} + \mathbf{e}, \ \mathbf{D}^T \mathbf{s} + \mathbf{e}_1 + \lceil q/2 \rceil \mu) \in \mathbb{Z}_q^{(\ell+2)m}$. Output the ciphertext $\mathbf{c_x}$.

- $\mathsf{D}_{\mathrm{FKHE}}(\mathsf{sk}_{y,f}, \mathbf{c})$: Let $\mathbf{c}$ be the encryption of μ under public key (x, g). If $x \neq y$ or f and g are not identical arithmetic circuits, output $\perp$. Otherwise, let $\mathbf{c} = (\mathbf{c}_{in}, \mathbf{c}_1, \ldots, \mathbf{c}_\ell, \mathbf{c}_{out}) \in \mathbb{Z}_q^{(\ell+2)m}$.

Set $\mathbf{c}_f = \mathsf{Eval}_{ct}\big(f,\ \{(x_i, \mathbf{B}_i, \mathbf{c}_i)\}_{i=1}^{\ell}\big) \in \mathbb{Z}_q^m$.

Let $\mathbf{c}_f' = (\mathbf{c}_{in}|\mathbf{c}_f) \in \mathbb{Z}_q^{2m}$ and output $\mathsf{Round}(\mathbf{c}_{out} - \mathbf{R}_f^{\mathsf{T}}\mathbf{c}_f') \in \{0, 1\}^m$.

Correctness. The correctness of the scheme follows from our choice of parameters and, in particular, from the requirement $\alpha_{\mathcal{F}}^2 \cdot m < \frac{1}{12} \cdot (q/\chi_{\max})$. Specifically, to show correctness, first note that when $f(\mathbf{x}) = y$ we know by the requirement on Eval_{ct} that $\mathbf{c}_f$ is in $E_{\mathbf{s},\Delta}(y, \mathbf{B}_f)$ so that $\mathbf{c}_f = y\mathbf{G} + \mathbf{B}_f^{\mathsf{T}}\mathbf{s} + \mathbf{e}$ with $\|\mathbf{e}\| < \Delta$. We show in the full version of this paper that in this case the secret key $\mathbf{R}_f$ correctly decrypts in algorithm $\mathsf{D}_{\mathsf{FKHE}}$.

Security. Next we prove that our FKHE is selectively secure for the family of functions $\mathcal{F}$ for which algorithms $(\mathsf{Eval}_{pk}, \mathsf{Eval}_{ct}, \mathsf{Eval}_{sim})$ are FKHE-enabling.

Theorem 4.2. *Given the three algorithms $(\mathsf{Eval}_{pk}, \mathsf{Eval}_{ct}, \mathsf{Eval}_{sim})$ for the family of functions $\mathcal{F}$, the FKHE system above is selectively secure with respect to $\mathcal{F}$, assuming the (n, q, χ)-LWE assumption holds where n, q, χ are the parameters for the FKHE.*

We provide the complete proof in the full version of the paper. Here we sketch the main idea which hinges on algorithms $(\mathsf{Eval}_{pk}, \mathsf{Eval}_{ct}, \mathsf{Eval}_{sim})$ and also employs ideas from [CHKP10, ABB10]. We build an LWE algorithm $\mathcal{B}$ that uses a selective FKHE attacker $\mathcal{A}$ to solve LWE. $\mathcal{B}$ is given an LWE challenge matrix $(\mathbf{A}|\mathbf{D}) \in \mathbb{Z}_q^{n \times 2m}$ and two vectors $\mathbf{c}_{in}, \mathbf{c}_{out} \in \mathbb{Z}_q^m$ that are either random or their concatenation equals $(\mathbf{A}|\mathbf{D})^{\mathsf{T}}\mathbf{s} + \mathbf{e}$ for some small noise vector $\mathbf{e}$.

$\mathcal{A}$ starts by committing to the target attribute vector $\mathbf{x} = (x_1^*, \ldots, x_{\ell}^*) \in \mathbb{Z}_q^{\ell}$. In response $\mathcal{B}$ constructs the FKHE public parameters by choosing random matrices $\mathbf{S}_1^*, \ldots, \mathbf{S}_{\ell}^*$ in $\{\pm 1\}^{m \times m}$ and setting $\mathbf{B}_i = \mathbf{A}\mathbf{S}_i^* - x_i^*\mathbf{G}$. It gives $\mathcal{A}$ the public parameters $\mathsf{mpk}_{\mathsf{FKHE}} = (\mathbf{A}, \mathbf{D}, \mathbf{B}_1, \ldots, \mathbf{B}_{\ell})$. A standard argument shows that each of $\mathbf{A}\mathbf{S}_i^*$ is uniformly distributed in $\mathbb{Z}_q^{n \times m}$ so that all $\mathbf{B}_i$ are uniform as required for the public parameters.

Now, consider a private key query from $\mathcal{A}$ for a function $f \in \mathcal{F}$ and attribute $y \in \mathbb{Z}_q$. Only functions f and attributes y for which $y^* = f(x_1^*, \ldots, x_{\ell}^*) \neq y$ are allowed. Let $\mathbf{B}_f = \mathsf{Eval}_{pk}\big(f, (\mathbf{B}_1, \ldots, \mathbf{B}_{\ell})\big)$. Then $\mathcal{B}$ needs to produce a matrix $\mathbf{R}_f$ in $\mathbb{Z}^{2m \times m}$ satisfying $(\mathbf{A}|\mathbf{B}_f) \cdot \mathbf{R}_f = \mathbf{D}$. To do so $\mathcal{B}$ needs a short basis for the lattice $\Lambda_q^{\perp}(\mathbf{F})$ where $\mathbf{F} = (\mathbf{A}|\mathbf{B}_f)$. In the real key generation algorithm this short basis is derived from a short basis for $\Lambda_q^{\perp}(\mathbf{A})$ using algorithm $\mathsf{ExtendRight}$. Unfortunately, $\mathcal{B}$ has no short basis for $\Lambda_q^{\perp}(\mathbf{A})$.

Instead, as explained below, $\mathcal{B}$ builds a low-norm matrix $\mathbf{S}_f \in \mathbb{Z}_q^{m \times m}$ such that $\mathbf{B}_f = \mathbf{A}\mathbf{S}_f - y^*\mathbf{G}$. Then $\mathbf{F} = (\mathbf{A} \mid \mathbf{A}\mathbf{S}_f - y^*\mathbf{G} + y\mathbf{G})$. Because $y^* \neq y$, algorithm $\mathcal{B}$ can construct the short basis $\mathbf{T}_{\mathbf{F}}$ for $\Lambda_q^{\perp}(\mathbf{F})$ using algorithm $\mathsf{ExtendLeft}((y - y^*)\mathbf{G}, \mathbf{T}_{G}, \mathbf{A}, \mathbf{S}_f)$ from Lemma 2.1 part 3. Using $\mathbf{T}_{\mathbf{F}}$ algorithm $\mathcal{B}$ can now generate the required key as $\mathbf{R}_f \leftarrow \mathsf{SampleD}(\mathbf{F}, \mathbf{T}_{\mathbf{F}}, \mathbf{D}, \sigma)$.

The remaining question is how does algorithm $\mathcal{B}$ build a low-norm matrix $\mathbf{S}_f \in \mathbb{Z}_q^{m \times m}$ such that $\mathbf{B}_f = \mathbf{A}\mathbf{S}_f - y^*\mathbf{G}$. To do so $\mathcal{B}$ uses Eval_{sim} giving it the secret matrices $\mathbf{S}_i^*$. More precisely, $\mathcal{B}$ runs $\mathsf{Eval}_{sim}(f, \big((x_i^*, \mathbf{S}_i^*)\big)_{i=1}^{\ell}, \mathbf{A})$ and obtains the required $\mathbf{S}_f$. This lets $\mathcal{B}$ answer all private key queries.

To complete the proof it is not difficult to show that $\mathcal{B}$ can build a challenge ciphertext $\mathbf{c}^*$ for the attribute vector $\mathbf{x} \in \mathbb{Z}_q^\ell$ that lets it solve the given LWE instance using adversary $\mathcal{A}$. An important point is that $\mathcal{B}$ cannot construct a key that decrypts $\mathbf{c}^*$. The reason is that it cannot build a secret key $\mathsf{sk}_{y,f}$ for functions where $f(\mathbf{x}^*) = y$ and these are the only keys that will decrypt $\mathbf{c}^*$.

Remark 4.3. We note that the matrix $\mathbf{R}_f$ in $\mathsf{KeyGen}_{\mathsf{FKHE}}$ can alternatively be generated using a sampling method from [MP12]. To do so we choose FKHE public parameters as we do in the security proof by choosing random matrices $\mathbf{S}_i, \ldots, \mathbf{S}_\ell$ in $\{\pm 1\}^{m \times m}$ and setting $\mathbf{B}_i = \mathbf{A}\mathbf{S}_i$. We then define the matrix $\mathbf{B}_f$ as $\mathbf{B}_f := \mathbf{A}\mathbf{S}_f$ where $\mathbf{S}_f = \mathsf{Eval}_{\mathsf{sim}}(f, ((0, \mathbf{S}_i))_{i=1}^\ell, \mathbf{A})$. We could then build the secret key matrix $\mathsf{sk}_{y,f} = \mathbf{R}_f$ satisfying $(\mathbf{A}|y\mathbf{G} + \mathbf{B}_f) \cdot \mathbf{R}_f = \mathbf{D}$ directly from the bit decomposition of $\mathbf{D}/y$. Adding suitable low-norm noise to the result will ensure that $\mathsf{sk}_{y,f}$ is distributed as in the simulation in the security proof. Note that this approach can only be used to build secret keys $\mathsf{sk}_{y,f}$ when $y \neq 0$ where as the method in $\mathsf{KeyGen}_{\mathsf{FKHE}}$ works for all y.

4.1 Evaluation Algorithms for Arithmetic Circuits

In this section we build the *FKHE-enabling* algorithms $(\mathsf{Eval}_{\mathsf{pk}}, \mathsf{Eval}_{\mathsf{ct}}, \mathsf{Eval}_{\mathsf{sim}})$ that are at the heart of the FKHE construction in Section 4. We do so for the family of polynomial depth, unbounded fan-in arithmetic circuits.

4.2 Evaluation Algorithms for Gates

We first describe Eval algorithms for single gates, i.e. when $\mathcal{G}$ is the set of functions that each takes k inputs and computes either weighted addition or multiplication:

$$\mathcal{G} = \bigcup_{\alpha, \alpha_1, \ldots, \alpha_k \in \mathbb{Z}_q} \left\{ g \mid g : \mathbb{Z}_q^k \to \mathbb{Z}_q, \begin{array}{c} g(x_1, \ldots, x_k) = \alpha_1 x_1 + \alpha_2 x_2 + \ldots + \alpha_k x_k \\ \text{or} \\ g(x_1, \ldots, x_k) = \alpha \cdot x_1 \cdot x_2 \cdot \ldots \cdot x_k \end{array} \right\}$$
(2)

We assume that all the inputs to a multiplication gate (except possibly one input) are integers in the interval $[-p, p]$ for some bound $p < q$.

We present all three deterministic Eval algorithms at once:

$\mathsf{Eval}_{\mathsf{pk}}(g \in \mathcal{G}, \vec{\mathbf{B}} \in (\mathbb{Z}_q^{n \times m})^k) \longrightarrow \mathbf{B}_g \in \mathbb{Z}_q^{n \times m}$

$\mathsf{Eval}_{\mathsf{ct}}(g \in \mathcal{G}, ((x_i, \mathbf{B}_i, \mathbf{c}_i))_{i=1}^k) \longrightarrow \mathbf{c}_g \in \mathbb{Z}_q^m$

$\mathsf{Eval}_{\mathsf{sim}}(g \in \mathcal{G}, ((x_i^*, \mathbf{S}_i))_{i=1}^k, \mathbf{A}) \longrightarrow \mathbf{S}_g \in \mathbb{Z}_q^{m \times m}$

– For a weighted **addition** gate $g(x_1, \ldots, x_k) = \alpha_1 x_1 + \cdots + \alpha_k x_k$ do:
  For $i \in [k]$ generate matrix $\mathbf{R}_i \in \mathbb{Z}_q^{m \times m}$ such that

$$\mathbf{G}\mathbf{R}_i = \alpha_i \mathbf{G} \; : \; \mathbf{R}_i = \mathsf{BD}(\alpha_i \mathbf{G}) \qquad \text{(as in Lemma 2.1 part 4).} \qquad (3)$$

Output the following matrices and the ciphertext:

$$\mathbf{B}_g = \sum_{i=1}^{k} \mathbf{B}_i \mathbf{R}_i, \qquad \mathbf{S}_g = \sum_{i=1}^{k} \mathbf{S}_i \mathbf{R}_i, \qquad \mathbf{c}_g = \sum_{i=1}^{k} \mathbf{R}_i^T \mathbf{c}_i \qquad (4)$$

– For a weighted **multiplication** gate $g(x_1, \ldots, x_k) = \alpha x_1 \cdot \ldots \cdot x_k$ do:
  For $i \in [k]$ generate matrices $\mathbf{R}_i \in \mathbb{Z}_q^{m \times m}$ such that

$$\mathbf{GR}_1 = \alpha \mathbf{G} \;:\; \mathbf{R}_1 = \mathsf{BD}(\alpha \mathbf{G}) \tag{5}$$

$$\mathbf{GR}_i = -\mathbf{B}_{i-1} \mathbf{R}_{i-1} \;:\; \mathbf{R}_i = \mathsf{BD}(-\mathbf{B}_{i-1} \mathbf{R}_{i-1}) \quad \text{for all } i \in \{2, 3, \ldots, k\} \tag{6}$$

Output the following matrices and the ciphertext:

$$\mathbf{B}_g = \mathbf{B}_k \mathbf{R}_k, \qquad \mathbf{S}_g = \sum_{j=1}^{k} \left(\prod_{i=j+1}^{k} x_i^* \right) \mathbf{S}_j \mathbf{R}_j, \qquad \mathbf{c}_g = \sum_{j=1}^{k} \left(\prod_{i=j+1}^{k} x_i \right) \mathbf{R}_j^T \mathbf{c}_j \tag{7}$$

For example, for $k = 2$, $\mathbf{B}_g = \mathbf{B}_2 \mathbf{R}_2$, $\mathbf{S}_g = x_2^* \mathbf{S}_1 \mathbf{R}_1 + \mathbf{S}_2 \mathbf{R}_2$, $\mathbf{c}_g = x_2^* \mathbf{R}_1^T \mathbf{c}_1 + \mathbf{R}_2^T \mathbf{c}_2$.

For multiplication gates, the reason we need an upper bound p on all but one of the inputs x_i is that these x_i values are used in (7) and we need the norm of $\mathbf{S}_g$ and the norm of the noise in the ciphertext $\mathbf{c}_g$ to be bounded from above. The next two lemmas show that these algorithms satisfy the required properties and are proved in the full version of the paper.

Lemma 4.4. *Let $\beta_g(m) = km$. For a* **weighted addition** *gate $g(\mathbf{x}) = \alpha_1 x_1 + \ldots + \alpha_k x_k$ we have:*

1. *If $\mathbf{c}_i \in E_{\mathbf{s}, \delta}(x_i, \mathbf{B}_i)$ for some $\mathbf{s} \in \mathbb{Z}_q^n$ and $\delta > 0$, then $\mathbf{c}_g \in E_{\mathbf{s}, \Delta}(g(\mathbf{x}), \mathbf{B}_g)$ where $\Delta \leq \beta_g(m) \cdot \delta$ and $\mathbf{B}_g = \mathsf{Eval}_{pk}(g, (\mathbf{B}_1, \ldots, \mathbf{B}_k))$.*
2. *The output $\mathbf{S}_g$ satisfies $\mathbf{A}\mathbf{S}_g - g(\mathbf{x}^*)\mathbf{G} = \mathbf{B}_g$ where $\|\mathbf{S}_g\|_2 \leq \beta_g(m) \cdot \max_{i \in [k]} \|\mathbf{S}_i\|_2$*
   and $\mathbf{B}_g = \mathsf{Eval}_{pk}(g, (\mathbf{A}\mathbf{S}_1 - x_1^* \mathbf{G}, \ldots, \mathbf{A}\mathbf{S}_k - x_k^* \mathbf{G}))$.

Lemma 4.5. *For a* **multiplication** *gate $g(\mathbf{x}) = \alpha \prod_{i=1}^{k} x_i$ we have the same bounds on $\mathbf{c}_g$ and $\mathbf{S}_g$ as in Lemma 4.4 with $\beta_g(m) = \frac{p^k - 1}{p - 1} m$.*

4.3   Evaluation Algorithms for Circuits

We will now show how using the algorithms for single gates, that compute weighted additions and multiplications as described above, to build algorithms for the depth d, unbounded fan-in circuits.

Let $\{\mathcal{C}_\lambda\}_{\lambda \in \mathbb{N}}$ be a family of polynomial-size arithmetic circuits. For each $\mathcal{C} \in \mathcal{C}_\lambda$ we index the wires of $\mathcal{C}$ following the notation in [GVW13]. The input wires are indexed 1 to ℓ, the internal wires have indices $\ell + 1, \ell + 2, \ldots, |\mathcal{C}| - 1$ and the output wire has index $|\mathcal{C}|$, which also denotes the size of the circuit. Every gate $g_w : \mathbb{Z}_q^{k_w} \rightarrow \mathbb{Z}_q$ (in $\mathcal{G}$ as per 2) is indexed as a tuple $(w_1, \ldots, w_{k_w}, w)$ where k_w is the fan-in of the gate. We assume that all (but possibly one) of the input values to the multiplication gates are bounded by p which is smaller than scheme modulus q. The "fan-out wires" in the circuit are given a single number. That is, if the outgoing wire of a gate feeds into the input of multiple gates, then all these wires are indexed the same. For some $\lambda \in \mathbb{N}$, define the family of functions $\mathcal{F} = \{f : f \text{ can be computed by some } \mathcal{C} \in \mathcal{C}_\lambda\}$.

We construct the required matrices inductively input to output gate-by-gate. Consider an arbitrary gate of fan-in k_w (we will omit the subscript w where it is clear from the context): $(w_1, \ldots, w_k, w)$ that computes the function $g_w : \mathbb{Z}_q^k \rightarrow \mathbb{Z}_q$. Each wire w_i caries a value x_{w_i}. Suppose we already computed $\mathbf{B}_{w_1}, \ldots, \mathbf{B}_{w_k}$, $\mathbf{S}_{w_1}, \ldots, \mathbf{S}_{w_k}$ and $\mathbf{c}_{w_1}, \ldots, \mathbf{c}_{w_k}$, note that if $w_1, \ldots, w_k$ are all in $\{1, 2, \ldots, \ell\}$ then these matrices and vectors are the inputs of the corresponding Eval functions. Using Eval algorithms described in Section 4.2, compute

$$\mathbf{B}_w = \mathsf{Eval}_{\mathrm{pk}}(g_w, (\mathbf{B}_{w_1}, \ldots, \mathbf{B}_{w_k}))$$

$$\mathbf{c}_w = \mathsf{Eval}_{\mathrm{ct}}(g_w, ((x_{w_i}, \mathbf{B}_{w_i}, \mathbf{c}_{w_i}))_{i=1}^k)$$

$$\mathbf{S}_w = \mathsf{Eval}_{\mathrm{sim}}(g_w, ((x_{w_i}^*, \mathbf{S}_{w_i}))_{i=1}^k, \mathbf{A})$$

Output $\mathbf{B}_f := \mathbf{B}_{|\mathcal{C}|}$, $\mathbf{c}_f := \mathbf{c}_{|\mathcal{C}|}$, $\mathbf{S}_f := \mathbf{S}_{|\mathcal{C}|}$. Correctness follows inductively for the appropriate choice of parameters (see the full version and paragraph 1.1).

5 ABE with Short Secret Keys for Arithmetic Circuits from LWE

The FKHE for a family of functions $\mathcal{F} = \{f : (\mathbb{Z}_q)^\ell \rightarrow \mathbb{Z}_q\}$ constructed in Section 4 immediately gives a key-policy ABE as discussed in Section 3. In this section we give a self-contained construction of the ABE system. Given FKHE-enabling algorithms $(\mathsf{Eval}_{\mathrm{pk}}, \mathsf{Eval}_{\mathrm{ct}}, \mathsf{Eval}_{\mathrm{sim}})$ for a family of functions $\mathcal{F}$ from Section 4.1, the ABE system works as follows:

- $\mathsf{Setup}(1^\lambda, \ell)$: Choose n, q, χ, m and σ as in "Parameters" in Section 4. Run algorithm $\mathsf{TrapGen}(1^n, 1^m, q)$ (Lemma 2.1, part 1) to generate $(\mathbf{A}, \mathbf{T_A})$. Choose random matrices $\mathbf{D}, \mathbf{B}_1, \ldots, \mathbf{B}_\ell \in \mathbb{Z}_q^{n \times m}$ and output the keys:

$$\mathsf{mpk} = (\mathbf{A}, \mathbf{D}, \mathbf{B}_1, \ldots, \mathbf{B}_\ell) \quad ; \quad \mathsf{msk} = (\mathbf{T_A}, \mathbf{D}, \mathbf{B}_1, \ldots, \mathbf{B}_\ell)$$

- $\mathsf{Keygen}(\mathsf{msk}, f)$: Let $\mathbf{B}_f = \mathsf{Eval}_{\mathrm{pk}}(f, (\mathbf{B}_1, \ldots, \mathbf{B}_\ell))$. Output $\mathsf{sk}_f := \mathbf{R}_f$ where $\mathbf{R}_f$ is a low-norm matrix in $\mathbb{Z}^{2m \times m}$ sampled from the discrete Gaussian distribution $\mathcal{D}_\sigma(\Lambda_q^{\mathbf{D}}(\mathbf{A}|\mathbf{B}_f))$ so that $(\mathbf{A}|\mathbf{B}_f) \cdot \mathbf{R}_f = \mathbf{D}$. To construct $\mathbf{R}_f$ build the basis $\mathbf{T_F}$ for $\mathbf{F} = (\mathbf{A}|\mathbf{B}_f) \in \mathbb{Z}_q^{n \times 2m}$ as $\mathbf{T_F} \leftarrow \mathsf{ExtendRight}(\mathbf{A}, \mathbf{T_A}, \mathbf{B})$ from Lemma 2.1 (part 2). Then run $\mathbf{R}_f \leftarrow \mathsf{SampleD}(\mathbf{F}, \mathbf{T_F}, \mathbf{D}, \sigma)$. Note that the secret key sk_f is always in $\mathbb{Z}^{2m \times m}$ independent of the complexity of the function f.

- Enc(mpk, $\mathbf{x} \in \mathbb{Z}_q^\ell$, $\mu \in \{0,1\}^m$): Choose a random vector $\mathbf{s} \leftarrow \mathbb{Z}_q^n$ and error vectors $\mathbf{e}_0, \mathbf{e}_1 \leftarrow \chi^m$. Choose ℓ uniformly random matrices $\mathbf{S}_i \leftarrow \{\pm 1\}^{m \times m}$ for $i \in [\ell]$. Set

$$\mathbf{H} = (\mathbf{A} \mid x_1 \mathbf{G} + \mathbf{B}_1 \mid \cdots \mid x_\ell \mathbf{G} + \mathbf{B}_\ell) \quad \in \mathbb{Z}_q^{n \times (\ell+1)m}$$

$$\mathbf{e} = (\mathbf{I}_m | \mathbf{S}_1 | \ldots | \mathbf{S}_\ell)^\mathsf{T} \cdot \mathbf{e}_0 \quad \in \mathbb{Z}_q^{(\ell+1)m}$$

Output $\mathbf{c} = (\mathbf{H}^T \mathbf{s} + \mathbf{e}, \; \mathbf{D}^T \mathbf{s} + \mathbf{e}_1 + \lceil q/2 \rceil \mu) \in \mathbb{Z}_q^{(\ell+2)m}$.

- Dec$\big(\mathsf{sk}_f, \; (\mathbf{x}, \mathbf{c})\big)$: If $f(\mathbf{x}) \neq 0$ output $\perp$. Otherwise, let the ciphertext $\mathbf{c} = (\mathbf{c}_{in}, \mathbf{c}_1, \ldots, \mathbf{c}_\ell, \mathbf{c}_{out}) \in \mathbb{Z}_q^{(\ell+2)m}$, set $\mathbf{c}_f = \mathsf{Eval}_{\mathsf{ct}}\big(f, \; \{(x_i, \mathbf{B}_i, \mathbf{c}_i)\}_{i=1}^\ell\big) \in \mathbb{Z}_q^m$.

Let $\mathbf{c}'_f = (\mathbf{c}_{in} | \mathbf{c}_f) \in \mathbb{Z}_q^{2m}$ and output $\mathsf{Round}(\mathbf{c}_{out} - \mathbf{R}_f^\mathsf{T} \mathbf{c}'_f) \in \{0,1\}^m$.

The proof of the following theorem is analogous to that of the FKHE system which is sketched in Section 4 and given in details in the full version of the paper.

Theorem 5.1. *For FKHE-enabling algorithms* $(\mathsf{Eval}_{pk}, \mathsf{Eval}_{ct}, \mathsf{Eval}_{sim})$ *for a family of functions $\mathcal{F}$ the ABE system above is correct and selectively-secure.*

6   ABE with Short Ciphertexts from Multi-linear Maps

We assume familiarity with multi-linear maps [BS02, GGH13a] and refer the reader to the full version for definitions.

Intuition. We assume that the circuits consist of AND and OR gates. To handle general circuits (with negations), we can apply De Morgan's rule to transform it into a monotone circuit, doubling the number of input attributes (similar to [GGH⁺13c]).

The inspiration of our construction comes from the beautiful work of Applebaum, Ishai, Kushilevitz and Waters [AIKW13] who show a way to compress the garbled input in a (single use) garbling scheme all the way down to size $|\mathbf{x}| + \mathsf{poly}(\lambda)$. This is useful to us in the context of ABE schemes due to a simple connection between ABE and *reusable* garbled circuits with authenticity observed in [GVW13]. In essence, they observe that the secret key for a function f in an ABE scheme corresponds to the garbled circuit for f, and the ciphertext encrypting an attribute vector $\mathbf{x}$ corresponds to the garbled input for $\mathbf{x}$ in the reusable garbling scheme. Thus, the problem of compressing ciphertexts down to size $|\mathbf{x}| + \mathsf{poly}(\lambda)$ boils down to the question of generalizing [AIKW13] to the setting of *reusable* garbling schemes. We are able to achieve this using multilinear maps.

Security of the scheme relies on a generalization of the bilinear Diffie-Hellman Exponent Assumption to the multi-linear setting (see the full version of our paper for the precise description of the assumption.) [1] The bilinear Diffie-Hellman Exponent Assumption was recently used to prove the security of the first broadcast

---

[1] Our construction can be converted to multi-linear graded-encodings, recently instantiated by Garg et al. [GGH13a] and Coron et al. [CLT13].

encryption with constant size ciphertexts [BGW05] (which in turn can be thought of as a special case of ABE with short ciphertexts.)

Theorem 6.1 (Selective security). *For all polynomials $d_{max} = d_{max}(\lambda)$, there exists a selectively-secure attribute-based encryption with ciphertext size $poly(d_{max})$ for any family of polynomial-size circuits with depth at most d_{max} and input size ℓ, assuming hardness of $(d + 1, \ell)$–Multilinear Diffie-Hellman Exponent Assumption.*

6.1 Our Construction

We describe the construction here, and refer the reader to the full version for correctness and security proofs.

- Params($1^\lambda, d_{max}$): The parameters generation algorithm takes the security parameter and the maximum circuit depth. It generates a multi-linear map $\mathcal{G}(1^\lambda, k = d + 1)$ that produces groups $(G_1, \ldots, G_k)$ along with a set of generators $g_1, \ldots, g_k$ and map descriptors $\{e_{ij}\}$. It outputs the public parameters $pp = (\{G_i, g_i\}_{i \in [k]}, \{e_{ij}\}_{i,j \in [k]})$, which are implicitly known to all of the algorithms below.
- Setup(1^ℓ): For each input bit $i \in \{1, 2, \ldots, \ell\}$, choose a random element q_i in $\mathbb{Z}_p$. Let $g = g_1$ be the generator of the first group. Define $h_i = g^{q_i}$. Also, choose α at random from $\mathbb{Z}_p$ and let $t = g_k^\alpha$. Set the master public key

$$\mathsf{mpk} := (h_1, \ldots, h_\ell, t)$$

and the master secret key as $\mathsf{msk} := \alpha$.
- Keygen(msk, C): The key-generation algorithm takes a circuit C with ℓ input bits and a master secret key msk and outputs a secret key sk_C defined as follows.
  1. Choose randomly $((r_1, z_1), \ldots, (r_\ell, z_\ell))$ from $\mathbb{Z}_q^2$ for each input wire of the circuit C. In addition, choose $((r_{\ell+1}, a_{\ell+1}, b_{\ell+1}), \ldots, (r_n, a_n, b_n))$ from $\mathbb{Z}_q^3$ randomly for all internal wires of C.
  2. Compute an $\ell \times \ell$ matrix $\tilde{M}$, where all diagonal entries (i, i) are of the form $(h_i)^{z_i} g^{r_i}$ and all non-diagonal entries (i, j) are of the form $(h_i)^{z_j}$. Append g^{-z_i} as the last row of the matrix and call the resulting matrix M.
  3. Consider a gate $\Gamma = (u, v, w)$ where wires u, v are at depth $j - 1$ and w is at depth j. If Γ is an OR gate, compute

$$K_\Gamma = \left(K_\Gamma^1 = g^{a_w}, K_\Gamma^2 = g^{b_w}, K_\Gamma^3 = g_j^{r_w - a_w r_u}, K_\Gamma^4 = g_j^{r_w - b_w r_v} \right)$$

Else if Γ is an AND gate, compute

$$K_\Gamma = \left(K_\Gamma^1 = g^{a_w}, K_\Gamma^2 = g^{b_w}, K_\Gamma^3 = g_j^{r_w - a_w r_u - b_w r_v} \right)$$

  4. Set $\sigma = g_{k-1}^{\alpha - r_n}$
  5. Define and output the secret key as

$$\mathsf{sk}_C := \left(C, \{K_\Gamma\}_{\Gamma \in C}, M, \sigma \right)$$

- Enc(mpk, $\mathbf{x}$, μ): The encryption algorithm takes the master public key mpk, an index $\mathbf{x} \in \{0,1\}^\ell$ and a message $\mu \in \{0,1\}$, and outputs a ciphertext $\mathbf{c_x}$ defined as follows. Choose a random element s in $\mathbb{Z}_q$. Let X be the set of indices i such that $x_i = 1$. Let $\gamma_0 = t^s$ if $\mu = 1$, otherwise let γ_0 be a randomly chosen element from G_k. Output ciphertext as

$$\mathbf{c_x} := \left(\mathbf{x}, \gamma_0, \ g^s, \ \gamma_1 = \Big(\prod_{i \in X} h_i \Big)^s \right)$$

- Dec(sk_C, $\mathbf{c_x}$): The decryption algorithm takes the ciphertext $\mathbf{c_x}$, and secret key sk_C and proceeds as follows. If $C(\mathbf{x}) = 0$, it outputs $\bot$. Otherwise,
  1. Let X be the set of indices i such that $x_i = 1$. For each input wire $i \in X$, using the matrix M compute $g^{r_i} \big(\prod_{j \in X} h_j \big)^{z_i}$ and then

$$g_2^{r_i s} = e\left(g^s, g^{r_i} \Big(\prod_{j \in X} h_j \Big)^{z_i} \right) \cdot e\left(\gamma_1, g^{-z_i} \right)$$

$$= e\left(g^s, g^{r_i} \Big(\prod_{j \in X} h_j \Big)^{z_i} \right) \cdot e\left(\Big(\prod_{j \in X} h_j \Big)^s, g^{-z_i} \right)$$

  2. Now, for each gate $\Gamma = (u, v, w)$ where w is a wire at level j, (recursively going from the input to the output) compute $g_{j+1}^{r_w s}$ as follows:
     - If Γ is an OR gate, and $C(\mathbf{x})_u = 1$, compute $g_{j+1}^{r_w s} = e(K_\Gamma^1, g_j^{r_u s}) \cdot e(g^s, K_\Gamma^3)$.
     - Else if $C(\mathbf{x})_v = 1$, compute $g_{j+1}^{r_w s} = e(K_\Gamma^2, g_j^{r_v s}) \cdot e(g^s, K_\Gamma^4)$.
     - Else if Γ is an AND gate, compute $g_{j+1}^{r_w s} = e(K_\Gamma^1, g_j^{r_u s}) \cdot e(K_\Gamma^2, g_j^{r_v s}) \cdot e(g^s, K_\Gamma^3)$.

  3. If $C(\mathbf{x}) = 1$, then the user computes $g_k^{r_n s}$ for the output wire. Finally, compute
$$\psi = e(g^s, \sigma) \cdot g_k^{r_n s} = e(g^s, g_{k-1}^{\alpha - r_n}) \cdot g_k^{r_n s}$$
  4. Output $\mu = 1$ if $\psi = \gamma_0$, otherwise output 0.

Acknowledgments. We thank Chris Peikert for his helpful comments and for suggesting Remark 4.3.

D. Boneh is supported by NSF, the DARPA PROCEED program, an AFO SR MURI award, a grant from ONR, an IARPA project provided via DoI/NBC, and Google faculty award. Opinions, findings and conclusions or recommendations expressed in this material are those of the author(s) and do not necessarily reflect the views of DARPA or IARPA.

S. Gorbunov is supported by Alexander Graham Bell Canada Graduate Scholarship (CGSD3).

G. Segev is supported by the European Union's Seventh Framework Programme (FP7) via a Marie Curie Career Integration Grant, by the Israel Science Foundation (Grant No. 483/13), and by the Israeli Centers of Research Excellence (I-CORE) Program (Center No. 4/11).

V. Vaikuntanathan is supported by an NSERC Discovery Grant, DARPA Grant number FA8750-11-2-0225, a Connaught New Researcher Award, an Alfred P. Sloan Research Fellowship, and a Steven and Renee Finn Career Development Chair from MIT.

References

[ABB10]   Agrawal, S., Boneh, D., Boyen, X.: Efficient lattice (H)IBE in the standard model. In: Gilbert, H. (ed.) EUROCRYPT 2010. LNCS, vol. 6110, pp. 553–572. Springer, Heidelberg (2010)

[ABV+12]   Agrawal, S., Boyen, X., Vaikuntanathan, V., Voulgaris, P., Wee, H.: Functional encryption for threshold functions (or fuzzy ibe) from lattices. In: Fischlin, M., Buchmann, J., Manulis, M. (eds.) PKC 2012. LNCS, vol. 7293, pp. 280–297. Springer, Heidelberg (2012)

[AFV11]   Agrawal, S., Freeman, D.M., Vaikuntanathan, V.: Functional encryption for inner product predicates from learning with errors. In: Lee, D.H., Wang, X. (eds.) ASIACRYPT 2011. LNCS, vol. 7073, pp. 21–40. Springer, Heidelberg (2011)

[AIKW13]   Applebaum, B., Ishai, Y., Kushilevitz, E., Waters, B.: Encoding functions with constant online rate or how to compress garbled circuits keys. In: Canetti, R., Garay, J.A. (eds.) CRYPTO 2013, Part II. LNCS, vol. 8043, pp. 166–184. Springer, Heidelberg (2013)

[Ajt99]   Ajtai, M.: Generating hard instances of the short basis problem. In: Wiedermann, J., Van Emde Boas, P., Nielsen, M. (eds.) ICALP 1999. LNCS, vol. 1644, pp. 1–9. Springer, Heidelberg (1999)

[ALdP11]   Attrapadung, N., Libert, B., de Panafieu, E.: Expressive key-policy attribute-based encryption with constant-size ciphertexts. In: Catalano, D., Fazio, N., Gennaro, R., Nicolosi, A. (eds.) PKC 2011. LNCS, vol. 6571, pp. 90–108. Springer, Heidelberg (2011)

[AP09]   Alwen, J., Peikert, C.: Generating shorter bases for hard random lattices. In: STACS (2009)

[BB11]   Boneh, D., Boyen, X.: Efficient selective identity-based encryption without random oracles. Journal of Cryptology 24(4), 659–693 (2011)

[BF03]   Boneh, D., Franklin, M.K.: Identity-based encryption from the Weil pairing. SIAM Journal on Computing 32(3), 586–615 (2003)

[BGW05]   Boneh, D., Gentry, C., Waters, B.: Collusion resistant broadcast encryption with short ciphertexts and private keys. In: Shoup, V. (ed.) CRYPTO 2005. LNCS, vol. 3621, pp. 258–275. Springer, Heidelberg (2005)

[BMR90]   Beaver, D., Micali, S., Rogaway, P.: The round complexity of secure protocols (extended abstract). In: STOC (1990)

[BNS]   Boneh, D., Nikolaenko, V., Segev, G.: Attribute-based encryption for arithmetic circuits. Cryptology ePrint Report 2013/669

[Boy13]   Boyen, X.: Attribute-based functional encryption on lattices. In: Sahai, A. (ed.) TCC 2013. LNCS, vol. 7785, pp. 122–142. Springer, Heidelberg (2013)

[BS02]   Boneh, D., Silverberg, A.: Applications of multilinear forms to cryptography. Contemporary Mathematics 324, 71–90 (2002)

[BSW11]   Boneh, D., Sahai, A., Waters, B.: Functional encryption: Definitions and challenges. In: Ishai, Y. (ed.) TCC 2011. LNCS, vol. 6597, pp. 253–273. Springer, Heidelberg (2011)

[BW07]   Boneh, D., Waters, B.: Conjunctive, subset, and range queries on encrypted data. In: Vadhan, S.P. (ed.) TCC 2007. LNCS, vol. 4392, pp. 535–554. Springer, Heidelberg (2007)

[BW13]   Boneh, D., Waters, B.: Constrained pseudorandom functions and their applications. In: Sako, K., Sarkar, P. (eds.) ASIACRYPT 2013, Part II. LNCS, vol. 8270, pp. 280–300. Springer, Heidelberg (2013)

[CHKP10]   Cash, D., Hofheinz, D., Kiltz, E., Peikert, C.: Bonsai trees, or how to delegate a lattice basis. In: Gilbert, H. (ed.) EUROCRYPT 2010. LNCS, vol. 6110, pp. 523–552. Springer, Heidelberg (2010)

[CLT13]   Coron, J.-S., Lepoint, T., Tibouchi, M.: Practical multilinear maps over the integers. In: Canetti, R., Garay, J.A. (eds.) CRYPTO 2013, Part I. LNCS, vol. 8042, pp. 476–493. Springer, Heidelberg (2013)

[Coc01]   Cocks, C.: An identity based encryption scheme based on quadratic residues. In: IMA Int. Conf. (2001)

[FN93]   Fiat, A., Naor, M.: Broadcast encryption. In: Stinson, D.R. (ed.) CRYPTO 1993. LNCS, vol. 773, pp. 480–491. Springer, Heidelberg (1994)

[GGH+]   Gentry, C., Gorbunov, S., Halevi, S., Vaikuntanathan, V., Vinayagamurthy, D.: How to compress (reusable) garbled circuits. Cryptology ePrint Report 2013/687

[GGH13a]   Garg, S., Gentry, C., Halevi, S.: Candidate multilinear maps from ideal lattices. In: Johansson, T., Nguyen, P.Q. (eds.) EUROCRYPT 2013. LNCS, vol. 7881, pp. 1–17. Springer, Heidelberg (2013)

[GGH+13b]   Garg, S., Gentry, C., Halevi, S., Raykova, M., Sahai, A., Waters, B.: Candidate indistinguishability obfuscation and functional encryption for all circuits. In: FOCS (2013)

[GGH+13c]   Garg, S., Gentry, C., Halevi, S., Sahai, A., Waters, B.: Attribute-based encryption for circuits from multilinear maps. In: Canetti, R., Garay, J.A. (eds.) CRYPTO 2013, Part II. LNCS, vol. 8043, pp. 479–499. Springer, Heidelberg (2013)

[GGP10]   Gennaro, R., Gentry, C., Parno, B.: Non-interactive verifiable computing: Outsourcing computation to untrusted workers. In: Rabin, T. (ed.) CRYPTO 2010. LNCS, vol. 6223, pp. 465–482. Springer, Heidelberg (2010)

[GGSW13]   Garg, S., Gentry, C., Sahai, A., Waters, B.: Witness encryption and its applications. In: STOC (2013)

[GHV10]   Gentry, C., Halevi, S., Vaikuntanathan, V.: A simple BGN-type cryptosystem from LWE. In: Gilbert, H. (ed.) EUROCRYPT 2010. LNCS, vol. 6110, pp. 506–522. Springer, Heidelberg (2010)

[GKP+13a]   Goldwasser, S., Kalai, Y.T., Popa, R.A., Vaikuntanathan, V., Zeldovich, N.: How to run turing machines on encrypted data. In: Canetti, R., Garay, J.A. (eds.) CRYPTO 2013, Part II. LNCS, vol. 8043, pp. 536–553. Springer, Heidelberg (2013)

[GKP+13b]   Goldwasser, S., Kalai, Y.T., Popa, R.A., Vaikuntanathan, V., Zeldovich, N.: Reusable garbled circuits and succinct functional encryption. In: STOC (2013)

[GKR08]   Goldwasser, S., Kalai, Y.T., Rothblum, G.N.: Delegating computation: interactive proofs for muggles. In: STOC (2008)

[GPSW06]   Goyal, V., Pandey, O., Sahai, A., Waters, B.: Attribute-based encryption for fine-grained access control of encrypted data. In: ACM CCS (2006)

[GPV08]   Gentry, C., Peikert, C., Vaikuntanathan, V.: Trapdoors for hard lattices and new cryptographic constructions. In: STOC (2008)

556   D. Boneh et al.

[GVW13]   Gorbunov, S., Vaikuntanathan, V., Wee, H.: Attribute-based encryption for circuits. In: STOC (2013)

[HW13]   Hohenberger, S., Waters, B.: Attribute-based encryption with fast decryption. In: Kurosawa, K., Hanaoka, G. (eds.) PKC 2013. LNCS, vol. 7778, pp. 162–179. Springer, Heidelberg (2013)

[KS08]   Kolesnikov, V., Schneider, T.: Improved garbled circuit: Free XOR gates and applications. In: Aceto, L., Damgård, I., Goldberg, L.A., Halldórsson, M.M., Ingólfsdóttir, A., Walukiewicz, I. (eds.) ICALP 2008, Part II. LNCS, vol. 5126, pp. 486–498. Springer, Heidelberg (2008)

[KSW08]   Katz, J., Sahai, A., Waters, B.: Predicate encryption supporting disjunctions, polynomial equations, and inner products. In: Smart, N.P. (ed.) EUROCRYPT 2008. LNCS, vol. 4965, pp. 146–162. Springer, Heidelberg (2008)

[LO13]   Lu, S., Ostrovsky, R.: How to garble ram programs. In: Johansson, T., Nguyen, P.Q. (eds.) EUROCRYPT 2013. LNCS, vol. 7881, pp. 719–734. Springer, Heidelberg (2013)

[LOS+10] Lewko, A., Okamoto, T., Sahai, A., Takashima, K., Waters, B.: Fully secure functional encryption: Attribute-based encryption and (hierarchical) inner product encryption. In: Gilbert, H. (ed.) EUROCRYPT 2010. LNCS, vol. 6110, pp. 62–91. Springer, Heidelberg (2010)

[LW12]   Lewko, A., Waters, B.: New proof methods for attribute-based encryption: Achieving full security through selective techniques. In: Safavi-Naini, R., Canetti, R. (eds.) CRYPTO 2012. LNCS, vol. 7417, pp. 180–198. Springer, Heidelberg (2012)

[MP12]   Micciancio, D., Peikert, C.: Trapdoors for lattices: Simpler, tighter, faster, smaller. In: Pointcheval, D., Johansson, T. (eds.) EUROCRYPT 2012. LNCS, vol. 7237, pp. 700–718. Springer, Heidelberg (2012)

[OT10]   Okamoto, T., Takashima, K.: Fully secure functional encryption with general relations from the decisional linear assumption. In: Rabin, T. (ed.) CRYPTO 2010. LNCS, vol. 6223, pp. 191–208. Springer, Heidelberg (2010)

[Pei09]   Peikert, C.: Public-key cryptosystems from the worst-case shortest vector problem. In: STOC (2009)

[PRV12]   Parno, B., Raykova, M., Vaikuntanathan, V.: How to delegate and verify in public: Verifiable computation from attribute-based encryption. In: Cramer, R. (ed.) TCC 2012. LNCS, vol. 7194, pp. 422–439. Springer, Heidelberg (2012)

[PTMW06] Pirretti, M., Traynor, P., McDaniel, P., Waters, B.: Secure attribute-based systems. In: ACM CCS (2006)

[Reg05]   Regev, O.: On lattices, learning with errors, random linear codes, and cryptography. In: STOC (2005)

[Sha84]   Shamir, A.: Identity-based cryptosystems and signature schemes. In: Blakely, G.R., Chaum, D. (eds.) CRYPTO 1984. LNCS, vol. 196, pp. 47–53. Springer, Heidelberg (1985)

[SW05]   Sahai, A., Waters, B.: Fuzzy identity-based encryption. In: Cramer, R. (ed.) EUROCRYPT 2005. LNCS, vol. 3494, Springer, Heidelberg (2005)

[Wat12]   Waters, B.: Functional encryption for regular languages. In: Safavi-Naini, R., Canetti, R. (eds.) CRYPTO 2012. LNCS, vol. 7417, pp. 218–235. Springer, Heidelberg (2012)

[Yao86]   Yao, A.C.: How to generate and exchange secrets (extended abstract). In: FOCS (1986)

Dual System Encryption via Doubly Selective Security: Framework, Fully Secure Functional Encryption for Regular Languages, and More

Nuttapong Attrapadung

National Institute of Advanced Industrial Science and Technology (AIST), Japan
n.attrapadung@aist.go.jp

Abstract. Dual system encryption techniques introduced by Waters in Crypto'09 are powerful approaches for constructing fully secure functional encryption (FE) for many predicates. However, there are still some FE for certain predicates to which dual system encryption techniques seem inapplicable, and hence their fully-secure realization remains an important problem. A notable example is FE for regular languages, introduced by Waters in Crypto'12.

We propose a generic framework that abstracts the concept of dual system encryption techniques. We introduce a new primitive called *pair encoding* scheme for predicates and show that it implies fully secure functional encryption (for the same predicates) via a generic construction. Using the framework, we obtain the first fully secure schemes for functional encryption primitives of which only selectively secure schemes were known so far. Our three main instantiations include FE for regular languages, unbounded attribute-based encryption (ABE) for large universes, and ABE with constant-size ciphertexts.

Our main ingredient for overcoming the barrier of inapplicability for the dual system techniques to certain predicates is a computational security notion of the pair encoding scheme which we call *doubly selective security*. This is in contrast with most of the previous dual system based schemes, where information-theoretic security are implicitly utilized. The doubly selective security notion resembles that of selective security and its complementary notion, co-selective security, and hence its name. Our framework can be regarded as a method for boosting doubly selectively security (of encoding) to full security (of functional encryption).

Besides generality of our framework, we remark that improved security is also obtained, as our security proof enjoys tighter reduction than previous schemes, notably the reduction cost does not depend on the number of all queries, but only that of *pre-challenged* queries.

1 Introduction

Dual system encryption techniques introduced by Waters [33] have been successful approaches for proving adaptive security (or called full security) for functional encryption (FE) schemes that are based on bilinear groups. These include adaptively-secure schemes for (hierarchical) id-based encryption (HIBE) [33,20,22,19],

P.Q. Nguyen and E. Oswald (Eds.): EUROCRYPT 2014, LNCS 8441, pp. 557–577, 2014.

attribute-based encryption (ABE) for Boolean formulae [24,28,23], inner-product encryption [24,28,1,29,30], and spatial encryption [1,17].

Due to structural similarities between these fully secure schemes obtained via the dual system encryption paradigm and their selectively secure counterparts previously proposed for the same primitive[1], it is perhaps a folklore that the dual system encryption approach can somewhat elevate the latter to achieve the former. This is unfortunately not so, or perhaps not so clear, as there are some functional encryption schemes that are only proved selectively secure at the present time and seem to essentially encounter problems when applying dual system proof techniques. A notable example is FE for regular languages proposed by Waters [34], for which fully secure realization remains an open problem.

In this paper, we affirmatively solve this by proposing the first fully secure functional encryption for regular languages. Towards solving it, we provide a generic framework that captures the core concept of the dual system encryption techniques. This gives us an insight as to why it was not clear in the first place that dual system encryption techniques can be successfully applied to certain primitives, but not others. Such an insight leads us not only to identify the obstacle when applying the techniques and then to find a solution that overcomes it, but also to improve the performance of security proofs in a generic way. Namely, our framework allows tighter security reduction.

We summarize our contributions below. We first recall the notion of functional encryption, formulated in [7]. Well-known examples of functional encryption such as ABE and the more recent one for regular languages can be considered as "public-index" predicate encryption, which is a class of functional encryption. We focus on this class in this paper.[2] A primitive in this class is defined by a predicate R. In such a scheme, a sender can associate a ciphertext with a ciphertext attribute Y while a secret key is associated with a key attribute X. Such a ciphertext can then be decrypted by such a key if $R(X, Y)$ holds.

1.1   Summary of Our Main Contributions

In this paper, we propose a generic framework that captures the concept of dual system encryption techniques. It is generic in the sense that it can be applied to *arbitrary* predicate R. The main component in our framework is a new notion called *pair encoding* scheme defined for predicate R. We formalize its security properties into two notions called *perfectly master-key hiding*, which is an information-theoretic notion, and *doubly selectively master-key hiding*, which is a computational notion. The latter consists of two notions which are *selective master-key hiding* and its complementary one called *co-selective master-key hiding* (and hence is named *doubly*). Our main results are summarized as follows.

Generic Construction. We construct a generic construction of fully secure functional encryption for predicate R from any pair encoding scheme for R which

---

[1] One explicit example is the fully secure HIBE of Lewko and Waters [20], which has the structure almost identical to the selectively secure HIBE by Boneh, Boyen, Goh [5].

[2] In this paper, the term "functional encryption" refers to this class.

is either perfectly master-key hiding or doubly selectively master-key hiding. Our construction is based on composite-order bilinear groups.

Instantiations. We give concrete constructions of pair encoding schemes for notable three predicates of which there is no known fully-secure functional encryption realization. By using the generic construction, we obtain fully secure schemes. These include the following.

- The first fully-secure functional encryption for regular languages. Only a selectively-secure scheme was known [34]. We indeed improve not only security but also efficiency: ours will work on *unbounded alphabet* universe, as opposed to *small universe* as in the original construction.
- The first fully-secure unbounded key-policy ABE with large universes. Such a system requires that no bound should be posed on the sizes of attribute set and policies. The available schemes are either selectively-secure [22,26] or small-universe [23] or restricted for multi-use of attributes [30].
- The first fully-secure key-policy ABE with constant-size ciphertexts. The available schemes are either only selectively-secure scheme [2], or restricted to small classes of policies [9].

Our three underlying pair encoding schemes are proved doubly selectively secure under new static assumptions, each of which is parameterized by the sizes of attributes in one ciphertext or one key, but *not* by the number of queries. These can be considered comparable to those assumptions for the respective selectively secure counterparts ([34,26,2], resp.).

Improved Security Reduction. By starting from a pair encoding scheme which is doubly selectively master-key hiding, the resulting functional encryption can be proved fully secure with tighter security reduction to subgroup decision assumptions (and the doubly selective security). More precisely, it enjoys reduction cost of $O(q_1)$, where q_1 is the number of *pre-challenged* key queries. This improves all the previous works based on dual system encryption (except only one recent work on IBE by [8]) of which reduction encumbers $O(q_{all})$ security loss, where q_{all} is the number of *all* key queries. As an instantiation, we propose an IBE scheme with $O(q_1)$ reduction, while enjoys similar efficiency to [20].

More Results. We also obtain some more results, which could not fit in the space here. These include a generic conversion for dual primitives (*i.e.*, key-policy to ciphertext-policy and vice-versa) for perfectly secure encoding, the first dual FE for regular languages, a unified treatment for existing FE schemes and improvements for ABE scheme of [24] (reducing key sizes to half for free, and a large-universe variant), a new primitive called key-policy over doubly spatial encryption, which unifies KP-ABE and (doubly) spatial encryption [17].

1.2   Related Work

Chen and Wee [8] recently proposed the notion of dual system groups. It can be seen as a *complementary* work to ours: their construction unifies group structures where dual system techniques are applicable (namely, composite-order and prime-order groups) but for specific primitives (namely, IBE and HIBE), while our construction unifies schemes for *arbitrary predicate* but over specific groups (namely, composite-order bilinear groups). It is also worth mentioning that the topic of functional encryption stems from many research papers: we list some more here [3,6,16,18,27,32]. Recent results give very general FE primitives such as ABE or FE for circuits [15,11,13,12], and for Turing Machines [14], but most of them might still be considered as proofs of concept, since underlying cryptographic tools such as multilinear maps [10] seem still inefficient. Constructing fully secure ABE for circuits *without complexity leveraging* is an open problem.

2   An Intuitive Overview of Our Framework

In this section, we provide an intuition for our formalization of the dual system techniques and describe how we define pair encoding schemes. In our framework, we view a ciphertext (C, C_0) (encrypting M), and a key K as

$$C = g_1^{c(s,h)}, \quad C_0 = Me(g_1, g_1)^{\alpha s}; \qquad K = g_1^{k(\alpha, r, h)}$$

where c and k are *encoding functions* of attributes Y, X associated to ciphertext and key, respectively. The bold font represents vectors. Our aim is to formalize such functions by providing sufficient conditions so that the scheme can be proved fully-secure in a generic way. We call such functions *pair encoding* for predicate R, since they encode a pair of attributes which are inputs to predicate R. They can be viewed as (multi-variate) polynomials in variables from s (which includes s), h, r, and α. Intuitively, α corresponds to a master key, h corresponds to parameter that will define public key g_1^h, and s, r correspond to randomness in ciphertexts and keys, respectively. We would require the following: (1) *correctness*, stating that if $R(X, Y) = 1$ then both encoding functions can be paired to obtain αs; and (2) *security*, which is the property when $R(X, Y) = 0$, and we show how to define it below. The key novelty of our abstraction stems from the way we define the security of encoding. Along the discussion, for a better understanding, a reader may think of the equality predicate and the Boneh-Boyen [4] IBE as a concrete example. Their encoding would be: $c(s, h) = (s, s(h_1 + h_2 Y))$ and $k(\alpha, r, h) = (\alpha + r(h_1 + h_2 X), r)$, where $h = (h_1, h_2)$.

We first recall how dual system encryption techniques can be used to achieve *adaptive security*. The idea is to mimic the functionality of the encryption scheme in the *semi-functional* space, and to define the corresponding parameter $\hat{h}$ in the semi-functional space to be independent from that of normal space, h. Adaptive security is then obtained by observing that $\hat{h}$ will not appear anywhere until the first query, which means that the reduction algorithm in the proof can adaptively deal with the adversary since it does not have to fix $\hat{h}$ in advance. This is in contrast with h, which is fixed in the public key g_1^h. In the case of composite-order groups, the semi-functional space is implemented in a subgroup $\mathbb{G}_{p_2}$ of a group $\mathbb{G}$ of composite order $p_1 p_2 p_3$ (and the normal space is in $\mathbb{G}_{p_1}$).

Our purpose of abstraction is to capture the above mechanism in a generic way, while at the same time, to incorporate the security of encoding. Our main

Table 1. Summary for properties used in each transition for C, K

Transition	Changes in $\mathbb{G}_{p_2}$	Indistinguishability under	Other properties of pair encoding
$C : 0 \to 1$	$g_2^{c(0,0)} \to g_2^{c(\hat{s},\hat{h})}$	subgroup decision	linearity, param-vanishing
$K : 0 \to 1$	$g_2^{k(0,0,0)} \to g_2^{k(0,\hat{r},\hat{h})}$	subgroup decision	linearity, param-vanishing
$K : 1 \to 2$	$g_2^{k(0,\hat{r},\hat{h})} \to g_2^{k(\hat{\alpha},\hat{r},\hat{h})}$	security of encoding	none
$K : 2 \to 3$	$g_2^{k(\hat{\alpha},\hat{r},\hat{h})} \to g_2^{k(\hat{\alpha},0,0)}$	subgroup decision	linearity, param-vanishing

idea for doing this is to define semi-functional types of ciphertexts and keys explicitly *in terms of pair encoding functions*, so that the scheme structure would be copied to the semi-functional space. More precisely, we define semi-functional ciphertexts and keys as follows: C_0 is unmodified, and let

$$
C = \begin{cases} g_1^{c(s,h)} \cdot g_2^{c(0,0)} & \text{(normal)} \\ g_1^{c(s,h)} \cdot g_2^{c(\hat{s},\hat{h})} & \text{(semi)} \end{cases}, \quad K = \begin{cases} g_1^{k(\alpha,r,h)} \cdot g_2^{k(0,0,0)} & \text{(normal)} \\ g_1^{k(\alpha,r,h)} \cdot g_2^{k(0,\hat{r},\hat{h})} & \text{(semi type 1)} \\ g_1^{k(\alpha,r,h)} \cdot g_2^{k(\hat{\alpha},\hat{r},\hat{h})} & \text{(semi type 2)} \\ g_1^{k(\alpha,r,h)} \cdot g_2^{k(\hat{\alpha},0,0)} & \text{(semi type 3)} \end{cases}
$$

where '·' denotes the component-wise group operation. The "semi-functional variables" (those with the hat notation) are defined to be independent from the normal part. (We neglect mask elements from $\mathbb{G}_{p_3}$ now for simplicity).

We then recall that the proof strategy for the dual system techniques uses hybrid games that modifies ciphertexts and keys from normal to semi-functional ones, and proves indistinguishability between each transition. By defining semi-functional types as above, we can identify which transition uses *security of encoding* and which one uses *security provided by composite-order groups* (namely, subgroup decision assumptions). We provide these in Table 1. In particular, we identify that the security of encoding is used in the transition from type 1 to type 2 semi-functional keys. We note that how to identify this transition was unclear in the first place, since in all the previous dual system based schemes (to the best of our knowledge), the indistinguishability of this form is *implicitly* employed inside another transition (*cf.* nominally semi-functional keys in [24]).

We explore both types of transitions and define properties needed, as follows.

Transition Based on the Security of Encoding. We simply define the security of encoding to be just as what we need for the transition definition. More precisely, the security of encoding (in the "basic" form) requires that, if $R(X, Y) = 0$, then the following distributions are indistinguishable:

$$
\left\{ g_2^{c(\hat{s},\hat{h})}, \ g_2^{k(0,\hat{r},\hat{h})} \right\} \quad \text{and} \quad \left\{ g_2^{c(\hat{s},\hat{h})}, \ g_2^{k(\hat{\alpha},\hat{r},\hat{h})} \right\},
$$

where the probability taken over random $\hat{h}$ (and others). We remark a crucial point that the fact that we define keys of *normal* types and semi-functional *type 3*

Table 2. Summary of approaches for defining the security of encoding

Indistinguishability between		Security	Implicit in
$\left\{ c(\hat{s},\hat{h}), k(0,\hat{r},\hat{h}) \right\}$, $\left\{ c(\hat{s},\hat{h}), k(\hat{\alpha},\hat{r},\hat{h}) \right\}$		info-theoretic	all but [23,8]
$\left\{ g_2^{c(\hat{s},\hat{h})}, g_2^{k(0,\hat{r},\hat{h})} \right\}$, $\left\{ g_2^{c(\hat{s},\hat{h})}, g_2^{k(\hat{\alpha},\hat{r},\hat{h})} \right\}$		computational	[23]
$\left\{ g_2^{c(\hat{s},\hat{h})}, \{g_2^{k_i(0,\hat{r}_i,\hat{h})}\}_{i\in Q} \right\}$, $\left\{ g_2^{c(\hat{s},\hat{h})}, \{g_2^{k_i(\hat{\alpha},\hat{r}_i,\hat{h})}\}_{i\in Q} \right\}$		computational	new

to not depend on $\hat{h}$ allows us to focus on the distribution corresponding to only *one key at a time*, while "isolating" other keys. (This is called key isolation feature in [23]). We provide more flavors of the definition below. Indeed, the computational variant is what makes our framework powerful.

Transitions Based on Subgroup Decision Assumptions. We require *all* pair encoding schemes to satisfy some properties in order to use subgroup decision assumptions. We identify the following two properties: *parameter-vanishing* and *linearity*.

(Param-Vanishing) $$k(\alpha, 0, h) = k(\alpha, 0, 0).$$

(Linearity) $$k(\alpha_1, r_1, h) + k(\alpha_2, r_2, h) = k(\alpha_1 + \alpha_2, r_1 + r_2, h),$$
$$c(s_1, h) + c(s_2, h) = c(s_1 + s_2, h).$$

Linearity makes it possible to indistinguishably change the randomness between 0 and $\hat{r}$ (in the case of k), and between 0 and $\hat{s}$ (in the case of c) under subgroup decision assumptions, but without changing the other variables (*i.e.,* $\hat{\alpha}, \hat{h}$). Parameter-vanishing can then "delete" $\hat{h}$ when $\hat{r} = 0$. The latter makes it possible to obtain the key isolation, required for the previous type of transition. A subgroup decision assumption states that it is hard to distinguish if $t_2 = 0$ or $t_2 \xleftarrow{\$} \mathbb{Z}_{p_2}$ in $T = g_1^{t_1} g_2^{t_2}$. The intuition of how to use this assumption in conjunction with linearity is, for example, to simulate a key as $g_1^{k(\alpha,0,h')} T^{k(0,r',h')}$, for known α, r', h' chosen randomly. This is a normal key if $t_2 = 0$ and semi-functional type-1 if $t_2 \xleftarrow{\$} \mathbb{Z}_{p_2}$. In doing so, we implicitly set $h = h' \bmod p_1$ and $\hat{h} = h' \bmod p_2$, but these are independent exactly due to the Chinese Remainder Theorem. (The last property is referred as parameter-hiding in prior work). We also note that linearity implies homogeneity: $c(0, 0) = 0$, $k(0, 0, 0) = 0$, and hence we can write the normal ciphertext and key as above.

Perfect Security of Pair Encoding. We identify three flavors for the security of encoding that imply the basic form of security defined above. We list them in Table 2. We refer the first notion as the *perfectly master-key hiding* security, which is an *information-theoretic* notion. All the previous dual system based schemes (except [23,8]) implicitly employed this approach. For some esoteric predicates (*e.g.,* the regular language functionality), the amount of information from $\hat{h}$ needed for hiding $\hat{\alpha}$ is not sufficient. This is exactly the reason why the "classical" dual system approach is inapplicable to FE for regular languages.

Computational Security of Pair Encoding. The second flavor (the second line of Table 2, which is exactly the same as the aforementioned basic form) employs *computational* security argument to hide $\hat{\alpha}$, and can overcome the obstacle of insufficient entropy, suffered in the first approach. This approach was introduced by Lewko and Waters [23] to overcome the obstacle of multi-use restriction in KP-ABE. We generalize their approach to work for any predicate.

When considering computational approaches, the ordering of queries from the adversary becomes important since the challenger is required to fix the value of $\hat{h}$ after receiving the first query. This is reminiscent of the notion of *selective security* for FE, where the challenger would fix public parameters after seeing the challenge ciphertext attribute. To this end, we refer this notion as *selective master-key hiding*, if a query for Y (corresponding to the encoding c) comes before that of X (for the encoding k), and analogously, *co-selective* master-key hiding if a query for X comes before that of Y, where we recall that co-selective security [1] is a complementary notion of selective security.[3]

Tighter Reduction. The classical dual system paradigm requires $O(q_{\mathrm{all}})$ transition steps, hence results in $O(q_{\mathrm{all}})$ loss for security reduction, where q_{all} is the number of all key queries. This is since each step is reduced to its underlying security: subgroup indistinguishability or the security of encoding. This is the case for all the previous works except the IBE scheme of [8].[4] To overcome this obstacle, we propose the third flavor for security of encoding, shown in the third line of Table 2. This new approach is unique to our framework (no implicit use in the literature before). The idea is to observe that, for the selective security proof, the reduction can program the parameter once by using the information of the ciphertext attribute Y, and after that, *any* keys for X such that $R(X, Y) = 0$ can be produced. Therefore, we can organize all the *post-challenged* keys into the correlated distribution (hence, in Table 2, we set Q to be this set of queries). This has a great benefit since we can define a new type of transition where all these *post-challenged* keys are simultaneously modified from semi-functional type-1 to type-2 *all at once*, which results in tighter reduction, $O(q_1)$, where q_1 is the number of *pre-challenged* queries. On the other hand, one could try to do the same by grouping also all the *pre-challenged* queries and mimicking co-selective security, so as to obtain tight reduction (with $O(1)$ cost). However, this will not work since the parameter must be fixed already after *only the first query*.

3 Preliminaries

3.1 Functional Encryption

Predicate Family. We consider a predicate family $R = \{R_\kappa\}_{\kappa \in \mathbb{N}^c}$, for some constant $c \in \mathbb{N}$, where a relation $R_\kappa : \mathbb{X}_\kappa \times \mathbb{Y}_\kappa \to \{0, 1\}$ is a predicate function

---

[3] As a result, this also clarifies why [23] uses selective security techniques of KP-ABE and *CP-ABE* to prove the full security of KP-ABE. This is since selective security of an FE (CP-ABE, in their case) resembles co-selective security of its *dual* (KP-ABE).

[4] The IBE of [8] used a technique from Naor and Reingold [25] PRFs for their computational argument, which is different from ours.

that maps a pair of key attribute in a space $\mathbb{X}_\kappa$ and ciphertext attribute in a space $\mathbb{Y}_\kappa$ to $\{0,1\}$. The family index $\kappa = (n_1, n_2, \ldots)$ specifies the description of a predicate from the family.

Predicate in Different Domains. We mandate the first entry n_1 in κ to specify some domain; for example, the domain $\mathbb{Z}_N$ of IBE (the equality predicate), where we let $n_1 = N$. In what follows, we will implement our scheme in composite-order groups and some relations among different domains in the same family will be used. We formalize them here. We omit κ and write simply R_N. We say that R is *domain-transferable* if for p that divides N, we have projection maps $f_1 : \mathbb{X}_N \to \mathbb{X}_p, f_2 : \mathbb{Y}_N \to \mathbb{Y}_p$ such that for all $X \in \mathbb{X}_N, Y \in \mathbb{Y}_N$:

- **Completeness.** If $R_N(X, Y) = 1$ then $R_p(f_1(X), f_2(Y)) = 1$.
- **Soundness.** (1) If $R_N(X, Y) = 0$ then $R_p(f_1(X), f_2(Y)) = 0$, *or* (2) there exists an algorithm that takes (X, Y) where (1) does not hold, and outputs a non-trivial factor F, where $p|F, F|N$.

The completeness will be used for correctness of the scheme, while the soundness will used in the security proof. All the predicates in this paper are domain-transferable. As an example, in the equality predicate (for IBE), R_N and R_p are defined on $\mathbb{Z}_N$ and $\mathbb{Z}_p$ respectively. The projective maps are simply modulo p. Completeness holds straightforwardly. Soundness holds since for $X \neq Y$ (mod N) but $X = Y$ (mod p), we set $F = X - Y$. The other predicates in this paper can be proved similarly and we omit them here.

Functional Encryption Syntax. A functional encryption (FE) scheme for predicate family R consists of the following algorithms.

- Setup$(1^\lambda, \kappa) \to$ (PK, MSK): takes as input a security parameter 1^λ and a family index κ of predicate family R, and outputs a master public key PK and a master secret key MSK.
- Encrypt$(Y, M, \text{PK}) \to$ CT: takes as input a ciphertext attribute $Y \in \mathbb{Y}_\kappa$, a message $M \in \mathcal{M}$, and public key PK. It outputs a ciphertext CT.
- KeyGen$(X, \text{MSK}, \text{PK}) \to$ SK: takes as input a key attribute $X \in \mathbb{X}_\kappa$ and the master key MSK. It outputs a secret key SK.
- Decrypt$(\text{CT}, \text{SK}) \to M$: given a ciphertext CT with its attribute Y and the decryption key SK with its attribute X, it outputs a message M or $\bot$.

Correctness. Consider all indexes κ, all $M \in \mathcal{M}$, $X \in \mathbb{X}_\kappa$, $Y \in \mathbb{Y}_\kappa$ such that $R_\kappa(X, Y) = 1$. If Encrypt$(Y, M, \text{PK}) \to$ CT and KeyGen$(X, \text{MSK}, \text{PK}) \to$ SK where (PK, MSK) is generated from Setup$(1^\lambda, \kappa)$, then Decrypt$(\text{CT}, \text{SK}) \to M$.

Security Notion. A functional encryption scheme for predicate family R is fully secure if no probabilistic polynomial time (PPT) adversary $\mathcal{A}$ has non-negligible advantage in the following game between $\mathcal{A}$ and the challenger $\mathcal{C}$. For our purpose of modifying games in next sections, we write some in the boxes. Let q_1, q_2 be the numbers of queries in Phase 1,2, respectively.

1 **Setup:** C runs [(1)] $\boxed{\mathsf{Setup}(1^\lambda, \kappa) \rightarrow (\mathsf{PK}, \mathsf{MSK})}$ and hands PK to $\mathcal{A}$.

2 **Phase 1:** $\mathcal{A}$ makes a j-th private key query for $X_j \in \mathbb{X}_\kappa$. C returns SK_j by computing [(2)] $\boxed{\mathsf{SK}_j \leftarrow \mathsf{KeyGen}(X_j, \mathsf{MSK}, \mathsf{PK})}$.

3 **Challenge:** $\mathcal{A}$ submits equal-length messages M_0, M_1 and a target ciphertext attribute $Y^\star \in \mathbb{Y}_\kappa$ with the restriction that $R_\kappa(X_j, Y^\star) = 0$ for all $j \in [1, q_1]$. C flips a bit $b \xleftarrow{\$} \{0, 1\}$ and returns the challenge ciphertext [(3)] $\boxed{\mathsf{CT}^\star \leftarrow \mathsf{Encrypt}(Y^\star, M_b, \mathsf{PK})}$.

4 **Phase 2:** $\mathcal{A}$ continues to make a j-th private key query for $X_j \in \mathbb{X}_\kappa$ under the restriction $R_\kappa(X_j, Y^\star) = 0$. C returns [(4)] $\boxed{\mathsf{SK}_j \leftarrow \mathsf{KeyGen}(X_j, \mathsf{MSK}, \mathsf{PK})}$.

5 **Guess:** The adversary $\mathcal{A}$ outputs a guess $b' \in \{0, 1\}$ and wins if $b' = b$. The advantage of $\mathcal{A}$ against the scheme FE is defined as $\mathsf{Adv}_\mathcal{A}^{\mathsf{FE}}(\lambda) := |\Pr[b = b'] - \frac{1}{2}|$.

3.2 Definitions for Some Concrete Functional Encryption

FE for Regular Languages (DFA-based FE). In this primitive, we have a key associated to the description of a deterministic finite automata (DFA) M, while a ciphertext is associated to a string w, and $R(M, w) = 1$ if the automata M accepts the string w. A DFA M is a 5-tuple $(Q, \Lambda, \mathcal{T}, q_0, F)$ in which Q is the set of states $Q = \{q_0, q_1, \ldots, q_{n-1}\}$, Λ is the alphabet set, $\mathcal{T}$ is the set of transitions, in which each transition is of the form $(q_x, q_y, \sigma) \in Q \times Q \times \Lambda$, $q_0 \in Q$ is the start state, and $F \subseteq Q$ is the set of accepted states. We say that M accepts a string $w = (w_1, w_2, \ldots, w_\ell) \in \Lambda^*$ if there exists a sequence of states $\rho_0, \rho_1, \cdots, \rho_n \in Q$ such that $\rho_0 = q_0$, for $i = 1$ to ℓ we have $(\rho_{i-1}, \rho_i, w_i) \in \mathcal{T}$, and $\rho_\ell \in F$. This primitive is important since it has a unique unbounded feature that one key for machine M can operate on input string w of *arbitrary* sizes. We note that it is wlog if we consider machines such that $|F| = 1$ (see the full version), and we will construct our scheme with this wlog condition.

Attribute Based Encryption for Boolean Formulae. Let $\mathcal{U}$ be a universe of attributes. In Key-Policy ABE, a key is associated to a policy, which is described by a boolean formulae Ψ over $\mathcal{U}$, while a ciphertext is associated to an attribute set $S \subseteq \mathcal{U}$. We have $R(\Psi, S) = 1$ if the evaluation of Ψ returns true when setting attributes in S as true and the others (in Ψ) as false.

ABE with *large-universe* is a variant where $\mathcal{U}$ is of super-polynomial size. *Unbounded* ABE is a variant where there is no restriction on any sizes of policies Ψ, attribute sets S, or the maximum number of attribute repetition in a policy. In a *bounded* ABE scheme, the corresponding bounds (*e.g.*, the maximum size of S) will be described as indexes inside κ for the predicate family.

A boolean formulae can be equivalently described by a linear secret sharing (LSS) scheme (A, π) over $\mathbb{Z}_N$, where A is a matrix in $\mathbb{Z}_N^{m \times k}$ and $\pi : [1, m] \rightarrow \mathcal{U}$, for some m, k. We briefly review the definition of LSS. It consists of two algorithms. First, Share takes as input $s \in \mathbb{Z}_N$ (a secret to be shared), and chooses $v_2, \ldots, v_k \xleftarrow{\$} \mathbb{Z}_N$, sets $\boldsymbol{v} = (s, v_2 \ldots, v_k)$, and outputs $A_i \boldsymbol{v}^\top$ as the i-th share, where A_i is the i-th row of A, for $i \in [1, m]$. Second, $\mathsf{Reconstruct}$ takes as input S such that (A, π) accepts S, and outputs a set of constants $\{\mu_i\}_{i \in I}$, where $I := \{ i \mid \pi(i) \in S \}$, which has a reconstruction property: $\sum_{i \in I} \mu_i (A_i \boldsymbol{v}^\top) = s$.

3.3   Bilinear Groups of Composite Order

In our framework, we consider bilinear groups $(\mathbb{G}, \mathbb{G}_T)$ of composite order $N = p_1p_2p_3$, where p_1, p_2, p_3 are distinct primes, with an efficiently computable bilinear map $e : \mathbb{G} \times \mathbb{G} \to \mathbb{G}_T$. For our purpose, we define a bilinear group generator $\mathcal{G}(\lambda)$ that takes as input a security parameter λ and outputs $(\mathbb{G}, \mathbb{G}_T, e, N, p_1, p_2, p_3)$. For each $d|N$, $\mathbb{G}$ has a subgroup of order d denoted by $\mathbb{G}_d$. We let g_i denote a generator of $\mathbb{G}_{p_i}$. Any $h \in \mathbb{G}$ can be expressed as $g_1^{a_1} g_2^{a_2} g_3^{a_3}$, where a_i is uniquely determined modulo p_i. We call $g_i^{a_i}$ the $\mathbb{G}_{p_i}$ component of h. We recall that e has the bilinear property: $e(g^a, g^b) = e(g, g)^{ab}$ for any $g \in \mathbb{G}$, $a, b \in \mathbb{Z}$ and the non-degeneration property: $e(g, h) \neq 1 \in \mathbb{G}_T$ whenever $g, h \neq 1 \in \mathbb{G}$. In a bilinear group of composite order, we also have orthogonality: for $g \in \mathbb{G}_{p_i}, h \in \mathbb{G}_{p_j}$ where $p_i \neq p_j$ we have that $e(g, h) = 1 \in \mathbb{G}_T$. The Subgroup Decision Assumptions 1,2,3 [33,20] and the 3DH assumption in a subgroup [23] are given below.

Definition 1 (Subgroup Decision Assumptions). *Subgroup Decision Problem 1,2,3 are defined as follows. Each starts with $(\mathbb{G}, \mathbb{G}_T, e, N, p_1, p_2, p_3) \xleftarrow{\$} \mathcal{G}(\lambda)$.*

1. *Given $g_1 \xleftarrow{\$} \mathbb{G}_{p_1}, Z_3 \xleftarrow{\$} \mathbb{G}_{p_3}$, and $T \in \mathbb{G}$, decide if $T = T_1 \xleftarrow{\$} \mathbb{G}_{p_1 p_2}$ or $T = T_2 \xleftarrow{\$} \mathbb{G}_{p_1}$.*

2. *Let $g_1, Z_1 \xleftarrow{\$} \mathbb{G}_{p_1}, Z_2, W_2 \xleftarrow{\$} \mathbb{G}_{p_2}, Z_3, W_3 \xleftarrow{\$} \mathbb{G}_{p_3}$. Given $g_1, Z_1 Z_2, Z_3, W_2 W_3$, and $T \in \mathbb{G}$, decide if $T = T_1 \xleftarrow{\$} \mathbb{G}_{p_1 p_2 p_3}$ or $T = T_2 \xleftarrow{\$} \mathbb{G}_{p_1 p_3}$.*

3. *Let $g_1 \xleftarrow{\$} \mathbb{G}_{p_1}, g_2, W_2, Y_2 \xleftarrow{\$} \mathbb{G}_{p_2}, Z_3 \xleftarrow{\$} \mathbb{G}_{p_3}$ and $\alpha, s \xleftarrow{\$} \mathbb{Z}_N$. Given $g_1, g_2, Z_3, g_1^\alpha Y_2, g_1^s W_2$, and $T \in \mathbb{G}_T$, decide if $T = T_1 = e(g_1, g_1)^{\alpha s}$ or $T = T_2 \xleftarrow{\$} \mathbb{G}_T$.*

We define the advantage of an adversary $\mathcal{A}$ against Problem i for $\mathcal{G}$ as the distance $\mathsf{Adv}_{\mathcal{A}}^{\mathsf{SD}i}(\lambda) := |\Pr[\mathcal{A}(\boldsymbol{D}, T_1) = 1] - \Pr[\mathcal{A}(\boldsymbol{D}, T_2) = 1]|$, where $\boldsymbol{D}$ denotes the given elements in each assumption excluding T. We say that the Assumption i holds for $\mathcal{G}$ if $\mathsf{Adv}_{\mathcal{A}}^{\mathsf{SD}i}(\lambda)$ is negligible in λ for any poly-time algorithm $\mathcal{A}$.

Definition 2 (3-Party Diffie Hellman Assumption, 3DH). *The 3DH Assumption in a subgroup assumes the hardness of the following problem: let $(\mathbb{G}, \mathbb{G}_T, e, N, p_1, p_2, p_3) \xleftarrow{\$} \mathcal{G}(\lambda), g_1 \xleftarrow{\$} \mathbb{G}_{p_1}, g_2 \xleftarrow{\$} \mathbb{G}_{p_2}, g_3 \xleftarrow{\$} \mathbb{G}_{p_3}, a, b, z \xleftarrow{\$} \mathbb{Z}_N$, given $\boldsymbol{D} = (g_2, g_2^a, g_2^b, g_2^z, g_1, g_3)$ and T, decide whether $T = g_2^{abz}$ or $T \xleftarrow{\$} \mathbb{G}_{p_2}$.*

Notation. In general, we treat a vector as a horizontal vector. For $g \in \mathbb{G}$ and $\boldsymbol{c} = (c_1, \ldots, c_n) \in \mathbb{Z}^n$, we denote $g^{\boldsymbol{c}} = (g^{c_1}, \ldots, g^{c_n})$. Denote '·' as the pairwise group operation on vectors. Consider $M \in \mathbb{Z}_N^{d \times n}$. We denote its transpose as $M^\top$. We denote by g^M the matrix in $\mathbb{G}^{d \times n}$ of which its (i, j) entry is $g^{M_{i,j}}$. For $Q \in \mathbb{Z}_N^{\ell \times d}$, we denote $(g^Q)^M = g^{QM}$. Note that from M and $g^Q \in \mathbb{G}^{\ell \times d}$, we can compute g^{QM} without knowing Q, since its (i, j) entry is $\prod_{k=1}^d (g^{Q_{i,k}})^{M_{k,j}}$. (This will be used in §4.3). For $g^{\boldsymbol{c}}, g^{\boldsymbol{v}} \in \mathbb{G}^n$, we denote $e(g^{\boldsymbol{c}}, g^{\boldsymbol{v}}) = e(g, g)^{\boldsymbol{c}\boldsymbol{v}^\top} \in \mathbb{G}_T$.

4   Our Generic Framework for Dual-System Encryption

4.1   Pair Encoding Scheme: Syntax

In this section we formalize our main component: pair encoding scheme. It follows the intuition from the overview in §2. We could abstractly define it purely by the described properties; however, we opted to make a more concrete definition, which seems not to lose much generality (we discuss this below).

Syntax. A pair encoding scheme for predicate family R consists of four deterministic algorithms given by $\mathsf{P} = (\mathsf{Param}, \mathsf{Enc1}, \mathsf{Enc2}, \mathsf{Pair})$:

- $\mathsf{Param}(\kappa) \to n$. It takes as input an index κ and outputs an integer n, which specifies the number of *common variables* in $\mathsf{Enc1}, \mathsf{Enc2}$. For the default notation, let $\boldsymbol{h} = (h_1, \ldots, h_n)$ denote the the list of common variables.
- $\mathsf{Enc1}(X, N) \to \boldsymbol{k} = (k_1, \ldots, k_{m_1})$ and m_2. It takes as inputs $X \in \mathbb{X}_\kappa$, $N \in \mathbb{N}$, and outputs a sequence of polynomials $(k_z)_{z \in [1, m_1]}$ with coefficients in $\mathbb{Z}_N$, and $m_2 \in \mathbb{N}$. We require that each polynomial k_z is a *linear combination of monomials* $\alpha, r_i, r_i h_j$, where $\alpha, r_1, \ldots, r_{m_2}, h_1, \ldots, h_n$ are variables.
- $\mathsf{Enc2}(Y, N) \to \boldsymbol{c} = (c_1, \ldots, c_{w_1})$ and w_2. It takes as inputs $Y \in \mathbb{Y}_\kappa$, $N \in \mathbb{N}$, and outputs a sequence of polynomials $(c_z)_{z \in [1, w_1]}$ with coefficients in $\mathbb{Z}_N$, and $w_2 \in \mathbb{N}$. We require that each polynomial c_z is a *linear combination of monomials* $s, s_i, s h_j, s_i h_j$, where $s, s_1, \ldots, s_{w_2}, h_1, \ldots, h_n$ are variables.
- $\mathsf{Pair}(X, Y, N) \to \boldsymbol{E}$. It takes as inputs X, Y, N, and output $\boldsymbol{E} \in \mathbb{Z}_N^{m_1 \times w_1}$.

Correctness. The correctness requirement is defined as follows.

1. For any $N \in \mathbb{N}$, let $(\boldsymbol{k}; m_2) \leftarrow \mathsf{Enc1}(X, N)$, $(\boldsymbol{c}; w_2) \leftarrow \mathsf{Enc2}(Y, N)$, and $\boldsymbol{E} \leftarrow \mathsf{Pair}(X, Y, N)$, we have that if $R_N(X, Y) = 1$, then $\boldsymbol{k}\boldsymbol{E}\boldsymbol{c}^\top = \alpha s$, where the equality holds symbolically.
2. For $p|N$, we have $\mathsf{Enc}i(X, N)_1 \bmod p = \mathsf{Enc}i(X, p)_1$, for $i = 1, 2$.

Note that since $\boldsymbol{k}\boldsymbol{E}\boldsymbol{c}^\top = \sum_{i \in [1, m_1], j \in [1, w_1]} E_{i,j} k_i c_j$, the first correctness amounts to check if there is a linear combination of $k_i c_j$ terms summed up to αs.

Remark 1. We mandate that the variables used in $\mathsf{Enc1}$ and those in $\mathsf{Enc2}$ are different except only those common variables in $\boldsymbol{h}$. We remark that in the syntax, all variables are only *symbolic*: no probability distributions have been assigned to them yet. (We will eventually assign these in the security notion and the generic construction). Note that m_1, m_2 can depend on X and w_1, w_2 can depend on Y. We also remark that each polynomial in $\boldsymbol{k}, \boldsymbol{c}$ has no constant terms.

Terminology. In what follows, we often omit N as input if the context is clear. We denote $\boldsymbol{k} = \boldsymbol{k}(\alpha, \boldsymbol{r}, \boldsymbol{h})$ or $\boldsymbol{k}_X(\alpha, \boldsymbol{r}, \boldsymbol{h})$, and $\boldsymbol{c} = \boldsymbol{c}(\boldsymbol{s}, \boldsymbol{h})$ or $\boldsymbol{c}_Y(\boldsymbol{s}, \boldsymbol{h})$, where we let $\boldsymbol{h} = (h_1, \ldots, h_n), \boldsymbol{r} = (r_1, \ldots, r_{m_2}), \boldsymbol{s} = (s, s_1, \ldots, s_{w_2})$. We remark that s in $\boldsymbol{s}$ is treat as a special symbol among the others in $\boldsymbol{s}$, since it defines the correctness. We always write s as the first entry of $\boldsymbol{s}$. In describing concrete schemes in §5, we often use symbols that deviate from the default notation (h_i, r_i, s_i in $\boldsymbol{h}, \boldsymbol{r}, \boldsymbol{s}$, respectively). In such a case, we will write $\boldsymbol{h}, \boldsymbol{r}, \boldsymbol{s}$ explicitly and omit writing the output m_2, w_2 since they merely indicate the sizes $m_2 = |\boldsymbol{r}|, w_2 = |\boldsymbol{s}| - 1$.

Remark 2. It is straightforward to prove that the syntax of pair encoding implies *linearity* and *parameter-vanishing*, symbolically. We opted to define the syntax this way (concrete, instead of abstract based on properties only) since for the generic construction (*cf.* §4.3) to work, we need one more property stating that $\boldsymbol{c}$ can be computed from $\boldsymbol{h}$ by a linear (or affine) transformation. This is for ensuring computability of ciphertext from the public key, since the public key will be of the form g_1^h and we can only do linear transformations in the exponent. This, together with linearity in s, prompts to define linear-form monomials in Enc2 as above. Contrastingly, there is no similar requirement for Enc1; however, we define linear-form monomials similarly so that the roles of both encoding functions can be exchangeable in the dual scheme conversion (see the full version).

4.2 Pair Encoding Scheme: Security Definitions

Security. We define the security notions of pair encoding schemes as follows.

(Perfect Security). The pair encoding scheme P is *perfectly master-key hiding* if the following holds. For $N \in \mathbb{N}$, if $R_N(X, Y) = 0$, let $(\boldsymbol{k}; m_2) \leftarrow \mathsf{Enc1}(X, N)$, $(\boldsymbol{c}; w_2) \leftarrow \mathsf{Enc2}(Y, N)$, then the following two distributions are identical:

$$\{\boldsymbol{c}(\boldsymbol{s}, \boldsymbol{h}), \ \boldsymbol{k}(0, \boldsymbol{r}, \boldsymbol{h})\} \qquad \text{and} \qquad \{\boldsymbol{c}(\boldsymbol{s}, \boldsymbol{h}), \ \boldsymbol{k}(\alpha, \boldsymbol{r}, \boldsymbol{h})\},$$

where the probability is taken over $\boldsymbol{h} \xleftarrow{\$} \mathbb{Z}_N^n, \alpha \xleftarrow{\$} \mathbb{Z}_N, \boldsymbol{r} \xleftarrow{\$} \mathbb{Z}_N^{m_2}, \boldsymbol{s} \xleftarrow{\$} \mathbb{Z}_N^{(w_2+1)}$.

(Computational Security). We define two flavors: *selectively secure* and *co-selectively secure master-key hiding* (SMH, CMH) in a bilinear group generator $\mathcal{G}$. We first define the game template, $\mathsf{Exp}_{\mathcal{G},\mathsf{G},b,\mathcal{A}}(\lambda)$, for the flavor $\mathsf{G} \in \{\mathsf{CMH}, \mathsf{SMH}\}$, $b \in \{0, 1\}$. It takes as input the security parameter λ and does the experiment with the adversary $\mathcal{A} = (\mathcal{A}_1, \mathcal{A}_2)$, and outputs b'. The game is defined as:

$$\mathsf{Exp}_{\mathcal{G},\mathsf{G},b,\mathcal{A}}(\lambda) : \ (\mathbb{G}, \mathbb{G}_T, e, N, p_1, p_2, p_3) \leftarrow \mathcal{G}(\lambda); \ g_1 \xleftarrow{\$} \mathbb{G}_{p_1}, g_2 \xleftarrow{\$} \mathbb{G}_{p_2}, g_3 \xleftarrow{\$} \mathbb{G}_{p_3},$$

$$\alpha \xleftarrow{\$} \mathbb{Z}_N, \boldsymbol{h} \xleftarrow{\$} \mathbb{Z}_N^n; \ \mathsf{st} \leftarrow \mathcal{A}_1^{\mathcal{O}_{\mathsf{G},b,\alpha,\boldsymbol{h}}^1(\cdot)}(g_1, g_2, g_3); \ b' \leftarrow \mathcal{A}_2^{\mathcal{O}_{\mathsf{G},b,\alpha,\boldsymbol{h}}^2(\cdot)}(\mathsf{st}),$$

where st denotes the state information and the oracles $\mathcal{O}_1, \mathcal{O}_2$ in each state are defined below. The subscripts $\alpha, \boldsymbol{h}$ for each oracle are omitted for simplicity.

- **Selective Security (SMH).** $\mathcal{O}^1$ can be queried once while $\mathcal{O}^2$ can be queried polynomially many times.

  $\mathcal{O}_{\mathsf{SMH},b}^1(Y^\star)$: $(\boldsymbol{c}; w_2) \leftarrow \mathsf{Enc2}(Y^\star, p_2); \boldsymbol{s} \xleftarrow{\$} \mathbb{Z}_{p_2}^{(w_2+1)}$; return $\boldsymbol{C} \leftarrow g_2^{\boldsymbol{c}(\boldsymbol{s}, \boldsymbol{h})}$.

  $\mathcal{O}_{\mathsf{SMH},b}^2(X)$: If $R_{p_2}(X, Y^\star) = 1$, then return $\perp$;

  $$\text{else, } (\boldsymbol{k}; m_2) \leftarrow \mathsf{Enc1}(X, p_2); \boldsymbol{r} \xleftarrow{\$} \mathbb{Z}_{p_2}^{m_2}; \text{ return } \boldsymbol{K} \leftarrow \begin{cases} g_2^{\boldsymbol{k}(0,\boldsymbol{r},\boldsymbol{h})} & \text{if } b = 0 \\ g_2^{\boldsymbol{k}(\alpha,\boldsymbol{r},\boldsymbol{h})} & \text{if } b = 1 \end{cases}$$

- **Co-selective Security (CMH).** Both $\mathcal{O}^1, \mathcal{O}^2$ can be queried once.

  $$\mathcal{O}_{\mathsf{CMH},b}^1(X^\star): (\boldsymbol{k}; m_2) \leftarrow \mathsf{Enc1}(X^\star, p_2); \boldsymbol{r} \xleftarrow{\$} \mathbb{Z}_{p_2}^{m_2}; \text{ return } \boldsymbol{K} \leftarrow \begin{cases} g_2^{\boldsymbol{k}(0,\boldsymbol{r},\boldsymbol{h})} & \text{if } b = 0 \\ g_2^{\boldsymbol{k}(\alpha,\boldsymbol{r},\boldsymbol{h})} & \text{if } b = 1 \end{cases}$$

  $\mathcal{O}_{\mathsf{CMH},b}^2(Y)$: If $R_{p_2}(X^\star, Y) = 1$, then return $\perp$;

  $\text{else, } (\boldsymbol{c}; w_2) \leftarrow \mathsf{Enc2}(Y, p_2); \boldsymbol{s} \xleftarrow{\$} \mathbb{Z}_{p_2}^{(w_2+1)}$; return $\boldsymbol{C} \leftarrow g_2^{\boldsymbol{c}(\boldsymbol{s}, \boldsymbol{h})}$.

We define the advantage of $\mathcal{A}$ in the game $\mathsf{G} \in \{\mathsf{SMH}, \mathsf{CMH}\}$ relative to $\mathcal{G}$ as $\mathsf{Adv}_{\mathcal{A}}^{\mathsf{G}}(\lambda) := |\Pr[\mathsf{Exp}_{\mathcal{G},\mathsf{G},0,\mathcal{A}}(\lambda) = 1] - \Pr[\mathsf{Exp}_{\mathcal{G},\mathsf{G},1,\mathcal{A}}(\lambda) = 1]|$. We say that the pair encoding scheme P is selectively (resp., co-selectively) master-key hiding in $\mathcal{G}$ if $\mathsf{Adv}_{\mathcal{A}}^{\mathsf{SMH}}(\lambda)$ (resp., $\mathsf{Adv}_{\mathcal{A}}^{\mathsf{CMH}}(\lambda)$) is negligible for all PPT attackers $\mathcal{A}$. If both hold, we say that it is *doubly selectively master-key hiding*.

Remark 3. The terms corresponding to parameter h (in particular, g_2^h) need *not* be given out to the adversary. Intuitively, this is since the security of encoding will be employed in the semi-functional space, and the parameter then corresponds to *semi-functional parameter* $\hat{h}$, which needs not be sent (*cf.* §2).

4.3   Generic Construction for Functional Encryption from Encoding

Construction. From a pair encoding scheme P for predicate R, we construct a functional encryption scheme for R, denoted FE(P), as follows.

- Setup($1^\lambda, \kappa$): Run $(\mathbb{G}, \mathbb{G}_T, e, N, p_1, p_2, p_3) \xleftarrow{\$} \mathcal{G}(\lambda)$. Pick generators $g_1 \xleftarrow{\$} \mathbb{G}_{p_1}$, $Z_3 \xleftarrow{\$} \mathbb{G}_{p_3}$. Run $n \leftarrow \mathsf{Param}(\kappa)$. Pick $h \xleftarrow{\$} \mathbb{Z}_N^n$ and $\alpha \xleftarrow{\$} \mathbb{Z}_N$. The public key is $\mathsf{PK} = (g_1, e(g_1, g_1)^\alpha, g_1^h, Z_3)$. The master secret key is $\mathsf{MSK} = \alpha$.
- Encrypt(Y, M, PK): Upon input $Y \in \mathbb{Y}_N$, run $(\boldsymbol{c}; w_2) \leftarrow \mathsf{Enc2}(Y, N)$. Pick $\boldsymbol{s} = (s, s_1, \ldots, s_{w_2}) \xleftarrow{\$} \mathbb{Z}_N^{w_2+1}$. Output the ciphertext as $\mathsf{CT} = (\boldsymbol{C}, C_0)$:

$$\boldsymbol{C} = g_1^{\boldsymbol{c}(\boldsymbol{s},h)} \in \mathbb{G}^{w_1}, \qquad C_0 = (e(g_1, g_1)^\alpha)^s M \in \mathbb{G}_T.$$

  Note that $\boldsymbol{C}$ can be computed from g_1^h and $\boldsymbol{s}$ since $\boldsymbol{c}(\boldsymbol{s}, h)$ contains only linear combinations of monomials $s, s_i, sh_j, s_i h_j$.
- KeyGen($X, \mathsf{MSK}, \mathsf{PK}$): Upon input $X \in \mathbb{X}_N$, run $(\boldsymbol{k}; m_2) \leftarrow \mathsf{Enc1}(X, N)$. Parse $\mathsf{MSK} = \alpha$. Recall that $m_1 = |\boldsymbol{k}|$. Pick $\boldsymbol{r} \xleftarrow{\$} \mathbb{Z}_N^{m_2}, \boldsymbol{R}_3 \xleftarrow{\$} \mathbb{G}_{p_3}^{m_1}$. Output SK as

$$\boldsymbol{K} = g_1^{\boldsymbol{k}(\alpha, \boldsymbol{r}, h)} \cdot \boldsymbol{R}_3 \in \mathbb{G}^{m_1}.$$

- Decrypt(CT, SK): Obtain Y, X from CT, SK. Suppose $R(X, Y) = 1$. Run $\boldsymbol{E} \leftarrow \mathsf{Pair}(X, Y)$. Compute $e(g_1, g_1)^{\alpha s} \leftarrow e(\boldsymbol{K}^{\boldsymbol{E}}, \boldsymbol{C})$, and obtain $M \leftarrow C_0 / e(g_1, g_1)^{\alpha s}$.

Correctness. For $R_N(X, Y) = 1$, we have $R_{p_1}(X, Y) = 1$ from the domain-transferability. Then, $e(\boldsymbol{K}^{\boldsymbol{E}}, \boldsymbol{C}) = e((g_1^{\boldsymbol{k}} \cdot \boldsymbol{R}_3)^{\boldsymbol{E}}, g_1^{\boldsymbol{c}}) = e(g_1, g_1)^{\boldsymbol{k} \boldsymbol{E} \boldsymbol{c}^\top} = e(g_1, g_1)^{\alpha s}$, where the last equality comes from the correctness of the pair encoding scheme.

Semi-functional Algorithms. These will be used in the proof only.

- SFSetup($1^\lambda, \kappa$): This is exactly the same as Setup($1^\lambda, \kappa$) except that it additionally outputs a generator $g_2 \xleftarrow{\$} \mathbb{G}_{p_2}$ and $\hat{h} \xleftarrow{\$} \mathbb{Z}_N^n$.
- SFEncrypt($Y, M, \mathsf{PK}, g_2, \hat{h}$): Upon inputs Y, M, PK, g_2 and $\hat{h}$, first run $(\boldsymbol{c}; w_2) \leftarrow \mathsf{Enc2}(Y)$. Pick $\boldsymbol{s} = (s, s_1, \ldots, s_{w_2}), \hat{\boldsymbol{s}} \xleftarrow{\$} \mathbb{Z}_N^{w_2+1}$ Output $\mathsf{CT} = (\boldsymbol{C}, C_0)$ as

$$\boldsymbol{C} = g_1^{\boldsymbol{c}(\boldsymbol{s},h)} g_2^{\boldsymbol{c}(\hat{\boldsymbol{s}},\hat{h})} \in \mathbb{G}^{w_1}, \qquad C_0 = (e(g_1, g_1)^\alpha)^s M \in \mathbb{G}_T.$$

- SFKeyGen($X, \mathsf{MSK}, \mathsf{PK}, g_2, \mathsf{type}, \hat{\alpha}, \hat{h}$): Upon inputs $X, \mathsf{MSK}, \mathsf{PK}, g_2$, and type $\in \{1, 2, 3\}$, $\hat{\alpha} \in \mathbb{Z}_N$, run $(\boldsymbol{k}; m_2) \leftarrow \mathsf{Enc1}(X)$. Pick $\boldsymbol{r}, \hat{\boldsymbol{r}} \xleftarrow{\$} \mathbb{Z}_N^{m_2}, \boldsymbol{R}_3 \xleftarrow{\$} \mathbb{G}_{p_3}^{m_1}$. Output SK as

$$\boldsymbol{K} = \begin{cases} g_1^{\boldsymbol{k}(\alpha, \boldsymbol{r}, h)} \cdot g_2^{\boldsymbol{k}(0, \hat{\boldsymbol{r}}, \hat{h})} \cdot \boldsymbol{R}_3 & \text{if type} = 1 \\ g_1^{\boldsymbol{k}(\alpha, \boldsymbol{r}, h)} \cdot g_2^{\boldsymbol{k}(\hat{\alpha}, \hat{\boldsymbol{r}}, \hat{h})} \cdot \boldsymbol{R}_3 & \text{if type} = 2 \\ g_1^{\boldsymbol{k}(\alpha, \boldsymbol{r}, h)} \cdot g_2^{\boldsymbol{k}(\hat{\alpha}, 0, 0)} \cdot \boldsymbol{R}_3 & \text{if type} = 3 \end{cases}$$

Note that the input $\hat{\alpha}$ (resp., $\hat{h}$) is not needed for type 1 (resp., type 3).

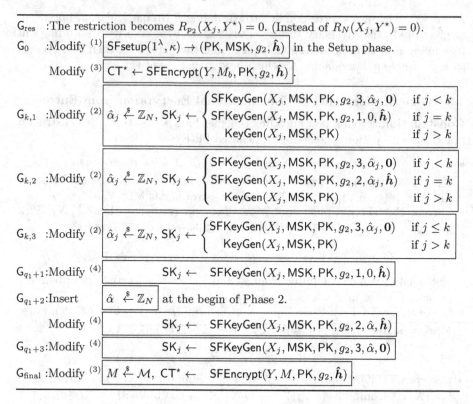

Fig. 1. The sequence of games in the security proof

Theorem 1. *Suppose that a pair encoding scheme* P *for predicate* R *is selectively and co-selectively master-key hiding in* $\mathcal{G}$, *and the Subgroup Decision Assumption 1,2,3 hold in* $\mathcal{G}$. *Also, suppose that* R *is domain-transferable. Then the construction* FE(P) *in* $\mathcal{G}$ *of function encryption for predicate* R *is fully secure. More precisely, for any PPT adversary* $\mathcal{A}$, *there exist PPT algorithms* $\mathcal{B}_1, \mathcal{B}_2, \mathcal{B}_3, \mathcal{B}_4, \mathcal{B}_5$, *whose running times are essentially the same as* $\mathcal{A}$, *such that for any* λ, *we have* $\mathsf{Adv}_{\mathcal{A}}^{\mathsf{FE}}(\lambda) \leq 2\mathsf{Adv}_{\mathcal{B}_1}^{\mathsf{SD1}}(\lambda) + (2q_1 + 3)\mathsf{Adv}_{\mathcal{B}_2}^{\mathsf{SD2}}(\lambda) + \mathsf{Adv}_{\mathcal{B}_3}^{\mathsf{SD3}}(\lambda) + q_1\mathsf{Adv}_{\mathcal{B}_4}^{\mathsf{CMH}}(\lambda) + \mathsf{Adv}_{\mathcal{B}_5}^{\mathsf{SMH}}(\lambda)$, *where* q_1 *is the number of queries in phase 1.*

Security Proof. We use a sequence of games in the following order:

$$
\begin{array}{ccccccccccc}
\mathsf{G}_{\text{real}} & \mathsf{G}_{\text{res}} & \mathsf{G}_0 & \mathsf{G}_{1,1} & & \mathsf{G}_{k-1,3} & \mathsf{G}_{k,1} & \mathsf{G}_{k,2} & \mathsf{G}_{k,3} & & \mathsf{G}_{q_1,3} & \mathsf{G}_{q_1+1} & \mathsf{G}_{q_1+2} & \mathsf{G}_{q_1+3} & \mathsf{G}_{\text{final}}
\end{array}
$$

$$
\begin{array}{cccccccc}
& \text{SD1,2} & \text{SD1} & & & \text{SD2} & \text{CMH} & \text{SD2} & & & \text{SD2} & \text{SMH} & \text{SD2} & \text{SD3}
\end{array}
$$

where each game is defined as follows. G_{real} is the actual security game, and each of the following game is defined exactly as *its previous game* in the sequence except the specified modification that is defined in Fig. 1. For notational purpose, let $\mathsf{G}_{0,3} := \mathsf{G}_0$. In the diagram, we also write the underlying assumptions used for indistinguishability between adjacent games. The proofs are in the full version.

We also obtain the theorem for the case where the encoding is perfectly secure.

Theorem 2. *Suppose that a pair encoding scheme* P *for predicate* R *is perfectly master-key hiding, and the Subgroup Decision Assumption 1,2,3 hold in* $\mathcal{G}$. *Suppose also that* R *is domain-transferable. Then* FE(P) *is fully secure. Indeed, let* $q_{all} = q_1 + q_2$ *be the number of all queries. For any PPT adversary* $\mathcal{A}$, *there exist PPT algorithms* $\mathcal{B}_1, \mathcal{B}_2, \mathcal{B}_3$, *whose running times are essentially the same as* $\mathcal{A}$, *such that for any* λ, $\mathsf{Adv}_{\mathcal{A}}^{\mathsf{FE}}(\lambda) \le 2\mathsf{Adv}_{\mathcal{B}_1}^{\mathsf{SD1}}(\lambda) + (2q_{all} + 1)\mathsf{Adv}_{\mathcal{B}_2}^{\mathsf{SD2}}(\lambda) + \mathsf{Adv}_{\mathcal{B}_3}^{\mathsf{SD3}}(\lambda)$.

5 Instantiations

5.1 Efficient Fully Secure IBE with Tighter Reduction

We first construct an encoding scheme for the simplest predicate, namely the equality relation, and hence obtain a new IBE scheme. This is shown as Scheme 1. It is similar to the Boneh-Boyen IBE [4] (and Lewko-Waters IBE [20]), with the exception that we have one more element in each of ciphertext and key. Their roles will be explained below. The encoding scheme can be proved perfectly master-key hiding due to the fact that $f(x) = h_1 + h_2 x$ is pairwise independent function (this is also used in [20]). The novelty is that we can prove the SMH security (with tight reduction to 3DH). Note that the CMH security is implied by perfect master-key hiding. Hence, from Theorem 1, we obtain a fully secure IBE with $O(q_1)$ reduction to SD2 (plus tight reduction to 3DH, SD1, SD3). [5]

Pair Encoding Scheme 1: IBE with Tighter Reduction
Param $\rightarrow$ 3. Denote $\boldsymbol{h} = (h_1, h_2, h_3)$.
$\mathsf{Enc1}(X) \rightarrow \boldsymbol{k}(\alpha, \boldsymbol{r}, \boldsymbol{h}) = (\alpha + r(h_1 + h_2X) + uh_3, \ r, \ u)$ where $\boldsymbol{r} = (r, u)$.
$\mathsf{Enc2}(Y) \rightarrow \boldsymbol{c}(\boldsymbol{s}, \boldsymbol{h}) = (s, \ s(h_1 + h_2Y), \ sh_3)$ where $\boldsymbol{s} = s$.

Theorem 3. *Scheme 1 is selectively master-key hiding under 3DH.*

Proof. Suppose we have an adversary $\mathcal{A}$ with non-negligible advantage in the SMH game against Scheme 1. We construct a simulator $\mathcal{B}$ that solves 3DH. $\mathcal{B}$ takes as an input the 3DH challenge, $\boldsymbol{D} = (g_2, g_2^a, g_2^b, g_2^z, g_1, g_3)$ and $T = g_2^{\tau + abz}$, where either $\tau = 0$ or $\tau \xleftarrow{\$} \mathbb{Z}_{p_2}$. $\mathcal{B}$ first gives (g_1, g_2, g_3) to $\mathcal{A}$.

Ciphertext Query (to $\mathcal{O}^1$). The game begins with $\mathcal{A}$ making a query for identity $Y^\star$ to $\mathcal{O}^1$. $\mathcal{B}$ picks $h'_1, h'_2, h'_3 \xleftarrow{\$} \mathbb{Z}_N$ and defines $\boldsymbol{h} = (h_1, h_2, h_3)$ by *implicitly* setting $g_2^{h_1} = g_2^{h'_1} g_2^{-Y^\star za}$, $g_2^{h_2} = g_2^{h'_2} g_2^{za}$, $g_2^{h_3} = g_2^{h'_3} g_2^z$. Note that only the last term is computable. $\mathcal{B}$ picks $s \xleftarrow{\$} \mathbb{Z}_N$ and computes $\boldsymbol{C} = g_2^{\boldsymbol{c}(s, \boldsymbol{h})} = (C_1, C_2, C_3)$ as: $C_1 = g_2^s, C_2 = g_2^{s(h'_1 + h'_2 Y^\star)}, C_3 = (g_2^{h_3})^s$. Obviously, C_1, C_3 are properly distributed. C_2 is properly distributed due to the cancellation of unknown za in the exponent: $h_1 + h_2 Y^\star = (h'_1 - Y^\star za) + (h'_2 + za)Y^\star = h'_1 + h'_2 Y^\star$.

---

[5] Compared to the recent IBE of [8], their scheme has the reduction cost that does not depend on the number of queries; they achieved $O(\ell)$ reduction to DLIN, while the public key size is $O(\ell)$, where ℓ is the identity length. Ours has $O(1)$ public key size.

Key Query (to $\mathcal{O}^2$). When $\mathcal{A}$ makes the j-th key query for $X_j (\neq Y^\star)$, $\mathcal{B}$ first computes a temporary key $\boldsymbol{K}' = (K_1', K_2', K_3')$ where $K_1' = T((g_2^b)^{\frac{1}{X_j - Y^\star}})^{h_1' + h_2' X_j}$, $K_2' = (g_2^b)^{\frac{1}{X_j - Y^\star}}$, and $K_3' = 1$. We then claim that $\boldsymbol{K}' = g_2^{\boldsymbol{k}_{X_j}(\tau, \boldsymbol{r}_j', \boldsymbol{h})}$, where $\boldsymbol{r}_j' = (r_j', u_j') = (\frac{b}{X_j - Y^\star}, 0)$. This holds since $K_1' = g_2^{(\tau + abz) + (\frac{b}{X_j - Y^\star})(h_1' + h_2' X_j)} = g_2^{\tau + (\frac{b}{X_j - Y^\star})((h_1' - Y^\star za) + (h_2' + za) X_j)} = g_2^{\tau + r_j'(h_1 + h_2 X_j)}$, where the unknown element abz in the exponent term $r_j'(h_1 + h_2 X_j)$ is simulated by using abz from T. A crucial point here is that $\boldsymbol{K}'$ is not properly distributed yet as r_j' is not independent among j (since all r_j' are determined from b). We re-randomize it by picking $r_j'', u_j'' \xleftarrow{\$} \mathbb{Z}_N$ and computing $K_1 = K_1' (g_2^{r_j''})^{h_1' + h_2' X_j} (g_2^z)^{u_j''}, K_2 = K_2' g_2^{r_j''}$, and $K_3 = K_3' g_2^{u_j''} (g_2^a)^{-r_j'' (X_j - Y^\star)}$. This is a properly distributed $\boldsymbol{K} = g_2^{\boldsymbol{k}_{X_j}(\tau, \boldsymbol{r}_j, \boldsymbol{h})}$ with $\boldsymbol{r}_j = (r_j, u_j) = (\frac{b}{X_j - Y^\star} + r_j'', u_j'' - ar_j'' (X_j - Y^\star))$.

Guess. The algorithm $\mathcal{B}$ has properly simulated $\boldsymbol{K} = g_2^{\boldsymbol{k}_{X_j}(\alpha, \boldsymbol{r}_j, \boldsymbol{h})}$ with $\alpha = 0$ if $\tau = 0$, and α is random if τ is random (since $\alpha = \tau$). $\mathcal{B}$ thus outputs the corresponding guess from $\mathcal{A}$. The advantage of $\mathcal{B}$ is thus equal to that of $\mathcal{A}$. $\quad\square$

Remark 4 (Randomizer Technique). Our proof much resembles the Boneh-Boyen technique [4], with a crucial exception that here we need to establish the indistinguishability in $\mathbb{G}$ (for our purpose of master-key hiding notion), instead of $\mathbb{G}_T$ (for the purpose of proving security for BB-IBE). Therefore, intuitively, instead of embedding only g^a to the parameter g^h as usual, we need to embed g^{az} so as to obtain the target element g^{abz} in $\mathbb{G}$ when combining with r (which uses b). This is in contrast to BB-IBE, where the target $e(g, g)^{abz}$ is in $\mathbb{G}_T$. Now that g^h contains non-trivial term g^{az}, we cannot re-randomize r in keys. To solve this, we introduce u as a "randomizer" via g^a. This is why we need one more element than BB-IBE. This technique is implicit in ABE of [23].

5.2 Fully Secure FE for Regular Languages

Waters [34] proposed a selective secure FE scheme for regular languages. No fully secure realization has been known so far.[6] Our scheme is built upon [34].

Motivation for Large Universe. Waters' scheme operates over *small-universe* alphabet sets, *i.e.*, $|\Lambda|$ is of polynomial size. We argue that this small-universe nature makes the system less efficient than other less-advanced FE for the same functionality. For example, we consider IBE, of which predicate determines equality over two identity $X, Y \in \{0, 1\}^\ell$. To construct DFA that operates over small-size universe to determine if $X = Y$ would require $\Theta(\log \ell)$ transition, which might not be so satisfactory for such a simple primitive.

Our Fully Secure FE for Regular Languages. We propose a new scheme which is *fully secure* and operates over *large-universe* alphabet sets, *i.e.*, $|\Lambda|$ is

---

[6] Waters also suggested that dual system techniques could be used, but only with the restricted version of the primitive where some bounds must be posed. This is not satisfactory since the bound would negate the motivation of having arbitrary string sizes for the ciphertext attribute. A recent work [31] proposes such a bounded scheme.

of super-polynomial size, namely we use $\Lambda = \mathbb{Z}_N$. This is also called *unbounded* alphabet universe (since the parameter size will not depend on the alphabet universe). Our encoding scheme is shown as Scheme 2.

Pair Encoding Scheme 2: FE for Regular Languages

Param	$\rightarrow 8$. Denote $\boldsymbol{h} = (h_0, h_1, h_2, h_3, h_4, \phi_1, \phi_2, \eta)$.

For any DFA $M = (Q, \mathbb{Z}_N, \mathcal{T}, q_0, q_{n-1})$, where $n = |Q|$, let $m = |\mathcal{T}|$, and parse $\mathcal{T} = \{(q_{x_t}, q_{y_t}, \sigma_t) | t \in [1, m]\}$.

Enc1$(M) \rightarrow \boldsymbol{k}(\alpha, \boldsymbol{r}, \boldsymbol{h}) = (k_1, k_2, k_3, k_4, k_5, \{k_{6,t}, k_{7,t}, k_{8,t}\}_{t \in [1,m]})$:

$$\left\{ \begin{array}{lll} k_1 = \alpha + r\phi_1 + u\eta, & k_2 = u, & k_3 = r, \\ k_4 = r_0, & k_5 = -u_0 + r_0 h_0, & k_{6,t} = r_t, \\ k_{7,t} = u_{x_t} + r_t(h_1 + h_2\sigma_t), & k_{8,t} = -u_{y_t} + r_t(h_3 + h_4\sigma_t) \end{array} \right\}$$

where $u_{n-1} := \phi_2 r$ and $\boldsymbol{r} = (r, u, r_0, r_1, \ldots, r_m, \{u_x\}_{q_x \in Q \setminus \{q_{n-1}\}})$.

For $w \in (\mathbb{Z}_N)^*$, let $\ell = |w|$, and parse $w = (w_1, \ldots, w_\ell)$.

Enc2$(w) \rightarrow \boldsymbol{c}(\boldsymbol{s}, \boldsymbol{h}) = (c_1, c_2, c_3, c_4, \{c_{5,i}\}_{i \in [0,\ell]}, \{c_{6,i}\}_{i \in [1,\ell]})$:

$$\left\{ \begin{array}{llll} c_1 = s, & c_2 = s\eta, & c_3 = -s\phi_1 + s_\ell\phi_2, \\ c_4 = s_0 h_0, & c_{5,i} = s_i, & c_{6,i} = s_{i-1}(h_1 + h_2 w_i) + s_i(h_3 + h_4 w_i) \end{array} \right\}$$

where $\boldsymbol{s} = (s, s_0, s_1, \ldots, s_\ell)$.

The correctness can be shown by providing linear combination of $k_\iota c_j$ which summed up to αs. When $R(M, w) = 1$, we have that there is a sequence of states $\rho_0, \rho_1, \cdots, \rho_n \in Q$ such that $\rho_0 = q_0$, for $i = 1$ to ℓ we have $(\rho_{i-1}, \rho_i, w_i) \in \mathcal{T}$, and $\rho_\ell \in F$. Let $(q_{x_{t_i}}, q_{y_{t_i}}, \sigma_{t_i}) = (\rho_{i-1}, \rho_i, w_i)$. Therefore, we have the following bilinear combination: $k_1 c_1 - k_2 c_2 + k_3 c_3 - k_4 c_4 + k_5 c_{5,0} + \sum_{i \in [1,\ell]} (-k_{6,t_i} c_{6,i} + k_{7,t_i} c_{5,i-1} + k_{8,t_i} c_{5,i}) = \alpha s$. This holds since for any $i \in [1, \ell]$, we have $-k_{6,t_i} c_{6,i} + k_{7,t_i} c_{5,i-1} + k_{8,t_i} c_{5,i} = s_{i-1} u_{x_{t_i}} - s_i u_{y_{t_i}}$. The sum of these terms for all $i \in [1, \ell]$ will form chaining cancelations and results in $s_0 u_{x_{t_1}} - s_\ell u_{y_{t_\ell}} = s_0 u_0 - s_\ell u_{n-1} = s_0 u_0 - s_\ell \phi_2 r$. Adding this to the rest, we obtain αs.

We prove that Scheme 2 does not satisfy the perfectly master-key hiding security, by using some basic properties of DFA (see the full version). We then prove its SMH security under a new static assumption, EDHE1 (see below), which is similar to the assumption for Waters' scheme [34]. A notable difference is that the target element will be in $\mathbb{G}$ instead of $\mathbb{G}_T$ (similar to [23]). This is analogous to our IBE, where we use 3DH. The proof strategy for SMH of our encoding naturally follows from the selective security proof of Waters'. The harder part is to prove the CMH security (under another new static assumption), where we use completely new techniques. This is since there has been no known selectively secure FE for the *dual predicate* of regular languages functionality. One of our techniques is that we construct the scheme in such a way that both terms related to transitions in DFA (*i.e.*, $k_{7,t}, k_{8,t}$) are functions of the corresponding alphabet σ_t. This is in contrast with Waters' scheme where only one of them is a function of σ_t. The intuition is to perform a certain type of cancellation that comes from both terms, in the CMH proof. We state here only the assumption and the theorem for SMH, and postpone those for CMH to the full version.

Definition 3 (ℓ-EDHE1). *The ℓ-Expanded Diffie-Hellman Exponent Assumption-1 in subgroup $\mathbb{G}_{p_2}$ is defined as follows. Let $(\mathbb{G}, \mathbb{G}_T, e, N, p_1, p_2, p_3) \xleftarrow{\$} \mathcal{G}(\lambda)$ and $g_i \xleftarrow{\$} \mathbb{G}_{p_i}$. Let $a, b, c, d_1, \ldots, d_{\ell+1}, f, z \xleftarrow{\$} \mathbb{Z}_N$. Suppose that an adversary is given g_1, g_2, g_3, T, and $\boldsymbol{D}$ consisting of the following: $g_2^a, g_2^b, g_2^{a/f}, g_2^{1/f}, g_2^{a^\ell c/z}$, $\forall_{i\in[1,\ell+1]}\, g_2^{a^i/d_i}, g_2^{a^i bf}$; $\forall_{i\in[0,\ell]}\, g_2^{a^i c}, g_2^{bd_i}, g_2^{bd_i/f}, g_2^{abd_i/f}$; $\forall_{i\in[1,2\ell+1],i\neq\ell+1,\, j\in[1,\ell+1]}$ $g_2^{a^i c/d_j}$; $\forall_{i\in[2,2\ell+2],\, j\in[1,\ell+1]}\, g_2^{a^i bf/d_j}$; $\forall_{i,j\in[1,\ell+1],i\neq j}\, g_2^{a^i bd_j/d_i}$. Then, it is hard for any PPT adversary to distinguish whether $T = g_2^{abz}$ or $T \xleftarrow{\$} \mathbb{G}_{p_2}$.*

Theorem 4. *Scheme 2 is selectively master-key hiding under ℓ-EDHE1 with tight reduction, where ℓ is the length of the ciphertext query $w^\star$.*

5.3   Fully Secure ABE

Fully-Secure Unbounded ABE with Large Universes. Our pair encoding scheme for unbounded KP-ABE with large universes is shown as Scheme 3. We can see that the parameter size is constant, and we can deal with any sizes of attribute policies, attribute sets, while the attribute universe is $\mathbb{Z}_N$. The structure of our scheme is similar to the selectively secure ABE of [26]. The correctness can be shown as follows. When $R((A, \pi), S) = 1$, let $I = \{\, i \in [1, m] \mid \pi(i) \in S \,\}$, we have reconstruction coefficients $\{\mu_i\}_{i\in I}$ such that $\sum_{i\in I} \mu_i A_i \boldsymbol{v}^\top = v_1 = r\phi_2$. Therefore, we have the following linear combination of the $k_i c_j$ terms: $k_1 c_1 - k_2 c_2 - k_3 c_3 + \sum_{i\in I} \mu_i (k_{4,i} c_4 - k_{5,i} c_{5,\pi(i)} + k_{6,i} c_{6,\pi(i)}) = \alpha s$.

Pair Encoding Scheme 3: Unbounded KP-ABE with Large Universes

Param	$\to 6$. Denote $\boldsymbol{h} = (h_0, h_1, \phi_1, \phi_2, \phi_3, \eta)$.

For LSS $A \in \mathbb{Z}_N^{m\times k}$, $\pi : [1, m] \to \mathbb{Z}_N$ (π needed not be injective).

$\mathsf{Enc1}(A, \pi) \to \boldsymbol{k}(\alpha, \boldsymbol{r}, \boldsymbol{h}) = \big(k_1, k_2, k_3, \{k_{4,i}, k_{5,i}, k_{6,i}\}_{i\in[1,m]}\big)$:

$$\left\{ \begin{array}{lll} k_1 = \alpha + r\phi_1 + u\eta, & k_2 = u, & k_3 = r, \\ k_{4,i} = A_i \boldsymbol{v}^\top + r_i \phi_3, & k_{5,i} = r_i, & k_{6,i} = r_i(h_0 + h_1\pi(i)) \end{array} \right\}$$

where $v_1 = r\phi_2$, $\boldsymbol{r} = (r, u, r_1, \ldots, r_m, v_2, \ldots, v_k)$, $\boldsymbol{v} = (v_1, \ldots, v_k)$.

For $S \subseteq \mathbb{Z}_N$.

$\mathsf{Enc2}(S) \to \boldsymbol{c}(\boldsymbol{s}, \boldsymbol{h}) = \big(c_1, c_2, c_3, c_4, \{c_{5,y}, c_{6,y}\}_{y\in S}\big)$:

$$\left\{ \begin{array}{lll} c_1 = s, & c_2 = s\eta, & c_3 = s\phi_1 + w\phi_2, \\ c_4 = w, & c_{5,y} = w\phi_3 + s_y(h_0 + h_1 y), & c_{6,y} = s_y \end{array} \right\}$$

where $\boldsymbol{s} = (s, w, \{s_y\}_{y\in S})$.

Fully-Secure ABE with Short Ciphertexts. Our encoding for this primitive is shown as Scheme 4. Denote by T the maximum size for attribute sets S. No further restriction is required. We can see that the ciphertext contains only 6 elements. The scheme is a reminiscent of the selectively secure ABE of [2]. The correctness can be shown as follows. When $R((A, \pi), S) = 1$, we have coefficients $\{\mu_i\}_{i\in I}$ similarly as above. Hence, we have $k_1 c_1 - k_2 c_2 - k_3 c_3 + \sum_{i\in I} \mu_i (k_{4,i} c_4 - k_{5,i} c_5 + (k_{6,i}(1, \boldsymbol{a})^\top) c_6) = \alpha s$, where $(1, \boldsymbol{a}) := (1, a_1, \ldots, a_T)$ and a_i is the coefficient of z^i in $p(z) = \prod_{y\in S}(z - y)$. Note that $\pi(i) \in S$ implies $p(\pi(i)) = 0$.

Pair Encoding Scheme 4: KP-ABE with Short Ciphertexts

$\mathsf{Param}(T) \rightarrow T + 6$. Denote $\boldsymbol{h} = (h_0, h_1, \ldots, h_{T+1}, \phi_1, \phi_2, \phi_3, \eta)$.

For LSS $A \in \mathbb{Z}_N^{m \times k}$, $\pi : [1, m] \rightarrow \mathbb{Z}_N$ (π needed not be injective).

$\mathsf{Enc1}(A, \pi) \rightarrow \boldsymbol{k}(\alpha, \boldsymbol{r}, \boldsymbol{h}) = (k_1, k_2, k_3, \{k_{4,i}, k_{5,i}, \boldsymbol{k}_{6,i}\}_{i \in [1,m]})$:

$$\left\{ \begin{array}{l} k_1 = \alpha + r\phi_1 + u\eta, \qquad k_2 = u, \qquad k_3 = r, \\ k_{4,i} = A_i \boldsymbol{v}^\top + r_i \phi_3, \qquad k_{5,i} = r_i, \\ \boldsymbol{k}_{6,i} = \left(r_i h_0, r_i(h_2 - h_1 \pi(i)), \ldots, r_i(h_{T+1} - h_1 \pi(i)^T) \right) \end{array} \right\}$$

where $v_1 = r\phi_2$, $\boldsymbol{r} = (r, u, r_1, \ldots, r_m, v_2, \ldots, v_k)$, $\boldsymbol{v} = (v_1, \ldots, v_k)$.

For $S \subseteq \mathbb{Z}_N$ such that $|S| \leq T$,
let a_i be the coefficient of z^i in $p(z) := \prod_{y \in S}(z - y)$.

$\mathsf{Enc2}(S) \rightarrow \boldsymbol{c}(\boldsymbol{s}, \boldsymbol{h}) = (c_1, c_2, c_3, c_4, c_5, c_6)$:

$$\left\{ \begin{array}{l} c_1 = s, \qquad c_2 = s\eta, \qquad c_3 = s\phi_1 + w\phi_2, \\ c_4 = w, \qquad c_5 = w\phi_3 + \tilde{s}(h_0 + h_1 a_0 + \cdots + h_{T+1} a_T), \qquad c_6 = \tilde{s} \end{array} \right\}$$

where $\boldsymbol{s} = (s, w, \tilde{s})$.

Both ABE schemes are special cases of our another new primitive called *key-policy over doubly spatial encryption*. We prove their SMH, CMH security under new static assumptions that are similar to those used for proving selective security of KP-ABE, CP-ABE of [26] respectively. Theses are provided in the full version. All the assumptions hold in the generic (bilinear) group model.

Acknowledgement. I would like to thank Michel Abdalla, Takahiro Matsuda, Shota Yamada, and reviewers for their helpful comments on previous versions.

References

1. Attrapadung, N., Libert, B.: Functional Encryption for Inner Product: Achieving Constant-Size Ciphertexts with Adaptive Security or Support for Negation. In: Nguyen, P.Q., Pointcheval, D. (eds.) PKC 2010. LNCS, vol. 6056, pp. 384–402. Springer, Heidelberg (2010)

2. Attrapadung, N., Libert, B., de Panafieu, E.: Expressive Key-Policy Attribute-Based Encryption with Constant-Size Ciphertexts. In: Catalano, D., Fazio, N., Gennaro, R., Nicolosi, A. (eds.) PKC 2011. LNCS, vol. 6571, pp. 90–108. Springer, Heidelberg (2011)

3. Bethencourt, J., Sahai, A., Waters, B.: Ciphertext-Policy Attribute-Based Encryption. In: IEEE Symposium on Security and Privacy 2007, pp. 321–334 (2007)

4. Boneh, D., Boyen, X.: Efficient Selective-ID Secure Identity-Based Encryption Without Random Oracles. In: Cachin, C., Camenisch, J.L. (eds.) EUROCRYPT 2004. LNCS, vol. 3027, pp. 223–238. Springer, Heidelberg (2004)

5. Boneh, D., Boyen, X., Goh, E.-J.: Hierarchical Identity-Based encryption with Constant Size Ciphertext. In: Cramer, R. (ed.) EUROCRYPT 2005. LNCS, vol. 3494, pp. 440–456. Springer, Heidelberg (2005)

6. Boneh, D., Hamburg, M.: Generalized Identity Based and Broadcast Encryption Schemes. In: Pieprzyk, J. (ed.) ASIACRYPT 2008. LNCS, vol. 5350, pp. 455–470. Springer, Heidelberg (2008)

7. Boneh, D., Sahai, A., Waters, B.: Functional Encryption: Definitions and Challenges. In: Ishai, Y. (ed.) TCC 2011. LNCS, vol. 6597, pp. 253–273. Springer, Heidelberg (2011)

8. Chen, J., Wee, H.: Fully (Almost) Tightly Secure IBE and Dual System Groups. In: Canetti, R., Garay, J.A. (eds.) CRYPTO 2013, Part II. LNCS, vol. 8043, pp. 435–460. Springer, Heidelberg (2013)

9. Chen, C., Chen, J., Lim, H.W., Zhang, Z., Feng, D., Ling, S., Wang, H.: Fully Secure Attribute-Based Systems with Short Ciphertexts/Signatures and Threshold Access Structures. In: Dawson, E. (ed.) CT-RSA 2013. LNCS, vol. 7779, pp. 50–67. Springer, Heidelberg (2013)

10. Garg, S., Gentry, C., Halevi, S.: Candidate multilinear maps from ideal lattices. In: Johansson, T., Nguyen, P.Q. (eds.) EUROCRYPT 2013. LNCS, vol. 7881, pp. 1–17. Springer, Heidelberg (2013)

11. Garg, S., Gentry, C., Halevi, S., Sahai, A., Waters, B.: Attribute-based encryption for circuits from multilinear maps. In: Canetti, R., Garay, J.A. (eds.) CRYPTO 2013, Part II. LNCS, vol. 8043, pp. 479–499. Springer, Heidelberg (2013)

12. Garg, S., Gentry, C., Halevi, S., Raykova, M., Sahai, A., Waters, B.: Candidate Indistinguishability Obfuscation and Functional Encryption for all circuits. In: FOCS 2013, pp. 40–49 (2013)

13. Goldwasser, S., Kalai, Y., Popa, R.A., Vaikuntanathan, V., Zeldovich, N.: Reusable garbled circuits and succinct functional encryption. In: STOC 2013, pp. 555–564 (2013)

14. Goldwasser, S., Kalai, Y., Popa, R.A., Vaikuntanathan, V., Zeldovich, N.: How to run Turing machines on encrypted data. In: Canetti, R., Garay, J.A. (eds.) CRYPTO 2013, Part II. LNCS, vol. 8043, pp. 536–553. Springer, Heidelberg (2013)

15. Gorbunov, S., Vaikuntanathan, V., Wee, H.: Attribute-based encryption for circuits. In: STOC 2013, pp. 545–554 (2013)

16. Goyal, V., Pandey, O., Sahai, A., Waters, B.: Attribute-based encryption for fine-grained access control of encrypted data. In: ACM CCS 2006, pp. 89–98 (2006)

17. Hamburg, M.: Spatial Encryption. Cryptology ePrint Archive: Report 2011/389

18. Katz, J., Sahai, A., Waters, B.: Predicate Encryption Supporting Disjunctions, Polynomial Equations, and Inner Products. In: Smart, N.P. (ed.) EUROCRYPT 2008. LNCS, vol. 4965, pp. 146–162. Springer, Heidelberg (2008)

19. Lewko, A.: Tools for Simulating Features of Composite Order Bilinear Groups in the Prime Order Setting. In: Pointcheval, D., Johansson, T. (eds.) EUROCRYPT 2012. LNCS, vol. 7237, pp. 318–335. Springer, Heidelberg (2012)

20. Lewko, A., Waters, B.: New Techniques for Dual System Encryption and Fully Secure HIBE with Short Ciphertexts. In: Micciancio, D. (ed.) TCC 2010. LNCS, vol. 5978, pp. 455–479. Springer, Heidelberg (2010)

21. Lewko, A., Waters, B.: Decentralizing Attribute-Based Encryption. In: Paterson, K.G. (ed.) EUROCRYPT 2011. LNCS, vol. 6632, pp. 568–588. Springer, Heidelberg (2011)

22. Lewko, A., Waters, B.: Unbounded HIBE and Attribute-Based Encryption. In: Paterson, K.G. (ed.) EUROCRYPT 2011. LNCS, vol. 6632, pp. 547–567. Springer, Heidelberg (2011)

23. Lewko, A., Waters, B.: New Proof Methods for Attribute-Based Encryption: Achieving Full Security through Selective Techniques. In: Safavi-Naini, R., Canetti, R. (eds.) CRYPTO 2012. LNCS, vol. 7417, pp. 180–198. Springer, Heidelberg (2012)

24. Lewko, A., Okamoto, T., Sahai, A., Takashima, K., Waters, B.: Fully Secure Functional Encryption: Attribute-Based Encryption and (Hierarchical) Inner Product Encryption. In: Gilbert, H. (ed.) EUROCRYPT 2010. LNCS, vol. 6110, pp. 62–91. Springer, Heidelberg (2010)
25. Naor, M., Reingold, O.: Number-Theoretic Constructions of Efficient Pseudo-Random Functions. Journal of ACM 51(2), 231–262 (2004)
26. Rouselakis, Y., Waters Practical, B.: constructions and new proof methods for large universe attribute-based encryption. In: ACM CCS 2013, pp. 463–474 (2013)
27. Sahai, A., Waters, B.: Fuzzy Identity-Based Encryption. In: Cramer, R. (ed.) EUROCRYPT 2005. LNCS, vol. 3494, pp. 457–473. Springer, Heidelberg (2005)
28. Okamoto, T., Takashima, K.: Fully secure functional encryption with general relations from the decisional linear assumption. In: Rabin, T. (ed.) CRYPTO 2010. LNCS, vol. 6223, pp. 191–208. Springer, Heidelberg (2010)
29. Okamoto, T., Takashima, K.: Adaptively Attribute-Hiding (Hierarchical) Inner Product Encryption. In: Pointcheval, D., Johansson, T. (eds.) EUROCRYPT 2012. LNCS, vol. 7237, pp. 591–608. Springer, Heidelberg (2012)
30. Okamoto, T., Takashima, K.: Fully Secure Unbounded Inner-Product and Attribute-Based Encryption. In: Wang, X., Sako, K. (eds.) ASIACRYPT 2012. LNCS, vol. 7658, pp. 349–366. Springer, Heidelberg (2012)
31. Ramanna, S.C.: DFA-Based Functional Encryption: Adaptive Security from Dual System Encryption. Cryptology ePrint Archive: Report 2013/638
32. Waters, B.: Ciphertext-Policy Attribute-Based Encryption: An Expressive, Efficient, and Provably Secure Realization. In: Catalano, D., Fazio, N., Gennaro, R., Nicolosi, A. (eds.) PKC 2011. LNCS, vol. 6571, pp. 53–70. Springer, Heidelberg (2011)
33. Waters, B.: Dual System Encryption: Realizing Fully Secure IBE and HIBE under Simple Assumptions. In: Halevi, S. (ed.) CRYPTO 2009. LNCS, vol. 5677, pp. 619–636. Springer, Heidelberg (2009)
34. Waters, B.: Functional Encryption for Regular Languages. In: Safavi-Naini, R., Canetti, R. (eds.) CRYPTO 2012. LNCS, vol. 7417, pp. 218–235. Springer, Heidelberg (2012)

Multi-input Functional Encryption*

Shafi Goldwasser[1,**], S. Dov Gordon[2], Vipul Goyal[3], Abhishek Jain[4],
Jonathan Katz[5,***], Feng-Hao Liu[5], Amit Sahai[7,†], Elaine Shi[5,‡],
and Hong-Sheng Zhou[9,§]

[1] MIT and Weizmann, Israel
shafi@csail.mit.edu
[2] Applied Communication Sciences, USA
sgordon@appcomsci.com
[3] Microsoft Research, India
vipul@microsoft.com
[4] Boston University and MIT, USA
abhishek@csail.mit.edu
[5] University of Maryland, USA
{jkatz,fenghao,elaine}@cs.umd.edu
[6] UCLA
sahai@cs.ucla.edu
[7] Virginia Commonwealth University, USA
hszhou@vcu.edu

* This conference proceedings publication is the result of a merge of two independent and concurrent works. The two papers were authored by Goldwasser, Goyal, Jain, and Sahai; and by Gordon, Katz, Liu, Shi, and Zhou.

** Research supported by NSFEAGER award # CNS1347364 DARPA award # FA8750-11-2-0225 and the Simons Foundation - Investigation Award.

*** Research supported by NSF awards #1111599 and #1223623, and by the US Army Research Laboratory and the UK Ministry of Defence under Agreement Number W911NF-06-3-0001. The views and conclusions contained herein are those of the authors and should not be interpreted as representing the official policies, either expressed or implied, of the US Army Research Laboratory, the U.S. Government, the UK Ministry of Defense, or the UK Government. The US and UK Governments are authorized to reproduce and distribute reprints for Government purposes notwithstanding any copyright notation hereon.

† Research supported in part from a DARPA/ONR PROCEED award, NSF grants 1228984, 1136174, 1118096, and 1065276, a Xerox Faculty Research Award, a Google Faculty Research Award, an equipment grant from Intel, and an Okawa Foundation Research Grant. This material is based upon work supported by the Defense Advanced Research Projects Agency through the U.S. Office of Naval Research under Contract N00014-11- 1-0389. The views expressed are those of the author and do not reflect the official policy or position of the Department of Defense, the National Science Foundation, or the U.S. Government.

‡ This work is partially supported by NSF award CNS-1314857 and a Google Research Award.

§ This work is partially supported by an NSF CI postdoctoral fellowship, and was mostly done while at the University of Maryland.

P.Q. Nguyen and E. Oswald (Eds.): EUROCRYPT 2014, LNCS 8441, pp. 578–602, 2014.

Abstract. We introduce the problem of Multi-Input Functional Encryption, where a secret key sk_f can correspond to an n-ary function f that takes multiple ciphertexts as input. We formulate both indistinguishability-based and simulation-based definitions of security for this notion, and show close connections with indistinguishability and virtual black-box definitions of obfuscation.

Assuming indistinguishability obfuscation for circuits, we present constructions achieving indistinguishability security for a large class of settings. We show how to modify this construction to achieve simulation-based security as well, in those settings where simulation security is possible.

1   Introduction

Traditionally, encryption has been used to secure a communication channel between a unique sender-receiver pair. In recent years, however, our networked world has opened up a large number of new usage scenarios for encryption. For example, a single piece of encrypted data, perhaps stored in an untrusted cloud, may need to be used in different ways by different users. To address this issue, the notion of functional encryption (FE) was developed in a sequence of works [19,13,7,14,15,6,16,18]. In functional encryption, a secret key sk_f can be created for any functions f from a class $\mathcal{F}$; such a secret key is derived from the master secret key MSK. Given any ciphertext c with underlying plaintext x, using SK_f a user can efficiently compute $f(x)$. The security of FE requires that the adversary "does not learn anything" about x, other than the computation result $f(x)$.

How to define "does not learn anything about" x is a fascinating question which has been addressed by a number of papers, with general formal definitions first appearing in [6,16]. The definitions range from requiring a strict *simulation* of the view of the adversary, which enlarges the range of applications, but has been shown to necessitate a ciphertext whose size grows with the number of functions for which secret keys will ever be released [1] (or a secret key whose size grows with the number of ciphertexts that will ever be released [6]), to an *indistinguishability* of ciphertexts requirement which supports the release of an unbounded number of function keys and short ciphertexts.

Functional encryption seems to offer the perfect non-interactive solution to many problems which arise in the context of delegating services to outside servers. A typical example is the delegation of spam filtering to an outside server as follows: Alice publishes her public key online and gives the spam filter a key for the filtering function; Users sending email to Alice will encrypt the email with her public key. The spam filter can now determine by itself, for each email, whether to pass it along to Alice's mailbox or to deem it as spam, but without ever learning anything about Alice's email (other than the fact that it was deemed a spam message or not). This example inherently requires computing a function f on a single ciphertext.

Multi-Input Functional Encryption. It is less clear, however, how to define or achieve functional encryption in the context of computing a function defined over *multiple* plaintexts given their corresponding ciphertexts, or further, the computation of functions defined over plaintexts given their ciphertexts each encrypted under a different key. Yet, these settings, which we formalize as *Multi-Input Functional Encryption*, encompass a vast landscape of applications, going way beyond delegating computation to an untrusted server or cloud.

Let us begin by clarifying the setting of Multi-Input Functional Encryption: Let f be an n-ary function where $n > 1$ can be a polynomial in the security parameter. We begin by defining multi-input functional encryption where the owner of a master secret key MSK can derive special keys SK_f whose knowledge enables the computation of $f(x_1, \ldots, x_n)$ from n ciphertexts $c_1, \ldots, c_n$ of underlying messages $x_1, \ldots, x_n$ with respect to the same master secret key MSK. We next allow the different ciphertexts c_i to be each encrypted under a different encryption key EK_i to capture the setting in which each ciphertext was generated by an entirely different party.

Let us illustrate a few settings in which one would want to compute a function over multiple plaintexts given the corresponding ciphertexts.

Example: Multi-input symmetric-key FE can be used for secure searching over encrypted data, where it can function in the same role as *order-preserving encryption* (OPE) [4,5] or, more generally, property-preserving encryption [17]. A direct application of our construction yields the first OPE scheme to satisfy the indistinguishability notion of security proposed by Boldyreva et al. [4], resolving a primary open question in that line of research. More specifically, consider a setting in which a client uploads several encrypted data items $c_1 = \mathsf{Enc}(x_1)$, $\ldots, c_n = \mathsf{Enc}(x_n)$ to a server. If at some later point in time the client wants to retrieve all data items less than some value t, the client can send $c^* = \mathsf{Enc}(t)$ along with a secret key SK_f for the (binary) comparison function. This allows the server to identify exactly which data items are less than the desired threshold t (and send the corresponding ciphertexts back to the client), without learning anything beyond the relative ordering of the data items. In fact, we can hide even more information than OPE: if the client tags every data item with a '0' (i.e., uploads $c_i = \mathsf{Enc}(0\|x_i)$) and tags the search term with a '1' (i.e., sends $c^* = \mathsf{Enc}(1\|t)$), then the client can send SK_f for the function

$$f(b\|x, b'\|t) = \begin{cases} x < t & b = 0, b' = 1 \\ 0 & \text{otherwise} \end{cases}$$

Thus, SK_f allows comparisons only between the data items and the threshold, but not between the data items themselves. More generally, the same approach can be followed to enable arbitrary searches over encrypted data while revealing only a minimal amount of information. We note also that the search query itself can remain hidden as well.

More generally, suppose Alice wishes to perform a certain class of general SQL queries over this database. If we use ordinary functional encryption, Alice would need to obtain a separate secret key for every possible valid SQL query, a potentially exponentially large set. Multi-input functional encryption allows us to address this problem in a flexible way. We highlight two aspects of how Multi-Input Functional Encryption can apply to this example:

- Let f be the function where $f(q, x)$ first checks if q is a valid SQL query from the allowed class, and if so $f(q, x)$ is the output of the query q on the database x. Now, if we give the secret key SK_f *and* the encryption key ek_1 to Alice, then Alice can choose a valid query q and encrypt it under her encryption key EK_1 to obtain ciphertext c_1. Then she could use her secret key SK_f on ciphertexts c_1 and c_2, where c_2 is the encrypted database, to obtain the results of the SQL query.
- Furthermore, if our application demanded that multiple users add or manipulate different entries in the database, the most natural way to build such a database would be to have different ciphertexts for each entry in the database. In this case, for a database of size n, we could let f be an $(n+1)$-ary function where $f(q, x_1, \ldots, x_n)$ is the result of a (valid) SQL query q on the database $(x_1, \ldots, x_n)$.

1.1   This Paper

This paper is a merge of two independent works, both of which can be found online [10,12]. These two works contain many overlapping results dedicated to the study of multi-input functional encryption, starting with formalizations of security. In them, the authors provide both feasibility results and negative results with respect to different definitions of security. Following the single-input setting, they consider two notions of security, namely, indistinguishability-based security (or IND security for short) and simulation-based security (or SIM security for short). Below we summarize only what appears in this proceedings, and refer the reader to the full versions for a more complete study of the subject.

Indistinguishability-Based Security. We start by considering the notion of indistinguishability-based security for n-ary multi-input functional encryption: Informally speaking, in indistinguishability security for multi-input functional encryption, we consider a game between a judge and an adversary. First, the judge generates the master secret key MSK, evaluation keys $\{\mathsf{EK}_1, \ldots, \mathsf{EK}_n\}$, and public parameters, and gives to the adversary the public parameters and a subset of evaluation keys (chosen by the adversary). Then the adversary can request any number of secret keys SK_f for functions f of the adversary's choice. Next, the adversary declares two "challenge vectors" of sets X^0 and X^1, where X_i^b is a set of plaintexts. The judge chooses a bit b at random, and for each $i \in [n]$, the judge encrypts every element of X_i^b using evaluation key ek_i to obtain a tuple of "challenge ciphertexts" C, which is given to the adversary. After this, the adversary can again request any number of secret keys SK_f for functions f of the adversary's choice. Finally, the adversary has to guess the bit b that the judge chose.

If the adversary has requested any secret key SK_f such that there exist vectors of plaintexts x^0 and x^1 where for every $i \in [n]$, either $x_i^b \in X_i^b$ or the adversary has EK_i, such that $f(x^0) \neq f(x^1)$, then we say that this function f

splits the challenge, and in this case the adversary loses – because the legitimate functionalities that he has access to already allow him to distinguish between the scenario where $b = 0$ and $b = 1$. If the adversary has never asked for any splitting function, and nevertheless the adversary guesses b correctly, we say that he wins. The indistinguishability-based security definition requires that the adversary's probability of winning be at most negligibly greater than $\frac{1}{2}$.

This definition generalizes the indistinguishability-based definition of (single-input) functional encryption, which was historically the first security formalization considered for functional encryption [19]. Informally speaking, this definition captures an information-theoretic flavor of security, where the adversary should not learn anything beyond what is information-theoretically revealed by the function outputs it can obtain.

With regard to the indistinguishability notion of security, we obtain the following results:

- **Indistinguishability-based security implies indistinguishability obfuscation, even for single-key security.** We show that the existence of a multi-input functional encryption scheme achieving indistinguishability-based security for all circuits implies the existence of an indistinguishability obfuscator [2] for all circuits, *even when security is only needed against an adversary that obtain a single secret key*, and where the adversary does not receive any evaluation keys. This stands in stark contrast to the single-input setting, where [18] showed how to obtain single-key secure (single input) functional encryption for all circuits, under only the assumption that public-key encryption exists. Indeed further research in single-key security for functional encryption has largely focused on efficiency issues [11] such as succinctness of ciphertexts, that enable new applications. In the setting of multi-input security, in contrast, even single key security must rely on the existence of indistinguishability obfuscation.

- **Positive Result, General Setting.** On the other hand, if we assume that an indistinguishability obfuscator for general circuits exists with sub-exponential security (the first candidate construction was recently put forward by [9]), and we assume that sub-exponentially secure one-way functions exist, then we obtain full indistinguishability-based security for any polynomial-size challenge vectors, with any subset of evaluation keys given to the adversary. Furthermore, our construction has security when the adversary can obtain any *unbounded* polynomial number of secret keys SK_f. Our result is obtained by first achieving *selective* security, where the adversary must begin by declaring the challenge vectors, using indistinguishability obfuscation and one-way functions (leveraging the results of [20]). Then we use complexity leveraging to obtain full security in a standard manner.

- **Positive Result, Symmetric Key Setting.** We consider a special case where the adversary is not given any of the evaluation keys, corresponding to a typical symmetric key setting. As an example, this can be useful in a scenario where a single user wishes to outsource their private dataset to one or more untrusted servers, issuing keys to facilitate searches over the data. In this setting, we give a construction with succinct ciphertexts whose size is dependent only on the security parameter, and not on the number of challenge plaintexts. We remark that the size of the public parameters, which are used in encryption and decryption, still grows with the number of challenge plaintexts. We refer the reader to the full versions [10,12] for ways to remove this dependency.

- **Positive Result, Isolated Time-steps.** We consider one last setting where each party encrypts a single plaintext in every *time-step*, and we modify the security definition to prevent the computation on ciphertexts from different time-steps. In this setting, as above, the adversary can request any subset of the evaluation keys. We give a construction that has succinct ciphertexts, dependent only on the security parameter, and independent of the number of time-steps or the number of challenge plaintexts. (The remark about the public parameters that appears above still applies.)

Simulation-Based Security. In simulation-based security, informally speaking, we require that every adversary can be simulated using only oracle access to the functions f for which the adversary obtains secret keys, even when it can obtain a set of "challenge" ciphertexts corresponding to unknown plaintexts – about which the simulator can only learn information by querying the function f at these unknown plaintexts. We highlight two natural settings for the study of simulation security for multi-input functional encryption: (1) the setting where an adversary has access to an encryption key (analogous to the public-key setting), and (2) the setting where the adversary does not have access to any encryption keys (analogous to the secret key setting). The security guarantees which are achievable in these settings will be vastly different as illustrated below.

Several works [6,1,3] have shown limitations on parameters with respect to which simulation-based security can be achieved for single-input functional encryption. For multi-input functional encryption, due to the connection to obfuscation discussed above, the situation for simulation-based security is more problematic. Indeed, it has been a folklore belief that n-ary functional encryption with simulation-based security would imply Virtual Black-Box obfuscation, which is known to be impossible [2]. We strengthen and formalize this folklore in three results:

- In the setting where the adversary receives only a single key for a single n-ary function, and receives no evaluation keys, and where the adversary can obtain a set of challenge ciphertexts that can (informally speaking) form a super-polynomial number of potential inputs to f, if simulation security is possible then virtual black-box obfuscation must be possible for arbitrary circuits, which is known to be impossible [2]. This follows immediately from the same construction that shows the connection of indistinguishability-based security to indistinguishability obfuscation mentioned above, and most directly formalizes the folklore belief mentioned above.
- In the setting where the adversary receives only a single key for a 2-ary function, and receives one evaluation key and one challenge ciphertext, if

simulation security is possible then virtual black-box obfuscation must be possible for arbitrary circuits, which is known to be impossible [2].

- The above results demonstrate that we cannot achieve simulation security for arbitrary multi-input functions. Looking at which functions we might support, we define a new notion of *learnable functions* and demonstrate that we can only achieve simulation-based security for this type of function. Informally, we call a 2-ary function, $f(\cdot, \cdot)$, *learnable* if, when given a description of f and oracle access to $f(x, \cdot)$, one can output the description of a function that is indistinguishable from $f_x(\cdot)$ (i.e. from the function obtained when restricting f to input x).

Positive Result. In light of these negative results, the only hope for obtaining a positive result lies in a situation where: (1) no evaluation keys are given to the adversary, and (2) the challenge ciphertexts given to the adversary can only form a polynomial number of potential inputs to valid functions. Assuming one-way functions and indistinguishability obfuscation, for any fixed polynomial bound on the size of these potential inputs we give a construction that achieves simulation-based security for multi-input functional encryption where the adversary obtains no evaluation keys, but can obtain some fixed polynomial number of secret keys SK_f before obtaining challenge ciphertexts, as well as an unbounded number of secret keys SK_f after obtaining challenge ciphertexts.

Finally, we complement this positive result by showing that even in the setting where the adversary obtains no evaluation keys and an unlimited number of challenge ciphertexts, simulation-based security is impossible if the adversary can ask for even one secret key SK_f before it obtains the challenge ciphertexts.

Our Techniques. We have several results in this work, but to provide some flavor of the kinds of difficulties that arise in the multi-input functional encryption setting, we now describe some of the issues that we deal with in the context of our positive result for indistinguishability-based security for multi-input functional encryption. (Similar issues arise in our other positive result for simulation-based security.)

The starting point for our construction and analysis is the recent single-input functional encryption scheme for general circuits based on indistinguishability obfuscation due to [9]. However, the central issue that we must deal with is one that does not arise in their context: Recall that in the indistinguishability security game, the adversary is allowed to get secret keys for any function f, as long as this function does not "split" the challenge vectors $\boldsymbol{X}^0$ and $\boldsymbol{X}^1$. That is, as long as it is *not* the case that there exist vectors of plaintexts $\boldsymbol{x}^0$ and $\boldsymbol{x}^1$ where for every $i \in [n]$, either there exists j such that $x_i^b \in X_j^b$ or the adversary has EK_i, such that $f(x^0) \neq f(x^1)$. A crucial point here is what happens for an index i where the adversary does *not* have EK_i. Let us consider an example with a 3-ary function, where the adversary has EK_1, but neither EK_2 nor EK_3.

Suppose the challenge ciphertexts $(\mathsf{CT}_1, \mathsf{CT}_2, \mathsf{CT}_3)$ are encryptions of either (y_1^0, y_2^0, y_3^0) or (y_1^1, y_2^1, y_3^1). Now, any function f that the adversary queries is required to be such that $f(\cdot, y_2^0, y_3^0) \equiv f(\cdot, y_2^1, y_3^1)$ and $f(y_1^0, y_2^0, y_3^0) = f(y_1^1, y_2^1, y_3^1)$.

However, there may exist an input plaintext (say) z such that $f(y_1^0, y_2^0, z) \neq f(y_1^1, y_2^1, z)$. This is not "supposed" to be a problem because the adversary does not have EK_3, and therefore it cannot actually query f with z as its third argument.

However, in the obfuscation-based approach to functional encryption of [9] that we build on, the secret key for f is essentially built on top of an obfuscation of f. Let CT^* denote an encryption of z w.r.t. EK_3. Then, informally speaking, in one of our hybrid experiments, we will need to move from an obfuscation that on input $(\mathsf{CT}_1, \mathsf{CT}_2, \mathsf{CT}^*)$ would yield the output $f(y_1^0, y_2^0, z)$ to another obfuscation that on the same input would yield the output $f(y_1^1, y_2^1, z)$. Again, while an adversary may not be able explicitly perform such a decryption query, since we are building upon *indistinguishability obfuscation* – which only guarantees that obfuscations of circuits that implement *identical* functions are indistinguishable – such a hybrid change would not be indistinguishable since we know that $f(y_1^0, y_2^0, z) \neq f(y_1^1, y_2^1, z)$ are not identical.

Solving this problem is the core technical aspect of our constructions and their analysis. At a very high level, we address this problem by introducing a new "flag" value that can change the nature of the function f that we are obfuscating to "disable" all plaintexts except for the ones that are in the challenge vectors. We provide more intuition in the full-versions.

Open Questions. Currently, our positive result for indistinguishability-based security requires that there to be a fixed polynomial limit on the size of challenge vectors, known at the time of setup. Unlike in the case of simulation security, we know of no corresponding lower bound showing that such a bound is necessary. Achieving full security without using complexity leveraging is another open question.

2 Multi-Input Functional Encryption

In this work, we study functional encryption for n-ary functions, where $n > 1$ (and in general, a polynomial in the security parameter). In other words, we are interested in encryption schemes where the owner of a "master" secret key can generate special keys SK_f that allow the computation of $f(x_1, \ldots, x_n)$ from n ciphertexts $\mathsf{CT}_1, \ldots, \mathsf{CT}_n$ corresponding to messages $x_1, \ldots, x_n$, respectively. We refer to such an encryption scheme as *multi-input* functional encryption. Analogously, we will refer to the existing notion of functional encryption (that only considers single-ary functions) as *single-input* functional encryption.

Intuitively, while single-input functional encryption can be viewed as a specific (non-interactive) way of performing two-party computation, our setting of multi-input functional encryption captures *multiparty* computation. Going forward with this analogy, we are interested in modeling the general scenario where the n input ciphertexts are computed by n *different* parties. This raises the following two important questions:

1. Do the parties (i.e., the encryptors) share the *same* encryption key or do they use *different* encryption keys EK_i to compute input ciphertexts CT_i.
2. Are the encryption keys secret or public?

As we shall see, these questions have important bearing on the security guarantees that can be achieved for multi-input functional encryption.

Towards that end, we present a general, unified syntax and security definitions for multi-input functional encryption. We consider encryption systems with n encryption keys, some of which may be public, while the rest are secret. When all of the encryption keys are public, then this represents the "public-key" setting, while when all the encryption keys are secret, then this represents the "secret-key" setting. Looking ahead, we remark that our modeling allows us to capture the intermediary cases between these two extremes that are interesting from the viewpoint of the security guarantees possible.

The rest of this section is organized as follows. We first present the syntax and correctness requirements for multi-input FE in Section 2.1). Then, in Section 2.2, we present our security definitions for multi-input FE. In Section 2.3 we give a construction that meets these definitions.

2.1   Syntax

Throughout the paper, we denote the security parameter by k. Let $\mathcal{X} = \{\mathcal{X}_k\}_{k \in \mathbb{N}}$ and $\mathcal{Y} = \{\mathcal{Y}_k\}_{k \in \mathbb{N}}$ be ensembles where each $\mathcal{X}_k$ and $\mathcal{Y}_k$ is a finite set. Let $\mathcal{F} = \{\mathcal{F}_k\}_{k \in \mathbb{N}}$ be an ensemble where each $\mathcal{F}_k$ is a finite collection of n-ary functions. Each function $f \in \mathcal{F}_k$ takes as input n strings $x_1, \ldots, x_n$, where each $x_i \in \mathcal{X}_k$ and outputs $f(x_1, \ldots, x_n) \in \mathcal{Y}_k$.

A multi-input functional encryption scheme $\mathcal{FE}$ for $\mathcal{F}$ consists of four algorithms (FE.Setup, FE.Enc, FE.Keygen, FE.Dec) described below.

- **Setup** FE.Setup$(1^k, n)$ is a PPT algorithm that takes as input the security parameter k and the function arity n. It outputs n encryption keys $\mathsf{EK}_1, \ldots, \mathsf{EK}_n$ and a master secret key MSK.
- **Encryption** FE.Enc(EK, x) is a PPT algorithm that takes as input an encryption key $\mathsf{EK}_i \in (\mathsf{EK}_1, \ldots, \mathsf{EK}_n)$ and an input message $x \in \mathcal{X}_k$ and outputs a ciphertext CT.
  In the case where all of the encryption keys EK_i are the same, we assume that each ciphertext CT has an associated label i to denote that the encrypted plaintext constitutes an i'th input to a function $f \in \mathcal{F}_k$. For convenience of notation, we omit the labels from the explicit description of the ciphertexts. In particular, note that when EK_i's are *distinct*, the index of the encryption key EK_i used to compute CT implicitly denotes that the plaintext encrypted in CT constitutes an i'th input to f, and thus no explicit label is necessary.
- **Key Generation** FE.Keygen(MSK, f) is a PPT algorithm that takes as input the master secret key MSK and an n-ary function $f \in \mathcal{F}_k$ and outputs a corresponding secret key SK_f.
- **Decryption** FE.Dec$(\mathsf{SK}_f, \mathsf{CT}_1, \ldots, \mathsf{CT}_n)$ is a deterministic algorithm that takes as input a secret key SK_f and n ciphertexts $\mathsf{CT}_i, \ldots, \mathsf{CT}_n$ and outputs a string $y \in \mathcal{Y}_k$.

Definition 1 (Correctness). *A multi-input functional encryption scheme $\mathcal{FE}$ for $\mathcal{F}$ is correct if for all $f \in \mathcal{F}_k$ and all $(x_1, \ldots, x_n) \in \mathcal{X}_k^n$:*

$$\Pr\left[\begin{array}{l} (\mathsf{EK}, \mathsf{MSK}) \leftarrow \mathsf{FE.Setup}(1^k)\,;\ \mathsf{SK}_f \leftarrow \mathsf{FE.Keygen}(\mathsf{MSK}, f)\,; \\ \mathsf{FE.Dec}\,(\mathsf{SK}_f, \mathsf{FE.Enc}\,(\mathsf{EK}_1, x_1)\,, \ldots, \mathsf{FE.Enc}\,(\mathsf{EK}_n, x_n)) \neq f(x_1, \ldots, x_n) \end{array} \right] = \mathsf{negl}(k)$$

where the probability is taken over the coins of $\mathsf{FE.Setup}$, $\mathsf{FE.Keygen}$ *and* $\mathsf{FE.Enc}$.

2.2 Security for Multi-Input Functional Encryption

We now present our security definitions for multi-input functional encryption. We provide the most general possible definition with respect to adversarial corruptions, allowing the adversary to choose which subset of parties he corrupts, and which evaluation keys he will learn as a consequence. In Section 3 we will consider more restricted definitions.

Following the literature on single-input FE, we consider two notions of security, namely, indistinguishability-based security (or IND-security, in short) and simulation-based security (or SIM-security, in short).

Notation. We start by introducing some notation that is used in our security definitions. Let N denote the set of positive integers $\{1, \ldots, n\}$ where n denotes the arity of functions. For any two sets $S = \{s_0, \ldots, s_{|S|}\}$ and $I = \{i_1, \ldots, i_{|I|}\}$ such that $|I| \leq |S|$, we let S_I denote the subset $\{s_i\}_{i \in I}$ of the set S. Throughout the text, we use the vector and set notation interchangeably, as per convenience. For simplicity of notation, we omit explicit reference to auxiliary input to the adversary from our definitions.

Indistinguishability-Based Security. Here we present an indistinguishability-based security definition for multi-input FE.

Intuition. We start by giving an overview of the main ideas behind our indistinguishability-based security definition. To convey the core ideas, it suffices to consider the case of 2-ary functions. We will assume familiarity with the security definitions for single-input FE.

Let us start by considering the natural extension of *public-key* single-input FE to the two-input setting. That is, suppose there are two public encryption keys EK_1, EK_2 that are used to create ciphertexts of first inputs and second inputs, respectively, for 2-ary functions. Let us investigate what security can be achieved for *one* pair of challenge message tuples (x_1^0, x_2^0), (x_1^1, x_2^1) for the simplified case where the adversary makes secret key queries after receiving the challenge ciphertexts.

Suppose that the adversary queries secret keys for functions $\{f\}$. Now, recall that the IND-security definition in the single-input case guarantees that an adversary cannot differentiate between encryptions of x^0 and x^1 as long as $f(x^0) = f(x^1)$ for every $f \in \{f\}$. We note, however, that an analogous security guarantee cannot be achieved in the multi-input setting. That is, restricting the functions $\{f\}$ to be such that $f(x_1^0, x_2^0) = f(x_1^1, x_2^1)$ is *not* enough since an adversary who knows both the encryption keys can create its own ciphertexts w.r.t. each encryption key. Then, by using the secret key corresponding to function f, it can learn additional values $\{f(x_1^b, \cdot)\}$ and $\{f(\cdot, x_2^b)\}$, where b is the challenge bit. In particular, if, for example, there exists an input x^* such that $f(x_1^0, x^*) \neq f(x_1^1, x^*)$, then the adversary can learn the challenge bit b! Therefore, we must enforce additional restrictions on the query functions f. Specifically, we must require that $f(x_1^0, x') = f(x_1^1, x')$ for *every* input x' in the domain (and similarly $f(x', x_2^0) = f(x', x_2^1)$). Note that this restriction "grows" with the arity n of the functions.

Let us now consider the secret-key case, where all the encryption keys are secret. In this case, for the above example, it suffices to require that $f(x_1^0, x_2^0) = f(x_1^1, x_2^1)$ since the adversary cannot create its own ciphertexts. Observe, however, that when there are *multiple* challenge messages, then an adversary can learn function evaluations over different "combinations" of challenge messages. In particular, if there are q challenge messages per encryption key, then the adversary can learn q^2 output values for every f. Then, we must enforce that for every $i \in [q^2]$, the i'th output value y_i^0 when challenge bit $b = 0$ is *equal* to the output value y_i^1 when the challenge bit $b = 1$.

The security guarantees in the public-key and the secret-key settings as discussed above are vastly different. In general, we observe that the *more* the number of encryption keys that are public, the *smaller* the class of functions that can be supported by the definition. Bellow, we present a unified definition that simultaneously captures the extreme cases of public-key and secret-key settings as well as all the "in between" cases.

Notation. Our security definition is parameterized by two variables t and q, where t denotes the number of encryption keys known to the adversary, and q denotes the number of challenge messages per encryption key. Thus, in total, the adversary is allowed to make $Q = q \cdot n$ number of challenge message queries.

To facilitate the presentation of our IND security definition, we first introduce the following two notions:

Definition 2 (Function Compatibility). *Let $\{f\}$ be any set of functions $f \in \mathcal{F}_k$. Let $\mathsf{N} = \{1, \ldots, n\}$ and $\mathsf{I} \subseteq \mathsf{N}$. Then, a pair of message vectors $\boldsymbol{X}^0$ and $\boldsymbol{X}^1$, where $\boldsymbol{X}^b = \{x_{1,j}^b, \ldots, x_{n,j}^b\}_{j=1}^q$, are said to be I-compatible with $\{f\}$ if they satisfy the following property:*

- *For every $f \in \{f\}$, every $\mathsf{I}' = \{i_1, \ldots, i_t\} \subseteq \mathsf{I} \cup \emptyset$, every $j_1, \ldots, j_{n-t} \in [q]$, and every $x'_{i_1}, \ldots, x'_{i_t} \in \mathcal{X}_k$,*

$$f\left(\left\langle x_{i_1, j_1}^0, \ldots, x_{i_{n-t'}, j_{n-t}}^0, x'_{i_1}, \ldots, x'_{i_t} \right\rangle\right) = f\left(\left\langle x_{i_1, j_1}^1, \ldots, x_{i_{n-t}, j_{n-t}}^1, x'_{i_1}, \ldots, x'_{i_t} \right\rangle\right),$$

where $\langle y_{i_1}, \ldots, y_{i_n} \rangle$ denotes a permutation of the values $y_{i_1}, \ldots, y_{i_n}$ such that the value y_{i_j} is mapped to the ℓ'th location if y_{i_j} is the ℓ'th input (out of n inputs) to f.

Definition 3 (Message Compatibility). *Let X^0 and X^1 be any pair of message vectors, where $X^b = \{x_{1,j}^b, \ldots, x_{n,j}^b\}_{j=1}^q$. Let $N = \{1, \ldots, k\}$ and $I \subseteq N$. Then, a function $f \in \mathcal{F}_k$ is said to be I-compatible with (X^0, X^1) if it satisfies the following property:*

- *For every $I' = \{i_1, \ldots, i_t\} \subseteq I \cup \emptyset$, every $j_1, \ldots, j_{n-t} \in [q]$ and every $x_{i_1}', \ldots, x_{i_t}' \in \mathcal{X}_k$,*

$$f\left(\langle x_{i_1,j_1}^0, \ldots, x_{i_{n-t},j_{n-t}}^0, x_{i_1}', \ldots, x_{i_t}'\rangle\right) = f\left(\langle x_{i_1,j_1}^1, \ldots, x_{i_{n-t},j_{n-t}}^1, x_{i_1}', \ldots, x_{i_t}'\rangle\right),$$

We are now ready to present our formal definition for (t, q)-IND-secure multi-input functional encryption.

Definition 4 (Indistinguishability-based security). *We say that a multi-input functional encryption scheme $\mathcal{FE}$ for for n-ary functions $\mathcal{F}$ is (t, q)-IND-secure if for every PPT adversary $\mathcal{A} = (\mathcal{A}_0, \mathcal{A}_1, \mathcal{A}_2)$, the advantage of $\mathcal{A}$ defined as*

$$\mathsf{Adv}_{\mathcal{A}}^{\mathcal{FE}, \mathsf{IND}}(1^k) = \left| \Pr[\mathsf{IND}_{\mathcal{A}}^{\mathcal{FE}}(1^k) = 1] - \frac{1}{2} \right|$$

is $\mathsf{negl}(k)$, where:

Experiment $\mathsf{IND}_{\mathcal{A}}^{\mathcal{FE}}(1^k)$:
$(I, st_0) \leftarrow \mathcal{A}_0(1^k)$ *where* $|I| = t$
$(\mathbf{EK}, \mathsf{MSK}) \leftarrow \mathsf{FE.Setup}(1^k)$
$(X^0, X^1, st_1) \leftarrow \mathcal{A}_1^{\mathsf{FE.Keygen}(\mathsf{MSK}, \cdot)}(st_0, \mathbf{EK_I})$ *where* $X^\ell = \{x_{1,j}^\ell, \ldots, x_{n,j}^\ell\}_{j=1}^q$
$b \leftarrow \{0, 1\}$; $\mathsf{CT}_{i,j} \leftarrow \mathsf{FE.Enc}(\mathsf{EK}_i, x_{i,j}^b) \; \forall i \in [n], \; j \in [q]$
$b' \leftarrow \mathcal{A}_2^{\mathsf{FE.Keygen}(\mathsf{MSK}, \cdot)}(st_1, \mathbf{CT})$
Output: $(b = b')$

In the above experiment, we require:

- **Compatibility with Function Queries:** *Let $\{f\}$ denote the entire set of key queries made by $\mathcal{A}_1$. Then, the challenge message vectors X_0 and X_1 chosen by $\mathcal{A}_1$ must be I-compatible with $\{f\}$.*
- **Compatibility with Ciphertext Queries:** *Every key query g made by $\mathcal{A}_2$ must be I-compatible with X^0 and X^1.*

Selective Security. We also consider selective *indistinguishability*-based security for multi-input functional encryption. Formally, (t, q)-sel-IND-security is defined in the same manner as Definition 4, except that the adversary $\mathcal{A}_1$ is required to choose the challenge message vectors X^0, X^1 *before* the evaluation keys **EK** and the master secret key MSK are chosen by the challenger. We omit the formal definition to avoid repetition.

Simulation-Based Security. Here we present a simulation-based security definition for multi-input FE. We consider the case where the adversary makes key queries *after* choosing the challenge messages. That is, we only consider *adaptive* key queries.

Our definition extends the simulation-based security definition for single-input FE that supports adaptive key queries[6,16,3,8]. In particular, we present a general definition that models both black-box and non-black-box simulation.

Intuition. We start by giving an overview of the main ideas behind our simulation-based security definition. To convey the core ideas, it suffices to consider the case of 2-ary functions. Let us start by considering the natural extension of *public-key* single-input FE to the two-input setting. That is, suppose there are two public encryption keys EK_1, EK_2 that are used to create ciphertexts of first inputs and second inputs, respectively, for 2-ary functions. Let us investigate what security can be achieved for *one* challenge message tuple (x_1, x_2).

Suppose that the adversary queries secret keys for functions $\{f\}$. Now, recall that the SIM-security definition in the single-input case guarantees that for every $f \in \{f\}$, an adversary cannot learn more than $f(x)$ when x is the challenge message. We note, however, that an analogous security guarantee cannot be achieved in the multi-input setting. Indeed, an adversary who knows both the encryption keys can create its own ciphertexts w.r.t. each encryption key. Then, by using the secret key corresponding to function f, it can learn additional values $\{f(x_1, \cdot)\}$ and $\{f(\cdot, x_2)\}$. Thus, we must allow for the ideal world adversary, aka simulator, to learn the same information.

In the secret-key case, however, since all of the encryption keys are secret, the SIM-security definition for single-input FE indeed extends in a natural manner to the multi-input setting. We stress, however, that when there are multiple challenge messages, we must take into account the fact that adversary can learn function evaluations over all possible "combinations" of challenge messages. Our definition presented below formalizes this intuition.

Similar to the IND-security case, our definition is parameterized by variables t and q as defined earlier. We now formally define (t, q)-SIM-secure multi-input functional encryption.

Definition 5 (Simulation-based Security). *We say that a functional encryption scheme $\mathcal{FE}$ for n-ary functions $\mathcal{F}$ is (t, q)-SIM-secure if for every PPT adversary $\mathcal{A} = (\mathcal{A}_0, \mathcal{A}_1, \mathcal{A}_2)$, there exists a PPT simulator $\mathcal{S} = (\mathcal{S}_0, \mathcal{S}_1, \mathcal{S}_2)$ such that the outputs of the following two experiments are computationally indistinguishable:*

Experiment $\mathsf{REAL}^{\mathcal{FE}}_{\mathcal{A}}(1^k)$:
  $(\mathrm{I}, \mathsf{st}_0) \leftarrow \mathcal{A}_0(1^k)$ *where* $|\mathrm{I}| = t$
  $(\mathbf{EK}, \mathsf{MSK}) \leftarrow \mathsf{FE}.\mathsf{Setup}(1^k)$
  $(\mathcal{M}, \mathsf{st}_1) \leftarrow \mathcal{A}_1(\mathsf{st}_0, \mathbf{EK}_\mathrm{I})$
  $\boldsymbol{X} \leftarrow \mathcal{M}$ *where* $\boldsymbol{X} = \{x_{1,j}, \ldots, x_{n,j}\}^q_{j=1}$
  $\mathsf{CT}_{i,j} \leftarrow \mathsf{FE}.\mathsf{Enc}(\mathsf{EK}_i, x_{i,j})\ \forall i \in [n],\ j \in [q]$
  $\alpha \leftarrow \mathcal{A}^{\mathsf{FE}.\mathsf{Keygen}(\mathsf{MSK}, \cdot)}_2(\mathbf{CT}, \mathsf{st}_1)$
  Output: $(\mathrm{I}, \mathcal{M}, \boldsymbol{X}, \{f\}, \alpha)$

Experiment $\mathsf{IDEAL}^{\mathcal{FE}}_{\mathcal{S}}(1^k)$:
  $(\mathrm{I}, \mathsf{st}_0) \leftarrow \mathcal{S}_0(1^k)$
  $(\mathcal{M}, \mathsf{st}_1) \leftarrow \mathcal{S}_1(\mathsf{st}_0)$
  $\alpha \leftarrow \mathcal{S}^{\mathsf{TP}(\mathcal{M}, \cdot, \cdot)}_2(\mathsf{st}_1)$
  Output: $(\mathrm{I}, \mathcal{M}, \boldsymbol{X}, \{g\}, \alpha)$

---

where the oracle $\mathsf{TP}(\mathcal{M}, \cdot, \cdot)$ *denotes the ideal world trusted party,* $\{f\}$ *denotes the set of queries of* $\mathcal{A}_2$ *to* $\mathsf{FE}.\mathsf{Keygen}$ *and* $\{g\}$ *denotes the set of functions appearing in the queries of* $\mathcal{S}_2$ *to* TP. *Given the message distribution* $\mathcal{M}$, TP *first samples a message vector* $\boldsymbol{X} \leftarrow M$, *where* $\boldsymbol{X} = \{x_{1,j}, \ldots, x_{n,j}\}^q_{j=1}$. *It then accepts queries of the form* $\left(g, (j_1, \ldots, j_{n-p}), \left(x'_{i'_1}, \ldots, x'_{i'_p} \right) \right)$ *where* $p \le t$, $\{i'_1, \ldots, i'_p\} \subseteq \mathrm{I} \cup \emptyset$ *and* $x'_{i'_1}, \ldots, x'_{i'_p} \in \mathcal{X}_k$. *On receiving such a query,* TP *outputs:*

$$g\left(\left\langle x_{i_1, j_1}, \ldots, x_{i_{n-p}, j_{n-p}}, x'_{i'_1}, \ldots, x'_{i'_p} \right\rangle \right),$$

where $\langle y_{i_1}, \ldots, y_{i_n} \rangle$ *denotes a permutation of the values* $y_{i_1}, \ldots, y_{i_n}$ *such that the value* y_{i_j} *is mapped to the* ℓ'*th location if* y_{i_j} *is the* ℓ'*th input (out of n inputs) to* g.

Remark 1 (On Queries to the Trusted Party). Note that when $t = 0$, then given the challenge ciphertexts $\mathbf{CT}$, intuitively, the real adversary can only compute values $\mathsf{FE}.\mathsf{Dec}\,(\mathsf{SK}_f, \mathsf{CT}_{1,j_1}, \ldots, \mathsf{CT}_{n,j_n})$ for every $j_i \in [q]$, $i \in [n]$. To formalize the intuition that this adversary does not learn anything more than function values $\{f\,(x_{1,j_1}, \ldots, x_{n,j_n})\}$, we restrict the ideal adversary aka simulator to learn exactly this information.

However, when $t > 0$, then the real adversary can compute values:

$$\mathsf{FE}.\mathsf{Dec}\left(\mathsf{SK}_f, \left\langle \mathsf{CT}_{i_1, j_1}, \ldots, \mathsf{CT}_{i_{n-t}, j_{n-t}}, \mathsf{CT}'_{i'_1}, \ldots, \mathsf{CT}'_{i'_t} \right\rangle \right)$$

for ciphertexts $\mathsf{CT}'_{i'_\ell}$ of its choice since it knows the encryption keys $\mathbf{EK}_\mathrm{I}$. In other words, such an adversary can learn function values of the form $f\left(\langle x_{i_1, j_1}, \ldots, x_{i_{n-t}, j_{n-t}}, \cdot, \ldots, \cdot \rangle \right)$. Thus, we must provide the same ability to the simulator as well. Our definition presented above precisely captures this.

Selective Security. We also consider *selective* simulation-based security for multi-input functional encryption. Formally, (t, q)-sel-SIM-security is defined in the same manner as Definition 5, except that in the real world experiment, adversary $\mathcal{A}_1$ chooses the message distribution $\mathcal{M}$ *before* the evaluation keys $\mathbf{EK}$ and the master secret key MSK are chosen by the challenger. We omit the formal definition to avoid repetition.

Remark 2 (SIM-security: Secret-key setting). When $t = 0$, *none* of the encryption keys are known to the adversary. In this "secret-key" setting, there is no difference between $(0, q)$-sel-SIM-security and $(0, q)$-SIM-security.

Impossibility of $(0, \mathsf{poly}(k))$-*SIM-security.* We note that the lower bounds of [6,3] already establish that it is impossible to achieve $(0, \mathsf{poly}(k))$-SIM-secure functional encryption for 1-ary functions. In particular, [6] prove their result for the IBE functionality, while the [3] impossibility result is given for almost all 1-ary functionalities (assuming the existence of collision-resistance hash functions). The positive results in this paper for SIM-secure multi-input FE are consistent with these negative results. That is, our constructions (for general functionalities) provide SIM security only for the case where the number of challenge messages q are a priori bounded.

2.3 A Construction for the General Case

Let $\mathcal{F}$ denote the family of all efficiently computable (deterministic) n-ary functions. We now present a functional encryption scheme $\mathcal{FE}$ for $\mathcal{F}$. Assuming the existence of one-way functions and indistinguishability obfuscation for all efficiently computable circuits, we prove the following security guarantees for $\mathcal{FE}$:

1. For $t = 0$, and any $q = q(k)$ such that $\binom{qn}{n} = \mathsf{poly}(k)$, $\mathcal{FE}$ is $(0, q)$-SIM-secure.[1] In this case, the size of the secret keys in $\mathcal{FE}$ grows linearly with $\binom{qn}{n}$.
2. For any $t \leq n$ and $q = \mathsf{poly}(k)$, $\mathcal{FE}$ is (t, q)-sel-IND-secure. In this case, the size of the secret keys is independent of q.

Note that by using standard complexity leveraging, we can extend the second result to show that $\mathcal{FE}$ is, in fact, (t, q)-IND-secure. Note that in this case, we would require the indistinguishability obfuscator $i\mathcal{O}$ (and the one-way function) to be secure against adversaries running in time $\mathcal{O}(2^M)$, where M denotes the total length of the challenge message vectors.

Notation. Let $(\mathsf{CRSGen}, \mathsf{Prove}, \mathsf{Verify})$ be a NIWI proof system. Let Com denote a perfectly binding commitment scheme. Let $i\mathcal{O}$ denote an indistinguishability obfuscator. Finally, let $\mathsf{PKE} = (\mathsf{PKE.Setup}, \mathsf{PKE.Enc}, \mathsf{PKE.Dec})$ be a semantically secure public-key encryption scheme. We denote the length of ciphertexts in PKE by $\mathsf{c\text{-}len} = \mathsf{c\text{-}len}(k)$. Let $\mathsf{len} = 2 \cdot \mathsf{c\text{-}len}$.

We now proceed to describe our scheme $\mathcal{FE} = (\mathsf{FE.Setup}, \mathsf{FE.Enc}, \mathsf{FE.Keygen}, \mathsf{FE.Dec})$.

Setup $\mathsf{FE.Setup}(1^k)$: The setup algorithm first computes a CRS $\mathsf{crs} \leftarrow \mathsf{CRSGen}(1^k)$ for the NIWI proof system. Next, it computes two key pairs – $(\mathsf{pk}_1, \mathsf{sk}_1) \leftarrow$

---

[1] Recall that when $t = 0$, there is no difference between selective security and standard security as defined in Section 2.2. See Remark 2.

PKE.Setup(1^k) and $(\mathsf{pk}_2, \mathsf{sk}_2) \leftarrow$ PKE.Setup(1^k) – of the public-key encryption scheme PKE. Finally, it computes the following commitments: (a) $Z_1^{i,j} \leftarrow$ Com(0^{len}) for every $i \in [n]$, $j \in [q]$. (b) $Z_2^i \leftarrow$ Com(0) for every $i \in [n]$.

For every $i \in [n]$, the i'th encryption key $\mathsf{EK}_i = \left(\mathsf{crs}, \mathsf{pk}_1, \mathsf{pk}_2, \left\{Z_1^{i,j}\right\}, Z_2^i, r_2^i\right)$ where r_2^i is the randomness used to compute the commitment Z_2^i. The master secret key is set to be $\mathsf{MSK} = \left(\mathsf{crs}, \mathsf{pk}_1, \mathsf{pk}_2, \mathsf{sk}_1, \left\{Z_1^{i,j}\right\}, \{Z_2^i\}\right)$. The setup algorithm outputs $(\mathsf{EK}_1, \ldots, \mathsf{EK}_n, \mathsf{MSK})$.

Encryption FE.Enc(EK_i, x): To encrypt a message x with the i'th encryption key EK_i, the encryption algorithm first computes $c_1 \leftarrow$ PKE.Enc(pk_1, x) and $c_2 \leftarrow$ PKE.Enc(pk_2, x). Next, it computes a NIWI proof $\pi \leftarrow$ Prove(crs, y, w) for the statement $y = \left(c_1, c_2, \mathsf{pk}_1, \mathsf{pk}_2, \left\{Z_1^{i,j}\right\}, Z_2^i\right)$:

- *Either* c_1 and c_2 are encryptions of the same message and Z_2^i is a commitment to 0, *or*
- $\exists\, j \in [q]$ s.t. $Z_1^{i,j}$ is a commitment to $c_1 \| c_2$.

A witness $w_{\mathsf{real}} = (m, s_1, s_2, r_2^i)$ for the first part of the statement, referred to as the *real witness*, includes the message m and the randomness s_1 and s_2 used to compute the ciphertexts c_1 and c_2, respectively, and the randomness r_2^i used to compute Z_2^i. A witness $w_{\mathsf{trap}} = (j, r_1^{i,j})$ for the second part of the statement, referred to as the *trapdoor witness*, includes an index j and the randomness $r_1^{i,j}$ used to compute $Z_1^{i,j}$.

The honest encryption algorithm uses the real witness w_{real} to compute π. The output of the algorithm is the ciphertext $\mathsf{CT} = (c_1, c_2, \pi)$.

Key Generation FE.Keygen(MSK, f): The key generation algorithm on input f computes $\mathsf{SK}_f \leftarrow i\mathcal{O}(\mathsf{G}_f)$ where the function G_f is defined in Figure 1. Note that G_f has the master secret key MSK hardwired in its description.

$\mathsf{G}_f(\mathsf{CT}_1, \ldots, \mathsf{CT}_n)$

1. For every $i \in [n]$:
   (a) Parse $\mathsf{CT}_i = (c_{i,1}, c_{i,2}, \pi_i)$.
   (b) Let $y_i = \left(c_{i,1}, c_{i,2}, \mathsf{pk}_1, \mathsf{pk}_2, \left\{Z_1^{i,j}\right\}, Z_2^i\right)$ be the statement corresponding to the proof string π_i. If Verify(crs, y_i, π_i) = 0, then stop and output $\bot$. Otherwise, continue to the next step.
   (c) Compute $x_i \leftarrow$ PKE.Dec($\mathsf{sk}_1, c_{i,1}$).
2. Output $f(x_1, \ldots, x_n)$.

Fig. 1. Functionality G_f

The algorithm outputs SK_f as the secret key for f.

Size of Function G_f. In order to prove that $\mathcal{FE}$ is $(0, q)$-SIM-secure, we require the function G_f to be padded with zeros such that $|\mathsf{G}_f| = |\mathsf{Sim}.\mathsf{G}_f|$, where the "simulated" functionality $\mathsf{Sim}.\mathsf{G}_f$ is described in the full version. In this case, the size of SK_f grows linearly with $\binom{qn}{n}$.

Note, however, that such a padding is *not* necessary to prove (t, q)-sel-IND-security for $\mathcal{FE}$. Indeed, in this case, the secret keys SK_f are independent of the number of message queries q made by the adversary.

Decryption $\mathsf{FE}.\mathsf{Dec}(\mathsf{SK}_f, \mathsf{CT}_1, \ldots, \mathsf{CT}_n)$: The decryption algorithm on input $(\mathsf{CT}_1, \ldots, \mathsf{CT}_n)$ computes and outputs $\mathsf{SK}_f(\mathsf{CT}_1, \ldots, \mathsf{CT}_n)$.

This completes the description of our functional encryption scheme $\mathcal{FE}$. The correctness property of the scheme follows from inspection. In the full version by Goldwasser et al. [10], we prove that $\mathcal{FE}$ is $(0, q)$-SIM-secure, and that $\mathcal{FE}$ is (t, q)-sel-IND-secure (and (t, q)-IND-secure via complexity leveraging).

3   Restricted Security Notions

In this section we present indistinguishability-based definitions and constructions for two restricted settings: the symmetric key setting in which the adversary does not learn any evaluation keys, and a setting in which all clients operate in fixed *time-steps*, encrypting only one plaintext in each time-step. In this latter setting, we do not allow functions to compute on ciphertexts from different time-steps. A full exposition appears in the full version by Gordon et al. [12].

3.1   The Symmetric-Key Setting

For simplicity, we focus on the binary-input setting in the symmetric key setting. However, we remark that our construction extends naturally to the n-ary setting. The only modification is to make the $i\mathcal{O}$ circuit accept more ciphertexts as inputs, and compute the function f over all decrypted values. The proof follows in a straightforward manner.

Definitions. Let $\mathcal{F} = \{\mathcal{F}_n\}_{n>0}$ be a collection of function families, where every $f \in \mathcal{F}_n$ is a polynomial time function $f : \{0,1\}^{m_1(n)} \times \{0,1\}^{m_2(n)} \to \Sigma$. A binary symmetric key FE scheme supporting $\mathcal{F}$ is a collection of 4 algorithms: (Setup, KeyGen, Enc, Eval). The first three algorithms are probabilistic, and Eval is deterministic. They have the following semantics, if we leave the randomness implicit:

> Setup: $(\mathsf{msk}, \mathsf{param}) \leftarrow \mathsf{Setup}(1^\kappa)$
> KeyGen: for any $f \in \mathcal{F}_n$, $\mathsf{TK}_f \leftarrow \mathsf{KeyGen}(\mathsf{msk}, f)$
> Enc: $\mathsf{CT} \leftarrow \mathsf{Enc}(\mathsf{msk}, x)$
> Eval: $\mathsf{ans} \leftarrow \mathsf{Eval}(\mathsf{param}, \mathsf{TK}_f, \mathsf{CT}_1, \mathsf{CT}_2)$

As usual, we must define the desired correctness and security properties. The correctness property states that, given $(\mathsf{msk}, \mathsf{param}) \leftarrow \mathsf{Setup}(1^\kappa)$, with overwhelming probability over the randomness used in Setup, KeyGen and Enc, it holds that $\mathsf{Eval}(\mathsf{KeyGen}(\mathsf{msk}, f), \mathsf{param}, \mathsf{Enc}(\mathsf{msk}, x), \mathsf{Enc}(\mathsf{msk}, y)) = f(x, y)$.

We now define security for IND-secure symmetric-key binary FE. In the full version by Gordon et al.[12] we provide the stronger, adaptive security definition. Unlike in the public key setting, here single-message security does not imply multi-message security, so we cannot prove a parallel to Lemma 1. (Technically, the problem arises in the reduction, where the simulator cannot create the necessary ciphertexts for the hybrid world without knowing the secret key.) Instead, we only define the multi-message variant.

Our construction below only achieves selective security, but we note that we can achieve adaptive security through standard complexity-leveraging techniques. (We omit the details.)

Selective security. An Ind-Secure scheme is said to be *selectively* IND-secure if for all PPT, *non-trivial* adversary $\mathcal{A}$, its probability of winning the following game is $\Pr[b = b'] < \frac{1}{2} + \mathsf{negl}(\kappa)$.

Ind-Secure-selective:

1. $\{(x_1, \ldots, x_n), (y_1, \ldots, y_n)\} \leftarrow \mathcal{A}(1^\kappa)$
2. $(\mathsf{msk}, \mathsf{param}) \leftarrow \mathsf{Setup}(1^\kappa)$
3. $b \leftarrow \{0, 1\}$
4. if $b = 0$: $\forall i \in [n]: \mathsf{CT}_i \leftarrow \mathsf{Enc}(\mathsf{msk}, x_i),$ else: $\forall i \in [n]: \mathsf{CT}_i \leftarrow \mathsf{Enc}(\mathsf{msk}, y_i).$

5. $b' \leftarrow \mathcal{A}^{\mathsf{KeyGen}(\cdot)}(\mathsf{param}, \mathsf{CT}_1, \ldots, \mathsf{CT}_n)$

An adversary is considered *non-trivial* if for every query f made to the $\mathsf{KeyGen}(\cdot)$ oracle, and for all $i, j \in [n]$, it holds that $f(x_i, x_j) = f(y_i, y_j)$. We note that this is a much weaker restriction on the adversary than the one used in the public key setting, which makes symmetric key schemes more difficult to construct.

A Construction

Scheme description. Our construction uses a SSS-NIZK scheme NIZK := (Setup, Prove, Verify) that is statistically simulation sound for multiple simulated statements an indistinguishable obfuscation scheme $i\mathcal{O}$, and a perfectly binding commitment scheme (commit, open), all of which are defined in the full version [12]. We also use a CPA-secure public-key encryption scheme $\mathcal{E} := (\mathsf{Gen}, \mathsf{Enc}, \mathsf{Dec})$ with perfect correctness. Our construction is as follows:
$\mathsf{Setup}(1^\kappa)$:

1. $\mathsf{crs} \leftarrow \mathsf{NIZK}.\mathsf{Setup}(1^\kappa)$
2. $\alpha, r \leftarrow \{0, 1\}^\kappa$; $\mathsf{com} = \mathsf{commit}(\alpha; r)$
3. $(\mathsf{pk}, \mathsf{sk}) \leftarrow \mathcal{E}.\mathsf{Gen}(1^\kappa),$ $(\mathsf{pk}', \mathsf{sk}') \leftarrow \mathcal{E}.\mathsf{Gen}(1^\kappa)$
4. Output $\mathsf{param} := (\mathsf{crs}, \mathsf{pk}, \mathsf{pk}', \mathsf{com})$, $\mathsf{msk} := (\mathsf{sk}, \mathsf{sk}', \alpha, r)$

Internal (hardcoded) state: param $= (\mathsf{crs}, \mathsf{pk}, \mathsf{pk}', \mathsf{com})$, sk, f

On input: $\mathsf{CT}_0, \mathsf{CT}_1$

- Parse CT_0 as $(c_0, c_0', \alpha_0, \pi_0)$ and CT_1 as $(c_1, c_1', \alpha_1, \pi_1)$. Let $\mathsf{stmt}_0 := (c_0, c_0', \alpha_0)$, and $\mathsf{stmt}_1 := (c_1, c_1', \alpha_1)$. Verify that $\alpha_0 = \alpha_1$ and $\mathsf{NIZK.Verify}(\mathsf{crs}, \mathsf{stmt}_0, \pi_0) = \mathsf{NIZK.Verify}(\mathsf{crs}, \mathsf{stmt}_1, \pi_1) = 1$. If fails, output $\bot$.
- Compute $x_0 = \mathcal{E}.\mathsf{Dec}(\mathsf{sk}, c_0)$ and $x_1 = \mathcal{E}.\mathsf{Dec}(\mathsf{sk}, c_1)$ output $f(x_0, x_1)$.

Fig. 2. Symmetric-key IND-secure binary FE: Program P

KeyGen(msk, f)

1. Using $\mathsf{msk} = (\mathsf{sk}, \mathsf{sk}', \alpha, r)$, construct a circuit C_f that computes program P as described in Figure 2.
2. Define $\mathsf{TK}_f := i\mathcal{O}(C_f)$, and output TK_f.

Enc(msk, x):

1. Parse msk as $(\mathsf{sk}, \mathsf{sk}', \alpha, r)$.
2. Compute $c = \mathcal{E}.\mathsf{Enc}(\mathsf{pk}; x; \rho)$ and $c' = \mathcal{E}.\mathsf{Enc}(\mathsf{pk}'; x; \rho')$ for random strings ρ and ρ' consumed by the encryption algorithm.
3. Output $\mathsf{CT} := (c, c', \alpha, \pi)$ where $\pi := \mathsf{NIZK.Prove}(\mathsf{crs}, (c, c', \alpha), (r, \rho, \rho', x))$ is a NIZK for the language $L_{\mathsf{pk},\mathsf{pk}',\mathsf{com}}$: for any statement $\mathsf{stmt} := (c, c', \alpha)$, $\mathsf{stmt} \in L_{\mathsf{pk},\mathsf{pk}',\mathsf{com}}$ if and only if $\exists (r, \rho, \rho', x)$ s.t. $(c = \mathcal{E}.\mathsf{Enc}(\mathsf{pk}; x; \rho)) \wedge (c' = \mathcal{E}.\mathsf{Enc}(\mathsf{pk}'; x; \rho')) \wedge (\mathsf{com} = \mathsf{commit}(\alpha; r))$.

Eval($\mathsf{param}, \mathsf{TK}_f, \mathsf{CT}_0, \mathsf{CT}_1$):

1. Interpret TK_f as an obfuscated circuit. Compute $\mathsf{TK}_f(\mathsf{CT}_0, \mathsf{CT}_1)$ and output the result.

In the full version we provide a proof of the following theorem [12].

Theorem 1. *If the $i\mathcal{O}$ is secure, the NIZK is statistically simulation sound, the commitment is perfectly binding and computationally hiding, and the encryption scheme is semantically secure and perfectly correct, then the above construction is selectively IND-secure, as defined in Section 3.1*

Instantiation and efficiency. If we use the approach described in our full version for constructing the SSS-NIZK, the ciphertext is succinct, and is $\mathsf{poly}(\kappa)$ in size [12]. For a scheme tolerant up to n ciphertext queries, the public parameter size, encryption time, decryption time are $O(n)\mathsf{poly}(\kappa)$. The reason for the dependence on n is due to the simulator's need to simultaneously simulate $O(n)$ SSS-NIZKs in the simulation, which increases the size of the crs. Removing the dependence on n remains an important open problem.

3.2   Time-dependent Setting

Definitions. Let $\mathcal{F} = \{\mathcal{F}_\ell\}_{\ell>0}$ be a collection of function families, where every $f \in \mathcal{F}_\ell$ is a polynomial time function $f : \mathcal{D}_\ell \times \cdots \times \mathcal{D}_\ell \to \Sigma$. A multi-client functional encryption scheme (MC-FE) supporting n users and function family $\mathcal{F}_\ell$ is a collection of the following algorithms:

Setup : $(\mathsf{msk}, \{\mathsf{usk}_i\}_{i\in[n]}) \leftarrow \mathsf{Setup}(1^\kappa, n)$, usk_i is a user secret key

Enc : $\mathsf{CT} \leftarrow \mathsf{Enc}(\mathsf{usk}_i, x, t)$, here $t \in \mathbb{N}$ denotes the current time step

KeyGen : $\mathsf{TK}_f \leftarrow \mathsf{KeyGen}(\mathsf{msk}, f)$.

Dec : $\mathsf{ans} \leftarrow \mathsf{Dec}(\mathsf{TK}_f, \{\mathsf{CT}_1, \mathsf{CT}_2, \ldots, \mathsf{CT}_n\})$.

Correctness. We say that an MC-FE scheme is correct, if given $(\mathsf{msk}, \{\mathsf{usk}_i\}_{i\in[n]}) \leftarrow \mathsf{Setup}(1^\kappa, n)$, given some $t \in \mathbb{N}$, except with negligible probability over randomness used in Setup, Enc, KeyGen, and Dec, it holds that $\mathsf{Dec}(\mathsf{KeyGen}(\mathsf{msk}, f), \mathsf{Enc}(\mathsf{usk}_1, x_1, t), \ldots, \mathsf{Enc}(\mathsf{usk}_n, x_n, t)) = f(x_1, x_2, \ldots, x_n)$.

Below we define a selectively secure indistinguishability-based security for binary FE. In the full version [12] we provide two other, stronger security definitions, both allowing adaptive plaintext challenges. There we prove the following Lemma stating that the two notions are equivalent.

Lemma 1. *Adaptive, multi-message indistinguishability security is equivalent to adaptive, single-message indistinguishability security.*

Our construction below only achieves selective security, but we note that we can achieve the stronger definitions through standard complexity-leveraging techniques [Folklore]. (We omit the details.)

Our definitions assume a *static corruption* model where the corrupted parties are specified at the beginning of the security game. How to support adaptive corruption is an interesting direction for future work.

Notations. We often use a shorthand $\boldsymbol{x}$ to denote a vector $\boldsymbol{x} := (x_1, x_2, \ldots, x_n)$. Let disjoint sets $G, \overline{G}$ denote the set of uncorrupted and corrupted parties respectively. $G \cup \overline{G} = [n]$. We use the short-hand $\overrightarrow{\mathsf{var}}_G$ to denote the vector $\{\mathsf{var}_i\}_{i\in G}$ for a variable var. Similarly, we use the short-hand $\mathbf{CT}_G \leftarrow \mathsf{Enc}(\mathbf{usk}_G, \boldsymbol{x}_G, t)$ to denote the following: $\forall i \in G : \mathsf{CT}_i \leftarrow \mathsf{Enc}(\mathsf{usk}_i, x_i, t)$. We use the shorthand $f(\boldsymbol{x}_G, \cdot) : \mathcal{D}^{|\overline{G}|} \to \Sigma$ to denote a function restricted to a subset G on inputs denoted $\boldsymbol{x}_G \in \mathcal{D}^{|G|}$. Let $h := f(\boldsymbol{x}_G, \cdot)$, then by our definition, $h(\boldsymbol{x}_{\overline{G}}) := f(\boldsymbol{x})$.

Selective security. We define a relaxation of the above security notion called selective security. Define the following single-challenge, selective experiment for a stateful adversary $\mathcal{A}$. For simplicity, we will omit writing the adversary $\mathcal{A}$'s state explicitly.

Define short-hand $K(\cdot) := \mathsf{KeyGen}(\mathsf{msk}, \cdot)$ to be an oracle to the KeyGen function. Define $E_G(\cdot)$ to be a *stateful* encryption oracle for the uncorrupted set G. Its initial state is the intial time step counter $t := 0$. Upon each invocation $E_G(\boldsymbol{x}_G)$, the oracle increments the current time step $t \leftarrow t + 1$, and returns $\mathsf{Enc}(\mathbf{usk}_G, \boldsymbol{x}_G, t)$.

1. $G, \overline{G}, (\boldsymbol{x}_G^*, \boldsymbol{y}_G^*) \leftarrow \mathcal{A}$.
2. $b \xleftarrow{\$} \{0, 1\}$, $(\mathsf{msk}, \{\mathsf{usk}_i\}_{i \in [n]}) \leftarrow \mathsf{Setup}(1^\kappa, n)$
3. "challenge" $\leftarrow \mathcal{A}^{K(\cdot), E_G(\cdot)}(\mathsf{usk}_{\overline{G}})$.
4. If $b = 0$: $\mathbf{CT}_G^* \leftarrow E_G(\boldsymbol{x}_G^*)$.   Else: $\mathbf{CT}_G^* \leftarrow E_G(\boldsymbol{y}_G^*)$.
5. $b' \leftarrow \mathcal{A}^{K(\cdot), E_G(\cdot)}(\mathbf{CT}_G^*)$.

We say $\mathcal{A}$ is *non-trivial*, if for any function f queried to the $\mathsf{KeyGen}(\mathsf{msk}, \cdot)$ oracle, $f(\boldsymbol{x}_G^*, \cdot) = f(\boldsymbol{y}_G^*, \cdot)$.

Definition 6 (Selective IND-security of MC-FE). *We say that an MC-FE scheme is selectively and indistinguishably secure, if for any polynomial-time, non-trivial adversary $\mathcal{A}$ in the above selective security game, $\left| \Pr[b' = b] - \frac{1}{2} \right| \leq \mathsf{negl}(\kappa)$.*

A Construction Intuition: In this setting, the adversary is allowed to corrupt some set $\overline{G}$. Our restriction on the adversary is that for challenge vectors $\boldsymbol{x}_G$ and $\boldsymbol{y}_G$, $f(\boldsymbol{x}_G, \cdots) = f(\boldsymbol{y}_G, \cdots)$, where $\boldsymbol{x}_G$ and $\boldsymbol{y}_G$ correspond to the plaintexts by the uncorrupted parties, and $\cdots$ denotes the plaintexts corresponding to the corrupted parties.

Recall that in the aforementioned single-client, symmetric-key setting, the sender must have a secret value α to encrypt. However, here we cannot give a single α to each party since the adversary can corrupt a subset of the parties. Instead, we would like to give each party their own α_i.

As before, there is a hybrid world in which the challenger must encrypt as $(\mathsf{Enc}(\boldsymbol{x}_G), \mathsf{Enc}(\boldsymbol{y}_G))$ in the two parallel encryptions. Later, in order for us to switch the decryption key in the $i\mathcal{O}$ from sk to sk', the two $i\mathcal{O}$'s (using sk and sk' respectively) must be functionally equivalent. To achieve this functional equivalence, we must prevent mix-and-match of simulated and honest ciphertexts. In the earlier single-client, symmetric-key setting, this is achieved by using a fake α value in the simulation, and verifying that all ciphertexts input into the $i\mathcal{O}$ must have the same α value. In the multi-client setting, a simple equality check no longer suffices, so we need another way to prevent mix-and-match of hybrid ciphertexts with well-formed ciphertexts. We do this by choosing a random vector $\boldsymbol{\beta}_G$ such that $\langle \boldsymbol{\beta}_G, \boldsymbol{\alpha}_G \rangle = 0$. We hard-code $\boldsymbol{\beta}_G$ in the $i\mathcal{O}$, and if the $\boldsymbol{\alpha}_G$ values in the ciphertexts are not orthogonal to $\boldsymbol{\beta}_G$, the $i\mathcal{O}$ will simply output $\bot$.

In the hybrid world, instead of using the honest vector $\boldsymbol{\alpha}_G$, the simulator uses another random $\boldsymbol{\alpha}_G'$ orthogonal to $\boldsymbol{\beta}_G$, and simulates the NIZKs. In this way, a mixture of honest and simulated ciphertexts for the set G will cause the $i\mathcal{O}$ to simply output $\bot$, since mixing the coordinates of $\boldsymbol{\alpha}_G$ and $\boldsymbol{\alpha}_G'$ will result in a vector *not* orthogonal to $\boldsymbol{\beta}_G$ (except with negligible probability over the choice of these vectors). In this way, except with negligible probability over the choice of these vectors, using either sk or sk' to decrypt in the $i\mathcal{O}$ will result in exactly the same input and output behavior.

Finally, in order for us to obtain faster encryption and decryption time, instead of encoding $\boldsymbol{\alpha}_G$ directly in the ciphertexts, we use a generator for a group that supports the Diffie-Hellman assumption and encode $g^{\boldsymbol{\alpha}_G}$ instead. As we will show later, this enables the simulator to simulate fewer NIZKs. In fact, with this trick, the simulator only needs to simulate NIZKs for the challenge time step alone. Therefore, the CRS and the time to compute ciphertexts will be independent of the number of time steps.

Let $\mathcal{G}$ denote a group of prime order $p > 2^n \cdot 2^\kappa$ in which Decisional Diffie-Hellman is hard. Let $H : \mathbb{N} \to \mathcal{G}$ denote a hash function modelled as a random oracle. Let $\mathcal{E} := (\mathsf{Gen}, \mathsf{Enc}, \mathsf{Dec})$ denote a public-key encryption scheme.

- $\mathsf{Setup}(1^\kappa, n)$: Compute $(\mathsf{pk}, \mathsf{sk}) \leftarrow \mathcal{E}.\mathsf{Gen}(1^\kappa)$, and $(\mathsf{pk}', \mathsf{sk}') \leftarrow \mathcal{E}.\mathsf{Gen}(1^\kappa)$. Run $\mathsf{crs} := \mathsf{NIZK}.\mathsf{Setup}(1^\kappa, n)$, where n is the number of clients. Choose a random generator $g \xleftarrow{\$} \mathcal{G}$. Choose random $\alpha_1, \alpha_2, \ldots, \alpha_n \in \mathbb{Z}_p$. For $i \in [n]$, let $g_i := g^{\alpha_i}$. Set $\mathsf{param} := (\mathsf{crs}, \mathsf{pk}, \mathsf{pk}', g, \{g_i\}_{i \in [n]})$. The secret keys for each user are: $\mathsf{usk}_i := (\alpha_i, \mathsf{param})$ The master secret key is: $\mathsf{msk} := (\{\alpha_i\}_{i \in [n]}, \mathsf{sk}, \mathsf{sk}')$.
- $\mathsf{Enc}(\mathsf{usk}_i, x, t)$: For user i to encrypt a message x for time step t, it computes the following. Let $h_t := H(t)$. Choose random ρ and ρ' as the random bits needed for the public-key encryption scheme. Let $c := \mathcal{E}.\mathsf{Enc}(\mathsf{pk}, x; \rho)$ and $c' := \mathcal{E}.\mathsf{Enc}(\mathsf{pk}', x; \rho')$. Let $d = h_t^{\alpha_i}$, Let statement $\mathsf{stmt} := (t, i, c, c', d)$; let witness $w := (\rho, \rho', x, \alpha_i)$. Let the NP language be defined as in Figure 3. Let $\pi := \mathsf{NIZK}.\mathsf{Prove}(\mathsf{crs}, \mathsf{stmt}, w)$. Informally, this proves that 1) the two ciphertexts c and c' encrypt consistent plaintexts using pk and pk' respectively; and 2) (h_t, g_i, d) is a true Diffie-Hellman tuple.
  The ciphertext is defined as: $\mathsf{CT} := (t, i, c, c', d, \pi)$.
  $\exists \, m, (\rho, \rho'), w$ s.t.

$$\mathsf{DH}(h_t, g_i, d, \omega) \wedge (c = \mathcal{E}.\mathsf{Enc}(\mathsf{pk}, m; \rho)) \wedge (c' = \mathcal{E}.\mathsf{Enc}(\mathsf{pk}', m; \rho'))$$

where $h_t = H(t)$ for the t defined by CT; $g_i := g^{\alpha_i}$ is included in the public parameters; (ρ, ρ') are the random strings used for the encryptions; and $\mathsf{DH}(A, B, C, \omega)$ is defined as the following relation that checks that (A, B, C) is a Diffie-Hellman tuple with the witness ω:

$$\mathsf{DH}(A, B, C, \omega) := ((A = g^\omega) \wedge (C = B^\omega)) \vee ((B = g^\omega) \wedge (C = A^\omega))$$

Our NP language $L_{\mathsf{pk}, \mathsf{pk}', g, \{g_i\}_{i \in [n]}}$ is parameterized by $(\mathsf{pk}, \mathsf{pk}', g, \{g_i\}_{i \in [n]})$ output by the Setup algorithm as part of the public parameters. A statement of this language is is of the format $\mathsf{stmt} := (t, i, c, c', d)$, and a witness is of the format $w := (\rho, \rho', x, \omega)$. A statement $\mathsf{stmt} := (t, i, c, c', d) \in L_{\mathsf{pk}, \mathsf{pk}', g, \{g_i\}_{i \in [n]}}$, iff

$$\exists \, x, (\rho, \rho'), \omega \quad \text{s.t.} \quad \mathsf{DH}(h_t, g_i, d, \omega) \wedge (c = \mathcal{E}.\mathsf{Enc}(\mathsf{pk}, x; \rho)) \wedge (c' = \mathcal{E}.\mathsf{Enc}(\mathsf{pk}', x; \rho'))$$

where $h_t = H(t)$ for the t defined by CT; $g_i := g^{\alpha_i}$ is included in the public parameters; (ρ, ρ') are the random strings used for the encryptions; and $\mathsf{DH}(A, B, C, \omega)$ is defined as the following relation that checks that (A, B, C) is a Diffie-Hellman tuple with the witness ω:

$$\mathsf{DH}(A, B, C, \omega) := ((A = g^\omega) \wedge (C = B^\omega)) \vee ((B = g^\omega) \wedge (C = A^\omega))$$

Fig. 3. NP language $L_{\mathsf{pk}, \mathsf{pk}', g, \{g_i\}_{i \in [n]}}$

Note that the NIZK π ties together the ciphertexts (c, c') with the term $d = H(t)^{\alpha_i}$. This intuitively ties (c, c') with the time step t, such that it cannot be mix-and-matched with other time steps.

- KeyGen(msk, f): To generate a server token for a function f over n parties' inputs compute token $\mathsf{TK}_f := i\mathcal{O}(P)$ for a Program P defined as in Figure 4:
- Dec($\mathsf{TK}_f, \mathsf{CT}_1, \ldots, \mathsf{CT}_n$): Interpret TK_f as an obfuscated program. Output $\mathsf{TK}_f(\mathsf{CT}_1, \mathsf{CT}_2, \ldots, \mathsf{CT}_n)$.

Program $P(\mathsf{CT}_1, \mathsf{CT}_2, \ldots, \mathsf{CT}_n)$:

Internal hard-coded state: param $= (\mathsf{crs}, \mathsf{pk}, \mathsf{pk}', g, \{g_i\}_{i \in [n]})$, sk, f

1. For $i \in [n]$, unpack $(t_i, j_i, c_i, c_i', d_i, \pi_i) \leftarrow \mathsf{CT}_i$. Check that $t_1 = t_2 = \ldots = t_n$, and that $j_i = i$. Let $\mathsf{stmt}_i := (t_i, j_i, c_i, c_i', d_i)$.
2. For $i \in [n]$, check that $\mathsf{NIZK.Verify}(\mathsf{crs}, \pi_i, \mathsf{stmt}_i) = 1$.
3. If any of these above checks fail, output $\perp$.
   Else: for $i \in [n]$, let $x_i \leftarrow \mathcal{E}.\mathsf{Dec}(\mathsf{sk}, c_i)$. Output $f(x_1, x_2, \ldots, x_n)$.

Fig. 4. MC-FE: Program P

Theorem 2. *Let $\mathcal{G}$ be a group for which the Diffie-Hellman assumption holds, and let H be a random oracle. If the $i\mathcal{O}$ is secure, the NIZK is statistically simulation sound, and the encryption scheme is semantically secure and perfectly correct, then the above construction is selectively, IND-secure, as defined in Section 3.2.*

Removing the random oracle. It is trivial to remove the random oracle if we choose $h_1, h_2, \ldots, h_T$ at random in the setup algorithm, and give them to each user as part of their secret keys (i.e., equivalent to embedding them in the public parameters). This makes the user key $O(n + T)\mathsf{poly}(\kappa)$ in size, where n denotes the number of parties, and T denotes an upper bound on the number of time steps.

Instantiation and efficiency. We can instantiate our scheme using the SSS-NIZK construction and the $i\mathcal{O}$ construction described by Garg et. al [9]. In this way, our ciphertext is succinct, and is only $\mathsf{poly}(\kappa)$ in size. Letting n denote the number of parties, the encryption time is $O(n)\mathsf{poly}(\kappa)$, and the decryption time is $O(n + |f|)\cdot\mathsf{poly}(\kappa)$. The dependence on n arises due to the need for the simulator to simulate $O(n)$ SSS-NIZKs. Each user's secret key is of size is $O(n)\mathsf{poly}(\kappa)$ for the version with the random oracle, and is $O(n + T)\mathsf{poly}(\kappa)$ for the version of the scheme without the random oracle. Note that due to our use of the Diffie-Hellman assumption, we have removed the dependence on T for encryption/decryption time in a non-trivial manner.

References

1. Agrawal, S., Gorbunov, S., Vaikuntanathan, V., Wee, H.: Functional encryption: New perspectives and lower bounds. In: Canetti, R., Garay, J.A. (eds.) CRYPTO 2013, Part II. LNCS, vol. 8043, pp. 500–518. Springer, Heidelberg (2013)
2. Barak, B., Goldreich, O., Impagliazzo, R., Rudich, S., Sahai, A., Vadhan, S.P., Yang, K.: On the (im)possibility of obfuscating programs. In: Kilian, J. (ed.) CRYPTO 2001. LNCS, vol. 2139, pp. 1–18. Springer, Heidelberg (2001)
3. Bellare, M., O'Neill, A.: Semantically-secure functional encryption: Possibility results, impossibility results and the quest for a general definition. In: Abdalla, M., Nita-Rotaru, C., Dahab, R. (eds.) CANS 2013. LNCS, vol. 8257, pp. 218–234. Springer, Heidelberg (2013)
4. Boldyreva, A., Chenette, N., Lee, Y., O'Neill, A.: Order-preserving symmetric encryption. In: Joux, A. (ed.) EUROCRYPT 2009. LNCS, vol. 5479, pp. 224–241. Springer, Heidelberg (2009)
5. Boldyreva, A., Chenette, N., O'Neill, A.: Order-preserving encryption revisited: Improved security analysis and alternative solutions. In: Rogaway, P. (ed.) CRYPTO 2011. LNCS, vol. 6841, pp. 578–595. Springer, Heidelberg (2011)
6. Boneh, D., Sahai, A., Waters, B.: Functional encryption: Definitions and challenges. In: Ishai, Y. (ed.) TCC 2011. LNCS, vol. 6597, pp. 253–273. Springer, Heidelberg (2011)
7. Boneh, D., Waters, B.: Conjunctive, subset, and range queries on encrypted data. In: Vadhan, S.P. (ed.) TCC 2007. LNCS, vol. 4392, pp. 535–554. Springer, Heidelberg (2007)
8. De Caro, A., Iovino, V., Jain, A., O'Neill, A., Paneth, O., Persiano, G.: On the achievability of simulation-based security for functional encryption. In: Canetti, R., Garay, J.A. (eds.) CRYPTO 2013, Part II. LNCS, vol. 8043, pp. 519–535. Springer, Heidelberg (2013)
9. Garg, S., Gentry, C., Halevi, S., Raykova, M., Sahai, A., Waters, B.: Candidate indistinguishability obfuscation and functional encryption for all circuits. In: FOCS (2013), http://eprint.iacr.org/2013/451
10. Goldwasser, S., Goyal, V., Jain, A., Sahai, A.: Multi-input functional encryption. Cryptology ePrint Archive, Report 2013/727 (2013), http://eprint.iacr.org/
11. Goldwasser, S., Kalai, Y.T., Popa, R.A., Vaikuntanathan, V., Zeldovich, N.: Reusable garbled circuits and succinct functional encryption. In: STOC (2013)
12. Gordon, S.D., Katz, J., Liu, F.-H., Shi, E., Zhou, H.-S.: Multi-input functional encryption. Cryptology ePrint Archive, Report 2013/774 (2013), http://eprint.iacr.org/
13. Goyal, V., Pandey, O., Sahai, A., Waters, B.: Attribute-based encryption for fine-grained access control of encrypted data. In: ACM Conference on Computer and Communications Security (2006)
14. Katz, J., Sahai, A., Waters, B.: Predicate encryption supporting disjunctions, polynomial equations, and inner products. In: Smart, N.P. (ed.) EUROCRYPT 2008. LNCS, vol. 4965, pp. 146–162. Springer, Heidelberg (2008)
15. Lewko, A., Okamoto, T., Sahai, A., Takashima, K., Waters, B.: Fully secure functional encryption: Attribute-based encryption and (hierarchical) inner product encryption. In: Gilbert, H. (ed.) EUROCRYPT 2010. LNCS, vol. 6110, pp. 62–91. Springer, Heidelberg (2010)
16. O'Neill, A.: Definitional issues in functional encryption. IACR Cryptology ePrint Archive, 2010 (2010)

17. Pandey, O., Rouselakis, Y.: Property preserving symmetric encryption. In: Pointcheval, D., Johansson, T. (eds.) EUROCRYPT 2012. LNCS, vol. 7237, pp. 375–391. Springer, Heidelberg (2012)
18. Sahai, A., Seyalioglu, H.: Worry-free encryption: functional encryption with public keys. In: ACM Conference on Computer and Communications Security, pp. 463–472 (2010)
19. Sahai, A., Waters, B.: Fuzzy identity-based encryption. In: Cramer, R. (ed.) EUROCRYPT 2005. LNCS, vol. 3494, pp. 457–473. Springer, Heidelberg (2005)
20. Sahai, A., Waters, B.: How to use indistinguishability obfuscation: Deniable encryption, and more. IACR Cryptology ePrint Archive, 2013 (2013)

Salvaging Indifferentiability
in a Multi-stage Setting

Arno Mittelbach

Darmstadt University of Technology, Germany

Abstract. The indifferentiability framework by Maurer, Renner and Holenstein (MRH; TCC 2004) formalizes a sufficient condition to safely replace a random oracle by a construction based on a (hopefully) weaker assumption such as an ideal cipher. Indeed, many indifferentiable hash functions have been constructed and could since be used in place of random oracles. Unfortunately, Ristenpart, Shacham, and Shrimpton (RSS; Eurocrypt 2011) discovered that for a large class of security notions, the MRH composition theorem actually does not apply. To bridge the gap they suggested a stronger notion called reset indifferentiability and established a generalized version of the MRH composition theorem. However, as recent works by Demay et al. (Eurocrypt 2013) and Baecher et al. (Asiacrypt 2013) brought to light, reset indifferentiability is not achievable thereby re-opening the quest for a notion that is sufficient for multi-stage games and achievable at the same time.

We present a condition on multi-stage games called *unsplittability*. We show that if a game is unsplittable for a hash construction then the MRH composition theorem can be salvaged. Unsplittability captures a restricted yet broad class of games together with a set of practical hash constructions including HMAC, NMAC and several Merkle-Damgård variants. We show unsplittability for the chosen distribution attack (CDA) game (Bellare et al., Asiacrypt 2009), a multi-stage game capturing the security of deterministic encryption schemes; for message-locked encryption (Bellare et al.; Eurocrypt 2013) a related primitive that allows for secure deduplication; for universal computational extractors (UCE) (Bellare et al., Crypto 2013), a recently introduced standard model assumption to replace random oracles; as well as for the proof-of-storage game given by Ristenpart et al. as a counterexample to the general applicability of the indifferentiability framework.

1 Introduction

The notion of indifferentiability, introduced by Maurer, Renner and Holenstein (MRH) [25] can be regarded as a generalization of indistinguishability tailored to situations where internal state is publicly available. It has found wide applicability in the domain of iterative hash functions which are usually built from a fixed-length compression function together with a scheme that describes how arbitrarily long messages are to be processed [26,16,30,23,11]. The MRH

P.Q. Nguyen and E. Oswald (Eds.): EUROCRYPT 2014, LNCS 8441, pp. 603–621, 2014.

$\mathbf{CDA}_{\mathcal{AE}}^{H^{\mathrm{h}},\mathcal{A}_1,\mathcal{A}_2}(1^\lambda)$	$\mathbf{CRP}_{p,s}^{H^{\mathrm{h}},\mathcal{A}_1,\mathcal{A}_2}(1^\lambda)$	$\mathbf{PRV\text{-}CDA}_{\mathrm{MLE}}^{H^{\mathrm{h}},\mathcal{A}_1,\mathcal{A}_2}(1^\lambda)$	$\mathbf{UCE}_{H^{\mathrm{h}}}^{\mathcal{S},\mathcal{D}}(1^\lambda)$
$b \leftarrow \{0,1\}$ $(pk,sk) \leftarrow \mathsf{KGen}(1^\lambda)$ $(\mathbf{m}_0,\mathbf{m}_1,\mathbf{r}) \leftarrow \mathcal{A}_1^{\mathrm{h}}(1^\lambda)$ $\mathbf{c} \leftarrow \mathcal{E}^{H^{\mathrm{h}}}(pk,\mathbf{m}_b;\mathbf{r})$ $b' \leftarrow \mathcal{A}_2^{\mathrm{h}}(pk,\mathbf{c})$ $\mathbf{return}\ (b=b')$	$M \leftarrow \{0,1\}^p$ $st \leftarrow \mathcal{A}_1^{\mathrm{h}}(M,1^\lambda)$ $\mathbf{if}\ |st| > n\ \mathbf{then}$ $\quad \mathbf{return\ false}$ $C \leftarrow \{0,1\}^c$ $Z \leftarrow \mathcal{A}_2^{\mathrm{h}}(st,C)$ $\mathbf{return}\ (Z = H^{\mathrm{h}}(M\|C))$	$P \leftarrow \mathcal{P}$ $b \leftarrow \{0,1\}$ $(\mathbf{m}_0,\mathbf{m}_1,Z) \leftarrow \mathcal{A}_1^{\mathrm{h}}(1^\lambda)$ $\mathbf{c} \leftarrow \mathcal{E}_P^{H^{\mathrm{h}}}(K_P(\mathbf{m}_b),\mathbf{m}_b)$ $b' \leftarrow \mathcal{A}_2^{\mathrm{h}}(P,\mathbf{c},Z)$ $\mathbf{return}\ (b=b')$	$b \leftarrow \{0,1\};\ k \leftarrow \mathcal{K}$ $L \leftarrow \mathcal{S}^{\mathrm{HASH}}(1^\lambda); b' \leftarrow \mathcal{D}(1^\lambda,k,L)$ $\mathbf{return}\ (b=b')$ $\mathrm{HASH}(x)$ $\mathbf{if}\ T[x] = \bot\ \mathbf{then}$ $\quad \mathbf{if}\ b=1\ \mathbf{then}\ T[x] \leftarrow H^{\mathrm{h}}(k,x)$ $\quad \mathbf{else}\ T[x] \leftarrow \{0,1\}^\ell$ $\mathbf{return}\ T[x]$

Fig. 1. Security Games. From left to right: the chosen distribution attack (CDA) game [4] capturing security in deterministic encryption schemes [3], the proof-of-storage challenge-response game (CRP) due to Ristenpart et al. [29] given as counter-example of the general applicability of the indifferentiability composition theorem, message locked encryption (MLE) [7], and universal computational extractors (UCE) [6] a standard model security assumption on hash-functions.

composition theorem formalizes a sufficient condition under which such a construction can safely instantiate a random oracle: namely indifferentiability of a random oracle. A different view on this is that with indifferentiability one can transfer proofs of security from one idealized setting into a different (and hopefully simpler) idealized setting. For example, proofs in the random oracle model (ROM) [8] imply proofs in the ideal cipher model if a construction from an ideal cipher that is indifferentiable from a random oracle exists.

Ristenpart, Shacham and Shrimpton (RSS) [29] gave the somewhat surprising result that the MRH composition theorem only holds in single-stage settings and does not necessarily extend to multi-stage settings where disjoint adversaries are split over several stages. As counterexample they present a simple *challenge-response game* (CRP, depicted in Figure 1): a file server that is given a file M can be engaged in a simple proof-of-storage protocol where it has to respond with a hash value $\mathcal{H}(M\|C)$ for a random challenge C while only being able to store a short state st (with $|st| \ll |M|$). The protocol can easily be proven secure in the ROM since, without access to file M, it is highly improbable for the server to correctly guess the hash value $\mathcal{H}(M\|C)$. The server can, however, "cheat" if the random oracle is replaced by one of several indifferentiable constructions. Here the server exploits the internal structure by computing an intermediate chaining value which allows it to later compute extended hash values of the form $H^{\mathrm{h}}(M\|\cdot)$. We refer to [29] for a detailed discussion.

To circumvent the problem of composition in multi-stage settings, RSS propose a stronger form of indifferentiability called *reset indifferentiability* [29], which intuitively states that simulators must be stateless and pseudo-deterministic [2]. While this notion allows composition in any setting, no domain extender can fulfill this stronger form of indifferentiability [17,24,2]. Demay et al. [17] present a second variant of indifferentiability called *resource-restricted indifferentiability* which models simulators with explicit memory restrictions and which lies somewhere in between plain indifferentiability and reset indifferentiability. However, they do not present any positive results such as constructions that achieve any form of resource-restricted indifferentiability or security games for which a resource-restricted construction allows composition.

The only positive results, we are aware of, is the analysis of RSS of the non-adaptive chosen-distribution attack (CDA) game [4], depicted in Figure 1. CDA captures a security notion for deterministic public-key encryption schemes [3], where the randomness does not have sufficient min-entropy. In the CDA game, the first-stage adversary $\mathcal{A}_1$ outputs two message vectors $\mathbf{m_0}$ and $\mathbf{m_1}$ together with a randomness vector $\mathbf{r}$ which, together, must have sufficient min-entropy independent of the hash functionality. According to a secret bit b one of the two message vectors is encrypted and given, together with the public key, to the second-stage adversary $\mathcal{A}_2$. The adversary wins if it correctly guesses b. For the non-adaptive CDA game, RSS give a direct security proof for the subclass of indifferentiable hash functions of the NMAC-type [18], i.e., hash functions of the form $H^{\mathbf{h}}(M) := \mathbf{g}(f^{\mathbf{h}}(M))$ where function $\mathbf{g}$ is a fixed-length random oracle independent of $f^{\mathbf{h}}$ which is assumed to be preimage aware. Note, while this covers some hash functions of interest, it does not, for example, cover chop-MD functions [15] (like SHA-2 for certain parameter settings) or Keccak (aka. SHA-3).

In the lights of the negative results on stronger notions of indifferentiability, we aim at salvaging the current notion; that is, we present tools and techniques to work with plain indifferentiability in multi-stage settings. For this, let us have a closer look at what goes wrong when directly applying the MRH composition theorem in a multi-stage setting.

Plain Indifferentiability in Multi-stage Settings. Consider the basic Merkle-Damgård construction[1] and consider a two stage game with adversaries $\mathcal{A}_1$ and $\mathcal{A}_2$. If adversary $\mathcal{A}_1$ makes an h-query $y_1 \leftarrow \mathbf{h}(m_1, \mathcal{IV})$ and passes on this value to adversary $\mathcal{A}_2$, then $\mathcal{A}_2$ can compute arbitrary hash values of the form $m_1 \| \ldots$ without having to know m_1. The trick in the MRH composition theorem is to exchange access to $\mathbf{h}$ with access to a simulator $\mathcal{S}$ when placing the adversary in a setting where it plays against the game with random oracle $\mathcal{R}$. If we apply this trick to our two-stage game we need two independent instances of this simulator, one for $\mathcal{A}_1$ and one for $\mathcal{A}_2$. Let's call these $\mathcal{S}^{(1)}$ and $\mathcal{S}^{(2)}$. The problem is now, that if $\mathcal{A}_1$ and $\mathcal{A}_2$ do not share sufficient state the same applies to the two simulator instances: they share exactly the same state that is shared between the two adversaries. Thus, if adversary $\mathcal{A}_2$ makes the query (y, m_2) simulator $\mathcal{S}^{(2)}$ does not know that y corresponds to query $(m_1, \mathcal{IV})$ from $\mathcal{A}_1$ and it will thus not be able to answer with a value y' such that $\mathbf{g}(y') = \mathcal{R}(m_1 \| m_2)$. This is, however, expected by $\mathcal{A}_2$ and would be the case if $\mathcal{A}_1$ and $\mathcal{A}_2$ had had access to the deterministic compression function $\mathbf{h}$.

Contributions. Our first contribution (Section 3) is to develop a model of hash functions based on directed, acyclic graphs that is rich enough to pinpoint and

---

[1] The basic MD function $H^{\mathbf{h}}(m_1, \ldots, m_\ell)$ is computed as $H^{\mathbf{h}}(m_1, \ldots, m_\ell) := \mathbf{h}(m_\ell, x_\ell)$ where $x_1 := \mathcal{IV}$ is some initialization vector and $x_{i+1} := \mathbf{h}(m_i, x_i)$.

argue about such problematic adversarial h-queries while at the same time allowing us to consider many different constructions simultaneously. Given this framework we define a property on games and hash functions called UNSPLITTABILITY (Definition 10). If a game is UNSPLITTABLE for a hash construction, this basically means that problematic queries as the one from the above example do not occur.

In Section 4 we then give a composition theorem for UNSPLITTABLE games which intuitively says that if a game is UNSPLITTABLE for an indifferentiable hash construction, then security proofs in the random oracle model carry over if the random oracle is implemented by that particular hash function. Assuming UNSPLITTABILITY, the main technical difficulty in proving composition is to properly derandomize the various simulator instances and make them (nearly) stateless. Note that simulators for indifferentiable hash constructions in the literature are mostly probabilistic and highly stateful. In a multi-stage setting the various instances of the simulator must, however, answer queries consistently, that is, in particular the same query by different adversaries must always be answered with the same answer independent of the order of queries. For this, we build on a derandomization technique developed by Bennet and Gill to show that the complexity classes $\mathcal{BPP}$ and $\mathcal{P}$ are identical relative to a random oracle [10]. One interesting intermediary result is that of a generic indifferentiability simulator that answers queries in a very restricted way.

In Section 5 we show how to prove UNSPLITTABILITY for all multi-stage security games depicted in Figure 1. We show that the CDA game (both, the non-adaptive and adaptive) is UNSPLITTABLE for Merkle-Damgård-like functions as well as for HMAC and NMAC (in the formulation of [5]) thereby complementing the results by RSS. Let us note that, that our results on CDA require less restrictions on the public-key encryption scheme (that is, the encryption scheme does not need to be IND-SIM [29]). Similarly, we show UNSPLITTABILITY for message locked encryption (MLE), a security definition for primitives that allow for secure deduplication [7]. MLE is closely related to CDA with the additional complication that the two adversaries here can communicate "in the clear" via state value Z (see Figure 1). For the RSS proof-of-storage (CRP) game given as counter-example for the general applicability of the MRH composition theorem, we show that it is UNSPLITTABLE for any so-called 2-round hash function. These are hash functions, such as Liskov's Zipper Hash [23] that process the input message twice for computing the final hash value. Finally, we resolve an open problem from [6]. Bellare, Hoang and Keelveedhi (BHK) introduce UCE a standard model assumption for hash constructions which is sufficient to replace a random oracle in a large number of applications [6]. At present the only instantiation of a UCE-secure function is given in the random oracle model and BHK left as open problem whether HMAC can be shown to meet UCE-security assuming an ideal compression function. We show that this is not just the case for HMAC but also for many Merkle-Damgård variants.

Finally, we want to note that we give the results for CDA, MLE and UCE via a meta-result that considers security games for keyed hash functions where the hash function key is only revealed at the very last stage. We show that all three security games can be subsumed under this class and we show that games from this class are UNSPLITTABLE for a large class of practical hash constructions including HMAC and NMAC and several Merkle-Damgård-like functions such as prefix-free or chop-MD [15]. This is particularly interesting as CDA and MLE are per se not using keyed hash functions, but can be reformulated in this setting and it seems that with keyed hash functions it is simpler to work with indifferentiability in a multi-stage scenario.

2 Preliminaries

If $n \in \mathbb{N}$ is a natural number then by 1^n we denote the unary representation and by $\langle n \rangle_\ell$ the binary representation of n (using ℓ bits). By $[n]$ we denote the set $\{1, 2, \ldots, n\}$. By $\{0,1\}^n$ we denote the set of all bit strings of length n while $\{0,1\}^*$ denotes the set of all finite bit strings. For bit strings $m, m' \in \{0,1\}^*$ we denote by $m \| m'$ their concatenation. If $\mathcal{M}$ is a set then by $m \leftarrow \mathcal{M}$ we denote that m was sampled uniformly from $\mathcal{M}$. If $\mathcal{A}$ is an algorithm then by $X \leftarrow \mathcal{A}(m)$ we denote that X was output by algorithm $\mathcal{A}$ on input m. As usual $|\mathcal{M}|$ denotes the cardinality of set $\mathcal{M}$ and $|m|$ the length of bit string m. Logarithms are to base 2. By $\mathrm{H}_\infty(X)$ we denote the min-entropy of variable X, defined as $\mathrm{H}_\infty(X) := \min_x \log(1/\Pr[X = x])$. We assume that any algorithm, game, etc. is implicitly given a security parameter as input, even if not explicitly stated. We call an algorithm *efficient* if its run-time is polynomial in the security parameter. Probability statements of the form $\Pr[\mathrm{step}_1; \mathrm{step}_2 : \mathrm{condition}]$ should be read as the probability that condition holds after the steps are executed in consecutive order. We use standard boolean notation and denote by $\wedge$ the AND by $\vee$ the OR of two values.

Hash Functions. A hash function is formally defined as a keyed family of functions $\mathcal{H}(1^\lambda)$ where each key k defines a function $H_k : \{0,1\}^* \to \{0,1\}^n$. "Practical" hash functions are usually built via domain extension from an underlying function $\mathbf{h} : \{0,1\}^d \times \{0,1\}^k \to \{0,1\}^s$ that is iterated through an iteration scheme H to process arbitrarily long inputs [26,16,30,23,1,21,31,11,20], with widely varying specifications. The underlying function $\mathbf{h}$ usually is a compression function— the first input taking message blocks and the second an intermediate chaining value—and we will state our results relative to compression functions. As an exception to this rule, the Sponge construction [12] (the design principle behind SHA-3, aka. Keccak [11]) iterates a permutation instead of a compression function. We discuss, how this fits into our model in the full version [27].

Indifferentiability. A hash function is called indifferentiable from a random oracle if no distinguisher can decide whether it is talking to the hash function and its ideal compression function or to an actual random oracle and a simulator. We here give the definition of indifferentiability from [15].

Definition 1. *A hash construction $H^h : \{0,1\}^* \to \{0,1\}^n$, with black-box access to an ideal function $h : \{0,1\}^d \times \{0,1\}^k \to \{0,1\}^s$, is called indifferentiable from a random oracle R if there exists an efficient simulator S^R such that for any distinguisher D there exists a negligible function* `negl`, *such that*

$$\left| \Pr\left[D^{H^h,h}(1^\lambda) = 1 \right] - \Pr\left[D^{R,S^R}(1^\lambda) = 1 \right] \right| \leq \texttt{negl}(\lambda) \ .$$

Game Playing. We use the game-playing technique [9,29] and present here a brief overview of the notation used. A game $G^{F,A_1,\ldots,A_m}$ gets access to adversarial procedures $A_1,\ldots,A_m$ and to one or more so called functionalities F which are collections of two procedures F.hon and F.adv, with suggestive names "honest" and "adversarial". Adversaries (i.e., adversarial procedures) access a functionality F via the interface exported by F.adv, while all other procedures access the functionality via F.hon. In our case, functionalities are exclusively hash functions which will be instantiated with iterative hash constructions H^h. The adversarial interface exports the underlying function h, while the honest interface exports plain access to H^h. We thus, instead of writing F.hon and F.adv usually directly refer to H^h and h, respectively. Adversarial procedures can only be called by the game's **main** procedure.

By $G^{F,A_1,\ldots,A_m} \Rightarrow y$ we denote that the game outputs value y. If the game is probabilistic or any adversarial procedure is probabilistic then $G^{F,A_1,\ldots,A_m}$ is a random variable and $\Pr\left[G^{F,A_1,\ldots,A_m} \Rightarrow y \right]$ denotes the probability that the game outputs y. By $G^{F,A_1,\ldots,A_m}(r)$ we denote that the game is run on random coins r.

For this paper we only consider the sub-class of functionality-respecting games as defined in [29]. A game is called *functionality respecting* if only adversarial procedures can call the adversarial interface of functionalities. We define $\mathcal{LG}$ to be the set of all functionality-respecting games. Note that this restriction is a natural restriction if a game is used to specify a security goal in the random oracle model since random oracles do not provide any adversarial interface.

3   A Model for Iterative Hash Functions

In the following we present a new model for iterated hash functions that allows to argue about many functions at the same time. A similar endeavor has been made by Bhattacharyya et al. [13] who introduce *generalized domain extension*. For our purpose, we need a more explicit model that allows us to talk about the execution of hash functions in great detail. Still, our model is general enough to capture many different types of constructions, ranging from the plain Merkle-Damgård over variants such as chop-MD [15] to more complex constructions such as NMAC, HMAC [5] or even hash trees. We give an overview over several hash constructions that are captured by our model in the full version of this paper [27].

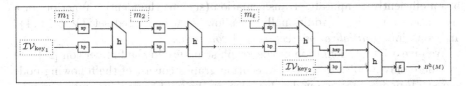

Fig. 2. Execution graph for NMAC for message $m_1 \| \ldots \| m_\ell := M$. Value $\mathcal{IV}_{\text{key}_1}$ is an initialization vector representing the first key in the NMAC-construction. Value $\mathcal{IV}_{\text{key}_2}$ is a constant representing the second key. The difference between initialization vectors and constants is that constants are used within the execution graph, i.e., in conjunction with interim values, while initialization vectors are used at the beginning of the graph.

Execution Graphs - An Introduction. We model iterative hash functions $H^{\mathtt{h}}$ as directed graphs where each message M is mapped to an execution graph which is constructed independently of a particular choice of function $\mathtt{h}$. Figure 2 presents the *execution graph* for a message $M := m_1 \| \ldots \| m_\ell$ for the NMAC construction [5]. For each input message M the corresponding execution graph represents how the hash value would be computed relative to some oracle $\mathtt{h}$, that is, we require that, relative to an oracle $\mathtt{h}$, a generic algorithm $\mathtt{EVAL}^{\mathtt{h}}$ on input the execution graph for M can then compute value $H^{\mathtt{h}}(M)$. Nodes in the execution graph are either *value-nodes* or *function-nodes*. A value node (indicated by dotted boxes) does not have ingoing edges and the outgoing edge is always labeled with the node's label (possibly prefixed by a constant). Function nodes represent functions and the outgoing edges are labeled with the result of the evaluation of the corresponding function taking the labels of the ingoing edges as input. An $\mathtt{h}$-node represents the evaluation of the underlying function $\mathtt{h}$. Outgoing edges can, thus, only be labeled relative to $\mathtt{h}$. Nodes labeled $\mathtt{mp}, \mathtt{hp}$ or $\mathtt{hmp}$ correspond to preprocessing functions (defined by the hash construction) which ensure that the input to the next $\mathtt{h}$-node is of correct length: $\mathtt{mp}$ processes message blocks, $\mathtt{hp}$ processes $\mathtt{h}$-outputs and $\mathtt{hmp}$, likewise, processes the output of $\mathtt{h}$-nodes but such that it can go into the "message slot" of an $\mathtt{h}$-node (see Figure 2). An execution graph contains exactly one $\mathtt{g}$-node with an unbound outgoing edge which corresponds to an (efficiently) computable transformation such as the identity or truncation.

Formalizing Hash Functions as Directed Graphs. We now formalize the above concept to model an iterative hash construction $H^{\mathtt{h}} : \{0,1\}^* \to \{0,1\}^n$ with a compression function of the form $\mathtt{h} : \{0,1\}^d \times \{0,1\}^k \to \{0,1\}^s$. For this let $\mathtt{pad} : \{0,1\}^* \to (\{0,1\}^b)^+$ be a padding function (e.g. Merkle-Damgård strengthening [16,26]) that maps strings to multiples of block size b. Let $\mathtt{mp} : \{0,1\}^* \to \{0,1\}^d$, $\mathtt{hp} : \{0,1\}^* \to \{0,1\}^k$ and $\mathtt{hmp} : \{0,1\}^* \to \{0,1\}^d$ be "preprocessing" functions that allow to adapt message blocks and intermediate hash values, respectively. We assume that $\mathtt{pad}, \mathtt{mp}, \mathtt{hp}$, and $\mathtt{hmp}$ are efficiently computable, injective, and efficiently invertible. Note that for many schemes these functions will be the identity function and $b = d$ and $s = k$. Let $\mathtt{g} : \{0,1\}^s \to \{0,1\}^n$

be an efficiently computable transformation (such as the identity function, or a truncation function).[2] Additionally we allow for a dedicated set $\mathcal{IV} \subset \{0,1\}^*$ and containing *initialization vectors* and *constants*.

We give a formal definition of the graph structure in the full version [27] and give here only a quick overview. Execution graphs consist of the following node types: $\mathcal{IV}$-nodes, message-nodes, h-nodes, mp, hp, and hmp-nodes and a single g-node. For each message block $m_1 \| \ldots \| m_\ell := \mathtt{pad}(M)$ the graph contains exactly one message-node. All outgoing edges must again be connected to a node, except for the single outgoing edge of the single g-node. An h-node always has two incoming edges one from an hp-node and one from either an mp or an hmp-node. Message nodes can be connected to mp-nodes. The outbound edges from h can be connected to either hp or hmp-nodes.[3] A *valid execution graph* is a non-empty graph that complies with the above rules. We require that for each message $M \in \{0,1\}^*$ there is exactly one valid execution graph and that there is an efficient algorithm that given M constructs the execution graph.

Besides valid execution graphs we introduce the concept of *partial execution graphs* which are non-empty graphs that comply to the above rules with the only exception that they do not contain a g-node. Hence, they contain exactly one unbound outgoing edge from an h-node. A partial execution graph is always a sub-graph of potentially many valid execution graphs. Given a valid execution graph a partial execution graph can be constructed by choosing an h-node and removing every node that can be reached via directed path from that h-node and then remove all unconnected components that do not have a directed path to the chosen h-node.

We define EVAL to be a generic, deterministic algorithm evaluating execution graphs relative to an oracle h. Let $\mathfrak{eg}$ be a valid execution graph for some message $M \in \{0,1\}^*$. To evaluate $\mathfrak{eg}$ relative to oracle h, algorithm $\mathtt{EVAL}^h(\mathfrak{eg})$ recursively performs the following steps: search for a node that has no inbound edges or for which all inbound edges are labeled. If the node is a function-node then evaluate the corresponding function using the labels from the inbound edges as input. If the node is a value-node, use the corresponding label as result. Remove the node from the graph and label all outgoing edges with the result. If the last node in the graph was removed stop and return the result. Note that $\mathtt{EVAL}^h(\mathfrak{eg})$ runs in time at most $\mathcal{O}(|V^2|)$ assuming that $\mathfrak{eg}$ contains $|V|$ many nodes. If $\mathfrak{pg}$ is a partial execution graph then $\mathtt{EVAL}^h(\mathfrak{pg})$, likewise, computes the partial graph outputting the result of the final h-node. We denote by $\mathfrak{g}(\mathfrak{pg})$ the corresponding execution graph where the single outbound h-edge of $\mathfrak{pg}$ is connected to a g-node. We call this the *completed* execution graph for $\mathfrak{pg}$.

We can now go on to define iterative hash functions such as Merkle-Damgård-like functions. Informally, an iterative hash function consists of the definitions

---

[2] We stress that g is efficiently computable and not an independent (ideal) compression function.

[3] The difference between hp and hmp is that hp outputs values in $\{0,1\}^k$ which hmp outputs values in $\{0,1\}^d$. Note that function h is defined as $\mathtt{h} : \{0,1\}^d \times \{0,1\}^k \to \{0,1\}^s$.

of the preprocessing functions, the padding function and the final transformation $g(\cdot)$. Furthermore, we require (efficient) algorithms that construct execution graphs as well as parse an execution graph to recover the corresponding message.

Definition 2. *Let $\mathcal{IV} \subset \{0,1\}^*$ be a set of named initialization vectors and $|\mathcal{IV}|$ be polynomial in the security parameter λ. We say $H^{h}_{g,mp,hp,hmp,pad} : \{0,1\}^* \rightarrow \{0,1\}^n$ is an iterative hash function if there exist deterministic and efficient algorithms* construct *and* extract *as follows:*

construct: *On input $M \in \{0,1\}^*$, algorithm* construct *outputs a valid execution graph containing one message-node for every block in $m_1 \| \ldots \| m_\ell :=$* pad$(M)$. *For all messages $M \in \{0,1\}^*$ it holds that $H^h(M) =$* EVAL$^h($construct$(M))$. *For any two $M, M' \in \{0,1\}^*$ with $|M| = |M'|$ it holds that graphs* construct(M) *and* construct(M') *are identical but for labels of message-nodes.*[4]
extract: *On input a valid execution graph* eg, *algorithm* extract *outputs message $M \in \{0,1\}^*$ if, and only if,* construct(M) *is identical to* eg. *On input a partial execution graph* pg, *algorithm* extract *outputs message $M \in \{0,1\}^*$ if, and only if, the completed execution graph $g($pg$)$ is identical to* construct(M). *Otherwise* extract *outputs $\perp$.*

When functions g, mp, hp, hmp and pad *are clear from context we simply write H^h.*

We give a detailed description of valid execution graphs, extensions to the model that, for example, cover keyed constructions, as well as several examples of hash constructions that are covered by Definition 2 in the full version [27].

3.1 Important h-Queries

Considering the execution of hash functions as graphs allows us to identify certain types of "important" queries by their position in the graph relative to a function h. Assume that $Q = (m_i, x_i)_{1 \leq i \leq p}$ is an ordered sequence of h-queries to compression function h. If we consider the i-th query $q_i = (m_i, x_i)$ then only queries appearing before q_i in Q are relevant for our upcoming naming conventions. We call q_i an *initial query* if, and only if, $hp^{-1}(x_i) \in \mathcal{IV}$. Besides initial queries we are interested in queries that occur "in the execution graph" and we call these *chained queries*. We call query q_i a *chained query* if given the queries appearing before q_i there exists a valid (partial) execution graph containing an h-node with its unbound edge labeled with value $hp^{-1}(x_i)$. Finally, we call query q_i result query for message M, if $g(q_i) = H^h(M)$ and q_i is a chained query. We define result queries in a broader sense and independent of a specific message by considering all possible partial graphs induced by query set Q and say that a query is a result query if it is a chained query and if its induced partial graph pg can be completed to a valid execution graph, that is, $g($pg$)$ is a valid execution graph. For a visualization of the query types see Figure 3.

---
[4] This condition ensures that the graph structure does not depend on the content of messages but only on its length.

Definition 3. *Let $Q = (m_i, x_i)_{1 \leq i \leq p}$ be a sequence of queries to $\mathrm{h} : \{0,1\}^d \times \{0,1\}^k \to \{0,1\}^s$. Let $q_i = (m_i, x_i)$ be the i-th query in Q and let $Q_{|1,\ldots,i}$ denote the sequence Q up to and including the i-th query. Let the predicate $\mathrm{init}(q_i) := \mathrm{init}(m_i, x_i)$ be true if, and only if, $\mathrm{hp}^{-1}(x_i) \in \mathcal{IV}$. We define the predicate $\mathrm{chained}^Q(m_i, x_i)$ to be true if, and only if,*

$$\mathrm{init}(m_i, x_i) \quad \vee \quad \exists\, j \in [i-1] : \Big(\mathrm{chained}^Q(m_j, x_j) \wedge \mathrm{hp}(\mathrm{h}(m_j, x_j)) = x_i\Big) \ .$$

Let $\mathfrak{pg}[\mathrm{h}, Q_{|1,\ldots,i}, q_i]$ denote the set of partial graphs such that for all $\mathfrak{pg} \in \mathfrak{pg}[\mathrm{h}, Q_{|1,\ldots,i}, q_i]$ it holds that all h queries occurring during the computation of $\mathrm{EVAL}^{\mathrm{h}}(\mathfrak{pg})$ are in $Q_{|1,\ldots,i}$ and that the final h-query equals q_i.[5] We define the predicate $\mathrm{result}^Q(m_i, x_i)$ to be true if, and only if,

$$\mathrm{chained}^Q(m_i, x_i) \quad \wedge \quad \exists\, \mathfrak{pg} \in \mathfrak{pg}[\mathrm{h}, Q_{|1,\ldots,i}, q_i] : \mathrm{g}(\mathfrak{pg}) \text{ is a valid execution graph}\,.$$

We drop the reference to the query set Q if it is clear from context.

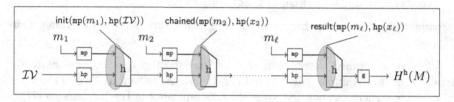

Fig. 3. Denoting queries in the Merkle-Damgård construction where value x_2 is computed as $x_2 := \mathrm{h}(\mathrm{mp}(m_1), \mathrm{hp}(\mathcal{IV}))$ and value x_l is computed recursively as $x_\ell := \mathrm{h}(\mathrm{mp}(m_\ell), \mathrm{hp}(x_{\ell-1}))$

3.2   Message Extractors and Missing Links

We now give two important lemmas concerning iterative hash functions. The first argues that if an adversary does not make all h-queries in the computation of $H^{\mathrm{h}}(M)$ for some message M, then its probability of computing the corresponding hash value is small. To get an intuition note that each h-node has a directed path to the final g-node. As we model the underlying function as ideal, an h-evaluation has s bits of min-entropy which are, so to speak, sent down the network to the final g-node. We refer to the full version [27] for the proof.

Lemma 1. *Let function $H^{\mathrm{h}} : \{0,1\}^* \to \{0,1\}^n$ be an iterative hash function and let $\mathrm{h} : \{0,1\}^d \times \{0,1\}^k \to \{0,1\}^s$ be a fixed-length random oracle. Let $\mathcal{A}^{\mathrm{h}}$ be an adversary that makes at most $q_{\mathcal{A}}$ many queries to h. Let $\mathrm{qry}^{\mathrm{h}}(\mathcal{A}^{\mathrm{h}}(1^\lambda; r))$ denote the adversary's queries to oracle h when algorithm $\mathcal{A}$ runs on randomness r and*

---

[5] If h is modeled as an ideal function then set $\mathfrak{pg}[\mathrm{h}, Q_{|1,\ldots,i}, q_i]$ contains with very high probability at most one partial graph as multiple graphs induce collisions on h.

by $\mathsf{qry}^{\mathbf{h}}(H^{\mathbf{h}}(M))$ denote the $\mathbf{h}$-queries during the evaluation of $H^{\mathbf{h}}(M)$. Then it holds that

$$\Pr_{r,\mathbf{h}}\left[(M,y) \leftarrow \mathcal{A}^{\mathbf{h}}(1^{\lambda};r) : \begin{array}{c} H^{\mathbf{h}}(M) = y \quad \wedge \\ \left(\mathsf{qry}^{\mathbf{h}}(H^{\mathbf{h}}(M)) \setminus \mathsf{qry}^{\mathbf{h}}(\mathcal{A}^{\mathbf{h}}(1^{\lambda};r))\right) \neq \emptyset \end{array}\right] \leq \frac{q_{\mathcal{A}}}{2^s} + \frac{1}{2^{\mathrm{H}_\infty(\mathsf{g}(U_s))}}$$

where $\setminus$ denotes the simple complement of sets and U_s denotes a random variable uniformly distributed in $\{0,1\}^s$. The probability is over the choice of random oracle $\mathbf{h}$ and the coins of $\mathcal{A}$.

Next, we show that given the sequence of $\mathbf{h}$-queries and corresponding answers of an adversary, there exists an efficient and deterministic extractor $\mathcal{E}$ that can reconstruct precisely the set of messages for which the adversary "knows" the corresponding hash value. We refer to the full version [27] for the proof.

Lemma 2. Let function $H^{\mathbf{h}} : \{0,1\}^* \to \{0,1\}^n$ be an iterative hash function and $\mathbf{h} : \{0,1\}^d \times \{0,1\}^k \to \{0,1\}^s$ a fixed-length random oracle. Let $\mathcal{A}^{\mathbf{h}}$ be an adversary making at most $q_{\mathcal{A}}$ queries to $\mathbf{h}$. Let $\mathsf{qry}^{\mathbf{h}}(\mathcal{A}^{\mathbf{h}}(1^{\lambda};r))$ denote the adversary's queries to oracle $\mathbf{h}$ (together with the corresponding oracle answer) when algorithm $\mathcal{A}$ runs on randomness r. Then there exists an efficient deterministic extractor $\mathcal{E}$ outputting sets $\mathcal{M}$ and $\mathcal{Y}$ with $|\mathcal{M}| = |\mathcal{Y}| \leq 3q_{\mathcal{A}}$, such that

$$\Pr_{r,\mathbf{h}}\left[\begin{array}{c} (M,y) \leftarrow \mathcal{A}^{\mathbf{h}}(1^{\lambda};r); \\ (\mathcal{M},\mathcal{Y}) \leftarrow \mathcal{E}(\mathsf{qry}^{\mathbf{h}}(\mathcal{A}^{\mathbf{h}}(1^{\lambda};r))) \end{array} : \begin{array}{c} \exists\, X \in \mathcal{M} : H^{\mathbf{h}}(X) \notin \mathcal{Y} \quad \vee \\ \left(H^{\mathbf{h}}(M) = y \wedge M \notin \mathcal{M}\right) \end{array}\right] \leq \frac{3q_{\mathcal{A}}^2}{2^{\mathrm{H}_\infty(g(U_s))}}.$$

Value U_s denotes a random variable uniformly distributed in $\{0,1\}^s$. The probability is over the coins r of $\mathcal{A}^{\mathbf{h}}$ and the choice of random oracle $\mathbf{h}$.

3.3 h-Queries during Functionality Respecting Games

We now define various terms that allow us to talk about specific queries from adversarial procedures to the underlying function $\mathbf{h}$ of iterative hash function $H^{\mathbf{h}}$ during game G. Recall that, as do Ristenpart et al. [29], we only consider the class of *functionality-respecting* games (see Section 2) where only adversarial procedures may call the adversarial interface of functionalities (i.e., the underlying function $\mathbf{h}$ in our case).

Definition 4. Let $G^{H^{\mathbf{h}},\mathcal{A}_1,\dots,\mathcal{A}_m}$ be a functionality respecting game with access to hash functionality $H^{\mathbf{h}}$ and adversarial procedures $\mathcal{A}_1,\dots,\mathcal{A}_m$. We denote by $\mathsf{qry}^{G,\mathbf{h}}$ the sequence of queries to the adversarial interface of $H^{\mathbf{h}}$ (that is, $\mathbf{h}$) during the execution of game G.

Note that $\mathsf{qry}^{G,\mathbf{h}}$ is a random variable over the random coins of game G. Thus, we can regard the query sequence as a deterministic function of the random coins. In this light, in the following we define subsequences of queries belonging to certain adversarial procedures such as the i-th query of the j-th adversarial procedure.

Game $G^{H^{\mathbf{h}},\mathcal{A}_1,\dots,\mathcal{A}_m}$ can call adversarial procedures $\mathcal{A}_1,\dots,\mathcal{A}_m$ in any order and multiple times. Thus, we first define a mapping from the sequence of adversarial procedure calls by the game's main procedure to the actual adversarial procedure $\mathcal{A}_i$. For better readability, we drop the superscript identifying game G in the following definitions and whenever the game is clear from context. We drop the superscript identifying oracle h exposed by the adversarial interface of functionality H^{h} if clear from context.

Definition 5. *We define* AdvSeq_i *(for $i \geq 1$) to denote the adversarial procedure corresponding to the i-th adversarial procedure call by game G. We set* $|\mathsf{AdvSeq}|$ *to denote the total number of adversarial procedure calls by G.*

We define sequence of h-queries made by the i-th adversarial procedure AdvSeq_i as:

Definition 6. *By* qry_i *we denote the sequence of queries to* h *by procedure* AdvSeq_i *during the i-th adversarial procedure call by the game's main procedure. By* $\mathsf{qry}_{i,j}$ *we denote the j-th query in this sequence.*

We also need a notion which captures all those queries executed before a specific adversarial procedure AdvSeq_i was called. For this, we will slightly abuse notation and "concatenate" two (or more) sequences, i.e., if S_1 and S_2 are two sequences, then by $S_1 \| S_2$ we denote the sequence that contains all elements of S_1 followed by all elements of S_2 in their specific order.

Definition 7. *By* $\mathsf{qry}_{<i}$ *we denote the sequence of queries to* h *before the execution of procedure* AdvSeq_i. *By* $\mathsf{qry}_{<i,j}$ *we denote the sequence of queries to* h *up to the j-th query of the i-th adversarial procedure call. Formally,*

$$\mathsf{qry}_{<i} := \overset{i-1}{\underset{k=1}{\|}} \mathsf{qry}_k \quad and \quad \mathsf{qry}_{<i,j} := \mathsf{qry}_{<i} \| \overset{j-1}{\underset{k=1}{\|}} \mathsf{qry}_{i,k}$$

Finally, we define the sequence of h-queries by procedure AdvSeq_i up-to the i-th adversarial procedure call by the game's main procedure. That is, in addition to queries qry_i we have all queries from previous calls to AdvSeq_i by the game's main procedure.

Definition 8. *By* $\mathsf{qry}_{<\mathcal{A}_i,j}$ *we denote the sequence of queries to procedure* h *by the i-th adversarial procedure* AdvSeq_i *up-to query* $\mathsf{qry}_{<i,j}$. *Formally,*

$$\mathsf{qry}_{<\mathcal{A}_i,j} := \underset{\substack{0<\ell<i, \\ \mathsf{AdvSeq}_\ell = \mathsf{AdvSeq}_i}}{\|} \mathsf{qry}_\ell \| \overset{j-1}{\underset{k=1}{\|}} \mathsf{qry}_{i,k} \; .$$

Bad Result Queries. Having defined queries to the adversarial interface of the hash functionality (i.e., underlying function h) occurring during a game G allows us to use our notation established in Section 3.1 on h-queries: initial queries, chained queries and result queries. For example, we can say that query $\mathsf{qry}_{i,j}$ is an initial query. With this, we now define a bad event corresponding to splitting up the evaluation of hash values via several adversarial stages (also refer to the introduction).

Informally, we call a query (m, x) to function $\mathsf{h}(\cdot, \cdot)$ badResult if it is a result query (cp. Definition 3) with respect to **all** previous queries during the game, but it is not a chained query (and thus not a result query) if we restrict the sequence of queries to that of the current adversarial procedure. Note that, whether or not a query is bad only depends on queries to h prior to the query in question and is not changed by any query coming later in the game. (Note the change in the underlying sequence for the two predicates in the following definition.)

Definition 9. *Let $G^{H^{\mathsf{h}}, \mathcal{A}_1, \dots, \mathcal{A}_m}$ be any game. Let $(m, x) := \mathsf{qry}_{i,j}$ be the j-th query to function h by adversary AdvSeq_i. Then query (m, x) is called badResult $^{\mathcal{A}_i}(\mathsf{qry}_{i,j})$ if, and only if: $\mathsf{result}^{\mathsf{qry}<i,j}(m, x)$ and $\neg\mathsf{chained}^{\mathsf{qry}<\mathcal{A}_i,j}(m, x)$.*

4 Unsplittable Multi-stage Games

The formalization of hash functions together with terminology on particular queries during a game allows us to define a property on games that will be sufficient to argue composition similar to that of the MRH composition theorem for indifferentiability. We call a game $G \in \mathcal{LG}$ UNSPLITTABLE for an iterative hash construction H^{h}, if two conditions hold: 1) For any adversary $\mathcal{A}_1, \dots, \mathcal{A}_m$ there exists adversary $\mathcal{A}_1^*, \dots, \mathcal{A}_m^*$ such that games $G^{H^{\mathsf{h}}, \mathcal{A}_1, \dots, \mathcal{A}_m}$ and $G^{H^{\mathsf{h}}, \mathcal{A}_1^*, \dots, \mathcal{A}_m^*}$ change only by a small factor, and 2) During game $G^{H^{\mathsf{h}}, \mathcal{A}_1^*, \dots, \mathcal{A}_m^*}$ we have that bad result queries only occur with small probability. Intuitively, this means that it does not help adversaries to split up the computation of hash values over several distinct adversarial procedures. After formally defining unsplittability we will then formulate the accompanying composition theorem which informally states that if a game is UNSPLITTABLE for an indifferentiable hash construction H^{h}, then security proofs in the ROM carry over if the random oracle is implemented by that particular hash function.

Definition 10. *Let H^{h} be an iterative hash function and let $\mathsf{h} : \{0,1\}^d \times \{0,1\}^k \to \{0,1\}^s$ be an ideal function. We say a functionality respecting game $G \in \mathcal{LG}$ is $(t_{\mathcal{A}^*}, q_{\mathcal{A}^*}, \epsilon_G, \epsilon_{\mathsf{bad}})$-UNSPLITTABLE for H^{h} if for every adversary $\mathcal{A}_1, \dots, \mathcal{A}_m$ there exists algorithm $\mathcal{A}_1^*, \dots, \mathcal{A}_m^*$ such that for all values y*

$$\Pr\left[G^{H^{\mathsf{h}}, \mathcal{A}_1, \dots, \mathcal{A}_m} \Rightarrow y \right] \leq \Pr\left[G^{H^{\mathsf{h}}, \mathcal{A}_1^*, \dots, \mathcal{A}_m^*} \Rightarrow y \right] + \epsilon_G .$$

Adversary $\mathcal{A}_i^*$ has run-time at most $t_{\mathcal{A}_i}^*$ and makes at most $q_{\mathcal{A}_i}^*$ queries to h. Moreover, it holds for game $G^{H^{\mathsf{h}}, \mathcal{A}_1^*, \dots, \mathcal{A}_m^*}$ that:

$$\Pr\left[\exists i \in [|\mathsf{AdvSeq}|], \exists j \in [q_{\mathcal{A}_i}^*] : \mathsf{badResult}^{\mathcal{A}_i}(\mathsf{qry}_{i,j}) \right] \leq \epsilon_{\mathsf{bad}} .$$

The probability is over the coins of game $G^{H^{\mathsf{h}}, \mathcal{A}^*_1, \dots, \mathcal{A}^*_m}$ and the choice of function h.

4.1   Composition for Unsplittable Multi-stage Games

We here give the composition theorem for UNSPLITTABLE games in the asymptotic setting. The full theorem with concrete advantages is given in the full version [27]. Due to space limitations, we here also only present a much shortened proof sketch.

Theorem 1 (Asymptotic Setting). *Let $H^h : \{0,1\}^* \to \{0,1\}^n$ be an iterative hash function indifferentiable from a random oracle $\mathcal{R}$ and let $h : \{0,1\}^d \times \{0,1\}^k \to \{0,1\}^s$ be an ideal function. Let game $G \in \mathcal{LG}$ be any functionality respecting game that is UNSPLITTABLE for H^h and let $\mathcal{A}_1, \ldots, \mathcal{A}_m$ be an adversary. Then, there exists efficient adversary $\mathcal{B}_1, \ldots, \mathcal{B}_m$ and negligible function* negl *such that for all values y*

$$\left| \Pr\left[G^{H^h, \mathcal{A}_1, \ldots, \mathcal{A}_m} \Rightarrow y \right] - \Pr\left[G^{\mathcal{R}, \mathcal{B}_1, \ldots, \mathcal{B}_m} \Rightarrow y \right] \right| \leq \texttt{negl}(\lambda) \ .$$

Proof (Proof Sketch). The proof consists of two steps. In a first step we are going to take the indifferentiability simulator for H^h and transform it into a simulator with a special structure that we call $\mathcal{S}_d$. Secondly, we take the UNSPLITTABILITY-property of game G to get a set of adversaries $\mathcal{A}_1^*, \ldots, \mathcal{A}_m^*$ such that during game $G^{\mathcal{F}, \mathcal{A}_1^*, \ldots, \mathcal{A}_m^*}$ bad result queries (cp. Definition 9) occur only with negligible probability. This property, together, with the structure of simulator $\mathcal{S}_d$ then allows to argue composition, similarly to RSS in their composition theorem for reset-indifferentiability: Theorem 6.1 in [28]. (Theorem 4 in the proceedings version [29]).

Construction of $\mathcal{S}_d$. We begin with the construction of simulator $\mathcal{S}_d$. Since H^h is indifferentiable from a random oracle there exists a simulator $\mathcal{S}$ such that no efficient distinguisher $\mathcal{D}$ can distinguish between talking to (H^h, h) or $(\mathcal{R}, \mathcal{S}^{\mathcal{R}})$. From this simulator we are going to construct a generic simulator $\mathcal{S}_*$ which keeps track of all queries internally constructing any potential partial graph for the query-sequence. We give a shortened description of simulator $\mathcal{S}_*$ in Figure 4. If a query corresponds to a result query (cp. Definition 3) it ensures to be compatible with the random oracle by picking a value from the preimage of $g^{-1}(\mathcal{R}(\texttt{extract}(\mathfrak{pg})))$ uniformly at random (see line 8), where $\mathfrak{pg}$ is the corresponding partial graph. Note that this ensures consistency with the answers of the random oracle. Otherwise, if the query is not a result query, it simply responds with a random value (line 9). The full construction and proof of indifferentiability is presented in the full version [27].

In a next step (the details are given in [27]) we derandomize simulator $\mathcal{S}_*$ using the random oracle and a derandomization technique by Bennet and Gill [10]. For any fixed value $t_{\mathcal{D}}$, this yields simulator $\mathcal{S}_d$ such that for any distinguisher $\mathcal{D}$ that runs in time at most $t_{\mathcal{D}}$ it holds that

$$\left| \Pr\left[\mathcal{D}^{H^h, h}(1^\lambda) = 1 \right] - \Pr\left[\mathcal{D}^{\mathcal{R}, \mathcal{S}_d^{\mathcal{R}}}(1^\lambda) = 1 \right] \right| \leq \texttt{negl}(\lambda) \ .$$

Fig. 4. Simulator $\mathcal{S}_*$ for proof of Theorem 1. $\mathcal{S}_*$ maintains a list of partial graphs that can be constructed from the query sequence. If query (m, x) is an initial query it constructs the corresponding partial graph and adds it to the temporary set $\mathcal{T}$. It then tries all existing partial graphs, if they can be extended by the current query. A query is answered either by a random value or (for result queries) by sampling a value uniformly at random from $\mathbf{g}^{-1}(\mathcal{R}(\mathtt{extract}(\mathfrak{pg}))$.

```
Simulator  S*(m, x) :
1  if M[m, x] ≠ ⊥ then return M[m, x]
2  T ← {}
3  if init(m, x) then
4      create partial graph from (m, x) and add to T
5  test all existing partial graphs, if any can be extended
6      by query(m, x). If so, add result to T
7  if ∃pg ∈ T : extract(pg) ≠ ⊥ then
8      M[m, x] ←$ g⁻¹(R(extract(pg)))
9  else M[m, x] ←$ {0, 1}ˢ
10 if |T| > 0 then
11     label output edge of any graph in T by M[m, x]
12     add all graphs in T to a list of partial graphs
13 return M[m, x]
```

Using $\mathcal{S}_d$ with UNSPLITTABLE *Games.* Let $\mathcal{A}_1^*, \ldots, \mathcal{A}_m^*$ be such that during game $G^{\mathcal{F}, \mathcal{A}_1^*, \ldots, \mathcal{A}_m^*}$ bad result queries occur only with negligible probability. We now set $\mathcal{B}_i := \mathcal{A}_i^{* \mathcal{S}_d^{(i)}}$ where every $\mathcal{S}_d^{(i)}$ denotes an independent copy of $\mathcal{S}_d$. The structure of $\mathcal{S}_d$ ensures that non-result queries (cp. Definition 3) are answered consistently over the several independent copies. Furthermore, the fact that result queries are with overwhelming probability not bad ensures that also these are answered consistently. We, thus, get that

$$\Pr\left[G^{H^{\mathbf{h}}, \mathcal{A}_1, \ldots, \mathcal{A}_m} \Rightarrow y\right] \approx \Pr\left[G^{H^{\mathbf{h}}, \mathcal{A}_1^*, \ldots, \mathcal{A}_m^*} \Rightarrow y\right] \approx \Pr\left[G^{\mathcal{R}, \mathcal{A}_1^{* \mathcal{S}_d^{(1)\mathcal{R}}}, \ldots, \mathcal{A}_m^{* \mathcal{S}_d^{(m)\mathcal{R}}}} \Rightarrow y\right]$$

which yields that $\Pr\left[G^{\mathcal{R}, \mathcal{B}_1, \ldots, \mathcal{B}_m} \Rightarrow y\right] \leq \mathtt{negl}$. □

5 Applications

We turn to the task of proving UNSPLITTABILITY for the various multi-stage games from the introduction: While for the RSS proof-of-storage game we will give a direct proof (which appears only in the full version [27]) we prove the results for CDA, MLE and UCE via a meta result on games using keyed hash functions (Theorem 2).

5.1 Unsplittability of Keyed-Hash Games

Let $\mathsf{qry}^{H^{\mathbf{h}}}\left[G^{H^{\mathbf{h}}, \mathcal{A}_1, \ldots, \mathcal{A}_m}(r)\right]$ be the list of queries by game G (running on random coins r) to the honest interface of the functionality (i.e., $H^{\mathbf{h}}$) and let

$$\mathsf{qry}^{\mathbf{h}}\left[G^{H^{\mathbf{h}}, \mathcal{A}_1, \ldots, \mathcal{A}_m}(r)\right] := \left\{(m, x) : \exists M \in \mathsf{qry}^{H^{\mathbf{h}}}\left[G^{H^{\mathbf{h}}, \mathcal{A}_1, \ldots, \mathcal{A}_m}(r)\right], (m, x) \in \mathsf{qry}^{\mathbf{h}}(H^{\mathbf{h}}(M))\right\}$$

be the list of queries by game G, when run on random coins r, to $\mathbf{h}$ triggered by queries to the honest interface of the functionality. (Note that the adversarial procedures $\mathcal{A}_1, \ldots, \mathcal{A}_m$ never query the honest interface.) For fixed random coins r and an adversarial $\mathbf{h}$-query $\mathsf{qry}_{i,j}$ during game $G^{H^{\mathbf{h}}, \mathcal{A}_1, \ldots, \mathcal{A}_m}(r)$ we set

$$G\text{-relevant}(\mathsf{qry}_{i,j}; r) \iff \mathsf{qry}_{i,j} \in \mathsf{qry}^{\mathbf{h}}\left[G^{H^{\mathbf{h}}, \mathcal{A}_1, \ldots, \mathcal{A}_m}(r)\right]$$

That is, we call an adversarial query G-relevant if the same query occurs during the honest computation of an $H^{\mathbf{h}}$ query by game G.

Let us observe that we can replace the adversarial interface $\mathbf{h}$ given to an adversarial procedure by one that differs from $\mathbf{h}$ on all points except for points that are also queried indirectly by the game (i.e., queries which are G-relevant), without changing the outcome of the game (or rather its distribution over the choice of ideal functionality $\mathbf{h}$).

Keyed-Hash Games. Hash functions can be considered in a keyed setting, where a key is included in the computation of every hash value. HMAC or NMAC were designed as keyed functions, other hash functions like Merkle-Damgård variants can be adapted to the keyed setting, for example, by requiring that the key is prepended to the message. In the following we write $H^{\mathbf{h}}(\kappa, M)$ to denote an iterative hash construction with an explicit key input (for further information on how keyed hash constructions are captured by our framework we refer to the full version [27]).

Many keyed constructions are designed such that the key is used in all initial queries. HMAC and NMAC are of that type, and also the adapted Merkle-Damgård variants such as chop-MD or prefix-free-MD [15] can be regarded of that type, if the key is always prepended to the message. We call such hash functions *key-prefixed hash functions*.

Definition 11. *A keyed iterative hash function $H^{\mathbf{h}}$ is called* key-prefixed, *if for all $\kappa \in \mathcal{K}$ and all $M \in \{0,1\}^*$*

$$\forall (m,x) \in \mathsf{qry}^{\mathbf{h}}(H^{\mathbf{h}}(\kappa, M)) : \neg\mathsf{init}(m,x) \vee \mathsf{mp}^{-1}(m) = \kappa \vee \mathsf{hp}^{-1}(x) = \kappa$$

where $\mathcal{K}$ denotes the key-space of function $H^{\mathbf{h}}$.

Now, consider games that only make keyed hash queries. By this we mean that either the game is defined using keyed hash functions directly, or it can be restated as such by identifying a part of each query as key, for example, because some parameter is prepended to every hash query.

Definition 12. *We call a game $G \in \mathcal{LG}$ a* keyed-hash game, *if G only makes keyed hash queries. We denote by $\mathcal{K}_G[H^{\mathbf{h}}, r]$ the set of keys used by G when run on coins r and with hash function $H^{\mathbf{h}}$, and require that $\mathcal{K}_G[H^{\mathbf{h}}, r]$ is polynomially bounded and chosen independently of the adversarial procedures.*

We now show that an interesting sub-class of *keyed-hash games* are UNSPLIT-TABLE for *key-prefixed hash functions*.

Theorem 2. *Let $G \in \mathcal{LG}$ be a keyed-hash game where adversarial procedures $\mathcal{A}_1, \ldots, \mathcal{A}_m$ are called exactly once and in this order. Let H^{h} be a key-prefixed iterative hash-function, that is indifferentiable from a random oracle. Let* $\text{h} : \{0,1\}^d \times \{0,1\}^k \rightarrow \{0,1\}^s$ *be an ideal function. Denote by* $\text{View}[\mathcal{A}_i; H^{\text{h}}, r]$ *the view of adversary $\mathcal{A}_i$, i.e., the random coins of $\mathcal{A}_i$ together with its input and answers to any of its oracle queries when game G is run with coins r and function H^{h}.*

If for every efficient extractor $\mathcal{E}$ and for every efficient adversary $\mathcal{A}_i$ (for $i = 1, \ldots, m-1$) there exists negligible function negl *such that*

$$\Pr_r\left[\, k \leftarrow \mathcal{E}(\text{View}[\mathcal{A}_i; H^{\text{h}}, r]) : k \in \mathcal{K}_G[H^{\text{h}}, r] \,\right] \leq \text{negl}(\lambda)$$

and adversary $\mathcal{A}_m$ gets $\mathcal{K}_G[H^{\text{h}}, r]$ as part of its input then G is UNSPLITTABLE *for H^{h}.*

The theorem can be applied to the CDA, the MLE and the UCE game (see Figure 1). Note that the CDA and the MLE game do not necessarily require keyed hash functions but in most constructions explicitly make only keyed hash queries by embedding the public key (for CDA) and the public parameter (for MLE) respectively in every hash query.[6] For the chosen distribution attack (CDA) game [3], which captures the security of deterministic PKE schemes, the only assumption is that the public-key cannot be guessed. For the adaptive version of the CDA game one needs the additional assumption that the PKE scheme does not leak the public-key within its ciphertexts. We call the corresponding property PK-EXT (short for public key extractability) and introduce it in the full version [27]. For message-locked encryption (MLE) [7] one needs to assume that the public parameter P cannot be guessed. Finally, UCE is stated directly for keyed-hash functions that is, here one needs to assume that the hash-key cannot be guessed. Note that this shows that HMAC is UCE-secure when assuming idealized compression functions which solves an open problem in [6]. We give introductions to the various notions, as well as, formal statements listing under which assumptions Theorem 2 applies to CDA, MLE and UCE in the full version of this paper [27].

Acknowledgments. I thank the anonymous reviewers for valuable comments. In particular, I would like to thank Paul Baecher, Christina Brzuska, Özgür Dagdelen, Pooya Farshim, Marc Fischlin, Tommaso Gagliardoni, Giorgia Azzurra Marson, and Cristina Onete for many fruitful discussions and support throughout the various stages of this work. This work was supported by CASED (www.cased.de).

References

1. Aumasson, J.P., Henzen, L., Meier, W., Phan, R.C.W.: SHA-3 proposal BLAKE. Submission to NIST (Round 3) (2010), http://131002.net/blake/blake.pdf

---

[6] For CDA, consider schemes Encrypt-With-Hash [3] and Randomized-Encrypt-With-Hash [4]. For MLE consider the convergent encryption (CE) scheme [7,19].

2. Baecher, P., Brzuska, C., Mittelbach, A.: Reset indifferentiability and its consequences. In: Sako, K., Sarkar, P. (eds.) ASIACRYPT 2013, Part I. LNCS, vol. 8269, pp. 154–173. Springer, Heidelberg (2013)

3. Bellare, M., Boldyreva, A., O'Neill, A.: Deterministic and efficiently searchable encryption. In: Menezes, A. (ed.) CRYPTO 2007. LNCS, vol. 4622, pp. 535–552. Springer, Heidelberg (2007)

4. Bellare, M., Brakerski, Z., Naor, M., Ristenpart, T., Segev, G., Shacham, H., Yilek, S.: Hedged public-key encryption: How to protect against bad randomness. In: Matsui, M. (ed.) ASIACRYPT 2009. LNCS, vol. 5912, pp. 232–249. Springer, Heidelberg (2009)

5. Bellare, M., Canetti, R., Krawczyk, H.: Keying hash functions for message authentication. In: Koblitz, N. (ed.) CRYPTO 1996. LNCS, vol. 1109, pp. 1–15. Springer, Heidelberg (1996)

6. Bellare, M., Hoang, V.T., Keelveedhi, S.: Instantiating random oracles via UCEs. In: Canetti, R., Garay, J.A. (eds.) CRYPTO 2013, Part II. LNCS, vol. 8043, pp. 398–415. Springer, Heidelberg (2013)

7. Bellare, M., Keelveedhi, S., Ristenpart, T.: Message-locked encryption and secure deduplication. In: Johansson and Nguyen [22], pp. 296–312

8. Bellare, M., Rogaway, P.: Random oracles are practical: A paradigm for designing efficient protocols. In: Ashby, V. (ed.) ACM CCS 1993, pp. 62–73. ACM Press (November 1993)

9. Bellare, M., Rogaway, P.: The security of triple encryption and a framework for code-based game-playing proofs. In: Vaudenay, S. (ed.) EUROCRYPT 2006. LNCS, vol. 4004, pp. 409–426. Springer, Heidelberg (2006)

10. Bennett, C.H., Gill, J.: Relative to a random oracle A, $P^A \neq NP^A \neq coNP^A$ with probability 1. SIAM Journal on Computing 10(1), 96–113 (1981)

11. Bertoni, G., Daemen, J., Peeters, M., Assche, G.V.: The keccak SHA-3 submission. Submission to NIST, Round 3 (2011), http://keccak.noekeon.org/Keccak-submission-3.pdf

12. Bertoni, G., Daemen, J., Peeters, M., Assche, G.V.: Cryptographic sponge functions (2011)

13. Bhattacharyya, R., Mandal, A., Nandi, M.: Indifferentiability characterization of hash functions and optimal bounds of popular domain extensions. In: Roy, B., Sendrier, N. (eds.) INDOCRYPT 2009. LNCS, vol. 5922, pp. 199–218. Springer, Heidelberg (2009)

14. Brassard, G. (ed.): CRYPTO 1989. LNCS, vol. 435. Springer, Heidelberg (1990)

15. Coron, J.S., Dodis, Y., Malinaud, C., Puniya, P.: Merkle-Damgård revisited: How to construct a hash function. In: Shoup, V. (ed.) CRYPTO 2005. LNCS, vol. 3621, pp. 430–448. Springer, Heidelberg (2005)

16. Damgård, I.: A design principle for hash functions. In: Brassard [14], pp. 416–427

17. Demay, G., Gazi, P., Hirt, M., Maurer, U.: Resource-restricted indifferentiability. In: Johansson and Nguyen [22], pp. 664-683

18. Dodis, Y., Ristenpart, T., Shrimpton, T.: Salvaging Merkle-Damgård for practical applications. In: Joux, A. (ed.) EUROCRYPT 2009. LNCS, vol. 5479, pp. 371–388. Springer, Heidelberg (2009)

19. Douceur, J.R., Adya, A., Bolosky, W.J., Simon, D., Theimer, M.: Reclaiming space from duplicate files in a serverless distributed file system. In: ICDCS, pp. 617–624 (2002)

20. Ferguson, N., Lucks, S., Schneier, B., Whiting, D., Bellare, M., Kohno, T., Callas, J., Walker, J.: The skein hash function family. Submission to NIST (Round 3) (2010), http://www.skein-hash.info/sites/default/files/skein1.3.pdf

21. Gauravaram, P., Knudsen, L.R., Matusiewicz, K., Mendel, F., Rechberger, C., Schläffer, M., Thomsen, S.S.: Grstl – a SHA-3 candidate. Submission to NIST (Round 3) (2011), http://www.groestl.info/Groestl.pdf
22. Johansson, T., Nguyen, P.Q. (eds.): EUROCRYPT 2013. LNCS, vol. 7881. Springer, Heidelberg (2013)
23. Liskov, M.: Constructing an ideal hash function from weak ideal compression functions. In: Biham, E., Youssef, A.M. (eds.) SAC 2006. LNCS, vol. 4356, pp. 358–375. Springer, Heidelberg (2007)
24. Luykx, A., Andreeva, E., Mennink, B., Preneel, B.: Impossibility results for indifferentiability with resets. Cryptology ePrint Archive, Report 2012/644 (2012), http://eprint.iacr.org/2012/644
25. Maurer, U.M., Renner, R., Holenstein, C.: Indifferentiability, impossibility results on reductions, and applications to the random oracle methodology. In: Naor, M. (ed.) TCC 2004. LNCS, vol. 2951, pp. 21–39. Springer, Heidelberg (2004)
26. Merkle, R.C.: One way hash functions and DES. In: Brassard [14], pp. 428–446
27. Mittelbach, A.: Salvaging indifferentiability in a multi-stage setting. Cryptology ePrint Archive, Report 2013/286 (2013), http://eprint.iacr.org/2013/286
28. Ristenpart, T., Shacham, H., Shrimpton, T.: Careful with composition: Limitations of indifferentiability and universal composability. Cryptology ePrint Archive, Report 2011/339 (2011), http://eprint.iacr.org/2011/339
29. Ristenpart, T., Shacham, H., Shrimpton, T.: Careful with composition: Limitations of the indifferentiability framework. In: Paterson, K.G. (ed.) EUROCRYPT 2011. LNCS, vol. 6632, pp. 487–506. Springer, Heidelberg (2011)
30. Rivest, R.: The MD5 Message-Digest Algorithm. RFC 1321 (Informational) (April 1992), http://www.ietf.org/rfc/rfc1321.txt (updated by RFC 6151)
31. Wu, H.: The hash function JH. Submission to NIST (round 3) (2011), http://www3.ntu.edu.sg/home/wuhj/research/jh/jh_round3.pdf

Déjà Q: Using Dual Systems to Revisit q-Type Assumptions

Melissa Chase[1] and Sarah Meiklejohn[2,*]

[1] Microsoft Research Redmond, USA
melissac@microsoft.com
[2] UC San Diego, USA
smeiklej@cs.ucsd.edu

Abstract. After more than a decade of usage, bilinear groups have established their place in the cryptographic canon by enabling the construction of many advanced cryptographic primitives. Unfortunately, this explosion in functionality has been accompanied by an analogous growth in the complexity of the assumptions used to prove security. Many of these assumptions have been gathered under the umbrella of the "uber-assumption," yet certain classes of these assumptions — namely, q-type assumptions — are stronger and require larger parameter sizes than their static counterparts. In this paper, we show that in certain bilinear groups, many classes of q-type assumptions are in fact implied by subgroup hiding (a well-established, static assumption). Our main tool in this endeavor is the *dual-system* technique, as introduced by Waters in 2009. As a case study, we first show that in composite-order groups, we can prove the security of the Dodis-Yampolskiy PRF based solely on subgroup hiding and allow for a domain of arbitrary size (the original proof only allowed a logarithmically-sized domain). We then turn our attention to classes of q-type assumptions and show that they are implied — when instantiated in appropriate groups — solely by subgroup hiding. These classes are quite general and include assumptions such as q-SDH. Concretely, our result implies that every construction relying on such assumptions for security (e.g., Boneh-Boyen signatures) can, when instantiated in appropriate composite-order bilinear groups, be proved secure under subgroup hiding instead.

1 Introduction

For the past decade, bilinear groups — i.e., groups equipped with a bilinear map, or pairing — have allowed for the efficient construction of a wide variety of advanced cryptographic primitives, including (but by no means limited to): signatures [10,3,5,35], group signatures [7,13,20], zero-knowledge proofs [21,22], (hierarchical) identity-based encryption [8,4,6,31], and functional and attribute-based encryption [29,33,34]. As such, pairings are now used as a standard general-purpose tool in cryptographic constructions.

---

* Work done as an intern at Microsoft Research Redmond.

P.Q. Nguyen and E. Oswald (Eds.): EUROCRYPT 2014, LNCS 8441, pp. 622–639, 2014.

Unfortunately, this growth in the complexity of cryptographic primitives has been accompanied by an analogous growth in the complexity of the assumptions required to prove security. While assumptions such as Bilinear Diffie Hellman (BDH) [8] and Decision Linear [7] have become relatively standard, the use of pairings has also ushered in various classes of assumptions such as q-type assumptions, in which the size of the assumption grows dynamically, or interactive assumptions, in which the adversary is given access to some oracle(s). For example, in the q-DBDHI (Decisional Bilinear Diffie Hellman Inversion) assumption, the adversary is given $(g, g^x, g^{x^2}, \ldots, g^{x^q})$ and is asked to produce $e(g,g)^{1/x}$. While the "uber-assumption" [6,12] generalizes many q-type assumptions (as well as many static assumptions) and provides a lower bound for their security in the generic group model [43], such assumptions nevertheless remain less understood than their static counterparts.

Beyond the understanding of such assumptions, the fact that they scale asymptotically with the security of the scheme can be problematic. In a reduction, the value of q is frequently tied to the number of queries that the adversary makes to an oracle. As a result, q must scale with some parameter of the system; e.g., for identity-based encryption, q must be at least as big as the number of parties that the adversary is able to corrupt. As it is typically the case that an assumption parameterized by q' implies the same assumption parameterized by q for $q' > q$ (as the assumption parameterized by q' gives out strictly more information), this means that the assumption gets stronger as the adversary is able to corrupt more parties. In some cases, this correlation is more striking. For example, Dodis and Yampolskiy [17] use the $2^{a(\lambda)}$-DBDHI assumption to prove the security of their pseudorandom function (PRF), where $a(\lambda)$ is the size of the domain of the PRF (and λ is the security parameter); as a result, the domain is restricted to be of logarithmic size. This correlation is furthermore not always an artifact of proof techniques, as Jao and Yoshida [24] showed that Boneh-Boyen signatures were in fact equivalent to the q-SDH assumption that they rely on for security. Finally, Cheon [16] showed that the time required to recover a secret key scales inversely with the size of q, so that if recovering a secret key takes time t when using $q = 1$ (e.g, it takes t steps to recover x given g and g^x), then it takes time $t/\sqrt{q}$ in the general case (e.g., given $(g, g^x, \ldots, g^{x^q})$). This means that constructions rely on asymptotically stronger assumptions to obtain stronger security guarantees, so the parameters must grow appropriately in order to maintain a constant level of security (e.g., 128-bit security).

On the positive side, one technique that has proved particularly effective at avoiding q-type assumptions — and boosting security as a result — is the dual-system technique, which was introduced by Waters [44] in 2009 and has been used extensively since [31,29,30,33,28,34]. Briefly, this technique takes advantage of subgroup hiding in bilinear groups [9]; i.e., the assumption, in a group of composite order $N = p_1 p_2$, that a random element of the full group is indistinguishable from a random element of order p_1. (Subgroup hiding can also be defined, albeit in a more complex way, for vector spaces over prime-order bilinear groups.) Using this core assumption, the dual-system technique begins with a scheme in a particular subgroup (for concreteness, the subgroup of elements of order p_1); i.e., a scheme in which all elements are contained solely within the subgroup. To prove security, a "shadow" copy of the original scheme is first added in a new subgroup (e.g., the subgroup of order p_2); the addition of this shadow copy goes unnoticed by subgroup hiding. Using a property called *parameter hiding* [28], this shadow copy is then randomized, so the value in the additional subgroup is now unstructured; in Waters' terminology, this object is now *semi-functional*. This randomness is then pushed back into the original subgroup, again using subgroup hiding, and is used to blind the structure of the original scheme; e.g., in an IND-CPA game it can be used to obscure all information about the challenge message.

Our Contributions. In this paper, we expand the usage of the dual-system technique. Rather than work at the level of constructions, we show directly that many q-type assumptions can be implied — with a crucial looseness of q — by subgroup hiding. In some sense, we thus interpret previous usages as *absorbing* rather than avoiding q-type assumptions, and believe our work takes a (perhaps surprising) step in expanding the power of the dual-system technique.

As a first exercise, we prove in Section 3 that the Dodis-Yampolskiy PRF — unmodified, but instantiated in a composite-order group — can be proved secure using only the subgroup hiding assumption. Because of the limitations (described above) in the original security proof, our result not only uses a static assumption, but also boosts security to allow for domains of arbitrary size, which is useful in and of itself for the many applications of the Dodis-Yampolskiy PRF [14,2,15,26].

Next, in Section 4, we look beyond cryptographic primitives and instead focus directly on the underlying assumptions, and in particular on the class of q-type assumptions that are instantiations of the uber-assumption. Here we show that many instantiations of the uber-assumption can be reduced — following a modified version of the dual-system technique, which still assumes subgroup hiding — to instantiations that are significantly weaker; in fact, in many cases we can reduce to an assumption so weak that it actually holds by a statistical argument. As examples, we revisit a number of well-known q-type assumptions. By applying our general theorem to these assumptions, we can reduce them to assumptions in which all secret information (e.g., the exponent x in q-DBDHI) is statistically hidden, so an adversary can do no better than a random guess and the security of the entire assumption collapses down to subgroup hiding.

Finally, in Section 5, we discuss the concrete implications of our work; i.e., in which concrete bilinear settings the abstract requirements of the dual-system technique (namely, subgroup hiding and parameter hiding) can be expected to hold. Due to current limitations in the parameter hiding supported by prime-order bilinear groups, our results can most generally be applied in asymmetric composite-order bilinear groups [11,37].

Putting it all together, we obtain the following concrete results:

- In a composite-order group (such as the target group of a composite-order pairing, or any composite-order elliptic curve group without a pairing), subgroup hiding implies any q-type assumption where the exponents are linearly independent rational functions.

- In an asymmetric composite-order bilinear group, subgroup hiding implies any q-type assumption where the exponents are linearly independent rational functions and the adversary must compute a value in the source group.

Related Work. As mentioned above, the dual-system technique was first introduced by Waters in 2009 [44], and was applied subsequently to achieve a wide variety of results [31,29,41,30,33,32,28,42], all involving randomized public-key primitives (e.g., identity-based encryption) in bilinear groups.

To the best of our knowledge, we are the first to systematically apply the dual-system technique directly to assumptions, and in particular to q-type assumptions. Boneh, Boyen, and Goh [6] analyzed the security of the uber-assumption — which includes many q-type assumptions — in the generic group model, and derived generic lower bounds on the runtime of an adversary that could break the uber-assumption; this work was later extended by Jager and Rupp [23], who showed the equivalence of many assumptions in the *semi-generic* group model. Our result is somewhat orthogonal to theirs, as we seek to show that in certain concrete (i.e., non-generic) settings these assumptions actually reduce to subgroup hiding. Anecdotally, several results use the dual-system technique to eliminate the requirement on q-type assumptions for specific primitives or constructions: Gerbush et al. [18] obtained Camenisch-Lysyanskaya signatures under static assumptions, as opposed to the interactive LRSW assumption; Attrapadung and Libert achieved the first identity-based broadcast encryption scheme with short ciphertexts [1]; and the original result of Waters [44] achieved the first secure HIBE under non-q-type assumptions.

2   Definitions and Notation

2.1   Preliminaries

If x is a binary string then $|x|$ denotes its bit length. If S is a finite set then $|S|$ denotes its size and $x \overset{\$}{\leftarrow} S$ denotes sampling a member uniformly from S and assigning it to x. $\lambda \in \mathbb{N}$ denotes the security parameter and 1^λ denotes its unary representation.

Algorithms are randomized unless explicitly noted otherwise. "PT" stands for "polynomial-time." By $y \leftarrow A(x_1, \ldots, x_n; R)$ we denote running algorithm A on inputs $x_1, \ldots, x_n$ and random coins R and assigning its output to y. By $y \overset{\$}{\leftarrow} A(x_1, \ldots, x_n)$ we denote $y \leftarrow A(x_1, \ldots, x_n; R)$ for some random coins R. By $[A(x_1, \ldots, x_n)]$ we denote the set of values that have positive probability of being output by A on inputs $x_1, \ldots, x_n$. Adversaries are algorithms.

We use games in definitions of security and in proofs. A game G has a MAIN procedure whose output is the output of the game. $\Pr[\mathsf{G}]$ denotes the probability that this output is true.

2.2   Bilinear Groups

We refer to a *bilinear group* as a tuple $\mathbb{G} = (N, G, H, G_T, e)$, where N can be either prime or composite, $|G| = |H| = kN$ and $|G_T| = \ell N$ for some $k, \ell \in \mathbb{N}$, and $e : G \times H \to G_T$ is a bilinear map, meaning it is (1) efficiently computable; (2) satisfies bilinearity: $e(x^a, y^b) = e(x, y)^{ab}$ for all $x \in G$, $y \in H$, and $a, b \in \mathbb{Z}/N\mathbb{Z}$; and (3) satisfies non-degeneracy: if $e(x, y) = 1$ for all $y \in H$ then $x = 1$ and if $e(x, y) = 1$ for all $x \in G$ then $y = 1$. When G and H are cyclic, we may include in $\mathbb{G}$ generators g and h of G and H respectively, and when the groups G and H decompose into subgroups $G = G_1 \oplus G_2$ and $H = H_1 \oplus H_2$, we may additionally include descriptions of these subgroups and/or their generators. In what follows, we use BilinearGen to denote the algorithm by which bilinear groups are generated, and provide it with an argument n that specifies the number of subgroups.

There are two additional structural properties of bilinear groups that are exploited in the dual-system technique: subgroup hiding and parameter hiding. Subgroup hiding is a computational assumption that requires that, if G (respectively H) decomposes into two subgroups, then distinguishing between a random element of the full group and a random element of one of the subgroups should be hard. (This is actually the specific simple case of subgroup hiding originally introduced by Boneh, Goh, and Nissim [9]; more general definitions exist as well [28,27].)

Assumption 2.1 (Subgroup hiding). *For a bilinear group* $\mathbb{G} = (N, G, H, G_T, e, g_1, g_2, h_1, h_2)$, *subgroup hiding* holds in $\mathbb{G}$ *if no PT adversary* $\mathcal{A}$ *has a non-negligible chance of distinguishing a random element of the subgroup* G_1 *from a random element of the group* G; *formally, define* $\mathbf{Adv}_{\mathcal{A}}^{sgh}(\lambda) = 2Pr[SGH_{\mu}^{\mathcal{A}}(\lambda)] - 1$, *where* $SGH_{\mu}^{\mathcal{A}}(\lambda)$ *is defined as follows for* $\mu \subseteq \{g_1, g_2, h_1, h_2\}$:

MAIN $SGH_{\mu}^{\mathcal{A}}(\lambda)$

$b \xleftarrow{\$} \{0, 1\}$; $(N, G, H, G_T, e, g_1, g_2, h_1, h_2) \xleftarrow{\$}$ BilinearGen$(1^\lambda, 2)$

if $(b = 0)$ *then* $T \xleftarrow{\$} G$

if $(b = 1)$ *then* $T \xleftarrow{\$} G_1$

$b' \xleftarrow{\$} \mathcal{A}((N, G, H, G_T, e), \mu, T)$

return $(b' = b)$

Then subgroup hiding *holds with respect to the auxiliary information* μ *if for all PT adversaries* $\mathcal{A}$ *there exists a negligible function* $\nu(\cdot)$ *such that* $\mathbf{Adv}_{\mathcal{A}}^{sgh}(\lambda) < \nu(\lambda)$.

There are often limits to the auxiliary information that can be provided to $\mathcal{A}$; e.g., if $\mathcal{A}$ is attempting to distinguish $T = g_1^r$ from $T = g^r$ for $r \xleftarrow{\$} \mathbb{Z}/N\mathbb{Z}$ and has access to a canceling pairing $e(\cdot, \cdot)$ — i.e., a pairing such that $e(G_1, H_2) = e(G_2, H_1) = 1$ — and $h_2 \in \mu$, it can easily distinguish between these elements by checking if $e(T, h_2) = 1$ or not. Thus, if an adversary is trying to distinguish between a random element of G_1 and a random element of $G_1 \oplus G_2$ (analogously, if it is trying to distinguish between G_2 and $G_1 \oplus G_2$), the problem becomes easy if μ includes h_2 (analogously, h_1).

Parameter hiding, unlike subgroup hiding, is a statistical property of the group that allows certain distributions across subgroups to be independent. In composite-order groups, for example, the Chinese Remainder Theorem tells us that the values of $x \bmod p_1$ and $x \bmod p_2$ are independent, so that given g_1^x, the value of g_2^x is unconstrained. In prime-order groups, Lewko [28] demonstrated how to support parameter hiding with respect to linear functions; i.e., how—using appropriate constructions of G_1 and G_2—the distribution of g_2^{ax} and g_2^r for $a, r \overset{\$}{\leftarrow} \mathbb{F}_p$ is identical, even given x and g_1^a. The first formal notion of parameter hiding with respect to these linear functions was later given by Lewko and Meiklejohn [27]; we generalize their notion as follows:

Definition 2.1 (Parameter hiding). *For a bilinear group* $\mathbb{G} = (N, G, H, G_T, e)$, *parameter hiding holds in G with respect to a family of functions $\mathcal{F}$ if the distribution* $\{g_1^{f(x_1,\ldots,x_n)} g_2^{f(x_1,\ldots,x_n)}\}_{f \in \mathcal{F}}$ *is identical to* $\{g_1^{f(x_1,\ldots,x_n)} g_2^{f(x_1',\ldots,x_n')}\}_{f \in \mathcal{F}}$ *for $g_1 \overset{\$}{\leftarrow} G_1$, $g_2 \overset{\$}{\leftarrow} G_2$, and $x_1, x_1', \ldots, x_n, x_n' \overset{\$}{\leftarrow} \mathbb{Z}/N\mathbb{Z}$. (And holds analogously in H using h_1 and h_2.)*

As a very simple example, if $\mathcal{F} = \{1, x_1\}$, for $g_1 \overset{\$}{\leftarrow} G_1$, $g_2 \overset{\$}{\leftarrow} G_2$, and $x_1, x_1' \overset{\$}{\leftarrow} \mathbb{Z}/N\mathbb{Z}$, the distributions $(g_1 g_2, g_1^{x_1} g_2^{x_1})$ and $(g_1 g_2, g_1^{x_1} g_2^{x_1'})$ are identical.

We also define a somewhat weaker condition, which requires distributions that are statistically close for any (potentially adaptively chosen) polynomial-sized subset of $\mathbb{F}$.

Definition 2.2 (Adaptive parameter hiding). *For a bilinear group* $\mathbb{G} = (N, G, H, G_T, e)$, *adaptive parameter hiding holds with respect to a family of functions $\mathcal{F}$ if for all $\lambda \in \mathbb{N}$ and all adaptively chosen sets $S \subseteq \mathcal{F}$ of size $\mathrm{poly}(\lambda)$, the distribution* $\{g_1^{f(x_1,\ldots,x_n)} g_2^{f(x_1,\ldots,x_n)}\}_{f \in S}$ *is statistically close to* $\{g_1^{f(x_1,\ldots,x_n)} g_2^{f(x_1',\ldots,x_n')}\}_{f \in S}$ *for $g_1 \overset{\$}{\leftarrow} G_1$, $g_2 \overset{\$}{\leftarrow} G_2$, and $x_1, x_1' \ldots, x_n, x_n' \overset{\$}{\leftarrow} \mathbb{Z}/N\mathbb{Z}$.*

We use these definitions in Sections 4, and discuss the different families of functions that can be supported in different types of bilinear groups in Section 5.

2.3 Pseudorandom Functions

A pseudorandom function family [19] F specifies the algorithms F.Pg, F.Keys, F.Dom, F.Rng, and F.Ev. Via $fp \overset{\$}{\leftarrow} \mathsf{F.Pg}(1^\lambda)$ one generates a description fp of a function $\mathsf{F.Ev}(1^\lambda, fp) \colon \mathsf{F.Keys}(1^\lambda, fp) \times \mathsf{F.Dom}(1^\lambda, fp) \to \mathsf{F.Rng}(1^\lambda, fp)$. The evaluation algorithm F.Ev is PT and deterministic.

Definition 2.3. *For a function family* F *and an adversary* $\mathcal{A}$*, let* $\mathbf{Adv}_{F,\mathcal{A}}^{prf}(\lambda) = 2\Pr[PRF_F^{\mathcal{A}}(\lambda)] - 1$*, where* $PRF_F^{\mathcal{A}}(\lambda)$ *is defined as follows:*

<u>MAIN $PRF_F^{\mathcal{A}}(\lambda)$</u>

$b \xleftarrow{\$} \{0,1\}; fp \xleftarrow{\$} \mathsf{F.Pg}(1^{\lambda}); sk \xleftarrow{\$} \mathsf{F.Keys}(1^{\lambda}, fp)$

$b' \xleftarrow{\$} \mathcal{A}^{\mathrm{FN}}(1^{\lambda}, fp)$

return $(b' = b)$

<u>*Procedure* $\mathrm{FN}_{sk}(x)$</u>

if $b = 0$ $y \xleftarrow{\$} \mathsf{F.Rng}(1^{\lambda}, fp)$

if $b = 1$ $y \leftarrow \mathsf{F.Ev}(1^{\lambda}, fp, sk, x)$

return y

Then F *is pseudorandom if for all PT algorithms* $\mathcal{A}$ *there exists a negligible function* $\nu(\cdot)$ *such that* $\mathbf{Adv}_{F,\mathcal{A}}^{prf}(\lambda) \le \nu(\lambda)$.

3   Pseudorandom Functions

In this section, we explore the security of the Dodis-Yampolskiy PRF [17]. First, we recall the Dodis-Yampolskiy PRF, instantiated for our purposes in a group of composite order $N = p_1 p_2$:[1]

- F.Pg(1^{λ}): Output $(N, G, H, G_T, e, g, h) \xleftarrow{\$} \mathsf{BilinearGen}(1^{\lambda}, 2)$. Then F.Keys = F.Dom = $\mathbb{Z}/N\mathbb{Z}$, and F.Rng = G_T.
- F.Ev($1^{\lambda}, fp, sk, x$): Output $y := e(g, h)^{\frac{1}{sk+x}}$. If $(sk + x)^{-1}$ is undefined in $\mathbb{Z}/N\mathbb{Z}$, then output $y := 1$.

Dodis and Yampolskiy originally showed that this was a *verifiable* random function—a more powerful primitive than a PRF, as it comes with the additional ability to prove that the PRF value was computed correctly—under the q-DBDHI assumption, which states that when given $(g, g^x, \ldots, g^{x^q})$, it should be hard to distinguish $e(g,g)^{1/x}$ from random. Their reduction, however, is quite loose: if the size of the PRF domain is $a(\lambda)$, then they use the $2^{a(\lambda)}$-DBDHI assumption, and show that $\mathbf{Adv}_{F,\mathcal{A}}^{\mathrm{pr\text{-}vrf}}(\lambda) \le 2^{a(\lambda)} \cdot \mathbf{Adv}_{\mathcal{A}}^{2^{a(\lambda)}\text{-}\mathrm{DBDHI}}(\lambda)$, which means that the scheme is provably secure only if the domain is restricted to be of logarithmic size (i.e., its size is logarithmic in the size of the security parameter).

We instead make two minor modifications to the PRF and show that

$$\mathbf{Adv}_{F,\mathcal{A}}^{\mathrm{prf}}(\lambda) \le q \cdot \mathbf{Adv}_{\mathcal{A}}^{\mathrm{sgh}}(\lambda)$$

for an adversary $\mathcal{A}$ that makes q queries to the PRF oracle; while the reduction is still not tight, our approach nevertheless allows for a domain of arbitrary size. Our first modification is to move the scheme into a subgroup: rather than use $e(g, h)$ for the full group generators, we switch to using $e(g_1, h_1)$, where g_1 and h_1 generate G_1 and H_1 respectively. (In a cyclic group, such as a composite-order

---

[1] To mirror the exposition of the original PRF, we use the target group G_T here, but note that in fact our analysis would work for *any* composite-order group in which subgroup hiding holds and there is no pairing.

target group, this could instead be accomplished using an additional application of subgroup hiding, and we can show that the function is a PRF even in the full group.) Our second modification is to use, rather than the "canonical" generator $e(g_1, h_1)$, a random generator $w_1 \in G_{T,1}$. We stress that these modifications are purely syntactical and do not fundamentally alter the spirit of the construction (and, in particular, do not affect its usage in applications). They do, however, allow us to prove the following theorem:

Theorem 3.1. *For all $\lambda \in \mathbb{N}$ and $fp \in [\mathsf{F.Pg}(1^\lambda)]$, if subgroup hiding holds in $\mathbb{G}$ and adaptive parameter hiding holds with respect to $\{\mathsf{F.Ev}(1^\lambda, fp, \cdot, x)\}_{x \in \mathsf{F.Dom}}$, then F is a pseudorandom function family.*

A proof of Theorem 3.1 can be found in the full version of the paper. Intuitively, our approach amplifies the only unknown value present in the PRF — namely, the sk value — as follows: first, this secret value is replicated in the $G_{T,2}$ subgroup, which is indistinguishable from the original by subgroup hiding. The secret value in the $G_{T,2}$ subgroup is then decoupled from the secret value in the $G_{T,1}$ subgroup, which is indistinguishable (in fact identical) by parameter hiding. Finally, the new secret value from the $G_{T,2}$ subgroup is moved back into $G_{T,1}$, which is again indistinguishable by subgroup hiding. At this point, we now have one additional secret value in the PRF values we return. By repeating the process, we can embed polynomially many secret values (in particular, we embed as many values as there are oracle queries), at which point we have enough entropy to argue that the values returned by the PRF are statistically indistinguishable from truly random values.

One interesting feature of our approach is that — because we are using a deterministic primitive — we do not need to follow the traditional dual-system structure and adhere to a "query hybrid," in which each query to the oracle must be treated separately. Nevertheless, we do need to add enough additional degrees of randomness to cover all of the adversary's queries, so we still end up with a looseness of q in our reduction (but where q is the number of queries, not the size of the PRF domain).

4   Reducing q-Type Assumptions to Subgroup Hiding

Our main result in this section is to show that — if subgroup hiding holds and parameter hiding holds with respect to certain functions in the exponent — certain q-type assumptions are equivalent to significantly weaker assumptions. In fact, these equivalent assumptions are often so weak that they hold by a purely statistical argument, so the original assumption is fully implied by subgroup hiding.

We begin by recalling the uber-assumption, which serves as an umbrella for many q-type assumptions. We then describe two approaches: roughly, the first reduces any uber-assumption to subgroup hiding, but only if the assumption gives out meaningful functions on one side of the pairing (or in the target group), and the second reduces any computational uber-assumption in the source group to subgroup hiding. Both of our reductions incur a looseness of q in the reduction, so we can think of them as "absorbing" the factor of q from the assumption rather than eliminating it outright.

4.1 The Uber-Assumption

We are able to examine many q-type assumptions at the same time using the "uber-assumption" [6,12], which was first introduced by Boneh, Boyen, and Goh as a way to reason generally about a wide variety of pairing-based assumptions. They prove that if the parameters of the uber-assumption meet certain independence requirements then the assumption is hard in the generic group model, which eliminates the need to prove generic lower bounds for every individual instantiation of the assumption that is introduced. Our motivation, on the other hand, is to prove that many common instantiations of the assumption are in fact implied — assuming subgroup hiding holds in the bilinear group — by weaker versions of the assumption.

Formally, for a bilinear group $\mathbb{G} = (N, G, H, G_T, e, g, h)$ (where N can be either prime or composite) the uber-assumption is parameterized by five values: an integer $c \in \mathbb{N}$, three sets R, S, and T of polynomials over $\mathbb{Z}/N\mathbb{Z}$ (which represent the values we are given in G, H, and G_T respectively), and a polynomial f over $\mathbb{Z}/N\mathbb{Z}$. For the sets of polynomials, we write $R = \langle \rho_1(x_1, \ldots, x_c), \ldots, \rho_r(x_1, \ldots, x_c) \rangle$ and as shorthand use $\rho_i(\vec{x}) = \rho_i(x_1, \ldots, x_c)$ and $g^{R(x_1,\ldots,x_c)} = \{g^{\rho_i(\vec{x})}\}_{i=1}^r$ (and similarly for S and T).

Assumption 4.1 (Computational). *For an adversary $\mathcal{A}$, define $\mathbf{Adv}_{\mathcal{A}}^{uber}(\lambda)$ $= Pr[c\text{-}UBER_{c,R,S,T,f}^{\mathcal{A}}(\lambda)]$, where $c\text{-}UBER_{c,R,S,T,f}^{\mathcal{A}}(\lambda)$ is defined as follows:*

MAIN $c\text{-}UBER_{c,R,S,T,f}^{\mathcal{A}}(\lambda)$

$(N, G, H, G_T, e, g, h) \xleftarrow{\$} \mathsf{BilinearGen}(1^\lambda, 2); x_1, \ldots, x_c \xleftarrow{\$} \mathbb{Z}/N\mathbb{Z}$

$y \xleftarrow{\$} \mathcal{A}(1^\lambda, (N, G, H, G_T, e, g, h), g^{R(x_1,\ldots,x_c)}, h^{S(x_1,\ldots,x_c)}, e(g,h)^{T(x_1,\ldots,x_c)})$
$return\ (y = e(g,h)^{f(x_1,\ldots,x_c)})$

Then the uber-assumption holds if for all PT algorithms $\mathcal{A}$ there exists a negligible function $\nu(\cdot)$ such that $\mathbf{Adv}_{\mathcal{A}}^{uber}(\lambda) < \nu(\lambda)$.

As an example, CDH in a symmetric group G uses $c = 2$, $R = S = \langle 1, x_1, x_2 \rangle$, $T = \langle 1 \rangle$, and $f(x_1, x_2) = x_1 x_2$, so that given (g, g^{x_1}, g^{x_2}), it should be hard to compute $g^{x_1 x_2}$. As long as R and S both include 1, the computational uber-assumption in the target group implies the computational uber-assumption in the source group, since given $X = g^{f(\vec{x})}$ one can always compute $e(X, h) = e(g, h)^{f(\vec{x})}$.

The game d-$UBER_{c,R,S,T,f}^{\mathcal{A}}(\lambda)$ for the decisional uber-assumption is defined analogously, except rather than compute $g^{f(x_1,\ldots,x_c)}$ at the end, the adversary has only to distinguish it from random. Unlike the computational version, the decisional uber-assumption in the source group implies the decisional uber-assumption in the target group, since one can use a decider between $e(g,h)^{f(\vec{x})}$

and R_T to decide between $g^{f(\vec{x})}$ and R by computing the pairing. Furthermore, the decisional uber-assumption (in either group) implies the computational uber-assumption, since the ability to compute the target value immediately implies the ability to distinguish it from random. The strongest version of the uber-assumption, and the one we therefore choose to aim for in the next section, is the decisional assumption in either of the source groups.

4.2   A First Approach: Functions on One Side of the Pairing

Our first approach shows that certain classes of the uber-assumption are equivalent to significantly weaker classes, and that in fact these weaker classes are so weak that the assumption holds by a statistical argument. The subclass of uber-assumptions we cover includes q-type assumptions such as exponent q-SDH (defined above), and implies that any schemes that currently rely on such assumptions can be instantiated so that they rely solely on subgroup hiding.

Our only modifications to the parameters of the uber-assumption are analogous to our modifications in Section 3, which are as follows: first, we assume G, H, and G_T all have two subgroups, and we initially operate solely in the first of these subgroups, so that $\mathcal{A}$ is given $(g_1^{R(x_1,\ldots,x_c)}, h_1^{S(x_1,\ldots,x_c)}, e(g_1, h_1)^{T(x_1,\ldots,x_c)})$ rather than values in the full group. Second, we again switch from the canonical generators g_1 and h_1 to random generators u_1 and v_1. To make our proofs cleaner, we phrase this requirement as follows: for every $\rho_i \in R$, there must exist an efficiently computable function $\hat{\rho}_i$ such that $g_1^{\rho_i(\vec{x})} = u_1^{\hat{\rho}_i(\vec{x})}$, and there must also exist an efficiently computable function $\hat{f}$ such that $g_1^{f(\vec{x})} = u_1^{\hat{f}(\vec{x})}$. Practically, suppose that $u_1 = g_1^r$. Then, using $x_1 = r$, our requirement is equivalent to the requirement that $\rho_i(x_1, \ldots, x_c) = x_1 \cdot \hat{\rho}_i(x_2, \ldots, x_c)$ (and the same for f). Again, we stress that this is just a base translation rather than a restriction on the parameters of the uber-assumption.

Theorem 4.2. *For a bilinear group* $\mathbb{G} = (N, G, H, G_T, e, g_1, g_2) \in [\mathsf{BilinearGen}(1^\lambda, 2)]$, *consider the decisional uber-assumption parameterized by* c, $R = \langle 1, \rho_1(\vec{x}_1), \ldots, \rho_r(\vec{x}_1) \rangle$, $S = T = \langle 1 \rangle$, *and* $f(\vec{x}_1)$. *Then, if subgroup hiding holds in* $\mathbb{G}$ *with respect to* $\mu = \{g_1, g_2\}$ *and parameter hiding holds with respect to* $R \cup \{f\}$, *this assumption is implied by the decisional uber-assumption parameterized by* ℓc, $R' = \langle 1, \sum_{i=1}^{\ell} \rho_1(\vec{x}_i), \ldots, \sum_{i=1}^{\ell} \rho_r(\vec{x}_i) \rangle$, S, T, *and* $f' = \sum_{i=1}^{\ell} f(\vec{x}_i)$ *for all* $\ell = poly(\lambda)$.

A proof of this theorem can be found in the full version of the paper, and also applies when $R = S = \langle 1 \rangle$ and only T contains meaningful functions, or more generally in the case when there might not be an efficiently computable pairing. Intuitively, the transitions rely on the same modified dual-system technique that we used in the proof of Theorem 3.1. First, all elements exist only in the G_1 subgroup, operating over the original set of variables $\vec{x}_1$. A shadow copy of these elements is then added into the G_2 subgroup, which goes unnoticed by subgroup hiding. This shadow copy is then switched to operate over a new set of variables $\vec{x}_2$, which is identical by parameter hiding. These new values are then folded back into the G_1 subgroup, which is again indistinguishable by subgroup hiding. Finally, the G_2 component is eliminated, which is once again indistinguishable by subgroup hiding. The result is now a G_1 component that operates over both $\vec{x}_1$ and $\vec{x}_2$, and the effect is analogous to the extra degree of randomness we obtain in the proof of Theorem 3.1. Repeating this process $\ell - 1$ more times proves the theorem.

To now show why this theorem is useful, we illustrate that the resulting game is often statistically hard, and thus the original uber-assumption is implied solely by subgroup hiding. To start, consider

$$
V = \begin{bmatrix}
1 & \rho_1(\vec{x}_1) & \rho_2(\vec{x}_1) & \cdots & \rho_q(\vec{x}_1) & f(\vec{x}_1) \\
1 & \rho_1(\vec{x}_2) & \rho_2(\vec{x}_2) & \cdots & \rho_q(\vec{x}_2) & f(\vec{x}_2) \\
\vdots & \vdots & & \ddots & \vdots & \vdots \\
1 & \rho_1(\vec{x}_\ell) & \rho_2(\vec{x}_\ell) & \cdots & \rho_q(\vec{x}_\ell) & f(\vec{x}_\ell)
\end{bmatrix}
\tag{1}
$$

We then have the following lemma, which relates the linear independence of the polynomials with the invertibility of the matrix:

Lemma 4.1. *For all $\lambda \in \mathbb{N}$, if the functions in $R \cup \{f\}$ are linearly independent and of maximum degree $poly(\lambda)$, $\ell = q+2$ for $q = poly(\lambda)$, and $N = p_1 \cdot \ldots \cdot p_n$ for distinct primes $p_1, \ldots, p_n \in O(2^{poly(\lambda)})$, then with all but negligible probability the matrix V is invertible.*

Proof. If the matrix V is invertible in $\mathbb{Z}/p_i\mathbb{Z}$ for each prime $p_i \mid N$, then it is also invertible in $\mathbb{Z}/N\mathbb{Z}$. To see that V is invertible (with all but negligible probability) in $\mathbb{Z}/p_i\mathbb{Z}$ for all i, define $F = \mathbb{Z}/p_i\mathbb{Z}$ (or, in the case that N is itself prime, define $F = \mathbb{Z}/N\mathbb{Z}$); then V is a matrix over F, where $|F|$ is exponential in λ. If we consider V instead as a matrix over the polynomial ring $F[x_{1,1}, \ldots, x_{1,c}, \ldots, x_{q+2,c}]$, then we can define its determinant to be the polynomial $D(\vec{x}_1, \ldots, \vec{x}_{q+2})$. By the definition of polynomial linear independence, the columns of V are linearly independent, so D is not the zero polynomial.

To consider the linear independence of the matrix over F, we must consider an assignment of concrete values $\vec{a}_1, \ldots, \vec{a}_{q+2}$ for the variables $\vec{x}_1, \ldots, \vec{x}_{q+2}$. To see that $D(\vec{a}_1, \ldots, \vec{a}_{q+2}) \neq 0$ with all but negligible probability — and thus the matrix V is invertible — consider $d = \max_{i=0}^{q}(d_i)$, where $d_0 = \deg(f)$ and $d_i = \deg(\rho_i)$ for all $\rho_i \in R$; then $\deg(D) \leq (q+1)d$. By the Schwartz-Zippel lemma, $\Pr[D(\vec{a}_1, \ldots, \vec{a}_{q+2}) = 0] \leq (q+1)d/|F|$ for $\vec{a}_1, \ldots, \vec{a}_{q+2} \xleftarrow{\$} F$. As $|F|$ is exponential in λ and both q and d are polynomial in λ, the probability is bounded by a negligible function in λ. $\qquad\square$

We then have the following corollary, which indicates when we can show that the original decisional assumption is implied by subgroup hiding.

Corollary 4.1. *The decisional uber-assumption parameterized by (c, R, S, T, f) holds with all but negligible probability if (1) subgroup hiding holds in $\mathbb{G}$ with* *respect to* $\mu = \{g_1, g_2\}$, *(2) parameter hiding holds with respect to* $R \cup \{f\}$, *(3)* $S = T = \langle 1 \rangle$, *and (4) the polynomials in* $R \cup \{f\}$ *are linearly independent.*

Proof. By requirements (1), (2), and (3), Theorem 4.2 tells us that the (c, R, S, T, f)-uber assumption is equivalent to the $(\ell c, R', S, T, f')$-uber-assumption. In this latter assumption, the adversary sees values with exponents of the form $\vec{y} = \vec{r} \cdot V$, where $\vec{r}$ is a random vector of length ℓ and V is the $\ell \times (q + 2)$ matrix defined in Equation 1. If we use $\ell = q + 2$, then by requirement (4), Lemma 4.1 tells us that V is invertible with all but negligible probability.

We can now use a bijection argument similar to the one in the proof of Theorem 3.1: $\vec{r}$ and $\vec{y}$ are both members of the set S containing all sets of size $q + 2$ over $\mathbb{Z}/N\mathbb{Z}$, so multiplication by V maps S to itself. As V is invertible, the map is invertible as well, and is thus a permutation over S. Sampling $\vec{r}$ uniformly at random and then multiplying by V thus yields a vector $\vec{y}$ that is distributed uniformly at random over $\mathbb{Z}/N\mathbb{Z}$.

An adversary $\mathcal{A}$ thus has no advantage in distinguishing between $\vec{y}$ and a uniformly random vector in S, as the distributions over the two are identical, and thus has no advantage in d-UBER$_{\ell c, R', S, T, f'}^{\mathcal{A}}(\lambda)$. □

As observed by Boneh, Boyen, and Goh, if f is not linearly independent from all polynomials in $R \cup T$, then the assumption becomes trivially false. It furthermore unnecessarily expands the size of the tuple to use polynomials in R or T that are linearly dependent, as, e.g., g^{2x} is redundant given g^x. We therefore believe that the requirement that the polynomials in $R \cup T \cup \{f\}$ be linearly independent is not restrictive, and in fact — to the best of our knowledge — it is satisfied by all existing instantiations of the uber-assumption.

As a concrete example, we finally examine the exponent q-SDH assumption, as introduced and used by Zhang et al. [45].

Example 4.1. For exponent q-SDH, $R = \langle 1, \alpha, \alpha^2, \ldots, \alpha^q \rangle$ and $f(\alpha) = \alpha^{q+1}$. Plugging these values into the matrix V gives a Vandermonde matrix, which is invertible. By Corollary 4.1, exponent q-SDH is thus implied by subgroup hiding, assuming parameter hiding holds with respect to the set $\{f_k(\alpha) = \alpha^k\}_{k=1}^{q+1}$ (which, given our discussion in Section 5, currently restricts us to composite-order groups).

4.3 A Second Approach: Computational Assumptions in the Source Group

Although our results in the previous section have potentially broad implications, the requirements for Theorem 4.2 — and in particular the requirement that $S = \langle 1 \rangle$ — are somewhat restrictive, as many q-type assumptions require meaningful functions on both sides of the pairing. We furthermore do not seem able to relax this requirement using our current proof strategy: briefly, the fact that we need subgroup hiding between both G_1 and $G_1 \times G_2$ and between $G_1 \times G_2$ and G_2 means that we cannot give out the subgroup generators h_1 and h_2 on the other side of the pairing. To get around this restriction and allow meaningful functions on both sides of the pairing, we now consider an alternate approach in which we require subgroup hiding only between G_1 and $G_1 \times G_2$, which allows us to give out h_1.

Theorem 4.3. *For a bilinear group* $\mathbb{G} = (N, G, H, G_T, e) \in [\mathsf{BilinearGen}(1^\lambda, 2)]$, *consider the computational uber-assumption parameterized by* c, $R = \langle 1, \rho_1(\vec{x})$, $\ldots, \rho_r(\vec{x}) \rangle$, S, T, *and* f. *Then, if subgroup hiding holds in* $\mathbb{G}$ *with respect to* $\mu = \{g_1, g_2, h_1\}$ *and parameter hiding holds with respect to* $R \cup \{f\}$, *this is implied by the following assumption for all* $\ell = poly(\lambda)$: *given*

$$(\mathbb{G}, u_1 g_2^{\sum_{i=1}^{\ell} r_i}, \{u_1^{\rho_k(\vec{x})} g_2^{\sum_{i=1}^{\ell} r_i \rho_k(\vec{x}_i)}\}_{k=1}^{r}, v_1^{S(x_1,\ldots,x_c)}, e(u_1, v_1)^{T(x_1,\ldots,x_c)})$$

for $\vec{x}, r_1, \vec{x}_1, \ldots, r_\ell, \vec{x}_\ell \xleftarrow{\$} \mathbb{Z}/N\mathbb{Z}$, *it is difficult to compute* $u_1^{f(\vec{x})} g_2^{\sum_{i=1}^{\ell} r_i f(\vec{x}_i)}$.

A proof of this theorem can be found in the full version of the paper. Intuitively, the starting point is the same as in our previous proofs: all elements exist only in the G_1 subgroup, operating over the original set of variables $\vec{x}$, and a shadow copy of these elements is added into the G_2 subgroup, which goes unnoticed by subgroup hiding. This shadow copy is then switched to operate over a new set of variables $\vec{x}_1$, which is identical by parameter hiding. Now, rather than attempt to move these new variables back into G_1, we simply repeat the process of adding and re-randomizing the original set of variables into the G_2 subgroup, until we end up with ℓ sets of variables there.

Once again, the usefulness of this theorem is revealed only when we examine what this more complex assumption provides. Interestingly, it is not clear how to show that the decisional assumption holds by a statistical argument, as the isolation of the $\vec{x}$ variables in the G_1 subgroup provides a potentially detectable distribution. Instead, we restrict our attention to computational assumptions in the source group, in which the adversary is required to compute $u_1^{f(\vec{x})} g_2^{\sum_{i=1}^{\ell} r_i f(\vec{x}_i)}$ rather than distinguish it from random. In this setting, we have the following corollary; as its proof is analogous to the proof of Corollary 4.1, we omit it here (but it can be found in the full version of the paper).

Corollary 4.2. *The computational uber-assumption parameterized by* (c, R, S, T, f) *holds in the source group with all but negligible probability if (1) subgroup hiding holds in* $\mathbb{G}$ *with respect to* $\mu = \{g_1, g_2, h_1\}$, *(2) parameter hiding holds with respect to* $R \cup \{f\}$, *(3) the polynomials in* $R \cup \{f\}$ *are linearly independent.*

To bring everything together, we examine the q-SDH assumption, as defined by Boneh and Boyen [5].

Example 4.2. The q-SDH assumption uses $R = \langle 1, \alpha, \ldots, \alpha^q \rangle$, $S = \langle 1, \alpha \rangle$, $T = \langle 1 \rangle$, and asks $\mathcal{A}$ to compute $(c, u^{\frac{1}{\alpha+c}})$. Using Theorem 4.3,[2] this is equivalent (under subgroup and parameter hiding) to an assumption in which $\mathcal{A}$ is

---

[2] Technically, this assumption doesn't meet the requirements of the theorem, as $\mathcal{A}$ produces a new value c rather than a function $f(\vec{x})$. The proof of the theorem can, however, be trivially extended to support assumptions of this type as well, as long as the group satisfies adaptive parameter hiding.

given $(u_1 g_2^{\sum_{i=1}^{q+2} r_i}, u_1^\alpha g_2^{\sum_{i=1}^{q+2} r_i \gamma_i}, \ldots, u_1^{\alpha^q} g_2^{\sum_{i=1}^{q+2} r_i \gamma_i^q}, v_1, v_1^\alpha)$, where $\gamma_1, \ldots, \gamma_{q+2} \xleftarrow{\$}$ $\mathbb{Z}/N\mathbb{Z}$, and is asked to compute $(c, u_1^{\frac{1}{\alpha+c}} g_2^{\sum_i \frac{r_i}{\gamma_i+c}})$. Applying the same analysis as above, we can ignore G_1 and focus on G_2, in which we use the matrix

$$A = \begin{bmatrix} 1 & \gamma_1 & \cdots & \gamma_1^q & \frac{1}{\gamma_1+c} \\ 1 & \gamma_2 & \cdots & \gamma_2^q & \frac{1}{\gamma_2+c} \\ \vdots & \vdots & \ddots & \vdots & \vdots \\ 1 & \gamma_\ell & \cdots & \gamma_\ell^q & \frac{1}{\gamma_\ell+c} \end{bmatrix}$$

Then, for its choice of c, $\mathcal{A}$ is given the first $q+1$ entries of $\vec{r} \cdot A$ and needs to compute the final entry. This matrix is invertible, so the same bijection argument as in Corollary 4.2 thus implies that $\mathcal{A}$ can produce the correct value with at most negligible probability, which implies (assuming parameter hiding holds with respect to $\{\rho_k(\alpha) = \alpha^k\}_{k=1}^q$) that q-SDH is implied by subgroup hiding.

5 Instantiating Our Results

Abstractly, our results provide quite a strong guarantee: as long as subgroup hiding and parameter hiding hold, many instantiations of the uber-assumption hold (as well as non-uber-assumptions, such as q-SDH), as they reduce to assumptions that hold by a statistical argument. Concretely, we need to examine which groups support these underlying assumptions.

Parameter Hiding. Our strongest requirement in our analysis was the generality of parameter hiding: to reason about any q-type assumption, we need a group where parameter hiding holds for all rational functions. While this seems hard to achieve in general, it does hold for any composite-order group (e.g., any group of order $N = p_1 p_2$ for primes p_1 and p_2), as the value of any exponent modulo p_1 is independent of its value modulo p_2.

Subgroup Hiding. In groups without a pairing — such as the target group of a bilinear tuple or a group over a non-pairing-friendly elliptic curve — subgroup decision is fairly straightforward. In groups with a pairing, however, the concerns mentioned in Section 2 (in which certain subgroup generators on the other side of the pairing could render subgroup decision easy) mean we have to be more careful. Our first approach in Section 4.2 relies on being unable to distinguish random elements of both G_1 and G_2 from $G_1 \times G_2$, even when given g_1 and g_2. This cannot hold, for example, in a symmetric bilinear group, so this assumption is reasonable only in the asymmetric setting. Our second approach in Section 4.3 requires that subgroup hiding holds even given h_1 and g_2, so it again requires an asymmetric pairing.

Instantiations. As mentioned above, our results in Sections 3 and 4 can be applied in any composite-order group where we can assume subgroup hiding.

Reasonable candidates for such a group include composite-order elliptic curve groups without efficient pairings, the target group of a composite-order bilinear group, or composite-order subgroups of finite fields.

In the case where we do have a pairing, we need an asymmetric composite-order bilinear group in order to make subgroup hiding a reasonable assumption. Although most composite-order bilinear groups are symmetric (as they are groups of points on supersingular curves), ordinary composite-order curves were first introduced by Boneh, Rubin, and Silverberg [11], and their applicability for cryptography — and in particular an examination of the nature of the resulting asymmetric composite-order bilinear group — was very recently explored by Meiklejohn and Shacham [37].

Applications. In asymmetric composite-order bilinear groups we can prove a wide range of constructions secure based on just subgroup hiding. For example, our examination of q-SDH means that the Boneh-Boyen signature, the Boneh-Boyen-Shacham group signature [7], and the attribute-based signature due to Maji et al. [36] can all be proved secure under subgroup hiding, and the fact that q-DHI [38] is also equivalent to subgroup hiding implies the Dodis-Yampolskiy VUF and the Jarecki-Liu PRF [25] can also both be proved secure based on subgroup hiding.

6   Conclusions and Open Problems

This paper demonstrated the applicability of the dual-system technique (and variants on it) by first proving the security of the Dodis-Yampolskiy PRF — using a domain of arbitrary size — under subgroup hiding, and then proving equivalence between many classes of the uber-assumption. This latter result further implies that many of these classes are in fact implied solely by subgroup hiding, as they reduce to assumptions that hold by a purely statistical argument. Our paper thus demonstrates that many common q-type assumptions — and the constructions that rely on them for security — can be implied directly by subgroup hiding when instantiated in the appropriate bilinear groups.

As our paper is a first step, many interesting directions and open problems remain. For example, we currently cannot prove anything about, e.g., decisional assumptions — such as q-DDHE — that require meaningful functions on both sides of the pairing. Perhaps the biggest open problem is obtaining more robust forms of parameter hiding in prime-order groups. Prime-order groups have the benefit of being significantly more efficient, and it is possible to construct groups with the appropriate subgroup hiding requirements using dual pairing vector spaces [39,40], as exemplified most recently by Lewko and Meiklejohn [27].

For parameter hiding in prime-order bilinear groups, however, it is currently known how to obtain parameter hiding only for linear functions. Papers that have focused on translating these structural properties into prime-order settings, however, have indicated that they focus on such simple functions to keep their "constructions...simple and tailored to the requirements that [they] need" [27], so we consider constructing parameter hiding for more robust functions in the prime-order setting an interesting open problem rather than an impossibility.

Acknowledgments. We thank Michael Naehrig for his valuable feedback, and the anonymous reviewers for their helpful suggestions.

References

1. Attrapadung, N., Libert, B.: Functional encryption for inner product: Achieving constant-size ciphertexts with adaptive security or support for negation. In: Nguyen, P.Q., Pointcheval, D. (eds.) PKC 2010. LNCS, vol. 6056, pp. 384–402. Springer, Heidelberg (2010)
2. Au, M.H., Susilo, W., Mu, Y.: Constant-size dynamic k-TAA. In: De Prisco, R., Yung, M. (eds.) SCN 2006. LNCS, vol. 4116, pp. 111–125. Springer, Heidelberg (2006)
3. Boldyreva, A.: Threshold signatures, multisignatures and blind signatures based on the gap-Diffie-Hellman-group signature scheme. In: Desmedt, Y.G. (ed.) PKC 2003. LNCS, vol. 2567, pp. 31–46. Springer, Heidelberg (2003)
4. Boneh, D., Boyen, X.: Secure identity based encryption without random oracles. In: Franklin, M. (ed.) CRYPTO 2004. LNCS, vol. 3152, pp. 443–459. Springer, Heidelberg (2004)
5. Boneh, D., Boyen, X.: Short signatures without random oracles. In: Cachin, C., Camenisch, J. (eds.) EUROCRYPT 2004. LNCS, vol. 3027, pp. 56–73. Springer, Heidelberg (2004)
6. Boneh, D., Boyen, X., Goh, E.-J.: Hierarchical identity based encryption with constant size ciphertext. In: Cramer, R. (ed.) EUROCRYPT 2005. LNCS, vol. 3494, pp. 440–456. Springer, Heidelberg (2005)
7. Boneh, D., Boyen, X., Shacham, H.: Short group signatures. In: Franklin, M. (ed.) CRYPTO 2004. LNCS, vol. 3152, pp. 41–55. Springer, Heidelberg (2004)
8. Boneh, D., Franklin, M.: Identity-based encryption from the Weil pairing. In: Kilian, J. (ed.) CRYPTO 2001. LNCS, vol. 2139, pp. 213–229. Springer, Heidelberg (2001)
9. Boneh, D., Goh, E.-J., Nissim, K.: Evaluating 2-DNF formulas on ciphertexts. In: Kilian, J. (ed.) TCC 2005. LNCS, vol. 3378, pp. 325–341. Springer, Heidelberg (2005)
10. Boneh, D., Lynn, B., Shacham, H.: Short signatures from the Weil pairing. In: Boyd, C. (ed.) ASIACRYPT 2001. LNCS, vol. 2248, pp. 514–532. Springer, Heidelberg (2001)
11. Boneh, D., Rubin, K., Silverberg, A.: Finding ordinary composite order elliptic curves using the Cocks-Pinch method. Journal of Number Theory 131(5), 832–841 (2011)
12. Boyen, X.: The uber-assumption family (invited talk). In: Galbraith, S.D., Paterson, K.G. (eds.) Pairing 2008. LNCS, vol. 5209, pp. 39–56. Springer, Heidelberg (2008)
13. Boyen, X., Waters, B.: Compact group signatures without random oracles. In: Vaudenay, S. (ed.) EUROCRYPT 2006. LNCS, vol. 4004, pp. 427–444. Springer, Heidelberg (2006)
14. Camenisch, J., Hohenberger, S., Lysyanskaya, A.: Compact e-cash. In: Cramer, R. (ed.) EUROCRYPT 2005. LNCS, vol. 3494, pp. 302–321. Springer, Heidelberg (2005)

15. Camenisch, J., Lysyanskaya, A., Meyerovich, M.: Endorsed e-cash. In: 2007 IEEE Symposium on Security and Privacy, pp. 101–115. IEEE Computer Society Press (May 2007)
16. Cheon, J.H.: Security analysis of the strong Diffie-Hellman problem. In: Vaudenay, S. (ed.) EUROCRYPT 2006. LNCS, vol. 4004, pp. 1–11. Springer, Heidelberg (2006)
17. Dodis, Y., Yampolskiy, A.: A verifiable random function with short proofs and keys. In: Vaudenay, S. (ed.) PKC 2005. LNCS, vol. 3386, pp. 416–431. Springer, Heidelberg (2005)
18. Gerbush, M., Lewko, A., O'Neill, A., Waters, B.: Dual form signatures: An approach for proving security from static assumptions. In: Wang, X., Sako, K. (eds.) ASIACRYPT 2012. LNCS, vol. 7658, pp. 25–42. Springer, Heidelberg (2012)
19. Goldreich, O., Goldwasser, S., Micali, S.: How to construct random functions. In: 25th FOCS, pp. 464–479. IEEE Computer Society Press (October 1984)
20. Groth, J.: Simulation-sound NIZK proofs for a practical language and constant size group signatures. In: Lai, X., Chen, K. (eds.) ASIACRYPT 2006. LNCS, vol. 4284, pp. 444–459. Springer, Heidelberg (2006)
21. Groth, J., Ostrovsky, R., Sahai, A.: Perfect non-interactive zero knowledge for NP. In: Vaudenay, S. (ed.) EUROCRYPT 2006. LNCS, vol. 4004, pp. 339–358. Springer, Heidelberg (2006)
22. Groth, J., Sahai, A.: Efficient non-interactive proof systems for bilinear groups. In: Smart, N.P. (ed.) EUROCRYPT 2008. LNCS, vol. 4965, pp. 415–432. Springer, Heidelberg (2008)
23. Jager, T., Rupp, A.: The semi-generic group model and applications to pairing-based cryptography. In: Abe, M. (ed.) ASIACRYPT 2010. LNCS, vol. 6477, pp. 539–556. Springer, Heidelberg (2010)
24. Jao, D., Yoshida, K.: Boneh-Boyen signatures and the strong Diffie-Hellman problem. In: Shacham, H., Waters, B. (eds.) Pairing 2009. LNCS, vol. 5671, pp. 1–16. Springer, Heidelberg (2009)
25. Jarecki, S., Liu, X.: Efficient oblivious pseudorandom function with applications to adaptive OT and secure computation of set intersection. In: Reingold, O. (ed.) TCC 2009. LNCS, vol. 5444, pp. 577–594. Springer, Heidelberg (2009)
26. Lee, M.Z., Dunn, A.M., Katz, J., Waters, B., Witchel, E.: Anon-pass: practical anonymous subscriptions. In: Proceedings of IEEE Symposium on Security and Privacy (2013)
27. Lewko, A., Meiklejohn, S.: A profitable sub-prime loan: Obtaining the advantages of composite-order in prime-order bilinear groups. Cryptology ePrint Archive, Report 2013/300 (2013), http://eprint.iacr.org/2013/300
28. Lewko, A.: Tools for simulating features of composite order bilinear groups in the prime order setting. In: Pointcheval, D., Johansson, T. (eds.) EUROCRYPT 2012. LNCS, vol. 7237, pp. 318–335. Springer, Heidelberg (2012)
29. Lewko, A., Okamoto, T., Sahai, A., Takashima, K., Waters, B.: Fully secure functional encryption: Attribute-based encryption and (hierarchical) inner product encryption. In: Gilbert, H. (ed.) EUROCRYPT 2010. LNCS, vol. 6110, pp. 62–91. Springer, Heidelberg (2010)
30. Lewko, A., Rouselakis, Y., Waters, B.: Achieving leakage resilience through dual system encryption. In: Ishai, Y. (ed.) TCC 2011. LNCS, vol. 6597, pp. 70–88. Springer, Heidelberg (2011)
31. Lewko, A., Waters, B.: New techniques for dual system encryption and fully secure HIBE with short ciphertexts. In: Micciancio, D. (ed.) TCC 2010. LNCS, vol. 5978, pp. 455–479. Springer, Heidelberg (2010)

32. Lewko, A., Waters, B.: Decentralizing attribute-based encryption. In: Paterson, K.G. (ed.) EUROCRYPT 2011. LNCS, vol. 6632, pp. 568–588. Springer, Heidelberg (2011)

33. Lewko, A., Waters, B.: Unbounded HIBE and attribute-based encryption. In: Paterson, K.G. (ed.) EUROCRYPT 2011. LNCS, vol. 6632, pp. 547–567. Springer, Heidelberg (2011)

34. Lewko, A., Waters, B.: New proof methods for attribute-based encryption: Achieving full security through selective techniques. In: Safavi-Naini, R., Canetti, R. (eds.) CRYPTO 2012. LNCS, vol. 7417, pp. 180–198. Springer, Heidelberg (2012)

35. Lu, S., Ostrovsky, R., Sahai, A., Shacham, H., Waters, B.: Sequential aggregate signatures and multisignatures without random oracles. In: Vaudenay, S. (ed.) EUROCRYPT 2006. LNCS, vol. 4004, pp. 465–485. Springer, Heidelberg (2006)

36. Maji, H.K., Prabhakaran, M., Rosulek, M.: Attribute-based signatures. In: Kiayias, A. (ed.) CT-RSA 2011. LNCS, vol. 6558, pp. 376–392. Springer, Heidelberg (2011)

37. Meiklejohn, S., Shacham, H.: New trapdoor projection maps for composite-order bilinear groups. Cryptology ePrint Archive, Report 2013/657 (2013), http://eprint.iacr.org/2013/657

38. Mitsunari, S., Saka, R., Kasahara, M.: A new traitor tracing. IEICE Transactions E85-A(2), 481–484 (2002)

39. Okamoto, T., Takashima, K.: Homomorphic encryption and signatures from vector decomposition. In: Galbraith, S.D., Paterson, K.G. (eds.) Pairing 2008. LNCS, vol. 5209, pp. 57–74. Springer, Heidelberg (2008)

40. Okamoto, T., Takashima, K.: Hierarchical predicate encryption for inner-products. In: Matsui, M. (ed.) ASIACRYPT 2009. LNCS, vol. 5912, pp. 214–231. Springer, Heidelberg (2009)

41. Okamoto, T., Takashima, K.: Fully secure functional encryption with general relations from the decisional linear assumption. In: Rabin, T. (ed.) CRYPTO 2010. LNCS, vol. 6223, pp. 191–208. Springer, Heidelberg (2010)

42. Ramanna, S.C., Chatterjee, S., Sarkar, P.: Variants of Waters' dual system primitives using asymmetric pairings. In: Fischlin, M., Buchmann, J., Manulis, M. (eds.) PKC 2012. LNCS, vol. 7293, pp. 298–315. Springer, Heidelberg (2012)

43. Shoup, V.: Lower bounds for discrete logarithms and related problems. In: Fumy, W. (ed.) EUROCRYPT 1997. LNCS, vol. 1233, pp. 256–266. Springer, Heidelberg (1997)

44. Waters, B.: Dual system encryption: Realizing fully secure IBE and HIBE under simple assumptions. In: Halevi, S. (ed.) CRYPTO 2009. LNCS, vol. 5677, pp. 619–636. Springer, Heidelberg (2009)

45. Zhang, F., Safavi-Naini, R., Susilo, W.: An efficient signature scheme from bilinear pairings and its applications. In: Bao, F., Deng, R., Zhou, J. (eds.) PKC 2004. LNCS, vol. 2947, pp. 277–290. Springer, Heidelberg (2004)

Distributed Point Functions
and Their Applications[*]

Niv Gilboa[1] and Yuval Ishai[2],[**]

[1] Dept. of Communication Systems Eng., Ben-Gurion University, Beer-Sheva, Israel
gilboan@bgu.ac.il
[2] Dept. of Computer Science, Technion, Haifa, Israel
yuvali@cs.technion.ac.il

Abstract. For $x, y \in \{0,1\}^*$, the point function $P_{x,y}$ is defined by $P_{x,y}(x) = y$ and $P_{x,y}(x') = 0^{|y|}$ for all $x' \neq x$. We introduce the notion of a *distributed point function* (DPF), which is a keyed function family F_k with the following property. Given x, y specifying a point function, one can efficiently generate a key pair (k_0, k_1) such that: (1) $F_{k_0} \oplus F_{k_1} = P_{x,y}$, and (2) each of k_0 and k_1 hides x and y. Our main result is an efficient construction of a DPF under the (minimal) assumption that a one-way function exists.

Distributed point functions have applications to private information retrieval (PIR) and related problems, as well as to worst-case to average-case reductions. Concretely, assuming the existence of a strong one-way function, we obtain the following applications.

- **Polylogarithmic 2-server binary PIR.** We present the first 2-server computational PIR protocol in which the length of each query is polylogarithmic in the database size n and the answers consist of a single bit each. This improves over the $2^{O(\sqrt{\log n})}$ query length of the protocol of Chor and Gilboa (STOC '97). Similarly, we get a polylogarithmic "PIR writing" scheme, allowing secure non-interactive updates of a database shared between two servers. Assuming just a standard one-way function, we get the first 2-server private keyword search protocol in which the query length is polynomial in the keyword size, the answers consist of a single bit, and there is no error probability. In all these protocols, the computational cost on the server side is comparable to applying a symmetric encryption scheme to the entire database.
- **Worst-case to average-case reductions.** We present the first worst-case to average-case reductions for PSPACE and EXPTIME complete languages that require only a constant number of oracle queries. These reductions complement a recent negative result of Watson (TOTC '12).

Keywords: Distributed point function, PIR, secure keyword search, worst-case to average-case reductions.

[*] Research received funding from the European Union's Tenth Framework Programme (FP10/2010-2016) under grant agreement no. 259426 ERC-CaC.
[**] Supported in part by ISF grant 1361/10 and BSF grant 2012378.

P.Q. Nguyen and E. Oswald (Eds.): EUROCRYPT 2014, LNCS 8441, pp. 640–658, 2014.

1 Introduction

For $x, y \in \{0,1\}^*$, the point function $P_{x,y}$ is defined by $P_{x,y}(x) = y$ and $P_{x,y}(x') = 0^{|y|}$ for all $x' \neq x$. Motivated by the goal of improving the efficiency of private information retrieval (PIR) [8,24] and related cryptographic primitives, we introduce and study the notion of a *distributed point function* (DPF). Informally speaking, a DPF is a representation of a point function $P_{x,y}$ by two keys k_0 and k_1. Each key individually hides x, y, but there is an efficient algorithm $Eval$ such that $Eval(k_0, x') \oplus Eval(k_1, x') = P_{x,y}(x')$ for every x'. Letting F_k denote the function $Eval(k, \cdot)$, the functions F_{k_0} and F_{k_1} can be viewed as an additive secret sharing of $P_{x,y}$.

A simple implementation of a DPF is to let k_0 specify the entire truth-table of a *random* function $F_{k_0} : \{0,1\}^{|x|} \to \{0,1\}^{|y|}$ and k_1 specify the truth-table of $F_{k_1} = F_{k_0} \oplus P_{x,y}$. Since each of k_0 and k_1 is random, this solution is perfectly secure. The problem with this solution is that the size of each key is exponential in the input size. Our main goal is to obtain a DPF with polynomial key size.

To demonstrate the usefulness of this new primitive, consider the goal of obtaining a 2-server secure keyword search protocol with low communication complexity. In such a protocol, two servers hold a large database $D = \{w_1, \dots, w_n\}$, where each w_i is an ℓ-bit keyword, and a user wishes to find whether $w \in D$ while hiding w from each server. Given a DPF scheme, the user creates keys (k_0, k_1) for the point function $P_{w,1}$ and sends one key to each server. Given a key k_b, $b \in \{0,1\}$, server b returns the answer bit $a_b = \bigoplus_{j=1}^n F_{k_b}(w_j)$. The user then computes $a_0 \oplus a_1$, which is equal to 1 if and only if $w \in D$. Essentially the same solution applies to 2-server PIR, where D is an n-bit database and the user wants to privately retrieve the i-th bit D_i.

The connection to PIR can be used to translate linear lower bounds on the communication complexity of 2-server PIR protocols with short answers [8,32] into an exponential lower bound of $2^{\Omega(|x|)}$ on the DPF key size if we require that each key hide x with information-theoretic security. However, this lower bound does not hold in the context of computational PIR (CPIR), where the security requirement is relaxed to computational security [7].

Based on the above discussion, we define a DPF to be a pair of PPT algorithms $(Gen, Eval)$, such that Gen receives x and y as input and creates the keys (k_0, k_1). In particular, the efficiency of Gen forces the key size to be polynomial in $|x| + |y|$. Each key individually must give no information in the computational sense on x, y. However, as described previously, $Eval(k_0, x') \oplus Eval(k_0, x') = P_{x,y}(x')$ for every x'.

Our Contribution. Our main result is establishing the feasibility of a DPF under the (minimal) assumption that a one-way function exists. Our construction uses a recursion that compresses the keys k_0 and k_1. The base scheme is the simple solution described above with each key of length $2^{|x|}|y|$. The recursion runs for $\lceil \log |x| \rceil$ steps. In each step of the recursion, the key is compressed to almost a square root of its former size. Random portions of the key are replaced with seeds for a pseudo-random generator (PRG) that can be expanded to longer strings that are pseudo-random. Carefully correlating the seeds in the two keys ensures that running $Eval$ on the two compressed keys and x' and then taking the XOR of the results still gives $P_{x,y}(x')$ as it does with the uncompressed keys.

Our construction looks quite attractive from a concrete efficiency point of view and may well give rise to the most practical solutions to date to PIR and related problems. The key size in our DPF is roughly $8\kappa \cdot |x|^{\log 3}$, where κ is the seed length of the underlying PRG and log is a base 2 logarithm. (This analytical bound is somewhat pessimistic; we present optimized key sizes for typical lengths of x in Table 1.)

Using the transformation described above, we get a 2-server CPIR protocol with query size equal to the DPF key size and a single bit answer from each server. The single bit answer feature is appealing in situations where the same user queries are used many times, say when the database is rapidly updated but the user's interests remain the same. We refer to a protocol that has this feature as *binary* CPIR.

Our protocol improves over the first CPIR protocol from [7], which implicitly relies on a DPF of super-polynomial complexity $|x|^{O(\sqrt{\log |x|})}$, and gives rise to the first polylogarithmic communication 2-server CPIR protocol based on (exponentially hard)[1] one-way functions, and the first *binary* polylogarithmic 2-server PIR protocol under any standard assumption.

In terms of computational cost on the server side, which typically forms the practical efficiency bottleneck in PIR, the computation of each server on a database of size n roughly corresponds to producing n pseudorandom bits.[2] (The computation on the client's side is negligible.) This is faster by orders of magnitude than the $\Omega(n)$ public-key operations required by known single-server CPIR protocols (cf. [24,29,10,25,17]).

Additional Applications. The above applications to 2-server PIR also apply to the related problem of private information storage [26] (aka "PIR writing"), where a client wants to non-interactively update entry i in a database D which is additively secret-shared between two servers without revealing i to each server. We get the first polylogarithmic solution to this problem (assuming exponentially strong OWFs). We note that single-server CPIR protocols or even stronger primitives such as fully homomorphic encryption [16] do not apply in this setting.

---

[1]   In this work we say that a one-way function is *exponentially hard* if it is hard to invert by circuits of size 2^{n^c}, for some $c > 0$. The proof of Theorem 5 shows that such a one-way function is necessary for the existence of binary 2-server CPIR protocols in which the query length is polylogarithmic in the database size n and security holds against $\text{poly}(n)$-time distinguishers. Alternatively, using the two-parameter definition of CPIR from [25] that limits the distinguisher to run in $\text{poly}(\kappa)$ time (independently of n), we get binary 2-server PIR with query length $\kappa \cdot \text{polylog}(n)$ assuming the existence of a standard one-way function.

[2]   A naive usage of a DPF requires a separate DPF evaluation for each nonzero entry of the database. In the full version we describe a method for amortizing this cost.

As the previous example demonstrates, DPF can be used to get qualitatively improvements over previous protocols for private keyword search [9,15,27]. Recall that in the two-server variant of this problem, two servers hold a set of words $\{w_1, \ldots, w_n\}$ and a user wishes to find out whether a word w is part of the set, while hiding w from each server. Previous solutions to this problem either make intensive use of public-key cryptography or alternatively involve data structures that have overhead in communication, round complexity, storage complexity, update cost, and error probability. Our protocol avoids all these disadvantages using only symmetric cryptography. It involves a single communication round, requires no data structures, has no error probability, and is the first private keyword search protocol we are aware of (under any standard assumption) that only requires one-bit answers. In more concrete terms, the query length of our protocol is $O(\kappa |w|^{\log 3})$ and the dominant computational cost involves a small number of PRG invocations (roughly corresponding to the DPF key size) for each keyword in the database. It can easily support database updates and be used in the streaming model of [27]. It can also be extended to support private keyword search with payloads, where the answer size of each server is equal to the size of the payload.

Finally, we present an application of DPFs to complexity theory. Assuming the existence of an exponentially hard one-way function, we get the first worst-case to average case reduction for PSPACE and EXPTIME languages which only makes $O(1)$ oracle calls. Concretely, we show a language L in PSPACE (or in EXPTIME) such that if an algorithm A decides L correctly on all but a δ fraction of the instances, then every language L' in PSPACE (or EXPTIME) admits a polynomial time oracle algorithm R such that R^A decides L' with good probability on *every* instance. The new feature of our reduction is that R makes only two calls to its oracle A. The best previous reductions required $\Omega(n/\log n)$ calls for inputs of length n [1,2]. A different version of the reduction applies to the case where A decides L correctly on all but a δ fraction of the instances, and on the other instances returns "don't know". In this case, R^A correctly decides any instance in L', with probability 1, while the expected number of calls to A is $O(1)$.

Alternatives and Related Work. In the information-theoretic setting for PIR, the best known 2-server protocol requires $O(n^{1/3})$ bits of communication [8]. However, in the case of *binary* 2-server PIR, the query size must be linear in n [8,32,3]. Much better protocols are known if there are 3 or more servers and security should only hold against a single server. The best known 3-server protocols [33,14,4] have queries of size $2^{O(\sqrt{\log n \cdot \log\log n})}$ and single-bit answers. Note that unlike our 2-server protocols, this communication complexity is super-polynomial in the bit-length of the user's input i. Polylogarithmic information-theoretic PIR protocols are known to exist only with $\Omega(\log n/\log\log n)$ servers [8]. A general technique from [5] can be used to convert a k-server binary PIR protocol with security against a single server into a k^t-server binary PIR protocol with security against t servers and comparable communication complexity. This technique can be applied to our 2-server protocol to yield t-private 2^t-server CPIR protocols with polylogarithmic communication.

While in this work we mainly focus on 2-server CPIR protocols, a better studied model for CPIR is the single-server model, introduced in [24]. Single-server protocols with polylogarithmic communication are known to exist under standard cryptographic assumptions [10,25,17,6].

Our two-server CPIR protocol has three main advantages over its single-server counterparts. First, as discussed above, our protocol is significantly more efficient in computation. Second, our protocol has single-bit answers, instead of answers that are at least the size of a security parameter (typically the ciphertext size in an underlying public-key encryption scheme). The third advantage is that our protocol relies on a much weaker cryptographic assumption, namely the existence of one-way functions. In contrast, single-server PIR protocols imply oblivious transfer [13], which in turn implies public-key encryption. We get even more significant advantages for the problems of private keyword search or PIR writing, where standard CPIR does not apply and alternative solutions have additional costs.

Organization. In Section 2 we present definitions and notation. Section 3 describes a construction for a distributed point function. Three applications of a distributed point function are presented in Section 4, a CPIR scheme in subsection 4.1, a scheme to privately retrieve information by keywords in subsection 4.2 and a worst case to average case reduction for EXPTIME and PSPACE languages in subsection 4.3. Finally, a proof that the existence of a DPF implies the existence of a one-way function appears in Section 6.

2   Definitions and Notation

Notation 1. *For $x, y \in \{0,1\}^*$, the* point function *$P_{x,y} : \{0,1\}^{|x|} \to \{0,1\}^{|y|}$ is defined by $P_{x,y}(x) = y$ and $P_{x,y}(x') = 0^{|y|}$ for all $x' \neq x$.*

Definition 1. *A* distributed point function *is a pair of PPT algorithms $DPF = (Gen, Eval)$ with the following syntax:*

- *$Gen(x, y)$, where $x, y \in \{0,1\}^*$, outputs a pair of keys (k_0, k_1). When y is omitted it is understood to be the single bit 1.*
- *$Eval(k, x', m)$, where $k, x' \in \{0,1\}^*$ and $m \in \mathbb{N}$, outputs $y' \in \{0,1\}^*$.*

DPF must satisfy the following correctness and secrecy requirements.
Correctness: *For all $x, x', y \in \{0,1\}^*$ such that $|x| = |x'|$*

$$Pr[(k_0, k_1) \leftarrow Gen(x, y) : Eval(k_0, x', |y|) \oplus Eval(k_1, x', |y|) = P_{x,y}(x')] = 1.$$

Secrecy: *For $x, y \in \{0,1\}^*$ and $b \in \{0,1\}$, let $D_{b,x,y}$ denote the probability distribution of k_b induced by $(k_0, k_1) \leftarrow Gen(x, y)$. There exists a PPT algorithm Sim such that the following distribution ensembles are computationally indistinguishable:*

1. *$\{Sim(b, |x|, |y|)\}_{b \in \{0,1\}, x, y \in \{0,1\}^*}$*
2. *$\{D_{b,x,y}\}_{b \in \{0,1\}, x, y \in \{0,1\}^*}$*

The above definition captures the intuitive security requirement that k_b reveals nothing except $b, |x|$, and $|y|$. We will also be interested in exponentially strong DPFs, which satisfy the stronger requirement that for some constant $c > 0$, the above two ensembles are $(2^{(|x|+|y|)^c}, 2^{-(|x|+|y|)^c})$-computationally indistinguishable.

Notation 2. *Let $\oplus$ denote bitwise exclusive-or and let $||$ denote concatenation of strings. We use $+$ to denote addition over a field or a vector space, as implied by the context.*

Notation 3. *Let $\mathbb{F}_{2^q}$ denote the finite field with 2^q elements and let $\mathbb{F}^n$ denote the vector space of dimension n over a field $\mathbb{F}$. The i-th unit vector of length n over $\mathbb{F}$ is denoted by e_i. The j-th element in a vector $v \in \mathbb{F}^n$ is denoted by $v[j]$.*

We sometimes view the input and output of *Gen* and *Eval* as elements of a finite field with an appropriate number of elements instead of as binary strings. The correctness requirement can be restated as $\Pr[(k_0, k_1) \leftarrow Gen(x, y) : Eval(k_0, x', |y|) + Eval(k_1, x', |y|) = P_{x,y}(x')] = 1$, with addition over $\mathbb{F}_{2^{|y|}}$.

3   Distributed Point Function

3.1   Initial Scheme

If we dispense with the requirement that *Gen* and *Eval* run in polynomial time then we can construct a fairly simple scheme for a DPF as follows. $Gen(x, y)$ outputs two keys k_0, k_1 such that $k_0, k_1 \in (\mathbb{F}_{2^{|y|}})^{2^{|x|}}$. Each key is regarded as a vector of length $2^{|x|}$ over the field $\mathbb{F}_{2^{|y|}}$ and is chosen randomly with the constraint that $k_0[x] + k_1[x] = y$, while $k_0[x'] + k_1[x'] = 0$, for all $x', x' \neq x$. $Eval(k, x', |y'|)$ returns $k[x']$ for every x'. Clearly, this scheme has both the correctness and secrecy properties required in a DPF.

The scheme we propose recursively compresses the keys k_0, k_1. Starting with the scheme above, which we denote $\text{DPF}_0 = (Gen_0, Eval_0)$, each recursion step compresses the length of the keys to slightly more than a square root of their length in the previous step. Repeating the process $\log |x|$ times results in polynomial length.

As an initial attempt towards constructing the next step, $\text{DPF}_1 = (Gen_1, Eval_1)$, we consider a simpler scheme $\text{DPF}_1^* = (Gen_1^*, Eval_1^*)$. The $2^{|x|}$ possible inputs x to the point function $P_{x,y}$ are arranged in a table with 2^m rows and 2^μ columns for some m, μ such that $m + \mu = |x|$. Each input x' is viewed as a pair $x' = (i', j')$, which represents the location of x' in the table.

Let $G : \{0,1\}^\kappa \longrightarrow \{0,1\}^{2^\mu |y|}$ be a pseudo-random generator. Let the representation of x as a pair be $x = (i, j)$. Gen_1^* first chooses uniformly at random and independently $2^m + 1$ seeds of length κ each, $s_1, \ldots, s_{i-1}, s_i^0, s_i^1, s_{i+1}, \ldots, s_{2^m}$. The output of Gen_1^* is a pair (k_0, k_1) defined by $k_0 = s_1, \ldots, s_{i-1}, s_i^0, s_{i+1}, \ldots, s_{2^m}$ and $k_1 = s_1, \ldots, s_{i-1}, s_i^1, s_{i+1}, \ldots, s_{2^m}$. Given input k, $x' = (i', j')$ and $|y'|$, the algorithm $Eval_1^*(k, x', |y'|)$ uses G to obtain $2^\mu \cdot |y|$ bits by computing $G(k[i'])$.

This expanded string is viewed as a vector of length 2^μ over $\mathbb{F}_{2^{|y'|}}$. $Eval_1^*$ $(k, x', |y'|)$ returns the j'-th entry of this vector, $G(k[i'])[j']$.

While DPF_1^* seems promising in terms of key length it is only partially correct. For each $x' = (i', j')$ such that $i' \neq i$, we have that:

$$Eval_1^*(k_0, x', |y'|) \oplus Eval_1^*(k_1, x', |y'|) = G(s_{i'})[j'] + G(s_{i'})[j'] = 0.$$

However, if $i' = i$, we have that

$$Eval_1^*(k_0, x', |y'|) \oplus Eval_1^*(k_1, x', |y'|) = G(s_i^0)[j'] + G(s_i^1)[j'],$$

and this value is wrong with overwhelming probability.

One possible approach to correct this deficiency of DPF_1^* is as follows. Associate each element in the vector space $\mathbb{F}_{2^{|y|}}^{2^\mu}$ with an element in the field $\mathbf{F}_{2^{|y|2^\mu}}$ in the natural way. Compute the element $CW \leftarrow (G(s_i^0) + G(s_i^1))^{-1} \cdot (ye_j)$ over $\mathbf{F}_{2^{|y|2^\mu}}$. Modify Gen_1^* by concatenating CW to both k_0 and k_1. Modify $Eval_1^*$ by computing $G(k[i']) \cdot CW$ over $\mathbf{F}_{2^{|y|2^\mu}}$, regarding the result as a vector over $\mathbb{F}_{2^{|y'|}}$ and returning the j'-th entry of this vector.

The actual approach we use in the next two algorithms, Gen_1 and $Eval_1$ is slightly more complex, involving two correction elements CW_0 and CW_1 instead of just one. This approach allows a recursion, further compressing the key size, which does not seem to be possible using a single CW.

In both Algorithm 1 implementing Gen_1 and Algorithm 2 we assume that $|y| \leq \kappa + 1$.

Algorithm 1. $Gen_1(x, y)$

1: Let $G : \{0,1\}^\kappa \longrightarrow \{0,1\}^{\kappa 2^{|x|/2}}$ be a pseudo-random generator.
2: **if** $(|y| \cdot 2^{|x|} \leq \kappa + 1)$ **then**
3:     Return $Gen_0(x, y)$.
4: Let $m \leftarrow \lceil \log((\frac{|y| \cdot 2^{|x|}}{\kappa + 1})^{1/2}) \rceil$ where κ is the length of the seeds.
5: $\mu \leftarrow \lceil \log((\frac{2^{|x|} \cdot (\kappa + 1)}{|y|})^{1/2}) \rceil$.
6: Choose $2^m + 1$ seeds $s_1, \ldots, s_i^0, s_i^1, \ldots, s_{2^m}$ randomly and independently from $\{0,1\}^\kappa$.
7: Choose 2^m random bits $t_1, \ldots, t_{2^m}$.
8: Let $t_i^0 \leftarrow t_i$ and $t_i^1 \leftarrow t_i \oplus 1$.
9: Choose two random vectors $r_0, r_1 \in \mathbb{F}_{2^{|y|}}^{2^\mu}$ such that $r_0 + r_1 = y \cdot e_j$.
10: Let $CW_b \leftarrow G(s_i^b) + r_b$, for $b = 0, 1$, with addition in $\mathbb{F}_{2^{|y|}}^{2^\mu}$.
11: Let $k_b \leftarrow s_1 || t_1, \ldots, s_i^b || t_i^b, \ldots, s_{2^m} || t_{2^m}, CW_0, CW_1$, for $b = 0, 1$.
12: Return (k_0, k_1).

We argue that DPF_1 is correct by looking at the following cases. If $(|y| \cdot 2^{|x|} \leq \kappa + 1)$ then Gen_1 executes Gen_0 and $Eval_1$ executes $Eval_0$ with correct results. Otherwise, if $i' \neq i$ then

---

Algorithm 2. $Eval_1(k, x', |y'|)$

1: Let $G : \{0,1\}^\kappa \longrightarrow \{0,1\}^{2^{x/2}\kappa}$ be a pseudo-random generator.
2: **if** $(|y'| \cdot 2^{|x'|} \le \kappa + 1)$ **then**
3:    Return $Eval_0(k, x', |y'|)$.
4: Let $m \leftarrow \lceil \log((\frac{|y'| \cdot 2^{|x'|}}{\kappa+1})^{1/2}) \rceil$ where κ is the length of the seeds.
5: $\mu \leftarrow \lceil \log((\frac{2^{|x'|} \cdot (\kappa+1)}{|y'|})^{1/2}) \rceil$.
6: Parse k as $k = s_1 || t_1, \ldots, s_{2m} || t_{2m}, CW_0, CW_1$.
7: Let the location of x' in the $2^m \times 2^\mu$ table be $x' = (i', j')$.
8: Let $v \leftarrow G(s_{i'}) + CW_{t_{i'}}$, with addition in $\mathbb{F}_{2^{|y|}}^{2^\mu}$.
9: Return $v[j']$.

$$Eval_1^*(k_0, x', |y'|) \oplus Eval_1^*(k_1, x', |y'|) \quad =$$
$$(G(s_{i'}) + CW_{t_{i'}})[j'] + (G(s_{i'}) + CW_{t_{i'}})[j'] = 0.$$

If $i' = i$ then

$$Eval_1^*(k_0, x', |y'|) \oplus Eval_1^*(k_1, x', |y'|) \quad =$$
$$(G(s_i^0) + CW_{t_i})[j'] + (G(s_i^1) + CW_{t_i \oplus 1})[j'] = r_0[j'] + r_1[j'].$$

By the choice of r_0 and r_1, if $j' \ne j$ then $Eval_1^*(k_0, x', |y'|) \oplus Eval_1^*(k_0, x', |y'|) = 0$, while if $j' = j$, i.e $x' = x$ then $Eval_1^*(k_0, x', |y'|) \oplus Eval_1^*(k_0, x', |y'|) = y$.

Intuitively speaking, DPF_1 is secret, because k_0 and k_1 are each pseudo-random. Note that the only parts of a key k_b which are not completely independent of the rest are s_i^b, CW_0 and CW_1. Together, these elements satisfy $CW_0 + CW_1 + G(s_i^b) + G(s_i^{1 \oplus b}) = y \cdot e_i$. However, since k_b does not include the seed $s_i^{1 \oplus b}$, the three elements s_i^b, CW_0 and CW_1 are polynomially indistinguishable from a random string.

If $|x|$ and $|y|$ are so small that $|y| \cdot 2^{|x|} \le (\kappa + 1)$ then Gen_1 has similar length output to Gen_0. Otherwise, the keys in DPF_1 are significantly smaller than the keys of DPF_0. Specifically, the total length of the seeds and additional bits (t_i) is $2^m(\kappa + 1)$. The total length of the correction words is $2 |y| \cdot 2^\mu$. The total length of a key is at most $6((\kappa + 1) |y| \cdot 2^{|x|})^{1/2}$, which is only about $6\kappa^{1/2}$ larger than a square root of the key size of DPF_0.

The computational complexity of Gen_1 and $Eval_1$ is proportional to the length of the keys and therefore slightly more than a square root of the complexity of the matching algorithms Gen_0 and $Eval_0$.

3.2 Full Scheme

While DPF_1 is a major improvement over DPF_0, the running time of Gen_1 (and that of $Eval_1$) is still exponential in $|x|$. Improving the scheme by repeating the compression step recursively requires the following two observations.

Gen_1 chooses r_0, r_1 randomly in line 9 so that $r_0, r_1 \in (\mathbb{F}_{2^{|y|}})^{2^\mu}$ and $r_0 + r_1 = y \cdot e_j$. Therefore, the pair (r_0, r_1) is distributed identically to the output of $Gen_0(j, y)$.

In addition, the keys k_0 and k_1 that Gen_1 creates have a list of seeds for G and associated bits. Specifically, k_b includes $\sigma_b \triangleq s_1 || t_1, \ldots, s_i^b || t_i^b, \ldots, s_{2^m} || t_{2^m}$ for $b = 0, 1$. Regarding σ_0 and σ_1 as vectors in $(\mathbb{F}_{2^{\kappa+1}})^{2^m}$ we have that $\sigma_0 + \sigma_1 = (s_i^0 || t_i^0 + s_i^1 || t_i^1) \cdot e_i$. If $s_i \triangleq s_i^0 \oplus s_i^1$ then $\sigma_0 + \sigma_1 = (s_i || 1) \cdot e_i$. Therefore, the pair (σ_0, σ_1) is distributed identically to the output of $Gen_0(i, s_i || 1)$.

The conclusion is that Gen_1 can be implemented by two calls to Gen_0. Similarly, we can define a pair of algorithms $Gen_\ell(x, y) = Gen(\ell, x, y)$ and $Eval_\ell(x, y) = Eval(\ell, x, y)$ by using recursive calls to $Gen_{\ell-1}(x, y)$ and $Eval_{\ell-1}(x, y)$. The scheme DPF_ℓ is defined as the pair of algorithms $Gen_{\ell-1}$ and $Eval_{\ell-1}$. Gen_ℓ is described in Algorithm 3 and $Eval_\ell$ is described in Algorithm 4. Setting $\ell = 1$ yields identical Gen_1 and $Eval_1$ algorithms to those defined in the previous sub-section.

In both the following algorithms, we assume that $|y| \leq \kappa + 1$.

Algorithm 3. $Gen_\ell(x, y)$

1: Let $G : \{0, 1\}^\kappa \longrightarrow \{0, 1\}^\alpha$ be a PRG (for α that will be determined in step 11).
2: **if** $(\ell = 0)$ or $(|y| \cdot 2^{|x|} \leq \kappa + 1)$ **then**
3:     Choose two random vectors $k_0, k_1 \in (\mathbb{F}_{2^{|y|}})^{2^{|x|}}$, such that $k_0 + k_1 = y \cdot e_x$.
4:     Return (k_0, k_1).
5: Let $m \leftarrow \lceil \log((\frac{|y| \cdot 2^{|x|}}{\kappa+1})^{1/2}) \rceil$.
6: Let $\mu \leftarrow |x| - m$.
7: Regard x as a pair $x = (i, j)$, $i \in \{0, 1\}^m, j \in \{0, 1\}^\mu$.
8: Choose a random κ-bit string s_i and let $t_i = 1$ be a bit.
9: Recursively compute $(\sigma_0, \sigma_1) \leftarrow Gen_{\ell-1}(i, s_i || t_i)$.
10: Let $s_i^0 || t_i^0 \leftarrow Eval_{\ell-1}(\sigma_0, i, \kappa + 1)$ and let $s_i^1 || t_i^1 \leftarrow Eval_{\ell-1}(\sigma_1, i, \kappa + 1)$.
11: Recursively compute $(r_0, r_1) \leftarrow Gen_{\ell-1}(j, y)$. Let $\alpha \leftarrow |r_0| (= |r_1|)$.
12: Let $CW_{t_i^b} \leftarrow G(s_i^b) + r_b$, for $b = 0, 1$, with addition in $\mathbb{F}_2^\alpha$.
13: Let $k_b \leftarrow \sigma_b || CW_0 || CW_1$, for $b = 0, 1$.
14: Return (k_0, k_1).

3.3 Analysis

We proceed to prove that $DPF_\ell = (Gen_\ell, Eval_\ell)$ is a distributed point function and analyze the complexity of Gen_ℓ and $Eval_\ell$. This analysis will determine the computational complexity of Gen_ℓ and $Eval_\ell$ and the size of the output of Gen_ℓ.

The reason to generalize DPF_1 to DPF_ℓ is to improve performance and specifically to obtain two algorithms Gen_ℓ and $Eval_\ell$ that run in polynomial time. Since Gen_ℓ outputs two keys (k_0, k_1), the length of the keys is a lower bound on its computational complexity. In the next proposition we provide an upper bound on the length of the output of Gen_ℓ.

Proposition 1. *For every $\kappa, \ell \in \mathbb{N}$ and every $x, y \in \{0, 1\}^*$, such that $|y| \leq \kappa + 1$, if (k_0, k_1) is a possible output of $Gen_\ell(x, y)$ then the length of k_0 and k_1 is at most $3^\ell (2^{|x|})^{\frac{1}{2^\ell}} \cdot (4(\kappa+1))^{\frac{2^\ell - 1}{2^\ell}} |y|^{\frac{1}{2^\ell}}$.*

Algorithm 4. $Eval_\ell(k, x', |y'|)$

1: Let $G : \{0,1\}^\kappa \longrightarrow \{0,1\}^\alpha$ be a PRG (for α that will be determined in step 7).
2: **if** $(\ell = 0)$ or $(|y'| \cdot 2^{|x'|} \le \kappa + 1)$ **then**
3:     Return $k[x']$.
4: Let $m \leftarrow \lceil \log((\frac{|y'| \cdot 2^{|x'|}}{\kappa+1})^{1/2}) \rceil$.
5: Let $\mu \leftarrow |x| - m$.
6: Regard x' as a pair $x' = (i', j'),\ i' \in \{0,1\}^m, j' \in \{0,1\}^\mu$.
7: Parse k as $k = \sigma || CW_0 || CW_1$. Let $\alpha \leftarrow |CW_0| (= |CW_1|)$.
8: Let $s_{i'} || t_{i'} \leftarrow Eval_{\ell-1}(\sigma, i', \kappa + 1)$.
9: Let $v \leftarrow G(s_{i'}) + CW_{t_{i'}}$, with addition in $\mathbb{F}_2^\alpha$.
10: Let $y' \leftarrow Eval_{\ell-1}(v, j', |y'|)$.
11: Return y'.

Proof. We prove the proposition by induction on ℓ. For $\ell = 0$, each key is chosen from $(\mathbb{F}_{2^{|v|}})^{2^{|x|}}$ and is therefore of length $2^{|x|} \cdot |y|$ which is exactly what is obtained by setting $\ell = 0$ in $3^\ell (|y| \, 2^{|x|})^{\frac{1}{2^\ell}} \cdot (4(\kappa+1))^{\frac{2^\ell-1}{2^\ell}}$.

For the induction step, let $\ell \ge 1$ and assume that the proposition is correct for $\ell - 1$. If $|y| \cdot 2^{|x|} \le \kappa + 1$ then Gen_ℓ runs the same algorithm as Gen_0 and the key size that Gen_ℓ outputs is $|y| \cdot 2^{|x|}$. Since $|y| \cdot 2^{|x|} \le \kappa + 1$, we deduce that $(|y| \cdot 2^{|x|})^{\frac{2^\ell-1}{2^\ell}} \le (4(\kappa+1))^{\frac{2^\ell-1}{2^\ell}}$ and therefore,

$$2^{|x|} \cdot |y| \le (2^{|x|})^{1/2^\ell} \cdot (4(\kappa+1))^{\frac{2^\ell-1}{2^\ell}} |y|^{1/2^\ell}.$$

If $|y| \cdot 2^{|x|} > \kappa + 1$ then Gen_ℓ outputs two keys k_0, k_1 such that $k_b = \sigma_b || CW_0 || CW_1$ for $b = 0, 1$. $Gen_\ell(x, y)$ computes σ_b by $(\sigma_0, \sigma_1) \leftarrow Gen_{\ell-1}(i, s_i || t_i)$. Since $i \in \{0,1\}^m$, the length of i is $\lceil \log(\frac{|y| \cdot 2^{|x|}}{\kappa+1})^{1/2} \rceil$. The length of $s_i || t_i$ is $\kappa + 1$. Therefore, by the induction hypothesis the length of σ_b is

$$3^{\ell-1} \cdot (2^{\lceil \log(\frac{|y| \cdot 2^{|x|}}{\kappa+1})^{1/2} \rceil})^{\frac{1}{2^{\ell-1}}} (4(\kappa+1))^{\frac{2^{\ell-1}-1}{2^{\ell-1}}} (\kappa+1)^{\frac{1}{2^{\ell-1}}} \le$$

$$3^{\ell-1} (2(\frac{|y| \cdot 2^{|x|}}{\kappa+1})^{1/2})^{\frac{1}{2^{\ell-1}}} 4^{\frac{2^{\ell-1}-1}{2^{\ell-1}}} (\kappa+1) =$$

$$3^{\ell-1} (|y| \cdot 2^{|x|})^{\frac{1}{2^\ell}} (4(\kappa+1))^{\frac{2^\ell-1}{2^\ell}}$$

CW_0 and CW_1 are the same length as r_0 and r_1. $Gen_\ell(x, y)$ computes r_0 and r_1 by $(r_0, r_1) \leftarrow Gen_{\ell-1}(j, y)$, where $j \in \{0,1\}^\mu$. The value of μ is set to $\mu \leftarrow \lceil \log(\frac{2^{|x|} \cdot (\kappa+1)}{|y|})^{1/2} \rceil$ and by the induction hypothesis, the length of each of

r_0 and r_1 is at most:

$$3^{\ell-1} \cdot (2^{\lceil \log(\frac{2^{|x|} \cdot (\kappa+1)}{|y|})^{1/2} \rceil}) 2^{\frac{1}{2^{\ell-1}}} (4(\kappa+1))^{\frac{2^{\ell-1}-1}{2^{\ell-1}}} |y|^{\frac{1}{2^{\ell-1}}} \le$$

$$3^{\ell-1}((\frac{4(\kappa+1) \cdot 2^{|x|}}{|y|})^{1/2}) 2^{\frac{1}{2^{\ell-1}}} 4^{\frac{2^{\ell-1}-1}{2^{\ell-1}}} |y|^{\frac{1}{2^{\ell-1}}} =$$

$$3^{\ell-1}(|y| \cdot 2^{|x|})^{\frac{1}{2^{\ell}}} (4(\kappa+1))^{\frac{2^{\ell}-1}{2^{\ell}}}$$

The length of k_b is the sum of the lengths of σ_b, CW_0 and CW_1, which is:

$$3 \cdot 3^{\ell-1}(|y| \cdot 2^{|x|})^{\frac{1}{2^{\ell}}} (4(\kappa+1))^{\frac{2^{\ell}-1}{2^{\ell}}} = 3^{\ell}(|y| \cdot 2^{|x|})^{\frac{1}{2^{\ell}}} (4(\kappa+1))^{\frac{2^{\ell}-1}{2^{\ell}}}.$$

□

Table 1 shows the length of a key k_b (either k_0 or k_1) for $|y| = 1$ and for some values of $|x|$ that are typical in applications of a distributed point function. The length of a key can be compared to the domain size, which is $2^{|x|}$. The leftmost column of the table shows the value of $|x|$. The next two columns show the depth of the recursion (ℓ) and the key size for after an actual execution of the algorithm that minimized the key size. The last two columns show the depth of the recursion and the key size as predicted by Proposition 1 for $\ell = \lceil \log |x| \rceil$.

Table 1. Key length in bytes for some values of $|x|$

$|x|$	ℓ (exact)	$\|k_b\|$ (exact)	ℓ (Prop. 1)	$\|k_b\|$ (Prop. 1)
20	2	1298	3	4513
40	4	5000	4	20003
80	5	18906	5	72941
160	6	61943	6	241256

Corollary 1. *In the special case of $y = 1$, by setting $\ell = \lceil \log |x| \rceil$ each key that Gen_ℓ outputs is of length at most $8(\kappa+1)|x|^{\log 3}$ bits.*

Proposition 2. *[Correctness] The scheme $DPF_\ell = (Gen_\ell, Eval_\ell)$ is correct as defined for a distributed point function, for every $\ell = 0, 1, \ldots$.*

The correctness claim for $DPF_\ell = (Gen_\ell, Eval_\ell)$ is proved using induction similarly to the correctness proof of $DPF_1 = (Gen_1, Eval_1)$.

The next step we take is analysis of the computational complexity of $Eval_\ell$ and Gen_ℓ. That complexity depends on the computational complexity of the PRG G.

Notation 4. *Since G is a PRG, it stretches a κ-bit seed s to an n-bit string $G(s)$ in polynomial time in n. Let $\gamma \ge 1$ be a constant such that computing $G(s)$ with additional $O(n)$ work can be done in time at most n^γ. We need γ as a* bound on the work that Gen_ℓ performs aside from its recursive calls. Therefore, it can be defined exactly such that n^γ is a bound on the work that $Gen_\ell(x, y)$ does in lines $1 - 10, 12$ and $14 - 16$, where n is the length of the output, i.e.

$$n = 2 \cdot 3^\ell (2^{|x|})^{\frac{1}{2^\ell}} \cdot (4(\kappa+1))^{\frac{2^\ell - 1}{2^\ell}} |y|.$$

Proposition 3. If $|y| \leq \kappa + 1$ then the computational complexity of $Eval_\ell(x, y)$ is at most $3^{\ell+1}[(2^{|x|})^{\frac{1}{2^\ell}} \cdot (4(\kappa+1))^{\frac{2^\ell-1}{2^\ell}} |y|^{\frac{1}{2^\ell}}]^\gamma$ for any $x \in \{0,1\}^*$ and $\ell \in \mathbb{N}$.

Proof Sketch. We prove the claim by induction on ℓ. For the base case, $\ell = 0$, the claim is obvious. For the induction step, the work that $Eval_\ell$ does can be divided into three parts. The first part is made up of the recursive call in line 8 to $Eval_{\ell-1}(\sigma, i', \kappa + 1)$, the second includes the recursive call in line 10 to $Eval_{\ell-1}(v, j', |y'|)$ and the third part of the algorithm is made up of all the operations apart from the two recursive calls. Most of the work in the third part is done in line 9, which includes an expansion of a seed by the PRG G.

By induction and the definition of γ, the computational complexity for each of the three parts is at most

$$3^\ell [(2^{|x|})^{\frac{1}{2^\ell}} \cdot (4(\kappa+1))^{\frac{2^\ell-1}{2^\ell}} |y|^{\frac{1}{2^\ell}}]^\gamma.$$

$\square$

Proposition 4. If $|y| \leq \kappa + 1$ then the computational complexity of $Gen_\ell(x, y)$ is at most $8 \cdot 3^{\ell+2}[(2^{|x|})^{\frac{1}{2^\ell}} \cdot (\kappa+1)]^\gamma$ any $x \in \{0,1\}^*$ and $\ell \in \mathbb{N}$.

The proof is omitted and will appear in a full version of the paper.

In the next part of the analysis we show that DPF_ℓ is secret. We do so by proving that each key k_b is pseudo-random and can therefore be simulated.

Notation 5. Let $L(Gen_\ell(x, y))$ denote the length of k_0 and k_1 induced by $(k_0, k_1) \leftarrow Gen_\ell(x, y)$. Let $T(Gen_\ell(x, y))$ denote the computational complexity of $Gen_\ell(x, y)$.

Notation 6. Let R denote the distribution induced on r_b and S denote the distribution induced on σ_b by the coin tosses of $Gen_\ell(x, y)$. Let U_n denote the uniform distribution on strings of length n and let $G(U_\kappa)$ denote the distribution induced by choosing a random string of length κ and extending it by G to $|r_b|$ bits.

Notation 7. Denote by K the distribution of the key k_b. Let $S||S'$ denote the distribution of $\sigma_b || s_i^{1-b}$. Let $CW^{(1)} \leftarrow G(s) + r_{1-b}$, where s is a uniformly random seed of length κ. Let $k_b^{(1)}$ be identical to k_b, except for replacing $CW_{t_i^{1-b}}$ by $CW^{(1)}$ and let $K^{(1)}$ denote the distribution induced by $k_b^{(1)}$. Let $CW^{(2)} \leftarrow u^{(2)} + r_{1-b}$, where $u^{(2)}$ is a uniformly random string of length $|r_{1-b}|$. Let $k_b^{(2)}$ be identical to $k_b^{(1)}$, except for replacing $CW^{(1)}$ by $CW^{(2)}$ and let $K^{(2)}$ denote the distribution induced by $k_b^{(2)}$. Let $CW^{(3)} \leftarrow G(s_i^b) + u^{(3)}$, where $u^{(3)}$ is a uniformly random string of length $|r_b|$. Let $k_b^{(3)}$ be identical to $k_b^{(2)}$, except for replacing $CW_{t_i^b}$ by $CW^{(3)}$ and let $K^{(3)}$ denote the distribution induced by $k_b^{(3)}$.

Proposition 5. *Let $\ell \in \mathbb{N}$, let $x \in \{0,1\}^*$ and let $G : \{0,1\}^\kappa \longrightarrow \{0,1\}^\alpha$ be a $T(\kappa), \varepsilon(\kappa)$-pseudo-random generator, for $\alpha = 4(\kappa + 1) \cdot 3^\ell(2^{|x|})^{\frac{1}{2^\ell}}$. Then, for $b = 0, 1$, the distribution K on the outputs k_b of $Gen_\ell(x,y)$ is $(T(\kappa) - T(Gen_\ell(x,y)), \frac{1}{2}(3^\ell - 1)\varepsilon(\kappa))$-computationally indistinguishable from $U_{L(Gen_\ell(x,y))}$.*

Proof Sketch: We use induction on ℓ to prove the statement. In the base of the induction, $\ell = 0$, the key k_b is distributed uniformly and therefore the claim is obvious. In the induction step, we use a hybrid argument on the ensembles induced from the distributions $K, K^{(1)}, K^{(2)}, K^{(3)}$ and $U_{|k_b|}$ when x ranges over $\{0,1\}^*$.

Proposition 6. *Let $x, y \in \{0,1\}^*$, let $\kappa = \max\{|x|, |y|\}$, let $\ell = \lceil \log|x| \rceil$ and let $G : \{0,1\}^\kappa \longrightarrow \{0,1\}^\alpha$ be a $T(\kappa), \varepsilon(\kappa)$-pseudo-random generator, for $\alpha = 4(\kappa + 1) \cdot 3^\ell(2^{|x|})^{\frac{1}{2^\ell}}$.*

1. *If G is a pseudo-random generator, i.e. $T(\kappa) \geq q(\kappa)$ and $\varepsilon(\kappa) \leq 1/q'(\kappa)$ for any two polynomials $q(\cdot), q'(\cdot)$ then $DPF_\ell = (Gen_\ell(x,y), Eval_\ell(x,y))$ satisfies the secrecy requirement for a distributed point function.*
2. *If G is an exponentially strong PRG G, i.e. $T(\kappa) = 2^{\kappa^c}$ and $\varepsilon(\kappa) = 2^{-\kappa^c}$ for some constant $c > 0$ then $DPF_\ell = (Gen_\ell(x,y), Eval_\ell(x,y))$ satisfies the exponential secrecy requirement for a distributed point function.*

Proof Sketch. For any polynomial $T'(\kappa)$ we have that $T(\kappa) = T'(\kappa) + T(Gen_\ell(x,y))$ is also a polynomial in κ. If G is a PRG, its output is $(T(\kappa), \varepsilon(\kappa))$-computationally indistinguishable from U_n for a negligible function $\varepsilon(\kappa)$. Setting $\varepsilon'(\kappa) = \frac{1}{2}(3^\ell - 1)\varepsilon(\kappa) \leq \frac{1}{2}(3|x|^{\log 3} - 1)\varepsilon(\kappa)$, we have by Proposition 5 that k_b, the output of $Gen_\ell(x,y)$, is $(T'(\kappa), \varepsilon'(\kappa))$-computationally indistinguishable from the uniform distribution, which satisfies the secrecy property. The exponential secrecy property is proved using a similar argument. □

Theorem 1. *The existence of a one-way function implies the existence of a DPF. If the one-way function is exponentially strong, so is the DPF.*

Proof. We show that the construction of $DPF_{\lceil \log|x| \rceil}$ is a DPF assuming the existence of a one-way function. By Proposition 2, DPF_ℓ is *correct* for any $\ell = 0, 1, \ldots$.

A series of works, beginning with [22] and currently culminating in [31] establish that the existence of one-way functions implies the existence of pseudorandom generators and furthermore that the existence of an exponentially hard one-way function implies the existence of an exponentially strong PRG.

Proposition 6 proves that given a security parameter $\kappa = \max\{|x|, |y|\}$, the scheme $DPF_{\lceil \log|x| \rceil}$ satisfies the secrecy requirement if G is a PRG and satisfies the exponential secrecy requirement if G is an exponentially strong PRG. Therefore, the existence of one-way functions implies that $DPF_{\lceil \log|x| \rceil}$ satisfies the secrecy requirement and the existence of an exponentially strong one-way function implies that $DPF_{\lceil \log|x| \rceil}$ satisfies the exponential secrecy requirement.

Propositions 4 and 3 prove that Gen_ℓ and $Eval_\ell$ are polynomial time algorithms for $\ell = \lceil \log|x| \rceil$. These results together satisfy Definition 1.

The converse of the first statement of Theorem 1, that DPF implies a one-way function is also true, see Theorem 5.

4   Applications

4.1   Computationally Private Information Retrieval

In the problem of private information retrieval (PIR) [8] a user wishes to retrieve the i-th bit of an n-bit string $z = (z_1, \ldots, z_n)$. This string, called the database, is held by several different non-colluding servers. The goal of the user is to obtain the bit z_i without revealing any information on i to any individual server. The index i can be hidden in an information-theoretical or computational sense, in which case the scheme is called a CPIR scheme. A formal definition of a two-server CPIR is as follows.

Definition 2. *A two-server CPIR protocol involves two servers S_0 and S_1, each holding the same n-bit database z, and a user. The protocol $\mathcal{P} = (Dom_Q, Dom_A, Q, A, M)$ consists of a query domain Dom_Q, an answer domain Dom_A, and three polynomial-time algorithms: a probabilistic query algorithm Q, an answering algorithm A and a reconstruction algorithm M. To retrieve z_i, the i-th bit of z, the user computes two queries $Q(n, i, r) = (q_0, q_1) \in (Dom_Q)^2$ using random coin tosses r. For each $b, b \in \{0, 1\}$, the server S_b receives q_b and computes an answer $a_b = A(b, z, q_b) \in Dom_A$. The user receives a_0 and a_1 and recovers z_i by applying the reconstruction algorithm $M(i, r, a_0, a_1)$. A two-server CPIR protocol must satisfy the following requirements:*

Correctness: *For every $n, n \in \mathbb{N}$, every $z \in \{0, 1\}^n$ and every $i \in \{1, \ldots, n\}$ and given a random string r*

$$Pr[(q_0, q_1) \leftarrow Q(n, i, r) : M(i, r, A(0, z, q_0), A(1, z, q_1)) = z_i] = 1.$$

Secrecy: *Let $D_{b, \lceil \log n \rceil, i}$, $b \in \{0, 1\}$, $n \in \mathbb{N}$ and $i \in \{1, \ldots, n\}$, denote the probability distribution on q_b induced by $(q_0, q_1) \leftarrow Q(n, i, r)$. There exists a PPT algorithm Sim such that the following distribution ensembles are computationally indistinguishable:*

1. *$\{Sim(b, \lceil \log n \rceil)\}_{b \in \{0,1\}, n \in \mathbb{N}}$*
2. *$\{D_{b, \lceil \log n \rceil, i}\}_{b \in \{0,1\}, n \in \mathbb{N}, i \in \{1, \ldots, n\}}$.*

The main measure of the efficiency of a PIR scheme is its communication complexity, which is the maximum number of bits exchanged between the user and servers over the choices of z, i and r. The query complexity is $\log |Dom_Q|$ and the answer complexity is $\log |Dom_A|$.

In the following theorem we show how to turn a DPF scheme into a two-server CPIR scheme.

Theorem 2. *Let* $DPF = (Gen, Eval)$ *be a distributed point function and let* $m(b, |x|, |y|) = \max\{|k_b| : b \in \{0, 1\}, (k_0, k_1) \leftarrow Gen(x, y)\}$. *There exists a CPIR scheme that for every* n *has query complexity* $m(b, \log n, 1)$, *answer complexity* 1 *and thus total communication complexity* $2m(b, \log n, 1) + 2$.

The full proof is omitted, but it relies on the procedure outlined in the introduction that involves computing $Eval(q_b, j, 1)$ separately for every $j = 1, \ldots, n$. The computational complexity of such a procedure is n times the computation required for a single invocation of $Eval$. Specifically, about $n \cdot |k_b|$ pseudo-random bits need to be computed. However, there is a more efficient alternative that for each node in the PRF tree rooted by k_b computes all of the node's children instead of a single one. This alternative results in computing less than $n + 2n^{1/2}$ pseudo-random bits.

By using the construction of $\mathrm{DPF}_{\lceil \log \log n \rceil}$ from Section 3, we get the following:

Corollary 2. *The existence of a one-way function* f *implies the existence of a two-server CPIR scheme with query complexity* $O(\kappa(\log n)^{\log 3})$ *and answer complexity* 1. *The term* $\kappa = \kappa(n)$ *is the length of a seed for a PRG* $G : \{0,1\}^{\kappa(n)} \rightarrow \{0,1\}^n$ *that is implied by* f *being a one-way function.*

4.2   Private Information Retrieval by Keywords

In the problem of Private Information Retrieval by Keywords [9,15] several servers hold a copy of the same set of n words, $w_1, \ldots, w_n$, of the same length ν. A user holds a word w and wishes to find out whether $w \in \{w_1, \ldots, w_n\}$ without providing information to any individual server on w.

Theorem 3. *The existence of a one-way function* f *implies the existence of a two-server scheme for private information retrieval by keywords with query length* $O(\kappa \nu^{\log 3})$ *and answer length* 1. *The term* $\kappa = \kappa(n)$ *is the length of a seed for a PRG* $G : \{0,1\}^{\kappa(n)} \rightarrow \{0,1\}^n$ *that is implied by* f *being a one-way function.*

Proof. The user generates two queries (q_0, q_1) by running $(q_0, q_1) \leftarrow Gen_{\lceil \log n \rceil}(w)$. Upon receiving a query q_b, the server S_b returns $a_b = \sum_{j=1}^{n} Eval(q_b, w_j) \bmod 2$ as its answer. The reconstruction algorithm M returns $a_0 + a_1 \bmod 2$. The correctness, secrecy and query length are proved in the same way as in Theorem 2.

The above protocol can be efficiently extended to the case where each keyword w_i has an associated nonzero payload p_i of length γ and the user should output p_i if w_i is in the database and output 0 otherwise. This is done by having each server respond with $a_b = \sum_{j=1}^{n} p_j \cdot Eval(q_b, w_j)$ where addition is in $\mathbb{F}_2^\gamma$. In the full version we will describe the application to PIR writing.

4.3   Worst-Case to Average-Case Reduction

A worst-case to average-case reduction transforms any average-case algorithm for one language L_2 into an algorithm that with good probability works on all inputs for another language L_1. We show how our scheme for a DPF translates into a worst-case to average-case reduction for languages in PSPACE and EXPTIME. Our result improves on known worst-case to average-case reductions for PSPACE and EXPTIME by requiring our worst-case algorithm to make only a constant number of queries to an average-case algorithm.

An interesting way to view our result is as a transformation of a heuristic algorithm to a worst-case algorithm. Given a heuristic algorithm A that correctly decides a certain language in PSPACE or EXPTIME on a $1 - \delta$ fraction of the inputs we show that for *any* language L in PSPACE or EXPTIME there exists an algorithm that decides L with good probability on *any* input and makes only two calls to the heuristic algorithm.

We complement a negative result from Theorem 3 of Watson's paper [30]. That theorem rules out a similar result where A is unbounded, thus applying to a reduction of "type 1" in his classification. We show that a reduction of "type 2" *is* possible (under standard assumptions), thus his negative result for type 1 reductions is tight.

We assume the existence of an exponentially hard one-way function. Given such a function there exists an exponentially strong PRG G [31].

Theorem 4. *Let $\delta < 1/2$ and assume the existence of an exponentially hard one-way function. Then,*

1. *There exist a language L_2 in EXPTIME (PSPACE) and a constant $c > 0$ such that if there is an algorithm A, which for any κ runs in time at most 2^{κ^c} and correctly decides a $1 - \delta$ fraction of the instances of $L_2 \cap \{0,1\}^\kappa$ then for any language L in EXPTIME (or PSPACE) there exists a probabilistic, polynomial time oracle algorithm R such that R^A decides any instance in $L \cap \{0,1\}^\kappa$ with error at most $2\delta + 2^{-\kappa^c}$ and with only two queries to A.*
2. *There exist a language L_2 in EXPTIME (PSPACE) and a constant $c > 0$ such that if there is an algorithm A running in time at most 2^{κ^c} that correctly decides a $1 - \delta$ fraction of the instances of $L_2 \cap \{0,1\}^\kappa$ and returns $\perp$ on any other instance then for any language L in EXPTIME (or PSPACE) there exists a probabilistic, polynomial time oracle algorithm R such that R^A decides any instance in $L \cap \{0,1\}^\kappa$ with only $1/(1 - 2\delta - 2^{-\kappa^c})$ expected queries to A.*

The proof is omitted and will appear in the full version of the paper

5   Efficient Implementation DPF with Large Output

Algorithms 3 and 4 assume that $|y| \leq \kappa + 1$. Given x and y, seeds must be chosen to be of length κ such that $|y| \leq \kappa + 1$. For concrete applications in which the length κ is given, a more efficient implementation is possible.

Let $DPF = (Gen, Eval)$ be a distributed point function for any $x \in \{0,1\}^*$ and any $y, |y| \leq \kappa + 1$. Define $DPF' = (Gen', Eval')$ on any $x, y \in \{0,1\}^*$ as follows. Let $G : \{0,1\}^\kappa \to \{0,1\}^{|y|}$ be a PRG. $Gen'(x,y)$ checks if y is the all-zero string. If it is, then $Gen'(x, y)$ executes $(k_0, k_1) \leftarrow Gen(x, 0^{\kappa+1})$, chooses a random element $r \in \mathbb{F}_{2^{|y|}}$ and outputs a key pair $(k'_0 = k_0 || r, k'_1 = k_1 || r)$. If y is not zero then $Gen'(x, y)$ chooses a random seed $s \in \{0, 1\}^\kappa$ and executes $(k_0, k_1) \leftarrow Gen(x, s)$. It then computes $r \leftarrow y \cdot (G(Eval(k_0, x, |y|)) + G(Eval(k_1, x, |y|)))^{-1}$ over $\mathbb{F}_{2^{|y|}}$ and outputs a key pair $(k'_0 = k_0 || r, k'_1 = k_1 || r)$.

$Eval'(k||r, x, |y'|)$ returns as its output $r \cdot G(Eval(k, x, |y'|))$ with computation over $\mathbb{F}_{2^{|y|}}$. The correctness is easy to verify and the secrecy of the DPF' follows from the secrecy of DPF and from G being a PRG.

6 DPF Implies OWF

In this section we show that the existence of a distributed point function implies the existence of a one-way function. As Theorem 2 proves, the existence of a DPF implies the existence of a binary two-server CPIR scheme with query length $o(n)$. We rely on the following lemma.

Lemma 1. *[19] Suppose there exist a pair of distribution ensembles $\{X_n\}_{n \in \mathbb{N}}$, $\{Y_n\}_{n \in \mathbb{N}}$ and a polynomial $p(\cdot)$ such that X_n and Y_n can be sampled in time polynomial in n; The statistical distance between X_n and Y_n is greater than $1/p(n)$ for all n, and X_n and Y_n are computationally indistinguishable. Then a one-way function exists.*

Theorem 5. *Suppose that there is a two-server CPIR protocol with query length $o(n)$ and binary answers. Then a one-way function exists.*

Proof. Denote the two servers by S_0, S_1 and define the following distribution ensembles:

- $X_n = (i, b, Q_b(n, i))$ where $i \in \{1, \dots, n\}$ is a random index, $b \in \{0, 1\}$ is a random server index, and $Q_b(n, i)$ is a random PIR query to server S_b on a database of size n and index i.
- $Y_n = (i, b, Q_b(n, i'))$ where $i' \in \{1, \dots, n\}$ is a random index picked independently of i.

The secrecy property of the PIR protocol implies that X_n and Y_n are indistinguishable. They are also efficiently samplable, since the query generation in the PIR protocol is efficient. It remains to show that they are statistically far.

Suppose towards contradiction that X_n, Y_n are $(1/n^2)$-close for infinitely many n. It follows that, for infinitely many n, there are no i, j, b such that $Q_b(n, i)$ and $Q_b(n, i')$ are more than 0.1-far. Thus, Q defines for infinitely many n an information-theoretic 2-server PIR protocol with statistical privacy error $\epsilon \leq 0.1$, sublinear-size queries, and binary answers. Such a protocol is known not to exist (see [32], Thm 8).

References

1. Beaver, D., Feigenbaum, J.: Hiding instances in multioracle queries. In: Choffrut, C., Lengauer, T. (eds.) STACS 1990. LNCS, vol. 415, pp. 37–48. Springer, Heidelberg (1990)

2. Babai, L., Fortnow, L., Nisan, N., Wigderson, A.: BPP has subexponential time simulations unless EXPTIME has publishable proofs. In: Proc. of the Sixth Annual Structure in Complexity Theory Conference, pp. 213–219 (1991)

3. Beigel, R., Fortnow, L., Gasarch, W.I.: A tight lower bound for restricted pir protocols. Computational Complexity 15(1), 82–91 (2006)

4. Beimel, A., Ishai, Y., Kushilevitz, E., Orlov, I.: Share Conversion and Private Information Retrieval. In: IEEE Conference on Computational Complexity 2012, pp. 258–268 (2012)

5. Barkol, O., Ishai, Y., Weinreb, E.: On Locally Decodable Codes, Self-Correctable Codes, and t-Private PIR. Algorithmica 58(4), 831–859 (2010)

6. Brakerski, Z., Vaikuntanathan, V.: Efficient Fully Homomorphic Encryption from (Standard) LWE. In: Proceedings of FOCS 2011, pp. 97–106 (2011)

7. Chor, B., Gilboa, N.: Computationally Private Information Retrieval. In: Proc. of the Twenty-Ninth Annual ACM Symposium on Theory of Computing (STOC 1997), pp. 304–313 (1997)

8. Chor, B., Goldreich, O., Kushilevitz, E., Sudan, M.: Private Information Retrieval. Journal of the ACM (JACM) 45(6), 965–981 (1998)

9. Chor, B., Gilboa, N., Naor, M.: Private information retrieval by keywords, TR CS0917, Dept. of Computer Science, Technion (1997)

10. Cachin, C., Micali, S., Stadler, M.: Computationally Private Information Retrieval with Polylogarithmic Communication. In: Stern, J. (ed.) EUROCRYPT 1999. LNCS, vol. 1592, pp. 402–414. Springer, Heidelberg (1999)

11. Desmedt, Y.: Society and Group Oriented Cryptography: A New Concept. In: Pomerance, C. (ed.) CRYPTO 1987. LNCS, vol. 293, pp. 120–127. Springer, Heidelberg (1988)

12. Desmedt, Y., Frankel, Y.: Threshold Cryptosystems. In: Brassard, G. (ed.) CRYPTO 1989. LNCS, vol. 435, pp. 307–315. Springer, Heidelberg (1990)

13. Di Crescenzo, G., Malkin, T., Ostrovsky, R.: Single Database Private Information Retrieval Implies Oblivious Transfer. In: Preneel, B. (ed.) EUROCRYPT 2000. LNCS, vol. 1807, pp. 122–138. Springer, Heidelberg (2000)

14. Efremenko, K.: 3-query locally decodable codes of subexponential length. In: Proc. of the 41st Annual ACM Symposium on Theory of Computing (STOC 2009), pp. 39–44 (2009)

15. Freedman, M.J., Ishai, Y., Pinkas, B., Reingold, O.: Keyword search and oblivious pseudorandom functions. In: Kilian, J. (ed.) TCC 2005. LNCS, vol. 3378, pp. 303–324. Springer, Heidelberg (2005)

16. Gentry, C.: Fully Homomorphic Encryption Using Ideal Lattices. In: Proc. of the 41st Annual ACM Symposium on Theory of Computing (STOC 2009), pp. 169–178 (2009)

17. Gentry, C., Ramzan, Z.: Single-Database Private Information Retrieval with Constant Communication Rate. In: Caires, L., Italiano, G.F., Monteiro, L., Palamidessi, C., Yung, M. (eds.) ICALP 2005. LNCS, vol. 3580, pp. 803–815. Springer, Heidelberg (2005)

18. Goldreich, O., Goldwasser, S., Micali, S.: How to construct random functions. Journal of the ACM (JACM) 33(4), 792–807 (1986)

19. Goldreich, O.: A Note on Computational Indistinguishability. Inf. Process. Lett. 34(6), 277–281 (1990)

20. Goldreich, O.: Foundations of Cryptography: Basic Tools. Cambridge University Press (2000)

21. Haitner, I., Harnik, D., Reingold, O.: Efficient pseudorandom generators from exponentially hard one-way functions. In: Bugliesi, M., Preneel, B., Sassone, V., Wegener, I. (eds.) ICALP 2006 Part II. LNCS, vol. 4052, pp. 228–239. Springer, Heidelberg (2006)

22. Hastad, J., Impagliazzo, R., Levin, L., Luby, M.: A Pseudorandom Generator from any One-way Function. SIAM J. Comput. 28(4), 1364–1396 (1999)

23. Holenstein, T.: Pseudorandom Generators from One-Way Functions: A Simple Construction for Any Hardness. In: Halevi, S., Rabin, T. (eds.) TCC 2006. LNCS, vol. 3876, pp. 443–461. Springer, Heidelberg (2006)

24. Kushilevitz, E., Ostrovsky, R.: Replication is NOT Needed: SINGLE Database, Computationally-Private Information Retrieval. In: Proc. of the 38th Symposium on Foundations of Computer Science (FOCS 1997), pp. 364–373 (1997)

25. Lipmaa, H.: An Oblivious Transfer Protocol with Log-Squared Communication. In: Zhou, J., López, J., Deng, R.H., Bao, F. (eds.) ISC 2005. LNCS, vol. 3650, pp. 314–328. Springer, Heidelberg (2005)

26. Ostrovsky, R., Shoup, V.: Private information storage. In: In Proceedings of the Twenty-Ninth Annual ACM Symposium on Theory of Computing, pp. 294–303. ACM (1997)

27. Ostrovsky, R., Skeith III, W.E.: Private Searching on Streaming Data. J. Cryptology 20(4), 397–430 (2007); Shoup, V.: Private information storage. In: Proceedings of the Twenty-Ninth Annual ACM Symposium on Theory of Computing, pp. 294–303. ACM (1997)

28. Shamir, A.: How to Share a Secret. CACM 22(11), 612–613 (1979)

29. Stern, J.P.: A New Efficient All-Or-Nothing Disclosure of Secrets Protocol. In: Ohta, K., Pei, D. (eds.) ASIACRYPT 1998. LNCS, vol. 1514, pp. 357–371. Springer, Heidelberg (1998)

30. Watson, T.: Relativized Worlds without Worst-Case to Average-Case Reductions for NP. Journal of ACM Transactions on Computation Theory (TOCT) 4(3), Article No. 8 (September 2012)

31. Vadhan, S., Zheng, C.: Characterizing pseudoentropy and simplifying pseudorandom generator constructions. In: Proc. of the 44th Annual ACM Symposium on the Theory of Computing (STOC 2012), pp. 817–836 (2012)

32. Wehner, S., de Wolf, R.: Improved Lower Bounds for Locally Decodable Codes and Private Information Retrieval. In: Caires, L., Italiano, G.F., Monteiro, L., Palamidessi, C., Yung, M. (eds.) ICALP 2005. LNCS, vol. 3580, pp. 1424–1436. Springer, Heidelberg (2005)

33. Yekhanin, S.: Towards 3-query locally decodable codes of subexponential length. In: Proc. of the 39th Annual ACM Symposium on Theory of Computing (STOC 2007), pp. 266–274 (2007)

A Full Characterization of Completeness for Two-Party Randomized Function Evaluation

Daniel Kraschewski[1], Hemanta K. Maji[2],
Manoj Prabhakaran[3], and Amit Sahai[4]

[1] Technion, Haifa, Israel
[2] Los Angeles, USA
[3] Univ. of Illinois, Urbana-Champaign, USA
[4] Univ. of California, Los Angeles, USA

Abstract. We settle a long standing open problem which has pursued a full characterization of completeness of (potentially randomized) finite functions for 2-party computation that is secure against active adversaries. Since the first such complete function was discovered [Kilian, FOCS 1988], the question of which finite 2-party functions are complete has been studied extensively, leading to characterization in many special cases. In this work, we completely settle this problem.

We provide a polynomial time algorithm to test whether a 2-party finite secure function evaluation (SFE) functionality (possibly randomized) is complete or not. The main tools in our solution include:

- A formal linear algebraic notion of *redundancy* in a general 2-party randomized function.
- A notion of *statistically testable games*. A kind of interactive proof in the information-theoretic setting where *both* parties are computationally unbounded but differ in their knowledge of a secret.
- An extension of the (weak) *converse of Shannon's channel coding theorem*, where an adversary can adaptively choose the channel based on its view.

We show that any function f, if complete, can implement any (randomized) circuit C using only $O(|C| + \kappa)$ calls to f, where κ is the statistical security parameter. In particular, for any two-party functionality g, this establishes a universal notion of its quantitative "cryptographic complexity" independent of the setup and has close connections to circuit complexity.

1 Introduction

Understanding the *complexity* of functions is central to theoretical computer science. While the most studied notion of complexity in this literature is that of computational complexity, there have also been other important aspects explored, most notably, *communication complexity* [35]. Another aspect of complexity of a (distributed) function is its *cryptographic complexity*, which seeks to understand the cryptographic utility of a function, stemming from how it hides and reveals information. While it is only recently that the term has been

P.Q. Nguyen and E. Oswald (Eds.): EUROCRYPT 2014, LNCS 8441, pp. 659–676, 2014.

explicitly used, cryptographic complexity theory has been vigorously pursued at least since Kilian introduced the notion of *completeness* of cryptographic primitives [23].

Completeness (of functions with finite domains) has been the first and most important question of cryptographic complexity: what properties of a function let all other cryptographic tasks (in the context of secure computation) be *reduced* to it. This question has been asked and answered several times [23,11,24,25,12,28,31] each time for a different class of functions, or restricted to different kinds of reductions (see Fig. 1 for a summary of the state of the art). These works produced several exciting ideas and advances, and brought together concepts from different fields. For instance, [25] used the Nash equilibrium in a zero-sum game defined using the function to obtain a secure protocol; earlier [11] identified the binary symmetric channel (noisy channel) as a complete function, paving the way to a fruitful and successful connection with information-theory literature.

However, these works left open what is arguably the hardest part of the characterization: completeness of *randomized* functions with finite domain under reductions that are secure against an *active* adversary (see Fig. 1). Indeed, even with a (usually simplifying) restriction that only one of the two parties receives an output from the function, it was not known which *randomized* functions are complete. In this work, we finally provide a full characterization of completeness of general[1] 2-party functions with finite domains. This work brings to close this rich line of investigation, but also introduces several new ideas and notions, and poses new questions regarding cryptographic complexity.

Prior to our work, the only completeness results known for randomized functions against active adversaries were for the very restricted case of channels [12], *i.e.* randomized functions that *only take input from one party*, and deliver the output to the other. Thus, in particular, before our work, no completeness characterization results against active adversaries were known for any randomized function classes that take input from both parties.

Also, along the way to our main construction, we generalize a result in another line of work, on black-box protocol constructions [20,19,22,9]. We give a black-box transformation from a passive-secure OT protocol *in a hybrid setting* (wherein the protocol has access to an ideal functionality) to a UC-secure OT protocol in the same hybrid setting, with access to the commitment functionality.[2] Our transformation relativizes with respect to any ideal functionality, as long as that functionality is "redundancy free" (see later). Though our focus is on information-theoretic security, we note that by considering ideal

---

[1] By a general function, we mean one without any restrictions on which parties have inputs and which parties have outputs. Earlier work on characterizing randomized functions considered only "symmetric" (both parties get same output) and "asymmetric" (only one party gets any output) functions. Beyond this, only specific examples were known, like correlated random variables considered by Beaver [1].

[2] It is interesting to note that, unlike in many other settings, a black-box transformation in the plain model does not imply a transformation in a hybrid model. That is, there is no analogue of universal composition for *black-box protocol compilation*.

functionalities that are *not* information-theoretically complete, our transformation implies black-box equivalence of related *computational assumptions*.

	Passive Completeness	Active Completeness
Deterministic	Symmetric: [24]-1991 Asymmetric: [3]-1999 General: [28]-2011	Symmetric: [24]-1991 Asymmetric: [25]-2000 General: [28]-2011
Randomized	Symmetric: [25]-2000 Asymmetric: [25]-2000 General: [31]-2012	Channels: [12]-2004 Symmetric/Asymmetric/General: **Open** *Settled in this paper*

Fig. 1. Summary of Completeness Characterization Results

Finally, our tools for analysis are novel in this line of work. In particular, we introduce the notion of **statistically testable games**, which is a kind of interactive proof in the information-theoretic setting where *both* parties can be computationally unbounded, but differ in their knowledge of some secret. We discuss these in more detail in Section 1.3 and in subsequent sections.

We also formulate and prove a new converse of Shannon's Channel Coding theorem to obtain a hiding property from a "channel." This is perhaps an unusual (but in hindsight, natural) use of a converse of the channel coding theorem, which was originally used to establish the optimality of the channel coding theorem.

1.1 Our Results

We provide the first *algorithmic* characterization of all finite 2-party (potentially randomized) functions that are complete for secure function evaluation against active adversaries: Namely, our results provide the first explicit algorithm (see Fig. 2 for an abridged version; the full figure is provided in the full version of the paper [27]) that can analyze any given (randomized) function f, and output whether or not f is complete against active adversaries.

The algorithm has two steps: finding what we call the "*core*" of a given function f and then checking if it is "*simple*" or not. A function f is complete if and only if its core is not simple.

Input: A 2-party randomized SFE f, given as a matrix $\mathfrak{P}^f$ of conditional probabilities $\mathfrak{p}^f[w, z | x, y]$.
Output: Whether f is UC-complete or not.
  1. Compute a core $\widehat{f}$ of f.
  2. Check if $\widehat{f}$ is simple or not (using combinatorial characterization in [31]).
  3. If $\widehat{f}$ is simple, then f is not complete.
  4. Else (i.e., $\widehat{f}$ is not simple), f is complete.

Fig. 2. This algorithm tests whether a function f is UC-complete or not. More detailed version is provided in [27].

We now provide a high-level intuitive explanation of our algorithmic characterization works, by considering some easy and well-known examples. This will help in understanding our exact characterization, which is somewhat more involved since it covers general randomized functions.

The *core* of f is computed by removing "redundant" parts of the function f. To develop some intuition for this, consider the one-sided OR function which takes two bits from Alice and Bob and outputs the logical OR of these two bits to only Bob. This function is *not* complete against active adversaries, and in fact is trivial: the reason is that a corrupt Bob can always choose his input to be "0" – and by doing so, it can always learn Alice's input, without Alice detecting this. (Thus, even a trivial protocol in which Alice sends her bit to Bob is indeed secure against active adversaries, since if Bob is corrupt, he could have learned Alice's input even in the ideal world.) Because of this, we say that Bob's input "1" is redundant from the adversary's point of view: the adversary is always better off using the input "0".

When extended to the setting of randomized functions, redundancy becomes more subtle. For instance, an input can become redundant because instead of using that input, an adversary could use a *distribution* over other inputs, without being detected. Another form of redundancy that appears for randomized functions is that of redundant outputs (for the same input). As an example, suppose in the above example, when Bob's input is 0, if Alice's input is 0 then he receives 0, but if her input is 1, he receives the output symbol α with probability $3/4$ and the symbol β with probability $1/4$. Here, we observe that the two outcomes α and β give Bob the same information about Alice's input, and could be merged into a single outcome. More generally, if two possible outputs that the adversary can obtain for the same input have identical conditional distributions for the other party's input-output pair, then the distinction between these two output values is redundant.

We provide a novel formal definition of redundancy that fully captures both these forms of redundancy: (1) it identifies inputs that are useless for the adversary; and (2) it identifies if the output can be compressed to remove aspects of the output that are useless for the adversary's goal of gaining information about the honest party's inputs. While the above intuition is useful, it is not exactly the motivation behind our formal definition. The formal definition balances the following two requirements on redundancy:

- Adding or removing redundancy does not change a function's complexity (as far as security against active corruption alone is concerned): in particular, f is complete if and only if its core is complete.
- A redundancy free function removes the possibility for a party to freely deviate from its interaction with a functionality without the rest of the system (the environment and the other party) detecting any difference.

The formal definition (based on Equation 1) is linear algebraic, inspired by simulatability considerations, and seemingly more general; but as will be discussed in Section 1.3 and later, this definition coincides with exactly the above two forms of redundancies. An explicit algorithm for removing redundancy and finding the "core" is given in the full version of the paper [27].

The second phase of our algorithm determines whether the core of f is *simple*, a notion defined earlier by [31] generalizing Kilian's condition for passive completeness [25]. Informally, a function g is simple if it preserves the independence of views. To develop intuition for this, consider a common randomness function that ignores the inputs of the two parties and simply outputs a uniform independent random bit to both parties. This function is intuitively useless because, at least in the passive-security setting, this function can be trivially realized by one party sampling this bit, and sending it to the other party. The formal notion of a simple function generalizes this to arbitrary randomized functions, by ensuring that if the parties start with independent inputs, then conditioned on the "common information" present after function evaluation, the views of the two players remain independent of each other (see the full version [27] for details). A natural explicit algorithm for determining whether a function is simple was already given by [31], which we use here.

Beyond the basic feasibility result, we also show that secure evaluation of any finite function g to a complete finite function f can be carried out, asymptotically, at "constant rate." That is, n copies of g can be evaluated with access to $O(n + \kappa)$ copies of f, and in fact, only $O(n + \kappa)$ communication, overall. Here κ is a statistical security parameter; that is, the error in security (simulation error) is negligible in κ. In fact, the total amount of communication in the protocol (including the interaction with copies of f) is also bounded by $O(n + \kappa)$. This leads to our main theorem:

Theorem 1. *A finite 2-party function is UC-complete (or equivalently, standalone-complete) against active adversaries if and only if its core is not simple. Further, if f is such a function, n copies of any finite 2-party function can be securely evaluated by a protocol in f-hybrid with communication complexity $O(n + \kappa)$, where κ is the security parameter.*

Connections to Circuit Complexity. An interesting measure of complexity of a function g (modeled as a 2-party function) is its "OT complexity" – the number of (1 out of 2, bit) OT instances needed for securely evaluating it.[3] As sketched below, the OT complexity of a function is closely related to its circuit complexity and may provide an approach to proving explicit circuit lowerbounds. Our results show that instead of OT complexity, one could consider f-complexity, for any f whose core is not simple. *This establishes "cryptographic complexity" as a fundamental complexity measure of (2-party) functions, independent of which complete finite 2-party function is used to securely realize it, just the same way circuit complexity is independent of which specific set of universal finite gates are used to implement it.*

Circuit complexity and OT complexity are closely related to each other as follows. By a simple protocol due to [16,17,18], we know that the OT complexity

---

[3] One may also define OT complexity to be the total amount of communication (possibly amortized) needed for securely evaluating g, in the OT-hybrid model.

of a function g (defined with respect to passive security) is $O(C(g))$, where $C(g)$ stands for the circuit complexity of g. This means that a super-linear lowerbound for OT complexity of g gives a super-linear lowerbound on $C(g)$. Of course, this only shows that it is a hard problem to lowerbound OT complexity. But interestingly, this connection does open up a new direction of approaching circuit complexity lowerbounds: the fact that most functions have exponential circuit complexity is an easy consequence of a counting argument due to Shannon; but *for OT complexity, even such an existential lowerbound is not known.* Resolving this could be an easier problem than finding explicit circuit lowerbounds, yet could lead to new insights to proving explicit OT complexity and circuit complexity lowerbounds.

The same argument applies for OT complexity defined with respect to active adversaries as well, due to the result of [22]. Note that it would be easier to lowerbound OT complexity when it is defined this way, than when defined with respect to passive adversaries. The relevance of our result is that instead of OT, one can consider any 2-party function f whose core is not simple. As we show that OT can be reduced to any such function at a constant rate, a super-linear lowerbound on (amortized) f-complexity will indeed translate to a super-linear lowerbound on circuit complexity. We discuss this more in the full version of our paper [27] and leave it as an important direction to study. Recently Beimel et al. [2] have shown that the OT-complexity of random functions is significantly lower than their (AND) circuit complexity, but still exponential in the input length, in the worst case.

1.2 Related Work

We briefly summarize the results on completeness from prior work (also refer to Fig. 1). The function oblivious transfer (OT) was identified independently by Wiesner and Rabin [32,34]. Brassard et al. [5] showed that various flavors of OT can be reduced to each other with respect to security against active adversaries. In a seminal work, Kilian identified OT as the first active-complete function [23]. Prior to this Goldreich and Vainish, and independently Micali and Haber, showed that OT is passive-complete [18,17]. Crépeau and Kilian then showed that the noisy channel is also active-complete [11]. The first characterization of completeness appeared in [24] where it was shown that among deterministic "symmetric" functions (in which both parties get the same output) a function f is active-complete if and only if there is an "OR minor" in the matrix representing f. Beimel, Malkin and Micali showed that among "asymmetric" functions (in which only one party gets the output), a function is passive-complete if and only if it is not "trivial" [3]. ([3] also concerned itself with the computational setting and asked cryptographic complexity questions regarding computational assumptions.) Kilian vastly generalized this by giving several completeness characterizations: active-complete deterministic asymmetric functions, passive-complete symmetric functions and passive-complete asymmetric functions [25]. Kilian's result for active-completeness was extended in two different directions by subsequent work: Crépeau, Morozov and Wolf [12] considered "channel functions" which are randomized asymmetric functions (only one party has output), but with the additional restriction that only one party has input; Kraschewski and Müller-Quade [28] considered functions in which both parties can have inputs and outputs, but restricted to deterministic functions.

Kilian's result for passive-completeness was extended to all functions in a recent work [31], which also presented a unification of all the prior characterizations and posed the question of completing the characterization. The full characterization we obtain matches the unified conjecture from [31].

A related, but different line of work investigated secure computability and completeness for *multi-party* computation (with more than 2 parties) (e.g., [8,4,33,29,26,14,13]). We restrict ourselves to 2-party functions in this work. Another direction of research considers whether a short protocol for f (instead of a black-box implementing f) is complete or not [30].

1.3   Technical Overview

An important ingredient of our result is a combinatorial/linear-algebraic characterization of "redundancy" in a general 2-party function. The importance of redundancy is two fold:

– Any function f is "equivalent" (or *weakly isomorphic*, as defined in [31]) to a "core" function $\hat{f}$ which is redundancy free, so that f is complete against active adversaries if and only if $\hat{f}$ is. Thus it is enough to characterize completeness for redundancy free functions.
– Our various protocols rely on being given access to a redundancy free function. Redundancy makes it possible for an adversary to deviate from a prescribed interaction with a function without any chance of being detected. Thus the statistical checks used to enforce that the adversary does not deviate from its behavior crucially rely on the protocol using only redundancy free functions.

While redundancy of special classes of 2-party functions have appeared in the literature previously, it turns out that for general 2-party functions, the nature of redundancy is significantly more intricate. Recall that we discussed redundancy informally by considering an adversary that tries to learn about the other party's input-output pair: any input it can avoid, and distinction between outputs (for the same input) that provide it with identical information are both redundant. However, the role of redundancy in showing completeness is somewhat different: redundancy in a function makes it hard (if not impossible) to use it in a protocol, as it allows an active adversary to *deviate* from behavior prescribed by a protocol, with no chance of being caught. Possible deviation includes replacing its prescribed input to the function by a probabilistically chosen input, *and* probabilistically altering the output it receives from the function before using it in the protocol, *at the same time*. The goal of this deviation is to minimize detectability by the other party (and the environment). Our formal definition of redundancy uses this point of view. We define *irredundancy* quantitatively

(Definition 1) as a lowerbound on the ratio of the detection advantage to the extent of deviation ("irredundancy = detection/deviation").

The first step in our characterization is to bridge the gap between these two formulations of redundancy. While the definition of irredundancy is what allows us to use a redundancy-free function in our protocols, to find the core of a function, we rely on the formulation in terms of redundancy of individual inputs – we shall reduce redundancy one input or output at a time, until we obtain a redundancy free function. Clearly when redundancy is present, irredundancy would be 0 (i.e., can deviate without being detected); but we show that conversely, when irredundancy is 0, then one of the two forms of redundancy must be present. We stress that *a priori*, it is not at all obvious that irredundancy cannot be 0 even if there is no redundancy (i.e., detection/deviation could approach 0 by a sequence of deviations that are smaller and smaller, achieving even smaller detectability). We provide a non-trivial linear algebraic analysis of irredundancy and show that this is not the case (Lemma 1).

Simple Function. Following [31], we define a simple function. First, we present a combinatorial characterization (given in Lemma 1 in [31]) of a simple function, which constitutes the algorithm for determining if a function is simple or not.

A 2-party randomized function f is described by a joint distribution over Alice-Bob output space $W \times Z$ for every Alice-Bob input pair in $X \times Y$. We consider the $|Y||Z| \times |X||W|$ matrix $\mathfrak{P}^f$, with rows indexed by $(y, z) \in Y \times Z$ and columns indexed by $(x, w) \in X \times W$, such that $\mathfrak{P}^f_{(y,z),(x,w)} = \mathsf{p}^f[w, z|x, y]$. The function f is simple if $\mathfrak{P}^f$ can be partitioned into a set of rank-1 minors such that no row or column of the matrix pass through two of these minors. Being of rank 1, each minor has all its rows (equivalently, columns) parallel to each other. (In [31], this is described in terms of a bipartite-graph in which each connected component is a complete bipartite graph, with weights on the edges being proportional to the product of the weights on the two end points of the vertex.)

To better understand what being simple means, we briefly explain how it is defined. The *kernel* of a function f is a symmetric function that provides both the parties with only the "common information" that f provides them with. A simple function is one which is "isomorphic" to its kernel: i.e., given just the output from the kernel, the rest of the information from f can be locally sampled by the two parties, independent of each other.

As stated in [31], the *passive*-complete functions are exactly those which are not simple. Our construction shows that *restricted to the class of redundancy free functions*, the same characterization holds for complete functions for active-security as well.

1.4   The Construction

Our main construction shows that any redundancy free function f which is not simple is also UC-complete. This construction separates into two parts:

- A protocol to UC-securely reduce the commitment functionality $\mathcal{F}_{\text{COM}}$ to f.

- A protocol in the $\mathcal{F}_{\text{COM}}$-hybrid model that UC-securely reduces OT to f, starting from a passive-secure reduction of OT to f (since f is passive-complete, such a protocol exists). That is, we compile (in a black-box manner) a passive-secure OT protocol using f, to a UC-secure OT protocol using f (and $\mathcal{F}_{\text{COM}}$).

In building the commitment functionality we rely on a careful analysis of functions that are redundancy free and not simple, to show that there will exist two or more *extreme views* for one party (which cannot be equivocated) that are *confusable* by the second party (provided it uses inputs from an "unrevealing distribution" — something that can be verified by the first party). We interpret the function invocations as a channel through which the first party transmits a message using the set of its extreme views as the alphabet. This message is encoded using an error correcting code of rate $1 - o(1)$ and $o(1)$ distance; the distance would be sufficient to prevent equivocation during opening. To argue hiding, we rely on a well-known result from information theory, namely the (weak) *converse of Shannon's Channel Coding Theorem*. We extend this theorem to the case of adaptively chosen channel characteristics, corresponding to the fact that the receiver can adaptively choose its input to the function and that determines the channel characteristics. Due to confusability, the capacity of this channel will be less than 1 (measured with the logarithm of the input alphabet size as the base). Since the rate of the code is higher than the capacity of the channel, this gives us some amount of hiding (which is then refined using an extractor).

The second part, which gives a compiler, is similar in spirit to prior protocols that established that a passive-secure OT protocol (in the plain model) can be converted to an active-secure OT protocol *in a black-box manner* [20,19,9]. In particular, its high-level structure resembles that of the protocol in [9]. However, the key difference in our protocol compared to these earlier protocols (which were all in the computational setting), is that the passive-secure OT protocol that we are given is not in the plain model, but is in the f-hybrid model. The technical difficulty in our case is in ensuring that a cut-and-choose technique can be used to verify an adversary's claims about what inputs it sent to a 2-party function and what outputs it received, when the verifier has access to only the other end of the function. This is precisely where the statistical testability of redundancy free functions (see below) is invoked.

Also, in contrast with the above mentioned compilers, we do not use a two-step compilation to first obtain security against active corruption of the receiver and then that of the sender. Instead, we directly obtain a somewhat "noisy" OT protocol that is secure against active corruption of either player, and use techniques from [22,21] to obtain the final protocol. In particular, we show how the result in [22] can be extended so that it works in a noisy OT-hybrid rather than a regular OT-hybrid. (A similar extension was used in [21], to allow using a noisy channel hybrid instead of a regular OT-hybrid.) These tools help us achieve a constant rate in implementing OTs from instances of f.

Statistically Testable Games. We introduce a formal notion of statistically testable game, which is an information-theoretic analogue of interactive proofs where both players can be computationally unbounded. Note that interactive proofs are not interesting in this information-theoretic setting (or if P=PSPACE). In a statistically testable game, the statements being proven (tested) are statements regarding the private observations of the prover in a system, which provides partial observations to the verifier as well. The non-triviality of such a proof system stems not from the computational limitations of the verifier, but from the fact that the verifier cannot observe the entire system. While such proofs have been implicitly considered in several special cases in many prior works (e.g. [11,12,22,21]), the class of games we consider is much more general than those implicitly considered in these earlier instances, and the soundness of the tests we consider is not at all obvious.

The game we consider is of 2-party function evaluation, in which the prover and the verifier interact with a (stateless) trusted third party which carries out a randomized function evaluation for them. The prover first declares a sequence of n inputs it will feed the function (the verifier chooses its inputs privately and independently). After n invocations of the function, the prover declares to the verifier the sequence of the n outputs it received from the invocations. A statistical test is a sound and complete proof system which convinces the verifier that the input and output sequences declared by the prover has a $o(1)$ fraction Hamming distance from the actual sequences in its interaction with the trusted party. Note that the verifier can use its local observations (its input-output sequences) to carry out the verification.

A major technical ingredient of our compiler is the following theorem:

> *Evaluation of a 2-party function f is statistically testable if and only if f is redundancy free.*

Clearly, if a function is not redundancy free, it admits no sound statistical test. But *a priori*, it may seem possible that even if no single input has redundancy, the prover can map the entire sequence of inputs and outputs to a different sequence, with only a small statistical difference in the verifier's view, such that this difference vanishes with the length of the sequence. We show that this is not the case: if the function is redundancy-free, then there is a lowerbound on the ratio of the "detection advantage" to "extent of deviation" that does not vanish with the number of invocations.

This naturally motivates our approach of compiling a passive-secure protocol in f-hybrid, where f is redundancy free, into one that is secure against active adversaries. We should be able to enforce honest behavior by "auditing" randomly chosen executions from a large number of executions, and the auditing would use the statistical tests. However, this idea does not work directly: the statistical test models a test by an *environment*: it lets the adversary arbitrarily interact with f and report back a purported output, but the purported input it sent to f was fixed by the environment before the adversary obtained the output from f. On the other hand, in a protocol, the honest party does not get to see the input to be sent to the functionality ahead of time. It is to solve this issue that we rely on the commitment functionality: the input each party should be sending to f is fixed *a priori* using commitments (and coin-tossing-in-the-well). When a session is chosen for auditing, the adversary could have sent a different input to f than it was supposed to, and it can lie about the output it received from f as well, but it cannot choose the purported input it sent to f after interacting with f.

2   Preliminaries

Matrix Definitions. In the following we shall refer to the following matrix norms: $\|A\|_\infty = \max_i \sum_j |a_{ij}|$ (maximum absolute row sum norm), and $\|A\|_{sum} = \sum_{i,j} |a_{ij}|$ (absolute sum norm). We shall also use the function $\max(A) = \max_{i,j} a_{ij}$ (maximum value among all entries); note that here we do not consider the absolute value of the entries in A. For a probability distribution $\mathfrak{p}^X$ over a space X (denoted as vectors), we define $\min(\mathfrak{p}^X) = \min_{x \in X} \mathfrak{p}^X[x]$, the minimum probability it assigns to an element in X. The norm $\|\cdot\|_\infty$ when applied to a column vector simply equals the largest absolute value entry in the vector. We say that a matrix P is a *probability matrix* if its entries are all in the range $[0,1]$ and $\|P\|_{sum} = 1$. We say that a matrix is a *stochastic matrix* (or row-stochastic matrix) if all its entries are in the range $[0,1]$ and every row sums up to 1. For convenience, we define the notation $\langle M \rangle_I$ for a square matrix M to be the diagonal matrix derived from M by replacing all non-diagonal entries by 0.

2-Party Secure Function Evaluation. A two-party randomized function (also called a secure function evaluation (SFE) functionality) is specified by a single randomized function denoted as $f : X \times Y \to W \times Z$. Despite the notation, the range of f is, more accurately, the space of probability distributions over $W \times Z$. The functionality takes an input $x \in X$ from Alice and an input $y \in Y$ from Bob and samples $(w, z) \in W \times Z$ according to the distribution $f(x, y)$; then it delivers w to Alice and z to Bob. Throughout, we shall denote the probability of outputs being (w, z) when Alice and Bob use inputs x and y respectively by $\mathfrak{p}^f[w, z|x, y]$. We use the following variables for the sizes of the sets W, X, Y, Z:

$$|X| = m \qquad |Y| = n \qquad |W| = q \qquad |Z| = r.$$

In this paper we shall restrict to function evaluations where m, n, q and r are constants, i.e. as the security parameter increases the domains do not expand. (But the efficiency and security of our reductions are only polynomially dependent on m, n, q, r, so one could let them grow polynomially with the security parameter. We have made no attempt to optimize this dependency.) W.l.o.g., we shall assume that $X = [m]$ (i.e., the set of first m positive integers), $Y = [n]$, $W = [q]$ and $Z = [r]$.

We consider standard security notions in the information-theoretic setting: UC-security, standalone-security and passive-security against computationally unbounded adversaries (and with computationally unbounded simulators). Using UC-security allows to compose our sub-protocols securely [7]. Error in security (simulation error) is always required to be negligible in the security parameter of the protocol, and the communication complexity of all protocols are required to be polynomial in the same parameter. However, we note that a protocol may invoke a sub-protocol with a security parameter other than its own (in particular, with a constant independent of its own security parameter).

Complete Functionalities. A two-party randomized function evaluation f is *standalone-complete* (respectively, *UC-complete*) against information theoretic adversaries if any functionality g can be standalone securely (respectively, UC securely) computed in f hybrid. We shall also consider passive-complete functions where we consider security against passive (semi-honest) adversaries.

3   Main Tools

In this section we introduce the three main tools used in our construction.

3.1   Characterizing Irredundancy

Redundancy in a function allows at least one party to deviate in its behavior in the ideal world and not be detected (with significant probability) by an environment. In our protocol, which are designed to detect deviation, it is important to use a function in a form in which redundancy has been removed. We define irredundancy in an explicit linear algebraic fashion, and introduce a parameter to measure the extent of irredundancy.

Irredundancy of a System of Stochastic Matrices. Let P_i, $i = 1, \ldots, m$ be a collection of $s \times q$ probability matrices (i.e., entries in the range $[0, 1]$, with $\|P_i\|_{\mathrm{sum}} = 1$). Consider tuples of the form $(j, \{M_i, \alpha_i\}_{i=1}^m)$, where $j \in [m]$, M_i are $q \times q$ stochastic matrices, and $\alpha_i \in [0, 1]$ are such that $\sum_i \alpha_i = 1$. Then we define the irredundancy of this system as

$$\mathfrak{D}(P_1, \ldots, P_m) = \inf_{(j, \{\alpha_i, M_i\}_{i=1}^m)} \frac{\|(\sum_{i=1}^m \alpha_i P_i M_i) - P_j\|_\infty}{1 - \alpha_j \|P_j \cdot \langle M_j \rangle_I\|_{\mathrm{sum}}} \tag{1}$$

where the infimum is over tuples of the above form. (Recall that $\langle M_j \rangle_I$ refers to the diagonal matrix with the diagonal entries of M_j.)

Intuitively, consider the rows of P_i to be probability distributions over a q-ary alphabet produced as the outcome of a process with the row index corresponding to a hidden part of the outcome, and the column index being an observable outcome. Then, irredundancy measures how well a P_j can (or rather, cannot) be approximated by a convex combination of all the matrices P_i, possibly with the observable outcome transformed using a stochastic matrix (corresponding to a probabilistic mapping of the observable outcomes); the denominator normalizes the approximability by how much overall *deviation* (probability of changing the process or changing the outcome) is involved. This excludes the trivial possibility of perfectly matching P_j by employing zero deviation (i.e., taking $\alpha_j = 1$ and $M_j = I$).

Irredundancy of a 2-Party Secure Function Evaluation Function. Recall that a 2-party SFE function f with input domains, $X \times Y$ and output domain $W \times Z$ is defined by probabilities $\mathfrak{p}^f[w, z | x, y]$. We define left and right redundancy of f as follows. Below, $|X| = m, |Y| = n, |W| = q, |Z| = r$.

To define left-redundancy, consider representing f by the matrices $\{P^x\}_{x \in X}$ where each P^x is an $nr \times q$ matrix with $P^x_{(y,z),w} = \mathfrak{p}^f[w, y, z | x]$. Here, $\mathfrak{p}^f[w, y, z | x]$ $\triangleq \frac{1}{n} \mathfrak{p}^f[w, z | x, y]$ (where we pick y independent of x, with uniform probability $\mathfrak{p}^f[y | x] = \frac{1}{n}$).

Definition 1. *For an SFE function $f : X \times Y \to W \times Z$, represented by matrices $\{P^x\}_{x \in X}$, with $P^x_{(y,z),w} = \Pr[w, y, z | x]$, we say that an input $\hat{x} \in X$ is left-redundant if there is a set $\{(\alpha_x, M_x) | x \in X\}$, where $0 \le \alpha_x \le 1$ with $\sum_x \alpha_x = 1$, and each M_x is a $q \times q$ stochastic matrix such that if $\alpha_{\hat{x}} = 1$ then $M_{\hat{x}} \ne I$, and $P^{\hat{x}} = \sum_{x \in X} \alpha_x P^x M_x$.*

We say $\hat{x}$ is strictly left-redundant if it is left-redundant as above, but $\alpha_{\hat{x}} = 0$. We say $\hat{x}$ is self left-redundant if it is left-redundant as above, but $\alpha_{\hat{x}} = 1$ (and hence $M_{\hat{x}} \ne I$).

We say that f is left-redundancy free if there is no $x \in X$ that is left-redundant.

Right-redundancy notions for inputs $\hat{y} \in Y$ are defined analogously. A function f is said to be *redundancy-free* if it is left-redundancy free and right-redundancy free. The main result about irredundancy is the following quantitative lemma:

Lemma 1. *Suppose a 2-party function $f : X \times Y \to W \times Z$ is left redundancy free. Let $\mathfrak{p}^Y$ be a probability distribution over Y. Let the probability matrices $\{P^x\}_{x \in X}$, be defined by $P^x_{(y,z),w} = \mathfrak{p}^f[w, z | x, y]\mathfrak{p}^Y[y]$. Then there is a constant $\epsilon_f > 0$ (depending only on f) such that $\mathfrak{D}(P^1, \ldots, P^m) \ge \epsilon_f \min(\mathfrak{p}^Y)$.*

The analogous statement holds for right redundancy.

3.2   Statistically Testable Function Evaluation

In this section we consider the notion of a statistically testable function evaluation game. (The notion is more general and could be extended to reactive systems, or multi-player settings; for simplicity we define it only for the relevant setting of 2-party functions.) We informally defined a statistical test in Section 1.3. As mentioned there, we shall show that *evaluation of a 2-party function is statistically testable if and only if the function is redundancy free.* For simplicity, we define a particular test and show that it is sound and complete for redundancy free functions (without formally defining statistical tests in general). (It is easy to see that functions with redundancy cannot have a sound and complete test. Since this is not relevant to our proof, we omit the details.)

Let f be redundancy free. Consider the following statistical test, formulated as a game between an honest challenger (verifier) and an adversary (prover) in the f-hybrid.

Left-Statistical-Test($f, \mathfrak{p}^Y; N$):

1. The adversary picks $\tilde{\mathbf{x}} = (\tilde{x}_1, \ldots, \tilde{x}_N) \in X^N$, and for each $i \in [N]$ the challenger (secretly) picks uniform i.i.d $y_i \in Y$, according to the distribution $\mathfrak{p}^Y$.
2. For each $i \in [N]$, the parties invoke f with inputs x_i and y_i respectively; the adversary receives w_i and the challenger receives z_i, where $(w_i, z_i) \xleftarrow{\$} f(x_i, y_i)$.
3. The adversary then outputs $\tilde{\mathbf{w}} = (\tilde{w}_1, \ldots, \tilde{w}_N) \in W^N$.

The adversary wins this game (breaks the soundness) if the following conditions hold:

1. Consistency: Let $\mu_{\tilde{w},\tilde{x},y,z}$ be the number of indices $i \in [N]$ such that $\tilde{w}_i = \tilde{w}, \tilde{x}_i = \tilde{x}, y_i = y$ and $z_i = z$. Also, let $\mu_{\tilde{x},y}$ be the number of indices $i \in [N]$ such that $\tilde{x}_i = \tilde{x}$ and $y_i = y$. The consistency condition requires that $\forall (w, x, y, z) \in W \times X \times Y \times Z$,

$$\mu_{\tilde{w},\tilde{x},y,z} = \mu_{\tilde{x},y} \times \mathfrak{p}^f[\tilde{w}, z | \tilde{x}, y] \pm N^{2/3}.$$

2. Separation: Let vectors $\mathbf{A}, \tilde{\mathbf{A}} \in (W \times X)^N$ be defined by $A_i := (w_i, x_i)$ and $\tilde{A}_i = (\tilde{w}_i, \tilde{x}_i)$. The separation condition requires that the Hamming distance between the vectors $\mathbf{A}$ and $\tilde{\mathbf{A}}$ is $\Delta(\mathbf{A}, \tilde{\mathbf{A}}) \geq N^{7/8}$.

The *Right-Statistical-Test*($f, \mathfrak{p}^X; N$) is defined analogously. The experiment *Statistical-Test*($f, \mathfrak{p}^X, \mathfrak{p}^Y; N$) consists of the left and right statistical tests, and the adversary wins if it wins in either experiment.

Before proceeding, we note that the above statistical test is indeed "complete": if the prover plays "honestly" and uses $\tilde{\mathbf{x}} = \mathbf{x}$ and $\tilde{\mathbf{w}} = \mathbf{w}$, then the consistency condition will be satisfied with all but negligible probability (for any choice of $\mathbf{x}$).

Lemma 2. *If f is redundancy free, and $\mathfrak{p}^X$ and $\mathfrak{p}^Y$ are constant distribution which have full support over X and Y respectively, then the probability that any adversary wins in Statistical-Test($f, \mathfrak{p}^Y, \mathfrak{p}^X; N$) is* negl($N$).[4]

3.3   A Converse of the Channel Coding Theorem

A converse of the channel coding theorem states that message transmission is not possible over a noisy channel at a rate above its capacity, except with a non-vanishing rate of errors (see, for e.g., [10]). We give a generalization of the (weak) converse of channel coding theorem where the receiver can adaptively choose the channel based on its current view. We show that if in at least a μ fraction of the transmissions, the receiver chooses channels which are noisy (i.e., has capacity less than that of a noiseless channel over the same input alphabet), then we can lower bound its probability of error in predicting the input codeword as a function of μ, an upper bound on the noisy channel capacities, and the rate of the code.

---

[4]   The distributions $\mathfrak{p}^X$ and $\mathfrak{p}^Y$ are constant while N is a growing parameter.

Lemma 3 (Weak Converse of Channel Coding Theorem, Generalization). *Let $\mathcal{F} = \{\mathcal{F}_1, \ldots, \mathcal{F}_K\}$ be a set of K channels which take as input alphabets from a set Λ, with $|\Lambda| = 2^\lambda$. Let $\mathcal{G} \subseteq [K]$ be such that for all $i \in \mathcal{G}$, the capacity of the channel $\mathcal{F}_i$ is at most $\lambda - c$, for a constant $c > 0$.*

Let $\mathcal{C} \subseteq \Lambda^N$ be a rate $R \in [0,1]$ code. Consider the following experiment: a random codeword $c_1 \ldots c_N \equiv \mathbf{c} \xleftarrow{\$} \mathcal{C}$ is drawn and each symbol $c_1 \ldots c_N$ is transmitted sequentially; the channel used for transmitting each symbol is chosen (possibly adaptively) from the set $\mathcal{F}$ by the receiver.

Conditioned on the receiver choosing a channel in $\mathcal{G}$ for μ or more transmissions, the probability of error of the receiver in predicting $\mathbf{c}$ is

$$P_e \geq 1 - \frac{1}{NR\lambda} - \frac{1 - c\mu/\lambda}{R}.$$

4 Main Construction

The main ingredient for the proof of Theorem 1 is the following result (details are provided in the full version [27]):

Theorem 2. *If f is a redundancy free 2-party function and f is passive-complete, then there is a constant rate UC-secure protocol for $\mathcal{F}_{\mathrm{OT}}$ in the f-hybrid model.*

Since f is passive-complete we know that OT does reduce to f against passive adversaries. We shall take such a passive-secure OT protocol in the f-hybrid, and convert it into a UC-secure protocol. For this we need two ingredients: first a UC-secure commitment protocol in the f-hybrid model, and secondly a compiler to turn the passive secure OT protocol in the f-hybrid model to a UC-secure protocol in the commitment-hybrid model. In building the UC-secure commitment protocol, we rely on the irredundancy of f as well as the combinatorial characterization that passive-complete functions are exactly those that are not simple (see Section 1.3).

4.1 A UC Secure Commitment Protocol

In this section we present the outline of a UC-secure commitment protocol in the f-hybrid model, for any 2-party randomized function f that is redundancy free (Definition 1) and is not simple (see Section 1.3).

The high-level structure of the protocol is as follows. The definition of the underlined terms cannot be accommodated due to lack of space. Interested readers should refer to [27].

1. Commitment phase:
   (a) The sender plays the role of (say) Alice in f, and the receiver plays the role of Bob in f. The sender invokes f several times, with random inputs $x \in X$; and the receiver will be required to pick its inputs from an *unrevealing distribution* p^Y.

(b) The sender checks if the frequencies of all the input-output pairs (x, w) it sees are consistent with the receiver using p^Y.

(c) The sender announces a subset of indices for which in the corresponding invocations, it obtained an _extreme_ input-output pair.

(d) The sender picks a random codeword from an appropriate code, and masks this codeword with the sequence of input-output pairs from the previous step, and sends it to the receiver.

(e) The sender also sends the bit to be committed masked by a bit extracted from the codeword in the previous step.

2. Reveal phase: The sender sends its view from the commitment phase. The receiver checks that this is consistent with its view and the protocol (in particular, the purported codeword indeed belongs to the code, and for each possible value (x, w) of the sender's input-output pair to f, the frequency of input-output pairs (y, z) on its side are consistent with the function). If so, it accepts the purported committed bit.

The delicate part of this construction is to show that there will indeed be a set of extreme input-output pairs and an unrevealing distribution as required above. We point out that _we cannot use our results on statistical testability of the function evaluation game from Section 3.2 directly_ to argue that binding would hold for all input-output pairs. This is because the game there requires the adversary to declare the input part of its purported view _before_ invoking the function. Indeed, once we have a commitment functionality at our disposal, we can exploit the binding nature of this game; but to construct our commitment protocol this is not helpful.

Due to lack of space, we provide rest of our construction in the full version of the paper [27].

Acknowledgments. We thank Vinod Prabhakaran for helpful discussions on the converse of the Channel Coding Theorem.

This work was done when Daniel Kraschewski was at KIT and Hemanta K. Maji was a CI Fellow at Univ. of California, Los Angeles. Manoj Prabhakaran was supported by NSF grants 07-47027 and 12-28856. Amit Sahai was supported in part from a DARPA/ONR PROCEED award, NSF grants 1228984, 1136174, 1118096, and 1065276, a Xerox Faculty Research Award, a Google Faculty Research Award, an equipment grant from Intel, and an Okawa Foundation Research Grant. This material is based upon work supported by the Defense Advanced Research Projects Agency through the U.S. Office of Naval Research under Contract N00014-11- 1-0389. The views expressed are those of the author and do not reflect the official policy or position of the Department of Defense, the National Science Foundation, or the U.S. Government.

References

1. Beaver, D.: Precomputing oblivious transfer. In: Coppersmith, D. (ed.) CRYPTO 1995. LNCS, vol. 963, pp. 97–109. Springer, Heidelberg (1995)

2. Beimel, A., Ishai, Y., Kumaresan, R., Kushilevitz, E.: On the cryptographic complexity of the worst functions (2013), http://www.cs.umd.edu/~ranjit/BIKK.pdf (retrieved October 16, 2013)

3. Beimel, A., Malkin, T., Micali, S.: The all-or-nothing nature of two-party secure computation. In: Wiener, M. (ed.) CRYPTO 1999. LNCS, vol. 1666, pp. 80–97. Springer, Heidelberg (1999)

4. Ben-Or, M., Goldwasser, S., Wigderson, A.: Completeness theorems for non-cryptographic fault-tolerant distributed computation (extended abstract). In: Simon, J. (ed.) STOC, pp. 1–10. ACM (1988)

5. Brassard, G., Crépeau, C., Robert, J.-M.: All-or-nothing disclosure of secrets. In: Odlyzko, A.M. (ed.) CRYPTO 1986. LNCS, vol. 263, pp. 234–238. Springer, Heidelberg (1987)

6. Canetti, R.: Universally composable security: A new paradigm for cryptographic protocols. Electronic Colloquium on Computational Complexity (ECCC) TR01-016 (2001); Previous version "A unified framework for analyzing security of protocols" available at the ECCC archive TR01-016. Extended abstract in FOCS 2001 (2001)

7. Canetti, R.: Universally composable security: A new paradigm for cryptographic protocols. Cryptology ePrint Archive, Report 2000/067 (2005); Revised version of [6]

8. Chaum, D., Crépeau, C., Damgård, I.: Multiparty unconditionally secure protocols. In: Simon, J. (ed.) STOC, pp. 11–19. ACM (1988)

9. Choi, S.G., Dachman-Soled, D., Malkin, T., Wee, H.: Simple, black-box constructions of adaptively secure protocols. In: Reingold, O. (ed.) TCC 2009. LNCS, vol. 5444, pp. 387–402. Springer, Heidelberg (2009)

10. Cover, T.M., Thomas, J.A.: Elements of information theory. Wiley-Interscience, New York (1991)

11. Crépeau, C., Kilian, J.: Achieving oblivious transfer using weakened security assumptions (extended abstract). In: FOCS, pp. 42–52. IEEE (1988)

12. Crépeau, C., Morozov, K., Wolf, S.: Efficient unconditional oblivious transfer from almost any noisy channel. In: Blundo, C., Cimato, S. (eds.) SCN 2004. LNCS, vol. 3352, pp. 47–59. Springer, Heidelberg (2005)

13. Fitzi, M., Garay, J.A., Maurer, U.M., Ostrovsky, R.: Minimal complete primitives for secure multi-party computation. J. Cryptology 18(1), 37–61 (2005)

14. Fitzi, M., Maurer, U.M.: From partial consistency to global broadcast. In: Frances Yao, F., Luks, E.M. (eds.) STOC, pp. 494–503. ACM (2000)

15. Goldreich, O.: Foundations of Cryptography: Basic Applications. Cambridge University Press (2004)

16. Goldreich, O., Micali, S., Wigderson, A.: How to play ANY mental game. In: Aho, A.V. (ed.) STOC, pp. 218–229. ACM (1987); See [15, Ch. 7] for more details

17. Goldreich, O., Vainish, R.: How to solve any protocol problem - an efficiency improvement. In: Pomerance, C. (ed.) CRYPTO 1987. LNCS, vol. 293, pp. 73–86. Springer, Heidelberg (1988)

18. Haber, S., Micali, S.: Unpublished manuscript (1986)

19. Haitner, I.: Semi-honest to malicious oblivious transfer - the black-box way. In: Canetti, R. (ed.) TCC 2008. LNCS, vol. 4948, pp. 412–426. Springer, Heidelberg (2008)

20. Ishai, Y., Kushilevitz, E., Lindell, Y., Petrank, E.: Black-box constructions for secure computation. In: STOC, pp. 99–108. ACM (2006)

21. Ishai, Y., Kushilevitz, E., Ostrovsky, R., Prabhakaran, M., Sahai, A., Wullschleger, J.: Constant-rate oblivious transfer from noisy channels. In: Rogaway, P. (ed.) CRYPTO 2011. LNCS, vol. 6841, pp. 667–684. Springer, Heidelberg (2011)

22. Ishai, Y., Prabhakaran, M., Sahai, A.: Founding cryptography on oblivious transfer - efficiently. In: Wagner, D. (ed.) CRYPTO 2008. LNCS, vol. 5157, pp. 572–591. Springer, Heidelberg (2008)

23. Kilian, J.: Founding cryptography on oblivious transfer. In: Simon, J. (ed.) STOC, pp. 20–31. ACM (1988)

24. Kilian, J.: A general completeness theorem for two-party games. In: Koutsougeras, C., Vitter, J.S. (eds.) STOC, pp. 553–560. ACM (1991)

25. Kilian, J.: More general completeness theorems for secure two-party computation. In: Frances Yao, F., Luks, E.M. (eds.) STOC, pp. 316–324. ACM (2000)

26. Kilian, J., Kushilevitz, E., Micali, S., Ostrovsky, R.: Reducibility and completeness in private computations. SIAM J. Comput. 29(4), 1189–1208 (2000)

27. Kraschewski, D., Maji, H.K., Prabhakaran, M., Sahai, A.: A full characterization of completeness for two-party randomized function evaluation. IACR Cryptology ePrint Archive, 2014:50 (2014)

28. Kraschewski, D., Müller-Quade, J.: Completeness theorems with constructive proofs for finite deterministic 2-party functions. In: Ishai, Y. (ed.) TCC 2011. LNCS, vol. 6597, pp. 364–381. Springer, Heidelberg (2011)

29. Kushilevitz, E., Micali, S., Ostrovsky, R.: Reducibility and completeness in multi-party private computations. In: FOCS, pp. 478–489. IEEE Computer Society (1994)

30. Lindell, Y., Omri, E., Zarosim, H.: Completeness for symmetric two-party functionalities - revisited. In: Wang, X., Sako, K. (eds.) ASIACRYPT 2012. LNCS, vol. 7658, pp. 116–133. Springer, Heidelberg (2012)

31. Maji, H.K., Prabhakaran, M., Rosulek, M.: A unified characterization of completeness in secure function evaluation. In: Galbraith, S., Nandi, M. (eds.) INDOCRYPT 2012. LNCS, vol. 7668, pp. 40–59. Springer, Heidelberg (2012)

32. Rabin, M.: How to exchange secrets by oblivious transfer. Technical Report TR-81, Harvard Aiken Computation Laboratory (1981)

33. Rabin, T., Ben-Or, M.: Verifiable secret sharing and multiparty protocols with honest majority. In: Johnson, D.S. (ed.) STOC, pp. 73–85. ACM (1989)

34. Wiesner, S.: Conjugate coding. SIGACT News 15, 78–88 (1983)

35. Yao, A.C.-C.: Some complexity questions related to distributive computing (preliminary report). In: STOC, pp. 209–213. ACM (1979)

On the Complexity of UC Commitments[*]

Juan A. Garay[1], Yuval Ishai[2,**], Ranjit Kumaresan[2], and Hoeteck Wee[3,***]

[1] Yahoo Labs
garay@yahoo-inc.com
[2] Department of Computer Science, Technion, Haifa, Israel
{yuvali,ranjit}@cs.technion.ac.il
[3] ENS, Paris, France
wee@di.ens.fr

Abstract. Motivated by applications to secure multiparty computation, we study the complexity of realizing universally composable (UC) commitments. Several recent works obtain practical UC commitment protocols in the common reference string (CRS) model under the DDH assumption. These protocols have two main disadvantages. First, even when applied to long messages, they can only achieve a small constant rate (namely, the communication complexity is larger than the length of the message by a large constant factor). Second, they require computationally expensive public-key operations for each block of each message being committed.

Our main positive result is a UC commitment protocol that simultaneously avoids both of these limitations. It achieves an optimal rate of 1 (strictly speaking, $1 - o(1)$) by making only few calls to an ideal oblivious transfer (OT) oracle and additionally making a black-box use of a (computationally inexpensive) PRG. By plugging in known efficient protocols for UC-secure OT, we get rate-1, computationally efficient UC commitment protocols under a variety of setup assumptions (including the CRS model) and under a variety of standard cryptographic assumptions (including DDH). We are not aware of any previous UC commitment protocols that achieve an optimal asymptotic rate.

A corollary of our technique is a rate-1 construction for *UC commitment length extension*, that is, a UC commitment protocol for a long message using a single ideal commitment for a short message. The extension protocol additionally requires the use of a semi-honest (stand-alone) OT protocol. This raises a natural question: can we achieve UC commitment length extension while using only inexpensive PRG operations as is the case for stand-alone commitments and UC OT? We answer this question in the negative, showing that the existence of a semi-honest OT protocol is necessary (and sufficient) for UC commitment length extension. This shows, quite surprisingly, that UC commitments are qualitatively different from both stand-alone commitments and UC OT.

[*] Research received funding from the European Union's Tenth Framework Programme (FP10/2010-2016) under grant agreement no. 259426 ERC-CaC.
[**] Supported in part by ISF grant 1361/10 and BSF grant 2012378.
[***] CNRS (UMR 8548) and INRIA. Part of this work was done at George Washington University, supported by NSF Award CNS-1237429.

P.Q. Nguyen and E. Oswald (Eds.): EUROCRYPT 2014, LNCS 8441, pp. 677–694, 2014.

Keywords: Universal composability, UC commitments, oblivious transfer.

1   Introduction

A *commitment scheme* is a digital analogue of a locked box. It enables one party, called the *committer*, to transfer a value to another party, called the *receiver*, while keeping it hidden, and later reveal it while guaranteeing to the receiver its originality. Commitment schemes are a fundamental building block for cryptographic protocols withstanding active adversarial attacks. As such, efficient implementations of the latter—particularly in realistic complex environments where they are to execute—crucially hinge on them. Such complex environments are today epitomized by the universal composability (UC) framework [6], which allows for a protocol to run concurrently and asynchronously with arbitrarily many others, while guaranteeing its security.

The first constructions of UC commitments were given by Canetti *et al.* [7,8] as a feasibility result. (It was also shown in [7] that it is impossible to construct UC commitments in the plain model, and that some setup such as a *common reference string* (CRS) is required.) Since then, and motivated by the above, a series of improvements (e.g., [14,13,28,19,33,4,1,25]) culminated in constructions achieving under various cryptographic assumptions *constant* communication rate and practical computational complexity, making it possible to commit to, say, L group elements by sending $O(L)$ group elements and performing $O(L)$ public-key operations (e.g., exponentiations).

Shortcomings—as well as ample room for improvement, however, remain, as the constant rate currently achieved is small and the computational cost per committed bit is high. This is the case even when committing to long messages and even when ignoring the cost of offline interaction that does not depend on the committed message. More concretely, the communication complexity is bigger than the length of the message by a large constant factor, and the online computation includes a large number of computationally expensive public-key operations for each block of the message being committed.[1] This is not satisfactory when considering concrete applications where UC commitments are used, such as UC secure computation and UC zero-knowledge. (See [4,28,1] for additional motivation on these applications.)

Our Results. We obtain both positive and negative results on the complexity of UC commitments. Our main positive result is a UC commitment protocol which simultaneously overcomes both of these limitations. Specifically, it achieves an *optimal rate* of 1 (strictly speaking, $1 - o(1)$) by making only few calls to an ideal oblivious transfer (OT) oracle and additionally making a black-box use

---

[1] Recent constructions [28,4] that work over standard DDH groups require at least 10 group elements and at least 20 public key operations per commitment instance. A very recent work by [25] (improving over [16]) requires 5 group elements in a bilinear group (assuming SXDH).

of a (computationally inexpensive) PRG. By plugging in known efficient protocols for UC-secure OT (e.g., [34]), we get rate-1, computationally efficient UC commitment protocols under a variety of setup assumptions (including the CRS model) and under a variety of standard cryptographic assumptions (including DDH). We are not aware of any previous UC commitment protocols which achieve an optimal asymptotic rate.

Our main idea is to use a simple code-based generalization of the standard construction of commitment from δ-Rabin-string-OTs [11,26,24,18]. The key observation is that the use of a rate-1 encoding scheme with a judicious choice of parameters yields a rate-1 construction of UC commitments.

Next, we show how to further reduce the computational complexity of the basic construction by using OT extension [2,23,24]. Our improvement ideally suits the setting where we need to perform a large number of commitments in a single parallel commit phase (with potentially several reveal phases), as with applications involving cut-and-choose. In particular, we show that the number of calls to the OT oracle can be made independent of the number of instances of UC commitments required. (Note that such a result does not follow from multiple applications of the basic construction.) We stress that when handling a large number of commitment instances (say, in garbled circuit applications of cut-and-choose), the number of public key operations plays a significant role (perhaps more than the communication) in determining efficiency. While current state-of-the-art UC commitment protocols [28,4] suffer from the need to many computationally expensive public-key operations, our result above enables us to obtain better computational as well as overall efficiency.

Lastly, another corollary of our technique is a rate-1 construction for *UC commitment length extension*, that is, a UC commitment protocol for a long message using a single ideal commitment for a short message. The extension protocol additionally requires the use of a semi-honest (stand-alone) OT protocol. This raises a natural question of whether we can achieve UC commitment length extension while using only inexpensive PRG operations as is the case for stand-alone commitments and UC OT. We answer this question in the negative, showing that the existence of a semi-honest OT protocol is necessary (and sufficient) for UC commitment length extension. This shows that UC commitments are qualitatively different from both stand-alone commitments and UC OT, which can be extended using any PRG [2], and are similar to adaptively-secure OT whose extension requires the existence of (non-adaptively secure) oblivious transfer [29].

We note that our constructions are only secure against a static (non-adaptive) adversary; we leave the extension to adaptive security for future work.

Related Work. We already mentioned above the series of results leading to constant-rate UC-commitments. Here we give a brief overview. Canetti *et al.* [7,8] were the first to construct (inefficient) UC commitments in the CRS model from general assumptions, and also achieve adaptive security. Shortly thereafter, Damgård and Nielsen [14] presented UC commitments with $O(1)$ exponentiations for committing to a single group element. Their construction is based on

N-residuosity and p-subgroup assumptions, and is also adaptively secure (without erasures), but requires a CRS that grows linearly with the number of parties. A construction of Damgård and Groth [13], also adaptively secure without erasures and based on the strong RSA assumption, requires a fixed-length CRS.

An important improvement in concrete efficiency was presented recently by Lindell [28]; this is achieved for static corruptions based on the DDH assumption in the CRS model. Blazy et al. [4] build on Lindell's scheme to achieve adaptive security (assuming erasures); they also obtain improvements in concrete efficiency. Fischlin et al. [16] also build on Lindell's scheme and present a non-interactive scheme using Groth-Sahai proofs [21]. Furthermore, they also provide an adaptively secure variant (with erasures) based on the DLIN assumption on symmetric bilinear groups. As mentioned above, none of these works achieve rate 1. We provide a concrete analysis of our protocol, with a comparison to [28,4] in Section 3.3.

A code-based construction of UC commitments from OT was recently used by Frederiksen et al. [18] as part of an efficient protocol for secure two-party computation. While this construction uses a similar high level technique as our basic construction, its suggested instantiation in [18] only achieves a small constant rate.

Our work also considers the extension of UC commitments. We mainly focus on the goal of *length extension*, namely using an ideal commitment to a short string for implementing a UC commitment to a long string. For standalone commitments, such a length extension is easy to implement using any PRG. This is done similarly to the standard use of a PRG for implementing a hybrid encryption scheme. It was previously shown by Kraschewski[27] that this simple extension technique does not apply to UC commitments. We strengthen this negative result to show that *any* extension protocol for UC commitments implies oblivious transfer. Similar negative results for adaptively secure OT extension were obtained by Lindell and Zarosim [29], and for reductions between finite functionalities by Maji et al. [30]. Negative results for statistical UC coin-tossing extension were obtained by Hofheinz et al. [22].

In an independent work [12], Damgård et al. also construct UC commitments using OT, PRG and secret sharing as the main ingredients. While the basic approach is closely related to ours, the concrete constructions are somewhat different, leading to incomparable results. In particular, a major goal in [12] is to optimize the asymptotic computational complexity as a function of the security parameter, achieving in one variant constant (amortized) computation overhead for the verifier. Moreover, they achieve both additive and multiplicative properties for UC commitments, which are not considered in our work.

Organization of the Paper. The rest of the paper is organized as follows. Model, definitions and basic functionalities are presented in Section 2. Our main construction—rate-1 UC commitment from OT—is presented in Section 3, together with the case of multiple commitment instances and a concrete efficiency analysis. Finally, the treatment of UC commitment extension—rate-1 construction and necessity of OT—is presented in Section 4. Due to space limitations, only proof sketches are presented in the main body; full proofs as well as complementary material are deferred to the full version.

2   Model and Definitions

In this section we introduce some notation and definitions that will be used throughout the paper. We denote the computational security parameter by κ, and the statistical security parameter by σ. A function μ is negligible if for every polynomial p there exists an integer N such that for every $n > N$ it holds that $\mu(n) < 1/p(n)$.

In this paper we will be concerned with efficient universally composable (UC) [6] realizations of functionalities such as commitments. Assuming already some familiarity with the framework, we note that it is possible to consider variants of the definition of UC security in which the order of quantifiers is "$\forall\mathcal{A}\exists\mathcal{S}\forall\mathcal{Z}$". Contrast this with our definition (and also the definition in [28]) in which the order of quantifiers is "$\exists\mathcal{S}\forall\mathcal{Z}\forall\mathcal{A}$". Both definitions are equivalent as long as $\mathcal{S}$, in the former definition makes only a blackbox use of $\mathcal{A}$ [6]. Indeed, this will be the case in our constructions. Therefore, as in [28], we demonstrate a single simulator $\mathcal{S}$ that works for all adversaries and environments, and makes only a blackbox use of the adversary. (In this case, one may also denote the ideal process by IDEAL$_{\mathcal{F},\mathcal{S}^{\mathcal{A}},\mathcal{Z}}$.)

We will sometimes explicitly describe the functionalities we realize. For instance, if a functionality $\mathcal{F}$ accepts inputs only of a certain length ℓ, then we will use the notation $\mathcal{F}[\ell]$ to denote this functionality. We let $cc(\mathcal{F})$ denote the communication cost, measured in bits, of realizing $\mathcal{F}$ in the *plain model*.

The multi-commitment ideal functionality $\mathcal{F}_{\text{MCOM}}$, which is the functionality that we UC realize in this work, is given in Figure 1. As mentioned above, $\mathcal{F}_{\text{MCOM}}[\ell]$ will explicitly denote that the functionality accepts inputs of length exactly ℓ. We will be giving our constructions in the OT-hybrid model.

Functionality $\mathcal{F}_{\text{MCOM}}$

$\mathcal{F}_{\text{MCOM}}$ with session identifier sid proceeds as follows, running with parties $P_1, \ldots, P_n$, a parameter 1^κ, and an adversary $\mathcal{S}$:

- Commit phase: Upon receiving a message (commit, $sid, ssid, s, r, m$) from P_s where $m \in \{0,1\}^\ell$, record the tuple $(ssid, s, r, m)$ and send the message (receipt, $sid, ssid, s, r$) to P_r and $\mathcal{S}$. (The length of the strings ℓ is fixed and known to all parties.) Ignore any future commit messages with the same $ssid$ from P_s to P_r.
- Decommit phase: Upon receiving a message (reveal, $sid, ssid$) from P_s: If a tuple $(ssid, s, r, m)$ was previously recorded, then send the message (reveal, $sid, ssid, s, r, m$) to P_r and $\mathcal{S}$. Otherwise, ignore.

Fig. 1. Functionality $\mathcal{F}_{\text{MCOM}}$ for multiple commitments

---

Functionality $\mathcal{F}_{\mathrm{OT}}^N$

$\mathcal{F}_{\mathrm{OT}}^N$ with session identifier sid proceeds as follows, running with parties $P_1, \ldots, P_n$, a parameter 1^κ, and an adversary $\mathcal{S}$:

- Upon receiving a message $(\mathsf{sender}, sid, ssid, s, r, x_1, \ldots, x_N)$ from P_i, where each $x_j \in \{0, 1\}^\ell$, record the tuple $(sid, ssid, s, r, x_1, \ldots, x_N)$. (The length of the strings ℓ is fixed and known to all parties.) Ignore any future sender messages with the same $sid, ssid$ pair from P_s to P_r.
- Upon receiving a message $(\mathsf{receiver}, sid, ssid, s, r, q)$ from P_r, where $q \in [N]$, send $(sid, ssid, s, r, x_q)$ to P_r and $(sid, ssid, s, r)$ to P_s, and halt. (If no $(\mathsf{sender}, sid, ssid, s, r, \ldots)$ message was previously sent, then send nothing to P_r.)

Fig. 2. Functionality $\mathcal{F}_{\mathrm{OT}}^N$ for 1-out-of-N oblivious transfer. We omit superscript N when $N = 2$.

Functionality $\mathcal{F}_{\mathrm{OT_R}}^\delta$

$\mathcal{F}_{\mathrm{OT_R}}^\delta$ with session identifier sid proceeds as follows, running with parties $P_1, \ldots, P_n$, parameters 1^κ and a real number δ, $0 < \delta < 1$, and an adversary $\mathcal{S}$:

- Upon receiving a message $(\mathsf{sender}, sid, ssid, s, r, x)$ from P_s, where $x \in \{0, 1\}^\ell$, record the tuple $(sid, ssid, s, r, x)$. (The length of the strings ℓ is fixed and known to all parties.)
- Upon receiving a message $(\mathsf{receiver}, sid, ssid, s, r)$ from P_r, set $y = x$ with probability δ, and $y = \bot$ with probability $1 - \delta$. Send $(sid, ssid, s, r, y)$ to P_r and $(sid, ssid, s, r)$ to P_r, and halt. (If no $(\mathsf{sender}, sid, ssid, s, r, \ldots)$ message was previously sent, then send nothing to P_r.)

Fig. 3. Functionality $\mathcal{F}_{\mathrm{OT_R}}^\delta$ for Rabin-OT with noise rate δ

The oblivious transfer functionality $\mathcal{F}_{\mathrm{OT}}^N$, capturing 1-out-of-$N$ OT for $N \in \mathbb{Z}$, is described in Figure 2. When $N = 2$, this is the standard 1-out-of-2 string-OT functionality, denoted by $\mathcal{F}_{\mathrm{OT}}$. The δ-Rabin-string-OT functionality, denoted $\mathcal{F}_{\mathrm{OT_R}}^\delta$, is described in Figure 3.

3   Rate-1 UC Commitments from OT

A recent line of work has focused on the practical efficiency of UC commitment in the CRS model [28,4,1,19,33]. In these works, a κ-bit string commitment is implemented by sending $O(1)$ group elements and computing $O(1)$ exponentiations in a DDH group of size $2^{O(\kappa)}$. We start this section by presenting a κ-bit UC-secure string commitment protocol in the $\mathcal{F}_{\text{OT}}$-hybrid model where the total communication complexity of each phase (including communication with the OT oracle) is $\kappa(1 + o(1))$. The above implies that if OT exists (in the plain model), then there is a UC-secure protocol for an N-bit string commitment in the CRS model which uses only $N + o(N)$ bits of communication.

Thus, our construction improves over previous protocols which achieve constant rate, but not rate 1. Using, for example, the DDH-based OT protocol of [34], we can get a rate-1 UC-commitment protocol in the CRS model which is quite efficient in practice; alternatively, if we wish to obtain a construction in the single global CRS model, we may instead start with the OT protocols given in [10,1]. We then address the setting where multiple UC commitments need to be realized, showing again a rate-1 construction where, in particular, the number of calls to the OT oracle is independent of the number of UC commitments required. We conclude the section with concrete efficiency analysis of our constructions.

On the "Optimality" of Our Construction. We note that our construction achieves essentially "optimal" rate. In any statistically binding commitment scheme as with our construction, the commit phase communication must be at least the message size. Moreover, any static UC secure commitment scheme must be equivocable, since the simulator for an honest sender does not know the message during the commit phase, and yet must be able to provide openings to any message. Therefore the communication in the decommit phase must be at least the message size, via an argument similar to the lower bound on secret key size in non-committing encryption [32].

3.1   Main Construction

Our idea is to use a simple code-based generalization of the standard construction of commitment from δ-Rabin-string-OTs [11,26,24,18]. Our key observation is that the use of a rate-1 encoding scheme with a judicious choice of parameters yields a rate-1 construction of UC commitments. We start off with the following reduction.

Rate-1 Rabin-OT from OT. We first show an efficient realization of Rabin-OT for a given $\delta \in (0,1)$, denoted $\mathcal{F}_{\text{OT}_{\text{R}}}^{\delta}$, in the $\mathcal{F}_{\text{OT}}$-hybrid model, making black-box use of a PRG.

Lemma 1 (Rabin-OT from OT [5,11,26,24]). *Let* $G : \{0,1\}^{\kappa_{\text{prg}}} \to \{0,1\}^{\ell}$ *be a secure PRG, and let* $\delta \in (0,1)$ *such that* $1/\delta$ *is an integer. Then, there exists a protocol which UC-realizes a single instance of* $\mathcal{F}_{\text{OT}_{\text{R}}}^{\delta}[\ell]$ *in the* $\mathcal{F}_{\text{OT}}[\kappa_{\text{prg}}]$*-hybrid model such that:*

- *The protocol has total communication complexity at most* $\ell + (1/\delta) + 3\kappa_{\text{prg}} \cdot 1/\delta$ *bits, including communication with* $\mathcal{F}_{\text{OT}}[\kappa_{\text{prg}}]$.

- *The protocol makes at most $1/\delta$ calls to the $\mathcal{F}_{\mathrm{OT}}[\kappa_{\mathrm{prg}}]$ functionality and requires each party to make a single invocation of G.*

The protocol works by implementing $\mathcal{F}^\delta_{\mathrm{OT_R}}[\ell]$ in the $\mathcal{F}^N_{\mathrm{OT}}[\ell]$-hybrid model for $N = 1/\delta$. Then $\mathcal{F}^N_{\mathrm{OT}}[\ell]$ is realized in the $\mathcal{F}_{\mathrm{OT}}[\kappa_{\mathrm{prg}}]$-hybrid model.

Rate-1 UC-Commitments from Rabin-OT. The construction is presented in the following lemma. Further construction and proof details can be found in the full version.

Encoding scheme Enc

Parameters: n', d, n such that $n' > d > n$.
Input: $m \in \{0,1\}^\ell$ for any $\ell > n \log(n + n')$.

- Parse $m \in \{0,1\}^\ell$ as $(m_1, \ldots, m_n) \in \mathbb{F}^n$ where $\mathbb{F}$ is such that $\log |\mathbb{F}| = \ell/n$.
- Let $e_1, \ldots, e_n$ and $\alpha_1, \ldots, \alpha_{n'}$ be $(n + n')$ distinct elements in $\mathbb{F}$.
- Pick random polynomial p of degree d such that $m_i = p(e_i)$ for all $i \in [n]$.
- Output encoding $m' = (p(\alpha_1), \ldots, p(\alpha_{n'})) \in \mathbb{F}^{n'}$.

Fig. 4. A rate-1 encoding scheme based on the multi-secret sharing scheme of [17]

Lemma 2. *Let σ be a statistical security parameter, and let n be such that there exists $\epsilon \in (0, 1/2)$ satisfying $n^{1-2\epsilon} = \sigma^{\Omega(1)}$. Then, for $\delta = (2n^\epsilon + 4)^{-1}$, and any $\ell > n \log(2n + 2n^{1-\epsilon})$, there exists a protocol that statistically UC realizes a single instance of $\mathcal{F}_{\mathrm{MCOM}}[\ell]$ in the $\mathcal{F}^\delta_{\mathrm{OT_R}}[\ell/n]$-hybrid model in the presence of static adversaries such that:*

- *The protocol has communication complexity $\ell(1 + 2n^{-\epsilon})$ bits in each phase, including communication with $\mathcal{F}^\delta_{\mathrm{OT_R}}[\ell/n]$.*
- *The protocol makes $n(1 + 2n^{-\epsilon})$ calls to the $\mathcal{F}^\delta_{\mathrm{OT_R}}[\ell/n]$ functionality.*

Proof. The protocol uses the randomized encoding scheme Enc described in Figure 4 with parameters n as in the Lemma, and $n' = n + 2n^{1-\epsilon}$ and $d = n + n^{1-\epsilon} - 1$. Note that $\delta = (d + 1 - n)/2n'$. Scheme Enc takes as input $m \in \{0,1\}^\ell$ and parses them as n elements from a field $\mathbb{F}$ and satisfies the following properties:

- it has rate $1 + 2n^{-\epsilon}$;
- any $(d + 1 - n)/n' = 2\delta$ fraction of the symbols reveal no information about the encoded message[2];
- any encodings of two distinct messages differ in $\Delta \stackrel{\text{def}}{=} n' - d$ positions (and we can efficiently correct $\Delta/2$ errors);

---

[2] We actually require a slightly stronger property to achieve equivocation, namely, that we can efficiently extend a random partial assignment to less than 2δ fraction of the symbols to an encoding of any message.

The construction realizing $\mathcal{F}_{\mathrm{MCOM}}[\ell]$ in the $\mathcal{F}_{\mathrm{OT_R}}^\delta[\ell/n]$-hybrid model is described in Figure 5. We first analyze the protocol's complexity:

Communication. In the commit phase, the sender transmits the encoding, i.e., $n(1+2n^{-\epsilon})$ symbols of $\mathbb{F}$ via $\mathcal{F}_{\mathrm{OT_R}}^\delta[\ell/n]$. Since $\log|\mathbb{F}| = \ell/n$, the communication complexity is $(n+2n^{1-\epsilon})\cdot\ell/n = \ell(1+2n^{-\epsilon})$ bits. In the reveal phase, the sender sends the encoding in the clear. It follows from the calculations above that the communication complexity of this phase is also $\ell(1+2n^{-\epsilon})$ bits.

Computation. In the commit phase, the sender makes $n(1+2n^{-\epsilon})$ calls to $\mathcal{F}_{\mathrm{OT_R}}^\delta[\ell/n]$.

We now turn to the proof of security. Note that $\delta = O(n^{-\epsilon})$ while $\Delta = O(n^{1-\epsilon})$. Simulating when no party is corrupted or both parties are corrupted is straightforward. We briefly sketch how we simulate a corrupted sender and a corrupted receiver:

Corrupt Sender. Here the simulator extracts the committed value by looking at the corrupted codeword $\mathbf{c}$ that P_s sends to the ideal OT functionality and compute the unique codeword $\mathbf{c}^*$ that differs from $\mathbf{c}$ in at most $\Delta/2$ positions. In addition, the simulator reveals each symbol of $\mathbf{c}$ to the honest receiver with probability δ. If $\mathbf{c}$ and $\mathbf{c}^*$ agree on all the positions that are revealed, then the committed value is the message corresponding to $\mathbf{c}^*$; else the committed value is $\perp$.

Next, suppose P_s sends a codeword $\mathbf{c}'$ in the reveal phase. We consider two cases:

- if $\mathbf{c}'$ and $\mathbf{c}$ differ in at most $\Delta/2$ positions, then $\mathbf{c} = \mathbf{c}^*$ and the simulator extracted the correct value;
- otherwise, the honest receiver accepts with probability at most $(1-\delta)^{\Delta/2}$, which is negligible in σ.

Corrupt Receiver. In the commit phase, the simulator acts as the ideal OT functionality and for each symbol of the encoding, decides with probability δ whether to send (and, thereby fix) a random element of $\mathbb{F}$ as that symbol to the receiver.

Next, the simulator receives the actual message m in the reveal phase. We consider two cases:

- As long as less than a 2δ fraction of the symbols are transmitted in the simulated commit phase above, the simulator can efficiently extend a random partial assignment implied by the transmitted symbols to the encoding of m;
- otherwise, the simulation of the reveal phase fails with probability at most $e^{-n'\delta/3}$, which is negligible in σ.

Putting things together:

Theorem 1 (Rate-1 UC commitments from OT). *Let κ be a computational security parameter, and let $\alpha \in (0, 1/2)$. Then, there is a protocol which UC-realizes a single instance of $\mathcal{F}_{\mathrm{MCOM}}[\kappa]$ using κ^α calls to $\mathcal{F}_{\mathrm{OT}}[\kappa^\alpha]$ and a black-box use of a PRG, where the total communication complexity of each phase (including communication with $\mathcal{F}_{\mathrm{OT}}$) is $\kappa(1+o(1))$.*

Realizing $\mathcal{F}_{\mathrm{MCOM}}$ in the $\mathcal{F}_{\mathrm{OT_R}}^{\delta}$-hybrid model

Let $\mathsf{Enc} : \mathbb{F}^n \to \mathbb{F}^{n'}$ be a randomized encoding scheme as in Figure 4.

Commit Phase.

1. Upon receiving input $(\mathsf{commit}, sid, ssid, s, r, m)$ with ℓ-bit input m, party P_s parses m as $(m_1, \dots, m_n) \in \mathbb{F}^n$. It then computes $m' = (m'_1, \dots, m'_{n'}) \leftarrow \mathsf{Enc}(m)$.

2. For each $j \in [n']$:
   - P_s sends $(\mathsf{sender}, sid, ssid \circ j, s, r, m'_j)$ to $\mathcal{F}_{\mathrm{OT_R}}^{\delta}$.
   - P_r sends $(\mathsf{receiver}, sid, ssid \circ j, s, r)$ to $\mathcal{F}_{\mathrm{OT_R}}^{\delta}$.
   - P_s and P_r receive $(sid, ssid \circ j, s, r)$ and $(sid, ssid \circ j, s, r, y_j)$ respectively from $\mathcal{F}_{\mathrm{OT_R}}^{\delta}$.

3. P_s keeps state $(sid, ssid, s, r, m, m')$.

4. P_r keeps state $(sid, ssid, s, r, \{y_j\}_{j \in [n']})$, and outputs $(\mathsf{receipt}, sid, ssid, s, r)$. Also, P_r ignores any later commitment messages with the same $(sid, ssid)$ from P_s.

Opening Phase.

1. Upon input $(\mathsf{reveal}, sid, ssid, P_s, P_r)$, party P_s sends $(sid, ssid, m')$, where $m' \in \mathbb{F}^{n'}$, to P_r. Let P_r receive $(sid, ssid, \widetilde{m}')$, where $\widetilde{m}' = (\widetilde{m}'_1, \dots, \widetilde{m}'_{n'})$.

2. Let J denote the set $\{j : y_j \neq \perp\}$. P_r outputs $\perp$ if any of the following checks fail:
   - $\widetilde{m}'$ is an (error-free) codeword;
   - for all $j \in J$, it holds that $y_j = \widetilde{m}'_j$.

   If both conditions hold, P_r decodes $\widetilde{m}'$ to obtain $\widetilde{m}$, and outputs $(\mathsf{reveal}, sid, ssid, s, r, \widetilde{m})$.

Fig. 5. A statistically UC-secure protocol for $\mathcal{F}_{\mathrm{MCOM}}$ in the $\mathcal{F}_{\mathrm{OT_R}}^{\delta}$-hybrid model

Proof. We set $\ell = \kappa$ and $\sigma = \kappa$. Then we pick $n, \epsilon \in (0, 1/2)$ such that $n^{1+\epsilon} = \kappa^{\alpha}/10$. Note that $\sigma, n, \epsilon, \ell$ satisfy conditions of Lemma 2. Further, setting $\kappa_{\mathrm{prg}} = \kappa^{\alpha}$, also ensures that $O(\kappa_{\mathrm{prg}} n^{1+\epsilon}) = o(\kappa)$. The security proof readily follows from composing the protocols given in the Lemmas 1 and 2. We just need to analyze the complexity of the resulting protocol.

Communication. By Lemma 1, to implement $n + 2n^{1-\epsilon}$ calls to $\mathcal{F}_{\mathrm{OT_R}}^{\delta}[\kappa/n]$, we need to communicate $(n + 2n^{1-\epsilon})((\kappa/n) + O(\kappa_{\mathrm{prg}} n^{\epsilon})) = \kappa + 2\kappa n^{1-\epsilon} + O(\kappa_{\mathrm{prg}} n^{1+\epsilon})$ bits in the $\mathcal{F}_{\mathrm{OT}}[\kappa_{\mathrm{prg}}]$-hybrid model. For $n, \epsilon, \kappa_{\mathrm{prg}}$ as set above, it follows that the communication cost of this phase is $\kappa(1 + o(1))$ bits in each phase. *Computation.* By Lemma 1, to implement the required $n + 2n^{1-\epsilon}$ calls to $\mathcal{F}_{\mathrm{OT_R}}^{\delta}[\kappa/n]$, we need to make blackbox use of PRG, and additionally $(n + 2n^{1-\epsilon}) \cdot (1/\delta) = 2n^{1+\epsilon} + 8n$, i.e., at most κ^{α} calls to the $\mathcal{F}_{\mathrm{OT}}[\kappa^{\alpha}]$ functionality.

3.2 Multiple Commitment Instances

Next, we show how to further reduce the computational complexity of the previous construction by using OT extension [2,23,24]. Our improvement here extends to the setting where we need to perform a large number of commitments in a single parallel commit phase (with potentially many reveal phases), as with applications involving cut-and-choose. In particular, we show that the number of calls to $\mathcal{F}_{OT}[\kappa_{prg}]$ can be made independent of the number of instances of UC commitments required. (Note that such a result does not follow from multiple applications of the protocol implied by Theorem 1.)

Theorem 2. *Let κ be a computational security parameter, and let $\alpha \in (0, 1/2)$. For all $c > 0$, there exists a protocol which UC-realizes κ^c instances of $\mathcal{F}_{MCOM}[\kappa]$ with rate $1+o(1)$ that makes κ^α calls to $\mathcal{F}_{OT}[\kappa^\alpha]$ and a blackbox use of correlation robust hash functions (alternatively, random oracle, or non-blackbox use of one-way functions).*

Proof. We repeat the protocol of Theorem 1 κ^c times to construct κ^c instances of $\mathcal{F}_{MCOM}[\kappa]$ using $\kappa^{c+\alpha}$ calls to $\mathcal{F}_{OT}[\kappa^\alpha]$. By Theorem 1, the communication cost of this construction is $\kappa^c(1 + o(1))$. We note that for each instance of this protocol, the commit phase has $o(\kappa)$ communication in addition to the cost involved in communicating with $\mathcal{F}_{OT}[\kappa^\alpha]$.

We then implement the required $\kappa^{c+\alpha}$ calls to $\mathcal{F}_{OT}[\kappa^\alpha]$ using the constant rate UC-secure OT extension protocol of [24] which makes blackbox use of correlation robust hash functions (alternatively, random oracle, or non-blackbox use of one-way functions). This implementation requires κ^α calls to the $\mathcal{F}_{OT}[\kappa^\alpha]$ functionality, and has communication complexity $O(\kappa^{c+2\alpha}) = o(\kappa^{c+1})$ bits for $\alpha \in (0, 1/2)$. Therefore, the total communication complexity of this protocol in each phase (including communication with the $\mathcal{F}_{OT}[\kappa^\alpha]$ functionality) is $\kappa^c(1 + o(1))$ for $c > 1$.

3.3 Concrete Efficiency Analysis

In this section, we provide an analysis of the concrete efficiency of our protocol, specifically requiring that the statistical security loss be $< 2^{-\sigma}$ for statistical security parameter σ, and the seedlength for PRG be 128. This reflects the state-of-the-art choices for similar parameters in implementations of secure computation protocols. In addition to the communication complexity, we will also be interested in the number of public key operations. (In practice, public-key operations (e.g., modular exponentiation) are (at least) 3-4 orders of magnitude slower than symmetric-key operations (e.g., AES).)

In the concrete instantiation of our UC commitment protocol in the CRS model, we will use (1) the protocol of Nielsen *et al.* [31] for OT extension in the RO model since it has better concrete security (cost $\approx 6 \cdot 128$ bits for each instance of 128-bit OT excluding the "seed" OTs) than the protocol of [24]), and (2) the protocol of Peikert *et al.* [34] to realize "seed" OTs in the CRS model (with concrete cost per OT instance equal to 5 modular exponentiations and 6 elements in a DDH group of size 256). Note that for realizing 128 instances of $\mathcal{F}_{OT}[128]$, the cost is $6 \cdot 128 \cdot 256 = 196608$ bits and the number of modular exponentiations is $5 \cdot 128 = 640$.[3] We stress that this cost is independent of parameters ℓ, σ, and number of commitment instances. In the following we summarize the cost of our construction for some parameters. Our costs are calculated by choosing concrete parameters for the encoding scheme Enc used in Lemma 2, and then apply the transformation of Lemma 1, and finally realizing $\mathcal{F}_{OT}$ using state-of-the-art protocols as discussed above.

For long strings, say of length $\ell = 2^{30}$, and for $\sigma = 30$, we can get concrete rate as low as 1.046^{-1} in each phase. However, the choice of parameters necessitate working over a field $\mathbb{F}$ with $\log |\mathbb{F}| = 2^{19}$. If we work over relatively smaller fields $\mathbb{F}$ with say $\log |\mathbb{F}| = 512$, then the rate of the encoding can be made 1.19^{-1} (resp. 2.01^{-1}), but the cost of realizing OTs (including OT extension) makes the total rate of the commit phase $\approx 9.58^{-1}$ (resp. 5.55^{-1}). Note, however, that there are standard techniques to reduce the communication cost of realizing OTs in our setting. For instance, by replacing Rabin-OT with d-out-of-n' OT (for d, n' as in Figure 4), we may then use standard OT length extension techniques. This however has the drawback that RS encodings need to be performed over large fields, and further the number of public-key operations increases with the number of commitment instances.

Consider the following alternative approach that ports our construction to work with smaller fields, and yet get concrete rate close to 1. First, the sender parse the message m as a matrix where each element of the matrix is now from the field of desired size. Next, the sender performs a row-wise encoding (using Enc) of this matrix, and sends each column of the encoded matrix via $\mathcal{F}^{\delta}_{OT_R}$. Later in the reveal phase, the sender simply transmits the encoded matrix. As noted earlier, the above approach lets us work over small fields, and the concrete rate would be as good as the concrete rate for encoding each row.

Next, we discuss the cost of our basic construction when committing to short strings. For short strings, say of length $\ell = 512$ (resp. 256) and $\sigma = 20$, while the rate of our reveal phase can be as low as 4.6^{-1} (resp. 8.12^{-1}), the rate of our commit phase can be very high ($\approx 1000^{-1}$). While we concede that this is not very impressive in terms of communication cost, we wish to stress that our constructions do offer a significant computational advantage over the protocols of [28,4] since we perform only a fixed number of public key operations independent of the number of commitment instances. In Appendix A, we propose efficient constructions to handle commitments over short strings in settings where a large number of such short commitments are used, e.g., in cut-and-choose techniques.

Efficiency in the preprocessing model. Our protocols can be efficiently adapted to the preprocessing model [3,31], and further, the online phase of our protocol can

---

[3] The protocol of [34] requires CRS of size m for m parties (cf. [10]). However, since CRS is a one-time setup, this does not affect our (amortized) communication cost. Alternatively, we could use the DDH based construction of [10] which uses a constant sized (6 group elements) global CRS for all parties and will only mildly increase (by a multiplicative factor ≈ 6) the cost of realizing the "seed" OTs).

be made free of cryptographic operations. First, note that any UC commitment protocol can be preprocessed, for example by committing to a random string in the offline model, and sending the real input masked with this random string in the online commit phase. Therefore, the online rate of the *commit* phase of the protocol in the preprocessing model can always be made 1. Next, the online rate in the *reveal* phase of our protocol is exactly the rate of the underlying encoding. Note that in the online reveal phase, we only need the receiver to check the validity of the encoding.

4 UC Commitment Extension

As a corollary of our technique above, we start this section by showing a rate-1 construction for *UC commitment length extension*, that is, a UC commitment protocol for a long message using a single ideal commitment for a short message. The extension protocol additionally requires the use of a semi-honest (stand-alone) OT protocol. We then show that the existence of a semi-honest OT protocol is necessary for UC commitment length extension.

4.1 Rate-1 UC Commitment Length Extension

In this setting, we want a secure realization of a single instance of UC commitment on a ℓ-bit string, for $\ell = \text{poly}(\kappa)$, while allowing the parties to access ideal functionality $\mathcal{F}_{\text{MCOM}}[\kappa]$ exactly once. We show that UC commitment length extension can be realized with rate $1 - o(1)$.

Theorem 3 (Rate-1 UC commitment length extension). *Let κ be a computational security parameter, and assume the existence of semi-honest standalone oblivious transfer. Then, for all $c > 0$, there exists a protocol which UC-realizes a single instance of $\mathcal{F}_{\text{MCOM}}[\kappa^c]$ with rate $1 - o(1)$ and makes a single call to $\mathcal{F}_{\text{MCOM}}[\kappa]$.*

Proof. The desired protocol is obtained by using the results of [15,9] to implement the necessary calls to the OT functionality in a protocol obtained by composing protocols of Lemma 2 and Lemma 1.

Using a single call to $\mathcal{F}_{\text{MCOM}}[\kappa]$, we can generate a uniformly random string (URS) of length κ. Interpreting this κ-bit string as a $\kappa^{1/2}$ instances of a $\kappa^{1/2}$-bit URS, and assuming the existence of semi-honest stand-alone OT, one can apply the results of Damgård et al. [15], or Choi et a. [9] to obtain κ^α instances of $\mathcal{F}_{\text{OT}}[\kappa^\alpha]$ with $p(\kappa^\alpha)$ invocations of a semi-honest stand-alone OT and communication cost $p(\kappa^\alpha)$, where $p(\cdot)$ is some polynomial, as long as $\alpha \leq 1/2$. We set $\alpha \in (0, 1/2)$ such that $p(\kappa^\alpha) = o(\kappa^c)$.

Using Lemma 2 with parameters $\sigma = \kappa$, and n, ϵ such that $n^{1+\epsilon} = \kappa^\alpha/10$, and $\ell = \kappa^c$, we can UC-realize $\mathcal{F}_{\text{MCOM}}[\kappa^c]$ by making $n + 2n^{1-\epsilon}$ calls to $\mathcal{F}^\delta_{\text{OT}_R}[\kappa^c/n]$ with $\delta = (2n^\epsilon + 4)^{-1}$. Then, setting $\kappa_{\text{prg}} = \kappa^\alpha$, we use Lemma 1 to UC-realize these $n + 2n^{1-\epsilon}$ calls to $\mathcal{F}^\delta_{\text{OT}_R}[\kappa^c/n]$ with communication complexity $(n + 2n^{1-\epsilon}) \cdot ((\kappa^c/n) + (1/\delta) + 3\kappa^\alpha \cdot (1/\delta))$ while making $2n^{1+\epsilon} + 8n$ calls to $\mathcal{F}_{\text{OT}}[\kappa_{\text{prg}}]$.

Thus, for parameters $n, \epsilon, \kappa_{\text{prg}}$ as described above, we see that the communication complexity is $\kappa^c(1+o(1))$ while making (at most) κ^α calls to $\mathcal{F}_{\text{OT}}[\kappa^\alpha]$. As described in the previous paragraph, these κ^α calls to $\mathcal{F}_{\text{OT}}[\kappa^\alpha]$ can be implemented with communication cost $o(\kappa^c)$. Therefore, a single instance of $\mathcal{F}_{\text{MCOM}}[\kappa^c]$ can be realized with communication cost $\kappa^c(1+o(1))$ in each phase.

For any setup where it is possible to construct UC-secure commitments on κ-bit strings (i.e., realize $\mathcal{F}_{\text{MCOM}}[\kappa]$), then assuming the existence of semi-honest stand-alone oblivious transfer, Theorem 3 implies that it is possible to realize UC-secure commitments on strings of arbitrary length (in particular, on κ-bit strings) with rate $1-o(1)$ in that model. We explicitly state this for the CRS model, where it is known that a protocol for UC commitments in the CRS model implies the existence of semi-honest stand-alone oblivious transfer [15].

Corollary 1. *If UC commitments exist in the CRS model, then they exist with rate $1 - o(1)$.*

4.2   UC Commitment Length Extension Implies OT

We now show that the existence of semi-honest stand-alone OT is necessary for the result above.

Theorem 4. *Let κ be a computational security parameter, and suppose there exists a protocol in which at most one party is allowed to make (at most) a single call to $\mathcal{F}_{\text{MCOM}}[\kappa]$ to UC-realize a single instance of $\mathcal{F}_{\text{MCOM}}[3\kappa]$. Then there exists a protocol for semi-honest stand-alone OT.*

Here we present only a proof sketch. The full proof is deferred to the full version.

Proof. We begin with a proof (sketch) for a weaker statement, namely, that UC commitment length extension from κ bits to 3κ bits implies key agreement. Recall that key agreement is implied by OT.

Key Agreement from Length Extension. Let Π denote the commitment protocol assumed to exist. We construct a bit agreement protocol between two parties, A and B, from Π as follows:

- A commits to a random 3κ-bit string m by acting as the honest sender in an execution of Π, and in addition, sends the query $q \in \{0,1\}^\kappa$ it makes to the short commitment oracle and a random $r \in \{0,1\}^\kappa$;
- B runs the UC straight-line extractor for Π to obtain m.

Both parties then agree on the Goldreich-Levin hard-core bit [20] $b = \langle m, r \rangle$ of m.

We now want to argue that an eavesdropper does not learn anything about b in two steps:

- First, if we ignore the query q, then the view of the eavesdropper is exactly the commitment-phase transcript for Π, which reveals no information about m, which means m has 3κ bits of *information-theoretic* entropy.

– The query q then reveals at most κ bits of information about m. Therefore, even upon revealing q, the message m still has $\approx 2\kappa$ bits of (min-)entropy. Then, the Goldreich-Levin hard-core bit works as a randomness extractor to derive a random bit from m.

Correctness is straightforward. To establish security against an eavesdropper, we crucially use the fact that a UC commitment scheme is equivocal, which allows us to essentially argue that m has 3κ bits of information-theoretic entropy. (Indeed, revealing κ bits of information about a 3κ-bit pseudorandom string could reveal the entire string, as is the case when we reveal the seed used to generate the output of a pseudorandom generator.)

Remark. For technical reasons, we will require that the equivocal simulator can simulate not only the public transcript of the protocol, but also the query q made to the short commitment oracle. The existence of such a simulator does not follow immediately from UC security, since the query q may not be revealed to the malicious receiver and the environment. To handle this issue, we basically proceed via a case analysis:

– If the honest sender always reveals q to the receiver either in the commit or the reveal phase, then the equivocal simulator must be able to simulate the query q since it is part of the public transcript.

– Otherwise, we show by a simple argument that a cheating receiver can break the hiding property of the commitment scheme. (See full version for details.)

We are now ready to show the OT implication.

OT from Length Extension. In the OT protocol, A holds (b_0, b_1), B holds σ, and B wants to learn b_σ. The protocol proceeds as follows:

– Alice runs two independent executions Π_0, Π_1 of the key agreement protocol for two random strings $m_0, m_1 \in \{0,1\}^{3\kappa}$ in parallel. In addition, A sends

$$z_0 = b_0 \oplus \langle m_0, r_0 \rangle, \quad z_1 = b_1 \oplus \langle m_1, r_1 \rangle.$$

– In the execution Π_σ, B behaves as in the key agreement protocol, which allows him to learn $\langle m_\sigma, r_\sigma \rangle$ and thus recover b_σ. In the other execution, B acts as the honest receiver in an execution of commitment scheme Π.

Correctness follows readily from that of key agreement. We argue security as follows:

– First, we claim that a corrupted semi-honest A does not learn σ. This follows from UC security of the commitment scheme against corrupted senders.

– Next, we claim that a corrupted semi-honest B does not learn $b_{1-\sigma}$. This follows essentially from a similar argument to that for the security of the key agreement protocol with two notable differences: (i) in the execution $\Pi_{1-\sigma}$, B acts as the honest receiver in Π (instead of running the extractor as in the key agreement protocol), and (ii) a semi-honest B learns the coin tosses of the receiver in Π, whereas an eavesdropper for the key agreementprotocol does not. Handling (i) is fairly straightforward albeit a bit technical; to handle (ii), we simply use the fact that the commitment phase transcript reveals no information about the committed value, even given the coin tosses of the honest receiver.

References

1. Abdalla, M., Benhamouda, F., Blazy, O., Chevalier, C., Pointcheval, D.: SPHF-friendly non-interactive commitments. In: Sako, K., Sarkar, P. (eds.) ASIACRYPT 2013, Part I. LNCS, vol. 8269, pp. 214–234. Springer, Heidelberg (2013)
2. Beaver, D.: Correlated pseudorandomness and the complexity of private computations. In: 28th Annual ACM Symposium on Theory of Computing (STOC), pp. 479–488. ACM Press (May 1996)
3. Bendlin, R., Damgård, I., Orlandi, C., Zakarias, S.: Semi-homomorphic encryption and multiparty computation. In: Paterson, K.G. (ed.) EUROCRYPT 2011. LNCS, vol. 6632, pp. 169–188. Springer, Heidelberg (2011)
4. Blazy, O., Chevalier, C., Pointcheval, D., Vergnaud, D.: Analysis and improvement of Lindell's UC-secure commitment schemes. In: Jacobson, M., Locasto, M., Mohassel, P., Safavi-Naini, R. (eds.) ACNS 2013. LNCS, vol. 7954, pp. 534–551. Springer, Heidelberg (2013)
5. Brassard, G., Crepeau, C., Robert, J.-M.: Information theoretic reduction among disclosure problems. In: FOCS, pp. 168–173 (1986)
6. Canetti, R.: Universally composable security: A new paradigm for cryptographic protocols. In: 42nd Annual Symposium on Foundations of Computer Science (FOCS), pp. 136–145. IEEE (October 2001)
7. Canetti, R., Fischlin, M.: Universally composable commitments. In: Kilian, J. (ed.) CRYPTO 2001. LNCS, vol. 2139, pp. 19–40. Springer, Heidelberg (2001)
8. Canetti, R., Lindell, Y., Ostrovsky, R., Sahai, A.: Universally composable two-party and multi-party secure computation. In: 34th Annual ACM Symposium on Theory of Computing (STOC), pp. 494–503. ACM Press (May 2002)
9. Choi, S.G., Dachman-Soled, D., Malkin, T., Wee, H.: Simple, black-box constructions of adaptively secure protocols. In: Reingold, O. (ed.) TCC 2009. LNCS, vol. 5444, pp. 387–402. Springer, Heidelberg (2009)
10. Choi, S.G., Katz, J., Wee, H., Zhou, H.-S.: Efficient, adaptively secure, and composable oblivious transfer with a single, global CRS. In: Kurosawa, K., Hanaoka, G. (eds.) PKC 2013. LNCS, vol. 7778, pp. 73–88. Springer, Heidelberg (2013)
11. Crépeau, C.: Equivalence between two flavours of oblivious transfers. In: Pomerance, C. (ed.) CRYPTO 1987. LNCS, vol. 293, pp. 350–354. Springer, Heidelberg (1988)
12. Damgård, I., David, B., Giacomelli, I., Nielsen, J.B.: Homomorphic uc commitments in uc (2013) (manuscript)
13. Damgård, I., Groth, J.: Non-interactive and reusable non-malleable commitment schemes. In: 35th Annual ACM Symposium on Theory of Computing (STOC), pp. 426–437. ACM Press (June 2003)
14. Damgård, I., Nielsen, J.B.: Perfect hiding and perfect binding universally composable commitment schemes with constant expansion factor. In: Yung, M. (ed.) CRYPTO 2002. LNCS, vol. 2442, pp. 581–596. Springer, Heidelberg (2002)
15. Damgård, I., Nielsen, J.B., Orlandi, C.: On the necessary and sufficient assumptions for UC computation. In: Micciancio, D. (ed.) TCC 2010. LNCS, vol. 5978, pp. 109–127. Springer, Heidelberg (2010)

16. Fischlin, M., Libert, B., Manulis, M.: Non-interactive and reusable universally composable string commitments with adaptive security. In: Lee, D.H., Wang, X. (eds.) ASIACRYPT 2011. LNCS, vol. 7073, pp. 468–485. Springer, Heidelberg (2011)

17. Franklin, M., Yung, M.: Communication complexity of secure computation. In: STOC, pp. 699–710 (1992)

18. Frederiksen, T., Jakobsen, T., Nielsen, J., Nordholt, P., Orlandi, C.: Minilego: Efficient secure two-party computation from general assumptions. In: Johansson, T., Nguyen, P.Q. (eds.) EUROCRYPT 2013. LNCS, vol. 7881, pp. 537–556. Springer, Heidelberg (2013)

19. Fujisaki, E.: A framework for efficient fully-equipped UC commitments. ePrint 2012/379 (2012)

20. Goldreich, O., Levin, L.A.: A hard-core predicate for all one-way functions. In: 21st Annual ACM Symposium on Theory of Computing (STOC), pp. 25–32. ACM Press (May 1989)

21. Groth, J., Sahai, A.: Efficient non-interactive proof systems for bilinear groups. In: Smart, N.P. (ed.) EUROCRYPT 2008. LNCS, vol. 4965, pp. 415–432. Springer, Heidelberg (2008)

22. Hofheinz, D., Müller-Quade, J., Unruh, D.: On the (im-)possibility of extending coin toss. In: Vaudenay, S. (ed.) EUROCRYPT 2006. LNCS, vol. 4004, pp. 504–521. Springer, Heidelberg (2006)

23. Ishai, Y., Kilian, J., Nissim, K., Petrank, E.: Extending oblivious transfers efficiently. In: Boneh, D. (ed.) CRYPTO 2003. LNCS, vol. 2729, pp. 145–161. Springer, Heidelberg (2003)

24. Ishai, Y., Prabhakaran, M., Sahai, A.: Founding cryptography on oblivious transfer - efficiently. In: Wagner, D. (ed.) CRYPTO 2008. LNCS, vol. 5157, pp. 572–591. Springer, Heidelberg (2008)

25. Jutla, C.S., Roy, A.: Shorter quasi-adaptive nizk proofs for linear subspaces. In: Sako, K., Sarkar, P. (eds.) ASIACRYPT 2013, Part I. LNCS, vol. 8269, pp. 1–20. Springer, Heidelberg (2013)

26. Kilian, J.: Founding cryptography on oblivious transfer. In: STOC, pp. 20–31 (1988)

27. Kraschewski, D.: Complete primitives for information-theoretically secure two-party computation (2013), http://digbib.ubka.uni-karlsruhe.de/volltexte/1000035100 (retrieved October 14, 2013)

28. Lindell, Y.: Highly-efficient universally-composable commitments based on the DDH assumption. In: Paterson, K.G. (ed.) EUROCRYPT 2011. LNCS, vol. 6632, pp. 446–466. Springer, Heidelberg (2011)

29. Lindell, Y., Zarosim, H.: On the feasibility of extending oblivious transfer. In: Sahai, A. (ed.) TCC 2013. LNCS, vol. 7785, pp. 519–538. Springer, Heidelberg (2013)

30. Maji, H., Prabhakaran, M., Rosulek, M.: Cryptographic complexity classes and computational intractability assumptions. In: ICS, pp. 266–289 (2010)

31. Nielsen, J., Nordholt, P., Orlandi, C., Burra, S.S.: A new approach to practical active-secure two-party computation. In: Safavi-Naini, R., Canetti, R. (eds.) CRYPTO 2012. LNCS, vol. 7417, pp. 681–700. Springer, Heidelberg (2012)

32. Nielsen, J.B.: Separating random oracle proofs from complexity theoretic proofs: The non-committing encryption case. In: Yung, M. (ed.) CRYPTO 2002. LNCS, vol. 2442, pp. 111–126. Springer, Heidelberg (2002)

33. Nishimaki, R., Fujisaki, E., Tanaka, K.: An eficient non-interactive universally composable string-commitment scheme. IEICE Transactions, 167–175 (2012)

694   J.A. Garay et al.

34. Peikert, C., Vaikuntanathan, V., Waters, B.: A framework for efficient and composable oblivious transfer. In: Wagner, D. (ed.) CRYPTO 2008. LNCS, vol. 5157, pp. 554–571. Springer, Heidelberg (2008)

A Efficient Commitments for Cut-and-Choose

While our rate 1 construction has good concrete efficiency for large string commitments, the case of short string commitments leaves a lot to be desired. An obvious approach to handle short strings is simply to concatenate these strings together to form one large string, and then use the rate 1 construction with this string as the input message. While this approach does provide a concrete rate close to 1 when the number of instances is large, it has the drawback that all instances of short strings must be opened simultaneously. In this section, we design more efficient commitment scheme for handling multiple instances of κ-bit strings with two opening phases (as required in techniques such as cut-and-choose). The extension to three or more opening phases is straightforward.

For $i \in [n]$, let the i-th κ-bit string be denoted by m_i, and let $m = (m_1, \ldots, m_n)$. Let p denote the number of opening phases, and for $j \in [p]$, let u_j denote the characteristic vector of the subset $S_j \subseteq [n]$ of the strings that need to opened in the j-th opening phase. Note that u_j is not known to the sender during the commit phase.

Our high level idea is as follows. As in our rate 1 construction, we let the sender encode m in to m' using the rate 1 encoding scheme. In addition, for each $i \in [p]$, the sender uses the rate $1/2$ encoding scheme (naturally derived from Enc) to encode the zero string $(0, \ldots, 0) \in \mathbb{F}^n$ twice using independent randomness to obtain codewords $z^{(1)}, z^{(2)}$ (each of length $2n'$). Next the sender prepares to send symbols through the Rabin-OT oracle. For this, it constructs $M_k = (m'_k, z^{(1)}_k, z^{(2)}_k)$ for $k \leq n'$, and symbols $M_k = (z^{(1)}_k, z^{(2)}_k)$ for $k \in \{n'+1, \ldots, 2n'\}$, as the k-th input to the Rabin-OT oracle. Then, it transmits M_k through Rabin-OT oracle with parameter $\delta' = \delta/2$ (where δ is the best parameter for obtaining commitments on strings of length $n\kappa$). Then, in the j-th opening phase, the receiver sends the randomness (alternatively, a seed to a PRG) to encode u_j into u'_j using the rate 1 encoding scheme. Now, denote the underlying polynomials (cf. Figure 4) for (1) the rate 1 encoding of m by q_m, (2) the rate $1/2$ encoding of $z^{(j)}$ as $q_z^{(j)}$, and (3) the rate 1 encoding of u_j by q_u^j. In the j-th opening phase, the sender simply reveals the polynomial $q^{(j)} = (q_m \cdot q_u^j) + q_z^{(j)}$. Now, let $\{\tilde{M}_k\}_{k \in J}$ denote the messages received by the receiver. The receiver checks if for all $k \in J \cap [n']$, it holds that $\tilde{M}_k = (\tilde{m}'_k, \tilde{z}^{(1)}_k, \tilde{z}^{(2)}_k)$ satisfies $q^{(j)}(k) = (\tilde{m}'_k \cdot q_u^j(k)) + \tilde{z}^{(j)}_k$. If the check succeeds, then the receiver computes $v_i = q^{(j)}(e_i)$, where e_i are the publicly known points as described in Figure 4. If for all $i \notin S_j$, it holds that $v_i = 0$, then receiver outputs $\{v_j\}_{j \in S_j}$ and terminates, else it outputs $\perp$ and terminates. Let c_1, c_2, c_3 represent our concrete cost of realizing commitments on strings of length $n\kappa$ in the offline, the online commit, and the online reveal phases respectively. It can be verified that the cost of the above scheme that implements n instances of κ-bit commitments with two opening phases is $\approx 8c_1, 2c_2, 2c_3$ in the offline, the online commit, and the online reveal phases respectively.

Universally Composable Symbolic Analysis for Two-Party Protocols Based on Homomorphic Encryption[*]

Morten Dahl and Ivan Damgård

Aarhus University, Denmark

Abstract. We consider a class of two-party function evaluation protocols in which the parties are allowed to use ideal functionalities as well
as a set of powerful primitives, namely commitments, homomorphic encryption, and certain zero-knowledge proofs. With these it is possible to
capture protocols for oblivious transfer, coin-flipping, and generation of
multiplication-triples.

We show how any protocol in our class can be compiled to a symbolic
representation expressed as a process in an abstract process calculus, and
prove a general computational soundness theorem implying that if the
protocol realises a given ideal functionality in the symbolic setting, then
the original version also realises the ideal functionality in the standard
computational UC setting. In other words, the theorem allows us to
transfer a proof in the abstract symbolic setting to a proof in the standard
UC model.

Finally, we have verified that the symbolic interpretation is simple
enough in a number of cases for the symbolic proof to be partly automated using the ProVerif tool.

Keywords: Cryptographic protocols, Security analysis, Symbolic analysis, Automated analysis, Computational soundness, Universal composition, Homomorphic encryption.

1 Introduction

Giving security proofs for cryptographic protocols is often a complicated and
error-prone task, and there is a large body of research targeted at this problem
using methods from formal analysis [AR02, BPW03, CH06, CC08, CKW11].
This is interesting because the approach could potentially lead to automated or
at least computer-aided (formal) proofs of security.

It is well known that the main difficulty with formal analysis is that it is
only feasible when enough details about the cryptographic primitives have been

---

[*] The authors acknowledge support from the Danish National Research Foundation
and The National Science Foundation of China (under the grant 61061130540) for
the Sino-Danish Center for the Theory of Interactive Computation, and also from
the CFEM research centre (supported by the Danish Strategic Research Council)
within which part of this work was performed.

P.Q. Nguyen and E. Oswald (Eds.): EUROCRYPT 2014, LNCS 8441, pp. 695–712, 2014.

abstracted away, while on the other hand this abstraction may make us "forget" about issues that make an attack possible. One solution is to show once and for all that a given abstraction is *computational sound*, which loosely speaking means that for any protocol, if we know there are no attacks on its abstract *symbolic* version then this (and some appropriate complexity assumption) implies there are no attacks on the original *computational* version. Such soundness theorems are known in some cases (see related work), in particular for primitives such as public-key encryption, symmetric encryption, signatures, and hash functions.

Another issue with formal analysis is how security properties should be specified. Traditionally this has been done either through trace properties or "strong secrecy" where two instances of the protocol running on different values are compared to each other[1]. This approach can be used to specify security properties such as authenticity and key secrecy. However, it is much less clear how it can capture security of protocols such as oblivious transfer where players take input from the environment. In the cryptographic community it is standard to give simulations-based definitions of security for such protocols, yet this approach have so far only received little attention in formal analysis.

Finally, making protocol (and in particular system) analysis feasible in general requires some way of breaking the task into smaller components which may be analysed independently. While also this has been standard in the cryptographic community for a while (in the form of, e.g., the UC framework [Can01]) it has not yet received much attention in the symbolic community (but see [CH06] for an exception).

1.1 Our Results

In this paper we make progress on expanding the class of protocols for which a formal analysis can be used to show security in the computational setting. We are particularly interested in two-party function evaluation protocols and the primitives used by many of these, namely homomorphic public-key encryption, commitments, and certain zero-knowledge proofs. We aim for proofs of UC security against an active adversary where one party may be (statically) corrupted.

Protocol Model. Besides the above primitives protocols are also allowed to use ideal functionalities and communicate over authenticated channels. We put some restrictions on how the primitives may be used. First, whenever a player sends a ciphertext he actually sends a package which also contains a zero-knowledge proof that the sender knows how the ciphertext was constructed: if the ciphertext was made from scratch then he knows the plaintext and randomness used, and if he constructed it from other ciphertexts using the homomorphic property then he knows randomness that "explains" the ciphertext as a function of

---

[1] For strong secrecy one runs the same protocol on two fixed but different inputs (or with one instance patched to give an independent output) and then ask if it is possible to tell the difference between the two executions. This can for instance be used to argue that a key-exchange protocol is independent of the exchanged key given only the transmitted messages.

that randomness and ciphertexts that were already known. We make a similar assumption on commitments and allow also zero-knowledge proofs that committed values relate to encrypted values in a given way. Second, we assume that honest players use the primitives in a black-box fashion, i.e. an honest player can run the protocol using a (private) "crypto module" that holds all his keys and handles encryption, decryption, commitment etc. This means that all actions taken by an honest player in the protocol may depend on plaintext sent or received but not, for instance, on the binary representation of ciphertexts. We emphasise that we make no such restriction on the adversary.

We believe that the assumptions we make are quite natural: it is well known that if a player provides input to a protocol by committing to it or sending an encryption then we cannot prove UC security of the protocol unless the player proves that he knows the input he provides. Furthermore, active security usually requires players to communicate over authenticated channels and prove that the messages they send are well-formed. We stress, however, that our assumptions do not imply that an adversary must be semi-honest; for instance, our model does not make any assumptions on what type and relationship checks the protocol must perform, nor on the randomness distributions used by a corrupted player.

Security Properties. We use *ideal functionalities* and *simulators* to specify and prove security properties. More concretely, we say that a *protocol ϕ is secure* (with respect to the ideal functionality $\mathcal{F}$) if no adversary can tell the difference between interacting with ϕ and interacting with $\mathcal{F}$ and simulator Sim, later written $\phi \sim \mathcal{F} \diamond Sim$ for concrete notions of indistinguishability. When this equivalence is satisfied we also say that the protocol *(UC) realises* the ideal functionality. We require that ideal functionalities only operate on plain values and do not use cryptography. Like honest players in protocols, our simulators will only use the primitives and their trapdoors in a black-box fashion which allows us to specify them on an abstract level.

Proof Technique. Our main result is quite simple to state on a high level: given a protocol ϕ, ideal functionality $\mathcal{F}$, and simulator Sim, we show how these may be compiled to symbolic versions such that if we are given a proof *in the symbolic world* that ϕ realises $\mathcal{F}$ then it follows that ϕ realises $\mathcal{F}$ *in the usual computational world* as well (assuming the crypto-system, commitment scheme and zero-knowledge proofs used are secure). As usual for UC security, we need to make a set-up assumption which in our case amounts to assuming a functionality that initially produces reference strings for the zero-knowledge proofs and keys for the crypto-system.

We arrive at our result as follows. First we define a simple programming language for specifying, on a rather high and abstract level, the programmes for honest players, ideal functionalities, and simulators that participate in a session of both the *real protocol* containing ϕ and the *ideal protocol* containing $\mathcal{F}$ and the simulator. The language is parameterised by the three corruption scenarios, indicated by which players are honest $\mathcal{H} \in \{AB, A, B\}$, and the class of protocols and properties we consider is implicitly defined as whatever can be described in it. We call such a set of programmes a *system* and may hence fully describe real and ideal protocols by system triples $(Sys^{AB}, Sys^{A}, Sys^{B})$.

We then define three different ways of interpreting such systems:

- *Real-world interpretation* $\mathcal{RW}(Sys)$: Assuming concrete instantiations of the cryptographic primitives this interpretation produces from system Sys a set of interactive Turing machines that fits in the usual UC model. For instance, if Sys_{real}^{AB} is the system for a real protocol in the scenario where both players are honest then $\mathcal{RW}(Sys_{real}^{AB})$ contains two ITMs M_A, M_B executing the player programmes.
- *Intermediate interpretation* $\mathcal{I}(Sys)$: This interpretation also produces a set of ITMs fitting into the UC model, but does not use concrete cryptographic primitives. Instead we postulate an ideal functionality $\mathcal{F}_{aux}$ that receives all calls from all parties to cryptographic functions and returns handles to objects such as encrypted plaintexts while storing these plaintexts in its memory. Players then send such handles instead of actual ciphertexts and commitments. In this interpretation, the adversary is limited to a certain benign cryptographic behaviour as he too can only access cryptographic objects through $\mathcal{F}_{aux}$.
- *Symbolic interpretation* $\mathcal{S}(Sys)$: This interpretation closely mirrors the intermediate interpretation but instead produces a set of *processes* described in a well-known process calculus.

Having defined these interpretations we define notions of equivalence of systems in each representation: $\mathcal{RW}(Sys_1) \overset{c}{\sim} \mathcal{RW}(Sys_2)$ means that no polynomial time environment can distinguish the two cases given only the public and corrupted keys, and may for instance be used to capture that a protocol UC-securely realises $\mathcal{F}$ in the standard sense; for the intermediate world $\mathcal{I}(Sys_1) \overset{c}{\sim} \mathcal{I}(Sys_2)$ means the same but in the $\mathcal{F}_{aux}$-hybrid model; finally, $\mathcal{S}(Sys_1) \overset{s}{\sim} \mathcal{S}(Sys_2)$ means the two processes are *observationally equivalent* in the standard symbolic sense.

We then prove two soundness theorems stating first, that $\mathcal{I}(Sys_1) \overset{c}{\sim} \mathcal{I}(Sys_2)$ implies $\mathcal{RW}(Sys_1) \overset{c}{\sim} \mathcal{RW}(Sys_2)$ and second, that $\mathcal{S}(Sys_1) \overset{s}{\sim} \mathcal{S}(Sys_2)$ implies $\mathcal{I}(Sys_1) \overset{c}{\sim} \mathcal{I}(Sys_2)$, so that in order to prove UC security of a protocol it is now sufficient to show equivalence in the symbolic model and this is the part we may automate using e.g. ProVerif [BAF05].

Finally, we note that in some cases (in particular when both players are honest) it is possible to use a standard simulator construction and instead check a different symbolic criteria along the lines of previous work [CH06]. This removes the manual effort required in constructing simulators.

Analysis Approach. Given the above, a protocol ϕ may be analysed as follows:

1. formulate in our model protocol ϕ and the ideal functionalities $\mathcal{F}_1, \ldots, \mathcal{F}_n$ it uses as a triple $(Sys_{real}^{AB}, Sys_{real}^{A}, Sys_{real}^{B})$
2. likewise formulate the target ideal functionality $\mathcal{G}$ and suitable simulators as a triple $(Sys_{ideal}^{AB}, Sys_{ideal}^{A}, Sys_{ideal}^{B})$
3. show in the symbolic model that $\mathcal{S}(Sys_{real}^{\mathcal{H}}) \overset{s}{\sim} \mathcal{S}(Sys_{ideal}^{\mathcal{H}})$ for all three $\mathcal{H}$

4. the soundness theorem then gives $\mathcal{RW}(Sys_{real}^{\mathcal{H}}) \overset{c}{\sim} \mathcal{RW}(Sys_{ideal}^{\mathcal{H}})$, and in turn that ϕ realises $\mathcal{G}$ under static corruption

Note that as usual in the UC framework we only need to consider one session of the protocol since the compositional theorem guarantees that it remains secure even when composed with itself a polynomial number of times. Note also that we may apply our result to a broader class of protocols through a hybrid-symbolic approach where the protocol in question is broken down into several sub-protocols and ideal functionalities analysed independently either within our framework or outside in an ad-hoc setting (possibly using other primitives).

We have tried to make the symbolic model suitable for automated analysis using current tools such as ProVerif, and although our approach requires the manual construction of a simulator for the symbolic version of the protocol, this is usually a very simple task. As a case study we have carried out a full analysis of the OT protocol from [DNO08] in the full version of this paper[2], where we also illustrate compositional analyses through a coin-flipping protocol, and that the model may express the preprocessing phase of the multi-party computation protocol in [BDOZ11][3].

1.2 Related Work

The main area of related work is *computational soundness* as discussed below (see also [CKW11] for an in-depth survey of this area), but there is also a large body of work on *symbolic modelling of security properties* which at this point has not given much attention to the simulation-based paradigm (see [DKP09, BU13] for two examples without computational soundness), as well as a substantial amount of work on the *direct approach* where the symbolic model is altogether avoided but instead used as inspiration for creating a computational model easier to analyse; this latter line of work includes [Bla08, BGHB11, MRST06, DDMR07] and while it is more expressive than the symbolic approach we have taken here, our focus has been on abstracting and automating as much as possible.

Computational Soundness. The line of work started by Backes et al. in [BPW03] and known as "the BPW approach" gives an ideal cryptographic library based on the ideas behind abstract Dolev-Yao models. The library is responsible for all operations that players and the adversary want to perform (such as encryption, decryption, and message sending) with every message being kept in a database by the library and accessed only through handles. Using the framework for reactive simulatability [PW01] (similar to the UC framework) the ideal library is realised using cryptographic primitives. This means that a protocol may be analysed relative to the ideal library yet exhibit the same properties when using the realisation instead. The original model supporting nested nonce generation, public-key

---

[2] Available at http://eprint.iacr.org/2013/296

[3] Due to limitations on expressibility of probabilistic choice in our model we analyse a slight variant of the protocol where the verification of the generated triples is pushed into the online phase.

encryption, and MACs has later been extended to support symmetric encryption [BP04] and a simple form of homomorphic threshold-encryption [LN08] allowing a single homomorphic evaluation. The approach has been used to analyse protocols for trace-based security properties such as authentication and key secrecy [BP03, BP06].

Comparing our work to the BPW approach we see that the functionality $\mathcal{F}_{aux}$ in our intermediate model corresponds to the ideal cryptographic library, and the real-world operation modules to the realisation. The difference lies in the supported operations, namely our more powerful homomorphic encryption and simulation operations – the former allows us to implement several two-party functionalities while the latter allows us to express simulators for ideal functionalities within the model. This not only allows us to capture an entirely different class of indistinguishability-based security properties[4] (such as the standard assumptions on OT with static corruption) but also to do modular and hybrid-symbolic analysis. The importance of this was elaborated on in [Can08].

The next line of closely related work is that started by Canetti et al. in [CH06] and building on [MW04, BPW03] but adding support for modular analysis. They first formulate a programming language for protocols using public-key encryption and give both a computational and symbolic interpretation. They then give a mapping lemma showing that the traces of the two interpretations coincide, i.e. the computational adversary can do nothing that the symbolic adversary cannot also do (except with negligible probability). This is used to give symbolic criteria for realising authentication and key-exchange functionalities, and show that ProVerif may be used to automate the analysis of the original Needham-Schroeder-Lowe protocol (relative to authenticity) and two of its variants (relative to key-exchange). Later work [CG10] again targets key-exchange protocols but adds support for digital signatures, Diffie-Hellman key-exchanges, and forward security under adaptive corruption.

Most importantly, our approach has been that of not fixing the target ideal functionalities but instead letting it be expressible in the model (along with the realising protocol and simulator). Hence it is relatively straight-forward to analyse protocols implementing other functionalities than what we have done here, whereas adapting [CH06] to other classes of protocols requires manually finding and showing soundness of a symbolic criteria. It is furthermore not clear which functionalities may be captured by symbolic criteria expressed as trace properties and strong secrecy. In particular, the target functionalities of [CH06] and [CG10] do not take any input from the players nor provide any security guarantees when a player is corrupt, and hence the criteria do not need to account for these case. Again we also show soundness for a different set of primitives.

---

[4] In principle the BPW model could be used as a stepping-stone to analyse cases where the simulator may simply run the protocol on constants. However, the simulator is sometimes required to use trapdoors in order to extract information needed to simulate an ideal functionality in the simulation-based paradigm. These cases cannot be analysed with the operations of the BPW model.

The final line of related work is showing soundness of indistinguishability-based (instead of trace-based) properties. This was started by Comon-Lundh et al. in [CC08] and, unlike the two previous lines of work, aims at showing that if the symbolic adversary cannot distinguish between two systems in the symbolic interpretation then the computational adversary cannot do so either for the computational interpretation. [CC08] showed this for symmetric encryption and was continued in [CHKS12] for public-key encryption and hash functions.

Our work obviously relates in that we are also concerned about soundness of indistinguishability. Again the biggest difference is the choice of primitives, but also that our framework seems more suitable for expressing ideal functionalities and simulators: although mentioned as an application, their model does not appear to be easily adapted to capturing the typical structure of a composable analysis framework such as the UC framework (private channels are not allowed for instance). To this end the result is closer to what might be achieved through the BPW approach. Note that the work in [CHKS12] does not require computable parsing (as we do through the NIZK proofs). However, for secure function evaluation in the simulation-based paradigm some form of computational extraction is typically required in general.

The work in [BMM10] is also somewhat related in that they also aim at analysing secure function evaluation, namely secure multi-party computations (MPC). However, they instead analyse protocols using MPC as a primitive whereas we are interested in analysing the (lower-level) protocols realising MPC. Moreover, they are again limited to trace properties.

Organisation. The rest of the paper is organised in a "top-down" approach of progressively removing cryptography and bitstrings, and ending up with an highly idealised model. Section 2 specifies our protocol class including the interface of the operation modules. Section 3 gives the preliminaries for the real-world interpretation in Section 4. The intermediate and symbolic worlds are given in Section 5 and 6 respectively together with their soundness statements. Further details including definitions and proofs are given in the full version of this paper.

2   Protocol Model

The specific form of protocols introduced here is an essential part of our soundness result in that it characterises the class of protocols for which the result holds. The model is parameterised by a finite domain of *values* $\{V_n\}$, two finite sets of *types* $\{T_i\}, \{U_j\}$, and two finite sets of arithmetic *expressions* $\{e_k\} \subseteq \{f_\ell\}$ which for simplicity we often assume to be over four variables.

Programmes are given in a simple programming language allowing input, output, conditionals, and invocation of operations. We consider three kinds of programmes, *plain*, *player*, and *simulator*, differing in what operations they may use and whether or not they accept cryptographic packages.

Plain programmes, such as ideal functionalities, may only use operations

$$\mathsf{isValue}(x) \to b, \ \mathsf{eqValue}(v, w) \to b, \ \mathsf{inType}_U(v) \to b, \ \mathsf{inType}_T(v) \to b,$$
$$\mathsf{peval}_f(v_1, v_2, w_1, w_2) \to v, \ \mathsf{isConst}(x) \to b, \ \mathsf{eqConst}_c(x) \to b,$$
$$\mathsf{isPair}(x) \to b, \ \mathsf{pair}(x_1, x_2) \to x, \ \mathsf{first}(x) \to x_1, \ \mathsf{second}(x) \to x_2$$

where for instance isValue determines if a message is a value, inType_U if a value belongs to type U, peval_f evaluates expression f on the four values, pair forms a pairing, and first projects the first component of a pairing. Their input command aborts if any cryptographic package is received.

Player programmes, in addition to those of plain programmes, may also use operations

$$\mathsf{isComPack}(x) \to b, \ \mathsf{isEncPack}(x) \to b, \ \mathsf{isEvalPack}(x) \to b,$$
$$\mathsf{commit}_{U,ck,crs}(v, r) \to d, \ \mathsf{encrypt}_{T,ek,crs}(v, r) \to c,$$
$$\mathsf{eval}_{e,ek,ck,crs}(c_1, c_2, v_1, r_1, v_2, r_2) \to c, \ \mathsf{decrypt}_{dk}(c) \to v,$$
$$\mathsf{verComPack}_{U,ck,crs}(d) \to b, \ \mathsf{verEncPack}_{T,ek,crs}(c) \to b,$$
$$\mathsf{verEvalPack}_{e,ek,ck,crs}(c, c_1, c_2, [d_1, d_2]) \to b$$

to respectively determine: whether a message is a cryptographic package and its kind; form a new commitment package under their own commitment key and CRS using the value and randomness supplied, and with a proof of plaintext membership in type U[5]; form a new encryption package under either encryption key and their own CRS using the value and randomness supplied, and with a proof of plaintext membership in type T; form a new evaluation package under the encryption key of the inputs and their own commitment key and CRS, with a fresh ciphertext, a proof that it was created through homomorphic evaluation of expression e on inputs c_1, c_2, v_1, v_2, and commitments to v_1, v_2 under the randomness supplied[6]; decrypt a ciphertext under their own encryption key; and finally verify cryptographic packages under the specified keys and, in case of evaluation packages, that the correct ciphertexts and (optional) commitments were used. Their input command aborts on cryptographic packages not created under the commitment key and CRS of the other player.

Finally, simulator programmes instead use simulation versions of the player operations

$$\mathsf{simcommit}_{U,ck,simtd}(v, r) \to d, \ \mathsf{simencrypt}_{T,ek,simtd}(v, r) \to c,$$
$$\mathsf{simeval}_{e,ek,ck,simtd}(c_1, c_2, v_1, r_1, v_2, r_2) \to c,$$
$$\mathsf{simeval}_{e,ek,ck,simtd}(v, c_1, c_2, d_1, d_2) \to c$$

---

[5] Note that the NIZK proofs allow us to realise an ideal commitment functionality with opening despite no explicit opening operation for commitments.

[6] Note that as an artefact from wanting a symbolic model easier to analysis with available tools, operation eval_e (unlike commit_U and $\mathsf{encrypt}_T$) only takes r_1, r_2 for commitments d_1, d_2 as input, and not an r for re-randomisation of the resulting ciphertext; instead, the implementations will choose fresh randomness internally.

for an honest player (and no decryption operation), and operations

$$\text{extractCom}_{extd}(d) \rightarrow v, \ \text{extractEnc}_{extd}(c) \rightarrow v,$$
$$\text{extractEval}_{1,extd}(c) \rightarrow v, \ \text{extractEval}_{2,extd}(c) \rightarrow v$$

for a corrupt player. The operations for an honest player are similar to those of a player programme except that less checks are performed and proofs are simulated. The operations for a corrupt player allows the programme to extract the plaintext value of commitment and encryption packages, and the two plaintext values of commitments in evaluation packages, as long as they were created under the CRS of the corrupt player. Their input command behaves as for player programmes.

As an example, consider the OT protocol from [DNO08]. Intuitively, the receiver gets a bit b from the environment, encrypts it as c_b under his own encryption key, and sends c_b to the sender along with a proof that it really contains either 0 or 1. After checking the proof, the sender uses the homomorphic property to evaluate expression $sel(b, v_0, v_1) = (1 - b) \cdot v_0 + b \cdot v_1$ on the received ciphertext and the values v_0, v_1 given by the environment. He then sends the resulting ciphertext c_v back to the receiver along with a proof that it was constructed correctly. Finally, the receiver checks the proof to ensure that c_v was created using c_b, and outputs the decrypted value.

In our protocol model we may express the two players as the programmes in Figure 1 with sender P_{OT}^S on the left and receiver P_{OT}^R on the right. Under the three scenarios of static corruption the real protocol may then be described by system triple

$$\left(\ P_{OT}^S \diamond Auth_{RS} \diamond Auth_{SR} \diamond P_{OT}^R \ , \quad P_{OT}^S \ , \quad P_{OT}^R \ \right)$$

where the first system for when both players are honest also have one authenticated channel in each direction (and no ideal functionalities), and the next two systems for when one player is corrupted contain just the honest player programme. Likewise we may describe the ideal protocol with an ideal OT functionality and simulators in the protocol model, obtaining system triple

$$\left(\ \mathcal{F}_{OT}^{SR} \diamond Sim_{OT}^{SR,R} \diamond Auth_{RS} \diamond Auth_{SR} \diamond Sim_{OT}^{SR,S} \ , \right.$$
$$\left. \mathcal{F}_{OT}^S \diamond Sim_{OT}^S \ , \quad \mathcal{F}_{OT}^R \diamond Sim_{OT}^R \ \right)$$

with simulators that respectively run the protocol on dummy values, use extraction to obtain b, and use extraction to obtain v_0, v_1. In our case analysis we use ProVerif to conclude for each of the three cases that the two corresponding systems are indistinguishable.

Note that the input command $\text{input}_{\mathcal{P}}[p : x]$ is specified with a set of ports $\mathcal{P}$ on which the programme is also listening but which will result in the programme aborting. The motivation for having these is that the symbolic soundness result requires that systems are *non-losing*, in the sense that whenever a programme

$\text{input}_\emptyset[\textit{receive}_{RS} : c_b];$
  $\text{if verEncPack}_{bit,ek_R,crs_R}(c_b) \text{ then}$
    $\text{output}[\textit{out}_{OT}^S : \texttt{getInput}];$
$\text{input}_\emptyset[\textit{in}_{OT}^S : (v_0, v_1)];$
  $\text{if isValue}(v_0) \text{ and isValue}(v_1) \text{ then}$
  $\text{let } c_v \leftarrow \text{eval}_{sel,R,S,S}(c_v, v_0, r_0, v_1, r_1);$
    $\text{output}[\textit{send}_{SR} : c_v];$
stop

$\text{input}_\emptyset[\textit{in}_{OT}^R : b];$
  $\text{if inType}_{bit}(b) \text{ then}$
  $\text{let } c_b \leftarrow \text{encrypt}_{bit,ek_R,crs_R}(b, r);$
    $\text{output}[\textit{send}_{RS} : c_b];$
$\text{input}_\emptyset[\textit{receive}_{SR} : c_v];$
  $\text{if verEvalPack}_{sel,R,S,S}(c_v, c_b) \text{ then}$
  $\text{let } v_b \leftarrow \text{decrypt}_{dk_R}(c_v);$
    $\text{output}[\textit{out}_{OT}^R : v_b];$
stop

$$\text{where eval}_{sel,R,S,S}(\dots) = \text{eval}_{sel,ek_R,ck_S,crs_S}(\dots)$$
$$\text{and verEvalPack}_{sel,R,S,S}(\dots) = \text{verEvalPack}_{sel,ek_R,ck_S,crs_S}(\dots)$$

Fig. 1. Player programmes for OT sender (left) and receiver (right)

sends a message on a closed port p the receiving programme must also be listening on p. This also accounts for the atypical specification of the sender programme above; making it explicit ask the environment for its input by sending `getInput` means we may use $\mathcal{P} = \emptyset$ for all input commands, thereby simplifying the symbolic analysis.

3 Computational Model and Cryptographic Primitives

Our computational model is that of the UC framework as described in [Can01]. In this model ITMs in a network communicate by writing to each others tapes, thereby passing on the right to execute. In other words, the scheduling is token-based so that any ITM may only execute when it is holding the token. Initially the special *environment* ITM $\mathcal{Z}$ holds the token. When it writes on a tape of an ITM M in the network it passes on the token and M is now allowed to execute. If the token ever gets stuck it goes back to the environment.

For environment $\mathcal{Z}$, adversary $\mathcal{A}$, and network N, we write $\text{Exec}_{\mathcal{Z},\mathcal{A},N}(\kappa, z)$ for the random variable denoting the output bit (guess) of $\mathcal{Z}$ after interacting with $\mathcal{A}$ and N, and denote ensemble $\{\text{Exec}_{\mathcal{Z},\mathcal{A},N}(\kappa, z)\}_{\kappa\in\mathbb{N}, z\in\{0,1\}^*}$ by $\text{Exec}_{\mathcal{Z},\mathcal{A},N}$. We may then compare networks as follows:

Definition 1 (Computational Indistinguishability). *Two networks of ITMs N_1 and N_2 are* computational indistinguishability *when no polynomial time adversary $\mathcal{A}$ may allow a polynomial time environment $\mathcal{Z}$ to distinguish between them with more than negligible probability, i.e. for all PPT $\mathcal{Z}$ and $\mathcal{A}$ we have $\text{Exec}_{\mathcal{Z},\mathcal{A},N_1} \overset{c}{\approx} \text{Exec}_{\mathcal{Z},\mathcal{A},N_2}$ which we write $N_1 \overset{c}{\sim} N_2$.*

By allowing different adversaries in the two networks we also obtain a notion of one network realising another, namely network N_1 *realises* network N_2

when, for any PPT $\mathcal{A}$, there exists a PPT *simulator Sim* such that for all PPT $\mathcal{Z}$ we have $N_1 \overset{c}{\sim} N_2$.

We require the following primitives and security properties:

Commitment Scheme. We assume two PPT algorithms $\mathbf{ComKeyGen}(1^\kappa) \to ck$ and $\mathbf{Com}_{ck}(V,R) \to D$ for key-generation and commitment, respectively. We require that the scheme is *well-spread, computationally binding* and *computationally hiding*. Intuitively, well-spread means that it is hard to predict the outcome of honestly generating a commitment.

Homomorphic Encryption Scheme. An *encryption scheme* is given by three PPT algorithms $\mathbf{EncKeyGen}(1^\kappa) \to (ek, dk)$, $\mathbf{Enc}_{ek}(V,R) \to C$, and $\mathbf{Dec}_{dk}(C) \to V$. A *homomorphic* encryption scheme furthermore contains a PPT algorithm $\mathbf{Eval}_{e,ek}(C_1, C_2, V_1, V_2, R) \to C$ for arithmetic expression $e(x_1, x_2, y_1, y_2)$ and randomness R for re-randomisation. We require that the scheme is *well-spread, correct, history hiding* (or *formula private*), and IND-CPA secure for the entire domain. Here, correct means that decryption almost always succeeds for well-formed ciphertexts, and history hiding that a ciphertext produced using $\mathbf{Eval}_{e,ek}$ is distributed as $\mathbf{Enc}_{ek}$ on the same inputs.

Non-Interactive Zero-Knowledge Proof-of-Knowledge Scheme. For binary relation $\mathcal{R}$ we assume PPT algorithms $\mathbf{CrsGen}_{\mathcal{R}}(1^\kappa) \to crs$, $\mathbf{SimCrsGen}_{\mathcal{R}}(1^\kappa) \to (crs, simtd)$, and $\mathbf{ExCrsGen}_{\mathcal{R}}(1^\kappa) \to (crs, extd)$ for CRS generation, PPT algorithms $\mathbf{Prove}_{\mathcal{R},crs}(x, w) \to \pi$, $\mathbf{SimProve}_{\mathcal{R},simtd}(x) \to \pi$, and $\mathbf{Ver}_{\mathcal{R},crs}(x, \pi) \to \{0, 1\}$ for respectively generating, simulating, and verifying proofs π, and finally deterministic polynomial time algorithm $\mathbf{Extract}_{\mathcal{R},extd}(x, \pi) \to w$ for extracting witnesses. We require that such schemes are *complete, computational zero-knowledge*, and *extractable*, and assume instantiations for:

- $\mathcal{R}_U = \left\{ (x, w) \,\middle|\, D = \mathbf{Com}_{ck}(V, R) \land V \in U \right\}$ with $x = (D, ck), w = (V, R)$
- $\mathcal{R}_T = \left\{ (x, w) \,\middle|\, C = \mathbf{Enc}_{ek}(V, R) \land V \in T \right\}$ with $x = (C, ek), w = (V, R)$
- $\mathcal{R}_e = \left\{ (x, w) \,\middle|\, C = \mathbf{Eval}_{e,ek}(C_1, C_2, V_1, V_2, R) \land D_i = \mathbf{Com}_{ck}(V_i, R_i) \right\}$
  with $x = (C, C_1, C_2, ek, D_1, D_2, ck)$ and $w = (V_1, R_1, V_2, R_2, R)$.

4 Real-World Interpretation

In the real-world model all messages sent between entities are annotated bit-strings BS of the following kinds: $\langle \mathtt{value} : V \rangle$ and $\langle \mathtt{const} : Cn \rangle$ for values and constants, $\langle \mathtt{pair} : BS_1, BS_2 \rangle$ for pairings, and $[\mathtt{comPack} : D, ck, \pi_U, crs]$, $[\mathtt{encPack} : C, ek, \pi_T, crs]$, $[\mathtt{evalPack} : C, C_1, C_2, ek, D_1, D_2, ck, \pi_e, crs]$ for commitment, encryption, and evaluation packages. In interpretation $\mathcal{RW}(Sys)$ of a system Sys each programme P is executed by ITM M_P with access to its own operation module $\mathcal{O}_P$ enforcing sanity checks on received messages and implementing the operations available to P as described in Section 2. These implementations follow straight-forwardly from the primitives.

The interpretation also contains a setup functionality $\mathcal{F}_{setup}$ connected to the operation modules of the cryptographic programmes. It is set to support either a real or an ideal protocol, is assumed to know the corruption scenario, and is responsible for generating and distributing the cryptographic keys and trapdoors, including leaking the public and corrupted keys to the adversary.

When a message is received by an M_P it is immediately passed to $\mathcal{O}_P$ which checks that every cryptographic package in it comes with a correct proof generated under the other player's CRS. The operation module also keeps a list σ of the ciphertexts received and generated by the player, so that it may enforce a policy of only accepting an evaluation package if it has first seen the ciphertexts it is supposedly constructed from, and rejecting certain ciphertexts that an honest player would never have produced and which cannot occur in the intermediate interpretation[7].

If the message was accepted by the operation module the machine gets back a reference through which it may access the message in the future. It then executes the operations as dictated by the programme and finally either halts or sends a message to another machine.

5   Intermediate Interpretation

The intermediate interpretation uses the same machines M_P for executing programmes as the real-world interpretation, however all operation modules and the setup functionality are now replaced with a single functionality $\mathcal{F}_{aux}$ offering operation implementations to the honest entities as well as a certain set of methods to the adversary. In effect, the cryptographic primitives and setup functionality has been replaced by a global memory with logical restrictions on how the adversary is allowed to access it.

All cryptographic messages passed around among the entities are uniformly random *handles* H of length κ associated to data objects in the global memory: commitment objects take form $(\mathsf{com} : V, R, ck)$, encryption objects $(\mathsf{enc} : V, R, ek)$, and proof objects[8] $(\mathsf{proof}_U : H_D, ck, crs)$, $(\mathsf{proof}_T : H_C, ek, crs)$, and $(\mathsf{proof}_e : H_C, H_{C_1}, H_{C_2}, ek, H_{D_1}, H_{D_2}, ck, crs)$. Note that the ck, ek, crs here are simply constants chosen by $\mathcal{F}_{aux}$ and indicating the creator and owner of the objects. For packages we have objects $(\mathsf{comPack} : H_D, ck, H_\pi, crs)$, $(\mathsf{encPack} : H_C, ek, H_\pi, crs)$, and $(\mathsf{evalPack} : H_C, H_{C_1}, H_{C_2}, ek, H_{D_1}, H_{D_2}, ck, H_\pi, crs)$.

The intermediate implementation of operations for honest entities follows the real-world implementation closely, yet of course using data objects instead of cryptographic bitstrings. One difference is that some guarantees are now provided by the model itself as a consequence of the adversary being limited in

---

[7] One example is if it receives two evaluation packages with the same C but with, say, different D_1; an honest player would have re-randomised the result thereby with overwhelming probability not produce the same C twice. As mentioned earlier, rejecting certain ciphertexts gives an easier-to-analyse symbolic interpretation.

[8] Note that proof objects do not have a randomness (or counter) component; we have gone with this option to simplify the symbolic model but it may easily be removed.

what he may do; for instance, it is not possible for him to construct packages with an invalid proof, and even adversarily evaluated ciphertexts are correctly re-randomised. This means that less checks are enforced through the σ list.

The methods offered to the adversary by $\mathcal{F}_{aux}$ essentially allows him to inspect and construct cryptographic packages, including decrypting ciphertexts for corrupted players, and compare arbitrary handles through a method $eq(H, H') \rightarrow \{0, 1\}$. These methods are determined by what is needed by translator[9] $\mathcal{T}_*$ in the soundness proof (see below and full paper).

5.1 Soundness of Intermediate Interpretation

Through a series of hybrid interpretations $\mathcal{T}[\mathcal{I}(Sys)]$, where leakage and influence ports of the authenticated channels are rewired to run through translator $\mathcal{T}$, we show that a real-world adversary cannot distinguish between $\mathcal{RW}(Sys)$ and $\mathcal{I}(Sys)$ for a well-formed system Sys.

Theorem 1 (Soundness of Intermediate Model). Let Sys_1 and Sys_2 be two well-formed systems. If $\mathcal{I}(Sys_1) \overset{c}{\sim} \mathcal{I}(Sys_2)$ then $\mathcal{RW}(Sys_1) \overset{c}{\sim} \mathcal{RW}(Sys_2)$.

Proof (overview). By a series of hybrid interpretations we first use the properties of the primitives to show that for any well-formed real or ideal protocol Sys we have $\mathcal{RW}(Sys) \overset{c}{\sim} \mathcal{T}_*[\mathcal{I}(Sys)]$ for a constructed PPT translator $\mathcal{T}_*$ using only the methods offered to the adversary by $\mathcal{F}_{aux}$. An important property here is that the identity of commitments and ciphertexts are preserved by the translation performed by each (hybrid-)translator. Next, by assumption no polynomially bounded ITM $\mathcal{Z}'$ can tell the difference between $\mathcal{I}(Sys_1)$ and $\mathcal{I}(Sys_2)$ using only the adversarial methods, and hence no $\mathcal{Z}' = \mathcal{Z} \diamond \mathcal{T}_*$ for a polynomially bounded ITM $\mathcal{Z}$ can tell the difference either. The result then follows.

Corollary 1. Let $(Sys_{real}^{\mathcal{H}})_{\mathcal{H}}$ specify a real protocol for ϕ and let $(Sys_{ideal}^{\mathcal{H}})_{\mathcal{H}}$ specify an ideal protocol with target functionality $\mathcal{F}$. If $\mathcal{I}(Sys_{real}^{\mathcal{H}}) \overset{c}{\sim} \mathcal{I}(Sys_{ideal}^{\mathcal{H}})$ for all three corruption cases $\mathcal{H}$ then ϕ is a realisation of $M_{\mathcal{F}}$ (with inlined operation module) under static corruption.

6 Symbolic Model and Interpretation

The symbolic model and interpretation is tailored to be a conservative approximation of the intermediate model and is based on the well-known dialect in [BAF05] of the applied-pi calculus [AF01], for which automated verification tools exist in the form of ProVerif.

We assume a modelling of the values v in the domain and a modelling of all constants plus **true, false, garbage**. Let *names* $\mathcal{N}$ be a countable set of atomic

---

[9] In UC-terms the translator is simply a simulator for $\mathcal{F}_{aux}$ used to show that the real-world interpretation is a realisation of the intermediate interpretation. However, we use this wording to avoid too much overload.

symbols used to model randomness r, secret key material $dk, extd$, and ports p. A term t is then build from names, a countable set of variables $x, y, z, \ldots$, and constructor symbols

$$\textbf{pair, ek, crs, com, enc, proof}_U, \textbf{proof}_T, \textbf{proof}_e,$$
$$\textbf{comPack, encPack, evalPack}$$

where the three $\textbf{proof}_{(\cdot)}$ constructors are unavailable to the adversary. The destructor symbols are

$$\textbf{isValue, eqValue, inType}_U, \textbf{inType}_T, \textbf{isConst, eqConst}_c, \textbf{equals,}$$
$$\textbf{isPair, first, second, isComPack, isEncPack, isEvalPack,}$$
$$\textbf{verComPack}_U, \textbf{verEncPack}_T, \textbf{verEvalPack}_e, \textbf{eval}_e, \textbf{peval}_f,$$
$$\textbf{dec, extractCom, extractEnc, extractEval}_1, \textbf{extractEval}_2,$$
$$\textbf{ckOf, ekOf, crsOf, comOf, encOf, encOf}_1, \textbf{encOf}_2, \textbf{comOf}_1, \textbf{comOf}_2$$

where only $\textbf{eval}_e$ is unavailable to the adversary. The reason for this is that in order to keep the symbolic model suitable for automated analysis, we do not wish to symbolically model the composition of randomness from encryptions when performing homomorphic evaluations; instead the private $\textbf{eval}_e$ destructor takes a name r as input and we give the adversary access to it only via an honest process that accepts inputs $c_1, c_2, v_1, r_1, v_2, r_2$, picks a fresh name for r, and applies the destructor before sending back the result. We also use t to range over terms with destructors.

Processes Q are built from grammar

$$\text{nil} \qquad \text{in}[p, x]; Q \qquad \text{let } x = t \text{ in } Q \text{ else } Q' \qquad Q \parallel Q'$$
$$\text{new } n; Q \qquad \text{out}[p, t]; Q \qquad \text{if } t = t' \text{ then } Q \text{ else } Q' \qquad !Q$$

where n is a name, p is a port, and x a variable. The nil process does nothing and represents a halted state. The new $n; Q$ process is used for name and port restriction. Intuitively, the let $x = t$ in Q else Q' process tries to evaluate t to t' by reducing it using our rewrite rules and (trivial) equational theory; if it is successful it binds it to x in Q and proceeds as this process, and if it fails then it proceeds as Q' instead. The if $t = t'$ then Q else Q' process is just syntactic sugar but intuitively proceeds as Q if t and t' can be rewritten to equivalent terms, and as Q' if not. Finally, $Q \parallel Q'$ denotes parallel composition, and $!Q$ unbounded replication.

An *evaluation context* $\mathcal{E}$ is essentially a process with a hole, built from $[\_]$, $\mathcal{E} \parallel Q$, and new $n; \mathcal{E}$. We obtain process $\mathcal{E}[Q]$ as the result of filling the hole in $\mathcal{E}$ with Q. The formal semantics of a process can then be given by a reduction relation $\rightarrow$ defined as the smallest relation closed under application of evaluation contexts and rules:

$$\text{out}[p, t]; Q_1 \parallel \text{in}[p, x]; Q_2 \rightarrow Q_1 \parallel Q_2\{t/x\}$$

$$\text{let } x = t \text{ in } Q \text{ else } Q' \rightarrow \begin{cases} Q\{t'/x\} & \text{when } t \Downarrow t' \\ Q' & \text{otherwise} \end{cases}$$

where $t \Downarrow t'$ indicates that t may be rewritten to some t' containing no destructors. We write $\to^*$ for the reflexive and transitive closure of reduction.

Our equivalence notion for formalising *symbolic indistinguishability* is observational equivalence [AF01]. Here we write $Q\downarrow_p$ when Q can send an observable message on port p; that is, when $Q \to^* \mathcal{E}[\mathsf{out}[p,t]; Q']$ for some term t, process Q', and evaluation context $\mathcal{E}$ that does not bind p.

Definition 2 (Symbolic indistinguishability). Symbolic indistinguishability, *denoted* $\overset{s}{\sim}$, *is the largest symmetric relation* $\mathcal{R}$ *on closed processes* Q_1 *and* Q_2 *such that* $Q_1 \mathcal{R} Q_2$ *implies:*

1. *if* $Q_1\downarrow_p$ *then* $Q_2\downarrow_p$
2. *if* $Q_1 \to Q_1'$ *then there exists* Q_2' *such that* $Q_2 \to^* Q_2'$ *and* $Q_1' \mathcal{R} Q_2'$
3. $\mathcal{E}[Q_1] \mathcal{R} \mathcal{E}[Q_2]$ *for all evaluation contexts* $\mathcal{E}$

Intuitively, a context may represent an attacker, and two processes are symbolic indistinguishable if they cannot be distinguished by any attacker at any step: every output step in an execution of process Q_1 must have an indistinguishable equivalent output step in the execution of process Q_2, and vice versa; if not then there exists an evaluation context that "breaks" the equivalence. Note that the definition uses an existential quantification: if $Q_1 \overset{s}{\sim} Q_2$ then we only know that a reduction of Q_1 can be matched by *some* reduction of Q_2.

6.1 Symbolic Interpretation

Using the model from above it is somewhat straight-forward to give a symbolic interpretation of a system $\mathcal{S}(Sys)$ by giving an interpretation of a programme P in the form of a process Q_P, as well as a symbolic implementation of its operation module. Doing this we obtain a process Q_h for the honest entities, and for the adversary's operations we get a process Q_{adv}, both of which depend on the corruption scenario $\mathcal{H}$. The symbolic interpretation of a protocol is hence given by the three processes

$$\mathcal{E}_{setup}^{AB}\left[Q_h^{AB} \parallel Q_{adv}^{AB}\right] \qquad \mathcal{E}_{setup}^{A}\left[Q_h^{A} \parallel Q_{adv}^{A}\right] \qquad \mathcal{E}_{setup}^{B}\left[Q_h^{B} \parallel Q_{adv}^{B}\right]$$

where $Q_h^{\mathcal{H}}$ and $Q_{adv}^{\mathcal{H}}$ are put together inside an evaluation context responsible for generating keys.

6.2 Soundness of Symbolic Interpretation

Since the symbolic model already matches the intermediate model quite closely, the main issue for the soundness theorem is to ensure that the two notions of equivalence coincide. This in turn boils down to ensuring that the scheduling that leads to symbolic equivalence coincides with the scheduling policy used in the computational interpretations. Our solution is to restrict systems such that they allow only one choice of symbolic scheduling, namely that of the computational model. It is enough to require that no message is lost, i.e. for any strategy of the adversary, if a programme sends a message on a port then the receiving programme is listening on that port. The motivation behind this is that the two models disagree on what happens when the receiver is not ready: in the computational model the message is lost (read but ignored by the receiver) while in the symbolic model the message hangs around (possibly blocking) until the receiver is ready; this may then lead to non-determinism and several scheduling choices.

Theorem 2. *Let Sys_1 and Sys_2 be two systems that do not allow messages to be lost. If $\mathcal{S}(Sys_1) \overset{s}{\sim} \mathcal{S}(Sys_2)$ then $\mathcal{I}(Sys_1) \overset{c}{\sim} \mathcal{I}(Sys_2)$.*

Proof (overview). By fixing the random bitstrings seen by $\mathcal{Z}$ when interacting with $\mathcal{I}(Sys_i)$ we obtain a deterministic execution that with overwhelming probability will be matched by the symbolic execution on some evaluation context; the only situation where this is not possible is if $\mathcal{Z}$ manages to guess a bitstring drawn uniformly at random from $\{0, 1\}^\kappa$. Symbolic indistinguishability between the two systems then implies that with overwhelming probability $\mathcal{Z}$ sees the same when interacting with $\mathcal{I}(Sys_1)$ and $\mathcal{I}(Sys_2)$.

Acknowledgements. We would like to thank Ran Canetti for valuable discussion and insights, and for hosting Morten at BU in the beginning of this work. We would also like to thank Hubert Comon-Lundh for discussion and clarification of his work, and Bogdan Warinschi for comments and valuable suggestions. Finally, we are thankful for the feedback provided by the anonymous reviewers, including mentioning of several places that needed clarification.

References

[AF01]   Abadi, M., Fournet, C.: Mobile values, new names, and secure communication. In: Symposium on Principles of Programming Languages (POPL 2001), pp. 104–115. ACM Press, New York (2001)

[AR02]   Abadi, M., Rogaway, P.: Reconciling two views of cryptography (the computational soundness of formal encryption). Journal of Cryptology 15, 103–127 (2002)

[BAF05]   Blanchet, B., Abadi, M., Fournet, C.: Automated Verification of Selected Equivalences for Security Protocols. In: Symposium on Logic in Computer Science (LICS 2005), pp. 331–340. IEEE (2005)

[BDOZ11] Bendlin, R., Damgård, I., Orlandi, C., Zakarias, S.: Semi-homomorphic encryption and multiparty computation. In: Paterson, K.G. (ed.) EUROCRYPT 2011. LNCS, vol. 6632, pp. 169–188. Springer, Heidelberg (2011)

[BGHB11] Barthe, G., Grégoire, B., Heraud, S., Béguelin, S.Z.: Computer-aided security proofs for the working cryptographer. In: Rogaway, P. (ed.) CRYPTO 2011. LNCS, vol. 6841, pp. 71–90. Springer, Heidelberg (2011)

[Bla08]   Blanchet, B.: A computationally sound mechanized prover for security protocols. IEEE Transactions on Dependable and Secure Computing 5(4), 193–207 (2008)

[BMM10]   Backes, M., Maffei, M., Mohammadi, E.: Computationally sound abstraction and verification of secure multi-party computations. In: Foundations of Software Technology and Theoretical Computer Science (FSTTCS 2010). LIPIcs, vol. 8, pp. 352–363. Schloss Dagstuhl (2010)

[BP03]   Backes, M., Pfitzmann, B.: A cryptographically sound security proof of the needham-schroeder-lowe public-key protocol. In: Pandya, P.K., Radhakrishnan, J. (eds.) FSTTCS 2003. LNCS, vol. 2914, pp. 1–12. Springer, Heidelberg (2003)

[BP04]   Backes, M., Pfitzmann, B.: Symmetric encryption in a simulatable dolev-yao style cryptographic library. In: Computer Security Foundations Workshop (CSFW 2004), pp. 204–218. IEEE (2004)

[BP06]   Backes, M., Pfitzmann, B.: On the cryptographic key secrecy of the strengthened yahalom protocol. In: Fischer-Hübner, S., Rannenberg, K., Yngström, L., Lindskog, S. (eds.) Security and Privacy in Dynamic Environments. IFIP, vol. 201, pp. 233–245. Springer, Boston (2006)

[BPW03]   Backes, M., Pfitzmann, B., Waidner, M.: A composable cryptographic library with nested operations. In: Computer and Communications Security (CCS 2003), pp. 220–230. ACM, New York (2003)

[BU13]   Böhl, F., Unruh, D.: Symbolic universal composability. In: Computer Security Foundations (CSF 2013), pp. 257–271. IEEE (2013)

[Can01]   Canetti, R.: Universally composable security: A new paradigm for cryptographic protocols. In: Foundations of Computer Science (FOCS 2001), pp. 136–145. IEEE Computer Society (2001)

[Can08]   Canetti, R.: Composable formal security analysis: Juggling soundness, simplicity and efficiency. In: Aceto, L., Damgård, I., Goldberg, L.A., Halldórsson, M.M., Ingólfsdóttir, A., Walukiewicz, I. (eds.) ICALP 2008, Part II. LNCS, vol. 5126, pp. 1–13. Springer, Heidelberg (2008)

[CC08]   Comon-Lundh, H., Cortier, V.: Computational soundness of observational equivalence. In: Computer and Communications Security (CCS 2008), pp. 109–118. ACM (2008)

[CG10]   Canetti, R., Gajek, S.: Universally composable symbolic analysis of diffie-hellman based key exchange. IACR Cryptology ePrint Archive, 2010:303 (2010)

[CH06]   Canetti, R., Herzog, J.C.: Universally composable symbolic analysis of mutual authentication and key-exchange protocols. In: Halevi, S., Rabin, T. (eds.) TCC 2006. LNCS, vol. 3876, pp. 380–403. Springer, Heidelberg (2006)

[CHKS12]   Comon-Lundh, H., Hagiya, M., Kawamoto, Y., Sakurada, H.: Computational soundness of indistinguishability properties without computable parsing. In: Ryan, M.D., Smyth, B., Wang, G. (eds.) ISPEC 2012. LNCS, vol. 7232, pp. 63–79. Springer, Heidelberg (2012)

[CKW11]   Cortier, V., Kremer, S., Warinschi, B.: A survey of symbolic methods in computational analysis of cryptographic systems. Journal of Automated Reasoning 46, 225–259 (2011)

[DDMR07]   Datta, A., Derek, A., Mitchell, J.C., Roy, A.: Protocol composition logic (PCL). Electronic Notes in Theoretical Computer Science 172, 311–358 (2007)

[DKP09]   Delaune, S., Kremer, S., Pereira, O.: Simulation based security in the applied pi calculus. In: Foundations of Software Technology and Theoretical Computer Science (FSTTCS 2009), vol. 4, pp. 169–180 (2009)

[DNO08]   Damgård, I., Nielsen, J.B., Orlandi, C.: Essentially optimal universally composable oblivious transfer. In: Lee, P.J., Cheon, J.H. (eds.) ICISC 2008. LNCS, vol. 5461, pp. 318–335. Springer, Heidelberg (2009)

[LN08]   Laud, P., Ngo, L.: Threshold homomorphic encryption in the universally composable cryptographic library. In: Baek, J., Bao, F., Chen, K., Lai, X. (eds.) ProvSec 2008. LNCS, vol. 5324, pp. 298–312. Springer, Heidelberg (2008)

[MRST06] Mitchell, J.C., Ramanathan, A., Scedrov, A., Teague, V.: A probabilistic polynomial-time process calculus for the analysis of cryptographic protocols. Theoretical Computer Science 353(1-3), 118–164 (2006)

[MW04]   Micciancio, D., Warinschi, B.: Soundness of formal encryption in the presence of active adversaries. In: Naor, M. (ed.) TCC 2004. LNCS, vol. 2951, pp. 133–151. Springer, Heidelberg (2004)

[PW01]   Pfitzmann, B., Waidner, M.: A model for asynchronous reactive systems and its application to secure message transmission. In: Proc. of IEEE Symposium on Security and Privacy, pp. 184–200 (2001)

Author Index